PHILOSOPHY

History & Problems

PHILOSOPHY

History & Problems

Third Edition

Samuel Enoch Stumpf
Vanderbilt University

McGraw-Hill Book Company
New York   St. Louis   San Francisco   Auckland
Bogotá   Hamburg   Johannesburg   London   Madrid
Mexico   Montreal   New Delhi   Panama
Paris   São Paulo   Singapore   Sydney
Tokyo   Toronto

PHILOSOPHY
History and Problems

Book I,
published as SOCRATES TO SARTRE,
copyright © 1982, 1975, 1966 by McGraw-Hill, Inc.
All rights reserved.

Book II,
published as PHILOSOPHICAL PROBLEMS,
copyright © 1983, 1971 by McGraw-Hill, Inc.
All rights reserved.

4567890DOCDOC8987654

ISBN 0-07-062181-0

This book was set in Laurel by Rocappi, Inc.
The editors were Kaye Pace and David Dunham;
the designer was Jo Jones;
the production supervisor was John Mancia.
R. R. Donnelley & Sons Company was printer and binder.

Library of Congress Cataloging in Publication Data

Stumpf, Samuel Enoch, date
     Philosophy, history and problems.

     Some of the material in this book appeared previously in the
author's Socrates to Sartre and Philosophical problems.
     Bibliography: p.
     Includes index.
     1. Philosophy—History.   2. Philosophy—Addresses, essays,
lectures.   I. Title.
B72.S788   1983   190   82-18005
ISBN 0-07-062181-0

TO JEAN
Paul   Sam, Jr.   Mark   Betsy

CONTENTS

BOOK II
PHILOSOPHICAL PROBLEMS

❋

PART FIVE   METAPHYSICS

PREFACE

A S in the earlier editions of this introduction to philosophy, this volume
presents two forms of philosophical literature: Book I is a narrative
history of Western philosophy and Book II is a selection of readings
dealing with the major problems of philosophy. While there is no substitute for reading the works of the leading philosophers in their original form, it
is helpful to have at hand a treatment of the unfolding of philosophical ideas in
the historical setting and sequence of their authors. Similarly, by reading only the
history of philosophy one will lack the first-hand acquaintance with each author's
literary style and the rigor of his systematic thought and argument. In this volume, then, the student will find both the original literature of philosophical authors and a historical treatment of the authors themselves and the development
of their ideas.

   This book is meant to have as much flexibility as the reader or instructor
desires. He or she may, for example, wish to begin with one of the problems, say,
Ethics, in Book II. The readings in the section on Ethics can be read in the order
in which they are arranged. Or the reader can read selections in more than one

problem area in any sequence he or she chooses. At the same time, in preparation for reading a selection in Book II, say, for example, Aristotle or Kant on Ethics, the reader can turn in Book I to the chapters dealing with the life and times and thought of Aristotle and Kant.

I had originally published the historical material in Book I under the title *Socrates to Sartre*. To this I have added selected readings in response to requests from those who have used *Socrates to Sartre* in order to combine in one volume both history and readings.

While substantially the same as the previous edition, this present edition contains some new material, including, in Book I, the addition of a new chapter on Rousseau, a treatment of Marx's theory of the "alienation of labor," a section on Heidegger, and an expansion of the philosophy of Sartre. In Book II several new readings have been added, including Sartre's entire essay "Existentialism and Humanism" and selections from A. J. Ayer on the verification principle; B. F. Skinner's *Walden Two* concerning human freedom; Rousseau's *Social Contract*; Marx's "Alienated Labor"; John Rawls' *A Theory of Justice*; Robert Nozick's *Anarchy, State and Utopia*; John Dewey's *A Common Faith*; Plato, Hume, and Kierkegaard concerning immortality; Bertrand Russell's reflections on metaphysics; and A. N. Whitehead's *Science and the Modern World*.

Samuel Enoch Stumpf

PHILOSOPHY

History & Problems

BOOK I
A HISTORY
OF PHILOSPHY

ONE

THE
ANCIENT PERIOD:
THE
SHAPING OF
THE
PHILOSOPHIC
MIND

Socrates' Predecessors: Philosophy and the Natural Order

Philosophy began with man's sense of wonder and curiosity expressed in the questions "What are things really like?" and "How can we explain the process of change in things?" What prompted these questions was the gradual recognition that things are not exactly what they seem to be, that "appearance" often differs from "reality." The facts of birth, death, growth, and decay—coming into being and passing away—raised not only the questions about personal destiny but also the larger questions of how things and persons come into existence, can be different at different times, pass out of existence only to be followed by other things and persons. Many of the answers given to these questions by the earliest philosophers are not as important as the fact that they focused upon just these questions and that they approached them with a fresh and new frame of mind that was in contrast to that of the great poets.

The birthplace of philosophy was the seaport town of Miletus, located across the Aegean Sea from Athens, on the western shores of Ionia in Asia Minor, and for this reason the first philosophers are called either Milesians or Ionians. By the time the Milesian philosophers began their systematic work, roughly around 585 B.C., Miletus had been a crossroads for both seaborne commerce and for cosmopolitan ideas. Its wealth made possible the leisure without which the life of art and philosophy could hardly develop, and the broad-mindedness and inquisitiveness of its people created a congenial atmosphere for the intellectual activity that was to become philosophy. Earlier, Ionia had produced the genius Homer, whose epic poetry projected upon the cosmic scene Mount Olympus, where the gods pursued lives not too different from their human counterparts on earth. This poetic view of the world also related the life of the gods to the life of humans, by describing various ways in which the gods intruded into or interfered with men's affairs. In particular, the Homeric gods would punish men for their lack of moderation and especially for their pride or insubordination, which the Greeks called *hubris*. It is not that Homer's gods are moral and require goodness; they are merely stronger than men and exact obedience. Moreover, when Homer suggests that there is a power that he calls "fate," a power to which even the gods are subject, he appears to be reaching for a way of describing a rigorous order in nature to which everyone and everything must be subordinate. But his poetic imagination is dominated so thoroughly by his thinking in human terms that his world is peopled everywhere with human types, and his conception of nature is that of capricious wills at work instead of the reign of physical natural laws. It was Hesiod, writing sometime in the eighth century B.C., who altered this concept of the gods and "fate" by removing from the gods all capriciousness, ascribing to them instead a moral consistency. Although Hesiod retains the notion that the gods control nature, he balances this personal element in the nature of things with an emphasis upon the impersonal operation of the moral law of the universe. The moral order, in Hesiod's view, is still the product of Zeus' commands, but these commands are neither capricious nor calculated, as Homer thought, to gratify the gods, but are rather fashioned for the good of man. For Hesiod the universe is a moral order, and from this idea it is a short step to say, without any reference to the gods, that there is an impersonal force controlling the structure of the universe and regulating its process of changes. It was this short step that the Milesians Thales, Anaximander, and Anaximenes took. Whereas Hesiod still thought in terms of traditional mythology with a peopled universe, philosophy among the Milesians began as an act of independent thought. To ask, as they did, "What are things really like?" and "How can we explain the process of change in things?" indicates a substantial departure from the poetry of Homer and Hesiod and a movement toward what we should call the temperament of science. Although the Milesians can rightly be called primitive scientists, it is a fact of the history of thought that science and philosophy were the same thing in the beginning and only later did various specific disciplines separate themselves from the field of philosophy, medicine being the first to do so. From the very beginning, however, Greek philosophy was an intellectual activity, for it was not a matter only of seeing or believing but of thinking, and philosophy meant thinking about basic questions in a mood of genuine and free inquiry.

WHAT IS PERMANENT IN EXISTENCE?

Thales We do not know as much as we should like about Thales of Miletus, and what we do know is rather anecdotal in nature. He left no writings. All that is available are fragmentary references to him made by later writers who recorded memorable incidents in his career. He was a contemporary of Solon and Croesus, and the years of his life are set between 624 and 546 B.C. During a military campaign against Persia, he apparently solved the difficult logistics problem of enabling the Lydian king's army to cross the wide Halys river by digging a channel that diverted part of the flow, thereby making two narrower rivers over which bridges could be built. While traveling in Egypt, Thales worked out a way of measuring the height of the pyramids, using the simple procedure of measuring a pyramid's shadow at that time of day when a man's shadow is equal to his height. It may have been during these Egyptian travels, too, that he became acquainted with the kinds of knowledge that enabled him to predict the eclipse of the sun on May 28, 585 B.C. In a practical vein, he constructed, while in Miletus, an instrument for measuring the distance of ships sighted at sea, and as an aid to navigation, he urged sailors to use the constellation Little Bear as the surest guide for determining the direction of the north.

It was probably inevitable that anecdotes should be attached to such an extraordinary man as Thales. Plato, in his *Theaetetus*, writes about "the jest which the clever witty Thracian handmaid is said to have made about Thales, when he fell into a well as he was looking up at the stars. She said that he was so eager to know what was going on in heaven that he could not see what was before his feet." Plato adds that "this is a jest which is equally applicable to all philosophers," apparently unaware of another incident in Thales' life that would seem to establish a very keen awareness of what was going on around him. In his *Politics*, Aristotle writes that "there is . . . the story which is told of Thales of Miletus. It is a story about a scheme for making money, which is fathered on Thales owing to his reputation for wisdom. . . . He was reproached for his poverty, which was supposed to show the uselessness of philosophy; but observing from his knowledge of meteorology (as the story goes) that there was likely to be a heavy crop of olives [during the next summer], and having a small sum at his command, he paid down earnest-money, early in the year, for the hire of all the olive-presses in Miletus and Chios; and he managed, in the absence of any higher offer, to secure them at a low rate. When the season came, and there was a sudden and simultaneous demand for a number of presses, he let out the stock he had collected at any rate he chose to fix; and making a considerable fortune, he succeeded in proving that it is easy for philosophers to become rich if they so desire, though it is not the business which they are really about." But Thales is famous not for his general wisdom or his practical shrewdness, but because he opened up a new area of thought for which he has rightly earned the title of the first philosopher.

Thales' novel inquiry concerned the nature of things. What is everything made of, or what kind of "stuff" goes into the composition of things? What

Thales was trying to get at with these questions was some way of accounting for the fact that there are many different kinds of things, such as earth, clouds, and oceans, and that some of these things change from time to time into something else and also that they resemble each other in certain ways. Thales' unique contribution to thought was his notion that in spite of the differences between various things there is, nevertheless, a basic similarity between them all, that *the many* are related to each other by *the One*. He assumed that some single element, some "stuff," a stuff which contained its own principle of action or change, lay at the foundation of all physical reality. To him this One, or this stuff, was *water*.

Although there is no record of how Thales came to the conclusion that water is the cause of all things, Aristotle writes that Thales might have derived it from observation of simple events, "perhaps from seeing that the nutriment of all things is moist, and that heat is generated from the moist and kept alive by it. . . . He got his notion from this fact and from the fact that the seeds of all things have a moist nature, and water is the origin of the nature of moist things." Other phenomena such as evaporation or freezing also suggest that water takes on different forms. But the accuracy of Thales' analysis of the composition of things is far less important than the fact that he raised the question concerning the nature of the world. His question had set the stage for a new kind of inquiry, one which could be debated on its merits and could either be confirmed or refuted by further analysis. In spite of his notion that "all things are full of gods," a notion that had apparently no theological significance for him and to which he turned in an attempt to explain the power in things, such as magnetic powers in stones, Thales shifted the basis of thought from a mythological base to one of scientific inquiry. And, again from his primitive starting point, others were to follow him with alternative solutions, but always with his problem before them.

Anaximander A younger contemporary and a pupil of Thales was Anaximander. He agreed with his teacher that there is some single basic stuff out of which everything comes. Unlike Thales, however, Anaximander said that this basic stuff is neither water nor any other specific or determinate element, arguing that water and all other definite things are only specific variations or offshoots of something which is more primary. It may very well be, he thought, that water or moisture is found in various forms everywhere, but water is only one specific thing among many other elements, and all these specific things require that there be some more elementary stuff to account for their origin. The primary substance out of which all these specific things come, said Anaximander, is an *indefinite* or *boundless* realm. Thus, Anaximander differentiates specific and determinate things from their origin by calling the primary substance the *indeterminate boundless*. Whereas actual things are specific, their source is indeterminate, and whereas things are finite, the original stuff is infinite or boundless.

Besides offering a new idea about the original substance of things, Anaximander advanced the enterprise of philosophy by attempting some explanation for his new idea. Thales had not dealt in any detail with the problem of explaining how the primary stuff became the many different things we see in the world, but Anaximander addressed himself precisely to this question. Although his explanation may seem strange, it represents an advance in knowledge in the sense that it is an attempt to deal with known facts from which hypotheses can be formulated instead of explaining natural phenomena in mythical and nondebatable terms. Still, what Anaximander has to say about the origin of things has the flavor of bold speculation, for in describing the indeterminate boundless as the unoriginated and indestructible primary substance, he speaks of this as also having eternal motion. As a consequence of this motion, the various specific elements come into being as a "separating off" from the original substance, and thus "there was an eternal motion in which the heavens came to be." But first *warm* and *cold* were separated off, and from these two came *moist*; then from these came *earth* and *air*. Anaximander then tried to account for the heavenly bodies and air currents around the earth in what appears to be a mechanical explanation of the orderly movement of the stars. He thought that the earth was cylindrical in shape in contrast to Thales, who thought it was flat as a disk and floated on the water. Coming to the origin of man, Anaximander said that all life, including man's, comes from the sea and that in the course of time, living things came out of the sea to dry land. He suggested that man evolved from creatures of a different kind, using as his argument the fact that other creatures are quickly self-supporting, whereas man alone needs prolonged nursing and that, therefore, man would not have survived if this had been his original form. Commenting on Anaximander's account of the origin of man, Plutarch writes that the Syrians "actually revere the fish as being of similar race and nurturing. In this they philosophize more suitably than Anaximander; for he declares, not that fishes and men came into being in the same parents, but that originally men came into being inside fishes, and that, having been nurtured there—like sharks—and having become adequate to look after themselves, they then came forth and took to the land." Returning again to the vast cosmic scene, Anaximander thought that there were many worlds and many systems of universes existing all at the same time, all of them perishable, there being the constant alternation between their creation and destruction. This cyclical process was for him a rigorous "necessity" as the conflict of opposite forces in nature caused what he called poetically an "injustice" requiring their ultimate destruction. In the only sentence from his writings that has survived, Anaximander gathers up his chief thought by saying, again somewhat poetically, that "From what source things arise, to that they return of necessity when they are destroyed; for they suffer punishment and make reparation to one another for their injustice according to the order of time."

Anaximenes The third and last of the Milesian philosophers was Anaximenes (about 585–528 B.C.), who was the young "associate" of Anaximander. As he considered Anaximander's answer to the question concerning the composition of natural things, he was dissatisfied with the notion of the *boundless* as being the source of all things, since it was too vague and intangible. He could understand why Anaximander chose this solution over Thales' notion that water is the cause of all things, because the boundless could help explain the "infinite" background to the wide variety of finite and specific things. Still, the indeterminate boundless had no specific meaning for Anaximenes, and he, therefore, chose to focus upon a definite substance the way Thales had done and, at the same time, tried to incorporate the advance achieved by Anaximander. To combine Thales' notion of a definite substance with Anaximander's new concept of the boundless in continued motion, Anaximenes designated *air* as the primary substance from which all things come. As the boundless, air is spread everywhere, but unlike the boundless, it is a specific and tangible material substance that can be identified. Moreover, the air's motion is a far more specific process than Anaximander's "separating off," for Anaximenes hit upon the highly respectable concepts of "rarefaction" and "condensation" as the specific forms of motion which lead to describable changes in air. Although air is invisible, men live only as long as they can breathe, and "just as our soul, being air, holds us together, so do breath and air encompass the whole world." But to explain how air is the origin of all things, Anaximenes introduced the important new idea that differences in "quality" are caused by differences in "quantity." The expansion and contraction of air represent quantitative changes, and these changes occurring in a single substance account for the multitude of different things. Expansion, or rarefaction, of air causes warming and, at the extreme, fire, whereas contraction, or condensation, causes cooling and the transformation of air into solids by way of a gradual transition where, as Anaximenes says, "air that is condensed forms winds . . . if this process goes further, it gives water, still further earth, and the greatest condensation of all is found in stones."

Although these Milesian philosophers appear to have proceeded with scientific concerns and temperaments, they did not form their hypotheses the way modern scientists would, nor did they devise any experiments to test their theories. Their ideas have a dogmatic quality, a mood of positive assertion, rather than the tentativeness of true hypotheses. But it must be remembered that the critical questions concerning the nature and limits of human knowledge had not yet been raised. Nor did the Milesians refer in any way to the problem of the relation between spirit and body. Their reduction of all reality to a material origin certainly raises this question, but it was recognized as a problem only later in the history of thought. Whatever may be the usefulness of their specific ideas about *water*, the *boundless*, and *air* as the primary substance of things, the real significance of the Milesians is, again, that they for the first time raised the question about the ultimate nature of things and made the first halting but direct inquiry into what nature really consists of.

THE MATHEMATICAL BASIS OF ALL THINGS

Pythagoras   Across a span of water from Miletus, located in the Aegean Sea, was the small island of Samos, which was the birthplace of a truly extraordinary and wise man, Pythagoras. From the various scraps of information we have about him and those who were his followers, an incomplete but still fascinating picture of his new philosophic reflections emerges. Apparently dissatisfied with conditions not only on Samos but generally in Ionia during the tyrannical rule of the rich Polycrates, Pythagoras migrated to southern Italy and settled there in the prosperous Greek city of Crotone, where his active philosophic life is usually dated from about 525 to 500 B.C.

We are told by Aristotle that "the Pythagoreans . . . devoted themselves to mathematics, they were the first to advance this study, and having been brought up in it they thought its principles were the principles of all things. . . ." In contrast to the Milesians, the Pythagoreans said that things *consist of numbers*. Although it is quite strange to say that everything consists of numbers, the strangeness, as well as the difficulty, of this doctrine is greatly overcome when we consider why Pythagoras became interested in numbers and what his conception of numbers was.

Pythagoras became interested in mathematics for what appear to be religious reasons. His originality could be said to consist in his conviction that the study of mathematics is the best purifier of the soul. He is, therefore, referred to as the founder both of a religious sect and at the same time a school of mathematics. What gave rise to the Pythagorean sect was the yearning among men for a deeply spiritual religion that could provide the means for purifying the soul and for guaranteeing its immortality. The Homeric gods were not gods in the theological sense, since they were as immoral as human beings and as such could be neither the objects of worship nor the source of any spiritual power to overcome the pervading sense of moral uncleanliness and the anxiety men had over the shortness of life and the finality of death. The religious movement that had earlier moved into this area of human concern was the religion of Dionysus, which became widespread during the seventh and sixth centuries B.C. The worship of Dionysus satisfied to some extent those yearnings for cleansing and immortality. Organized into small, secret, and mystical societies, the devotees would worship Dionysus under various animal forms. Working themselves into a frenzy of wild dances and song, they would drink the blood of these animals, which they had torn apart in a state of intoxication, and would finally drop in complete exhaustion, convinced that at the height of their frenzy, their bodies had been entered by the spirit of Dionysus, purifying them and conferring his own immortality upon their souls.

The Pythagoreans were clearly concerned with the mystical problems of purification and immortality, and it was for this reason that they turned to science and mathematics, the study of which they considered the best purge for the soul. In scientific and mathematical thought they saw a mode of life that more than any other kind was "pure." Thought and reflection represent a clear contrast to the life of trade and competition for various honors. It was Pythagoras who first distinguished the three different kinds of lives, and by implication the three divisions of the soul, by saying that there are three different kinds of men who go to the Olympian games. The lowest class is made up of those who go there to buy and sell, to make a profit. Next are those who go there to compete, to gain honors. Best of all, he thought, are those who come as spectators, who reflect upon and analyze what is happening. Of these three, the spectator illustrates the thinker, whose activity as a philosopher liberates him from the involvements of daily life and its imperfections. To "look on" is one of the meanings of the Greek word "theory." Theoretical thinking, or pure science and pure mathematics, was considered by the Pythagoreans as a purifier of the soul, particularly as mathematical thought could liberate men from thinking about particular things and lead their thought, instead, to the permanent and ordered world of numbers. The final mystical triumph of the Pythagorean is his liberation from "the wheel of birth," from the migration of his soul to animal and other forms in the constant progress of death and birth, for thus the spectator achieves a unity with god and shares his immortality.

To connect this religious concern with the philosophical aspects of the Pythagoreans, mention should be made first of all of their interest in *music*. They considered music highly therapeutic for certain nervous disorders, seeing as they did some relation between the harmonies of music and the harmony of man's interior life. But their true discovery in the field of music was that the musical intervals between the notes could be expressed in numerical terms. They discovered that the length of the strings of a musical instrument is proportionate to the actual interval of the sounds they produce. They could demonstrate that a string making a sound an octave lower than another string was twice as long as that string, the ratio here being 2:1. All the other intervals could similarly be expressed in numerical ratios, and music became, for the Pythagoreans, a formidable example of the pervasive relevance of numbers in all things, leading Aristotle to say about them that "since they saw that the attributes and the ratios of the musical scales were expressible in numbers; since then all other things seemed in their whole nature to be modeled after numbers, and numbers seemed to be the first things in the whole of nature, and the whole heaven to be a musical scale and a number."

What must have facilitated the development of their doctrine that all things *are* numbers was the Pythagorean practice in counting or their way of writing numbers. Apparently they built numbers out of individual units, using pebbles to count. The number *one* was therefore a single pebble and all other numbers were created by the addition of pebbles, somewhat like our present practice of representing numbers on dice by the use of dots. But the significant point is that the Pythagoreans discovered a relation between arithmetic and geometry. A single pebble, as a point is *one*, but *two* is made up of two pebbles or two points, and these two points make a line. Three points, as in the corners of a triangle, create a plane or area and four points can represent a solid. This suggested to the Pythagoreans a close relationship between number and magnitude, and Pythagoras is credited with discovering that the square of the hypotenuse is equal to the squares of the other two sides of a right-angled triangle. This correlation between numbers and magnitude provided immense consolation to those who were seeking evidence of a principle of structure and order in the universe, and it is understandable that the possibly apocryphal story should have arisen that Hippasus was drowned in the Hellespont for letting out the secret, which anybody could have figured out, that this principle does not hold true in the case of the isosceles right-angled triangle, where the relation between its hypotenuse and its sides cannot be expressed by any numerical ratio, only by an irrational number.

The importance of the relation between number and magnitude was that numbers, for the Pythagoreans, meant certain "figures," such as a triangle, square, rectangle, and so forth. The individual points were "boundary stones" which marked out "fields." Moreover, these "triangular numbers," "square numbers," "rectangular numbers," and "spherical numbers" were differentiated by the Pythagoreans as being "odd" and "even," thereby giving them a new way of treating the phenomenon of the conflict of opposites. In all these forms, numbers were, therefore, far more than abstractions—they were specific kinds of entities. To say, then, as the Pythagoreans did, that all things *are* numbers meant for them that there is a numerical basis for all things which possess shape and size; thus they moved from arithmetic to geometry and then to the structure of reality. All things had numbers, and their odd and even values explained such opposites in things as one and many, square and oblong, straight and curved, rest and motion. Even light and dark are numerical opposites, as are male and female and good and evil.

This way of understanding numbers led the Pythagoreans to formulate their most important philosophical notion, which was, therefore, their most significant contribution to philosophy; namely, the concept of *form*. The Milesians had conceived the idea of a primary *matter* or stuff out of which everything was constituted, but they had no coherent concept of how specific things are differentiated from this single matter. They all spoke of an unlimited stuff, whether it be water, air, or the indeterminate boundless, by which they all meant some primary *matter*. It was the Pythagoreans who now came forth with the conception of *form*. For them, form meant *limit*, and limit is understandable especially in numerical terms. It is no wonder that the two arts in which the Pythagoreans saw the concept of limit best exemplified were music and medicine, for in both of these arts the central fact is harmony, and harmony is achieved by taking into account proportions and limits. In *music* there is a numerical ratio by which different notes must be separated in order to achieve concordant intervals. Harmony is the form that the limiting structure of numerical ratio imposes upon the unlimited possibilities for sounds possessed by the strings of a musical instrument. In *medicine* the Pythagoreans saw the same principle at work, health being the harmony or balance or proper ratio of certain *opposites* such as hot and cold, wet and dry, and the volumetric balance of various specific elements later known as biochemicals. Indeed, the Pythagoreans looked upon the body as they would a musical instrument, saying that health is achieved when the body is "in tune" and that disease is a consequence of undue tensions or the loss of proper tuning of the strings. The concept of number was frequently used, when translated to mean "figure," in connection with health and disease in the literature of early medicine, especially pertaining to the constitution of the human body. The *true* number, or figure, therefore, refers to the proper balance of all the elements and

Acropolis (*Royal Ontario Museum, Toronto*)

functions of the body. Number, then, represents the application of *limit* (form) to the unlimited (matter), and the Pythagoreans referred to music and medicine only as vivid illustrations of their larger concept, namely, that all things *are* numbers.

The brilliance of Pythagoras and his followers is measured to some extent by the enormous influence they had upon later philosophers and particularly upon Plato. There is much in Plato that first came to light in the teachings of Pythagoras, including the importance of the soul and its threefold division and the importance of mathematics as related to the concept of form and the Forms.

ATTEMPTS TO EXPLAIN CHANGE

Heraclitus Whereas earlier philosophers concentrated upon describing what things consist of, Heraclitus shifted attention to a new problem, the problem of *change*. His chief idea was that "all things are in flux," and he expressed this concept of constant change by saying that "you cannot step twice into the same river." The river changes because "fresh waters are ever flowing in upon you." This concept of *flux*, thought Heraclitus, must apply not only to rivers but to all things, including the soul of man. Rivers and men exhibit the fascinating fact of becoming different and yet remaining the same. We return to the "same" river although fresh waters have flowed into it, and the man is still the same person as the boy. Things change and thereby take on many different forms, but, nevertheless, they contain something which continues to be the same throughout all the flux of change. Between these many forms and the single continuing element, between the many and the one, there must be, said Heraclitus, some basic *unity*. Developing his novel and influential philosophy around 504–501 B.C., this nobleman from Ephesus described the process of change as a unity in diversity, and he did this with such imaginative skill that although some of his ideas may seem fanciful, much of what he had to say found an important place in the later philosophies of Plato and the Stoics and was deeply admired by Hegel and Nietzsche.

Flux and Fire   To describe change as unity in diversity, Heraclitus assumed that there must be *something* which changes and he argued that this something is *fire*. But he did not simply substitute the element of fire for Thales' water or Anaximenes' air. What led Heraclitus to fasten upon fire as the basic element in things was that fire behaves in such a way as to suggest how the process of change operates. Fire is simultaneously a deficiency and a surplus; it must constantly be fed and it constantly gives off something either in the form of heat, smoke or ashes. Fire is a process of transformation, then, whereby what is fed into it is transformed into something else. For Heraclitus it was not enough simply to point to some basic element, such as water, as the basic nature of reality, because this would not answer the question of how this basic stuff could change into different forms. When, therefore, Heraclitus fastened upon fire as the basic reality, he not only identified the *something* which changes but thought he had discovered the principle of change itself. To say that everything is in flux meant for Heraclitus that the world *is* an "ever-living Fire" whose constant movement is assured by "measures of it kindling and measures going out." These "measures" meant for Heraclitus a kind of balance between what kindles and what goes out of the fire, and he describes this balance in terms of financial exchange, saying that "all things are an exchange for Fire, and Fire for all things, even as wares for gold and gold for wares." With this explanation of exchange, Heraclitus sought to make the point that nothing is really ever lost in the nature of things. If gold is exchanged for wares, both the gold and the wares still continue to exist although they are now in different hands. Similarly, all things continue to exist although they exchange their form from time to time.

There is a stability in the universe because of the orderly and balanced process of change or flux, the same "measure" coming out as going in, as if reality were a huge fire that inhaled and exhaled equal amounts, preserving all the while an even inventory in the world. This inventory represents the widest array of things, all of them being simply different forms of fire. Flux and change consist of the movements of fire, movements which Heraclitus called the "upward and downward paths." The downward path of fire explains the coming into being of the things we experience so that when fire is condensed it becomes moist and this moisture under conditions of increased pressure becomes water and water, in turn, when "congealed" becomes earth. On the upward path this process is reversed, the earth being transformed into liquid and from this water come the various forms of life. Nothing is ever lost in this process of transformation because, as Heraclitus says, "fire lives the death of earth, and air the death of fire; water lives the death of air, earth that of water." With this description of the constant transformation of things in fire, Heraclitus thought he had explained the rudiments of the unity between the *one* basic stuff and the *many* diverse things in the world. But there was another significant idea that Heraclitus added to his concept of Fire, namely, the idea of *reason* as the universal law.

Reason as the Universal Law   The process of change is not a haphazard movement but the product of God's universal Reason (*logos*). This idea of *Reason* came from Heraclitus' religious conviction that the most real thing of all is the soul, and the soul's most distinctive and important attribute is wisdom or thought. But when Heraclitus speaks about God and the soul, he does not have in mind separate personal entities. For him there is only one basic reality, namely, Fire, and it is this material substance, Fire, which Heraclitus calls the One, or God. Inevitably, Heraclitus was a pantheist, since all things according to him were Fire. The soul in man is a part of God, for God is in everything. As wisdom is God's most important attribute, wisdom or thought is also man's chief activity. But inanimate things also contain the principle of reason, since they are also permeated with the fiery element. Because God *is* Reason and since God is the One, permeating all things, Heraclitus believed that God is the universal Reason which holds all things in unity and orders all things to move and change in accordance with thought or principles, and these principles and thought constitute the essence of *law*. God, as Reason, is, therefore, the universal law immanent in all things. All men share this universal law insofar as they possess God or Fire in their own natures and thereby possess the capacity for thought.

Logically, this account of man's rational nature would mean that all of man's thoughts are God's thoughts, since there is a unity between the One and the many, between God and men. All men must share in a common stock of knowledge since they all have a similar relation to God, just as, considering a different aspect of the world, all stones partake in that part of God's Reason which makes them all equally behave according to the "law" of gravity. But men notoriously disagree and often try to make inconsistent kinds of worlds in which to live. Recognizing this fact about human disagreement, Heraclitus said that "those awake have one ordered universe in common, but in sleep every man turns away to one of his own." Just how it is possible for men to "sleep," by which Heraclitus must mean to be thoughtless or even ignorant, if their souls and minds are part of God, is not explained. Still, this concept of a common universe available to all thoughtful men, this participation by all men in God's universal Reason or universal law, was one of the truly significant contributions of Heraclitus to human thought. It was this concept which provided the basis for the Stoics' idea of cosmopolitanism, the idea that all men are equally citizens of the world precisely because they all share in the One, in God's Reason, and contain in themselves some portion of the Fire, sparks of the divine. It was this concept, too, which formed the foundation for the classic theory of natural law, which, with some variations, has had a continuous impact upon Western thought and political practices, as it was preached by the Stoics, was adapted by early and medieval Christian theologians, became a dynamic force in the American Revolution, and is even in modern times a vital theory of the nature of law.

The Conflict of Opposites Although men can know the eternal wisdom that directs all things, they do not pay attention to this wisdom and, therefore, "prove to be uncomprehending" of the reasons for the way things happen to them. Men are distressed by what appear to them to be meaningless disorders in the world. They are overwhelmed by the presence of good and evil and long for the peace that means the end of strife. But Heraclitus sought to account for strife by saying that it is the very essence of change itself. The conflict of opposites is not a calamity but the permanent condition of all things. If we could visualize the whole process of change, we should know, says Heraclitus, that "war is common and justice is strife and that all things happen by strife and necessity." From this perspective, he says, "what is in opposition is in concert, and from what differs comes the most beautiful harmony." Even death is no longer a calamity, for "after death things await men which they do not expect or imagine." Throughout his treatment of the problem of strife and disorder, Heraclitus emphasizes again and again that the many find their unity in the One, so that what appear to be disjointed events and contradictory forces are in reality intimately harmonized. For this reason he says that "men do not know how what is at variance agrees with itself. It is an attunement of opposite tensions, like that of the bow and the lyre." Fire itself exhibits this tension of opposites and indeed depends upon it. Fire *is* its many tensions of opposites. In the One, the many find their unity so that in the One "the way up and the way down is the same," "good and ill are one," and "it is the same thing in us that is quick and dead, awake and asleep, young and old." This solution of the conflict of opposites rests upon Heraclitus' major assumption that nothing is ever lost but merely changes its form, that the eternal Fire moves with measured pace following the direction of Reason, that change requires opposites and diverse things. Still, "to God all things are fair and good and right, but men hold some things wrong and some right." Heraclitus came to this conclusion not because he believed that there was a personal God whose judgment it was that all things are good, but simply because he thought that "it is wise to agree that all things are one," that the One takes shape and appears in many forms.

Parmenides A younger contemporary of Heraclitus and the founder of the Eleatic school of philosophy was Parmenides, whose chief philosophical contribution was a radically novel interpretation of the phenomenon of change. Parmenides rejected Heraclitus' attempt to explain change as a unity in diversity and at the same time criticized the Milesian philosophers' theories about the origin of things. Both the Heraclitean and Milesian philosophies assumed that all things emerge out of something else, that although there is only one basic stuff in the world, this stuff is the source of a variety of things and that the process by which the One becomes many is the process of change. Parmenides, on the other hand, rejected the very notion of change, resting his argument on at least two grounds: namely, that if there is a single substance behind all things, the concept of change is absurd logically, and that the phenomenon of change is basically an illusion.

For Parmenides, the concept of change was logically neither thinkable nor expressible. He maintained that whatever exists "must *be* absolutely, or not at all." To exist in an "absolute" way meant for Parmenides that whatever is, simply *is*. We can never admit, he said, that "anything should come into being . . . out of not-being." It was this concept of "coming into being" or "becoming" which struck him as absurd, for he maintained that something either ". . . is or it is not." How can you say of anything that it came into being, that it *changed* from not-being to being? You cannot say about anything that *it* ever had non-being, for if you can think of an "it," it already exists and, consequently, there is no process of change because there is no "non-being" from which or into which a thing or a state of a thing could change. Parmenides said that "it is the same thing that can be thought that can be"; he expressed this more directly when he wrote, "you will not find thinking without being to which it refers." To think is to think about something and for this reason you cannot think of anything changing or coming into being. To think of change requires one to attempt to do the impossible; namely, to think of something in terms of what it is not. Being, or reality, is what it is and not something else. For this reason it is impossible to think of change in any clear way since the only thing one can think about is *being*, or what actually is. It follows, therefore, that *being* is absolute, that being is not divisible, since all being is alike, and, says Parmenides, ". . . all is full of being. Therefore, it is altogether continuous; for being is close to being." To make this point with greater force, Parmenides tried to show the absurdity of the concept of becoming or change by drawing out the implications of saying that something comes to be.

Wherein lies the absurdity of saying that "something comes into being"? It lies, said Parmenides, in the impossibility of saying consistently or coherently that something can *arise* either out of being or out of non-being. The assumption behind the concept of change, or of becoming, is just this, that something changes from non-being to being or from being to being. But for Parmenides this assumption made no sense for the following reason: If one says that something arises out of being, as Thales and the other Milesians did, there cannot then be any coming-into-being, for, if it arises out of being, it already is. Similarly, if something is said to arise out of non-being, one assumes that non-being is some-thing. But to say that non-being is something is clearly a contradiction since every something has being. The problem of explaining change was, according to Parmenides, equally impossible whether one had in mind explaining the large question of the origin of the total structure of reality or simply some small, particular thing. In either case, the problem is the same, namely, that some form of being must come from being or non-being. But, again, if it comes from being, then it already is, and hence there is no change or becoming, and if it comes from non-being, it is necessary to treat non-being as something in order to avoid the contradiction of saying that something comes from nothing. In either case, if there is any movement, it is from being to being, in which case there is no change, because before the "change" occurs something *is* and after the change it still *is*, in which case there was no change or movement after all.

Speaking of all reality as *It*, Parmenides says that "one path only is left for us to speak of, namely, that *It is*. In this path are very many tokens that what is, is uncreated and indestructible, for it is complete, immovable and without end." There cannot be different shades of being, because either *It* is or *It* is not, and since there is no becoming, being is not divisible. There is as much being in one place as in another, and there is no empty space. From these considerations, Parmenides argued that the *It* or reality is material in nature and is finite. Reality is a spherical, material, motionless, and fully occupied plenum, a continuous mass where there is no reality to emptiness and beyond which there is nothing. Because there is no change, reality is uncreated and is also indestructible and is, therefore, eternal and motionless.

To demonstrate the logical absurdity of the concept of change was not enough to dispel this concept from common sense. Everywhere the average man sees things in flux, and to him this represents genuine change. But Parmenides rejected the common-sense notion of change by his distinction between appearance and reality. Change, he said, is the confusion of appearance with reality, and, therefore, change is simply an illusion. What lay behind this distinction between appearance and reality was Parmenides' equally important distinction between opinion and truth. Appearance cannot produce more than opinion, whereas reality is the basis of truth. Although common sense would say that things appear to be in flux and, therefore, in a continuous process of change, this opinion based on sensation must, says Parmenides, yield to the activity of reason, which is able to discern the truth about things, and reason tells us that if there is a single substance of which everything consists, then there can be no movement or change. To some extent, the earliest philosopher, Thales, had made a similar point when he said that everything derives from water, as if to say that the appearance of things does not give us the true constitution or stuff of reality. But it was Parmenides who explicitly emphasized these distinctions, which were to become of such decisive importance in Plato's philosophy. Plato took the basic idea of Parmenides regarding the unchangeability of being and on the basis of this developed his distinction between the intelligible world and the visible world. Plato also derived from Parmenides' unchangeable being his objective and permanent Idea.

Parmenides was born about 510 B.C. and lived most of his life in Elea, a colony founded by refugee Greeks in the southwest of Italy. He flourished there in more than one capacity, giving the people of Elea laws and establishing a new school of philosophy whose followers became known as Eleatics. At the age of sixty-five, he went to Athens accompanied by his chief pupil Zeno, and there is the tradition that on this visit he conversed with the young Socrates. His rigorous attempt to draw out the logical implications of the assumption that reality consists of a single substance led him to conclude that in spite of what our senses tell us, there can be no motion or change. This severe conclusion inevitably brought forth critical challenges and ridicule, and it was Parmenides' ablest pupil Zeno whose task it became to defend his master's position against his attackers.

Zeno   Born in Elea about 489 B.C., Zeno was over forty years old when his master Parmenides was about sixty-five and when Socrates was a very young man. As a major Eleatic philosopher, Zeno was chiefly concerned with answering Parmenides' critics by showing that their own assumptions led to conclusions even more ridiculous than the ones they were criticizing. The Pythagoreans, for example, rejected the basic assumption Parmenides had accepted; namely, the assumption that reality is One. Instead, they believed in a plurality of things, that there exist a quantity of separate and distinct things and that, therefore, motion and change are real. Their argument seemed to accord more closely with common sense or the testimony of the senses. But the Eleatic approach that Zeno followed required a distinction between appearance and reality. To philosophize, according to Parmenides and Zeno, one must not only look at the world but must also think about it in order to understand it. This emphasis upon the logical relation of ideas to each other is the central characteristic of the Eleatic philosophers, and this is particularly evident in Zeno's arguments.

That the senses give us no clue to reality but only to appearance and, therefore, do not give us reliable knowledge but only opinion was demonstrated by Zeno to his own satisfaction by his reference to the millet seed. If one takes a millet seed, said Zeno, and drops it to the ground, it will not make a sound. But if one takes a half-bushel of millet seeds and lets them fall to the ground, there will be a sound. From this difference, Zeno concluded that our senses have deceived us, for either there is a sound when the single seed falls or there is not a sound when the many seeds fall. To get at the truth of things it is more reliable, then, to go by way of thought instead of sensation.

Zeno's Four Arguments or Paradoxes   In answering the critics of Parmenides, Zeno fashioned his arguments in the form of paradoxes. What he wanted to show was that it is no more possible to demonstrate the reality of motion and change in a world of many things than in the world of the One. Either way, said Zeno, there are insuperable difficulties, but the difficulties connected with proving the reality of motion on the assumption that many things exist are greater than those connected with Parmenides' view. To be sure, the casual observer of events thinks he is observing genuine motion as, for example, when he is a spectator at a race or when he sees someone shoot an arrow. But, says Zeno, this is all an illusion, for although it *appears* that there is motion, it is not possible to *think* what motion really is or to account for it rationally. To prove the impossibility of motion in a world composed of divisible reality or of multiple units, Zeno formulated the following four arguments:

1. *The racecourse.* Parmenides had said that the One is indivisible and therefore consisted of a single continuous plenum. Against this the Pythagoreans argued for a pluralistic world, saying that the world is divisible into units. If one were to consider, says Zeno, the distance around a racecourse as the Pythagoreans did, he would say that this distance must be divisible into units. According to this example of motion, the runner traverses a series of units of distance from the beginning to the end of the racecourse. But Zeno asks, just what takes place in this example? Is there really any motion? In order to traverse the racecourse, the runner, according to the Pythagorean hypothesis, would have to traverse an infinite number of points, and he would have to do this in a finite number of moments. But the critical question is, how can he traverse an infinite number of points in a finite amount of time? The reason he confronts an infinite number of points is that on the Pythagorean assumption everything is divisible; hence the distance from the beginning to the end of the racecourse is divisible. Thus, the runner cannot reach the end of the course until he first reaches the dividing line at the halfway point; but the distance from the beginning to the halfway point can also be divided in half, and he must first reach that point, the one-quarter mark, before he can reach the halfway point. Likewise, the distance between the beginning and the one-quarter point is divisible, and this process of division must go on to infinitude since there is always a remainder and every such unit is divisible. If, then, the runner cannot reach any point without first reaching its previous midpoint, and if there are an infinite number of points, it is impossible to traverse this infinite number of points in a finite amount of time. For this reason, Zeno concludes that motion does not exist.

2. *Achilles and the tortoise.* In this example, Zeno is not presenting a constructive argument of his own but is simply demonstrating where the Pythagorean premise of plural units leads one. Imagine a race between the swift Achilles and a slow tortoise where Achilles is pursuing the tortoise. Because he is a sport, Achilles gives the tortoise a head start. Zeno argues that Achilles cannot ever overtake the tortoise because he must always reach the point which the tortoise has passed so that logically the tortoise will always be ahead. The distance between Achilles and the tortoise will always be divisible and, as in the case of the racecourse, no point can be reached before the previous point has been reached, and the effect is that there can be no motion at all, and Achilles, on these assumptions, could never overtake the tortoise. What Zeno thought he had demonstrated here was, again, that although the Pythagoreans claimed the reality of motion, their theory of the plurality of the world made it impossible to think of the idea of motion in a coherent way.

3. *The arrow.* Does an arrow move when the archer shoots it at the target? Here again the Pythagoreans, who had argued for the reality of space and therefore of its divisibility, would have to say that the arrow must occupy a particular position in space. But for an arrow to occupy a position in space equal to its length is precisely what is meant when one says that the arrow is at rest. Since the arrow must always occupy such a position in space equal to its length, the arrow must always be at rest. Moreover, since any quantity, as we saw in the

FIGURE 1   FIGURE 2

example of the racecourse, is infinitely divisible, the space occupied by the arrow is infinite and as such it must coincide with everything else, in which case everything must be One instead of many. Motion, therefore, is an illusion.

4. *The relativity of motion.* Imagine three passenger cars of equal length on tracks parallel to each other, each car having eight windows on a side. One car is stationary, and the other two are moving in opposite directions at the same speed.

In Figure 1, car A is stationary, and cars B and C are moving in opposite directions at the same speed until they reach the positions indicated in Figure 2. In order to reach the positions in Figure 2, the front of car B would go past four of car A's windows while the front of car C would go past all eight of car B's windows. Each window represents a unit of distance, and each such unit is passed in an equal unit of time. Since car B went past only four of A's windows while car C went past eight of B's windows, and since each window represents the same unit of time, it would have to follow that four units of time are equal to eight units of time or that four units of distance equal eight units of distance, which is absurd. Whatever may be the inner complications of this argument, Zeno's chief point was that motion has no clear definition, that it is a relative concept.

In all these arguments, Zeno was simply counterattacking the adversaries of Parmenides, taking seriously their assumption of a pluralistic world, a world where, for example, a line or time is divisible. Instead of proving thereby that motion is real, Zeno thought he had demonstrated that the assumption of a pluralistic world lands one into insoluble absurdities and paradoxes. He, therefore, reiterated the Eleatic thesis that change and motion are illusions and that there is only one being, continuous, material, and motionless. Still, the persistence in common sense of the view that things really do move and that there is indeed change brought forth a new attempt to deal with the problem of the One and the many, and this new attempt is found in the philosophy of Empedocles.

Empedocles For Empedocles the arguments for as well as the arguments against motion and change had some merit. Instead of taking either side, however, he ingeniously combined both points of view in what was the first attempt at synthesizing the major philosophical contributions of his predecessors. He thereby discovered a consistent way of saying that there is change and at the same time affirming that reality is fundamentally changeless. He was an impressive figure in his native Agrigentum, Sicily, where he lived probably from 490 to 430 B.C. His interests and activities ranged from politics and medicine to religion and philosophy. His desire to be remembered as godlike gave rise to the tradition that he ended his life by leaping into the crater of Mt. Etna, hoping thereby to leave no trace of his body so that the people would think that he had gone up to heaven. He wrote his philosophy in the form of poetry, of which only a small portion has survived. From it one discovers not an original or new philosophy but, rather, a new way of putting together what his predecessors had already said.

Empedocles agreed with Parmenides that being is uncreated and indestructible, that it simply *is*, saying that "from what in no wise exists, it is impossible for anything to come into being; and for being to perish completely is incapable of fulfillment and unthinkable; for it will always be there, wherever any one may place it on any occasion." But unlike Parmenides, he did not agree that being consists simply of the One. To accept the notion of the One would require him to deny the reality of motion, but to Empedocles the phenomenon of motion was both too obvious and compelling to deny. He therefore rejected the idea of the One and argued instead that although Parmenides was correct in saying that being is uncreated and indestructible, being is not One but many. It is *the many* which are changeless and eternal. What Empedocles meant was that the objects we see and experience do in fact come into being and are also destroyed, and this change and motion are possible because objects are composed of many material particles. Thus, although objects can change, as Heraclitus had said, the particles of which they are composed do not change but are, as Parmenides had said about being, changeless. It is not the many *objects* that are changeless but the many *particles* of which the objects are composed that have this changeless attribute. But of what did these particles consist?

Empedocles described the particles of which objects are composed as being eternal kinds of material elements. This idea he developed by reinterpreting the philosophies of the Milesians Thales and Anaximenes. Thales had said that the stuff of which everything is composed is water, whereas Anaximenes had designated this stuff as air. Both these philosophers had tried to explain the relation between the One and the many by tracing the many to the One, by saying, for example, as Thales had done, that water becomes the various kinds of objects, as if to say that one kind of matter was transformed into other kinds of matter. Against this view, Empedocles now said that there must be certain forms of matter, such as water and air, to which he then added fire and earth, these four, which are changeless and eternal and are themselves never transformed into something else. This notion that there are four basic kinds of particles is not to be confused with the later theory of Democritus, who argued that all things consist of various arrangements of atoms. What explains the coming into being of objects is therefore not the transformation of any of these basic material elements but simply their mixture, for there is "only a mingling and interchange of what has

been mingled." Earth, air, fire, and water, though they are unchangeable particles, do mingle together to form objects and thereby make possible what in
common experience we see as change.

Empedocles thought it necessary not only to describe the basis for change
in objects through the intermingling of the various types of eternal material
particles, but also to designate the specific forces that animate the process of
change. The Ionians had assumed that the stuff of nature simply transformed
itself into various objects. Only Anaximenes had made any detailed attempt to
analyze the process of change with his theory that air becomes different things
through the process of condensation and rarefaction.

By contrast, Empedocles assumed that there are in nature positive forces,
which he called Love and Hate, or Harmony and Discord. These physical and
material forces are what cause the four elements to intermingle and later to
separate. The force of Love causes elements to be attracted to each other and to
be built up into some particular form or person, and the force of Hate causes the
decomposition of things. Expressing this never-ending cycle in his poetic style,
Empedocles writes that "this process is clearly to be seen throughout the mass of
mortal limbs: sometimes through love all the limbs which the body has as its lot
come together into one, in the prime of flourishing life; at another time again,
sundered by evil feuds, they wander severally by the breakers of the shore of life.
Likewise too with shrub plants and fish in their watery dwelling, and beasts with
mountain lairs and diver birds that travel on wings." At the beginning of each
cycle of change, the four elements are fully mingled together and are held in
Harmony by the governing principle of Love. At the same time, the force of Hate
is lurking nearby and when it invades things, the particles fall into Discord and
begin to separate until all the air particles, earth particles, and fire and water
particles have each been separated into their own four groups, ready again to
begin a new cycle as the force of Love returns to attract the elements into
harmonious combinations, and this process continues without end.

Anaxagoras   A major development in philosophy occurred when Anaxagoras
(500–428 B.C.) introduced a novel interpretation of the process by which matter
takes on the form of particular things. His major contribution was the concept of
mind (nous), which he distinguished from matter. Anaxagoras agreed with Empedocles that all coming into and going out of being consists merely in the
mixture and separation of already existing substances. But he rejected Empedocles' account that the formation of the objects of an experience is the product of
the forces of Love and Hate. The process of change called for a more adequate
explanation, according to Anaxagoras, than one based on the ambiguous and
quasimythical elements of Love and Hate. The world and all its objects appeared
to him a well-ordered and intricate structure requiring as a principle of explanation a being with knowledge and power. Such a rational principle is what Anaxagoras proposed in his concept of *mind* or *nous* as the principle that provides
matter with its order.

According to Anaxagoras, the nature of reality is best understood as consisting of *mind* and *matter*. Before mind has influenced the shape and behavior of matter, matter exists, as a mixture of various kinds of material substances, all uncreated and imperishable. Even when this original mass of matter is divided into actual objects, each part contains all "things" (*spermata*, seeds). Snow, for example, contains the opposites of black and white and is called white only because white predominates in it. In a sense, then, each part contains what is in the whole of reality, each thing having a special "portion" of everything in it.

The process by which this matter was formed into things is, according to Anaxagoras, the process of "separation." This separation was originally achieved (and continues always to occur) through the power of mind. Specifically, mind produced a rotary motion causing a vortex which spread out so as to encompass more and more of the original mass of matter, forcing a "separation" of various substances. This rotary motion originally caused a separation of matter into two major divisions, a mass which contained the warm, light, rare, and dry, and another mass which contained the cold, dark, dense, and moist. This process of separation is continuous, and there is constant progress in the process of separation. Particular objects are always combinations of substances in which some particular substance predominates. Describing this process in one of the preserved fragments of his last book, Anaxagoras says that "Nous set in order all things that were to be and are now and that will be, and this revolution in which now revolve the stars and the sun and the moon and the air and the aether which are separated off." Continuing, he says, "the revolution itself caused the separating off, and the dense is separated off from the rare, the warm from the cold, the bright from the dark, and the dry from the moist. And there are many portions of many things." Emphasizing the continued mixture of things, he says that "no thing is altogether separated off from anything else except Nous." Forces set in motion in the vortex account for the appearance of the thick and moist at the center and the thin and warm at the circumference, that is, of the earth and the atmosphere. The forces of rotation also caused red-hot masses of stones to be torn away from the earth and to be thrown into the ether, and this is the origin of the stars. The earth, originally mud, was dried by the sun and fertilized by germs contained in the air. Everything, even now, is animated by mind, including life in plants and sense perception in human beings. Mind is everywhere, or as Anaxagoras says, nous is "there where everything else is, in the surrounding mass."

Although Anaxagoras considered nous the moving or controlling force in the cosmos and in human bodies, his account of the actual role of nous was limited. For one thing, the nous was not for Anaxagoras the *creator* of matter, since he held that matter is eternal. Moreover, he did not see in nous the source of any *purpose*. His explanation of the origin of particular things in the process of "separation" appears to be a mechanical explanation. Things still appear to be the products of the action of material causes, and mind appears to have no distinctive role apart from starting motion. Aristotle, who later was so concerned to distinguish the different kinds of causes, expressed a double evaluation of Anaxagoras' views. Comparing Anaxagoras to his predecessors, who were willing "to entrust so great a matter [i.e. the origin of things] to spontaneity and chance," Aristotle wrote that "when [Anaxagoras] said . . . that reason was present—as in animals, so throughout nature—as the cause of order and of all arrangement, he seemed like a sober man in contrast with the random talk of his predecessors." But, adds Aristotle, Anaxagoras made use of his concept of nous only "to a small extent." His criticism was that "Anaxagoras uses reason as a *deus ex machina* for making the world, and when he is at a loss to tell from what cause something necessarily is, then he drags reason in, but in all other cases ascribes events to anything rather than reason." Anaxagoras seemed to provide only an explanation of how matter acquired its rotary motion, leaving the rest of the order of nature to be a product of that motion. Still, what Anaxagoras had to say about reason was of great consequence in the history of philosophy because he thereby introduced a mental principle into the nature of things. He differentiated mind and matter. While he may not have described mind as completely immaterial, he did nevertheless distinguish mind from the matter it had to work with, saying that mind, unlike matter, "is mixed with nothing, but is alone, itself by itself." What made mind different from matter was that it is "the finest of all things and the purest, and it has all knowledge about everything and the greatest power. . . ." Thus, while matter is composite, mind is simple. But Anaxagoras did not distinguish two different worlds, that of mind and that of matter, but saw these two as always interrelated, since mind is "there where everything else is. . . ." Although he had not worked out all the possibilities of his concept of nous, this concept was nevertheless destined to have enormous influence in later Greek philosophy.

THE ATOMISTS

Leucippus and Democritus formulated a theory about the nature of things that bears an astonishing resemblance to some twentieth-century scientific views. The atomist philosophy that they elaborated was the final answer to Thales' question before philosophy took a new turn at the hands of Socrates, Plato, and Aristotle. Although it is difficult now to disentangle the individual contribution Leucippus and Democritus each made to this atomistic theory, inasmuch as their writings are lost for the most part, it is known that Leucippus was the founder of the atomist school and that Democritus supplied much of the detailed elaboration of it. Leucippus was a contemporary of Empedocles (490–430 B.C.), whereas Democritus, born in Abdera, Thrace, is reputed to have lived one hundred years, from 460 to 360 B.C. Through his immense learning and painstaking attempt to state with clarity his abstract theory of atomism, Democritus inevitably overshadowed Leucippus, to whom, nevertheless, the credit must be given for the insight that everything is made up of atoms moving in space.

Atoms and the Void The philosophy of atomism originated, according to Aristotle, as an attempt to overcome the logical consequences of the Eleatic denial of space. Parmenides had denied that there could be many independent things because everywhere there was *being*, in which case the total reality would be

One. Specifically, he denied the existence of non-being or the void, because to say that there *is* the void is to say that the void *is something*. It is impossible, he thought, to say that there *is* nothing. Yet, in order to prove that there is motion and change it is necessary to assume that there is empty space in which things can move. But empty space is nothing, yet to say that it *is* meant for Parmenides that space is part of the total *Is*. By arguing that there is only the One, since there could be no areas of non-being between things to give things separate spheres of existing, Parmenides thought he had proved that there could be no motion or change. It was precisely to reject this Eleatic treatment of space or the void that Leucippus formulated his new theory.

Leucippus affirmed the reality of space and thereby prepared the way for a coherent theory of motion and change. What had complicated Parmenides' concept of space was his thought that whatever exists must be *material*, wherefore space, if it existed, must also be material. Leucippus, on the other hand, thought it possible to affirm that space exists without having to say at the same time that it is material. Thus, he described space as something like a receptacle that could be empty in some places and full in others. As a receptacle, space, or the void, could be the place where objects move, and Leucippus apparently saw no reason for denying this characteristic of space. Without this concept of space, it would have been impossible for Leucippus and Democritus to develop that part of their philosophy for which they are best known, namely, that all things consist of atoms.

According to Leucippus and Democritus, the nature of things consists of an infinite number of particles or units called atoms. To these atoms both Leucippus and Democritus ascribed the characteristics that Parmenides had ascribed to the One, namely, indestructibility and, therefore, eternity. Whereas Parmenides had said reality consists of a single One, the atomists now said that there are an infinite number of atoms, each one being completely full, containing no empty spaces, therefore being completely hard and indivisible. These atoms exist in space and differ from each other in shape and size, and because of their small size, they are invisible. Since these atoms are eternal, they did not have to be created. Nature consists, therefore, of two things only: namely, *space*, which is a vacuum, and *atoms*. The atoms move about in space, and their motion leads them to form the objects we experience.

The atomists did not think it was necessary to account for the origin of this motion of the atoms in space. The original motion of these atoms, they thought, was similar to the motion of dust particles as they dart off in all directions in a sunbeam even when there is no wind to impel them. Democritus said that there is no absolute "up" or "down," and since he did not ascribe *weight* to atoms, he thought atoms could move in any and all directions. Things as we know them have their origin in the motion of the atoms. Moving in space, the atoms originally were single individual units, but inevitably they began to collide with each other, and in cases where their shapes were such as to permit them to interlock, they began to form clusters, or what Anaxagoras had called *vortices*. In this the atomists resembled the Pythagoreans, who had said that all things are numbers.

Things, like numbers, are made up of combinable units, and things, for the atomists, were simply combinations of various kinds of atoms. Mathematical figures and physical figures were, therefore, thought to be similar.

In the beginning, then, there were atoms in space. Each atom is like the Parmenidean One, but though they are indestructible, they are in constant motion. The stuff about which Thales, Anaximenes, Heraclitus, and Empedocles spoke, namely, water, air, fire, and earth, these the atomists described as different clusters of changeless atoms, the product of the movement of originally single atoms. These four elements were not the primeval "roots" of all other things but were themselves the product of the absolutely original stuff, the atoms.

The atomists had produced a mechanical conception of the nature of things. For them, everything was the product of the collision of atoms moving in space. Their theory had no place in it for the element of *purpose* or *design*, and their materialistic reduction of all reality to atoms left no place, and in their minds no need, for a creator or designer. They saw no need to account either for the origin of the atoms or for the original motion impelling the atoms, since the question of origins could always be asked, even about God. For them, to ascribe eternal existence to the material atoms seemed as satisfactory as any other solution.

So formidable was this atomistic theory that, although it went into a decline after Aristotle and during the Middle Ages, it was revived and provided science with its working model for centuries to come. Sir Isaac Newton (1642–1727) still thought in atomistic terms when he wrote his famous *Principia*, in which, having deduced the motion of the planets, the comets, the moon, and the sea, he wrote in 1686, "I wish we could devise the rest of the phenomena of Nature by the same kind of reasoning from mechanical principles, for I am induced by many reasons to suspect that they may all depend upon certain forces by which the particles of bodies, by some causes hitherto unknown, are either mutually impelled towards one another and cohere in regular figures, or are repelled and recede from one another." Although Newton assumed God had set things in motion, his physical analysis of nature was restricted to the mechanical principles of matter moving in space. What Leucippus and Democritus had envisioned, therefore, had a long and influential history. Their materialism was soon rejected in the metaphysical theories of Plato and Aristotle, but the theory of bodies in motion as the explanation of nature was revived in the sixteenth century and held sway until the quantum theory and Einstein gave the twentieth century a new conception of matter, denying the attribute of indestructibility to the atoms.

Democritus was concerned with two other philosophical problems besides describing the structure of nature: namely, the problem of knowledge and the problem of human conduct. This portion of his philosophy developed as a reaction to issues raised by Protagoras concerning the nature of knowledge and by the Sophists, who doubted the possibility of any stable rules for ethics. Although Democritus' views on these subjects derive their force only when seen in relation to the views of Protagoras and the Sophists, with which we shall deal later, it can be said now that Democritus tried to deal with these subjects in a way consistent with his mechanical view of nature.

Being a thorough materialist, Democritus held that *thought* can be explained in the same way that any other phenomenon can, namely, as the movement of atoms. He distinguished between two different kinds of perception, one of the senses and one of the understanding, both of these being physical processes. When the eye sees something, this something is an "effluence" or the shedding of atoms by the object, forming an "image." These atomic images of things enter the eyes (and other organs of sense) and make an impact upon the soul, which is itself made up of atoms. Whereas Protagoras said that our senses are all equally reliable, that everything we sense really is what we sense it to be, Democritus disagreed, saying that "there are two forms of knowledge, the trueborn and the bastard. To the bastard belong all these: sight, hearing, smell, taste, touch. The trueborn is quite apart from these."

What distinguishes these two modes of thought is that whereas "trueborn" knowledge depends only on the object, "bastard" knowledge is affected by the particular conditions of the body of the person involved. This is why two persons can agree that what they have tasted is an apple (trueborn) and still disagree about the taste (bastard knowledge), one saying the apple is sweet and the other saying it is bitter, so that, concludes Democritus, "by the senses we know in truth nothing sure, but only something that changes according to the disposition of the body and of the things that enter into it or resist it." Still, Democritus had to say that both sensation and thought are the same type of mechanical process.

When Democritus came to the other problem, however, the problem of ethics, he appears to have departed from his mechanical view of things. For one thing, if all reality is mechanically interlocked, there would hardly be any point in giving advice on how to behave, since each person's movements would be determined by the movement of other things, and conduct would not be within a person's control. In spite of this technical contradiction in his philosophy, Democritus developed a very lofty set of rules for human behavior, urging moderation in all things along with the cultivation of culture as the surest way of achieving the most desirable goal of life, namely, cheerfulness.

With the emergence of ethics as its primary concern, philosophy reached one of its major watersheds, closing out the first era where the principal question had been about the natural physical order. Now men would ask more searching questions about how they should behave.

2

Socrates
and the Sophists:
the Problems
of Truth and
Goodness

The first philosophers had focused their attention upon nature; the Sophists and Socrates shifted the concerns of philosophy to the study of man. Instead of asking the large cosmic questions about the ultimate principle of things, philosophy became preoccupied with questions relating more directly to man's behavior. This transition from predominantly scientific concerns to basic ethical questions is explained in part by the failure of the pre-Socratics to arrive at any uniform conception of the cosmos. Inconsistent interpretations of nature had been proposed, and there appeared to be no way of reconciling them. Heraclitus had said that nature consists of a plurality of substances and that everything is in a process of constant change or flux, whereas Parmenides took the opposite view, arguing that reality is a single, static substance, the One, and that motion and change are illusions cast upon our senses by the appearances of things. Had these contradictory cosmologies produced simply an intellectual fatigue by virtue of the sheer difficulty of deciphering the secrets of nature, or an impatience and disinterest in pursuing a philosophic activity that gave no promise of a successful outcome, philosophy might have stopped at this point. As it was, the controversy over the ultimate principle of things had generated a mood of skepticism about the ability of human reason to discover the truth about nature. But this very mood, this skepticism, provided the impulse for a new direction for philosophy, for skepticism itself became the subject of serious concern.

Instead of debating about alternative theories of nature, philosophers now addressed themselves to the problem of human knowledge, asking whether it was possible for the human mind to discover any universal truth. This question had been further aggravated by the disclosure of cultural differences between various races and peoples so that the question about truth became deeply implicated with the problem of goodness. Could there be a universal concept of goodness if men were incapable of knowing any universal truth? The principal parties to this new debate were the Sophists and Socrates.

THE SOPHISTS

The three most outstanding Sophists who emerged in Athens sometime during the fifth century B.C. were Protagoras, Gorgias, and Thrasymachus. They were part of a group who had come to Athens either as traveling teachers or, as in the case of Hippias of Elis, as ambassadors, and they called themselves Sophists or "intellectuals." Coming as they did from different cultures, Protagoras from Abdera in Thrace, Gorgias from Leontini in southern Sicily, and Thrasymachus from Chalcedon, they took a fresh look at Athenian thought and customs and asked searching questions about them. They became the great spokesmen of the Greek enlightenment by forcing the Athenians to consider whether their ideas and customs were founded upon truth or simply upon conventional ways of behaving. Was their distinction between Greeks and barbarians, they asked, as well as that between masters and slaves, based upon evidence or simply upon prejudice? Not only had the Sophists lived in different countries with their different customs, but they had also gathered a wide fund of information based upon the observation of a multitude of cultural facts. Their encyclopedic knowledge of different cultures made them skeptical about the possibility of attaining any absolute truth by which a society might order its life. They forced upon thoughtful Athenians the question whether Hellenic culture was based upon man-made rules or upon nature, whether their religious and moral codes were conventional and, therefore, changeable or *natural* and, therefore, permanent. In a decisive way, the Sophists set the stage for a more deliberate and careful consideration of the nature of man, how he acquires knowledge, and how he might order his behavior.

The Sophists were primarily practical men, and the circumstances of Athenian democracy under Pericles were such that their practical skills were quickly put to use. It was their interest and competence in prose and grammar as well as their skill in discourse that made them uniquely pertinent to the current scene. Under Pericles, the aristocracy had been replaced by democracy, and this had the effect of intensifying political life in Athens by drawing the free citizens into political discussion and making them eligible for leadership. But the older aristocratic education had not prepared men for the new conditions of democratic life, for that education had been founded for the most part upon family tradition. There had been no disciplined and theoretical training in the areas of religion, grammar, and the careful interpretation of the poets. The Sophists moved into this cultural vacuum, and their practical interest in teaching filled an urgent need. They became popular lecturers and were the chief source of the new education. What made them particularly sought after was that they professed, above all, to teach the art of *rhetoric*, the art of persuasive speech. The power of persuasion had become a political necessity in the democratic Athens for anyone who hoped to rise to the level of leadership. Because of their extensive knowledge of grammar and their fund of information about various cultures as well as their wide experience derived from their travels and teaching in many places, the Sophists possessed all that was needed to train the emerging new Athenian citizen.

The reputation of the Sophists was at first very favorable. They rendered an immense service by training men to present their ideas clearly and forcefully. Clear speech and the power of persuasion were especially indispensable in a popular assembly where it would be disastrous to permit debate among unskilled speakers who could neither present their own ideas effectively nor discover the errors in their opponents' arguments. But rhetoric became somewhat like a knife in that it could be employed for good or ill use, to cut bread or to kill. One who possessed the power of persuasion could use that power either to cut through a difficult problem and through psychological resistance to a good idea on the one hand, or, on the other, he could use it to put over an idea in which he had a special interest, the intrinsic goodness of which was questionable. The shift from the one use of rhetoric to the other was greatly facilitated by the inherent skepticism of the Sophists. It was their skepticism and relativism that made them suspect. No one would have criticized them for training lawyers, as they did, to be able to argue either side of a case. Surely a person deserves to have his defense presented with as much skill as the prosecutor uses against him. As long as the art of persuasion was linked to the pursuit of truth there could be no quarrel with the Sophists. But since they looked upon truth as a relative matter, it was inevitable that they should be charged with teaching young men how to make a bad case look good or to make the unjust cause appear to be just. Furthermore, they developed the reputation of gathering together young men from good families only to lead them in a critical and destructive analysis of their traditional religious and ethical views. To add further to their ill repute, they departed from the earlier image of the philosopher as a disinterested thinker who did not engage in philosophy for gain. The Sophists, by contrast, charged fees for their teaching and appeared to seek out the rich, who were able to pay these fees. Socrates had studied under the Sophists, but because of his poverty could only afford their "shorter course." This practice of charging fees for their teaching prompted Plato to disparage them as "shopkeepers with spiritual wares."

Protagoras   Among the Sophists who had come to Athens, Protagoras of Abdera was the oldest and, in many ways, the most influential. He is best known for his statement that "man is the measure of all things, of the things that are, that they are, and of the things that are not, that they are not." To say that man is the measure of all things apparently meant to Protagoras that whatever knowledge man could achieve about anything would be limited to his human capacities. He dismissed any discussion of theology, saying that "About the gods, I am not able to know whether they exist or do not exist, nor what they are like in form; for the factors preventing knowledge are many: the obscurity of the subject, and the shortness of human life." Knowledge, said Protagoras, is limited to our various perceptions and these perceptions will differ with each person. If two persons were to observe the same object, their sensations would be different, because each would occupy a different position in relation to it. Similarly, the same breeze blowing at one person would feel cool to him, while it would be warm to another. Whether the breeze is or is not cold cannot be answered in a simple way. It is in fact cold for one person and warm for the other. To say that man is the measure of all things is, therefore, to say that our knowledge is measured by what we perceive, and if there is something about each person that makes him perceive things in a different way, there is no standard for testing whether one person's perception is right and another person's wrong. Protagoras thought that the objects men perceive by their various senses must possess all the properties that different men perceive as belonging to them. For this reason, it is impossible to discover what is the "true" nature of anything; a thing has as many characteristics as there are people perceiving it. There is no way to distinguish between "appearance" and "reality"; for the person who says that the breeze is cold it really *is* cold and does not simply appear so just because it feels warm to somebody else. On this theory of knowledge, it would be impossible to build any scientific knowledge, because it rejects the possibility of discovering what nature is really like since there are built-in differences in each observer leading each one to see things differently. Protagoras concluded, therefore, that knowledge is relative to each person.

When he turned to the subject of ethics, Protagoras maintained that moral judgments are relative. He was willing to admit that the idea of law reflects a general desire in each culture for a moral order among men. But he denied that there was any uniform law of nature pertaining to human behavior that all peoples everywhere could discover. He distinguished between nature and custom or convention and said that laws and moral rules are based, not upon nature, but upon convention. Each society has its own laws and its own moral rules, and there is no way, apart from certain common-sense observations about their relative "soundness," of judging some to be true and others wrong. But Protagoras did not carry this moral relativism to the extreme revolutionary position of saying that because moral judgments are relative, every individual can decide what is moral. Instead, he took the conservative position that the state makes the laws and that these laws should be accepted by everyone because they are as good as any that can be made. Other communities might have different laws, and individuals within a state might think of different laws, but in neither case are these better laws; they are only different. In the interests of a peaceful and orderly society, then, men should respect and uphold the customs, laws, and moral rules their tradition had carefully nurtured. In matters of religion, Protagoras took a similar view, saying that the impossibility of knowing with certainty about the existence and nature of the gods should not prevent anyone from participating in the worship of the gods. The curious outcome of Protagoras' relativism was his conservative conclusion that young men should be educated to accept and support the tradition of their society, not because this tradition is true but because it makes possible a stable society. Still, there could be no question that Protagoras' relativism had seriously dislodged men's confidence in the possibility of discovering true knowledge and had brought upon his skepticism the heavy criticism of Socrates and Plato.

Gorgias   Gorgias came to Athens from Sicily as ambassador from his native city of Leontini in 427 B.C. He took such a radical view regarding truth that he eventually gave up philosophy and turned instead to the practice and teaching of rhetoric. This radical view differed from Protagoras' in that while Protagoras said that everything is true, that truth is relative to persons and circumstances, Gorgias denied that there is any truth at all. With hair-splitting keenness, employing the mode of reasoning used by the Eleatic philosophers Parmenides and Zeno, Gorgias propounded the extraordinary notions (1) that nothing exists, (2) that if anything exists it is incomprehensible, and (3) that even if it is comprehensible, it cannot be communicated. Taking this third notion, for example, he argued that we communicate with words, but words are only symbols or signs and no symbol can ever be the same as the thing it symbolizes. For this reason, knowledge can never be communicated. By this mode of close reasoning, Gorgias thought he could prove all three of his propositions, or at least that his reasoning was as coherent as any used by those who disagreed with him. He was convinced, consequently, that there could be no reliable knowledge and certainly no truth.

Abandoning philosophy, Gorgias turned to rhetoric and tried to perfect it as the art of persuasion. It is said that he developed, in this connection, the technique of deception, making use of his knowledge of psychology and of the powers of suggestion. Having earlier concluded that there is no truth, he was willing to employ the art of persuasion for whatever practical ends he chose.

Thrasymachus   In the *Republic*, Thrasymachus is portrayed as the Sophist who asserted that injustice is to be preferred to the life of justice. He did not look upon injustice as a defect of character. On the contrary, Thrasymachus considered the unjust person as positively superior in character and intelligence. Indeed, he said that "injustice pays," not only at the meagre level of the pickpocket, although there is profit in that too, but especially in the case of those who carry injustice to perfection and make themselves masters of whole cities and nations. Justice, he said, is pursued by simpletons and leads to weakness. Thrasymachus held that a person should aggressively pursue his own interests in a virtually unlimited form of self-assertion. He regarded justice as being the inter-est of the stronger and believed that "might is right." Laws, he said, are made by the ruling party for its own interest. These laws define what is right. In all states alike "right" has the same meaning for "right" is the interest of the party estab-lished in power. So, says Thrasymachus, "the sound conclusion is that what is 'right' is the same everywhere: the interest of the stronger party."

Here, then, is the reduction of morality to power, an inevitable logical consequence of the progressive radicalism of the Sophists which led them to a nihilistic attitude toward truth and ethics. It was Socrates' chief concern to unravel the logical inconsistencies of the Sophists and to rebuild some notion of truth and also establish some firm foundation for moral judgments.

SOCRATES

Many Athenians had mistaken Socrates for a Sophist. The fact is that Socrates was one of the Sophists' keenest critics. That Socrates should have been identi-fied with them was due in part to his relentless analysis of any and every subject, a technique employed also by the Sophists. But between the Sophists and Socra-tes there was a fundamental difference. The Sophists split hairs to show that equally good arguments could be advanced on either side of any issue. They were skeptics who doubted that there could be any certain or reliable knowledge. Moreover, they concluded that since all knowledge is relative, moral ideas and ideals are also relative. Socrates, on the other hand, had a different motivation for his constant argumentation. He was committed to the pursuit of truth and con-sidered it his mission to seek out the basis for stable and certain knowledge. He was also attempting to discover the foundation for the good life. As he pursued his mission, Socrates devised a method for arriving at truth, linking *knowing* and *doing* to each other in such a way as to argue that to know the good is to do the good, that "knowledge is virtue." Unlike the Sophists, then, Socrates engaged in argumentation, in "dialectic," not for ends destructive of truth or to develop pragmatic skills among lawyers and politicians, but to achieve creative concepts of truth and goodness.

Socrates' Life   Seldom has there been a time and place so rich in men of genius as the Athens into which Socrates was born in 470 B.C. By this time, Aeschylus had written some of his great dramatic works. Euripides and Sophocles were young boys who were to produce great tragedies that Socrates may very well have attended. Pericles, who was to usher in a great age of democracy and the flowering of art, was still a young man. Socrates could have seen the Parthenon and the statues of Phidias started and completed during his lifetime. By this time, too, Persia had been defeated, and Athens had advanced toward becoming a naval power with control over much of the Aegean Sea. Athens had reached a level of unprecedented power and splendor. But though Socrates grew up in a golden age, his declining years were to see Athens defeated in war and his own

Socrates (*The Bettmann Archive*)

life brought to an end in prison where, in 399 B.C., at the age of seventy-one, he drank the hemlock in compliance with the death sentence meted out by the court that tried him.

Socrates wrote nothing. Most of what we know about him has been preserved by three of his famous younger contemporaries, Aristophanes, Plato, and Xenophon. From these sources Socrates emerges as an intense genius who along with his extraordinary rational rigor possessed a personal warmth and a fondness for humor. He was a robust man with great powers of physical endurance. In his playful comedy, *The Clouds*, Aristophanes depicts Socrates as a strutting waterfowl, poking fun at his habit of rolling his eyes and referring impishly to his "pupils" and "thinking shop." But from Xenophon comes the portrait of a loyal soldier who has a passion for discussing the requirements of morality and who inevitably attracted the younger men to seek out his advice. Plato confirmed Xenophon's portrait and in addition pictured Socrates as a man with a deep sense of mission and absolute moral purity. In the *Symposium*, Plato relates how Alcibiades, a fair youth, expected to win the amorous affections of Socrates, contriving in various ways to be alone with him, but, says Alcibiades, ". . . nothing of the sort occured at all: he would merely converse with me in his usual manner, and when he had spent the day with me he would leave me and go his way." In military campaigns, Socrates could go without food longer than anyone else, and while others wrapped themselves up with "prodigious care" against the bitter cold of winter, using "felt and little fleeces" over their shoes, Socrates, says Alcibiades, "walked out in that weather, clad in just such a coat as he was always wont to wear, and he made his way more easily over the ice unshod than the rest of us did in our shoes."

Socrates was capable of intense and sustained concentration. On one occasion during a military campaign, he stood in deep contemplation for a day and night, "till dawn came and the sun rose: then walked away after offering a prayer to the sun." This may have been the occasion on which he experienced what he considered a mandate to pursue the mission of prophetic concern over the moral life of his fellow men. He had frequently received messages or warnings from a mysterious "voice" or what he called his *daimon*. Although this "supernatural sign" invaded his thoughts from early childhood, it suggests more than anything else Socrates' sensitivity as a "visionary," particularly his sensitivity to the moral qualities of human actions that make life worth living. He must have been familiar with the natural science of the earlier Ionian philosophers and Anaxagoras, although he does say in the *Apology* that "the simple truth is, O Athenians, that I have nothing to do with physical speculations." For him, such speculations had to give way to the more urgent questions about human nature, about truth, and about goodness. The decisive event that confirmed his mission as a moral philosopher was the reply of the Delphic Oracle. When Chaerophon asked the Oracle whether there was any living person who was wiser than Socrates, the Oracle replied that there was not. Socrates interpreted this reply to mean that he was the wisest because he realized and admitted his own ignorance. In this mood, Socrates set out on his quest for abiding truth and wisdom.

Socrates as a Philosopher   Because Socrates left no writings of his own, there is today some disagreement over what philosophical ideas can be properly attributed to him. Our most extensive sources of his thought are the *Dialogues* of Plato, in which he is, especially in the earlier dialogues, the leading character. But the persistent question is whether Plato is here reporting what Socrates had actually taught or expressing his own ideas through the figure of Socrates. There are those who argue that the Socrates found in Plato's dialogues is the historically correct Socrates. This would mean that Socrates must get all the credit for the novel philosophical activity these dialogues contain, giving Plato credit only for the literary form he devised for preserving, elaborating, and lending precision and color to Socrates' thought. On the other hand, Aristotle distinguished between the philosophical contributions made by Socrates and Plato. To Socrates Aristotle gave the credit for "inductive arguments and universal definitions," and to Plato he ascribed the development of theory of Forms, the notion that universal Ideas, or Forms, exist independently of the particular things that embody them. The argument, for the most part, is over whether Socrates or Plato developed the theory of Forms. Since Aristotle was himself particularly interested in this subject, having discussed it at length with Plato in the Academy, it seems reasonable to suppose that his distinction between Socrates' and Plato's ideas is accurate. At the same time, some of the early dialogues are clearly accurate representations of Socrates' own thought, as in the case of the *Apology* and the *Euthyphro*. The most plausible solution to the problem, therefore, would be to accept portions of both views, agreeing that the earlier dialogues are portrayals of Socrates' philosophic activity whereas the later dialogues represent Plato's own philosophic development, including his formulation of the metaphysical theory of the Forms. On this basis, Socrates is seen as an original philosopher who developed a new method of intellectual inquiry.

If Socrates was to be successful in overcoming the relativism and skepticism of the Sophists, he had to discover some immovable foundation upon which to build the edifice of knowledge. This foundation Socrates discovered not in the facts of the world outside of man but within man. The interior of man, said Socrates, is the seat of a unique activity, the activity of knowing, which leads to the practical activity of doing. To describe this activity, Socrates created the conception of the soul, the *psyche*. For him the soul was not any particular faculty, nor was it any special kind of substance, but was rather the capacity for intelligence and character; it was man's conscious personality. Socrates further described what he meant by the soul as "that within us in virtue of which we are pronounced wise or foolish, good or bad." By describing it in these terms, Socrates identified the soul with the normal powers of intelligence and character instead of as some ghostly substance. The soul was the structure of personality. However difficult it may have been for Socrates to describe exactly what the soul is, what he was sure of was that the activity of the soul is to *know* and to influence or even direct and govern a person's daily conduct. Although for Socrates the soul was not a *thing*, he could say that man's greatest concern should be the proper care of his soul so as to "make the soul as good as possible." One takes best care of his soul when he understands the difference between fact and fancy and builds his thought upon a knowledge of what human life is really like. Having attained such knowledge, the man who has the proper care of his soul in mind will conduct his behavior in accordance with his knowledge of the true moral values. Socrates was primarily concerned with *the good life* and not with mere contemplation.

The immovable point in this conception of the soul was, for Socrates, man's conscious awareness of what some words mean. To know that some things contradict others, that justice cannot mean harming others, represented for Socrates a typical example of the kind of knowledge the soul can attain just by using its powers to know. To act in defiance of this knowledge, to harm someone even when one knows that such behavior is contrary to one's knowledge of justice, is to do violence to one's nature as a human being. Socrates was certain that men could attain sure and reliable knowledge and that only such knowledge could be the proper basis of morality. His first major task was, therefore, to clarify for himself and his followers just how one attains reliable knowledge.

Socrates' Theory of Knowledge: Intellectual Midwifery   Socrates was convinced that the surest way to attain reliable knowledge was through the practice of disciplined conversation, acting as an intellectual midwife, a method he called *dialectic*. This was a deceptively simple technique. It would always begin with a discussion of the most obvious aspects of any problem. Socrates believed that through the process of dialogue, where each party to the conversation was forced to clarify his ideas, the final outcome of the conversation would be a clear statement of what was meant. Although the technique appeared simple, it was not long before anyone upon whom Socrates employed it could feel its intense rigor as well as the discomfort of his irony. In the earliest dialogues in which this method is displayed, as, for example, in the *Euthyphro*, Socrates would feign ignorance about a subject and try to draw out from the other person the fullest possible knowledge about it. He considered this method of dialectic a kind of intellectual midwifery. His assumption was that by progressively correcting incomplete or inaccurate notions, one could coax the truth out of anyone. His reliance was solely upon the permanent structure of the soul, on man's capacity for knowing and for recognizing lurking contradictions. If the human mind was incapable of knowing something, Socrates would want to demonstrate that, too, believing that no unexamined idea is worth having any more than the unexamined life is worth living. Some dialogues therefore end inconclusively, since Socrates was not concerned with imposing a set of dogmatic ideas upon a listener but with leading him through an orderly process of thought.

A good example of Socrates' method is found in his dialogue with Euthyphro. The scene is in front of the Hall of King Archon, where Socrates is waiting in the hope of discovering who has brought suit against him for *impiety*, which was a capital offense. He wants to know what that charge means. When young Euthyphro arrives upon the scene, Socrates discovers that he has come to prosecute a suit of his own, charging that his father was guilty of impiety. With devastating irony, Socrates expresses relief at his good fortune in meeting him, for Euthyphro is making the identical charge against his father that has been made against Socrates. Sarcastically, Socrates says to Euthyphro that "not every one could rightly do what you are doing; only a man who is well advanced in wisdom." Only someone who knew exactly what impiety meant would charge anyone with such a serious offense, and to bring such a charge against one's *father* would only corroborate the assumption that the accuser knew what he was talking about. Socrates professes ignorance of the meaning of impiety and asks Euthyphro to explain what it means, since he has charged his father with this offense.

Euthyphro answers Socrates by defining piety as "prosecuting the wrongdoer" and impiety as not prosecuting him. To this Socrates replies that "I did not ask you to tell me one or two of all the many pious actions that there are; I want to know what is the idea of piety which makes all pious actions pious." Since his first definition was unsatisfactory, Euthyphro tries again, this time saying that "what is pleasing to the gods is pious." But Socrates refers to the stories of quarrels among the gods, indicating that the gods disagree among themselves about what is better and worse. The same act, then, can be pleasing to some gods and not pleasing to others, wherefore Euthyphro's second definition is also inadequate. Trying to repair the damage, Euthyphro offers a new definition, saying that "piety is what *all* the gods love, and impiety is what they *all* hate." But, asks Socrates, "do the gods love an act because it is pious, or is it pious because the gods love it?" In short, what is the *essence* of piety? Trying again, Euthyphro says that piety is "that part of justice which has to do with the attention which is due to the gods. . . ." Again, Socrates presses for a clearer definition by asking what kind of attention is due to the gods. By this time, Euthyphro is hopelessly adrift, and Socrates says to him that "it cannot be that you would ever have undertaken to prosecute your aged father for the murder of a laboring man unless you had known exactly what is piety and impiety." And when Socrates presses him once more for a clearer definition. Euthyphro answers, "Another time . . . Socrates. I am in a hurry now, and it is time for me to be off."

Though the dialogue thus ends inconclusively, as far as the subject of piety is concerned, it is a vivid example of Socrates' method of dialectic and a portrayal of his conception of the philosophical life. More specifically, it illustrates Socrates' unique concern with *definition* as the instrument of clear thought.

Definition   Nowhere is Socrates' approach to knowledge more clearly displayed than in his preoccupation with the process of definition. For him, a definition was a clear and fixed concept. What impressed Socrates was that although particular events or things varied in some respects or passed away, there was something about them that was the same, that never varied and never passed away, and this was their definition or their essential nature. It was this permanent meaning that Socrates wanted Euthyphro to give him when he asked for that "idea of piety by which pious acts are pious." In a similar way, Socrates sought the Idea of *Justice* by which acts become just or the Idea of *Beauty* by which particular things are said to be beautiful and the Idea of *Goodness* by which we recognize human acts to be good. No particular thing is perfectly beautiful, but insofar as it is beautiful it is because it partakes of Beauty. Moreover, when a beautiful thing passes away, the Idea of Beauty remains. Socrates was struck by the ability of the mind to think about general ideas and not only about particular things. In some way, the mind, he thought, thinks of two different kinds of objects whenever it thinks about anything. A beautiful flower is at once this particular flower and at the same time a single example or partaker of the general or universal meaning of Beauty. The process of definition was for Socrates the process by which the mind could distinguish or sort out these two objects of thought, namely, the particular (this beautiful flower) and the general or universal (the Idea of Beauty of which this flower partakes so as to make it a beautiful flower). If Socrates asked, "What is a beautiful flower?" or "What is a pious act?" he would not be satisfied with your pointing to this flower or this act. For, although Beauty is in some way connected with something, that thing does not either equal or exhaust the Idea of Beauty. Moreover, although various beautiful things differ from each other, whether they be flowers or persons, they are each called beautiful because in spite of their differences, they share in common that element by which they are called beautiful. Only by the rigorous process of definition does the mind finally grasp the distinction between a particular thing (this beautiful flower) and the general fixed notion (Beauty or beautiful). The process of definition, as Socrates worked it out, was a process for arriving at clear and fixed concepts.

Through his technique of definition, Socrates indicated that true knowledge is more than simply an inspection of facts. Knowledge has to do with the power of the mind to discover in facts the abiding elements that remain after the facts disappear. Beauty remains after the rose fades. To the mind an imperfect triangle suggests *the* Triangle and imperfect circles are seen as approximations to the perfect Circle, the definition of which produces the clear and fixed notion of Circle. Facts can produce a variety of notions, for no two flowers are the same. By the same token, no two persons or no two cultures are the same. If one limited his knowledge simply to uninterpreted facts, he would conclude that everything is different, that there are no universal likenesses. The Sophists did just this, arguing from the facts they had collected about other cultures that all ideas of justice and goodness are relative. But Socrates would not accept this conclusion. To him the factual differences between men, the differences in their height, strength, and mental ability, did not obscure the equally certain fact that they were all men. By his process of definition, he cut through the obvious factual differences about them to discover what caused all these men to be men in spite of their differences. His clear concept of *Man* provided him with a firm basis for thinking about men. Similarly, though cultures differ, though their actual laws and moral rules differ, still, said Socrates, the Ideas of Law, Justice, and Goodness can be defined as rigorously as the Idea of Man. Instead of leading to intellectual skepticism and moral relativism, Socrates believed that the manifold of facts could yield clear and fixed concepts if one employed the technique of analysis and definition.

Behind the world of facts, then, Socrates believed there was an order in things that the mind could discover. This led him to introduce into philosophy a way of looking at everything in the universe that was more fully developed by Plato and by Aristotle, and this was the *teleological* conception of things, the view that things have a function or purpose. To say that something—for example, a man—has a definable nature is also to say that there is an activity appropriate to his nature. If man is a rational being, acting rationally is the behavior appropriate to human nature. From this it is a short step to saying that a man *ought* to act rationally. By discovering the essential nature of everything, Socrates believed that he could thereby also discover the intelligible order in everything. In this view, things had not only their own specific natures and functions, but these functions had some additional purpose in the whole scheme of things. There are many kinds of things in the universe, not because of some haphazard mixture, but because each thing does one thing best and all of them acting together make up the orderly universe. Clearly, Socrates could distinguish two levels of knowledge, one based upon the *inspection* of facts and the other based upon an *interpretation* of facts, one based upon particular things and the other based upon general or universal Ideas or conceptions. That universal Ideas, such as Beauty, Straight, Triangle, and Man, were always used in discourse certainly suggested that there was some basis in reality for their use. The big question soon to arise was whether these universal Ideas or words refer to some existing reality in the same way that particular words do. If the word *John* refers to a person existing in a particular place, does the word *Man* also refer to some reality someplace? Whether Socrates dealt with this problem of the metaphysical status of universals depends upon whether we consider Plato or Socrates to be the author of the doctrine of the Forms, of the *theory of Ideas*. Plato certainly taught that these Ideas, whatever they are, are the most real things there are, and that they have a separate existence from the particular things we see, which partake of these Ideas. Aristotle rejected this theory of the separate existence of Ideas, arguing that in some way these universal Ideas exist only in the actual things we experience. He indicated, too, that Socrates had not "separated off" these Ideas from things. If Socrates was not the author of the theory of Ideas found in the Platonic dialogues, he was, nevertheless, the one who had fashioned the concept of an intelligible order lying behind the visible world.

Socrates' Moral Thought   For Socrates, knowledge and virtue were the same thing. If virtue has to do with "making the soul as good as possible," it is first necessary to know what makes the soul good. Goodness and knowledge are, therefore, closely related. But Socrates said more than simply that goodness and knowledge are related. He identified these two, saying that to know the good is to do the good, that knowledge is virtue. By identifying knowledge and virtue, Socrates meant also to say that vice, or evil, is the absence of knowledge. Just as knowledge is virtue, so, too, vice is ignorance. The outcome of this line of reasoning was Socrates' conviction that no one ever indulged in vice or committed an evil act knowingly. Wrongdoing, he said, is always involuntary, being the product of ignorance.

To equate virtue with knowledge and vice with ignorance may seem to contradict the most elementary experience of most human beings. Our common sense tells us that we frequently indulge in acts that we know to be wrong, so that wrongdoing for us is a deliberate and voluntary act. Socrates would have readily agreed that men commit acts that can be called evil. He denied, however, that anybody deliberately did an evil act because he knew it to be evil. When someone commits an evil act, said Socrates, he always does it thinking that it is good in some way.

When he equated virtue and knowledge, Socrates had in mind a particular conception of virtue. For him, virtue meant fulfilling one's function. As a rational being, a man's function is to behave rationally. At the same time, every human being has the inescapable desire for happiness or the well-being of his soul. This inner well-being, this "making the soul as good as possible," can be achieved only by certain appropriate modes of behavior. Because man has a desire for happiness, he chooses his acts with the hope that they will bring him happiness. Which acts, or what behavior, will produce happiness? Socrates knew that some forms of behavior *appear* to produce happiness, but in *reality* do not. For this reason, men frequently choose an act that may in itself be questionable but that they, nevertheless, think will bring them happiness. A thief may know that stealing as such is wrong, but he steals in the hope that it will bring him happiness. Similarly, men pursue power, physical pleasure, and property, which are the symbols of success and happiness, confusing these with the true ground of happiness.

The equating of vice with ignorance is not so contrary to common sense after all, for the ignorance Socrates speaks of refers not to the act itself but to its ability to produce happiness. It is ignorance about one's soul, about what it takes to "make the soul as good as possible." Wrongdoing is, therefore, a consequence of an inaccurate estimate of modes of behavior. It is the inaccurate expectation that certain kinds of things or pleasures will produce happiness. Wrongdoing, then, is the product of ignorance simply because it is done with the hope that it will do what it cannot do. Ignorance consists in not knowing that certain behavior cannot produce happiness. It takes a true knowledge of human nature to know what it requires to be happy. It also takes a true knowledge of things and types of behavior to know whether they can fulfill the human requirements for happiness. And it requires knowledge to be able to distinguish between what *appears* to give happiness and what *really* does.

To say, then, that vice is ignorance and is involuntary is to say that no one ever deliberately chooses to damage, disfigure, or destroy his human nature. Even when one chooses pain, he does so with the expectation that this pain will lead to virtue, to the fulfillment of human nature, a nature that seeks its own well-being. One always thinks he is acting rightly, but whether his actions are right depends upon whether they harmonize with the true nature of man, and this is a matter of true knowledge. Moreover, because Socrates believed that the fundamental structure of human nature is constant, he believed also that certain ways of behaving and, therefore, certain moral values are also constant. This was the basis for his great triumph over the Sophists' skepticism and relativism. Socrates set the direction that moral philosophy would take throughout the history of Western civilization. His thought was modified by Plato, Aristotle, and the Christian theologians, but it remained the dominant intellectual and moral tradition around which other variations developed.

Socrates' Trial and Death   Convinced that the care of the human soul should be a man's greatest concern, Socrates spent most of his time examining his own life and the life and thought of his fellow Athenians. While Athens was a secure and powerful democracy under Pericles, Socrates could pursue his calling as a "gadfly" without serious opposition. His relentless quest for the stable and constant moral order underlying man's fitful behavior proved alternately irritating and amusing, giving him the reputation of an intellectual dealing in paradoxes and, worse still, of thinking freely on matters about which many Athenians believed that discussion should be closed. But what Socrates could do without penalty when the economic and military position of Athens was strong, he could no longer do in the days of crisis and defeat. To develop the dialectic skill among the young men from leading families, the skill of raising searching questions about customs in moral, religious, and political behavior, did raise suspicions about Socrates earlier, but his actions were not considered a clear and present danger until Athens was at war with Sparta.

A series of events connected with this war eventually led to the trial and sentence of Socrates. One event was the traitorous actions of Alcibiades, whom the Athenians knew was Socrates' pupil. Alcibiades had actually gone to Sparta and had given valuable advice to the Spartans in their war with Athens. Inevitably many Athenians concluded that Socrates must in some way be responsible for what Alcibiades had done. In addition, Socrates found himself in serious disagreement with the Committee of the Senate of Five Hundred, of which he was a member. The issue before them was the case of eight military commanders who were charged with negligence at a naval battle off the islands of Arginusae, a battle that the Athenians won in the end but at the staggering cost of 25 ships and 4,000 men. It was decided that the eight generals involved in this expensive campaign should be brought to trial and that their guilt should be determined not individually but as a group by a single vote. At first the Committee resisted this move, holding it to be a violation of the regular constitutional procedures. But when the prosecutors threatened to add the names of the Committee members to the list of generals, only Socrates stood his ground, and the rest of the Committee capitulated. The generals were then found guilty, and the six of them who were in custody were immediately put to death. This had occurred in 406 B.C., and in 404 B.C., with the fall of Athens, Socrates once again found himself in opposition to a formidable group. Under pressure from the Spartan victor, a Commission of Thirty was set up in order to fashion legislation for the new government of Athens. Instead, this group became a violent oligarchy, arbitrarily executing former stalwarts of Pericles' democratic order and taking property for themselves. Within a year, this oligarchy was removed by force, and a democratic order was restored. But unfortunately for Socrates, some of the members of the revolutionary oligarchy had been his close friends, particularly Critias and Charmides. This was another occasion of guilt by association, as in the case of Alcibiades, where Socrates was put in the position of being a teacher of traitors. By this time, irritation had developed into distrust, and in 400/399, Socrates was brought to trial on the charge, as Diogenes Laertius recorded it, "(1) of not worshipping the gods whom the State worships, but introducing new and unfamiliar religious practices; (2) and, further, of corrupting the young. The prosecutor demands the death penalty."

Socrates could have gone into voluntary exile upon hearing the charges against him. Instead, he remained in Athens and defended himself before a court whose jury numbered about five hundred. His defense, as recorded in Plato's *Apology,* is a brilliant defense of his intellectual activities and a powerful exposure of his accusers' motives and inadequate grounds for their charges. He made much of his devotion to Athens, including references to his military service and his actions in upholding constitutional procedures in the trial of the generals. His defense is a model of forceful argument, resting wholly upon a recitation of facts and upon the requirements of rational discourse. When he was found guilty, he was given the opportunity to suggest his own sentence. Being convinced not only of his innocence but of the great value his mode of life and teachings had contributed to Athens, he proposed that Athens should reward him by giving him what he deserved. Comparing his life with someone "who has won victory at the Olympic games with his horse or chariots," Socrates said, "such a man only makes you seem happy, but I make you really happy." Therefore, he said, his reward should be "public maintenance in the prytaneum," an honor bestowed upon eminent Athenians, generals, Olympian winners, and other outstanding men. Affronted by his arrogance, the jury sentenced him to death.

His friends tried to the end to make possible his escape, but Socrates would have none of it. Just as he refused to play on the emotions of the jury by calling attention to his wife and young children, so now he was not impressed by Crito's plea that he should think of his children. How could he undo all he had taught others and unmake his conviction that he must never play fast and loose with the truth? Socrates was convinced that to escape would be to defy and thereby injure Athens and its procedures of law. That would be to strike at the wrong target. The laws were not responsible for his trial and sentence; it was his accusers, Anytus and Meletus, who were at fault. Accordingly, he confirmed his respect for the laws and its procedures by complying with the court's sentence.

Describing Socrates' last moments after he drank the poisonous potion, Plato writes in his *Phaedo* that "Socrates felt himself, and said that when it came to his heart, he should be gone. He was already growing cold . . . and spoke for the last time. Crito, he said, I owe a cock to Asclepius; do not forget to pay it. . . . Such was the end, Echecrates, of our friend, a man, I think, who was, of all the men of his time, the best, the wisest and the most just."

3

Plato

In Plato, the Greek genius was realized with extraordinary completeness. So powerful was Plato's comprehensive treatment of knowledge that his philosophy became the most influential strand in the history of Western thought. Unlike his predecessors who focused upon single main problems, Plato brought together all the major concerns of human thought into a coherent organization of knowledge. The earliest philosophers, the Milesians, were concerned chiefly with the constitution of physical nature, not with the foundations of morality. Similarly, the Eleatic philosophers Parmenides and Zeno were interested chiefly in arguing that reality consists of a changeless, single reality, the One. Heraclitus and the Pythagoreans, on the other hand, described reality as always changing, full of flux, and consisting of a vast multitude of different things. Socrates and the Sophists showed less interest in physical nature and, instead, steered philosophy into the arena of morality. Plato's great influence stems from the manner in which he brought all these diverse philosophic concerns into a unified system of thought.

Plato began with the common-sense recognition of the variety of things that pass in parade before our view. To make sense out of these many things, he realized that the mind must discover reasons for the way these physical things behave. This pursuit led him to a world behind the world of things. It was the world of thought and Ideas, the world of science. Physical things, he thought, lead the mind to the science of physics. To understand the science of physics requires, moreover, the intellectual grasp of mathematics, for to understand the behavior of things—not these particular things only, but any and all such things under similar circumstances—the mind must discover the principles and rules that things in their behavior obey. The model for thinking about such rules is the model of mathematics, for mathematics is a way of thinking without being tied to particulars.

Inevitably, mathematics led Plato into the field of metaphysics. If physics is made possible by the mind's emancipation from the world of appearances, by the mind's operation in the world of Ideas "above" or "behind" the world of visible things, one cannot avoid the question whether this world of Ideas *exists* or is *real*. Indeed, Plato was to argue in time that, contrary to common sense, it was this world of Ideas and not the visible world of actual things that is most real, that the Idea *Two*, for example, has a timeless quality, whereas two apples disappear.

At this point, Plato argued that the reason for disagreements between men concerning truth was that they confused these two worlds; only the world of timeless Ideas could produce true knowledge, whereas the world of appearances could produce only opinion. Here Plato followed his great master Socrates in repudiating the skepticism of the Sophists, whose denial that true knowledge can be attained about anything would have made science impossible. Similarly, Plato rejected the moral relativism of the Sophists, arguing that his theory of knowledge formed a reliable bridge from metaphysics to ethics. If, that is, we have knowledge about the true nature of things, of reality, including the true nature of man, we have also the basic clue to how men should behave. Human behavior is at once a personal matter, a matter involving one's fellowman, and, finally, a matter raising the question of one's ultimate destiny. For Plato, these three facets of human concern were to be dealt with through the separate but related disciplines of ethics, politics, and religion. When we consider, then, that Plato rather systematically brought together his theory of knowledge, physics, metaphysics, ethics, politics, and religion, as well as a theory of art, we can all the more appreciate how it was that, along with Aristotle, he shaped the mind of Western man, that the moral philosophy and the scientific tradition of Western civilization are essentially the achievements of Plato's thought.

Plato was born in Athens in 428/27 B.C., one year after the death of Pericles and when Socrates was about forty-two years old. Athenian culture was flourishing, and as Plato's family was one of the most distinguished in Athens, his early training must have included the rich ingredients of that culture in the arts, politics, and philosophy. His father traced his lineage to the old kings of Athens and before them to the god Poseidon, while his mother, Perictione, was the sister of Charmides and the cousin of Critias, both of whom were leading personalities in the short-lived oligarchy which followed the fall of Athens in the Peloponnesian War. When his father died, early in Plato's childhood, his mother married Pyrilampes, who had been a close friend of Pericles. Such close ties with eminent public figures had long distinguished Plato's family, especially on his mother's side, where an early relative had been a friend of the great giver of law, Solon, and another distant member of the family was the archon, or the highest magistrate, in 644 B.C.

In such a family atmosphere, it was inevitable that Plato would learn much about public life and develop at an early age a sense of responsibility for public political service. But Plato's attitude toward Athenian democracy was also influenced by what he saw during the last stages of the Peloponnesian War. He saw the inability of this democracy to produce great leaders and saw also the way it treated one of its greatest citizens, Socrates. Plato was present at Socrates' trial and had expressed willingness to guarantee payment of his fine. The collapse of Athens and the execution of his master Socrates could well have led Plato to despair of democracy and to begin formulating a new conception of political leadership in which authority and knowledge are appropriately combined. Plato had concluded that as in the case of a ship, where the pilot's authority rests upon his knowledge of navigation, so also the ship of state should be piloted by one who has adequate knowledge, a theme which he developed at length in his *Republic*.

Plato was aware of the various modes of philosophy circulating in Athens, but the decisive influence in the formation of his thought was the life and teaching of Socrates. Plato had known Socrates from his early youth, and from his friendship with him had discovered a new meaning for philosophy. Philosophy was for Plato, as for Socrates, not merely a specialized and technical activity but a way of life. Since philosophy would range over all questions both in science and in the realm of human behavior, it would require not only intellectual ability but also certain moral qualities that one associates with the pursuit of truth and of goodness. The purpose of relating all branches of knowledge was, for Plato, to enable men to understand how they fit into the scheme of the universe. Ultimately, by philosophic activity, by the continuous and passionate exercise of the mind, men could relate themselves to the world and also achieve an inner integrity of all their powers and capacities.

Plato did not assume that he had discovered perfect knowledge or absolute truth, any more than Socrates had. What he was certain about was that the surest way of going after knowledge is the dialectic method, the method of dialogue in which a premise or hypothesis is continuously subjected to counterargument. This was Socrates' method, and life. With genuine humility and intellectual receptivity, Socrates pursued an unending quest for just the right way to understand and adjust to those conditions that alone could produce the good life. Though he really never had "pupils," he, nevertheless, became the model for Plato's philosophic life. But whereas Socrates wrote nothing, Plato became a prolific writer. Moreover, while Plato preserved Socrates' dialectic method by casting his writings into dialogue form, he embellished Socrates' moral concern by building around it his metaphysical system, his philosophy of nature and reality.

At the height of his powers, around 387 B.C., after he had written most of his dialogues and when he was about forty years old, Plato founded the Academy at Athens. This was, in a sense, the first university to emerge in the history of Western Europe, and for twenty years, Plato administered its affairs as its director. The chief aim of the Academy was to pursue scientific knowledge through original research. Although Plato was particularly concerned with educating

Plato (*The Bettmann Archive*)

statesmen, he was convinced that their education must consist of rigorous intellectual activity, by which he meant scientific study, including mathematics, astronomy, and harmonics.

The scientific emphasis at the Academy was in sharp contrast to the activities of Plato's contemporary Isocrates, who also engaged in training young men for public life. Isocrates had little use for science, holding that pure research had no practical value or humanistic interest. Instead, he set out to teach techniques of clear and effective expression and persuasion, developing in his students the ability to expound dominant opinions or some particular point of view. But Plato put mathematics into the center of his curriculum, arguing that the best preparation for those who will wield political power is the disinterested pursuit of truth or scientific knowledge. Here the mind is trained to cut through opinion and emotion and by hard thinking to confront the facts of reality and to base judgments on knowledge. Plato's emphasis upon rigorous mathematical and scientific study at once repudiated the superficial approach of the Sophists and attracted some of the ablest thinkers to the Academy. A brilliant group of scholars associated with the Academy made significant advances over the mathematical knowledge of the older Pythagoreans, and this activity caused the famous mathematician Eudoxus to bring his own School from Cyzicus to unite with Plato's Academy in Athens.

Plato, it is said, lectured at the Academy without the use of any notes. These lectures were on subjects and ways of treating subjects which were different from what we find in his written *Dialogues*. Plato's lectures were never published because they were never written, although his hearers' notes were circulated. Aristotle entered the Academy in 367 B.C., when he was eighteen years old, and took notes of Plato's lectures. Later, unlike Plato, Aristotle lectured from a written manuscript but never published popular works, which Plato's *Dialogues* were, for the most part, apparently meant to be.

Plato's dialogues number more than twenty—an extensive literary production—and, as mentioned above, most of them were written by the time he had founded the Academy, that is, by the time he was around forty years old. These include, first, a group of early writings, usually called Socratic dialogues because of their preoccupation with ethics, consisting of the *Apology, Crito, Charmides, Laches, Euthyphro, Euthydemus, Cratylus, Protagoras,* and *Gorgias*; the second, or middle, group in which the theory of Ideas and metaphysical doctrines are expounded include the *Meno, Symposium, Phaedo, Republic,* and *Phaedrus*. Later in life, Plato wrote some more technical dialogues dealing with the structure of nature and representing at once the views of one who has had much time to reflect on problems and a mood of deepening religious conviction, these dialogues being the *Theaetetus, Parmenides, Sophist, Statesman, Philebus, Timaeus,* and the *Laws*.

Although the execution of Socrates had deeply disillusioned Plato about politics to the extent of diverting him personally from an active life of public service, Plato nevertheless continued to teach that rigorous knowledge must be the proper training of the ruler. He gained a wide reputation for this view and was invited to Syracuse, a place he traveled to at least three times, to give instruction to a young tyrant, Dionysius II. His efforts did not meet with success since his student's education was started too late and his character was too weak. Plato continued to write in his ripe years, and while still active in the Academy, died in 348/47 B.C. at the age of eighty.

Plato's complete works constitute a full system of philosophy. But Plato did not himself organize his thoughts into such an explicit system, for to him system building seemed artificial. Although his many dialogues do contain the elements of a full system, there is no one work to which we can go to find a schematic arrangement of his thought. Plato wanted to preserve the freedom of his mind so that he could restate his ideas if new insights came to him. He never closed out future discussion of any subject just because he had once written about it. Accordingly, his dialogues reflect his intellectual development and display changes in emphasis and insight. Still, certain clear topics and unique ways of treating them emerge from Plato's works, and to deal with Plato's philosophy we turn now to some of these major topics.

PLATO'S THEORY OF KNOWLEDGE

Plato described how the human mind achieves knowledge, and indicated what knowledge consists of, by means of (1) his allegory of the *Cave*, (2) his metaphor of the *Divided Line*, and (3) his doctrine of the *Forms*.

The Cave   Plato asks us to imagine some men living in a large cave where from childhood they have been chained by the leg and by the neck so that they cannot move. Because they cannot even turn their heads, they can only see what is in front of them. Behind them is an elevation that rises abruptly from the level where the prisoners are seated. On this elevation there are other persons walking back and forth carrying artificial objects, including the figures of animals and human beings made out of wood and stone and various other materials. Behind these walking persons is a fire, and farther back still is the entrance to the cave. The chained prisoners can look only forward against the wall at the end of the cave and can see neither each other nor the moving persons nor the fire behind them. All that the prisoners can ever see is the shadows on the wall in front of them, which are projected as persons walk in front of the fire. They never see the objects or the men carrying them, nor are they aware that the shadows are shadows of other things. When they see a shadow and hear a person's voice echo from the wall, they assume that the sound is coming from the shadow, since they are not aware of the existence of anything else. These prisoners, then, recognize as reality only the shadows formed on the wall.

What would happen, asks Plato, if one of these prisoners were released from his chains, were forced to stand up, turn around, and walk with eyes lifted up toward the light of the fire? All of his movements would be exceedingly painful. Suppose he were forced to look at the objects being carried, the shadows of which he had become accustomed to seeing on the wall. Would he not find these actual objects less congenial to his eyes, and less meaningful, than the shadows? And would not his eyes ache if he looked straight at the light from the fire itself? At this point he would undoubtedly try to escape from his liberator and turn back to the things he could see with clarity, being convinced that the shadows were clearer than the objects he was forced to look at in the firelight.

Suppose this prisoner could not turn back, but was instead dragged forcibly up the steep and rough passage to the mouth of the cave and released only after he had been brought out into the sunlight. The impact of the radiance of the sun upon his eyes would be so painful that he would be unable to see any of the things that he was now told were real. It would take some time before his eyes became accustomed to the world outside the cave. He would first of all recognize some shadows and would feel at home with them. If it were the shadow of a man, he would have seen that shape before as it appeared on the wall of the cave. Next, he would see the reflections of men and things in the water, and this would represent a major advance in his knowledge, for what he once knew only as a solid dark blur would now be seen in more precise detail of line and color. A flower makes a shadow which gives very little, if any, indication of what a flower really looks like, but its image as reflected in the water provides the eyes with a clearer vision of each petal and its various colors. In time, he would see the flower itself. As he lifted his eyes skyward, he would find it easier at first to look at the heavenly bodies at night, looking at the moon and the stars instead of at the sun in daytime. Finally, he would look right at the sun in its natural positions in the sky and not at its reflection from or through anything else.

This extraordinary experience would gradually lead this liberated prisoner to conclude that the sun is what makes things visible. It is the sun, too, that accounts for the seasons of the year, and for that reason the sun is the cause of life in the Spring. Now he would understand what he and his fellow prisoners saw on the wall, how shadows and reflections differ from things as they really are in the visible world, and that without the sun there would be no visible world.

How would such a person feel about his previous life in the cave? He would recall what he and his fellow prisoners there took to be wisdom, how they had a practice of honoring and commending each other, giving prizes to the one who had the sharpest eye for the passing shadows and the best memory for the order in which they followed each other so that he could make the best guess as to which shadow would come next. Would the released prisoner still think such prizes were worth having, and would he envy the men who received honors in the cave? Instead of envy he would have only sorrow and pity for them.

If he went back to his former seat in the cave, he would at first have great difficulty, for going suddenly from daylight into the cave would fill his eyes with darkness. He could not, under these circumstances, compete very effectively with the other prisoners in making out the shadows on the wall. While his eyesight was still dim and unsteady, those who had their permanent residence in the darkness could win every round of competition with him. They would at first find this situation very amusing and would taunt him by saying that his sight was perfectly all right before he went up out of the cave and that now he has returned with his sight ruined. Their conclusion would be that it is not worth trying to go up out of the cave. Indeed, says Plato, "if they could lay hands on the man who was trying to set them free and lead them up, they would kill him."

Most of mankind, this allegory would suggest, dwell in the darkness of the cave. They have oriented their thoughts around the blurred world of shadows. It is the function of *education* to lead men out of the cave into the world of light. Education is not simply a matter of putting knowledge into a person's soul that does not possess it, any more than vision is putting sight into blind eyes. Knowledge is like vision in that it requires an organ capable of receiving it. Just as the prisoner had to turn his whole body around in order that his eyes could see the light instead of the darkness, so also it is necessary for the entire soul to turn away from the deceptive world of change and appetite that causes a blindness of the soul. Education, then, is a matter of *conversion,* a complete turning around from the world of appearance to the world of reality. "The conversion of the soul," says Plato, is "not to put the power of sight in the soul's eye, which already has it, but to insure that, instead of looking in the wrong direction, it is turned the way it ought to be." But looking in the right direction does not come easily. Even the "noblest natures" do not always want to look that way, and so Plato says that the rulers must "bring compulsion to bear" upon them to ascend upward from darkness to light. Similarly, when those who have been liberated from the cave achieve the highest knowledge, they must not be allowed to remain in the higher world of contemplation, but must be made to come back down into the cave and take part in the life and labors of the prisoners.

Arguing, as Plato did, that there are these two worlds, the dark world of the cave and bright world of light, was his way of rejecting the skepticism of the Sophists. For Plato knowledge was not only possible, but it was virtually infallible. What made knowledge infallible was that it was based upon what is most *real.* The dramatic contrast between the shadows, reflections, and the actual objects was for Plato the decisive clue to the different degrees to which human beings could be enlightened. Plato saw the counterparts of shadows in all of human life and discourse. Disagreements between men concerning the meaning of justice, for example, were the result of each one's looking at a different aspect of the reality of justice. One person might take justice to mean whatever the rulers in fact command the people to do, on the assumption that justice has to do with rules of behavior laid down by the ruler. Just as a shadow bears some relation to the object of which it is the shadow, so this conception of justice has some measure of truth to it, for justice does have some connection with the ruler. But different rulers command different modes of behavior, and there could be no single coherent concept of justice if men's knowledge of justice were derived from the wide variety of examples of it. The Sophists were skeptical about the possibility of true knowledge because they were impressed by the variety and constant change in things, and, they argued, since our knowledge comes from our experience, our knowledge will reflect this variety and will, therefore, be relative to each person. Plato agreed that such knowledge as is based upon our sense experiences would be relative and not absolute, but he would not accept the Sophists' notion that *all* knowledge is relative. "The ignorant," writes Plato, "have no single mark before their eyes at which they must aim in all the conduct of their lives. . . ." If all we could know were the shadows, we could never have reliable knowledge, for these shadows would always change in size and shape depending upon the, to us, unknown motions of the real objects. Plato was convinced that the human mind could discover that "single mark," that "real" object behind all the multitude of shadows, so that the mind could attain true knowledge. There is, he believed, a true Idea of Justice, an Idea that can be blurred by rulers and communities. This line of reasoning lay behind Plato's distinction between the world of sense and the world of thought, between the visible world and the intelligible world. Whereas the allegory of the Cave illustrates these distinctions in dramatic terms, Plato's metaphor of the Divided Line sets forth the stages or levels of knowledge in more systematic form.

The Divided Line   In the process of discovering true knowledge, the mind, says Plato, moves through four stages of development. At each stage, there is a parallel between the kind of object presented to the mind and the kind of thought this object makes possible. These objects and their parallel modes of cognition can be diagramed as follows:

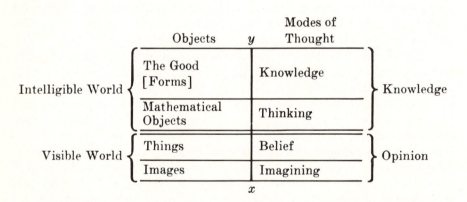

The vertical line from x to y is a continuous one, suggesting that there is some degree of knowledge at every point. But as the line passes through the lowest forms of reality to the highest, there is a parallel progression from the lowest degree of truth to the highest. The line is divided, first of all, into two unequal parts. The upper and larger part represents the intelligible world and the smaller, lower part the visible world. This unequal division symbolizes the lower degree of reality and truth found in the visible world as compared with the greater reality and truth in the intelligible world. Each of these parts is then subdivided in the same proportion as the whole line, producing four parts, each one representing a clearer and more certain mode of thought than the one below.

Recalling the allegory of the Cave, we can think of this line as beginning in the dark and shadowy world at *x* and moving up to the bright light at *y*. Going from *x* to *y* represents a continuous process of the mind's enlightenment. The objects presented to the mind at each level are not four different kinds of real objects: rather, they represent four different ways of looking at the same object.

Imagining   The most superficial form of mental activity is found at the lowest level of the line. Here the mind confronts images, or the least amount of reality. The word *imagining* could, of course, mean the activity of penetrating beyond the mere appearances of things to their deeper reality. But here Plato means by *imagining* simply the sense experience of appearances wherein these appearances are taken as true reality. An obvious example is a shadow, which can be mistaken for something real. Actually, the shadow *is* something real; it is a real shadow. But what makes imagining the lowest form of knowing is that at this stage the mind does not know that it *is* a shadow or an image that it has confronted. If a person knew that it was a shadow, he would not be in the state of imagining or illusion. The prisoners in the cave were trapped in the deepest ignorance because they were unaware that they were seeing shadows.

Besides shadows, there are other kinds of images which Plato considered deceptive. These are the images fashioned by the artist and the poet. The artist presents images that are at least two steps removed from true reality. Suppose an artist paints a portrait of Socrates. Socrates represents a specific or concrete version of the Ideal Man. Moreover, the portrait represents only the artist's own view of Socrates. The three levels of reality here are, then, (1) the Idea of Man, (2) the embodiment of this Idea in Socrates, and (3) the image of Socrates as represented on canvas. Plato's criticism of art is that it produces images that, in turn, stimulate illusory ideas in the observer. Again, it is when the image is taken as a perfect version of something real that illusion is produced. For the most part, men know that an artist puts on canvas his own way of seeing a subject. Still, artistic images do shape men's thoughts, and if men restrict their understanding of things to these images with all their distortions and exaggerations, they will certainly lack an understanding of things as they really are.

What concerned Plato most were the images fashioned by the art of using words. Poetry and rhetoric were for him the most serious sources of illusion. Words have the power of creating images before the mind, and the poet and rhetorician have great skill in using words to create such images. Plato was particularly critical of the Sophists, whose influence came from this very skill in the use of words. They could make either side of an argument *seem* as good as the other. In a discussion of justice, for example, the Sophist, or any other artist with words, could create the same distortion that we found in the portrait. Justice as understood in Athens could be taken by a pleader and distorted in favor of a special client. This special pleader's version of justice could be a distortion of the Athenian view; also, the Athenian view might very well be a distortion of the Ideal Justice. If someone heard only the special pleader's version of justice, he would be at least twice removed from the true Idea of Justice. There is no illusion if the special pleader's distortions of Athenian justice are recognized as such. Moreover, it would be possible for some citizens to recognize that Athenian law itself represented some deviations from the true concept of Justice. Everything depends upon what the mind has access to as its object. The special pleader does present some degree of truth about Justice but in a very distorted form, just as a shadow gives some evidence of some reality. Imagining, however, implies that a person is not aware that he is observing an image, and, therefore, imagining amounts to illusion and ignorance.

Belief   The next stage after imagining is belief. It may strike one as strange that Plato should use the world *believing* instead of *knowing* to describe the state of mind induced by seeing actual objects. We tend to feel a strong sense of certainty when we observe visible and tangible things. Still, for Plato, seeing constitutes only believing, because visible objects depend upon their context for many of their characteristics. There is, then, a degree of certainty that seeing gives us, but this is not absolute certainty. If the water of the Mediterranean looks blue from the shore but turns out to be clear when taken from the sea, one's certainty about its color or composition is at least open to question. That all bodies have weight because we see them fall may seem a certainty, but this testimony of our vision must also be adjusted to the fact of the weightlessness of bodies in space at certain altitudes. Plato therefore says that believing, even if it is based upon seeing, is still in the stage of opinion. The state of mind produced by visible objects is clearly on a level higher than imagining, because it is based upon a higher form of reality. But although actual things possess greater reality than their shadows, they do not by themselves give us all the knowledge we want to have about them. Again, justice may be seen in a particular context, but to find justice defined in a different way in another culture does raise the question about the true nature of Justice. Whether it be color, weight, or justice, these properties of things and acts are experienced under particular circumstances. For this reason, our knowledge about them is limited to these particular circumstances. But the mind is unsatisfied with this kind of knowledge, knowing that its certainty could very well be shaken if the circumstances were altered. The scientist and the jurist, therefore, do not want to confine their understanding to these particular cases, but look for principles behind the behavior of things.

Thinking   When a person moves from believing to thinking, he moves from the visible world to the intelligible world, from the realm of opinion to the realm of knowledge. The state of mind that Plato calls *thinking* is particularly characteristic of the scientist. The scientist deals with visible things but not simply with his vision of them. For him, visible things are symbols of a reality that can be thought but not seen. Plato illustrates this kind of mental activity by referring to the mathematician. The mathematician engages in the act of "abstraction," of drawing out from the visible thing what that thing symbolizes. When a mathematician sees the diagram of a triangle, he thinks about *triangularity* or triangle-in-itself. He distinguishes between the *visible* triangle and the *intelligible* triangle.

By using visible symbols, science provides a bridge from the visible to the intelligible world. Science forces one to think, because the scientist is always searching for laws or principles. Although the scientist may look at a particular object, a triangle or a brain, he goes beyond this particular triangle or brain and thinks about *the* Triangle or *the* Brain. Science requires that we "let go" our senses and rely instead upon our intellects. The mind knows that two and two equal four no matter two of what. It knows also that the angles of an equilateral triangle are all equal, regardless of the size of the triangle. Thinking, therefore, represents the power of the mind to abstract from a visible object that property which is the same in all objects in that class even though each such actual object will have other variable properties: we can, in short, think the Idea *Man* whether we observe small, large, dark, light, young, or old persons.

Thinking is characterized not only by its treatment of visible objects as symbols, but also by reasoning from *hypotheses*. By an hypothesis Plato meant a truth which is taken as self-evident but which depends upon some higher truth: "You know," says Plato, "how students of subjects like geometry and arithmetic begin by postulating odd and even numbers, or the various figures and the three kinds of angle. . . . These data they take as known, and having adopted them as assumptions, they do not feel called upon to give any account of them to themselves or to anyone else but treat them as self-evident." Using hypotheses, or "starting from these assumptions, they go on until they arrive, by a series of consistent steps, at all the conclusions they set out to investigate." For Plato, then, an hypothesis did not mean what it means to us, namely, a temporary truth. Rather, he meant by it a firm truth but one that is related to a larger context. The special sciences and mathematics treat their subjects as if they were independent truths. All Plato wants to say here is that if we could view all things as they really are, we should discover that all things are related or connected. Thinking or reasoning from hypotheses does give us knowledge of the truth, but it does still bear this limitation, that it isolates some truths from others, thereby leaving the mind still to ask *why* a certain truth is true.

Perfect Intelligence The mind is never satisfied as long as it must still ask for a fuller explanation of things. But to have perfect knowledge would require that the mind should grasp the relation of everything to everything else, that it should see the unity of the whole of reality. Perfect intelligence represents the mind as completely released from sensible objects. At this level, the mind is dealing directly with the *Forms*. The Forms are those intelligible objects, such as Triangle and Man, that have been abstracted from the actual objects. The mind is now dealing with these pure Forms without any interference from even the symbolic character of visible objects. Here, also, the mind no longer uses hypotheses, because they represent limited and isolated truths. This highest level of knowledge is approached to the extent that the mind is able to move beyond the restrictions of hypotheses toward the unity of all Forms. It is by the faculty or power of *dialectic* that the mind moves toward its highest goal, for this is the power of seeing at once the relation of all divisions of knowledge to each other.

Perfect intelligence therefore means the *synoptic* view of reality and this, for Plato, implies the unity of knowledge.

Plato concludes his discussion of the Divided Line with the summary statement, "now you may take, as corresponding to the four sections, these four states of mind: *intelligence* for the highest, *thinking* for the second, *belief* for the third and for the last *imagining*. These you may arrange as the terms in a proportion, assigning to each a degree of clearness and certainty corresponding to the measure in which their objects possess truth and reality." The highest degree of reality, he argued, was possessed by the *Forms*, as compared with shadows, reflections, and even the visible objects. Just what he meant by the Forms we must now explore in greater detail.

The Platonic Doctrine of Forms or Ideas Plato's theory of the *Forms* or *Ideas* represents his most significant philosophic contribution. However obscure and unsatisfactory his theory may be to us, it gathers around itself the novel insights that led Plato's philosophy beyond anything that had been thought before him. Basically, the *Forms* or *Ideas* are those changeless, eternal, and nonmaterial essences or patterns of which the actual visible objects we see are only poor copies. There is the Form of *the* Triangle and all the triangles we see are mere copies of that Form. This tentative description of the Forms as nonmaterial realities already indicates what was so novel about this Platonic doctrine: Whereas the pre-Socratic philosophers thought of reality as material stuff of some sort, Plato now designated the nonmaterial Ideas or Forms as the true reality. Similarly, whereas the Sophists thought that all knowledge is relative because the material order, which is all they knew, is constantly shifting and changing, Plato argued that knowledge is absolute because the true object of thought is not the material order but the changeless and eternal order of the Ideas or Forms. Although Socrates anticipated this view by holding that there is an absolute Good, which makes possible our judgments of particular goods, Plato went beyond Socrates' ethical concern by adding to the concept of Good a theory of metaphysics, an explanation of the whole structure of reality and the place of morality in it. Moreover, Plato had fashioned with this theory of Forms a novel explanation of the relation between the One and the many, avoiding Parmenides' conclusion that everything is One and Heraclitus' conclusion that everything is in flux. He was aided by the Pythagorean concept of form as it derived from mathematics. In the end, however, Plato's doctrine of Ideas was something new and became the central concept in all of his philosophy.

The doctrine of Forms represents a serious attempt to explain the nature of existence. We have certain kinds of experiences that raise the question about existence for us. For example, we make judgments about things and behavior, saying about a thing that it is beautiful and about an act that it is good. This suggests that there is somewhere a standard of beauty, which *is* different from the thing we are judging, and that there *is* a standard of good, which is somehow separate from the person or his act that we judge. Moreover, visible things change—they come and go, generate and perish. Their existence is brief. Compared with things, Ideas such as Good and Beautiful seem timeless. They have more *being* than things. Plato concluded, therefore, that the real world is not the visible world but rather the intelligible world. The intelligible world is most real, said Plato, because it consists of the eternal Forms.

There are at least five questions that one might want to ask about the Forms. And although they cannot be answered with precision, the replies to them that are found in his various writings will provide us with Plato's general theory of the Forms.

What Are the Forms? We have already suggested Plato's answer to this question by saying that Forms are eternal patterns of which the objects that we see are only copies. A beautiful person is a copy of Beauty. We can say about a person that she is beautiful because we know the Idea of Beauty and recognize that a person shares more or less in this Idea. In his *Symposium*, Plato suggests that we normally apprehend beauty first of all in a particular object or person. But having discovered beauty in this limited form, we soon "perceive that the beauty of one form is akin to another," and so we move from the beauty of a particular body to the recognition that beauty "in every form is one and the same." The effect of this discovery that all modes of beauty have some similarity is to loosen one's attachment to the beautiful object and to move from the beautiful physical object to the concept of Beauty. When a person discovers this general quality of Beauty, says Plato, "he will abate his violent love of the one, which he will . . . deem a small thing and will become a lover of all beautiful forms; in the next stage he will consider that the beauty of the mind is more honourable than the beauty of outward form." Then, "drawing towards and contemplating the vast sea of beauty, he will create many fair and noble thoughts and notions in boundless love of wisdom; until on that shore he grows and waxes strong, and at last the vision is revealed to him of a single science, which is the science of beauty everywhere." Plato appears to be saying that beautiful things in their multiplicity point toward a Beauty from which everything else derives its beauty. But this Beauty is not merely a concept: Beauty has objective reality. Beauty is a Form or Idea. Things *become* beautiful: but Beauty always *is*. Accordingly, Beauty has a separate existence from those changing things which move in and out of Beauty.

In the *Republic*, Plato shows that the true philosopher is concerned to know the essential nature of things. When he asks what is justice or beauty, he does not want examples of just and beautiful things. He wants to know what makes these things just and beautiful. The difference between opinion and knowledge is just this, that one who is at the level of opinion can recognize a just act but cannot tell you why it is just. He does not know the essence of Justice, which the particular act shares. Knowledge is not concerned simply with passing facts and appearances, with the realm of *becoming*. Knowledge seeks what truly *is*: its concern is with *Being*. What really is, what has Being, is the essential nature of things: these *essences*, such as Beauty and Goodness, which make it possible for us to judge things as good or beautiful, these are eternal Forms or Ideas.

It would seem that besides the Forms of Beauty and Goodness, there would be many other Forms. Plato speaks of the Ideal Bed of which the beds we see are mere copies. But this raises the question whether there are as many Forms as there are essences or essential natures. Although Plato is not sure that there are Ideas or Forms of dog, water, and other things, he indicates in the *Parmenides* that there are "certainly not" Ideas of mud and dirt. Clearly, if there were Forms behind all classifications of things, there would have to be a duplicate world. These difficulties increase as one tries to specify how many and which Forms there are. Nevertheless, what Plato means by the Forms is clear enough, for he considers them to be the essential archetypes of things, having an eternal existence, apprehended by the mind and not the senses, for it is the mind that beholds "real existence, colorless, formless and intangible, visible only to the intelligence."

Where Do the Forms Exist?   If the Forms are truly real, if they embody Being, it would seem that they must be someplace. But how can the Forms, which are immaterial, have a location? It could hardly be said that they are spatially located. Plato's clearest suggestion on this problem is that the Forms are "separate" from concrete things; they exist "apart from" the things we see. To be "separate" or "apart from" must mean simply that the Forms have an independent existence; they persist even though particular things perish. Forms have no dimension, but the question of their location comes up as a consequence of our language, which implies that Forms, being something, must be someplace in space. It may be that nothing more can be said about their location than the fact that the Forms have an independent existence. But there are two additional ways in which this is emphasized by Plato. For one thing, in connection with his theory of the preexistence of the soul, he says that the soul of man was acquainted with the Forms before it was united with the body. Secondly, in the process of creation, the Demiurge or God used the Forms in fashioning particular things, suggesting that the Forms had an existence prior to their embodiment in things. Furthermore, these Forms seem to have originally existed in the "mind of God" or in the supreme principle of rationality, the One. Aristotle says in his *Metaphysics* that "the Forms are the cause of the essence of all other things, and the One is the cause of the Forms." In our treatment of Plato's metaphor of the Divided Line, we showed how Plato traced the journey of the mind from the lowest level of images to the highest level, where the Idea of the Good contained the perfect vision of *reality*. And just as the sun in the allegory of the Cave was at once the source of light and life, so also, said Plato, the Idea of the Good is "the universal author of all things beautiful and right, parent of light and of the lord of light in this world, and the source of truth and reason in the other." Whether the Forms truly exist in the mind of God is a question, but that the

Forms are the agency through which the principle of reason operates in the universe seems to be just what Plato means.

What Is the Relation of Forms to Things? A Form can be related to a thing in three ways, which may be three ways of saying the same thing. First, the Form is the *cause* of the essence of a thing. Next, a thing may be said to *participate* in a Form. And, finally, a thing may be said to imitate or *copy* a Form. In each case, Plato implies that although the Form is separate from a thing, that the Idea of Man is different from Socrates, still, every concrete or actual thing in some way owes its existence to a Form, in some degree participates in the perfect model of the class of which it is a member, and is in some measure an imitation or copy of the Form. Later on, Aristotle was to argue that form and matter are inseparable and that the only real good or beautiful was found in actual things. But Plato would only allow participation and imitation as the explanation of the relation between things and their Forms. He accentuated this view by saying that it was the Forms through which order was brought into the chaos, indicating the separate reality of form and matter. Aristotle's criticism of Plato's view was formidable, since there seems to be no coherent way of accounting for the existence of the Forms apart from actual things. Still, Plato would ask him what makes it possible to form a judgment about the imperfection of something if the mind does not have access to anything more than the imperfect thing.

What Is the Relation of Forms to Each Other? Plato says that "we can have discourse only through the weaving together of Forms." Thinking and discussion proceed for the most part on a level above particular things. We speak in terms of the essences or universals that things illustrate, so we speak of queens, dogs, and carpenters. These are definitions of things and as such are universals or Forms. To be sure, we also refer to specific things in our experiences, such as dark and beautiful and person, but our language reveals our practice of connecting Forms with Forms. There is the Form Animal and such subclasses of Forms as Man and Horse. Forms are, therefore, related to each other as genus and species. In this way Forms tend to interlock even while retaining their own unity. The Form Animal seems to be present also in the Form Horse, so that one Form partakes of the other. There is therefore a hierachy of Forms representing the structure of reality, of which the visible world is only a reflection. The "lower" one comes in this hierarchy of Forms, the closer he comes to visible things and therefore the *less* universal is his knowledge, as when one speaks of "red apples." Conversely, the higher he goes, or the more abstract the Form, as when one speaks of Apple in general, the broader his knowledge. The discourse of science is the most abstract, but for that very reason, because it has achieved such independence from particular cases and particular things, it possesses the highest form of knowledge. The botanist who has proceeded in knowledge from *this rose* to Rose and to Flower has achieved the kind of abstraction or independence from particulars of which Plato was here thinking. This does not mean, however, that

Plato thought that all Forms could be related to each other: he only meant to say that every significant statement involves the use of some Forms and that knowledge consists of understanding the relations of the appropriate Forms to each other.

How Do We Know the Forms?   Plato indicates at least three different ways in which the mind discovers the Forms. First there is *recollection:* before it was united with the body, the soul was acquainted with the Forms. Men now recollect what their souls knew in their prior state of existence. Visible things remind them of the essences previously known. Education is actually a process of reminiscence. Secondly, men arrive at the knowledge of Forms through the activity of *dialectic*, which is the power of abstracting the essence of things and discovering the relations of all divisions of knowledge to each other. And third, there is the power of *desire*, love (*eros*), which leads men step by step, as Plato described in the *Symposium*, from the beautiful object to the beautiful thought and then to the very essence of Beauty itself.

The doctrine of Forms leaves many questions as well as problems. Plato's language gives the impression that there are two distinct worlds, but the relationship of these worlds is not easily conceived. Nor is the relation between Forms and their corresponding objects as clear as one would wish. Still, his argument is highly suggestive, particularly as he seeks to account for our ability to make judgments of value. To say a thing is better or worse implies some standard, which obviously is not there as such in the thing being evaluated. The doctrine of the Forms also makes possible scientific knowledge, for clearly the scientist has "let go" of actual visible particulars and deals with essences or universals, that is, with "laws." The scientist formulates "laws," and these laws tell us something about *all* things, not only the immediate and particular things. Although this whole doctrine of the Forms rests upon Plato's metaphysical views, that ultimate reality is nonmaterial, it goes a long way toward explaining the more simple fact of how it is possible for us to have ordinary conversation. Any discourse between human beings, it would seem, illustrates our independence from particular things. Conversation, Plato would say, is the clue that leads us to the Forms, for conversation involves more than seeing. The eye can see only the particular thing, but the thinking that animates conversation departs from specific things as thought "sees" the universal, the Form. There is, in the end, a stubborn lure in Plato's theory, even though it ends inconclusively.

PLATO'S MORAL PHILOSOPHY

There is a natural progression from Plato's theory of Forms to his philosophy of ethics. If a person can be deceived by appearances in the natural physical world, he can be equally deceived by appearances in the moral realm. The kind of knowledge that helps one to distinguish between shadows, reflections, and real objects in the visible world is just the kind of knowledge that man needs to discriminate between the shadows and reflections of the genuinely good life. Plato believed that just as there could be no science of physics if our knowledge were limited to visible things, so also there could be no knowledge of a universal Idea of Good if we were limited to the experiences we have of particular cultures. The well-known skepticism of the Sophists illustrated to both Socrates and Plato this connection between knowledge and morality. For the Sophists, believing that all knowledge is relative, denied that man can discover any stable and universal moral standards. Their skepticism led the Sophists to some inevitable conclusions regarding morality, namely (1) that moral rules are fashioned deliberately by each community and have relevance and authority only for the people in that place; (2) that moral rules are unnatural, that men obey them only because of the pressure of public opinion, and that if their acts could be done in private, even the "good" men would not follow the rules of morality; (3) that the essence of justice is power, or that "might is right"; and (4) that in answer to the basic question "what is the good life?" one would have to say that it is the life of pleasure. Against this formidable teaching of the Sophists, Plato brought forth the Socratic notion that "knowledge is virtue" and supplied it with a philosophical elaboration the chief ingredients of which were (1) the concept of the *soul* and (2) the theory of *virtue* as function.

Concept of the Soul In the *Republic*, Plato describes the soul as having three parts, which he calls *reason, spirit,* and *appetite*. He derived this tripartite conception of the soul from the common experience of internal confusion and conflict that all men share. When he analyzed the nature of this conflict, he discovered that there are three different kinds of activity going on in a person. First, there is an awareness of a goal or a value, and this is the act of reason. Secondly, there is the drive toward action, the spirit, which is neutral at first but responds to the direction of reason. Last, there is the desire for the things of the body, the appetites. What made him ascribe these activities to the soul was his assumption that the soul is the principle of life and movement. The body by itself is inanimate, and, therefore, when it acts or moves, it must be moved by the principle of life, the soul. That the soul has three parts followed, Plato thought, from the fact that man's internal conflict indicated different springs of action at work. The reason could suggest a goal for behavior only to be overcome by sensual appetite, and the power of the spirit could be pulled in either direction by these sensual desires. Plato illustrated this condition of man by his striking figures in the *Phaedrus*, where he portrays the charioteer driving two horses. One horse, says Plato, is good, "needs no touch of the whip, but is guided by word and admonition only." The other is bad, "the mate of insolence and pride . . . hardly yielding to whip and spur." Though the charioteer has a clear vision of where to go and the good horse is on course, the bad horse "plunges and runs away, giving all manner of trouble to his companion and the charioteer. . . ."

The spectacle of horses moving in opposite directions and the charioteer standing helpless as his commands go unheeded strikes the imagination with particular force because it exhibits so clearly the breakdown of order. The charioteer, by being what he is, namely, the one who holds the reins, has the duty, the right, the function to guide and control the horses. In the same way, the rational part of the soul has the right to rule the spirited and appetitive parts. To be sure, the charioteer cannot get anywhere without the two horses, and for this reason these three are linked together and must work together to achieve their goals. The rational part of the soul has this same sort of relation to its other parts, for the powers of appetite and spirit are indispensable to life itself. Reason works with and upon spirit and appetite, and these two also move and affect the reason. But the relation of reason to spirit and appetite is determined by what reason is: namely, a goal-seeking and measuring faculty. Of course, the passions also engage in goal seeking, for they constantly seek the goal of pleasure. Pleasure is a legiti-mate goal of life, but the passions, being simply drives toward the things that give pleasure, are incapable of distinguishing between objects that provide higher or longer-lasting pleasure and those that only appear to provide these pleasures. The peculiar function of the rational part of the soul is to seek the true goal of human life, and it does this by evaluating things according to their true nature. Although the passions or appetites might lead us into a world of fantasy and deceive us into believing that certain kinds of pleasures will bring us happiness, it is the unique role of reason to penetrate the world of fantasy, to discover the true world and thereby direct the passions to objects of love that are capable of producing true pleasure and true happiness. Unhappiness and the general disorder of the human soul are the result of man's confusing appearance with reality. This confusion occurs chiefly when the passions override the reason. This is why Plato argued, as Socrates had before him, that moral evil is the result of *ignorance.* Just as there can be order between the charioteer and the horses only if the charioteer is in control, so also with the human soul—it can achieve order and peace only if the rational part is in control of the spirit and appetites.

Throughout his account of the moral experience of men, Plato alternates between an optimistic view of man's capacity for virtue and a rather negative opinion about whether men will fulfill their potentiality for virtue. This double attitude rests upon Plato's theory of moral evil. We have already said that evil or vice is caused by ignorance, by false knowledge. False knowledge occurs when the passions influence the reason to think that what appears to bring happiness will do so, although in reality it cannot. When the appetites thus overcome the reason, the unity of the soul is adversely affected. While there is still a unity, this new unity of the soul is inverted, since now the reason is subordinated to the appetites and has thereby lost its rightful place. What makes it possible for this disordered unity to occur, or what makes false knowledge possible? In short, what is the cause of moral evil?

The cause of evil is discovered in the very nature of the soul and in the relation of the soul to the body. Before it enters the body, says Plato, the soul has a prior existence. As we have seen, the soul has two main parts, the rational and the irrational. This irrational part in turn is made up of two sections, the spirit and the appetites. Each of the two original parts has a different origin. The rational part of the soul is created by the Demiurge out of the same receptacle as the World Soul, whereas the irrational part is created by the celestial gods, who also form the body. Thus, even before it enters the body, the soul is composed of two different kinds of ingredients. In the soul's prior existence, the rational part has a clear vision of the Forms, of truth, though at the same time, the spirit and appetites already, by their very nature, have a tendency to descend. If one asks why it is that the soul descends into a body, Plato says that it is simply the tendency of the irrational part, the part of the soul that is not perfect, to be unruly and to pull the soul toward the earth. For Plato says that "when perfect and fully winged she [the soul] soars upward . . . whereas the imperfect soul, losing her wings and drooping in her flight at last settles on the solid ground—there, finding a home, she receives an earthly frame . . . and this composition of soul and body is called a living and mortal creation." The soul "falls," and that is how it comes to be in a body. But the point is that the soul has an unruly and evil nature in its irrational parts even before it enters the body, so that in one sense the cause of evil is present even in the soul's preexistent state. It is in "heaven" that the soul alternates between seeing the Forms or the truth and "forgetting" this vision, whereupon its decline sets in. The soul has the inherent possibility of disorder, so that when in fact disorder does occur in the soul, the cause of evil is to be located within the soul itself, being the product of ignorance and forgetfulness of the vision of reality. Evil, in this view, is not a positive thing but is rather a characteristic of the soul wherein the soul is "capable" of forgetfulness, and it is those souls only that do forget the truth that in turn descend, being dragged down by the attraction for earthly things. The soul, then, is perfect by nature, but one aspect of its nature is this possibility to lapse into disorder, for the soul also contains the principle of imperfection as do other parts of creation. Upon its entrance into the body, however, the difficulties of the soul are greatly increased.

Plato believed that the body stimulated the irrational part of the soul to overcome the rulership of reason. The soul's entrance into the body, therefore, is a further cause of disorder or the breakdown of the harmony between the various parts of the soul. For one thing, when the soul leaves the realm of the Forms and enters the body, it moves from the realm of the One to the realm of the many. Now the soul is adrift in the bewildering sea of the multiplicity of things and subject to all sorts of errors because of the deceptive nature of these things. In addition, the body stimulates such activities in the irrational part of the soul as the indiscriminate search for pleasure, exaggerating such appetites as hunger, thirst, and the desire to create offspring, which in turn can become lust. In the body the soul experiences sensation, desire, pleasure, and pain as well as fear and anger. There is love, too, for a wide range of objects varying from the simplest morsel that can satisfy some taste to a love of truth or beauty that is pure and eternal. All this suggests that the body acts as a sluggish encumbrance to the soul, that the spirit and appetites of the soul are peculiarly susceptible to the workings of the body. In this way, then, the body disturbs the harmony of the soul, for the body exposes the soul to stimuli that deflect the reason from true knowledge or that prevent the reason from recalling the truth it once knew.

In the world of people, error is perpetuated whenever a society has the wrong values causing individuals to accept as their own these wrong values. Every society inevitably acts as a teacher of its members, and for this reason its values will become the values of individuals. Moreover, societies tend to perpetuate the evils and errors committed by earlier generations. Plato underscored this notion by suggesting that in addition to such a social transmission of evil, human souls would reappear via a transmigration, bringing into a new body their earlier errors and judgments of value. It is the body, in the last analysis, that accounts for ignorance, rashness, and lust, for the body disturbs that clear working of the reason, spirit, and appetites by exposing the soul to a cascade of sensations.

Looking back upon Plato's account of man's moral condition, we have seen that he begins with a conception of the soul as existing first of all independently of the body. In this state, the soul enjoys a basic harmony between its rational and irrational parts, a harmony wherein the reason controls the spirit and appetites through its knowledge of the truth. But since the irrational part of the soul has the possibility of imperfection, it expresses this possibility by being attracted through its appetites to the lower regions, dragging with it the spirit and reason. Upon entering the body, the original harmony of the parts of the soul is further disrupted, former knowledge is forgotten, and the inertia of the body obstructs the recovery of this knowledge.

For Plato, morality consists in the recovery of man's lost inner harmony. It means reversing the process by which the reason has been overcome by the appetites and the stimuli of the body. The reason must regain its control over the irrational parts of the self. Only knowledge can produce virtue because it is ignorance or false knowledge that has produced evil. Men always think that whatever they do will in some way give them pleasure and happiness. No one, says Plato, ever knowingly chooses an act that will be harmful to himself. He may do "wrong" acts, such as murder or lying, and even admit the wrongness of these and other acts, but he always assumes that *he* will somehow benefit from them. This is false knowledge, a kind of ignorance, which men must overcome in order to be moral. To say, then, that "knowledge is virtue" means that false knowledge must be replaced with an accurate appraisal of things or acts and their values.

Before one can go from false to true knowledge, he must somehow become aware that he is in a state of ignorance. It is as if one must be awakened from a "sleep of ignorance." A person can be awakened either by something that is happening within himself or by something external to him or by someone else. Similarly, with regard to knowledge and particularly moral knowledge, man's awakening works in these two ways. Assuming, as Plato does, that knowledge is lodged deeply in the mind's memory, this latent knowledge will from time to time come to the surface of consciousness. What the soul once knew is raised to present awareness by the process of *recollection*. Recollection begins first of all when the mind experiences difficulties with the seeming contradictions of sense experience. As one tries to make sense out of the multiplicity of things, he begins to go "beyond" the things themselves to ideas, and this action of the mind is set in motion by one's experience of a problem that needs to be solved. Besides this internal source of awakening, there is Plato's notion of the external agent. In his allegory of the Cave, Plato depicted how men moved from darkness to light, from ignorance to knowledge. But in this allegory he portrays the mood of self-satisfaction among the prisoners; they do not know that they are prisoners, that they are chained by false knowledge and dwell in the darkness of ignorance. Their awakening must come through some external agent. As Plato says, "their release from the chains and the healing of their unwisdom" is brought about by their being "forced suddenly to stand up, turn . . . and walk with eyes lifted to the light." That is, someone must break off the prisoner's chains and turn him around. Then, having been forcibly released, he can be led step by step out of the cave.

Socrates, with the power of his irony and the persistence of his dialectic method, was one of history's most effective awakeners of men from their sleep of ignorance. But besides awakening one, or breaking off his chains, the effective teacher must turn the prisoner around so that he will shift his gaze from shadows to the real world. As we have already noticed, the liberated prisoner will move from shadows to actual objects, to mathematical objects, and finally to a knowledge of the Good. Along this arduous trek, he passes through the realm of opinion, where imagining and belief are the modes of knowing, until he crosses over the divide into the intelligible world, where thinking and true knowing are achieved. As the mind moves progressively from the lower to the higher levels of knowledge, it recalls more of what it once knew and what it must know to achieve inner harmony. One's moral development parallels his intellectual ascent, for one's growing knowledge intensifies his love for Truth, Beauty, and Goodness. Inevitably, one's behavior begins to respond to his expanded knowledge. As the liberated prisoner reflects upon his previous life in the cave where people won prizes for predicting what shapes the shadows would take upon the wall, he now realizes that when he was there he did not even know that these were shadows. Moreover, in light of his new knowledge, those games and prizes seem trivial. Plato was convinced that in real life true knowledge would have the same power to sort out trivial and worthwhile pursuits. Trival pursuits would be incapable of producing a genuine sense of well-being and happiness, whereas worthwhile behavior would lead to such happiness and virtue. Again, virtue means knowledge, a true knowledge of the true consequences of all acts. But to say that knowledge is virtue does not mean that virtue is merely the knowledge of a list of truths. Virtue for Plato has the broader meaning of the fulfillment of a unique function.

Virtue as Fulfillment of Function   Throughout his discussions of morality, Plato viewed the good life as the life of inner harmony, of well-being, of happiness. The key words of morality, namely, *virtue* and *goodness,* had been obscured by the Sophists, who thought that each culture could give these words whatever meanings it wished. For Plato, however, goodness and virtue were intimately connected with the mode of behavior that produced well-being and harmony. For him, harmony could be achieved only if the parts of the soul were doing what the nature of each required that it do. Each part of the soul has a special function and, says Plato, "a thing's function is the work that it alone can do, or can do better than anything else." Here Plato wanted to show that virtue is not a matter of custom or opinion but is rather grounded in the very nature of the soul. It is the very nature of reason to know and to direct the spirit and appetites. Reason has a function, and reason is good only when it is acting as reason should. Clearly, one's reason is not fulfilling its function if it is pushed around by passion. At the same time, spirit has a function, and so do the appetites, and the good life is achieved only when every part is fulfilling its function.

Plato frequently compared the good life to the efficient functioning of things. A knife is good, he said, when it cuts efficiently, that is, when it fulfills its function. We say of a physician that he is a good physician when he fulfills the function of doctoring. Plato then asks, "Has the soul a function that can be performed by nothing else?" The physician's function is the art of doctoring and the musician, in his own way, engages in an art. Living, said Plato, is likewise an art, and the soul's unique function is the art of living. Comparing the art of music with the art of living, Plato saw a close parallel, for in both cases the art consists of recognizing and obeying the requirements of limit and measure. When a musician tunes his instrument, he knows that each string should be tightened just so much, no more and no less, for each string has its specific pitch. The musician's art consists, therefore, in acknowledging the limit beyond which a string should not be tightened and, in playing the instrument, observing the "measure" between intervals. In a similar way, the sculptor must be ruled by a vivid awareness of measure and limit, for as he works with his mallet and chisel, he must regulate the force of each stroke by the form he wants to accomplish. His strokes will be heavy as he begins to clear away the larger sections of marble, but as he works around the head of the statue he must have a clear vision of the limits beyond which his chisel must not go, and his strokes must be gentle as he fashions the delicate features of the face.

Similarly, the art of living requires a knowledge of limits and of measure. The soul has various functions, but these functions must operate within the limits set by knowledge or intelligence. Because the soul has various parts, each part will have a special function, and since virtue is the fulfillment of function, there will be as many virtues as there are functions. Corresponding to the three parts of the soul are three virtues, which are achieved when those parts are respectively fulfilling their functions. When, therefore, the appetites are kept within limits and in their measure, avoiding excesses so that they do not usurp the position of the other parts of the soul, this moderation in pleasures and desires leads to the virtue of *temperance*. Also, when the energy of will, which issues from the spirited part of the soul, is kept within limits, avoiding rash or headlong action and becoming instead a trustworthy power in aggressive and defensive behavior, the virtue of *courage* is achieved. Reason, when it remains undisturbed by the onrush of appetites and continues to see the true ideals in spite of the constant changes experienced in daily life, achieves the virtue of *wisdom*. Between these three virtues there are interconnections, for temperance is the rational control of the appetites, and courage is the rational ordering of the spirit. At the same time, each part of the soul has its own function, and when each is in fact fulfilling its special function, a fourth virtue, *justice*, is attained, for justice means giving to each its own due. Justice, then, is the general virtue, which reflects a person's attainment of well-being and inner harmony, which, in turn, is achieved only when every part of the soul is fulfilling its proper function.

By grounding morality in the various functions of the soul, Plato felt that he had overcome the skepticism and relativism of the Sophists. Morality, argued Plato, is not the product of public opinion, nor is right simply a question of might. To be sure, some cultures and some men do in fact believe this to be the case. But Plato would respond by saying that just as the proper function of a hammer is discovered not by opinion but by analyzing the nature and capacities of a hammer, so also the proper behavior for man is not prescribed by opinion but is rather required by the very character of the parts of the soul. Although men try to evade the clear limits and measures that the parts of the soul must obey, they cannot avoid the consequences of their acts. Everyone wants to achieve well-being and happiness, and whenever a person chooses a mode of behavior, he always assumes that his act will bring such well-being. But well-being in human nature is the product only of inner harmony, of balance, of a proper order between the parts of the soul. Virtue, therefore, is attained only when each part of the soul is fulfilling its own function. The appetites and the spirit must therefore be subject to the sovereignty of the rational element, which directs one's dynamic capacities and orders the desires and affections according to intelligence.

PLATO'S POLITICAL PHILOSOPHY

In Plato's thought, political theory is closely connected with moral philosophy. Indeed, Plato considered the state as being "man writ large." As justice is the general virtue of the moral man, so also it is justice that characterizes the good society. But Plato does not simply say that there is an interesting or coincidental connection between the just man and the just society. He argues, rather, that there is a structural and natural as well as logical relation between man and the state. In the *Republic* Plato argues that the best way to understand the just man is to analyze the nature of the state. "We should begin," he says, "by inquiring what justice means in a state. Then we can go on to look for its counterpart on a smaller scale in the individual." He describes someone who wants to inquire about the just or good man as "a rather short-sighted person told to read an inscription in small letters from some way off. He would think it a godsend if someone pointed out that the same inscription was written up elsewhere on a bigger scale."

The State as Man Writ Large We have reversed Plato's sequence and have considered the just man first. Although Plato would begin with a study of the state, his whole argument was that the state grows out of the nature of the individual, so that the individual comes logically prior to the state. The state, said Plato, is a natural institution, natural because it reflects the structure of human nature. The origin of the state is a reflection of man's economic needs, for, says

Plato, "a state comes into existence because no individual is self-sufficing; we all have many needs." Our many needs require many skills, and no one possesses all the skills needed to produce food, shelter, and clothing, to say nothing of the various arts. There must, therefore, be a division of labor, for "more things will be produced and the work more easily and better done, when every man is set free from all other occupations to do, at the right time, the one thing for which he is naturally fitted." Man's needs are not limited to his physical requirements, for his goal is not simply survival but a life higher than an animal's. Still, the healthy state soon becomes affected by a wide range of desires and becomes "swollen up with a whole multitude of callings not ministering to any bare necessity." Now there will be "hunters and fishermen . . . artists in sculpture, painting and music; poets with their attendant train of professional reciters, actors, dancers, producers; and makers of all sorts of household gear, including everything for women's adornment. And we shall want more servants . . . lady's maids, barbers, cooks and confectioners." This desire for more things will soon exhaust the resources of the community and before long, says Plato, "we shall have to cut off a slice of our neighbor's territory . . . and they will want a slice of ours." At this rate, neighbors will inevitably be at war. Wars have their "origin in desires which are the most fruitful source of evils both to individuals and states." With the inevitability of war, it will now be necessary to have "a whole army to go out to battle with any invader, in defence of all this property and of the citizens. . . ." Thus emerge the guardians of the state, who, at first, represent the vigorous and powerful men who will repel the invader and preserve internal order. Now there are two distinct classes of men, those who fill all the crafts—farmers, artisans, and traders—and those who guard the community. From this latter class are then chosen the most highly trained guardians, who will become the rulers of the state and will represent a third and elite class.

The relation between the individual and the state now becomes plain, for the three classes in the state are an extension of the three parts of the soul. The craftsmen or artisans represent as a class the lowest part of the soul, namely, the appetites. The guardians embody the spirited element of the soul. And the highest class, the rulers, represent the rational element. So far, this analysis seems to have logical rigor, for it does not strain the imagination to see the connection (1) between the individual's appetites and the class of workers who satisfy these appetites, (2) between the spirited element in man and the large-scale version of this dynamic force in the military establishment, and (3) between the rational element and the unique function of leadership in the ruler. But Plato was aware that it would not be simple to convince people to accept this system of classes in the state, particularly if they found themselves in a class that might not be the one they would choose if they had the chance. The assignment of all persons to their respective classes would come only after extensive training, where only those capable of doing so would progress to the higher levels. Although theoretically each person would have the opportunity to reach the highest level, he would in fact stop at the level of his natural aptitudes. To make everyone satisfied with his lot, Plato thought it would be necessary to employ a "convenient fiction . . .

a single bold flight of invention." He writes, "I shall try to convince, first the Rulers and the soldiers, and then the whole community, that all that nurture and education which we gave them was only something they seemed to experience as it were in a dream. In reality they were the whole time down inside the earth, being molded . . . and fashioned . . . and at last when they were complete, the earth sent them up from her womb into the light of day."

This "noble lie" would also say that the god who fashioned all men "mixed gold in the composition" of those who were to rule and "put silver in the guardians, and iron and brass in the farmers and craftsmen." This would imply that by nature some would be rulers and others craftsmen and that this would provide the basis for a perfectly stratified society. But whereas later societies in Europe assumed that the children born into such a stratified society would stay at the level at which they were born, Plato recognized that children would not always have the same quality as their parents. He said, therefore, that among the injunctions laid by heaven upon the rulers "there is none that needs to be so carefully watched as the mixture of metals in the souls of children. If a child of their own is born with an alloy of iron or brass, they must, without the smallest pity, assign him the station proper to his nature and thrust him out among the farmers and craftsmen." Similarly, if a child with gold or silver is born to craftsmen, "they will promote him according to his value. . . ." Most important of all, Plato thought that everyone should agree on who is to be the ruler and agree also on the reason why the ruler should be obeyed.

The Philosopher-King To Plato it seemed natural that competence should be the qualification for authority. The ruler of the state should be the one who has the peculiar abilities to fulfill that function. Disorder in the state is caused by the same circumstances that produce disorder in the individual, namely, the attempt on the part of the lower elements to usurp the role of the higher faculties. In both the individual and the state the uncontrolled drives of the appetites and spirited action lead to internal anarchy. At both levels, the rational element must be in control. Who should be the captain of a ship—should it be the most "popular" man, or the one who knows the art of navigation? Who should rule the state— should it be someone whose training is in war or commerce? The ruler, said Plato, should be the one who has been fully educated, one who has come to understand the difference between the visible world and the intelligible world, between the realm of opinion and the realm of knowledge, between appearance and reality. The philosopher-king is one whose education, in short, has led him up step by step through the ascending degrees of knowledge of the Divided Line until at last he has a knowledge of the Good, that synoptic vision of the interrelation of all truths to each other. To reach this point, the philosopher-king will have progressed through many stages of education. By the time he is eighteen years old, he will have had training in literature, music, and elementary mathematics. His literature would be censored, for Plato accused certain poets of outright falsehood and of impious accounts of the behavior of the gods. Music also would be prescribed so that seductive music would be replaced by a more wholesome, martial meter. For the next few years there would be extensive physical and military training, and at age twenty a few would be selected to pursue an advanced course in mathematics. At age thirty, a five-year course in dialectic and moral philosophy would begin. The next fifteen years would be spent gathering practical experience through public service. Finally, at age fifty, the ablest men would reach the highest level of knowledge, the vision of the Good, and would then be ready for the task of governing the state.

The Virtues in the State   Whether justice could ever be achieved in a state would depend, Plato thought, upon whether the philosophic element in society could attain dominance. He wrote that "I was forced to say in praise of the correct philosophy that it affords a vantage-point from which we can discern in all cases what is just for communities and for individuals," and he believed that "the human race will not be free of evils until either the stock of those who rightly and truly follow philosophy acquire political authority, or the class who have power in the cities be led by some dispensation of providence to become real philosophers." But justice, as we have already seen, is a general virtue. It means that all parts are fulfilling their special functions and are achieving their respective virtues. Justice in the state will be attained only when and if the three classes fulfill their functions.

As the craftsmen embody the element of the appetites, they will also reflect the virtue of temperance. Temperance is not limited to the craftsmen but applies to all the classes, for it indicates, when it is achieved, the willingness of the lower to be ruled by the higher. Still, temperance applies in a special way to the craftsmen insofar as they are the lowest and must be subordinate to the two higher levels.

The guardians, who defend the state, manifest the virtue of courage. To assure the state that these guardians will always fulfill their function, special training and provision are made for them. Unlike the craftsmen who marry and own property, the guardians will have both property and wives in common. Plato considered these arrangements essential if the guardians were to attain true courage, for courage means knowing what to fear and what not to fear. The only real object of fear for the guardian should be fear of moral evil. He must never fear poverty or privation, and for this reason his mode of life should be isolated from possessions. Although wives will be held in common, this was by no means to suggest any form of promiscuity. On the contrary, Plato believed that men and women were equal in respect to certain things, saying, for example, that "a man and a woman have the same nature if both have a talent for medicine." This being the case, they should both be assigned to the same task whenever they possess the appropriate talent. For this reason, Plato believed that women could be guardians as well as men. In order to preserve the unity of the members of the class of guardians, the permanent individual family would be abolished, and the whole class would become a single family. Plato's reasoning here was that the guardians must be free not only from the temptation to acquire property, but free also from the temptation to prefer the advantages of one's family to those of the state. Moreover, he thought it rather foolish to take such pains in breeding racing dogs and horses and at the same time rely upon pure chance in producing the guardians and rulers of the state. For this reason, sexual relations would be strictly controlled and would be limited to the special marriage festivals. These festivals would occur at stated times, and the partners, under the illusion that they had been paired by drawing lots, would, instead, be brought together through the careful manipulation of the rulers to ensure the highest eugenic possibilities. Plato does say that "young men who acquit themselves well in war and other duties, should be given, among other rewards and privileges, more liberal opportunities to sleep with a wife," but only for the utilitarian purpose, that "with good excuse, as many as possible of the children may be begotten of such fathers." As soon as children are born to the guardians, they will be taken in charge by officers appointed for that purpose and will be reared in a creche in the care of nurses living in a special part of the city. Under these circumstances, thought Plato, the guardians would be most likely to fulfill their true function of defending the state without being deflected by other concerns, and would thereby achieve their appropriate virtue of courage.

Justice in the state is therefore just the same as justice in the individual. It is the product of everyone's staying in his place and doing his special task. Justice is the harmony of the virtues of temperance, courage, and wisdom. Since the state is made up of individuals, it will also be necessary for each of these virtues to be attained by each person. For example, even the craftsman must have the virtue of wisdom, not only to keep his appetites in check but also to know that he rightly belongs where he is and must obey the rules. Similarly, as we have seen, the guardians must have sufficient wisdom in order to know what to fear and what not to fear so that they can develop genuine courage. Most important of all, the ruler must come as close as possible to a knowledge of the Good, for the well-being of the state depends upon his knowledge and character.

The Decline of the Ideal State   If the state is "man writ large," then, said Plato, a state will reflect the kind of people a community has become. What he had in mind was that although the nature of man is fixed, in that all men possess a tripartite soul, the kind of men people become will depend upon the degree of internal harmony they achieve. The state will therefore reflect these variations in human character. For this reason, Plato argued that "constitutions cannot come out of stocks and stones; they must result from the preponderance of certain characters which draw the rest of the community in their wake. So if there are five forms of government, there must be five kinds of mental constitution among individuals." And these five forms of government are *aristocracy, timocracy, plutocracy, democracy,* and *despotism.*

Plato considered the transition from aristocracy to despotism as a step-by-step decline in the quality of the state corresponding to a gradual deterioration of the moral character of the rulers and the citizens. His ideal state was, of course, aristocracy, in which the rational element embodied in the philosopher-king was supreme and where each person's reason controlled his appetites. Plato emphasized that this was only an Ideal, though significant, nevertheless, as a target to aim at. He was deeply disenchanted with politics, particularly because of the way Athens had executed Socrates and had failed to produce consistently good leaders. "As I gazed upon the whirlpool of public life," he said, "[I] saw clearly in regard to all States now existing that without exception their system of government is bad." Still, the norm for a state is *aristocracy*, for in that form is found the proper subordination of all classes.

Even if this Ideal were achieved, however, there would be a possibility for change, since nothing is permanent, and aristocracy would decline first of all into a *timocracy*. This represents a degeneration, for timocracy represents the love of honor, and insofar as an ambitious member of the ruling class loves his own honor more than the common good, the spirited part of his soul has usurped the role of reason. Although this is only a small break in the structure of the soul, it does begin a process whereby the irrational part assumes a progressively larger role. From love of honor to the desire for wealth is a short step, for it means allowing the appetites to rule.

Even under a timocracy there would be the beginning of a system of private property, and this desire for riches paves the way for a system of government called *plutocracy*, where power resides in the hands of men whose main concern is wealth. And, says Plato, "as the rich rise in social esteem, the virtuous sink." What is serious about plutocracy, according to Plato, is that it breaks the unity of the state into two contending classes, the rich and the poor. Moreover, the plutocrat is a consumer of goods, and when he has used up his money, he becomes dangerous because he wants more of what he has become accustomed to. The plutocrat is like the person who seeks constant pleasure. But the very nature of pleasure is that it is momentary and must therefore be repeated. There can never be a time of perfect satisfaction; the seeker of pleasure can never be satisfied any more than a leaky pail can be filled. Still, though the plutocrat is torn between many desires, "his better desires will usually keep the upper hand over the worse," and so the plutocrat, says Plato, "presents a more decent appearance than many."

Democracy is a further degeneration, said Plato, for its principles of equality and freedom reflect the degenerate human characters whose whole range of appetites are all pursued with equal freedom. To be sure, Plato's concept of democracy, and his criticism of it, were based upon his firsthand experience with the special form democracy took in the small city-state of Athens. Here democracy was direct in that all citizens had the right to participate in the government. The Athenian Assembly consisted, theoretically at least, of all citizens over eighteen years of age. Thus, Plato did not have in mind modern liberal and representative democracy. What he saw in his day was rather a mode of direct popular government that clearly violated his notion that the rulership of a state should be in the hands of those with the special talent and training for it. What produced this spirit of equality was the legitimizing of all the appetites under the plutocracy where the aim of life was to become as rich as possible and, said Plato, "this insatiable craving would bring about the transition to democracy," for "a society cannot hold wealth in honour and at the same time establish self-control in its citizens." Even the dogs in a democracy exhibit equality and independence by refusing to move out of the way in the streets. It is, however, when the rich and poor find themselves in a contest under plutocracy that the turning point is reached, for "when the poor win, the result is a democracy." Then, "liberty and free speech are rife everywhere; anyone is allowed to do what he likes." Now, "you are not obliged to be in authority . . . or to submit to authority, if you do not like it. . . ." All this political equality and freedom stem from a soul whose order has been shattered. It is a soul whose appetites are now all equal and free and act as a "mob" of passions. The life of liberty and equality declares that "one appetite is as good as another and all must have their equal rights."

But the continuous indulgence of the appetites leads one inevitably to the point where a single master passion will finally enslave the soul. One cannot yield to every craving without finally having to yield to the strongest and most persistent passion. At this point we say that a person is under the tyranny of his master passion. Likewise, in the state, the passion for money and pleasures leads the masses to plunder the rich. As the rich resist, the masses seek out a strong man who will be their champion. But this man demands and acquires absolute power and makes the people his slaves, and only later do the people realize to what depths of subjugation they have fallen. This is the unjust society, the enlargement of the unjust soul. The natural end of democracy is *despotism*.

PLATO'S VIEW OF THE COSMOS

Although Plato's most consistent and sustained thought centered around moral and political philosophy, he also turned his attention to science. His theory of nature, or physics, is found chiefly in the *Timaeus*, a dialogue he wrote when he was about seventy years old. Plato had not deliberately postponed this subject, nor had he chosen to deal with moral matters instead of promoting the advancement of science. On the contrary the science of his day had reached a blind alley, and there seemed to be no fruitful direction to take in this field. Earlier, according to Plato, Socrates had had "a prodigious desire to know that department of philosophy which is called the investigation of nature; to know the causes of things . . ." but he was disillusioned by the conflicting answers and theories put forward by Anaximander, Anaximenes, Leucippus and Democritus, and others. Plato shared this same disappointment. Moreover, as his own philosophy took shape, some of his theories about reality cast doubt upon the possibility of a strictly accurate scientific knowledge. Physics, he thought, could never be more than "a likely story." It was particularly his theory of the Forms that rendered science as an exact mode of knowledge impossible. The real world, he said, is the world of Forms, whereas the visible world is full of change and imperfection. Yet, it is about the visible world of things that science seeks to build its theories. How can one formulate accurate, reliable, and permanent knowledge about a subject matter which is itself imperfect and full of change? At the same time, Plato clearly felt that his theory of Forms or Ideas as well as his notions of morality, evil, and truth required that he provide some view of the cosmos in which all these elements of his thought could be brought together in a coherent way. Recognizing, then, that his account of the material world was only "a likely story," or at best probable knowledge, he nevertheless was convinced that what he had to say about the world was as accurate as the subject matter would allow.

Plato's first thought about the world is that, though it is full of change and imperfection, it nevertheless exhibits order and purpose. He rejected the explanation given by Democritus, who had argued that all things came into being through the accidental collision of atoms. When Plato considered, for example, the orbits of the planets, he observed that they were arranged according to a precise series of geometrical intervals, which, when appropriately calculated, produced the basis for the harmonic scale. Plato made much of the Pythagorean use of mathematics in describing the world, though instead of saying, as the Pythagoreans did, that things are numbers, he said that things participate in numbers, that they are capable of a mathematical explanation. This mathematical characteristic of things suggested to Plato that behind things there must be not merely chance and subsequent mechanism but rather thought and purpose. The cosmos must therefore be the work of *intelligence*, since it is the mind that orders all things. Man and the world bear a likeness to each other, for both contain first an intelligible and eternal element, and second a sensible and perishing element. This dualism is expressed in man by the union of soul and body. Similarly, the world is a soul in which the things as we know them are arranged.

Although Plato said that *mind* orders everything, he did not develop a doctrine of creation. The doctrine of creation holds that things are created *ex nihilo*, out of nothing. But Plato's explanation of the origin of the visible world bypasses this doctrine of creation. Although Plato does say that "that which becomes must necessarily become through the agency of some cause," this agent, which he calls the divine Craftsman or Demiurge, does not bring new things into being but rather confronts and orders what already exists in chaotic form. We have, then, a picture of the Craftsman with the material upon which he will work. Thus, in explaining the generation of things as we know them in the visible world, Plato assumes the existence of all the ingredients of things, namely, that out of which things are made, the Demiurge who is the Craftsman, and the Ideas or Forms or *patterns* after which things are made.

Plato departed from the materialists who thought that all things derived from some original kind of matter, whether in the form of earth, air, fire, or water. Plato did not accept the notion that matter was the basic reality: matter itself, said Plato, must be explained in more refined terms as the composition not of some finer forms of matter but of something other than matter. What we call matter, whether in the form of earth or water, is a reflection of an Idea or Form, and these Forms are expressed through a medium. Things are generated out of what Plato calls the *receptacle*, which he considered the "nurse of all becoming." The receptacle is a "matrix" or a medium that has no structure but that is capable of receiving the imposition of structure by the Demiurge. Another word Plato uses for the *receptacle* is *space*, which, he says, "is everlasting, not admitting destruction; providing a situation for all things that come into being, but itself apprehended without the senses by a sort of bastard reasoning, and hardly an object of belief." There is no explanation of the origin of the receptacle, for in Plato's thought it is underived, as are the Forms and the Demiurge. The receptacle is where things appear and perish.

To an unreflective person, earth and water may appear as solid and permanent modes of matter. But Plato said that they are constantly changing and therefore do not hold still long enough "to be described as 'this' or 'that' or by any phrase that exhibits them as having permanent being." What the senses consider "matter" or "substance" when they apprehend the elements of earth and water are only *qualities*, which appear through the medium of the receptacle "in which all of them are always coming to be, making their appearance and vanishing out of it." Material objects are composed of nonmaterial compounds. Here Plato is again influenced by the Pythagorean perspective when he argues that solid objects of matter are described and defined in geometric terms according to their surfaces. Any surface, he said, can be resolved by triangles, and, in turn, any triangle can be divided into right triangles. These shapes, these triangular surfaces, are irreducible and must therefore be the ingredients of the compound known as matter. The simplest solid, for example, would be a pyramid that consists of four triangular surfaces. Similarly, a cube could be made of six square surfaces, where each square surface is composed of two half squares, that is, two triangles. What we normally call "solid" never contains anything more than "surfaces," so that one can say that "body" or "molecules" are geometric figures. Indeed, the whole universe could be thought of in terms of its geometrical diagram—and could be defined simply as what is happening in space, or as space reflecting various forms. What Plato wanted particularly to establish was the notion that matter is only the appearance of something more basic.

If various kinds of triangles represent the basic constituents of all things, how can one account for the variations in things as well as their stability? What, in short, makes it possible to have the kind of world and universe that we know? Here again Plato was forced to assume that all things must be ordered by mind, that the cosmos is the activity of the World Soul in the receptacle. The world of things is the world of *phenomena,* which is the Greek word for appearances. What is presented to our perception is the multitude of appearances, which, when analyzed, are found to consist of geometric surfaces. These surfaces, again, are primary and irreducible and are found as "raw material" in the receptacle and require some organizing agency to arrange them into triangles and then into phenomena. All this activity is achieved by the World Soul. The World Soul is eternal, though at times Plato appears to say that it is the creation of the Demiurge. Although the World Soul is eternal, the world of appearance is full of change, just as in man the soul represents the eternal element whereas the body contains the principle of change. The world of matter and body changes because it is composite and always tends to return to its basic constituents, "going into" and "going out of" space. But insofar as the World Soul is eternal, there is, in spite of all the change in the world of our experience, an element of stability and permanence, a structure, a discernible universe.

There is evil in the world, says Plato, because there are obstacles in the way of the Demiurge. The world is not perfectly good even though the Demiurge sought to make it as much like its pattern as possible. Although the Demiurge represents divine reason and the agency that fashioned the order of the universe, "the generation of this cosmos," says Plato, "was a mixed result of the combination of Necessity and Reason." Necessity in this context signifies unwillingness to change and when applied to the "raw material" of the *receptacle* it indicates a recalcitrance as though impervious to the ordering of *mind*. In this sense, *necessity* is one of the conditions of evil in the world, for evil is the breakdown of purpose, and purpose is characteristic of mind. Whatever, then, frustrates the working of mind contributes to the absence of order, which is the meaning of evil. This suggests that in human life, too, the circumstance of a recalcitrant body and lower parts of the soul produces evil insofar as mind is not in control. Necessity is expressed in various modes, such as inertia and irreversibility, and reason, even God's reason, must cope with these obstacles while trying to order the world according to a definite purpose.

Finally, there is the question about *time*. According to Plato, time comes to be only after phenomena are produced. Not until there are things as we know them, as imperfect and changing, can there be time. Until then, by definition, whatever is, is eternal. The very meaning of time is change, and therefore in the absence of change there could be no time. Whereas the Forms are timeless, the various copies of them in the receptacle constantly "go in" and "go out," and this going in and out is the process of change, which is the cause of time. Still, time represents the double presence in the cosmos of time and eternity; since the cosmos is ordered by mind, it contains the element of eternity, and since the cosmos consists of temporary combinations of surfaces, it contains the element of change and time. And since change is not capricious but regular, the very process of change exhibits the presence of eternal mind. This regularity of change, as exhibited, for example, by the regular change or motion of the stars and planets, makes possible the measurement of change and makes it possible to "tell time."

Plato's "likely story" about the cosmos consisted, then, of an account of how the Demiurge fashioned things out of the receptacle using the Forms as patterns. The World Soul is produced by the Demiurge and is the energizing activity in the receptacle, producing what to us appears to be substance or solid matter though in reality is only qualities caused by the arrangement of geometric surfaces. Evil and time are, in this account, the product of imperfection and change. The world as we know it depends upon an agency and "raw material" that are not found in the physical world as we know it, this agency being mind and the raw material being explained chiefly in terms of mathematics.

At this point one would wish to engage in a sustained and critical appraisal of Plato's vast system of philosophy. But in a sense, the history of philosophy represents just such a large-scale dialogue where thinkers arise to agree and disagree with what he taught. So powerful was the mold into which he had cast the enterprise of philosophy that for centuries to come his views dominated the intellectual scene. Indeed, Whitehead once remarked that "the safest general characterization of the European philosophical tradition is that it consists of a series of footnotes to Plato." Many of these footnotes, it might be added, were written by Plato's prodigious successor, Aristotle, to whom we now turn.

4

Aristotle

Aristotle was born in 384 B.C. in the small town of Stagira on the northeast coast of Thrace. His father was the physician to the king of Macedonia. It could be that Aristotle's great interest in biology and science in general was nurtured in his early childhood as it was the custom, according to Galen, for families in the guild of the Asclepiadae to train their sons in the art of dissection. When he was seventeen years old, Aristotle went to Athens to enroll in Plato's Academy, where he spent the next twenty years as a pupil and a member. At the Academy, Aristotle had the reputation of being the "reader" and "the mind of the school." He was profoundly influenced by Plato's thought and personality even though eventually he was to break away from Plato's philosophy in order to formulate his own version of certain philosophical problems. Still, while at the Academy, he wrote many dialogues in a Platonic style, which his contemporaries praised for the "golden stream" of their eloquence. He even reaffirmed, in his *Eudemus*, the very doctrine so central to Plato's thought, the doctrine of the Forms or Ideas, which he later criticized so severely.

There is no way now to reconstruct with exactness just when Aristotle's thought diverged from Plato's. Plato's own thought, it must be remembered, was in process of change while Aristotle was at the Academy. Indeed, it is usually said that Aristotle studied with Plato during Plato's "later" period, a time when Plato's interests had shifted toward mathematics, method, and natural science. During this time, also, specialists in various sciences, such as medicine, anthropology, and archeology, came to the Academy. This meant that Aristotle was exposed to a vast array of empirical facts, which, because of his temperament, he found useful for research and for his mode of formulating scientific concepts. It may be, therefore, that the intellectual atmosphere of the Academy marked by some of Plato's latest dominant concerns and the availability of collected data in special fields provided Aristotle with a direction in philosophy that was congenial to his scientific disposition.

The direction Aristotle took did eventually cause him to depart from some of Plato's doctrines, though the degree of difference between Plato and Aristotle is still a matter of careful interpretation. But even when they were together at the Academy, certain temperamental differences must have been apparent. Aristotle, for example, was less interested in mathematics than Plato and more interested in empirical data. Moreover, as time went on, Aristotle's gaze seemed to be more firmly fixed upon the concrete processes of nature, so that he considered his abstract scientific notions to have their real habitat in this living nature. By contrast, Plato separated the world of thought from the world of flux and things, ascribing true reality to the Ideas and Forms, which, he thought, had an existence separate from the things in nature. It could be said, therefore, that Aristotle oriented his thought to the dynamic realm of *becoming*, whereas Plato's thought was fixed more upon the static realm of timeless *Being*. Whatever differences there were between these two great minds, the fact is that Aristotle did not break with Plato personally, as he remained at the Academy until Plato's death. Moreover, throughout Aristotle's later major treatises, unmistakable influences of Plato's thought are to be found in spite of Aristotle's unique interpretations and style. But his distinctly "Platonist" period came to an end upon Plato's death, when the direction of the Academy passed into the hands of Plato's nephew Speusippos, whose excessive emphasis upon mathematics was uncongenial to Aristotle, for which reason, among others, Aristotle withdrew from the Academy and left Athens.

It was in 348/47 B.C. that Aristotle left the Academy and accepted the invitation of Hermeias to come to Assos, near Troy. Hermeias had formerly been a student at the Academy and was now the ruler of Assos. Being somewhat of a philosopher-king, he had gathered a small group of thinkers into his court, and here Aristotle was able for the next three years to write, teach, and carry on research. While at Hermeias' court, he married this ruler's niece and adopted daughter, Pythias, who bore him a daughter. Later, when they had returned to Athens, his wife died and Aristotle then entered into a relationship with Herpyllis, which was never legalized but which was a happy, permanent, and affectionate union from which there came a son, Nicomachus, after whom the *Nicomachean Ethics* was named. After his three years in Assos, Aristotle moved to the neighboring island of Lesbos, settling there for the time being in Mitylene, where he taught and continued his investigations in biology, studying especially the many forms of marine life. Here he also became known as an advocate of a united Greece, urging that such a union would be more successful than independent city-states in resisting the might of Persia. Then, in 343/42, Philip of Macedon invited Aristotle to become the tutor of his son Alexander, who was then thirteen years old. As a tutor to a future ruler, Aristotle's interests included politics, and it is possible that it was here that he conceived the idea of collecting and comparing various constitutions, a project he later carried out by collecting digests of the constitutions of 158 Greek city-states. When Alexander ascended the throne after his father Philip's death, Aristotle's duties as tutor had come to an end, and after a brief stay in his home town of Stagira, he returned to Athens.

Upon his return to Athens in 335/34, Aristotle embarked upon the most productive period of his life. Under the protection of the Macedonian statesman Antipater, Aristotle founded his own school. His school was known as the Lyceum, named after the groves where Socrates was known to have gone to think and which were the sacred precincts of Apollo Lyceus. Here Aristotle and his

Aristotle (*Scala/Editorial Photocolor Archives*)

pupils walked in the Peripatos, a tree-covered walk, and discussed philosophy, for which reason his school was called *peripatetic*. Besides these peripatetic discussions, there were also lectures, some technical for small audiences and others of a more popular nature for larger audiences. Aristotle is also said to have formed the first great library by collecting hundreds of manuscripts, maps, and specimens, which he used as illustrations during his lectures. Moreover, his school developed certain formal procedures whereby its leadership would alternate among members. Aristotle formulated the rules for these procedures as he also did for the special common meal and symposium once a month when a member was selected to defend a philosophical position against the critical objections of the other members. For twelve or thirteen years Aristotle remained as the head of the Lyceum, not only teaching and lecturing, but above all formulating his main ideas about the classification of the sciences, fashioning a bold new science of logic, and writing his advanced ideas in every major area of philosophy and science, exhibiting an extraordinary command of universal knowledge.

When Alexander died in 323, a wave of anti-Macedonian feeling arose, making Aristotle's position in Athens very precarious because of his close connections with Macedonia. As Socrates before him, Aristotle was charged with "impiety," but, as he is reported to have said, "lest the Athenians should sin twice against philosophy," he left the Lyceum and fled to Chalcis where he died in 322 of a digestive disease of long standing. In his will he expressed sensitive human qualities by providing amply for his relatives, preventing his slaves from being sold and providing that some of his slaves should be emancipated. As with Socrates and Plato, Aristotle's thought was of such decisive power that it was to influence philosophy for centuries to come. From the vast range of his philosophy, we shall consider some aspects of his logic, metaphysics, ethics, politics, and aesthetics.

LOGIC

Aristotle invented formal logic. He also invented the idea of the separate sciences. For him, there was a close connection between logic and science, inasmuch as he considered logic to be the instrument (*organon*) with which to formulate language properly when analyzing what a science involves. Although formal logic is concerned with the forms of human thinking, Aristotle did not limit his interest in logic to the relations of propositions to each other or simply to the consistency of language with itself. His chief interest was with the forms of proof, and for this reason he was particularly concerned with what we can state in precise language about reality, about *what* things exist and *why* they are as they are. Science, as Aristotle understood it, consisted of true statements that accounted for the reasons why things behave as they do and why they *have* to be as they are. In this sense, science consists in the knowledge of the *fact that* and of the *reason why*. It includes both observation *and* a theory that explains what is observed. For example, one can observe steam coming from a kettle on the stove, but this mere observation does not by itself enable us to define "steam" in any systematic or scientific manner. A scientific statement about this observation would reflect a careful sorting out of the essential elements of this observation, setting aside all irrelevant details or "accidents" such as the particular fuel used for the fire and the kind of vessel used for the water, focusing squarely upon the special kind of event this is, the production of steam, and giving reasons for the occurrence of this event by relating heat, water, and steam in such a way that one can know, have proof, why and under what conditions heat and water produce steam. The most important thing about science is therefore the language in which it is formulated. Scientific language must indicate as precisely as possible what constitutes the distinctive subject matter of a science, and it must describe why things act the way they do. Logic, then, is a study of words or language, but not the way a grammarian would study these. Aristotelian logic is the study of the thought for which words are signs; it is an attempt to get at truth by an analysis of the thought that reflects our apprehension or understanding of the nature of things. In short, for Aristotle, logic was the instrument of analysis of human thought as it thinks about reality. To be sure, thought does not always reflect reality accurately, but it is the function of logic always to work toward a more adequate relation between language and reality.

The Categories and the Starting Point of Reasoning   Before one can demonstrate or prove something, he must have a clear starting point for his reasoning process. For one thing, he must specify the subject matter he is discussing, the specific "kind" of thing he is dealing with. To this he must add the properties and causes that are related to that kind of thing. In this connection, Aristotle developed his doctrine of the *categories,* which explains how we think about things. Whenever we think of a distinct subject matter, we think of a subject and its predicates, or of some *substance* and its accidents. *We think the word* man *and* also connect the word *man* with such predicates as *tall* and *able.* The word *man* is here a substance, and Aristotle indicates that there are about nine *categories* (meaning predicates) that can be connected with a substance, including *quantity* (e.g., six feet tall), *quality* (e.g., articulate), *relation* (e.g., double), *place* (e.g., at the school), *date* (e.g., last week), *posture* (e.g., standing), *possession* (e.g., clothed), *action* (e.g., serves), and *passivity* (e.g., is served). *Substance* itself can be considered a category, since we, for example, say "he is a man," in which case *man* (a substance) is a *predicate.* These categories represented for Aristotle the classification of concepts that are used in scientific knowledge. They represent the specific ways in which whatever exists does exist or is realized. In our thinking, we arrange things into these categories, classifying such categories into genera, species, and the individual thing. We see the individual as a member of the species and the species as related to the genus. Aristotle did not consider these categories or these classifications as artificial creations of the mind. He thought that they were actually in existence outside the mind and in things. Things, he thought, fall into various classifications by their very nature, and we think of their being members of a species or genus because they *are.* Thinking, as Aristotle saw it, was connected with the way things are, thereby indicating a close relation between logic and metaphysics. Thinking is always about some specific individual thing, a substance. But a thing never simply exists; it exists some*how* and has a reason *why*.

There are always predicates (categories) related to subjects (substances). Some predicates are intrinsic to a thing; such predicates or categories belong to a thing simply because it is what it is. A horse is thought of as having certain predicates *because* it is a horse; it has in common these predicates with all other horses. It also has other predicates, not so intrinsic but rather "accidental," such as color, place, size, and other determinations affecting its relation to other material objects. What Aristotle wants to underscore is that there is a sequence that leads to "science," this sequence being, first of all, the *existence* of things and their processes; secondly, our *thinking* about things and their behavior; and, finally, the transformation of our thought about things into *words*. Language is the instrument for formulating scientific thought. Logic, then, is the analysis of language, of the process of reasoning, of the way language and reasoning are related to reality.

Since scientific language attempts to demonstrate accurately how things behave, such language is concerned both with proof and truth. Proof requires that the process of reasoning rest upon the proper, i.e., valid, relation of terms and propositions to each other. However, Aristotle was concerned not only with consistency, i.e., showing that conclusions validly follow from certain premises. He was also concerned that the premises be true, so that the conclusions would have demonstrative value concerning reality. Aristotle said that "the proper object of unqualified scientific knowledge is something which cannot be other than it is." We have scientific knowledge, he said, "when we think that we know the cause on which the fact depends, as the cause of that fact and no other, and, further, that the fact could not be other than it is." To relate causes and effects involves the multiple acts of observing, judging, and concluding. Observation by itself does not provide us with the definition of things, nor does it give us science as such. What science requires is, first of all, the discovery of a premise, a starting point for reasoning. This premise is a product of *induction*. Our mind, says Aristotle, has a better knowledge of the things close to our senses than of things farther from our senses. For this reason, our minds move from a knowledge of particular things discovered by observation to universal or class ideas, which we do not as such sense. We observe particular men and then form the general idea of Man. Having formulated premises by induction, our mind can then employ these premises deductively or demonstratively. Although Aristotle said that "we must get to know the primary premises by induction," he did not develop this aspect of knowledge with its corollaries of hypothesis and experimentation. His emphasis was upon deduction and demonstrative reasoning. The basic elements of this form of reasoning were analyzed and systematically organized for the first time by Aristotle through his doctrine of *syllogism*.

The Syllogism Aristotle defines the syllogism as "discourse in which certain things being stated, something other than what is stated follows of necessity from their being so." This is the principle of implication, and Aristotle was particularly concerned that scientific discourse should proceed from one valid step to another with precision. He wanted to discover the rules that would guarantee that conclusions were rightly inferred from their premises. How, then, could one be sure that a conclusion follows from its premises; or, what makes it possible for us, assuming that we have two propositions, to derive from these a third proposition? Aristotle thought he had discovered the answer to these questions in the basic structure of the syllogism.

The syllogism is a special form of connected language. Scientific demonstrations are possible because certain words stand for certain properties, qualities, or characteristics of things. Such words stand for *essential* properties as compared with *accidental* properties. To say that a man is mortal is to describe one of his essential properties, whereas to say that he has red hair is to describe something accidental, since to be a man it is not necessary or essential that one have red, or even any, hair. But it is "essential" to his being a man that he be mortal, and it is such essential properties of things that scientific propositions contain. Still, when we ask why it is that men are mortal, a fact we already know from experience, we are asking for a scientific or technical "reason why." It is at this point that the specially connected language of the syllogism comes into operation, for the syllogism represents the linking of propositions about essential properties in such a way that the conclusion necessarily follows. And what makes the conclusion follow is that a particular term is found in both of the premises, linking these premises together so that the conclusion necessarily follows. The term that serves this function of linking propositions is called by Aristotle the *middle,* saying that "I call that term middle which is itself in another and contains another in itself; in position also it comes in the middle." Hence, the "reason why" it is true that "all men are mortal" is that this is a conclusion from two other premises that are linked together by a middle term, as follows: We say first that "all animals are mortal" and next that "all men are animals" and from this it follows that "all men are mortals." The middle term here is *animals,* and this term is linked to the predicate *mortal* and to the subject *all men,* thereby producing the implication that "all men are mortal."

In a formal way, Aristotle sets up the structure of the syllogism as follows:

If *A* is predicated of all *B*
and *B* is predicated of all *C*
then *A* is necessarily predicated of all *C*

Here Aristotle has provided a purely formal instrument for orderly reasoning and in this formal sense it is like mathematics. What it consists of is a major and minor premise and a conclusion:

Major premise   If *A* is predicated of all *B* (e.g., all animals are mortal)

Minor premise   and *B is* is predicated of all *C* (e.g., all men are animals)

Conclusion   then *A* is necessarily predicated of all *C* (e.g., all men are mortal)

Although Aristotle's doctrine of the syllogism is a tool for determining which relationships between premises and conclusion have consistency, his chief interest in developing the syllogism was not simply to assure consistent reasoning. His aim was to provide an instrument for scientific demonstration, and for this reason, again, he emphasized the relation between logic and metaphysics, between our way of knowing and what things are and how they behave. That is, he thought that words and propositions are linked together because the things which language mirrors are also linked together. For this reason, Aristotle recognized that it is entirely possible to employ the syllogism consistently without necessarily arriving at science or truth if the premises did not rest upon valid assumptions (i.e., if they did not reflect true reality). Accordingly, Aristotle distinguished between three kinds of reasoning, each of which might use the instrument of the syllogism, but with different results: these are, first, *dialectical* reasoning, which is reasoning from "opinions that are generally accepted"; second, there is *eristic* or contentious reasoning, which begins with opinions that seem to be generally accepted but are really not; and, third, there is what Aristotle calls *demonstrative* reasoning, where the premises from which reasoning starts are true and primary.

The value of syllogistic reasoning depended for Aristotle upon the accuracy of the premises. If true scientific knowledge is to be achieved, it is necessary that the premises one uses be more than opinion or even probable truth. Demonstrative reasoning moves backward, as it were, from conclusions to those premises that constitute the necessary beginnings of the conclusion. When we say that "all men are mortal," we in effect move back to those causes and properties in animals that indicate their mortality. We then link men with these properties by including them in the class of animals. Demonstrative reasoning must therefore lay hold of reliable premises, principles, or what Aristotle calls *archai*, i.e., "first things." Demonstrative reasoning is reasoning from true *archai*, that is, accurately defined properties of any thing, class, or distinctive area of subject matter. Valid reasoning therefore presupposes the discovery of true *archai* from which conclusions can be drawn.

How are these first principles or *archai* arrived at? Aristotle answers that we learn these *archai* from observation and induction. When we observe certain facts many times, "the universal that is there," he says, "becomes plain." Whenever we observe any particular "that," our memory stores it away and after observing many similar "thats," there is generated from all these particular "thats" a general term with a general meaning. The mind discovers the universal within the particulars by the process of induction, a process that results in the discovery of additional meanings in the particular "thats" observed.

If one then asks the additional question whether and how we can know that the *archai* or principles are true, Aristotle says we know they are true simply because the mind, working with certain facts, recognizes and "sees" their truth. These *archai* or primary premises are not in turn demonstrated: If it were necessary to demonstrate every premise, this would involve an infinite regress, since each prior premise would also have to be proved, in which case the enterprise of knowledge could never get started. Aristotle, referring again to the *archai* or primary premises, said that "not all knowledge is demonstrative: on the contrary, knowledge of the immediate premises is independent of demonstration." Scientific knowledge, he said, rests upon knowledge that is not itself subject to the same proof as scientific conclusions, so that "besides scientific knowledge there is its originative source which enables us to *recognize* the definitions." Here Aristotle used the word *recognize* in contrast to Plato's use of the word *recollect* or *remember* to explain how we know certain truths. To "recognize" a truth is to have a direct intuitive grasp of it, as when we know that two and two equal four. It may be that the occasion for "recognizing" this truth of arithmetic was the act of adding particular things such as bricks or stones. Still, from these specific factual cases the mind "sees" or "recognizes" the truth that certain things belong to a species or genus and that certain relations exist between them, such as two and two equal four. Thus, Aristotle argued that science rests upon primary premises, which are arrived at by intellectual intuition (*nous*). Once these primary premises and definitions of the essential natures of things are in hand, it is then possible to engage in demonstrative reasoning. Insofar as these premises accurately grasp aspects of reality, syllogistic reasoning assures linking of major and minor premises through the agency of the middle term, thereby producing valid conclusions.

METAPHYSICS

In his work entitled *Metaphysics* (a term that indicates the position of this work among his other writings, namely, *beyond*, or coming after, *Physics*) Aristotle develops what he called the science of *first philosophy*. Throughout his *Metaphysics*, he is concerned with a type of knowledge that he thought could be most rightly called *wisdom*. He begins this work with the statement that "All men by nature desire to know." This innate desire, says Aristotle, is not only a desire to know in order to do or make something. In addition to these pragmatic motives, there is in man a desire to know certain kinds of things simply for the sake of knowing. An indication of this, says Aristotle, is "the delight we take in our senses; for even apart from their usefulness they are loved for themselves" inasmuch as our seeing "makes us know and brings to light many differences between things."

There are different levels of knowledge. Some men know only what they experience through their senses, as, for example, when they know that fire is hot. But, says Aristotle, we do not regard what we know through the senses as wisdom. To be sure, our most authoritative knowledge of particular things is acquired through our senses. Still, this kind of knowledge tells us only the "that" of anything and not the "why"; it tells us, for example, *that* fire is hot but not *why*. Similarly, in medicine, some men know only *that* medicines heal certain illnesses. This knowledge, based upon specific experiences, is, according to Aristotle, on a lower level than the knowledge of the medical scientist who knows not only "that" a medicine will heal but knows also the reason "why." In the various crafts, the master craftsmen "know in a truer sense and are wiser than the manual workers, because they know the *causes* of the things that are done."

Wisdom is, therefore, more than that kind of knowledge obtained from sensing objects and their qualities. It is even more than knowledge acquired from repeated experiences of the same kinds of things. Wisdom is similar to the knowledge possessed by the scientist who begins by looking at something, then repeats these sense experiences, and finally goes beyond sense experience by thinking about the *causes* of the objects of his experiences. There are as many sciences as there are definable areas of investigation, and Aristotle deals with many of them, including physics, ethics, politics, and aesthetics. In each case, the respective science is concerned with discovering the causes or reasons or principles underlying the activity of its special subject matter; thus, for example, in physics one asks what causes material bodies to move, in ethics what causes the good life, in politics what causes the good state, and in aesthetics what causes a good poem. Sciences differ not only in their subject matter but also in their relation to each other. Some sciences depend upon others, as when the physicist must rely upon the science of mathematics. In the hierarchy of sciences, Aristotle says that "the science which knows to what end each thing must be done is the most authoritative of the sciences, and more authoritative than any ancillary science." In addition to the specific sciences, then, there is another science, *first philosophy*, or what we now call *metaphysics*, which goes beyond the subject matter of the other sciences and is concerned with "first principles and causes." These "first principles and causes" are the true foundation of *wisdom*, for they give us knowledge not of any particular object or activity, but rather knowledge of true reality.

Metaphysics deals with knowledge at the highest level of abstraction. This knowledge is abstract because it is about what is universal instead of what is particular. Every science has its own level of abstraction inasmuch as it deals with the first principles and causes of its subject matter, as when the physicist talks about the principles of motion in general as distinguished from describing the motion of this planet or that pendulum. Wisdom has to do, then, with the abstract levels of knowledge and not with the levels of visible things, for, as Aristotle says, "sense-perception is common to all, and therefore easy and no mark of Wisdom." True wisdom, first philosophy, or metaphysics is the most abstract and also the most exact of all the sciences because it tries to discover the truly first principles from which even the first principles of the various sciences are derived. True knowledge is therefore found in what is most knowable, and, says Aristotle, "the first principles and the causes are most knowable . . . and from these, all other things come to be known. . . ." We are led, then, to consider more specifically the subject matter of metaphysics.

The Problem of Metaphysics Defined   The various sciences seek to find the first principles and causes of specific kinds of things, such as material bodies, the human body, the state, a poem, and so on. Unlike these sciences, which ask, "What is such-and-such a thing like and why?" metaphysics asks a far more general question, a question that each science must ultimately take into account, namely, "What does it mean to be anything whatsoever?" What, in short, does it mean *to be?* It was precisely this question that concerned Aristotle in his *Meta-*

physics, making metaphysics for him "the science of any existent, as existent." The problem of metaphysics as he saw it was therefore the study of Being and its "principles" and "causes."

Aristotle's metaphysics was to a considerable extent an outgrowth of his views on logic and his interest in biology. From the viewpoint of his logic, "to be" meant for him to be *something* that could be accurately defined and that could therefore become the subject of discourse. From the point of view of his interest in biology, he was disposed to think of "to be" as something implicated in a dynamic process. "To be," as Aristotle saw the matter, always meant to be *something.* Hence, all existence is individual and has a determinate nature. All the categories Aristotle dealt with in his logical works, categories (or predicates) such as *quality, relation, posture, place,* and so on, presuppose some subject to which these predicates can apply. This subject to which all the categories apply Aristotle called *substance (ousia).* To be, then, is to be a particular kind of substance. Also, "to be" means to be a substance as the product of a dynamic process. In this way, metaphysics is concerned with *Being* (i.e., existing substances) and its *causes* (i.e., the processes by which substances come into being).

Substance as the Primary Essence of Things   A major clue to what Aristotle means by substance is discovered, he thought, in the way we know a thing. Having in mind again the categories or predicates, Aristotle says that we know a thing better when we know *what it is* than when we know the color, size, or posture it has. The mind separates a thing from all its qualities and focuses upon what a thing really is, upon its *essential nature.* We recognize that all men are *men* in spite of their different sizes, colors, or ages. *Something* about each concretely different man makes him a man in spite of the unique characteristics that make him this particular man. At this point, Aristotle would readily agree that these special characteristics (categories, predicates) also exist, have some kind of being. But the being of these characteristics is not the central object of metaphysical inquiry. The central concern of metaphysics is the study of substance, the essential nature of a thing. In this view, substance means "that which is not asserted of a subject but of which everything else is asserted." Substance, that is, is what we know as basic about something, *after* which we can say other things about *it.* Whenever we define something, we get at its essence *before* we can say anything about it, as when we speak of a large table or a healthy man. Here table and man are understood in their "essence," in what makes them a table or a man, before they are understood as large or healthy. To be sure, we can know only specific and determinate things, actual individual tables and men. At the same time, the essence, or substance, of a table or a man has its existence peculiarly separate from its categories or its qualities. This does not mean that a substance is ever in fact found existing separately from its qualities. Still, if we can know the essence of a thing, "tableness" let us say, as "separable" from these particular qualities, round, small, and brown, there must be some universal essence that is found wherever one sees a table; and this essence or substance must be independent of its particular qualities inasmuch as the essence is the same even though in the case of each actual table the qualities are different. What Aristotle seems to be saying is that a thing is more than the sum of its particular qualities. There is something "beneath" (*sub stance*) all the qualities; thus, any specific thing is a combination of qualities, on the one hand, and a substratum to which the qualities apply, on the other. With these distinctions in mind, Aristotle was led, as was Plato before him, to consider just how this essence, or universal, was related to the particular thing. What, in short, makes a substance a substance; is it *matter* as a substratum or is it *form*?

Matter and Form   Although Aristotle distinguished between *matter* and *form*, he nevertheless said that we never find matter without form or form without matter in nature. Everything that exists is some concrete individual thing, and every *thing* is a unity of matter and form. Substance, therefore, is a composite of form and matter.

Plato, it will be recalled, argued that Ideas or Forms, such as Man or Table, had a separate existence. Similarly, he treated *space* as the material substratum or the stuff out of which individual things were made. For Plato, then, this primary stuff of space was molded by the eternally existing Forms into individual shapes. This was Plato's way of explaining how there could be many individual things that all have one and the same, that is, universal, nature or essence while still being individual. This universal, Plato said, is the Form, which exists eternally and is separate from any particular thing and is found in each thing only because the thing (this table) *participates* in the Form (tableness, or Ideal Table).

Aristotle rejected Plato's explanation of the universal Forms, rejecting specifically the notion that the Forms existed separately from individual things. Of course, Aristotle did agree that there are universals, that universals such as Man and Table are more than merely subjective notions. Indeed, Aristotle recognized that without the theory of universals, there could be no scientific knowledge, for then there would be no way of saying something about all members of a particular class. What makes scientific knowledge effective is that it discovers classes of objects (for example, a certain form of human disease), so that whenever an individual falls into this class, other facts can be assumed also to be relevant. These classes, then, are not merely mental fictions but do in fact have objective reality. But, said Aristotle, their reality is to be found not anywhere else than in the individual things themselves. What purpose, he asked, could be served by assuming that the universal Forms existed separately? If anything, this would complicate matters, inasmuch as everything, that is, not only individual things but also their relationships, would have to be reduplicated in the world of Forms. Moreover, Aristotle was not convinced that Plato's theory of Forms could help us know things any better, saying that "they help in no wise towards the knowledge of other things. . . ." Since presumably the Forms are motionless, Aristotle concluded that they could not help us understand things as we know them, which are full of motion, nor could they, being immaterial, explain objects of which we have sense impressions. Again, how could the immaterial Forms be related to any particular thing? That things *participate* in the Forms was not a satisfactory explanation for Aristotle, leading him to conclude that "to say that they are patterns and that other things share in them, is to use empty words and poetical metaphors."

When we use the words *matter* and *form* to describe any specific thing, we seem to have in mind the distinction between what something is made of and what it is made into. This, again, disposes our minds to assume that what things are made of, matter, exists in some primary and unformed state until it is made into a thing. But, again, Aristotle argues that we shall not find anywhere such a thing as "primary matter," that is, matter without form. Consider the sculptor who is about to make a statue of Venus out of marble. He will never find marble without some form; it will always be this marble or that, a square piece or an irregular one, but he will always work with a piece in which form and matter are already combined. That he will give it a different form is another question. The question here is, how does one thing become another thing? What, in short, is the nature of *change?*

The Process of Change: The Four Causes   In the world around us we see things constantly changing. Change is one of the basic facts of our experience. For Aristotle, the word *change* means many things, including motion, growth, decay, generation, and corruption. Some of these changes are *natural,* whereas others are the products of *human art.* Things are always taking on new form; new life is born and statues are made. Because change always involves taking on new form, several questions can be asked concerning the process of change. Of anything, says Aristotle, we can ask four questions, namely (1) what is it? (2) what is it made of? (3) by what is it made? and (4) for what end is it made? The four responses to these questions represent Aristotle's four *causes.* Although the word *cause* refers in modern use primarily to an event prior to an effect, for Aristotle it meant an *explanation.* His four causes represent therefore a broad pattern or framework for the total explanation of anything or everything. Taking an object of art, for example, the four causes might be (1) a statue (2) of marble (3) by a sculptor (4) for a decoration. Distinguished from objects produced by human art, there are those things which are produced *by nature.* Although nature does not, according to Aristotle, have "purposes" in the sense of "the reason for," it does always and everywhere have "ends" in the sense of having built-in ways of behaving. For this reason, seeds sprout and roots go down (not up!) and plants grow and in this process of change move toward their "end," i.e., their distinctive function or way of being. In nature, then, change will involve these same four elements. Aristotle's *four causes* are therefore (1) the *formal* cause, which determines *what* a thing is, (2) the *material* cause, or that out of which it is made, (3) the *efficient* cause, by what a thing is made, and (4) the *final* cause, the "end" for which it is made.

Aristotle looked at life through the eyes of a biologist. For him, nature is *life.* All things are in motion, in the process of becoming and dying away. The process of reproduction was for him a clear example of the power inherent in all living things to initiate change, and to reproduce their kind. Summarizing his causes, Aristotle said that "all things that come to be come to be by some agency and from something, and come to be something." From this biological viewpoint, Aristotle was able to elaborate his notion that form and matter never exist separately. In nature, generation of new life involves, according to Aristotle, first of all an individual who already possesses the specific form which the offspring will have (the male parent); there must then be the matter capable of being the vehicle for this form (this matter being contributed by the female parent); from this comes a new individual with the same specific form. In this example, Aristotle indicates that change does not involve bringing together formless matter with matterless form. On the contrary, change occurs always in and to something that is already a combination of form and matter and that is on its way to becoming something new or different.

Potentiality and Actuality   All things, said Aristotle, are involved in processes of change. Each thing possesses a power to become what its form has set as its end. There is in all things a dynamic power of striving toward their "end." Some of this striving is toward external objects, as when a man builds a house. But there is also the striving to achieve ends that pertain to one's internal nature, as when a man fulfills his nature as a man by the act of thinking. This self-contained end of anything Aristotle called its *entelechy*. All things have their own entelechy.

That things have ends led Aristotle to consider the distinction between *potentiality* and *actuality*. This distinction is used by Aristotle to explain the processes of change and development. If the *end* of an acorn is to be a tree, in some way the acorn is only potentially a tree but not actually so at this time. A fundamental mode of change, then, is the change from potentiality to actuality. But the chief significance of this distinction is that Aristotle argues for the priority of actuality over potentiality. That is, although something actual emerges from the potential, there could be no movement from potential to actual if there were not first of all something actual. A boy is potentially a man, but before there could be a boy with that potentiality, there had to be prior to him an actual man.

As all things in nature are similar to the relation of a boy to a man, or an acorn to a tree, Aristotle was led to see in nature different levels of being. If everything were involved in change, in generation and corruption, everything would partake of potentiality. But, as we have seen, for there to be something potential, there must already be something actual. To explain the existence of the world of potential things, Aristotle thought it was necessary to assume the existence of some actuality at a level above potential or perishing things. He was led to the notion of a Being that is pure actuality, without any potentiality, at the highest level of being. Since change is a kind of motion, Aristotle saw the visible world as one composed of things in motion. But motion, a mode of change, involves potentiality. Things are potentially in motion but must be moved by something that is actually in motion. Again, to explain motion ultimately led Aristotle to speak of the Unmoved Mover.

The Unmoved Mover For Aristotle, the Unmoved Mover did not mean the same thing as a *first* mover, as though motion could be traced back to a *time* when motion began. Nor was the Unmoved Mover considered by him a *creator* in the sense of later theology. From his previous distinction between potentiality and actuality, Aristotle concluded that the only way to explain how motion or change can occur is to assume that something actual is *logically* prior to whatever is potential. The fact of change must imply the existence of something actual, something *purely* actual without any mixture of potentiality. This *Mover* is not, according to Aristotle, an *efficient* cause in the sense of exerting a power or force, or as expressing a *will*. Such acts would imply potentiality, as when one says that God "willed" to create the world. This would mean that *before* God created the world, he was potentially capable or intended to create it. Aristotle did not think of the Unmoved Mover as a Being that *thinks* or prescribes *purposes* for the world. In a sense, the Unmoved Mover does not know anything precisely because it is not a kind of being as much as it is a way of explaining the fact of motion. All of nature is full of striving toward fulfilling all of its particular entelechies. Each thing is aiming at perfecting its possibilities and its *end*, aiming, that is, at becoming the perfect tree, the perfectly good man, and so on. The aggregate of all these strivings constitutes the large-scale processes of the world order so that it can be said that all of reality is in the process of change, moving from its potentialities and possibilities to the ultimate perfection of these potentialities. To explain this comprehensive or general motion, to make it intelligible, Aristotle referred to the Unmoved Mover as the "reason for" or the "principle of" motion. For this reason, the Unmoved Mover stood for him as the actual, and, because there is here no potentiality, the *eternal* principle of motion. Since this explanation of motion implies an eternal activity, then, there was never a "time" when there was not a world of things in process. For this reason, too, Aristotle denied that there was a "creation" in time. Although there are passages in Aristotle that have a distinctly religious and theistic flavor, the dominant mood of his thought on this matter is less religious than it is scientific. Still, to speak of an Unmoved Mover involved Aristotle in certain metaphorical language. In explaining how an Unmoved Mover can "cause" motion, he compared it to a beloved who "moves" the lover just by being the object of love, by the power of attraction and not by force. In a more technical way, Aristotle considered the Unmoved Mover as the *form* and the world as the substance. From the point of view of his four causes, Aristotle considered the Mover as the *final* cause, in the way that the *form* of man is in the boy, directing the motion of his change toward a *final*, that is, fixed or appropriate, natural *end*. By being a final cause, the Unmoved Mover thereby, in relation to the world, becomes also *efficient* cause, through the power of attraction, by being desired and loved, by inspiring the striving toward natural ends, a process that goes on eternally. What in Aristotle's thought was the unconscious principle of motion and immanent form of the world, the Unmoved Mover, became, especially at the hands of Aquinas in the thirteenth century, the philosophical description of the God of Christianity. Aristotle's Unmoved Mover could be said to be pure understanding, pure *nous*, and since it must think the best, it "thinks itself . . . and its thinking is a thinking of thinking . . . throughout all eternity." Such a "God" is not the religious God who becomes involved in the affairs of man. Aristotle's "God" is immanent in the world, making the world an intelligible order.

THE PLACE OF MAN:
PHYSICS, BIOLOGY, AND PSYCHOLOGY

Aristotle placed man in the nature of things in such a way as to distinguish his position in the hierarchy of being from inanimate things and animals. He points out in his *Physics* that "of things that exist, some exist by nature, some from other causes. 'By nature' the animals and their parts exist, and the plants and the simple bodies (earth, fire, air and water)." In the order of nature, there are, then, first of all, simple bodies, plants, and animals. What is significant about all these things in nature is, as Aristotle states, that they all "present a feature in which they differ from things which are *not* constituted by nature. Each of them has *within* itself a principle of motion and of rest. . . ." This internal motion is the decisive aspect of things, for through this motion Aristotle explains the whole process of generation and corruption.

Physics   Limiting our concern only to the question of how things come to be in the natural world, Aristotle begins with the notion of *prime matter*. We have already said that Aristotle rejected the position that either pure forms or pure matter could exist separately. There is no *primary matter* existing by itself anywhere. By *prime matter* Aristotle must have meant the substratum in things that is capable of changing, of becoming other substances or things, of assuming novel forms. The processes of nature, then, involve the continuous transformation of matter from one form to another. When the sculptor makes a statue, his material, let us say marble, already has some form, and he will now transform it. In this same sense, Aristotle says that there are certain materials out of which *nature* makes things and he calls these *simple bodies,* namely air, fire, earth, and water. In one way or another, he says, all things are analyzable down to these. Still, when these bodies combine with one another, they form novel substances. Unlike the statue, however, the genesis of these new forms is a product of nature itself, since these bodies have within themselves a "principle of motion and rest." For this reason, fire tends to rise and become air, water to fall and become earth, the solid to become liquid, and the wet to become dry. In any case, to say that things *change* is to say that these basic simple bodies are constantly being transformed into things through their internal principle of motion and by the motion of other things.

Biology   What confers life upon certain kinds of bodies? Aristotle accounts for the transition from inorganic to organic bodies by considering the nature of the *soul.* All bodies, he says, are a combination of the primary elements, but some have life and others do not. By life Aristotle means "self-nutrition and growth (with its correlative decay)." Matter as such is not the principle of life, since material substance is said to be only potentially alive. Matter is always potentiality, whereas form is actuality. A body, then, that is actually alive has its life from the source of actuality, namely, *form.* The soul, then, is the form of an organized body. Neither can exist without the other, nor are they identical, and, says Aristotle, "that is why we can wholly dismiss as unnecessary the question whether the soul and body are one: it is as meaningless as to ask whether the wax and the shape given to it by the stamp are one. . . ." The soul, as Aristotle defines it, is "the first grade of actuality of a natural organized body." When a body is "organized," its parts have set motions to perform: thus, in a living plant, "the leaf serves to shelter the pericarp, the pericarp to shelter the fruit, while the roots of plants are analogous to the mouth of animals . . . serving for the absorption of food." The soul is "the definitive formula of a thing's essence." The soul exists when there is a particular kind of body, namely, "one having *in itself* the power of setting itself in movement and arresting itself." Soul and body are not two separate things but are rather the matter (body) and form (soul) of a single unity; and, "from this it indubitably follows that the soul is inseparable from its body. . . ." Without the body, the soul could not exist, any more than there could be vision without an eye.

Aristotle distinguished between three types of soul in order to indicate the three different ways a body can be organized. He called these the *vegetative, sensitive,* and *rational* souls. They represent various capacities of a body for activity, the first being simply the act of living, the second both living and sensing, and the third a body that includes living, sensing, and thinking.

Psychology   The sensitive soul is found at the animal level. Its chief characteristic lies in its power to absorb qualities and *forms* of things without taking in their *matter.* This is in contrast to the lower nutritive soul, which takes in the *matter* (e.g., food) but has no capacity to absorb its *form.* The basic sense is tactile, or touch, and is capable of absorbing what all bodies have in common. For the other senses, Aristotle says that "each sense has one kind of object which it discerns, and never errs in reporting that what is before it is color or sound." Again, the sensitive soul absorbs only the form and not the matter, "in the way," says Aristotle, "in which a piece of wax takes on the impress of a signet ring without the iron or gold . . . in a similar way the sense is affected by what is coloured or flavoured or sounding, but it is indifferent to what in each case the *substance* is."

Just how the sensitive soul senses was explained by Aristotle by a special interpretation of *potentiality.* The sense organs must be capable of sensing many different forms. They must therefore by potentially capable of adjusting to any quality. The eye, for example, must be composed of material that potentially can become blue and that in fact does become blue when a certain kind of object is sensed. This neutral material of the eye must possess potentially all colors as well as all shapes. Our various other senses have similar potentialities with respect to other qualities. Moreover, the five senses have a way of combining their information into a unified whole, reflecting the single object or world from which these "sensibles" come. Errors are possible, as when something will "look" hard but "feel" soft. The qualities we sense can continue even after we are no longer directly perceiving an object, and this Aristotle explains in terms of *memory* and also *imagination*. Much of what we remember retains its associations with other things, suggesting that neither sensation nor memory is a random act but rather tends to reproduce what in fact exists in the real world. From the power of memory and imagination comes finally the higher form of soul, the human or the rational soul.

Human Rationality   The human soul combines in itself all the lower forms of soul, the vegetative, nutritive, and sensitive, having in addition to these the *rational soul*. The rational soul has the power of scientific thought. The *reason* is capable not only of distinguishing between different kinds of things, which is the power of analysis, it is able also to understand the relationships of things to each other. Besides scientific thought, the rational soul has the power of *deliberation*. Here the mind not only discovers what truth is in the nature of things, it discovers the guides for human behavior.

Again, for Aristotle, the soul forms the *entelechy*, the definitive form, of the body. Without the body, the soul could neither be nor exercise its functions. This is in sharp contrast to Plato's explanation of the body as the prison house of the soul. By contrast, Aristotle says that the body and soul together form one substance. Because he separated soul and body, Plato could speak of the preexistence of the soul. He could also describe knowledge or learning as the process of recollection of what the soul knew in its previous state. Moreover, Plato could also speak of the immortality of the individual soul. Aristotle, on the other hand, tied soul and body so closely together that with the death of the body, the soul, its organizing principle, also perished. Also, for him the mind begins as a blank tablet.

The rational soul of man, as the sensitive soul, is characterized by potentiality. Just as the eye is capable of seeing a red object but will only see it when it actually confronts a red object, so, also, the rational soul is capable of understanding the true nature of things. But reason has its knowledge only potentially; it must reason out its conclusions. Human thought, in short, is a possibility and not a continuous actuality, for if it is *possible* for the human mind to attain knowledge, it is also possible for it not to attain knowledge. Human thought is therefore intermittent between *actually* and *potentially* knowing. Truth is never continuously present in the human intellect.

The continuity of truth is implied by the continuity of the world. What the human mind has as potential knowledge must therefore be perfect and continuous knowledge in some mind. Aristotle had spoken of the Unmoved Mover as the soul (*nous*) of the world and its intelligible principle. In his *De Anima* he speaks of the Active Intellect, saying that "*Nous* does not at one time function and at another not." Here he appears to compare the individual human intellect, which knows only intermittently, with the Active Intellect, which is in some sense independent of particular men and is eternal. If this intellect is indeed purely active, it possesses no potentiality. But this is what Aristotle had described as the Unmoved Mover. The distinctive activity of the Unmoved Mover is pure act, which is an exercise of the mind in complete harmony with the truth about the whole of reality. The whole system of Forms taken as the intelligible structure of all things must therefore constitute the continuous knowledge of the *nous* of the world, the Unmoved Mover, the Active Intellect. This Intellect is immortal, and to the extent that our passive and potential intellects know any truth, they have in them what the Active Intellect always knows. What is immortal when a man dies is what belongs to the Active Intellect, but as this is not a part of *him*, his own individual soul perishes with the matter for which it was the form. Only what is pure act is eternal, and man's substance, being an admixture of potentiality, does not survive.

ETHICS

Aristotle's theory of morality centers around his belief that man, as everything else in nature, has a distinctive "end" to achieve or a function to fulfill. For this reason, his theory is rightly called *teleological*. He begins his *Nicomachean Ethics* by saying that "every art and every inquiry, and similarly every action and pursuit, is thought to aim at some good. . . ." If this is so, the question for ethics is, "What is the *good* at which human behavior aims?" Plato had answered this question by saying that man aims at a knowledge of the Idea of the Good. For him this supreme principle of Good was separated from the world of experience and from individual men and was to be arrived at by the mind's ascent from the visible world to the intelligible world. For Aristotle, on the other hand, the principle of good and right was imbedded within each man; moveover, this principle could be discovered by studying the essential nature of man and could be attained through his actual behavior in daily life. Aristotle warns his reader, however, not to expect more precision in a discussion of ethics than "the subject-matter will admit." Still, just because this subject is susceptible of "variation and error" does not mean, said Aristotle, that ideas of right and wrong "exist conventionally only, and not in the nature of things." With this in mind, Aristotle set out to discover the basis of morality in the structure of human nature.

Types of "Ends" Aristotle sets the framework for his ethical theory with a preliminary illustration. Having said that all action aims toward an end, he now wants to distinguish between two major kinds of ends, which can be called *instrumental* ends (acts that are done as *means* for other ends) and *intrinsic* ends (acts that are done for their own sake). These two types of ends are illustrated, for example, in "every action connected with war." When we consider step by step what is involved in the total activity of a war, we find, says Aristotle, that there is a series of special kinds of acts, which have their own ends but which, when they are completed, are only means by which still other ends are to be achieved. There is, for one thing, the art of the bridle maker. When the bridle is completed, its maker has achieved his end as a bridle maker. But the bridle is a means for the horseman to guide his horse in battle. Also, a carpenter builds a barrack, and when it is completed, he has fulfilled his function as a carpenter. The barracks also fulfill their function when they provide safe shelter for the soldiers. But the ends here achieved by the carpenter and the building are not ends in themselves but are instrumental in housing soldiers until they move on to their next stage of action. Similarly, the builder of ships fulfills his function when the ship is successfully launched, but again this end is in turn a means for transporting the soldiers to the field of battle. The doctor fulfills his function to the extent that he keeps the soldiers in good health. But the "end" of health in this case becomes a "means" for effective fighting. The officer aims at victory in battle, but victory is the means to peace. Peace itself, though sometimes taken mistakenly as the final end of war, is the means for creating the conditions under which men, *as men,* could fulfill their function as men. When we discover what men aim at, not as carpenters, doctors, or generals, but as *men,* we will then arrive at action *for its own sake,* and for which all other activity is only a means, and this, says Aristotle, "must be the Good of Man."

How shall the word *good* be understood? As Plato before him, Aristotle tied the word *good* to the special function of a thing. A hammer is good if it does what hammers are expected to do. A carpenter is good if he fulfills his function as a builder. This would be true for all the crafts and professions. But here Aristotle distinguishes between a man's craft or profession and his activity as a man. To be a good doctor, for example, did not for Aristotle mean the same thing as being a good man. One could be a good doctor without being a good man, and vice versa. There are two different functions here, the function of doctoring and the function of acting as a man. To discover the good at which a man should aim, Aristotle said we must discover the distinctive function of human nature. The good man, according to Aristotle, is the man who is fulfilling his function as a man.

The Function of Man Aristotle asks, "Are we then to suppose that while carpenter and cobbler have certain works and courses of action, Man as Man has none, but is left by Nature without a work?" Or, if "the eye, hand, foot and in general each of the parts evidently has a function, may one lay it down that man similarly has a function apart from all these?" Surely, man too has a distinctive mode of activity, but what is it? Here Aristotle analyzes man's nature in order to discover his unique activity, saying, first of all, that man's end "is not mere life," because that plainly is shared with him even by vegetables, and, says Aristotle, "we want what is peculiar to him." Next there is the life of sensation, "but this again manifestly is common to horses, oxen and every animal." There remains then "an active life of the element that has a rational principle . . . if the function of man is an activity of soul which follows or implies a rational principle . . . then the human good turns out to be activity of soul in accordance with virtue. . . ."

Since man's function as a man means the proper functioning of his soul, Aristotle sought to describe the nature of the soul. The soul is the form of the body. As such, the soul refers to the total person. Accordingly, Aristotle said that the soul has two parts, the irrational and the rational. The irrational part in turn is composed of two subparts, the vegetative and the desiring or "appetitive" parts. For the most part, these are "something contrary to the rational principle, resisting and opposing it." The conflict between the rational and irrational elements in man is what raises the problems and subject matter of morality.

Morality involves action, for nothing is called *good* unless it is functioning. Thus Aristotle says that "as at the Olympic games it is not the finest and strongest men who are crowned, but they who enter the lists, for out of these the prize-men are selected; so too in life, of the honourable and good, it is they who act who rightly win the prizes." The particular kind of action implied here, if one has in mind Aristotle's analysis of the soul, is the rational control and guidance of the irrational parts of the soul. Moreover, the good man is not the one who does a good deed here or there, now and then, but whose whole life is good, "for as it is not one swallow or one fine day that makes a spring, so it is not one day or a short time that makes a man blessed and happy."

Happiness as the End   Human action should aim at its proper end. Everywhere men aim at pleasure, wealth, and honor. But none of these ends, though they have value, can occupy the place of the chief good for which man should aim. To be an ultimate end an act must be *self-sufficient* and *final*, "that which is always desirable in itself and never for the sake of something else," and it must be *attainable by man.* Aristotle seems certain that all men will agree that *happiness* is the end that alone meets all the requirements for the ultimate end of human action. Indeed, we choose pleasure, wealth, and honor only because we think that "through their instrumentality we shall be happy." Happiness, it turns out, is another word or name for *good,* for like good, happiness is the fulfillment of our distinctive function; or, as Aristotle says, "Happiness . . . is a working of the soul in the way of excellence or virtue. . . ."

How does the soul work to attain happiness? The general rule of morality is "to act in accordance with Right Reason." What this means is that the rational part of the soul should control the irrational part. That the irrational part of the soul requires guidance is obvious when we consider what it consists of and what its mechanism is. Referring now only to the appetites, or the "appetitive" part of the soul, we discover first that it is affected or influenced by things outside of the self, such as objects and persons. Also, there are two basic ways in which the appetitive part of the soul reacts to these external factors, these ways being *love* and *hate,* or through the *concupiscent* and *irascible* "passions." The concupiscent passion leads one to desire things and persons, whereas the irascible passion leads one to avoid or destroy them. It becomes quickly apparent that these passions or capacities for love and hate, attraction or repulsion, creation or destruction, taken by themselves could easily "go wild." In themselves they do not contain any principle of measure or selection. What should a person desire? How much? Under what circumstances? How should he relate himself to things, wealth, honor, and other persons?

We do not automatically act the right way in these matters; as Aristotle says, "none of the moral virtues arises in us by nature; for nothing that exists by nature can form a habit contrary to its nature." Morality has to do with developing habits, the habits of right thinking, right choice, and right behavior.

Virtue as the "Golden Mean"   Since the passions are capable of a wide range of action, all the way from too little to too much, a person must discover the proper meaning of excess and defect and thereby discover the appropriate *mean*. Virtue is concerned with our various feelings and actions, for it is in them that there can be excess and defect. For example, it is possible, says Aristotle, to feel the emotion of fear, confidence, lust, anger, compassion, pleasure, and pain, too much or too little, and in either case wrongly. To feel these when we ought to, on which occasions, toward whom, and as we should is the *mean;* that is the best state for man to be in, and this is *virtue*. Vice, again, is either extreme, excess or defect, and virtue is the mean. It is through the rational power of the soul that the passions are controlled and action is guided. The virtue of *courage*, for example, is the mean between two vices: namely, fear (defect) and foolhardiness (excess). Virtue, then, is a state of being, "a state apt to exercise deliberate choice, being in the relative mean, determined by reason, and as the man of practical wisdom would determine."

The mean is not the same for every person, nor is there a mean for every act. Each mean is relative to each person inasmuch as the circumstances will vary. In the case of eating, the mean will obviously be different for an adult athlete and a little girl. But for each person, there is nevertheless a proportionate or relative mean, *temperance,* clearly indicating what extremes—namely, gluttony (excess) and starvation (defect)—would constitute vices for them. Similarly, when one gives money, *liberality,* as the mean between prodigality and stinginess, is not an absolute figure but is relative to one's assets. Moreover, for some acts there is no mean at all; their very nature already implies badness, such as spite, envy, adultery, theft, and murder. These are bad in themselves and not in their excesses or deficiencies. One is always wrong in doing them.

Deliberation and Choice   There are in the rational soul two kinds of reasoning. The first is theoretical, giving us knowledge of fixed principles or philosophical wisdom. The other is practical, giving us a rational guide to our action under the particular circumstances in which we find ourselves, and this is practical wisdom. What is important about the role of reason is that without this rational element, man would not have any moral capacity. Again, Aristotle stressed that although man has a natural capacity for *right* behavior, he does not act rightly *by nature*. A man's life consists of an indeterminate number of possibilities. Goodness is in man *potentially;* but unlike the acorn out of which the oak will grow with almost mechanical certitude, man must move from what is potential in him to its actuality by knowing what he must do, deliberating about it, and then choosing in fact to do it. Unlike Plato and Socrates, who thought that to know the good was sufficient to do the good, Aristotle saw that there must be deliberate choice in addition to knowledge. Thus, Aristotle said that "the origin of moral action—its efficient, not its final cause—is choice, and (the origin) of choice is desire and reasoning with a view to an end." There cannot be *choice* without reason. And again, "intellect itself . . . moves nothing, but only the intellect which aims at an end and is practical."

Morality and moral choice imply human responsibility. If some ways of behaving are right and others wrong, it is necessary to discover why a person acts in a wrong instead of right way. If we are to praise or blame, praise virtue and blame vice, a person must be truly capable of making a choice. Aristotle assumed that an act for which a person could be held responsible must be a *voluntary* act. A genuine choice is a voluntary action. But not all our actions are voluntary. Thus, Aristotle said that "praise and blame arise upon such as are voluntary, while for the involuntary allowance is made, and sometimes compassion is excited." The distinction, as he saw it, between voluntary and involuntary acts was in general this: *Involuntary* acts are those for which a person is not responsible because it is (1) done out of ignorance of particular circumstances, or (2) a result of external compulsion, or (3) done to avoid a greater evil. *Voluntary* acts are those for which a person is responsible because none of these three extenuating circumstances obtain.

The Virtues In a general way we have already defined virtue as the fulfillment of man's distinctive function, and as the mean between extremes. Another way to describe Aristotle's concept of virtue is to consider each virtue as the product of the rational control of the passions. In this way we can combine all aspects of human behavior. Human nature consists for Aristotle not simply in rationality but in the full range covered by the vegetative, sensitive or appetitive, and the rational souls. Virtue does not imply the negation or rejection of any of these natural capacities. The moral man employs all his capacities, *physical* and *mental*. Corresponding to these two broad divisions in man there are two functions of reason, the intellectual and the moral, and each has its own virtues. There are accordingly *intellectual virtues* and *moral virtues*.

The intellectual virtues are philosophical wisdom and understanding and owe their birth and growth to teaching and learning. Moral virtue comes about as a result of habit, whence comes the name *ethics* (*ethike*), "formed by a slight variation from the word *ethos* (habit)." All the moral virtues have to be learned and practiced, and they become virtues only through action, for "we become just by doing just acts, temperate by doing temperate acts, brave by doing brave acts." The "cardinal" moral virtues are courage, temperance, justice, and wisdom. In addition to these, Aristotle considered also the virtues of magnificence, liberality, friendship, and self-respect. And although he acknowledged the central role of reason as a guide to practical and moral action, he nevertheless concluded that philosophic wisdom is superior to practical wisdom, that *contemplation* is most likely to lead to happiness.

Contemplation Aristotle concludes that if happiness is the product of our acting according to our distinctive nature, it is reasonable to assume that it is acting according to our highest nature, and "that this activity is contemplative we have already said." This activity is the best, says Aristotle, "since not only is reason the best thing in us, but the objects of reason are the best of knowable objects." Moreover, contemplation "is most continuous, since we can contemplate truth more continuously than we can *do* anything." Finally, "we think happiness has pleasure mingled with it, but the activity of philosophic wisdom is admittedly the pleasantest of virtuous activities."

POLITICS

In his *Politics*, as in his *Ethics*, Aristotle stresses the element of purpose. The state, as man, is endowed by nature with a distinctive function. Combining these two ideas, Aristotle says that "it is evident that the State is a creature of nature, and that man is by nature a political animal." So closely does he relate man and the state as to conclude that "he who is unable to live in society, or who has no need because he is sufficient for himself, must be either a beast or a god." Not only is man by nature destined to live in a state, but the state, as every other community, "is established with a view to some good," exists for some end. The family exists primarily to preserve life. The state comes into existence in the first instance to preserve life for families and villages, which in the long run are not self-sufficing. But beyond this economic end, the function of the state is to ensure the supreme good of man, namely, his moral and intellectual life.

Unlike Plato, Aristotle did not create a blueprint for an ideal state. Even though Aristotle viewed the state as the agency for enabling men to achieve their ultimate goals as human beings, he nevertheless realized that any practical theory of the state must take note of "what kind of government is adapted to particular states . . . [that] the best is often unattainable . . ." and that the legislator must be acquainted with "which is best relatively to circumstances . . . how a state may be constituted under any given conditions . . . [and] how it may be longest preserved," concluding that "political writers, although they have excellent ideas, are often unpractical." For these reasons, Aristotle had little patience with Plato's most radical ideas. Ridiculing Plato's arrangement for the abolition of the family for the guardian class and providing a public nursery for their children, Aristotle said that "there is no reason why the so-called father should care about the son, or the son about the father, or brothers about one another." The communal ownership of property would likewise destroy certain basic human pleasure as well as engender inefficiency and endless disputes.

Types of States   Aristotle was willing to recognize that under appropriate circumstances, a community could organize itself into at least three different kinds of government. The basic difference between them is primarily the number of rulers each has. A government can have as its rulers either *one*, a *few*, or *many*. But each of these forms of government can have a true or a perverted form. When a government is functioning rightly, it governs for the common good of all the people. A government is perverted when its rulers govern for their own private gain or interests. The true forms of each type of government, according to Aristotle, are *monarchy (one)*, *aristocracy (few)*, and *polity (many)*. The perverted forms are *tyranny (one)*, *oligarchy (few)*, and *democracy (many)*. His own preference was aristocracy, chiefly because even though ideally an individual of exceptional excellence would be desirable, such persons do not exist with sufficient frequency. In an aristocracy, there is the rule of a group of men whose degree of excellence, achievement, and ownership of property makes them responsible, able, and capable of command.

Differences and Inequalities   Because he relied so heavily upon his observation of things, it was inevitable that Aristotle would make some mistakes. Nowhere is this more true than in his estimate of slavery. Observing that slaves invariably were strong and large, he concluded that slavery was a product of nature. "It is clear," said Aristotle, "that some men are by nature free, and others slaves, and that for these slavery is both expedient and right." To be sure, Aristotle took great care to distinguish between those who become slaves by nature, a mode he accepted, and those who became slaves by military conquest, a mode he rejected. He rejected slavery by conquest on the highly defensible grounds that to overpower someone does not mean that one is superior to him in nature. Moreover, the use of force may or may not be justified, in which case enslavement could very well be the product and extension of an unjust act. At the same time, speaking of the "proper treatment of slaves," he proposed that "it is expedient that liberty should be always held out to them as the reward of their services." The fact is that in his own last will and testament, Aristotle provided for the emancipation of some of his slaves.

   Aristotle also believed in the inequality of citizenship. He held that the basic qualification for citizenship was a person's ability to take his share in ruling and being ruled in turn. A citizen had the right and the obligation to participate in the administration of justice. Since a citizen would therefore have to sit in the assembly and in the law courts, he would have to have both ample time as well as an appropriate temperament and character. For this reason, Aristotle did not believe that laborers should be citizens, as they had neither the time nor the appropriate mental development, nor could they benefit from the experience of sharing in the political process.

Good Government and Revolution   Over and over again Aristotle made the point that the state exists for the sake of man's moral and intellectual fulfillment. "A state," he said, "exists for the sake of a good life, and not for the sake of life only"; also, "the state is the union of families and villages in a perfect and self-sufficing life, by which we mean a happy and honourable life." Finally, he said, "our conclusion . . . is that political society exists for the sake of noble actions, and not mere companionship." Still, whether a state produces the good life depends upon how its rulers behave. We have already said that the perverted forms of government are distinguished from the true forms by this, that the good rulers seek to achieve the good of all, whereas the perverted rulers seek their own private gain.

Whatever form a government has, it will rest upon some conception of justice and proportionate equality. But these conceptions of justice can bring disagreement and ultimately revolution. Democracy, as Aristotle knew it, arises out of the assumption that those who are equal in any respect are equal in all respects; "because men are equally free, they claim to be absolutely equal." On the other hand, Aristotle said *oligarchy* is based upon the notion that "those who are unequal in one respect are in all respects unequal." Hence, "being unequal . . . in property, they suppose themselves to be unequal absolutely." For these reasons, whenever the democrats or oligarchs are in the minority and the philosophy of the incumbent government "does not accord with their preconceived ideas, [they] stir up revolution. . . . Here then . . . are opened up the very springs and fountains of revolution."

Aristotle concludes that "the universal and chief cause of this revolutionary feeling [is] the desire of equality, when men think they are equal to others who have more than themselves." He did not overlook other causes such as "insolence and avarice" as well as fear and contempt. Knowing these causes of revolution, Aristotle said that each form of government could take appropriate precautions against it; for example, a king must avoid despotic acts, an aristocracy should avoid the rule by a few rich men for the benefit of the wealthy class, and a polity should provide more time for its abler members to share in the government. Another precaution is to guard against the beginning of change. Most important of all, Aristotle urged that "there is nothing which should be more jealously maintained than the spirit of obedience to law." In the end, men will always criticize the state unless their conditions of living within it are such that they can achieve happiness in the form of what they consider the good life.

PHILOSOPHY OF ART

Aristotle had a far more sympathetic interest in art than did Plato. For Plato, as for Aristotle, art was essentially a matter of imitation, an imitation of nature. What made Plato so contemptuous of some forms of art was his notion that a work of art is at least three steps removed from truth. The true reality of man, let us say, is the eternal Form of Man. A poor copy of this Form would be any particular man—Socrates, for example. A statue or portrait of Socrates would then be a copy of a copy. Plato was particularly concerned with the cognitive aspect of art, feeling that it had the effect of distorting knowledge because it was removed several steps from reality. Aristotle, on the other hand, believing that the universal Forms exist only in particular things, felt that the artist is dealing directly with the universal when he studies things and translates them into art forms. For this reason Aristotle affirmed the cognitive value of art, saying that since art does imitate nature, it therefore communicates information about nature.

In his *Poetics*, he stresses the cognitive aspect of poetry by contrasting poetry with history. Unlike the historian, who is concerned only with particular persons and events, the poet deals with basic human, and therefore universal, experience. The true difference between them is that history relates what has happened, whereas poetry considers what may happen. "Poetry, therefore," says Aristotle, "is a more philosophical and a higher thing than history: for poetry tends to express the universal, history the particular." By universality, Aristotle means "how a person of a certain type will on occasion speak or act, according to the law of probability or necessity," and it is "this universality at which poetry aims. . . ."

In addition to its cognitive value, art has in Aristotle's view considerable psychological significance. For one thing, art reflects a deep facet of human nature by which man is differentiated from animals, this being his implanted instinct for imitation. Indeed, from earliest childhood learning takes place through imitation. In addition to this instinct, there is also the fact of pleasure men feel upon confronting art. Thus, "the reason men enjoy seeing a likeness is, that in contemplating it they find themselves learning or inferring, and saying perhaps, 'Ah, that is he'."

Although Aristotle gave detailed analyses of *epic, tragedy,* and *comedy,* indicating what each consists of and what its function is, it was his remarks about tragedy that became most famous in subsequent thought. He particularly emphasized the emotional aspect of tragedy, centering upon the notion of *catharsis.* "A tragedy," says Aristotle, "is the imitation of an action that is serious and also, as having magnitude, complete in itself; in language with pleasurable accessories, each kind brought in separately in the parts of the work; in a dramatic, not a narrative form; with incidents arousing pity and fear, *wherewith to accomplish its catharsis of such emotions.*" Does the term *catharsis* imply that through tragedy we "get rid of" our feelings? Or, does it mean that we are given an occasion to express or give vent to our deepest emotions in a vicarious way? In either case, what Aristotle seems to be saying is that the artistic representation of deep and great suffering arouses in the audience genuine terror and pity, thereby purging and in a sense purifying the hearers' spirit. Thus, Aristotle says that "tragedy is an imitation of an action . . . through pity and fear effecting the proper purgation of these emotions."

5

Classical Philosophy After Aristotle

After Aristotle had completed his great speculative system, philosophy moved toward a new emphasis. Four groups of philosophers helped to shape this new direction, namely, the Epicureans, the Stoics, the Skeptics, and the Neoplatonists. They were, of course, greatly influenced by their predecessors, so we find that Epicurus relied upon Democritus for his atomic theory of nature, the Stoics made use of Heraclitus' notion of a fiery substance permeating all things, the Skeptics built a method of inquiry upon the Socratic form of doubt, and Plotinus drew heavily upon Plato. What made their philosophy different, however, was not so much its subject matter as its mood and its emphasis. Its emphasis was practical, and its mood was self-centered. Philosophy became more practical by emphasizing the art of living. To be sure, each of these new movements of thought did involve speculative descriptions of the structure of the universe. But instead of working out blueprints for the ideal society and fitting individuals into large social and political organizations, as Plato and Aristotle had done, these new philosophers led people to think primarily of themselves and how they as individuals in a scheme of nature could achieve the most satisfactory personal life.

These new directions in ethics were brought about to a great extent by the historical conditions of the times. After the Peloponnesian War and with the fall of Athens, Greek civilization declined. With the breakdown of the small Greek city-state, individual citizens lost the sense of their own importance and their ability to control or perfect their social and political destiny. Individuals increasingly felt this loss of personal control over collective life as they were absorbed into the growing Roman Empire. When Greece became a mere province of Rome, men lost interest in pursuing the speculative questions concerning the ideal society. What was needed was a practical philosophy to give life direction under changing conditions. And at a time when events overwhelmed people, it seemed idle to try to change history. But if history was beyond man's control, at least his own life could be managed with some success. Philosophy, therefore, shifted to this practical emphasis in a mood of increasing concern for the more immediate world of the individual.

The Epicureans turned in the direction of apathy, what they called *ataraxia* or tranquillity of soul, the Stoics sought to control their reactions to inevitable events, while the Skeptics sought to preserve personal freedom by refraining from any basic commitment to ideals whose truth was doubtful, and Plotinus promised salvation in a mystical union with God. They looked to philosophy for a source of meaning for human existence, and it is no wonder that their philosophy, particularly Stoicism, was later to compete with religion for the allegiance of men. They sought to discover ways in which individual persons could successfully achieve happiness or contentment in a world that was not altogether friendly and filled with many pitfalls.

EPICURUS: PERFECTING THE PLEASURE PRINCIPLE

Epicurus was born about seven or eight years after Plato's death, when Aristotle was forty-two years old. Born in 342 or 341 B.C. on the island of Samos in the Aegean Sea, he was exposed in his teens to the writings of Democritus, whose ideas about nature had a permanent influence upon his own philosophy. When the Athenians were driven out of Samos, Epicurus went to Asia Minor, where he became a teacher in several schools. About the year 306 B.C. he moved to Athens and here founded his own school. The meeting place of his school was his own garden, which in time ranked with Plato's Academy, Aristotle's Lyceum, and Zeno's Stoa as one of the influential schools of ancient times. Here Epicurus attracted a close group of friends, who were attached to him by deep affection and reverence, and to each other by the love of cultivated conversation. In spite of the loss of the bulk of his prolific writings there emerged from this school a definite approach to philosophy, which survived Epicurus' death in 270 B.C. The lasting impact of his teaching is shown by its continuous appearance in Athens and its spread to Rome, where the poet Lucretius (98–55 B.C.) embodied the major thoughts of Epicurus in his memorable poem *On the Nature of Things* (*De Rerum Natura*), which has survived to our day.

Epicurus was a practical philosopher. He thought that ideas should have as much effect upon the control of life as medicine has upon the health of the body. Indeed, he considered philosophy as the medicine of the soul. He did not deal at length with the intricate aspects of questions such as "what is the world made of?" The picture of the world as consisting of atoms, or bits of matter, which had been developed by Democritus, seemed to Epicurus a reasonable answer. If that is what the world consists of, thought Epicurus, what consequences follow from that for human behavior?

To Epicurus, the chief aim of human life is pleasure. But it is ironic that his name should be linked even today with the indulgent gourmand or voluptuary, for nothing could be further from the teaching of Epicurus than the notion that pleasure consists in the triple formula of eat, drink, and be merry. Instead, he took great pains to distinguish between various types of pleasures as, for example, between those that are intense but last only a short while and those that are not so intense but last longer, or, between those pleasures which have a painful aftermath and those which bestow a sense of calm and respose. He tried to refine the principle of pleasure as the basis of conduct.

Physics and Ethics   What made Epicurus turn to the pleasure principle was the "science" or physics he had inherited from Democritus. Building upon this "atomic theory," Epicurus concluded that everything that exists must be made up of eternal atoms, small, indestructible bits of hard matter. Apart from these clusters of atoms, nothing else exists. This would mean that if God or gods exist, they too must be material beings. Most important of all, God is not the source or the creator of anything but is himself the result of a purposeless and random event.

The origin of everything is explained by the notion that there is no beginning to the atoms. Atoms have always existed in space. As raindrops, they were at one time separately falling in space, and since they encountered no resistance, they always remained the same distance apart from each other. During this vertical drop, thought Epicurus, one atom instead of falling perfectly straight had developed a slight easing to one side, a lateral "swerve." In time, this atom moved into the path of an oncoming atom, and the resulting impact forced both of these atoms into the paths of other atoms, thereby setting in motion a whole series of collisions until all the atoms had been formed into clusters. These clusters or arrangements of atoms are the things we see even now, including rocks, flowers, animals, human beings, in short, the world. Since there was an infinite number of atoms, there must now be an infinite number of worlds. In any case, human beings are not part of a created or purposeful order caused or ruled by God but rather the accidental product of the collision of atoms.

God and Death   With this explanation of the origin of human beings, and for that matter of all beings including "divine beings," Epicurus thought that he had liberated man from the fear of God and from the fear of death. One no longer had to fear God because God did not control nature or human destiny, and was, therefore, unable to intrude into man's life. As for death, this, said Epicurus, need not bother anyone, because only a living person has sensation either of pain or pleasure. After death, there is no sensation, since the atoms that make up both the body and mind come apart, so there is no longer this particular body or mind but only a number of distinct atoms that return, as it were, to the primeval inventory of matter to continue the cycle of new formations. Only matter exists, and in human life all we know is this body and this present moment of experience. The composition of human nature includes atoms of different sizes and shapes, the larger atoms making up our bodies, with the smaller, smoother, and swifter atoms accounting for sensation and thinking. No other principle is needed to explain man's nature, no God and, therefore, no afterlife. To be liberated from the fear of God and of death sets the stage for a way of life completely under a person's own control.

This was a new direction in moral philosophy, for it focused upon the individual and his immediate desires for bodily and mental pleasures instead of upon abstract principles of right conduct or considerations of God's commands. Just as his physical theory made the individual atom the final basis of all being, so also Epicurus singled out the individual person as the arena of the moral enterprise.

The Pleasure Principle   Although he portrayed the origin of all things in a mechanical way and had placed man into the nature of things as just another small mechanism whose nature led him to seek pleasure, Epicurus, nevertheless, reserved for man both the power and the duty to regulate the traffic of his desires. Even though he had liberated men from the fear of God's providence, he had no intention, thereby, of opening the floodgates of passion and indulgence. He was certain that pleasure was the standard of goodness, but he was equally certain that not every kind of pleasure had the same value.

If one were to ask Epicurus how he knew that pleasure was the standard of *goodness,* he would answer simply that all men have an immediate feeling of the difference between pleasure and pain and of the desirability of pleasure, "For we recognize pleasure as the first good innate in us, and from pleasure we begin every act of choice and avoidance, and to pleasure we return again." Feeling, Epicurus said, is as immediate a test of goodness or badness as sensation is the test of truth. To our senses, pain is always bad and pleasure always good, just as seeing tells us whether something is in front of us or not.

Still, Epicurus laid his greatest emphasis upon the distinction between various kinds of pleasures in order to guide men to the happiest life. To him it was clear that some desires were both natural and necessary, as in the case of food; others natural but not necessary, as in the case of some types of sexual pleasure; and still others neither natural nor necessary, as, for example, any type of luxury or popularity. It was because he could make these clear distinctions that he concluded that "when . . . we maintain that pleasure is the end, we do not mean the pleasures of the profligates and those that consist of sensuality, as is supposed by some who are either ignorant or disagree with us or do not understand, but freedom from pain in the body and from trouble in the mind. For it is not continuous drinkings and revelings, nor the satisfaction of lusts, nor the enjoyment of fish and other luxuries of the wealthy table, which produces a pleasant life, but sober reasoning, searching out of motives of all choice and avoidance, and banishing mere opinions, to which are due the greatest disturbance of the spirit."

Epicurus did not mean to deprecate the pleasures of the body but meant only to emphasize that too great a concern with these pleasures was both unnatural and the surest way to unhappiness and pain. Certain kinds of bodily pleasures could never be fully satisfied, he said, and if such pleasures required continuous indulgence it followed that a person pursuing such a pleasure would by definition always be unsatisfied and would, therefore, constantly suffer some pain. If, for example, a person wanted more money, or more public acclaim, or more exotic foods, or a higher position, he would always be dissatisfied with his present situation and would suffer some internal pain. The wise man, on the other hand, is able to determine what is the minimum his nature requires, and is able easily and quickly to satisfy these needs. When these needs are satisfied, a person's constitution is in balance. The wise man's diet of bread and water is far more likely to bring happiness than the gourmet's surplus of fancy foods, for the wise man has learned not only to consume little but, also, and this is the clue, to need little.

The ultimate pleasure human nature seeks is repose, by which Epicurus means the absence of bodily pain and the gentle relaxation of the mind. This sense of repose can be most successfully achieved by scaling down our desires, overcoming useless fears, and, above all, turning to the pleasures of the mind, which have the highest degree of permanence. In a sense these pleasures of the mind are physical pleasures inasmuch as they have the effect of preventing overindulgence in matters of the flesh and, therefore, preventing their ensuing pain.

Individual Pleasure versus Social Duty   In the end, Epicurus had fashioned a self-centered moral philosophy, for his concern was not primarily with human society but with individual pleasure. Even the life of the philosopher is looked upon as a means to avoiding pain and not as an influence for creating a good society. Just as Epicurus sought to detach himself from the tyranny of exotic foods, so also did he seek to detach himself from entanglements with other people and particularly with poor people, whose needs and problems are many. For him the good life was not to be found in service to one's fellow man but in the pleasant, decent company of intellectually fascinating friends. The only function of civil society that Epicurus would recognize was to deter those who might inflict pain upon individuals. His theory of physics, which rules out all purpose and any realm of rational order, left him without a firm idea of justice. There was, for Epicurus, no higher value than the absence of pain and the control of desires by the mind. We shall see that for centuries to come this moral philosophy fashioned by Epicurus challenged and in turn was challenged by alternative concepts of the moral life.

STOICISM: DISTINGUISHING BETWEEN WHAT WE CAN AND CANNOT CONTROL

Stoicism as a school of philosophy includes some of the most distinguished intellectuals of antiquity. Founded by Zeno (334–262 B.C.), who assembled his school on the Stoa (Greek for *porch,* hence the term *stoic*), this philosophical movement attracted Cleanthes (303–233 B.C.) and Aristo in Athens and later found such advocates in Rome as Cicero (106–43 B.C.), Epictetus (60–117 A.D.), Seneca (4 B.C. ? – 65 A.D.), and the Emperor Marcus Aurelius (121–180 A.D.). Zeno had been inspired as a youth by the ethical teachings and particularly by the courageous death of Socrates. This influence helped to fix the overwhelming emphasis of Stoic philosophy upon ethics, although the Stoics addressed themselves to all three divisions of philosophy formulated by Aristotle's Academy, namely, logic, physics, and ethics.

Wisdom and Control versus Pleasure In their moral philosophy, the Stoics aimed at happiness, but unlike the Epicureans they did not expect to find it in

Stoa (*Agora Excavations, American School of American Studies at Athens*)

pleasure. Instead, the Stoics sought happiness through wisdom, a wisdom by which to control what lay within human power and to accept with dignified resignation what had to be. They were profoundly influenced by Socrates, who had faced death with serenity and courage. This example of superb control over the emotions in the face of the supreme threat to one's existence, the threat of death, provided the Stoics with an authentic model after which to pattern their lives. Centuries later the Stoic Epictetus said that "I cannot escape death, but cannot I escape the dread of it?" Developing this same theme in a more general way, he wrote, "Demand not that events should happen as you wish; but wish them to happen as they do happen, and you will go on well." We cannot, that is, control all events, but we can control our attitude toward what happens. It is useless to fear future events, for they will happen in any case. But it is possible by an act of will to control our fear. We should not, therefore, fear events—in a real sense we have "nothing to fear but fear itself."

There is an elegant simplicity to this moral philosophy, and yet it was a philosophy for an intellectual elite. The conclusion was simple enough, to control one's attitudes, but how did the Stoics arrive at this conclusion in a philosophical way? They did it by creating a mental picture of what the world must be like and how man fits into this world. The world, they said, is an orderly arrangement where man and physical things behave according to principles of *purpose*. They saw throughout all of nature the operation of *reason* and *law*. The Stoics relied upon a special idea of God to explain this view of the world, for they thought of God as a rational substance existing not in some single location but in all of nature, in all things. It was this kind of God, a pervading substantial form of *reason* that controls and orders the whole structure of nature, that the Stoics said determines the course of events. Herein lay the basis for moral philosophy, but the direction in which Stoic thought moved on these matters was set by their theory of the nature of knowledge.

Stoic Theory of Knowledge The Stoics went into great detail to explain how human beings are able to achieve knowledge. They did not entirely succeed in doing this, but their theory of knowledge was nevertheless important for at least two reasons. First, it laid the foundation for their materialistic theory of nature, and, secondly, it provided the basis for their conception of truth or certainty.

Both of these consequences of the Stoics' theory of knowledge stem from their account of the origin of ideas. Words, they said, express thoughts, and thoughts are originated by the impact of some object upon the mind. The mind is blank at birth and builds up its store of ideas as it is exposed to objects. These objects make impressions upon the mind through the channel of the senses. A tree, for example, impresses its image upon the mind through the sense of vision in the same way that a seal leaves its imprint in wax. Repeated exposure to the world of things increases the number of impressions, develops our memory, and enables us to form more general conceptions beyond the objects immediately before us.

The real problem the Stoics faced was how to explain this last point, that is, how to account for our general ideas. They had to show how our thinking is related to our sensations. It is one thing to prove that our idea of a tree comes from our vision of trees. But how can we account for general ideas, ideas that refer to things beyond our senses as, for example, the idea of goodness? To this the Stoics in effect replied that all thought is in some way related to the senses, even thoughts that represent judgments and inferences. A judgment or an inference, that something is good or true, is the product of the mechanical process of impressions. Our thinking in all its forms starts with impressions, and some of our thinking is based upon impressions that start from within us, as in the case of feelings. Feelings can, therefore, give us knowledge; they are the source of "irresistible perceptions," which, in turn, are the ground of our sense of certainty. As the Skeptics later pointed out, this explanation could not stand up to all the critical questions one could raise against it. But the Stoics not only found in it a basis for truth, they had also, through this theory of knowledge, imposed a most distinctive slant upon their general philosophy. For, to argue as they did, that all thought derives from the impact of objects on the senses is to affirm that nothing real exists except things that possess some material form. Stoic logic had cast Stoic philosophy into a materialistic mold.

Matter as the Basis of All Reality   This materialism provided Stoicism with an ingenious conception of the physical world and the nature of man. The broad picture the Stoics drew of physical nature followed from their logic that all that is real is material. Everything in the whole universe is, therefore, some form of matter. But the world is not just a pile of inert or passive matter—it is a dynamic, changing, structured, and ordered arrangement. Besides inert matter, there is force or power, which represents the active shaping and ordering element in nature. This active power or force is not different from matter but is rather a different form of matter. It is a constantly moving, subtle thing, like an air current or breath. The Stoics said it was fire, and this fire spread to all things providing them with vitality. This material fire had the attribute of rationality, and since this was the highest form of being, it was inevitable that the Stoics should understand this rational force to be God.

God in Everything   The pivotal idea of Stoicism was the notion that God is in everything. To say that God is fire, or force, or logos or rationality and then to say that God is in everything is to conclude that all of nature is filled with the principle of reason. In a detailed manner the Stoics spoke of the permeability of matter, by which they meant that different types of matter are mixed up together. The material substance of God, they said, was mixed with what would otherwise be motionless matter. Matter behaves the way it does because of the presence in it of the principle of reason. The continued behavior of matter in accordance with this principle is what is meant by natural law, the law or principle of a thing's nature. When we recall that the Stoics ascribed the origin of nature to God, the warm, fiery matrix of all things, and that all things immediately receive the impress of God's structuring reason and continue to behave as they were arranged to behave, we can see how the Stoics also developed from these ideas their other notions of fate and providence.

Fate and Providence To the Stoics, *providence* meant that events occur the way they do because all things and persons are under the control of the logos, or God. The order of the whole world is based upon the unity of all its parts, and what unifies the whole structure of matter is the fiery substance that permeates everything. Nothing "rattles" in the universe, for nothing is loose. It was against this background of a material universe that is totally controlled that the Stoics fashioned their moral philosophy.

Human Nature The Stoics knew that to build a moral philosophy it is necessary to have a clear view of what human nature is like. They shaped their view of human nature by simply transferring to the study of man the very same ideas they had used in describing nature at large. Just as the world is a material order permeated by the fiery substance called reason or God, so also man is a material being who is permeated by this very same fiery substance. When the Stoics said that man contains a spark of the divine within him, they meant that in a real sense man contains part of the substance of God. God is the soul of the world, and man's soul is part of God. This spark of the divine is a very fine and pure material substance that permeates man's body, causing it to move and to be capable of all sensations. The soul is corporeal, comes from God, and is transmitted by parents to children in a physical way. The Stoics thought that the soul was centered in the heart and that it circulated through the blood stream. What the soul added to the body was the delicate mechanisms of the five senses as well as the powers of speech and reproduction. But since God is the logos or reason, the soul of man is also rooted in reason and consequently human personality finds its unique expression in its rationality. For the Stoics, however, human rationality did not mean simply that man is able to think, or to reason about things, but rather that man's nature participates in the rational structure and order of the whole of nature. Human rationality represents man's awareness of the actual order of things and of his place in this order. It is the awareness that all things obey law. To relate human behavior to this order of law was the chief concern of Stoic moral philosophy.

Ethics and the Human Drama Moral philosophy in Stoic thought rested upon a simple insight, wherein man was viewed as an actor in a drama. What Epictetus meant when he used this image was that an actor does not choose his role, but on the contrary it is the author or director of the drama who selects people to play the various roles. In the drama of the world, it is God or the principle of reason who determines what each man shall be and how he will be situated in history. Human wisdom, said the Stoics, consists in recognizing what one's role in this drama is and then performing the part well. Some people have "bit parts," while others are cast into leading roles. "If it be [God's] pleasure that you should act a poor man, see that you act it well; or a cripple or a ruler, or a private citizen. For this is your business" says Epictetus, "to act well the given part." The actor develops a great indifference to those things over which he has no control, as, for example, the shape and form of the scenery as well as who the other players will be. He especially has no control over the story or its plot. But there is one thing the actor can control, and that is his attitude and emotions. He can sulk because he has just a bit part, or he can be consumed with jealousy because someone else was chosen to be the hero, or he can feel terribly insulted because the makeup artist put a particularly ugly nose on his face. But neither sulking nor jealousy nor feeling insulted can in any way alter the fact that he has a bit part, is not a hero, and must wear an ugly nose. All these feelings can do is rob him of his happiness. If he can remain free from these feelings, or develop what the Stoics called apathy, he will achieve a serenity and happiness that are the mark of a wise man. The wise man is the one who knows what his role is.

The Problem of Freedom   There is, however, a persistent problem in Stoic moral philosophy, and this concerns the nature of human freedom. The whole Stoic analysis of the structure of nature as being fixed, that is, caused or ordered, by God's reason, is rather easy to follow, especially when we think of this grand scheme as a cosmic drama. It may be true that actors do not choose their roles. But what is the difference between choosing your role in the drama, on the one hand, or choosing your attitude on the other? If you are not free to choose one, how can you be free to choose the other? It could very well be that God not only chose you to be a poor man, but also cast you as a particularly disgruntled poor man. Do attitudes float freely waiting to be chosen by the passing parade of mankind, or are they as much a part of a person as the color of his eyes?

The Stoics stuck doggedly to their notion that attitudes are under the control of man's choice, that by an act of will we can decide how we shall react to events. But they never provided a satisfactory explanation for the fact that providence rules everything while at the same time providence does not rule our attitudes. The closest they came to an explanation was to imply that whereas everything in the whole universe behaves according to law or reason, or logos, it is the special feature of human beings that they behave according to their knowledge of the law. For example, water evaporates from the heat of the sun and later condenses and returns in the form of rain. But one drop never says to the other, "here we go again," as if to register disgust at being uprooted from the blue sea. A human being undergoes a similar process of change when he begins to age and face death; but a man knows what is happening, for in addition to the mechanical process of aging, he *knows* that it is happening. No amount of additional knowledge will change the fact that he is mortal, but the Stoics built their whole moral philosophy on the conviction that if a man knows the rigorous law and understands his role as inevitable, he will not strain against the inevitable but will move cheerfully with the pace of history. Happiness is not a product of choice; it is rather a quality of existence, which follows from acquiescing or agreeing to what has to be. Freedom, therefore, is not the power to alter our destiny but rather the absence of emotional disturbance.

Cosmopolitanism and Justice   It was inevitable that the Stoics should have also developed a strong notion of cosmopolitanism, the idea that all men are citizens of the same human community. To look at the world process as a drama was to admit that everyone had a role in it. Human relations were viewed by the Stoics as having the greatest significance, for human beings were the bearers of the divine spark. What related man to his fellow man was the fact that each person shared a common element. It was as though the logos were a main telephone line and each person had his own phone and the entire circuit was on a party line, thereby connecting God to all men and all men to each other. Or, as Cicero put it: " . . . since reason exists both in man and God, the first common possession of man and God is reason. But those who have reason in common must also have right reason in common. And since right reason is Law, we must believe that men have Law also in common with the Gods. Further, those who share Law must also share Justice, and those who share these are to be regarded as members of the same commonwealth." Universal brotherhood and the doctrine of a universal natural law of justice were among the most impressive contributions made to the Western mind by the Stoics. They had injected basic themes into the stream of thought that were to have a decisive impact, particularly upon the development of Christian philosophy in the next period.

Although Stoicism shared many of the characteristics of Epicurean philosophy, it had made some radical innovations. With the Epicureans, the Stoics put their chief emphasis upon the practical concerns of ethics, regarded self-control as the center of ethics, viewed all of nature in materialistic terms, and sought happiness as the end. The most significant variation injected by the Stoics was that they viewed the world not as the product of chance but as the product of an ordering mind or reason. This view involved the Stoics in a highly optimistic attitude regarding the possibilities of human wisdom. Yet it was against this claim to wisdom, a claim that we can know so much about the detailed operation of the world, that there developed the critical philosophy of the Skeptics.

SKEPTICISM: HOW TO BEHAVE WITHOUT A CRITERION OF TRUTH

Today we refer to skeptics as men whose basic mood is that of doubt. But the old Greek word, *skeptikoi*, from which *skeptics* is derived, meant something rather different, namely, *seekers* or *inquirers*. To be sure, the Skeptics were doubters, too. They doubted that Plato and Aristotle had succeeded in discovering the truth about the world, and they had these same doubts about the Epicureans and Stoics. But for all their doubt, they were nevertheless seekers after a method for achieving a tranquil life. Their founder was Pyrrho (361–270 B.C.), and early Skepticism was known also as Pyrrhonism. They were also known as *Academics*, after Arcesilaus (ca. 316–241 B.C.) who became head of Plato's Academy in the third century, rejected Plato's metaphysics, and developed the doctrine of probabilism. Among the many other notable Skeptics the names Carneades (214–129

B.C.) and Sextus Empiricus (ca. 200 A.D.) are outstanding. As Skepticism moved through its different periods of development, it took on many variations in its point of view. While many of the original documents written by the Skeptics are now lost, some of the works of the authoritative codifier of Greek Skepticism, Sextus Empiricus, have survived. In the early sections of his *Pyrrhonic Sketches,* Sextus offers an illuminating account of the meaning and purposes of the viewpoint of Skepticism.

What gave rise to Skepticism? Sextus says that Skepticism originated in the hope of attaining mental peace or calmness. Men have been disturbed, he says, by the contradiction in things and plagued by doubt as to which alternative they should believe. Accordingly the Skeptics thought that if they could by investigation determine truth from falsehood they could then attain tranquillity of mind. The Skeptics were struck, however, by the different conceptions of truth different philosophers had proposed. They also noticed that men who searched for truth could be placed into three groups, those who think they have discovered the truth (and these the Skeptics called *dogmatists*), those who confess they have not found it and also assert that it cannot be found (and this they also considered a dogmatic position), and finally those who persevere in the search for it. Unlike the first two, says Sextus, "the Skeptics keep on searching." Skepticism is not a denial of the possibility of finding truth, nor is it a denial of the basic facts of human experience. It is rather a continuous process of inquiry in which every explanation of experience is tested by a counterexperience. The fundamental principle of Skepticism, says Sextus, is that to every proposition an equal proposition is opposed. It is in consequence of this principle, he says, that "we end by ceasing to dogmatize."

The Skeptics were greatly impressed by the fact that "appearances" call forth such a variety of explanations from those who experienced them. They discovered also, says Sextus, that arguments opposed to each other seem to have equal force. By equality of force he meant equality in respect of the credibility of probability of alternative explanations. Accordingly, the Skeptics were led to suspend judgment and to refrain from denying or affirming anything. From this suspension of judgment they hoped to achieve an undisturbed and calm mental state.

Clearly, the Skeptics did not give up the enterprise of vigorous thought and debate. Nor did they deny the evident facts about life, that men become thirsty and hungry and that they are in peril when they come near a precipice. That men must be careful about their behavior was very clear to the Skeptics. They had no doubt that they lived in a "real" world. They only wondered whether this world had been accurately described. No one, says Sextus, will dispute that objects have this or that appearance; the question is whether "the object is in reality such as it appears to be." Therefore, even though the Skeptics refused to live dogmatically, they did not deny the evident facts about experience. "We pay due regard to appearances," says Sextus. Daily life seemed to the Skeptics to require careful recognition of four items, which Sextus calls (1) the guidance of nature, (2) the constraint of the feelings, (3) the tradition of laws and customs, and (4) the instruction of the arts. Each of these contributes to successful and peaceful living and not one of them requires any dogmatic interpretation or evaluation, only acceptance. Thus, it is by Nature's guidance that we are naturally capable of sensation and thought. Also, it is by the force of the feelings that hunger drives us to food and thirst to drink. And it is the tradition of laws and customs that constrains us in everyday life to accept piety as good and impiety as evil. Finally, says Sextus, it is by virtue of the instruction of the arts that we engage in those arts in which we choose to participate.

There can be no doubt, therefore, that the Skeptics were far from denying the evident facts of sense perception. Indeed, Sextus says that those who say that the Skeptics deny appearances "seem to me to be unacquainted with the statements of our School." They did not question appearances but only "the account given of appearances," As an example, Sextus says that honey appears to be sweet, and "this we grant, for we perceive sweetness through the senses. . . ." But the real question is whether it is really, in essence, sweet. Thus, the arguments of the Skeptics about appearances are expounded not with the intention of denying the reality of appearance but in order to point out the "rashness" of the "Dogmatists." The moral Sextus drew from this treatment of the objects of sense was that if human reason can be so easily deceived by appearances, "if reason is such a trickster as to all but snatch away the appearances from under our very eyes," should we not be particularly wary of following reason in the case of nonevident matters and thus avoid rashness?

Nonevident matters had a central place in the great philosophical systems of Plato, Aristotle, and the Stoics. Here the Skeptics found elaborate theories, especially about the nature of physical things. But how can any theory of physics, an inquiry which deals with nonevident matters, give us reliable truth? The Skeptics had a double attitude toward the study of physics. On the one hand, they refused to theorize about physics as if to give "firm and confident opinions on any of the things in physical theory about which firm doctrines are held." Nevertheless, they did touch on physics "in order to have for every argument an equal argument to oppose it, and for the sake of mental tranquillity." Their approaches to matters of ethics and logic were similar. In each case their pursuit of mental tranquillity was not a negative approach, a refusal to think, but rather an active approach. Their mode of "the suspension of judgment" involved the activity of "setting things in opposition." As Sextus says, "we oppose appearances to appearances, or thoughts to thoughts, or appearances to thoughts."

The Skeptics, then, distinguished between two types of inquiry, between those dealing with evident and nonevident matters. Evident matters, such as whether it is night or day, raise no serious problems of knowledge. In this category, too, are evident requirements for social and personal tranquillity, for we know that customs and laws bind society together. But nonevident matters, as, for example, whether the stuff of nature is made of atoms or some fiery substance, do raise intellectual controversies. Whenever we go beyond the sphere of what is evident in human experience, our quest for knowledge should proceed under the influence of creative doubt. Thus, if we ask how we know what the universe is like, the Skeptics would answer that we do not yet know. It may be, they said, that men can attain the truth; it may also be that they are in error. But whether they have the truth or are in error cannot be decided, because there is available as yet no reliable criterion for determining the truth in nonevident matters.

The Senses Are Deceptive   If, as the Stoics had argued, our knowledge comes to us from our experience or sense impressions, all the more reason is there to doubt the adequacy of all knowledge. For the fact is that our senses give us different information about the same object at different times and under different circumstances. From a distance, a square building looks round. Landscape looks different at different times of day. To some people honey is bitter. Painted scenery at a theater gives the impression of real doors and windows when only lines exist on a flat surface. That we do have impressions is certain, as, for example, when we "see" a bent oar in the water. But what we can never be certain about is whether in fact the oar is bent. Although the oar can be taken out of the water and the error of perception discovered, not every perception affords such an easy test for its accuracy and truth. Most of our knowledge is based upon perceptions for which we have no criterion of truth. The conclusion of the Skeptic, therefore, is that we cannot be certain that our knowledge of the nature of things is true or not true.

Moral Rules Raise Doubts   Moral conceptions as well as physical objects are subject to doubt. People in different communities have different ideas of what is good and right. Customs and laws differ with each community and in the same community at different times. The Stoics said that there is a universal reason in which all men share, leading to a general consensus of all men regarding human rights. The Skeptics challenged both the theory and the fact, saying that there was no proof that all men have the capacity to agree upon the truth of universal moral principles and adding that there is no evidence that men in fact exhibit this universal agreement. The fact is that men disagree. Moreover, those who disagree can each make an equally strong case for their own point of view. On matters of morality there is no absolute knowledge; there is only opinion. Whereas the Stoics had argued that on certain matters the test for truth was the "irresistible perception," the Skeptics responded by saying that the sad fact is that however strongly an opinion is held, it is, after all, still only an opinion, and one can with as much evidence support an opposite opinion. When men take a dogmatic stand, their conclusions always seem to them to be irresistible, but this is no guaranty that their conceptions are true.

The outcome of this skeptical attitude toward our knowledge of the nature of things and of our knowledge of moral truth is that we have a right to doubt the validity of knowledge. Since we lack sure knowledge, it behooves us to withhold judgment on all matters. But there is a matter about which it is difficult for men to withhold judgment, and that is the matter of ethics. When one faces a problem of behavior, he wants to know what is the right thing to do, and this requires knowledge of the right. It would appear, therefore, that the Skeptics had made ethics impossible and had removed from men any guide for human behavior.

Morality Possible without Intellectual Certainty The Skeptics argued, however, that it was not necessary to have knowledge in order to behave sensibly. It is enough, they said, to have reasonable assurance, or what they called *probability*. There could never be absolute certainty, but if there was a strong probability that our ideas would lead us to a life of happiness and peacefulness, we should be justified in following these ideas. We are able from daily experience to distinguish between notions that are not clear and those that have a high degree of clarity. When notions of right have a high degree of clarity, they create in us a strong belief that they are right, and this is all we need to lead us to action. For this reason customs, the laws of the land, and our basic appetites are for the most part reliable guides. But even here the Skeptic wants to retain a certain amount of caution, so that we will not mistake appearance for reality and above all avoid fanaticism and dogmatism. Although we are able to act enthusiastically even without a criterion of truth, our psychological safety requires that we leave open the channels of inquiry. The only safe attitude to take is one of doubt about the absolute truth of any idea. And if one can maintain a sense of imperturbability under this mood of doubt, he has the best chance of achieving the happy life.

If we ask whether the Skeptics had a "system," Sextus answers "No," if by a system is meant "an adherence to a number of dogmas which are dependent both on one another and on appearances" and where "dogma" is taken to mean "assent to a non-evident proposition." But if by a system is meant "a procedure which, in accordance with appearance, follows a certain line of reasoning . . . indicating how it is possible to seem to live rightly . . . ," then the Skeptic did have a system. For, as Sextus says, "we follow a line of reasoning which . . . points us to a life conformable to the customs of our country and its laws and institutions, and to our own instinctive feelings."

PLOTINUS: SALVATION IN MYSTICAL UNION WITH GOD

At the culmination of classical philosophy stands the influential figure of Plotinus (ca. 204–270 A.D.). He lived at a time when there was no single compelling philosophical doctrine that could satisfy the special concerns of his age. The great variety of religious cults attested to the desperate attempt by men in the second and third centuries of the Roman world to lay hold of an explanation of life and its destiny. It was an age of syncretism, when ideas were taken from several sources and put together as philosophies and religions. The cult of Isis combined Greek and Egyptian ideas of the gods; the Romans developed the Imperial Cult and worshiped their emperors, living and dead; devotees of the Mithraic cult worshiped the sun; and there was the Phrygian worship of the Great Mother of the Gods. Christianity was still considered a cult, even though there had already emerged some Christian thinkers, such as Justin Martyr (100–165), Clement of Alexandria (ca. 150–220), Tertullian (ca. 160–230), and Origen (185–254), who sought to give the Christian faith a systematic character and an intellectual defense. Origen had tried to provide a Platonic and Stoic framework for Christianity. Earlier, Clement of Alexandria had also tried to join Christian thought with philosophic ideas. But Christian theology would not achieve its full strength until Augustine had formulated his powerful synthesis of Christian and Platonic thought. The decisive bridge between classical philosophy and Augustine would be the writings of Plotinus. But Plotinus nowhere mentions Christianity; his original contribution consisted of a fresh version of Plato's philosophy, and for this reason is known as Neoplatonism.

Plotinus was born in Egypt about 204 A.D. He was the pupil of Ammonius Saccas in Alexandria. Alexandria was at this time an intellectual crossroads of the ancient world, and here Plotinus developed a wide grasp of classical philosophy, including the ideas of Pythagoras, Plato, Aristotle, Epicurus, and the Stoics. Out of all these strands he selected Platonism as the surest source of truth and indeed criticized the others by using his version of Plato's thoughts as his standard. From Alexandria he went, at the age of forty, to Rome, where the atmosphere was charged by considerable chaos in morality and religion and by social and political unrest. At Rome he opened his own school, to which he attracted some of that city's elite, including the emperor and his wife. For a while he planned to develop a city based upon the doctrines of Plato's *Republic* to be called Platonopolis, but this plan was never realized. He wrote fifty-four treatises with no particular order and in a style less eloquent than his speech. These treatises were assembled after Plotinus' death by his ablest pupil, Porphyry, who arranged them into six sets of nines, or, as they are now called, *Enneads*. Plotinus had been a brilliant lecturer and at the same time a man of spiritual idealism. Indeed, it was his moral and spiritual force combined with his intellectual rigor that influenced not only his contemporaries but especially St. Augustine. Later, Augustine said that Plotinus would have to change "only a few words" to become a Christian. In any case, the thought of Plotinus became a major strand in most of medieval philosophy.

What made Plotinus' philosophy distinctive was that he combined a speculative description of the system of reality with a religious doctrine of salvation. He not only described the world, but also gave an account of its source, of man's place in it, and of how man overcomes his moral and spiritual difficulties in it. In short, Plotinus developed a doctrine about God as the source of all things and as that to which man must return. In formulating his thought, Plotinus successively analyzed and rejected as inadequate the views of the Stoics, Epicureans, Pythagoreans, and Aristotelians. Among his objections to these schools of thought was his conviction that they did not understand the true nature of the soul. The Stoics had described the soul as a material body, a physical "breath." But Plotinus argued that neither the Stoics nor Epicureans, both materialists, understood the essential independence of the soul from the material body. Likewise, the Pythagoreans, who had said that the soul is the "harmony" of the body, would have to admit that when the body is not in harmony, it has no soul. Finally, Aristotle's notion that the soul is the form of the body, that it cannot exist without a body, was rejected by Plotinus on the ground that if part of the body loses its form, this would mean that to that extent the soul would also be deformed. This would make the body primary, whereas, said Plotinus, it is the soul that is primary, that gives life to the body as a whole. Everything for Plotinus turned upon the accurate understanding of man's essential nature.

To understand man's nature, Plotinus pursued the line of thought Plato had set forth in his vivid myths and allegories. He was struck by Plato's comprehensive treatment of reality, including his account of the Demiurge fashioning matter into the world, the doctrine that the Idea of the Good is like the rays of light emanating from the sun, the notion that the soul has an existence before it enters the body, is a prisoner in the body, and struggles to escape from this captivity and return to its source, and that the true reality is to be found not in the material but in the spiritual world. Plotinus took these basic ideas, emphasizing particularly the central Platonic theme that only the spirit is true reality, and reformulated Plato's ideas into a new kind of Platonism.

God as the One   The material world, with its multiplicity of things, cannot be the true reality, Plotinus thought, because it is always changing. Only that can really *be* that does not change, and this unchanging reality must therefore be something different from the material world. The true reality is God, about whom nothing specifically descriptive can be said except that He absolutely transcends or lies beyond everything in the world. For this reason God is not material, is not finite, is not divisible, has no specific form either as matter, soul, or mind, each of which undergoes change, cannot be confined to any idea or ideas of the intellect and for this reason cannot be expressed in any human language, and is accessible to none of the senses but can be reached only in a mystical ecstasy that is independent of any rational or sense experience. For this reason, Plotinus spoke of God as the One, signifying thereby that in God there is absolutely no complexity, that God is Absolute Unity. The One signifies, moreover, that God does not change, is indivisible, has no variety, is uncreated, and is in every way unalterable.

The One cannot be the sum of particular things because it is precisely these things whose finite existence requires explanation and a source. Plotinus held that the One "cannot be any existing thing, but is prior to all existents." There are no positive attributes that we can ascribe to the One because all our ideas of attributes are derived from finite physical things. It is not possible therefore to say that God is this and not that since this procedure would fasten upon God certain limits. To say, then, that God is One is to affirm that God *is*, that God transcends the world, that He is simple, without any duality, potentiality, or material limitation, and that He transcends all distinctions. In a sense, God cannot engage in any self-conscious activity since this would imply complexity through thinking *particular* thoughts *before* and *after,* thus implying change. God in no way resembles man. He is indeed simply One, Absolute Unity.

The Metaphor of Emanation   If God is One, He cannot create, for creation is an act, and activity, said Plotinus, implies change. Then how can we account for the many things of the world? Striving to maintain a consistent view of the Unity of God, Plotinus explained the origin of things by saying that they come from God, not through a free act of creation but through necessity. To express what he meant by "necessity," Plotinus used several metaphors, especially the metaphor of *emanation.* Things emanate, they flow from God, the way light emanates from the sun, the way water flows from a spring that has no source outside itself. The sun is never exhausted, it does not *do* anything, it just *is;* and being what it is, it necessarily emanates light. In this way, God is the source of everything, and everything manifests God. But nothing is equal to God, any more than the rays of light equal in any way the sun. Plotinus, in short, is not a pantheist. On the contrary, his theory of emanation formed the basis for the hierarchic view of nature. Just as the light closest to the sun is the brightest, so also the highest form of being is the first emanation. Plotinus described this first emanation from the One as *Mind* (*nous*). It is most like the One, but is not absolute and can therefore be said to have a specific attribute or character. This nous is *Thought* or *universal intelligence* and signifies the underlying rationality of the world. It is the nature of rationality to have no spatial or temporal boundaries. But rationality does imply multiplicity in that thinking contains the ideas of all particular things.

The World Soul   Just as light emanates from the sun in ever-diminishing intensity, so also the gradations of being, which emanate from God, represent a decline in the degrees of perfection. Moreover, each succeeding emanation is the cause of the next-lower emanation, as if there were a principle at work requiring that every nature bring into being that which is immediately subordinate to it. In this way, the nous is in turn the source of the Soul. The Soul of the World has two aspects: looking upward, as it were, toward nous or pure rationality, the Soul strives to contemplate the eternal ideas of all things; looking downward, it emanates by reasoning one thing at a time, providing thereby the life principle to all of nature, bridging the gap between the ideas of things and the actual realm of the natural order. The activity of the Soul accounts for the phenomenon of *time,* since now there is the emergence of things, and the relations of things to each other results in events, and events come *after* one another, and this relationship of events is what is meant by time. To be sure, the One, the nous and the World Soul are all coeternal; it is that below the World Soul lies the realm of nature, of particular things, reflecting in a changing way, in time, the eternal ideas.

The Human Soul   The human soul is an emanation from the World Soul. Like the World Soul, it also has two aspects. Again, looking upward, the human soul shares in the nous or universal reason, and looking downward, the soul becomes connected with, but is not identical with, the body. Here Plotinus reaffirmed Plato's doctrine of the preexistence of the soul, believing also that the union of the soul with the body is a product of a "fall." Moreover, after death the soul survives the body, conceivably enters a sequence of transmigrations from one body to another, and being spiritual and therefore truly real, it will not be annihilated but will join all other souls again in the World Soul. While in the body, it is the soul that provides the power of rationality, sensitivity, and vitality.

The World of Matter   At the lowest level in the hierarchy of being, that is, at the farthest remove from the One, is matter. Recalling that there is a principle at work in emanation, which requires that the higher grades of being overflow in accordance with the next realm of possibilities, it follows, then, that after ideas and souls comes the world of material objects organized into a mechanical order whose operation or movement is the work of reason, subjecting all objects to the laws or rules of cause and effect. Once again, the material world displays a higher and lower aspect, the higher being its susceptibility to the laws of motion but the lower, its bare material nature, being a dark world of gross matter moving aimlessly with sluggish discord toward collision and extinction. Plotinus compared matter to the dimmest, the farthest reach, of light, the most extreme limit of light, which is darkness itself. Darkness, clearly, is the very opposite of light; similarly, matter is the opposite of spirit and is therefore the opposite of the One. Again, insofar as matter exists in conjunction with the soul, either the individual or the World Soul, to this extent matter is not complete darkness. But just as light tends to emanate finally to the point of utter darkness, so also matter stands at the boundary line of nothingness, where it tends to disappear into non-being.

What Causes Evil?   By the doctrine of emanation, Plotinus argued that God necessarily overflows in order to share His perfection as much as possible. Since God could not reduplicate Himself perfectly, He did so in the only possible way, namely, by representing, in the emanations, all the possible degrees of perfection. For this reason, it was necessary to have not only the nous but also the lowest level of being, matter. Still, there is moral evil, sin, pain, and the continued warfare of the passions, and, finally, death and sorrow. How could the Perfect One, from whom everything ultimately emanates, permit this kind of imperfection to exist among human beings? Plotinus explained the problem of evil in various ways. For one thing, he said that evil in its own way occupies a place in the hierarchy of perfection, since without evil something would be lacking in the scheme of things. Evil is like the dark shadings of a portrait, which greatly enhance the beauty of the image. Moreover, all events occur with rigorous necessity, as the Stoics had argued earlier, so that the good man does not look upon them as evil, whereas for the sinner they could be considered just punishment. But Plotinus finds the best explanation of evil in his account of matter.

For Plotinus, matter is the necessary and final reach of the emanation from the One. The very nature of emanation as we have seen is that the higher levels necessarily move toward the lower, that the One generates the nous, and, finally, that the individual soul generates a body, matter. Matter itself, however, continues the process of emanation, as if moving farther and farther from the One, the way the light grows dimmer and dimmer, the farther it moves from the sun. There is, then, the tendency for matter to move beyond, or separate itself from, the activity of the soul and to engage in motion that is not rationally directed. Again, as matter faces upward, it encounters the soul or the principle of rationality; for objects in nature this accounts for the orderliness of their movements, whereas for an individual person it means that the body responds to the activity of the soul at the levels of rationality, sensitivity, appetite, and vitality. But as matter faces downward, which is its natural tendency because of the downward momentum of emanation, it encounters darkness itself and at this point matter is separated from rationality.

The clue to the problem of moral evil is, then, that the soul is now united with a material body, and, in spite of the rational character of the soul, it must contend with the body, whose material nature disposes it to move downward and away from rational control. When the body reaches the level below rationality, it becomes subject to an indefinite number of possible ways of acting. Now the passions move the body to respond to all kinds of appetites. Evil is the discrepancy between the soul's right intentions and its actual behavior; it is an imperfection in the soul-body arrangement, and much of the cause for this imperfection is ascribed to the final irrational movement of the material body.

Matter, or body, is the principle of evil in the sense that matter is at the fringe of emanation, where the absence of rationality results in formlessness and the least degree of perfection. But since matter comes from God in the sense that everything emanates from the One, it could be said that God is the source of evil. Still, evil, for Plotinus, is not a positive destructive force; it is not a "devil" or rival god contending with the good God; nor, as the Persians thought, is it a contest between the coequal forces of light and darkness. Evil, for Plotinus, is simply the absence of something, the lack of perfection, the lack of form for the material body, which is not itself essentially evil. Man's moral struggle is therefore a struggle not against some outside force but against the tendency to be undone within, to become disordered, to lose control of the passions. Evil, again, is no *thing*, but rather the absence of order. The body *as such* is not evil. Evil is the formlessness of matter as darkness is the absence of light. Throughout his analysis, Plotinus tries simultaneously to argue that the soul is responsible for its acts and that all events are determined. Just how these two views can be reconciled is not exactly clear. At the same time, much of Plotinus' appeal came from the promise of salvation, which he thought his philosophy could provide.

Salvation   Plotinus moved from his philosophical analysis of emanation to the religious and mystical program of salvation. Unlike the mystery cults of his day, which offered a swift fulfillment of man's desire to unite with God, Plotinus described the soul's ascent to unity with God as a difficult and painful task. This ascent required that a person develop successively the moral and intellectual virtues. Since the body and the physical world were not considered evil per se, it was not necessary to reject them altogether. The key insight was rather that the physical things of the world must not distract the soul from its higher aims. The world is therefore renounced as a means of facilitating the soul's ascent to intellectual activity as in philosophy and science. One must discipline himself in rigorous and correct thinking. Such thinking lifts a person out of his individuality and, through a broad knowledge of things, tends to relate the self to the whole arrangement of the world. But all the steps up the ladder of knowledge lead toward the final union of the self with the One or with God in a state of ecstasy, where there is no longer any consciousness of the self's separation from God. This ecstasy is the final result of right conducts, correct thinking, and the proper disposition of the affections.

To achieve this union, said Plotinus, could require many incarnations of each soul. Finally the soul is refined and purified in its love, as Plato had indicated in his *Symposium,* and is capable of the fullest self-surrender. At this point the process of emanation is fully reversed, and the self merges once again with the One. For many, Plotinus' Neoplatonism had all the power of a religion and represented a strong alternative to Christianity. Although its intricate intellectual scheme prevented it from becoming widely popular, Neoplatonism made a considerable impact upon the emerging Christian theology of this era. It was St. Augustine who saw in the *Enneads* of Plotinus a strikingly new explanation of evil and of salvation through orderly love. Through Augustine, Neoplatonism became a decisive element in the intellectual expression of the Christian faith during the Middle Ages.

✿TWO✿

THE
MEDIEVAL PERIOD:
THE CONFLUENCE
OF PHILOSOPHY
AND THEOLOGY

6

St. Augustine's Christian Philosophy

S t. Augustine's intense concern over his personal destiny provided the driving force for his philosophic activity. From his early youth, he suffered from a deep moral turmoil, which drove him to a life-long quest for true wisdom and spiritual peace. He was born in Tagaste in the African province of Numidia in 354 A.D. His father was a pagan, but his mother, Monica, was a devout Christian. At the age of sixteen, Augustine began the study of rhetoric in Carthage, a port city given to licentious ways. Though his mother had instilled in him the ways of Christian thought and behavior, he threw off this religious faith and morality, taking at this time a mistress by whom he had a son and with whom he lived for a decade. At the same time, his thirst for knowledge impelled his extremely able mind to rigorous study, and he became a successful student of rhetoric.

A series of personal experiences led him to his unique approach to philosophy. He was nineteen years old when he read the *Hortensius* of Cicero, which was an exhortation to achieve philosophical wisdom. These words of Cicero kindled his passion for learning, but he was left with the problem of where to find intellectual certainty. His Christian ideas seemed unsatisfactory to him. He was particularly perplexed by the ever-present problem of moral evil. How can one explain the existence of evil in human experience? The Christians had said that God is the creator of all things and also that God is good. How, then, is it possible for evil to arise out of a world that a perfectly good God had created? Because Augustine could find no answer in the Christianity he learned as a youth, he turned to a group called the Manichaeans, who were sympathetic to much of Christianity but who, boasting of their intellectual superiority, rejected the basic monotheism of the Old Testament and with it the doctrine that the Creator and Redeemer of man are one and the same. Instead, the Manichaeans taught a doctrine of dualism, according to which there were two basic principles in the universe, the principle of light or goodness, on the one hand, and the principle of darkness or evil, on the other. These two principles were held to be equally eternal and were seen as eternally in conflict with each other. This conflict was reflected in human life in the conflict between the soul, composed of light, and the body, composed of darkness. At first this theory of dualism seemed to provide the answer to the problem of evil; it overcame the contradiction between the presence of evil in a world created by a good God. Augustine could now attribute his sensual desires to the external power of darkness. Although this dualism seemed to solve the contradiction of evil in a God-created world, it raised new problems. For one thing, how could one explain why there are two conflicting principles in nature? If no convincing reason could be given, is intellectual certitude possible? Far more serious was his awareness that it did not help to solve his moral turmoil to say that it was all engendered by some external force. The presence of fierce passion was no less unsettling just because the "blame" for it had been shifted to something outside of himself. What had originally attracted him to the Manichaeans was their boast that they could provide him with truth that could be discussed and made plain, not requiring, as the Christians did, "faith before reason." He therefore broke with the Manichaeans, feeling that "those philosophers whom they call Academics [Skeptics] were wiser than the rest in thinking that we ought to doubt everything, and that no truth can be comprehended by man." He was now attracted to Skepticism, though at the same time he retained some belief in God. He maintained a materialistic view of things and on this account doubted the existence of immaterial substances and the immortality of the soul.

Hoping for a more effective career in rhetoric, Augustine left Africa for Rome and shortly thereafter moved to Milan, where he became municipal professor of rhetoric in 384. Here he was profoundly influenced by Ambrose, who was then Bishop of Milan. From Ambrose Augustine derived not so much the techniques of rhetoric, but somewhat unexpectedly a greater appreciation of Christianity. While in Milan, Augustine took another mistress, having left his first one in Africa. It was here also that Augustine came upon certain forms of Platonism, especially the Neoplatonism found in the *Enneads* of Plotinus. There was much in Neoplatonism that caught his imagination, particularly the conception of an immaterial world totally separate from the material world and the belief that man possesses a spiritual sense that enables him to know God and the immaterial world. Moreover, from Plotinus Augustine derived the conception that evil is not a positive reality but is rather a matter of privation, the absence of good. Above all, Neoplatonism overcame Augustine's former skepticism, materialism, and dualism. Through Platonic thought he was able to understand that not all activity is physical, that there is a spiritual as well as a physical reality. He could now see the unity of the world without having to assume the existence of two principles behind soul and body, for Plotinus had presented the picture of reality as a single graduated system in which matter is simply on a lower level.

Intellectually, Neoplatonism provided what Augustine had been looking for, but it left his moral problem still unsolved. What he needed now was moral strength to match his intellectual insight. This he found by way of Ambrose's sermons. Neoplatonism had finally made Christianity reasonable to him, and now he was also able to exercise the act of faith and thereby derive the power of the spirit without feeling that he was lapsing into some form of superstition. His dramatic conversion occurred in 386, when he gave "real assent" to abandoning his profession of rhetoric and giving his life totally to the pursuit of philosophy, which, for him, also meant the knowledge of God. He now saw Platonism and Christianity as virtually one, seeing in Neoplatonism the philosophical expression of Christianity, saying that "I am confident that among the Platonists I shall find what is not opposed to the teachings of our religion." He therefore set out on what he called "my whole program" of achieving wisdom, saying that "from this moment forward, it is my resolve never to depart from the authority of Christ, for I find none that is stronger." Still, he emphasized that "I must follow after this with the greatest subtlety of reason."

For Augustine, true philosophy was inconceivable without a confluence of faith and reason. To him, wisdom was Christian wisdom. Reason without revelation was certainly possible, but it would never be complete. This was true particularly for Augustine, since he came to believe that there is no such thing as a purely natural man without some ultimate spiritual destiny. Consequently, to understand the concrete condition of man, he must be considered from the point of view of the Christian faith, and this in turn requires that the whole world be considered from the vantage point of faith. There could be, for Augustine, no distinction between theology and philosophy. Indeed, he believed that one could not properly philosophize until his will was transformed, that clear thinking was possible only under the influence of God's grace. In this way, Augustine set the dominant mood and style of Christian wisdom of the Middle Ages, although Aquinas in the thirteenth century altered some of its assumptions.

It is therefore not possible to discuss Augustine's philosophy without at the same time considering his theological viewpoint. Indeed, Augustine wrote no purely philosophical works in the contemporary sense of that term. He was an incredibly prolific writer, and as he became a noted leader in the Catholic Church, he was inevitably involved in writing as a protagonist of the faith and a defender against heresy. In 396 he became Bishop of Hippo, the seaport near his native town of Tagaste. Among his many opponents was Pelagius, with whom he

Augustine (*Scala/Editorial Photocolor Archives*)

entered into a celebrated controversy. Pelagius had taught that all men possess the natural ability to achieve a righteous life, thereby denying the doctrine of original sin. This led, according to Augustine, to misunderstanding the true nature of man by assuming that man's will is of itself capable of achieving his salvation and thereby minimizing the function of God's grace. This controversy illuminates Augustine's mode of thought perfectly, for it indicates again his insistence that all knowledge upon all subjects must take into account the revealed truth of Scripture along with the insights of philosophy. Since all knowledge aimed at helping man understand God, this religious dimension had clearly a priority in his reflections. As Aquinas said about him later, "Whenever Augustine, who was imbued with the doctrine of the Platonists, found in their writings anything consistent with the faith, he adopted it; and whatever he found contrary to the faith, he amended." Still, it was Platonism that had rescued Augustine from skepticism, made the Christian faith reasonable and, indeed, powerful for him, and set off one of the great literary achievements in theology and philosophy. As if to symbolize his tempestuous life, Augustine died in 430 at the age of seventy-five in the posture of reciting the Penitential Psalms, as the Vandals besieged Hippo.

HUMAN KNOWLEDGE

Overcoming Skepticism Augustine had taken the Skeptics (Academics) seriously for a time, agreeing with them that "no truth can be comprehended by man." But after his conversion, his problem was no longer *whether* man can attain certainty, but rather *how* he can attain it. Augustine therefore sought to answer the Skeptics, and he did this first of all by showing that human reason does indeed have certainty about various things. Specifically, human reason is absolutely certain of the principle of contradiction. We know that a thing cannot both be and not be at the same time. Using this principle, we can be certain, for example, that there is either one world or many worlds; that if there are many, their number is either finite or infinite. What we know here is simply that both alternatives cannot be true. This is not yet any substantive knowledge, but it meant for Augustine that the mind is not hopelessly lost in uncertainty. Not only does the mind know that both alternatives cannot be true simultaneously, it knows also that this is always, eternally, the case. In addition, he said that even the Skeptics would have to admit that the act of doubting is itself a form of certainty, for a person who doubts is certain that he doubts. Here, then, is another certainty, the certainty that I exist, for if I doubt, I must exist. Whatever else one can have doubts about, he cannot doubt that he doubts. To object, as the Skeptics did, that a person could be asleep and only dreaming that he sees things or is aware of himself, did not seem to Augustine to be a formidable argument, for in reply he said "whether he be asleep or awake he lives." Any conscious person is certain that he exists, that he is alive, and that he can think, "for we are," says Augustine, "and we know we are, and we love our being and our knowledge of it. . . . These truths stand without fear in the face of the arguments of the Academics." Unlike Descartes, who formulated a similar argument in his classic "I think, therefore I am" and then proceeded to use it as a foundation for his system of philosophy, Augustine was content merely to derive from the fact of doubt a refutation of the Skeptics' basic premise. Instead of proving the existence of external objects, Augustine referred to these objects chiefly in order to describe in some detail how the mind achieves knowledge in relation to things.

Knowledge and Sensation When a person senses objects, he derives some knowledge from this act of sensation. But according to Augustine, such sense knowledge is at the lowest level of knowing. Still, the senses do give us a kind of knowledge. What puts sense knowledge at the lowest level is that it gives us the least amount of certainty. What reduces the certainty of sense knowledge is two things: first, that the objects of sense are always changing, and, second, that the organs of sense change. For these two reasons, sensation varies from time to time and between persons. Something can taste sweet to one person and bitter to another, warm to one and cold to another. Still, Augustine believed that the senses are always accurate as such. It is unjust, he said, to expect or demand more from the senses than they can provide. For example, there is nothing wrong with our senses when the oar in the water appears bent to us. On the contrary, there would be something wrong if the oar appeared straight, since under these circumstances the oar ought to seem bent. The problem arises when we have to make a judgment about the actual condition of the oar. One would be deceived if he gave assent to the notion that the oar was in fact bent. To avoid this error, says Augustine, "don't give assent to more than the fact of appearance, and you won't be deceived." In this way, Augustine affirmed the reliability of the senses while also indicating their limitations. Just how the senses give us knowledge Augustine indicated by analyzing the nature or mechanics of sensation.

What happens when we sense an object? To answer this question Augustine relied upon his Platonic interpretation of man. Man is a union of body and soul. He even suggested that the body is the prison of the soul. But when he described how the soul attains knowledge, he departed from the Platonic theory of recollection. Knowledge is not an act of remembering. It is an act of the soul. When we see an object, the soul (mind) fashions out of its own substance an image of the object. The object cannot make a physical "impression" upon the mind the way a signet ring leaves its mark in wax because the soul is spiritual, not material. Accordingly, it is the mind itself that produces the image. Moreover, when we sense an object, we not only sense an image but also make a judgment. We look at a person and say that she is beautiful. This act of judgment indicates that I not only see the person with my senses, but also compare her with a standard to which my mind has access in some realm other than that in which I sense the person. Similarly, when I see seven boys and three boys I know that they can be added to make ten boys. As other things in nature are mutable, these ten boys, being mortal, will eventually pass away. But we are able to separate the numbers from the boys and discover that seven and three do not depend upon the boys or any other things and that their making ten by addition is always and necessarily true.

Sensation, then, gives us some knowledge, but its chief characteristic is that it necessarily points beyond its objects. From the sensation of an oar we are moved to think about straightness and bentness, from the person to beauty, and from the boys to the eternal truths of mathematics. Here the description of man becomes again decisive, since the explanation of the mechanics of sensation leads to a distinction between body and soul. Sensation involves the body insofar as some physical organ is required to sense things, but, unlike animals, men not only sense things, they have some rational knowledge of them and make rational judgments about them. When a rational person makes such judgments, he is no longer dependent solely upon the senses but has directed his mind to other objects, such as Beauty and the truths of mathematics. A careful analysis shows therefore that the act of human sensation involves at least four elements, namely (1) the object sensed, (2) the bodily organ upon which sensation depends, (3) the activity of the mind in formulating an image of the object, and (4) the immaterial object, e.g., Beauty, which the mind uses in making a judgment about the sensed object. What emerges from this analysis is that there are two different kinds of objects that human beings encounter, namely, the objects of the bodily sense and the objects of the mind. With the physical eye man sees things, and with the mind he apprehends eternal truths. These different objects account for the different degrees of intellectual certainty, for a person will derive less reliable truth when his mutable sense organs are directed toward changing physical objects than when his mind is contemplating eternal truths independently of the senses. Also, sensation directs the trail of knowledge to an activity within man and not to things outside of him. Knowledge moves from the level of sensed things to the higher level of general truth. The highest level of knowledge is for Augustine the knowledge of God. Sensation plays its part in attaining this knowledge in that it directs the mind upward. Hence, Augustine says that we move toward God "from the exterior to the interior, and from the inferior to the superior."

The Doctrine of Illumination In his account of the relation between sensation and knowledge, Augustine was left with the problem of how the mind could make judgments involving eternal and necessary truths. What makes it possible for the mind to know that seven and three, which at first the mind confronts in relation to things, always and necessarily make ten? Why, as a matter of fact, is there a problem here? The problem exists because so far in his account of human knowledge, all the elements involved are mutable or imperfect, hence finite and not eternal. The sensed objects are mutable, and the bodily organs of sense are also subject to change. The mind itself is a creature and is therefore finite and not perfect. How, then, can these elements be deployed in such a way as to rise above their own imperfection and mutability and discover eternal truths about which the mind has no doubts, truths that indeed confront the mind with the coercive power of certitude, truths so superior to what the human mind could produce that the mind must adjust or conform to them? Plato had answered this question by his doctrine that knowledge is recollection, whereby the soul is made to remember what it once knew before it entered the body. Aristotle, on the other hand, argued that the eternal universal ideas were abstracted by the intellect from particular things. Augustine accepted neither one of these solutions, though he did follow Plato's other insight contained in the analogy between the sun in the visible world and the Idea of the Good in the intelligible world.

Augustine was not so much concerned with the origin *as with our awareness of the certitude* of some of our ideas. Rejecting recollection and some form of innate Ideas, he came closer to the notion of abstraction. Actually, Augustine says that man is made is such a way that when the eye of his body sees an object, the mind can form an image of it provided the object is bathed in light. Similarly, the mind is capable of "seeing" eternal objects provided that they too are bathed in their own appropriate light. As Augustine says, we ought to believe "that the nature of the intellectual mind was so made that, by being naturally subject to intelligible realities, according to the arrangement of the Creator, it sees these truths [such as mathematical truth] in a certain incorporeal light of a unique kind, just as the eye of the body sees the things all around it in this corporeal light." The human mind, in short, requires illumination if it is to "see" eternal and necessary truths. We cannot anymore "see" the intelligible objects or truths of the intellect without some illumination than we can see the things in the world without the light of the sun.

Augustine states his doctrine of *illumination* in succinct form when he says that "there is present in [us] . . . the light of eternal reason, in which light the immutable truths are seen." Just what he means by this doctrine is not altogether clear. What is clear is that for Augustine the illumination comes from God just as light is shed abroad by the sun. If this analogy or metaphor is taken seriously, the divine light must illuminate something that is already there. By the light of the sun we can see the trees and houses. If the divine light performs the same kind of function, this light must also illuminate something—our ideas. This light is not so much the source of our ideas as much as it is the condition under which we recognize the quality of truth and eternity in our ideas. In short, divine illumination is not a process by which the content of ideas is infused into our minds; it is, rather, the illumination of our judgment whereby we are able to discern that certain ideas contain necessary and eternal truth. God, the source of this light, is perfect and eternal, and the human intellect operates under the influence of God's eternal ideas. It could not be said that the human mind knows God, but the doctrine of illumination does mean that the limitations of knowledge caused by the mutability of physical objects and the finitude of man's mind are overcome by the divine illumination. With this doctrine, then, Augustine solved to his satisfaction the problem of how the human intellect is able to go beyond sense objects and make judgments about necessary and eternal truths.

GOD

Augustine was not interested in mere speculations about the existence of God. His philosophical reflections about God were the product of his intense pursuit of wisdom and spiritual peace. His deep involvement in sensual pleasures had given him dramatic evidence that the soul cannot find its peace among the pleasures of flesh or sensation. Similarly, in his quest for certainty of knowledge, he discovered that the world of things was full of change and impermanence. His mind, too, he discovered, was imperfect, since it was capable of error. At the same time, he had the experience of knowing certain truths that were eternal. He was able to compare the experience of contemplating truth with the experience of having pleasure and sensations. Of these two experiences he found that the activities of the mind could provide more lasting and profound peace. When he considered the technical question of how it was that his finite human mind was capable of attaining knowledge beyond the capacity of his mind, he concluded that this knowledge could not have come from finite things outside of him; nor could it be produced fully by his own mind. Since the knowledge available to him was superior to the workings of his mind, that is, since this knowledge was eternal and could not come from his limited or finite mind, he was led to believe that immutable truth must have its source in God. What led to this conclusion was the similarity between the characteristics of some of his knowledge and the attributes of God, namely, that both are eternal and true. The existence of eternal truth meant for Augustine the existence of the Eternal Truth, which God is. In this way, Augustine moved through various levels of personal experience and spiritual quest to what amounted to a "proof" of the existence of God.

Since God is Truth, God in some sense is within man, but since God is eternal, He also transcends man. But what else can man say by way of describing God? Actually, Augustine found it easier to say what God is not than to define what He is. Still, to say that God is superior to finite things was a major step. Taking the scriptural name for God given to Moses, namely, "I Am That I Am," Augustine transposed this to mean that God is *being itself*. As such He is the highest being, not the beingless One of Plotinus but the "something than which nothing more excellent or more sublime exists," a phrase that influenced Anselm to formulate his famous ontological argument. As the highest being, God is perfect being, which means that He is self-existent, immutable, and eternal being. As perfect, He is also "simple," in that whatever plural attributes are assigned to Him turn out to be identical; His knowledge, wisdom, goodness, and power are all one and constitute His essence. Further, Augustine reasoned that the world of everyday things reflects the being and activity of God. Although the things we see are mutable in that they gradually cease to be, nevertheless insofar as they exist they have a definite form, and this form is eternal and is a reflection of God. Indeed, that things possess any being at all is ascribed by Augustine to God, who is the source of all being.

But unlike the things of the world, God, as Augustine says, "is . . . in no interval or extension of place" and similarly "is in no interval or extension of time." In short, Augustine described God as pure or highest being, suggesting thereby that in God there is no change either from non-being to being or from being to non-being. God *is*; "I Am That I Am." Again, the force of this line of thought is to be found not so much in its philosophic rigor, though Augustine was convinced it had that too, as in its relevance in solving Augustine's spiritual problem. God as the source of being and truth and the one eternal reality now became for Augustine the legitimate object both of thought and affection. From God there comes both enlightenment for the mind and strength for the will. Moreover, all other knowledge is possible because God is the standard for truth. His essence is to be, and to be is to act, and to act is to know, and being both eternal and all-knowing, God always knew all the possible ways in which He could be reflected in creation. For this reason, the various forms in which the world is shaped were always in God as Exemplars. All things therefore are finite reflections of God's eternal thought. If God's thought is "eternal," difficulties arise in our language when it is said that God "foresees" what will happen. What is important to Augustine, however, is that the world and God are intimately related, that the world reflects God's eternal thought even though God is not identical with but transcends the world. Because there is this relation between God and the world, to know one is to know something of the other. This is why Augustine was so convinced that the person who knew most about God could understand most deeply the true nature of the world and especially the true nature and destiny of man. Finally, although Augustine saw everywhere evidences of the Trinity, his language about God revolves chiefly around the Father, since the other persons, the Word and the Spirit, being of the same substance, are one and share the same being.

THE CREATED WORLD

Even though Augustine concluded that God is the most appropriate object of thought and affection and that the physical, mutable world could not provide man with true knowledge or spiritual peace, he nevertheless paid considerable attention to the material world. After all, human life must be lived in the physical world, and one needs to know how to understand this world in order to relate himself appropriately to it. From what he had already said about the nature of knowledge and about God, it was inevitable that Augustine should see the world as the creation of God. Wherever one looks, says Augustine in his *Confessions,* all things, for example, the flowers, say, "We made not ourselves, but He made us that abideth forever." Finite things, that is, demand that there should be some permanent being to explain how they could come into existence. Just how God is related to the world was explained by Augustine in his unique theory of creation.

Creatio Ex Nihilo Augustine's distinctive doctrine was that God created all things *ex nihilo,* out of nothing. This was in contrast to Plato's account of the world which was not "created" but was the Demiurge's combining of the Forms and the receptacle, which always existed independently. Augustine also departed from the Neoplatonic theory of Plotinus, which explained the world as an emanation from God. Plotinus had said that there was a *natural necessity* in God to overflow, since the Good must necessarily diffuse itself. Moreover, this theory held that there is a continuity between God and the world, that the world is merely an extension of God. Against all these notions, Augustine stressed that the world is the product of God's free act, whereby He brings into being, out of nothing, all the things that make up the world. All things, then, owe their existence to God. There is, however, a sharp distinction between God and the things He created. Whereas Plotinus saw the world as the overflowing and therefore continuation of God, Augustine speaks of God as bringing into being what did not exist before. He could not have created out of an existing matter because matter, even in a primary form, would already be something. To speak of a formless matter is really to refer to nothing. Actually, according to Augustine, everything, including matter, is the product of God's creative act. Even if there were some formless matter that was capable of being formed—even this would have its origin in God and would have to be created by Him out of nothing. That matter is created by God meant for Augustine that matter is good, because nothing evil is created by God. The essential goodness of matter was to play an important role in Augustine's theory of morality, for this doctrine was in sharp contrast to the teachings of the Manichaeans, who said that the body was composed of darkness and therefore embodied the principle of evil. Indeed, Augustine was to reject the notion that anything in the created order can be intrinsically evil since everything is created by the goodness of God.

The Rationes Seminales   Augustine was struck by the fact that the various species in nature never produce new species. Horses produce horses, and flowers produce flowers; at the human level, parents produce more children. What fascinated Augustine about all this was its relevance to the general question about *causality*. Although in a sense the parents are the cause of the children and the flowers the cause of the new flowers, still, none of these things is able to introduce new forms into nature. In the created order, existing things are able only to animate existing forms into completed beings. Augustine drew from this fact (for which he admittedly did not have decisive empirical information) the conclusion that the causality behind the formation of all things is God's intelligence. There is no original causal power in things capable of fashioning new forms. How then do things, animals, and men produce anything? Augustine's answer was that in the act of creation, God had implanted seminal principles (*rationes seminales*) into matter, thereby setting into nature the potentiality for all species to emerge. These *rationes seminales* are the germs of things; they are invisible and have causal power. Thus, all species bear the invisible, potential power to become what they are not yet at the present time. When species begin to exist, their seminal principle, that is, their potentiality, is fulfilled, and subsequently actual seeds transmit the continuation of the fixed species from potentiality to actuality. Originally, God, in a single act of complete creation furnished the germinating principles of all species.

   With this doctrine, Augustine explained the origin of species, locating their cause in the mind of God, whence came the seminal principles. By this doctrine of *rationes seminales,* Augustine thought he also solved a problem in the Scriptures, where it is said in *Genesis* that God created the world in six days. That God should have to create step by step seemed inconsistent with Augustine's view of God. There was some question, too, about what is meant here by six days, especially since the sun was not "created" until the fourth day. What the doctrine of *rationes seminales* enabled Augustine to say was that God had created all things at once, meaning by this that he had implanted the seminal principles of all species simultaneously. But, since these germs are principles of potentiality, they are the bearers of things that are to be but that have not yet "flowered." Accordingly, though all species were created at once, they did not all exist fully formed simultaneously. They each fulfilled their potentiality in a sequence of points in time. Although Augustine did not try to do so, his notion of seminal principles could conceivably be extended into a doctrine of the evolution of species.

MORAL PHILOSOPHY

Every philosophical notion developed by Augustine pointed in one way or another to the problem of man's moral condition. For him, therefore, moral theory was not some special or isolated subject. Everything culminates in morality, in clarifying for man the sure road to happiness, which is the goal of human behavior. In fashioning his ideas about morality, then, Augustine brought to bear his major insights about the nature of human knowledge, the nature of God, and the doctrine of creation. From the vantage point of these ideas, he focused upon the nature of man's moral constitution.

Man's moral quest is the inevitable outcome of his specific and concrete condition. Man's condition is that he is made in such a way that he seeks happiness. Although the ancient Greeks had also considered happiness as the culmination of the good life, Augustine's theory provided a novel estimate of what constitutes happiness and just how it is to be achieved. What differentiated him from, say, Aristotle was that whereas Aristotle said that happiness is achieved when a person fulfills his natural functions through a well-balanced life, Augustine held that happiness required that man go beyond the natural to the supernatural. He expressed this view both in religious and philosophical language. In his *Confessions* he wrote, "Oh God Thou hast created us for Thyself so that our hearts are restless until they find their rest in Thee." In more philosophical language he makes this same point by saying that human nature is so made that "it cannot itself be the good by which it is made happy." There is, in short, no purely "natural" man. The reason there is no purely natural man, says Augustine, is that nature did not produce man. God did. Consequently, man always bears the marks of his creation, which means, among other things, that there are some permanent relations, actual and possible, between man and God. It is not by accident that man *seeks* happiness. That he seeks it is a consequence of his incompleteness, his finitude. That he can find happiness only in God is also no accident, since he was made by God to find happiness only in God. Augustine elaborates this aspect of man's nature through his doctrine of love.

The Role of Love   Man inevitably loves. To love is to go beyond oneself and to fasten one's affection upon an object of love. What makes it inevitable that man will love is, again, his incompleteness. There is a wide range of objects that man can choose to love, reflecting the variety of ways in which man is incomplete. A person can love (1) physical objects, (2) other persons, or even (3) himself. From those he can derive satisfaction for some of his desires and passions. Augustine stressed that all things in the world are good because all things come from God, who is goodness itself. Consequently, all things are legitimate objects of love. Everything that man loves will provide him with some measure of satisfaction and happiness. Nothing is evil in itself; evil is not a positive thing but the absence of something. Man's moral problem consists not so much in loving or even in the objects he loves as in the *manner* in which he attaches himself to his objects of love and in his *expectations* regarding the outcome of his love. Everyone expects to achieve happiness and fulfillment from love, yet men are miserable, unhappy, and restless. Why? Augustine lays the blame upon man's "disordered" love.

Evil and Disordered Love   Each object of love is different, and for this reason the consequences of loving them will be different. Similarly, the human needs which prompt the act of love are also different. Augustine thought that there is some sort of correlation between various human needs and the objects that can satisfy them. Love is the act that harmonizes these needs and their objects. What constitutes the chief fact about man is that the range of his needs includes not only (1) objects, (2) other persons, and (3) himself, but also, and most of all, (4) God. There is no way to unmake this fact about man. Augustine formulates this point in virtually quantitative terms. Each object of love can give only so much satisfaction and no more. Each of man's needs likewise has a measurable quantity. Clearly, satisfaction and happiness require that an object of love contain a sufficient amount of whatever it takes to fulfill or satisfy the particular need. Thus, we love food and we consume a quantity commensurate with our hunger. But our needs are not all physical in that primary sense. We love objects of art too for the aesthetic satisfaction they give. At a higher level we have the need for love between persons. Indeed, this level of affection provides quantitatively and qualitatively more in the way of pleasure and happiness than mere physical things, such as the various forms of property, can. From this it becomes clear that certain human needs cannot be met by an interchange of objects; the deep human need for human companionship cannot be met any other way than by a relationship with another person. Things can't be a substitute for a person because things do not contain within themselves the unique ingredients of a human personality. Therefore, although each thing is a legitimate object of love, one must not expect more from it than its unique nature can provide. The basic need for human affection cannot be satisfied by things. But this is particularly the case with man's spiritual need. Man was made, said Augustine, to love God. God is infinite. In some way, then, man's nature was made so that only God, the infinite, can give him ultimate satisfaction or happiness. "When," says Augustine, "the will which is the intermediate good, cleaves to the immutable good . . . man finds therein the blessed life," for, "to live well is nothing else but to love God. . . ." To love God is, then, the indispensable requirement for happiness, because only God, who is infinite, can satisfy that peculiar need in man that is precisely the need for the infinite.

If objects are not interchangeable, if things cannot substitute for a person, neither can any finite thing or person substitute for God. Yet, all men confidently expect that they can achieve true happiness by loving objects, other persons, and themselves. While these are all legitimate objects of love, man's love of them is disordered when these are loved for the sake of ultimate happiness. Disordered love consists in expecting more from an object of love than it is capable of providing. Disordered love produces all forms of pathology in human behavior. Normal self-love becomes pride, and pride is the cardinal sin that affects all aspects of man's conduct. The essence of pride is the assumption of self-sufficiency. Yet the permanent fact about man is precisely that he is not self-sufficient, neither physically, emotionally, nor spiritually. Man's pride, which turns him away from God, leads him to many forms of overindulgence, since he tries to satisfy an infinite need with finite entities. He therefore loves things more than he should in relation to what they can do for him. His love for another person can become virtually destructive of the other person, since he tries again to derive from that relationship more than it can possibly give. Appetite flourishes, passion multiplies, and there is a desperate attempt to achieve peace by satisfying all desires. The soul becomes seriously disfigured and is now implicated in envy, greed, jealously, trickery, panic, and a pervading restlessness. It does not take long for disordered love to produce a disordered person, and disordered persons produce a disordered community. No attempt to reconstruct an orderly or peaceful community or household is possible without reconstructing each human being. The rigorous and persistent fact is that personal reconstruction, salvation, is possible only by reordering love, by loving the proper things properly. Indeed, Augustine argued that we can love a person properly only if we love God first, for then we will not expect to derive from human love what can be derived only from our love of God. Similarly, we can love ourselves properly only as we subordinate ourselves to God, for there is no other way to overcome the destructive consequences of pride than by eliminating pride itself.

Free Will as the Cause of Evil   Augustine did not agree with Plato that the cause of evil is simply ignorance. To be sure, there can be some circumstances under which a person does not know the ultimate good, is not aware of God. Still, Augustine says that "even the ungodly" have the capacity to "blame and rightly praise many things in the conduct of men." The overriding fact is that in daily conduct men understand praise and blame only because they already understand that they have an obligation to do what is praiseworthy and to abstain from what is blameworthy. Under these circumstances, man's predicament is not that he is ignorant but that he stands in the presence of alternatives. He must choose to turn toward God or away from God. He is, in short, free. Whichever way man chooses, he does so with the hope of finding happiness. He is capable of directing his affections exclusively toward finite things, persons, or himself and away from God. Augustine says that "this turning away and this turning to are not forced but voluntary acts." Evil, or sin, is a product of the will. It is not, as Plato said, ignorance, nor, as the Manichaeans said, the work of the principle of darkness permeating the body. In spite of the fact of original sin, all men still possess the freedom of their will. This freedom (*liberum*) of the will is not, however, the same as spiritual freedom (*libertas*), for true spiritual liberty is no longer possible in its fullness in this life. Man now uses his free will to choose wrongly; but even when man chooses rightly, he does not, says Augustine, possess the spiritual power to do the good he has chosen. He must have the help of God's grace. Whereas evil is caused by an act of free will, virtue, on the other hand, is the product not of man's will but of God's grace. The moral law tells man what he must do, but in the end it really shows him what he can't do. Hence, Augustine concludes that "the law was . . . given that grace might be sought; grace was given that the law might be fulfilled." He also says that "sin is quelled when it is beaten down by the love of God, which none but He gives, and He only, by Jesus Christ the Mediator of God and Man, who made Himself mortal that we might be made eternal."

JUSTICE

For Augustine, public or political life was under the same rule of the moral law as man's individual or personal life. There is a single source of truth for both realms, and this truth he considered "entire, inviolate and not subject to changes in human life." All men recognize this truth and know it, for the purposes of conduct, as natural law or natural justice. Augustine considered natural law as man's intellectual sharing in God's truth, or God's *eternal law*. Augustine's notion of *eternal law* had already been anticipated by the Stoics when they spoke of the diffusion of the principle of reason throughout all of nature, ascribing to this reason the role and power of ruling everything. Their theory was that *nous*, the principle of reason, constituted the laws of nature. Whereas the Stoics, then, considered the laws of nature to be the working of the *impersonal* force of rational principles in the universe, Augustine interpreted the eternal law as the reason and will of the personal Christian God, saying that "the eternal law is the divine reason and the will of God which commands the maintenance (observance) of the natural order of things and which forbids the disturbance of it." Since *eternal law* is God's reason commanding orderliness, man's intellectual grasp of the eternal principles is called *natural law*. When a political state makes a law, said Augustine, such temporal laws must be in accord with the principle of natural law, which in turn is derived from the eternal law.

Augustine's chief argument regarding law and justice was that the political state is not autonomous, that in making laws the state does not merely express its power to legislate; the state must also follow the requirements of justice. Justice is a standard, moreover, which precedes the state and is eternal. What made Augustine's argument unique was his novel interpretation of the meaning of justice. He accepted the formula that said that "justice is a virtue distributing to every one his due." But, he asked, what is "due" to anyone? He rejected the notion that justice is conventional, that it will differ with each society. For him, justice was to be discovered in the structure of human nature with its relation to God. Hence, he said that justice is "the habit of the soul which imparts to every man the dignity due him. . . . Its origin proceeds from nature . . . and this notion of justice . . . is not the product of man's personal opinion, but something implanted by a certain innate power." To require the state to follow such a standard was obviously to place heavy moral limitations upon political power. Indeed, Augustine argued that if the laws of the state were out of harmony with natural law and justice, they would not have the character of laws, nor would there be a state. He said, "If then a commonwealth be an estate of the people, and that they be no people that are not united in one consent of the law: nor is that a law which is not grounded in justice: then it must follow, where no justice is, there no commonwealth is."

By relating justice to the moral law, Augustine argued that justice is not limited merely to the relations between man and man. The primary relationship in justice is between man and God. For this reason, Augustine said, "if man serve not God what justice can be thought to be in him? seeing that if he serve not Him the soul has neither lawful sovereignty over the body nor the reason over the affections." Moreover, collective justice is impossible apart from this individual justice, for "if this justice is not found in one man, no more then can it be found in a whole multitude of such like men. Therefore, amongst such there is not that consent of law which makes a multitude of people." Again, "Is he not [unjust who] takes himself away from his Lord God, and gives himself to the service of the devil?" To serve God is to love God, but this means also to love one's fellow man. Still, "what justice is that which takes man from the true God . . . ?" To serve God and to love one's fellow man are, among other things, to recognize that all men should also have this inviolate right and opportunity to love and serve God. All of ethics, then, is based upon man's love for God and his love for his fellow man. Love is the basis of justice.

Although Augustine's thoughts about law raised the church and religion to a position of superiority over the temporal state, he did concede to the state the right to use coercive force. Indeed, the state is the product of man's sinful condition and therefore exists as a necessary agency of control. Even so, Augustine would never concede that the principle of force was higher than the principle of love, for he says that ". . . a society cannot be ideally founded unless upon the basis and by the hand of faith and strong concord, where the object of love is the universal good which in its highest and truest character is God Himself and where men love one another with complete sincerity in Him, and the ground of their love for one another is the love of Him from whose eyes they cannot conceal the spirit of love." The earthly state still has a function even though its force cannot match the creative power of love, for the state's action can at least mitigate some evils: "When the power to do hurt is taken from the wicked," says Augustine, "they will carry themselves better being curbed." For this reason, the state "had not been designed in vain."

THE TWO CITIES AND HISTORY

Augustine made the love of God the central principle of morality. He also accounted for evil by his doctrine of disordered love. From this he concluded that the human race can be divided between those who love God, on the one hand, and those who love themselves and the world, on the other. These groups form in their own way a society, since they are, so Augustine says, "an association of rational beings united by a unanimous agreement upon the things they love." There being two basically different kinds of love, there are, then, two opposing societies. Those who love God Augustine called the *City of God,* and those who love self and the world he called the *City of the World.*

These two cities were not considered by Augustine to be identical with the church and state, respectively. Having stressed that the decisive element in the formation of a society is the dominant love of its members, he pointed out that those who love the world are found both in the state and in the church. It does not follow therefore that the church contains the whole society called the City of God. Similarly, there are in the state those who love God. These two cities therefore cut across both church and state and have an independence of them in an invisible way. Hence, wherever those people are who love God, there will be the City of God, and wherever there are those who love the world, there will be the City of the World.

History Augustine saw in the conflict between the two cities the clue to a philosophy of history. What he meant by a *philosophy* of history was that history has a meaning. The early Greek historians saw no pattern in the events of man other than, perhaps, the fact that kingdoms rise and fall and that there are cycles of repetition. Aristotle, it will be recalled, considered history as hardly capable of teaching men any important knowledge about humanity because, unlike drama, history deals with individual persons, nations, and events, whereas drama deals with universal conditions and problems. But Augustine thought that the greatest drama of all is human history. Its author, moreover, is God. History begins with Creation, is punctuated by such decisive events as the Fall of man and the Incarnation of God in Christ. The present historic moment is involved in the tension between the City of God and the City of the World. Nothing happens without reference to God's ultimate providence. Moreover, what happens is a consequence of human actions, particularly actions of sin and vice. Thus, when the barbarian Goths sacked Rome in 410, the pagans laid the blame upon the Christians, saying that their excessive emphasis upon loving and serving God had the effect of diluting patriotism and weakening the defenses of the state. To answer such charges and many others, Augustine wrote his book *The City of God* in 413. In it he argued that the fall of Rome was due not to the subversive activities of the Christians but, on the contrary, to the rampant vice throughout the Empire, which the Christian faith and love of God could have prevented. The fall of Rome was for Augustine just another example of God's providential intrusion into history, whereby He was seeking to establish the City of God and curb the City of the World. In this drama there was for Augustine a universal meaning and relevance, for all men must know that their own destinies, as well as the destinies of their societies, are inevitably linked with the two cities and with the providence of God. There is an all-embracing destiny for man and the world, and it will be achieved in God's good time and when the love of God reigns. With these views, Augustine took what he considered otherwise random persons and events and supplied them with a comprehensive meaning, a "philosophy of history."

Philosophy in the Dark Ages: Boethius, Pseudo-Dionysius, Erigena

The fall of the Roman Empire in 476 ushered in a period of intellectual darkness. The barbarians who destroyed the political might of Rome also shattered the institutions of culture in Western Europe. Learning came almost to a halt. Virtually the whole body of ancient literature was lost. For the next five or six centuries, philosophy was kept alive by Christian scholars who became the channels through which the works of the ancient Greeks were transmitted to the West.

BOETHIUS

One of the most prominent philosophic figures in the early Middle Ages was Anicius Manlius Severinus Boethius (ca. 480–524), of Rome and Pavia, Italy. He grew up in the kingdom of Theodoric as a Christian. At an early age he was sent to Athens, where he mastered the Greek language and encountered Aristotelianism, Neoplatonism, and Stoicism. Later, in 510, he was elevated to the position of consul in the court of Theodoric and was eventually showered with honors. In spite of his fame and his impressive political status, he was suspected of high treason, stripped of his honors, subjected to a long imprisonment, and, in 524, finally executed. During his imprisonment, in Pavia, he wrote his famous *The Consolation of Philosophy,* a book that was widely circulated in the Middle Ages and had such lasting influence that Chaucer translated it and patterned some of his *Canterbury Tales* on its contents. In the early pages of this book Boethius offered an allegorical description of philosophy, which can still be seen carved on the façades of many cathedrals in Europe. What led him to see philosophy in these allegorical terms was his attempt to overcome his melancholy by writing poetry as he languished in prison. At this point he was struck by a new vision of philosophy, which he set down with considerable imaginative force. Philosophy came to him as a noble woman with eyes of such keenness as to suggest that philosophy has powers higher than human nature. She gives the impression of having no specific age, indicating that philosophy is perennial. On her robe appear the Greek letters phi (ϕ), symbolizing practical philosophy, and theta (θ), symbolizing theoretical philosophy, and a ladder between them indicates the ascent on the steps to wisdom. Boethius is consoled by philosophy when he discovers from it that no earthly goods and pleasures can give him true happiness, that one must turn to the Supreme Good to whom philosophy leads. But in addition to this allegorical interpretation, Boethius formulated a more technical definition of philosophy, calling it the *love of wisdom.* The word *wisdom* carried the whole freight of his definition. To him *wisdom* meant a reality, something that exists in itself. Wisdom is the living thought that causes all things. In loving wisdom, one loves the thought and cause of all things. In the end, the love of wisdom is the love of God.

Boethius became the most important channel through which Greek thought, especially some of Aristotle's works, was transmitted to the West in the early Middle Ages. Being an accomplished student of the Greek language, he had originally intended to translate the works of Plato and Aristotle into Latin and to show how their apparent differences could be harmonized. Although he did not accomplish this ambitious project, he nevertheless did leave a considerable legacy of philosophical writings, consisting of translations of some of Aristotle's works, commentaries on these works, and some original treatises. In addition he was the author of theological works of considerable importance, as well as of treatises concerning each of the four liberal arts—arithmetic, geometry, astronomy, and music—to which he gave the name *quadrivium* to distinguish them from the other three liberal arts, the *trivium,* consisting of grammar, logic, and rhetoric.

Boethius translated Aristotle's logical treatises, including the *Prior* and *Posterior Analytics,* the *Topics,* and the *Categories.* He also translated Porphyry's *Introduction (Isagoge) to Aristotle's Categories.* His commentaries were on Porphyry's *Isagoge,* on Aristotle's *Categories, Topics,* and *De Interpretation.* In addition, he wrote a commentary on Cicero's *Topics.* His original treatises covered several aspects of logic. He also wrote on mathematics and music, and his aforementioned *The Consolation of Philosophy,* a dialogue between himself and a personification of philosophy, ranged over the subjects of God, fortune, freedom, and evil.

In his original treatises, Boethius drew upon a wide variety of authors, indicating his familiarity with Plato, Aristotle, the Stoics, Plotinus, Augustine, and others, though clearly under the dominant influence of Aristotle. His works achieved the status of classics and were later used by the leading philosophers, including St. Thomas Aquinas, as authoritative guides for interpreting ancient authors and basic philosophic problems. In particular, Boethius became the great interpreter of Aristotle's thought, exhibiting in this work his own immense philosophical skill. In his original treatises, Boethius worked out with great care some preliminary formulations of problems that later received more elaborate treatment. These problems covered such significant topics as the proof for God's existence, the problem of universals, and the nature of *being*, which ultimately became the center of Aquinas' philosophy. Though he wrote some specifically theological works, he tried to distinguish between faith and reason, and in his *Consolation* he makes no mention of Christianity but rather formulates a natural theology based upon what the unaided human reason can provide. At the same time, he considered the problem of knowledge, somewhat unexpectedly accepting Plato's doctrine of reminiscence, which held that learning consists in the soul's recovery of what it once knew but forgot. Boethius also departed from Aristotle's theory of universals, saying that we do not abstract the universal from particular things, that the mind is able to think universals "separate from bodies." At the same time, Boethius gave evidence of being a student of St. Augustine, employing some of his insights concerning evil and the cause of human restlessness, the relation between human freedom and God's providence, and our intuitive consciousness of God.

What Boethius gave the early Middle Ages in the form of translations, commentaries, and original treatises gave him a stature comparable to Aristotle and Augustine for centuries to come. His chief significance lies in his having taught this period the fundamentals of Aristotle's thought and in formulating the basic philosophical definitions and terms that were destined to become the keys to the intellectual activity of the West.

PSEUDO-DIONYSIUS THE AREOPAGITE

A large and influential body of Neoplatonic writing, whose origin has been traced to the Byzantine world but whose author is still unknown, appeared in the West around 500 A.D. For a while, these writings were attributed to the disciple of St. Paul, Dionysius the Areopagite. But since their contents embody ideas developed by Proclus (ca. 410–485) and were appealed to at the Council of 533, it is now thought that they were written probably in Syria close to 500 and that the author used a pseudonym. The treatises of Pseudo-Dionysius attempt to relate Christian thought systematically with Neoplatonic philosophy. These works consist of *The*

Divine Names, The Celestial Hierarchy, The Ecclesiastical Hierarchy, The Mystical Theology, and also ten letters. They were all translated into Latin frequently, and several commentaries were written on them. The influence of Pseudo-Dionysius was very great throughout the Middle Ages. Philosophers and theologians concerned with quite different problems made considerable use of his writings. The mystics drew heavily upon his elaborate theory of the hierarchy of beings, as it afforded a rich source for describing the ascent of the soul to God. Aquinas used his theories in accounting for the great chain of being and the analogical relation between man and God. Above all, he was one of the most powerful sources of Neoplatonism, influencing philosophical thought regarding the origin of the world, the knowledge of God, and the nature of evil.

Pseudo-Dionysius gave an account of the relation of the world to God in which he combined the Neoplatonic theory of *emanation* and the Christian doctrine of *creation.* He wanted to avoid the pantheism latent in the theory that says that all things are emanations from God. At the same time he wanted to establish that whatever exists comes from God, though he apparently had no clear conception of God's creative act as an act of free will. The world, nevertheless, is the object of God's providence. God has placed between Himself and man a virtual ladder or hierarchy of beings called heavenly spirits. From the lowest level of being to the highest, where God is at the summit, there are various degrees of being. Though he came close to pantheism and monism because of this continuous scale or chain of being, which he sometimes described as a shaft of light, Dionysius did maintain a pluralistic view of things. God is the goal of all created things. He attracts all things to Himself by His goodness and the love He inspires.

The knowledge of God, says Dionysius, can be approached in two ways, a *positive* and a *negative* way. When the mind takes the positive way, it ascribes to God all the perfect attributes discovered by a study of creatures. In this way the *divine* can be given such *names* as goodness, light, being, unity, wisdom, and life. Dionysius indicates that these names belong in their perfection to God and only in a derivative sense to man, depending upon the degree to which the creature participates in these perfections. Dionysius thought it was fair to assume that these attributes would be found actually to exist in God in the literal sense, since surely God *is* goodness, life, wisdom, and so on. By contrast, men *have* these to a lesser degree. Still, God and man are more alike than God and a stone, about which it cannot be said that it is good, wise, and alive.

More important, however, was the *negative* way, which Dionysius developed under the influence of Proclus. Dionysius himself considered it more significant than the positive way, and St. Thomas Aquinas made considerable use of it in the thirteenth century. In the negative way, the mind considers God's nature by denying of God whatever seems least compatible with Him, such as "drunkenness and fury." Then, by a process of "remotion," various categories of attributes are "removed" from our conception of God. Dionysius was aware that men unavoidably develop anthropomorphic conceptions of God, and for this reason he undertook to remove from God all the attributes of creatures. To him it was obvious that what characterized God was precisely that He did not have the attributes of finite creatures. Step by step he removed from the conception of God all the things we say about creatures. Since all we know is the world of creatures, the negative process of "remotion" leads the human mind not to a clear conception of God but only to a "darkness of unknowing," the only positive aspect of which is the assurance of knowing what God is *not* like. Because God is no object, He is beyond the knowable. This view became of paramount influence among the later mystics, who believed that as men ascended closer to God, the ordinary forms of human knowledge were annihilated by the blindness caused by the excess of God's light.

In Neoplatonic terms, Dionysius denied the positive existence of *evil*. If evil were something positive, had some substantial being, it would have to be traced back to God as its cause, for all being is from God. For Dionysius, being and goodness were identical terms, for whatever is, is good, and something that is good, certainly is. In God goodness and being are one, and therefore whatever comes from God (and everything that is *does* come from God) is therefore good. The corollary would not necessarily be true, namely, that evil is synonymous with non-being. Still, it is in fact non-being in the sense of the absence or "privation" of being *where it rightly belongs* that constitutes evil. The absence of being amounts to evil because it means the absence of good. An evil person is good in all the ways in which he possesses positive being but is evil in whatever respect he is lacking some form of being, particularly in the operation of his will. Ugliness and disease in physical nature are called evil for the same reason that acts in the province of morality are, namely, because they suffer deficiency in form or the absence of some being. Blindness is the absence of sight and not the presence of some evil force.

All three of these doctrines refined by Pseudo-Dionysius in an attempt to combine Neoplatonism and Christianity were to play a strong role in the rest of medieval philosophy, as writers continued to speculate about the origin of the world, about what can be known of God's nature, and about how to account for the presence of evil.

JOHN SCOTUS ERIGENA

Three centuries passed from the time of Boethius and Pseudo-Dionysius before another philosopher of stature appeared in the West. He was a remarkable Irish monk, John Scotus Erigena, who produced the first full-scale philosophical system in the Middle Ages. Born in Ireland in 810, he studied in a monastery and was one of the few scholars of his day who had mastered Greek, as the study of Greek in the ninth century was virtually limited to the Irish monasteries. Even the great educator from York, Alcuin, who crossed the Channel to become headmaster in the Palace School under Charlemagne and who sought to restore the school system of Western Europe, which had been destroyed by the barbarians, knew very little Greek. By any standard, Erigena was an unusually able Greek scholar, and given the philosophical material at his disposal at that time, his systematic writing set him apart as the most impressive thinker of his century.

Erigena left Ireland and appeared in the court of Charles the Bald around 851. His studies at this time were devoted chiefly to Latin authors, especially St. Augustine and Boethius, on whose *The Consolation of Philosophy* he wrote a commentary. At the request of Charles the Bald, Erigena translated the Greek texts of Pseudo-Dionysius into Latin in 858 and in addition wrote commentaries on these texts. He also translated works by Maximus the Confessor and St. Gregory of Nyssa. After this work of translation, Erigena produced his celebrated treatise on *The Division of Nature,* a book written in dialogue form around 864. In this work, Erigena undertook the complicated task of expressing Christian thought and Augustine's philosophical views in terms of the Neoplatonism of Pseudo-Dionysius. Although it became a landmark in medieval thought, it attracted little attention from Erigena's contemporaries. Various later writers appealed to this book to corroborate theories, such as pantheism, that were inimical to orthodoxy, leading Pope Honorius III to condemn Erigena's *The Division of Nature* on January 25, 1225, and order it to be burned, in spite of which several manuscript copies have survived even to the present time.

The Division of Nature   The complicated argument of Erigena's *The Division of Nature* revolves around his special understanding of the two words in the title of his book. First of all, by *Nature* Erigena meant "everything there is." In this sense Nature includes both God and creatures. Secondly, when he talks about the *division* of Nature, he has in mind the ways in which the whole of reality, God and creatures, is divided. In addition, the word *division* has a special meaning. Erigena says that there are two ways of understanding the structure of reality; one is by *division and the other by analysis.* By *division* he means moving from the more universal to the less universal, as when one divides *substance* into *corporeal* and *incorporeal.* In turn, *incorporeal* can be divided into *living* and *inanimate,* and so on. On the other hand, by *analysis* the process of division is reversed, and the elements divided off from substance are worked back into the unity of substance. Underlying Erigena's method of division and analysis was his conviction that the human mind works in accordance with the metaphysical realities. The mind is not simply dealing with *concepts* when it "divides" and "analyzes"; it is describing how things really exist and behave. If God is the ultimate unity, things and the world are divisions of this basic unity, and analysis is the process by which things return to God. The laws of thought, according to Erigena, parallel the laws of reality.

With these distinctions in mind, Erigena argued that there is only one true reality and that all other things depend upon it and return to it, and this reality is God. Within the total reality of Nature, a fourfold division is possible as follows: there is, first, nature that creates and is not created; second, nature that is created and creates; third, nature that is created and does not create; and fourth, nature that neither creates nor is created. Erigena goes into considerable detail to elaborate each of these divisions, using Christian, Augustinian, and especially Neoplatonic concepts to formulate his philosophy about them. Some of his central ideas about each division will indicate the mode of his thought.

Nature That Creates and Is Not Created   By this Erigena meant God, who is the cause of all things but does not Himself need to be caused. He brought all creatures into existence out of nothing. Our knowledge of God, following the distinction made by Pseudo-Dionysius, is *negative,* since none of the attributes we derive from objects in our experience apply in any proper sense to God, who possesses all the perfections in His infinity. To make sure that not even the likely attributes of wisdom and truth are ascribed to God without qualification, Erigena adds the term *super* to them, so that about God one would say that He is superwisdom and supertruth. None of Aristotle's predicates or categories applies to God, for these predicates assume some form of substance—as, for example, "quantity" implies dimension—but God does not exist in a definable place. Most of what Erigena says about God's nature and of creation "out of nothing" follows generally along Christian and Augustinian lines. But as he pursues the subject of the relation between God and creatures, his Neoplatonism seems to become dominant, and it is difficult to avoid the conclusion that for Erigena there is no sharp distinction between God and creatures. "When we hear that God made all things," says Erigena, "we should understand nothing else but that God is in all things. . . ." This follows because only God "truly is" and therefore whatever is in anything is God.

Nature That is Created and Creates   This division refers to the divine Ideas, which become the prototypes of all created things. They are the *exemplary causes* of all the created species. To say that they are *created* does not mean, according to Erigena, that they come to be at some point of time. He has in mind a logical and not a chronological sequence. In God there is the full knowledge of everything, including the primordial causes of all things. These primordial causes are the divine Ideas and prototypes of things, and they are said to *create* in the sense that all creatures "participate" in them, as, for example, man's wisdom participates in superwisdom. Though he uses the word *creation* here, his Neoplatonism once again dominates, particularly since creation for Erigena does not occur in time but is an eternal relation between God's Ideas and creatures.

Nature That Is Created and Does Not Create   This is the world of things as we experience it. Technically, it refers to the collective external effects of the primordial causes. These effects, whether incorporeal (for example, angels or intelligence) or corporeal (such as man and things), are *participations* in the divine Ideas. Erigena emphasizes that these things, this full range or hierarchy of beings, contain God as their essence, even though specific things give the impression of being individual. He compares this apparent plurality of things to the many varied reflections of light on the feathers of a peacock. Each color is a real one, but it depends upon the feathers, and therefore, in the end, the color is not an independent reality. In the created world, each individual is real by virtue of its primordial cause, which is in God's mind. But God is, if anything, a unity, and to speak of Ideas, prototypes, and archetypes in His mind is to speak metaphorically, for these all constitute a unity. For this reason, the world is also a unity, as the peacock, and between the world and God, finally, there is also a comprehensive unity, since God is in everything. All things depend upon and are infused with the suprasensible; they exhibit a rhythm of "going out" into species and genera, but only as reflections, as the colors, of the divine Ideas and then "returning." What Erigena appears to say is that the divine *Ideas* stand midway between God and creatures, as though they could look "up" toward God and "down" toward these externalized forms. But in the end his Neoplatonism leads him to erase the "spaces" between the *Ideas* and God and creatures, fusing them all into a unity and eventually a pantheism.

Nature That Neither Creates Nor Is Created This last division refers to God again, this time as the goal or end of the created order. As all things proceed from God, they also all return to God. Using Aristotle's metaphor, Erigena compares God to a beloved who without moving attracts the lover. Whatever starts from a principle returns again to this same principle, and in this way the universal cause draws to itself the multitude of things that have risen from it. With this return there is an end to all evil, and man finds his union with God.

Erigena's *The Division of Nature* displayed his wide knowledge of Neoplatonism but also his inevitable pantheism. Again, his book did not receive immediate attention or acclaim but became, nevertheless, one of the decisive documents in the development of medieval philosophy. This book, along with his translations of Pseudo-Dionysius, Maximus, and Gregory of Nyssa, amounted to a substantial contribution by Erigena to the tradition of theology and philosophy.

8

Early Statements
of Major Problems

With the aggressive revival of learning under Charlemagne and with the appearance of Erigena's large-scale and systematic work *The Division of Nature*, it might have been expected that philosophy had emerged from the Dark Ages and that it would soon flourish again in Western Europe. This early promise of continued revival was delayed, however, by several historical events. After Charlemagne's death, the Empire was decentralized into feudal divisions, the papacy entered a period of moral and spiritual weakness, the monasteries exerted no effective leadership in their special province of education and learning, and the invasions by the Mongols, Saracens, and Norsemen added to these forces making for cultural darkness. For almost a hundred years, during most of the 900s, very little philosophical activity was carried on. When philosophy did revive in the next century, its main feature for the next two hundred years, from about 1000 to 1200, was its preoccupation with particular problems, including the problems of universals, of proving God's existence, and of relating the domains of faith and reason. In the discussion of these problems, several sources of philosophy were stimulated, producing a confluence of Greek, Christian, Jewish, and Arabian thought.

THE PROBLEM OF UNIVERSALS

The problem of universals, by no means a new one, struck the medieval thinkers as fundamental, because in their judgment the enterprise of thought rested to a great extent upon its solution. The central issue in this problem is how to relate the objects of human thought and the objects that exist outside the mind. Objects outside the mind are individual and many, whereas objects in the mind are single or universal. For example, in human discourse we use words such as *tree* or *man*, but such words refer to the actual and particular trees and men that we observe with our senses. To *see* a tree is one thing; to *think* it is another. We see particulars but we think universals. When we see a particular thing, our minds place it into either a species or genus. We never see *tree* or *man*, only "this oak" or "John." *Tree* stands in our language for all the actual trees, oak, elm, and so on, whereas *man* includes John, James, and every other specific person. What, then, is the relation between these words and these trees and persons? Is the word *tree only* a word, or does it refer to something that exists someplace? If the word *tree* refers to something in this oak that belongs to all trees, the word refers to something universal. The universal, then, is a general term, but the objects that exist outside our mind are single or particular and specific. If the universal is merely an idea in our mind, what is the connection between the way we think, on the one hand, and the actual particular objects outside our mind, on the other? How does the mind go about forming a universal concept? Is there anything *outside* the mind corresponding to the universal idea *in* the mind?

Boethius States the Problem   Boethius had translated Porphyry's *Introduction (Isagoge) to Aristotle's Categories*. There he found a discussion of the problem of universals in terms of certain questions raised by Porphyry. These questions centered around the relation between generic and specific notions. What, in short, is the relation between genera or species and specific objects? Porphyry raised these three questions: (1) Do genera and species really exist in nature, or are they merely constructions of the mind? (2) If they are realities, are they material or immaterial? (3) Do they exist apart from sensible things or somehow in them? While Porphyry did not answer his own questions, Boethius formulated a solution chiefly in terms of Aristotle's approach to the problem.

Boethius was aware of the immense difficulty of the problem. If the issue is to discover whether human thought conforms to realities outside the mind, we can quickly discover some ideas in our mind for which there is no corresponding external object. We can think of a centaur, but such a combination of man and horse does not exist. Or, again, we can think of a line, the way a geometer does. But we do not find this kind of line existing as such anywhere. What is the difference between the idea of the centaur and of the line? One can say about the concept of the centaur that it is *false*, whereas the concept of the line is *true*. What Boethius wants to illustrate here is that there are two fundamentally different ways in which the mind forms concepts, namely, by *composition* (putting together horse and man) and *abstraction*, by drawing from a particular object some of its predicates. He wanted to say that universal ideas, such as genera and species, are abstracted by the mind from actual individual things and are, therefore, *true* ideas.

Saying that universals are abstracted from individuals led Boethius to conclude that genera or species *exist in* the individual things and that they are universals when they are *thought* by the mind. In this way, universals (not only genera and species, to which Boethius limited his analysis, but other qualities such as *just, good, beautiful*) are simultaneously in the object and in the mind, *subsisting* in the thing and *thought* in the mind. What makes two trees both trees is that, as objects, they resemble each other because they contain a universal or the same substance or foundation to their being; at the same time, they can both be *thought* as trees because the mind discovers the same universal element in both of them. This, then, was Boethius' way of answering the first question, namely, whether universals exist in nature or only in the mind. For him, they exist both in things and in the mind. To the second question, whether the universals are material or immaterial, he could now say that they exist concretely in things and immaterially or abstractly in the mind. Similarly, his reply to the third question, whether universals exist apart from individual objects or are realized in them, was that they exist both in things and apart from them in the mind.

When these questions, which were formulated by Porphyry and answered by Boethius, came under discussion almost five hundred years later, they precipitated a vigorous debate for centuries to come. Although the issues were formulated in relatively restricted and seemingly unimportant terms, the participants saw serious theological as well as philosophical consequences hinging on the outcome of the debate. At least three major approaches were developed to this problem of universals.

Exaggerated Realism   The problem had resolved itself into the simple question of whether a universal is a real *thing* or not. Those who said universals are in fact real things are known as *exaggerated realists*. These men said that genera or species exist in reality and that individual things *share* in these universals. They did not go so far as Plato, who said, in addition, that the universals were Forms or Ideas and existed separately from individual things. Rather, he said, for example, that *humanity* and *man* exist but that these exist in the plurality of men.

Why should this form of realism seem such an important matter? One answer is found in the works of Odo of Taurnai, who taught in the Cathedral School of Tours, founded the Abbey of St. Martin, was Bishop of Cambrai, and died in the Monastery at Anchin in 1113. For him realism was the foundation of certain orthodox theological doctrines. For example, the doctrine of original sin, according to him, requires the realistic description of human nature. Realism says that there exists a universal substance, which is contained in every member of a species. If we are to understand the condition of human nature accurately, he said, we must realize that in the sin of Adam and Eve, the universal substance of *man* or *humanity* was affected and infected so that all subsequent generations have inherited the consequence of their acts. If one denied *realism*, what Adam and Eve did would pertain only to themselves, in which case the force of the doctrine of original sin would be lost. In a similar way, St. Anselm (1033–1109) thought that the doctrine of the Trinity required the viewpoint of *realism*. If one denied that an identical substance exists in several members, the Trinity would amount to tritheism, where each member is a totally separate and different being. Replying to this line of reasoning developed by Roscellinus (1050–1125), Anselm, an advocate of exaggerated realism, said that "He who does not understand how many men are specifically one only man cannot understand that several persons, each one of which is God, are one only God."

Another exaggerated realist was Guillaume de Champeaux (1070–1121), who had formulated two different views: first in his *identity* theory he held that the universal, say *humanity,* is identical in all members, in this case in all men. The *whole* reality of the universal is contained in each man. What differentiates James and John is merely certain secondary or accidental modifications of their essence or substance. Abelard (1079–1142), ridiculed this line of reasoning by saying that if each man is the whole human species, humanity exists in Socrates in Rome and in Plato in Athens. If Socrates is present wherever the human essence is found, and since it is both at Rome and Athens, Socrates must be at the same moment in Rome and in Athens, and this, said Abelard, is not only absurd but leads to pantheism. Guillaume was forced by this and other criticisms to adopt a second theory, that of *indifferentism,* an antirealist view, in which he now argued that the individuals of a species are the same thing not through some common essence but because in certain respects they are not different, they are *indifferent.*

Nominalism   One of the most formidable critics of exaggerated realism was Roscellinus (1050–1125), who was born in Compiègne, traveled to England, Rome, and Tours; taught at Taches, Compiègne, and Besançon; and was a teacher of Abelard. His central argument was that only individuals exist in nature. Species and genera are not real things. A general term, a universal, such as word does not refer to anything; it is only a word (*voces*), or a name (*nomen*), composed of letters and expressed as a *vocal emission* and is therefore only air. Logic, in Roscellinus' view, deals only with words. For this reason, discussions about universals are about words and not real things. Roscellinus was willing to draw certain obvious conclusions from his argument, particularly that the three persons of the Trinity are three separate beings and that all they have in common is a word but nothing really essential, hence they can be considered three Gods. For these views he was accused by the council at Soissons (1092) of tritheism, and when he was threatened with excommunication, he denied this doctrine. Nevertheless, Roscellinus served a decisive function in the history of the problem of universals in that he deflected thought from exaggerated realism by holding that universals, or any kind of abstraction, must not be made into a thing.

Conceptualism or Moderate Realism Roscellinus seemed to be as extreme in his nominalism as others had been in their realism. Both were exaggerated views. Avoiding both of these extremes was the position developed by Peter Abelard, who was born in Le Pallet in 1079 of a military family. During his tempestuous life, he quarreled with his teachers, had a celebrated romance with Heloïse, was abbot of the monastery in Brittany, was a famous lecturer in Paris, was condemned for his heretical teachings by Innocent II, and finally retired at Cluny, where he died in 1142.

On the problem of universals, Abelard said that universality must be ascribed principally to words. A word is *universal* when it is applied to many individuals. The word *Socrates* is not universal because it applies only to one person, whereas the word *man* is universal because it can be applied to all persons. The function of a universal term, says Abelard, is to denote individual things in a special way. The question then is, how does it come about that we formulate these universal terms? To this Abelard answers that certain individual things, because of the *way* they exist, cause anyone observing them to conceive a likeness in all these individuals. This so-called likeness is not what the realists called an *essence* or *substance*. It consists simply in the way things agree in likeness. When we experience an individual, we *see* it but also *think* or *understand* it. Unlike the eye, which requires an object, the mind does not require a physical object since it can form *conceptions*. Thus, the mind is capable of doing two things, namely, forming concepts of individuals, Plato or Socrates, and forming concepts of universals, such as *man*. The conception of the individual is clear, whereas the conception of the universal is blurred. We cannot clearly focus on the precise meaning of the universal even though we do in fact know what it means. As conceptions of the mind, the universals exist apart from the individual sensible bodies; but as words applied to these individuals they exist only in these bodies. The same word can be applied commonly to several individuals because each individual already exists in such a way as to cause it to be conceived the way others like it are conceived. The universal is therefore abstracted from the individual. The process of abstraction tells us how we understand the universal but not how the universal subsists. We understand things properly insofar as we abstract from them those properties that they truly possess. Abelard concluded, therefore, that the universal is a word and concept representing some reality that supplies the ground for this concept. This ground is the way similar things exist and strike our minds. To this extent, there is an objective ground for the universals, but this ground is not, as the realist held, something *real* in the sense of a *thing*. Nor would Abelard agree with the strict nominalist who would say that the universal is *only* a subjective idea or word for which there is no objective ground.

Abelard's theory of universals carried the day, defeating both extremes of realism and nominalism. For the most part, St. Thomas Aquinas accepted Abelard's moderate realism. Using Avicenna's formulation of the status of universals,

Aquinas, following Abelard, agreed that universals exist outside of things (*ante rem*) but as such only as the divine Ideas in God's mind, in things (*in re*) as the concrete individual essence in all members of a species, and in the mind (*then post rem*) after abstracting the universal concept from the individual. The problem of universals had one more major treatment in the Middle Ages, and this time it was given a different solution by William of Ockham.

PROVING THE EXISTENCE OF GOD: ANSELM'S ONTOLOGICAL ARGUMENT

St. Anselm is famous in the history of thought primarily for his celebrated *ontological* argument for the existence of God. He was born in Piedmont in 1033, entered the Benedictine Order, and eventually became Archbishop of Canterbury, where he died in 1109. For Anselm, there was no clear line between philosophy and theology. Like Augustine before him, he was particularly concerned with providing rational support for the doctrines of Christianity, which he already accepted as a matter of faith. He was convinced that faith and reason lead to the same conclusions. Moreover, Anselm believed that human reason can create a natural theology or metaphysics that is rationally coherent and does not depend upon any authority other than rationality. This did not mean, however, that Anselm denied any connection between natural theology and faith. On the contrary, his view was that natural theology consists of giving a rational version of what is believed. In this he was thoroughly Augustinian, saying that he was not trying to *discover* the truth about God through reason alone, but wanted rather to employ reason in order to *understand* what he was believing. His method therefore was *faith seeking understanding;* "I do not seek to understand in order that I may believe," he said, "but I believe in order that I may understand." He made it particularly clear that his enterprise of proving God's existence could not even begin unless he had already believed in His existence. The human mind cannot penetrate into the profundity of God, "for I deem my intellect in no way sufficient thereunto. . . ." From the rational proof of God's existence, Anselm had a limited expectation, as he said that "I desire only a little understanding of the truth which my heart believes and loves."

Before he composed the ontological argument, which appears in his book entitled *Proslogion,* he formulated three other arguments in an earlier book called *Monologion.* These three arguments indicate his philosophical orientation, namely, his acceptance of *realism* and his rejection of *nominalism.* His realism comes out in his belief that words are not simply sounds or grammatical conventions but stand for real things outside of the mind. Stated briefly, his three early arguments proceed as follows: (1) Men seek to enjoy what they consider *good.* Since we can compare things with each other as being *more* or *less* good, these things must share in one and the same goodness. This goodness must be good-in-itself and as such the supreme good. One could use the same argument as applied to *greatness.* There must therefore be something which is the best and greatest of all. (2) Everything that exists, exists either through something or through nothing. Obviously, it cannot come out of nothing. The only remaining alternative, then, is to say that a thing is caused either by something else or by itself. It cannot be caused by itself because before it is, it is nothing. To say that it is caused by something else could mean that things cause each other, which is also absurd. There must therefore be one thing that alone is from itself and that causes all other things to be, and this is God. (3) There are various *degrees* or *levels* of being, whereby animals have a *higher* being than plants, and men have a higher being than animals. Using a line of reasoning similar to his first argument, he concluded that unless one continued to move up through an infinite number of levels, he must arrive at a *highest* and most perfect being, than which there is no more perfect. All three of these arguments start from an existing finite thing and move up through a hierarchy until it reaches the summit of the scale of Being. Again, Anselm's realism is evident here, as is the influence of Plato and Augustine, since he assumes throughout that when a finite thing shares in what our language calls *good, great, cause, being,* these words refer to some existing reality; finite things therefore share not only in a *word* but in *being,* which somewhere exists in maximum perfection. Still, Anselm was aware that these arguments did not have the clarity or power of a mathematical proof. Moreover, his fellow monks wondered whether he could simplify these arguments. Accordingly, after much thought on the matter, Anselm thought he had discovered a single, clear, and virtually flawless argument which he published in the *Proslogion; or, Faith Seeking Understanding.*

Ontological Argument The first thing to notice about this proof is that Anselm's thought proceeds from within his mind, rather than starting, as Aquinas did, with the assumption that each proof must begin with some empirical evidence from which the mind can then move logically to God. Anselm followed Augustine's doctrine of divine illumination, which gave him direct access to certain truths. Indeed, Anselm asks the reader, before beginning the ontological argument, to "enter the inner chamber of your mind" and to "shut out all things save God and whatever may aid you in seeking God." Clearly, Anselm is assured of the existence of God before he begins, saying, again, that "unless I believe, I shall not understand."

The argument itself moves swiftly. We believe, says Anselm, that God is "that than which nothing greater can be thought." The question then is, does this than which nothing greater can be thought really exist? There are those who would deny God's existence. Anselm quotes Psalms 14:1, where it says that "The fool has said in his heart: There is no God." What is meant by the word *fool* in this context? It means that one who denies God's existence is involved in a flat contradiction. For when the fool hears the words "something than which nothing greater can be thought," he understands what he hears, and what he understands can be said to be in his intellect. But it is one thing for something to be in the intellect; it is another to understand that something actually exists. A painter, for example, thinks in advance what he is about to portray. At this point, there is in his intellect an understanding of what he is about to make, though not an understanding that the portrait, which is still to be made, actually exists. But when he has finally painted it, he both has in his understanding and understands as existing the portrait he has finally made. What this proves is that something can be in the intellect even before the intellect knows it to exist. There is, then, in the fool's intellect an understanding of what is meant by the phrase "something than which nothing greater can be thought," even though he does not yet necessarily understand that this something does in fact exist. It is in his intellect because when the fool hears this phrase, he understands it, and whatever is understood is in the understanding. Hence, even the fool knows that there is at least in his intellect a being than which nothing greater can be thought. This brings Anselm to the crux of his argument, which is this: Anyone, even the fool, can think of something greater than a being which is only in the intellect as an *idea*, and this something is the *actual existence* of that than which there is no greater. The contradiction in which the fool finds himself is in understanding what is meant by the word *God*, namely, a being than which nothing greater can be thought, realizing that its actual existence is greater than just having an idea of it in the intellect, and still denying that God exists. Therefore, says Anselm, "there exists beyond doubt something than which a greater cannot be thought, both in understanding and in reality." In a concluding prayer, Anselm thanks God "because through your divine illumination I now so understand that which, through your generous gift, I formerly believed. . . ."

Gaunilon's Rebuttal   In the Abbey of Marmontier near Tours, another Benedictine monk, Gaunilon, came to the defense of the "fool." Gaunilon did not want to deny God's existence but simply to argue that Anselm had not constructed an adequate proof. For one thing, Gaunilon argued that the first part of the "proof" is impossible to achieve: It requires that there be in the understanding an idea of God, that upon hearing this word the fool is expected to have a conception of that than which there is no greater. But, says Gaunilon, the fool cannot form a concept of such a being since there is nothing among other realities he experiences from which this concept can be formed, in addition to which Anselm has already argued that there is no reality like Him. Actually, if the human mind could form such a concept, no "proof" would be necessary, for one would then already connect existence as an aspect of a perfect being. Gaunilon's other major objection is that we often think of things that in fact do not exist. We can imagine a perfect island, an island than which no greater can exist, but there is no way to prove that such a perfect island exists.

Anselm's Reply to Gaunilon   Anselm gave two replies. First, he said that we, along with the fool, are able to form a concept of that than which there is no greater. We do this whenever we compare different degrees of perfection in things and move upward to the maximum perfection, than which there is no more perfect. Secondly, he thought Gaunilon's reference to a perfect island showed that he had missed the point of the argument. Anselm points out that we can move from an idea to its necessary existence in only one case, namely, in the case of that Being whose nonexistence cannot be thought. An island does not *have to be,* it is a *possible* or *contingent* kind of being. This would be similarly true of every finite thing. There is only one something through which everything else has its being but that is itself not derived from anything else but has its existence necessarily from itself, and this is God.

FAITH AND REASON IN ARABIAN AND JEWISH THOUGHT

Most of medieval thought is an attempt to reconcile the domains of philosophy and theology, of faith and reason. The leading writers were Christians, who wrote philosophy with an admixture of theology. Their religious orientation stemmed from the mainstream of the Christian tradition and was therefore, for the most part, the same for all of them. Their philosophical orientation, however, was quite diverse, since at different times and at different places they were exposed to different philosophers. Even when they relied upon the same philosopher—Aristotle, for example—they were exposed to different interpretations of his writings. What makes the Arabian philosophers highly important in the Middle Ages is that they had produced influential commentaries on Aristotle upon which many Christian writers depended for their understanding of Aristotle. As it turned out, these Arabian interpretations of Aristotle were the source of much knowledge about Aristotle but also the cause of serious difficulties in harmonizing the domains of faith and reason.

Arabian Philosophy   Under the leadership of Mohammed (570–632) there was established the vast Moslem Empire with cultural centers in Persia and Spain, where during the ninth through the twelfth centuries significant philosophic activity took place. During these centuries, the Moslem world was far more advanced in its knowledge of Greek philosophy, science, and mathematics than was the Christian world. Moreover, the Moslem world had access to the chief works of Aristotle centuries before Western Europe finally received them. Many texts of the Greek philosophers had been translated into the Arabic, from which later Latin translations were made in the West. By 833, philosophy was well established in Baghdad, where a school had been established for translating Greek manuscripts on philosophy and science, and for creative scholarship as well. A distinguished line of thinkers worked here, especially Avicenna (980–1037). The other focal point of Moslem culture was Cordova, Spain, where the other leading Arabian philosopher, Averroës, wrote much of his philosophy. Although Avicenna and Averroës wrote in Arabic and were Moslems, they were not Arabs. Avicenna was a Persian, and Averroës a Spaniard. Both of them wrote interpretations of Aristotle's philosophy. These interpretations were accepted by some Christian writers as the authentic doctrines of Aristotle. Because these interpretations showed Aristotle to be at variance with Christian doctrine, some medieval writers, such as Bonaventura, thought it necessary to reject Aristotle to avoid

errors. St. Thomas Aquinas, on the other hand, contended with the leading exponent at the University of Paris of Averroës' views, Siger de Brabant, but Aquinas
had access to other versions of Aristotle. For this reason, Aquinas' debates with
Brabant were not to reject Aristotelianism but to interpret Aristotle in a way
compatible with Christian doctrine. The significance of the Arabian philosophers
was therefore twofold in that they were transmitters of Aristotle and other Greek
thinkers to the West and were also the authors of interpretations of Aristotle that
became the basis of controversy in medieval philosophy.

Avicenna   Avicenna, born in Persia in 980, was a phenomenal scholar. He had
studied geometry, logic, jurisprudence, the Koran, physics, theology, and medicine, becoming a practicing physician at the age of sixteen. He was the author of
many works, and although his thought centered around Aristotle, it shows some
Neoplatonic influences as well as original formulations of problems.

Of particular importance was Avicenna's formulation of the doctrine of
creation. Here he combined Aristotelian and Neoplatonic views and arrived at a
theory that was hotly debated in the thirteenth century. Avicenna begins with
the assumption that whatever begins to be (as is the case with everything we
experience) must have a cause. Things that require a cause are called *possible*
beings. A cause which is also a *possible* being must be caused by a prior being.
This too must have a cause, but there cannot be an infinite series of such causes.
There must therefore be a First Cause, whose being is not simply *possible* but is
necessary, having its existence in itself and not from a cause, and this is God.
(Aquinas would later make much of this line of reasoning in his *third proof*.)

God is at the apex of Being, has no beginning, always is in act (i.e., is
always expressing His full Being), and therefore has always created. According to
Avicenna, then, creation is both necessary and eternal. This conclusion struck
Bonaventura in the thirteenth century as a serious error and in conflict with the
Biblical notion of creation, whose two chief features were that creation is a
product of God's free will, not of necessity, and that creation occurred at a point
in time, not from eternity. Aquinas would agree, however, that philosophically
there is no way to decide whether creation occurred in time or from eternity,
that this must ultimately be a matter of faith.

If Avicenna's metaphysics caused Christian philosophers difficulties because of his doctrine of creation, his psychology caused even more serious concern. In his psychology, Avicenna wanted particularly to account for men's intellectual activity. Central to his theory was the distinction between the *possible*
intellect and the *Agent Intellect*. To account for this distinction, Avicenna employed his Neoplatonic view of the gradations of beings, placing man under the
lowest level of angelic beings or Intelligences. That is, God creates a single effect,
and this effect is called an *Intelligence*, the highest angel, but this Intelligence in
turn creates a subordinate Intelligence. There are nine such Intelligences in descending order, each one creating (1) the one below it and (2) the soul of the
successive sphere. The ninth Intelligence, then, creates the tenth and final Intelligence, and this is the Agent Intellect. It is the Agent Intellect that creates the

four elements of the world and the individual souls of men. The Agent Intellect not only creates the souls or minds of men, it also "radiates forms" to these created minds.

What Avicenna was saying is that since a person's mind has a beginning, it is a *possible* being; therefore, man has a *possible intellect*. Here Avicenna made a sharp distinction between existence and essence, saying that there are two different things in creatures. That is, because a creature's essence is distinct from his existence, his *essence* is not automatically fulfilled, and it is certainly not given existence by itself. The essence of the human mind is to know, but it does not always know. The intellect is capable of knowing, its essence is to know, but its knowing is only *possible*. The intellect is actually created without any knowledge but with an essence or possibility for knowledge. The *existence* of knowledge in the human intellect requires two elements, namely, (1) the bodily senses through which we perceive sensible objects externally and the powers of retaining images of objects in the memory or imagination internally, and (2) the power to discover the essence or universal in individual things through the power of abstraction. But, and here was Avicenna's unique point, this abstraction is not performed by the human intellect but is the work of the Agent Intellect, which illuminates the human mind to enable it to *know,* thereby adding existence to the mind's essence. Since the Agent Intellect is the creator of the souls of all men and, in addition, is the active power in human knowledge, there is, then, only one active intellect in all men, in which all men share.

What concerned Bonaventura so much about this psychology, which Siger de Brabant was teaching at the University of Paris, was that it threatened the notion of the discrete individuality of each person. Avicenna had not meant to imply this, for he actually had a doctrine of the immortality of each soul, since each returned to its source, the Agent Intellect. Still, Christian writers tended to see in the doctrine of the Agent Intellect the annihilation of the individual soul as well as serious separation between man and God, since the Agent Intellect, and not God, confers enlightenment upon the human intellect. The individual person exists only insofar as matter is formed into his body, and his soul is the form of his body. But, again, the active part of the intellect is not *his*. In these ways then, Avicenna injected into medieval philosophy some very provocative themes, including (1) the eternity and necessity of creation, (2) the gradations and emanations of a hierarchy of beings, (3) the doctrine of the Agent Intellect who both creates the human soul and illuminates the *possible intellect,* and (4) the distinction between essence and existence as related to possible and necessary being.

Averroës   Like Avicenna before him, Averroës was a prodigious scholar. He was born in 1126 in Cordova, Spain, where he studied philosophy, mathematics, jurisprudence, medicine, and theology. After serving, as his father had, as a judge, he became a physician, but spent much of his time writing his famous commentaries, for which reason he became known in the Middle Ages as The Commentator. He spent his last days in Morocco, where he died in 1198 at the age of seventy-two.

Averroës considered Aristotle the greatest of all philosophers, going so far as to say that nature had produced him as the model of human perfection. For this reason, Averroës structured all his work around Aristotle's texts and ideas. At some points he disagreed with Avicenna. For one thing, whereas Avicenna argued that creation is eternal and necessary, Averroës denied altogether the idea of creation, saying that philosophy knows no such doctrine, that this is merely a teaching of religion. Averroës also rejected the distinction between essence and existence, saying that there is no *real* distinction between them (such as led Avicenna to distinguish between the *possible* and *active intellects*), but only a logical distinction for purposes of analysis. Moreover, Averroës held that the form of man is the soul, but that the soul is a material and not a spiritual form. As such, the material soul has the same mortality as the body, so that upon death nothing survives. What confers special status to man among animals is that, unlike the lower animals, man is united through knowledge with the Agent Intellect. Unlike Avicenna, who said that each man has a possible intellect, a spiritual power, unique to himself, whereas for all men there was one and the same Agent Intellect, Averroës denied that men have separate *possible* intellects. He therefore explicitly located human knowledge in the universal Agent Intellect and denied the doctrine of immortality. It is no wonder that the Christian thinkers thought his teachings impious. But his influence was immense, and Aquinas frequently quotes from his works. Still, Averroës had little respect for theology and went to great lengths to distinguish the domains of philosophy and theology, of faith and reason.

Philosophy and theology each have a function, said Averroës, because there are different kinds of people whom they respectively serve. He envisioned three groups of men. (1) The majority of men live by imagination and not by reason. They are kept virtuous through fear communicated by eloquent preachers. By contrast, the philosopher needs no threat, but is motivated by his knowledge. Although religion and philosophy work generally for the same end, they communicate different contents and, in this sense, different truths. These truths do not necessarily contradict each other; they simply are different kinds. Hence, the first group is composed of those who are governed more by dramatic forms of thought than by reason. (2) The second group is of theologians, who differ from the first group only in that while they have the same religious beliefs, they attempt to devise intellectual supports for them as their justification. But, having prejudiced their thinking by resting it upon inflexible assumptions, they cannot arrive at truth even though they have some notion of the power of reason. (3) The third and superior group consists of the philosophers, who constitute a small minority. They are able to appreciate the truth for which religious persons and rational theologians are seeking, but they see no reason for trying to see this truth *through* the unavoidably indirect perspective of religion. The philosophers know truth directly. Actually, Averroës thought that religious beliefs had a social function in that they made philosophical truths accessible to minds that were incapable of philosophical thought. He thought, however, that the theologians, as compared with the masses, should have known better than to employ the powers of sophisticated reasoning upon a subject matter, religion, that is by nature a deviation from, though not necessarily contrary to, reason.

Jewish Philosophy: Moses Maimonides   Both Jewish and Arabian thought were more advanced than and therefore superior to Christian thought in the twelfth century. The reason is that at this time the Christian philosophers did not have access to the rich apparatus of Greek philosophic concepts. As we have seen, the Arabians had been working with Aristotle's texts since the ninth century. The great Jewish philosopher Maimonides owed his acquaintance with Aristotle to the Arabians. Both the Arabian and Jewish philosophers exerted a powerful influence upon the development of thirteenth-century scholastic philosophy because they had worked out some preliminary solutions to the major philosophical problems and had, moreover, transmitted considerable learning to that century. Maimonides had a special influence upon the succeeding generations of Christian thinkers because he shared with them a common belief in the Old Testament. And Maimonides' attempt to harmonize Old Testament thought with Greek philosophy and science served as a model for Thomas Aquinas in reconciling Biblical and secular learning.

Moses ben Maimonides was born in 1135 at Cordova and was a contemporary of Averroës who was also born there. He was forced to leave Spain, and he went first to Morocco and then to Egypt, where he earned his livelihood by practicing medicine. He died in Cairo in 1204 at the age of sixty-nine. His principal work was his book entitled *Guide of the Perplexed*. In it he set out to prove that the teachings of Judaism harmonize with philosophic thought and, in addition, that Biblical thought offers certain valid insights that reason alone cannot discover. To accomplish this end, Maimonides drew on an astonishing amount of literature, being dominated, however, by the works of Aristotle. Again, that he had so effectively utilized Aristotle as a rational foundation for Jewish theology had a strong influence upon others, notably Aquinas, who undertook the similar task of harmonizing Christian thought with philosophy.

Apart from expressing many of Aristotle's views, which others had also learned and taught, Maimonides proposed certain distinctive notions. Among these are the following: *First,* Maimonides believed that there can be no basic conflict between theology, philosophy, and science, between faith and reason. His *Guide of the Perplexed* was addressed principally to those believing Jews who had studied the sciences of the philosophers and had become perplexed by the literal meaning of the Law. The science of the Law (Torah) and philosophy, he said, are distinct forms of knowledge. Although they do not conflict, their range and content are not the same. For this reason, not every religious doctrine will have a rational or philosophical explanation.

Second, the doctrine of the creation of the world is a matter of religious belief. Although Aristotle's philosophy suggests that the world existed from eternity, that there was no creation in time, Maimonides points out that on this matter the philosophic proof is not decisive; that is, philosophically the arguments for and against the doctrine of creation are of equal weight. Aquinas later took this same view, saying, as Maimonides had, that on this matter, the religious view must prevail, since it does not conflict with rational thought.

Third, Maimonides thought that conflicts between faith and reason were produced by two things, namely, the anthropomorphic language of religion and the disorderly way in which the problems of faith are approached by the perplexed. One must proceed step by step, moving from mathematics, the natural sciences, to the study of the Law, and then to metaphysics or technical philosophical theology. With this kind of methodical training it becomes easier to understand the allegorical nature of much Biblical language. But to reduce the anthropomorphic element in religious language one must be trained in the categories of scientific and philosophical concepts.

Fourth, Maimonides agreed with Avicenna regarding the structure of human nature. Like Avicenna, he accepted the theory of the Agent Intellect as the source of man's substantive knowledge. Each man has only a *possible* or *passive* intellect belonging uniquely to him. Each person *acquires* an active intellect, which *is* the Agent Intellect, or comes from the Agent Intellect in varying degrees, depending upon each man's degree of merit. Upon death, man's soul, which is the form of his body, perishes, and the only element that survives is the active intellectual ingredient that came from the Agent Intellect and that now returns to it. If this is a doctrine of immortality, it is one in which the unique characteristics of each individual have been greatly diminished.

Fifth, Maimonides anticipated three of Aquinas' proofs for the existence of God. Using portions of Aristotle's *Metaphysics* and *Physics,* he proved the existence of a Prime Mover, the existence of a *necessary* Being (relying here also on Avicenna), and the existence of a primary cause. Whether the world was created out of nothing or existed from eternity did not, Maimonides thought, affect the enterprise of natural theology. But having proved the existence of God, Maimonides, unlike Aquinas, rejected the possibility of saying *what* God is like. No positive attributes can be ascribed to God but only negative ones, by saying what God is not like.

Sixth, the goal of human life is to achieve man's appropriate perfection. The philosophers, says Maimonides, have made it clear there are four kinds of perfections that man can attain; there are, in ascending order, the perfection of possessions, the perfection of the bodily constitution and shape, the perfection of the moral virtues, and, finally, the highest, which is the acquisition of the rational virtues. By rational virtues, says Maimonides, "I refer to the conception of intelligibles, which teach true opinions concerning the divine things. That is in true reality the ultimate end; thus what gives the individual true perfection . . . through it man is man." This rational account of man's perfection had its counterpart also in faith, for Maimonides concluded by saying that "the prophets too have explained the self-same notions—just as the philosophers have interpreted them." Faith and reason are in harmony.

9

The Apex of Medieval Philosophy: The Scholastic System of St. Thomas Aquinas

The great achievement of St. Thomas Aquinas (1225–1274) was that he brought together into a formidable synthesis the insights of classical philosophy and Christian theology. More specifically, Aquinas "Christianized" the philosophy of Aristotle. Although his philosophical orientation was dominated by Aristotle, he was aware of the vast scope of thought produced by the ancients, the Christian fathers, and the earlier medieval writers, including the Arabian and Jewish writers. By the time he began his literary work, a large part of Plato's and Aristotle's writings had become available in Western Europe. Augustine had formulated an earlier synthesis of philosophy and theology by combining the Christian faith with elements of Plato's thought, which he had discovered in the writings of the Neoplatonist Plotinus. Shortly after Augustine, in the sixth century, Boethius made a portion of Aristotle's works available in Latin for the first time and thereby stimulated philosophical speculation again. From about the seventh to the thirteenth century there were several lines of development, leading toward differences and controversies between Platonists and Aristotelians. This conflict continued after the thirteenth century as a controversy between Augustinians and Thomists, insofar as each of these theologians built his thought around Plato and Aristotle, respectively. In these formative centuries, medieval thinkers wrestled with the problem of relating philosophy and theology, expressing this problem as the relation between faith and reason. There was also the problem of *universals*, which not only reflected the different viewpoints of Plato and Aristotle but also had important ramifications for the Christian faith. On all these matters, Aquinas now exerted a decisive influence by clarifying the precise questions involved, acknowledging alternative solutions offered by different authorities, and answering the major objections to his Aristotelian-Christian solutions. In this way, Aquinas perfected the "scholastic method."

The term *scholasticism* in this context is derived from the intellectual activity carried on in the medieval cathedral *schools*, and its proponents were called *doctores scholastici*. Eventually, scholasticism came to refer to the dominant system of thought developed by the doctors in the schools and to the special method they utilized in teaching philosophy. Scholastic philosophy was an attempt to put together a coherent system of *traditional* thought rather than a pursuit of genuinely novel forms of insight. The content of this system was for the most part a fusion of Christian theology and the philosophies of Plato and especially Aristotle. Most distinctive in scholasticism was its *method,* a process relying chiefly upon strict logical deduction, taking on the form of an intricate *system* and expressed in a *dialectical* or disputational form in which theology dominated philosophy.

Thomas was born in 1225 near Naples. His father was a Count of Aquino who had hoped that his son would someday enjoy high ecclesiastical position. For this reason, Thomas was placed in the Abbey of Monte Cassino as a boy of five, and for the next nine years he pursued his studies in this Benedictine abbey. At the age of fourteen, he entered the University of Naples, but while in that city he was fascinated by the life of some Dominican friars at a nearby convent and decided to enter their Order. As the Dominicans were particularly dedicated to teaching, Thomas had, upon entering their Order, resolved to give himself to a religious and also a teaching vocation. Four years later, in 1245, he entered the University of Paris, where he came under the influence of a prodigious scholar whose enormous intellectual achievements had earned him the names "Albert the Great" (Albertus Magnus) and the "Universal Teacher." During his long and intimate association with Albert both at Paris and Cologne, Thomas' mind was shaped in decisive ways by the vast range of Albert's learning and by his views on particular problems.

Albert had recognized the significance of philosophy and science for grounding Christian faith and for developing the capacities of the human mind. While other theologians looked askance at secular learning, Albert concluded that the Christian thinker must master philosophical and scientific learning in all its forms. He had respect for all intellectual activity, and his writings attest to his acquaintance with a vast amount and variety of learning. He knew virtually all the ancient, Christian, Jewish, and Arabian writers. His mind was encyclopedic rather than creative. Still, it was Albert who had recognized the fundamental

Aquinas (*The Bettmann Archive*)

difference between philosophy and theology, sharpening more accurately than his predecessors had the boundaries between them. Albert thought that such writers as Anselm and Abelard, for example, had ascribed too much competence to reason, not realizing that from a rigorous point of view much of what they ascribed to reason was in fact a matter of faith. Albert's particular objective was to make Aristotle clearly understandable to all of Europe, hoping to put into Latin all of Aristotle's works. He considered Aristotle the greatest of all philosophers, and much of the credit for the dominance of Aristotle's thought in the thirteenth century must be given to him. It was inevitable, under these circumstances, that his pupil Thomas Aquinas would also see in Aristotle the most significant philosophical support for Christian theology.

Unlike Albert, who did not change anything in the philosophers he quoted in his works, Thomas used Aristotle more creatively, systematically, and with a more specific recognition of the harmony between what Aristotle said and the Christian faith. After an interval of teaching under the auspices of the Papal Court from 1259 to 1268, Thomas returned once again to Paris and became involved in the celebrated controversy with the Averroists. In 1274, Pope Gregory X called him to Lyons to participate in a council, and while on his way there, he died in a monastery between Naples and Rome, at the age of forty-nine.

Thomas left a huge literary legacy, the vastness of which is all the more remarkable when one recalls that it was all composed within a twenty-year span. Among his principal works are his commentaries on many of Aristotle's writings, careful arguments against the errors of the Greeks and the Averroists, a brilliant early work on essence and existence, a political treatise on rulers, and many other notable works. His most renowned literary achievements are his two major theological works, the *Summa contra Gentiles* and *Summa Theologica*.

The University of Paris   The first universities grew out of what were called "cathedral schools." The University of Paris evolved from the Cathedral School of Notre Dame, its formal rules of organization and procedures being approved officially by the Papal representative in 1215. Originally, like all early universities, Paris consisted of masters and students without any special buildings or other features we now associate with universities, such as libraries and endowments. These were added in the fourteenth and fifteenth centuries. But the most important ingredients were there, namely, masters and students with a passion for learning. Being originally church institutions, universities shared a common theological doctrine. This meant, too, that of the four faculties, theology, law, medicine, and arts, the theological faculty enjoyed undisputed supremacy.

Besides its theological orientation, the University of Paris had a receptivity to universal knowledge. This accounts for the gradual acceptance and triumph of Aristotle's philosophy at Paris. It is easily apparent, however, that the invasion of Aristotelianism would raise problems of orthodoxy. There was, however, not only the concern over the impact of Aristotle's philosophy upon Christian thought, but also serious questions over whether Aristotle had been faithfully and accurately interpreted by the Arabians. In addition, whereas Augustine and Platonism had triumphed at Oxford, this mode of thought, although not dominant at Paris, was nevertheless strongly represented there at this time by Bonaventura, a contemporary of Aquinas. Bonaventura was critical of Aristotle, holding that by denying the Platonic doctrine of Ideas, Aristotle's thought would, if incorporated into theology, produce serious errors. For example, to deny the Platonic Ideas would mean that God does not possess in Himself the Ideas of all things and would therefore be ignorant of the concrete and particular world. In turn, this would deny God's providence or His control over the universe. This would also mean that events occur either by chance or through mechanical necessity. Even more serious was Bonaventura's charge that if God does not think the Ideas of the world, He could not have created it. On this point Aquinas was later to have serious difficulties with the church authorities, for in following Aristotle, he could discover no decisive reason for denying that the world always existed instead of being created at a point in time. But, said Bonaventura, if the world always existed, there must have existed an infinite number of human beings, in which case there must be either an infinite number of souls, or, as Averroists argued, there is only one soul or intellect, which all human beings share. If this Averroist argument were accepted, it would annul the doctrine of personal immortality. This was strongly urged by the leading Averroist of the thirteenth century, Siger de Brabant, who said that there is only one eternal intellect and that while individual men are born and die, this intellect or soul remains and always finds another human being in which to carry out its functions of organizing the body and the act of knowing. In short, there is only one intellect, which all men have in common.

Against Aristotelian philosophy, which Bonaventura considered dangerous to Christian faith because of all these errors it engendered, he offered the insights of Augustine and Platonism. Still, because Aristotle's thought was so formidable and so systematic, particularly concerning matters of nature and science, its forward march was irresistible, and its triumph virtually inevitable. If most parts of the University were to be oriented to Aristotle's thought, the theologians could not avoid coming to terms with this monumental thinker. If Aristotle was to be accepted, the specific task of the theologians would now be to harmonize his philosophy with Christianity, that is, they would have to "Christianize" Aristotle. This is what Aquinas set out to do, contending at the same time against Bonaventura's Augustinianism and Siger de Brabant's version of Aristotle.

PHILOSOPHY AND THEOLOGY

Aquinas thought and wrote as a Christian. He was primarily a theologian. At the same time, he relied heavily upon the philosophy of Aristotle in writing his theological works. That he brought together philosophy and theology did not mean that he confused these two disciplines. On the contrary, it was his view that philosophy and theology played complementary roles in man's quest for truth. Like his teacher Albert the Great, Aquinas went to great pains to delineate the boundaries between faith and reason, indicating what philosophy and theology respectively could and could not provide to the human mind. That he wished to combine the insights of these two disciplines reflected the dominant religious orientation of thirteenth-century thought, in that knowledge of God was considered of decisive importance. What made the correct knowledge of God so essential was that any basic errors on this subject could affect the direction of a person's life, directing him either toward or away from God, who is man's ultimate end. Philosophy and theology were therefore viewed in relation to man's end, being distinguished by their different ways of contributing to man's knowledge of God. Philosophy proceeds from principles discovered by human reason, whereas theology is the rational ordering of principles received from authoritative revelation and held as a matter of faith. Aquinas' philosophy, then, consists for the most part in that portion of his theology that we should call *natural theology* and that Aquinas considered rationally demonstrable.

Aquinas saw specific differences between philosophy and theology, between reason and faith. For one thing, philosophy begins with the immediate objects of sense experience and reasons upward to more general conceptions until, as in Aristotle's case, the mind fastens upon the highest principles or first causes of being, ending in the conception of God. Theology, on the other hand, begins with a faith in God and interprets all things as creatures of God. There is here a basic difference in method, since the philosopher draws his conclusions from his rational description of the essences of things, whereas the theologian rests the demonstration of his conclusions upon the authority of revealed knowledge. Again, theology and philosophy do not contradict each other, but not everything that philosophy discusses is significant for man's religious end. Theology deals with what man needs to know for his salvation, and to ensure this knowledge, it was made available through revelation. Some of the truths of revelation could not ever be discovered by natural reason, whereas other elements of revealed truth could be known by reason alone but were revealed to ensure their being known. For this reason, there is some overlapping between philosophy and theology. For the most part, however, philosophy and theology are two separate and independent disciplines. Wherever reason is capable of knowing something, faith, strictly speaking, is unnecessary, and what faith uniquely knows through revelation cannot be known by natural reason alone. Both philosophy and theology deal with God, but the philosopher can only infer that God exists and cannot by reflecting upon the objects of sensation understand God's essential nature. There is, nevertheless, a coalescence of the object of philosophy and theology since they are both concerned with truth. Aristotle had considered the object of philosophy the study of first principles and causes, the study of being and its causes, and this led to a First Mover, which he understood as the ground of truth in the universe. This is the philosophical way of saying what the theologian has set as his object of knowledge, namely, God's being and the truth this reveals about the created world. To discover the chief aspects of Aquinas' philosophy, then, it is necessary to take from his theological writings those portions of it in which he attempts to demonstrate truths in a purely rational way. His philosophical approach is particularly evident in his attempts to demonstrate the existence of God.

PROOFS OF GOD'S EXISTENCE

Aquinas formulated five *proofs* or ways of demonstrating the existence of God. His approach was the opposite of Anselm's. Anselm began his proof with the *idea* of a perfect being "than which no greater can be conceived," from which he inferred the existence of that being inasmuch as the actual existence is greater than the mere idea of a perfect being. By contrast, Aquinas said that all knowledge must begin with our experience of sense objects. Instead of beginning with innate ideas of perfection, Aquinas rested all five of his proofs upon the ideas derived from a rational understanding of the ordinary objects that we experience with our senses. The chief characteristic of all sense objects is that their existence requires a *cause*. That every event or every object requires a cause is something the human intellect knows as a principle whenever, but not until, it comes in contact with experience. By the light of natural reason, the intellect knows, by experiencing events, that for every effect there must be a cause, that *ex nihilo nihil fit*, nothing comes from nothing. To demonstrate that God exists, Aquinas relied, then, first upon his analysis of sense objects and secondly upon his notion that the existence of these objects requires a finite series of causes and ultimately a First Cause, or God.

Proof from Motion   We are certain, because it is evident to our senses, that in the world some things are in motion. It is equally clear to us that whatever is in motion was moved by something else. If a thing is at rest, it will never move until something else moves it. When a thing is at rest, it is only potentially in motion. Motion occurs when something potentially in motion is moved and is then actually in motion; motion is the transformation of *potentiality* into *actuality*. Imagine a series of dominoes standing next to each other. When they are set up in a row, it can be said that they are all potentially in motion, though actually at rest. Consider a particular domino. Its potentiality is that it will not move until it is knocked over by the one next to it. It will move only if it is moved by something actually moving. From this fact, Aquinas drew the general conclusion that nothing can be transformed from a state of potentiality by something that is also in a mere state of potentiality. A domino cannot be knocked over by another domino that is standing still. Potentiality means the absence of something and is therefore *nothing;* for this reason, potential motion in the neighboring domino cannot move the next one because it is *nothing,* and you cannot derive motion from nonmotion. As Aquinas says, "nothing can be reduced from potentiality to actuality except by something in a state of actuality." Moreover, it is not possible for the same thing, for example a domino, to be *at the same time* in actuality and potentiality regarding motion. What is actually at rest cannot be simultaneously in motion. This means that the particular domino cannot be simultaneously the thing that is moved and also the mover. Something potentially in motion cannot move itself. Whatever is moved must be moved by another. The last domino to fall was potentially in motion, but so was the next to the last. Each domino could become a *mover* only after it had been moved by the one prior to it. Here we come to Aquinas' decisive point: If we are to account for motion, we cannot do so by going back in an infinite regress. If we must say about each mover in this series that it in turn was moved by a prior mover, we would never discover the source of motion, because every mover would then be only potentially in motion. Even if such a series went back infinitely, each one would still be only potential, and from that no actual motion could ever emerge. The fact is, however, that there *is* motion. There must therefore be a Mover, which is able to move things but which does not itself have to be moved, and this, says Aquinas, "everyone understands to be God."

Two things need to be noticed about this proof. First, Aquinas does not limit his concept of motion to things such as dominoes, that is, to locomotion. He has in mind the broadest meaning of motion so as to include the idea of *generation* and creation. Secondly, for Aquinas the First Mover is not simply the first member of a long series of causes, as though such a Mover was just like the others, its only distinction being that it is the first. Clearly, this could not be the case, for then this Mover would also be only potentially in motion. The First Mover must therefore be pure Actuality without potentiality and is therefore First not in the series but in actuality.

Proof from Efficient Cause   We experience various kinds of effects, and in every case we assign an efficient cause to each effect. The efficient cause of the statue is the work of the sculptor. If we took away the activity of the sculptor, we should not have the effect, the statue. But there is an order of efficient causes; the parents of the sculptor are his efficient cause. Workers in the quarry are the efficient cause of this particular piece of marble's availability to the sculptor. There is, in short, an intricate order of efficient causes traceable in a series. Such a series of causes is demanded because no event can be its own cause; the sculptor does not cause himself, and the statue does not cause itself. A cause is prior to an effect. Nothing, then, can be prior to itself; hence, events demand a prior cause. Each prior cause must itself have its own cause, as parents must have their own parents. But it is impossible to go backward to infinity, because all the causes in the series depend upon a first efficient cause that has made all the other causes to be actual causes. There must then be a first efficient cause "to which everyone gives the name of God."

Proof from Necessary versus Possible Being   In nature we find that things are possible to be and not to be. Such things are *possible* or *contingent* because they do not always exist; they are *generated* and are *corrupted*. There was a time when a tree did not exist; it exists, and finally it goes out of existence. To say, then, that it is *possible* for the tree to exist, must mean that it is also possible for it *not* to exist. The possibility for the tree *not* to exist must be taken two ways; first, it is possible for the tree *never* to come into existence, and secondly, once the tree is in existence, there is the possibility that it will go out of existence. To say, then, that something is *possible* must mean that at both ends of its being, that is, before it comes into being and after it goes out of being, it does not exist. *Possible* being has this fundamental characteristic, namely, that it can *not-be*. It can *not-be* not only after having existed but more importantly *before* it is generated, caused, or moved. For this reason something that is possible, which can not-be, in fact "at some time is not."

All *possible* beings, therefore, at one time did not exist, will exist for a time, and will finally pass out of existence. Once possible things *do* come into existence, they can cause other similar possible beings to be generated, as when parents beget children, and so on. But Aquinas is making this argument, namely, that possible beings do not have their existence in themselves or from their own essence; and that if *all* things in reality were only *possible*, that is, if about *everything* one could say that it could not-be *both* before it is and after it is, then at one time there was nothing in existence. But if there was a time when nothing existed then nothing could start to be, and even now there would be nothing in existence, "because that which does not exist begins to exist only through something already existing." But since our experience clearly shows us that things do exist, this must mean that not all beings are *merely possible.* Aquinas concludes from this that "there must exist something the existence of which is necessary." We must therefore admit, he says, "the existence of some being having of itself its own necessity, and not receiving it from another, but rather causing in others this necessity. This all men speak of as God."

Proof from the Degrees of Perfection   In our experience we find that some beings are more and some less good, true, and noble. But these and other ways of comparing things are possible only because things resemble in their different ways something that is the maximum. There must be something that is truest, noblest, and best. Similarly, since it can be said about things that they have more or less being, or a lower or higher form of being, as when we compare a stone with a rational creature, there must also be "something which is most being." Aquinas then argues that the maximum in any genus is the cause of everything in that genus, as fire, which is the maximum of heat, is the cause of all hot things. From this, Aquinas concludes that "there must also be something which is to all beings the cause of their being, goodness, and every other perfection; and this we call God."

Proof from the Order of the Universe   We see that things such as parts of the natural world or parts of the human body, which do not possess intelligence, behave in an orderly manner. They act in special and predictable ways to achieve certain ends or functions. Because these things act to achieve ends always, or nearly always, in the same way and to achieve the best results, "it is plain that they achieve their end, not fortuitously, but designedly." But things that lack intelligence, such as an ear or a lung, cannot carry out a function unless it be directed by something that does have intelligence, as the arrow is directed by the archer. Aquinas concludes, therefore, that "some intelligent being exists by whom all natural things are directed to their ends; and this being we call God."

Summary The two major characteristics of these five proofs are (1) their foundation in sense experience and (2) their reliance upon the notion of causality. In addition, the first three proofs do not as obviously lead to the idea of what all men call God, a personal being. These are, however, proofs that Aquinas considered philosophical corroborations of the religious notion of God, and they, it must be remembered, were composed in the context of his theological task. Moreover, many of Aquinas' illustrations, as, for example, that fire is the maximum of heat, and his assumptions, that order, for example, presupposes an intelligence independent of the natural process, raise for the modern mind critical questions. Still, Aquinas was deliberately employing the insights he had derived from Aristotle, Maimonides, and Albert the Great in order, by means of these philosophical arguments, to make the religious claim of God's existence intellectually defensible. His own view was that the argument from motion was the most obvious of all. The third one, comparing possible and necessary being, appears, however, to contain the most philosophical rigor and the basic assumption of all the other proofs, namely, that possible beings must derive their existence from something that has its existence necessarily in itself.

KNOWLEDGE OF GOD'S NATURE

To prove *that* God is does not tell us positively *what* God is. There is a vast gulf between the powers of human knowledge and the infinitude of God's nature. Aquinas was always aware of this virtually unbridgeable gulf, saying that "the divine reality surpasses all human conceptions of it." But each of the five proofs adds something to the conception of God. As First Mover, God is seen as unchangeable and therefore eternal. As First Cause, God is seen all powerful to create. To say that God is necessary rather than possible being is to say that God is pure actuality. As the ultimate truth and goodness, God is perfection itself. And as the orderer or designer of the universe, God is the supreme intelligence directing things.

The Negative Way (*Via Negativa*) The knowledge about God derived from the five proofs does not clarify positively what the essence of God is. We know what we do about God only in a negative way by knowing what God is not. The proof shows only that God is *un*moved, and that therefore he must be *un*changeable. This must mean that God is *not* in time, and is therefore eternal. Similarly, to account for motion, it is necessary that there be something that does *not* have potentiality—it is matter in particular that has potentiality—therefore, in God there is nothing material. God is pure act and *im*material. Since there is neither matter nor potentiality in God, He is then *simple, without* any composition. This idea of God's *simplicity* is achieved not by our direct apprehension of it but via the negative way, whereby we *remove* from our conception of God such notions as compositeness and corporeality. Philosophically, God's simplicity means that unlike creatures that possess both potentiality and actuality, God is simply pure act. Whereas a creature *has* its being, God *is* His being. Whereas in creatures existence is one thing and essence another, God's essence is His existence. But even these positive-sounding attributes of God are in the end ways of saying what God is not, saying that God is other than creatures.

Knowledge by Analogy   All human language is inevitably derived from our experience with things in our sensed world. For this reason, as Aquinas realized, the names men apply to God are the same ones they use when describing human beings and things. These names, such as *wise* or *loving,* certainly cannot mean the same thing when applied to finite man on the one hand and to the infinite God on the other. If, then, these names and words mean different things to us when we use them respectively to describe creatures and God, the critical question is whether we can know anything at all about God from our knowledge about creatures.

Aquinas distinguishes between three ways in which God might be related to human beings. The first type of relation would be *univocal,* in which case words, such as *wise,* used about God and men would mean exactly the same thing and would imply that God and man are alike in nature. This clearly cannot be the case since God and man are not alike. God is infinite, and man is finite. A second type of relation might be what Aquinas calls *equivocal,* where terms applied to both would mean totally different things for each, implying that God and man are totally unlike. In this case our knowledge of man would give us no knowledge whatsoever about God. Aquinas insists, however, that insofar as man is a creature of God, he must in some degree, even though imperfectly, reflect the nature of God. The third and final possibility is that man and God are neither totally alike nor totally unlike, that their relationship is *analogical.* When a word such as *wise* is used to describe both God and man, it does not mean that God and man are wise in exactly the same sense, nor does it mean that they are wise in completely different ways.

Analogy for Aquinas is an ontological term; it means that what is in God is also in man. This is more than mere metaphor or simile. To say that there is an analogical relationship between God and man is to say that man resembles God. *Resembles* here means that man has in some degree or certain proportion what God uniquely is. For example, Aquinas says that man *has* a certain mode or degree of being. God, on the other hand, *is* Being. What makes the relationship between God and man analogical is, therefore, the fact that God and man are linked together by common attributes. Man derives his very existence from God, and this fact accounts for the common elements in both God and man. When we use a word such as *wise,* we refer to (but do not fully comprehend) an attribute perfectly realized in God and only partially realized in man. Wisdom is something that exists both in God and man, and the relationship between the two wisdoms is analogical, which is midway between univocal and equivocal. What makes wisdom different in man is that his mind is located in his physical body and is dependent upon the senses. When man thinks and speaks, he does so discursively, saying and thinking a word or an idea at a time. God, being pure act with no material substance, knows all things simultaneously. Analogy would mean, then, that man knows what God knows but not everything that God knows and not the way God knows it. Again, what makes this analogical relation possible is that God's creatures bear a likeness to God. Analogy means, then, that man is simultaneously like and unlike God. To know what man is like is to have *some* degree of knowledge about God. For this reason, names and terms that men formulate first of all about human beings have some meaning when applied to God, provided that the meanings in each case are adjusted to reflect the different degrees and modes of being of God and man.

CREATION

Throughout his discussion of the proofs of God's existence and of God's nature, Aquinas assumes the doctrine of creation. The objects of our sense experience, according to the proofs, cannot derive their existence from themselves but must have it from the First Mover, First Cause, Necessary Being, Perfect Being, and Orderer of the Universe. There are, however, certain specific problems concerning the doctrine of creation that Aquinas considers from a philosophical point of view.

Is the Created Order Eternal? According to Biblical revelation, creation occurred at a point in time. How could this doctrine of faith be supported by philosophical reasoning? Aquinas did not think that it is possible to decide in a philosophical manner whether the world has existed from eternity or whether it was created in time. That it was created must follow from the revealed nature of God. Being pure act and free, God willed to create. Creation, as a free act, is distinguished by Aquinas from a *necessary* emanation, as taught by Plotinus. But since God is pure act, He could have acted to create the world from eternity. In short, there is no contradiction in saying that God created and that He created eternally. There might be a more serious question of contradiction if one argued that God created in time, since this could imply potentiality in God in that before He created things He was potentially a creator. That Aquinas was somewhat inconclusive on this point raised questions about his orthodoxy. But he maintained that Aristotle, who had argued that God had created from eternity, could not be refuted, in spite of Bonaventura's attempts to do so. In the end, Aquinas settled the question by accepting the authority of revelation, concluding that philosophically either solution is possible.

Ex Nihilo What does it mean to say that God creates out of nothing, *ex nihilo?* Again, Aquinas thought that if God is the source of all being, there cannot be any other source of being. There is, in short, no useful comparison between God and an artist at this point. An artist rearranges already existing materials, as when a sculptor fashions a statue. Prior to creation there is only God: God does not act upon any existing material since no such primary matter exists. Only God exists originally, and whatever comes to be derives its existence from God. Everything, then, is related to God, is a creature of God because it came ultimately from God, there being no independent source of being other than God.

Is This the Best Possible World?   Aquinas argued that to answer such a question requires that one bear in mind two things. First, unlike God, who is infinite, man is finite, and man's perfection will therefore be less than God's. Secondly, the universe cannot be any better than or any different from what creatures are capable of by their nature. Throughout this discussion, Aquinas stresses that certain limitations must pervade the universe only because to create certain kinds of beings sets limits on others. The world is the best only in the sense that it contains the best arrangement possible of the kinds of things that have been created.

Evil as Privation   The problem of evil is aggravated by the argument that everything that exists comes from God. Since there is evil in the world, it would appear that evil, too, comes from God. But Aquinas accepted Augustine's solution of the problem of evil, saying that evil is not anything positive. God is not the cause of evil because evil is not a thing. Moral evil represents the absence or privation in something that in itself is good. In this sense, absence or privation consists of an inappropriate mode of action where the action as such is not evil. The act of the adulterer, says Aquinas, is evil not in its physical aspects but in that which makes it adultery, namely, the absence of propriety. Similarly, in the natural order evil is not a positive thing but a privation, as in the case of blindness, which consists in the absence of sight. Still, in the moral realm, there appear to be those who choose to indulge in ways that are obviously wicked. As Plato, Aquinas argues that men always will their acts, however diabolical they may seem, under the assumption, and with the hope, that some good will come out of them. The adulterer never wills his acts solely as an evil but rather for that aspect of his act that is good and affords pleasure. The question remains, however, why God should permit defects both in physical nature and in man's moral behavior. Aquinas replies that the perfection of the universe required the existence of various kinds of beings, including corruptible as well as incorruptible beings, thus providing the possibility, but not the necessity, for defect and suffering. But having created corruptible things, there will be corruption, that is, alteration in things.

     In the moral order, the primary fact is that man possesses freedom. Without freedom men could not love God; with freedom they possess the capacity to choose for or against God, right, just, and good. Evil is the possibility for wrong choice that accompanies man's freedom. Its actual occurrence was not willed by God even though God willed that man should have freedom. The possibility of evil is the unavoidable corollary of the greater good that comes from man's freedom to love and serve God. Aquinas therefore concludes that God is not the cause of evil even though by creating human beings with freedom He permitted the possibility of it. Moral evil, under these circumstances, is the product of the will whereby the essentially good element in the willed act lacks its true end.

The Range of Created Being: the Chain of Being Aquinas describes the universe as consisting of a full range, or hierarchy, of different things, as if there existed a great *chain of being*. These beings differ in species and in the degree of their being. That such a full range of beings exists is required so that God's perfection can be most adequately represented in the total created order. Because no single creature could ever reflect God's perfection suitably, God created many levels of being, which overlap in such a way that there are no gaps in the structure of being. Thus, below God is the hierarchy of angels. Aquinas calls these *intelligences* and says that they are immaterial. These can be known to exist both by revelation (the Bible speaks of them in various terms, such as *principles, powers, seraphim,* etc.) and reason. Reason requires their existence in order to account for the full continuity of beings from the lowest to the highest without any unaccounted-for spaces. Below these angels are human beings, whose nature includes both material and spiritual aspects. Then come animals, plants, and finally the four elements of air, earth, fire, and water.

Aquinas points out that there are no gaps between the various levels of beings: they interlock like links in a chain. For example, the lowest species of animals overlap with the highest forms of plants, the highest forms of animals correspond to the lowest form of human nature, and the highest element in man (intelligence) corresponds to what uniquely constitutes angels. What distinguishes the beings on all these levels is their particular composite nature, or the way their form and matter are related. In man, the soul is the form, and the body is the material substance. Angels have no material substance, and because they do not possess the kind of matter that designates the particular qualities of a specific individual, each angel is its own species. Each angel, then, occupies a separate grade in the hierarchy of being, differing from other angels in the degree or amount of its being. The highest angel is nearest God and the lowest nearest man, and below man are the animals, plants, and single elements, all representing the full range of created beings.

MORALITY AND NATURAL LAW

Aquinas built upon Aristotle's theory of ethics. Like Aristotle, he considered ethics or morality a quest for happiness. Moreover, following Aristotle's lead, Aquinas argued that happiness is connected closely with man's end or purpose. To achieve happiness one must fulfill his purpose. But whereas Aristotle envisioned a *naturalistic* morality whereby men could achieve virtue and happiness by fulfilling their natural capacities or end, Aquinas added to this his concept of man's *supernatural* end. As a Christian, Aquinas viewed human nature as having both its source and ultimate end in God. For this reason, human nature does not contain its own standards of fulfillment. It is not enough for a man simply to be a man and to exercise his natural functions and abilities in order to achieve perfect happiness. Aristotle thought such a naturalistic ethics was possible. Aquinas agreed with most of this claim, adding only that the Aristotelian ethics is incomplete. Aquinas therefore argued that there is a double level to morality corresponding to man's natural end and to his supernatural end.

The ingredients of man's moral experience are provided by man's nature. For one thing, the fact that man has a body inclines him to certain kinds of acts. His senses become the vehicle for appetites and passions. His senses also give him a certain level of knowledge about sensible objects so that he is attracted to some objects, which he perceives as pleasurable and good (concupiscent appetite), and repels some objects, which he perceives as harmful, painful, or bad (irascible appetite). This attraction and rejection are the rudiments of man's capacity for love and pleasure, and hate and fear.

In animals these irascible and concupiscent appetites immediately control and direct behavior. In man, however, the will, in collaboration with the power of reason, consummates the human act. The will is the agency that inclines man toward the achievement of good. That is, man's full range of appetites seeks to be satisfied, and in man the process of satisfaction requires that choices be made between alternative objects. This choice must be made by the will under the direction of reason. If the right choices are made, a person achieves happiness. But not every choice is a correct one. For this reason, the will by itself cannot always make the right move; the intellect must be the guide. Nor is the intellect the final source of knowledge, for man's supernatural end requires God's grace and revealed truth. Still, the will represents man's appetite for the good and right, whereas the intellect has the function and capacity for apprehending the general or universal meaning of what is good. The intellect is man's highest faculty, and man's natural end requires that the intellect, as well as all the other faculties, seek its appropriate object. The appropriate object of the intellect is truth, and truth in its fullness is God. When the intellect directs the will, then, it helps the will choose the good. The intellect knows, however, that there is a hierarchy of goods, that some goods are limited and must not be mistaken for man's most appropriate and ultimate good. Riches, pleasure, power, and knowledge are all goods and are legitimate objects of the appetites, but they cannot produce man's deepest happiness because they do not possess the character of the universal good that man's soul seeks. The perfect happiness is found not in created things but in God, who is the supreme good.

Man's moral constitution consists, then, of sensuality, appetites, the will, and reason. What confers upon man the attributes of morality is that these elements are the ingredients of *free* acts. If a man were moved to act by his appetites in a mechanical or rigorously determined way, his acts would not be free and could not be considered from a moral point of view. Not only is freedom a prerequisite for an act to be considered *moral;* Aquinas adds that an act is *human* only if it is free. For freedom is possible only where there is knowledge of alternatives and the power of will to make choices. Virtue, or goodness, consists in making the right choices, the mean between extremes. Aquinas agreed with Aristotle that the virtues of the natural man are achieved when the appetites are duly controlled by the will and reason. The dominant or cardinal natural virtues are courage, temperance, justice, and prudence. In addition to these particular virtues, the natural end of man is further realized through man's knowledge of the natural law or the moral law.

Natural Law   Morality, as Aquinas viewed it, is not an arbitrary set of rules for behavior. The basis of moral obligation, he thought, is found, first of all, in the very nature of man. Built into man's nature are various inclinations, such as the preservation of his life, the propagation of his species, and, because he is rational, the inclination toward the search for truth. The basic moral truth is simply to "do good and avoid evil." As a rational being, then, man is under a basic natural obligation to protect his life and health, in which case suicide and carelessness are wrong. Secondly, the natural inclination to propagate the species forms the basis of the union of man and wife, and any other basis for this relation would be wrong. And thirdly, because man seeks for truth, he can do this best by living in peace in society with his fellow men who are also engaged in this quest. To ensure an ordered society, human laws are fashioned for the direction of the community's behavior. All these activities of preserving life, propagating the species, forming an ordered society under human laws, and pursuing the quest for truth—all these, again, pertain to man at his natural level. The moral law is founded upon human nature, upon the natural inclinations toward specific modes of behavior, and upon the reason's ability to discern the right course of conduct. Because human nature has certain fixed features, the rules for behavior that correspond to these features are called *natural law*.

　　Much of this theory of natural law was already developed by Aristotle. In his *Ethics*, Aristotle distinguished between natural justice and conventional justice. Some forms of behavior, he said, are wrong only because, and only after, a law has been made to regulate such behavior. To use a modern example, it is wrong to drive a vehicle at certain speeds only because a speed limit has been set, but there is nothing in nature that requires that vehicles travel at that speed. Such a law is therefore not natural but conventional, because before the law was passed, there was nothing wrong with traveling at speeds exceeding the new limit. On the other hand, there are some laws the precepts of which are derived from nature, so that the behavior they regulate has always been wrong, as in the case of murder. But Aquinas did not limit his treatment of natural law to the simple notion that in some way man's reason is able to discover the natural basis for human conduct. Instead, he reasoned that if man's existence and nature can be fully understood only when seen in relation to God, then natural law must be described in metaphysical and theological terms, as the Stoics and St. Augustine had done.

　　Law, says Aquinas, has to do primarily with reason. The rule and measure of acts is the reason, because it belongs to reason to direct a man's whole activity toward his end. Law consists of these rules and measures of human acts and therefore is based upon reason. The natural law is dictated by the reason. But Aquinas argues that since God created all things, human nature and the natural law are best understood as the product of God's wisdom or reason. From this standpoint, Aquinas distinguishes *four* kinds of law.

Eternal Law   This law refers to the fact that "the whole community of the universe is governed by Divine Reason. Wherefore the very Idea of the government of things in God the Ruler of the universe, has the nature of a law. And since the Divine Reason's conception of things is not subject to time but is eternal . . . therefore it is that this kind of law must be called eternal."

Natural Law   For Aquinas, natural law consists of that portion of the eternal law that pertains particularly to man. His reasoning is that "all things partake somewhat of the eternal law . . . from its being imprinted on them" and from this all things "derive their respective inclinations to their proper acts and ends." This is particularly true of man, because his rational capacity "has a share of the Eternal Reason, whereby it has a natural inclination to its proper act and end." And, says Aquinas, "this participation of the eternal law in the rational creature is called the natural law," and, again, "the natural law is nothing else than the rational creature's participation of the eternal law." We have already indicated the basic precepts of the natural law as being the preservation of life, propagation and education of offspring, and pursuit of truth and peaceful society. Thus the natural law consists of broad general principles that reflect God's intentions for man in creation.

Human Law   This refers to the specific statutes of governments. These statutes or human laws are derived from the general precepts of natural law. Just as "we draw conclusions of the various sciences" from "naturally known indemonstrable principles," so also "from the precepts of the natural law . . . the human reason needs to proceed to the more particular determination of certain matters." And "these particular determinations, devised by human reason, are called human laws. . . ." What was so far-reaching about this conception of human law was that it repudiated the notion that a law was a law only because it was decreed by a sovereign. Aquinas argued that what gives a rule the character of law is its moral dimension, its conformity with the precepts of natural law, its agreement with the moral law. Taking St. Augustine's formula, namely, that "that which is not just seems to be no law at all," Aquinas said that "every human law has just so much of the nature of law, as it is derived from the law of nature." But, he adds, "if in any point it deflects from the law of nature, it is no longer a law but a perversion of law." Such laws no longer bind in conscience, but are sometimes obeyed to prevent an even greater evil. Aquinas went further than simply denying the character of law to a command of a government that violated the natural moral law; such a command, he said, should not be obeyed. Some laws, he said, "may be unjust through being opposed to the Divine Good: such are the laws of tyrants inducing to idolatry, or to anything else contrary to the Divine Law. . . ." He concluded that "laws of this kind must nowise be observed, because . . . *we ought to obey God rather than men.*"

Divine Law   The function of law, said Aquinas, is to direct man to his proper end. Since man is ordained to an end of eternal happiness, in addition to his temporal happiness, there must be a kind of law that can direct him to that supernatural end. Here, in particular, Aquinas parted company with Aristotle, for Aristotle knew only about man's natural purpose and end, and for this purpose the natural law known by man's reason was considered a sufficient guide. But the eternal happiness to which man is ordained, said Aquinas, is "in proportion to man's natural faculty." Therefore, "it was necessary that besides the natural and the human law, man should be directed to his end by a law given by God." The *divine law,* then, is available to man through revelation and is found in the Scriptures. It is not the product of man's reason but is given to man through God's grace to ensure that men know what they must do to fulfill both their natural and, especially, their supernatural ends. The difference between the natural law and divine law is this: The natural law represents man's rational knowledge of the good, by which the intellect directs the will to control man's appetites and passions, leading men to fulfill their natural end by achieving the cardinal virtues of justice, temperance, courage, and prudence. The divine law, on the other hand, comes directly from God through revelation, a gift of God's grace, whereby men are directed to their supernatural ends, having obtained the higher or theological virtues of faith, hope, and love, not through any of man's natural powers, for these virtues are "infused" into man by God's grace. In this way, Aquinas completed and surpassed the naturalistic ethics of Aristotle, showed how the natural desire of man to know God can be assured, indicated how revelation becomes the guide for reason, and described the manner in which man's highest nature is perfected through God's grace.

THE STATE

The state, said Aquinas, is a natural institution. It is derived from the nature of man. In this view, Aquinas was following the political theory of Aristotle, from whom he had taken the phrase that "man is by nature a social animal." But insofar as Aquinas had a different view of human nature, he was bound to have a somewhat different political philosophy also. The difference lay in the two conceptions of the role or task of the state. Aristotle supposed that the state could provide for all the needs of man because he knew only about man's natural needs. Aquinas, on the other hand, believed that in addition to his material or natural needs, man also has a supernatural end. The state is not equipped to deal with this more ultimate end of man. It is the church that directs man to this end. But Aquinas did not simply divide these two realms of human concern, giving one to the state and the other to the church. Instead, he looked upon the state, and explained its origin, in terms of God's creation.

The state, in this view, is willed by God and has its God-given function. It was required because of the social nature of man. The state is not, for Aquinas, as it was for Augustine, a product of man's sinfulness. On the contrary, Aquinas says that even "in the state of innocence man would have lived in society." But even then, "a common life could not exist, unless there were someone in control, to attend to the common good." The state's function is to secure the common good by keeping the peace, organizing the activities of the citizens into harmonious pursuits, providing for the resources to sustain life, and preventing, as far as possible, obstacles to the good life. This last item concerning threats to the good life gives to the state not only a function tied to man's ultimate end; it also accounts for the state's position in relation to the church.

The state is subordinate to the church. To say this did not mean that Aquinas considered the church a superstate. Aquinas saw no contradiction in saying that the state has a sphere in which it has a legitimate function and that at the same time it must subordinate itself to the church. Within its own sphere the state is autonomous. But, insofar as there are aspects of human life that bear upon man's supernatural end, the state must not put arbitrary hindrances in the way to frustrate man's spiritual life. The church does not challenge the autonomy of the state; it only says that the state is not absolutely autonomous. Within its own sphere, the state is what Aquinas calls a "perfect society," having its own end and the means for achieving it. But the state is like man; neither the state nor man has only a natural end. Man's spiritual end cannot be achieved, as Aquinas says, "by human power, but by divine power." Still, because man's destiny does include attaining to the enjoyment of God, the state must recognize this aspect of human affairs: in providing for the common good of the citizens, the sovereign must pursue his community's end with a consciousness of man's spiritual end. Under these circumstances, the state does not become the church, but it does mean that the sovereign "should order those things which lead to heavenly beatitude and prohibit, as far as possible, their contraries." In this way, Aquinas affirmed the legitimacy of the state and its autonomy in its own sphere, subordinating it to the church only to ensure that the ultimate spiritual end of man be taken into account.

As the state rules the behavior of its citizens through the agency of law, the state is in turn limited by the requirements of just laws. Nowhere is Aquinas' rejection of the absolute autonomy of the state so clearly stated as when he describes the standards for the making of human or positive law. We have already analyzed the different types of law, eternal, natural, human and divine. The state is particularly the source of human law. Each government is faced with the task of fashioning specific statutes to regulate the behavior of its citizens under the particular circumstances of its own time and place. Lawmaking, however, must not be an arbitrary act but must be done under the influence of the natural law, which is man's participation in God's eternal law. Positive laws must consist of particular rules derived from the general principles of natural law. Any positive human law that violates the natural law loses its character as law, is a "perversion of law," and loses its binding force in the consciences of men. The lawmaker has his authority to legislate from God, the source of all authority, and to God he is responsible. If the sovereign decrees an unjust law by violating God's divine law, such a law, says Aquinas, "must nowise be observed."

The political sovereign has his authority from God, and the purpose of his authority is to provide for the common good. Authority is never to be used as an end in itself or for selfish ends. Nor must the common good be interpreted in such a way that the individual is lost sight of in the collective whole. The common good must be the good of concrete persons. Thus Aquinas says that "the proper effect of law is to lead its subjects to their proper virtue . . . to make those to whom it is given good. . . ." The only "true ground" of the lawgiver is his intention to secure "the common good regulated according to divine justice," and thus it follows that "the effect of the law is to make men good. . . ." This is to say that the phrase *common good* has no meaning for Aquinas except insofar as it results in the good of individuals. At the same time, Aquinas says that "the goodness of any part is considered in comparison with the whole. . . . Since then every man is a part of the state, it is impossible that a man be good unless he be well proportionate to the common good." The entire scheme of society and its laws is characterized by the rational elements in it. Law itself, says Aquinas, is "an ordinance of reason for the common good, made by him who has care of the community, and promulgated." Thus, although the sovereign has authority and power, the laws must not reflect this power in a naked sense but as domesticated by reason and aimed at the common good.

MAN AND KNOWLEDGE

Man   Aquinas had a distinctive conception of man. Man, he said, is a physical substance. What made this a unique conception was that Aquinas insisted upon the *unity* of human nature. Plato had talked about the soul as being imprisoned in the body. Similarly, Augustine considered the soul as a spiritual substance. Both Plato and Aristotle agreed that the soul is the form of the body but did not see, as Aquinas thought he did, that the soul of man is as dependent upon the body as the body is upon the soul. To say, as Aquinas did, that man is a physical substance underscored the substantial unity of man. Man *is* his unity of body and soul. Without the soul, the body would have no form. Without the body, the soul would not have its required organs of sense through which to gain its knowledge. As a physical substance, man is a composite of soul and body. The angels are pure intelligence and have no body, but although man, too, is a rational creature, his special attribute is to exist and function as man only when unified as body and soul. Since the soul confers upon man his form, it is the soul that gives man his life, understanding, and special physical functions. The soul accounts also for man's capacity for sensation and the powers of intellect and will. Man's highest capacity is located in his intellect, making him a rational animal and conferring upon him the means by which to attain the contemplation of God.

Knowledge   Aquinas followed Aristotle's theory of knowledge. He was especially impressed with Aristotle's answer to those who doubted that the human mind could arrive at certainty on any subject. Some ancient philosophers had argued that since man's knowledge is limited to sense perception, there could be no certainty because each man senses things differently and the objects of sense are always in flux. Plato agreed with this estimate of sense knowledge saying that it could give us no certainty. But he avoided intellectual pessimism by assuming the existence of a separate world, the intelligible world, contrasting it with the visible world, saying that in it there existed Ideas or Forms, which possess eternal being and provide the basis for knowledge. St. Augustine adapted this Platonic theory of Ideas to Christian thought by saying that God possesses these Ideas in His mind and that human beings are able to know the truth insofar as these Ideas illumine their minds through the divine light. But Aquinas accepted Aristotle's approach, saying that the human mind knows what it does through its confrontation with actual concrete objects. The mind is able to grasp what is permanent and stable within sensible things. When we sense things or persons, we *know* their essence, for example, *tree* and *man,* even though they are in the process of change. What we know about them, given the fact that they are in flux, is that they are either more or less a tree or a man, but we are not in doubt about what they are. In short, the intellect *sees* the universal *in* the particular thing; it *abstracts* the universal from the particular. The mind does not possess any innate ideas, but is rather in potentiality to knowledge. Unlike angelic intelligences, the human mind, set in the composite of soul and body, has as its natural object of knowledge the essential properties of physical things. Man's active intellect is able, says Aquinas, to recognize the intelligible aspect of sense objects, discovering in individual things the universal essence. Aquinas denied that the universal, for example *man,* has any existence separate from particular concrete men. There is only the abstracted concept, not an existing Idea, which the actual intellect formulates and which makes knowledge possible. It was Aquinas's view that there could be no knowledge without sense experience, for nothing could be in the intellect that was not first in the senses (*nihil in intellectu quod prius non fuerit in sensu*).

SOME REACTIONS TO AQUINAS: VOLUNTARISM, NOMINALISM, AND MYSTICISM

If Aquinas' most important achievement was to synthesize theology and philosophy, the most significant reactions to his work were those that tended to dissolve this synthesis. Among those whose thinking led to the gradual dissolution of the thirteenth-century synthesis was John Duns Scotus (1265–1308), William of Ockham (ca. 1280–1349) and Johannes Eckhart (ca. 1260–1327). These men did not disagree with everything Aquinas had taught. Indeed, on many matters they were in general agreement with his ideas. At the same time, they each set forth a basic criticism that had the effect of driving a wedge between philosophy and theology, between faith and reason. Against Aquinas' notion of the supremacy of reason, Scotus argued that in God the will is supreme, and this became known as the doctrine of *voluntarism*. Against Aquinas' notion that universals as such have some form of existence, Ockham argued that universals are only words, and this view became known as *terminism* or *nominalism*. And against the highly rational and technical articulation of theology as he found it in both Albert the Great and Aquinas, Eckhart urged the more immediate experience of the divine reality in the spiritual exercise of *mysticism*.

Why should these three developments have the effect of separating philosophy and theology? The problem becomes at once clear when we consider some of the implications of voluntarism. Aquinas had argued that both in man and God the will is subordinate to the intellect, that reason guides or determines the will. Scotus maintained, however, that if God's will were subordinate to reason, or were limited by an eternal truth, God Himself would appear to be limited. He cannot do whatever He wills since He is bound or *determined* by a norm in some sense *above* Him. If God is to be *free,* He must be conceived as having an absolutely free will, in which case His will is His dominant faculty.

The consequence of saying that God's will, and not His intellect, is primary is that God's actions and moral commands are acts of will and as such irrational. If God's actions in creation and in the giving of the moral law do not represent His adherence to the standards of rationality, the created world is not the embodiment of God's rational nature. God, in this view, could have willed any kind of universe and whatever moral rules He chose. Again, Aquinas said that God commands certain moral rules *because they are good* and His wisdom recognizes them as good. Scotus, on the contrary, maintained that a moral rule is good *because God willed or commanded it.* Morality therefore cannot be discovered rationally. Aquinas had made much of the point that moral principles are known by a *natural light,* that men habitually contain these principles in their conscience. Most important of all, Aquinas assumed that morality is capable of an intellectual discipline insofar as the principles of good can be discovered rationally. Scotus and Ockham both argued, however, that morality is grounded not in reason but in will. Consequently, morality cannot be a subject of philosophy, of rational inquiry, but only a matter of faith and acceptance.

Nor could there be a *natural theology* whereby, for example, human reason could discover a rational order in which cause and effect are linked in such a way that reason could move reliably, by inference, from effect to cause. Aquinas had assumed that his demonstrations had rational rigor and were therefore valid. Scotus, on the other hand, would not agree that reason could discover a rational relationship between the world of experience and God. The existence of God, apart from merely *probable* demonstrations, became for Scotus and Ockham a matter of faith, and the domain of reason was limited to the empirical world. In this way, the subject matter and the concerns of philosophy were separated from those of theology. Religious *knowledge* was now seen again more in Platonic and Augustinian terms as a product of divine illumination or *revelation* and not attainable by philosophical discovery.

In a similar way, Ockham's nominalism separated faith and reason. Ockham had raised critical questions about the status of universal terms. The central question was whether such terms as *man* refer to any reality other than particular men, James and John. Is there a *substance* in addition to these *particular* men to which the *universal* term *man* refers? To a keen logician such as Ockham these critical questions had far-reaching consequences. Most important of all was his conclusion that in using universal terms, the mind is not doing anything more than thinking in an orderly way about particular things. Only concrete individual things exist. Universal terms such as *man* refer equally to James and John not because there is some real substance of "man-ness" in which both James and John *share* or *participate,* but only because the nature that is James is like the nature that is John. Universal terms such as *man* are simply *signs* or *names* (hence *nominalism*) for designating those concepts that particular things engender in human reason. Human reason, then, is limited to the world of individual things. Ockham's view was genuinely empirical. The mind, he said, does not know anything more than individual things and their qualities even though the mind is able to use universal terms. Such terms are nothing more than terms or names for classes of individual things: above all, universal terms do not refer to a realm of reality *above* or *beyond* the world of concrete individual things.

How did this view differ from Aquinas' treatment of the problem of universals? For the most part Ockham's view was in harmony with what Aquinas had said, inasmuch as Aquinas argued that universals are found *in re,* in particular things, and are abstracted from things *post rem,* after our experiences of them. But Aquinas also accorded universals a metaphysical status when he said that they exist before individual things do as Ideas in the mind of God, as universals *ante rem.* If universals exist in the mind of God, two men are alike because they share in this metaphysical reality in God's mind. Also, the human mind, when it thinks universals, shares in some way in God's thought. This was the point Ockham wished to reject. He rejected the doctrine of divine Ideas for the same reason Scotus had, holding that in God the will has supremacy. Men are what they are because God chose to make them that way and not because they reflect an eternal pattern that exists in God's mind as an Idea. Hence, says Ockham, "no universal is anything existing in any way outside the [mind of man]. . . ."

If man's thought is restricted to individual things in experience, his knowledge of these things does not lead him in any logical way to any reality beyond experience. Those who believed that universal terms signified something real as existing beyond individual things were confident that their use of such terms gave them reliable knowledge about reality beyond the empirical scene. And if one assumed that universals were Ideas in God's mind, he would conclude that philosophical reasoning about the origin, nature, and relationships of individual things could lead to various theological truths. There could be a *natural,* that is, rational, theology. But Ockham's strict interpretation of universals had the effect of severing philosophy from metaphysics, making out of philosophy something more like science. Theology and religious truth could not be achieved by philosophy or science. Indeed, his position implied the doctrine of *double truth*, that one kind of truth is available through science or philosophy, and another kind of truth is received through revelation. The first truth is the product of human reason, and the other is a matter of faith. One kind of truth, moreover, cannot influence the other kind. The ultimate consequence of the double-truth doctrine was that theological and philosophical truths were not only independent and not derivable from each other but that these different truths could even contradict each other. This was the explicit teaching of the followers of Averroës who held, for example, that while it is true in philosophy that there is no personal immortality, such a doctrine is false for theology. Ockham had not gone that far in separating faith and reason. He had, nevertheless, set the stage for an empirical and scientific way of thinking about the facts of experience. His nominalism had the effect of separating science from metaphysics. The study of natural things became more and more independent of metaphysical or theological explanations. His celebrated formula, which we know as *Ockham's razor*, stated one of his guiding principles, namely, that "what can be explained on fewer principles is explained needlessly by more." Thus, universal terms, he felt, can be adequately explained as being simply names for concepts that similar individual things engender in the human mind. Such terms do not refer to reality beyond visible things. Hence, the combined force of Ockham's nominalism and Scotus' voluntarism did much to dismantle the medieval synthesis by separating philosophy and theology, faith and reason.

Finally, Eckhart's mysticism shifted the medieval emphasis from reason to feeling. Actually, he appeared simply to carry to a further extreme what Albert the Great and Thomas Aquinas had done. While these great masters, especially Aquinas, constructed elaborate rational systems of theology, Eckhart attempted to articulate as far as possible his deep feeling of piety. Eckhart was not a careful systematic philosopher. Though he considered in great detail many systematic questions concerning God's nature, creation, and the nature of man, he was primarily a mystic who wanted to share with others his rich experiences of unity with God. In translating his piety into theological language, he made many bold statements, as for example that God is "above being," and that apart from God there is "nothing." More important was his notion that *being* and *knowledge* are one. If therefore God is above being, He is also above knowledge; He is particularly beyond human concepts and categories. Consequently, the union of man and God is an experience beyond rationality, and Eckhart is forced to use such terms as *wilderness* or *darkness* to express this mystical union. And this union cannot be reached except by liberating oneself from the objects of the world. Whereas Aquinas built his demonstrations of God's existence upon his explanation of finite things, Eckhart urged men to pass beyond sensory knowledge, which is after all limited to material objects. But union with God is not achieved by human effort. Only through God's grace and illumination is union consummated, and only in the deepest reaches of the soul does one grasp God in His fullness. When this happens, says Eckhart, man becomes one with God, for "we are transformed totally into God and are converted into Him in a similar manner as in the sacrament the bread is converted into the body of Christ."

Eckhart's teachings contained many contradictions; he was not a precise philosopher or a highly systematic theologian. His use of earlier ideas gained from Albert and Aquinas shows the strong influence of Neoplatonism into which he cast most of his thought. What is significant about his writings is that they focused upon the inner world of mysticism, where faith and piety are dominant. There followed after Eckhart a flowering of mystical writers, among whom some of the more notable were Tauler (1300–1361), Heinrich Suso (1300–1366), and Ruysbroeck (1293–1381). The element of feeling that mysticism exalted and the scientific mood that the empiricism of Ockham required received new emphasis as the Middle Ages merged into the Renaissance.

Engraved by W. Holl.

*❈*THREE*❈*

THE
MODERN PERIOD:
PHILOSOPHY
AND THE
UNFOLDING WORLD
OF SCIENCE

10

The Renaissance Interlude

For most philosophers in the Middle Ages, the sky hung low, suggesting a close bond between heaven and earth, and, accordingly, between philosophy and theology. Indeed, philosophy in the Middle Ages was virtually the handmaiden of theology, supplying religious thought with a reasoned account of its various doctrines. To be sure, Plato and Aristotle had also concerned themselves with the question of how the daily affairs of men could and should be related to the permanent structures of reality and to God. But the synthesis of theology and philosophy in the Middle Ages was a precarious one. For one thing, there was some serious question about the compatibility, for example, of Aristotle's nontheistic philosophy and the belief in a personal God in Christianity. Moreover, much of Aristotle's thought was made available at this time through Moslem Arabian thinkers, who had construed Aristotle in ways that could hardly be accepted by Christians. Aquinas sought to reinterpret and Christianize Aristotle to overcome this incompatibility. Yet, philosophy now found itself to a great extent doing a task that it had not originally set out to do, namely, providing an intellectual and metaphysical foundation for revealed religion. Nor had philosophy been previously domesticated, as it were, by an institution the way it was by the church in the Middle Ages. To be sure, philosophers were from the earliest days in mortal jeopardy when their teachings threatened the *status quo*. Socrates was, after all, put to death for just this reason, and in Aristotle's case Athens almost "sinned against philosophy a second time." Generally, classical philosophy had been free to move wherever the pursuit of truth led it. Philosophy could dwell upon the subjects of man, nature, ethics, God, and political authority by referring only to what human thought discovered about these matters. The spirit of medieval philosophy was different in that its starting point was now virtually fixed by the doctrines of Christian theology. In addition, the whole cultural atmosphere was affected by the predominance of the church so that moral theory, political doctrine, the institutions of society such as the family and work, the arts and literature, and much of science—all these bore the imprint of theology.

Just how closely daily life followed the ideals of this synthesis in the Middle Ages is not altogether clear. That there was a widening gap between the set structure of thought of Christendom and man's yearning for a freer encounter with all the possibilities of life, art, and thought is attested by the eventual decline of the medieval synthesis. Within the church itself, the debates over the appropriateness of employing philosophy as the handmaiden of theology led finally to the conclusion that as a discipline philosophy is wholly separate from theology and religion. Accordingly, religion was reconceived as primarily a matter of faith, a point of view that found its great culmination in the Reformation, and philosophy was reinstated, most dramatically by the father of modern philosophy, Descartes, as an autonomous discipline. It may be argued that Descartes had not really created a new foundation for philosophy after all, but what is significant at this point is that he thought he had.

With the dissolution of the synthesis between Aristotle's philosophy and Christian theology, Aristotle became only one thinker among many to whom men would now turn. During this period called the Renaissance, spanning roughly the fifteenth and sixteenth centuries, there was a revival of classical learning, and many of the philosophies of antiquity once again became available. Although the Middle Ages had known Plato through the Neoplatonists and especially Augustine, Plato was now being read for himself without particular reference to theology. Stoicism became widespread again, influencing such eminent writers as Montaigne and Charron. Even the skepticism of Sextus Empiricus and of Pyrrho became strongly felt and in some cases employed as a ground for viewing religion as a matter of faith rather than reason. The separation of philosophy from theology also brought about a far greater accent upon the strictly human dimensions of life. Artists now paid more attention to the human body and form. Nature itself became the object of fresh and free inquiry. This humanism and natural science did not involve the rejection of religion but only the affirmation that areas of humanity and nature could be fruitfully studied by methods and assumptions not directly derived from religion. Philosophical thought in the Renaissance centuries, then, included Platonism, Aristotelianism, Skepticism, Epicureanism, Stoicism, humanism, and the influence of those natural philosophers, including Copernicus, Kepler, and Galileo, who were so influential in ushering in the enterprise of modern science.

The Renaissance was a time of discovery and emancipation. On every hand new worlds were being opened. While Columbus' bold adventure led him to discover a new continent, others opened up new worlds of the mind and spirit. Giotto's (ca. 1276–1337) paintings and Dante's (1265–1321) literature had earlier facilitated the transition from medieval symbolism to the exaltation of nature. Petrarch (1304–1374) turned to a description of the joys and sorrows of natural man, expressing deep dimensions of feeling as opposed to the brittle logic of doctrine. Boccaccio (1313–1375) was even more frank in his account of man's sensual capacities. Curiosity and the desire for beauty led others to explore the structure and subtleties of the human body. Even while serving the church with the genius of his art, Michelangelo (1475–1564) managed to give strong expression to the new humanism of the time. His painting of Adam is a striking description of physical beauty and strength all the more powerful in its unashamed nakedness and resolute poise toward light and life. Leonardo da Vinci (1452–1519), that universal genius, looked behind beauty with care to the more minute ingredients of man's anatomy, a mode of curiosity that later led Harvey (1578–1657) to discover the circulation of the blood.

Such concern with natural man led also to a new-found basis of man's dignity. In his *Oration on the Dignity of Man*, Pico della Mirandola (1463–1494) imagined God as saying to man, his creation, that ". . . we have set thee at the world's center that thou mayest from thence more easily observe whatever is in the world . . . so that with freedom of choice and with honor, as though the maker and molder of thyself, thou mayest fashion thyself in whatever shape thou shalt prefer. . . ." Enhancing the dignity of the individual was his ready access to information. There was much enthusiasm over the discovery of original texts of classical writers, which could now be read in place of garbled translations and revised versions which had been rearranged to suit special purposes. Greek manuscripts were brought back from Athens to Rome. In Florence, Cosimo de' Medici founded an academy where Plato's philosophy was the chief subject of study. This academic influence, reinforced by similar academies in Naples and Rome, further diluted the preeminence of Aristotelian thought and scholastic methodology. Direct access to texts also created a deep fascination for language.

The discovery of ancient Greek and Roman literature had the effect of encouraging a new style of writing, which was less formal than the original texts of medieval authors and had its expression increasingly in the vernacular. With the use of vernacular, literature became more and more the property of the people. Wycliffe's rendering of the Bible into the vernacular would in time set off widespread reverberations in religious thought as the masses acquired direct access to the contents of the Scriptures. The extensive diffusion of culture was most effectively facilitated by Johann Gutenberg's invention in the 1440s of movable type, which made books readily available, smaller and easier to handle, and cheaper to buy. Printing presses soon appeared in Paris, London, Madrid, and in Italy at the monastery of Subiaco. The making of books and the use of vernacular inevitably affected the mode of writing philosophy in that the sense of liberation implied in these activities led philosophers to engage more in original formulations rather than in writing commentaries on authoritative thinkers. In time, the modern philosophers would write their treatises in the language of their own people, so that Locke and Hume would write in English, Voltaire and Rousseau in French, and Kant in German.

If the Renaissance were regarded simply as the decisive influence of classical literature upon the modern world, one might be tempted to say that Erasmus *was* the Renaissance. But the Renaissance was not limited to literary activity. Equally important, as we have seen, was the new art with its preoccupation with human nature and its purely natural qualities. At the same time, new theories of political authority and behavior were fashioned, particularly by Machiavelli, who shifted the base of political thought away from the moral ground prepared by Thomas Aquinas' theory of natural law toward a new secular theory of the state. Religion, the chief element in the medieval synthesis, took a sharp turn in this period when the Reformers added immense power to a view already suggested by Scotus and Ockham that Christianity is a matter of faith and not reason. Although the crosscurrents of thought in this period were still in somewhat unsystematic disarray, many of the new modes of thinking were gathered up in the extraordinary person of Michel de Montaigne. And inevitably, the new intellectual mood of the Renaissance engendered a new mode of analyzing the structure of nature. Natural science was now to be born in its modern form with its stress upon observation and mathematics, an approach employed chiefly by Copernicus, Kepler, and Galileo. The Renaissance was, therefore, a time when many individuals from many lands exhibited many new modes of freedom and expression, causing at points some discontinuity with the past while changing the emphasis in areas in which continuity with the past was preserved. Although the extraordinary richness of the Renaissance can hardly be captured in this brief space, some additional comments can be made concerning the impact of Erasmus, the Reformation, Machiavelli, Montaigne, and the scientists upon the unfolding of modern thought.

ERASMUS AND LUTHER

Born in Rotterdam in 1466 as the illegitimate son of a priest, Erasmus had a considerable influence upon the development of humanism. He was the foe of scholastic theology though he had no intention of rejecting the Christian faith. Through his humanistic learning, especially in the Greek language, he sought to uncover the pure and simple elements of Christianity that had been overlaid and obscured by the excessive rationalism of scholastic doctrine. His earliest training began in the school of the Brethren of the Common Life, from which he later entered the Augustinian monastery of Steyn. At the monastery, life was miserable for Erasmus as he was unfitted mentally, physically, and temperamentally for a regime that offered little physical comfort and virtually no intellectual freedom. Through good fortune, he was invited by the Bishop of Cambrai to become his Latin secretary. The Bishop sent him to study for a while at the Collège Montaigue in Paris, where again he felt only contempt for scholastic methods of instruction. It was here, nevertheless, that his enthusiasm for classical literature was stimulated, and it was here, too, that he began his first book, which would in time become one of his famous volumes, a book of proverbs entitled *Adagiorum Chiliades.* In 1499, Erasmus visited England, where he soon came under the influence of Colet, a Biblical scholar, and Sir Thomas More. Erasmus thought it strange that Colet should lecture on the Bible without a knowledge of Greek. He therefore set out to become proficient in this language, eventually publishing a widely accepted Greek Testament with a new Latin translation. During a second visit to England in 1511, Erasmus became a member of the academic community of Cambridge, where he had been appointed Lady Margaret Professor. He had little respect for his colleagues, whom he called "Cyprian bulls and dung-eaters," nor did he have any good words for the English beer or climate. After a few years he went to Basel, where he made his home until his death in 1536 at the age of seventy.

Erasmus made several contributions to the spirit of the Renaissance. His enthusiasm for classical learning was a decisive influence at this time. He realized that the invention of printing now made it possible to popularize the ancient classics by bringing inexpensive editions within the reach of large numbers of intelligent readers. These books opened up new worlds of classical learning that had not been available in the Middle Ages. But Erasmus was not simply an editor, even though his work in making available these classic Greek and Latin editions would have secured his reputation and significance in the history of thought. More important was his contribution to the development of a new style of literary expression. Erasmus loved words and spent much thought in selecting just the right word or phrase to express his insights. As painters would display genius in their use of colors, Erasmus, long a foe of the incredible lifelessness of scholastic discourse, found deep joy and freedom in fashioning a new and pure literary style marked by the elegance of each phrase.

Erasmus criticized scholastic jargon not only because of its lack of elegance but even more because it obscured the true teachings of the Gospels. It appeared to Erasmus that the ideas of the great classical writers were in basic harmony with the Gospels. In particular, he saw a close similarity between Plato's philosophy and the teachings of Christ. He sensed a deep incongruity between the simple teachings of Christ and the opulence and arrogance of the Papal Court. This moved him to write the satirical *Julius Exclusus* in which Pope Julius II is forbidden by St. Peter to enter the heavenly gates. His own earlier experience with life in the monasteries prompted him to write a trenchant criticism of the clergy in a book called *Praise of Folly,* which Luther made much use of in his decisive argument with the church. But Erasmus was neither a religious skeptic nor did he become a Lutheran. His was a lover's quarrel with the church. He wished to harmonize the church's teachings with the new humanistic learning. He wanted also to challenge the assumption that religious truth is accessible to many only through the rigorous exercise of his rational faculties.

Erasmus' *Praise of Folly* was both an ironic and a serious treatment of two kinds of folly. It was the clergy's folly that felt the weight of Erasmus' irony and invective as he lashed out at the priests for their intricate calculations over pardons and indulgences and the exact duration of a soul's residence in purgatory. He ridiculed the disputations of the theologians as they struggled valiantly with each other over the doctrines of the Incarnation, Trinity, and transubstantiation. His chief complaint was that the whole point of religion had been lost, that too much emphasis was being put on trivial and irrelevant details, especially in the monasteries where matters of dress and minutiae of discipline deflected men from the central aim of Christianity. Imagining how these priests would stand before the judgment seat seeking to enter heaven by calling attention to all their good works, Erasmus, going beyond good humor to invective, describes a priest who points to "so many bushels of prayers, another brags of not having touched a penny without at least two pairs of gloves on. . . ." To all these Christ answers, "I left you but one precept, of loving one another, which I do not hear anyone plead that he has faithfully discharged." Closely connected with this criticism of monastic life was Erasmus' abiding dislike of the hair-splitting logic of scholastic doctrine. Whereas his praise of the priests' folly was ironic, he now quite seriously praised that other kind of folly that he identified with the simplicity of faith. True religion, he felt, is a matter of the heart and not of the head, a view that became central for the Reformers and was again expressed with great force by Pascal, who wrote that "the heart has reasons which the reason does not know."

But while Luther became a passionate Reformer, Erasmus remained only a critic. In his moderate book *Essay on Free Will* he expressed the Renaissance view that man has great capacities for moral improvement. To this book Luther replied with his bristling *De Servo Arbitrio*, affirming the Pauline doctrine of the corruption of human nature and dismissing Erasmus as a "babbler," a "skeptic," or "some other hog from the Epicurean sty." In this debate Erasmus was the great exponent of the spirit of the Renaissance. With unfaltering optimism he continued to believe that education would eventually conquer stupidity and ignorance. His interest in classical literature and philosophy did not lead him to formulate a new scholasticism or to subordinate Christian faith to the philosophy of Plato. Rather, he used his knowledge of the classical languages to discover the real words of the Gospels, saying that "if there is any fresh Greek to be had, I had rather pawn my coat than not get it, especially if it is something Christian, as the Psalms in Greek or the Gospels." As it turned out, Erasmus exerted an enormous influence simultaneously upon the development of humanistic learning and, though he remained a son of the church, upon the Reformation.

If Erasmus looked back to antiquity for the treasure of the classics, the Reformers, particularly Luther, looked back to the primitive community of Christians for the original spirit of Christianity. In this way the Renaissance and the Reformation both epitomized a revival of the past. Though Erasmus and Luther could agree on many points in their mutual attacks upon the state of Christianity in the sixteenth century, Luther pushed his argument to the point of causing a sundering explosion within the church. The significance of Luther's vigorous revolt was that it altered the mode of thought for a substantial number of people in Western civilization. Whereas Erasmus could balance classical humanistic learning with a simplified Christian faith, Luther's exaltation of faith had the effect of throwing serious doubt upon the capacity of human reason to lead men to salvation.

Luther had been deeply influenced philosophically by William of Ockham, whom he called "my beloved Master William." It was Ockham who had earlier rejected St. Thomas Aquinas' impressive system of natural theology based primarily upon the notion of causality. Natural reason, said Aquinas, leads us to God by way of an analysis of the causal relations of all things, an analysis that ends by requiring a First Cause, which is God. Ockham had developed a strictly empirical and, in a sense, skeptical view regarding knowledge. He argued that "from the fact that one thing is known to exist, it cannot be inferred that another thing exists." To say that some things are caused by other things gives one no warrant to argue that God is the cause of the natural order. Ockham concluded not that we can know nothing about God but only that the unaided reason cannot discover God. Knowledge of God is a gift of grace and is assured by an act of faith. Luther built on this foundation, finding impressive support for this view in the writings of St. Augustine.

From St. Augustine Luther also drew his heavy emphasis upon the Pauline conception of sin, which located man's predicament not in ignorance or undeveloped reason but rather in the bondage of the will. It is therefore *faith*, not reason, that overcomes man's predicament. Moreover, said Luther, "it is the quality of faith that it wrings the neck of reason." What seems impossible to reason becomes feasible to faith. The difficulty with reason is that being the faculty of finite man it tends to reduce everything to its own limited perspective. This is especially true when the natural reason contemplates the nature and capacities of God. Here human reason tends to limit God to strictly human estimates of what God is and can do. Luther was particularly struck by the intellectual difficulties faced by Abraham when God promised that from his barren wife Sarah he would give him seed. "There is no doubt," said Luther, that "faith and reason mightily fell out in Abraham's heart about this matter, yet at last did faith get the better, and overcame and strangled reason, that all-cruelest and most fatal enemy of God." The element of faith reveals the limited scope not only of reason but also of so-called "good works."

Luther's version of the Christian life had the effect therefore of challenging not only the medieval system of scholastic theology but also those optimistic visions of individual and social perfection based upon man's good works. Luther said, "all manner of works, even contemplation, meditation and all that the soul can do, avail nothing." Only one thing is necessary for righteousness, liberty, and the Christian life, and "that one thing is the most holy word of God, the Gospel of Christ." If someone asks "what then is this word of God, and how shall it be used, since there are so many words of God?" Luther answers, "the Apostle explains that in Romans I:17 'The just shall live by faith.' . . . It is clear then that a Christian man has in his faith all that he needs, and needs no works to justify him."

Luther's emphasis upon faith in religious matters had its counterpart in his political thought. Government, according to Luther, is ordained of God. For this reason, he viewed the functions of government as the "preservation of the peace." The recalcitrance of men caused by their sinful nature requires a strong ruler, and for this reason "God has subjected them to the sword, so that even though they would do so, they cannot practice their wickedness. . . ." The counterpart of faith in the political realm was therefore the attitude of obedience. The individual must obey the ruler in spite of what the ruler commands, since his commands are directed toward the preservation of peace and order. Without the power of the ruler, self-centered men would produce anarchy "and thus the world would be reduced to chaos." Man's life upon earth is in any case not the most important consideration; what counts most is the salvation of one's soul. Whatever a ruler or sovereign does "cannot harm the soul but only the body and property. . . ." Consequently, said Luther, "the temporal power is a very small thing in God's sight, and far too slightly regarded by Him, that for its sake, whether it do right or wrong, we should resist, become disobedient and quarrel." Indeed, says Luther, "to suffer wrong destroys no one's soul, nay, it improves the soul, although it inflicts loss upon the body and property. . . ." This is a far cry from the medieval view that St. Thomas formulated when he said that if a positive law of the state is contrary to the natural law, it is not a law but a perversion of the law and need not be obeyed. Still, Luther thought that he had given a theological basis for his justification of the power of the temporal ruler and his laws. It was Machiavelli who went the next step and shifted political thought to a thoroughly secular base, anticipating the modern theories of sovereignty and power politics.

MACHIAVELLI (1469–1527)

Niccolò Machiavelli, the son of an Italian lawyer, was a young man in his twenties when the great preacher Savonarola was at the height of his influence in Florence. That such an influential man came to such a miserable end taught Machiavelli an early lesson about the relative power of good and evil forces in society. During his own career in government and diplomacy, and with the restoration of the Medici in 1512, he gave considerable thought to the rules or principles of effective political behavior, recording his unsystematic thoughts in two books, *The Prince* and *The Discourses*. In *The Discourses*, Machiavelli writes approvingly of the Roman Republic, expressing enthusiasm for self-government and liberty. In *The Prince*, however, his emphasis is upon the need for an absolute monarch. The clue to Machiavelli's thought lies in the reason for his apparent inconsistency in these two books. By expressing a preference for an absolute monarch in *The Prince*, he had not intended to reject the desirability of self-government about which he spoke so approvingly in *The Discourses*. His argument was, rather, that given the condition of moral decay in Italy when he was writing *The Prince* (1513), the kind of popular government exemplified in the Roman Republic could not be successfully established.

If Machiavelli urged rulers to develop the art of deception, it was because he was convinced that only the shrewdest and most crafty individuals could survive in the precarious art of governing. Basing his thought upon a very close inspection of the actual behavior of his contemporaries, he quickly concluded that to think of political behavior in moral terms would be to expose oneself to all the dangers that clever opponents could create. For this reason he developed an indifference to the claims of morality. Indeed he argued that "our religion places the supreme happiness in humility, lowliness and a contempt for worldly objects, whilst the . . . [religion of antiquity] on the contrary places the supreme good in grandeur of soul, strength of body and all such other qualities as render men formidable. . . ." His chief criticism against Christian ethics was that it had "made men feeble, and caused them to become an easy prey to evil-minded men. . . ."

That men are evil was a fact only too obvious to Machiavelli. There was corruption at the highest levels; even the popes of his day were of such bad repute that Machiavelli could write that "we Italians then owe to the Church of Rome and to her priests our having become irreligious and bad. . . ." But he was particularly struck by the general social decadence of Italy in his day. "In fact," he says, "it is vain to look for anything good from those countries which we see nowadays so corrupt, as is the case above all others with Italy." This fact of human corruption was therefore the decisive starting point for Machiavelli's political thought. A basically corrupt society requires a strong government, preferably in the hands of a single man since it happens rarely or not at all that a republic or kingdom is well-ordered or reformed "if this is not done by one man." It is therefore necessary that "there should be one man alone who settles the method and on whose mind any such organization depends." In short, there is a need for an absolute legislator.

Machiavelli envisioned a double standard of behavior, one for rulers and the other for the people. Although he thought it would be disastrous for the rulers to adapt their acts to Christian ethics, he considered religion to be a very important element for uniting people in peace and order. This was a cynical and pragmatic view of religion, since Machiavelli was not particularly concerned with its truth but only with its social usefulness. The ruler, on the other hand, must have the freedom to adjust his acts to the requirements of each occasion without feeling bound to any objective moral rules. There is some question whether *The Prince* was in any sense intended to be a *philosophy* of politics. Since it grew out of the particular circumstances of Machiavelli's day, the recommendations to rulers contained therein constitute instead a practical program of action for existing rulers. Still, the drift of Machiavelli's thought is in the direction of equating the right with the expedient. The ruler should keep faith only if his best interests are served thereby. He will at times therefore be faithless, "but it is necessary," says Machiavelli, "to be able to disguise this character well, and to be a great feigner and dissembler. . . ." Thus, while it is not necessary for the ruler to have all the virtues, "it is very necessary to seem to have them." Even ruthlessness has its place. Machiavelli speaks approvingly of Caesar Borgia's treatment of Ramiro d'Orco, a subordinate whose stern treatment of the people caused him, and therefore Caesar Borgia, to become unpopular. To overcome the damage which d'Orco's unpopularity might have upon him, Caesar Borgia "caused him to be executed and left on the Piazza at Cesaria, with the block and a bloody knife at his side. The barbarity of this spectacle caused the people to be at once satisfied and dismayed."

Machiavelli was well aware of the shifting mood of the people and believed that their inconstancy must be matched by shrewdness and swift adaptability on the part of the ruler. Moreover, he said, "men are ungrateful, fickle, false, cowards, covetous and as long as you succeed they are yours entirely. . . ." But when the ruler really needs help, "they turn against you." Machiavelli was therefore repelled by any notions that would require the ruler to be domesticated by morality. He recognized no higher law such as Aquinas had propounded but urged a thoroughly secular approach to politics. He valued skill in cunning higher than moral conviction. But again, Machiavelli was not unmindful of the desirability of certain political ends. His chief point was, however, that the ruler should choose only those means that could guarantee that the ends be in fact achieved. In the context of unscrupulous and egotistical men, morality must give way to sheer power if the ruler is to succeed. Only those elements in society that have superior power can prevail.

Machiavelli thought his views were supported by past history, where political "Machiavellianism" was far more prevalent than idealistic theorists would be candid enough to admit. It was one of Machiavelli's achievements that he translated politics into the vernacular and anticipated others, notably Thomas Hobbes, who would amplify with more philosophical sophistication the secular and totalitarian implications of Machiavelli's reflections. Unhappily, too, history in the twentieth century produced rulers who carried Machiavelli's recommendations to extremes he might never have imagined.

MICHEL DE MONTAIGNE (1533–1592)

In his celebrated *Essays*, Montaigne expressed for the Renaissance a captivating version of classical Skepticism. Montaigne had discovered in the ancient writings of the Skeptics a prescription for an emancipated mode of daily life. The Skeptics of antiquity, such as Pyrrho, Skepticism's founder, and Sextus Empiricus, meant by *skepticism* something quite different from what that word means in modern usage. The word *skepticism* has over the centuries come to mean chiefly the mood of doubt, a doubt that anything can ever be known with certainty. The corollary of such doubt is an indifference to the drift of events and, in extreme cases, an indifference to the physical conditions of life, not unlike the Stoic sense of resignation. But these were not the chief characteristics of classical Skepticism or of Montaigne's thought. Pyrrho had formulated no strict doctrine about what man could or could not know, what did or did not exist. Central to classical Skepticism was the mood of inquiry coupled with a desire to live a thoroughly exemplary human life. This also was Montaigne's chief concern. He was particularly attracted to a way of life that permitted him constantly to discover new insights and at the same time enjoy all the powers he possessed as a human being.

Montaigne (The Bettmann Archive)

LE SEIGNEVR DE MONTAIGNE

Montaigne wrote that "Pyrrho did not want to make himself into a stone; he wanted to make of himself a living man, discoursing and reasoning, enjoying all pleasures and natural commodities, using all of his corporeal and spiritual parts regularly and properly." Above all, Montaigne looked upon himself, as he said, as "an unpremeditated philosopher," one who was not confined intellectually to some rigid set of ideas within which his thought and life must be expressed. His desire to live a happy life could not be fulfilled if he committed himself to doctrines about which perfectly reasonable objections could be raised. Many problems, he felt, had no clear solutions. On such questions as what is the true nature of things, which so preoccupied the pre-Socratics, Montaigne accepted the judgment of the Skeptics, who said that there is "no more likelihood that this is true than that that is true." But, again, this formula of skepticism was not intended to deny what common sense tells us is the case. In a curious way Montaigne saw in skepticism a liberating force, which would in the end make doubt superfluous because one would never make any permanent commitment to any doctrines but would assume a perpetual mood of inquiry. Contentment, said Montaigne, is possible only as one achieves tranquillity of mind. What disturbs this tranquillity is the attempt to go beyond our ordinary experiences and penetrate the inner nature of things. The saddest spectacle of all is to find men formulating final answers on questions that are far too subtle and variable for such treatment. The final folly of this attempt to capture the perfect and permanent truth is the mood of fanaticism and dogmatism.

Montaigne knew well the frightful outcome of fanaticism. In his lifetime he saw wars and fierce religious persecution. He wrote of his "neighborhood grown so old in riot" that he wondered whether his society could be held together. "I saw," he wrote, "common and general behavior so ferocious, above all in inhumanity and treachery, that I cannot think of it without blenching in horror." This he blamed upon the fires of fanaticism. The loss of inner peace of mind would in time, he felt, be reflected in social turmoil. He genuinely believed that the mood of constructive skepticism could prevent such outbursts of cruelty. In the mood of true skepticism, men's energies would be directed toward manageable subjects and purposes. Rather than struggling with riddles about the universe and its destiny, Montaigne would counsel men to start their philosophy of life by reflecting upon matters close at hand.

A good place to begin, said Montaigne, is with one's own personal experiences: "Every man carries within himself the whole condition of humanity." For this reason he was convinced that whatever proved useful to himself might also serve usefully for someone else. In the true spirit of the Renaissance, Montaigne sought an open and clear form of expression about the most natural and normal actions of men, rejecting the obscurity of technical jargon. "My page," he writes, "makes love and knows what he is doing. But read to him Leo Hebraeus or Ficino where they speak of the actions and thoughts of love, and he can't make head or tail of it." Montaigne complained that "I can't recognize most of my daily doings when they appear in Aristotle. They are decked out or hidden in another cloak for the benefit of schoolmen." What Montaigne thought was needed was to "do as much to make art natural as they do to make nature artificial." The art of life is to recognize what it means to be human, he says, for "there is nothing so handsome as to play the man properly and well. Of all our diseases, the worst is to despise our own being." Nothing disfigures human nature more than a man's attempt to think higher of himself that he should. Whenever this happens, says Montaigne, "I have always observed a singular accord between supercelestial ideas and subterranean behavior." Whenever men "would flee from themselves and escape from being men [they] engage in folly. Instead of transforming themselves into angels, they turn themselves into beasts."

For Montaigne, skepticism did not mean either pessimism as a mood or license as a rule for behavior. On the contrary, he saw in skepticism a source for a positive affirmation of all the facets of human life. Although he saw serious limits to the power of technical reason, he glorified the human capacity for judgment. To be a human being in the deepest sense, he thought, is to have fully conscious experiences, experiences in which a person consciously weighs alternatives and controls his behavior through an act of judgment. Judgment, in contrast to reason, permits a fuller expression of the faculties of man, including the affections and emotions, and is far more willing to allow the soul to be "warned and awakened by occasions foreign, present and fortuitous," inasmuch as "agitation is [the soul's] life and its grace." But although Montaigne could say that "chance has a greater right over me" than the stricture of doctrine, he nevertheless thought it to be a matter of good judgment to accept the basic conditions of life as he found them. He thought that "for men the height of wisdom is to take things as they are, and look upon the rest with confidence."

He adopted as his own the central insight of classical Skepticism, using this formula: "I stop—I examine—I take for my guide the ways of the world and the experience of the senses." The senses give man sufficiently reliable information about himself and the physical world to ensure physical survival and genuine pleasure. The ways of the world also have value almost irrespective of their objective rightness or truth. Religion and laws are positive facts about the world, and to deny or reject them is virtually the same as saying that one is in no danger as he stands at the edge of a precipice. Practical judgment requires one to accept the formal conditions and organization of the country of which he is a citizen. Again, judgment can distinguish between appropriate and inappropriate restrictions upon one's life. For these reasons, Montaigne's skepticism did not lead him to revolutionary or anarchic behavior. He became a true conservative who believed that social change must not be abrupt, that since there are no absolute truths, there are no specific ends toward which society must be forced to move. Custom acquires therefore a higher claim upon the allegiance of men. In matters of religion also the man of good judgment will respect the authority of tradition, seeing in the stability of the organized religious community the condition for continued inquiry that anarchy would render impossible.

Thus Montaigne sought to remind his generation that wisdom lies in accepting life as it is and realizing how difficult it is to know anything with certainty. He wanted particularly to direct men's attention to the richness of human life that respectful acceptance of human capacities could make possible. In this he was a true representative of the main current of the Renaissance. It was not long, however, before Descartes once again saw philosophy's task as the quest for certainty and thereby employed human doubt for purposes quite foreign to Montaigne's intentions. Moreover, Montaigne's preoccupation with human instead of cosmic questions did not deflect other Renaissance thinkers from pursuing questions about the physical world. Indeed, one of the significant aspects of the Renaissance was the gradual emergence during this period of the method of modern science.

SCIENCE

The scientists of the Renaissance brought about the most fundamental alterations in the world of thought, and they accomplished this feat by devising a new method for discovering knowledge. Unlike the medieval thinkers who proceeded for the most part by reading traditional texts, the early modern scientists laid greatest stress upon observation and the formation of temporary hypotheses. The method of observation implied two things: namely, that traditional explanations of the behavior of nature should be empirically demonstrated, the new assumption being that such explanations could very well be wrong, and that new information could be available to scientists if they could penetrate beyond the superficial appearances of things. Men now began to look at the heavenly bodies with a new attitude, hoping not solely to find the confirmation of Biblical statements about the firmament but, further, to discover the principles and laws that describe the movements of bodies. Observation was directed not only upon the stars but also in the opposite direction, toward the minutest constituents of physical substance.

To enhance the exactness of their observations, they invented various scientific instruments. Tippershey, a Dutchman, invented the telescope in 1608, although Galileo was the first to make dramatic use of it. In 1590 the first compound microscope was created. The principle of the barometer was discovered by Galileo's pupil Torricelli. The air pump, which was so important in creating a vacuum for the experiment that proved that all bodies regardless of their weight or size fall at the same rate when there is no air resistance, was invented by Guericke (1602–1686). With the use of instruments and through the use of imaginative hypotheses, fresh knowledge began to unfold. Galileo discovered the moons around Jupiter, and Leeuwenhoek (1632–1723) discovered spermatozoa, protozoa, and bacteria. Whereas Copernicus (1473–1543) formed a new hypothesis of the rotation of the earth around the sun, Harvey (1578–1657) discovered the circulation of the blood. Gilbert (1540–1603) wrote a major work on the magnet, and Boyle (1627–1691), the father of chemistry, formulated his famous law concerning the relation of temperature, volume, and pressure of gases. Added to these inventions and discoveries was the decisive advance made in mathematics, especially by Sir Isaac Newton and Leibniz, who independently invented the differential and integral calculus. The method of observation and mathematical calculation now became the hallmarks of modern science.

The new scientific mode of thought in time influenced philosophic thought in two important ways. First, the assumption that the basic processes of nature are observable and capable of mathematical calculation and description had the effect of engendering another assumption, namely, that everything consists of bodies in motion, that everything conforms to a mechanical model. The heavens above and the smallest particles below all exhibit the same laws of motion. Even human thought was soon explained in mechanical terms, not to mention the realm of human behavior, which the earlier moralists described as the product of *free will.*

A second consequence of scientific thought was a new estimate of the place of man in the universe. Medieval thought had placed man at the apex of creation, locating him upon the earth, which stood in the center of the universe. But the ancient Ptolemaic astronomy, which had envisioned an earth-centered universe, was shattered in the Renaissance. The Polish astronomer Nicolaus Copernicus formulated a new hypothesis in his *De Revolutionibus Orbium Coelestium,* which said that the sun is at the center of the universe and that the earth rotates daily and revolves around the sun annually. Copernicus was a faithful son of the church and had no thought of contradicting any orthodox Biblical doctrines. His work expressed rather his irrepressible desire to work out a theory of the heavens that would conform to the available evidence. As an hypothesis, it was startling enough, but more facts were required before confirmation could be achieved. Tycho Brahe (1546–1601) made additional and corrective observations, and his young associate Kepler (1571–1630) formulated three important laws of planetary motion in which he added mathematical equations to support mere observation. It was Galileo (1564–1642) who provided the greatest theoretical precision to the new astronomy and, in the course of this endeavor, formulated his important laws of acceleration and dynamics, which Newton (1642–1727) refined in his own famous laws of motion. Although Newton still spoke of God as the one who created the machine of nature, it became increasingly unnecessary to refer to God when explaining the phenomena of nature. The whole drift of the new scientific method was toward a new conception of man, of nature, and of the whole mechanism of human knowledge.

As the universe was now viewed as a system of bodies in motion, so now all other aspects of nature were described as bodies in motion. Man himself and human thought also were soon to be viewed in mechanical terms. If all things consist of bodies in motion, this mechanical behavior, it was thought, must be capable of mathematical description. Thus, again, observation and the use of mathematics emerged in the Renaissance as the ingredients of the new method of scientific thought. With this method, it was assumed that new knowledge could be discovered. It was the view of Renaissance scientists that medieval thinkers had simply worked out explanatory systems for what men already knew but had provided no method for discovering new information. But the spirit of discovery, dramatized by Columbus' discovery of a new continent and by the discovery of new worlds in the arts, in literature, and in the unused faculties and capacities of man, was now impelling the scientists to open up new worlds in the structure of nature. And it was this new attitude of science that had the most immediate effect upon the development of modern philosophy, especially upon Francis Bacon and Thomas Hobbes, to whom we now turn.

Advocates
of the Method
# of Science:
Bacon and Hobbes

As the world of science began to open, it was inevitable that philosophy would be affected by this new way of discovering facts. Among the early modern thinkers who saw in the methods of science a fresh way of developing knowledge and who therefore sought to utilize these methods for the enterprise of philosophy were Sir Francis Bacon and Thomas Hobbes. The old and the new ways of thinking had not yet been clearly separated, so science still clung to some traditional ways of thinking and philosophy had not adjusted itself to the methods and assumptions of science. What had to be done now was to make science and philosophy consistent with each other, and it was in doing just this that Bacon and Hobbes launched philosophy upon its modern course.

FRANCIS BACON: METHOD AS THE KEY TO KNOWLEDGE

Francis Bacon assigned himself the task of reforming the philosophy and science of his day. His central criticism was that learning had become stagnant. Science was identified with learning, and learning meant reading ancient texts. The study of medicine, for example, was chiefly literary and was practiced by poets, rhetoricians, and clergymen, whose qualification to practice was their ability to quote Hippocrates and Galen. Philosophy was still dominated by Plato and Aristotle, whose teachings Bacon denounced as "shadows" and "phantoms." Because he emphasized the utility of knowledge, having said that "Knowledge is power," he was particularly agitated by the "uselessness" of traditional learning. What made this learning useless was that science had become mixed up with "superstition," unguided speculation, and theology. Bacon challenged this approach to science as having no adequate method for discovering what nature and its workings are really like. The one ancient writer for whom he did have respect was Democritus, whose materialism he adopted. But the teachings of the Schoolmen of the Middle Ages he considered as "degenerate" versions of Aristotle and of no merit because, instead of deriving substantial evidence from the actual nature of things, they worked upon their own imaginations and as spiders brought forth "cobwebs of learning, admirable for the fineness of thread and work, but of no substance or profit."

Bacon advocated wiping the slate of human knowledge clean and starting over again, using a new method for assembling and explaining facts. He was convinced that he had discovered such a method, which would unlock all the secrets of nature. He was aware of other attempts to correct the inadequacies of traditional learning, particularly attempts by Gilbert, Copernicus, and Galileo to amend Aristotle's physics. But what impressed him most was Galileo's construction and use of telescopes, an event he considered one of the most important in the history of astronomy because it made possible an advancement of learning. Whereas the ancients did not know the composition of the Milky Way, the telescope made it evident that the Milky Way is a collection of distant stars. Bacon considered the mind as being like a glass or mirror, which had been made rough and uneven both by natural tendencies of passions as well as by the errors of traditional learning. In such a condition, the mind cannot reflect truth accurately. Bacon's method, and his hope, was to make the mind's surface clean and smooth and to supply it with new and adequate instruments so that it could observe and understand the universe accurately. To achieve this, he would have to free science from entrenched and traditional learning, separate scientific truth from revealed truths of theology, and fashion a new philosophy based upon a new method of observation and a new interpretation of nature.

By birth and breeding, Bacon was destined to live, work, and think in a style befitting one in high station. He was born in 1561, the son of Sir Nicholas Bacon, who was then Lord Keeper of the Great Seal. He entered Cambridge at the age of twelve and at the age of sixteen was admitted at a relatively senior status to the legal world of Gray's Inn. Through the succeeding years, he was honored by Queen Elizabeth and King James I as a member of Parliament, the House of Lords, and in time became Solicitor-General, Lord Keeper, and finally Lord Chancellor. When one considers that Bacon engaged in a full legal and political career and in addition wrote philosophical works of great breadth and significance, among which his *Advancement of Learning* and *Novum Organum* are the best known, his precocious nature can be all the more appreciated. But he was aware that his political life had interfered with his primary objectives as a thinker, saying that "I reckoned that I was by no means discharging my duty, when I was neglecting that by which I could of myself benefit man. . . ." To add further misery to his last years, he was, shortly after being named Lord Chancellor, accused of accepting bribes and was thereupon fined, sentenced to a short imprisonment, and barred from public office forever. The end came when, pursuing his zeal for experimentation, wondering whether the putrefaction of flesh could be halted by freezing, he went out in the cold and stuffed a chicken with snow, getting badly chilled, from which affliction he died in a few days in 1626 at the age of sixty-five.

Bacon's ideal objective was, as he said, "the total reconstruction of the sciences, arts and all human knowledge," and this he called his "great instauration." But before he could proceed with his creative task, he leveled some fierce criticisms against Oxford, Cambridge, and universities in general, and also against the reigning schools of philosophy, denouncing them for their slavish attachment to the past. It was Bacon who gathered up the rising discontent with medieval philosophy and sounded the call for a break with the lingering influence of Aristotle. The mood in which Bacon carried out his attack upon the past ways of thinking can best be discovered in his treatment of the "distempers of learning" and the *Idols* that proceed from the mind of man, which "is not sincere, but of an ill and corrupt nature."

Distempers of Learning   Bacon named the three distempers of learning, *fantastical* learning, *contentious* learning, and *delicate* learning. These he considered the vices or major diseases of learning, and he described how they distort knowledge. In fantastical learning, men concern themselves with words, emphasizing texts, languages, and style, and "hunt more after words than matter, and more after choiceness of phrase . . . than after the weight of matter." Contentious learning is even worse, he said, because it begins with the fixed positions or points of view taken by earlier thinkers, and these views are used as the starting point in contentious argumentation. Finally, there is delicate learning, wherein earlier authors, who claim more knowledge than can be proved, are accepted by readers as knowing as much as they claim, and this accounts for the acceptance of Aristotle, for example, as the dictator of science. These three diseases, he argued, must be cured in order to relieve the mind of the errors they engender.

Idols of the Mind   Likewise, the human mind is corrupted by *Idols*. Bacon refers to four Idols, which he metaphorically calls the Idols of the *Tribe*, the *Cave*, the *Market Place*, and the *Theatre*. These Idols, or "false phantoms," are distortions of the mind, like distortions of beams of light reflected from an uneven mirror: "For from the nature of a clear and equal glass, wherein the beams of things should reflect according to their true incidence, it is rather like an enchanted glass, full of superstition and imposture. . . ." The only way to correct this wayward mode of thought is through observation and experimentation, through the inductive method. These idols, or "false opinions," "dogmas," "superstitions" and "errors," distort knowledge in many ways.

The Idols of the Tribe are man's preoccupation with opinions, following from "the false assertion that the sense of man is the measure of things." Here Bacon wanted to make the point that simply looking at things is no guarantee we shall see them as they really are, because we all bring our hopes and fears, prejudices, and impatience to things and thereby affect our understanding of them.

The Idols of the Cave were taken by Bacon from the Platonic allegory and again suggest the limitations of the untrained mind, which is shut in the cave of its own environment of customs and opinions, reflecting the kinds of books one reads, the ideas he considers significant, and the intellectual authorities to whom he defers.

The third class of idols is very aptly designated as the Idols of the Market Place, for it stands for the words men use in the commerce of daily life, words that are common coin in daily conversation. In spite of their usefulness, words can weaken knowledge, because they are not created with care or precision but framed so that the common man will understand their use. And even philosophers are diverted by these idols, for they often give names for something that exists only in their imagination and, in addition, fashion names for abstractions derived from things, such as *element of fire* or *fortune*, or such names of qualities as *heavy, rare*, or *dense*.

Finally, the Idols of the Theatre are the grand systematic dogmas of long philosophic treatises, "representing worlds of their own creation after an unreal and scenic fashion." Bacon wants to include here not only whole systems, but all principles or axioms in science that "by tradition, credulity and negligence have come to be received."

Inductive Method   Having duly warned his generation that the understanding can be distorted by these *Idols*, Bacon set forth a new method for acquiring knowledge. In order to "penetrate into the inner and further recesses of nature," he said, "it is necessary that our notion . . . be derived from things in a more sure and guarded way." This way would include ridding oneself of his prejudices ("unless one become as a child") and looking at things as they are: "We must lead men to the particulars themselves, and their series and order." To guide and help observation it is necessary to supply "rectifications to correct its errors; and this I endeavour to accomplish not so much by instruments as by *experiments*. For the subtlety of experiments is far greater than that of sense itself. . . ."

Bacon's concept of experiment and his method of observation, however, did not lead to what we today know as the scientific method. He relied too much upon pure induction, that is, upon the possibility of deriving "laws" from the simple observation of particulars and their series and order. Bacon knew the limitations of "induction by simple enumeration," for example, concluding that all horses are black because the first eighteen counted were black; but in going beyond this type of induction, he ironically lapsed back into a search for a "substance," a procedure more appropriate to an Aristotelian.

The example he gave of his inductive method was the outline of how one could investigate the cause of heat. The first step is to draw up a list of all the forms in which we encounter heat, producing a *Table of Essence and Presence.* Next, another list must be compiled to include items that resemble those on the first list but that do not have heat, and this second list he called the *Table of Deviation.* Thus, the first list would include the sun, and the second would include the moon. A third, the *Table of Comparison*, is a further attempt to discover the nature of heat by analyzing the different degrees of heat to be found in different things, "as in fishes, quadrupeds, serpents, birds, . . . man, . . . planets." The fourth step is the *Process of Exclusion*, whereby, setting "induction to work," we try to find some "nature" that is present whenever there is heat and absent when heat is absent. Is light the cause of heat? No, because the moon is bright but is not hot. This process of exclusion was central to Bacon's method of science, and this process he called "the foundation of true induction." He assumed that "the Form of a thing is to be found in each and all the instances, in which the thing itself is to be found." Applying this assumption to the problem of heat, Bacon concluded that "from a survey of all instances, all and each, the nature of which heat is a particular case appears to be Motion." This conclusion has an Aristotelian sound when Bacon says that ". . . Heat itself, its essence and quiddity, is Motion and nothing else," for essences are what Aristotle talked about. This suggests that Bacon's break with Aristotle was not complete, for he clung to the concept of substance. The final step, however, does have a modern ring, for Bacon wanted to verify his conclusions by checking them against all the items produced in his tables.

The major weakness in Bacon's method is that he had no grasp of what modern scientists mean by an hypothesis. Bacon assumed that if one simply looked at enough facts, an hypothesis would suggest itself, whereas a modern scientist knows it is necessary to have an hypothesis before one inspects facts in order to have some guide in the selection of facts relevant to the experiment. Furthermore, only if one begins with an hypothesis does deduction as well as induction play a large part in science. Bacon also underestimated the importance of mathematics for science. But he had, nevertheless, dislodged the grip of scholastic thought and provided the impetus for making philosophy scientific. The addition of mathematical and deductive reasoning to scientific philosophy was achieved in England by Bacon's friend and countryman, Thomas Hobbes.

THOMAS HOBBES: A SINGLE METHOD FOR KNOWING MATTER, MAN, AND THE STATE

The life of Thomas Hobbes spans ninety-one eventful years, from 1588 to 1679. He was born at Westport near Malmesbury, England, the son of a vicar. His education at Oxford stirred in him a fascination for classical literature, whereas his exposure to Aristotelian logic left him bored. In 1608 he left Oxford and had the good fortune of becoming the tutor of the Earl of Devonshire, William Cavendish. This association with the Cavendish family was to influence Hobbes' development significantly, as it afforded him the opportunity to travel widely on the Continent and to meet many leading thinkers and personages of the day. In Italy he met Galileo, and in Paris he formed a lasting friendship with Descartes' admirer Mersenne and also Descartes' antagonist Gassendi. There is some question whether he ever met Descartes in person, but his carefully reasoned objections to the *Meditations* indicate Hobbes' close familiarity with Descartes' philosophy. In England, Hobbes was much admired by Bacon, who, as Lord Chancellor, enjoyed conversation with him and frequently dictated his thoughts to Hobbes during "delicious walkes at Gorambery." Hobbes' early interest in classics led him to translate Thucydides, but his discovery of Euclid's *Elements* in his early forties shifted his interest to mathematics and analysis. The next stage of his development, which was to persist for the rest of his life, witnessed the publication of his brilliant philosophical treatises, among which the most renowned is his *Leviathan*.

Influence of Geometry upon Hobbes's Thought   Although the *Leviathan* is primarily a book on social and political philosophy, Hobbes had not intended to restrict his attention to that subject. Caught up in the rising tide of scientific discovery, he was deeply impressed by the precision of science and above all by the certainty of scientific knowledge. The intellectual atmosphere of the sixteenth and seventeenth centuries had been undergoing a radical alteration as one area of inquiry after another yielded to the probing method of science. Copernicus (1473–1543) had called into question the traditional view of astronomy, which had remained virtually unchanged and unchallenged since Ptolemy (second century, Egypt) had argued that the earth is the center of the universe. Against this Ptolemaic view, Copernicus held, "at length by much and long observation" of the "motions of the other planets," and having "calculated as for the revolution of that planet [the earth]," that the earth revolves on its axis and moves in a circular path around the sun, thus making the sun the center, instead of the earth. This was a major development, but equally important was the method Copernicus had employed, a method characterized by two salient features, namely, the observation of moving bodies and the mathematical calculation of the motion of bodies in space.

By the time Hobbes appeared on the intellectual scene, what Copernicus had begun was now considerably refined by Kepler (1571–1630) and particularly by Galileo (1564–1642), who not only emphasized the importance of observation, which led to his discovery of the satellites around the planet Jupiter, but who sought to give astronomy the precision of geometry. By using the model of geometry for his reasoning about astronomy, Galileo assumed that he could demonstrate the accuracy of his conclusions if he could, as one does in geometry, produce basic axioms from which to deduce his conclusions. Moreover, he assumed that empirical facts correspond to geometric axioms, or that the axioms

Hobbes, title-page of *Leviathan* (*The Bettmann Archive*)

that the mind formulates correspond to the actual characteristics of observable moving bodies. To think in terms of geometry is to know how things actually behave. Specifically, Galileo formulated, for the first time, a geometric representation of the motion of bodies and their acceleration. Galileo helped to perfect a method that, in their own way, Francis Bacon in his *Novum Organum* (1620) and Descartes in his *Discourse on Method* (1637) had attempted. What most of these thinkers had in common was their belief that human knowledge about the nature of things is available to anyone who used the appropriate method in its pursuit. Instead of looking back to tradition or to the testimony of ancient authorities, individuals can have direct access to the truth about nature, and this truth would most likely be discovered if one took the information he received through observation and organized it into a system of axioms.

Hobbes caught the spirit of the times. His initial fascination for mathematics came from his encounter with Euclid's *Elements*, a book that "made [him] in love with geometry." Hobbes joined that small but eloquent company of thinkers who saw in geometry the key to the study of nature. With a razor-sharp intellect and a fervor that caused him to exaggerate the possibilities of this method, Hobbes undertook to recast the whole gamut of knowledge in accordance with this single approach. Hobbes assumed that it mattered little what the object of study was, that the method of observation and deductive reasoning from axioms, formed from observation, would yield exact knowledge. He therefore set out an ambitious project, which was to recast the study of physical nature, the nature of man, and the nature of human society, using the same method throughout. He published *De Cive (The Citizen)* in 1642, *De Corpore (Concerning Body)* in 1655, and *De Homine (Concerning Man)* in 1658. In the end, it was his political philosophy that made him famous, for it was here that his application of rigorous logic and the scientific method produced startling new results.

As a political philosopher, Hobbes is frequently, though not accurately, called the father of modern totalitarianism. His books *De Cive* and *Leviathan* read like grammars of obedience. He describes the relation between citizen and sovereign in such severe terms that it is no wonder he brought upon himself widespread criticism. Two considerations led Hobbes to formulate his unique theory of political obligation. The first was the political turbulence of his times, which saw Cromwell preparing to lead his men in a savage civil war. This experience of violence growing out of deep disagreements between men on political matters contrasted sharply in Hobbes' mind with the relatively quick agreements men achieved in mathematical and scientific matters. Secondly, Hobbes looked at political philosophy as a variation of the science of physics. He assumed that from a thoroughly materialistic view of human nature, in which human behavior could be explained simply in terms of bodies in motion, he could formulate an accurate political philosophy. It was his hope that if political theory could be formulated with logical precision, men would be more likely to achieve agreement between themselves and thereby arrive at what Hobbes longed for most of all, namely, peace and order. There is some question whether Hobbes was logically consistent in his systematic political philosophy, and there is even greater question about his assumption that men would become orderly in their relations to each other just because they had been provided a logical plan for harmonious behavior. In any case, his theory of man and society took its novel turn mainly because he built it according to a mechanical model, the chief ingredients of which were bodies and motion. And because Hobbes' political theory depends so much upon his unique theory of knowledge and his mechanical model of reality, these aspects of his philosophy need to be considered in some detail as the background to his views on political community.

Bodies in Motion: The Object of Thought Philosophy, according to Hobbes, is concerned chiefly with the causes and characteristics of bodies. There are three major types of bodies, physical bodies such as stones, the human body, and the body politic. Philosophy is concerned with all three types, inquiring into their causes and characteristics. There is one principal characteristic that all bodies share and that alone makes it possible to understand how they came to be and do what they do, and that characteristic is motion. Motion is a key concept in Hobbes' thought. Equally important is the assumption Hobbes makes that only bodies exist, that knowable reality consists solely of bodies. He will not admit that anything such as *spirit* or *God* exists if these terms refer to beings that have no bodies, or are incorporeal. Of God's existence, Hobbes writes that "by the visible things in this world, and their admirable order, a man may conceive there is a cause of them, which men call God: and yet not have an idea or image of him in his mind." Hobbes was willing to concede *that* God exists but argued that men do not know *what* God is. Still, it made no sense to Hobbes that there could be something with an *incorporeal substance*, as the theologians characterized God. Substance, he argued, could be only corporeal, wherefore God would possess some form of body. But Hobbes did not wish to pursue theological subtleties and appears to have dealt with God's nature in this connection only to make the broader point that whatever exists is corporeal and that the scope of philosophy is limited to the study of bodies in motion.

Hobbes set out to explain both physical and mental events as nothing more than bodies in motion. "Motion," says Hobbes, "is a continual relinquishing of one place and acquiring of another." Anything that moves is changing its location, and, similarly, whatever is caused to move changes its place. If something is at rest, it will always be at rest unless something moves it. Only a moving body can cause a resting body to move, for "by endeavoring to get into its place by motion [it] suffers it no longer to remain at rest." Similarly, a body in motion tends to stay in motion unless its movement is halted by some other body. This account of motion appears to be restricted to locomotion, for such concepts as inertia, force, impetus, resistance, and endeavor, terms that Hobbes uses to describe motion, all seem to apply to things in space that occupy or change their location. But since Hobbes started with the premise that only bodies exist, it was inevitable that he would have to explain all of reality and all processes in terms of moving bodies. Motion is therefore not only locomotion in the simple sense but is also what we know as the process of change. Things become different because something in them has been moved by something else, and this refers not only to physical but also to mental change.

Besides the kind of motion Galileo described as he charted the course of the stars and planets, or the more obvious modes of locomotion, Hobbes refers to two kinds of motion that are peculiar to animals or men, namely, *vital* and *voluntary* motions. Vital motions begin with the process of birth, continue through life and include such motions as pulse, nutrition, excretion, the course of the blood, and breathing, "to which motions there needs no help of imagination." On the other hand, voluntary motions, such as going, speaking, and the deliberate movement of our limbs, are first of all movements in our minds, and "because *going*, *speaking* and the like voluntary motions, depend always upon a precedent thought of *whither*, *which way*, and *what*; it is evident that the imagination is the first internal beginning of all voluntary motion." Imagination is the cause of voluntary acts, but imagination itself and the human activity we call *thought* are also explained as being effects of prior causes, as being consequences of prior motions.

Mechanical View of Human Thought   The human mind works in various ways, ranging from *perception, imagination, memory*, to *thinking*. All of these modes of mental activity are fundamentally the same because they are all motions in our bodies. That perception, imagination, and memory are alike was particularly obvious to Hobbes. Perception, by which he meant our ability to "sense" things, is our basic mental act, and the others are "derived from that original." The whole structure and process of human thought is explained as bodies in motion, and the variations in mental activity are accounted for by designating the location of each type of mental act along a describable causal chain. Thus, the thought process begins when a body external to us moves and causes a motion inside of us, as when we *see* a tree, and seeing the tree is *perception* or *sensation*. When we look at an object, we see what Hobbes called a *phantasm*. A phantasm is the image within us caused by an object outside of us. Perception is not the sensation *of* motion, or the sensation of the exact qualities an object actually possesses. We see the green tree, but *green* and *tree* are two *phantasms*, a *quality* and an *object*, and these represent the *ways* we experience the motion caused by the body external to us. The initial impact upon us caused by an external object creates not only our immediate sensation but more lasting effects as well, just as on the ocean, though the wind cease, "the waves give not over rolling for a long time after." And, "so also it happeneth in that motion, which is made in the internal parts of man . . . for after the object is removed, or the eye shut, we still retain an image of the thing seen, though more obscure than when we see it. . . ." This retention of the image within us after the object is removed is what Hobbes means by imagination. Thus, imagination is simply a lingering, or what Hobbes called a *decaying*, sensation. When, later, we wish to express this decay and indicate that the sense is fading, we call this memory, "so that imagination and memory are but one thing, which for divers considerations hath divers names. . . ."

It would appear that thinking, as when we have conversation with each other, is something quite different from sensation and memory. In sensation the sequence of images in our mind is determined by what is happening, moving, outside of us, whereas in thinking we seem to put ideas together whichever way we wish. But, using his mechanical model, Hobbes explained thinking in exactly the same terms that he used in his account of sensation, so that thinking, for him, is a variation of sensation. Ideas, he said, follow each other in thought because they first followed each other in sensation, for "those motions that immediately succeeded one another in sense, continue also together after sense. . . ." Our ideas have a firm relationship to each other for the reason that in any form of continued motion, and thought is such a motion, "one part follows another by cohesion." But the mechanism of thought is not all that perfect, and men are always thinking in ways that do not mirror their past sensations exactly. Hobbes was aware of this, but he tried to explain even the broken sequences as the invasions of more dominant sensations into the stream of imagination and memory, as when the thought of the civil war might remind him of a personal experience and thereby break the chain of events for which the civil war stood in his memory. He wanted to establish the view that nothing happens in thinking that cannot be accounted for by sensation and memory.

Still, there is a difference between the mind of an animal and the mind of a human being, even though both animal and man have sensation and memory. What distinguishes them is that men are able to form *signs* or *names* to mark their sensations. With these names men are able to recall their sensations. Moreover, science and philosophy are possible because of man's capacity to formulate words and sentences. Knowledge, then, takes on two different forms, one being knowledge of *fact* and the other knowledge of *consequences*. Knowledge of fact is simply memory of past events. Knowledge of consequences is hypothetical or conditional, but still based upon experience, for it affirms that *if A* is true, *B* will also be true, or, using Hobbes' illustration, "If the figure shown be a circle, then any straight line through the center shall divide it into two equal parts." Scientific knowledge, or philosophy in the broad sense, is possible only because of man's capacity to use words and speech. Although Hobbes spoke of signs and names as "word(s) taken at pleasure to serve for a mark," these words represent our experiences. Words and sentences point to the actual way things behave. Reasoning with words is therefore not the same as playing with words, for once the meaning of words is established, certain consequences follow for their use, mirroring the reality they help our imaginations recall. Thus, to say that *man is a living creature* is a true proposition for the two reasons that the word *man* already includes the idea of living and that the word *man* is a mark for the sensation we have when we see an actual human being. The relation of words to each other is based upon the relations between the events for which the words stand as representations. Reasoning, then, is "nothing but *reckoning*, that is adding and subtracting, of consequences of general names. . . ." And even if the word *man* does not refer to any general or universal reality but only to particular men, Hobbes still maintains that we have reliable knowledge, that although "experience concludeth nothing universally," science, based on experience, does "conclude universally."

This is Hobbes' *nominalism*, which led him to say that universal terms such as *man* are merely words and point to no general reality, and his *empiricism*, which led him to argue that we can know things about all men because of what we know from our experience about some men.

Political Philosophy and Morality When we turn directly to Hobbes' political philosophy, we find that he employed as much of his theory of motion and his logic, as well as the method of geometry, as this subject would permit. Just as he looked to the concepts of motion and bodies to describe the nature of men, and particularly to describe human knowledge, so also he now analyzes the structure and nature of the state in terms of moving bodies. Moreover, his account of the state is the most impressive example of his conception of philosophy, for if philosophy is a matter of "*reckoning*, that is adding and subtracting, of consequences of general names," it is preeminently in his political philosophy that he exhibits his skill and rigor with the meanings of words.

What strikes one first about Hobbes' theory of state is that he approaches the subject not from an historical point of view but from the vantage point of logic and analysis. He does not ask, "*when* did civil societies emerge?" but asks rather, "*how* do you explain the emergence of society?" He is concerned to discover the *cause* of civil society, and in harmony with his general method sets out to explain the cause of the state by describing the motion of bodies. His thought about political philosophy resembles the method of geometry only in the sense that from axiomlike premises he deduces all the consequences or conclusions of his political theory, and most of these premises cluster around his conception of human nature.

The State of Nature Hobbes describes men, first of all, as they appear in what he calls the *state of nature*, which is the condition of men before there is any state or civil society. In this state of nature all men are equal and equally have the right to whatever they consider necessary for their survival. Equality here means simply that anyone is capable of hurting his neighbor and taking what he judges he needs for his own protection. Differences in strength can in time be overcome and the weak can destroy the strong. The "right of all to all" which prevails in the state of nature does not mean that one man has a right whereas others have corresponding duties. The word *right* in the bare state of nature is a man's *freedom* "to do what he would, and against whom he thought fit, and to possess, use and enjoy all that he would, or could get." The driving force in man is the will to survive, and the psychological mood pervading all men is fear, the fear of death and particularly the fear of violent death. In the state of nature all men are relentlessly pursuing whatever acts they think will secure their safety. The picture one gets of this state of nature is of men moving against each other, bodies in motion, or the anarchic condition Hobbes called "the war of all against all."

Why do men behave this way? Hobbes analyzes human motivation by saying that all men possess a twofold *endeavor*, namely *appetite* and *aversion*. These two endeavors account for man's motions to and from persons or objects, and have the same meanings as the words *love* and *hate*. Men are attracted to what they think will help them survive, and they hate whatever they judge to be a threat to them. The words *good* and *evil* have whatever meaning each individual will give them, and each person will call *good* whatever he loves and *evil* whatever he hates, "there being nothing simply and absolutely so." Men are fundamentally egotistical in that they are concerned chiefly about their own survival and identify goodness with their own appetites. It would appear therefore that in the state of nature there is no obligation for men to respect others or that there is no morality in the traditional sense of goodness and justice. Given this egotistical view of human nature, it would appear also that men did not possess the capacity to create an ordered and peaceful society.

But Hobbes argued that several logical conclusions or consequences can be deduced from man's concern for his survival, among these being what Hobbes called *natural laws.* Even in the state of nature, men *know* these natural laws, which are logically consistent with man's principal concern for his own safety. A natural law, said Hobbes, "is a precept, or general rule, found out by reason," telling what to do and what not to do. If the major premise is that I want to survive, I can logically deduce, even in the state of nature, certain rules of behavior that will help me to survive. The first law of nature is therefore that every man ought to "seek peace and follow it." Now this law that urges me to seek peace is natural because it is a logical extension of my concern for survival. It is obvious that I have a better chance to survive if I help to create the conditions of peace. My desire for survival therefore impels me to seek peace. From this first and fundamental law of nature is derived the second law, which states that "a man be willing, when others are so too, as farforth as for peace, and defense of himself he shall think it necessary, to lay down his right to all things; and be contented with so much liberty against other men, as he would allow other men against himself. . . ."

Obligation in the State of Nature   If men know these and other natural laws even in the state of nature, do they have an obligation to obey them? Hobbes answers that these laws are always binding, in the state of nature as well as in civil society. But he distinguishes between two ways in which these natural laws are applicable in the state of nature, saying that "the laws of nature oblige *in foro interno*; that is to say, they bind to a desire they should take place: but *in foro externo*; that is, to putting them in act, not always." Thus, it isn't as if there were no obligation in the state of nature; rather, the circumstances for living by these laws in the state of nature are not always present. Men have a right to all things in the state of nature not because there is no obligation, but because if a man were modest, tractable, and kept his promises "in such time and place where no man else should do so, [he] should but make himself a prey to others, and procure his own ruin, contrary to the ground of all laws of nature, which tend to nature's preservations." And even when men act to preserve themselves, they are not free from rational natural laws, for even in the state of nature they ought to act in good faith: ". . . if any man *pretend* somewhat to tend necessarily to his preservation, which yet he himself doth not confidently believe so, he may offend against the laws of nature."

Hobbes was aware that the logical outcome of egotistical individuals all deciding how best to survive would be anarchy, where there were "no arts; no letters; no society; and which is worst of all, continual fear, and danger of violent death; and the life of man, solitary, poor, nasty, brutish, and short. . . ." To avoid such a condition of anarchy, the chief cause of which is the conflict of individual and egotistical judgments of right, men, following the dictates of natural law, seeking peace, renounce some of their rights or freedoms and enter into a social contract and thereby create an artificial man, that great *leviathan*, called a *commonwealth*, or *state*.

The Social Contract The contract by which men avoid the state of nature and enter civil society is an agreement between individuals, "as if every man should say to every man, *I authorize and give up my right of governing myself, to this man, or to this assembly of men, on this condition, that thou give up thy right to him, and authorize all his actions in like manner.*" Two things stand out clearly in this contract. First, the parties to the contract are individuals who promise each other to hand over their right to govern themselves to the sovereign; it is not a contract between the sovereign and the citizens. The sovereign has absolute power to govern and is in no way subject to the citizens. Secondly, Hobbes clearly states that the sovereign can be either "this man" or "this assembly of men," suggesting that in theory, at least, his view of sovereignty was not identified with any particular form of government. It may be that he had a preference for a single ruler with absolute power, but he recognized the possible compatibility of his theory of sovereignty with "democracy." But whatever form the sovereign would take, it is clear that Hobbes saw the transfer of the right to rule from the people to the sovereign as both absolute and irrevocable.

Hobbes was particularly anxious to demonstrate with logical rigor that sovereign power is indivisible. Having shown that in the state of nature anarchy is the logical consequence of independent individual judgments, he concluded that the only way to overcome such anarchy is to make a single body out of the several bodies of the citizens. The only way to transform multiple wills into a single will is to agree that the sovereign's single will and judgment represent the will and judgment of all the citizens. In effect, this is what the contract says when men agree to hand over their right to govern themselves. The sovereign now acts not only on behalf of the citizens but *as if* he embodied the will of the citizens, thereby affirming an identity between the wills of the sovereign and citizens. Resistance against the sovereign by a citizen is therefore illogical on two counts, first because it would amount to resistance to himself, and secondly, to resist is to revert to independent judgment, which is to revert to the state of nature or anarchy. The power of the sovereign must therefore be absolute in order to secure the conditions of order, peace, and law.

Civil Law versus Natural Law Law begins only when there is a sovereign. This is a logical truism, for in the judicial or *legal* sense, a law is defined as a command of the sovereign. It follows that where there is no sovereign, there is no law. To be sure, Hobbes affirmed that even in the state of nature men have knowledge of the natural law, and in a special sense the natural law is binding even in the state of nature. But only after there is a sovereign can there be a legal order, because only then is there the apparatus of law in which the power of enforcement is central. Without the power to enforce, said Hobbes, covenants are "mere words." Hobbes identifies law with sovereign command and makes the additional point that "there can be no unjust law."

Nowhere does Hobbes' severe authoritarianism express itself in more startling form than when he argues that there can be no unjust law. It appears that justice and morality begin with the sovereign, that there are no principles of justice and morality that precede and limit the acts of the sovereign. Hobbes affirmed this in a notable passage: "To the care of the sovereign, belongeth the making of good laws. But what is a good law? By good law, I mean not a just law: for no law can be unjust." Hobbes gives two reasons for saying no law can be unjust: first, because justice means obeying the law, and this is why justice comes into being only after a law has been made and cannot itself be the standard for law; secondly, when a sovereign makes a law, it is as though the people were making the law, and what they agree upon cannot be unjust. Indeed, the third natural law Hobbes speaks of is *that men perform their covenants made*," and he indicated that this is the "fountain of justice." Hence, to keep the contract in which you agreed to obey the sovereign is the essence of Hobbesian justice.

It is evident that Hobbes forces the reader to take each word seriously and "reckon" all the "consequences" that can be deduced from it. If law means the sovereign's command and if justice means obeying the law, there can be no *unjust* law. But there can be a *bad* law, for Hobbes was enough of an Aristotelian to recognize that a sovereign has a definite purpose "for which he was trusted with the sovereign power, namely, the procuration of *the safety of the people*; to which he is obliged by the law of nature, and to render an account thereof to God. . . ." But even in such a case, where the sovereign has commanded a "bad" law, the citizens are not the ones to judge it as such, nor does this justify their disobedience. The sovereign has the sole power to judge what is for the safety of the people; if the people disagreed with him, they would revert to anarchy. If the sovereign engages in iniquitous acts, this is a matter between the sovereign and God, not between the citizens and the sovereign. And because he feared anarchy and disorder so deeply, Hobbes pushed his logic of obedience to the point of making religion and the church subordinate to the state. To the Christian who felt that the sovereign's command violated the law cf God, Hobbes gave no comfort but insisted that if such a person could not obey the sovereign, he must "go to Christ in martyrdom. . . ."

With these bold strokes, Hobbes altered the course of philosophy. He was among the first to apply the methods of science to the study of human nature, providing novel explanations for human knowledge and moral behavior, departing also from the medieval notion of natural law, and arriving in the end at a highly authoritarian concept of sovereignty. Although Hobbes did not win widespread approval in his day, and even though there is much in his philosophy to question and criticize, his enduring influence was assured by the precision of his formulation of the problems of philosophy.

12

Rationalism on the Continent: Descartes, Spinoza, and Leibniz

Although philosophy rarely alters its direction and mood with radical suddenness, there are times when its new concerns and emphases clearly separate it from its immediate past. Such was the case with seventeenth-century Continental rationalism, whose founder was René Descartes and whose new program initiated what is called *modern philosophy*. In a sense, much of what the Continental rationalists set out to do had already been attempted by the medieval philosophers and by Bacon and Hobbes. But Descartes, Spinoza, and Leibniz fashioned a new ideal for philosophy. Influenced by the progress and success of science and mathematics, their new program was an attempt to provide philosophy with the exactness of mathematics. They set out to formulate clear rational principles that could be organized into a system of truths from which accurate information about the world could be deduced. Their emphasis was upon the rational capacity of the human mind, which they now considered the source of truth both about man and about the world. Although they did not reject the claims of religion, they did consider philosophical reasoning something independent of supernatural revelation. Although they saw little value in subjective feeling and enthusiasm as means for discovering truth, they did believe that the mind of an individual is structured in such a way that simply by operating according to the appropriate method it can discover the nature of the universe. This was an optimistic view of human reason, which offset the recent attempts, by Montaigne and Charron, at reviving ancient skepticism. The rationalists assumed that what they could think clearly with their minds did in fact exist in the world outside their minds. Descartes and Leibniz even argued that certain ideas are innate in the human mind, that, given the proper occasion, experience would cause these innate truths to become self-evident. That the highly optimistic program of rationalism was not altogether successful is indicated by the differences in the three systems it produced. To be sure, all the rationalists finally interpreted the natural world after the mechanical model of physics and ascribed determinism to all physical events. But Descartes described reality as a dualism consisting of two basic substances, thought and extension; Spinoza proposed a monism, saying that there is only a single substance, Nature, which has various attributes and modes; Leibniz was a pluralist, saying that although there is only one kind of substance, the monad, there are nevertheless different kinds of monads accounting for the various elements in nature. The British empiricists, Locke, Berkeley, and Hume, who can be considered a second group of modern philosophers following closely after the rationalists, asked some searching questions about the premises of the rationalists; some of these questions have not been satisfactorily answered to this day.

DESCARTES

René Descartes, usually called the "father of modern philosophy," was born in Touraine in 1596. His father, Joachim Descartes, was a councillor of the Parliament of Brittany. From 1604 to 1612 young Descartes studied in the Jesuit college of La Flèche, where his education included mathematics, logic, and philosophy. He was most impressed, during these years, with the certainty and precision of mathematics, as compared with philosophy whose teachings invariably produced doubts and disputes. For a time he was a soldier in the army of Maximilian of Bavaria. After traveling widely throughout Europe, he decided, in 1628, to settle down in Holland, and it was here that Descartes wrote his principal works, including his *Discourse on Method* (1637), *Meditations on First Philosophy* (1641), *Principles of Philosophy* (1644), and *The Passions of the Soul* (1649). He went to Sweden in 1649 at the invitation of Queen Christina, who wanted Descartes to instruct her in his philosophy. As the queen could see him only at five o'clock in the morning, this unaccustomed encounter with the bitter cold of that hour made him easy prey to illness. Within a few months he suffered an attack of fever, and in February, 1650, he died at the age of fifty-four.

Descartes was concerned chiefly with the problem of intellectual certainty. He had been educated, as he says, "at one of the most celebrated schools in Europe. . . ." And yet, "I found myself embarrassed with . . . many doubts and errors. . . ." Looking back on his studies, he saw that ancient literature provided him charming fables that stimulated his mind but could not guide his behavior, because these fables portrayed behavior beyond the power of human beings to perform. He spoke kindly of poetry, saying that the poet gives us knowledge through his "imaginative force," even making truth "shine forth the more brightly" than could the philosophers. Still, poetry is a gift of the mind and not the fruit of study and therefore gives us no method for consciously discovering truth. Though he honored theology, he concluded that its "revealed truths . . . are quite above our intelligence" and that if one were to be successful in thinking about them, "it was necessary to have some extraordinary assistance from above and to be more than a mere man." He did not want to deny these truths, for he apparently remained a pious Catholic to the end, but he did not find in theology a method by which these truths could be arrived at solely through the powers of human reason. Nor was the philosophy he learned at college any more helpful in this regard, for "no single thing is to be found in it which is not subject of dispute, and in consequence which is not dubious. . . ."

His quest for certainty led Descartes to turn from his books to that "great book of the world," where through travel he met "men of diverse temperaments and conditions" and collected "varied experiences." It was his thought that among men of the world, he would discover more exact reasoning, since in practical life, as compared with scholarly activity, a mistake in reasoning has harmful consequences. But, he says, he found as much difference of opinion among practical men as among philosophers. From this experience with the book of the world, Descartes decided "to believe nothing too certainly of which I had only been convinced by example and custom. . . ." He resolved to continue his search for certainty, and on a memorable night, November 10, 1619, he had three dreams, which unmistakably convinced him that he must construct the system of true knowledge upon the powers of human reason alone.

Descartes broke with the past and gave philosophy a fresh start. In particular, since his system of truth would have to be derived from his own rational powers, he would no longer rely on previous philosophers for his ideas, nor would he accept any idea as true only because it was expressed by someone with authority. Neither the authority of Aristotle's great reputation nor the authority of the church could suffice to produce the kind of certainty he sought. Descartes was determined to discover the basis of intellectual certainty in his own reason. He therefore gave philosophy a fresh start by using only those truths he could know through his own powers as the foundation for all other knowledge. He was well aware of his unique place in the history of philosophy, for he writes that "although all the truths which I class among my principles have been known from all time and by all men, there has been no one up to the present, who, so far as I know, has adopted them as the principles of philosophy . . . as the sources from which may be derived a knowledge of all things else which are in the world. This is why it here remains to me to prove that they are such."

His ideal was to arrive at a system of thought whose various principles were true and were related to each other in such a clear way that the mind could move easily from one true principle to another. But in order to achieve such an organi-

Descartes (*The Bettmann Archive*)

cally connected set of truths, Descartes felt that he must make these truths "conform to a rational scheme." With such a scheme he could not only organize present knowledge but could "direct our reason in order to discover those truths of which we are ignorant." His first task therefore was to work out his "rational scheme," his *method*.

Descartes' Method   Descartes' method consists of harnessing the powers of the mind with a special set of rules. He insisted upon the *necessity* of method, upon systematic and orderly thinking. He was appalled at scholars who sought aimlessly for truth, comparing them to men who, "burning with an unintelligent desire to find treasure, continuously roam the streets, seeking to find something that a passerby might have chanced to drop. . . . It is very certain that unregulated inquiries and confused reflections of this kind only confound the natural light and blind our mental powers." Our minds naturally possess two powers, namely, *intuition* and *deduction*, "mental powers by which we are able, entirely without fear of illusion, to arrive at the knowledge of things." But by themselves these powers can lead us astray unless they are carefully regulated. Method consists, therefore, in those rules by which our powers of intuition and deduction are guided in an orderly way.

The Example of Mathematics Descartes looked to mathematics for the best example of clear and precise thinking. "My method," he writes, "contains everything which gives certainty to the rules of arithmetic." Indeed, Descartes wanted to make all of knowledge a "universal mathematics." For he was convinced that mathematical certainty is the result of a special *way of thinking,* and if he could discover this *way,* he would have a method for discovering true knowledge "of whatever lay within the compass of my powers." Mathematics is not *itself* the method but merely exhibits the method Descartes is searching for; geometry and arithmetic, he says, are only "examples" or "the outer covering" and not "the constituents" of his new method. What then is there about mathematics that led Descartes to find in it the basis of his own method?

In mathematics, Descartes discovered something fundamental about the operation of the human mind. Specifically, he fastened upon the mind's ability to apprehend directly and clearly certain basic truths. He was not so much concerned with explaining the mechanics of the formation of our ideas from experience as he was with affirming the fact that our minds are capable of knowing some ideas with absolute clarity and distinctness. Moreover, mathematical reasoning showed him that we are able to discover what we do not know by progressing in an orderly way from what we do know. If we can discover the mathematical values of certain terms (e.g., the degree of an angle) from our knowledge of other terms (e.g., the length of lines and degrees of other angles in a triangle), why can we not use this same method of reasoning in other fields as well? Descartes was convinced that we could, for he claimed that his method contained "the primary rudiments of human reason" and that with it he could elicit the "truths in every field whatsoever." To him all the various sciences are merely different ways in which the same powers of reasoning and the same method are used. In each case it is the orderly use of intuition and deduction.

Intuition and Deduction Descartes placed the whole edifice of knowledge upon the foundation of intuition and deduction, saying that "these two methods are the most certain routes to knowledge," adding that any other approach should be "rejected as suspect of error and dangerous. . . ." By *intuition,* Descartes means an intellectual activity or vision of such clarity that it leaves no doubt in the mind. Whereas the fluctuating testimony of our senses and the imperfect creations of our imaginations leave us confused, intuition provides "the conception which an unclouded and attentive mind gives us so readily and distinctly that we are wholly freed from doubt about that which we understand. . . ." Intuition gives us not only clear notions but also some truths about reality, as for example, that *I think*, that *I exist*, and that *a sphere has a single surface*, truths that are basic, simple, and irreducible. Moreover, it is by intuition that we grasp the connection between one truth and another: for example, that two things equal to a thing are equal to each other (if $A = B$ and $C = B$, then $A = C$) is made clear to us by intuition.

By *deduction* Descartes means something similar to intuition, describing it as "all necessary inference from facts that are known with certainty." What makes intuition and deduction similar is that both involve truth: by intuition we grasp a simple truth completely and immediately, whereas by deduction we arrive at a truth by a process, a "continuous and uninterrupted action of the mind. . . ." By tying deduction so closely with intuition, Descartes gave a new interpretation of deduction, which up to his time had been identified with a mode of reasoning called the syllogism. Deduction, as Descartes described it, is different from a syllogism, for whereas a syllogism indicates the relationship of *concepts* to each other, deduction for Descartes indicates the relation of *truths* to each other. It is one thing to move from a fact that is known with certainty to a conclusion that that fact implies, as Descartes indicates we must do by deduction. But it is something different to go from a *premise* to a conclusion as one does in a syllogism. Descartes emphasized this difference between reasoning from a *fact* and from a *premise*, for the central point of his method was at stake here. Descartes was aware that one can reason *consistently* from a premise but argued that the value of the conclusion would depend upon whether the premise was *true* or not. His quarrel with earlier philosophy and theology was that conclusions were drawn syllogistically from premises that were either untrue or else based only upon authority. Descartes wanted to rest knowledge upon a starting point that had absolute certainty in the individual's own mind. Knowledge requires the use, therefore, of intuition and deduction, where "first principles are given by intuition alone while the remote conclusions . . . are furnished only by deduction." Still, Descartes' *method* does not consist only of intuition and deduction, but also in the rules he formulated for their guidance.

Rules of Method   The chief point of Descartes' rules is to provide a clear and orderly procedure for the operation of the mind. It was his conviction that "method consists entirely in the order and disposition of the objects toward which our mental vision must be directed if we would find out any truth." The mind must begin with a simple and absolutely clear truth and must move step by step without losing clarity and certainty along the way. Descartes spent many years at the task of formulating rules for helping the mind choose appropriate starting points for reasoning and to direct the mind in the ordered process of reasoning. Of the twenty-one rules found in his *Rules for the Direction of the Mind*, the following are among the most important. Rule III: When we propose to investigate a subject, "our inquiries should be directed, not to what others have thought, nor to what we ourselves conjecture, but to what we can clearly and perspicuously behold and with certainty deduce. . . ." Rule IV: This is a rule requiring that other rules be adhered to strictly, for "if a man observe them accurately, he shall never assume what is false as true, and will never spend his mental efforts to no purpose. . . ." Rule V: We shall comply with the method exactly if we "reduce involved and obscure propositions step by step to those that are simpler, and then starting with the intuitive apprehension of all those that are absolutely simple, attempt to ascend to the knowledge of all others by precisely similar steps. . . ." Rule VIII: "If in the matters to be examined we come to a step in the series of which our understanding is not sufficiently well able to have an intuitive cognition, we must stop short there."

In a similar way, Descartes formulated four precepts in his *Discourse on Method*, which he believed were perfectly sufficient, "provided I took the firm and unwavering resolution never in a single instance to fail in observing them": "The *first* was never to accept anything for true which I did not clearly know to be such; . . . to comprise nothing more in my judgment than what was presented to my mind so clearly and distinctly as to exclude all ground of doubt. The *second*, to divide each of the difficulties under examination into as many parts as possible, and as might be necessary for its adequate solution. The *third*, to conduct my thoughts in such order that by commencing with objects the simplest and easiest to know, I might ascend by little and little, and, as it were, step by step, to the knowledge of the more complex. . . . And the *last*, in every case to make enumerations so complete, and reviews so general, that I might be assured that nothing was omitted."

Compared with Bacon and Hobbes, Descartes puts very little emphasis in his method upon sense experience and experiment in achieving knowledge. How is it that we know the essential qualities, for example, of a piece of wax, Descartes asks? At one time a piece of wax is hard, has a certain shape, color, size, and fragrance. But when we bring it close to the fire its fragrance vanishes, its shape and color are lost, and its size increases. What remains in the wax that permits us still to know it is wax? "It cannot," says Descartes, "be anything that I observed by means of the senses, since everything in the field of taste, smell, sight, touch, and hearing are changed, and still the same wax nevertheless remains." It is "nothing but my understanding alone which does conceive it . . . solely an inspection by the mind," which enables me to know the true qualities of the wax. And, says Descartes, "what I have said here about the wax can be applied to all other things external to me." He relies for the most part upon the truths contained in the mind, "deriving them from [no] other source than certain germs of truth which exist naturally in our souls." Descartes assumed that we possess certain innate ideas, in the sense that we are "born with a certain disposition or propensity for contracting them." Because we can know these truths, we can be assured of a reliable foundation for our deductions. Descartes was confident that he could start from the beginning and rethink and rebuild all of philosophy by having recourse solely to his own rational powers, and directing them in accordance with his rules. He therefore set out to show that we can have certainty of knowledge not only about mathematical concepts but also about the nature of reality.

Methodic Doubt Descartes used the method of doubt in order to find an absolutely certain starting point for building up our knowledge. Having set out in his *Rules* that we should never accept anything about which we can entertain any doubt, Descartes now tries to doubt everything, saying that "because I wished to give myself entirely to the search after truth, I thought it was necessary for me . . . to reject as absolutely false everything concerning which I could imagine the least ground of doubt. . . ." His intention is clear, for he wants to sweep away all his former opinions, "so that they might later on be replaced, either by others which were better, or by the same, when I had made them conform to the uniformity of a rational scheme."

By this method of doubt, Descartes shows how uncertain our knowledge is, even of what seems most obvious to us. What can be clearer than "that I am here, seated by the fire . . . holding this paper in my hands. . . ." But when I am asleep, I dream that I am sitting by the fire, and this makes me realize that "there are no conclusive indications by which waking life can be distinguished from sleep. . . ." Nor can I be sure that *things* exist for I cannot tell when I am imagining or really knowing, for "I have learned that [my] senses sometimes mislead me." But surely arithmetic, geometry, or sciences that deal with things must contain some certainty, for "whether I am awake or asleep, two and three together will always make the number five." Here Descartes refers to his long-held belief that there is a God who can do anything: but "how can I be sure but that [God] has brought it about that there is no earth, no sky, no extended bodies . . . and that nevertheless I have impressions of these things. . . . And . . . that I am always mistaken when I add two and three. . . ." We cannot be certain that God is supremely good, for "He may be an evil genius not less powerful than deceitful," so that all things I experience "are nothing but illusions and dreams": Descartes is therefore "constrained to confess that there is nothing in what I formerly believed to be true which I cannot somehow doubt."

Reversal of Doubt At this point, Descartes says that "if I am fortunate enough to find a single truth which is certain and indubitable," that will suffice to reverse doubt and establish a philosophy. Like Archimedes, who demanded only an immovable fulcrum to move the earth from its orbit, Descartes searched for his one truth and found it in the very act of doubting.

Cogito and the Self Though I can doubt that my body exists, or that I am awake, or that I am being deceived, in short that all is illusion or false, one thing remains about which I can have no doubt at all, that *I think*. To doubt is to think, and "it must necessarily be that I who [think am] something; and remarking that this truth, *I think*, therefore I am [*cogito ergo sum*], was so solid and so certain that all the most extravagant suppositions of the skeptics were incapable of upsetting it, I judged that I could receive it without scruple as the first principle of the philosophy that I sought." So clear was the truth of his own existence that again Descartes says, "this conclusion, *I think, therefore I am*, is the first and most certain of all which occur to one who philosophizes in an orderly way." Accordingly, Descartes employed this basic truth for reversing his doubts about the self, things, true ideas, and God.

At first, nothing more is proved by this truth, *I think, therefore I am*, than the existence of my thinking self. My doubts still remain about the existence of my own body and about anything else that is other than my thinking. To say *Cogito ergo sum* is to affirm *my* existence: "But what then am I? A thing which thinks. What is a thing which thinks? It is a thing which doubts, understands, affirms, denies, wills, refuses and which also imagines and feels." Throughout, Descartes assumes that because thinking is a fact, there must also be a thinker, "a thing which thinks." This "thing" is not the body, for "I knew that I was a substance the whole nature of which is to think, and that for its existence there is no need of any place, nor does it depend on any material thing." This much then seems absolutely certain, namely, that I, an ego, exist, "for it is certain that no thought can exist apart from a thing which thinks. . . ." But so far, the thinker is alone, a Robinson Crusoe, enclosed in his ideas.

Criterion of Truth   To go beyond the certainty of his own existence as a thinking being, Descartes asks again how we know something to be true: "What," he asks, "is required in a proposition for it to be true and certain?" What is there about the proposition, *Cogito ergo sum* that makes it certain? "I came to the conclusion that I might assume as a general rule that the things which we conceive very *clearly* and *distinctly* are all true." In this context *clear* means "that which is present and apparent to an attentive mind," in the same way that objects are clear to our eyes, and *distinct* refers to "that which is so precise and different from all other objects that it contains within itself nothing but what is clear." The reason, then, that the proposition *I think, therefore I am*, is true is simply that it is clear and distinct to my mind. This is the reason, too, that mathematical propositions are true, for they are so clear and distinct that we cannot help accepting them. But to guarantee the truth of our clear and distinct ideas, Descartes had to prove that God exists and that He is not a deceiver who makes us think that false things are true.

The Existence of God   Descartes cannot use Aquinas' proofs for the existence of God because those proofs are based upon the very facts which are still subject to Descartes' doubt, namely, facts about the external world such as *motion* and *cause* among physical things. Instead, Descartes must prove God's existence solely in terms of his rational awareness of his own existence and internal thoughts. He therefore begins his proof by examining the various ideas that pass through his mind.

Two things strike him about these ideas, that they are caused, and that according to their content they differ markedly from each other. Ideas are effects, and their causes must be discovered. Some of our ideas seem to be "born with me," some "invented" by me, whereas others "come from without." Our reason tells us that "something cannot be derived from nothing" and also that "the more perfect . . . cannot be a consequence of . . . the less perfect." Our ideas possess different degrees of reality, but "it is manifest by natural light that there must be at least as much reality in the efficient and total cause as in the effect." Some of our ideas, judging by the degree of their reality, could have their origin in myself. But the idea of God contains so much "objective reality" that I wonder whether I could have produced that idea by myself. For "by the name God I understand a substance which is infinite, independent, all-knowing, all-powerful and by which I myself and everything else, if anything else exists, have been created." How can I, a finite substance, produce the idea of an infinite substance? Indeed, how could I know that I am finite unless I could compare myself with the idea of a perfect being? The idea of perfection is so clear and distinct that I am convinced that it could not proceed from my imperfect nature. Even if I were *potentially* perfect, the idea of perfection could not come from that potentiality, for an actual effect must proceed from a being that *actually* exists. For these reasons, Descartes concludes that since ideas have causes, and since the cause must have at least as much reality as the effect, and finally since he is finite and imperfect, it must be that the cause of his idea of a perfect and infinite Being comes from outside himself, from a perfect Being who exists, from God. In addition, Descartes concludes that God cannot be a deceiver, "since the light of nature teaches us that fraud and deception necessarily proceed from some defect," which could hardly be attributed to a perfect Being.

In addition to this argument from causation, by which he proved the existence of God, Descartes, following Augustine and Anselm, offered his version of the ontological argument. Whereas in the argument from causation he reasoned that his idea of a perfect Being could not have come from himself because of his own known imperfection, in the ontological argument Descartes sought to demonstrate the existence of God by exploring what the very idea of God implies. He says that if "all which I know clearly and distinctly as pertaining to this object really does belong to it, may I not derive from this an argument demonstrating the existence of God?" How is it possible to move from an analysis of an idea to the certainty that God exists?

Some of our ideas, says Descartes, are so clear and distinct that we immediately perceive what they imply. One cannot, for example, think of a triangle without at once thinking of its lines and angles. Although one cannot think about a triangle without also thinking about its attributes of lines and angles, it does not follow that to think about a triangle implies that it exists. But just as the idea of a triangle implies certain attributes, so also the idea of God implies attributes, and specifically the attribute of existence. The idea of God signifies a perfect Being. But the very idea of perfection implies existence. To speak of a nonexistent perfection is to engage in contradiction. One cannot coherently conceive of a Being who is supremely perfect in all respects and at the same time nonexistent. Just as one cannot think the idea of triangle without recognizing its attributes, so also one cannot think the idea of God, says Descartes, without recognizing that this idea clearly implies the attribute of existence. Descartes says, "That which we clearly and distinctly understand to belong to the true and immutable nature of anything, its essence or form, can be truly affirmed of that thing. But after we have with sufficient accuracy investigated the nature of God, we clearly and distinctly understand that to exist belongs to His true nature. Therefore we can with truth affirm of God that He exists." Against this line of reasoning, Descartes' critic Gassendi said that perfection does not imply existence, since existence is not a necessary attribute of perfection. To lack existence, he said, implies no impairment of perfection, only the lack of reality. Kant, as we shall see, went into considerably greater detail in his criticism of these attempts to prove the existence of God.

Existence of Things From his own existence, Descartes has proved God's existence. Along the way he has also established the criterion of truth and provided thereby the foundation for mathematical thought and for all rational activity. Now, Descartes takes another look at the physical world, at his own body, and other things, and asks whether he can be certain that they exist. To be a thinking thing does not of itself prove that my body exists, for my thinking self "is entirely and absolutely distinct from my body and can exist without it." How then can I know that my body and other physical things exist?

Descartes answers that we all have the clear and distinct experiences of changing our position and moving about, activities that imply a body, or what he calls "an extended substance." We also receive sense impressions, of sight, sound, and touch, frequently even against our will, and these lead us to believe that they come from bodies other than our own. This overwhelming inclination to believe that these impressions "are conveyed to me by corporeal objects" must come from God; otherwise, He could not "be defended from the accusation of deceit if these ideas were produced by causes other than corporeal objects. Hence we must allow that corporeal objects exist." For Descartes, then, knowledge of the self is prior to knowledge of God, and both the self and God are prior to our knowledge of the external world.

Descartes has now reversed all his doubts and has satisfied himself absolutely that the self, things, and God exist. He has concluded that there are thinking things and things that are extended, have dimension. Since a person has both a mind and body, Descartes is left with the problem of indicating how body and mind are related.

Mind and Body The whole drift of Descartes' thought is in the direction of dualism—the notion that there are two different kinds of substances in nature. We know a substance by its attribute, and since we clearly and distinctly know two quite different attributes, namely, *thought* and *extension*, there must be two different substances, the spiritual and the corporeal, mind and body. Because Descartes defines a substance as "an existent thing which requires nothing but itself to exist," he considers each substance as thoroughly independent of the other. To know something about the mind, therefore, we need make no reference to the body, and similarly, the body can be thoroughly understood without any reference to mind. One of the consequences of this dualism was that Descartes hereby separated theology and science and assumed that there need be no conflict between them. Science would study physical nature in isolation of any other discipline, since material substance possessed its own sphere of operation and could be understood in terms of its own laws.

If thought and extension are so distinct and separate, how can one account for living things? Descartes reasoned that because living bodies partake of extension, they are part of the material world. Consequently, living bodies operate according to the same mechanical and mathematical laws that govern other things in the material order. Speaking, for example, of animals, Descartes considered them to be automata, saying that "the greatest of all prejudices we have retained from infancy is that of believing that brutes think." We assume animals think, says Descartes, only because we see them act as humans do on occasion, as when dogs do acrobatic tricks. Because *men* have two principles of motion, one physical and the other mental, we assume that when animals perform humanlike acts, their physical movements are caused by their mental powers. But Descartes saw no reason for attributing mental powers to animals, because all of their motions, or actions, can be accounted for by mechanical considerations alone, since it is "nature which acts in them according to the disposition of their organs, just as a clock, which is only composed of wheels and weights. . . ." Thus animals are machines or automata. But what about human beings?

Many activities of the human body, said Descartes, are as mechanical as those of animals. Such physical acts as respiration, circulation of the blood, and digestion are automatic. The workings of the human body could be reduced, he thought, to physics. Every physical event can be adequately accounted for by a consideration of mechanical or efficient causes; there is no need to consider a final cause when describing the physical processes of the body. Moreover, as Descartes believed that the total quantity of motion in the universe is constant, he was led to conclude that the movements of the human body could not *originate* in the human mind or soul; the soul, he said, could only affect or alter the direction of the motion in certain elements and parts of the body. Just how the mind could do this was difficult to explain precisely, because thought and extension, mind and body, were for Descartes such different and separate substances. He said that the soul does not move the various parts of the body directly but, having "its principal seat in the brain," in the pineal gland, comes first of all in contact with the "vital spirits," and through these the soul interacts with the body. Clearly, Descartes tried to give the human body a mechanical explanation and at the same time preserve the possibility of the soul's influence, through the activity of the will, upon human behavior. Man, therefore, unlike an animal, is capable of several kinds of activities; he can engage in pure thought, his mind can be influenced by physical sensations and perceptions, his body can be directed by his mind, and his body is moved by purely mechanical forces.

But Descartes' strict dualism made it difficult for him to describe how the mind and body could interact upon each other. If each substance is completely independent, the mind must dwell in the body as a pearl in an oyster, or, to use Descartes' own metaphor, as a pilot in a ship. Scholastic philosophy had described man as a unity, in which mind is the form and body is the matter and said that without one there could not be the other. Hobbes had reduced mind to bodies in motion and achieved the unity of man in that way. But Descartes aggravated the separation of mind and body by his novel definition of "thinking," for he included in the act of thinking some experiences that had traditionally been referred to the body, namely, the whole sphere of sense perceptions, for example, "feeling." When Descartes defines "what I am" as "a thing which thinks," he makes no mention of the body, for everything is included in "thinking": a thinking thing "is a thing which doubts, understands, affirms, denies, wills, refuses, and which also imagines and *feels*." Presumably the self could feel heat without a body. But here Descartes cannot, apparently, accept his own dualism, for he admits that "nature also teaches me by these sensations of pain, hunger, thirst, etc., that I am not lodged in my body as a pilot in a vessel, but that I am very closely united to it, and, so to speak, so intermingled with it that I seem to compose with it one whole." He even tried to locate the mind in the pineal gland, though even there the technical problem of interaction remains, for if there is interaction, there would have to be contact, and so mind would have to be extended. On this problem, his rules of method did not lead him to any clear and distinct conclusion.

Some of Descartes' followers struggled with this mind-body problem and proposed some ingenious solutions. Among them, Arnold Geulincx is most notable for his theory of *occasionalism* or *parallelism*. Geulincx maintained Descartes' strict dualism and denied that there is any interaction between mind and body, for they are two separate substances. Still, it is a fact that when I *decide* or *will* to move my arm, it actually moves. But, said Geulincx, my will did not *cause* my arm to move. Rather, there are two parallel series of acts going on simultaneously, one physical and the other mental. When I will to move my arm, on that occasion God moves it and thereby creates an action parallel to my thought. It may even be, he said, that God has decreed this parallelism from the beginning of time. However cumbersome this explanation may seem, it does no violence to Descartes' thought, for Descartes was willing to accept a deterministic explanation of physical nature and also animal nature, and there seems to be nothing to prevent the inclusion here of human nature.

SPINOZA

Spinoza was the greatest of Jewish philosophers. His originality of mind is suggested by his expulsion from the Synagogue of Amsterdam for his unorthodox views. His refusal to accept the chair of philosophy at Heidelberg was further evidence of his desire to preserve his freedom to pursue his ideas wherever the search for truth might lead him. Though he was content to live in simplicity, to earn a modest living grinding lenses, his fame as a thinker spread abroad and aroused both admiration and condemnation. Baruch Spinoza was born in Amsterdam in 1632 in a family of Portuguese Jews who had fled from persecution in Spain. He was trained in the study of the Old Testament and the Talmud and was familiar with the writings of the Jewish philosopher Maimonides. Having been forced to leave Amsterdam, he eventually went, in 1663, to The Hague, where he carried on his literary career, of which his *Ethics* is the crowning work. In 1677 he died of consumption at the age of forty-five.

Spinoza was influenced by Descartes' rationalism, by his method, and by his choice of the major problems of philosophy. But their similarity of interest and even terminology does not mean that Spinoza was a follower of Descartes. At many points Spinoza brought something new to Continental rationalism, which Descartes had begun.

Method   In common with Descartes, Spinoza thought that we can achieve exact knowledge of reality by following the method of geometry. Descartes had worked out the basic form of this method for philosophy, starting with clear and distinct first principles and attempting from these to deduce the whole content of knowledge. What Spinoza added to Descartes' method was a highly systematic arrangement of principles and axioms. Whereas Descartes' method was simple, Spinoza almost set out literally to write a geometry of philosophy, that is, a complete set of axioms or theorems (about 250 altogether) that would explain the whole system of reality the way geometry explains the relations and movement of things. In geometry, conclusions are demonstrated, and Spinoza believed that our theory of the nature of reality could also be demonstrated. Hobbes questioned whether Spinoza had accomplished anything by arranging his vast number of axioms and theorems into a system of knowledge. Hobbes argued that it is certainly possible to draw consistent conclusions from axioms but that since these axioms consist of nothing more than arbitrary definitions, they do not tell us about reality. Spinoza would not agree that his definitions were arbitrary, for he believed, as did Descartes, that our rational powers are capable of forming ideas that reflect the true nature of things: "Every definition or clear and distinct idea," says Spinoza, "is true." It must follow, therefore, that a complete and systematic arrangement of true ideas will give us a true picture of reality, for "the order and connection of ideas is the same as the order and connection of things."

The order of things also provides the pattern for the order in which the philosopher should arrange his subjects. It is of utmost importance to observe this order carefully if we are to understand the various aspects of nature accurately. If, for example, we say that things depend for their nature upon God, we must first know all that we can about God before we can understand things. For this reason Spinoza could find little value in Francis Bacon's method, which consisted of enumerating observations of visible events and drawing conclusions from these observations by induction. Nor would he use Aquinas' method of accounting for the existence of God by first of all analyzing the nature of our ordinary experience with things and persons. At this point, too, Spinoza rejects Descartes' approach, for Descartes started with a clear and distinct idea of his *own* existence and from the formula *I think, therefore I am*, proceeded to deduce the other parts of his philosophy. Because in the true nature of things God is prior to everything else, Spinoza believed that philosophy must formulate ideas about God first so that these ideas could appropriately affect the conclusions we draw about such matters as man's nature, his way of behaving, and the relation of his mind and body. And because Spinoza had such novel things to say about God, it was inevitable that he would say novel things also about human nature. Spinoza, therefore, begins his philosophy with the problem of the nature and existence of God.

God   Spinoza offered a strikingly unique conception of God, in which he identified God with the whole cosmos. His famous formula was *Deus sive Natura*, God or Nature, as if to say that these two words are interchangeable. Although this pantheism could be found in such Biblical descriptions of God as He "in whom we live and move and have our being," Spinoza stripped the idea of God of earlier meanings by emphasizing not the *relation* between God and man but a basic *unity* between them: "Whatever is," he said, "is in God, and nothing can exist or be conceived without God." The clue to Spinoza's unique conception of God is found in his definition: "God I understand to be a being absolutely infinite, that is, a substance consisting of infinite attributes, each of which expresses eternal and infinite essence." Spinoza's special thoughts revolve around the ideas of *substance* and its *attributes*.

Substance and Attributes   Through an intricate sequence of arguments Spinoza arrives at the conclusion that the ultimate nature of reality is a single substance. This substance is infinite. That such a substance does exist and that it is infinite follow from our ability to think certain ideas clearly and distinctly. Spinoza defines substances as "that which is in itself and is conceived through itself: I mean that the conception of which does not depend on the conception of another thing from which it must be formed." Substance, then, has no external cause but has the cause of itself within itself. So far this is only a *conception*, an idea of a self-caused infinite substance. This idea, however, includes not only what this substance is like but also that it exists. The very idea of substance includes its existence, for "existence appertains to substance," and "therefore from its mere definition its existence can be concluded." This resembles Anselm's *ontological* argument and raises the same problems. Still, Spinoza was certain that we can go with assurance from our idea of this perfect substance to its existence, saying that "if anyone says that he has a clear and distinct, that is, a true idea of substance and nevertheless doubts whether such a substance exists, he is like one who says that he has a true idea and yet doubts whether it may not be false." That this substance is one and infinite follows from the previous definition Spinoza has given of substance. There is therefore a single substance with infinite attributes.

An attribute, says Spinoza, is "that which an intellect perceives as constituting the essence of substance." If God is defined as a "substance consisting of infinite attributes," it would appear that there would be an infinite number of substances or that God would possess infinite essence. But Spinoza could very well mean here that since an attribute is "that which an intellect perceives," it is possible for the intellect to perceive the single substance in an infinite number of ways. Actually, says Spinoza, we can know only two attributes of substance, namely, thought and extension. Descartes thought that these two attributes indicated the existence of two substances, thereby leading him to affirm the dualism of mind and body. Spinoza saw these two attributes as different ways of expressing the activity of a single substance. God is therefore substance perceived as infinite thought and infinite extension. Being infinite, God contains everything.

God and the World: The Modes   Spinoza does not contrast God and the world as if they were as different and distinct as cause and effect, as though God were the immaterial cause and the world the material effect. He has already established that there is only one substance and that the word *God* is interchangeable with *Nature*. But Spinoza does distinguish between two aspects of Nature, using for this purpose the two expressions *natura naturans* and *natura naturata*. By *natura naturans* Spinoza means substance and its attributes, or God insofar as He is considered to act by the requirements of His own nature. On the other hand, by *natura naturata*, he means "everything which follows from the necessity of the nature of God, or of any one of God's attributes." Further, "by *natura naturata* I understand . . . all the modes of God's attributes in so far as they are considered as things which are in God, and which without God can neither be nor can be conceived." What in earlier language was called the *world*, Spinoza now calls the *modes* of God's attributes. The *world* is not distinct from God but *is* God expressed in various modes of thought and extension, of thought and corporeality.

Modes and Necessity   As the *world* consists of the modes of God's attributes, everything in the world acts in accordance with necessity, that is, everything is determined. For the modes in which thought and extension take form in the world are determined by God's substance, or, as Spinoza says, these modes represent "everything which follows from the necessity of the nature of God." Spinoza gives us a picture of a tight universe where every event unfolds in the only possible way in which it can occur, for "in the nature of things nothing contingent is granted, but all things are determined by the necessity of divine nature for existing and working in a certain way." In a special way God is free, not that He could have created a different kind of world but that though He had to create just what He did, He was not forced to do this by some external cause, only by His own nature. On the other hand, man is not even that free, for he is determined to exist and behave according to God's substance, of whose attributes man is a mode. All modes of God's attributes are fixed from eternity, for "things could not have been produced by God in any other manner or order than that in which they were produced." All the things we experience "are nothing else than modifications of the attributes of God [Nature], or modes by which attributes are expressed in a certain and determined manner." Thus, everything is intimately connected, the infinite substance providing a continuity through all things, particular things being simply modes or modifications of the attributes of substance, or Nature, or God.

No Final Cause   Because everything is eternally as it must be, and because particular events are simply finite modifications of substance, there is no direction toward which things are moving, no *end*, no *purpose*, no final cause. From our human vantage point, men try to explain events as either fulfilling or frustrating some purpose of history. Ideas of purpose, says Spinoza, are derived from our tendency to act with an end in view. From this habit we tend to look at the universe as though it too had some goal. But this is a wrong way of looking at the universe and indeed at our own behavior. For neither the universe nor human beings are pursuing purposes; they are only doing what they must. This "truth might have lain hidden from the human race through all eternity, had not mathematics, which does not deal with final causes but with the essences of things, offered to men another standard of truth." And the truth is that all events are a continuous and necessary set of modifications of the eternal substance, which simply *is*. Thus Spinoza reduced the biological to the mathematical.

The Levels of Knowledge   But how can Spinoza claim to know the ultimate nature of reality? He distinguishes between three levels of knowledge and describes how we can move from the lowest to the highest. We begin with the things most familiar to us, and, says Spinoza, "the more we understand individual things the more we understand God." By refining our knowledge of things, we can move from (1) *imagination*, to (2) *reason*, and finally to (3) *intuition*.

At the level of *imagination* our ideas are derived from sensation, as when we see another person. Here our ideas are very concrete and specific, and the mind is passive. Though our ideas on this level are specific, they are vague and inadequate, for we know things only as they affect our senses—I know that I *see* a person, but as yet I do not know simply by looking at him what his essential nature is. I can form a general idea, such as *man*, by seeing several men, and the ideas I form from experience are useful for daily life, but they do not give me true knowledge.

The second level of knowledge goes beyond imagination to *reason*. This is scientific knowledge. All men can participate in this kind of knowledge because it is made possible by man's sharing in the attributes of substance, in God's thought and extension. There is in man what is in all things, and since one of these common properties is mind, man's mind shares in the mind that orders things. At this level man's mind can rise above immediate and particular things and deal with abstract ideas, as he does in mathematics and physics. At this level, knowledge is *adequate* and *true*. If we ask Spinoza how we know that these ideas of reason and science are true, he replies in effect that truth validates itself, for "he who has a true idea knows at the same time that he has a true idea, nor can he doubt concerning the truth of the thing."

The third and highest level of knowledge is *intuition*. Through intuition we can grasp the whole system of nature. At this level we can understand the particular things we encountered on the first level in a new way, for at that first level we saw other bodies in a disconnected way, and now we see them as part of the whole scheme. This kind of knowing "proceeds from an adequate idea of the formal essence of certain attributes of God to the adequate knowledge of the essence of things." When we reach this level we become more and more conscious of God and hence "more perfect and blessed," for through this vision we grasp the whole system of Nature and see our place in it, giving us an intellectual fascination with the full order of Nature, of God.

Mind and Body   Descartes was left with the difficult problem of explaining how the mind interacts with the body. This was for him virtually insoluble because he assumed that mind and body represent two distinct substances. For Spinoza, however, this was no problem at all because he viewed mind and body as attributes of a single substance. There is only one order of Nature, to which both the body and mind belong. Man is a single mode. It is only because we are able to consider man as a mode of extension that we speak of his body, and as a mode of thought that we speak of his mind. There can be no separation of mind and body because they are aspects of the same thing. For every body there is a corresponding idea, and, in general, Spinoza says that the mind is the idea of the body, which is his way of describing the relationship of the mind to the body. The structure within which the mind and body operate is the same. Thus, man is a finite version of God, for he is a mode of God's attributes of thought and extension. This interpretation of both man and God set the stage for Spinoza's distinctive theory of ethics.

Ethics   The central feature of Spinoza's account of human behavior is that he treats man as an integral part of Nature. When Spinoza says that he looks upon "human actions and desires exactly as if I were dealing with lines, planes, and bodies," his point is that human behavior can be explained just as precisely in terms of causes, effects, and mathematics as any other natural phenomenon. Although men think they are *free* and are able to make *choices*, they are victims of an illusion, for it is only human ignorance that permits us to think we possess freedom of the will. Men like to think that in some special way they stand outside the rigorous forces of cause and effect, that though their wills can cause actions, their wills are themselves not affected by prior causes. But Spinoza argued for the unity of all Nature, with man as an intrinsic part of it. Spinoza therefore develops a naturalistic ethics whereby all human actions, both mental and physical, are said to be determined by prior causes.

All men possess as a part of their nature the *endeavor* to continue or persist in their own being, and this endeavor Spinoza calls *conatus*. When this *conatus* refers to the mind and body, it is called *appetite*, and insofar as appetite is conscious, it is called *desire*. As we become conscious of higher degrees of self-preservation and perfection, we experience pleasure, and with a reduction of such perfection, we experience pain. Our ideas of good and evil are related to our conceptions of pleasure and pain, for as Spinoza says, "By good I understand here all kinds of pleasure and whatever conduces to it, and more especially that which satisfies our fervent desires, whatever they may be. By bad I understand all kinds of pain, and especially that which frustrates our desires." There is no intrinsic *good* or *bad*, for we call something *good* if we desire it and *bad* if we dislike it. Goodness and badness reflect a subjective evaluation. But because our desires are determined, so are our judgments.

If all our desires and actions are determined by external forces, how can there be any occasion for morality? Here Spinoza resembles the Stoics, who also argued that all events are determined. The Stoics called for resignation and acquiescence to the drift of events, saying that though we cannot control events, we can control our attitudes. In a similar way, Spinoza tells us that through our knowledge of God we can arrive at "the highest possible mental acquiescence." Morality, therefore, consists of improving our knowledge by moving from the level of confused and inadequate ideas up to the third level of intuition, where we have clear and distinct ideas of the perfect and eternal arrangement of all things in God. Only knowledge can lead us to happiness, for only through knowledge can we be liberated from the bondage of our passions. We are enslaved by passions when our desires are attached to perishable things and when we do not fully understand our emotions. The more we understand our emotions, the less excessive will be our appetites and desires. And "the mind has greater power over the emotions and is less subject thereto, in so far as it understands all things as necessary." We must study not only our emotions but the whole order of Nature, for it is only from the perspective of eternity that we can really understand our own particular lives, for then we see all events through the idea of God as cause. Spiritual unhealthiness, says Spinoza, can always be traced to our "excessive love for something which is subject to many variations and which we can never be masters of." But we possess by nature the desire for and the capacity for higher degrees of perfection, and we achieve levels of perfection through our intellectual powers. Passions enslave us only when we lack knowledge. But "from this kind of knowledge necessarily arises the intellectual love of God. From this kind of knowledge arises pleasure accompanied by the idea of God as cause, that is, the love of God; not in so far as we imagine Him as present, but in so far as we understand Him to be eternal; this is what I call the intellectual love of God." This love of God is of course not the love of a divine person but is more akin to the mental pleasure we have when we understand a mathematical formula or a scientific operation. That the way to morality described here is "exceedingly hard" Spinoza was willing to admit, adding that "all things excellent are as difficult as they are rare."

LEIBNIZ

From his early youth, Leibniz showed unmistakable signs of a brilliant mind. At the age of thirteen, he was reading difficult scholastic treatises with the same ease that others would be reading novels. He discovered the infinitesimal calculus and published his results three years before Sir Isaac Newton, who claimed to have made the discovery first, had released his manuscript to the printers. He was a man of the world, courting the favor and receiving the patronage of eminent people. He was personally acquainted with Spinoza, whose philosophy impressed him, though he departed from Spinoza's ideas in decisive ways. Leibniz engaged in extensive correspondence with philosophers, theologians, and men of letters. Among his grand projects were attempts to achieve a reconciliation between Protestantism and Catholicism and an alliance between Christian states, which in his day would have meant a United States of Europe. He became the first president of the Society of the Sciences at Berlin, which was later to become the Prussian Academy.

Gottfried Wilhelm von Leibniz was born at Leipzig in 1646 and entered the university there at the age of fifteen. At Leipzig he studied philosophy, going next to Jena to study mathematics and then to Altdorf, where he completed the course in jurisprudence and received the doctorate in law at the age of twenty-one. With extraordinary vigor he lived actively in the two worlds of action and thought. He was the author of several significant works, including *New Essays on Human Understanding*, in which he examines systematically Locke's *Essay*, *Essays in Theodicy*, which deals with the problem of evil, *Discourse on Metaphysics*, the *New System of Nature and the Interaction of Substances*, and the *Monadology*. He was in the service of the House of Hanover, but when George I became King of England, Leibniz was not invited to go with him, possibly because of his quarrel with Newton. His public influence declined, and in 1716, neglected and unnoticed even by the learned society he founded, he died at the age of seventy.

Substance   Leibniz was dissatisfied with the way Descartes and Spinoza had described the nature of substance, because he felt they had distorted our understanding of human nature, freedom, and the nature of God. To say, as Descartes did, that there are two independent substances, thought and extension, was to produce the impossible dilemma of trying to explain how those two substances could interact as body and mind either in man or in God. Spinoza had tried to solve the dilemma by saying that there is only one substance with two knowable attributes, thought and extension. But to reduce all reality to a single substance was to lose the distinction between the various elements in nature. To be sure, Spinoza spoke of the *world* as consisting of many *modes*, in which the attributes of thought and extension appear. Still, Spinoza's monism was a pantheism in which God was everything and everything was part of everything else. To Leibniz, this conception of substance was inadequate because it blurred the distinctions between God, man, and nature, each of which Leibniz wanted to keep separate. Paradoxically, Leibniz accepted Spinoza's single-substance theory and his mechanical model of the universe but presented such a unique theory of this one substance that he was able to speak of the individuality of persons, the transcendence of God, and the reality of purpose and freedom in the universe.

Extension versus Force   Leibniz challenged the fundamental assumption upon which both Descartes and Spinoza had built their theory of substance, namely, that *extension* implies actual size and shape. Descartes assumed that *extension* refers to a material substance that is extended in space and is not divisible into something more primary. Spinoza, too, considered extension as an irreducible material attribute of God or Nature. Leibniz disagreed. Observing that the bodies or things we see with our senses are divisible into smaller parts, why can we not assume, asked Leibniz, that all things are compounds or aggregates? "There must be," he said, "simple substances, since there are compound substances, for the compound is only a collection or *aggregatum* of simple substances."

There is nothing new in saying that things must be made of simple substances, for Democritus and Epicurus had argued centuries before that all things consist of small atoms. But Leibniz rejected this notion of atoms, because Democritus had described these atoms as extended bodies, as irreducible bits of matter. Such a particle of matter would have to be considered lifeless or inert and would have to get its motion from something outside itself. Rejecting the idea of matter as primary, Leibniz argued that the truly simple substances are the *monads*, and these are "the true atoms of nature . . . the elements of things." The monads differ from atoms in that atoms were viewed as extended bodies, whereas Leibniz described the monad as being *force* or *energy*. Leibniz therefore said that matter is not the primary ingredient of things but that monads with their element of force constitute the essential substance of things.

Monads Leibniz wanted to emphasize that substance must contain life or a dynamic force. Whereas Democritus' material atom would have to be acted upon from outside itself in order to move or become a part of a large cluster, Leibniz said that simple substance, the monad, is "capable of action." He added that "*compound* substance is the collection of *monads*. *Monas* is a Greek word which signifies unity, or that which is one. . . . Simple substances, lives, souls, spirits are unities. Consequently all nature is full of life."

Monads are unextended, they have no shape or size. A monad is a point, not a mathematical or a physical point but a metaphysically existent point. Each monad is independent of other monads, and monads do not have any causal relation to each other. It is difficult to imagine a *point* that has no shape or size, yet Leibniz wanted to say just this in order to differentiate the monad from a material atom. Actually his thinking here resembles the twentieth-century notion that physical particles are reducible to energy, or that particles are a special form of energy. Essentially Leibniz was saying that monads are logically prior to any corporeal forms. True substances, then, are monads, and these Leibniz also calls *souls* to emphasize their nonmaterial nature. Each monad is different from the others, and each possesses its own principle of action, its own force, and, says Leibniz, "there is a certain sufficiency which makes them the source of their internal actions and, so to speak, incorporeal automata." Monads are not only independent and different. They also contain the source of their activity within themselves. Moreover, in order to emphasize that the rest of the universe does not affect their behavior, Leibniz says that the monads are *windowless*. But there must be some relation between all the monads which make up the universe, some explanation for their orderly actions. This explanation Leibniz finds in his idea of a *preestablished harmony*.

Preestablished Harmony   Each monad behaves in accordance with its own created purpose. These *windowless* monads, each following its own purpose, form a unity or the ordered universe. Even though each is isolated from the other, their separate purposes form a large-scale harmony. It is as though several clocks all struck the same hour because they keep perfect time. Leibniz compares all these monads to "several different bands of musicians and choirs, playing their parts separately, and so placed that they do not see or even hear one another . . . nevertheless [they] keep perfectly together, by each following their own notes, in such a way that he who hears them all finds in them a harmony that is wonderful, and much more surprising than if there had been any connection between them." Each monad, then, is a separate world, but all the activities of each monad occur in harmony with the activities of the others. In this way it can be said that each monad mirrors the whole universe (but from a unique perspective), in the sense that if anything "were taken away or supposed different, all things in the world would have been different" from what they are like at present. Such a harmony as this could not be the product of an accidental assortment of monads but must be, said Leibniz, the result of God's activity, whereby this harmony is preestablished.

God's Existence   To Leibniz, this fact of a universal harmony of all things provided a "new proof of the existence of God." He had accepted, for the most part, the earlier attempts to prove God's existence, saying that "nearly all of the means which have been employed to prove the existence of God are good and might be of service, if we would perfect them. . . ." But he was particularly impressed by "this perfect harmony of so many substances which have no communication with each other," saying that this harmony pointed to the existence of God with "surprising clearness," because a harmony of many windowless substances "can only come from a common cause." This resembles the argument from design and from a first cause although Leibniz modified the argument from cause with his principle of *sufficient reason*.

Principle of Sufficient Reason   Any event, said Leibniz, can be explained by referring to a prior cause. But that prior cause must itself be explained by a still earlier cause. If all the causes we refer to are alike in that they must be caused, we could never truly explain the reason for any event. It is not sufficient to point to the immediate or proximate cause, for we are left with the problem of explaining *its* existence. Only by referring to some cause outside the series of causes, or outside the complex organization of the universe, can the solution be found for the existence of any particular thing. The final reason, or the sufficient reason, for all things is found in a substance whose own existence is necessary, whose existence requires no cause or further explanation, a Being "whose essence involves existence, for this is what is meant by a necessary Being." The sufficient reason for the ordinary things we experience in the world of fact lies therefore in a Being outside the series of obvious causes, in a Being whose very nature or essence is a sufficient reason for its own existence, requring no prior cause, and this Being is God.

Evil and the Best of All Possible Worlds

Evil and the Best of All Possible Worlds   The harmony of the world led Leibniz to argue not only that God had preestablished it but also that in doing this God has created the best of all possible worlds. Whether this is the best or even a good world is open to question because of the disorder and evil in it. Indeed, Schopenhauer thought that this is, if anything, the worst of all possible worlds and that consequently we are not justified in concluding that God exists or that the world with all its evil is the creation of a good God. Leibniz was aware of the fact of evil and disorder but considered it compatible with the notion of a benevolent Creator. In his perfect knowledge, God could consider all the possible kinds of worlds he could create, but his choice must be in accord with the moral requirement that the world should contain the greatest possible amount of good. Such a world would not be without imperfection. On the contrary, the world of creation consists of limited and imperfect things, "for God could not give the creature all without making it God; therefore there must needs be . . . limitations also of every kind." The source of evil is not God but rather the very nature of things God creates, for as these things are finite or limited, they are imperfect. Evil, then, is not something substantial but merely the absence of perfection. Evil for Leibniz is privation. This is why Leibniz could say that "God wills *antecedently* the good and *consequently* the best," since the most that God can do, in spite of his goodness, is to create the best possible world. As a final consideration, Leibniz agrees that we cannot rightly appraise evil if we consider only the particular evil thing or event. Some things that in themselves appear to be evil turn out to be the prerequisites for good, as when "sweet things become insipid if we eat nothing else; sharp, tart and even bitter things must be combined with them, so as to stimulate the taste." Again, events in our lives, taken by themselves, lose their true perspective. Leibniz asks, "If you look at a very beautiful picture, having covered up the whole of it except a very small part, what will it present to your sight, however thoroughly you examine it . . . but a confused mass of colors, laid on without selection and without art? Yet if you remove the covering, and look at the whole picture from the right point of view, you will find that what appeared to have been carelessly daubed on the canvas was really done by the painter with very great art."

Freedom

Freedom   How can there be any freedom in the determined world Leibniz portrays, where God preestablishes an orderly arrangement by infusing specific purposes into the several monads? Each monad is involved in developing its built-in purpose, and "every present state of a simple substance is naturally a consequence of its preceding state, in such a way that its present is big with its future." Each person, whose identity centers around a dominant monad, his soul, must represent in this mechanical view an unfolding of a life that has been set from the beginning. Yet, since the basic nature of this person is thought, his development through life consists in overcoming confused thoughts and arriving at true ideas, which lie in all of us in the murky form of potentiality seeking to become actual. When our potentialities become actual, we see things as they really are, and this, says Leibniz, is what it means to be free. For him freedom does not mean volition, the power of choice, but rather self-development, so that although one is determined to act in specific ways, it is his own internal nature that determines his acts and not outside forces. Freedom in this sense means the ability to become what one is destined to be without obstructions, and it also means a quality of existence whereby one's knowledge has passed from confusion to clarity. The free man is one who knows why he does what he does. It was along these lines that Leibniz thought he had succeeded in reconciling his deterministic view of nature with freedom.

Whether Leibniz succeeded in reconciling his world of monads with the notion of freedom is certainly questionable. Although he does at one point speak of freedom in terms of "choice in our will" and say that "free and voluntary mean the same thing," still his dominant emphasis appears to be upon determinism, upon the notion of a mechanical-like universe, a spiritual machine. Actually, Leibniz does not use the mechanical model in describing the universe, for if he did, he would have to say that the various parts of the universe act upon each other the way parts of a clock affect the movements of each other. In a sense, Leibniz's explanation is even more rigorously deterministic than the mechanical model suggests, for his monads are all independent of each other, are not affected by each other, but behave in accordance with their original purpose which they received from the beginning through God's creation. This kind of determinism is more rigorous because it does not depend upon the vagaries of external causation but upon the given and permanently fixed internal nature of each monad.

Knowledge and Nature   This deterministic view of nature is further supported by Leibniz's theory of knowledge. A person, for example, is for Leibniz similar to a subject in the grammatical sense. For any true sentence or proposition, the predicate is already contained in the subject. Thus, to know the subject is already to know certain predicates. "All men are mortal" is a true proposition because the predicate *mortal* is already contained in the notion of *men*. Leibniz therefore says that in any true proposition "I find that every predicate, necessary or contingent, past, present, or future, is comprised in the notion of the subject. . . ." Similarly, in the nature of things, all substances are, so to speak, subjects, and the things they do are their predicates. Just as grammatical subjects contain their predicates, so also existing substances already contain their future behavior. Thus, Leibniz concludes that "in saying that the individual notion of Adam involves all that will ever happen to him, I mean nothing else but what all philosophers mean when they say that the predicate is in the subject of a true proposition." Leibniz patterned his theory of substance or metaphysics after his theory of knowledge or logic. At the center of his argument is his special treatment of the notion of truth.

Leibniz distinguished between truths of reason and truths of fact. We know truths of reason purely by logic, whereas we know truths of fact by experience. The test of a truth of reason is the law of contradiction, and the test for a truth of fact is the law of sufficient reason. A truth of reason is a necessary truth in that to deny it is to be involved in a contradiction. Truths of fact, on the other hand, are contingent, and their opposite is possible. A truth of reason is a necessary truth because the very meaning of the terms used and the mode of human understanding require that certain things be true. For example, that a triangle has three sides is true because to have three sides is what a triangle means. To say that a triangle has four sides is clearly to be involved in a contradiction. That 2 and 2 equals 4, that A is A, that A is not not-A, that heat is not cold—all these propositions are true because to deny their truth would be contradictory. Truths of reason are tautologies, because in such propositions the predicate simply repeats what is already contained in the subject. Once the subject is clearly understood, there needs to be no further proof about the truth of the predicate. Truths of reason do not require or affirm that the subject of the proposition exists. It is true, for example, that a triangle has three sides even though one does not refer to any specific existing triangle. Truths of reason tell us what would be true in any case where a subject, in this case triangles, is involved. They deal with the sphere of the possible. That a triangle should be a square is never possible, would be contradictory, and therefore cannot be true.

Mathematics is a striking example of the truths of reason, since its propositions are true when they pass the test of the law of contradiction. Thus Leibniz says that "the great foundation of mathematics is the principle of contradiction . . . that is, that a proposition cannot be true and false at the same time. . . . This single principle is sufficient to demonstrate every part of arithmetic and geometry. . . ." In short, truths of reason are self-evident truths. They are *analytic* propositions, the predicate of which is contained already in the subject, and to deny the predicate is to be involved in a contradiction.

What about truths of fact? These truths are known through experience. They are not necessary propositions. Their opposites can be considered possible without contradiction, and for this reason their truth is contingent. The statement "Mary exists" is not a truth of reason; its truth is not a priori. There is nothing in the subject *Mary* that necessarily implies, or makes it possible for us to deduce, the predicate *exists*. We know the predicate that she exists only *a posteriori*, after an experience. This truth of fact, as is the case with all truths of fact, is based upon the law of sufficient reason, which says that "nothing happens without a reason why it should be so rather than otherwise." As it stands, the proposition "Mary exists" is contingent upon some sufficient reason. In the absence of any sufficient reason, it would be just as true to say that "Mary does not exist." When a sufficient reason is present, other propositions have a basis of truth, so that we say "if A, then B." This hypothetical character of A indicates that although there may be a necessary connection between A and B, it is not absolutely necessary that A exist. The existence of A is contingent, that is, is *possible.* Whether it will in fact exist depends upon whether there is or will be a sufficient reason for it to exist. About every truth of fact one can think of its opposite as possible without contradiction.

When one considers all the possibilities that propositions about facts imply, a principle of limitation emerges. Whereas some events can be considered possible, simply as the opposite of others, they cannot be possible once certain other possibilities have become actual. That is, some possibilities are *compossible* with some events though not with others. Thus Leibniz says that "not all possible species are compossible in the universe, great as it is, and that this holds not only in regard to things which exist contemporaneously but also in regard to the whole series of things."

The universe of facts, as we know it, is only a collection of certain kinds of compossibles, that is, the collection of all the existent possibles. There could be other combinations of possibles than the ones our actual universe contains. The relation of the various possibles to each other requires us to understand the sufficient reason that connects each event to another event. Physical science, unlike mathematics, cannot, however, be a deductive discipline. The truths of mathematics are analytic. But in propositions concerning facts, the subject does not contain the predicate. The law of sufficient reason, which governs truths of fact, requires that these truths be verified. But this verification is always partial, since each preceding event in the causal chain of events must also be verified. However, no human being is able to account for the infinite sequence of causes. If the cause of *A* is *B*, it is then necessary to account for the cause of *B* and to go back as far as the beginning. The first fact about the universe is like any other fact; it does not contain, so far as the power of human analysis is capable of discovering, any clearly necessary predicate. To know its truth requires that we discover the sufficient reason for its being what it is.

The final explanation of the world, says Leibniz, is that "the true cause why certain things exist rather than others is to be derived from the free decrees of the divine will. . . ." Things are as they are because God willed them to be that way. Having willed some things to be what they are, He limited the number of other possibilities and determined which events can be compossible. God could have willed other universes, other combinations of possibilities. But having willed this universe, there now exist certain necessary connections between specific events. Although from the perspective of human reason, propositions concerning the world of facts are *synthetic*, or require experience and verification, if we are to know their truth, these propositions are, from God's perspective, *analytic*. Only God can deduce all the predicates of any substance. And only our ignorance prevents us from being able to see in any particular person all the predicates that are connected with him. In the end, truths of fact are also analytic, according to Leibniz. A person does already contain his predicates, so that if we really comprehended the complete notion of a person, we could deduce these predicates, as, for example, "the quality of king, which belongs to Alexander the Great. . . ." Thus, "God, seeing the individual notion of Alexander, sees in it at the same time the foundation and the reason of all the predicates which can be truly attributed to him, as, for example, whether he would conquer Darius and Porus, even to knowing *a priori* [and not by experience] whether he died a natural death or by poison which we [with our limited human intellects] can only know by history."

For Leibniz, then, logic is a key to metaphysics. From the grammar of propositions, he inferred conclusions about the real world. In the end, he argued that all true propositions are analytic. For this reason, substances and persons are for Leibniz equivalent to subjects of an analytic proposition; they really contain, he said, all their predicates. He also applies his *law of continuity* to his notion of substance in order to confirm his theory that each substance unfolds its predicates in an orderly and (from God's perspective) predictable way. The *law of continuity* states that "Nature makes no leaps." Among created things, every possible position is occupied, so that all change is continuous. According to the law of continuity rest and motion are aspects of each other, merging into each other through infinitesimal changes, "so much so that the rule of rest ought to be considered as a particular case of the rule of motion." The *windowless* monads, then, bear in themselves all their future behavior. And as this is true of each monad, all the combinations and possibilities of events already contained in the world also contain the whole future of the world, and the sufficient reason for this order is ". . . the supreme reason, which does everything in the most perfect way." Although the human mind cannot know all reality as God knows it, still, says Leibniz, it contains certain innate ideas, self-evident truths. A child does not know all these truths at once but must wait until maturity and for specific occasions in experience when these ideas are called forth. That these ideas become known only on such occasions makes them *virtually* innate. Still, this doctrine of innate ideas, along with Leibniz's general treatment of the relation of logic to reality, reflected his optimistic appraisal of the capacity of reason to know reality and his belief that from innate self-evident truths considerable knowledge of the real world could be deduced.

Empiricism in Britain: Locke, Berkeley, and Hume

Although the school of empiricism came upon the scene in an unpretentious way, it was destined to alter the course and concerns of modern philosophy. Whereas Bacon aimed at "the total reconstruction of . . . all human knowledge," Locke, who was the founder of empiricism in Britain, aimed at the more modest objective of "clearing the ground a little, and removing some of the rubbish that lies in the way to knowledge." But in the process of "clearing" and "removing," Locke hit upon a bold and original interpretation of how the mind works and from this described the kind and extent of knowledge we can expect from the human mind.

The scope of our knowledge, Locke said, is limited to, and by, our experience. This was not a new insight, for others before him had said much the same thing. Both Bacon and Hobbes had urged that knowledge should be built upon observation, and to this extent they could be called empiricists. But neither Bacon nor Hobbes raised any critical question about the intellectual powers of man. Although both uncovered and rejected modes of thought that they considered fruitless and erroneous, they nevertheless accepted without challenge the general view that the mind is capable of producing certainty of knowledge about nature provided only that the proper method is used. Similarly, Descartes assumed that there was no problem that human reason could not solve if the correct method was employed. This was the assumption Locke called into critical question, namely, the assumption that the human mind has capabilities that enable it to discover the true nature of the universe. David Hume pushed this critical point even further and asked whether any secure knowledge at all is possible. In their separate ways, the British empiricists Locke, Berkeley, and Hume challenged not only their English predecessors but also the Continental rationalists, who had launched modern philosophy upon an optimistic view of man's rational powers that the empiricists could not accept.

LOCKE

John Locke was born in 1632 at Wrington, Somerset, and died seventy-two years later in 1704. He grew up in a Puritan home, trained in the virtues of hard work and the love of simplicity. After a thorough training in the classics at Westminster School, Locke became a student at Oxford University, where he took the Bachelor's and Master's degrees and was appointed Senior Student and later Censor of Moral Philosophy. He spent thirty years of his life in the city of Oxford. Though he continued his studies of Aristotle's logic and metaphysics, he was gradually drawn toward the newly developing experimental sciences, being influenced in this direction particularly by Sir Robert Boyle. His scientific interests led him to pursue the study of medicine, and in 1674 he obtained his medical degree and was licensed to practice. As he pondered what direction his career might take, there was added to the considerations of medicine and Oxford Tutor an alternative, diplomacy. He actually served in various capacities, eventually becoming the personal physician and confidential adviser to the Earl of Shaftesbury, one of the leading politicians of London. But earlier influences, among them his reading of Descartes' works while at Oxford, confirmed his desire to devote his creative powers to working out a philosophical understanding of certain problems that perplexed his generation. He wrote on such diverse topics as *The Reasonableness of Christianity, An Essay Concerning Toleration,* and the *Consequences of the Lowering of Interest and Raising the Value of Money,* indicating his active participation in the public affairs of his day.

In 1690, when he was fifty-seven years old, Locke published two books, which were to make him famous as a philosopher and as a political theorist: *An Essay Concerning Human Understanding* and *Two Treatises of Civil Government.* Although other philosophers before him had written about human knowledge, Locke was the first one to produce a full-length inquiry into the scope and limits of the human mind. Similarly, others had written important works on political theory, but Locke's second of the *Two Treatises* came at a time when it could shape the thoughts of an era and later affect the course of events. The *Two Treatises* and *Essay* indicate Locke's way of combining his practical and theoretical interests and abilities. The *Two Treatises* were expressly formulated to justify the revolution of 1688. Some of its ideas took such strong hold upon succeeding generations that phrases contained in it, as for example, that men are "all equal and independent" and possess the natural rights to "life, health, liberty and possessions," worked their way into the Declaration of Independence and affected the shaping of the American Constitution. Regarding his *Essay*, he tells us that it grew out of an experience that occurred about twenty years before this work was published. On that occasion, five or six friends met to discuss a point in philosophy, and before long they were hopelessly snarled, "without coming any nearer a resolution of those doubts which perplexed us." Convinced that the discussion had taken a wrong turn, Locke decided that before one could move directly into such a subject as "the principles of morality and revealed religion," it was necessary "to examine our own abilities, and see what *objects* our understandings were, or were not, fitted to deal with." From this examination Locke eventually composed his *Essay on Human Understanding*, which became the foundation of empiricism in Britain.

Locke (*New York Public Library Picture Collection*)

Locke's Theory of Knowledge Locke set out "to enquire into the origin, certainty, and extent of human knowledge. . . ." He assumed that if he could describe what knowledge consists of and how it is obtained, he could determine the limits of knowledge and decide what constitutes intellectual certainty. His conclusion was that knowledge is restricted to *ideas*, not Plato's Ideas or Forms, but ideas that are generated by objects we experience. The origin of ideas is *experience*, and experience takes two forms, *sensation* and *reflection*. Without exception, then, all our ideas come to us through the senses, whereby we experience the world external to us, and through reflection upon these ideas, which is an experience internal to us. What Locke wanted to make quite clear was that we cannot have the experience of *reflection* until we have had the experience of *sensation*. For reflection means simply the mind's taking notice of its own operations; but its operations begin when the mind is provided with ideas, and these ideas come from without through the senses. This means that each person's mind is in the beginning like a blank sheet of paper upon which experience alone can subsequently write knowledge. Before he could elaborate these conclusions, Locke felt that he must lay to rest the persisting theory of innate ideas, the notion that in some way we all come into the world with a standard stock of ideas built into the mind.

No Innate Ideas It is obvious that if Locke is going to say that all ideas come from experience, he must reject the theory of innateness. He points out that "It is an established opinion among some men, that there are in the understanding certain innate principles . . . stamped upon the mind of man, which the soul receives in its very first beginning, and brings into the world with it." Not only does Locke reject this as not true, but he considers this doctrine a dangerous tool in the hands of those who could misuse it. If a skillful ruler could convince people that certain principles are innate, this could "take them off from the use of their own reason and judgment, and put them on believing and taking them upon trust without further examination," and "in this posture of blind credulity, they might be more easily governed. . . ." But there were those whose interest in the theory of innate ideas was not so malignant, as in the case of Cudworth, the Cambridge Platonist, who published *The True Intellectual System of the Universe* in 1678, just at the time when Locke was trying to sort out his thoughts on these problems. Cudworth took the position that the demonstration of the existence of God rested upon the premise that certain principles are innate in the human mind. It was his contention that the famous empiricist formula that "nothing exists in the intellect which was not first in the senses" leads to atheism. He reasoned that if knowledge consists solely of information supplied to the mind by objects external to it, the external world existed before there was knowledge. In that case, knowledge could not have been the cause of the world. Locke disagreed with this view, saying that it was indeed possible to prove the existence of God without recourse to the notion of innate principles. He was particularly concerned to expose the groundless claim for innate ideas in order to keep clear the distinction between prejudice, enthusiasm, and opinion, on the one hand, and knowledge on the other. He therefore set out a series of arguments against this claim to innate ideas.

Those who argued for the theory of innate ideas did so on the grounds that men universally accept as true and certain various rational principles. Among these are the principles that "What is, is," which is the principle of identity, and that "It is impossible for the same thing to be, and not to be," which is the principle of noncontradiction. But are these innate? Locke denies that they are, though he does not question their certainty. These principles are certain not because they are innate but because the mind, reflecting on the nature of things as they are, will not let us think otherwise. To enforce this line of reasoning, Locke suggests first of all that even if it were true that these principles were accepted as true by all men, this would not prove that they were innate, provided that an alternative explanation could be given for this universal consent. Moreover, there is some question whether there is universal knowledge of these principles. "Seldom," says Locke, are these general principles "mentioned in the huts of Indians, much less are they found in the thoughts of children. . . ." If it is argued that such principles can be apprehended only after the mind matures, then why call them innate? If they were truly innate, they must always be known, for "No proposition can be said to be in the mind, which it never yet knew, which it never yet was conscious of." As Locke saw the matter, the doctrine of innate ideas was superfluous because it contained nothing that he could not explain in terms of his empirical account of the origin of ideas.

Simple and Complex Ideas   Locke assumed that knowledge could be explained by discovering the raw materials out of which it was made. Of these ingredients he spoke this way: "Let us then suppose the mind to be, as we say, white paper, void of all characters, without any ideas:—How comes it to be furnished? . . . Whence has it all the *materials* of reason and knowledge? To this I answer, in one word, from EXPERIENCE." Experience gives us two sources of ideas, sensation and reflection. From the senses we receive into our minds several distinct perceptions and thereby become conversant about objects external to us. This is how we come to have the ideas of yellow, white, heat, cold, soft, hard, bitter, sweet, and all other sensible qualities. Sensation is the "great source of most of the ideas we have. . . ." The other facet of experience is reflection, an activity of the mind that produces ideas by taking notice of previous ideas furnished by the senses. Reflection involves perception, thinking, doubting, believing, reasoning, knowing, willing, and all those activities of the mind that produce ideas as distinct as those we receive from external bodies affecting our senses. All the ideas men have can be traced either to sensation or to reflection, and these ideas are either simple or complex.

Simple ideas constitute the chief source of the raw materials out of which our knowledge is made. These ideas are received passively by the mind through the senses. When we look at an object, ideas come into our minds single file. Even though an object has several qualities blended together, such as a white lily that has the qualities of whiteness and sweetness without any separation, the mind receives the ideas of *white* and *sweet* separately, because each idea enters through a different sense, namely the sense of sight and the sense of smell. But even if different qualities entered by the same sense, as when both the hardness and coldness of ice come through the sense of touch, the mind sorts out the difference between them because there are in fact two different qualities involved. Simple ideas originate first of all, then, in sensation. But they also originate in reflection. Just as the senses are affected by objects, so also the mind is *aware* of the ideas it has received. In relation to the ideas received through the senses, the mind can develop other simple ideas by reasoning and judging, so that a simple idea of reflection might be pleasure or pain, or the idea of power obtained from observing the effect natural bodies have on one another.

Complex ideas, on the other hand, are not received passively but are rather put together by the mind as a compound of simple ideas. Here the emphasis is upon the activity of the mind, which takes three forms as the mind *joins* ideas, *brings* ideas together but holds them separate, and *abstracts*. Thus, the mind joins the ideas of whiteness, hardness, and sweetness to form the complex idea of a lump of sugar. The mind also brings ideas together but holds them separate for the purpose of thinking of relationships, as when we say the grass is greener than the tree. Finally, the mind can separate ideas "from all other ideas that accompany them in their real existence [as when we separate the idea of *man* from John and Peter]; and thus all its general ideas are made."

Primary and Secondary Qualities   To describe in even more detail how we get our ideas, Locke turned his attention to the problem of how ideas are related to the objects that produce them. Do our ideas reproduce exactly the objects we sense? If, for example, we consider a snowball, what is the relation between our ideas that the snowball engenders in our minds and the actual nature of the snowball? We have such ideas as round, moving, hard, white, and cold. To account for these ideas, Locke says that objects have *qualities*, and he defines a quality as "the power [in an object] to produce any idea in our mind." The snowball, then, has qualities that have the power to produce ideas in our minds.

Locke attempts here an important distinction between two different kinds of qualities in order to answer the question of how ideas are related to objects. He terms these qualities *primary* and *secondary*. Primary qualities are those that "really do exist in the bodies themselves"; thus our ideas, caused by primary qualities, resemble exactly those qualities that belong inseparably to the object. The snowball looks round and *is* round, appears to be moving and *is* moving. Secondary qualities, on the other hand, produce ideas in our mind that have no exact counterpart in the object. We have the idea of *cold* when we touch the snowball and the idea *white* when we see it. But there is no whiteness or coldness in the snowball; what *is* in the snowball is the quality, the power to create in us the ideas of cold and white. Primary qualities, then, refer to solidity, extension, figure, motion or rest, and number, or qualities which belong to the object. Secondary qualities, such as colors, sounds, tastes, and odors, do not belong to or constitute bodies except as powers to produce these ideas in us.

The importance of Locke's distinction between primary and secondary qualities is that through it he sought to distinguish between appearance and reality. Locke did not invent this distinction. Democritus had long ago suggested something similar when he said that colorless atoms are the basic reality and that colors, tastes, and odors are the results of particular organizations of these atoms. Descartes also separated secondary qualities from the basic substance he called *extension*. Locke's distinction reflected his interest in the new physics and the influence of the "judicious Mr. Newton's incomparable book" upon his thought. Newton explained the appearance of *white* as the motions of invisible minute particles. Reality, then, is found not in whiteness, which is only an effect, but in the motion of something, which is the cause. His discussion of primary and secondary qualities assumed throughout that there was *something* that could possess these qualities, and this he called *substance*.

Substance   Locke approached the question of substance from what he regarded as a common-sense point of view. How can we have ideas of qualities without supposing that there is something, some substance, in which these qualities subsist? If we ask what has shape or color, we answer something solid and extended. *Solid* and *extended* are primary qualities, and if we ask in what they subsist, Locke answers *substance*. However inevitable the idea of substance may be to common sense, Locke was unable to describe it with precision, admitting that "if any one will examine himself concerning his notion of pure substance in general, he will find he has no other idea of it at all, but only a supposition of he knows not what support of such qualities which are capable of producing simple ideas in us." Still, Locke saw in the concept of substance the explanation of sensation, saying that sensation is caused by substance. Similarly, it is substance that contains the powers that give regularity and consistency to our ideas. Moreover it is substance, Locke held, that constitutes the object of sensitive knowledge.

Locke was impelled by the simple logic of the matter, that if there is motion, there must be something that moves, that qualities cannot float around without something that holds them together. We have ideas of *matter* and of *thinking*, but "we shall never be able to know whether any mere material being thinks or no." But if there is thinking, there must be something that thinks. We also have an idea of God, which, like the idea of substance in general, is not clear and distinct. Yet, "if we examine the idea we have of the incomprehensible supreme being, we shall find that we come by it in the same way, and that the complex ideas we have both of God and separate spirits are made up of the simple ideas that we receive from reflection." The idea of God, as the idea of substance, is inferred from other simple ideas and is the product not of immediate observation but of demonstration. But the idea of substance, being "something we know not what," does raise for Locke the question of just how far our knowledge extends and how much validity it has.

The Degrees of Knowledge   How far our knowledge extends and how much validity it has depend, according to Locke, upon the relations our ideas have to each other. Indeed, Locke finally defines knowledge as nothing more than "the perception of the connexion of and agreement, or disagreement and repugnancy of any of our ideas." Our ideas enter single file into our minds, but once they are inside they can become related to each other in many ways. Some of the relations our ideas have to each other depend upon the objects we experience. At other times, our imagination can rearrange our simple and complex ideas to suit our fancy. Whether our knowledge is fanciful or valid depends upon our *perception* of the relationships of our ideas to each other. There are three modes of perception, namely, *intuitive, demonstrative*, and *sensitive*, and each one leads us to a different degree of knowledge regarding reality.

Intuitive knowledge is immediate, leaves no doubt, and is "the clearest and most certain that human frailty is capable of." Such knowledge "like sunshine forces itself immediately to be perceived as soon as ever the mind turns its view that way." Instantly we know that a circle is not a square or that 6 is not 8, because we can perceive the repugnancy of these ideas to each other. But besides these formal or mathematical truths, intuition can lead us to a knowledge of what exists. From intuition we know that we exist: "Experience then convinces us, that we have intuitive knowledge of our own existence, and an internal infallible perception that we are."

Demonstrative knowledge occurs when our minds engage in trying to discover the agreement or disagreement of ideas by calling attention to still other ideas. Ideally, each step of the demonstration must have intuitive certainty. This is particularly the case in mathematics, but again Locke thought that demonstration is a mode of perception that leads the mind to a knowledge of some form of existing reality. Thus "man knows, by an intuitive certainty, that bare nothing can no more produce any real being than it can be equal to two right angles." From this starting point Locke argued that since there are in fact existing things that begin and end in time, and since a "nonentity cannot produce any real being, it is an evident demonstration, that from eternity there has been something." Reasoning in a similar way, he concludes that this eternal Being is "most knowing" and "most powerful" and that "it is plain to me we have a more certain knowledge of the existence of God, than of anything our senses have not immediately discovered to us."

Sensitive knowledge is not knowledge in the strict sense of the term; it only "passes under the name of knowledge." Locke did not doubt that things outside of us exist, for, otherwise, where did we get our simple ideas? But sensitive knowledge does not give us certainty, nor does it extend very far. We sense that we see another man and have no doubt that he exists, but when he leaves us, we are no longer sure of his existence: "For if I saw such a collection of simple ideas as is wont to be called *man*, existing together one minute since, and am now alone, I cannot be certain that the same man exists now, since there is no *necessary connexion* of his existence a minute since with his existence now." And therefore, "though it be highly probable that millions of men do now exist, yet, whilst I am alone, writing this, I have not that knowledge of it which we strictly call knowledge; though the great likelihood of it puts me past doubt. . . ." Since experience simply makes us aware of qualities, we have no assurance of the connections between qualities, and in particular sensitive knowledge does not assure us that qualities which appear to our senses to be related are *necessarily* connected. We simply sense things as they are, and as we never sense *substance*, we never know from sensation how things are *really* connected. Nevertheless, sensitive knowledge gives us *some* degree of knowledge but not certainty. Intuitive knowledge gives us certainty that we exist, demonstrative knowledge indicates that God exists, and sensitive knowledge assures us that other selves and things exist but only as they are when we experience them.

Locke's Moral and Political Theory   Locke placed our thought about morality into the category of demonstrative knowledge. To him morality could have the precision of mathematics: "I am bold to think that morality is capable of demonstration, as well as mathematics: since the precise real essence of the things moral words stand for can be perfectly known, and so the congruity and incongruity of the things themselves be perfectly discovered." The key word in ethics, namely *good*, is perfectly understandable, for everybody knows what the word *good* stands for: "Things are good or evil only in reference to pleasure or pain. That we call good which is apt to cause or increase pleasure, or diminish pain in us. . . ." Certain kinds of behavior will bring us pleasure, whereas other kinds will bring us pain. Morality, then, has to do with choosing or willing the good.

As a further definition of ethics, Locke says that "moral good and evil, then, is only the conformity or disagreement of our voluntary actions to some law," and he speaks of three kinds of laws, namely, the *law of opinion*, the *civil law*, and the *divine law*. The real issue here is to ask how Locke knows that these laws exist and also how he understands the relation of all three of them to each other. Bearing in mind that he saw no difficulty in demonstrating the existence of God, he now wants to draw further deductions from that demonstrative knowledge, saying that ". . . the idea of a supreme being infinite in power, goodness and wisdom, whose workmanship we are and on whom we depend, and the idea of ourselves as understanding rational beings, being such as are clear in us, would, I suppose, if duly considered and pursued, afford such foundations of our duty and rules of actions, as might place morality amongst the sciences capable of demonstration: wherein I doubt not but from self-evident principles, by necessary consequences, as incontestable as those in mathematics, the measures of right and wrong might be made out to anyone that will apply himself with the same indifferency and attention as he does to the other of those sciences."

Locke is here suggesting that by the light of nature, that is, by our reason, we can discover the moral rules that conform to God's law. He did not elaborate this program into a system of ethics, but he did indicate what relation the different kinds of laws should have to each other. The law of opinion represents a community's judgment of what kind of behavior will lead to happiness: conformity to this law is called virtue, though it must be noticed that different communities have different ideas of what virtue consists of. The civil law is set by the commonwealth and enforced by the courts. This law tends to follow the first, for in most societies the courts enforce those laws that embody the opinion of the people. The divine law, which men can know either through their own reason or revelation, is the true rule for human behavior: "That God has given a rule whereby men should govern themselves, I think there is nobody so brutish as to deny." And "this is the only true touchstone of moral rectitude." In the long run, then, the law of opinion and also the civil law should be made to conform to the divine law, the "touchstone of moral rectitude." The reason there is a discrepancy between these three kinds of laws is that men everywhere tend to choose immediate pleasures instead of choosing those that have more lasting value. However ambiguous this moral theory may seem to us, Locke believed that these moral rules were eternally true, and upon the insights derived from the divine law he built his theory of natural rights.

The State of Nature In his *Second Treatise of Government*, Locke begins his political theory as Hobbes did, with a treatment of "the state of nature." But he described this condition in a very different way, even making Hobbes the target of his remarks. For Locke, the state of nature is not the same as Hobbes' "war of all against all." On the contrary, Locke says that "men living together according to reason, without a common superior on earth with authority to judge between them is properly the state of nature." According to Locke's theory of knowledge, men were able even in the state of nature to know the moral law. He said that "reason, which is that law, teaches all mankind who will but consult it, that, being all equal and independent, no one ought to harm another in his life, health, liberty or possessions." This natural moral law is not simply the egotistical law of self-preservation but the positive recognition of each man's value as a person by virtue of his status as a creature of God. This natural law implied natural rights with correlative duties, and among these rights Locke emphasized particularly the right of private property.

Private Property For Hobbes, there could be a right to property only after the legal order had been set up. Locke said that the right to private property precedes the civil law, for it is grounded in the natural moral law. The justification of private ownership is labor. Since a man's labor is his own, whatever he transforms from its original condition by his own labor becomes his, for his labor is now mixed with those things. It is by mixing his labor with something that a man takes what was common property and makes it his private property. There is consequently also a limit to that amount of property one can accumulate, namely, "as much as anyone can make use of to any advantage of life before it spoils, so much he may by his labour fix a property in. . . ." Locke assumed also that as a matter of natural right a person could inherit property, for "every man is born with . . . a right, before any other man, to inherit with his brethren his father's goods."

Civil Government If men have natural rights and also know the moral law, why do they desire to leave the state of nature? To this question Locke answered that "the great and chief end of men's uniting into commonwealths and putting themselves under government is the preservation of their property." By the term *property* Locke meant men's "lives, liberty and estates, which I call by the general name, property." It is true that men know the moral law in the state of nature, or rather they are capable of knowing it if they turn their minds to it. But through indifference and neglect they do not always develop a knowledge of it. Moreover, when disputes arise, every man is his own judge and tends to decide in his own favor. It is desirable therefore to have both a set of written laws and also an independent judge to decide disputes. To achieve those ends, men create a political society.

Locke put great emphasis on the inalienable character of men's rights, and this led him to argue that political society must rest upon the *consent* of men, for "men being . . . by nature all free, equal and independent, no one can be put out of this estate and subjected to the political power of another without his consent." But to what do men consent? They consent to have the laws made and enforced by society, but since "no rational creature can be supposed to change his condition with an intention to be worse," these laws must be framed so as to confirm those rights that men have by nature. They consent also to be bound by the majority, since "it is necessary the body should move that way whither the greater force carries it, which is the consent of the majority." For this reason Locke considered absolute monarchy as "no form of civil government at all." Whether in fact there was a time when men entered a compact is considered by Locke to be of no great consequence, for the important thing is that logically our behavior indicates that we have given our consent, and this Locke calls "tacit consent." For if we enjoy the privilege of citizenship, own and exchange property, rely upon the police and the courts, we have in effect assumed also the responsibilities of citizenship and consent to the rule of the majority. The fact that a person stays in his country, for after all he could leave and go to another one, confirms his act of consent.

Sovereignty   Locke gives us a different picture of the sovereign power in society from the one we find in Hobbes. Hobbes' sovereign was absolute. Locke agrees that there must be a "supreme power," but he carefully placed this in the hands of the legislature, for all intents the majority of the people. He emphasized the importance of the division of powers chiefly to ensure that those who execute or administer the laws do not also make them, for "they may exempt themselves from obedience to the laws they make, and suit the law, both in its making and execution, to their own private advantage. . . ." The executive is therefore "under the law." Even the legislature is not absolute, although it is "supreme," for legislative power is held as a *trust* and is therefore only a fiduciary power. Consequently, "there remains still in the people a supreme power to remove or alter the legislative when they find the legislative act contrary to the trust reposed in them." Locke would never agree that men had irrevocably transferred their rights to the sovereign. The right to rebellion is retained, though rebellion is justified only when the government is *dissolved*. For Locke, government is dissolved not only when it is overthrown by an external enemy but also when internally there has been an alteration of the legislature. The legislative branch can be altered, for example, if the executive substitutes his law for the legislature's or if he neglects the execution of the official laws; in these cases rebellion against him is justified. Whereas Hobbes placed the sovereign under God's judgment, Locke stated that "the people shall judge."

BERKELEY

George Berkeley was born in Ireland in 1685. At the age of fifteen he entered Trinity College, Dublin, where he studied mathematics, logic, languages, and philosophy. He became a Fellow of the College a few years after he took his B.A. degree and was also ordained a clergyman in the Church of England, becoming a bishop in 1734. Beginning his famous literary career in his early twenties, his most important philosophical works include, among others, his *Essay towards a New Theory of Vision* (1709), *A Treatise Concerning the Principles of Human Knowledge* (1710), and *Three Dialogues between Hylas and Philonous* (1713). He traveled in France and Italy, and in London became friends with Steele, Addison, and Swift. While in London he sought to interest Parliament in his project of creating a college in Bermuda, whose purpose would be "the reformation of manners among the English in our western plantations, and the propagation of the Gospel among the American savages." With his recent bride he sailed in 1728 for America and for three years stayed in Newport, Rhode Island, making plans for his college. As the money for his college was never raised, Berkeley returned to London, leaving his influence upon American philosophy through frequent associations with Jonathan Edwards. Shortly thereafter he returned to Ireland, where for eighteen years he was Bishop of Cloyne. At the age of sixty-seven, he settled down in Oxford with his wife and family and a year later, in 1753, he died and was buried in Christ Church Chapel in Oxford.

It is ironic that Locke's common-sense approach to philosophy should have influenced Berkeley to formulate a philosophical position that at first seems so much at variance with common sense. He became the object of severe criticism and ridicule for denying what seemed most obvious to anyone. Berkeley had set out to deny the existence of matter. Dr. Samuel Johnson must have expressed the reaction of many when he kicked a large stone and said about Berkeley, "I refute him thus."

Berkeley's startling and provocative formula was that "to be is to be perceived," *esse est percipi*. Clearly this would mean that if something were not perceived, it would not exist. Berkeley was perfectly aware of the potential nonsense involved in this formula, for he says, "Let it not be said that I take away Existence. I only declare the meaning of the word so far as I comprehend it." Still, to say that the existence of something depends upon its being perceived does raise for us the question whether it exists when it is not being perceived. For Berkeley the whole problem turned on how we interpret or understand the word *exists*: "The table I write on I say exists; that is, I see and feel it: and if I were out of my study I should say it existed; meaning thereby that if I were in my study

I might perceive it, or that some other spirit actually does perceive it." Here Berkeley is saying that the word *exists* has no other meaning than the one contained in his formula, for we can know no instance where the term *exists* is used without at the same time assuming that a mind is perceiving something. To those who argued that material things have some kind of *absolute* existence without any relation to their being perceived, Berkeley replied, "that is to me unintelligible." To be sure, he said, "the horse is in the stable, the books in the study as before, even if I am not there. But since we know of no instance of anything's existing without being perceived, the table, horse, and books *exist* even when I do not perceive them because someone does perceive them."

How did Berkeley come upon this novel view? In his *New Theory of Vision* he argued that all our knowledge depends upon actual vision and other sensory experiences. In particular Berkeley argued that we never sense *space* or *magnitude*; we only have different visions or perceptions of things when we see them from different perspectives. Nor do we *see* distance; the distance of objects is *suggested* by our experience. All that we ever see is the qualities of an object that our faculty of vision is capable of sensing. We do not see the *closeness* of an object; we only have a different vision of it when we move toward or away from it. The more Berkeley considered the workings of his own mind and wondered how his ideas were related to objects outside of his mind, the more certain he was that he could never discover any object independent of his ideas. "When we do our utmost to conceive the existence of external bodies," he said, "we are all the while contemplating our own ideas." Nothing seems easier for us than to imagine trees in a park or books in a closet without anyone's looking at them. But what is all this, says Berkeley, except "framing in your mind certain ideas which you call *books* and *trees.* . . . But do not *you* yourself perceive or think of them all the while?" It is impossible, he concluded, ever to think of *anything* except as related to a mind. We never experience something that exists outside of us and separate from us as our ideas of *close* and *far* might suggest. There is nothing *out there* of which we do not have some perception.

It was Locke's philosophy that had raised doubts in Berkeley's mind about the independent existence of things, about the reality of matter. Locke had failed to push his own theory of knowledge to conclusions that to Berkeley seemed inevitable. When Locke spoke of substance as "something we know not what," he was only a short step from saying that it was nothing, which Berkeley did say. Locke's treatment of the relation between ideas and things assumed there is a real difference between primary and secondary qualities, between an object's size and shape on the one hand and its color, taste, and smell on the other. He assumed that whereas color exists only as an idea in the mind, size has to do with an object's *substance*, that reality that exists "behind" or "under" such secondary qualities as color and is therefore independent of a mind, is inert matter.

Berkeley, however, argued that size, shape, and motion "abstracted from all other qualities, are inconceivable." What, for example, is a cherry? It is soft, red, round, sweet, and fragrant. All these qualities are ideas in the mind that the cherry has the power to produce through the senses, so that the softness is felt, the color is seen, the roundness is either felt or seen, the sweetness is tasted, and the fragrance smelled. Again, the very existence of all these qualities consists in their being perceived. And, apart from these qualities, there is no sensed reality, in short, nothing else. The cherry, then, consists of all the qualities we perceive; the cherry (and all things) represents a complex of sensations. To say that besides the qualities perceived by the senses there are more primary qualities such as shape and size is to assume, says Berkeley, that primary and secondary qualities can be divided. It is impossible, he said, even to conceive of shape or size as independent of perception and therefore independent of secondary qualities. Is it possible, he asks, to separate primary and secondary qualities "even in thought"? He adds, "I might as easily divide a thing from itself. . . . In truth, the object and the sensation are the same thing, and cannot therefore be abstracted from each other." A thing *is*, therefore, the sum of its perceived qualities, and it is for this reason that Berkeley argued that to be is to be perceived. Since substance, or matter, is never perceived or sensed, it cannot be said to exist. If substance does not exist and if only sensed qualities are real, then only thinking or, as Berkeley says, *spiritual* beings exist.

Besides leading Locke's empirical philosophy to what he thought were obvious conclusions, Berkeley was also contending with a complex of problems, to which he referred in his *Principles of Human Knowledge* as ". . . *the chief causes of error and difficulty in the Sciences, with the grounds of Scepticism, Atheism and Irreligion, . . . inquired into.*" It was the notion of *matter* that caused all the difficulties, for if an inert material substance is admitted as really existing, where is there any place for spiritual or immaterial substances in such a universe? Also, would not scientific knowledge, based upon general ideas drawn from the behavior of things, give us a complete philosophy without requiring the idea of God, leading to "the monstrous systems of atheists"? This is not to say that Berkeley arbitrarily denounced the idea of matter because of these theological consequences but that he had additional reasons for pressing his views, which, he was convinced, were intrinsically right.

Matter a Meaningless Term Locke had said that substance, or matter, *supports* or acts as a *substrate* to the qualities we sense. In Berkeley's *First Dialogue between Hylas and Philonous*, Hylas expresses Locke's view: ". . . I find it necessary to suppose a material *substratum*, without which [qualities] cannot be conceived to exist." Philonous replies that the word *substratum* has no clear meaning for him and that he would want to "know any sense, literal or not literal, that you understand in it." But Hylas admits that he cannot assign any definite meaning to the term *substratum*, saying, "I declare I know not what to say." From this the conclusion is drawn that "The *absolute* existence of unthinking things [matter] are words without meaning." This is not to say that sensible things do not possess reality but only that sensible things exist only insofar as they are perceived. This of course implies that only ideas exist, but Berkeley adds that "I hope that to call a thing 'idea' makes it no less real." Aware that his idealism can be ridiculed, Berkeley writes: "What therefore becomes of the sun, moon, and stars? What must we think of houses, rivers, mountains, trees, stones; nay even of our own bodies? Are all these so many chimeras and illusions of fancy?" By his principles, he says, "we are not deprived of any one thing in nature. Whatever we see, feel, hear, or any wise conceive or understand, remains as secure as ever, and is as real as ever. There is a *rerum natura*, and the distinction between realities and chimeras retains its full force." If this is the case, why say that only *ideas*, instead of *things*, exist? In order, says Berkeley, to eliminate the useless concept of matter: "I do not argue against the existence of any one thing that we can apprehend, either by sense or reflexion. . . . The only thing whose existence we deny, is that which philosophers call matter or corporeal substance. And in doing of this, there is no damage done to the rest of mankind, who, I dare say, will never miss it."

Science and Abstract Ideas   Since it was the science of his day, particularly physics, that relied so heavily upon the notion of matter, Berkeley had to come to terms with its assumptions and methods. Science had assumed that we can, and must, distinguish between appearance and reality. The sea appears blue but is really not. Berkeley challenged the scientist to show whether there is any other reality than the sensible world. In this analysis Berkeley was pursuing the principle of empiricism and was trying to refine it. Physicists, he said, were obscuring science by including metaphysics in their theories: They used such words as *force, attraction, gravity* and thought they referred to some real physical entity. Even to speak of minute particles, whose motions cause the quality of color, is to engage in a rational and not empirical analysis. What disturbed Berkeley most was that scientists used general or abstract terms as though these terms accurately referred to real entities, particularly to an underlying material substance in nature. Nowhere, Berkeley argues, do we ever come upon such a substance, for substance is an abstract idea. Only sensed qualities really exist, and the notion of substance is a misleading inference drawn from observed qualities: "As several of these [qualities] are observed to accompany each other, they come to be marked by one name, and so to be reputed as one *thing*. Thus, for example, a certain colour, taste, smell, figure and consistence having been observed to go together, are accounted one distinct thing, signified by the name apple; other collections of ideas constitute a stone, a tree, a book and the like sensible things." Similarly, when scientists observe the operations of things, they use such abstract terms as *force* or *gravity* as though these were things or had some real existence in things. But *force* is simply a word describing our sensation of the behavior of things and gives us no more knowledge than our senses and reflections give us.

Berkeley did not mean to destroy science any more than he wanted to deny the existence of the "nature of things." What he did want to do was to clarify what scientific language was all about. Terms such as *force, gravity,* and *causality* refer to nothing more than clusters of ideas, which our minds derive from sensation. We experience that heat melts wax, but all we know from this experience is that what we call *melting wax* is always accompanied by what we call *heat*. We have no knowledge of any single thing for which the word *cause* stands. Indeed, the only knowledge we have is of particular experiences. But even though we do not have firsthand knowledge of the causes of all things, we do know the order of things. We experience order, that *A* is followed by *B*, even though we have no experience of *why* this occurs. Science gives us a description of physical behavior, and many mechanical principles can be accurately formulated from our observations that are useful for purposes of prediction. Thus Berkeley would leave science intact, but he would clarify its language so that nobody would think that science was giving us more knowledge than we can derive from the sensible world. And the sensible world shows us neither substance nor causality.

God and the Existence of Things   Since Berkeley did not deny the existence of things or their order in nature, it was necessary for him to explain how things external to our minds exist even when *we* don't perceive them and how they achieve their order. Thus, elaborating his general thesis that to be is to be perceived, Berkeley says that "When I deny sensible things an existence out of the mind, I do not mean my mind in particular, but all minds. Now it is plain they have an existence exterior to my mind, since I find them by experience to be independent of it. There is therefore some other mind wherein they exist, during the intervals between the time of my perceiving them." And because all human minds are intermittently diverted from things "there is an *omnipresent eternal Mind*, which knows and comprehends all things, and exhibits them to our view in such a manner and according to such rules as he himself hath ordained, and are by us termed the *Laws of Nature*." The existence of things therefore depends upon the existence of God, and God is the cause of the orderliness of things in nature.

Again, Berkeley did not want to deny, for example, that even if I left the room, the candle would still be there, and that when I returned after an interval of time, it would have burned down. But this meant for Berkeley only that experience has a certain regularity that makes it possible for us to predict what our future experiences will be. To say that candles burn even when *I* am not in the room still does not prove that material substance exists independently from a mind. It seemed a matter of common sense to Berkeley to say that one can know about the candle only because he actually experiences a perception of it. In a similar way, one knows that he exists because he has an awareness of his mental operations.

If, then, I try to describe or interpret reality in terms of my experience, I come first to the conclusion that there are other persons like myself who have minds. From this it can be assumed that as I have ideas other persons likewise have ideas. Apart from my finite mind and the finite minds of others, there is a greater Mind analogous to mind, and this is God's Mind. God's ideas constitute the regular order of nature. The ideas that exist in men's minds are God's ideas, which He communicates to men so that the objects or things that we perceive in daily experience are caused not by *matter* or *substance* but by God. It is God, too, who coordinates all experiences of finite minds, assuring regularity and dependability in experience, which, in turn, enables us to think in terms of the "laws of nature." Thus the orderly arrangement of ideas in God's mind is communicated to the finite minds or spirits of men, allowance being made for the differences in competence between the Divine and finite minds. The ultimate reality, then, is spiritual, God, and not material, and the continued existence of objects when *we* are not perceiving them is explained by God's continuous perception of them.

To say, as Berkeley does, that men's ideas come from God implies a special interpretation of causation. Again, Berkeley did not deny that we have an insight into causation; he only insisted that our sense data do not disclose to us a unique causal power. We do not, for example, when considering how and why water freezes, discover any power in cold that forces water to become solid. We do, however, understand causal connections through our mental operations. We are, for example, aware of our volition: we can will to move our arm, or, what is more important here, we can produce imaginary ideas in our minds. Our power to produce such ideas suggests that perceived ideas are also caused by a mental power. But whereas imaginary ideas are produced by finite minds, perceived ideas are created and caused to be in us by an infinite Mind.

Berkeley was confident that through his treatment of the formula *esse est percipi* he had effectively undermined the position of philosophical materialism and religious skepticism. Locke's empiricism inevitably implied skepticism insofar as he insisted that knowledge is based upon sense experience and that substance, or the reality behind appearances, could never be known. Whether Berkeley's arguments for the reality of God and spiritual beings successfully refuted materialism and skepticism remains a question, for his arguments contained some of the flaws he held against the materialist. His influence was nevertheless significant, but it was his empiricism and not his idealism that had lasting influence. Building upon Locke's empiricism, Berkeley made the decisive point that the human mind reasons only and always about particular sense experiences, that abstract ideas refer to no equivalent reality. Hume, who was to carry empiricism to its fullest expression, spoke of Berkeley as "a great philosopher [who] has disputed the received opinion in this particular, and has asserted that all general ideas are nothing but particular ones. . . . I look upon this to be one of the greatest and most valuable discoveries that has been made of late years in the republic of letters."

HUME

David Hume took the genuinely empirical elements in the philosophy of Locke and Berkeley, rejected some lingering metaphysics from their thought, and gave empiricism its clearest and most rigorous formulation. Born in Edinburgh in 1711 of Scottish parents, his early interest in literature soon indicated to his family that he would not follow their plan for him to become a lawyer. Though he attended the University of Edinburgh, he did not graduate. He was a gentle person with a tough mind who regarded "every object as contemptible except the improvement of my talents in literature," feeling "an insurmountable aversion to everything but the pursuits of philosophy and general learning." He spent the years 1734–1737 in France, under conditions of "rigid frugality," composing his *A Treatise of Human Nature*. When this book appeared in 1739, Hume was disappointed in its reception, remarking later that "never literary attempt was more unfortunate," for the book "fell deadborn from the press. . . ." His next book, *Essays Moral and Political*, published in 1741–1742, was an immediate success. Hume then revised his *Treatise* and eventually gave it the new title *An Enquiry Concerning Human Understanding*, by which it is known today. Besides his extensive books on the history of England, Hume wrote three other works that were to enhance his fame, namely, *Principles of Morals, Political Discourses*, and the book published after his death, *Dialogues on Natural Religion*.

Hume played a part in public life, going to France in 1763 as secretary to the British ambassador. His books had given him a wide reputation on the Continent, and among his European friends was the philosopher Rousseau. For two years, 1767 to 1769, he was Under-Secretary of State, and in 1769 he returned to Edinburgh, where his house became the center for the most distinguished persons of that society. Being now "very opulent," he lived a quiet and contented life among friends and admirers among whom Adam Smith was included. He died in Edinburgh in 1776.

Hume wanted to build a *science of man*, to study human nature by using the methods of physical science. His wide acquaintance with literature had shown him how often conflicting opinions are offered to readers on all subjects. He considered this conflict of opinions the symptom of a serious philosophical problem: How can we know the true nature of things? If artful authors can lead readers to accept conflicting ideas about morality, religion, and the true nature of physical reality, are these ideas equally true, or is there some method by which to discover the reason for this conflict of ideas? Hume shared the optimism of his day, which saw in scientific method the means for solving all the problems of the universe. He believed that such a method could lead us to a clear understanding of human nature and in particular of the workings of the human mind.

As it turned out, Hume discovered that this optimism about the possibilities of using scientific methods for describing the mechanics of human thought could not be justified. His early faith in reason led, in the end, to skepticism. For as he traced the process by which ideas are formed in the mind, he was startled to discover how limited is the range of human thought. Both Locke and Berkeley had come to this same point, but neither one took his own account of the origin of ideas seriously enough to rest his theory of knowledge wholly upon it. They still had recourse to the "common-sense" beliefs of men, which they were not willing to give up entirely. Although they argued that all our ideas come from experience, they felt confident that experience can give us certainty of knowledge on many subjects. Hume, on the other hand, concluded that if we take seriously the premise that all our ideas come from experience, we must accept the limits to knowledge that this explanation of ideas forces upon us, no matter what our customary beliefs may suggest.

Hume's Theory of Knowledge　The only way, says Hume, to solve the problem of disagreements and speculations regarding "abstruse questions" is to "enquire seriously into the nature of human understanding, and show from an exact analysis of its powers and capacity, that it is by no means fitted for such remote and abstruse subjects." Accordingly, Hume carefully analyzed a series of topics that led him to his skeptical conclusion, beginning with an account of the contents of the mind.

Contents of the Mind　Nothing seems more unbounded, says Hume, than man's thought. Although our body is confined to one planet, our mind can roam instantly into the most distant regions of the universe. Nor, it may seem, is the mind bound by the limits of nature or reality, for without difficulty the imagination can conceive the most unnatural and incongruous appearances, such as flying horses and gold mountains. But, though the mind seems to possess this wide freedom, it is, says Hume, "really confined within very narrow limits." In the last analysis, the contents of the mind can all be reduced to the materials given us by the senses and experience, and those materials Hume calls *perceptions*. The perceptions of the mind take two forms, which Hume distinguishes as *impressions* and *ideas*.

Impressions and *ideas* make up the total content of the mind. The original stuff of thought is an *impression*, and an *idea* is merely a copy of an impression. The difference between an impression and an idea is only the degree of their vividness. The original perception is an impression, as when we hear, see, feel, love, hate, desire, or will. These impressions are "lively" and clear when we have them. When we reflect upon these impressions, we have ideas of them, and those ideas are less-lively versions of the original impressions. To feel pain is an impression, whereas the memory of this sensation is an idea. In every particular, impressions and their corresponding ideas are alike, differing only in their degree of vivacity.

Besides merely distinguishing between impressions and ideas, Hume argues that without impressions there can be no ideas. For if an idea is simply a copy of an impression, it follows that for every idea there must be a prior impression. Not every idea, however, reflects a corresponding impression, for we have never seen a flying horse or a golden mountain even though we have ideas of them. But Hume explains such ideas as being the product of the mind's "faculty of compounding, transposing, or diminishing the materials afforded us by the senses and experience." When we think of a flying horse, our imagination joins two ideas, wings and horse, which we originally acquired as impressions through our senses. If we have any suspicion that a philosophical term is employed without any meaning or idea, we need, says Hume, "but enquire, *from what impression is that supposed idea derived?* And if it be impossible to assign any, this will serve to confirm our suspicion." Hume subjected even the idea of God to this test and concluded that it arises from reflecting on the operations of our own minds "augmenting without limit" the qualities of goodness and wisdom that we experience among human beings. But if all our ideas follow from impressions, how can we explain what we call *thinking*, or the patterns by which ideas group themselves in our minds?

Association of Ideas   It is not by mere chance that our ideas are related to each other. There must be, says Hume, "some bond of union, some associating quality, by which one idea naturally introduces another." Hume calls it "a gentle force, which commonly prevails . . . pointing out to every one those simple ideas, which are most proper to be united in a complex one." It is not a special faculty of the mind that associates one idea with another, for Hume has no impression of the structural equipment of the mind. But by observing the actual patterns of our thinking and analyzing the groupings of our ideas, Hume thought he discovered the explanation of the association of ideas.

His explanation was that whenever there are certain qualities in ideas, these ideas are associated with each other. These qualities are three in number: resemblance, contiguity in time or place, and cause and effect. Hume believed that the connections of all ideas to each other could be explained by these qualities and gave the following examples of how they work: "A picture naturally leads our thoughts to the original [*resemblance*]: the mention of one apartment in the building naturally introduces an enquiry . . . concerning the others [*contiguity*]: and if we think of a wound, we can scarcely forebear reflecting on the pain which follows it [*cause and effect*]." There are no operations of the mind that differ in principle from one of these three examples of the association of ideas. But of these, the notion of cause and effect was considered by Hume to be the central element in knowledge. He took the position that the causal principle is the foundation upon which the validity of all knowledge depends. If there is any flaw in the causal principle, we can have no certainty of knowledge.

Causality   Hume's most original and influential ideas deal with the problem of causality. Neither Locke nor Berkeley challenged the basic principle of causality; though Berkeley did say that we cannot discover efficient causes *in* things, his intention was to look for the cause of phenomena in God.

For Hume, the very idea of causality is suspect, and he approaches the problem by asking the question, "What is the origin of the idea of causality?" Since ideas are copies of impressions, Hume asks what impression gives us the idea of causality. His answer is that there is no impression corresponding to this idea. How then does the idea of causality arise in the mind? It must be, said Hume, that the idea of causality arises in the mind when we experience certain relations between objects. When we speak of cause and effect, we mean to say that A causes B. But what kind of a relation does this indicate between A and B? Experience furnishes us three relations: first, there is the relation of *contiguity*, for A and B are always close together; secondly, there is *priority in time*, for A, the "cause," always precedes B, the "effect"; and third, there is *constant conjunction*, for we always see A followed by B. But there is still another relation that the idea of causality suggests to common sense, namely, that between *A* and *B* there is a "necessary connexion." But neither contiguity, priority, nor constant conjunction implies "necessary" connection between objects. There is no object, says Hume, that implies the existence of another when we consider objects individually. No amount of observation of oxygen can ever tell us that when mixed with hydrogen it will give us water. We know this only after we have seen the two together: "It is therefore by *experience* only that we can infer the existence of one object from another." While we do have impressions of contiguity, priority, and constant conjunction, we do *not* have any impression of *necessary connections*. Thus, causality is not a quality in the objects we observe but is rather a "habit of association" in the mind produced by the repetition of instances of *A* and *B*.

Insofar as Hume assumed that the causal principle is central to all kinds of knowledge, his attack on this principle undermined the validity of all knowledge. He saw no reason for accepting the principle that *whatever begins to exist must have a cause of existence* as either intuitive or capable of demonstration. In the end, Hume considered thinking or reasoning "a species of sensation," and as such our thinking cannot extend beyond our immediate experiences.

What Exists External to Us?   Hume's extreme empiricism led him to argue that there is no rational justification for saying that bodies or things have a continued and independent existence external to us. Our ordinary experience suggests that things outside of us do exist. But if we take seriously the notion that our ideas are copies of impressions, the philosophical conclusion must be that all we know is impressions. Impressions are internal subjective states and are not clear proof of an external reality. To be sure we always act as though there is a real external world of things, and Hume was willing to "take for granted in all our reasonings" that things do exist. But he wanted to inquire into the reason why we think there is an external world.

Our senses do not tell us that things exist independent of us, for how do we know that they continue to exist even when we interrupt our sensation of them? And even when we sense something, we are never given a double view of it whereby we can distinguish the thing from our impression of it; we have only the impression. There is no way for the mind to reach beyond impressions or the ideas they make possible: ". . . let us chase our imagination to the heavens, or to the utmost limits of the universe; we never advance a step beyond our selves, nor can we conceive any kind of existence, but those perceptions which have appeared in that narrow compass. This is the universe of the imagination, nor have we any idea but what is there produced."

Constancy and Coherence   Our belief that things exist external to us, says Hume, is the product of our imagination as it deals with two special characteristics of our impressions. From impressions our imagination becomes aware of both *constancy* and *coherence*. There is a constancy in the arrangement of things when, for example, I look out of my window: there are the mountain, the house, and the trees. If I shut my eyes or turn away and then later look at the same view again, the arrangement is still the same, and it is this constancy in the contents of my impressions that leads my imagination to conclude that the mountain, house, and trees exist whether I think of them or not. Similarly, I put a log on the fire before I leave the room, and when I return it is almost in ashes. But even though a great change has taken place in the fire, I am accustomed to find this kind of change under similar circumstances: "this coherence . . . in their changes is one of the characteristics of external objects. . . ." In the case of the mountain, there is a constancy of our impressions, whereas in respect to the fire our impressions have a coherent relation to the processes of change. For these reasons, the imagination leads us to believe that certain things continue to have an independent existence external to us. But this is a *belief* and not a rational proof, for the assumption that our impressions are connected with things is "without any foundation in reasoning." Hume extends this skeptical line of reasoning beyond objects or things to consider the existence of the *self, substance*, and *God*.

The Self   Hume denied that we have any idea of *self*. This may seem paradoxical, that *I* should say that I do not have an idea of myself, yet here again Hume wants to test what we mean by a self by asking, "from what impression could this idea be deriv'd?" Is there any continuous and identical reality which forms our ideas of the self? Do we have any one impression that is invariably associated with our idea of *self*? "When I enter most intimately into what I call *myself*," says Hume, "I always stumble on some particular perception or other, of heat or cold, love or hatred, pain or pleasure. I never can catch *myself* at any time without a perception and never can observe anything but the perception." Hume denies the existence of a continuous self-identity and says about the rest of mankind that "they are nothing but a bundle or collection of different perceptions." How then do we account for what we think is the self? It is our power of memory that gives the impression of our continuous identity. Hume compares the mind to "a kind of theatre where several perceptions successively make their appearance," but adds that "we have not the most distant notion of the place where these scenes are represented. . . ."

Substance   What led Hume to deny the existence of a continuous self that in some way retains its identity through time was his thorough denial of the existence of any form of *substance*. Locke retained the idea of substance as that *something*, which has color or shape, and other qualities, though he spoke of it as "something we know not what." Berkeley denied the existence of substance underlying qualities but retained the idea of spiritual substances. Hume denied that substance in any form exists or has any coherent meaning. If what is meant by the *self* is some form of substance, Hume argued that no such substance can be derived from our impressions of sensation. If the idea of substance is conveyed to us by our senses, Hume asked, ". . . which of them; and after what manner? If it be perceiv'd by the eyes, it must be a colour; if by the ears, a sound; if by the palate, a taste. . . . We have therefore no idea of substance, distinct from that of a collection of particular qualities. . . ."

God   It was inevitable that Hume's rigorous premise, that "our ideas reach no further than our experience," would lead him to raise skeptical questions about the existence of God. Most attempts to demonstrate the existence of God rely upon some version of causality. Among these, the argument from *design* has always made a powerful impact upon the mind. Hume is aware of the power of this argument, but he quickly sorts out the elements of the problem, leaving the argument with less than its usual force.

The argument from design begins with the observance of a beautiful order in nature. This order resembles the kind of order the human mind is able to impose upon unthinking materials. From this preliminary observation, the mind concludes that unthinking materials do not contain the principle of orderliness within themselves: "throw several pieces of steel together, without shape or form; they will never arrange themselves so as to compose a watch. . . ." Order, it is held, requires the activity of a mind, an orderer. Our experience tells us that neither a watch nor a house can come into being without a watchmaker or an architect. From this it is inferred that the natural order bears an analogy to the order fashioned by human effort, and that just as the watch requires an ordering cause, so the natural order of the universe requires one. But such an inference, says Hume, "is uncertain; because the subject lies entirely beyond the reach of human experience."

If the whole argument from design rests upon the proposition *"that the cause or causes of order in the universe probably bear some remote analogy to human intelligence,"* then, says Hume, the argument cannot prove as much as it claims. Hume's criticism of the idea of causality has particular force here. Since we derive the idea of cause from repeated observations of the contiguity, priority, and constant conjunction of two things, how can we assign a cause to the universe when we have never experienced the universe as related to anything we might consider a cause. The use of analogy does not solve the problem, since the analogy between a watch and the universe is not exact. Why not consider the universe the product of a vegetative process instead of a rational designer? And even if the cause of the universe is something like an intelligence, how can moral characteristics be ascribed to such a being? Moreover, if analogies are to be used, which one should be selected? Houses and ships are frequently designed by a group of designers: should we say there are many gods? Sometimes experimental models are built with no present knowledge of what the finished form will be like: Is the universe a trial model or the final design? By this line of probing, Hume wished to emphasize that the order of the universe is simply an empirical fact and that we cannot infer from it the existence of God. This does not make Hume an atheist. He is simply testing our idea of God the way he had tested our ideas of the *self* and *substance* by his rigorous principle of empiricism. He ends, to be sure, as a skeptic, but finally makes the telling point that "to whatever length any one may push his speculative principles of scepticism, he must act and live and converse like other men. . . . It is impossible for him to persevere in total scepticism, or make it appear in his conduct for a few hours."

ETHICS

Hume's skepticism did not prevent him from taking ethics seriously. On the contrary, in the opening passage of the third book of his *Treatise of Human Nature* Hume writes that "morality is a subject that interests us above all others." His interest in ethics was so strong that he hoped to do for that subject what Galileo and Newton did for natural science, saying in the first section of his *Enquiry Concerning the Principles of Morals* that "moral philosophy is in the same condition as . . . astronomy before the time of Copernicus." Just as the older science with its abstract general hypotheses had to give way to a more experimental method, so also the time had come, Hume writes, when philosophers "should attempt a like reformation in all moral disquisitions; and reject every system of ethics, however subtle or ingenious, which is not founded on fact and observation."

For Hume, the central fact about ethics is that moral judgments are formed not by reason alone but by the sentiment of sympathy. There is no doubt that reason plays a considerable role in our discussions about ethical decisions. But, says Hume, reason "is not sufficient alone to produce any moral blame or approbation." What limits the role of reason in ethics is that reason makes judgments concerning *matters of fact* and *relations* whereas moral judgments of good and evil are not limited to matters of fact or relations.

Why, for example, do we judge murder to be a crime? Or, to use Hume's words, "where is that matter of fact which we here call *crime?*" If you describe the action, the exact time at which it occurred, the weapon used, in short, if you assemble all the details about the event, the faculty of reason would still not isolate that fact to which the label of crime is attached. After all, this act cannot always and in all circumstances be considered a crime. The same action might be called self-defense or official execution. The judgment of good or evil is made *after* all the facts are known. The goodness or badness of an act is not a new fact discovered or deduced by reason. Nor is moral discourse similar to mathematical reasoning. From a few facts about a triangle or circle, additional facts and relations can be inferred. But goodness, like beauty, is not an additional fact inferred or deduced by reason. "Euclid has fully explained all the qualities of the circle," says Hume, "but has not in any proposition said a word of its beauty. The reason is evident. The beauty is not a quality of the circle. It lies not in any part of the line, whose parts are equally distant from a common center. It is only the effect which that figure produces upon the mind, whose peculiar fabric of structure renders it susceptible of such sentiments."

Hume presses this point by asking us to "see if you can find that matter of fact, or real existence, which you call *vice*," and he argues that "in whichever way you take it, you find only certain passions, motives, volitions and thoughts. There is no other matter of fact in the case. . . . You can never find it, till you turn your reflection into your own breast and find a sentiment of disapprobation which arises in you toward this action. Here is a matter of fact; but it is the object of feeling, not reason. It lies in yourself, not in the object."

Hume realized that to build a system of ethics upon the faculty of feeling, sentiment, or sympathy is to run the risk of reducing ethics to a matter of taste where moral judgments are subjective and relative. Moreover, to designate feeling or sentiment as the source of praise or blame is to imply that our moral judgments flow from a calculus of our individual self-interest or self-love. Hume rejects these assumptions by affirming that moral sentiments are found in all men, that men praise or blame the same actions and that praise or blame are not derived from a narrow self-love. The sentiment of sympathy, or fellow-feeling, writes Hume, must be acknowledged as a "principle in human nature beyond which we cannot hope to find any principle more general." It is through this human capacity, he writes, that "we frequently bestow praise on virtuous actions, performed in very distant ages and remote countries; where the utmost subtilty of imagination would not discover any appearance of self-interest, or find any connection of our present happiness and security with events so widely separated from us." Moreover, adds Hume, "a generous, a brave, a noble deed, performed by an adversary, commands our approbation; while in its consequences it may be acknowledged prejudicial to our particular interest." Hume was convinced that this capacity for sympathy provides a complete explanation for our judgments of praise or blame.

Hume's conception of moral sentiment and sympathy is in sharp contrast to the traditional ethical theory which holds that morality consists in the relation of actions to a rule of right. That theory defines an action as good or evil depending upon whether the action agrees or disagrees with the rule. But Hume rejects the hypothesis that there are moral rules, saying that such an hypothesis is "abstruse" and "can never be made intelligible." By contrast, Hume offers an alternative hypothesis for ethics which, he says, "defines virtue to be *whatever mental action or quality gives to a spectator the pleasing sentiment of approbation; and vice the contrary.*" Among those qualities which give the spectator the pleasing sentiment of approbation are "discretion, caution, enterprise, industry, economy, good-sense, prudence and discernment." Also, there is virtually universal agreement, even among the most cynical men of the world, concerning "the merit of temperance, sobriety, patience, constancy, considerateness, presence of mind, quickness of conception and felicity of expression." What is there about these qualities which generates our praise? It is, says Hume, that these qualities are *useful* and *agreeable.* But useful for what? Hume replies, "for somebody's interest, surely. Whose interest then? Not our own only: For our approbation frequently extends farther. It must, therefore, be the interest of those, who are served by the character or action approved of." *Usefulness* is defined by Hume as "a tendency to a natural end." He also argues that the distinction between what is useful and what is pernicious is the essential moral distinction. Therefore, says Hume, "if usefulness . . . be a source of moral sentiment, and if this usefulness be not always considered with reference to self; it follows, that everything which contributes to the happiness of society, recommends itself directly to our approbation and good-will. Here is a principle which accounts in great part for the origin of morality: And what need we seek for abstruse and remote systems, when there occurs one so obvious and natural?"

Hume acknowledges the intermingling of self-interest and sympathy in his analysis of justice. Indeed, he argues that justice, which he describes as "a general peace and order" or "a general abstinence from the possessions of others," reflects the self-interest of each person who desires to be secure in person and property. This security and happiness can be achieved only in society, in an arrangement of justice. To this extent, justice is a reflection of self-interest. The usefulness of justice is that it satisfies self-interest. For this reason, Hume is able to say that public utility is the *sole* origin of justice, and that reflections on the beneficial consequences of this virtue are the *sole* foundation of its merit." But although social utility or self-interest drive men into society or into a scheme of justice, it is something besides self-interest which provides the *moral* basis for justice. What gives justice the quality of a moral virtue and injustice that of vice is not self-interest but rather the sentiment of sympathy. We condemn injustice not only when our own personal interests are involved but whenever it produces pain or disagreeableness in others which we can share through sympathy. "Thus," says Hume, "self-interest is the original motive to the establishment of justice: but a sympathy with public interest is the source of the moral approbation which attends that virtue."

14

Rousseau:
A Romantic
in the
Age of Reason

Rousseau's career unfolded during the French Enlightenment, that Age of Reason which in eighteenth-century France was dominated by Voltaire (1694–1778), Montesquieu (1689–1755), Diderot (1713–1784), Condorcet (1743–1794) d'Holbach, and others who were known as *philosophes*. These men were, for the most part, dissident voices who challenged the traditional modes of thought concerning religion, government, and morality. Believing that human reason provides the most reliable guide to man's destiny, they held that "Reason is to the *philosophe* what grace is to the Christian." This was the theme of that remarkable *Encyclopédie* (1751–1780) which contained the distinctive ideas of the *philosophes* and which, under the editorship of Diderot and d'Alembert, consisted by 1780 of thirty-five volumes. Into this vigorous intellectual climate Rousseau entered with the most unlikely credentials. Despite little formal education, he fashioned a set of ideas about human nature with such compelling power that his thought ultimately prevailed over the most impressive thinkers of his time.

Jean-Jacques Rousseau was born in Geneva in 1712. His mother died a few days after his birth, and his father, a watchmaker, left him at age ten in the care of an aunt who had raised him. After two years in a boarding school where, he says in his *Confessions,* "we were to learn . . . all the insignificant trash that has obtained the name of education," he was recalled to his aunt's household and thus, at the age of twelve, his formal education came to an end. After a short apprenticeship as an engraver of watchcases, he left Geneva and wandered from place to place meeting a series of people who alternately helped him make a meager living or referred him to still other potential benefactors. Along the way he read books and developed his skills in music. Eventually he wandered into France and there came under the care of a noblewoman, Mme. de Warens, who sought to further his formal education, an attempt which failed, and to arrange for his employment. His most consistent work was copying music, though he was for a while tutor to the children of M. de Mably, who was grand provost of Lyons and later he was secretary to the French Ambassador to Venice. He was a precocious child and learned to read at an early age. In his twenties he read portions of the classic works of Plato, Virgil, Horace, Montaigne, Pascal, and

Rousseau (*The Bettmann Archive*)

Voltaire, which in their variety strongly influenced his imagination. From Lyons he went armed with letters of introduction from the Mablys to Paris where he met some of the most influential persons of this capitol city. Here he was struck by the contrast of noble wealth and sweaty artisans, the majesty of cathedrals and bishops who read the heretical ideas of Voltaire, the gaiety of the salons and the tragic themes of Racine's plays. Although he met many notables, including Diderot, and moved increasingly in the upper circles of French society, he retained his childhood shyness, especially with women, and in 1746 eventually formed a lifelong relationship with an uneducated young servant girl, Thérèse Levasseur, whom he finally married in 1768.

Rousseau's literary career began with his prize-winning essay entitled *Discourse on the Arts and Sciences* (1750). With strong emotional power he argued that morals had been corrupted by the replacement of religion by science, by sensuality in art, by licentiousness in literature, and by the emphasis upon logic at the expense of feeling. The essay made Rousseau instantly famous, leading Diderot to say that "never was there an instance of a like success." There followed in 1752 an operetta, *Le Devin du Village,* performed before the King and his court at Fontainebleau, and a comedy, *Narcisse,* played by the Comédie-Française. Two important works appeared in 1755, his Discourse on *What Is the Origin of the Inequality Among Men, and Is It Authorized by Natural Law?,* and a *Discourse on Political Economy* which appeared in the *Encyclopédie.* In 1761 Rousseau published a love story, *Julie, ou La Nouvelle Héloïse,* which became the most celebrated novel of the eighteenth century. His book *Émile,* published in 1762, offered an elaborate proposal for a new approach to education and contained also a provocative section, "The Confession of Faith of a Savoyard Vicar," which was critical of institutional religion while advocating the importance of religion to mankind. In the same year he published his most famous work, *The Social Contract,* in which he sought to describe the passage from the "state of nature" to the civil state and to answer why it is that laws governing men are legitimate.

Rousseau's last days were unhappy as he was in failing health and suffered from profound paranoia. Moreover, his books were severely criticized by the leaders of both church and state, and word went out that "J.-J. Rousseau shall be apprehended and brought to the Concierge prison in the Palace [of Justice]." He became a fugitive, and at one point he accepted David Hume's invitation to visit him in England where he spent sixteen months. He returned to France convinced that his enemies were plotting to defame him. When he was told that Voltaire was dying, he said, "Our lives were linked to each other; I shall not survive him long." In July, 1778, Rousseau died at the age of sixty-six. His remarkably frank and detailed autobiography was published after his death in his *Confessions.*

THE PARADOX OF LEARNING

When Rousseau read the announcement by the Academy of Dijon that a prize would be given for the best essay on the question "Whether the restoration of the arts and sciences has had the effect of purifying or corrupting morals?", he reacted with passionate excitement at the prospect of writing just such an essay. Looking back upon that moment, he said, "I felt myself dazzled by a thousand sparkling lights. Crowds of vivid ideas thronged into my mind with a force and confusion that threw me into unspeakable agitation." He was already thirty-eight years old, had read widely in classical and contemporary literature, had traveled in Switzerland, Italy, and France, had observed the ways of different cultures, and had spent enough time in the social circles of Paris to have nothing but contempt for that sophisticated society. "If ever I could have written a quarter of what I saw and felt," he continued, "with what clarity I should have brought out all the contradictions of our social system." What he did set out to show was that "man is by nature good, and that only our institutions have made him bad." This turned out to be the underlying theme of Rousseau's future writings. But in this essay, this theme lacked precision and clarity, for, as Rousseau himself admitted, "though full of force and fire, [this first *Discourse*] was absolutely wanting in logic and order . . . and it is the weakest in reasoning of all the works I ever wrote." For this reason, Rousseau's *Discourse on the Arts and Sciences* was an easy target for his critics. It was inevitable that his readers would have difficulty with his paradoxical argument that civilization is the cause of unhappiness or that the corruption of society is caused by learning in the arts and sciences.

Rousseau begins his *Discourse* with high praise for the achievements of human reason, saying that "it is a noble and beautiful spectacle to see man raising himself . . . from nothing by his own exertions; dissipating by the light of reason all the thick clouds by which he was by nature enveloped." Only a few sentences later, his essay becomes a slashing attack upon the arts, literature and sciences which, he says, "fling garlands of flowers over the chains which weight men down" in their common life and "stifle in men's hearts that sense of original liberty for which they seem to have been born." Rousseau recognizes that human nature was not really any better in earlier times but believed that the arts and sciences produced some significant changes making men worse. Before art and literature molded our behavior and taught our passions to speak an artificial language, our morals, says Rousseau, were rude but natural. Modern manners have made everyone conform in speech, dress, and attitude, always following the laws of fashion, never the promptings of our own nature, so that we no longer dare appear to be what we really are. The herd of mankind all act exactly alike and thus we never know even among our friends with whom we are dealing. Human relationships are now full of deceptions, whereas earlier men could easily see through one another, an advantage which prevented their having many vices.

Rousseau directed his attack also against luxury and against political leaders who emphasized the economic aspects of politics. He reminded his contemporaries that "the politicians of the ancient world were always talking about morals and virtue; ours speak of nothing but commerce and money." His argument against luxury was that it could produce a brilliant but not a lasting society, for although money "buys everything else, it cannot buy morals and citizens." Artists and musicians pursuing luxury will lower their genius to the level of the times, composing mediocre works that will be immediately admired. This is the evil consequence of learning in the arts and sciences where morals no longer have their rightful place and where taste has been corrupted. One way to confront this matter is to acknowledge the role of women for, says Rousseau, "men will always be what women choose to make them. If you wish then they should be noble and virtuous, let women be taught what greatness of soul and virtue are." But, says Rousseau, the question is no longer whether a man is honest but whether he is clever, not whether a book is useful but whether it is well-written. Rewards are lavished on ingenuity, but virtue is left unhonored.

Rousseau pointed to historical evidence for the notion that progress in the arts and sciences always leads to the corruption of morals and the decay of society. Egypt, he said not altogether correctly, was "the mother of philosophy and the fine arts; soon she was conquered by Cambyses, and then successively by the Greeks, the Romans, the Arabs and finally the Turks." Similarily, Greece, once peopled by heroes, "always learned, always voluptuous, and always a slave, has experienced amid all its revolutions no more than a change of masters." It was for this reason that in Greece "not all the eloquence of Demosthenes could breathe life into a body which luxury and the arts had once enervated." Rome developed a great empire when she was a nation of barbarians and soldiers, but when she relaxed the stoic discipline and fell into epicurean indulgence, she was scorned by other nations and derided even by the barbarians. Only Sparta, where patriotism was the supreme virtue and where arts, artists, science, and scholars were not tolerated, emerged as Rousseau's ideal state.

To see Rousseau praising ignorance during the height of the Enlightenment is an astonishing spectacle. But he did not mean to say that philosophy and science had no value. He quoted approvingly the words of Socrates who also had praised ignorance. For Athens had its sophists, poets, orators, and artists who had made extravagant claims to knowlege while in fact they knew very little, whereas, says Socrates, "I am at least in no doubt of my ignorance." What Rousseau was concerned about was the danger to morals and society caused by the confusion of contending theories or points of view. If everyone is allowed to pursue his own thoughts about moral values or even about scientific truth, it is inevitable that there will be serious differences of opinion. If differences of opinion are to be found everywhere, it will not be long before a deep skepticism will spread throughout the population.

A stable society is based upon a set of opinions or values which the majority accept as the rule for their thought and behavior. Rousseau believed that these firmly held opinions can be undermined by philosophy and science for several reasons. For one thing, each society is unique and its genius is its special local set of values. But science and philosophy seek to discover universal truth. The very pursuit of such universal truth exposes the local opinion as less than the truth and thereby destroys its authority. To compound this problem, science emphasizes the requirement of proof and evidence, yet the dominant opinions about the most important subjects cannot be demonstrated beyond doubt and therefore they lose their binding force. Moreover, science requires an attitude of doubt which is contrary to the mood of ready acceptance of opinion. What keeps society together is faith not knowledge. Both the scientist and the philosopher suspend faith during their pursuit of knowledge. So long as this suspension of faith is restricted to certain special individuals there is no great harm. What disturbed Rousseau was the damage done by the wide diffusion among the population of the spirit of doubt which culminates in skepticism. The step from skepticism to the loosening of morality in turn inevitably causes a weakening of public virtue, which Rousseau understood chiefly as the virtue of patriotism. The very spirit of science undermines patriotism since the scientist tends to be a cosmopolitan, whereas the patriot has a strong attachment to his own society. To counteract these disintegrating trends in society, strong governments become necessary and this, according to Rousseau, paves the way to despotism.

In the end, Rousseau's quarrel was not so much with philosophy and science as with the attempt to popularize these disciplines. He had great respect for Sir Francis Bacon, Descartes, and Sir Isaac Newton, whom he considered great teachers of mankind. But, he said, "It belongs only to a few to raise monuments to the glory of human learning," and it is proper to allow some men to apply themselves to the study of the arts and sciences. His attack was upon those who would distort knowledge by trying to make it popular, "those compilers who have indiscreetly broken open the door to the sciences and introduced into their sanctuary a populace unworthy to approach it." Men need to know, said Rousseau, that "nature would have preserved them from science, as a mother snatches a dangerous weapon from the hands of her child." Ordinary men should build their happiness upon the opinions which "we can find in our own hearts." Virtue, says Rousseau, is the "sublime science of simple minds," for the true philosophy is to "listen to the voice of conscience."

THE SOCIAL CONTRACT

Although Rousseau compares natural man in the "state of nature" with man as a citizen of a civil society, he admits that he cannot give a specific account of how the transition from the earlier condition to the later one occurred. The purpose of his book *The Social Contract* is therefore not to describe the change from man's natural state to his subsequent membership in a political society but rather to provide an answer to the question why it is that a person ought to obey the laws of government. Thus, Rousseau begins his book with the famous phrase that "Man is born free; and everywhere he is in chains." "How," he continues, "did this change come about? I do not know. What can make it legitimate? That question I think I can answer."

In the state of nature, man was happy, not because he was an angel but because he lived entirely for himself and therefore possessed an absolute independence. Rousseau rejected the doctrine of original sin and instead believed that the origin of evil is to be found in the later stages of man's development in society. In the state of nature, says Rousseau, man is motivated by "a natural sentiment [*amour de soi*] which inclines every animal to watch over his own preservation, and which, directed in man by reason and pity, produces humanity and virtue." By contrast, as man develops social contacts, he also develops vices, for now he is motivated by "an artificial sentiment [*amour propre*] which is born in society and which leads every individual to make more of himself than every other," and " this inspires in men all the evils they perpetrate on each other . . . ," including intense competition for the few places of honor, envy, malice, vanity, pride, and contempt. Ultimately, it was impossible to live alone, for in all probability, says Rousseau, it was the steady growth in numbers that first brought men together into society. How, then, were men to reconcile the independence into which they were born with the inevitability that they would have to live together? The problem, says Rousseau, is "to find a form of association which will defend and protect with the whole common force the person and goods of each associate, and in which each, while uniting himself with all, may still obey himself alone." The solution to this problem is "the total alienation of each associate, together with all his rights, to the whole community." While this solution appears on the surface to be a prescription for despotism, Rousseau was convinced that it was the road to freedom.

The idea of a "social contract" seems to imply that such a contract was entered into at some point in the historic past. Rousseau did not view the contract in historical terms since he admitted that there is no way to discover evidence for such an event. For him, the social contract is a living reality which will be found to be present wherever there is a legitimate government. This living contract is the fundamental principle underlying a political association; this principle helps to overcome the lawlessness of absolute license and assures liberty, because everyone willingly adjusts his conduct to harmonize with the legitimate freedom of others. What man loses by the social contract is his "natural liberty" and an unlimited right to everything; what he gains is "civil liberty" and a property right in what he possesses. The essence of the social contract, says Rousseau, is that "each of us puts his person and all his power in common under the supreme direction of the general will, and, in our corporate capacity, we receive each member as an indivisible part of a whole." This contract tacitly assumes that whoever refuses to obey the *general will* shall be compelled to do so by the whole body; in short, "this means that he will be forced to be free."

What is the justification for saying that citizens can be "forced to be free"? The law is, after all, the product of the "general will." In turn, the general will is, says Rousseau, the will of the "sovereign." For Rousseau, the sovereign consists of the total number of citizens of a given society. The general will of the sovereign is therefore the single will which reflects the sum of the wills of all the individual citizens. The many wills of the citizens can be considered one general will because everyone who is a party to the social contract (as every citizen is) has agreed to direct his actions (to limit his actions) to achieving the common good. Each citizen by thinking of his own good realizes that he should refrain from any behavior that would cause others to turn upon and injure him. In this way, each citizen understands that his own good and his own freedom is connected with the common good. Ideally, therefore, each individual's will is identical with every other individual's since they are all directed to the same purpose, namely, the common good. Because in this ideal setting all the individual wills are identical or at least consistent, it can be said that there is only one will, the general will. For this reason it can also be said that if laws are the product of the sovereign general will, each individual is really the author of those laws and in this way each person obeys only himself. The element of force or compulsion enters Rousseau's formula only when someone refuses to obey a law.

Rousseau distinguishes between the "general will" and the "will of all," saying that "there is often a great deal of difference between the will of all and the general will." What differentiates these two forms of the collective wills is the purpose each attempts to achieve. If the "will of all" had the same purpose as the "general will," namely, the common good or justice, there would be no difference between them. But, says Rousseau, there is often a different purpose pursued by the "will of all," where "all" refers to the voters of a group, even if by chance they are in the majority. Such a deviant purpose reflects special or private interests as opposed to the common good. When this happens, society no longer has a general will; it now has as many wills as there are groups or "factions." If, therefore, the general will is to be able to express itself, there must not be factions or partial societies within the state. Rousseau was convinced that if the people were given adequate information and had the opportunity to deliberate, and even if the citizens had no communication with one another and simply thought their own thoughts, they would arrive at the general will. They would choose the path leading to the common good or justice. Only the common good would provide the setting for the greatest possible freedom for each citizen.

At this point there could be someone who chooses not to obey the law. If the law was made with the common good or justice in mind, as opposed to special interests, then the law truly expresses the general will. The person who votes against this law or chooses to disobey it is in error: "When therefore the opinion that is contrary to my own prevails, this proves neither more nor less than that I was mistaken, and that what I thought to be the general will was not so." When a law is proposed, the citizens are not asked to approve or reject the proposal: they are asked to decide whether it is in conformity with the general will, that is, with the common good or justice. Only when the question is put this way can it be said that "the general will is found by counting the votes." Only under these circumstances is there any justification for forcing someone to obey the law. In effect he is then being forced to behave in accordance with a law he would have been willing to obey if he had accurately understood the requirements of the common good which alone provides him with the greatest amount of freedom. Only under these circumstances, says Rousseau, is it legitimate to say that "he will be forced to be free."

Rousseau was under no illusion that it would be easy to establish all the conditions for making just laws in the modern world. For one thing, much of his thought reflected the conditions in his small native Geneva where participation by the citizens could be more direct. In addition, his vision included certain assumptions that would require considerable human virtue. If everyone were required to obey the laws, then everyone would be entitled to participate in deciding upon those laws. When making the laws, those persons involved in the decisions would have to overcome special interests or the concerns of factions and self-consciously think of the common good. Rousseau also believed that all the citizens should be equally involved in the making of the laws, that the laws should not be made even by representatives, for "the people cannot, even if it wishes, deprive itself of this incommunicable right. . . ." But as the modern state has continued to grow in size and complexity, a development that Rousseau had already seen happening in his own day, his assumptions and conditions for achieving the just society appeared to be more of an ideal than an immediate possibility.

Taken as a whole, Rousseau's writings represented an attack on the Age of Reason, gave impetus to the Romantic movement by emphasizing feeling (leading Goethe to say that "feeling is all"), revived religion even though he had doubts about some traditional teachings, provided a new direction for education (his book *Émile* was considered by some the best work on education since Plato's *Republic*), inspired the French Revolution, made a unique impact upon political philosophy, and, more than any of his contemporaries, he influenced several subsequent philosophers, especially Immanuel Kant. On one occasion Kant was so absorbed in reading Rousseau's *Émile* that he forgot to take his celebrated daily walk. While Kant admitted that it was David Hume who awakened him from his dogmatic slumbers regarding the theory of knowledge, it was Rousseau who showed him the way to a new theory of morality. So impressed was Kant by the insights of Rousseau that he hung a picture of him on the wall of his study, convinced that Rousseau was the Newton of the moral world.

15

Kant:
Critical Mediator
Between
Dogmatism
and Skepticism

Immanuel Kant lived all of his eighty years (1724–1804) in the small provincial town of Königsberg in East Prussia. His parents were of modest means, and their religious spirit, nurtured by a sect known as Pietists, was to have a permanent influence upon Kant's thought and personal life. His education began at the local Collegium Fredericianum, whose director was also a Pietist, and in 1740 Kant entered the University of Königsberg. At the university he studied the classics, physics, and philosophy. The German universities were at this time dominated by the philosopher Christian von Wolff (1679–1754), who was neither a great nor an original thinker but whose achievement was that he stimulated philosophic activity by developing a comprehensive system of philosophy along the lines of Leibniz's rationalism and metaphysics. Kant's professor at Königsberg, Martin Knutzen, had come under the influence of this Wolff-Leibnizian approach to philosophy, and inevitably Kant's university training laid much emphasis upon the power of human reason to move with certainty in the realm of metaphysics. Although Martin Knutzen had thus slanted Kant's early thought toward the tradition of Continental rationalism, it was also Knutzen who stimulated Kant's interest in Newtonian physics, an interest that played a very important part in the development of Kant's original and critical philosophy. Upon completion of his university course, Kant spent about eight years as a family tutor, and in 1755 became a lecturer at the university. In 1770 he was appointed to the chair of philosophy that had been held by Knutzen.

Although Kant's personal life contains no remarkable events, as he did not travel and developed no notable political or social connections, he was, nevertheless, immensely successful as a lecturer and was an interesting conversationalist and charming host. He is often pictured as an old bachelor whose every activity was scheduled with such precision that neighbors could set their watches when he stepped out of his house each day at half past four to walk up and down his small avenue eight times. Without this discipline, however, he could hardly have produced such a striking succession of famous books as his monumental *Critique of Pure Reason* in 1781, *Prolegomena to Any Future Metaphysics* in 1783, *Principles of the Metaphysics of Ethics* in 1785, *Metaphysical First Principles of Natural Science* in 1786, the second edition of the *Critique of Pure Reason* in 1787, the *Critique of Practical Reason* in 1788, the *Critique of Judgment* in 1790, *Religion within the Limits of Mere Reason* in 1793, and the small work *Perpetual Peace* in 1795.

THE SHAPING OF KANT'S PROBLEM

Kant revolutionized philosophy. What prompted this revolution in Kant's mind was his profound concern over a problem that the philosophy of his day could not deal with successfully or adequately. The elements of his problem are suggested by his famous comment that "two things fill the mind with ever new and increasing admiration and awe . . . *the starry heavens above and the moral law within.*" To him the starry heavens were a reminder that the world, as pictured earlier by Hobbes and Newton, is a system of bodies in motion, where every event has a specific and determinate cause. At the same time, all men experience the sense of moral duty, an experience which implies that men, unlike some other elements of nature, possess freedom in their behavior. The problem, then, was how to reconcile the two seemingly contradictory interpretations of events, one holding that all events are the product of *necessity* and the other saying that in certain aspects of human behavior there is *freedom.*

As Kant viewed the drift of scientific thought, he saw in it an attempt to include *all* of reality, including human nature, in its mechanical model. This would mean that all events, being parts of a unified mechanism, could be explained in terms of cause and effect. Moreover, this scientific approach would eliminate from consideration any elements that could not fit into its method, a method that placed greatest emphasis upon limiting knowledge to the realm of actual sense experience and to generalizations that could be derived by induction from such experience. Pursuing this method, science would have no need for, nor could it account for, such notions as freedom and God.

Kant was impressed by the obvious success and the constant advance of scientific knowledge. What the success of Newtonian physics did for Kant was to raise some serious questions about the adequacy of the philosophy of his day. The two major traditions of his day were Continental rationalism and British empiricism, and Newtonian physics enjoyed an independence from both of these philosophical systems. Since Continental rationalism had been built upon a mathematical model, this mode of philosophizing emphasized the relation of *ideas* to each other and therefore had no clear connection with things as they really are. Rationalism could not produce the kind of knowledge Newtonian physics represented, and for this reason its metaphysical speculations about reality beyond experience were considered dogmatic. Kant was to say with some respect that Christian Wolff, whose Leibnizian metaphysics had influenced Kant's prerevolutionary thought, was "the greatest of all dogmatic philosophers." This contrast between rationalism and science raised for Kant the question whether metaphysics can increase our knowledge the way science obviously can. The dogmatic character of metaphysics was made clear particularly by the variety of conclusions to which metaphysicians had come in their systems of thought, as indicated by the differences between Descartes, Spinoza, and Leibniz. But the heart of the matter was that the scientists were proceeding successfully in unraveling the nature of reality and were showing less and less concern about such metaphysical notions as freedom and God and the possibility of moral and valuational truth.

At the same time, science proceeded independently of the other major philosophical tradition of Kant's day, namely, British empiricism. Hume's most striking philosophical argument was that since all our knowledge comes from experience, we cannot have any knowledge of "causality" or necessary connections because we do not experience causality, and, therefore, we cannot infer or predict any future event from our experience of the present. What we call *causality,* said Hume, is simply our habit of associating two events because we experience them together, but this does not justify the conclusion that these events have any necessary connection. Thus, Hume denied inductive inference. And yet, it is precisely upon the notion of causality and inductive inference that science is built, for it assumes that our knowledge of particular events in the present gives us reliable knowledge about an indefinite number of similar events in the future. The logical outcome of Hume's empiricism was that there cannot be any scientific knowledge, and this leads to philosophical skepticism. Kant was left, therefore, with great admiration for science but with serious questions about philosophy because of the dogmatism of rationalism and the skepticism of empiricism.

Although Newtonian physics impressed Kant, science itself raised two major questions for him. The first we have already mentioned, namely, that as the scientific method was applied to the study of all of reality including human behavior, the whole realm of moral values with its attendant notions of freedom and God was threatened by absorption into a mechanical universe. A second problem raised by science for Kant was how to explain, or to justify, scientific knowledge. That is, did the scientist give an adequate explanation of what makes his understanding of nature possible? As it turned out, these two problems were very closely related, because Kant discovered that in principle scientific knowledge is similar to metaphysical knowledge, and, therefore, the justification or explanation of scientific thought on the one hand and metaphysical thought concerning freedom and morality on the other are the same. Kant, therefore, rescued metaphysics not by attacking science but by discovering that what the scientist is doing in describing nature is similar to what the metaphysician is doing when he discusses freedom and morality. Both in science and in metaphysics, the mind starts with some given datum, which gives rise to a judgment in human reason. For this reason, says Kant, "the genuine method of metaphysics is fundamentally the same kind which Newton introduced into natural science and which was there so fruitful." By thus interpreting the nature of scientific and moral thought, Kant provided a new function and a new life for philosophy. This function is suggested by the title of Kant's major work, the *Critique of Pure Reason,* for now the task of philosophy became the critical appraisal of the capacities of human reason. In pursuing this new critical function, Kant achieved what he called his Copernican revolution in philosophy.

KANT'S CRITICAL PHILOSOPHY AND HIS COPERNICAN REVOLUTION

The turning point in Kant's intellectual development was his encounter with Hume's empiricism. He tells us that "I openly confess, the suggestion of David Hume was the very thing, which many years ago first interrupted my dogmatic slumber and gave my investigations in the field of speculative philosophy quite a new direction." Hume had argued that all our knowledge is derived from experience and that therefore we cannot have knowledge of any reality beyond our experience. This argument struck at the very foundation of rationalism, whose advocates had argued confidently that human reason can derive knowledge about realities beyond experience simply by moving from one idea to another as one does in mathematics. The rationalist proofs for the existence of God were a case in point, and Spinoza's and Leibniz's explanation of the structure of reality were another. Kant eventually turned his back on rationalist metaphysics, calling it "rotten dogmatism," but he did not accept Hume's entire argument, saying that "I was far from following him in the conclusions at which he arrived. . . ."

Kant refused to follow Hume all the way not merely because this would lead to skepticism but because he felt that although Hume was on the right track, he had not completed the task of explaining how knowledge is acquired. Nor did Kant wish to give up some of the subjects that concerned the rationalist metaphysicians, such as freedom and God, about which it is impossible to be "indifferent," even though he was prepared to say that we cannot have demonstrative knowledge of objects beyond our experience. Kant, therefore, sought to build upon what he thought was significant both in rationalism and empiricism and to reject what could not be defended in these systems. He did not simply combine the insights of his predecessors, but rather embarked upon a genuinely new approach, which he called *critical philosophy.*

The Way of Critical Philosophy Kant's *critical* philosophy consists of an analysis of the powers of human reason, by which he meant "a critical inquiry into the faculty of reason with reference to all the knowledge which it may strive to attain independently of all experience." The way of critical philosophy is, therefore, to ask the question "What and how much can understanding and reason know, apart from all experience?" Thus, whereas earlier metaphysicians engaged in disputes about the nature of the supreme being and other subjects that took them beyond the realm of immediate experience, Kant asked the critical question whether the human reason possessed the powers to undertake such inquiries. From this critical point of view Kant thought it foolish for metaphysicians to engage in attempts to construct systems of knowledge even before they had inquired into whether by pure reason alone one can apprehend what is not given to him in experience. Critical philosophy for Kant was therefore not the negation of metaphysics but rather a preparation for it. If metaphysics has to do with knowledge that is developed by reason alone, that is, prior to experience, or a priori, the critical question is how is such a priori knowledge possible.

The Nature of a Priori Knowledge Kant affirmed that we possess a faculty that is capable of giving us knowledge without an appeal to experience. He agreed with the empiricists that our knowledge begins with experience, but he added that "though our knowledge begins *with* experience, it does not follow that it all arises *out* of experience." This was the point that Hume had missed, for Hume had said that all our knowledge consists of a series of impressions, which we derive through our senses. Yet we clearly possess a kind of knowledge that does not come *out of* experience even though it begins *with* experience. Hume was right that we do not, for example, experience or sense *causality,* but Kant rejected his explanation that *causality* is simply a psychological habit of connecting two events that we call cause and effect. Kant believed that we have knowledge about causality and that we get this knowledge not from sense experience but directly from the faculty of rational judgment and, therefore, a priori.

What, more specifically, is a priori knowledge? Kant replies that "if one desires an example from the sciences, one needs only to look at any proposition in mathematics. If one desires an example from the commonest operations of the understanding, the proposition that every change must have a cause can serve one's purposes." What makes a proposition of mathematics, or the proposition that every change must have a cause, a priori knowledge? It is, says Kant, that this kind of knowledge cannot be derived from experience. Experience cannot show us that *every* change must have a cause since we have not yet experienced every change. Nor can experience show us that connections between events are *necessary,* for the most experience can tell us is "that a thing is so and so, but not that it cannot be otherwise." Experience, then, cannot give us knowledge about

necessary connections or about the *universality* of propositions. Yet we do in fact
have this kind of knowledge about causality and universality for these are the
notions that characterize mathematics and scientific knowledge. We confidently
say that all heavy objects will fall in space or that all instances of five added to
seven will equal twelve. That there is such a priori knowledge is clear, but what
concerned Kant was how such knowledge can be accounted for. How, in short,
can Hume's skepticism be answered? But it was not simply a question of how a
priori knowledge is possible, but how "synthetical judgments *a priori*" are possible. To answer this question, Kant had first to discover what constitutes a synthetical judgment a priori.

The Synthetic a Priori Kant distinguishes between two kinds of judgments, the
analytic and the *synthetic*. A judgment, he said, is an operation of thought
whereby we connect a subject and predicate, where the predicate qualifies in
some way the subject. When we say that "The building is tall," we make a
judgment, for the mind is able to understand a connection between the subject
and the predicate. Subjects and predicates are connected to each other in two
different ways, thereby leading the mind to make two different kinds of judgments.

In *analytic judgments,* the predicate is already contained in the concept of
the subject. The judgment that all triangles have three angles is an analytic
judgment. Because the predicate is already implicit in the subject of an analytic
judgment, such a predicate does not give us any new knowledge about the subject. Again, the judgment that "all bodies are extended" is analytic, for the idea
of extension is already contained in the idea of body. An analytic judgment is
true only because of the logical relation of subject and predicate. To deny an
analytic judgment would involve a logical contradiction.

A *synthetic judgment* differs from the analytic in that its predicate is not
contained in the subject. Thus, in a synthetic judgment the predicate adds something new to our concept of the subject. To say that "the apple is red" joins two
independent concepts, for the concept apple does not contain the idea of redness. Similarly, for Kant "all bodies are heavy" is an example of a synthetic
judgment, for the idea of heaviness is not contained in the concept of body, that
is, the predicate is not contained in the subject.

At this point, Kant makes a further distinction, this time between judgments that are a priori and judgments that are a posteriori. All analytic judgments
are a priori: their meaning does not depend upon our experience of any particular cases or events since they are independent of any observations, as in the case
of mathematics. As "necessity and strict universality are sure marks of *a priori*
knowledge," Kant has no trouble showing that analytic judgments represent a
priori knowledge. Synthetic judgments, on the other hand, are for the most part
a posteriori, that is, they occur after an experience of observation. To say, for
example, that all boys in school *X* are 6 feet tall is a synthetic judgment a
posteriori, for this proposition regarding their height is contingently and not
necessarily true of all the present or future members of that school. That judg-

ment cannot be made without experience with the particular details of this school. Thus, while all analytic judgments are a priori, most synthetic judgments are a posteriori.

There is, however, still another kind of judgment besides the analytic a priori and the synthetic a posteriori, and this is the *synthetic a priori*. This is the kind of judgment Kant was most concerned about because he was certain that we

Kant (*The Bettmann Archive*)

make these judgments and yet there was the persistent question how such judgments are possible. The question arises because by definition synthetic judgments are based upon experience, but if that is the case, how can they be called a priori, since this implies independence of experience? Still, Kant showed that in mathematics, physics, ethics, and metaphysics, we do make judgments that are not only a priori but also synthetic. For example, the judgment $7 + 5 = 12$ is certainly a priori because it contains the marks of necessity and universality; that is, 7 plus 5 *has* to equal 12, and it *always* has to do so. At the same time, this judgment is synthetic and not analytic because 12 cannot be derived by a mere analysis of the numbers 7 and 5. The act of intuition is necessary in order to achieve a synthesis of the concepts 7, 5, and plus. Kant shows that in propositions of geometry also the predicate is not contained in the subject even though there is a necessary and universal connection between subject and predicate. Thus, propositions of geometry are at once a priori and synthetic: For example, says Kant, "that a straight line between two points is the shortest, is a synthetic proposition. For my concept of *straight* contains no notion of quantity, but only of quality. The concept of *the shortest* is thus wholly an addition, and it cannot be derived by any analysis from the concept of a straight line. Intuition must, therefore, lend its aid here, by means of which alone is this synthesis possible." In physics, too, we find synthetic a priori judgments; Kant says that "natural science contains within itself synthetic *a priori* judgments as principles." The proposition "in all changes of the material world the quantity of matter remains unchanged" is a priori, for we make this judgment before we have experienced every change, and it is synthetic, for the idea of permanence is not discoverable in the concept of matter. In metaphysics, we assume that we are extending or increasing our knowledge. If this is so, the propositions of metaphysics, such as the judgment "man is free to choose" must be synthetic, for here the predicate adds new knowledge to the concept of the subject. At the same time, this metaphysical judgment is a priori, for the predicate *is free* is connected to our idea of all men even before we have experience of all men.

What Kant wanted to show by these illustrations is that it is not only in metaphysics but also in mathematics and physics that we make synthetic a priori judgments. If these judgments create difficulties in metaphysics, they create the same ones for mathematics and physics. Kant believed, therefore, that if synthetic a priori judgments could be explained or justified in mathematics and physics, they would, thereby, also be justified in metaphysics.

Kant's Copernican Revolution   Kant solved the problem of the synthetic a priori judgment by substituting a new hypothesis concerning the relation between the mind and its objects. It was clear to him that if we assume, as Hume did, that the mind, in forming its concepts, must conform to its objects, there could be no solution to the problem. Hume's theory would work for our ideas of things we have actually experienced, but these are a posteriori judgments. If I ask, "How do I know that the chair is brown?" my answer is that I can see it; and if my assertion is challenged, I refer to my experience. When I thus refer to my experience, that settles the question, because we all agree that experience gives us a kind of knowledge that conforms to the nature of things. But a synthetic *a priori* judgment cannot be validated by experience; if I say, for example, that every straight line is the shortest way between two points, I certainly cannot say that I have had experience of every possible straight line. What makes it possible for me to make judgments about events before they even occur, judgments that are universally true and can always be verified? If, as Hume believed, the mind is passive and simply receives its information from the objects, it follows that the mind would have information only about that particular object. But the mind makes judgments about all objects, even those that it has not yet experienced, and, in addition, objects do in fact behave in the future according to these judgments we make about them. This scientific knowledge gives us reliable information about the nature of things. But since this knowledge, which is both synthetic and a priori, could not be explained on the assumption that the mind conforms to its objects (how could it conform to every straight line . . . every change?), Kant was forced to try a new hypothesis regarding the relation between the mind and its objects.

Kant's new hypothesis was that it is the objects that conform to the operations of the mind, and not the other way around. He came to this hypothesis with a spirit of experimentation, consciously following the example of Copernicus, who, "failing of satisfactory progress in explaining the movements of the heavenly bodies on the supposition that they all revolved round the spectator, he tried whether he might not have better success if he made the spectator to revolve and the stars to remain at rest." Seeing an analogy here with his own problem, Kant says that "hitherto it has been assumed that all our knowledge must conform to objects. But all our attempts to extend our knowledge of objects by establishing something in regard to them *a priori* by means of concepts, have, on this assumption, ended in failure. We must, therefore, make trial whether we may not have more success in the tasks of metaphysics, if we suppose that objects must conform to our knowledge. . . . If intuition must conform to the constitution of the objects, I do not see how we could know anything of the latter *a priori;* but if the object (as object of the senses) must conform to the constitution of our faculty of intuition, I have no difficulty in conceiving such a possibility."

Kant did not mean to say that the mind creates objects, nor did he mean that the mind possesses innate ideas. His Copernican revolution consisted rather in his saying that the mind brings something to the objects it experiences. With Hume, Kant agreed that our knowledge begins with experience, but unlike Hume, Kant saw the mind as an active agent doing something with the objects it experiences. The mind, says Kant, is structured in such a way that it imposes its way of knowing upon its objects. By its very nature, the mind actively organizes our experiences. That is, thinking involves not only receiving impressions through our senses but also making judgments about what we experience. Just as a person who wears colored glasses sees everything in that color, so every human being, having the faculty of thought, inevitably thinks about things in accordance with the natural structure of the mind.

THE STRUCTURE OF RATIONAL THOUGHT

Kant says that "there are two sources of human knowledge, which perhaps spring from a common but to us unknown root, namely sensibility and understanding. Through the former objects are *given* to us; through the latter they are *thought*." Knowledge is, therefore, a cooperative affair between the knower and the thing known. But, although I am able to distinguish the difference between myself as a knower and the thing I know, I can never know that thing as it is in itself, for the moment I know it, I know it as my structured mind permits me to know it. If colored glasses were permanently fixed to my eyes, I should always see things in that color and could never escape the limitations placed on my vision by those glasses. Similarly, my mind always brings certain ways of thinking to things, and this always affects my understanding of them. What does the mind bring to the *given* raw materials of our experience?

The Categories of Thought and the Forms of Intuition   The distinctive activity of the mind is to synthesize and to unify our experience. It achieves this synthesis first by imposing on our various experiences in the "sensible manifold" certain forms of intuition: space and time. We inevitably perceive things as being in *space* and *time*. But space and time are not ideas derived from the things we experience, nor are they concepts. Space and time are encountered immediately in intuition and are, at the same time, a priori or, to speak figuratively, lenses through which we always see objects of experience.

In addition to space and time, which deal particularly with the way we sense things, there are certain categories of thought, which deal more specifically with the way the mind unifies or synthesizes our experience. The mind achieves this unifying act by making various kinds of judgments as we engage in the act of interpreting the world of sense. The manifold of experience is judged by us through certain fixed forms or concepts such as *quantity, quality, relation,* and *modality*. When we assert *quantity*, we have in mind one or many; when we make a judgment of *quality*, we make either a positive or negative statement; when we make a judgment of *relation*, we think of cause and effect, on the one hand, or of the relation of subject and predicate on the other; and when we make a judgment of *modality*, we have in mind that something is either possible or impossible. All these ways of thinking are what constitute the act of synthesis through which the mind strives to make a consistent single world out of the manifold of sense impressions.

The Self and the Unity of Experience   What makes it possible for us to have a unified grasp of the world about us? From his analysis of the way our minds work, Kant's answer is that it is the mind that transforms the raw data given to our senses into a coherent and related set of elements. But this leads Kant to say that the unity of our experience must imply a unity of the self, for unless there was a unity between the several operations of the mind, there could be no knowledge of experience. To have such knowledge involves, in various sequences, sensation, imagination, memory, as well as the powers of intuitive synthesis. Thus, it must be the same self that at once senses an object, remembers its characteristics, imposes upon it the forms of space and time and the category of cause and effect. All these activities must occur in some single subject; otherwise, there could be no knowledge, for if one subject had only sensations, another only memory, and so on, the sensible manifold could never be unified.

Where and what is this single subject that accomplishes this unifying activity? Kant calls it the "transcendental unity of apperception," what we should call the *self*. He uses the term *transcendental* to indicate that we do not experience the self directly even though such a unity, or self, is implied by our actual experience. Thus, the idea of this self is a priori as a necessary condition for the experience we do have of having knowledge of a unified world of nature. In the act of unifying all the elements of experience, we are conscious of our own unity, so that our consciousness of a unified world of experience and our own self-consciousness occur simultaneously. Our self-consciousness, however, is affected by the same faculties that affect our perception of external objects. I bring to the knowledge of myself the same apparatus and, therefore, impose upon myself as an object of knowledge the same "lenses" through which I see everything. Just as I do not know things as they are apart from the perspective from which I see them, so also I do not know the nature of this "transcendental unity of apperception" except as I am aware of the knowledge I have of the unity of the field of experience. What I am sure of is that a unified self is implied by any knowledge of experience.

Phenomenal and Noumenal Reality   A major impact of Kant's critical philosophy was his insistence that human knowledge is forever limited in its scope. This limitation takes two forms. In the first place, knowledge is limited to the world of experience. Secondly, our knowledge is limited by the manner in which our faculties of perception and thinking organize the raw data of experience. Kant did not doubt that the world as it appears to us is not the ultimate reality. He distinguished between *phenomenal* reality, or the world as we experience it, and *noumenal* reality, which is purely intelligible, or nonsensual, reality. When we experience a thing, we inevitably perceive it through the "lenses" of our a priori categories of thought. But what is a thing like when it is not being perceived? What is a thing-in-itself (*Ding an sich*)? We can obviously never have an experience of a nonsensuous perception. All objects we know are sensed objects. Still, we know that the existence of our world of experience is not produced by the mind. The mind, rather, imposes its ideas upon the manifold of experience, which is derived from the world of things-in-themselves. This means that there is a reality external to us that exists independently of us but that we can know only as it appears to us and is organized by us. The concept of a thing-in-itself does not, then, increase our knowledge but reminds us of the limits of knowledge.

Transcendental Ideas of Pure Reason as Regulative Concepts   Besides the general concept of the noumenal realm, there are three regulative ideas that we tend to think about, ideas that lead us beyond sense experiences but about which we cannot be indifferent because of our inevitable tendency to try to unify all our experience. These are the ideas of the *self,* of the *cosmos,* and of *God.* They are *transcendental* because they correspond to no object in our experience. They are produced not by intuition but by pure reason alone. They are, however, prompted by experience in the sense that we think those ideas in our attempts to achieve a coherent synthesis of all our experience. Kant says that "the first [regulative] idea is the 'I' itself, viewed simply as thinking nature or soul . . . endeavoring to represent all determinations as existing in a single subject, all powers, so far as possible, as derived from a single fundamental power, all change as belonging to the states of one and the same permanent being, and all *appearances* in space as completely different from the actions of thought." In this way our pure reason tries to synthesize the various psychological activities we are aware of into a unity, and it does this by formulating the concept of the *self.*

Similarly, pure reason tries to create a synthesis of the many events in experience by forming the concept of the *world,* so that "the second regulative idea of merely speculative reason is the concept of the world in general. . . . The absolute totality of the series of conditions . . . an idea which can never be completely realized in the empirical employment of reason, but which yet serves as a rule that prescribes how we ought to proceed in dealing with such series. . . . The cosmological ideas are nothing but simply regulative principles, and are very far from positing . . . an actual totality of such series. . . ."

Kant continues, "the third idea of pure reason, which contains a merely relative supposition of a being that is the sole and sufficient cause of all cosmological series, is the idea of *God.* We have not the slightest ground to assume in an absolute manner the object of this idea. . . . It becomes evident that the idea of such a being, like all speculative ideas, seems only to formulate the command of reason, that all connection in the world be viewed in accordance with the principles of a systematic unity—*as if* all such connection had its source in one single all-embracing being as the supreme and sufficient cause."

Kant's use of these regulative ideas exemplifies his way of mediating between dogmatic rationalism and skeptical empiricism. With the empiricists, Kant agrees that we can have no knowledge of reality beyond experience. The ideas of the self, the cosmos, and God cannot give us any theoretical knowledge of realities corresponding to these ideas. The function of these ideas is simply and solely regulative. As regulative ideas, they give us a reasonable way of dealing with the constantly recurring questions raised by metaphysics. To this extent Kant acknowledged the validity of the subject matter of rationalism. His critical analysis of the scope of human reason, however, led him to discover that earlier rationalists had made the error of treating *transcendental* ideas as though they were ideas about *transcendent* or actual beings. Kant emphasizes that "there is a great difference between something given to my reason as an *object absolutely,* or merely as an *object in the idea.* In the former case our concepts are employed to determine the object [transcendent]; in the latter case there is in fact only a scheme for which no object, not even a hypothetical one, is directly given, and which only enables us to represent to ourselves other objects in an indirect manner, namely in their systematic unity, by means of their relation to this idea. Thus, I say, that the concept of a highest intelligence is a mere idea [transcendental]. . . ."

The Antinomies and the Limits of Reason   Because regulative ideas do not refer to any objective reality about which we can have knowledge, we must consider these ideas as being the products of our pure reason. As such we cannot bring to these ideas the a priori forms of time and space or the category of cause and effect since these are imposed by us only upon the sensible manifold. Science is possible because all men, having the same structure of mind, will always and everywhere order the events of sense experience the same way; that is, we all bring to the *given* of sense experience the same organizing faculties of understanding. But there can be no science of metaphysics because there is not the same kind of *given* when we consider the ideas of self, cosmos, and God as when we consider "the shortest distance between two points." What *is* given in metaphysics is the felt need to achieve a synthesis of the wide variety of events in experience at ever-higher levels and of discovering an ever-wider explanation of the realm of phenomena.

There is a difference for Kant between a priori or theoretical scientific knowledge, on the one hand, and speculative metaphysics on the other. The difference is that we can have scientific knowledge of phenomena but cannot have scientific knowledge of the noumenal realm, or the realm that transcends experience. Our attempts to achieve a "science" of metaphysics, says Kant, are doomed to failure. Whenever we try to discuss the self, the cosmos, or God as though they were objects of experience, the inability of the mind ever to do so successfully is indicated by what Kant calls the *antinomies* into which we fall. These four antinomies show us that when we discuss the nature of the world beyond experience, we can argue with equal force on opposite sides of various propositions, namely, that (1) the world is limited in time and space, or that it is unlimited; that (2) every composite substance in the world is made up of simple parts, or that no composite thing in the world is made up of simple parts since there nowhere exists in the world anything simple; that (3) besides causality in accordance with the laws of nature there is also another causality, that of freedom, or that there is no freedom since everything in the world takes place solely in accordance with the laws of nature; and, finally, that (4) there exists an absolutely necessary being as a part of the world or as its cause, or an absolutely necessary being nowhere exists.

These antinomies reflect the disagreements generated by dogmatic metaphysics, disagreements that occur only because they are based upon "non-sense," that is, upon attempts to describe a reality about which we have, and can have, no sense experience. Kant did, however, believe that these antinomies have positive value; namely, that they provide an additional argument for saying that the world of space and time is phenomenal only and that in such a world freedom is a coherent idea. This follows because if the world were a thing-in-itself, it would have to be either finite or infinite in extent and divisibility. But the antinomies show that there can be no demonstrative proof that either alternative is true.

Insofar, then, as the world is phenomenal only, we are justified in affirming moral freedom and human responsibility.

As regulative ideas, the concepts of the self, the world, and God have a legitimate function, for they help us to synthesize our experience. Also, to speak of a noumenal realm, or the realm of the thing-in-itself, is to respond to certain given experiences and tendencies of our thought. For this reason we can think of a person in two different ways, as a phenomenon and as a noumenon. As a phenomenon, a person can be studied scientifically as a being in space and time and in the context of cause and effect. At the same time, our experience of moral obligation suggests that a person's noumenal nature, what he is like beyond our sense perception of him, is characterized by freedom. In this context, the concept of freedom, as the idea of the self, or God, is a regulative idea. There can never be any demonstrative proof either that man is free or that God exists, for these concepts refer us beyond sense experience where the categories of the mind have no data upon which to work.

Proofs of God's Existence   With this critical estimate of the powers and scope of human reason, it was inevitable that Kant would reject the traditional proofs for the existence of God, namely, the *ontological, cosmological,* and *teleological* proofs. His argument against the *ontological* proof is that it is all a verbal exercise, for the essence of this proof is the assertion that since we have the idea of a most perfect being, it would be contradictory to say that such a being does not exist. Such a denial would be contradictory because the concept of a perfect being necessarily includes the predicate of *existence.* A being, that is, that does not exist can hardly be considered a perfect being. But Kant argues that this line of reasoning is "taken from judgments, not from things and their existence," that the idea of God is made to have the predicate of existence by simply fashioning the concept in such a way that existence is made to be included in the idea of a perfect being. This argument nowhere indicates why it is necessary to have the subject, *God.* There would be a contradiction if a perfect being did exist and we denied that such a being was omnipotent. But to say that we avoid a contradiction by agreeing that a supreme being is omnipotent does not by itself demonstrate that such a being exists. Moreover, to deny that God exists is not simply to deny a predicate but to abandon the subject and thereby all the predicates that go with it, and "if we reject subject and predicate alike, there is no contradiction; for nothing is then left to be contradicted." Kant concluded, therefore, that "all the trouble and labour bestowed on the famous ontological or cartesian proof of the existence of a supreme Being from concepts alone is trouble and labour wasted. A man might as well expect to become richer in knowledge by the aid of mere ideas as a merchant to increase his wealth by adding some noughts to his cash account."

Whereas the ontological proof begins with an idea (of a perfect being), the *cosmological* proof "takes its stand on experience," for it says that "I exist, therefore, an absolutely necessary being exists," on the assumption that if anything exists an absolutely necessary being must also exist. The error of this argument according to Kant is that while it begins with experience, it soon moves beyond experience. Within the realm of sense experience it is legitimate to infer a cause for each event, but "the principle of causality has no meaning and no criterion for its application save only in the sensible world." Here is the direct application of Kant's critical method, for he argues that we cannot employ the *a priori* categories of the mind in trying to describe realities beyond sense experience. The cosmological argument cannot, therefore, securely lead us to a first cause of all things, for the most we can infer from our experience of things is a regulative idea of God. Whether there actually is such a being, a ground of all contingent things, raises the same question posed by the ontological argument, namely, whether we can successfully bridge the gap between our idea of a perfect being and demonstrative proof of its existence.

Similarly, the *teleological* argument begins with considerable persuasiveness, for it says that "in the world we everywhere find clear signs of an order in accordance with a determinate purpose. . . . The diverse things could not of themselves have cooperated, by so great a combination of diverse means, to the fulfillment of determinate final purposes, had they not been chosen and designed for these purposes by an ordering rational principle in conformity with underlying ideas." To this argument Kant replies that it may very well be that our experience of order in the universe suggests an orderer, but order in the world does not demonstrate that the material stuff of the world could not exist without an orderer. The most this argument from design can prove, says Kant, "is an *architect* of the world who is always very much hampered by the adaptability of the material in which he works, not a *creator* of the world to whose idea everything is subject." To prove the existence of a creator leads us back to the cosmological argument with its idea of causality, but since we cannot use the category of causality beyond the things in experience, we are left simply with an idea of a first cause or creator, and this takes us back to the ontological argument, with its deficiencies. Kant's conclusion, therefore, is that we cannot use transcendental ideas or theoretical principles, which have no application beyond the field of sense experience, to demonstrate the existence of God.

It follows from Kant's critical remarks about the "proofs," however, that just as we cannot demonstrate God's existence, neither can we demonstrate that God does not exist. By pure reason alone we can neither prove nor disprove God's existence. If, therefore, the existence of God cannot be effectively dealt with by the theoretical reason, which Kant has gone to such lengths to show has relevance only in the realm of sense experience, some other aspect of reason must be considered as the source of the idea of God. Thus, the idea of God has importance in Kant's philosophy, as do other regulative ideas.

PRACTICAL REASON

Besides the "starry heavens above," it was also the "moral law within" that filled Kant with wonder. He was aware that human beings not only gaze upon a world of things but become participants in a world of action. Reason is, therefore, alternately concerned with theory about things and with practical behavior. But there is "ultimately only one and the same reason which has to be distinguished in its application," says Kant, and of the objectives of reason, "the first is *theoretical*, the second *practical* rational knowledge." It was Kant's way of explaining the scope and powers of pure theoretical reason that made possible his account of the practical reason.

The tendency of the scientific thought of Kant's day was to identify reality with what we can know from sense experience, from appearance. If this were a true account of reality, knowledge would consist only of a sensible manifold understood as things strictly related to each other by causality. Reality would then be viewed as a large mechanism whose every activity was the product of prior causes, and man would also be viewed as a part of this mechanical system. If this were the case, says Kant, "I could not . . . without palpable contradiction say of one and the same thing, for instance the human soul, that its will is free and yet is subject to natural necessity, that is, not free." Kant avoided this contradiction by saying that man's phenomenal self, or the self we can observe, is subject to natural necessity or causality, whereas his noumenal self as a thing-in-itself possesses freedom. It is in a negative way, by limiting the scope of theoretical reason to the sensible manifold, that Kant made way for the positive use of practical reason: insofar as "our Critique limits speculative reason, it is indeed *negative*, but since it thereby removes an obstacle which stands in the way of the employment of practical reason, nay threatens to destroy it, it has in reality a positive and very important use." Morality becomes possible because even though we cannot know things-in-themselves, or objects in the noumenal realm, "we must yet be in a position at least to *think* them as things-in-themselves; otherwise we should be landed in the absurd conclusion that there can be appearance without anything that appears." But "if our Critique is not in error in teaching that the object [e.g., a human being] is to be taken *in a twofold sense*, namely as appearance and as a thing-in-itself . . . then there is no contradiction in supposing that one and the same will is, in the appearance, that is, in visible acts, necessarily subject to the law of nature, and so far not free, while yet, as belonging to a thing-in-itself, is not subject to that law, and is, therefore *free*." To be sure, the soul cannot be *known* by speculative reason as being free, "but though I cannot *know*, I can yet *think* freedom. . . ." Kant has, therefore, provided the basis for moral and religious discourse by distinguishing two kinds of reality, the phenomenal and the noumenal, and by limiting the scope of science to the phenomenal and justifying the use of practical reason in connection with the noumenal world.

The Basis of Moral Knowledge   The task of moral philosophy, according to Kant, is to discover how we are able to arrive at principles of behavior that are binding upon all men. He was sure that we cannot discover these principles simply by studying the actual behavior of people, for although such a study would give us interesting anthropological information about how people *do* behave, it would not tell us how they *ought* to behave. Still, we do make moral judgments when we say, for example, that we ought to tell the truth, and the question is how we arrive at such a rule of behavior. For Kant, the moral judgment that "we ought to tell the truth" is on principle the same as the scientific judgment that "every change must have a cause." What makes them similar is that both of these judgments come from our reason and not from the objects we experience. Just as our theoretical reason brings the category of causality to visible objects and thereby explains the process of change, so also the practical reason brings to any given moral situation the concept of duty or ought. Both in science and in moral philosophy we use concepts that go beyond any particular facts we experience at any one time. Experience in both cases is the occasion for triggering the mind to think in universal terms. When we experience a given example of change, our minds bring to this event the category of causality, which makes it possible to explain the relation of cause and effect not only in this case but in all cases of change. Similarly, in the context of human relations, the practical reason is able to determine how we should behave not only at this moment but what should be the principle of our behavior at all times. Like scientific knowledge, moral knowledge is based upon a priori judgments. Just as Kant discovered that scientific knowledge is possible because of the a priori categories that the mind brings to experience, so he now says that "the basis of obligation must not be sought in human nature or in the circumstances of the world in which [man] is placed, but *a priori* simply in the concepts of reason."

Morality for Kant is, therefore, an aspect of rationality and has to do with our consciousness of rules or "laws" of behavior, which we consider both universal and necessary. The qualities of *universality* and *necessity* are the marks of a priori judgments, and this further confirms Kant's view that the principles of behavior are derived by the practical reason a priori. Instead of searching for the quality of "goodness" in the effects of our actions, Kant focuses upon the rational aspect of our behavior.

Morality and Rationality   As a rational being, I not only ask the question "What shall I do?" but am also conscious of being under an obligation to act in particular ways, that I "ought" to do something. These rational activities reflect the powers of practical reason, and I can assume that all rational beings are aware of the same problems. When I consider what I must do, therefore, I am also considering what all rational beings must do, for if a moral law or rule is valid for me as a rational being, it must be valid for all rational beings. A major test of a morally good act is, therefore, whether its principle can be applied to all rational beings and applied consistently. Moral philosophy is the quest for these principles that apply to all rational beings and that lead to behavior that we call *good*.

"Good" Defined as the Good Will   Kant says that "Nothing can possibly be conceived in the world, or even out of it, which can be called good, without qualification, except a good will." He would admit, of course, that other things can be considered good, such as moderation of the passions, "and yet one can hardly call them unreservedly good . . . for without the principles of a good will they may become evil indeed. The cold-bloodedness of a villain not only makes him far more dangerous, but also directly makes him seem more despicable to us than he would have seemed without it." Kant's chief point is that the essence of the morally good act is the principle that a person affirms when he wills an act. "The good will is good not because of what it causes or accomplishes, not because of its usefulness in the attainment of some set purpose, but alone because of the willing, that is to say, it is good of itself."

A rational being strives to do what he *ought* to do, and this Kant distinguishes from an act that a person does either from *inclination* or *self-interest*. We can all compare the differences in these motives, for to act either from inclination or self-interest appears to us to be on a different level morally from acting out of *duty* to the moral law. The reason Kant makes the rather startling statement that the "good will is good not because of what it accomplishes" is that he wants to emphasize the dominant role of the will in morality. It is not enough for the effects or consequences of our behavior to *agree with* the moral law; the truly moral act is done *for the sake of the moral law,* "for all these effects—even the promotion of the happiness of others—could have been also brought about by other causes, so that for this there would have been no need of the will of a rational being. . . ." The seat of moral worth is in the will, and the good will is one that acts out of a sense of duty; and "an action done from duty must wholly exclude the influence of inclination, and with it every object of the will, so that nothing remains which can determine the will except objectively the *law* and subjectively *pure respect* for this practical law. . . ."

Duty implies that we are under some kind of obligation, a moral law, and Kant says that as rational beings we are aware of this obligation as it comes to us in the form of an *imperative.* Not all imperatives or commands are connected with morality, for they are not in every case directed to all men and therefore lack the quality of universality that a moral rule requires. There are, for example, *technical* imperatives or rules of skill, which command us to do certain things *if* we want to achieve certain ends: *if* we want to build a bridge across the river, we *must* use materials of certain strength. But we do not absolutely have to build a bridge. We can either build a tunnel or use surface craft to get to the other side. Similarly, there are certain *prudential* imperatives, which say, for example, that if I want to be popular with certain people, I *must* say or do certain things. But again, it is not absolutely necessary that I achieve this popularity. The technical and prudential imperatives are, therefore, *hypothetical* imperatives because they command us only if we decide to enter their sphere of operation.

The Categorical Imperative   Unlike the technical and prudential imperatives, which are hypothetical in nature, the truly moral imperative is *categorical.* This categorical imperative applies to all men and commands "an action as necessary of itself without reference to another end, that is, as objectively necessary." It commands certain conduct immediately, without having any other purpose as a condition. Actually, the categorical imperative commands a law that forms the basis of particular actions. It is *categorical* because it instantly applies to all rational beings, and it is *imperative* because it is the principle on which we *ought to act*. The basic formulation of the categorical imperative is this: "*Act only on that maxim whereby thou canst at the same time will that it should become a universal law.*" Kant had said that "everything in nature works according to laws. Rational beings alone have the faculty of acting according *to the conception of laws. . . .*" Now he wants to indicate that the categorical imperative is our conception of the law of nature as it pertains to human behavior, and, therefore, he expresses the imperative of duty in an alternate way, namely, "*Act as if the maxim of thy action were to become a universal law of nature.*"

It is clear that the categorical imperative does not give us specific rules of conduct, for it appears to be simply an abstract formula. Still, this was precisely what Kant thought moral philosophy should provide us in order to guide our moral behavior, for once we understand the fundamental principle of the moral law, we can then apply it to specific cases. To illustrate how the categorical imperative enables us to discover our moral duties, Kant gives the following example: A man "finds himself forced by necessity to borrow money. He knows that he will not be able to repay it, but sees also that nothing will be lent to him unless he promises stoutly to repay it in a definite time. He desires to make this promise, but he has still so much conscience as to ask himself: Is it not unlawful and inconsistent with duty to get out of a difficulty in this way? Suppose, however, that he resolves to do so, then the maxim of his action would be expressed thus: When I think myself in want of money, I will borrow money and promise to repay it, although I know that I never can do so. Now this principle of self-love or of one's own advantage may perhaps be consistent with my whole future welfare; but the question now is, Is it right? I change then the suggestion of self-love into a universal law, and state the question thus: How would it be if my maxim were a universal law? Then I see at once that it could never hold as a universal law of nature, but would necessarily contradict itself. For supposing it to be a universal law that everyone when he thinks himself in a difficulty should be able to promise whatever he pleases, with the purpose of not keeping his promise, the promise itself would become impossible, as well as the end that one might have in view in it, since no one would consider that anything was promised to him, but would ridicule all such statements as vain pretenses."

If one were still to ask why he must tell the truth, or why he should avoid the contradiction involved in a false promise, Kant answers that there is something about a human being that makes him resist and resent being treated as a *thing* instead of a *person*. What makes us persons is our rationality, and to be a person, or a rational being, is therefore an end in itself. We become a thing when some one uses us as a means for some other end, as when one tells us a lie; but however necessary such use of us may be at times, we nevertheless consider ourselves as being of absolute intrinsic worth as persons. The individual human being as possessing absolute worth becomes the basis for the supreme principle of morality: "the foundation of this principle is: *rational nature exists as an end in itself.* All men everywhere want to be considered persons instead of things for the same reason that I do, and this affirmation of the absolute worth of the individual leads to a second formulation of the categorical imperative which says: *So act as to treat humanity, whether in thine own person or in that of any other, in every case as an end withal, never as means only."*

There is a third formulation of the categorical imperative, which is already implied in the first two but which Kant wants to make explicit by saying that we should "always so act that the *will could regard itself at the same time as making universal law through its own maxim."* Here Kant speaks of the *autonomy* of the will, that each person through his own act of will legislates the moral law. He distinguishes autonomy from *heteronomy,* the determination (of a law or action) by someone or something other than the self. Thus an heteronomous will is influenced or even determined by desires or inclination. An autonomous will, on the other hand, is free and independent, and as such is the "supreme principle of morality." Central to the concept of the autonomy of the will is the idea of *freedom,* the crucial regulative idea, which Kant employed to distinguish between the worlds of science and morality, the phenomenal and noumenal worlds; he says that "the *will* is a kind of causality belonging to living beings in so far as they are rational, and *freedom* would be this property of such causality that it can be efficient, independently of foreign causes determining it; just as *physical necessity* is the property that the causality of all irrational being has of being determined to activity by the influence of foreign causes." And again, ". . . I affirm that we must attribute to every rational being which has a will that it has also the idea of freedom and acts entirely under this idea. For in such a being we conceive a reason that is practical, that is, has causality in reference to its objects." The categorical imperative, therefore, speaks of the universality of the moral law, affirms the supreme worth of each rational person, and assigns freedom or autonomy to the will. Our experience of the moral law suggested to Kant some further insights concerning the postulates of freedom, immortality, and God.

The Moral Postulates Kant did not think it possible to prove or demonstrate that God exists or that the human will is free. Freedom is an idea that it is necessary to assume because of our experience of moral obligation, that is, "because I must, I can." Though we cannot demonstrate that our wills are free, we are intellectually compelled to assume such freedom, for freedom and morality "are so inseparably united that one might define practical freedom as independence of the will of anything but the moral law alone." How could a person be responsible or have a duty if he were not able or free to fulfill his duty or respond to the moral command? Freedom must be assumed, and as such it is the first postulate of morality.

A second moral postulate for Kant is *immortality.* The line of reasoning by which Kant was led to postulate immortality begins with his conception of the supreme good, or the *summum bonum.* Although virtue is the supreme good, we as rational beings are fully satisfied only when there is a union between virtue and happiness. Though it does not always happen so, we all assume that virtue ought to produce happiness. Kant had rigorously maintained that the moral law commands us to act not so that we be happy, but so that our actions will be *right*. Still, the full realization of a rational being requires that we think of the supreme good as including both virtue and happiness. But our experience indicates that there is no necessary connection between virtue and happiness. If we were to limit human experience to this world, it would then appear impossible to achieve the supreme good in its fullness. Still, the moral law does command us to strive for perfect good, and this implies an indefinite progress toward this ideal, "but this endless progress is possible only on the supposition of the unending duration of the existence and personality of the same rational being, which is called the immortality of the soul."

The moral universe also compels us to postulate the existence of God as the grounds for the necessary connection between virtue and happiness. If we mean by happiness "the state of a rational being in the world with whom in the totality of his experience *everything goes according to his wish and will*," then happiness implies a harmony between man's will and physical nature. But man is not the author of the world, nor is he capable of ordering nature so as to effect a necessary connection between virtue and happiness. But since we do conclude from our conception of the supreme good that virtue and happiness must go together, we must postulate "the existence of a cause of the whole of nature which is distinct from nature and which contains the ground of this connection, namely, of the exact harmony of happiness with morality," and thus "it is morally necessary to assume the existence of God." This is not to say that there cannot be morality without religion, for Kant has already indicated that a person can recognize his moral duty without the idea of God and that he must obey the law simply out of respect for the law, "for duty's sake." But Kant does say that "through the idea of the supreme good as object and final end of the pure practical reason the moral law leads to religion, that is to the recognition of all duties as divine commands, not as sanctions, that is, as arbitrary commands of an alien will . . . but as essential laws of every free will in itself, which, however, must be looked on as commands of the supreme Being, because it is only from a morally perfect and at the same time all-powerful will . . . that we hope to attain the highest good, which the moral law makes it our duty to take as the object of our endeavor."

Whether Kant succeeded in reaching the objectives he set for his new critical philosophy, his achievement was monumental. It may very well be that his mistakes along the way were more important than most men's successes, but what is beyond question is that although it is not necessary to accept everything Kant said, it is nevertheless virtually impossible to philosophize today without taking his views into account.

16

Hegel:
Absolute
Idealism

Hegel's historical significance lies in the fact that he accomplished with extraordinary and systematic thoroughness what Kant had so recently said could not be done. Kant had argued that metaphysics is impossible, that it is impossible for the human mind to achieve theoretical knowledge about all of reality. Hegel, on the other hand, set forth the general proposition that "what is rational is real and what is real is rational," and from this concluded that everything that is, is knowable. Here was an elaborate metaphysics, which provided a new basis for thinking about the very structure of reality and about its manifestations in morality, law, religion, art, history, and above all thought itself. It might be argued that the eventual decline of Hegelian philosophy was more a matter of abandonment than of studied attack, more like deserting a mansion than capturing a stronghold. But to imply that Hegel's successors merely decided to ignore his elaborate metaphysical system is to misjudge the impact and grip his ideas had upon the generations that followed him. The power of Hegel's thought can be measured by the fact that most twentieth-century philosophy represents ways of revising or rejecting aspects of his absolute idealism.

Hegel was born at Stuttgart in 1770 and lived through Germany's most brilliant intellectual period. This was the year when Beethoven was born and when the poet-scientist Goethe, that "complete civilization in himself," was twenty years old. Kant was forty-six years old and had not yet written his classic philosophical works. The Englishman Wordsworth was also born in this year, and his poetry in time formed a part of that romanticism that shared some of the attitudes of German idealism. At an early age, Hegel was deeply impressed by the Greek writers, coming eventually to believe that Plato and Aristotle were not only the sources of modern philosophy but even now its life-giving roots. After

Hegel (*The Bettmann Archive*)

being a rather ordinary pupil at school in Stuttgart, Hegel enrolled at age eighteen in the theological school at the University of Tübingen. Here he became friends with Hölderlin and Schelling and was caught up in lively discussions over the issues of the French Revolution. During his five years at Tübingen his interest gradually turned to the relation between philosophy and theology. It was after he left the university that his interest in philosophy finally flowered. He became a family tutor for six years, in Berne and in Frankfurt, and during these years wrote some minor works that nevertheless contained germs of the major problems he eventually made central in his philosophical works.

By this time German idealism had found two influential spokesmen in Fichte and Schelling. In 1801, when Hegel was appointed to the faculty of the University of Jena, he published his first work, on the *Difference between the Philosophical Systems of Fichte and Schelling*, in which he expressed a dislike of Fichte's identification of the ego and non-ego in the Absolute. While he was more sympathetic with Schelling in these early days, it was not long before his independent and original approach to philosophy was made public in his first major work, *The Phenomenology of Mind*, which, he says, he finished at midnight before the Battle of Jena in 1807. As this battle closed his university, Hegel supported himself and his wife, whom he married in 1811, by becoming rector of the secondary school at Nürnberg, where he remained until 1816. It was here that he wrote his influential *Science of Logic*, which brought him invitations from several universities. In 1816 he joined the faculty at Heidelberg, where in the following year he published his *Encyclopaedia of the Philosophical Sciences in Outline*, the work in which Hegel presents the grand structure of his philosophy in its threefold aspect, namely, logic, philosophy of nature, and philosophy of mind. Two years later, Hegel was given the chair of philosophy at the University of Berlin, where he remained until his death from cholera in 1831 at the age of sixty-one. At Berlin Hegel's writing was massive, although most of it was published after his death. His works during this period included his *Philosophy of Right* and lectures posthumously published on *Philosophy of History, Aesthetics, Philosophy of Religion,* and *History of Philosophy.*

DEALING WITH THE LEGACY OF KANT

Following closely upon Kant's *critical* philosophy was the movement of nineteenth-century German *idealism* as formulated by Fichte, Schelling, and Hegel. Kant had reacted against the pretensions of the rationalist metaphysicians who assumed that human reason could penetrate the secrets of ultimate reality. Against these assumptions Kant set forth his critical conception of philosophy, which consisted in describing the limits beyond which the human mind could never proceed. His argument was that the mind is structured in such a way that it is forever barred from going beyond the realm of sense experience, the realm of phenomena or appearances. Moreover, our interpretation of the world of experience is permanently fixed by the categories that the mind imposes upon the objects of experience. These categories, such as cause and effect, existence and negation, and others—all these, said Kant, are concepts that the mind possesses prior to experience and employs in relation to objects, and this is what makes knowledge possible.

The impact of Kant's critical method, however, derived from his argument that in addition to the world of experience, the world of phenomena, there is also the world "behind" phenomena called the *noumenal* world. The noumenal aspect of any object is what that object is *as such,* what the object is like when the categories of the mind are not imposed on it. We experience only the *appearance* of the red apple but not what the apple is *as such.* We can *never* experience anything except the appearance of a thing. Still, Kant said, we can *think* of that aspect of objects that *has* the appearances. Behind the redness of the apple there must be something to which the color red is related or which can *have* the color red. But, again, though we can say there is, besides the appearance of the red apple, the thing-as-such, we can never know anything about this thing-in-itself. We cannot *know* anything about the thing-in-itself because the categories of the mind apply only to the phenomenal world and not to the thing-in-itself. Since knowledge is possible, according to Kant, only when the categories of the mind are imposed upon the objects we experience through our senses, and since we do not sense the thing-in-itself, we cannot have any knowledge about it. Finally, since ultimate reality was for Kant the thing-in-itself, to say that we cannot have knowledge about it meant that we cannot have knowledge about reality.

The idealists, especially Fichte, quickly recognized the glaring contradiction in Kant's argument concerning the thing-in-itself. How is it possible to say that something exists but that we can know nothing about it? Do we not already know something about it when we say that it exists? Moreover, Kant had asserted the existence of the thing-in-itself in order to account for our experiences of sensation, saying in effect that the thing-in-itself is the *cause* of any given sensation. But he had clearly argued that the categories of the mind, such as cause and effect, could not be used to give us knowledge about the noumenal world. For Kant to say, then, that the thing-in-itself is the cause of our sensations is to contradict his own rule for limiting the use of the categories to our judgments about the objects of sense experience. Even to say that the thing-in-itself *exists* is to go beyond the limits Kant had set for knowledge because *existence* is a category of the mind, a concept, which applies only to objects that we experience through our senses. Indeed, Kant's strongest argument against the earlier metaphysicians was that they had wrongly ascribed *existence* to supposed beings and realities beyond sense experience. Now with his doctrine of the thing-in-itself, Kant appeared to have retained just what his critical philosophy was supposed to eliminate. Not only is it impossible, on Kant's terms, to ascribe the category of existence to the thing-in-itself, it is also a clear contradiction to say that there can be something in existence that is unknowable. We can, of course, distinguish between something that is at the moment unknown (but knowable) and what is unknowable. But to say that something is unknowable is contradictory, because such a statement implies that we already know that something *is* and to that extent it is knowable. The conception of the thing-in-itself collapsed, therefore, because it violated Kant's own rules for limiting the categories of cause and existence to objects of sense experience.

Now the idealists put forward the opposite thesis, namely, that whatever is, is knowable. At the same time, the first idealist, Fichte, had no intention of reverting to the kind of metaphysics Kant had rejected. Fichte believed that Kant had achieved genuine progress in philosophy, and he intended to carry forward what Kant had begun. What Fichte tried to do, therefore, was to use Kant's method, now stripped of the concept of the unknowable thing-in-itself, and transform Kant's critical idealism into a metaphysical idealism. That is, Fichte and the other German idealists took Kant's theory that the mind imposes its categories upon experience and transformed this into the theory that every object and therefore the entire universe is a product of mind.

Hegel joined with Fichte and Schelling in the enterprise of transforming Kant's critical philosophy into a metaphysical idealism. But each of these philosophers approached this enterprise in his own and somewhat different way. What they did agree on, however, was that there can be no unknowable thing-in-itself. Moreover, knowledge, as Kant had shown, was possible because the mind itself produced the forms of knowledge through its various categories. But while Kant had assumed that these forms of knowledge received their material content from the *given* of our experience, from an external thing-in-itself, the idealists now argued that the content as well as the forms of knowledge must be the product of mind. In this way, they came to the conclusion that every object of knowledge, including *things,* is the product of mind. This would mean also, as Hegel did assert, that every reality is rational and that the rational is real. And, since there can be nothing unknowable, the idealists were confident that they could know the inner secrets of absolute reality. This reality must be some form of rationality because it had just been argued that there is no independent and essentially unknowable external thing-in-itself that causes consciousness, that only mind produces the objects of knowledge. We do experience a world of things external to us, which we recognize as existing independently of us and which we did not create. If all objects of our knowledge are the products of mind, but not *our* minds, it must be assumed that they are the products of an intelligence other than that of a finite individual. The idealists concluded that all objects of knowledge, and therefore all objects, and indeed the whole universe, are the products of an absolute subject, an Absolute Mind.

Whereas for Kant the categories of the mind merely make knowledge possible, for Hegel the categories have a mode of *being* independent of any individual's mind. Again, for Kant, the categories represented the mental process of an individual and provided for Kant the critical explanation of the modes and limits of human knowledge. The categories, he said, are concepts in the human mind that the mind brings to experience and by which the mind can understand the world of experience. Hegel, on the other hand, considered the categories not only as mental processes but as objective realities possessing being independent of the thinking individual. The transformation of Kant's critical philosophy into metaphysical idealism consisted in Hegel's saying that the categories, which Kant thought were merely concepts of the human mind, had objective status, that is, possessed a mode of being independent of any individual's thought. The categories, said Hegel, have their being in the Absolute Mind. But, as we shall see, Hegel did not mean to say that there were categories or ideas, on the one hand, and things, such as chair and apples, on the other. Such a distinction would suggest that ideas have a separate existence and that things have a separate existence and that knowledge consists in somehow fitting the appropriate idea to the appropriate thing, the way Plato connected his Forms to things. Hegel, unlike Plato, did not ascribe any independent existence to the categories or universals. What he said was that they have *being* and have their being independently of a person's mind or thought. Hegel wanted to say that the real world is more than the subjective conceptions of men's minds. At the same time, he was saying that reality is rationality, or Thought.

Take, for example, a chair. What is a chair, or what does it consist of? Hegel said that if we take seriously the conclusion that there can be no unknowable thing-in-itself, as we must, a chair must consist of the sum of the ideas we can have about it. On this basis a chair must consist of all the universals we find in it when we experience it. We say that the chair is hard, brown, round, and small. These are all universal ideas, and when they are related to each other this way, they are a chair. These universals have their being in the chair; universals or categories never exist singly or independently. Since there is no unknowable aspect of the chair, that is, nothing in addition to the qualities we experience, it follows that the chair *is* what we know about it, and what we know about it is that it consists of a combination of universals or ideas. To say, then, that the categories and universals have objective status means that they have their being independent of the knowing subject. At the same time, as the example of the chair indicates, Hegel says that the object of thought consists after all in thought itself. There is, he said, an identity between knowing and being. Knowing and being are simply two sides of the same coin. To be sure, Hegel recognized that there is a subject and an object, a person and the world. But the essence of his idealism consisted in his notion that the object of our consciousness, the *thing* we experience and think about, is itself *thought*. In the end, Hegel arrived at the notion that reality is to be found in the Absolute Idea.

So far, two major points in Hegel's argument have been set forth, namely, that we must reject the notion of an unknowable thing-in-itself and that the nature of reality is thought, rationality, and that ultimate reality is the Absolute Idea. To indicate some of the steps by which Hegel came to this conclusion that reality is Thought, we turn next to a few of the basic elements in his intricate system of philosophy.

THE NATURE OF REALITY

Hegel looked upon the world as an organic process. We have already seen that for him the truly real is what he called the Absolute. In theological terms, this

Absolute is called God. But Hegel was particularly concerned to indicate that he was not here referring to a Being separate from the world of nature or even from individual persons. Whereas Plato made a sharp distinction between appearance and reality, Hegel argued in effect that appearance *is* reality. Nothing, said Hegel, is unrelated. For this reason, whatever we experience as separate things will, upon careful reflection, lead us to other things to which they are related until at last the process of dialectical thought will end in the knowledge of the Absolute. Still, the Absolute is not the unity of separate things. Hegel rejected the premise of materialism, which held that there are separate, finite particles of hard matter, which, when arranged in different formations, make up the whole nature of things. Nor did Hegel accept the extreme alternative put forward in the ancient world by Parmenides and more recently by Spinoza, namely, that everything is One, a single substance with various modes and attributes. Hegel described the Absolute as a dynamic process, as an organism having parts but nevertheless unified into a complex system. The Absolute is therefore not some entity separate from the world but *is* the world when viewed in a special way.

Hegel believed that the inner essence of the Absolute could be reached by human reason because the Absolute is disclosed in Nature as well as in the working of the human mind. What connects these three, the Absolute, Nature, and man's mind, is Thought itself. A person's way of thinking is, as it were, fixed by the structure of Nature, by the way things actually behave. Things behave as they do, however, because the Absolute is expressing itself through the structure of Nature. Thus, a person thinks about Nature the way the Absolute expresses itself in Nature. Just as the Absolute and also Nature are dynamic processes, so also human thought is a process, a dialectic process.

Logic and the Dialectic Process   Hegel laid great stress upon logic. To be sure, he understood logic to mean virtually the same thing as metaphysics. This was inevitable in his case inasmuch as he believed that knowing and being coincide. Still, it was Hegel's view that we can know the essence of reality by moving logically step by step and avoiding all self-contradiction along the way. Descartes had advocated a similar method, whereby certainty in knowledge would follow from the movement from one clear idea to the next. Unlike Descartes, however, whose emphasis was upon the relations of ideas to each other, Hegel argued that thought must follow the inner logic of reality itself. That is, since Hegel had identified the rational with the actual, he concluded that logic and logical connections must be discovered *in* the actual and not in some "empty ratiocination." He argued that "since philosophy is the exploration of the rational, it is for that very reason the apprehension of the present and the actual, not the erection of a beyond, supposed to exist, God knows where. . . ." Logic, then, is the process by which we deduce, from our experiences of the actual, the categories that describe the Absolute. This process of deduction is at the very heart of Hegel's dialectic philosophy.

Hegel's dialectic process exhibits a *triadic* movement. Usually this triadic structure of the dialectic process is described as a movement from *thesis* to *antithesis* and finally to *synthesis,* after which the synthesis becomes a new thesis, and this process continues until it ends in the Absolute Idea. What Hegel emphasized in his dialectic logic was that thought *moves* and that *contradiction,* rather than bringing knowledge to a halt, acts as a positive moving force in human reasoning.

To illustrate Hegel's dialectic method, we can take the first basic triad of his logic, namely, the triad of *Being, Nothing,* and *Becoming.* Hegel said that the mind must always move from the more general and abstract to the specific and concrete. The most general concept we can form about things is that they are. Although various things have specific and different qualities, they all have one thing in common, namely, their being. Being, then, is the most general concept the mind can formulate. Also, Being must be logically prior to any specific thing, for things represent determinations or the shaping of what is originally without features. Thus, logic (and reality) begins with the indeterminate, with "the original featurelessness which precedes all definite character and is the very first of all. And this we call Being." Hegel's system begins, therefore, with the concept of Being, and this is the thesis. The question now is, how can thought move from such an abstract concept to any other concept? More important still is the question, how is it possible to *deduce* any other concept from such a universal idea as Being?

It was here that Hegel believed he had discovered something new about the nature of thought. Ever since the time of Aristotle, logicians had thought that nothing could be deduced from a category that was not contained in that category. To deduce *B* from *A* requires that in some way *B* already be contained in *A.* Hegel accepted this. But what he rejected in Aristotelian logic was the assumption that nothing could be deduced from a *universal* term. For example, Aristotle argued that everything is a distinct thing and that logic, therefore, provides us only with specific universal terms from which no other universal terms could be deduced. Thus, for example, there is either *blue* or *not-blue;* there is no way to deduce any other color from blue. If blue is blue, you cannot at the same time say that it is something else, a non-blue. This principle of noncontradiction is very important in any formal logic. Still, Hegel believed that it is not true that a universal does not contain another concept. Returning, then, to the concept of Being, Hegel said that we have here an idea which contains none of the particular qualities or characteristics of the many things that have being. The idea of Being has no content, for the moment you give it some content, it would no longer be the concept of pure Being but the concept of something. Unlike Aristotle, however, Hegel believed that from this concept of Being it is possible to deduce another concept. He argued that because pure Being is mere abstraction, it is therefore absolutely negative. That is, since the concept of Being is wholly indeterminate, it passes into the concept of not-Being. Whenever we try to think of Being without any particular characteristics, the mind moves from Being to not-Being. This, of course, means that in some sense Being and not-Being are the same. Hegel was aware, as he said, that "the proposition that Being and Nothing are the same is so paradoxical to the imagination or understanding, that it is perhaps taken for a joke." Indeed, to understand Being and Nothing as the same, said Hegel, "is one of the hardest things thought expects itself to do." Still, Hegel's point is that Nothing is deduced from Being. At the same time, the concept of Nothing easily leads the mind back to the concept of Being. Of course Hegel is not implying here that we can say of particular things that they simultaneously are the same as nothing. His argument is limited to the concept of pure Being, which, he says, contains the idea of Nothing. He has, then, deduced the concept of Nothing from the concept of Being. The antithesis, Nothing, is contained in the thesis, Being. In Hegel's logic, the antithesis is always deduced from, because it is contained in, the thesis.

The movement of the mind from Being to Nothing produces a third category, namely *Becoming*. The concept of Becoming is formed by the mind when it understands that Being, for the reasons already mentioned, is the same as Nothing. Becoming, says Hegel, is "the unity of Being and Nothing." It is, he says, "*one* idea." Becoming is therefore the *synthesis* of Being and Nothing. If we ask how something can both be and not be, Hegel would answer that it can both be and not be when it becomes.

Throughout his vast and intricate system, Hegel employs this same dialectic method of logic. At each step, he sets forth a thesis from which is deduced its antithesis; this thesis and antithesis then find their unity in a higher synthesis. In the end, Hegel arrives at the concept of the Absolute Idea, which he describes, in accordance with his dialectic method, as Becoming, as a process of self-development. Beginning, then, at the lowest level of knowledge, with the sensation of qualities and characteristics of particular things, Hegel sought to expand the scope of knowledge by discovering the ever-widening interrelationships of all things, always making sure that the mind takes no flight of fancy but rather moves rigorously by way of deduction from one concept to the other that the mind finds as categories in actuality. Single facts, for Hegel, are irrational; only when such single facts are seen as aspects of the whole do they become rational. Thinking is forced to move from one fact to another by the very nature of each concept that facts engender. As an example, which does not accurately illustrate Hegel's point but does suggest how single facts acquire a rational quality, one can consider the parts of an engine. By itself, a spark plug has no rational character; what confers rationality upon it is its relation to the other parts of the engine. To discover the essence of the spark plug is, thus, to discover truth about the other parts and eventually the entire engine. The human mind, then, moves dialectically, constantly embracing an ever-increasing scope of reality discovering the truth of anything only after discovering its relation to the whole, to the *Idea*.

The *Idea* of which Hegel speaks is deduced in his logic by the same method that yielded Becoming out of Being. The category of *subjectivity* is deduced from the fact that a person can have a notion of a thing, make a judgment about it, and be able to reason out logical connections. But from *subjectivity* there can be deduced its opposite, namely, *objectivity*. That is, the notion of subjectivity already contains the idea of objectivity. To say that I am a self (subjectivity) implies that there is not-self (objectivity). Subjectivity consists of thought in its formal sense. Objectivity, on the other hand, is thought that is, as it were, *outside* itself and *in* things. Describing the objective character of a person's notion, Hegel says that it consists of *mechanism, chemism,* and *teleology.* What a subject knows about nature as mechanical laws, for example, objects express in their behavior. The synthesis of the subjective and the objective, says Hegel, is their unity in the Idea. That is, in the Idea, the subjective (formal) and the objective (material) are brought together in unity. The Idea, however, contains its own dialectic, namely, life, cognition, and the Absolute Idea. Thus, the Idea is the category of self-consciousness; it knows itself in its objects. The whole drift of Hegel's logic, therefore, has been to move from the initial concept of Being finally to the notion of the Idea. But this Idea must also be understood as being in a dynamic process, so that the Idea is itself in a continuous process of self-development toward self-perfection.

The Philosophy of Nature   From the Idea is derived the realm of Nature. As Hegel puts it, Nature represents the Idea "outside itself." This expression is somewhat misleading, because it implies that the Idea exists independently of the world. In addition, Hegel ascribes "absolute freedom" to the Idea as it "goes forth freely out of itself as Nature." Recalling, however, Hegel's premise that the real is rational, it must follow here that Nature is simply rationality, or the Idea, in *external* form, somewhat the way a watchmaker's idea is found outside of himself in the watch. But Hegel's view is more subtle than the relation of the watchmaker to the watch would suggest inasmuch as Hegel does not really refer to two separately existing things, Idea and Nature. Ultimate reality is a single organic and dynamic whole. Hegel's distinction between the logical Idea "behind" all things, on the one hand, and Nature, on the other, is his attempt simply to distinguish between the "inner" and "outer" aspects of the self-same reality. Nature, in short, is the opposite, the antithesis, of the rational Idea (thesis). Our thought moves dialectically from the rational (Idea) to the nonrational (Nature). The concept of Nature leads our thought finally to a synthesis represented by the unity of Idea and Nature in the new concept of Spirit (*Geist,* translated as either Spirit or Mind). What drives our thought from Nature back to Spirit is the dialectic movement within the concept of Nature. Just as logic begins with the most abstract concept, namely, Being, so the philosophy of Nature begins with the most abstract thing, which is, says Hegel, space. Space is empty (just as Being is indeterminate). At one "end," then, Nature touches emptiness. At the other end, it passes over into Spirit. Between space and Spirit is the diversity of particular things, which is what Nature is. Nature exhibits the laws of mechanics, physics, and organics. Each of these aspects of Nature is in turn analyzed by Hegel into its dialectic terms.

Much of what Hegel says about Nature is somewhat outmoded by the developments of science since his day. But it was not his intention to take over the work of the scientists. He was concerned, rather, to discover through the philosophy of Nature a rational structure and pattern in all of reality. At the same time, he tried to show what is the difference between *freedom* and *necessity*, saying that Nature is the realm of necessity whereas Spirit is freedom. Nature, says Hegel, "is to be considered as a system of stages, of which one proceeds necessarily from the other." Freedom, on the other hand, is the act of Spirit. There is, then, a dialectic opposition between Spirit and Nature, between freedom and necessity. Indeed, the "career" of reality, the teleological movement of history, represents the gradual and continuous unfolding of the Spirit, of the Idea of freedom.

The Philosophy of Spirit   The third part of Hegel's system, following his logical Idea and his philosophy of Nature, is the philosophy of Spirit or Mind. Here again, Hegel sets forth the elements of his dialectic in which the thesis is subjective spirit, the antithesis is objective spirit, and the synthesis is Absolute Spirit. He goes into considerable detail, piling triad upon triad to illustrate that the Absolute is Spirit and that this Spirit finds its manifestation in the minds of individuals, in the social institutions of family, civil society, and the state, and finally in art, religion, and philosophy. The subjective spirit refers to the inner workings of the human mind, whereas the objective spirit represents the mind in its external embodiment in the social and political institutions. At the apex of knowledge are art, religion, and philosophy, which are the achievement of Absolute Spirit.

Most of what made Hegel's philosophy famous was that portion of his thought that he developed around his concept of objective spirit. Here we come upon the unity of Hegel's thought as he now attempts to connect his moral, social, and political thought with the rest of his system. The whole sphere of human behavior, both individual and collective, is described by him as part of the actual and therefore is essentially rational. Moreover, as part of the actual this objective side of the Spirit is seen as involved in the dialectic process. Human behavior and social and political organisms contain or embody the Spirit, just as Nature is the objective embodiment of the Absolute Idea. For this reason, Hegel looked upon institutions not as the creations of man, but as the product of the dialectic movement of history, of the objective manifestation of rational reality. Speaking, for example, about his book on the *Philosophy of Right*, Hegel writes that "containing as it does the science of the state, [it] is to be nothing other than the endeavor to apprehend and portray the state as something inherently rational. As a work of philosophy, it must be poles apart from an attempt to construct a state as it ought to be." This identification of the actual state with the very grounds of reality is what caused Hegel's political theory to have such a captivating influence among those who wished to think about the state in totalitarian or at least nondemocratic terms. We turn, then, to some of the "moments" in the dialectic process by which Hegel seeks to indicate the natural movement from the individual's concept of right to the state's authority over society. The basic triadic movement here is from *right* (thesis) to *morality* (antithesis) and then to *social ethics* (synthesis).

ETHICS AND POLITICS

The Concept of Right   Human behavior must, of course, be understood first of all as the actions of individuals. The individual, says Hegel, is aware of his freedom. He expresses his freedom most concretely by an act of will. Hegel looked upon will and reason as virtually synonymous, saying that "only as thinking intelligence, will is free will." A person expresses his freedom chiefly in relation to material things, appropriating them, using them, and exchanging them. "To appropriate," says Hegel, "is at bottom only to manifest the majesty of my will towards things, by demonstrating that they are not self-complete and have no purpose of their own." The basis of the right to property is for Hegel the free will of the individual in the act of appropriation. Inasmuch as this will resides in the individual, property is a private right. Free men, however, are able to "alienate" themselves from property, and this they do through "contract." A contract is the product of two free wills agreeing to exchange property. It also indicates the development of a duty, which the terms of the contract now embody. Hegel's central point here is that insofar as individual persons act rationally, their free acts conform to the rationality of the universe. Their individual wills harmonize with the universal will. But among free men, the harmony of wills is precarious. Thus, there is always the possibility of the opposite of right; the negation of right is exemplified in violence and fraud. "Wrong" consists in the breakdown of harmony between the individual will and the universal will. The dialectic relation between "right" and "wrong" produces the tension between the way the "wrong" will acts and the way the will should act in order to be universal, that is, rational. This tension or conflict between right and wrong is what gives rise to morality.

Morality, said Hegel, is fundamentally a matter of purpose and intention in the ethical life of man. There is more to "goodness," in other words, than merely obeying laws and keeping contracts. Morality has to do with those deeds for which men can themselves be held responsible. Only those consequences that a person intends and that constitute the purpose of his act can affect the goodness or badness of his act. It appears, then, that for Hegel the essence of morality is found internally in a person's intention and purpose. But Hegel argues that although moral responsibility begins with those acts that can be assigned to a free will, a will that intends the act, the full scope of morality is not exhausted by this subjective aspect of the act. After all, human behavior takes place always in a context, especially in a context of other persons, hence other wills. Moral duty or responsibility is therefore broader than the concerns or intentions of the individual. Moral duty derives from the requirement of identifying a person's individual will with the universal will. Although it is perfectly legitimate for a person to be concerned with his own happiness and welfare, the principle of rationality requires that he must exercise his own will in such a way that the wills of other persons, also acting freely, can achieve their welfare as well. Morality is therefore an element in the dialectic process: the thesis is the abstract right of each individual; the antithesis is morality, for morality represents the duties that the universal will raises as limitations to the individual will. The relation between these two wills is the relation between freedom and duty, subjectivity and objectivity. The dialectic process in this ethical sphere is constantly moving toward a greater harmony between the subjective and objective, and in this regard Hegel described the *good* as "the realization of freedom, the absolute final purpose of the world." But the realization of freedom, for Hegel, had to occur within the limits of duty. In this sense the freest man is the one who most completely fulfills his duty. It was inevitable, then, that Hegel should discover the synthesis of the individual's freedom and right on the one hand, and the universal will, on the other, in the concrete institutions of mankind, particularly in the state.

The State　Between the individual and the state there are two dialectic steps according to Hegel, namely, the *family* and *society*. The family is, as it were, the first stage of the objective will. In marriage two persons give up their individual wills to some degree in order to become one person. Because the family is a single unit, its property becomes a common possession even though, for legal reasons, the husband might be said to own it. Again, the family, united by the bond of feeling or love, constitutes the logically first moment of the embodiment of the universal will. At the same time, the family contains its own antithesis, namely, individuals who will eventually grow up, leave the family, and enter into that larger context of similar individuals that is called *civil society*. These individuals now chart out their own lives and have their own purposes. We need to remember at this point that Hegel is here analyzing the dialectic development of the state and is not giving an historical account of its emergence. The state is the synthesis of the family and of civil society. The family, in this analysis, stands for the embodied universal, whereas civil society represents particularity insofar as each individual, unlike the members of a family, sets his own goals. These two elements, universality and particularity, cannot exist independently, for they are contained in each other; their unity, therefore, is found in the state, which is the synthesis of universality and particularity. The state is a unity in difference. This does not seem to be a genuine deduction, but Hegel does conclude that the synthesis of the universal and the particular consists in the individual. In this context, the state is conceived as an individual, the true individual, an organic unity of partial individuals.

　　　Hegel did not conceive of the state as an authority imposed from the outside upon the individual. Nor did he consider the state the product of the general or majority will. The state, said Hegel, "is absolutely rational—substantial will," and again, "the state is the actuality of the ethical idea." Hegel conferred upon the state the characteristic of a person, saying that the state represents universal self-consciousness. A particular individual, he said, is conscious of himself insofar as he is a part of this larger self. And, says Hegel, "since the state is mind objectified, it is only as one of its members that the individual himself has objectivity, genuine individuality, and an ethical life." A person's spiritual reality is also found in the state, for as Hegel says, a human being's "spiritual reality consists in this, that his own essence—Reason—is objectively present to him, that it has objective immediate existence for him. . . ." Recalling that Hegel was not interested in formulating a theory of the *ideal* state, his descriptions of the *actual* state are all the more striking. It was the actual living state about which he said that "the state is the embodiment of rational freedom," and most striking of all, that "the State is the Divine Idea as it exists on earth."

All these highly exalting descriptions of the state would make it appear that Hegel had advocated the totalitarian state. Hegel did insist, however, that insofar as the state is the synthesis of particularity and universality, of the family and the individual, there will be the preservation by the state of the individual's liberty, that liberty which the individual possesses as a member of civil society. Neither the family nor civil society is destroyed by the state; they continue to exist within the state. The laws of the state and in general the legislative and executive arms of the state do not issue arbitrary commands. Laws are universal rules, which have their application in individual cases involving individual persons. Moreover, laws must be rational and directed at rational persons. The reason for laws is that men, in their ability to make free choices, are capable of choosing ends that harm others. Insofar as their acts harm others, their behavior is irrational. The function of law is therefore to bring rationality into behavior. What makes an act rational is that it at once achieves a person's private good as well as the public good. Only a person who acts rationally can be free, because only rational acts can be permitted in society, because only rational acts avoid social harm. The function of the state is therefore not to compound personal harm or misery by issuing arbitrary and therefore irrational commands, but rather to increase, through its laws, the aggregate of rational behavior. The state is thus an organism that is seeking to develop the Idea of freedom to its maximum, and to achieve objective freedom only as its individual members do. In this way, the laws of the state, rather than being arbitrary, are rational rules of behavior that the individual himself would choose if he were acting rationally. The only limitation upon the individual will that reason allows is the limitation required by the existence of other wills. The sovereign acts in the name of the universal will and reason and not arbitrarily. The state then, "is the Idea of Spirit in the external manifestation of human Will and its Freedom."

When it comes to the relations between states, Hegel emphasizes the autonomy and absolute sovereignty of each state. The relation of one state to another is different for Hegel from the relation of one person to another in civil society. Above two persons who disagree in society, there is the state as a higher power capable of resolving the dispute. But as between two states, there is no higher entity. Each nation, says Hegel, "is mind in its substantive rationality and immediate actuality and is therefore the absolute power on earth." For this reason, "every state is sovereign and autonomous against its neighbors. It is a fundamental proposition of international law that obligations between states ought to be kept." But, says Hegel, "states are . . . in a state of nature in relation to each other," and for this reason there is no universal will binding upon them. The "rights of states are actualized only in their particular wills," insofar as there are no constitutional powers over them. There is no one to judge between states.

Why Hegel did not carry his dialectic movement to the next level at which individual states would be united into a community of nations is not clear. He was of course aware that Kant had an idea of securing "perpetual peace" by a League of Nations to adjust every dispute. But he said that such an arrangement could not work because it would still be necessary for each state to *will* to obey the international tribunal. But a state will always *will* its own welfare. Indeed, says Hegel, "welfare is the highest law governing the relation of one state to another." There can be no moral limitations upon the state, for the state *is* "the ethical substance." It follows, says Hegel, that "if states disagree and their particular wills cannot be harmonized, the matter can only be settled by war."

World History   In Hegel's view, the history of the world is the history of nations. The dynamic unfolding of history represents the "progress in the consciousness of freedom." This progress is not a matter of mere chance but is rather a rational process. "Reason," says Hegel, "dominates the world and . . . world history is thus a rational process." In a special way, the state is the bearer of reason, and it was for this reason that Hegel had said that the state is "the Idea of Spirit" in external form and that the state is "the Divine Idea as it exists on earth." But the dialectic of the historical process consists in the opposition between states. Each state expresses a national spirit and indeed the world spirit in its own collective consciousness. To be sure, only individual minds are capable of consciousness. Still, the minds of a particular people develop a spirit of unity, and for this reason it is possible to speak of a "national spirit." Each national spirit represents a moment in the development of the world spirit, and the interplay between national spirits represents the dialectic in history.

The conflict between nations is inevitable inasmuch as the historical process is the very stuff of reality, is the gradual working out of the *Idea of Freedom*. Nations are carried along by the wave of history, so that in each epoch a particular nation is "the dominant people in world history for this epoch. . . ." A nation cannot choose when it will be great, for "it is only once that it can make its hour strike." At decisive points in history, says Hegel, special world-historical persons emerge as agents of the world spirit. These persons lift nations to a new level of development and perfection. Hegel thought that such individuals could hardly be judged in terms of a morality that belonged to the epoch out of which a nation is being led, that the value of such persons consists in their creative responsiveness to the unfolding Idea of Freedom.

The time process of history was for Hegel the logical process of the dialectic. History is moving toward a purposive end, namely, freedom. To illustrate the dialectic of history, Hegel used examples of various peoples, which, he thought, indicated the three *moments* in the development of freedom. The Orientals, he thought, knew nothing of freedom except that the potentate alone could do what he wished. Although the Greeks and Romans knew the concept of citizenship, they limited this status only to a few and regarded others as being by nature slaves. It was the *Germanic* peoples who, under the influence of Christianity, developed the insight that man as such is free. Thus, Hegel says that "The East knew and to the present day knows, only that *One* is free; the Greek and Roman world, that *some* are free; the German world knows that *All* are free." The highest freedom, we have seen, occurs, according to Hegel, when the individual acts according to the universal, rational will of the whole society.

ABSOLUTE SPIRIT

Hegel's philosophy has its culmination in man's knowledge of the Absolute. In the process of dialectic, knowledge of the Absolute is the synthesis of subjective spirit and objective spirit. Because reality is rationality, Thought, Idea, it followed for Hegel that man's knowledge of the Absolute is actually the Absolute knowing itself through the finite spirit of man. Just how this moment of self-consciousness of the Absolute occurs in the spirit of man is described by Hegel in a final dialectic.

Our consciousness of the Absolute, says Hegel, is achieved progressively as the mind moves through the three stages from art, to religion, and finally to philosophy. Art provides "a sensuous semblance of the Idea" by providing the mind with an object of sense. In the object of art, the mind apprehends the Absolute as beauty. The object of art, moreover, is the creation of Spirit and as such contains some aspect of the Idea. Hegel saw in the movement from Oriental symbolic art to classical Greek art and finally to romantic Christian art an ever-deepening insight into the Absolute.

Art leads beyond itself to religion. What differentiates religion from art is that religion is an activity of thought, whereas an aesthetic experience is primarily a matter of feeling. Although art can direct consciousness toward the Absolute, religion comes closer to it precisely because the Absolute is Thought. At the same time, religious thought, said Hegel, is pictorial thought. In early religions this pictorial element looms large. "The Greek God," for example, "is the object of naïve intuition and sensuous imagination. His shape is therefore the bodily shape of man." At the apex of religion is Christianity, which is the religion of the Spirit.

Hegel regarded Christianity as the pictorial representation of philosophy. He believed that religion and philosophy have basically the same subject matter, that both represent "knowledge of that which is eternal, of what God is, and what flows out of his nature," so that "religion and philosophy come to the same things." Philosophy leaves behind the pictorial forms of religion and rises to the level of pure thought. But philosophy does not offer man the knowledge of the Absolute at any particular moment, for such knowledge is the product of the dialectic process. Philosophy itself has a history, a dialectic movement, where the major periods and systems of philosophy are not mere haphazard developments. These systems in the history of philosophy represent the necessary succession of ideas required by the progressive unfolding of the Idea. The history of philosophy is for Hegel, therefore, the development of the Absolute's self-consciousness in the mind of man.

Comte:
The Rise
of Positivism
in France

Although Auguste Comte is called the founder of *positive philosophy,* he did not discover this mode of thought, for as John Stuart Mill has said, positivism was "the general property of the age." Comte had begun his serious thinking in an age and at a place that were characterized by intellectual confusion and social instability. It was the France of the early nineteenth century to which Comte brought his perceptive and independent mind. Born at Montpellier in 1798, he was educated at the École Polytechnique, for some years was secretary to the noted socialist Saint-Simon, and in his early twenties published a series of books of which his *Système de politique positive* (1824) is the best known and which, as it turned out, was an early sketch of his major work *Cours de philosophie positive,* which was written in several volumes over the period from 1830 to 1842. His deep romantic involvement with Clotilde de Vaux, which lasted two years, 1844–1846, and ended with her tragic death, led Comte to declare the all-important role the element of affection must play in life. This emphasis upon love, which became central in his new "Religion of Humanity," was to contrast sharply with the strictness of his views concerning the scientific understanding of human society. He admits that there is such a contrast between his earlier and later ideas, claiming that he was an Aristotle in the early period of his career and a St. Paul in the later.

Even though Comte's major philosophical contribution centered around his conception of the positive sciences and the positivistic theory of knowledge, it was also his concern to show that his new philosophy could provide the basis of true religion. But although his positive philosophy did attract devoted adherents, many of them, notably John Stuart Mill, regretted Comte's attempt to found a secularized version of the Roman Catholic Church from which all supernatural elements had been removed and of which he made himself the High Priest, all of which led Mill to say that "an irresistible air of ridicule" surrounds Comte's religion and while "others may laugh . . . we could far rather weep at this melancholy decadence of a great intellect." Comte blamed the severe specialization of university scholars for their refusal to provide him a post for teaching the history of the sciences. Living off the voluntary contributions of the friends of positivism, he continued to work in Paris in a little house only a short distance from the place at the Sorbonne where there now stands a statue of him, and from this meager setting emerged Comte's other major books, his second *Le système de politique positive* (1851–1854), *Catéchisme positiviste* (1852), and the *Synthèse subjective* (1856). Before he could complete his projected series on ethics, the system of positive industrial organization, and other philosophical works, his career ended in 1857, when he died at the age of fifty-nine.

Comte's chief objective was the total reorganization of society. But he was convinced that this practical objective required first of all the reconstruction or at least reformation of the intellectual orientation of his era. As he saw the situation, the Scientific Revolution, which had been unfolding since the discoveries of Galileo and Newton, had not been sufficiently assimilated in other fields, particularly in social, political, moral, and religious thought. The achievements of science in France had been outstanding, including the work of men such as Ampère and Fresnel in physics, Chevreul and Dumas in chemistry, Magendie in physiology, and Lamarck, Saint-Hilaire, and Cuvier in biology and zoology. What commanded so much respect about the work these men were doing was that their discoveries could be employed in solving problems of everyday life, leading to new methods in medicine and surgery, and making possible new industrial techniques and transportation. Gaining a sense of authority from its spectacular accomplishments, science challenged other ways of thinking, which could not in their field match these successes. Inevitably, questions that had been raised earlier about the relation between science and religion, about the freedom of the will, about the value of metaphysics, and about the possibility of discovering objective moral standards now took on a greater degree of intensity and urgency.

This was an age, too, when the state of philosophy in France was being influenced by internal political events and external systems of thought. The French Revolution had been, for Saint-Simon as well as for Comte, a dramatic example of anarchy. There developed, accordingly, some antirevolutionary philosophies especially in the writings of de Maistre and de Bonald. Some saw in the

Revolution a contest of power whose effect was to destroy the legitimate power and authority both of the government and of the church, an effect that could only result in the further destruction of the institutions of the family and of private property. The cross-fire of thought that followed this event consisted of theories of society where some argued that society rests upon the consent of the governed as expressed in a social contract as against those who held the notion that society is a reality that lies beyond or above particular individuals. Added to these internal differences in thought was the gradual importation of philosophies from other lands, which dealt not only with social philosophy but treated the problems of the theory of knowledge and metaphysics in such a way as to engender not a clear new trend in philosophy but rather the atmosphere of vigorous debate. Frenchmen were now reading such varied authors as Kant, Hegel, Fichte, Schelling, Strauss, Feuerbach, and Goethe. Advocates of materialism, idealism, and new metaphysical systems entered the lists, and grandiose doctrines of Humanity, Absolute, and Progress were put forth. Karl Marx was also among the social thinkers of the day.

To overcome the anarchy that political revolution brings to pass, and even more to overcome the anarchy of philosophic thought that makes political anarchy inevitable, Auguste Comte set out to reform both society and philosophy by developing a science of society, *sociology*, built upon a scientifically oriented philosophy, positive philosophy or *positivism*. He offered positivism, therefore, not simply as a way of thought, but as a major solution to the problem of society, for the issue was how to maintain social unity and order at a time when theological beliefs were no longer accepted as supports for political authority. Where beliefs are no longer held in common and when anarchy of ideas threatens anarchy in society, the only solution, as Comte saw it, unless people accepted positivism, was a dictatorship of naked power. None of the usual arguments against dictatorship seemed satisfactory to Comte, for against those who would seek to reinstate the earlier balance of temporal and spiritual powers as they were before the Revolution, Comte answered that it is not possible to reverse the course of historical progress; and against those who advocated the methods of democracy, he argued that their concepts of *equality* and *rights of man* and especially *sovereignty of the people* were metaphysical abstractions and dogmas. Only the method of positivism, he declared, can guarantee social unity. His task of reorganizing society, therefore, required that he first of all bring about an intellectual reformation, which in turn led him to formulate his classic theory of positivism.

POSITIVISM DEFINED

Positivism is best defined as a general attitude of mind, a spirit of inquiry, an approach to the facts of human existence. Its central feature is first of all negative in that it rejects the assumption that nature has some ultimate purpose or end. Secondly, positivism gives up any attempt to discover either the "essence" or the internal or secret causes of things. On the positive side, its spirit is expressed in the attempt to study facts by observing the constant relations between things and formulating the laws of science simply as the laws of constant relations between various phenomena. In this spirit, Newton had described the phenomena of physics without going beyond useful limits in asking questions about the essential nature of things; before him Galileo made great strides in understanding the movements and relations of stars without inquiring into their physical constitution; Fourier had discovered mathematical laws of the diffusion of heat without any theoretical assumption concerning the essential nature of heat; and the biologist Cuvier had worked out some laws concerning the structure of living things without any hypothesis about the nature of life. A corollary of this spirit of research and inquiry was the assumption that knowledge derived from science can be used in the material and social life. This was positivism's great appeal, for it promised an effective means for dealing not only with physical reality—as, for example, the disorders of the body, which concerned medicine—but with the disorders of the body politic, which must become the concern of the scientist of society, the sociologist.

The initial rigor of positivism is suggested by Comte's clear statement that "any proposition which does not admit of being ultimately reduced to a simple enunciation of fact, special or general, can have no real or intelligible sense." Counting himself a positivist and using much of Comte's own language, John Stuart Mill described the general outlook of positivism in these terms: "We have no knowledge of anything but Phenomena, and our knowledge of phenomena is relative, not absolute. We know not the essence, nor the real mode of production, of any fact, but only its relations to other facts in the way of succession or of similitude. These relations are constant; that is, always the same in the same circumstances. The constant resemblances which link phenomena together, and the constant sequences which unite them as antecedent and consequent, are termed their laws. The laws of phenomena are all we know respecting them. Their essential nature, and their ultimate causes, either efficient or final, are unknown and inscrutable to us." This was the intellectual mood and spirit that Comte and his followers brought to the study of society and religion, saying that in the end every subject must utilize the same approach to truth for only in that way could unity be achieved in thought as well as social life. To be sure, this method had its own assumptions, the foremost of them being that there is an order in the nature of things whose laws we can discover. Comte also assumed that we can overcome the pitfalls of subjectivity by "transforming the human brain into a perfect mirror of the external order." His optimism for achieving his objectives came from his interpretation of the history of ideas and from his study of the development of the various sciences, which he believed clearly pointed to the inevitability and the validity of positivism.

THE LAW OF THE THREE STAGES

The history of ideas, said Comte, indicates that there has been a clear movement of thought through three stages, each stage representing a different way of discovering truth. These stages are the *theological,* in which phenomena are explained as being caused by divine powers, the *metaphysical*, in which anthropocentric concepts of divinity are replaced by impersonal and abstract forces, and the *positivistic* or scientific, in which only the constant relations between phenomena are considered and all attempts to explain things by references to beings beyond our experience are given up. He called this evolution from one state to another the *law* of the three stages, because he thought he could find this threefold development at work not only in thought in general but in each particular science. Moreover, this law could be said to be at work in the political order, too, for since the structure of a society reflects the philosophical orientation of an epoch, any major change in philosophic thought will bring about a change in the political order. For example, the theological explanation of the physical world either in Greek mythology or in orthodox Christianity with frequent instances of the intervention of the gods or of God had its counterpart in political theory in the doctrines of the divine right of kings or the "two kingdoms." But this theological approach is superseded by metaphysics, which speaks of a *necessary being* or *ground of being* as the explanation for the existence of finite beings such as men and things. This concept of necessary being, says Comte, is abstract and impersonal, and although it goes beyond the idea of some capricious being acting upon the physical world, it does not overcome the uselessness of dogmatism. Its counterpart in political thought is the attempt to formulate abstract principles such as the *rights of man* or the *sovereignty of the people*. Comte's harsh judgment was that slavery and the military state go along with the theological stage and that the assumptions of liberal democracy, which he rejected as dogmas, are an outgrowth of the metaphysical stage. Such palpable dogmas as *the equality of all men*, thought Comte, must now give way to the clear scientific fact that men are unequal and have different capacities and must, therefore, have different functions in society. To deal effectively with such questions of political order required a carefully worked out science of society, which Comte did not find already available and which he, therefore, set out to create, calling it *sociology*.

Comte's creation of sociology illustrates his account of the development of knowledge, for in his theory the movement of thought is from decreasing generality to increasing complexity and from the abstract to the concrete. He makes much of the fact that of the five major sciences, mathematics came first, then in order came astronomy, physics, chemistry, and biology. In this sequence he saw the movement from generality and simplicity to complexity and concreteness, for mathematics deals with quantities of a general kind; to quantity, astronomy adds the elements of mass and force and some principles of attraction; physics differentiates between types of forces when it deals with gravity, light, and heat; chemistry makes quantitative and qualitative analyses of materials; and biology adds the structure of organic and animal life to the material order. A sixth science, sociology, deals with the relations of human beings to each other in society, and as such it is the necessary outcome of the previous stage of science. Dramatically, Comte indicates that mathematics and astronomy came early in the ancient world, whereas physics as a true science had to wait for Sir Isaac Newton in the seventeenth century, that chemistry begins with Lavoisier, biology with Bichat, and that it is now his own task to usher in the science of sociology. For him sociology is the queen of the sciences, the summit of knowledge, for it makes use of all previous information and coordinates it all for the sake of a peaceful and orderly society.

COMTE'S SOCIOLOGY AND "RELIGION OF HUMANITY"

Unlike revolutionary thinkers who called for a radical reconstruction of society, or idealists who fancied utopian communities, Comte moved along lines that he thought were clearly visible to the scientific mind and that referred to the actual conditions of history. Two things in particular dominate his sociological theory, namely, what he calls the *static* and the *dynamic* components of social existence. The static component consists of certain stable elements of society, such as the family, private property, language, and religion. Since these are virtually permanent, he does not advocate any revolutionary change in them. At the same time, he does recognize a dynamic component, which he understands as the force of progress. His theory of "the law of the three stages" contains the technical elaboration of this dynamic force. Progress has to do, therefore, not with any basic alteration of the social elements but simply with a continual refinement of our understanding of how we should utilize these stable structures in an optimum way. Just as the stars and constellations do not change as we move from the theological to the metaphysical and finally to the scientific way of accounting for their behavior, neither should the structures of society change as far as their basic elements are concerned. The family, for example, must remain, and indeed Comte sees in this institution the fundamental building blocks of society. But what the dynamic influence of positivism would bring to the family would be, for example, the conferring upon women of a new and spiritually defensible status. Similarly, property should be utilized in such a way as to call forth the highest instincts of altruism instead of greed and envy. Religion is the key to the whole system, but instead of the worship of a supernatural being, religion should consist of the cult of *humanity*. Positivism also calls for a political organization that utilizes both temporal and spiritual powers in such a way that these two do not compete but rather harmoniously complement each other.

Comte frequently refers to the Middle Ages as a time when the relation between the static and dynamic components of society were most adequately attuned to each other. Indeed, he uses the medieval community as his model for the new society. He would, of course, reject the theological aspects of this period, but what struck him about it was the intimate relation between religion and society, between a body of thought and the organization of the structures of society in medieval Europe. The family, property, and government, all of these elements had a justification in and derived their motivations from a set of beliefs held in common. The key to the reorganization of nineteenth-century society is therefore not to destroy old structures and create new ones but rather to bring the permanent elements of society up to date and to overcome the contemporary anarchy by reestablishing the contact between religion and the institutions of society. Only by reorganizing the dynamic forces at work, the fact of intellectual and technological progress, could this contact between religion and society be reestablished. Much of the anarchy of this period, both intellectual and political, stemmed, as Comte saw it, from the breakdown of theological authority brought on by the rise of science. To reestablish this earlier grip of theology upon contemporary minds was, he said, impossible. Moreover, the legacy of the Enlightenment, which was the exaltation of each person's own ideas and opinions, could not lead to any unity. Only a new religion, based upon ideas and realities that would be so clearly obvious to everyone as to achieve universal agreement, could create the unity between all the people and between their thinking and their ways of living. The Middle Ages had the correct approach to social organization, but, says Comte, they had the wrong intellectual orientation. On the other hand, contemporary Europe seemed to him to have the right philosophy in scientific positivism but not an adequate organization. Although science had seriously shaken the hold of theology, it had not yet completely eliminated it. The ensuing debates over the relation between science and religion also raised the specific question of the comparative roles of intellect and feeling, the mind and the heart. Comte's enormous task, therefore, was to reconceive the whole nature of religion in terms of science, bind the new religion to the structures of society, and unify the powers of reason and affection in each individual's life and thereby infuse man's every act with a sense of purpose or direction. Proceeding with this task, Comte said that "Love, then, is our principle; Order our basis; and Progress our end."

What his new society would be like is indicated first of all by what he did not want it to be. Although the theological stage had now been passed, new dogmas created by metaphysics still lingered, and these would have to be rejected. To achieve the new society every old fiction would have to be given up, whether it be the theistic God or the metaphysical dogma of equality or popular sovereignty. Since the function of the mind now would be to *mirror* the truly real state of things, the contents of the new religion must be drawn from such an objectively real source, and this, says Comte, is *humanity* itself. It is, after all, from humanity that we all draw our material, intellectual, spiritual, and moral resources. But although he did not want to retain past dogmas, he nevertheless built his new *religion of humanity* as though it were a secularized version of Catholicism. Instead of God, Comte substituted humanity, which he called *Grand-Être*, the Supreme Being; he became his own High Priest, instituted a calendar of saints, mostly renowned scientists, created a catechism at the end of which Comte says, "Humanity definitely occupies the place of God," adding that "she does not forget the services which the idea of God provisionally rendered"; the sacraments become "social" and include *Presentation* (Baptism); *Initiation* at age fourteen; *Admission,* when at age twenty-one a person is authorized to serve humanity; *Destination* or choice of career at twenty-eight; *Marriage* for men at twenty-eight and for women at twenty-one; and *Retirement* at age sixty-three.

Although there is no doubt that Comte had from the beginning of his systematic thought considered the goal of his positive science the creation, as he says, of a "sound philosophy, capable of supplying the foundation of true religion," there is equally no doubt that his later writings were influenced by his emotional crisis following his intense love affair with Clotilde de Vaux, his "incomparable angel." Having in his earlier career emphasized the role of the intellect, he now argued for the supremacy of the affections, claiming that "greater distinctness . . . is given to the truth that the affective element predominates in our nature." For this reason he now states that "where the moral excellence of true Religion is illustrated, feeling takes the first place. The disastrous revolt of Reason against Feeling will never be terminated till the new Western priesthood can fully satisfy the claims of the modern intellect. But this being done, moral requirements at once reassume the place that belongs to them; since in the construction of a really complete synthesis, Love is naturally the one universal principle." In light of this supremacy of feeling, it becomes the function of positive philosophy to fashion "a system which regulates the whole course of our private and public existence, by bringing Feeling, Reason and Activity into permanent harmony." As love is the supreme moral principle, all thought or acts of the intellect must become subordinate to it, thereby making scientists philosophers, and philosophers priests, wherein all of life becomes "a continuous and intense act of worship," and "live for others" becomes the truly human moral standard. The scientists will organize and rule society and the philosopher-priests will exercise their influence over society by the organization of public worship and by controlling education. In this way, Comte tried to achieve a modern version of the medieval separation between the spiritual and temporal powers. In this way, too, morals would be independent of politics and would instead be a constructive influence upon the political and economic order.

The civil order will also reflect the forces of dynamic progress, particularly as this process indicates the movement from a *military* to an *industrial* basis. Comte considered that the military phase of history had much to do with developing the industrial power and organization of the modern state by forcing men to bring together otherwise isolated material resources and human labor for the sake of survival. But now the habits of industry and discipline must be used for the sake of peace and internal order and civilization.

The central aim of all human effort, said Comte, must be the amelioration of the order of nature. Science helps us to understand nature so that we can alter it. Humanity, the new God, is worshiped not in the former posture of solemn inactivity, for in *positive religion*, "the object of worship is a Being [Humanity] whose nature is relative, modifiable and perfectible." Through such worship is *progress* achieved, for progress is "the development of Order under the influence of Love." Putting so much emphasis upon human effort was Comte's way of replacing the theological doctrine of *providence*, for he says that "we must look to our own unremitting activity for the only providence by which the rigour of our destiny can be alleviated."

Translating this concept of providence into more specific detail, Comte said that human providence has four main divisions: Women are the *moral provi-*

dence, the priesthood the *intellectual providence,* the patriciate or capitalists the *material providence,* and the proletariat the *general providence.* "The people," said Comte, "represent the activity of the Supreme Being, as women represent its sympathy, and philosophers its intellect." Of the capitalists, Comte said that they are "the nutritive reservoirs, the social efficiency of which mainly depends on their being concentrated in few hands," adding that only the influence of moral persuasion can regulate "their foolish and immoral pride." Inevitably, Comte's society would require that each person fulfill his special function by staying in the place most suited to his powers. Above all, there must be the supremacy of the intellectual elite, since the technical problems of administering a complex society can be understood only by specialists. For this reason, Comte thought it was just as senseless to permit free inquiry or discussion about matters of social and political administration by the masses as to allow them to voice their opinions about some technical matter in chemistry, a field in which they lack proper information, and, therefore, he called for the abolition of the "vagabond liberty of individual minds."

Again, the success of the *religion of humanity* would require the stability of the family and the inculcation by the family of the spirit of altruism and love. Comte would not accept the earlier theological appraisal of the depravity of man or the notion that altruism is uncongenial to human nature. To Comte, the altruistic instincts were a matter of scientific fact, citing the founder of phrenology Gall, who claimed to show that there is an "organ" of benevolence in the brain. In addition, just as the women preserved the claims of morality after the synthesis of the medieval period came apart and when men became preoccupied with practical and material ends, so now women would continue to exert their creative function in the family and would spontaneously consecrate their "rational and imaginative faculties to the service of feeling." For Comte, the very symbol of humanity on the *flag of positivism* was to be a young mother with her infant son, a final analogy between Christianity and the Religion of Humanity.

The more Comte concerned himself with the creation of a new religion, the further he seemed to depart from the very principles of the positivism he was so concerned to delineate and advocate. In the end, Comte seemed to be indicating the goal toward which society *ought* to be moving instead of describing the course which history *is* in fact taking. To be sure, Comte tried to derive his objectives from his scientific studies, from the "law of the three stages" and his hierarchical classification of the sciences. Although Comte's influence was soon to be eclipsed by the politically more captivating theories of Karl Marx, he is still to be considered a leading figure in that impressive line of thinkers that began with Bacon and Hobbes and the empiricists Locke, Berkeley, and Hume, who came before him, and included the students of scientific method such as Mach and Poincaré, as well as Russell and the other logical positivists of the present.

18

Utilitarianism of Bentham and Mill

For more than a hundred years, the moral and political philosophy of Jeremy Bentham and John Stuart Mill influenced the thinking and political action of Englishmen. Rarely has a way of thinking captured the imagination of generations of men so completely as did this philosophy called *utilitarianism*. What attracted people to it was its simplicity and its way of confirming what most men already believed, for it set forth the general thesis that pleasure and happiness are what everyone desires. From this simple fact that everyone desires pleasure and happiness, the utilitarians inferred that the whole moral idea of what is "good" can be best understood in terms of the principle of happiness, which they spoke of as "the greatest good of the greatest number," and by which they meant that "good" is achieved when the aggregate of pleasure is greater than the aggregate of pain. An act is good, therefore, if it is useful in achieving pleasure and diminishing pain.

Such a swift account of what is good had not only the merit of simplicity but had, according to Bentham and Mill, the additional virtue of scientific accuracy. Whereas earlier theories of ethics, which defined the good as the commands of God, or the dictates of reason, or the fulfillment of the purposes of human nature, or the duty to obey the categorical imperative, all raised vexing questions as to just what these commands, dictates, purposes, and imperatives consist of, the principle of utility seemed to measure every act by a standard everyone knows, namely, pleasure. To bypass the moral teachings of theology and the classical theories of Plato and Aristotle as well as the recently formulated ethics of Kant, the utilitarians followed in the philosophical footsteps of their own countrymen, the British empiricists.

Hobbes had already tried to construct a science of human nature and had turned his back upon traditional moral thought, emphasizing instead the selfish concern of every man for his own pleasure. Hume also had rejected the intricacies of traditional philosophy and theology and had instead built his system of thought around the individual, denying that men can know universal moral laws any more than they can know universal laws of physics. For Hume, the whole enterprise of ethics had to do with our capacity for "sympathy," a capacity that all men share and by which we "touch a string to which all mankind have an accord. . . ." Sympathy, said Hume, is the pleasure we feel when we consider the pleasures of others, and for this reason our moral sentiments direct us to judge acts as worthy of approval if they produce pleasure and minimize pain. In similar words John Locke also said that "what has an aptness to produce pleasure in us is what we call good, and what is apt to produce pain in us we call evil."

In moral philosophy, Bentham and Mill were, therefore, not innovators, for the principle of utilitarianism had already been stated in its general form by their predecessors. What makes Bentham and Mill stand out as the most famous of the utilitarians is that they, more than the others, had succeeded in connecting the principle of utility with the many problems of their age, thereby providing nineteenth-century England with a philosophical basis not only for moral thought but also for practical reform.

JEREMY BENTHAM

Born in Red Lion Street, Houndsditch, London, in 1748, Bentham showed early signs of his unusual intellectual capacities. While only four years old, he was already studying Latin grammar, and at eight he was sent off to Westminster School, where, he said later, the instruction "was wretched." He entered Queen's College in Oxford when he was twelve years old, and after three years, which were not particularly happy ones as he disapproved of the vice and laziness of his fellow students, he took his B.A. degree in 1763 and entered Lincoln's Inn, in accordance with his father's wish, to prepare for a career in the legal profession. That same year he returned to Oxford for one of the decisive experiences of his intellectual life, for he went to hear the lectures on law given by Sir William Blackstone. What made this such a significant event was that as he listened to these lectures with deep concentration, he says he "immediately detected Blackstone's fallacy respecting natural rights," and this experience crystallized his own theory of law, in which he rejected the theory of "natural rights" as "rhetorical

Bentham (*The Bettmann Archive*)

nonsense—nonsense on stilts.'' He took his M.A. degree in 1766 and again re-turned to London, but he never developed any affection for the legal profession and decided against being a lawyer. Instead, he was drawn into a vigorous liter-ary career in which he tried to bring order and moral defensibility into what he considered the deplorable state both of the law and the social realities that the law made possible.

Bentham was therefore chiefly a reformer. His philosophical orientation had been provided, for the most part, by the empiricists Locke, whose enlight-ened and free thought gave Bentham a powerful weapon against ideas based upon prejudice, and Hume, whose *Treatise on Human Nature* Bentham read with such profit that he said it was "as if scales fell" from his eyes regarding moral philosophy. His first book, *Fragment on Government,* appeared in 1776 and was an attack upon Blackstone. This *Fragment* was also in sharp contrast to another document that appeared in that year, namely the Declaration of Independence, which Bentham thought was a confused and absurd jumble of words in which the authors had all along assumed the natural rights of man, which was what they wanted to demonstrate. Among his later writings were a *Defence of Usury* (1787), his famous *Introduction to the Principles of Morals and Legislation* (1789), *A Plea for the Constitution* (1803), and *Catechism of Parliamentary Reform* (1809). With these writings and his personal involvement in the social and political problems of his day, Bentham remained a powerful public figure for most of his long life until his death in 1832 at the age of eighty-four.

The Principle of Utility   Bentham begins his *Introduction to the Principles of Morals and Legislation* with the classic sentence: "Nature has placed mankind under the governance of two sovereign masters, *pain* and *pleasure*. It is for them alone to point out what we ought to do, as well as determine what we shall do." To be subject to pleasure and pain is a fact we all recognize, and that we desire pleasure and want to avoid pain is also a fact. But in a few sentences, without indicating just how he does it, Bentham moves from the *fact* that we *do* desire pleasure to the *judgment* that we *ought* to pursue pleasure, or from a psychological fact to the moral principle of utility. By the *principle of utility* he means "that principle which approves or disapproves of every action whatsoever, according to the tendency which it appears to have to augment or diminish . . . happiness. . . ." In Bentham's language to *approve* or *disapprove* is the same as saying about an act that it is *good* or *bad,* or *right* or *wrong*. Between saying that men desire pleasure and saying that they *ought* to or that it is *right* that they should, there is a gap that Bentham does not fill with any careful argument. Still, he says that only about an action "that is conformable to the principle of utility [can] one always say either that it is one that ought to be done . . ." or that ". . . it is a right action. . . ." Tying *ought* to *pleasure*, says Bentham, is the only way "the words *ought*, and *right* and *wrong*, and others of that stamp have a meaning: when, otherwise, they have none." Bentham was aware that he had not proved that happiness is the basis of "good" and "right," but this was not an oversight. It is rather the very nature of the principle of utility, he says, that one cannot demonstrate its validity: "Is it susceptible to any proof? It should seem not: for that which is used to prove every thing else, cannot itself be proved: a chain of proofs must have their commencement somewhere. To give such proof is as impossible as it is needless."

But if Bentham could not *prove* the validity of the principle of utility, he felt that he could at least demonstrate that so-called "higher" theories of morality were either reducible to the principle of utility or else were inferior to this principle because they had no clear meaning or could not be consistently followed. As an example, Bentham takes the social-contract theory as an explanation for our obligation to obey the law. Apart from the difficulty of determining whether there ever was such a contract or agreement, Bentham argues that the obligation to obey, even in the contract theory itself, rests upon the principle of utility, for it really says that the greatest happiness of the greatest number can be achieved only if we obey the law. This being the case, why develop an involved and scientifically dubious theory when the whole problem can be swiftly solved by saying simply that obedience is better because disobedience does more harm than good? The case is the same when others say that goodness and right in an act are determined by our *moral sense* or *understanding* or *right reason* or the *theological principle* of the will of God. All of these, says Bentham, are similar to each other and are reducible to the principle of utility. For example, "The principle of theology refers everything to God's pleasure. But what is God's pleasure? God does not, he confessedly does not now, either speak or write to us. How then are we to know what is his pleasure? By observing what is our own pleasure and pronouncing it to be his." Only pains and pleasures, therefore, give us the real value of actions, and in private and public life we are in the last analysis all concerned with maximizing happiness.

The Sanctions   Just as pleasure and pain give the real values to acts, so do they also constitute the efficient causes of our behavior. Bentham distinguishes four sources from which pleasures and pains can come and identifies these as causes of our behavior, calling them *sanctions.* A sanction is what gives binding force to a rule of conduct or to a law, and these four sanctions are termed the *physical,* the *political,* the *moral,* and the *religious* sanctions. Bentham indicates the special character of each sanction by an example where "A man's goods, or his person, are consumed by fire. If this happened to him by what is called accident, it was a calamity: if by reason of his own imprudence (for instance, from his neglecting to put his candle out), it may be styled a punishment of the *physical* sanction: if it happened to him by the sentence of the political magistrate, a punishment belonging to the *political* sanction; that is, what is commonly called a punishment: if for want of any assistance which his *neighbor* withheld from him out of some dislike to his moral character, a punishment of the *moral* sanction: if by an immediate act of *God's* displeasure, manifested on account of some *sin* committed by him . . . a punishment of the *religious* sanction."

In all these areas, then, the sanction, or the efficient cause of behavior, is the threat of pain. In public life, the legislator understands that men feel bound to do certain acts only when such acts have some clear sanction connected with them, and this sanction consists of some form of pain if the mode of conduct prescribed by the legislator is violated by the citizen. The legislator's chief concern is, therefore, to decide what forms of behavior will tend to increase the happiness of society and what sanctions will be most likely to bring about such increased happiness. The word *obligation* was given concrete meaning by Bentham's concept of *sanction,* for obligation now meant not some undefined duty but the prospect of pain if one did not obey the moral or legal rule. Unlike Kant, who argued that the morality of an act depends upon having the right motive and not upon the consequences of the act, the utilitarians took the opposite position, saying that morality depends directly upon the consequences. Bentham admits that some motives are more likely than others to lead to more useful conduct, that is, conduct which increases happiness, but it is still pleasure and not the motive that confers the quality of morality upon the act. Moreover, Bentham took the position that, especially in the social arena where the law is at work, the law can punish only those who have actually inflicted pain, whatever their motive may be, though some exceptions were admitted. While it may be true that the legislator cannot always take account of motives, this whole question of motives does loom large in morality. Bentham, however, seemed to regard both the moral and legal obligations as being similar in that in both cases the external consequences of the action were considered more important than the motives behind them.

The Pleasure-Pain Calculus Each individual and each legislator is concerned with avoiding pain and achieving pleasure. But pleasures and pains differ from each other and therefore have different values. With an attempt at mathematical precision, Bentham speaks of units, or what he called *lots*, of pleasure or pain, suggesting that before we act, we should, and really do, calculate the values of these lots. Their value, taken by themselves, will be greater or less depending, says Bentham, upon a pleasure's *intensity, duration, certainty*, and *propinquity* or nearness. When we consider not only the pleasure by itself but what consequences it can lead to, other circumstances must be calculated, such as a pleasure's *fecundity,* or its chances of being followed by more of the same sensations, that is, by more pleasure, and its *purity,* or the chances that pleasure will not be followed by pleasure but by pain. The *seventh* circumstance is a pleasure's *extent,* that is, the number of persons to whom it *extends* or who are affected by it.

As this calculus indicates, Bentham was interested chiefly in the quantitative aspects of pleasure, so that all actions are equally good if they produce the same amount of pleasure. Therefore, we "sum up all the values of all the *pleasures* on the one side, and those of all the pains on the other. The balance, if it be on the side of pleasure, will give the *good* tendency of the act . . . if on the side of pain, the *bad* tendency. . . ." Whether we actually do engage in this kind of calculation was a question Bentham anticipated, and he replies that "there are some, perhaps, who . . . may look upon the nicety employed in the adjustment of such rules as so much labor lost: for gross ignorance, they will say, never troubles itself about laws, and passion does not calculate. But the evil of ignorance admits of cure: and . . . when matters of such importance as pain and pleasure are at stake, and these in the highest degree . . . who is there that does not calculate? Men calculate, some with less exactness, indeed, and some with more: but all men calculate."

Law and Punishment It was particularly in connection with law and punishment that Bentham made impressive use of the principle of utility. As it is the function of the legislator to discourage some acts and encourage others, how shall he classify those that should be discouraged as against those that should be encouraged?

The Object of Law   Bentham's method of legislation was first of all to measure the "mischief of an act," and this mischief consisted in the consequences, the pain or evil inflicted by the act, and acts that produce evil must be discouraged. There are, says Bentham, both primary and secondary evils that concern the legislator. A robber inflicts an evil upon his victim, who loses his money, and this is a case of primary evil. But robbery creates a secondary evil because successful robbery suggests that theft is easy. This suggestion is evil because it weakens respect for property, and property becomes insecure. From the point of view of the legislator, the secondary evils are frequently more important than the primary evils because, taking the example of robbery again, the actual loss to the victim may very well be considerably less than the loss in stability and security in the community as a whole.

The law is concerned with augmenting the total happiness of the community, and it must do this by discouraging those acts that would produce evil consequences. A criminal act or offense is by definition one that is clearly detrimental to the happiness of the community, and only an act that in some specific way does in fact inflict some sort of pain and thereby diminish the pleasure of some specific individual or group—only such an act ought to be the concern of the law. For the most part, the government accomplishes its business of promoting the happiness of society by punishing men who commit offenses that the principle of utility has clearly measured as evil. It was Bentham's confirmed belief that if the legislator used only the principle of utility in deciding which acts should be considered "offenses," many acts that the laws of his day controlled would have to be considered a matter of private morals to be subject only to the sanction of opinion. Utilitarianism had the effect, then, of requiring a reclassification of behavior to determine what is and is not appropriate for the government to regulate. In addition, the principle of utility provided Bentham with a new and simple theory of punishment, a theory that he thought could not only be justified more readily than the older theories but could achieve the purposes of punishment far more effectively.

Punishment   "All punishment," said Bentham, "is in itself evil" because it inflicts suffering and pain. At the same time, the "object which all laws have in common, is to augment the total happiness of the community." If punishment is to be justified from a utilitarian point of view, it must be shown, said Bentham, that the pain inflicted by punishment must in some way prevent or exclude some greater pain. Punishment must therefore be "useful" in achieving a greater aggregate of pleasure and happiness and has no justification if its effect is simply to add still more units or *lots* of pain to the community. The principle of utility would clearly call for the elimination of pure "retribution," where someone is made to suffer only because his act caused his victim pain, for no useful purpose is served by adding still more pain to the sum total society suffers. This is not to say that utilitarianism rejects the category of punishment but only that the principle of utility, particularly in the hands of Bentham, called for a reopening of the question of why society should punish offenders and urged a reclassification of cases that are "meet" and "unmeet" for punishment. Punishment should not be inflicted (1) where it is *groundless*, where, for example, there is an offense that admits of compensation and where there is virtual certainty that compensation is forthcoming; (2) where it must be *inefficacious* in that it cannot prevent a mischievous act, as when a law made after the act is retroactive, or ex post facto, or where a law has already been made but not been announced. Punishment would be inefficacious also where an infant, an insane person, or a drunkard was involved, though Bentham admitted that neither infancy nor intoxication was sufficient grounds for "absolute impunity." Nor should punishment be inflicted (3) where it is *unprofitable* or too *expensive*, "where the mischief it would produce would be greater than what it prevented," or (4) where it is *needless*, "where the mischief may be prevented, or cease of itself, without it: that is at a cheaper rate," particularly in cases "which consist in the disseminating pernicious principles in matters of duty," since in these cases persuasion is more efficacious than force.

Whether a given kind of behavior should be left to *private ethics* instead of becoming the object of *legislation* was a question Bentham answered by simply applying the principle of utility. If to involve the whole legislative process and the apparatus of punishment does more harm than good, the matter should be left to private ethics. He was convinced that attempts to regulate sexual immorality would be particularly unprofitable, since this would require intricate supervision, as would "such offenses as ingratitude or rudeness, where the definition is so vague that the judge could not safely be entrusted with the power to punish." Duties that we owe to ourselves could hardly be the concern of law and punishment, nor must we be "coerced" to be "benevolent," though we can be liable on certain occasions for failing to help. But the main concern of law must be to encourage those acts that would lead to the greatest happiness of the community. There is, then, a justification for punishment, which is that through punishment the greatest good for the greatest number is most effectively secured.

Besides providing a rationale for punishment, the principle of utility also gives us some clue to what punishment should consist of. Bentham describes the desirable properties of each unit or *lot* of punishment by considering "the proportion between punishments and offenses," and he gives the following rules: The punishment must be great enough to outweigh the profit that the offender might get from the offense; the greater the offense, the greater the punishment: where two offenses come in competition, the punishment for the greater offense must be sufficient to induce a man to prefer the less; punishments should be variable and adaptable to fit the particular circumstances, although each offender should get the same punishment for the same offense; the amount of punishment should never be greater than the minimum required to make it effective; the more uncertain that an offender will be caught, the greater should be the punishment; and if an offense is habitual, the punishment must outweigh not only the profit of the immediate offense but of the undiscovered offenses. These rules led Bentham to conclude that punishment should be *variable* to fit the particular case, *equable* so as to inflict equal pain for similar offenses, *commensurable* in order that pun-ishments for different classes of crimes be proportional, *characteristic* so as to impress the imagination of potential offenders, *frugal* so as not to be excessive, *reformatory* in order to correct faulty behavior, *disabling* in order to deter future offenders, *compensatory* to the sufferer, and, in order not to create new problems, punishment should have *popular* acceptance and be capable of *remittance* for sufficient cause.

Bentham's Radicalism   It was inevitable that Bentham would discover elements in the law and the general social structure of England that did not fit the require-ments set by the principle of utility. Bentham wanted the legislative process to operate on the principle of utility with practically the same rigor with which the stars obey the principle of gravitation. To systematic thought he wanted to add systematic action, so that wherever he found a discrepancy between the actual legal and social order on the one hand and the principle of utility on the other, he wanted to press for reforms. He traced most of the evils of the legal system to the judges who, he charged, "made the common law. Do you know how they make it? Just as a man makes laws for his dog. When your dog does anything you want to break him of, you wait till he does it and then beat him . . . this is the way judges make laws for you and me." Having exposed one monstrous evil after another, Bentham was impelled by his zeal to reform these evils and to become an aggressive philosophical radical.

Bentham laid the cause for the breakdown of the principle of utility to the very structure of the aristocratic society of his day. Why should social evils and evils of the legal system persist even after he had demonstrated that certain new modes of behavior would produce the "greatest happiness of the greatest num-ber"? The answer, he thought, was that those in power did not want the "great-est happiness of the greatest number." The rulers were more concerned with their own interests. Bentham was acutely aware that men seek their own happi-ness. The object of government, however, is to help achieve the greatest happi-ness of the greatest number. Whenever those in power represent only a class or a small group, their self-interest will be in conflict with the proper end of govern-ment. The way to overcome this conflict or contradiction is to identify the rulers and the ruled, or to put the government into the hands of the people. If there is an identity between the rulers and the ruled, their interests will be the same, and the greatest happiness of the greatest number will be assured. This identity of interest cannot, by definition, be achieved under a monarchy, for the monarch acts in his own interests or at best aims at the happiness of a special class grouped around him. It is in a democracy where the greatest happiness of the greatest number is most apt to be realized, for the rulers are the people, and representa-tives of the people are chosen precisely because they promise to serve the great-est good. The application of the principle of utility clearly required, as Bentham saw it, the rejection of monarchy with all its corollaries, and so he would do away with king, house of peers, and the established church and would prefer to construct a democratic order after the model of the United States. Since "all government is in itself one vast evil," its only justification is to apply evil in order to prevent or exclude some greater evil.

Bentham's radicalism consisted in his desire to press for major social reforms in order to put his philosophical principles into practice, and his reforms were required in order to construct the kind of society and legal process that could most likely contribute the greatest happiness to the greatest number.

JOHN STUART MILL

The principle of utilitarianism had one of its ablest advocates in John Stuart Mill. His father, James Mill, had been closely associated with Bentham and more than anyone had helped to give shape and form to Bentham's philosophical doctrine. Later, young Mill wrote in his *Autobiography* that "it was my father's opinions which gave the distinguishing character to the Benthamic or Utilitarian propagandism . . . ," and his father's ideas flowed into the thought of early nineteenth-century England through various channels, of which, says Mill, "one was through me, the only mind directly formed by his instructions, and through whom considerable influence was exercised over various young men. . . ." John Stuart Mill had shared not only his father's ideas but through him was exposed to the thinking of some of the leading men of the day. He had known and visited the political economist Ricardo, but "of Mr. Bentham I saw much more, owing to the close intimacy which existed between him and my father." Mill adds that "my father was the earliest Englishman of any great mark, who thoroughly understood, and in the main adopted, Bentham's general views of ethics, government and law. . . ." And when young Mill read Bentham's principal work on law and administration, *Introduction to the Principles of Morals and Legislation,* it was "one of the turning points in my mental history." What impressed him most was that Bentham's "greatest happiness principle" rendered attempts to deduce morality and legislation from phrases such as *law of nature, right reason,* the *moral sense,* or *natural rectitude* unnecessary if not impossible. As he read Bentham, Mill says that "the feeling rushed upon me, that all previous moralists were superseded, and that here indeed was the commencement of a new era of thought." Upon finishing Bentham's book, he became a different person, for "the 'principle of utility' understood as Bentham understood it . . . gave unity to my conceptions of things. I now had opinions, a creed, a doctrine, a philosophy; in one among the best senses of the word, a religion; the inculcation and diffusion of which could be made the principal outward purpose of a life." When Bentham died, Mill was twenty-six years old, but already he was developing certain convictions of his own about utilitarianism, which were to distinguish his approach from Bentham's in a significant way.

John Stuart Mill was born in 1806, and between the ages of three and fourteen he was the object of a rigorous "educational experiment" imposed upon him by his father. So intense was this personal tutoring in the classics, languages, and history that he could say later that "through the training bestowed on me by my father, I started, I may fairly say, with an advantage of a quarter of a century over my contemporaries." But this intense learning with its emphasis not only upon memorizing but also upon critical and analytical thinking took its toll upon young Mill, and at the age of twenty he fell into "a dull state of nerves." He attributed his breakdown to the overemphasis upon analysis without a parallel development of the emotional qualities, of feeling. There had been at this time an underrating of expressions of feeling, and Mill points out that "Bentham himself . . . used to say that 'all poetry is misrepresentation.'" But "the habit of analysis has a tendency to wear away the feelings . . . [and] I was thus, as I said to myself, left stranded at the commencement of my voyage, with a well equipped ship and a rudder, but no sail. . . ." He belatedly turned, therefore, to such writers as Coleridge, Carlyle, and Wordsworth, who were to affect his thought so deeply that he could later say that "the cultivation of the feelings became one of the cardinal points in my ethical and philosophical creed." His long romance with Mrs. Taylor, which began when he was twenty-five and which later led to their marriage, further confirmed his high valuation of the role of feeling among human faculties. His literary achievements reflect his attempt to maintain a balance among the wide range of human faculties, starting with the rigorous *System of Logic* (1843) and including *Principles of Political Economy* (1848), the essay *On Liberty* (1859), *Considerations on Representative Government* (1861), the essay *Utilitarianism* (1861), and his *Autobiography* and *Three Essays on Religion*, which were published after he died in 1873 at the age of sixty-seven.

Mill's Version of Utilitarianism   Mill's purpose in writing his famous essay on *Utilitarianism* was to defend the *principle of utility*, which he learned from his father and Bentham, against their critics. In the course of his defense, however, he made such important modifications of this theory that his version of utilitarianism turned out to be different from Bentham's in several ways. His definition of the doctrine of utility was perfectly consistent with what Bentham had taught: Mill writes that "The creed which accepts as the foundation of morals Utility, or the greatest Happiness Principle, holds that actions are right in proportion as they tend to promote happiness, wrong as they tend to produce the reverse of happiness. By 'happiness' is intended pleasure, and the absence of pain; by 'unhappiness,' pain, and the privation of pleasure." But even though he started with the same general ideas as Bentham did, especially relating *happiness* with *pleasure*, Mill soon took a different tack by his novel treatment of the role of pleasure in morality.

Qualitative versus Quantitative Approach   Bentham had said that pleasures differ only in their amount, that is, that different ways of behaving produce different *quantities* of pleasure. He had also said that "pushpin is as good as poetry," by which he meant that the only criterion for goodness is the amount of pleasure an act can produce. It would have to follow on this calculation that all modes of behavior that produce the same amount of pleasure would be equally good, whether such behavior be the game of "pushpin" or the writing or enjoyment of poetry. Bentham was so committed to the simple quantitative measurement of pleasure as the chief test of the morality of an act that he even suggested that "there ought to be a moral thermometer." Just as a thermometer measures the different degrees of heat or temperature, so also a "moral thermometer" could measure the degrees of happiness or unhappiness. This analogy reveals Bentham's exclusive emphasis upon quantity in his treatment of goodness and pleasure, for just as it is possible to achieve the same degree of heat whether one burns coal, wood, or oil, so also it is possible to achieve equal quantities of pleasure through pushpin, poetry, or other modes of behavior. Goodness, for Bentham, is not connected with any particular *kinds* of behavior but only with the amounts of pleasure as measured by his "calculus." Inevitably, the utilitarians were accused of being moral relativists who had rejected all moral absolutes in favor of each person's subjective opinion about what is good. John Stuart Mill sought to defend utilitarianism against these charges, but in the course of his defense he was drawn into the position of altering Bentham's quantitative approach to pleasure by substituting instead a qualitative approach.

Whereas Bentham had said that "pushpin is as good as poetry," Mill said that he would "rather be Socrates dissatisfied than a fool satisfied," or that "it is better to be a human being dissatisfied than a pig satisfied." Pleasures, said Mill, differ from each other in kind and quality, not only in quantity. He took his stand with the ancient Epicureans, who had also been attacked for their "degrading" emphasis upon pleasure as the end of all behavior. To their accusers the Epicureans replied that it was they, the accusers, who had a degrading conception of human nature, for *they* assumed that the only pleasures men are capable of are those of which only swine are capable. But this assumption is obviously false, said Mill, because "human beings have faculties more elevated than the animal appetites, and when once conscious of them, do not regard anything as happiness which does not include their gratification." The pleasures of the intellect, of feelings and imagination, and of the moral sentiments have a higher value than the pleasures of mere sensation. Though Mill had referred to these higher pleasures originally in order to answer the critics of utilitarianism, his concern over higher pleasures led him to criticize the very foundation of Bentham's doctrine of utility: he said that "it would be absurd that . . . the estimation of pleasures should be supposed to depend on quantity alone." For Mill, the mere quantity of pleasure produced by an act was of secondary importance when a choice had to be made between pleasures. If a person, says Mill, is acquainted with two different kinds of pleasures and places one of these far above the other in his preference, "even though knowing it to be attended with a greater amount of discontent, and would not resign it for any quantity of the other pleasure which [man's] nature is capable of, we are justified in ascribing to the preferred enjoyment a superiority in quality, so far outweighing quantity as to render it, in comparison, of small account."

The qualitative aspect of pleasure, Mill thought, was as much an empirical fact as was the quantitative element on which Bentham placed his entire emphasis. Mill departed even further from Bentham by grounding the qualitative difference between pleasures in the structure of human nature, thereby focusing upon certain human faculties whose full use, instead of pleasure only, were to be the criterion of true happiness and, therefore, of goodness. For this reason, says Mill, "few human creatures would consent to be changed into any of the lower animals, for a promise of the fullest allowance of a beast's pleasures; no intelligent human being would consent to be a fool, no instructed person would be an ignoramus, no person of feeling and conscience would be selfish and base, even though they should be persuaded that the fool, the dunce, or the rascal is better satisfied with his lot than they are with theirs." Pleasures, according to Mill, have to be graded not for their quantity but for their quality. But if pleasures must be graded for their quality, pleasure is no longer the standard of morality; if, that is, only the full use of our higher faculties can lead us to true happiness, the standard of goodness in behavior has to do not with pleasure directly but with the fulfillment of our human faculties. Mill went beyond mere quantitative hedonism, to a qualitative hedonism wherein the moral value of life is found in the higher pleasures of man's higher faculties. But if it is better to be Socrates dissatisfied than a pig satisfied, morality is proportionate to the happiness we find in being truly human and not in the amount of pleasure we experience. The higher happiness, then, is the aim of all human life, a life "exempt as far as possible from pain, and as rich as possible in enjoyments. . . ."

Pleasure-pain Calculus Impossible   By preferring the higher quality of happiness over a mere quantity of pleasure, Mill struck at another of Bentham's important assumptions, namely, that pleasures and pains can be calculated or measured. Whereas Bentham based his pleasure-pain calculus on simple quantitative considerations, saying that pleasures can be measured as to their duration, intensity, or extent, Mill argued that there is no way to measure either the quantity or quality of pleasures. Whenever we have to make a choice between two pleasures, we can express a preference wisely only if we have experienced both possibilities. Mill asks, "what means are there of determining which is the acutest of two pains, or the intensest of two pleasurable sensations, except the general [feeling] of those who are familiar with both? . . . What is there to decide whether a particular pleasure is worth purchasing at the cost of a particular pain, except the feelings and judgment of the experienced?" The main reason that pleasures and pains cannot be calculated along the lines Bentham suggested, says Mill, is that "neither pains nor pleasures are homogeneous, and pain is always heterogeneous with pleasure." Instead of calculating, men simply express a preference, and apart from this act of preference, "there is no other tribunal."

Moral Obligation: Desire versus Desirable   Bentham had simply assumed that we *ought* to choose those acts that produce for us the greatest quantity of pleasure. He also assumed that we should naturally help other people achieve happiness because in that way we should secure our own, and this was his *greatest-happiness principle.* Mill accepted this point but added the quality of *altruism* to this principle, saying that "the happiness which forms the utilitarian standard of what is right in conduct, is not the agent's own happiness, but that of all concerned." Mill modified Bentham's egoistic pleasure seeking by indicating that "as between his own happiness and that of others, utilitarianism requires [us] to be as strictly impartial as a disinterested and benevolent spectator." Mill thus gives the impression that the true utilitarian interprets the greatest-happiness principle to mean not *my* greatest happiness but the greatest happiness of the greatest number. It is not surprising, therefore, that he could say that "in the golden rule of Jesus of Nazareth, we read the complete spirit of the ethics of utility. To do as one would be done by, and to love one's neighbor as oneself, constitute the ideal of utilitarian perfection." Mill is here trying to defend utilitarian ethics from the charge of egoism; and to emphasize further the "golden rule" character of utilitarianism, he adds that "utility would enjoin, first, that laws and social arrangements should place the happiness, . . . or the interest of every individual, as nearly as possible in harmony with the interest of the whole; and secondly, that education and opinion, which have so vast a power over human character, should so use that power as to establish in the mind of every individual an indissolvable association between his own happiness and the good of the whole . . . so that a direct impulse to promote the general good may be in every individual one of the habitual motives of action. . . ."

The further Mill pursues his argument, the less utilitarian it sounds. To emphasize, as he does, that it is not merely the quantity of pleasures but their quality that counts, and, moreover, that it is not my pleasures but the "good of the whole" that we must seek, all this suggests that the ground of obligation is somewhere other than simply in our pleasures. Still, he wants to say that happiness is at the center of the moral life, that happiness is the most desirable goal of human conduct. The word *desirable* for Mill means something we *ought* to choose, and, therefore, to say that happiness is desirable is to say that it is our moral duty to pursue happiness. The words *right* and *good* are also involved here, since, according to the utilitarian principle, an act is good or right insofar as it produces happiness. When Mill was asked why we *ought* to pursue pleasure, his answer was that *we do.* This is the critical point, or even the fallacy, in his whole argument, for he tried to build a system of morality, of what men ought to do, upon what in fact they already do.

Nowhere is Mill's difficulty with the problem of moral obligation and choice more apparent than when he deals with the question of what is the *desirable* mode of conduct for man. Upon this question, Mill thought, hangs the basic principle of utilitarianism, for to answer it requires some proof that this principle is correct or that happiness is indeed the ultimate end of human conduct. But how can we prove that happiness is the true and desirable end of human life and conduct? Mill answers that "the only proof capable of being given that an object is visible, is that people actually see it. The only proof that a sound is audible, is that people hear it; and so of the other sources of our experience. In like manner, I apprehend, the sole evidence it is possible to produce that anything is desirable, is that people do actually desire it. . . ." No reason can be given why the general happiness is desirable except that "each person, so far as he believes it to be attainable, desires his own happiness."

Clearly, however, there is no similarity between the examples Mill has here given, since *desirable* is not related to *desired* in the same way that *visible* is to *seen*. The difference between these two terms turns upon an important moral distinction, for whereas *visible* means simply that something is *capable of being seen*, *desirable* implies that something is *worthy of being desired*, that, moreover, it *ought* to be desired. For this reason, it is quite true that a thing's being seen proves that it is visible, but it does not follow that because a thing is desired it is for that reason desirable. The logical difficulties here seem to be insurmountable, and the more so as Mill seemed to go beyond mere pleasure as the criterion of goodness to the internal region of "conscience" as the agency of moral sanction. Not happiness alone but a sense of *duty* directs our moral thought, and so Mill speaks of "The internal sanction of duty . . . a feeling in our own mind; a feeling of pain more or less intense, attendant on violation of duty. . . .This feeling, when . . . connecting itself with the pure idea of duty . . . is the essence of conscience . . . all encrusted over with collateral associations, derived from sympathy, from love and still more from fear; from all the forms of religious feeling, from the recollections of childhood and all of our past life; from self-esteem, desire of the esteem of others, and occasionally even self-abasement." Mill thus departed from Bentham's external standard of goodness and turned inward, concluding that the basis of morality is a "powerful natural sentiment" and "a subjective feeling in our own minds" and, finally, "the conscientious feelings of mankind."

Liberty Mill was as much concerned with the problems of society as was Bentham. The principle of the greatest happiness inevitably led all utilitarians to consider how the individual and the government should be related. Bentham had put his faith in democracy as the great cure for social evils inasmuch as in a democracy the interests of the rulers and the ruled are the same because the rulers are the ruled. But Mill did not have the same implicit faith in democracy that Bentham had. Although Mill agreed that democracy is the best form of government, he set forth in his essay *On Liberty* certain dangers inherent in the democratic form of government. Principally, he warned that the will of the people is most often the will of the majority, and it is entirely possible for the majority to oppress the minority. In addition, there is in a democracy the tyranny of opinion, a danger as great as oppression. Even in a democracy, therefore, it is necessary to set up safeguards against the forces that would deny men their free and full self-development. In this respect, in his concern to eliminate clear social evils, Mill reflected Bentham's desire for reform. But Mill was particularly concerned to preserve liberty by setting limits to the actions of government.

Mill argued that "the sole end for which mankind are warranted, individually or collectively, in interfering with the liberty of action of any of their number, is self-protection. That the only purpose for which power can be rightly exercised over any member of a civilized community, against his will, is to prevent harm to others." There is, of course, a legitimate role for government, but, said Mill, no government should interfere with its subjects (1) when the action can be done better by private persons; (2) when, although the government could possibly do the action better than private individuals, it is desirable for the individuals to do it for their development and education; and (3) when there is danger that too much power will unnecessarily accrue to the government. Mill's argument for liberty was, therefore, an argument for individualism. Let each individual pursue his happiness in his own way. Even in the realm of ideas, men must be free to express their thoughts and beliefs, because truth is most quickly discovered when opportunity is given to refute falsehoods. Mill took the position that "there is the greatest difference between presuming an opinion to be true because, with every opportunity for contesting it, it has not been refuted, and assuming its truth for the purpose of not permitting its refutation." He assumed, however, that it is important that the truth be known, and his whole concept of liberty, unlike Bentham's, was conceived as the precondition for developing the full possibilities of human nature.

As he considered the ideal goal of man, Mill asked "what more or better can be said of any condition of human affairs than that it brings human beings themselves nearer to the best thing they can be?" But is it the function of government to make human beings the best thing they can be? Mill had a deep dislike for the totalitarian state even though he lived too soon to see its ugliest manifestations. When he set forth the limits beyond which the government must not go, Mill argued forcefully that a man must not, except to prevent harm, be subject to the power of government, and especially "his own good, either physical or moral, is not a sufficient warrant."

Still, Mill had departed sufficiently from Bentham's version of utilitarianism to set in motion subtle forces that moved Mill from his clear individualism to tepid forms of collectivism. If he was concerned with quality instead of quantity in pleasures, and if this quality is based upon human beings' being "the best thing they can be," and, finally, if only those persons who have experienced the higher pleasures can know them, there is the natural urge for those who know these qualitatively higher pleasures to want others to have them also. But what is to be done if those who do not know and appreciate the higher values do not want them? It is not surprising that in this situation Mill advocated, for example, compulsory education, thereby reversing his earlier view that men must not interfere with the liberty of any member of mankind even for "his own good." It is most often in the name of man's good that the state moves into the area of man's freedom. What Mill said about liberty has particular relevance in the twentieth century, which has witnessed the encroachment of government upon the actions and thoughts of men everywhere. But the difficulties of stating utilitarianism as a consistent philosophy are nowhere better seen than in Mill's own attempts to defend its principle.

FOUR

THE CONTEMPORARY PERIOD: THE RESHAPING OF THE PHILOSOPHIC MIND

19

Nietzsche

F riedrich Nietzsche died on August 25, 1900, at the age of fifty-five, leaving a legacy of brilliant writings whose impact and influence were delayed until the twentieth century. His life was full of sharp contrasts. The son and grandson of Lutheran ministers, he was nevertheless the herald of the judgment that "God is dead" and undertook a "campaign against morality." He was nurtured in an environment thoroughly dominated by females yet advocated the most masculine philosophy of the superman. He called for the fullest expression of human vitality in the name of the Will to Power and yet believed that sublimation and control are the truly human characteristics. His writings rank among the most lucid ever written, yet he ended his days in hopeless insanity.

Named after the reigning King of Prussia, Friedrich Wilhelm Nietzsche was born in Röcken, in the province of Saxony, on October 15, 1844. His father died when he was four years old, and he grew up in a household consisting of his mother, sister, grandmother, and two maiden aunts. At age fourteen he was sent to the famed boarding school at Pforta, where for six years he underwent rigorous intellectual discipline, excelling particularly in the classics, religion, and German literature. It was here that he came under the spell of the Greek genius, discovering it especially in Aeschylus and Plato. In October of 1864 he went to the University of Bonn but stayed only one year as he was unimpressed by the caliber of his fellow students and decided to follow his excellent teacher of classics and philology, Friedrich Ritschl, who was invited to accept a chair at the University of Leipzig. While at Leipzig he came upon the main work of Schopenhauer, whose atheism and antirationalism deeply influenced Nietzsche for a while and confirmed his own revolt against contemporary European culture, which he had come to despise as decadent. It was here also that Nietzsche came under the spell of Wagner's music. "I could not have stood my youth without Wagner's music," Nietzsche said later. "When one wants to rid oneself of an intolerable pressure, one needs hashish. Well, I needed Wagner."

Nietzsche (*The Bettmann Archive*)

When the University of Basel was looking for someone to fill the chair of philosophy, Nietzsche's name figured prominently. He had not yet completed his doctor's degree, but some of his published papers had attracted notice for their exceptional scholarship. On the additional strength of his teacher Ritschl's enthusiastic recommendation, Nietzsche was appointed a university professor at the age of twenty-four. After the University of Basel confirmed his appointment, the University of Leipzig conferred the doctor's degree upon Nietzsche without examination. In May, 1869, he delivered his inaugural lecture on *Homer and Classical Philology*. During his years at Basel, Nietzsche visited Richard Wagner frequently at his villa on Lake Lucerne. While this friendship was not destined to last, Wagner did exert an influence upon Nietzsche's thought in his first book (1872), *The Birth of Tragedy from the Spirit of Music*. Of longer duration was Nietzsche's friendship with his older colleague Jacob Burckhardt, the eminent historian, with whom he shared a common fascination for ancient Greece and Renaissance Italy. Nietzsche's wretched health and his dislike of his duties at the university led him to resign his professorship in 1879 at the age of thirty-four. For the next decade, he wandered through Italy, Switzerland, and Germany searching for some place where his health might be restored. In spite of his poor health, he wrote several books during the six-year period 1881–1887 including *The Dawn of Day, Joyful Wisdom*, the famous *Thus Spake Zarathustra, Beyond Good and Evil*, and *A Genealogy of Morals*.

In 1888, when he was forty-four, Nietzsche felt a brief period of respite from his prolonged cycle of sickness and recovery and during a span of six months produced with incredible speed five books, among which are to be found some of his best, *The Case Wagner, Twilight of Idols, Antichrist, Ecce Homo*, and *Nietzsche contra Wagner*. Shortly thereafter, in January, 1889, Nietzsche collapsed on a street in Turin. He was taken back to Basel to a clinic from which he was sent to an asylum in Jena and finally to the care of his mother and sister. For the last eleven years of his life, Nietzsche was irretrievably insane as a result of an infection that affected his brain. He was thus unable to complete his projected major work, the *Revaluation of All Values*. Nietzsche's books have great vivacity of style and are written with a passionate intensity; even though some of his latter works show signs of impending difficulties, it is generally agreed that his writings cannot be discounted because of his subsequent mental collapse.

"GOD IS DEAD"

Nietzsche wrote philosophy in a manner calculated more to provoke serious thought than to give formal answers to questions. In this regard he resembled Socrates and Plato more than Spinoza, Kant, or Hegel. He produced no formal system because system building, he thought, assumes that one has at hand self-evident truths upon which to build. It was his conviction that building a system is to lack integrity, since honest thought must challenge precisely these self-evident truths upon which most systems are built. One must engage in dialectic and be willing at all times to declare himself against his previous opinions. Moreover, most philosophic system builders, he thought, try to solve all problems at once by acting as the "unriddler of the universe." Nietzsche believed that the philosopher must be less pretentious, pay more attention to questions of human values than to abstract systems, and concern himself with immediate human problems with an attitude of fresh experimentation and a freedom from the dominant values of his culture. Because he took a variety of positions on important problems, it was inevitable that Nietzsche's ideas should be interpreted in contradictory ways. Moreover, he expressed his views on issues with brief aphorisms instead of detailed analyses, leaving the impression of ambiguity and ambivalence. Still, Nietzsche formulated many distinctive views, which emerge from his writings with considerable clarity.

While others saw in nineteenth-century Europe the symbols of power and security, Nietzsche grasped with prophetic insight the imminent collapse of the traditional supports of the values to which modern men had committed themselves. The Prussian army had made Germany a great power on the Continent, and the mood of optimism was further animated by the astonishing advances of science and technology, yet Nietzsche boldly prophesied that power politics and vicious wars were in store for the future. What he sensed was an approaching period of *nihilism,* the seeds of which had already been sown. The greatest fact for him was neither the military power of Germany nor the unfolding advances of science but rather the incontrovertible fact that belief in the Christian God had drastically declined to the point where he could say that "God is dead."

Although Nietzsche was by temperament an atheist, he contemplated the "death" of God with mixed reactions. He was appalled at the consequences that would follow once everyone had become fully aware of all the implications of the death of God, a cultural event that he said has not yet become apparent to modern man. Contemplating simultaneously the collapse of religious faith and the mounting belief in the Darwinian notion of a relentless evolution of the species, he could see in this combination the destruction of any basic distinction between man and animal. If this is what people will be asked to believe, he said, then nobody should be surprised if in the arena of the future there will be wars such as have never been seen on earth. At the same time, the death of God meant for Nietzsche the opening of a new day, a day when the essentially life-denying ethics of Christianity could be replaced with a life-affirming philosophy. "At last," he said, "the sea, *our* sea, lies open before us. Perhaps there has never been so open a sea." His ambivalent reaction to the nihilistic consequences of the death of God turned Nietzsche's mind to the central question of human values. In his search for a new foundation for values in a day when God could no longer be the goal and sanction of human conduct, Nietzsche turned to the aesthetic dimension of human nature as the most promising alternative to religion. Only as an aesthetic phenomenon, he said, are existence and the world eternally justified. It was the Greek genius, he believed, that had originally discovered the true meaning and mode of human endeavor. He initially drew his fundamental insights about man from the Greek conceptions of Apollo and Dionysus.

APOLLONIAN VERSUS DIONYSIAN

What concerned Nietzsche at first was whether in light of the encircling nihilism it was inevitable that men must become pessimistic about life and therefore renounce it, as Schopenhauer did, or whether there was some reason nevertheless for affirming life, as one of Nietzsche's idols, Goethe, had done in his career. Nietzsche found in Homer's account of Apollo and Dionysus that the birth of tragedy, that is, the emergence of art and the fullest development of the aesthetic element in man, is the result of a fusion between the two principles that these gods respectively represent and embody. Dionysus was for Nietzsche the symbol of the dynamic stream of life, which knows no restraints or barriers and defies all limitations. In the worship of Dionysus, the individual would lapse into a drunken frenzy and thereby lose his own identity in the larger ocean of life. Apollo, on the other hand, was the symbol of order, restraint, and form, the power to create beauty through art. If the Dionysian mood was best expressed in the feeling of abandonment in some types of music, the Apollonian form-giving force found its highest expression, according to Nietzsche, in Greek sculpture. Thus Dionysus symbolized man's unity with life where his own individuality is absorbed in the larger reality of the life force, whereas Apollo was the symbol of the "principle of individuation," that power that controls and restrains the dynamic processes of life in order to create a formed work of art or a controlled personal character. From another point of view, the Dionysian represents the negative and destructive dark powers of the soul, which culminate, when unchecked, in "that disgusting mixture of voluptuousness and cruelty" typical of "the most savage beasts of nature." Again, the Apollonian represents the power to deal with the powerful surge of vital energy, to harness destructive powers and to transmute these into a creative act.

Greek tragedy, according to Nietzsche, is a great work of art. It represents the conquest of Dionysus by Apollo. But from this account Nietzsche drew the conclusion that man is not faced with a choice between the Dionysian and the Apollonian. To assume even that one has such a choice to make is to misunderstand the true nature of the human condition. The fact is that human life inevitably includes the dark and surging forces of passion. What Greek tragedy illustrates, according to Nietzsche, is that instead of abandoning oneself to the flood of impulse, instinct, and passion, the awareness of these driving forces becomes the occasion for producing a work of art, whether in one's own character through moderation or in literature or the plastic arts through the imposition of form upon a resisting material. Nietzsche saw the birth of tragedy or the creation of art as a response of the basically healthy element in man, the Apollonian, to the challenge of the diseased frenzy of the Dionysian. In this view art could not occur without the stimulus of the Dionysian; at the same time, if the Dionysian were considered either the only element in human nature or the dominant element, one might very well despair and come finally to a negative attitude toward life. But for Nietzsche the supreme achievement of human nature occurred in Greek culture where the Dionysian and Apollonian elements were brought together. To deny, as nineteenth-century culture seemed to do, that the Dionysian element had a rightful place in life was to postpone, as Nietzsche saw, to some later date the inevitable explosion of vital forces, which cannot be permanently denied expression. To ask whether life should dominate knowledge or knowledge dominate life is to provoke the question which of these two is the higher and more decisive power. There is no doubt, said Nietzsche, that life is the higher and dominating power, but raw vital power is finally life-defeating. For this reason, Nietzsche looked to the Greek formula, the fusion of the Dionysian and Apollonian elements, by which human life is transformed into an aesthetic phenomenon. Such a formula, thought Nietzsche, could provide modern culture with a relevant and workable standard of behavior at a time when religious faith was unable to provide a compelling vision of man's destiny. What disqualified religious faith in Nietzsche's mind was the essentially life-denying negativeness of the Christian ethics.

MASTER MORALITY VERSUS SLAVE MORALITY AND THE WILL TO POWER

Nietzsche rejected the notion that there is a universal and absolute system of morality that everyone must equally obey. People are different, he thought, and to conceive of morality in universal terms is to disregard basic differences between individuals. It is unrealistic to assume that there is only one kind of human nature whose direction can be prescribed by one set of rules. There is, however, one thing that does characterize all human beings, says Nietzsche, and that is the drive to dominate the environment. This drive, so central to human nature, is the *Will to Power*. This Will to Power is more than simply the will to survive. It is, rather, an inner drive to express a vigorous affirmation of all of man's powers. As Nietzsche says, "the strongest and highest Will to Life does not find expression in a miserable struggle for existence, but in a Will to War. A Will to Power, a Will to Overpower!" Whenever someone proposes a universal moral rule, he invariably seeks really to deny the fullest expression of man's elemental vital energies. In this respect, Christianity along with Judaism is the worst offender, for the Judeo-Christian ethics is so contrary to man's basic nature that its antinatural morality debilitates man and produces only "botched and bungled" lives.

How did human beings ever produce such unnatural systems of morality? There is, says Nietzsche, a "twofold early history of good and evil," which shows the development of two primary types of morality, namely, the *master morality* and the *slave morality*. In the *master morality* "good" has always meant "noble" in the sense of "with a soul of high calibre," and "evil" meant "vulgar" or "plebeian." The noble type of man regards himself as the creator and determiner of values. He does not look outside of himself for any approval of his acts. He passes judgment upon himself. His morality is one of self-glorification. This noble individual acts out of a feeling of power, which seeks to overflow. He may help the unfortunate, but not out of pity, rather from an impulse generated by an abundance of power. He honors power in all its forms and takes pleasure in subjecting himself to rigor and toughness and has reverence for all that is severe and hard. By contrast, the *slave morality* originates with the lowest elements of society, the abused, the oppressed, the slaves, and those who are uncertain of themselves. For the slave, "good" is the symbol for all those qualities that serve to alleviate the existence of sufferers, such as "sympathy, the kind helping hand, the warm heart, patience, diligence, humility and friendliness. . . ." This slave morality, says Nietzsche, is essentially the morality of utility, where goodness refers to whatever is beneficial to those who are weak and powerless. Whereas for the slave morality the man who arouses fear is "evil," according to the master morality it is precisely the "good" man who is able to arouse fear.

The challenge to the master morality resulted from a deep-seated *resentment* on the part of the "slaves," a resentment, says Nietzsche, "experienced by creatures who, deprived as they are of the proper outlet of action, are forced to find their compensation in an imaginary revenge." This revenge took the form of translating the virtues of the noble aristocrat into evils. Nietzsche's great protest against the dominant Western morality was that it exalted the mediocre values of the "herd," which "knows nothing of the fine impulses of great accumulations of strength, as something high, or possibly as the standard of all things." Incredibly, the "herd mentality" in time overcame the master morality by succeeding in making all the noble qualities appear to be vices and all the weak qualities appear to be virtues. The positive affirmation of life in the master morality was made to seem "bad" and something for which one should have a sense of "guilt." The fact is, says Nietzsche, that "men with a still natural nature, barbarians in every terrible sense of the word, men of prey, still in possession of unbroken strength of will and desire for power, threw themselves upon weaker, more moral, more peaceful races. . . . At the commencement, the noble caste was always the barbarian caste: their superiority did not consist first of all in their physical, but in their psychical power—they were *complete* men. . . ." But the power of the master race was broken by the undermining of its psychic strength. Against the natural impulse to exert aggressive strength, the weak races had erected elaborate psychic defenses. New values, new ideals, such as peace and equality were put forward under the guise of "the fundamental principle of society." This, said Nietzsche, was a not-so-subtle desire on the part of the weak to undermine the power of the strong. The weak have created a negative psychic attitude toward the most natural drives of man. This slave morality is, says Nietzsche, "a Will to the *denial* of life, a principle of dissolution and decay." But a skillful psychological analysis of the herd's resentment and its desire to exact revenge against the strong will show, says Nietzsche, what must be done, namely, that one must "resist all sentimental weakness: life is essentially appropriation, injury, conquest of the strange and weak, suppression, severity, obtrusion of peculiar forms . . . and at the least, putting it mildest, exploitation. . . ." Nietzsche wanted particularly to emphasize that "exploitation" is not some depraved act, that it does not belong to an imperfect or primitive society. It belongs, he said, "to the nature of the living being as a primary function." Exploitation is, he said, "a consequence of the intrinsic Will to Power, which is precisely the Will to Life—a *fundamental fact* of all history. . . ." Come now, he said, "let us be so far honest toward ourselves!"

European morality, by denying the primacy of the Will to Power, was basically dishonest, in Nietzsche's view. He assigned primary responsibility for this dishonest morality to Judaism and Christianity. With utter directness he said that "I regard Christianity as the most fatal and seductive lie that has ever yet existed—as the greatest and most *impious lie*. . . ." He was appalled that Europe should be subjected to the morality of that small group of wretched outcasts who clustered around Jesus. Imagine, he said, "the *morality of paltry people* as the measure of all things. . . ." This he considered "the most repugnant kind of degeneracy that civilization has ever brought into existence." Worse yet was the fact that New Testament ethics is still hanging, under the name of "God," over men's heads. To Nietzsche it was incredible that in the New Testament "the least qualified people . . . have their say in its pages in regard to the greatest problems of existence." With what impudent levity "the most unwieldy problems are spoken of here (life, the world, God, the purpose of life) as if they were not problems at all, but the most simple things which these little bigots know all about!!!" Christianity contradicts nature when it requires us to love our enemies, for Nature's injunction is to *hate* your enemy. Moreover, the natural origin of morality is denied by requiring that before man can love anything, he must first love God. To inject God into men's affections, said Nietzsche, is to subvert the immediate, natural moral standard of utility. All the vital energies of the strong are diluted by routing men's thinking toward God. Again, this is the revenge that the resentment of the weak has engendered. Among men there is always a surplus of "dejective, diseased, degenerating, infirm, and necessarily suffering individuals." These are the "failures," which the Judeo-Christian religions seek to keep alive and preserve. Nietzsche was willing to admit that the "spiritual men" of Christianity had rendered invaluable services to Europe by offering comfort and courage to the suffering. But at what price was Christian charity achieved? asked Nietzsche. The price, he said, was "the deterioration of the European race." It was necessary "to *reverse* all estimates of value—*that* is what they had to do! And to shatter the strong, to spoil great hopes, to cast suspicion on the delight in beauty, to break down everything autonomous, manly, conquering, and imperious." In addition, all instincts that are natural to the full "men" had to be transmuted into "uncertainty, distress of conscience, and self-destruction." Christianity succeeded in inverting "all love of the earthly and of supremacy over the earth into hatred of the earth and earthly things. . . ."

Nietzsche was willing for the weak and the herd to have their own morality, provided that they did not impose it upon the higher ranks of men. Why should men of great creative powers be reduced to the common level of mediocrity characteristic of the herd? When Nietzsche spoke of rising "beyond good and evil," he had in mind simply rising above the dominant herd morality of his day. He envisioned a new day, when once again the truly complete man would achieve new levels of creative activity and thereby become a higher type of man.

This new man will not reject morality; he will reject only the negative morality of the herd. Again, Nietzsche argued that the morality based upon the Will to Power is only an honest version of what the slave morality has carefully disguised. If the superman is "cruel," said Nietzsche, one must recognize that, actually, almost everything that we now call "higher culture" is simply a spiritualized intensification of cruelty. "This is my thesis," he said, that "the 'wild beast' has not been slain at all, it lives, it flourishes, it has only been—transfigured." He refers to the Romans' pleasures in the arena, the Christian ecstasy of the cross, the Spaniard's delight at the gory sight of the bull fight, the Parisian workman's homesickness for a bloody revolution and the Wagnerienne who "with unhinged will" *undergoes* a performance of Tristan and Isolde. "What all these enjoy and strive with mysterious ardour to drink in," said Nietzsche, "is the philtre of the great Circe 'cruelty'. . . ." Looked at from the vantage point of the master morality, the word *cruelty* refers simply to the basic Will to Power, which is a natural expression of strength. Men are differentiated into ranks, and it is, he says, "quanta of power, and nothing else, which determine and distinguish ranks." For this reason such ideals as equality among men are nonsensical. There can be no equality where there are in fact different quanta of power. Equality can only mean the leveling downward of everyone to the mediocrity of the herd. Nietzsche wanted to preserve the natural distinction between the two ranks or types of men, namely, between that "type which represents ascending life and a type which represents decadence, decomposition, weakness." To be sure, a higher culture will always require as its basis a strongly consolidated mediocre herd, but only to make possible the development and emergence of the higher type of man, the "superman." If the superman is to emerge, he must go beyond good and evil as conceived by the lower ranks of men.

REVALUATION OF ALL MORALS

What would Nietzsche want to put in the place of the traditional morality, which he believed was clearly dying? His positive prescriptions are not so clear as his critical analysis. Much of the content of his new values can, however, be inferred from his rejection of the slave morality. If the slave morality originated in resentment and revenge, there must again occur a *revaluation* of all values. By *revaluation* Nietzsche did not intend the creation of a new table of moral values. He meant rather to declare war upon the presently accepted values, as Socrates, "applying the knife vivisectionally to the very virtues of the time. . . ." Since traditional morality is a perversion of original natural morality, *revaluation* must consist in rejecting traditional morality in the name of honesty and accuracy. Revaluation implies, said Nietzsche, that all the "stronger motives are still extant, but that now they appear under false names and false valuations, and have not yet become conscious of themselves." It is not necessary to legislate new values but only to reverse values once again. Just as "Christianity was a revaluation of all the values of antiquity," so today the dominant morality must be rejected in favor of man's original and deepest nature. Thus Nietzsche's program of *revaluation* was essentially a critical analysis of modern man's ideals. He showed that what modern man called "good" was not at all virtuous, that his so-called truth was disguised selfishness and weakness, and that his religion was a skillful creation of psychological weapons with which moral pygmies domesticated natural giants. Once the disguise is removed from modern morality, he thought, the true values will emerge.

Moral values must in the last analysis be built upon the true nature of man and his environment. Unlike Darwin, who laid great stress upon external circumstances when describing the evolution of the species, Nietzsche focused upon the internal power within man, which is capable of shaping and creating events, "a power which *uses* and *exploits* the environment." Nietzsche's grand hypothesis was that everywhere and in everything the Will to Power is seeking to express itself. "This world," he says, "is the Will to Power—and nothing else." Life itself is a plurality of forces, "a lasting form of processes of assertions of force. . . ." Man's psychological makeup shows that his preoccupation with pleasure and pain reflects a striving after an increase of power. Pain can be the spur for exerting power to overcome an obstacle, whereas pleasure can represent a feeling of increased power.

THE SUPERMAN

The Will to Power has its greatest relevance for Nietzsche's philosophy in his notion of the *superman*. We have already seen that Nietzsche rejected the concept of equality. He also indicated that morality must suit each rank of man. Even after the *revaluation* of all values, the "common herd" will not be intellectually capable of reaching the heights of the "free spirits." There can, in short, be no "common good." Great things, says Nietzsche, remain for the great, "everything rare for the rare." The superman will be rare, but he is the next stage in human evolution. History is moving not toward some abstract developed "humanity" but toward the emergence of some exceptional men: "*Superman* is the goal," says Nietzsche. But the superman will not be the product of a mechanical process of evolution. Only when superior individuals have the courage to revalue all values and respond with freedom to their internal Will to Power can the next stage be reached. "Man is something to be surpassed," and it is the superman who represents the highest level of development and expression of physical, intellectual, and emotional strength. The superman will be the truly free man for whom nothing is forbidden except what obstructs the Will to Power. He will be the very embodiment of the spontaneous affirmation of life.

Nietzsche did not contemplate that his superman would be a tyrant. To be sure, there would be much of the Dionysian element in him. But his passions would be controlled and his animal nature harmonized with his intellect, giving style to his behavior. Such a superman is not to be confused with a totalitarian bully. Nietzsche had in mind as a model his hero Goethe, suggesting also as an ideal "the Roman Caesar with Christ's soul." As Nietzsche's thought matured, his

ideal man would have to possess a balanced unity of the Dionysian and Apollonian elements. Earlier, when his thought was influenced by Wagner and Schopenhauer, Nietzsche had criticized Socrates for having caused Western man to
take a wrong turn in history, the turn toward rationality. Even at the end, Nietzsche believed that knowledge and rationality must be used in the service of life
and that life must not be sacrificed for knowledge. Still, Socrates was important
historically precisely because he saved men from self-destruction, which would
have occurred if, says Nietzsche, "this whole incalculable sum of energy [in
human striving was] *not* employed in the service of knowledge. . . ." The lust for
life, he says, would then have led to wars of annihilation. The Dionysian element
by itself leads to pessimism and destruction. That it was necessary to harness
man's vital energies already suggested a basic decadent tendency in man, which
could be halted only by the kind of influence Socrates represented. But while the
Apollonian element could subvert the vital streams of life, Nietzsche did not see
how, in the end, life could be lived without its form-giving guidance. Socrates
became important for Nietzsche precisely because this ancient philosopher was
the first to see the proper relation between thought and life. Socrates recognized,
said Nietzsche, that thought serves life while for previous philosophers life served
thought and knowledge. Here, then, was Nietzsche's ideal, the passionate man
who has his passions under control.

Two Twentieth-Century Metaphysicians: Bergson and Whitehead

Just when modern science was reaching its most impressive heights of achievement, two bold speculative philosophers called into question the basic assumptions of the scientific mode of thought. Neither Bergson nor Whitehead wished to deny that the scientific method had given man considerable control over nature and to that extent was a brilliantly successful enterprise. What concerned them primarily was a philosophical question, namely, whether reality, the basic nature of things, was what science assumed it to be. As late as the second half of the nineteenth century, and the early decades of the twentieth, the major assumption of science was that nature consists of material objects located in space. Matter, it was held, is the final irreducible stuff out of which all things are formed. The model for thinking about the contents and behavior of nature was the model of a machine. All the particular things in nature were thought to be parts of a large mechanism. This meant that the behavior of each part could in time be described with mathematical exactness, since material objects moved in space in accordance with precise rules or laws. Moreover, as parts of a mechanism, things were related to each other in a tight sequence of cause and effect. Human nature was also viewed in these material and mechanical terms. As parts of a tightly organized cosmic machine, men were no longer thought of as being "free," as possessing freedom of the will.

Each of these assumptions raised serious philosophical problems for Bergson and Whitehead. They wondered whether nature really does consist of inert material objects located in space and whether the intellect is capable of discovering "out there" such an orderly and mechanical arrangement of things as the logical and mathematical reasoning of science portrays. How, moreover, can there be any genuine novelty in nature if the basic reality is material and its various parts organized in a tight mechanism? Can a world made of material things ever become anything more than these same objects simply rearranged from time to time? How, in short, can inert matter overcome its static status and "evolve"? How can the concrete experience of life be explained in terms of a lifeless nature? And how can human freedom be explained in a thoroughly mechanical universe? Science itself had recently been developing new concepts, as for example, the theory of evolution, which made the mechanical model of nature less and less plausible.

Whitehead pointed out that late in the nineteenth century, the "men of science were quite unaware that the ideas they were introducing, one after the other, were finally to accumulate into a body of thought inconsistent with the Newtonian ideas dominating their thoughts and shaping their modes of expression." Whitehead moved, as it were, from within science to his metaphysics, drawing out many of the implications of the emerging new physics. Similarly, Bergson had no intention of rejecting science but thought, rather, that metaphysics and science could enrich each other. His view was that "philosophy ought then to follow science, in order to superpose on scientific truth a knowledge of another kind, which may be called metaphysical. Thus combined, all our knowledge, both scientific and metaphysical, is heightened." What Bergson and Whitehead did challenge in science, however, was the assumption that the scientific mode of thought could be the sole comprehensive source of knowledge. Accordingly, they sought to show just what the limits of science are and what unique insights could be provided by metaphysics.

BERGSON

Henri Bergson was born in Paris in 1859, the brilliant son of a Polish father and an English mother. This same year saw the publication of Darwin's *On the Origin of Species by Means of Natural Selection* and the birth of John Dewey. Bergson's rise in the academic world was rapid. At the age of twenty-two he became professor of philosophy at the Angers Lycée, and by 1900 he was appointed to the distinguished chair of modern philosophy at the Collège de France. With uncommon lucidity and a captivating style, Bergson wrote a series of works that won wide attention and stimulated considerable discussion, including *Time and Free Will* (1889), *Matter and Memory* (1897), *An Introduction to Metaphysics*

Bergson (*New York Public Library Picture Collection*)

(1903), *Creative Evolution* (1907), and *The Two Sources of Morality and Religion* (1932). These last three works gained particular fame and contain his most distinctive ideas. Their publication assured him of a worldwide reputation and attracted people from many countries to hear his lectures in Paris where he lived until his death in 1941 at the age of eighty-two.

Analysis versus Intuition   At the center of Bergson's philosophy is his conviction that there are "two profoundly different ways of knowing a thing." The first way, he says, "implies that we move around the object," and the second, that "we enter into it." Knowledge derived in the first way depends upon the vantage point from which we observe an object, and therefore this mode of knowledge will be different for each observer and on that account *relative*. Moreover, knowledge derived by observation is expressed in symbols, where the symbol used can refer not only to this specific object but any and all similar objects. The second kind of knowledge, however, is *absolute*, says Bergson, because in this case, by "entering" the object, we overcome the limitations of any particular perspective and grasp the object as it really is.

Bergson illustrates these two modes of knowing with several examples. First, there is the example of the movement of an object in space. My observation of this object, he says, will vary with the point of view, moving or stationary, from which I observe it. When I try to describe this motion, my expression of it will vary with the points of reference to which I relate it. Both in observing and describing the moving object, I am placed outside of it. In describing the object's motion, I think of a line that is divided into units and express this through the symbol of a graph with its axes, a series of points through which the object is thought to move. By contrast to this attempt to plot and chart movement in terms of discrete units of space, there is, says Bergson, the true movement, a continuous flow, where there are in reality no points being crossed. Suppose, says Bergson, that you were inside the object as it moved. You would then know the object as it really is and moves and not only as translated into the symbolic language of points and units of distances, for "what I experience will depend neither on the point of view I may take up in regard to the object, since I am inside the object itself, nor on the symbols by which I may translate the motion, since I have rejected all translations in order to possess the original." Instead of trying to grasp the movement from where I stand, from my static position, I must try to grasp the object's motion from where *it* is, from within, as the motion is in the object itself. When a person raises his arm, he has a simple and single perception of the movement he has created; he has an "absolute" knowledge of this movement. But, says Bergson, for me, "watching it from the outside, your arm passes through one point, then through another, and between these points there will be still other points. . . . Viewed from the inside, then, an absolute is a simple thing; but looked at from the outside, that is to say, relatively to other things, it becomes, in relation to these signs which express it, the gold coin for which we never seem able to finish giving small change."

The case is the same when we take a character in a novel. The author takes great pains to describe his traits and to make him engage in action and dialogue. But, says Bergson, "all this can never be equivalent to the simple and indivisible feeling which I should experience if I were able for an instant to identify myself with the person of the hero himself." The reason why descriptive traits do not help me know this particular hero is that such traits are merely symbols, "which can make him known to me only by so many comparisons with persons or things I know already." Such symbols take me outside of him, and "they give me only what he has in common with others and not what belong to him alone." It is not possible, says Bergson, to perceive what constitutes a person's "essence" from without, because by definition his essence is internal and therefore cannot be expressed by symbols. Description and analysis require the use of symbols, but symbols are always "imperfect in comparison with the object of which a view has been taken, or which the symbols seek to express." Not all the photographs of Paris, taken from every conceivable point of view, and not even motion pictures, would ever be equivalent to the solid Paris in which we live and move. Not all the translations of a poem could render the inner meaning of the original. In every example, there is the original, which we can know absolutely only by entering into it, compared with the "translation" or copy, which we know only relatively depending upon our vantage point and the symbols we use for expression.

What, more precisely, does it mean to "go around" an object and to "enter into it"? To go around an object is what Bergson means by that special activity of the intellect that he calls *analysis*. By contrast, to enter into an object is what is implied by his use of the term *intuition*. By intuition Bergson means "the kind of *intellectual sympathy* by which one places oneself within an object in order to coincide with what is unique in it and consequently inexpressible." The basic contrast between science and metaphysics turns upon the difference between *analysis* and *intuition*.

Bergson contended that in the end scientific reasoning, insofar as it is based upon analysis, falsifies the nature of whatever object it analyzes. This follows, he said, from the fact that "analysis . . . is the operation which reduces the object to elements already known, that is, to elements common both to it and other objects." Therefore, "to analyze . . . is to express a thing as a function of something other than itself." To analyze a rose is to take it apart and discover its constituents. From such an analysis we do in fact derive knowledge of the rose, but in such a state of analysis, the rose is no longer the living thing it was in the garden. Similarly, the science of medicine discovers much knowledge of the human anatomy by dissecting it into parts.

In every case, says Bergson, the analytic intellect learns, ironically, by destroying the object's essence. Its essence is its dynamic, thriving, pulsing, living, continuing existence—its *duration*. Analysis, however, interrupts this essential duration; it *stops* life and movement; it separates into several independent and static parts what in true life is a unified, organic, and dynamic reality.

The language of analytic science tends, moreover, to exaggerate even further this static and disjointed conception of things through its use of symbols.

Each new object is described by science by using as many symbols as there are ways of looking at a thing. And the content of each such perception is, says Bergson, *abstracted,* that is, drawn or lifted out from the object. Thus, the intellect forms a series of concepts about a thing, "cutting out of reality according to the lines that must be followed in order to act conveniently upon it." Since we think in terms of our language, that is, in terms of single concepts, we tend to analyze things into as many concepts as there are ways of looking at, moving around, an object. This is, says Bergson, the ordinary function of scientific analysis, namely, to work with symbols. Even the sciences concerned with life "confine themselves to the visible form of living beings, their organs and anatomical elements. They make comparisons between these forms, they reduce the more complex to the more simple; in short, they study the workings of life in what is, so to speak, only its visual symbol." There seem to be, says Bergson, a "symmetry, concord and agreement" between our intellect and matter, as though our intellect were made to analyze and utilize matter. Indeed, he says, "our intelligence is the prolongation of our senses"; even before there was either science or philosophy, "the role of intelligence was already that of manufacturing instruments and guiding the action of our body on surrounding bodies." If, then, the intellect has been made to utilize matter, "its structure has no doubt been modelled upon that of matter." But it is precisely for this reason that the intellect has a limited function; its very structure and function fit it for analysis, for separating what is unified into its parts. Even when it comes to the study of the most concrete reality, namely, the *self,* the intellect, proceeding analytically, is never capable of discovering the true self. As all other sciences, psychology analyzes the self into separate "states" such as sensations, feelings, and ideas, which it studies separately. To study the self by studying separately the various psychical states is, says Bergson, like trying to know Paris by studying various sketches all of which are labelled *Paris.* The psychologists claim to find the "ego" in the various psychical states, not realizing that "this diversity of states has itself only been obtained . . . by transporting oneself outside the ego altogether. . . ." And "however much they place the states side by side, multiplying points of contact and exploring the intervals, the ego always escapes them. . . ."

But there is another way, says Bergson, of knowing the self, and that is by *intuition.* As he says, "there is one reality, as least, which we all seize from within, by intuition and not by simple analysis. It is our own personality through time—our self which endures." As Descartes, Bergson founded his philosophy upon the immediate knowledge of the self. But whereas Descartes built a system of rationalism upon his self-knowledge, Bergson set forth the method of intuition, which was in sharp contrast to rationalism. Intuition, Bergson argued, is a kind of intellectual sympathy. It enables one's consciousness to become identified with an object; intuition "signifies . . . immediate consciousness, a vision which is scarcely distinguishable from the object seen, a knowledge which is contact or even coincidence." Most important of all, says Bergson, "to think intuitively is to think in *duration.*" This is the difference between analytic and intuitive thought.

Analysis begins with the static and reconstructs movement as best it can with immobilities in juxtaposition. By contrast, "intuition starts from movement, posits it, or rather perceives it as reality itself, and sees in immobility only an abstract moment, a snapshot taken by our mind. . . ." Ordinarily, analytic thought pictures the new as a new arrangement of what already exists; although nothing is ever lost, neither is anything ever created. But "intuition, bound up to a duration which is growth, perceives in it an uninterrupted continuity of unforeseeable novelty; it sees, it knows that the mind draws from itself more than it has, that spirituality consists in just that, and that reality, impregnated with spirit, is creation." Intuition, then, discovers that the self is a duration, a continuous flux.

The inner life of the self is compared by Bergson to a continual rolling up, "like that of a thread on a ball, for our past follows us, it swells incessantly with the present that it picks up on its way; and consciousness means memory." An even better way of thinking about the self, he says, is to imagine an infinitely small elastic body, which is gradually drawn out in such a manner that from that original body comes a constantly lengthening line. While even this image is not satisfactory to him, Bergson does see in it an analogy to human personality in that the drawing out of the elastic body is a continuous action representing the duration of the ego, the pure mobility of the self. But whatever images are used to describe it, "the inner life is all this at once: variety of qualities, continuity of progress, and unity of direction. It cannot be represented by images." "No image can replace the intuition of duration."

Bergson centered his attention upon the process in all things that he called *duration.* His criticism of classical schools of philosophy was that they failed to take duration, or becoming, seriously. For the most part, philosophers such as Plato, Descartes, and Kant sought to interpret the world through fixed structures of thought. This was particularly the case with Plato, whose notion of the Forms provides us with a static structure of reality. Even the empiricists, in spite of their preoccupation with experience, analyzed experience into static components, as in the case of Hume, who described knowledge in terms of individual "impressions." Neither the rationalists nor the empiricists, Bergson charged, took the matter of mobility, development, becoming, and duration seriously. Just how this metaphysical notion of duration could be employed in scientific knowledge Bergson did not make entirely clear. But he was certain that to "think in duration" is to have a true grasp of reality. Such thought also gives us a more accurate notion of *time,* real, continuous time, as compared with the "spatialized" time created by the intellect.

Only when we think of time and motion in such "spatialized" terms do we encounter the paradoxes Zeno spoke of. Zeno, it will be recalled, said that a flying arrow really does not move, because at each instant the arrow occupies a single point in space, which would mean that at each instant the arrow is at rest since otherwise it would not occupy a given space at a given instant of time. Zeno's argument would be unassailable, says Bergson, if his assumption about space and time were correct. But he argues that Zeno was in error in assuming that there are real positions in space and discrete units of times: these so-called positions are, says Bergson, merely *suppositions* of the intellect, and the units of time are only the artificial segments into which the analytic intellect slices what in reality is a continuous flow. What Zeno's paradoxes show us is that it is impossible to construct mobility out of static positions or true time out of instants. Although the intellect is capable of comprehending static parts, it is incapable of grasping movement or duration. Only intuition can grasp duration. And reality is duration. Reality, says Bergson, does not consist of *things*, but only of "things in the making, not self-maintaining *states*, but only changing states. . . ." Rest is only apparent, for all reality "is tendency, if we agree to mean by tendency an incipient change of direction."

The "Élan Vital" Is not the doctrine of evolution an example of how science can successfully understand duration and becoming? After examining the major conceptions of evolution, Bergson concludes that none of these scientific theories are adequate and therefore offers a theory of his own. The particular inadequacy he found in the other theories was their inability to give a convincing account of how the transition is made through the gap that separates one level from a higher level. Darwin referred to variations among members of a species, and DeVries spoke of mutations as the conditions leading some members to possess variations favorable for survival. But neither Darwin nor DeVries explained how such variations in a species could occur; both of them inferred that either slowly or suddenly a change occurs, presumably in some part of the organism. This overlooks the functional unity of an organism, which requires that any variation in one part must be accompanied by variations throughout the organism. Just how this can occur neither Darwin nor DeVries explained, leaving unanswered the question of how there can be a continuity of function in spite of successive changes of form. The neo-Lamarckian theory attributed evolution to the special "effort" employed by certain organisms, causing them to develop capacities favorable to survival. But can such acquired characteristics be transmitted from one generation to the next? Bergson insisted that although "effort" had some promising implications, it was too haphazard a notion to explain the overall process of development. Nor was Spencer's theory of the transmission of acquired characteristics such as habits satisfactory, since, again, this seemed to Bergson to be an unsuccessful attempt to construct movement or evolution out of unchanging parts.

Evolution, said Bergson, is best explained in terms of a vital impulse, the *élan vital*, which drives all organisms toward constantly more complicated and higher modes of organization. The *élan vital* is the essential interior element of all living beings—and is the creative power that moves in unbroken continuity through all things. Since the intellect can grasp only static things, it is not capable of grasping the *élan vital*, as this is the essence of duration, of movement, and "all change, all movement, [is] . . . absolutely indivisible." Knowing, for Bergson, is a secondary activity; more basic and therefore primary is living. Intuition and consciousness, not analytic intellect, grasp this primary life and discover it to be a continuous and undivided process of which all things are expressions and not parts. All things are motivated by this *élan vital;* the *élan vital* is the fundamental reality. We discover it first through the immediate awareness of our own continuous self: we discover that we *endure.*

Here finally is where intuition must challenge intellect, for intellect by its natural function transforms, and thereby falsifies, movement into static states. The truth that intuition discovers about reality is that it is continuous, that it cannot be reduced to parts, and that the creative process caused by the *élan vital* is irreversible. "To get a notion of this irreducibility and irreversibility," says Bergson, "we must do violence to the mind, go counter to the natural bent of the intellect. But that is just the function of philosophy."

Whereas the intellect would describe evolution as a single, steady line moving upward through measurable levels, intuition suggests divergent tendencies at work. The vital impulse, says Bergson, moved in three discernible directions, producing vegetative beings, anthropods, and vertebrates including finally man. Distinguishing intellect and intuition, he says that the emergence of intellect and matter occurred together, and these were intended to work together: "our intellect in the narrow sense of the word, is intended to secure the perfect fitting of our body to its environment, to represent the relations of external things among themselves—in short, to think matter." Moreover, "matter is weighted with geometry." But neither matter nor geometrical figures represent ultimate reality. The *élan vital* must itself resemble consciousness, from whence emerges life and all its creative possibilities. Evolution is creative precisely because the future is open, there is no preordained "final" goal; duration constantly endures, producing always genuinely novel events like an artist who never knows precisely what he will create until he has created his work. Bergson finally refers to the creative effort of the *élan vital* as being "of God, if it is not God himself."

Morality and Religion   There are, says Bergson, two sources of morality. The first is the sheer feeling of the necessity for solidarity, and to achieve such social solidarity, a society formulates certain rules of obligation. The second source lies in a deeper seat of feeling, which is touched by the example of great moral men whose emotional appeal transcends particular cultural groups. These two sources, the pressure of social necessity and the aspiration toward higher modes of life, reflect the differences between intellect and intuition. The intellect thinks in particular terms, directing specific rules to specific people to achieve specific ends. To this extent, the intellect tends to restrict morality to a closed society. Bergson was aware that the Stoics saw in reason a source of universal morality. Still, it takes intuition, a breadth of sympathy and feeling, to develop a morality that extends beyond a closed society. Moral progress occurs, says Bergson, only when mystics and saints, obscure heroes of moral life, appear, men who raise humanity to a new destiny, "who see in their mind's eye a new social atmosphere, an environment in which life would be more worth living. . . ." Even when the intellect formulates laws for all people, the intuition opens up richer sources of emotional power, at once inducing aspiration and providing creative power to embrace new modes of life. Thus morality moves constantly from a consideration of the self and of one's society to the larger field of humanity.

The difference between intellect and intuition is reflected also in the two modes of religion, which Bergson calls *static* and *dynamic*. Since we find that all men are religious in one way or another, religion must be due to some inherent aspect of human structure. Moreover, since the intellect is formed to aid man in preserving his survival, the intellect must be the source of religion, inasmuch as religion presumes to answer certain basic demands of life. Religious concepts seek to provide security, confidence, and a defense against fear. But these concepts soon become institutionalized, are converted into belief to protect them against critical reason, are surrounded by ceremonies and disciplines, and tend to become embedded in the social structure. This is static religion, the religion of social conformity. Dynamic religion, on the other hand, is more in the nature of mysticism. Bergson's definition of mysticism follows closely his notion of intuition, when he says that "the ultimate end of mysticism is the establishment of a contact, consequently of a partial coincidence, with the creative effort which life itself manifests." Just as intuition grasps reality more completely than intellect does, so does dynamic religion discover God more vividly. For, says Bergson, we must consider static religion "as the crystallization, brought about by a scientific process of cooling, of what mysticism had poured, white hot, into the soul of man."

WHITEHEAD

Whitehead reacted, as Bergson had, against the analytic mode of thought, which assumed that facts exist in isolation from other facts. His main theme was that "connectedness is the essence of all things." What science tends to separate, philosophy must try to see as an organic unity. Thus, "the red glow of the sunset should be as much a part of nature as are the molecules and electric waves by which men of science would explain the phenomenon." The function of natural philosophy, he thought, is "to analyze how these various elements of nature are connected." Describing Wordsworth's romantic reaction against the scientific mentality, Whitehead says that "Wordsworth was not bothered by any intellectual antagonism. What moved him was moral repulsion." He was repulsed by the fact that scientific analysis had left something out, "that what had been left out comprised everything that was most important," namely, moral intuitions and life itself. Whitehead, agreeing with Wordsworth, went on to say that "neither physical nature nor life can be understood unless we fuse them together as essential factors in the composition of really real things whose interconnections and individual characters constitute the universe." And, he says, "it is important therefore to ask what Wordsworth found in nature that failed to receive expression in science. I ask this question in the interest of science itself." Whitehead was convinced that "the status of life in nature . . . is the modern problem of philosophy and science." Although he shared these same problems with Bergson,

Whitehead brought a different intellectual background to their solution and produced therefore a different and novel speculative metaphysics.

Alfred North Whitehead had three careers, two in England and one in America. Born in the village of Kent in 1861, he was educated at Sherborn School and at Trinity College in Cambridge. For twenty-five years he taught mathematics at Trinity. It was here, too, that Whitehead collaborated with Bertrand Russell on their famed *Principia Mathematica,* which went to the press in 1910. From Trinity he moved to London, eventually becoming associated with the University of London as a member of its faculty of science and later as the dean of this faculty. During these thirteen years at London, he also developed a strong interest in the problems of higher education, being concerned particularly with the impact of modern industrial civilization upon the enterprise of learning. But his major writings while at London represented an attempt to replace Issac Newton's concept of nature with his own empirically grounded theory. These works on the philosophy of science include his *Enquiry Concerning the Principles of Natural Science* (1919), *The Concept of Nature* (1920), and *The Principle of Relativity* (1922).

When Whitehead was sixty-three years old and nearing retirement, he was appointed professor of philosophy at Harvard and embarked upon the third and, in many ways, most important of his careers. To his achievements as a logician, mathematician, and philosopher of science he added his works as a metaphysician, writing at this time his *Science and the Modern World* (1925), *Process and Reality* (1929), and *Adventures of Ideas* (1933). What motivated Whitehead to write these books was his conviction that scientific knowledge had arrived at a point in its history that called for a new scheme of ideas to reflect more adequately the new developments in science. Since scientific thought always relies upon some scheme of ideas, he said, the importance of philosophy is to make such schemes explicit so that they can be criticized and improved. Though his chief speculative work, *Process and Reality,* is a massive and intricate statement, Whitehead acknowledges in the preface that "there remains the final reflection, how shallow, puny, and imperfect are efforts to sound the depths in the nature of things. In philosophical discussion, the merest hint of dogmatic certainty as to finality of statement is an exhibition of folly." His metaphysical writings combine, then, a bold and creative mind tempered with a sensitive humility. In 1937, Whitehead retired but continued to live near Harvard Yard until his death in 1947 at the age of eighty-seven.

Whitehead was convinced that Newtonian physics was based upon a fallacy, consisting in the doctrine of *simple location,* and he called it the *fallacy of misplaced concreteness.* Newton had followed Democritus in assuming that the nature of things consists of individual bits of matter existing in space. What is fallacious about that? Whitehead says that "to say that a bit of matter has *simple location* means that, in expressing its spatio-temporal relations, it is adequate to state that it is where it is in a definite region of space and throughout a definite duration of time, apart from any essential reference of the relations of that bit of matter to other regions of space and to other durations of time." Against this view, Whitehead argues that "among the primary elements of nature as apprehended in our immediate experience, there is no element whatsoever which possesses this character of simple location." The concept of an isolated atom, he says, is the product of intellectual *abstraction.* By a process of abstraction we can, he admits, "arrive at abstractions which are the simply-located bits of material. . . ." But these abstractions, by definition, represent the lifting out of a thing from its concrete environment. To mistake the abstraction for the concrete *is* the error that Whitehead calls the fallacy of misplaced concreteness. Such things as instants of time, points in space, or independent particles of matter are helpful concepts for scientific thought, but when they are taken as descriptions of ultimate reality, they are distortions of concrete reality.

When it came to giving his own account of concrete reality, Whitehead developed a novel form of atomism. He sought to draw out the implications of the recent developments in quantum physics, the theory of relativity, and evolution. His units of reality differed from the atoms of Democritus and Newton in two ways, namely, in their *content* and in their *relations* to each other. Whitehead discarded the word *atom* because historically this term meant that the content of the atom is hard, lifeless matter and that, being hard, atoms never penetrate each other; hence their relations to each other are always external. For the term *atoms,* Whitehead therefore substituted the term *actual entities* or its equivalent *actual occasions.* Unlike lifeless atoms, Whitehead's actual entities are "chunks in the life of nature." As such, they never exist in isolation but are intimately related to the whole field of life that throbs around them. Whereas atomistic materialism gives us a mechanical view of nature, Whitehead's actual occasions permit us to view nature as a living *organism.* Thus, whether we speak of God or "the most trivial puff of existence," there is the same principle of life in all things, for "actual entities—also termed 'actual occasions'—are the final real things of which the world is made up."

Whitehead saw in our own self-consciousness a good example of an actual occasion. He felt that the "direct evidence as to the connectedness of [my] immediate present occasion of experience with [my] immediately past occasions, can be validly used to suggest . . . the connectedness of all occasions in nature." Because an actual occasion is not a material thing, it is best understood as an experience. These occasions do not exist, they happen. The difference is that merely to exist implies no change, whereas to happen suggests a dynamic alteration. Whitehead's actual occasions represent continually changing entities, this change coming about through the impact of entities upon each other. Consider what occurs when a person has an experience. We usually think that in this case there is on the one hand a permanent subject and then something "out there" that the subject experiences. Whitehead argues that the subject and the object are both in a continual process of change, that every experience the subject has affects the subject. If it is true, as Heraclitus said, that one cannot step into the same river twice, it is also true that no person can think the same way twice, because after each experience he is a different person. And this is true of all of nature as it consists of actual occasions or aggregates of actual occasions. Thus, if all of reality is made up of actual occasions, drops of experience, nature is a throbbing organism undergoing constant change throughout. "The universe is thus a creative advance into novelty. The alternative to this doctrine is a static morphological universe."

The doctrine of actual occasions enabled Whitehead to account for the relation of body and mind and for the presence of feeling and purpose in the universe. Democritus had not satisfactorily described how it is possible to have sensation, feeling, thinking, purpose, and life in a universe consisting solely of lifeless material atoms. Nor could Descartes ever join together his two substances, thought and extension. Leibniz did recognize that from lifeless matter it was impossible to derive life, and so he described nature as consisting of monads, which, though they resembled the atoms of Democritus in some ways, were thought by Leibniz to be individual "souls" or centers of energy. Although the Leibnizian monad was a somewhat more satisfactory concept than the atom of Democritus, Whitehead considered it inadequate. Leibniz had described the monads as "windowless," meaning thereby that each monad was completely closed or locked up within itself, that its relation to other monads was purely external, that its behavior was determined by a preestablished harmony, and although the monad was thought to undergo change, this change did not signify any truly novel process, no evolution, no creativity, but only the running of its predetermined course. By contrast, Whitehead's actual entities have no permanent identity or history. They are always in the process of becoming. They feel the impact of other actual occasions and absorb them internally. In this process actual occasions come into being, take on a determinate form or character, and, having become an actual occasion, they perish. To "perish" signifies that the creativity of the universe moves on to the next birth and that in this process an actual occasion loses its unique character but is preserved in the flow of the process. Perishing, says Whitehead, is what we mean by memory or causality, that with the passage of time something of the past is preserved in the present.

We do not ever experience a single isolated actual entity but only aggregates of these entities; an aggregate of actual entities Whitehead calls either a *society* or *nexus* (plural nexūs) in which the entities are united by their *prehensions*. These are some of the novel words Whitehead invented to explain his novel ideas. "In the three notions—actual entity, prehension, nexus—[says Whitehead] an endeavor has been made to base philosophical thought upon the most concrete elements in our experience. . . . The final facts are, all alike, actual entities; and these actual entities are drops of experience, complex and interdependent." Whitehead visualized reality as a continual process in which actual entities are constantly becoming, a process in which *what* an actual entity becomes depends upon *how* it becomes. His emphasis is upon the notion of *creativity* as the fundamental characteristic of the process of nature. Creativity is the ultimate principle by which the many enter into complex unity. If we took each actual entity separately, we should have a disjoined universe, but the creative unity of the many constitutes the conjoined universe. And "the production of novel togetherness," says Whitehead, "is the ultimate notion embodied in the term 'concrescence'. . . ." But the meaning of the term *concrescence* is closely related to the activity that Whitehead calls *prehension.*

Whitehead uses the term *prehension* to describe how the elements of actual entities are related to each other and how these entities are further related to other entities. Nothing in the world is unrelated; in a sense, every actual occasion absorbs, or is related to, the whole universe. Actual entities are brought together by the creative process into sets, or societies, or nexūs. In this process of becoming, actual entities are formed through the concrescence of prehensions. Every prehension, says Whitehead, consists of three factors: first, the "subject" that is prehending; second, the "datum which is prehended"; and third, the "subjective form," which is *how* the subject prehends the datum. There are various species of prehensions: *positive prehensions,* which are termed *feelings,* and *negative prehensions,* which are said to "eliminate from feeling." The subjective forms, or the ways data are prehended, are of many species, including emotions, valuations, purposes, and consciousness. Thus, for Whitehead, emotional feeling is the basic characteristic of concrete experience. Even in the language of physics it is appropriate, according to Whitehead, to speak of *feelings,* for *physical feelings* are the physicist's idea that energy is transferred. Both physical feelings and conceptual feelings are positive prehensions, or internal relations of the elements of actual entities.

The distinction between physical and conceptual feelings does not imply the older dualism of body and mind. It is of course still meaningful to use the terms *body* and *mind.* But Whitehead insists that to assume that these terms imply a basic metaphysical difference such as Descartes urged between his terms *thought* and *extension* is to commit again the fallacy of misplaced concreteness. This fallacy, it will be recalled, is committed when one mistakes an abstraction for the concrete. Both body and mind are for Whitehead societies or nexūs—they are sets of actual entities. The only concrete reality is an actual entity, but actual entities can be organized into different kinds of societies, such as body and mind. But in each case, the actual entities possess the same characteristic, namely, the capacity for prehension, for feeling, for internal relations. Body and mind are both abstractions in the sense that their mode of existence, their reality, is dependent upon the peculiar organization of the actual entities; hence, body and mind are not permanently or ultimately different. To speak of the body as an abstraction is similar to speaking of the *body politic* as an abstraction where only the individual citizens are the concrete reality. Whitehead insisted that "The final facts are, all alike, actual entities," and all of these are capable of being interconnected in a stream of experience.

One might ask at this point just how Whitehead accounts for the underlying process of reality, the process of creativity, which brings actual entities into being and organizes them into societies and preserves what to our experience appears as the endurance of things. Here Whitehead's thought displays a strong Platonic influence. What makes an actual entity what it is, he says, is that the entity has been stamped with a definiteness of character by certain *eternal objects.* These *eternal objects,* resembling Plato's Forms, are uncreated and are eternal; they are patterns and qualities, such as roundness or squareness, greenness or blueness, courage or cowardice. An actual occasion acquires a definite character and not other possible characters because it selects *these* eternal objects and rejects *those.* Hence, an actual event is constituted by the togetherness of various eternal objects in some particular pattern.

Eternal objects, says Whitehead, are *possibilities*, which, as the Platonic Forms, retain their self-identity independent of the flux of things. The relation between the eternal object and an actual entity is described as *ingression,* which means that once the actual entity has selected an eternal object, the latter *ingresses,* that is, stamps its character upon the actual entity. Thus, "the functioning of an eternal object in the self-creation of an actual entity is the 'ingression' of the eternal object in the actual entity." Simple eternal objects stamp their character upon actual entities, whereas complex eternal objects give definiteness, or the status of fact, to societies or nexūs.

To speak of eternal objects as *possibilities* required that Whitehead describe how and where these possibilities exist and how they become relevant to actual occasions. Since only actual occasions exist, what is the status of eternal objects? Whitehead designated one actual entity as being timeless, and this entity he called God. For him God is not a creator, he is "not *before* all creation, but *with* all creation." God's nature is to grasp conceptually all the possibilities that constitute the realm of eternal objects. This realm of eternal objects differs from Plato's system of Forms in that whereas Plato visualized one perfect order for all things, Whitehead's God grasps virtually unlimited possibilities, "all possibilities of order, possibilities at once incompatible and unlimited with a fecundity beyond imagination." What makes the creative process of the world orderly and purposive is the availability of eternal objects, of possibilities. These possibilities exist in God as his primordial nature. God, moreover, is the active mediator between the eternal objects and the actual occasions. It is God who selects the relevant possibilities from the realm of eternal objects. God does not impose the eternal objects upon actual entities. Rather, God presents these possibilities as *lures* of what might be. Persuasion, not compulsion, characterizes God's creative activity. That God always presents relevant possibilities is no guarantee that actual entities will select them. When God's persuasive lure is accepted, the result is order, harmony, and novel advance. When it is rejected, the result is discord and evil. God is the ultimate principle striving toward actualizing all relevant possibilities. What we experience as the stable order in the world and in our intuition of the permanent rightness of things shows forth God's "consequent nature." "God's role," says Whitehead, "lies in the patient operation of the overpowering rationality of his conceptual harmonization. He does not create the world, he saves it: or, more accurately, he is the poet of the world, with tender patience leading it by his vision of truth, beauty and goodness."

21

Pragmatism

Pragmatism emerged at the end of the nineteenth century as the most original contribution of American thought to the enterprise of philosophy. This movement was given its initial theoretical formulation by Charles S. Peirce; it was given wide and popular circulation through the brilliant and lucid essays of William James; and it was methodically implemented into the daily affairs of American institutions by John Dewey. Each of these men expressed a different aspect, or even a different kind, of pragmatism. Peirce was initially interested in logic and science, James wrote about psychology and religion, and Dewey was absorbed with the problems of ethics and social thought, which he expressed especially through his philosophy of education. These men were all contemporaries, they all came from New England, and, in spite of their common concern with the practical aspects of daily life, they were all highly skilled academic men. What united them was their conviction that there must be a close connection between thinking and doing. The popular notion that pragmatism exalts the "practical" man who disdains theoretical thought and prefers to "get things done" is only a half-truth. The pragmatist philosophers, to be sure, saw little value in modes of thinking that did not somehow make a difference in daily life. At the same time, as Socrates, who thought that "the unexamined life is not worth living," they concluded that behavior that did not rest upon thought was lacking an important ingredient. For the original pragmatists, therefore, the term *practical* meant *the way thought works in action*.

As a movement in philosophy, pragmatism was founded for the purpose of mediating between two divergent tendencies in nineteenth-century thought. On the one hand, there was the cumulative impact of empiricism, utilitarianism, and science, to which Darwin's theory of evolution had given the most recent and striking claim to authoritative thought about man. The drift of this tradition was in the direction of looking at the world and man as parts of a mechanical or biological process in which the mind occupied the status either of observer or reflector of these natural physical processes. The mind, in short, was on the edge of things, molded by influences external to it, and was not a creative instrument capable of fashioning thought and directing history. On the other hand, there was the tradition stemming from Descartes' rationalistic philosophy and moving through the critical idealism of Kant, the absolute idealism of Hegel, and the romantic and revised idealism of the late-nineteenth-century neo-Hegelians. In this tradition, the human mind was, for the most part, accorded enormous power, so that philosophers proceeded to construct theories about the whole nature of things, the block universe.

Between these two traditions there was an ever-widening gulf. From the scientific point of view, much of the rationalistic and idealistic philosophy was rejected as lacking in objective evidence. From the rational and idealistic points of view, the assumptions of science constituted a threat to the distinctively human aspects of man, to his moral and religious convictions, which had provided man with a sense of purpose and a reason for expending his energies. Pragmatism sought to mediate between these traditions and to combine what was most significant in each of them. With the empirical tradition, the pragmatists agreed that we have no conception of the whole of reality, that we know things from many perspectives, and that we must settle for a pluralistic approach to knowledge. With the rationalists and idealists, they agreed that morality and religion and, in short, the whole realm of values constituted a significant aspect of human experience. But now, the pragmatists concluded, discussions about God, goodness, free will, and similar subjects must be approached not solely from an "intellectualistic" point of view, where one is concerned chiefly with verbal consistency; the pragmatic *maxim* would ask instead what difference it would make to accept one theory rather than another, what difference it would make to say, for example, that man possesses free will or that he does not.

The argument could be made that pragmatism represented an attempt to justify or to provide the grounds for theoretical thinking, requiring only that thought terminate in action of some sort. In this way, the legitimate claims of science regarding empirical evidence and the observation of facts could be coupled with the human enterprises of volition and belief. One would no longer face the bleak choice of either being a scientist and renouncing as pure subjectivity all moral and religious thought, on the one hand, or, on the other hand, accepting both science and moral and religious claims but refusing to consider any contradictions between them, assuming that if such contradictions did exist they must be ignored. In short, pragmatism unified for men the realms of fact and value, making it possible for them to utilize both science and philosophy in a coherent and creative way.

CHARLES SANDERS PEIRCE (1839–1914)

Peirce (pronounced *purse*), was born in Cambridge, where his father was a noted Harvard professor of mathematics. His early training consisted of rigorous work in mathematics, science, and philosophy both at home under his father's discipline and at Harvard College, where he was a student between the ages of sixteen and twenty. Later, after receiving an M.A. in mathematics and chemistry, he worked for three years at the Harvard astronomical observatory and published his photometric researches in 1878. For thirty years, from 1861 to 1891, he was associated with the United States Coastal and Geodetic Survey. He was also for a short period a lecturer in logic at the Johns Hopkins University. But Peirce was never a full-time member of a university faculty, presumably because his brilliance was overshadowed by personal eccentricities. Without an academic position he encountered resistance and indifference from publishers, so that very little of his total literary output was published during his lifetime and he received virtually none of the fame to which his abilities entitled him. Decades after his death, his works were collected and organized into several volumes, which stand now as a prodigious achievement of creative thought. In his declining years, Peirce was in financial difficulties, failing health, and virtual social rejection. His loyal friend throughout these difficulties was William James, who not only assisted him, but became the channel through which Peirce's original thoughts about pragmatism found their way into the language and thought of a whole generation throughout the world.

A Theory of Meaning At the heart of Peirce's pragmatism is a new explanation of how words acquire their meanings. He coined the word *pragmatism* from the Greek word *pragma* (meaning act or deed) in order to emphasize the fact that words derive their meanings from actions of some sort. Our ideas are clear and distinct only when we are able to translate them into some mode of operation. For example, the adjectives *hard* and *heavy* have meaning only because we are able to conceive of some specific effects that are associated with these terms. Thus, *hard* means that which cannot be scratched by many other substances, and *heavy* means that which will fall if we let go of it. To underscore the decisive role of *effects* in the meanings of words, Peirce argued that there would be absolutely no difference between a hard thing and a soft thing as long as they did not test differently. From such simple examples, Peirce sought to generalize about the nature of meaning and knowledge in general. His basic point was that "our idea of anything *is* our idea of its sensible effects. . . ." That is, if words are to have any meaning, one must be able to use the operational formula, which says "if *A* then *B*," which is to say that such an object or such qualities imply that such effects can be expected. If a word refers to an object or a quality about which no practical effects can be conceived, such a word has no meaning.

Peirce was, of course, highly influenced by the language of science, for it is particularly scientific language that satisfies this pragmatic test for meaning. What he was arguing against was the kind of rationalism Descrates had firmly fixed in the theories of knowledge. To be sure, the earlier empiricists had sought to show the shortcomings of rationalism, but Peirce found the assumptions of rationalism still very much alive. Descartes had localized all thought within the mind of each individual. Intellectual certainty for him consisted in "clear and distinct" ideas, which the mind grasped by intuition. For Descartes, the mind was a purely theoretical instrument that could operate successfully in isolation from environmental circumstances. Thinking, for him, was chiefly a matter of self-consciousness. Against all these assumptions Peirce argued that thinking always occurs in a context, not in isolation from it. Meanings are derived not by intuition but by experience or experiment. For these reasons, meanings are not individual or private but social and public. Again, if there is no way of testing ideas by their effects or public consequences, such ideas are meaningless. To be able to distinguish between meaningful and meaningless is particularly important, Peirce thought, when various and opposing systems of thought are urged upon a person.

The Role of Belief Peirce looked upon belief as occupying the very important middle position between thought and action. Beliefs guide our desires and shape our actions. But beliefs are "unfixed" by doubts. It is when the "irritation of doubt" causes a struggle to attain belief that the enterprise of thought begins. Through thought, we try to fix our beliefs so that we shall have a guide for action. There are several ways in which we can fix our beliefs, according to Peirce. There is the method of *tenacity*, whereby people cling to beliefs, refusing to entertain doubts about them or to consider arguments or evidence for another view. Another method is to invoke *authority*, as when persons in authority require the acceptance of certain ideas as true on pain of punishment. Still another method is that of the metaphysician or philosopher such as Plato, Descartes, or Hegel, who, according to Peirce, would settle questions of belief by asking whether an idea was "agreeable to *reason*." With all these methods Peirce found himself in disagreement precisely because they could not, in his view, achieve their intent, namely, to fix or settle belief. What they all lacked was some connection with experience and behavior.

Peirce therefore offered a fourth method, the method of *science*, whose chief virtue, he thought, was its realistic basis in experience. Unlike the methods of *tenacity, authority,* and *reason,* all of which rest upon what a person possesses within his own mind as a consequence solely of his thinking, the method of science is built on the assumption that there are real things, the characteristics of which are entirely independent of our opinions about them. Moreover, because these real things affect our senses according to regular laws, we can assume that they will affect each observer the same way. Beliefs that are grounded in such real things can therefore be verified, and their "fixation" can be a public act rather than a private one. There is in fact no way to agree or disagree with a conclusion arrived at by means of the first three methods since they refer to nothing whose consequences or real existences can be tested. The method of tenacity is clearly irrational; the method of authority precludes argument; and the method of *a priori* reasoning, because it occurs in isolation from facts, permits the affirmation of several different explanations of things, as was the case with the alternative metaphysical systems produced by the Continental rationalists.

The Elements of Method   What commended the scientific method to Peirce for settling the conflicts between alternative beliefs were those elements of this method that would overcome and avoid individual prejudice. For one thing, the method of science requires that a person state not only what truth he believes but also how he arrived at it. The procedures he follows should be available to anyone who cares to retrace the same steps to test whether the same results will occur. Peirce again and again emphasized this public or community character of the method of science. Secondly, the method of science is highly self-critical. It subjects its conclusions to severe tests, and wherever indicated, the conclusions of a theory are adjusted to fit the new evidence and new insights. This, says Peirce, ought also to be the mental attitude of anyone in relation to his beliefs. Thirdly, Peirce felt that science requires that there be a high degree of coopera- tion between all members of the scientific community. This element of the method, this cooperation, is yet another force that prevents any individual or group from shaping truth to fit its own interests. Conclusions of science must be conclusions that all scientists can draw. Similarly, in questions of belief and truth, it should be possible for anyone to grasp the same conclusions. Here Peirce laid down the method of empirical inquiry as the basis for any cooperative approach to belief. This meant that in the last analysis, there would have to be some practical consequence, that is, some consequence in practice, of any idea. As he pointed out, "the final upshot of thinking is the exercise of volition." The essence of science, as Peirce understood it, though not the way all scientists understand it, is that science is a method of doing something. For this reason, Peirce consid- ered all thinking a way of doing something. But before men are able to *do*, they must have a *belief*; a belief, in turn, requires *thought*. Peirce had argued that only thought that is tested by the criteria of experience and experiment could provide men with the surest basis for belief, which in turn would establish their habit of action.

WILLIAM JAMES (1842–1910)

The rich flavor of William James' writings reflects the equally rich quality and breadth of his life. Born in New York City, he grew up in a highly cultured family, which produced not only the most outstanding American philosopher, but also his brother Henry James, the gifted novelist. William studied at Harvard and traveled to universities throughout Europe acquiring a broad outlook both culturally and intellectually. He received his M.D. degree from the Harvard Medical School in 1869 and was appointed to its faculty in 1872 as an instructor in physiology. From medicine, William James moved to psychology and philosophy, producing in 1890 his famous *Principles of Psychology*. He was a member of the illustrious Harvard department of philosophy, which included George Santayana and Josiah Royce. Although he did not write any philosophical treatise comparable in scope to his famous book on psychology, he published a great many definitive essays, which singly and as collections in book form were read throughout the world. By the time of his death in 1910 at the age of sixty-eight, William James had fashioned a new approach to philosophy and had managed to communicate his pragmatic principles to an unusually wide audience of readers. Starting from the work already done by Peirce, he took a fresh look at pragmatism and developed it along novel lines. Among the important topics to which James turned his attention were the questions of (1) the pragmatic method, (2) the pragmatic theory of truth, (3) the role and status of the human will, and (4) the relevance of the will to believe.

Pragmatism as a Method   William James thought that "the whole function of philosophy ought to be to find out what definite difference it will make to you and me, at definite instants of our life, if this world-formula or that world-formula be the true one." His emphasis was upon the concrete concerns of life, upon facts, upon action as it affects and displays power, and upon power and action as they affect *my* life *now* and in the determinate future. But pragmatism as such contained no substance or content, no special information about human purpose or destiny. As a philosophy, pragmatism did not have its own creed; it did not as such offer a world-formula.

"Pragmatism," said James, "is a method only." Still, as a method, pragmatism assumed that human life has a purpose and that rival theories about man and the world would have to be tested against this purpose. There is in fact no single definition of man's purpose; the understanding of human purpose is part of the activity of thinking. Philosophical thinking arises when men want to understand things and the setting in which they live; purpose derives its meaning from a sense of being at home in the universe. As a method, pragmatism rejected rationalism chiefly because, said James, it was dogmatic and presumed to give conclusive answers about the world in terms that frequently left the issues of life untouched. By contrast, pragmatism "has no dogmas and no doctrines save its method." As a method, pragmatism hovered close to life, refusing to close the process of thought prematurely, taking its cue from the proved facts of life, willing to be led to new conceptions of purpose as deeper facets of human emotion and expectations were discovered. Again, as a method, pragmatism did not specify any *particular* results, though it did orient thinking around results, fruits, and consequences. No formulation either in science, theology, or philoso-

William James (*The Bettmann Archive*)

phy should be taken as final; all formulations of theory are only approximations. In the last analysis, the meanings of all these theories are to be found not in their internal verbal consistency, but in their capacity to solve problems.

Instead of mere consistency, said James, "you must bring out of each word its practical cash value." Although pragmatism stands for no particular results, as a method in practice its essence is precisely to assure *results*. When it finds a theory that does not *make* a difference one way or another for practical life, such a theory is abandoned. If, for example, there is a dispute over whether God exists, pragmatism has no preconceived creed to offer; but it does ask whether it makes a difference to believe in God's existence. To raise that question could very well lead one to see the "truth" in the claim of God's existence even though the same person might have rejected a "rational proof" of the existence of God. By asking always what difference an idea makes, James had virtually reduced the pragmatic method to the formula "does it work?" But supporting that formula was the combined methodological apparatus, as James said, of "nominalism—in always appealing to particulars; [of] utilitarianism in emphasizing practical aspects; [of] positivism in its disdain for verbal solutions, useless questions and metaphysical abstractions." It was inevitable that such a method should raise the question whether to say about an idea that "it works" is the same as saying that "it is true."

The Pragmatic Theory of Truth   James made the startling statement that "truth *happens* to an idea." What was so startling about this statement was that the more traditional theories of truth took virtually the opposite view, namely, that truth is a property or quality of an idea. James was rejecting what he called the *copy-view* of truth. This theory assumes that an idea "copies" *reality*, and an idea is therefore true if it copies what is "out there" accurately. Truth is that quality an idea has when it copies accurately. The assumption of the "intellectualists" who hold this theory, said James, is that "truth means essentially an inert static relation. When you've got your true idea of anything, there's an end of the matter. You're in possession; you *know*. . . ." Against this theory, James brought the whole arsenal of his pragmatism. Truth must be the cash value of an idea. What other motive could there be for saying that something is true or not true than to provide workable guides to practical behavior? James would ask, "what concrete difference will its being true make in anyone's actual life?"

By tying truth to life, to action, James rejected the view that truth is a *stagnant* property in ideas. Ideas *become* true; they are *made* true by events. That is why he wanted to say that truth *happens* to ideas. In addition, to say that truth happens to ideas is to make truth a part of experience. Whereas the *copy-view* of truth assumes that ideas really do copy what is out there, pragmatism says that there rarely is exact copying. Consider, he says, a clock on the wall. We consider it to be a clock not because we have a *copy-view* of it: we see only its face and hands, but not its internal mechanism, which makes it a clock. Still, our notion of it passes for true, not because our idea of it is an accurate copy, but because we *use* it as a clock and as such it *works*, enabling us to end a lecture "on time" and to catch the train. To be sure, we could check our idea to verify whether it is indeed a clock. But *verifiability* is as good as verification. We do not in fact verify every idea. Indeed, says James, "for one truth-process completed there are a million in our lives that function in this state of nascency." For this reason truth lives "on a credit system." We do not require in every instance of truth that we should, as it were, see the wheels of the clock. What more would be added to the truth of our idea that that is a clock than we already have in the successful regulation of our behavior?

Ideas become true insofar as they help us to make successful connections between various parts of our experience. Truth is therefore part of the process of experience, of *living*. As part of a process, truth is *made* by the process of successful experience; successful experience *is* the verification process. To say that a truth always is, that it absolutely obtains, would mean that the clock on the wall is a clock whether anyone sees it or not. But what James wants to show is that the question about the "truth" of the clock arises only in actual life when we live "as if" that thing on the wall is a clock, and the truth that it is a clock is *made* by our successful behavior. On this theory, says James, there are many, *plural* truths, as many truths as there are concrete successful actions. Moreover, James would say that truth is bound up with the personal interests of concrete individuals. By this he meant that truth is not something *capricious*. As bound up with personal interests, the "truth" must lead to successful action; it must *work*. In the long run a true belief must work beneficially, just as an "untrue" one will work destructively.

If the pragmatist is asked why anyone *ought* to seek the truth, James answers that "our obligation to seek the truth is part of our general obligation to do what pays," just as one ought to seek health because it pays to be healthy. Above all, James thought that the pragmatic theory of truth could render a desperately needed service to philosophy by providing a means for settling disputes. Some disputes cannot be resolved if each party simply affirms that his views are true. James would ask, which theory fits the facts of real life? One such dispute, which has exercised philosophers through the ages, is the question of freedom versus determinism.

The Role and Status of the Will   William James was convinced that it is not possible to "prove" by any rational mode of argument that the will of man is either free or determined. Apparently equally good arguments could be given for each case. But he was nevertheless convinced that he could put the problem in a new light by applying the pragmatic method, by asking what difference it makes in actual life to accept one or the other side of the dispute. And the dispute was worth undertaking because it implied something momentous about life—either men were driven by external forces or they possessed "freedom" to choose their mode of behavior and therefore possessed the power to shape their lives and, thus, history.

The central issue in this dispute, said James, "relates solely to the existence of possibilities," of things that may, but need not, be. The determinist says that there are no possibilities, that what will be will be: " . . . those parts of the universe already laid down absolutely appoint and decree what the other parts shall be. The future has no ambiguous possibilities in its womb. . . ." On the other hand, the indeterminist says that there is a certain amount of "loose play" in the universe, so that the present existence of certain facts and arrangements does not necessarily determine what the future shall be; he says that there are genuine alternatives in the future from which an actual choice can be made. Here then are two contradictory points of view. What divides us into *possibility* men and *antipossibility* men, asks James. It is, he says, the postulates of rationality. For some men it seems more rational to say that all events are set down from eternity, whereas for others it seems more rational to assume that men can engage in genuine choice. If both of these points of view seem equally rational to their respective proponents, how can the dispute be resolved?

This was not for James simply an interesting puzzle. His whole philosophical orientation revolved around this problem of the role and status of the will. With his basic concern about action and choosing those ideas and modes of behavior with the highest cash value, he inevitably saw philosophy in terms of human striving, and this, he was convinced, implied a certain kind of universe. His solution of the problem, therefore, was to ask the simply pragmatic question, what does a deterministic world imply? If, that is, one says that all events without exception are rigorously determined from the beginning of time so that they could not have happened in any other way, what kind of universe must this be? Using a metaphor, one could only answer that such a universe is like a machine, where each part fits tightly and all the gears are interlocked, so that the slightest motion of one part causes a motion of every other part. There is no loose play in the machine. How can such a metaphor be applied to men, James asks. A man is different from a mechanical part in a machine. What makes a man different is his consciousness. For one thing, a man is capable of a "judgment of regret." But how can one "regret" what could not have been otherwise? The determinist must define the world as a place where what "ought to be" is impossible. Still, we are always making not only judgments of regret, but of approval and disapproval. Moreover, we seek to persuade others to do or refrain from doing certain actions. In addition, men are punished or rewarded for certain actions. All these forms of judgment imply that a man is constantly facing genuine choices; a "forced" or "determined" act is not a *choice*.

The capacity of choice involves the capacity to recognize alternative influences upon one, to hold these alternatives in momentary suspense and then select one or the other. If one denies such a capacity for choice, the only alternative is the mechanical explanation. But no human beings ever consciously act as if this were a mechanically determined universe. Most of our language and thought processes suggest just the opposite; they suggest that at many points each person in fact faces genuine possibilities, options, real choices. James did not want to deny the reality of causal relations. Indeed, his pragmatism rested upon the operational formula that *"if* we do A, B will happen." But the word *if* is the clue; we are not forced to do A, and therefore B will happen only if we decide to choose A. James realized that if the determinist charged that his ideas about free will were determined, that his assumptions about genuine possibilities were part of the block universe, that such charges would indeed bring an end to rational discourse, that the problem could no longer be discussed. What would remain, however, would be human beings with their hopes, fears, and regrets, and in the arena of daily life the assumptions of mechanical determinism would be abandoned, and the pragmatic question would come to the forefront, the question "what should I do?" or "which alternative would be better or wiser for me?"

In actual practical life, we see ourselves and others as vulnerable. Men are capable of lying, stealing, and murdering. We judge these to be wrong, not only in retrospect, but wrong because they were not rigorously inevitable when they were done; persons doing these things "could have" done otherwise. James concludes, in this vein, by saying that this problem is finally a "personal" one, that he simply cannot conceive of the universe as a place where murder *must* happen; it is a place where murder *can* happen and *ought not*. If this reflects only his "instinct" concerning the kind of universe this is, then, says James, "there are *some* instinctive reactions which I, for one, will not tamper with." As men, we remain the same whatever side of the dispute we choose. But, said James, the only consistent way to represent what in fact men do when they help, hinder, injure, hope, judge, and regret is to see the universe as one with real possibilities, where individual effort can make a difference in life and history. This was the basic theme in his classic essay on *The Will to Believe*.

The Relevance of the Will to Believe   James raised this question: "Can our will either help or hinder our intellect in its perceptions of truth?" In answering this question, James did not intend to propose the fanciful thesis that "wishing will make it true." His intention was to give a defense of "our right" to believe something of which our purely logical intellect may not have been persuaded. Religious questions in particular have a way of running ahead of evidence. But if the evidence for God's existence is lacking, there is, nevertheless, the fact of human behavior. James put great store by the concrete fact that men engage in moral discourse and also religious practice. It is necessary to recognize this fact of religious behavior when considering the issue of religious truth. Moreover, pragmatism recognized the close relation between thinking and doing and therefore between belief and action. This made belief an important element in life, and what James wanted to do was to discover just how relevant the will to believe is in relation to truth.

James said that the will to believe is relevant only under highly restricted conditions. One cannot will to believe just anything under any and all circumstances. First of all, there must be a clear *hypothesis* that is proposed for our belief. Such an hypothesis must be *live* rather than *dead*; that is, it must, as an electric wire, make a connection with my life. If an American Protestant is asked to believe in the Mahdi, this makes no connection with him and arouses no credibility at all and could, therefore, be only a dead hypothesis. Further, there must be an *option*. James argued that a genuine option requires that both alternative hypotheses be *live* and not dead; the option must be *forced* and not avoidable; and it must be *momentous* and not trivial. The will to believe, then, is relevant and can operate only when we are confronted with an option that (1) is *forced* upon us, in that it is impossible not to choose one way or the other, (2) is a *living* option because both hypotheses make a genuine appeal, and (3) is a *momentous* option because the opportunity to choose might not present itself again. And, moreover, belief is relevant only where reason alone cannot settle the matter.

Having stated these conditions, James then argues that it is frequently the case that our wills influence our convictions. The clearest example, he thought, was our postulate that there is truth and that our minds can attain it. How do we know there is truth? We don't, says James; our belief that there is truth is but a "passionate affirmation of desire." We want to have truth, and we want to believe that our experiments will unfold more truth, and in this desire we have the support of the community. For these reasons, James says that "our passionate nature not only lawfully may, but must, decide an option between propositions, whenever it is a genuine option that cannot by its nature be decided on intellectual grounds; for to say, under such circumstances, 'Do not decide, but leave the question open,' is itself a passional decision . . . and is attended with the . . . risk of losing the truth."

Just how the will to believe becomes relevant, what its function really is, is suggested by the last phrase, where James speaks of the "risk of losing the truth." James argues that certain kinds of truths become possible only when we put ourselves in the position for the truth fully to materialize itself. If we fail to make ourselves "available," we risk losing the truth. Suppose a young man wants to know whether a certain young lady loves him. Let us also suppose that objectively it is a fact that she loves him but he does not *know* it. If he assumes that she does not, if, that is, he does not will to believe that she loves him, his doubt will prevent him from saying or doing what would cause her to reveal her love. In this case, he would "lose the truth." His will to believe would not necessarily create the love; that is already there. Belief has the effect of making what is already there come full circle. If the young man required evidence before he could know the truth, he would never know it, because the evidence he is looking for can become available only after he willed to believe it is true. In this case, the will to believe would have discovered a fact that already existed. Projecting this method deeper into the realm of religious experience, James did not want to argue that the will to believe would "create" the existence of God as the product of mere wish. He rather thought that the truth of religion and the power of God in human experience is the discovery, through the will to believe, of what is in fact "there." Some truths forever escape us until we plunge into the stream of experience.

Besides *discovering* facts, the will to believe can *create* facts. An individual, says James, frequently gains a promotion chiefly because he believed he could achieve it and acted resolutely on that belief. Taking his estimate of his powers as true, such a person *lives* by it, sacrifices for its sake, and takes risks. His faith *creates* its own verification. In a political campaign, the will to believe can provide the psychic energy for creating a majority for a candidate. When one person is impressed by the optimism of another, he is energized to express the same optimism about the outcome of the election, and this *energy* can eventually create the majority vote. James gives the illustration of the passengers on a train, all of whom are individually brave, but when held up by robbers each one is afraid that if he resists he will be shot. If they believed that the others would arise, resistance could begin. The robbers know that they can count on each other. The passengers, on the other hand, are paralyzed. Though they possess superior force, they are not *sure* their fellows would support their resistance. But if one passenger actually arose, that evidence could influence the others, and this will to believe would help to create the fact of total resistance.

In the end, religious experience was for James a fact that is both discovered and created through the will to believe. His pragmatism led him to distinguish between organized religion and that firsthand religion whose cash value could be realized only when a person put himself into a position to be affected by it. Religion grows out of the deep personal experience of the fragmentary or broken character of life, and this awareness leads one to discover a power that can overcome this sense of incompleteness. James thought of God in these terms, as a power able to reconstruct human life. For this reason, James concluded that "the universe is no longer a mere *It* to us, but a *Thou*, if we are religious; any relation that may be possible from person to person might be possible here."

JOHN DEWEY (1859–1952)

If William James was the most brilliant of the pragmatists, John Dewey was in the final analysis the most influential. By the time of his death at the age of ninety-two, Dewey had brought about a reconstruction of philosophy and had influenced the workings of many American institutions, particularly the schools and the legislative and judicial processes. His influence was felt beyond the boundaries of the United States, especially in Japan and China, where his lectures made a lasting impression. Born in Burlington, Vermont, John Dewey was educated at the University of Vermont and at the Johns Hopkins University, where he received his Ph.D. in philosophy in 1884. For the next ten years, except for one year when he was at Minnesota, he taught at the University of Michigan, and for the next decade at the University of Chicago, where he gained renown for his pragmatic concepts of education. As director of the Laboratory School for children at the University of Chicago, he experimented with a more permissive and creative atmosphere for learning, setting aside the more traditional and formal method of learning by listening and encouraging instead the pupil's initiative and individual involvement in projects. From 1904 to 1929 he was a member of the faculty at Columbia University. He produced an enormous number of writings even after his retirement in 1929. His interests covered a wide range, and he wrote on logic, metaphysics, and the theory of knowledge. But as Dewey's chief expressions of pragmatism were in the social rather than individual realm, his most influential works related to education, democracy, ethics, religion, and art.

The Spectator versus Experience   Dewey's chief quarrel with earlier philosophy was that it had confused the true nature and function of knowledge. For the most part, he said, the empiricists had assumed that thinking refers to fixed things in nature, that for each idea there is a corresponding something in reality. It is as though knowing is modeled after what is supposed to happen when we look at something. This he called "a spectator theory of knowledge." Thus, to see something is to have an idea of it. But the reverse process was also thought to be true, namely, that to have a clear idea is to guarantee, as the rationalists argued, that the object of thought exists in reality. In either case, the mind was viewed as an instrument for considering what is fixed and certain in nature. Nature is one thing and the mind another, and knowing is the relatively simple activity of looking, as a spectator does, at what is there.

Dewey considered this view of knowledge, admittedly more intricate than his oversimplification, as too static, for one thing, and too mechanical for another. Influenced as he was by Darwin's theories, Dewey looked upon man as a biological organism. As such, man can best be understood in relation to his environment. As any other biological organism, man struggles for survival. Although Dewey gave up his early Hegelian orientation, he still looked upon man as enmeshed in a dialectic process, not Hegel's conflict of ideas, but a conflict in the material or natural environment. Dewey's grand concept was therefore *experience*, a concept he employed for the purpose of connecting man as a dynamic biological entity with man's precarious environment. If both man and his environment are dynamic, it is clear that a simple spectator-type theory of knowledge will not work. The mind, or more specifically *intelligence*, is for Dewey not a fixed substance, and knowledge is not a set of static concepts. Intelligence is the power man possesses to cope with his environment. Thinking is not an individual act carried on in private, in isolation from practical problems. Thinking, or active intelligence, arises in "problem situations"; thinking and doing are intimately related.

All thinking, says Dewey, has two aspects, namely, "a perplexed, troubled, or confused situation at the beginning and a cleared-up, unified, resolved situation at the close. . . ." He gave his theory the name *instrumentalism* to emphasize that thinking is always instrumental in solving problems. The mind does not know simply individual things; it functions as a mediator between man as an organism and his environment. The mind spreads itself over a range of things as these bear upon the person's desires, doubts, and dangers. Knowing may very well consist of a "cognitive act," of an activity in the mind, but the full description of knowing must include the environmental origin of the problem or situation that calls forth the cognitive act. In this way, instrumentalism differs from empiricism and rationalism. Whereas the latter two theories of knowledge separate thinking and doing, instrumentalism holds that reflective thought is always involved in transforming a practical situation.

Thinking, therefore, is not a quest for the "truth," as though the truth were a static and eternal quality in things. Thinking, rather, is the act of trying to achieve an adjustment between man and his environment. The best test of the value of any philosophy, says Dewey, is to ask, "Does it end in conclusions which, when referred back to ordinary life-experiences and their predicaments, render them more significant, more luminous to us and make our dealings with them more fruitful?"

Habit, Intelligence, and Learning   Dewey built his theory of instrumentalism, his problem-solving theory of knowing, around his special view of human nature. Even though Dewey emphasized the social aspect of man, he did nevertheless recognize in individual men certain inherited structures. There are, for example, certain basic human instincts. At the same time, these instincts are not a fixed inheritance, but are "highly flexible." Dewey says that "any impulse may become organized into almost any disposition according to the way it interacts with surroundings." For example, *fear* may become cowardice, reverence for superiors, the cause for accepting superstitions, and so on. Just what an impulse will result in depends, says Dewey, upon the way an impulse is interwoven with other impulses and upon the inhibitions and outlets supplied by the environment. Dewey's central point here is that there is in fact a human psychological structure, that human nature possesses certain inherited capacities. At the same time, these capacities are flexible, so that given natural impulses will work differently under different social conditions. When impulses tend to result in the same response, this does not mean that for a given impulse there can be only that particular response. This was Dewey's decisive argument, for he seemed to reject the simple mechanical stimulus-response account of behavior. If an impulse reflects itself always in the same way time after time, said Dewey, this is not a mechanical necessity but only the product of *habit*. But habit and impulse need to be clearly distinguished. *Habit* is only the way a person deals with certain classes of "stimuli, standing predilections and aversions." But since habit is only *one* way of responding to the stimuli of one's impulses, clearly there is no *necessary* connection between a person's natural impulses and any *particular* response. This means that responses are acquired or learned through the interaction between human nature and culture. If this is the case, habits do not represent eternal forms of human behavior. They can be singled out, analyzed, and appraised. Habits can be tested for their usefulness, the criterion being whether they support life and generally facilitate the successful adaptation of man to his environment.

Most important of all is the new insight this analysis gave Dewey of the nature of social and human "evil." Evil is not the product of some permanent instinct or impulse in human nature that cannot be altered. Evil is, rather, the product of the special ways a culture has shaped and conditioned man's impulses. On this view, evil is the product of the "inertness of established habit." *Intelligence* itself is a habit by which the human organism adjusts its relation to its environment. Habits therefore include not only ways of reacting to certain stimuli but also ways of thinking about the environment. Since all habits are only *established* but *not necessary* modes of behavior, the clue to overcoming personal and social evil is to alter a society's habits, its habits of response and its habits of thought.

Nothing is more important than *education* in remolding a society. If man is a creature of habit, education should provide the conditions for developing the most useful and creative habits. Dewey regretted that in the past progress was achieved only when some catastrophe or major social upheaval broke the spell of long-standing habits. He would prefer a more controlled approach to change, and nothing, he thought, provides man with more power to control than knowledge. Instead of revolution, therefore, change should be achieved through the skillful alteration of habits through education. He was convinced that "the chief means of continuous, graded, economical improvement and social rectification lies in utilizing the opportunities of educating the young to modify prevailing types of thought and desire." The spirit of education should be *experimental*, because the mind is fundamentally a problem-solving instrument, and it is therefore more important to try alternative means for successfully solving problems than to pursue neat theoretical formulations.

Dewey's instrumentalism was governed by the presuppositions of science. Like science, education should recognize the intimate connection between action and thought, between experiment and reflection. Achieving knowledge is a continuous process; it is a struggle to fashion theory in the context of experiment and thought. But if education is the key to social improvement, and if experiment is the best way to discover the instrumental *means* for solving problems, the crucial questions concern the problem of *ends*. Improvement assumes a scale of values, and means are employed toward ends. How does man or a society discover its ends or the foundations of its values? Dewey addressed himself to this difficult problem of relating facts to value, science to morality, and in the process fashioned a new theory of value.

Value in a World of Fact   Dewey's theory of value followed his general theory of knowledge. The mind discovers values the way it discovers facts, namely, in experience. Values do not exist as eternal entities someplace to be discovered by the theoretical mind. Every person experiences the problem of choosing between two or more possibilities. The question about values arises in these experiences where choices have to be made. Choices are most often made regarding means for achieving ends. Where an end is already clear, the value judgment concerning the means can be pursued with scientific rigor. Science, or intelligent reflection, always asks how a given act will terminate. The act that will terminate most successfully is by definition the most "valuable" act. Much of Dewey's theory can be understood through the simple example of a leaking roof. For one thing, the problem of the leaking roof raises *all at once* the questions of both *ends* and *means*. A person quickly realizes that a leaky roof calls for action. Before action is begun, intelligence is used to sort out the various possibilities for stopping the leak. The function of intelligence is to appraise the consequences of various alternatives, using knowledge based upon past experience or experiment. The human intelligence did not have to be endowed or supplied with either a theory of "ultimate ends" or an elaborate "hierarchy of values" in order to deal effectively with the problem. All that was needed to solve this problem could be discovered by the functioning of intelligence. One does not need a theory of value to know that fixing a leaky roof is both desired and desirable. To a great extent Dewey would solve the problem of values by saying that intelligence can discover the best solution when the problem is analyzed in its specific practical context.

Dewey's novel approach was his rejection of any theory of values that said that the standard of value, whether moral, social, political, or economic, is to be found either in the "essences" of things or in some form of transcendent eternal truth. There is no way to grasp in any neat formula just how any act will terminate. Value must always mean that behavior or consequences are *satisfactory*. But it is not possible to decide *beforehand* upon a limited number of consequences that will be called *good*. Life is too dynamic and the circumstances of behavior too diverse to permit the making of any kind of *list* of rules. Moreover, there is, says Dewey, "only relative, not absolute, impermeability and fixity of structure," and "new individuals with novel ends emerge. . . ." This shows Darwin's influence upon Dewey's thinking about value; for value, as Dewey conceived it, is the quality of satisfactoriness of an act that one performs in the Darwinian world, in the pursuit of successfully controlling life in his environment.

Dewey was so concerned to set the problem of values into the concrete events of daily life that he refused to consider the question of ultimate ends and the so-called hierarchy of values. He apparently assumed the ends concerning human existence could be discovered as easily as the notion that leaky roofs must be fixed. Since intelligence is the agency for bridging the gap between *any* problem and its solution, he assumed that this same experimental and instrumental approach could successfully resolve the problems of individual and social destiny. His optimism rested, of course, upon the spectacular successes of the sciences. He was convinced that science could also provide the standard for value judgments. Indeed, in asking where men could discover regulating norms for life if they gave up the traditional moral and religious standards, Dewey answered, for the most part "from the findings of the natural sciences."

In principle, the seat of value must be located in human desire and its satisfaction. Science can tell us not only that men have desires but also that these desires can be satisfied in various ways. By employing the scientific method in value problems, Dewey sought to go beyond the theory of utilitarianism. For the most part, the utilitarians concluded that something is desirable because in fact it is desired. Men ought to maximize pleasure because they desire pleasure. At first glance this seems to be Dewey's approach also, especially because he had given up the classic theory of "truth" and the theory of ultimate ends by which to test or appraise what men in fact do desire. But Dewey added a rigorous element to his procedure of evaluation. For him, desire was only the starting point. It is necessary, he said, to engage in critical inquiry before one makes a choice. A moral choice will admittedly begin with a person's or a society's desire, but a desire must be submitted to the critical power of intelligence. What intelligence does under these circumstances is to consider the consequences of any given form of satisfaction of desire. Value is therefore not simply satisfaction of desire, but rather the satisfactory solution of the problem reflected by desire.

By this activity of critical intelligence, Dewey sought to achieve two purposes: first, to say that value is something that must be worked out in concrete experience and, second, to say that values are not wholly relative and subjective, but must be subject to critical scrutiny. In the end, Dewey's theory appears to rest on the assumption that experience gives a person or society the ends toward which life and behavior should move. Each generation should formulate its own ends in the context of democracy. Democracy itself represented Dewey's *faith* in the capacities of human intelligence. Dewey believed that apart from "pooled and cooperative experience" there is no reliable source of knowledge, wisdom, or guides for collective action.

22

Karl Marx: Dialectical Materialism

For at least one-third of the world's population in the second half of the twentieth century, Marxism provides the official philosophical point of view, or the systematic articulation of beliefs about the world and man's destiny in it. That the views of Karl Marx should have achieved such immense influence is all the more remarkable when one considers that he spent a considerable portion of his adult life in relative obscurity. He rarely spoke in public, and when he did, he displayed none of the attributes of the captivating orator. He was primarily a thinker, thoroughly absorbed in the task of elaborating the intricate details of a theory whose broad outlines he had grasped as a young man still in his twenties. He rarely mingled with the masses whose status and future occupied the center of his theoretical concern. Although he wrote an enormous amount, his writings were not read extensively during his lifetime. One finds no reference to Marx, for example, in the social and political writings of his famed contemporary John Stuart Mill. Nor was what Marx had to say entirely original. Much of his economic thought can be found in Ricardo, some of his philosophical assumptions and apparatus in Hegel and Feuerbach, the view that history is shaped by the conflict between social classes in Saint-Simon, and the labor theory of value in John Locke. But what was original in Marx was that out of all these sources he distilled a unified scheme of thought, which he fashioned into a powerful instrument of social analysis and social revolution.

Karl Heinrich Marx was born in Trier, Germany, in 1818, the oldest son of a Jewish lawyer and the descendant of a long line of rabbis. In spite of his Jewish lineage, he was brought up as a Protestant since his father had become a Lutheran, for apparently prudent reasons rather than religious convictions. The elder Marx had a strong influence on his son's intellectual development through his own rational and humanitarian inclinations. Young Marx was also influenced by Ludwig von Westphalen, a neighbor and a distinguished Prussian government official and his future father-in-law, who stimulated his interest in literature and a lifelong respect for the Greek poets and tragedians, Dante, and Shakespeare. After high school in Trier, Marx went to the University of Bonn in 1835 and began the study of law at the age of seventeen. A year later he transferred to the University of Berlin, giving up the study of law and pursuing instead the study of philosophy. Three years later, at the age of twenty-three, he received his doctoral degree from the University of Jena, for which he wrote a dissertation entitled *On the Difference between the Democritean and Epicurean Philosophies of Nature.*

At the University of Berlin, the dominant intellectual influence was the philosophy of Hegel, and accordingly Marx was for the time being deeply impressed by Hegel's idealism and his dynamic view of history. He became a member of a group of young radical Hegelians who saw in Hegel's approach to philosophy the key to a new understanding of man, the world, and history. Hegel had centered his thought around the notion of *Spirit* or *Mind.* To him, Absolute Spirit or Mind is God. God is the whole of reality. God is identical with all of Nature, and therefore God is found also in the configurations of culture and civilization. History consists in the gradual self-realization of God in the sequence of time. What makes Nature knowable is that its essence is Mind, and what produces history is the continuous struggle of Mind or Spirit or Idea to realize itself in perfect form. Thus, God and the world are one. The basic reality is therefore Spirit or Mind. For this reason, Hegel had concluded that the rational is real and the real is rational. Moreover, the rational basis of reality, the Idea, is in a continuous process of unfolding from lower to higher degrees of perfection, and this is the process we know as history. History is a dialectic process moving in a triadic pattern from *thesis* to *antithesis* and finally to *synthesis.*

Whether Marx ever accepted Hegel's idealism in all its fullness is not certain, but what did strike him with force was Hegel's method of identifying God and Nature or the world. Hegel had said that "Spirit [God] is alone reality. It is the inner being of the world, that which essentially is and is *per se.*" Whatever there is, and whatever there is to know, exists as the world of Nature; besides the world and its history there is nothing. This rejection of the older theology, which had separated God and the world, is what struck Marx as being so novel and significant. Although Hegel had not intended his views to destroy the foundations of religion, the radical young band of Hegelians at the University of Berlin undertook a "higher citicism" of the Gospels. David Strauss wrote a critical *Life of Jesus* in which he argued that much of Jesus' teaching was a purely mythical invention, particularly those portions which referred to another world. Bruno Bauer went even further by denying the historical existence of Jesus. Using the Hegelian method of identifying God and the world, these radical writers shattered the literal interpretation of the language of the Gospels and considered its only value to lie in its pictorial power, not in its truth. The inevitable drift of Hegelianism was to identify God with man, since man, among all things in Nature, embodies the element of Spirit or Mind in a unique way. It was then only another step, which Hegel had not taken, but which the young radicals, among them Marx, did take, to the position of philosophical atheism.

What began to take shape in Marx's mind from his exposure to Hegelianism was (1) the notion that there is only one reality and this can be discovered as the embodiment of rationality in the world, (2) the recognition that history is a process of development and change from less to more perfect forms in all of reality, including physical nature, social and political life, and human thought, and (3) the assumption that the thoughts and behavior of men at any given time and place are caused by the operation in them of an identical spirit or mind, the spirit of the particular time or epoch. Although these were the general themes which Hegelianism seemed to be engendering in Marx's mind, other influences moved into his thought, causing him to reject portions of Hegel's philosophy and to reinterpret these three themes of Hegelianism accordingly. In particular, the appearance of Ludwig Feuerbach's writings, shortly after Marx had finished his doctoral dissertation, had a decisive effect upon the young radical Hegelians and especially upon Marx.

Feuerbach seemed to take the Hegelian viewpoint to its extreme conclusion and thereby criticized the very foundation of Hegelianism itself. He did this by rejecting Hegel's idealism, substituting instead the view that the basic reality is material. In short, Feuerbach had revived philosophical materialism, and Karl Marx instantly saw in this view a far more useful assumption than Hegel's idealism for explaining human thought and behavior. Whereas Hegel saw the thought and behavior of a particular epoch as the working in all men of an identical spirit, Feuerbach now contended that, on the contrary, the generating influence of men's thoughts was the total sum of the material circumstances of any historic time.

Feuerbach's view had the effect of inverting the Hegelian assumption of the primacy of Spirit and Idea, substituting for it the primacy of the material order. One finds this "inversion" developed with particular force in the *Essence of Christianity*, in which Feuerbach argued that it is man and not God who is the basic reality. When our ideas of God are analyzed, said Feuerbach, we find that apart from human feelings and wants there are no ideas of God. All so-called knowledge of God, he said, is man's knowledge about himself. God, therefore, is man. That is, the Spirit or our ideas of God—these are simply reflections of the modes of man's existence. God is the product of man's thought and not the other way around. In this way, Feuerbach had inverted Hegel's idealism, and the resulting materialism struck fire in Marx's mind, providing him with one of the most decisive and characteristic elements in his own philosophy.

Marx now acknowledged that Feuerbach was the pivotal figure in philosophy. Most important of all, Feuerbach had shifted from God to man the focal point of historic development. That is, whereas Hegelian thought said that it was Spirit or Idea that was progressively realizing itself in history, Feuerbach said that it is really man who is struggling to realize himself. Man, and not God, was in some way alienated from himself, and history has to do with man's struggle to overcome his self-alienation. Clearly, if this was in fact the condition of man, Marx thought, the world should be changed in order to facilitate man's self-realization. This is what led Marx to say that hitherto "the philosophers have only *interpreted* the world differently: the point is, however, to *change* it." Marx had grounded his thought in two major insights, Hegel's dialectic view of history and Feuerbach's emphasis on the primacy of the material order. Now he was ready to embark upon a program of forging these ideas into a full-scale instrument of social analysis and, most important of all, to undertake a vigorous and practical program of action.

At the age of twenty-five, Marx left Berlin and went to Paris, where he and some friends undertook the publication of the radical periodical *Deutsch-Französiche Jahrbücher*. In Paris, Marx met many radical revolutionaries and utopian thinkers and confronted the ideas of such men as Fourier, Proudhon, Saint-Simon, and Bakunin. Of lasting significance was his meeting with Friedrich Engels, the son of a German textile manufacturer, with whom Marx was to have a long and intimate association. Apart from his progressively deeper involvement in practical social action through his journalism, Marx was greatly preoccupied in Paris with the question of why the French Revolution had failed. He wanted to know whether it was possible to discover any reliable laws of history in order to avoid mistakes in the future in revolutionary activity. He read extensively on this subject and discovered several promising answers, being particularly impressed by Saint-Simon's account of class conflict, which led Marx to focus upon the classes not only as the parties to conflict but also as the bearers of the material and economic realities in which their lives are set. What Marx began to see was that revolutions do not succeed if they consist only in romantic ideas while overlooking the realities of the material order. But it was only a year after he arrived in Paris that Marx was expelled from the city, and for the next three years, from 1845 to 1848, Marx and his family settled in Brussels. Here he helped to organize a German Worker's Union, which in 1847, at a meeting in London, united with several other similar groups in Europe to form an international Communist League, whose first secretary was Engels. By this group Marx was asked to formulate a statement of principles, a statement that appeared in 1848, shortly before the Paris revolution, as *The Manifesto of the Communist Party*. From Brussels he returned to Paris briefly to participate in some revolutionary activities and was again required to leave, and this time, in the autumn of 1849, he went to London, where he would spend the rest of his life.

Marx (*Culver Pictures*)

England at this time was in no sense ripe for revolutionary activities, since there was no widespread organization of the mass of workers. Marx himself became an isolated figure, prodigiously studying and writing. Each day he went to the reading room of the British Museum, working there from nine in the morning until seven at night with additional hours of work after he returned to his bleak two-room apartment in the cheap Soho district of London. While his poverty was deeply humiliating, he was driven with such single-mindedness to produce his massive books that he could not deviate from this objective to provide his family with more adequate facilities. In addition to his poverty, he was afflicted with a liver ailment and, as Job, was plagued with boils. In this environment his six-year-old son died, and his beautiful wife's health failed. Some financial help came from Engels and from his writing regular articles on European affairs for the *New York Daily Tribune*. Under these incredible circumstances, Marx produced many notable works, including his first systematic work on economics, which he called the *Critique of Political Economy* (1859) and his massive *Capital*, whose first volume he published in 1867 and whose second and third volumes were assembled from his manuscripts after his death and published by Engels in 1885 and 1894. Although Marx supplied the theoretical basis for the Communist movement, he participated less and less in the practical activities he had urged. Still, he had a lively hope that the great revolution would come and that his prediction of the downfall of capitalism would become a fact. But in the last decade of his life, as his name became famous around the world, he became less productive. Two years after his wife died and only two months after his eldest daughter's death, Karl Marx died in London on March 14, 1883, of pleurisy at the age of sixty-five.

Marx had often protested that he was not a "Marxist." Not every idea or every strategy utilized by world communism can rightly be ascribed to him. There is, nevertheless, a central core of thought, which constitutes the essence of Marxist philosophy and which Karl Marx had formulated in the highly charged intellectual atmosphere of the mid–nineteenth-century Europe of which he was a part. This core of Marxist thought consists in the analysis of three basic elements, namely (1) the major epochs of history, (2) the causal power of the material order, and (3) the source and role of ideas. This analysis was meant not only to uncover what each of these three elements means but more importantly to show how they are related to each other.

THE EPOCHS OF HISTORY: MARX'S DIALECTIC

Already in his *Communist Manifesto*, Marx had formulated his basic doctrine, which he considered in many ways original. "What I did that was new," he said, "was to prove (1) that the *existence of classes* is only bound up with particular historic phases in the development of production; (2) that the class struggle necessarily leads to the dictatorship of the proletariat; (3) that the dictatorship itself only constitutes the transition to the *abolition of all classes* and to a classless society." Later, while in London, he worked out in painstaking detail his argument, which he thought provided scientific support for the more general pronouncements in his *Manifesto*. Accordingly, he stated in the preface to his *Capital*, that "it is the ultimate aim of this work, to lay bare the economic law of motion of modern society." This law of motion became his theory of dialectical materialism.

The Five Epochs   Marx indicated that the class struggle is bound up with "particular historic phases." He distinguished five such phases, dividing history into five separate epochs. These he called (1) the primitive communal, (2) slave, (3) feudal, (4) capitalist, and, as a prediction of things to come, (5) the socialist and communist phases. For the most part, this was a more or less conventional division of Western social history into its major periods. But what Marx wanted to do was to discover the "law of motion," which could explain not only *that* history had produced these various epochs but the *reasons why* these particular epochs unfolded as they did. If he could discover history's law of motion, he could not only explain the past but predict the future. He had assumed that the behavior of individuals and societies is subject to the same kind of analysis as are the objects of physical and biological science. He considered the commodity and value products of economics as being "of the same order as those [minute elements] dealt with in microscopic anatomy." When he analyzed the structure of each historic epoch, he either imposed upon it or abstracted from it the fact of class conflict as the decisive force at work. In time, this conflict itself would have to be analyzed in more detail. Now he looked upon history as the product of conflict and relied heavily upon the Hegelian concept of *dialectic* to explain it. He, of course, had rejected Hegel's idealism but had accepted the general theory of the dialectic movement of history, which Hegel had proposed. Hegel had argued that ideas develop in a dialectic way, through the action and reaction of thought, describing this dialectic process as a movement from *thesis* to *antithesis* and then to *synthesis*, where the synthesis becomes a new thesis and the process goes on and on. In addition, Hegel had said that the external social, political, and economic world is simply the embodiment of men's (and God's) ideas. The development or the movement of the external world is the result of the prior development of ideas. Marx, again, considered Hegel's notion of dialectic a most important tool for understanding history, but, through the powerful influence of Feuerbach, Marx supplied a materialistic basis for the dialectic. Accordingly, Marx said that "my dialectic method is not only different from the Hegelian, but is its direct opposite. To Hegel, the process of thinking . . . is the [creator] of the real world . . . with me, on the contrary, the ideal is nothing else than the material world reflected by the human mind, and translated into forms of thought." History, according to Marx, was to be seen therefore as a movement caused by conflicts in the material order, and for this reason history is a *dialectical materialism*.

Change: Quantitative and Qualitative   What history shows is that social and economic orders are in a process of change. The effect of Marx's dialectical materialism was to show, also, that since the material order is primary, since it is the basis of what is truly real, there are no stable fixed points in reality because everything is involved in the dialectic process of change. With this view, Marx had rejected the notion that somewhere there are stable, permanent structures of reality or certain "eternal verities." Materialism meant to Marx that the world as we see it is all there is, that the materialist outlook on the world "is simply the conception of nature as it is, without any reservations." Moreover, with Engels he agreed that all of nature, "from the smallest thing to the biggest, from a grain of sand to the sun . . . to man, is in . . . a ceaseless state of movement and change." History is the process of change from one epoch to another in accordance with the rigorous and inexorable laws of historical motion.

For Marxism, change is not the same as mere growth. A society does not simply mature the way a boy becomes a man. Nor does nature simply move in an eternally uniform and constantly repeated circle. It passes through a real history. Change means the emergence of new structures, novel forms. What causes change is simply the *quantitative* alteration of things, which leads to something *qualitatively* new. For example, as one increases the temperature of water, it not only becomes warmer, but finally reaches the point at which this quantitative change changes water from a liquid into vapor. Reversing the process, by gradually decreasing the temperature of water, one finally changes it from a liquid to a solid, to ice. Similarly, a large pane of glass can be made to vibrate, the range of the vibrations increasing as the quantity of force applied to it is increased. But finally, a further addition of force will no longer add to the quantity of vibration but will, instead, cause a qualitative change, the shattering of the glass. Marx thought that history displays this kind of change by which certain quantitative elements in the economic order finally force a qualitative change in the arrangements of society. This is the process that has moved history from the primitive communal to the slave, and in turn to the feudal and capitalist epochs. Indeed, Marx's prediction that the capitalist order would fall was based upon this notion that the changes in the quantitative factors in capitalism would inevitably destroy capitalism. With the low-key expression of one who was describing how water will turn into steam as the heat is increased, Marx wrote in his *Capital* that "while there is a progressive diminution in the number of capitalist magnates, there is of course a corresponding increase in the mass of poverty, enslavement, degeneration and exploitation, but at the same time a steady intensification of the role of the working class." Then "the centralization of the means of production and the socialization of labor reach a point where they prove incompatible with their capitalist husk. This bursts asunder. The knell of private property sounds. The expropriators are expropriated." This, on the social level, is what Marx describes as the *quantitative leap*, which is "the leap to a new aggregate state . . . where consequently quantity is transformed into quality."

Determinism or Inexorable Law   There is a basic difference between the transformation of water into steam as a laboratory experiment and the movement of society from feudalism to capitalism and finally from capitalism to socialism. The difference is that one can *choose* to raise or not to raise the temperature of the water. But there are no such hypothetical qualifications surrounding history.

Though one can say "*if* the temperature is raised," he cannot say "*if* the social order is thus and so." Marxism holds that there *is* a fundamental "contradiction within the very essence of things" causing the dialectic movement, and though there are ways of delaying or accelerating this inner movement in the nature of things, there is no way to prevent its ultimate unfolding. All things are related to each other *causally*; nothing floats freely. For this reason there are no isolated events either in physical nature or human behavior or, therefore, in history. That there is a definite and inexorable process of movement and change at work producing "history" is as certain as the plain fact that nature exists.

This scientific notion that all things behave in accordance with a principle of regularity and predictability, according to "the laws of science," requires that Marxism make some careful distinctions. The laws of physics, for example, describe "mechanical determinism." History, on the other hand, displays a law of determinism but not in a strictly mechanical way. The movement of one billiard ball by another is the typical example of the mechanical mode of determinism. If one can locate an object in space and measure its distance from another object whose velocity can also be measured, it would then be possible to predict the time of the impact and the subsequent trajectories and rates of motion. This mechanical determinism is hardly applicable to such a complex phenomenon as a social order, which does not have the same kind of location in space and time. But society is nevertheless the result of necessary causation and determinism, and its new forms are capable of prediction just as the submicroscopic particles are determined in quantum mechanics, even though there is only "probable" prediction regarding particular particles. Thus, although the specific history of a particular person could not be predicted with any high degree of accuracy, the future state of a social order can be plotted. On the basis, therefore, of his analysis of the various epochs of history, Marx thought he had discovered the built-in law of change in nature, a kind of inexorable inner logic in events, causing history to move from one epoch to the next with a relentless determinism. From this basis, he predicted that capitalism would inevitably fall and would be transformed by the wave of the future, giving way to the qualitatively different social order of socialism and communism.

The End of History   For Marx, history would have an end with the emergence of socialism and finally communism. Here, again, he followed Hegel's theory in an inverted way. For Hegel, the dialectic process comes to an end when the Idea of freedom is perfectly realized, for by definition this would mean the end of all conflict and struggle. Marx, on the other hand, seeing that the dialectic or struggle of opposites is in the material order and therefore in the struggle between the classes, predicted that when the inner contradictions between the classes were resolved, the principle cause of movement and change would disappear, a classless society would emerge where all the forces and interests would be in perfect balance, and this equilibrium would be perpetual. For this reason there could be no further development in history, inasmuch as there would no longer be any conflict to impel history on to any future epoch.

Marx's theory of the dialectic development of the five epochs of history rested upon the distinction between the order of material reality, on the one hand, and the order of human thought on the other. He was convinced that the only way to achieve a realistic understanding of history, and therefore to avoid errors in the practical program of revolutionary activity, was to assess properly the roles of the material order and the order of human thought. Accordingly, Marx made a sharp distinction between the *substructure* and the *superstructure* of society. The *substructure* is the material order, containing the energizing force that moves history, whereas the *superstructure* consists in men's ideas and simply reflects the configurations of the material order.

THE SUBSTRUCTURE: THE MATERIAL ORDER

To Marx, materialism meant the sum total of the natural environment, and this included for him all of inorganic nature, the organic world, social life, and human consciousness. Unlike Democritus, who defined matter in terms of irreducible tiny particles, atoms, Marx defines matter as "objective reality existing outside the human mind. . . ." Again, unlike Democritus, who considered the atoms as the "bricks of the universe." Marxist materialism did not take this approach of trying to discover a single form of matter in all things. The chief characteristic of Marxist materialism is that it recognizes a wide diversity in the material world without reducing it to any one form of matter. The material order contains everything in the natural world that exists outside our minds; the notion that any spiritual reality, God for example, exists outside our minds and as something other than nature is denied. That human beings possess minds means only that organic matter has developed to the point where the cerebral cortex has become the organ capable of the intricate process of reflex action called human thought. Moreover, the human mind has been conditioned by the labor activity of man as a social being. For this reason, relying upon the Darwinian notion of the evolution of man, Marxism affirms the primacy of the material order and regards mental activity as a secondary by-product of matter. The earliest forms of life were without mental activity until man's ancestors developed the use of their forelimbs, learned to walk erect, and began to use natural objects as tools to procure food and to protect themselves against harm. The big transformation from animal to human being came with the ability to fashion and use tools and to control such forces as fire, which, in turn, made possible a wider variety of food and the further development of the brain. Even now the complex material order is the basic reality, whereas the mental realm is derivative from it. In particular, the material order consists of (1) the *factors* of production and (2) the *relations* of production.

The Factors of Production　The basic fact of human life is that in order to live, men must secure food, clothing, shelter, and in order to have these material things, men must produce them. Wherever we find any society of men, there is always at hand those factors of production, the raw materials, instruments as well as the experienced labor skill, by which things are produced to sustain life. But these factors or forces of production represent chiefly the way men are related to these material things. Of greater importance is the way men are related to each other in the process of production. What Marx wanted to emphasize was that production always takes place as a social act, where men struggle against and utilize nature not as individuals but as groups, as societies. The static analysis of what goes into production was for Marx, therefore, not as important as the dynamic relations of men to each other as a producing society. To be sure, the factors of production were seen by Marx as affecting the relations of production, inasmuch as such circumstances as the scarcity of raw materials or the ownership by some of the instruments of production could have a considerable effect upon the way men would become related to each other in the process of production. In any case, Marx centered his analysis of the material order upon the way men engaged in the act of production, upon the *relations of production*.

The Relations of Production   Marx considered his analysis of the relations of production to be virtually the core of his social analysis. It was here that he thought he had located the energizing force of the dialectic process. The key to the relations of production was the status of property or its ownership; that is, what determined how men were related to each other in the process of production was their relation to property. Under the slave system, for example, the slave owner owned the means of production, even owning the slave, whom he could purchase or sell. The institution of slavery was a necessary product of the dialectic process, since it arose at a time when advanced forms of tools made possible more stable and sustained agricultural activity and a division of labor. But in the slave epoch, as well as in the subsequent historical epochs, the laborer, slave or hired, is "exploited" in that he shares in neither the ownership nor in the fruits of production. The basic struggle between the classes is seen already in the slave system, for the ownership of property divides the society between those who have and those who have not. In the feudal system, the feudal lord owns the means of production: the serf rises above the level of the former slaves, has some share in the ownership of tools, but still works for the feudal lord and, says Marx, feels exploited and struggles against his exploiter. In capitalism, the workers are free as compared with the slaves and the serfs, but they do not own the means of production, and in order to survive, they must sell their labor to the capitalist.

The shift from slave to feudal to capitalist relations of production is not the result of rational design but a product of the inner movement and logic of the material order. Specifically, the impelling force to survive leads to the creation of tools, and, in turn, the kinds of tools created affect the way men become related to each other. Thus, whereas certain tools permit independent existence, such as the bow and arrow, the plough, on the other hand, logically implies a division of labor. Similarly, whereas a spinning wheel can be used in the home or small shops, heavier machinery requires large factories and the new concentration of workers in a given locality. Such is the survey Marx makes of the unfolding of the epochs of history, emphasizing that this process moves in a deterministic way, impelled by basic economic drives whose direction is set by the technological requirements of the moment. The thoughts and behavior of all men are determined by their relations to each other and to the means of production. Although in all periods there is a conflict and struggle between the different classes, the class struggle is particularly violent under capitalism.

There are at least three characteristics of the class struggle under capitalism. First, the classes have now been reduced basically to two, the owners, or bourgeoisie, and the workers, or the proletariat. Secondly, the relations of those classes to each other rest upon a fundamental contradiction, namely, that although both classes participate in the act of production, the mode of distribution of the fruits of production does not correspond to the contribution made by each class. The reason for this discrepancy is that the price of labor in the capitalist system is determined by the forces of supply and demand, and the large supply of workers tends to send wages down to a subsistence level. But the products created by labor can be sold for more than it costs to hire the labor force. Marx's analysis assumed the labor theory of value, that the value of the product is created by the amount of labor put into it. From this point of view, since the product of labor could be sold for more than the cost of labor, the capitalist would then reap the difference, which Marx called *surplus value*. The existence of surplus value constituted the contradiction in the capitalistic system for Marx. For this reason, Marx argued that in the capitalistic system exploitation was not merely an isolated occurrence here or there, now or then, but always and everywhere, because of the manner in which the iron law of wages operates. Still, Marx made no moral judgment of this condition, saying that as a matter of fact the worker received what he was worth if the determination of the wage through the supply and demand of labor is the norm. "It is true," he said, "that the daily maintenance of labor power costs only half a day's labor, and that nevertheless the labor power can work for an entire working day, with the result that the value which its use creates during a working day is twice the value of a day's labor power. So much the better for the purchaser, but it is nowise an injustice to the seller [worker]."

In a sense, Marx did not "blame" the capitalist for this arrangement any more than he would attribute to him the organization of the laborers into a self-conscious and powerful group. These are rather the consequences of the material forces of history, which have determined the existence of these arrangements. Labor became a coherent group only because large-scale machinery required large factories, and suddenly the multitude of workers who were required to run the machines found themselves living close together. That history had produced the capitalist system was one thing, but that it rested upon a contradiction was something else. For this reason, Marx "excused" the capitalist but argued that for "scientific reasons" he must say that the class conflict caused by this contradiction of surplus value would force the dialectic movement to the next stage in history, namely, socialism and finally communism.

The third characteristic of this class struggle was the prediction that the condition of the workers in capitalism would become progressively more wretched, that the poor would become poorer and more numerous while the rich would become richer and fewer until the masses would take over all the means of production. As a matter of historic fact, Marx could not have been more wrong than he was at this point, since it is precisely the workers whose condition has improved most dramatically in the highly developed capitalistic economies. Still, Marx argued that as long as the means of production remained in the hands of a few, the class struggle would continue inexorably until the contradiction was resolved, ending the dialectic movement. Meanwhile, the workers' lives would be terribly dehumanized by what Marx calls "the alienation of labor".

THE ALIENATION OF LABOR

While still in his twenties, Marx produced a brief series of manuscripts called the *Economic and Philosophical Manuscripts of 1844,* first published in 1932. The key concept of these manuscripts is that of *alienation,* a theme which moves throughout the whole system of Marx's thought. Although Marx was by no means the first to develop a theory of alienation, his views on this theme were unique, because they were based upon his particular economic and philosophical assumptions which formed the basis of his criticism of capitalism.

If man is alienated, that is, estranged or separated, he must be alienated from something. As early as biblical times, man was seen as alienated from God through "the fall." In a legal sense, alienation means selling or giving something away, or as Kant says, "the transference of one's property to someone else is its alienation." In the course of time almost everything became a saleable object. Kant spoke of the process by which a person could be used as a thing, while Balzac said ironically that "even the Holy Spirit has its quotation on the Stock Exchange." Rousseau insisted upon some severe limits to alienation. He held that although upon entering the Social Contract there is "the total alienation of each associate . . . to the whole community," Rousseau held that man cannot alienate his freedom. In addition, Rousseau decried the dehumanizing effect upon man of certain social values, of "civilization," saying that social corruption has introduced "from outside" various vices "alien to man's constitution" and destructive of the "original goodness of man." For Marx there is something about man that is essential to his nature and from which he can be alienated. What is novel about Marx's concept of alienation is the manner in which he identifies the causes of the alienation of labor within capitalism.

Marx calls attention to four aspects of alienation, saying that man is alienated (1) from *nature,* (2) from *himself,* (3) from his *species-being,* and (4) from *other men.* He begins with the fundamental relation of a worker to the product of his labor. Originally, man's relation to the product of his labor is identical with the relation of man to the *sensuous external world,* to the objects of nature. Man's relation to nature is intimate because man lives from inorganic nature, for as Marx says, "nature is his *body* with which he must remain in continuous interchange in order not to die." To say that man's relation, both physical and mental, is intimately related to nature, to the objects of nature, means that nature is interdependent with itself, because man is a part of nature. This intimate relation between man and nature, between man's activity and the objects of nature, is the "right" relationship between man and the objects of nature. The worker is not capable of creating without nature, that is, without the sensual external world. That world is the material into which he invests his labor, through which he produces things, and without which he cannot live. But in capitalism this relationship is broken, man is alienated from nature, from the products of his activity or work.

The contemporary economic fact is, says Marx, that the object produced by labor now stands as an "alien being" to the worker. Man's labor is embodied in an object and is turned into a physical thing; this product is an "objectification of labor." The objectification of labor represents a loss to the worker as well as "servitude to the object." In short it is the alienation of the worker from what he produces. Moreover, in the productive process, man's labor becomes as much an object as the physical material being worked upon, since labor is now bought and sold. The more objects the worker produces the fewer he can personally possess and therefore the greater is his loss. This follows from the fact that the worker is related to the product of his labor as to an alien object. What is embodied, "objectified," in the product, part of himself, his labor, is no longer his own. "The worker," says Marx, "puts his life into the object, and his life then belongs no longer to himself but to the object." And the object is appropriated, owned, by someone else. In this way, the original relation between man and nature is destroyed through the alienation from man of the products of his labor.

Man is alienated not only from the products of his labor but also from himself through the *process* of production. The nature of labor's productive activity results in man's self-alienation. This comes about because work is *external* to, that is, not part of the nature of, the worker. His work is not voluntary but is imposed upon him; he has a feeling of misery instead of well being; rather than fulfilling himself, he must deny himself; he does not freely develop his physical and mental capacities but is instead physically exhausted and mentally debased. As a consequence, the worker feels like a human being only during his leisure hours. Most important of all the worker is alienated from his work because it is not his own work but rather work for someone else. In this sense, the worker does not belong to himself but to someone else. The result is that "man [the worker] feels himself to be freely active only in his animal functions—eating, drinking and procreating—or at most also in his dwelling and personal adornment—while in his human functions he is reduced to an animal." Although eating, drinking and procreating are genuine human functions, they become animal functions when separated, alienated, from other human functions.

At still another level, man is alienated from his *species-being*, from his truly human nature. The character of any species resides in the type of life activity it expresses. The species-character of human beings is "free, conscious activity." By contrast, an animal cannot distinguish itself from its activity. The animal *is* its activity. But, says Marx, "man makes his life activity itself an object of his will and consciousness." It is true that animals can produce nests and dwellings as in the case of bees, ants and beavers. But their production of these things is limited to what is strictly required for themselves or their young. Man, on the other hand, produces universally, that is, in a manner that is applicable and understandable to all human beings. Also, whereas animals produce only under the compulsion of specific physical need, man produces his most distinctive products only when he is free from physical need. Animals reproduce only themselves whereas man can produce a whole world, a world of art, of science and literature. Animals are limited in their activity to the standards of the species to which they belong. Man, on the other hand, knows how to produce in accordance with the standards of every species. For these reasons, the whole object of man's labor is to objectify, that is, impose upon the world of nature, his species life, his free, spontaneous and creative activity. In this way man reproduces himself in the things he creates not only intellectually, in the realm of ideas, but also actively, seeing his own reflection in the world which he has created. This unique character of human species-life is lost when man's labor is alienated. Just as the object of labor is no longer his, so also man is shorn of his free and spontaneous activity and creativity. His consciousness is now deflected from creativity and is transferred into simply a means to his individual existence. Thus alienated labor turns the species life of man into an alien being and alienates his mental life and his human life.

Inevitably the alienation of man from the product of his labor, from his productive or life activity and from his species life—all this leads to man's alienation from other men. The breakdown in man's relation to his fellow human beings is similar to the alienation of man from the objects of his labor. In an environment of alienated labor all men look upon other men from the point of view of workers who see other workers as objects whose labor is bought and sold, and not as full members of the human species. To say, then, that man's species nature is alienated or estranged from him means that "each man is estranged from the other, as each of them is from man's essential nature."

Marx asks, "if the product of labor is alien to me . . . to whom does it belong?" In an earlier age, when temples were built in Egypt and India, it was thought that the product belonged to the gods. But, says Marx, the alienated product of labor can belong only to man himself. If it does not belong to the worker, it must belong to a man other than the worker. Thus, as a result of alienated labor the worker produces a new relationship between another man and labor, this other man being the capitalist. The final product of alienated labor is private property. Private property is both a product of alienated labor and also the means by which labor is alienated. In the wage system entailed by private property labor finds itself not as an end but as the servant of wages. Nor would a forced increase in wages restore to either the workers or to their work their human significance or value. As a statement of eventual redemption, Marx concludes that the emancipation of society from private property involves the emancipation of the workers which in turn will lead to the emancipation of humanity as a whole.

The general matter-of-fact tone of Marx's analysis of capitalism is in sharp contrast to the shrill voice of world communism. Marx was himself capable on occasion of the severest denunciation of the conditions of the capitalism to which he was exposed. He was convinced, moreover, that the dialectic process inevitably involved tragic conflicts, wars, and revolutions. He saw in history the deep tension between forces that were in the last analysis incompatible, each exerting its power to overcome the other. The use of revolutionary force could hardly be avoided, but force could not bring into being simply any desired utopian system. Only the relations of production toward which the inner logic of the material order was driving in a determined way could be the objective of revolution. Even when a society is aware of the so-called "natural laws of its movement," this society, says Marx, "can neither clear by bold leaps, nor remove by legal enactments, the obstacles offered by the successive phases of its normal development." What, then, is the function of the revolutionary activities of the working classes? It is, says Marx, to "shorten and lessen the birth-pangs."

With this rigorous view of the nature of the class struggle, Marx had clearly assigned to the substructure, to the material order, the supreme significance in the dialectic process of history. What, then, is the status and role of human thought? Do ideas have power and consequences? For Marx, ideas represented a mere reflection of the basic material reality, and for this reason, he described the enterprise of human thought as the *superstructure*.

THE SUPERSTRUCTURE: THE ORIGIN AND ROLE OF IDEAS

Each epoch, said Marx, has its dominant ideas. Men formulate ideas in the areas of religion, morality, and law. Hegel had argued that men agreed for the most part in their religious, moral, and juristic thought because there was at work in them a universal Spirit, the Idea. Marx, on the contrary, said that the ideas of each epoch grow out of and reflect the actual material conditions of the historic period. For this reason, thinking comes *after* the material order has affected men's minds. Thus, Marx accounted for the relationship between man's conscious life and his material environment by saying that "it is not the consciousness of men that determines their being, but, on the contrary, their social being that determines their consciousness."

The source of ideas is rooted in the material order. Such ideas as justice and goodness and even religious salvation, says Marx, are only various modes of rationalizing the existing order. Justice, for the most part, represents the will of the economically dominant class and its desire to "freeze" the relations of production as they are. Marx had been impressed during his early years as a law student with the teachings of the jurist Savigny, who had defined law as the "spirit" of each epoch. Savigny argued that law is like language and is therefore different for each society. As Savigny, but now for different reasons, Marx rejected the notion of a universal and eternal norm of justice. Indeed, he thought it followed with logical rigor that if ideas simply reflect the inner order of the relations of production, each successive epoch will have its own set of ideas, its own dominant philosophy.

The conflict of ideas within a society at a given time is due to the dynamic nature of the economic order. The dialectic process, which is a struggle of opposites, has its material aspect but also its ideological side. Since members of a society are related to the dialectic process by belonging to different classes, their interests are different, and therefore their ideas are opposed. Moreover, the greatest error, according to Marx, is to fail to realize that ideas that accurately reflected the material order at an earlier time no longer do so because, in the meantime, the substructure of reality has moved on. Those who hold on to old ideas do not realize that there is no longer any reality corresponding to them, and their desire to reverse the order of things to fit these ideas makes them "reactionaries." On the other hand, an astute observer can discover the direction in which history is moving and will adjust his thinking and behavior to it. The fact is, says Marx, that the dialectic process involves the disappearance of some things and the birth of new things; that is why one epoch dies and another is born, and there is no way to stop the process. Those who assume the objective reality of "eternal principles" of justice, goodness, and righteousness do not realize that such notions cannot refer to reality since the material order, which is the only reality, is constantly changing. "The sum total of the productive relations," says Marx, "constitutes the economic structure of society—the real foundation on which rise legal and political superstructures . . . [and which] determines the general character of the social, political and spiritual processes of life."

Because he believed that ideas were chiefly a reflection of the material order, Marx attributed a limited role or function to them. Ideas are particularly useless when they bear no relationship to the economic reality. Marx's impatience with reformers, do-gooders, and utopians was intense. He argued that ideas cannot determine the direction of history, that they can only hinder or accelerate the inexorable dialectic. For this reason, Marx thought that his own ideas about capitalism did not constitute a moral condemnation. He did not say that capitalism was either wicked or due to human folly; it was caused by the "law of motion of society." In the end, Marx assumed that he was proceeding in his analysis as a scientist, limiting his thought to objective reality, abstracting from it the laws of motion.

Almost every aspect of Marx's thought raises serious critical questions. He was, for one thing, apparently unaware that at the time he was writing his *Capital* the nature of English capitalism was undergoing modifications. His scientific style was not adequately supported with empirical observations. Marx clearly expressed a metaphysical belief in the existence of a predetermined goal for all history. His theory of knowledge solved some problems but created new ones, particularly the problem of accounting for the diversity of ideas and of erroneous ideas. If ideas reflected reality, reality and thought would have to correspond.

But how does one account for the emergence of utopian thought? Moreover, to say that force is a necessary element of revolution showed that Marx had not understood how a society could move through self-criticism and change, and even revolution, without physical violence. What did come as a genuine contribution from Marx was his insight that the economic order is capable of creating an ideology whereby some are led to believe that the *status quo* rests upon eternal and immutable principles. His insistence upon self-reflection to discover the subtle disguise of self-interest was an important aspect of social analysis. Still, it is a matter of fascination that Marxism as a philosophy should have spread chiefly among underdeveloped peoples rather than in the advanced capitalist states where, presumably, it was supposed to have its greatest relevance.

23

Analytic
Philosophy

The dominant movement of philosophical activity in the contemporary English-speaking world is known as *analytic philosophy*. To call it a *movement* rather than a *school* underscores the fact that although analytic philosophy has certain clear distinguishing characteristics, the sources out of which it emerged, the changes it has undergone, and the variety of ways in which it is pursued are many. What unifies all analytic philosophers is their agreement concerning the central task of philosophy. The task of philosophy, they say, is to clarify the meaning of language. In his early work, the *Tractatus Logico-Philosophicus*, Wittgenstein had said that "the object of philosophy is the logical clarification of thoughts" so that "the result of philosophy is not a number of philosophical propositions, but to make propositions clear." The full force of this new way of doing philosophy is found in the negative and positive aspects of its task.

On the negative side, to say that the philosopher does not formulate "philosophical propositions" meant for the early analysts that there must be a self-imposed limit upon the scope of philosophic activity. Specifically, this meant that, in contrast to the immediately past tradition of nineteenth-century idealism, especially Hegelianism, whose practitioners engaged in constructing complete systems of thought regarding the whole universe, the analysts would now undertake the more modest task of working upon individual problems. Not only would these problems be single and manageable, they would all fit into a single class; they would all be problems revolving around the meanings and usages of language. For this reason, it would no longer be the task of the philosopher to investigate the nature of reality, to build complete systems that seek to explain the universe, or to fashion moral, political, and religious philosophies of behavior. Philosophy, in this new key, "is not a doctrine but an activity" and as such it can produce "no ethical propositions," said Wittgenstein. The philosopher is no longer to consider himself capable of discovering unique forms of information about the world and man. The discovery of facts is the task of the scientist. There are no facts left over for the philosophers after all the sciences have done their work.

On the positive side, the new assumption was that the philosopher can render a genuine service by carefully unpacking complex problems whose origin is found in the imprecise use of language. Scientists themselves, it was felt, had discussed their findings in language that was often misleading and in certain ways ambiguous. That is, scientific language contained ambiguities of logic, not of physical discovery, and the clarification of these logical ambiguities was required. It was assumed, also, that rigorous linguistic analysis could *prevent* the use or abuse of language in ways that would cause us, as A. J. Ayer said, "to draw false inferences, or ask spurious questions, or make nonsensical assumptions." What concerned Ayer was that we often use propositions about nations as though nations were persons, we talk about material things as though we believed in a physical world "beneath" or "behind" visible phenomena, and we use the word *is* in relation to things whose existence we could not possibly want to infer. Philosophy is called upon to remove these dangers from our use of language, said Ayer. In a somewhat similar vein, Gilbert Ryle wrote about "Systematically Misleading Expressions," saying that, although he would rather allot to philosophy "a sublimer task than the detection of the sources in linguistic idioms of recurrent misconstructions and absurd theories," still, philosophical analysis consists in inquiring about "what it really means to say so and so." In this way, the new philosophy became closely related to the enterprises of science, not as a rival discipline offering propositions of what reality is like but as the proofreader of the scientists' expressions, checking the literature of science for its clarity and logical meaningfulness. It would no longer be the function of the philosopher either to propound vast systems of thought after the manner of Plato, Aristotle, and Hegel or to tell people how they ought to behave. He would instead analyze statements or propositions to discover the causes of ambiguities and the foundations of meaning in language.

What caused this dramatic shift in the enterprise of philosophy? At Cambridge, Bertrand Russell and G. E. Moore had reacted in the early decades of the twentieth century against the system building of the Hegelian philosophers such as F. H. Bradley, Bernard Bosanquet, and J. E. McTaggart, who had been engaged in ambitious metaphysical speculation. They reacted to the extravagance of the metaphysical language these Hegelians used and wondered just what could be meant by these interpretations of the whole universe. Although Moore did not necessarily want to give up metaphysics, he was especially disturbed by the contrast between metaphysical language and so-called "common sense." To him certain statements, as for example McTaggart's famous notion that "Time is unreal," seemed "perfectly monstrous." Moore was inspired to analyze language particularly to clarify ordinary language and to make language fit the test of common sense in its meaning. Bertrand Russell, on the other hand, was a brilliant mathematician, trained in precise thought, and in comparison with the language of mathematics, metaphysical language seemed to him loose and obscure. He did not want to reject metaphysics, any more than Moore did, but he did want to tighten up the language of metaphysics. While Moore set out to analyze common-sense language, Russell tried to analyze "facts" for the purpose of inventing a new language, *logical atomism,* which would have the exactness and rigor of mathematics because this new language would be made to correspond exactly to the "facts." Although neither Moore nor Russell gave up the attempt to understand reality, the way they went about their task emphasized the fact that philosophy is concerned not with discovery but with clarification and, therefore, in a sense, not with truth but with meaning.

Across the channel, a group of mathematicians, scientists, and philosophers formed a group in Vienna in the 1920s describing themselves as *logical positivists* and known as the "Vienna Circle." Their orientation was rigorously empirical, and they proceeded to reject the whole enterprise of metaphysics. Their ideal for philosophy was the unification of the sciences, hoping thereby to produce a unified system of meaningful and valid knowledge. Among this group were such men as Moritz Schlick, Rudolph Carnap, Friedrich Waismann, Herbert Feigl, Otto Neurath, and Kurt Gödel. A young former student of Bertrand Russell's, Ludwig Wittgenstein, lived nearby, and though he was not a member of the Circle, he had conversations with them, since his early book, *Tractatus Logico-Philosophicus* (1919), was considered by the Vienna Circle to express its philosophical point of view with great accuracy. Not only had Wittgenstein said that "whatever can be said at all can be said clearly," he concluded his book by saying that "whereof one cannot speak, thereof one must be silent." This dictum was less harsh than Hume's rigorous conclusion in his *Enquiry,* where, following the implicit logic of his principles of empiricism, he wrote: "When we run over libraries, persuaded of these principles, what havoc we must make? If we take in our hand any volume; of divinity or school metaphysics, for instance; let us ask, Does it contain any abstract reasoning concerning quantity or number? No. Does it contain any experimental reasoning concerning matter of fact and existence? No. Commit it then to the flames: for it can contain nothing but sophistry and illusion." The Vienna Circle thought of themselves as the twentieth-century heirs of Hume's empirical tradition. To this tradition they now sought to apply the rigorous apparatus of mathematics and science. If their ideal was to clarify the language of science and the sciences, their first task would have to be the formulation of a standard for clarity, and this resulted in their famous *verification principle*. This principle would in time be shown to suffer from certain defects and require attempts at modification. These internal difficulties with their central principle as well as with other aspects of their philosophic concerns, and the scattering of the members to British and American universities in the 1930s, dissolved the Vienna Circle, and gradually led to the decline of *logical positivism*.

What followed next in the history of analytic philosophy was the decisive work of the "new" Wittgenstein. Between his *Tractatus Logico-Philosophicus* (1919) and the posthumous publication of his famed *Philosophical Investigations* (1953), his thought had acquired a radically new character, and it is this version of his way of doing philosophy that has dominated the contemporary philosophic scene in the English-speaking world. The major facets of analytic philosophy are to be found, then, in Bertrand Russell's *logical atomism*, the Vienna Circle's *logical positivism*, and the later Wittgenstein's *philosophical analysis*. We shall also consider the work of Gilbert Ryle and John Austin.

LOGICAL ATOMISM

Bertrand Russell's point of departure in philosophy was his admiration for the precision of mathematics. Accordingly, he announced that "the kind of philosophy that I wish to advocate, which I call logical atomism, is one which has forced itself upon me in the course of thinking about the philosophy of mathematics." He wanted to set forth "a certain kind of logical doctrine and on the basis of this a certain kind of metaphysics." Russell thought that since it was possible to construct a logic by which the whole of mathematics could be derived from a small number of logical axioms, as he had already done with A. N. Whitehead in their *Principia Mathematica*, then why could not this logic form the basis of a language that could accurately express everything that could be clearly stated? His assumption was, recalling that in the quotation above he connected "logical atomism" and "a certain kind of metaphysics," that the world would correspond to his specially constructed logical language. The vocabulary of the new logic would, for the most part, correspond to particular objects in the world. To accomplish this task of creating a new language, Russell set out first of all to analyze certain "facts," which he differentiated from "things."

"The things in the world," said Russell, "have various properties, and stand in various relations to each other. That they have these properties and relations are *facts*. . . ." Facts constitute for Russell the complexity of the relations of things to each other, and therefore "it is with the analysis of *facts* that one's consideration of the problem of complexity must begin." Russell's basic assumption was that "facts, since they have components, must be in some sense complex, and hence must be susceptible of analysis." The complexity of facts is matched by the complexity of language. For this reason, the aim of analysis is to make sure that every statement represents an adequate picture of the reality, of the facts, of the world.

Language, according to Russell, consists of a unique arrangement of words, and the meaningfulness of language is determined by the accuracy with which these words represent facts. Words, in turn, are formulated into propositions. "In a logically perfect language," said Russell, "the words in a proposition would correspond one by one with the components of the corresponding facts." By analysis, certain *simple* words are discovered. These are words that cannot be further analyzed into something more primary and can therefore be understood only by knowing what they symbolize. The word *red*, for example, is not capable of further analysis and is therefore understood as a simple *predicate*. Other words, similarly simple, refer to particular things, and as symbols of these things they are *proper names*. Language consists in part, then, of words, which in their simplest form refer to a particular thing and its predicate, as for example a *red*

Bertrand Russell (*The Bettmann Archive*)

rose. A. proposition states a fact. When a fact is of the simplest kind, it is called an *atomic fact.* Propositions that state atomic facts are called *atomic propositions.* If our language consisted only of such atomic propositions, it would amount only to a series of reports regarding atomic facts. This is what Wittgenstein said in his *Tractatus,* when he wrote that "the world is everything that is the case. . . . What is the case, the fact, is the existence of atomic facts."

It is clear that in our language atomic propositions are put together into more complex propositions. When two or more atomic propositions are linked together with such words as *and* and *or,* the result is what Russell calls a *molecular* proposition. However, there are no "molecular" *facts,* only atomic facts. For this reason, molecular propositions cannot correspond to molecular facts. How can one test the truth or falsity, then, of molecular propositions? Their truth depends upon the truth or falsity of the atomic propositions of which they are made up. Language, on this account, consists of an indefinite number of atomic propositions, whose correspondence with actual facts is settled by empirical methods and techniques. Nothing can be said about the world that is not analyzable down to an atomic proposition, which, in turn, corresponds to an atomic fact. The grammatical independence of each atomic proposition indicates the metaphysical independence of each atomic fact. Again, in an ideal language words and propositions would correspond to facts. Moreover, it was assumed that after a careful analysis of words and propositions and their corresponding atomic facts, one would arrive at the basic character of language and of the world, and that apart from these facts there would be no residue. Thus, the ideal language would express all there is to say about the world. All of reality, on this theory, could be described in statements such as "That is green."

Underlying this thought of an ideal language for describing reality was Russell's recent work in logic and mathematics. He had devised various symbolic notations for the foundations of mathematics. Now he would try to use similar notations for metaphysical language. A proposition or statement is either true or false. Using symbolic notations, a true proposition can be called p, and a false proposition is *not-p.* A molecular proposition consists of two or more atomic propositions (p, q, and so on) linked together with logical connectives, such as *and* and *or.* A proposition such as p *and* q [for which symbols any facts can be supplied, such as (p) he is tall and (q) he is dark) is true, says Russell, only if the atomic propositions p and q are each true. The entire molecular proposition is what Russell calls a *truth function.* There is no single atomic fact corresponding to the entire proposition. Its truth or falsity can be determined only from the truth or falsity of each of its component atomic propositions. To say that "he is tall and dark" is therefore a truth function of "he is tall" and "he is dark." The propositions p and q (and an indefinite additional number n) are capable of a wide variety and intricacy of relationships. But these relationships can all be stated symbolically, and since the logical forms of language correspond to reality, it is possible to discover through the logically correct relations of propositions a true essence of things or the world.

Difficulties developed in the program of logical atomism first of all when

Russell and others tried to account for *general* facts. It is one thing to say "that is a white horse," whose truth or falsity is checked by connecting the *words* "white" and "horse" with the atomic *facts* of this white color and this animal, the horse. It is another thing to say "all horses are white." How would one test the truth or falsity of such a statement? According to logical atomism, one should analyze this statement into its atomic propositions and test *their* truth or falsity. There is no atomic fact corresponding to "all horses . . . ," for this means more than just this horse and that horse, namely all horses, and this is a *general* fact. But the whole argument of logical atomism was that only atomic facts exist, and the theory had no way of dealing adequately with so-called "general" facts unless general facts were accepted as a form of atomic facts. Still, if one were disposed to consider only the particular things recorded by our senses as the basis of our language, as Hume did, singular atomic facts would be the only facts available for human discourse, and language would therefore consist solely of atomic and molecular propositions.

As the revived interest in Hume's empiricism was more and more felt by the logical atomists, it was difficult for their theory to retain its metaphysical character. In addition, Wittgenstein pointed out in his *Tractatus* that, from the point of view of logical atomism, propositions could be stated *significantly* only if they could correspond to an atomic fact or be truth functions of propositions that did. Therefore, only atomic or molecular propositions could be stated significantly. But most of the propositions of logical atomism were peculiar in that they said things *about* facts rather than stating facts. If only propositions that state facts are significant or sensible, the conclusion had to be that language *about* facts, as when one tries to account for the relation between words and facts, is senseless and insignificant. This would, of course, make most of philosophy insignificant, and Wittgenstein was deeply aware of this upshot of logical atomism. For this reason, he concluded that "my propositions are elucidatory in this way: he who understands me finally recognizes them as senseless, when he has used them to climb out beyond them. (He must so to speak throw away the ladder, after he has climbed up on it)." Wittgenstein became more and more convinced that philosophy must reject the metaphysical elements in logical atomism. The right method of philosophy would be "to say nothing except what can be said, i.e., the propositions of science. . . ." This is for the most part just what logical positivism took as its basic theme.

LOGICAL POSITIVISM

The men who formed the Vienna Circle were by temperament attracted to the methods of science and mathematics. They were disposed to reject metaphysics, as had the earlier positivists who considered metaphysics, as Comte did, as outdated by science. Now they had the additional argument, because of Russell's work in logic and Wittgenstein's powerful formulation of the relation of logic and language in the *Tractatus,* that metaphysics is impossible as shown by the logical and essential character of language. To differentiate themselves from the earlier Comtean positivists and to emphasize that they would combine the rigorous techniques of the new logic with the empirical temper of Hume, they called themselves *logical positivists,* or sometimes *logical empiricists.* For the English-speaking world, A. J. Ayer, in his brilliantly lucid and powerfully argued book *Language, Truth and Logic* (1936) did, as he later said with considerable under-statement, "something to popularize what may be called the classic position of the Vienna Circle."

This position called for a blanket rejection of metaphysics, and the grounds for this rejection were to be found in the Vienna Circle's famous *verification principle.*

Rudolph Carnap   Among the foremost members of the Vienna Circle was the eminent positivist Rudolph Carnap. Born in Germany in 1891, he taught in Vienna and Prague from 1926 to 1935. After arriving in the United States in 1936, he taught for many years at the University of Chicago, and since 1954 until his death in 1970 he was associated with the University of California at Los Angeles. "The only proper task of Philosophy," Carnap wrote in his *Philosophy and Logical Syntax,* "is Logical Analysis." It is the function of logical analysis, he said, to analyze all knowledge, all assertions of science and of everyday life, in order to make clear the sense of each such assertion and the connections between them. The purpose of logical analysis is to discover how we can become certain of the truth or falsehood of any proposition. One of the principal tasks of the logical analysis of a given proposition is, therefore, to discover the method of verification of that proposition.

For Carnap, the method of verification of a proposition is either direct or indirect. If a proposition asserts something about a perception I am having, for example, that I see a house, this proposition is effectively tested or verified by my present perception. On the other hand, there are propositions which cannot be verified so directly. To say, for example, that "this key is made of iron" requires an indirect method of verification. For one way to verify the assertion that the key is made of iron is to place it near a magnet which enables one to perceive that the key is attracted. It now becomes possible to arrange a series of proposi-tions in a tight logical sequence leading to verification as follows: a verified physical law holds that "if an iron thing is placed near a magnet it is attracted;" another verified proposition asserts that "this metal bar is a magnet"; it is verified through direct observation that "the key is placed near the bar." When the key is finally attracted by the magnet, the verification is complete. Carnap concludes that a proposition which is not directly verifiable can only be verified by the direct verification of those propositions, as indicated in the preceding example, which can be clearly and logically deduced from the original proposition together with other propositions already empirically verified. If a proposition is phrased as a prediction, as in the proposition "The key will be attracted by the magnet," its verification requires observation of the completed attraction. If the key is at-tracted by the magnet, there is a considerable degree of certainty about the truth of the description of the key. Statements of predictions, however, are only *hypotheses* since there is always the possibility of finding in the future a negative instance. For this reason, even though the degree of certainty is sufficient for most practical purposes, the original proposition cannot ever be completely verified in order to produce *absolute* certainty.

These two forms of verification, direct and indirect, are central to scientific method, for in the field of science every proposition, says Carnap, either asserts something about present perceptions or about future perceptions. In both cases verification is either through direct perception or by the logical connection of already verified propositions. Thus, if a scientist were to make an assertion from which no proposition verified by perception could be deduced, it would be no assertion at all. To say, for example, that there is not only a gravitational field but also a *levitational field* could not be verified. While propositions concerning gravity can be verified by observable effects upon bodies, there are no observable effects or laws describing levitation. Assertions about levitation are, says Carnap, no assertions at all because they do not speak about anything. They are nothing but a series of empty words—expressions with no sense.

When logical analysis is applied to metaphysics, Carnap concludes that metaphysical propositions are not verifiable, or, if an attempt at verification is made the results are always negative. If one takes, for example, the proposition propounded by Thales that "the principle of the World is Water," one cannot deduce any propositions asserting any perceptions whatever which may be expected in the future. Such a proposition therefore asserts nothing at all. It is inevitable, says Carnap, that metaphysicians cannot avoid making their propositions nonverifiable because if they made them verifiable they would belong to the realm of empirical science since their truth or falsehood would depend upon experience. Carnap therefore rejects metaphysics by saying in Chapter I of his *Philosophy and Logical Syntax:* "Metaphysical propositions are neither true nor false, because they assert nothing, they contain neither knowledge nor error, they lie completely outside the field of knowledge, of theory, outside the discussion of truth or falsehood. But they are, like laughing, lyrics, and music, expressive. They express not so much temporary feelings as permanent emotional or volitional dispositions. . . .The danger lies in the *deceptive* character of metaphysics; it gives the illusion of knowledge without actually giving any knowledge. This is the reason why we reject it."

Normative ethics and value judgments in general belong, according to Carnap, to the realm of metaphysics. When he applies his method of logical analysis to the propositions of normative ethics, these propositions predictably turn out to be meaningless for him. There can of course be a science of ethics in the form of psychological or sociological or other empirical investigations about the actions of human beings and their effects upon other people. But the philosophy of moral values or moral norms does not rest upon any facts since its purpose is to state norms for human action or for making judgments about moral values. The value statement "Killing is evil" has the grammatical form of an assertive proposition. But, says Carnap, "a value statement is nothing else than a command in a misleading grammatical form. It may have effects upon the actions of men, and these effects may be in accordance with our wishes or not; but it is neither true nor false. It does not assert anything and can neither be proved nor disproved."

Carnap was convinced that the propositions of psychology belong to the region of empirical science in just the same way as do the propositions of biology and chemistry. He was aware that many would consider it an offensive presumption to place psychology, "hitherto robed in majesty as the theory of spiritual events," into the domain of the physical sciences. Yet that is what he proceeded to do, saying in his essay on *Psychology and Physical Language* that *"every sentence of psychology may be formulated in physical language."* What he meant by this was that "all sentences of psychology describe physical occurences, namely, the physical behavior of humans and other animals." This is an extension of the general thesis of physicalism which Carnap described as holding that "physical language is a universal language, that is, a language into which every sentence may be translated." In effect, Carnap would make psychology an aspect of physics since all science would become physics and the various domains of science would become parts of unified science. In this manner, propositions in psychology were to be tested by the criterion of verifiability by translating them into physical language. Thus, the statement "John is in pain" is translated into a statement describing the observable state S of John's body. This process of translation requires only that there be a scientific law stating that someone is in pain if and only if his bodily condition is in a particular state S. It is then meaningful to say that "John is in pain" and "John's body is in state S" since, while not equivalent, these are interchangeable translations. Only those statements which could be verified or translated into verifiable statements were thought to have meaning. Neither metaphysics, some aspects of psychology, theories of "reality," nor the philosophy of normative values could satisfy the criterion of verifiability and were therefore rejected as meaningless.

In time there were objections to Carnap's early formulation of the criterion of verifiability, as we shall indicate shortly. Reacting to criticisms from Reichenbach, Popper, Lewis, and Nagel, Carnap shifted his ground from verification to *confirmation.* Carnap agreed that if verification is taken to mean a complete and definitive establishment of the truth then the laws of science could never be verified. The number of instances to which the laws, say of biology or physics, apply is infinite and if strict verification required personal observation of every instance then obviously there could not be verification as so defined. Though the universal scientific law cannot be verified in its universal application, single instances in the form of particular sentences derived from the law and from other sentences previously established can be verified. In this way, *verification* in the strict sense gives way to the gradually increasing *confirmation* of scientific laws.

As a further aid to logical clarity, Carnap made a distinction in his book *The Logical Syntax of Language* between what he called the *material* and the *formal* modes of language. It was his contention that the *material* mode, commonly used in philosophy, frequently leads to the ambiguities and errors of metaphysicians and in general is the source of meaningless philosophical controversy.

To overcome these dangers, he felt it necessary to translate sentences from the material idiom into the more accurate *formal* idiom. He gives the following example: the sentence "The moon is a thing" is cast in the material mode. It can be translated into the formal mode in this sentence: "The word 'moon' is a thing-designation." Every sentence which states "such and such is a *thing*" belongs in the material mode. Carnap holds that many other words, such as "quality," "relation," "number," and "event" also function the same way as the word "thing." Another example of this distinction is the manner in which the sentence "7 is not a thing but a number," expressed in the material mode, is translated into the formal mode by saying "The sign 7 is not a thing sign but a numerical sign." The way to avoid the "dangerous material mode," says Carnap, is to avoid the word "thing" and use instead the syntactical term "thing-designation." Similarly, instead of using the word "number" one should use the term "numerical-designation," instead of "quality," "quality-designation," instead of "event," "event-designation" and so forth. Other examples would include the translation of Wittgenstein's sentence "There is also the inexpressible" in the material mode to "There are also words which are not words" in the formal mode. Or, "He lectured about Babylon" is translated into "The word Babylon occured in his lecture." It was Carnap's hope that by this method of translation of sentences into the formal mode "we free logical analysis from all reference to extra-linguistic objects themselves" being then concerned only with the form of linguistic expressions, with *syntax.* It would appear from his distinction between the material and formal modes of language that Carnap implied that one could never speak about anything besides words. This is, of course, true to the extent that Carnap's conclusion applies to *Logical analysis.* But, says Carnap, " . . . there is no question of eliminating reference to objects themselves from object-sciences. On the contrary, these sciences are really concerned with objects themselves, with things, not merely with thing-designations." In short, statements are not merely syntactical, they are also semantic.

The Principle of Verification If the charge against metaphysics was that its language, its propositions or sentences, was *meaningless* or, as Wittgenstein said in the *Tractatus, senseless,* such a charge required the use of some criterion by which to test which sentences did and which did not express a genuine proposition about a matter of fact. Accordingly, the logical positivists formulated the verification principle as the basic criterion for the meaningfulness or the literal significance of a proposition. If a proposition fulfilled the requirements of this criterion, it was considered meaningful, and if a proposition failed to do so, it was considered meaningless.

The *verification principle* consisted in the notion that *the meaning of a statement is the method of its verification.* The assumption behind this principle was that verification must always rest upon empirical observation, that is, in sense experience. Any proposition, therefore, that could not be verified by the method of observation would be said to have no meaning. The case of mathematical propositions was treated in a special way, but it was clear that with such a rigorous criterion, metaphysical language could not pass the test of meaningful-ness.

The positivists, following the tradition of Hume and Kant, distinguished two types of statements, namely, *analytic* and *synthetic*. Each of these types has a different ground for its meaningfulness. Analytic statements derive their mean-ingfulness from the definitions of their words or symbols. To say that "all men are mortals" has literal significance because the word *men* is defined in such a way as to include the idea *mortals*. In general, in analytic statements the subject already contains or implies the predicate. For the most part, analytic statements do not increase our knowledge, and for this reason they are *tautologies*. Moreover, their meaning does not depend upon experience, only upon the consistent use of their clearly defined terms. If words with clearly defined terms are used inconsistently, the result is a *contradiction*. A statement, then, that is necessarily true, true because of the meanings of its terms, is a tautology, whereas a statement that is necessarily false is a contradiction. An analytic proposition that is also a tautology is always and in every case necessarily true, because its only test is the meanings of the terms. Similarly, a contradiction is always and necessarily a false proposi-tion since its falseness is determined by the inconsistent use of terms. Thus, the truth or falsity of an analytic proposition turns on the logical analysis of mean-ings. On the other hand, *synthetic* propositions are either true or false in each case, and their truth or falsity can be discovered only by reference to some nonlogical or nonlinguistic datum, a fact. Unlike analytic statements, which are *necessarily* either tautologies or contradictions, synthetic statements may be ei-ther true or false. Synthetic statements require some sense experience of the object that such a statement refers to in order to advance from its possible to its actual truth.

From this distinction between analytic and synthetic propositions, the posi-tivists formulated their conception of *cognitive meaning* or *literal significance*. Analytic propositions, they said, have a *formal* meaning, since their meaning derives not from facts but from the logical implications of words and ideas, as in mathematics, logic, and the formal sciences. On the other hand, synthetic propo-sitions have a factual meaning, because their meaning is based upon the empiri-cal observation of the objects referred to in these statements. Synthetic state-ments are the language of the factual sciences, physics, biology, psychology, and so on. It was at this point that the principle of verification had its decisive application. For now the positivists concluded that there could be only two kinds of statements that could have any meaning at all, namely, *analytic* statements, which are universally and necessarily true because the consistent use of words would never allow them to be anything else, and *synthetic* statements, which are judged as true or false by using the verification principle. Statements that are neither analytic nor synthetic have no cognitive meaning or literal significance; they are simply *emotive*. It takes only brief reflection to realize that into this category of *emotive* or *noncognitive* language would fall not only metaphysics but also ethics, aesthetics, and religion.

W. V. O. Quine   The distinction between analytic and synthetic truths was challenged by W. V. O. Quine who was himself sympathetic to the original ideal of the Vienna Circle. In his essay "Two Dogmas of Empiricism" (Chapter II of his *From A Logical Point of View*), Quine argued that "a boundary between analytic and synthetic statements simply has not been drawn. That there is such a distinction to be drawn at all is an unempirical dogma of empiricists, a metaphysical article of faith." The other dogma is that of *reductionism* which holds that every meaningful statement can be translated into a statement about immediate experience. Quine was aware that to reject these dogmas would mean abandoning, or at least "blurring the supposed boundary between speculative metaphysics and natural science." Not only is the notion of "analyticity" difficult to clarify, apart from some limited logical statements. Even synthetic statements do not live up to their empirical verifiability as clearly as they are supposed to. After a rigorous and sustained analysis of the many ways others have sought to establish the truth of both analytic and synthetic statements, Quine draws the conclusion that "no statement is immune to revision." This would mean that both analytic and synthetic propositions contain only contingent truth and to that extent they do not differ. Even logical statements, presumably true "no matter what," can be revised, as once proposed for example as a means of simplifying quantum mechanics. Quine asks: "What difference is there in principle between such a shift [in logic] and the shift whereby Kepler superseded Ptolemy, or Einstein, Newton, or Darwin, Aristotle?" As an empiricist, Quine believes that conceptual schemes, including science and logic, are tools. Indeed, the total range of our knowledge, he says, "is a man-made fabric which impinges upon experience only along the edges." Any conflict between a statement we hold to be true and a new experience at variance with it requires an adjustment not only of that one statement but ultimately of all the interconnected concepts. Just where certainty seems greatest, in the physical realm, a serious reminder must be made to the effect that physical bodies are themselves only a convenient conceptual tool. Indeed, Quine says that physical objects are simply "irreducible posits," comparing them to the gods of Homer. As an empiricist he believes that it would be an error not to believe in physical objects instead of in Homer's gods. "But," he says, "in point of epistemological footing the physical objects and the gods differ only in degree and not in kind." To argue in this manner clearly undercuts the distinction between analytic and synthetic and between metaphysics and science. In the end, this leads Quine to settle for a strongly pragmatic conception of truth, saying, "Each man is given a scientific heritage plus a continuing barrage of sensory stimulation; and the considerations which guide him in warping his scientific heritage to fit his continuing sensory promptings are, where rational, pragmatic." Besides Quine's technical argument against the analytic-synthetic distinction, a variety of reactions to the clearly iconoclastic movement of positivism emerged. Some were appalled at the incredible denial of meaning to moral language. Others took comfort in the fact that the verification principle had simply formulated the requirements whereby an utterance could be rightly called a *statement*. That is, the only consequence that followed from the inability of an utterance to be verified by sense experience was that it could not be called a genuine statement. But this, it was felt, was of little consequence, since it meant at most that the designation *statement* would merely be reserved for a special class of utterances. Still, there could be little comfort in this, since the positivists made two things very clear along the way, namely, first, that their choice of utterances to be designated as statements was not at all arbitrary, but must be those utterances that could be empirically verified, and second, that only statements have cognitive meaning. At the same time, this rigorous interpretation of the verification principle encountered serious difficulties, not from its external critics but from some inherent defects, which the positivists themselves recognized.

Among the difficulties encountered was, first of all, the serious question of what constituted verification. To answer "sense experience" raised the further question "whose experience?" The assumption behind the verification principle was that whatever could be said meaningfully would be stated in atomic or elementary statements. Scientific language would be reducible ultimately to *observational statements*. But what is the "fact" that an observation statement reports? Is it a subjective experience about a physical object, or is it a pure picture of that object? The technical problem was whether it is ever possible to translate a person's internal experience into a statement about a physical object, or vice versa. This is the problem of solipsism, the view that the self is the only object of real knowledge and that therefore the experiences of one person cannot be the same as those of another. Each person's experience is different, and all of their experiences are different from the objectively real world. If this is the case, what does the verification principle amount to in the end? Verification statements would mean one thing to one person and something else to others.

In the second place, it was in the very area where this principle was presumed to have its greatest relevance, in the sciences, that its greatest difficulty arose. Scientific knowledge is frequently expressed in the form of universal laws. These "laws" are the basis for scientific *prediction*. But the problem the positivists faced was whether to consider scientific statements meaningful. How can a statement that makes a prediction be verified? Can my present experience, or experiment, tell me anything about the future? Obviously, literal significance or meaning is one thing when we verify the statement "There is a black cow in Smith's barn" and quite another thing when we say, as the scientist does, for example, that when a moving body is not acted upon by external forces, its direction will remain constant. The first case is specific and verifiable. The second involves an indefinite number of cases, and any single case in the future can falsify that statement. Since there is no single fact that can verify *now* the future truth of a general scientific statement, such a statement, by a rigorous application of the verification principle, would be meaningless. Schlick had said of certain utterances, "If not conclusively verifiable in principle, then not propositions." This would have to apply to scientific as well as other forms of language. For this reason, a compromise in the rigorous application of the principle was proposed, thus giving rise to the distinction between the *strong* and *weak* forms of the verification principle. The weak form said simply that a statement must be at least "verifiable in principle," or *capable* of verification, that is, confirmed in some degree by the observation of something physical.

In the third place, it turned out that the verification principle was not itself verifiable. Critics asked why it should be that the criterion of meaning should be sense experience. The Vienna Circle did not answer this question in any formal way. It may be that for them the verification principle was clearly suggested by the difference between scientific procedures, on the one hand, and metaphysical speculation on the other. Being oriented chiefly to science, the positivists assumed that only language that referred to physical objects and their interrelationships could have cognitive meaning. Moreover, the techniques of logic as they understood them implied the correspondence between words and facts and between the logical structure of language and the logical relation of facts. The positivists assumed, furthermore, that through *physicalism,* their doctrine that called for the coupling of all statements to physical facts, they could achieve the *unity of science,* and that such a unified knowledge would give sciences a common language and tell us all there is to say. But the internal defects of the verification principle, namely, the difficulty of formulating the criterion of sense experience without falling into solipsism, and the impossibility of verifying general scientific statements, gradually led not only to a weak form of verification but also to the recognition that statements reflect many forms of experience. For this reason, the initial iconoclastic intensity of positivism was toned down. The blanket rejection of metaphysics and morals was reversed. Instead, analysts began to ask what kind of problem the metaphysicians and moralists were driving at. Ayer described this new temper by saying that "the metaphysician is treated no longer as a criminal but as a patient: there may be good reasons why he says the strange things he does." Ethics, on this view, is no longer nonsense but a discipline whose language is analyzed both for its relation to fact and for its value in pointing to a problem. As it turns out, ethical language is, as R. M. Hare has argued, not *descriptive* but is rather *imperative.* C. L. Stevenson has also elaborated the emotive theory of ethics, showing that ethical statements express approval and disapproval and are used particularly for purposes of persuasion. What positivism came ultimately to say about ethics was that it is not possible to derive normative statements, what *ought* to be done, from a description of facts, from what *is.* But even though the analyst still holds that it is not his function as a philosopher to *prescribe* or *exhort* any particular form of behavior, he does accept the task of creatively analyzing moral language for the purpose of clarifying it. That he reserves the right to make value judgments as a *person* underscores the growing recognition that there are modes of human experience besides simply the observation of physical objects and their interrelationships that have meaning and literal significance. Although logical positivism in its classical form dissolved from the weight of its inner difficulties, its impact continues in the analytic movement, which is still concerned overwhelmingly with the usages and analysis of language.

THE "NEW" WITTGENSTEIN

With the appearance of Ludwig Wittgenstein's *Philosophical Investigations* (1953) analytic philosophy adjusted itself to a new point of view. It was still concerned with language, as were logical atomism and logical positivism. But now the analyst would see the nature of language in a different light. Wittgenstein, who had provided the most impressive systematic statement of logical atomism in his *Tractatus Logico-Philosophicus* (1919), had shortly thereafter repudiated a considerable portion of that book on the grounds that his theory of language upon which that book was based was now seen as inadequate. It was inadequate because it assumed that language has really only one function, namely, to state facts. It was further assumed that sentences for the most part derive their meanings from stating facts. More seriously, Wittgenstein had assumed, as did also Rudolph Carnap, that the skeleton of all language is a logical one. What struck Wittgenstein now was the somewhat obvious point that language has *many* functions besides simply "picturing" objects. Language always functions in a *context* and therefore has as many purposes as there are contexts. Words, he said, are like "tools in a tool-box; there is a hammer, pliers, a saw, a screwdriver, a rule, a glue-pot, glue, nails and screws.—The function of words is as diverse as the functions of these objects." What made him think earlier that language had only one function? He had been "held captive" by a "picture" of language as being the giving of names, as if by Adam, to all things. We are all the victims, he said, of "the bewitchment of our intelligence by means of language." Our incorrect picture of language is "produced by grammatical illusions." To analyze grammar might lead one to discover some logical structure in language. But would that justify the conclusion that all language has essentially the same rules, functions, and meanings? It occurred to Wittgenstein that the assumption that all language states facts and contains a logical skeleton was derived not by observation but by "thought." It was simply assumed that all language, in spite of certain superficial differences, is alike, the way all games are alike. Wittgenstein uncovered the flaw in this analogy by taking the case of games and asking, "What is common to them all?—Don't say: There *must* be something common, or they would not be called 'games'—but *look and see* whether there is anything common at all.—For if you look at them you will not see something that is common to *all*, but similarities, relationships, and a whole series of them at that. To repeat: don't think, but look." He was apparently saying that logical atomism was the product of thought, of theory, and not of careful observation of the way in fact language operates and is used. Wittgenstein therefore shifted the program of analysis from a preoccupation with logic and the construction of a "perfect" language to the study of the ordinary usages of language. He moved away from what Russell and Carnap were doing and turned now in the direction of G. E. Moore's earlier emphasis upon the analysis of ordinary language, testing it by the criterion of "common sense." Wittgenstein was now of the opinion that language does not contain one single pattern alone, that it is as variable as life itself. Indeed, he said that "to imagine a language means to imagine a form of life." For this reason, analysis should consist not in the *definition* of language or its meanings but rather in a careful *description* of its uses: "We must do away with all explanation, and *description alone* must take its place." We must, said Wittgenstein, "stick to the subjects of everyday thinking, and not go astray and imagine that we have to describe extreme subtleties." Confusions arise not when our language is "doing work," but only when it is "like an engine idling."

By recognizing the diversity of the functions of language, Wittgenstein inevitably altered the task of philosophy. For one thing, unlike the positivists, he would not reject the statements of metaphysics outright. Since the new mood was to consider the metaphysician a patient instead of a criminal the function of philosophy could now be considered as "therapeutic." Metaphysical language can indeed create confusion, and the central concern of philosophy is to deal with problems that baffle and confuse us because of the lack of clarity. Philosophy is a "battle against the bewitchment of our intelligence by means of language." Bewitchment causes confusion, and so "A philosophical problem has the form: 'I don't know my way about.'" Philosophy helps one to find his way, to survey the scene. "What we do," said Wittgenstein, "is to bring words back from their metaphysical to their everyday usage." His aim in philosophy, he said, was "to show the fly the way out of the fly-bottle." When the fly is out of the bottle, and when words are brought back from metaphysics to their everyday usage, and when the person who didn't know his way about now does know the way, what has happened? Wittgenstein says that philosophy "leaves everything as it is." Philosophy does not provide men with new or more information, but adds clarity by a careful description of language. It is as though one could see all the parts of a jigsaw puzzle but was baffled by how to put it together; he is actually looking at everything he needs to solve the problem. Philosophical puzzlement is similar and can be removed by a careful description of language as we ordinarily use it. What makes us feel trapped as a fly in a bottle is the use of language in ways other than their ordinary use. Hence, "the results of philosophy are the uncovering of one or another piece of plain nonsense." By *nonsense* Wittgenstein did not necessarily mean the language of metaphysics, for, again, he had a basic sympathy for what some metaphysicians were trying to do. If metaphysics displayed resistance or a prejudice that obscures the ordinary usage of words, he agreed that this is "not a *stupid* prejudice." He saw in the confusions of metaphysics a deep human condition, saying that "the problems arising through a misinterpretation of our forms of language have the character of *depth*. They are deep disquietudes; their roots are as deep in us as the forms of our language and their significance is as great as the importance of our language."

How, more specifically, does one who doesn't know his way about find it, or how does the fly escape from the fly-bottle? One must not expect from Wittgenstein any single systematic answer to this question. He is too sensitive to the suppleness and variability of life and language to force upon them the straitjacket of a single method. "There is not *a* philosophical method," he says, "though there are indeed methods, like different therapies." Because philosophical problems grow out of language, it is necessary to acquire a basic familiarity with the usages of the language out of which each problem arises. As there are many kinds of games, there are many sets of rules of the games. Similarly as there are many languages (that is, the many forms of ordinary language of work, play, worship, science, and so forth), there are many *usages*. Under these circumstances, "the work of the philosopher consists in *assembling reminders* for a particular purpose." In his *Philosophical Investigations,* Wittgenstein "does philosophy" by taking many problems and assembling many reminders of the way language is used as a means of clarifying these problems. But the philosopher, in addition to assembling these uses of language, selects and arranges them in order to get a picture of the landscape. In other words, philosophy does not consist in giving crisp abstract answers to questions. A person who has lost his way about wants, rather, a map of the terrain, and this is supplied by the selection and arrangement of concrete examples of the actual use of language in ordinary experience.

But it is not enough to just look at these examples of usage, any more than it is sufficient simply to look at the pieces of the jigsaw puzzle. There must be selection and rearrangement. Then, everything is before one that he needs for solving his problem. Still, says Wittgenstein, we frequently "fail to be struck by what, once seen, is *most* striking and most powerful." The most important things are hidden "because of their simplicity and familiarity." But what does it mean to "fail to be struck"? There is no sure method according to Wittgenstein to guarantee that one will "be struck" and thereby find his way. Apparently the fly can frequently pass the opening of the jar without escaping. In any case, what Wittgenstein sought to do was to shift philosophy's concern from meanings, from the assumption that words carried in them as so much freight "pictures" of objects in the world. Instead, he directed attention, through the assembling, selecting, and arranging of relevant examples, to the actual usages of words. Because most *philosophical* problems were assumed to arise from puzzlements about words, the scrupulous description of their ordinary uses would, it was assumed, eliminate this puzzlement. It was in this manner also that Gilbert Ryle (1900–1976), whose teaching at Oxford began in 1924, defined the task of the new style of philosophy.

GILBERT RYLE

An impressive example of philosophical analysis is Gilbert Ryle's book *Concept of Mind,* published in 1949, four years before Wittgenstein's *Philosophical Investigations.* While these two books have substantially the same objectives, Ryle's book is distinctive in that it focuses in a sustained manner upon a single family of philosophical problems, namely, the many facets of the mind-body problem, to which he applies his method of philosophical analysis. As early as 1932, Ryle had already established his commitment to this new style in philosophy in his vigorous essay "Systematically Misleading Expressions" in which he wrote that to enquire "what it means to say so and so . . . is what philosophical analysis is, and . . . this is the sole and whole function of philosophy." Philosophy, says Ryle in the introduction to *The Concept of Mind,* does not give new information about minds, or for that matter about any other subject. "The philosophical arguments which constitute this book," he writes, "are not intended to increase what we know about minds, but to rectify the logical geography of the knowledge which we already possess."

The Ghost in the Machine   Ryle contends that the "official doctrine" about the nature and the place of minds is unsound and contradicts virtually everything we know about minds. In its simplest form, the official doctrine holds that every human being has both a mind and a body, that these two are coordinated, but that upon the death of the body the mind may continue both to exist and exert its powers. Not only is this basic theory of mind-body incorrect, says Ryle, but it also leads to many other serious errors as one elaborates the implications of this doctrine.

It must follow from the official doctrine that each person has two collateral histories, one consisting of the events of his body and the other consisting of what transpires in and to his mind. Whereas human bodies are in space and are governed by mechanical physical laws, minds do not exist in space and are not subject to mechanical laws. A person's bodily life is publicly observable while the activities of the mind are not accessible to external observers and are therefore private. At this point a rather serious difficulty is encountered since the contrast between the public character of the body and the private status of the mind requires one to say that the workings of the body are external whereas the workings of the mind are internal. It is then a short step to say that the mind is *in* the body. Although this language describing the place of the mind may be "metaphorical," since the mind which occupies no space could hardly be in any particular place, it is Ryle's contention that for the most part the contrast between the outer and inner realms is taken literally. Theorists in various disciplines take this contrast between "inner" and "outer" for granted. Stimuli are assumed to come from "outside" and from far distances generating responses inside the skull. Activity of the mind is said to produce external events such as a motion of the hand or eye; smiles suggest activities of the mind. All this suggests, too, some mode of transaction between the mind and body, but there is no method for either observing or reporting just how these transactions between mind and body take place. No laboratory experiment can discover this relationship and physiologists and psychologists alternate in designating physical bases and mental behavior as possible explanations of how these polar oppositions are brought together. Self-analysis and introspection are special modes of perception requiring no physical eye and are so private as to be a special privilege of the mind itself to which no one else has direct access. Even though one were to assume that minds similar to one's own are located in other human bodies, there is no way to discover what they do or undergo, and so, says Ryle, "Absolute solitude is on this showing the ineluctable destiny of the soul. Only our bodies can meet." Accordingly, our language which presumes to describe someone's mental activities such as knowing, hoping, dreading, or intending must be construed as signifying special events in the secret histories of people. No one has direct access to these mental operations, neither biographer, teacher, critic, or friend. But because we know how to use mental-conduct words and to use them with general correctness, earlier philosophers constructed their theories of the nature and place of minds in conformity with the official doctrine. They sought to identify the logical geography of their mental-conduct concepts and thus arose what Ryle has called the basically incorrect "dogma of the Ghost in the Machine."

The Category-Mistake What Ryle finds wrong with the official doctrine of the Ghost in the Machine is not that some details here and there are ambiguous but that the very principle on which the theory rests is false. It is not even a series of particular mistakes. It is, says Ryle, one big mistake of a unique kind and this he calls a "category-mistake." The big mistake consists in representing the facts of mental life as if they belonged to one and the same logical category whereas in fact they belong to quite different and separate ones. The official doctrine is therefore a "myth" and it is necessary to "rectify the logic of mental-conduct concepts."

To indicate what is meant by a category-mistake, Ryle describes the imaginary visit of a foreigner to Oxford for the first time. The visitor is shown the playing fields, museums, scientific laboratories, and some of the colleges. Having seen these various places, the vistor asks, "But where is the University?" The question assumes that the University is yet another institution, a counterpart to the colleges and laboratories, another entity that can be seen in the same way as the others. Actually, the University is simply the way all he has already seen is coordinated. Thus, the visitor's mistake consists in his assumption that one can correctly speak of the Bodleian Library, the Ashmolean Museum, All Souls College *and* the University as if the University was the same kind of member in the class to which the others belong. In short, the visitor mistakenly placed the University into the wrong category, a category in which it does not belong. In a similar illustration Ryle speaks of the mistake made by a child watching a military parade in which a division is marching by. Having been told that he was seeing battalions, batteries, and squadrons, the child wanted to know when the division was going to appear. Again, he assumed that the division is another unit similar to the others, not realizing that in seeing the battalions, batteries, and squadrons he had already seen the division. His mistake was in thinking it correct to speak of battalions, batteries, squadrons, *and* a division. He placed the division in the wrong category. The category-mistake indicates an inability to use certain elements in the English language correctly. What is more significant, says Ryle, is that people who are perfectly capable of applying concepts are nevertheless liable in their abstract thinking to allocate these concepts to logical categories to which they do not belong.

What Ryle has sought to do through these illustrations is to show, as he says, that "a family of radical category-mistakes is the source of the double-life theory." The notion that a person is a ghost mysteriously ensconced in a machine is a consequence of thinking that because a person's feeling, thinking, and purposive activity cannot be described solely in terms of physics, they must be described in a set of counterpart idioms. Moreover, because mental conduct differs so from bodily activities, the official theory sought to invest mind with its own status, though made of a different stuff and having a different structure, and possessing its own complex organization. Body and mind were thought to be separate fields of causes and effects, the body's being mechanical and the mind's nonmechanical.

How did this category-mistake originate? Although Ryle designates Descartes as the major culprit of this error, it is obvious that the mind-body dualism has a history extending very much farther back than the seventeenth century. Still, Descartes's special formulation of this official doctrine for modern philosophy, says Ryle, followed Gallileo's assertion that his methods of scientific discovery were capable of providing a mechanical theory which would be applicable to every occupant in space. From a strictly scientific point of view, Descartes was impressed with the mechanical description of nature, but as a religious and moral person he was reluctant to agree with the claim that human nature in its mental aspects differs only in degree of complexity from a machine. Consequently, Descartes and subsequent philosophers wrongly construed mental-conduct words to signify nonmechanical processes and concluded that nonmechanical laws must explain the nonspatial workings of minds. But what this explanation retained was the assumption that mind, though different from body, was nevertheless a member of the categories of "thing," "stuff," "state," "process," "cause," and "effect." Thus, just as the visitor expected the University to be another extra unit, so Descartes and his heirs treated minds as additional though special centers of the causal process. From these conclusions a host of theoretical difficulties arose. How are the mind and body related? How do they cause effects in each other? If the mind is governed by strict laws analogous to the laws governing the body, does this not imply a determinism in which case such notions as responsibility, choice, merit, and freedom make no sense? Worst of all, only negative terms could be used to speak of the mind as compared with the body since minds are not in space, have no motions, are not aspects of matter, and are not observable. For these and other reasons Ryle concludes that the entire argument of the ghost in the machine is "broken-backed."

In a sustained and careful analysis of several assertions "about the mind," Ryle seeks to clarify these assertions by arguing in each case that mental-conduct words do indeed refer to mental acts but not to minds. The acts of knowing, exercising intelligence, understanding, willing, feeling, imagining, and the like, all these according to the official theory, were considered as being unconnected with the body and as occurring, when referred to in the present tense, in the mind. Refuting this, Ryle holds that virtually in every assertion about the mind some facts about bodily behavior are relevant. For example, in speaking of human emotions one does not infer the working of some interior and obscure forces. In favorable circumstances, says Ryle, "I find out your inclinations and your moods more directly than this. I hear and understand your conversational avowals, your interjections and your tones of voice; I see and understand your gestures and facial expressions." Or, if we consider that the act of theorizing is the distinctive act of human intelligence and that this supports the dogma of the Ghost in the Machine, Ryle gives various rejoinders, including that "to find that most people have minds . . . is simply to find that they are able and prone to do certain sorts of things, and this we do by witnessing the sorts of things they do." Or, "overt intelligent performances are not clues to the workings of minds; they are those workings." Ryle says, further, that "In opposition to this entire dogma, I am arguing that in describing the workings of a person's mind we are not describing a second set of shadowy operations. We are describing his one career; namely we are describing the ways in which parts of his conduct are managed." And again, in speaking about the act of *understanding,* Ryle says, "It is being maintained throughout this book that when we characterize people by mental predicates, we are not making untestable inferences to any ghostly processes occurring in streams of consciousness which we are debarred from visiting; we are describing the ways in which those people conduct parts of their predominantly public behavior." Assertions ostensibly about the mind are therefore made true or false not by inner private events but by what has or will happen publicly. To say of someone that he is intelligent appears to be an assertion about his mind, but Ryle argues that it is rather our knowledge of his public performance.

What Ryle has sought to achieve through his analysis is a new theory of mind. It may appear that he is arguing that only bodies exist, that mental-conduct words are really statements about bodily behavior and that there is no independent private inner life. It was his intention in his *Concept of Mind* to "dissipate the contrast between Mind and Matter," not by reducing the one to the other but by demonstrating that the polar opposition between Mind and Matter can be solved by rejecting the assumption that they are terms of the same logical type. In any case, The *Concept of Mind* represents one of the outstanding attempts to deal with a classic problem through the analysis of linguistic idioms wherein misconstructions and absurd theories might be detected and clarified.

JOHN AUSTIN

Another philosopher concerned with the analysis of language was the Englishman John Austin. During his brilliant but brief career, Austin fashioned a new way of doing philosophy. Born in 1911 and educated at Oxford, he later became a powerful figure as a scholar at Oxford through the sheer force of his intellect. At his untimely death at the age of forty-nine in 1960, he had achieved immense respect as an original thinker even though he had not yet produced what others might consider a monumental work. That he did not publish extensively was only partly a consequence of his brief life. He once said that he had to decide early on whether he was going to write books or teach people to do philosophy in a way that he had found so useful and satisfying in his own work and life. That his style of doing philosophy has not become as widespread as other more familiar ones might be due to the greater difficulty of transferring to others his unique capacities, his interests, rigorous classical training, and patient temperament. Nevertheless, his mode of linguistic analysis has been highly influential and, though it is not easy to imitate, it is not difficult to understand and appreciate. One detects an unusually pleasant mood and a sense of fascination as Austin goes about his special way of doing philosophy. Early in his significant essay on "A Plea for Excuses" he tells the reader that doing it provided for him what philosophy is so often barren of, namely, "the fun of discovery, the pleasure of cooperation and the satisfaction of reaching agreement." With relief and humor he tells how his research enabled him to consider various words and idioms "without remembering what Kant thought" and to move on by degrees to discuss "deliberation without for once remembering Aristotle or self-control without Plato." In contrast to heavy and grim philosophizing, Austin exhibited a deceptive simplicity as expressed, for example, in the opening sentence of his William James Lectures at Harvard, *How to Do Things with Words*, where he wrote, "What I shall have to say here is neither difficult nor contentious: the only merit I should like to claim for it is that of being true, at least in parts."

Austin centered his work on the analysis of ordinary language. He was aware that the use of such phrases as "the analysis of language," or "analytic philosophy" or even "ordinary language" could lead to the misunderstanding that such analysis was *only* and *solely* concerned with words. It is not only words, says Austin, "but also . . . the realities we use the words to talk about" that concerned him: "we are using a sharpened awareness of words to sharpen our perception of, though not the final arbiter of, the phenomena." He even wondered in passing whether his way of doing philosophy might not more usefully be called "linguistic phenomenology," a notion he gave up as being "rather a mouthful." Actually, Austin had little interest in criticising the methods of other philosophers or putting excessive emphasis upon his own style. He had discovered a technique for studying the nature of language and found it successful in dealing with various philosophical problems. Turning to his essay on "A Plea for Excuses" we find in it some flavor of his fruitful analysis of ordinary language.

Before Austin analyzes the many uses of the word "excuses," he elaborates in some detail just how and why he philosophizes about words. For one thing, Austin felt that philosophy can be "done" in a wide variety of ways. Unlike one of the sciences, whose subject matter and methods are highly organized, philosophy functions in those spheres where no one is sure just what is the best way to resolve a particular problem. Austin therefore developed the technique of selecting some area of discourse of interest to philosophers. For him the word "excuses" provided a rich field for the study of language as well as human behavior. Through the analysis of this word Austin discovers distinctions of various degrees, sometimes minute, between words closely connected with "excuses." Moreover, his analysis uncovers interesting insights to human behavior as suggested by the distinctions between a web of interrelated words.

At the outset, the word "excuses" turns out to be a term surrounded by other significant words such as "defence," "justification," or "plea." It is necessary, says Austin, to give a complete and clear account and to consider the largest number possible of cases of the use of the chosen word. An excuse involves in general a situation where one is *accused* of having done something wrong, or "bad," or "inept," and he either tries to defend his conduct or establish his innocence. He can admit that he *did* the action of which he is accused but then argue that under the prevailing circumstances it was either the right or acceptable or at least understandable thing to do. This would be to "justify" the action. A quite different way to proceed would be for the accused to admit that the act was a bad one but that it would be unfair to say without qualification that he *did* it. It could be that his action was unintentional, an accident or precipitated by some other event. The word "responsibility" becomes significantly related to "he did it" and to "excuses." And the distinction between an "excuse" for an action and a "justification" of it turns out to be an important one. Moreover, if the charge happens to be "murder," a plea for the accused could rest on the justification of self-defence or excused as accidental. Words with finer degrees of distinction could be employed here, including "mitigation" and "extenuation." And what about the language of a defendant who says, "I didn't do it—something in me made me do it." An act can also be the result of a "fit of anger" as distinguished from a "deliberate act."

Why go through this analysis of the word "excuses" or any other term of discourse? Apart from the fact that the fashioning of excuses has occupied such an important role in human affairs and is on that account worthy of careful study, Austin believed that moral philosophy could benefit by this analysis for two reasons. For one thing, such an analysis could facilitate in developing a more accurate and up-to-date version of human conduct. Secondly, as a corollary, it could contribute toward the correction of older and prematurely settled theories. And inasmuch as moral philosophy is the study of the rightness and wrongness of conduct or the doing of actions, it becomes crucial to understand what it means to "do something" before one can properly say about it that it is either right or wrong.

"Doing an action," says Austin, is a very abstract expression. Do we mean by it "to think something," "to say something," or "to try to do something"? It is just as inaccurate, says Austin, to think that all our actions are of the same nature as to think that all "things" are of the same kind, that winning a war, as an action, is the same as sneezing, that a horse as a thing is equal to a bed as a thing. Do we *do* an action when we breathe or see? For what, then, is the phrase "doing an action" an appropriate substitute? What rules are there for the proper word signifying "the" action for which a person is responsible or for which he manufactures excuses? Can human actions be divided in order to attribute one part to the actor and the remainder to someone or something else? Moreover, is an action a simple event? Austin here emphasizes rather the complex nature of a human act, even the mere motion of the body which could involve intentions, motives, response to information, the reflection upon rules, a studied control of the motion of a limb, or a shove from someone else.

Austin believed that the questions just raised and the problems posed can be illumined by the analysis of the word excuses. For one thing, an excuse implies that a certain mode of behavior went wrong in some way. To determine the nature of the wrongness involves a clarification of the right. The abnormal frequently clarifies the normal. The careful study of excuses provides the opportunity to determine when excuses are appropriate, what actions can be classified as excusable, what particular abnormalities of behavior are truly "actions" and in a more intricate manner determine what constitutes the very structure or mechanism of human behavior. The study of excuses can also resolve some traditional mistakes or inconclusive arguments in moral philosophy. High on the list is the problem of Freedom. Here Austin compares the words "freedom" and "truth," pointing out that just as "truth" is not a name characterizing assertions, neither is "freedom" a name characterizing actions. Freedom, says Austin, is "the name of the dimension in which action is assessed." He then says, "in examining all the ways in which each action may not be 'free', i.e. the cases in which it will not do to say simply 'X did A,' we may hope to dispose of the problem of freedom." This is, of course, just the beginning of Austin's meticulous analysis of the word excuses but it suffices to suggest his style.

Besides throwing light on moral philosophy, the study of excuses provides Austin with a concrete application for his philosophical method. He begins with "ordinary language" through which he expects to discover "what we should say when" and therefore "why and what we should mean by it." Underlying his faith in the fruitfulness of the analysis of ordinary language is his conviction that such an analysis can clear up the uses and misuses of words and in that manner avoid the traps in which one can be caught by imprecise language. The analysis of ordinary language also emphasizes the differences between words and things and enables one to remove the words from the realities we use words to talk about and in that way get a fresh look at those realities. Most of all, Austin believed that "our common stock of words embodies all the distinctions men have found worth drawing, and the connections they have found worth making, in the lifetimes of many generations." This stock of words in ordinary language must, he felt, be more sound and more subtle than any we could think up for the purpose of philosophizing inasmuch as they have stood up to the test of time and the competition of other possible words. Moreover, ordinary language provides the philosopher "a good site for fieldwork." It makes possible a different climate of philosophical discourse by disengaging individuals from frozen and rigid philosophical positions. How much easier it is to agree on the uses of words or even on how to reach agreement. Austin hoped that this method could someday be applied in the turbulent field of aesthetics, saying, "if only we could forget for awhile about the beautiful and get down to the dainty and the dumpy."

Austin was aware that ordinary language, as a basis for analysis, could present certain problems. For one thing, there is a certain "looseness" in ordinary language so that one person's usage may not be the same as another's. To this Austin replies that there is not as much disagreement in the use of words as one might think. Surface differences tend to disappear when, through analysis, it is discovered that it was not really the *same* situation about which different persons have been speaking: "the more we imagine the situation in detail," says Austin, "the less we find we disagree about what we should say." Sometimes, however, there are disagreements in the use of words, but even here, says Austin, "we can find *why* we disagree," and "the explanation can hardly fail to be illuminating." Another question about ordinary language, besides its looseness, is whether it should be construed as the "last word" on matters. While ordinary language does not claim to be the last word, it is significant that it embodies the inherited experience and insights of many generations. And although these insights have been focused particularly upon the practical affairs of men, that fact further strengthens the claim for its accuracy. For if the distinctions of words work well in ordinary life "then there is something in it," says Austin. To be sure, scholars may have interests other than those whose language pertains to ordinary life. And there is no reason to believe that error and superstition cannot survive for long periods of time in a language. To this extent, Austin readily concedes that "ordinary language is *not* the last word: in principle it can everywhere be supplemented and improved upon and even superseded." But for Austin it *is* the first word in his program of analysis.

Austin recommended three resources which one can utilize in undertaking a full scale analysis of the word "excuses." Similar resources and methods would presumably be available for the analysis of other words as well. First he advocated using the dictionary. A concise one would do, and he suggested reading through it entirely and listing all the relevant words, remarking that it would not take as long as many would suppose. Or one could make a list of obviously relevant words first and consult the dictionary to discover their various meanings, a process which would then lead to other germane words until the relevant list is complete. A second source for this purpose would be the law. Here one would be provided with a vast number of cases along with a wide variety of pleas for excuses along with many analyses of the circumstances of the particular conduct in question. The third source is psychology. The use of psychology is an interesting example of how ordinary language is supplemented and even superseded inasmuch as psychology classifies some varieties of behavior or gives explanations of ways of acting which may not have been noticed by laymen nor captured by ordinary language. Given these resources "and with the aid of imagination," Austin was confident that the meanings of a vast number of expressions would emerge and that a large number of human actions could be understood and classified thereby achieving one of the central purposes of this whole process, namely, "explanatory definition."

24

Existentialism

Existentialism emerged in its contemporary form in Paris following World War II. At first it appeared to be a philosophical fad whose practitioners expounded their thoughts in cafés far removed from the professional precincts of university philosophers. Like most fads, it was expected that this one too would soon pass into oblivion. But existentialism has, if anything, gained momentum by invading virtually every form of human thought and expression, including the novel, theater, poetry, art, and theology. In the sheer scope of its influence existentialism has achieved a far wider response than any other mode of philosophy in current times, and this influence does not appear to be waning.

What appeared after World War II in the essays, plays, and novels of Jean Paul Sartre and Albert Camus was for the most part a brilliant and popular version of a mood and mode of thought that earlier philosophers had seized upon but that evoked widest response only in the historic circumstances of the twentieth century. Existentialism was one of the major currents of thought in Germany under the Weimar Republic, with Heidegger and Jaspers among its leaders. In the middle of the nineteenth century its main themes had already been worked out by the melancholy Dane Sören Kierkegaard with variations found in the works of Schelling and Marx. That writers with such diverse philosophical orientations should all have become identified with existentialism is an important reminder that existentialism has many forms and that among existentialists there are probably more differences than similarities. Even William James, Bergson, Nietzsche, the German mystic Jacob Böhme, and Pascal must be counted among those who contributed to the existentialist theme. What all these philosophers had in common was a concern about existence, human existence, the conditions and quality of the existing human individual.

Existentialism was bound to happen. The individual had over the centuries been pushed into the background by systems of thought, historical events, and technological forces. The major systems of philosophy had rarely paid attention to the uniquely personal concerns of individuals. Although Aristotle, for example, wrote a major treatise on ethics, Montaigne could say that "I can't recognize most of my daily doings when they appear in Aristotle." Nietzsche also wrote that "to our scholars, strangely enough, the most pressing question does not occur: to what end is their work . . . useful?" To be sure, Socrates had focused upon just these matters with his insistence that all thought and activity should be directed toward enhancing the meaning of human existence. St. Augustine also engaged in profound introspective psychological analysis to discover the source of man's personal insecurity and anxiety. Still, philosophy for the most part dealt with the technical problems of metaphysics, ethics, and the theory of knowledge in a general and objective manner, which bypassed the intimate concerns of men about their personal destiny. Historical events, particularly wars, showed a similar disregard for the feelings and aspirations of individuals. And technology, which arose as an aid to man, soon gathered a momentum of its own, forcing men to fit their lives into the rhythm of machines. Everywhere men were losing their peculiarly human qualities. They were being converted from "persons" into "pronouns," from "subjects" into "objects," from an "I" into an "it."

Inevitably, dehumanized Western man began to exhibit all the symptoms of his dehumanization. If learning, even philosophy and theology, talked in abstract generalities and skirted around the personal perplexities of individuals, it would be only a question of time before men would conclude that there is no expressible meaning for any human being's existence. If wars overwhelmed men in spite of their frantic efforts to forestall such calamities, life would be regarded as precarious, ambiguous, and insecure, and man would develop deep anxiety and the feeling of being abandoned in an insensitive and random universe. If technology removed much of the human dimension of existence by harnessing men to machines and requiring them to work as "organization men," men would find fewer occasions for expressing their existence as persons.

Religion, the traditional source of man's sense of worth, meaning, and moral guidance, was itself suffering from the critical impact of rational and scientific thought. Dostoevsky experimented with the implications of a nonreligious estimate of man, wondering whether one could successfully maintain that "since there is no God, everything is permitted." For Nietzsche, the bankruptcy of religious faith appeared to be the decisive cultural fact of his day. He did not hesitate to proclaim that for all intents and purposes "God is dead." This fact, he urged, should be accepted with courage, and upon it should be built a new conception of human existence. Atheism had become an important cause of the problems that gave rise to existentialism, since the breakdown of the religious tradition of Europe greatly aggravated the growing sense of life's worthlessness and meaninglessness. In their struggle against this meaninglessness, some existentialists took a frankly atheistic position and drew out all the consequences of such a position in formulating their approach to life. Others turned once again to religion in order to rediscover there what they believed had been missed by rational and scientific thinkers.

Whether they were theists or atheists, the existentialists all agreed that traditional philosophy was too academic and remote from life to have any adequate meaning for them. They rejected systematic and schematic thought in favor of a more spontaneous mode of expression in order to capture the authentic concerns of concrete existing individuals. Although there is no "system" of existentialist philosophy, its basic themes can, nevertheless, be discovered in some representative existentialist thinkers.

KIERKEGAARD

Many of the themes of contemporary existentialism were first expressed in the writings of Sören Kierkegaard. Born in Copenhagen in 1813, he spent his short life in a brilliant literary career, producing an extraordinary number of books before his death in 1855 at the age of forty-two. Although his books were soon forgotten after his death, they made an enormous impact upon their rediscovery by some German scholars in the early decades of the twentieth century. At the University of Copenhagen Kierkegaard was trained in Hegel's philosophy and was not favorably impressed by it. When he heard Schelling's lectures at Berlin, which were critical of Hegel, Kierkegaard agreed with this attack upon Germany's greatest speculative thinker. "If Hegel had written the whole of his Logic and then said . . . that it was merely an experiment in thought," wrote Kierkegaard, "then he could certainly have been the greatest thinker who ever lived. As it is, he is merely comic." What made Hegel comic for Kierkegaard was that this great philosopher had tried to capture all of reality in his system of thought, yet in the process lost the most important element, namely, *existence*. For Kierkegaard, the term *existence* was reserved for the individual human being. To exist, he said, implies being a certain kind of individual, an individual who strives, who considers alternatives, who chooses, who decides, and who, above all, commits himself. Virtually none of these acts were implied in Hegel's philosophy. Kierkegaard's whole career might well be considered as a self-conscious revolt against abstract thought and an attempt on his part to live up to Feuerbach's admonition: "Do not wish to be a philosopher in contrast to being a man . . . do not think as a thinker . . . think as a living, real being . . . think in Existence."

To "think in Existence" meant for Kierkegaard to recognize that one is faced with personal choices. Men find themselves constantly in an "existential situation." For this reason, their thinking ought to deal with their own personal situation with a view to coming to terms with the problem of alternatives and choices. Hegel's philosophy falsified man's understanding of reality because it shifted attention away from the concrete individual to the concept of universals. It called upon men *to think* instead of *to be*, to think the Absolute Thought instead of being involved in decisions and commitments. Kierkegaard drew the distinction between the *spectator* and the *actor*, arguing that only the actor is involved in existence. To be sure, the spectator can be said to exist, but the term *existence* does not properly belong to inert or inactive things, whether these be spectators or stones. Kierkegaard illustrated this distinction by comparing two kinds of men in a wagon, one who holds the reins in his hands but is asleep and the other who is fully awake. In the first case, the horse goes along the familiar road without any direction from the sleeping man, whereas in the other case the man is truly a driver. Surely, in one sense it can be said that both men exist, but Kierkegaard insists that *existence* must refer to a quality in the individual, namely, his conscious participation in an act. Only the conscious driver exists, and so, too, only a person who is engaged in conscious activity of will and choice can be truly said to exist. Thus, while both the spectator and the actor exist in a sense, only the actor is involved in existence.

Kierkegaard's criticism of rational knowledge was severe. He revolted against the rational emphasis in Greek wisdom, which, he charged, had permeated subsequent philosophy and Christian theology. His specific argument was that Greek philosophy had been too greatly influenced by a high regard for mathematics. Although he did not want to reject either mathematics or science in their proper uses, he did reject the assumption that the mode of thought characteristic of science could be successfully employed when trying to understand human nature. Mathematics and science have no place for the human individual, only for the general, the universal. Likewise, Platonic philosophy emphasizes the universal, the Form, the True, the Good. Plato's whole assumption was that if one *knew* the Good he would do it. Kierkegaard thought that such an approach to ethics was a falsification of man's real predicament. What Kierkegaard wanted to underscore was that even when a person has knowledge, he is still in the predicament of having to make a decision. The grand formulations of philosophical systems are, in the long run, only prolonged detours, which eventually come to nothing unless they lead attention back once again to the individual. To be sure, there are problems that can be solved by mathematics and science as well as by ethics and metaphysics. But over against such universal or general problems stands life, each person's life, making demands upon the individual, and at these critical moments general and abstract thought do not help. Kierkegaard saw in the Biblical story of Abraham the typical condition of man: and "God did tempt

Abraham and said unto him, Abraham: and he said, here I am. And he said, take now thy son, thine only son, Isaac, whom thou lovest." What kind of knowledge can help Abraham decide whether to obey God, to sacrifice his son? The most poignant moments in life are personal, where the individual becomes aware of himself as a subject. This subjective element is obscured if not denied by rational thought, which considers only man's objective characteristics, those characteristics that *all* men have in common. But subjectivity is what makes up each person's unique existence. For this reason, objectivity cannot give the whole truth about the individual self. That is why rational, mathematical, and scientific thought are incapable of guiding man to genuine existence.

Truth, said Kierkegaard, *is* subjectivity. By this strange notion he meant that for existing, striving, deciding persons there is not available "out there" a prefabricated truth. Anticipating the pragmatic view of William James, who said that "truth is made" by an act of will, Kierkegaard wrote that what is "out there" is "an objective uncertainty"; he argued that "the highest truth attainable for an Existing individual" is simply "an objective uncertainty held fast in the most passionate personal experience. . . ." Whatever may have been his criticism of Plato, he did nevertheless find in Socrates' claim to ignorance a good example of this notion of truth, saying that "the Socratic ignorance which Socrates held fast with the entire passion of his personal experience, was thus an expression of the principle that the eternal truth is related to the Existing individual." This would suggest that the cultivation of the mind is not the only important or decisive thing in life. Of more consequence is the development and maturity of personality.

In describing man's *existential situation,* Kierkegaard distinguished between man's present estate, that is, what he now *is,* and what he *ought* to be, or what he is *essentially.* There is, says Kierkegaard, a movement in the life of man from his *essential* to his *existential* condition, a movement from *essence* to *existence.* The traditional explanation of this movement in theology is made in terms of the doctrine of sin, of the Fall. Kierkegaard translated this doctrine into a profound psychological analysis, in which he isolated man's anxiety over his own finitude as the cause of his estrangement or alienation from his essential being. Sensing his insecurity and finitude, a person tries to "do something" to overcome his finitude, and invariably what he does only aggravates his problem by adding guilt and despair to his anxiety. Kierkegaard has in mind throughout his analysis the Christian understanding of man. Man's *essential* nature entails his relation to God, the infinite. His *existential* condition is a consequence of his alienation from God. If, then, a person's actions drive him even further from God, his alienation and despair are compounded. This is why it is not of any help to lose oneself in a crowd. Whatever be the nature of a crowd or collectivity, whether rich or poor or political in makeup, or even a congregation in a church—in every case, says Kierkegaard, "a crowd in its very concept is the untruth, by reason of the fact that it renders the individual completely impenitent and irresponsible, or at least weakens his sense of responsibility by reducing it to a fraction." Being in a crowd, in short, unmakes one's nature as an individual by diluting the self. From the point of view of Christian faith, being thus immersed in a crowd appears as an attempt upon man's part to derive some meaning for his existence. But this is a wrong attempt, for "to relate oneself to God is a far higher thing than to be related to" any other thing, whether a person, race, or even church. Until man does actualize his essential self in God, says Kierkegaard, his life is full of anxiety. His anxiety is caused by his awareness, however obscure, of a deep alienation of his existential from his essential self. This alienation creates in man a dynamic drive to recover his essential self. In describing this dynamic movement, Kierkegaard speaks of the "stages on life's way."

Kierkegaard's analysis of the "three stages" represents a sharp contrast to Hegel's theory of the gradual development of a person's self-consciousness. Whereas Hegel expounded the dialectic movement of the mind as it moves from one stage of intellectual awareness to another through the process of thinking, Kierkegaard described the movement of the self from one level of existence to another through an act of will, an act of choice. Hegel's dialectic moves gradually toward a knowledge of the universal, whereas Kierkegaard's dialectic involves the progressive actualization of the individual. Whereas Hegel overcomes the antithesis by a conceptual act, Kierkegaard overcomes it by the act of personal commitment.

The first stage in this dialectic process, says Kierkegaard, is the *aesthetic stage*. At this level, a person behaves according to his impulses and emotions. Although he is not simply sensual at this stage, he is for the most part governed by his senses. For this reason, the aesthetic person knows nothing of any universal moral standards. He has no specific religious belief. His chief motivation is a desire to enjoy the widest variety of pleasures of the senses. His life has no principle of limitation except his own taste; he resents anything that would limit his vast freedom of choice. At this stage an individual can *exist* inasmuch as he deliberately chooses to be an aesthetic man. But even though *existence* can be achieved at this level, Kierkegaard injects the element of *quality* into the matter of existence. Later existentialists were to speak of this quality in terms of *authenticity*. That is, an individual on the aesthetic level is aware, notwithstanding his variety of sense experiences, that his life consists, or *ought* to consist, of more than his emotive and sense experiences. Kierkegaard distinguishes between man's capacity to be *spirit* on the one hand and *sensuousness* on the other, calling the first the *building* and the second the *cellar*. Man, he ways, "prefers to dwell in the cellar." To be able to make this distinction about someone else is one thing; but for each individual to have an awareness of these two possibilities within himself is what triggers the dialectic movement in the individual. The antithesis of the sensual drive is the lure of the spirit. In experience, this conflict produces anxiety and despair when the individual discovers that he is in fact living in the "cellar" but that life at this level cannot possibly produce his *authentic* self, cannot result in *true existence*. The individual is now face to face with an *either-or*; either he remains on the aesthetic level with its fatal attractions, whose limitations he knows, or he moves to the next stage. This transition, says Kierkegaard, cannot be made by thinking alone but must be achieved by making a decision, or by an act of will, by a commitment.

The second level is the *ethical stage*. Unlike the aesthetic man, who has no universal standards but only his own taste, the ethical man does recognize and accept rules of conduct that reason formulates. Moral rules give the ethical man's life the elements of form and consistency. Moreover, the ethical man accepts the limitations upon his life that moral responsibility imposes. Kierkegaard illustrates the contrast between the aesthetic man and the ethical man in their attitude toward sexual behavior, saying that whereas the former yields to his impulses wherever there is an attraction, the ethical man accepts the obligations of marriage as an expression of reason, the universal reason of man. If Don Juan exemplifies the aesthetic man, it is Socrates who typifies the ethical man or the reign of the universal moral law. The ethical man has the mood of moral self-sufficiency; he takes a firm stand on moral questions and, as Socrates argued, assumes that to know the good is to do the good. For the most part, the ethical man considers moral evil as being a product either of ignorance or of weakness of will. But the time comes, says Kierkegaard, when the dialectic process begins to work in the consciousness of the ethical man. He begins to realize that he is involved in something more profound than an inadequate knowledge of the moral law or insufficient strength of will. He is, in short, doing something more serious than merely making mistakes. The ethical man ultimately comes to realize that he is in fact incapable of fulfilling the moral law, that he deliberately violates that law and therefore he becomes conscious of his guilt. Guilt, or the sense of sin, says Kierkegaard, becomes the dialectic element, the antithesis, which places before man a new *either-or*. Now he must either remain at the ethical level and try to fulfill the moral law, or he must respond to his new awareness, the awareness of his own finitude and estrangement from God to whom he belongs and from whom he must derive his strength. Again, man's movement from the ethical to the next stage cannot be achieved by thinking alone but by an act of commitment, by a *leap* of faith.

The difference between faith and reason is particularly striking for Kierkegaard when man arrives at the third level, or the *religious stage*. Man's movement from the aesthetic to the ethical level required an act of choice and commitment; it ushered man into the presence of reason inasmuch as the moral law is an expression of the universal reason of man. But the movement from the ethical to the religious level is quite different. The leap of faith does not bring one into the presence of a God who can be philosophically or rationally described as the Absolute and Knowable Truth (and therefore objective) but into the presence of a Subject. The secret of religious consciousness, says Kierkegaard, is that the existing individual cannot pursue God in an "objective way," or "bring God to light objectively." This, says Kierkegaard, "is in all eternity impossible because God is subject, and therefore exists only for subjectivity in inwardness." At the ethical level, it is possible for the existing individual to give his life, as Socrates did, for the moral law that he rationally understands. But when it is a question of man's relation to God, there is available no rational or conceptual or objective knowledge about this relationship. The relationship between God and each individual is a unique and subjective experience. There is no way, prior to the actual relationship, to get any knowledge about it. Any attempt to get such objective knowledge about it is, says Kierkegaard, entirely an *approximation process*. Only an act of faith can assure the existing individual of his personal relation to God. That he must find his self-fulfillment in God becomes clear to him as he discovers the inadequacy of his existence at the aesthetic and ethical levels. Through despair and guilt he is brought to the decisive moment in life when he confronts the final *either-or* of faith. The existence of God is suggested to man in his awareness of his self-alienation, that subjective awareness of the contrast between his existential and his essential self. That God has disclosed Himself in Christ is a further complication, indeed a *paradox*. To say, as Christian faith does, that God, the infinite, is revealed in Christ, the finite, is an extraordinary affront to human reason, "to the Jews a stumbling block and to the Greeks foolishness." But Kierkegaard wanted to maintain that the only way to cross the span between man and God, that "infinite qualitative distinction between time and eternity," is not through speculative reason, not even Hegel's, but through faith. Again, truth for Kierkegaard was a subjective matter, a consequence of commitment. Without risk, said Kierkegaard, there is no faith. And with faith, the existing individual realizes his true self.

Kierkegaard's existentialism can be summed up in his statement that: "Every human being must be assumed in essential possession of what essentially belongs to being a man." This being the case, "the task of the subjective thinker is to transform himself into an instrument that clearly and definitely expresses in existence whatever is essentially human." This is Kierkegaard's central point, namely, that each person possesses an essential self, which he *ought* to actualize. This essential self is fixed by the very fact that man must inescapably become related to God. To be sure, man can *exist* at any one of the three stages along life's way. But the experience of despair and guilt creates in man an awareness of qualitative differences in various modes of existence, that some modes of human existence are more authentic than others. But arriving at authentic existence is not a matter of the intellect; it is a matter of faith and commitment, a continuous process of choice by the existing individual in the presence of varieties of *either-or*.

HUSSERL'S PHENOMENOLOGY

A major source of contemporary existentialism is the phenomenology of Edmund Husserl. The connection between existentialism and phenomenology is not always obvious since so much of Husserl's philosophy is cast in technical and even special scientific language, whereas existentialism focuses upon the immediate human concerns of man's daily existence. Phenomenology is rationalistic whereas existentialism is concerned with such practical issues as making choices, decisions, and personal commitments. Moreover, a significant element in Husserl's phenomenology is the act of detachment, of standing back from the realm of experienced existence in order to understand it, whereas existentialism urges a life of thorough-going engagement and involvement as the surest way of creating meaning for human existence. Although there are these and other differences between existentialism and phenomenology, it is the spectacular spread of existentialism that has has brought Husserl's thought before a wider audience. Husserl can rightly be called the "father" of phenomenology, but he is also the first in a line of thinkers who together encompass many modes of existentialism and phenomenology. Among those influenced by Husserl's insights in various ways were the philosophers Heidegger, Merleau-Ponty, and Sartre.

Edmund Husserl was born in the Moravian province of Prossnitz in 1859, the same year in which were born Henri Bergson and John Dewey. After his early education in that province, he went to the University of Leipzig where during 1876 to 1878 he studied physics, astronomy and mathematics and found time to attend lectures by the philosopher Wilhelm Wundt. Husserl continued his studies at the Friederich Wilhelm University in Berlin and later, in 1881, he went to the University of Vienna where, in 1883, he earned his Ph.D. for his dissertation on "Contributions to the Theory of the Calculus of Variations." During 1884 to 1886, he attended the lectures of Franz Brentano (1838–1917) who became a most significant influence in Husserl's philosophical development especially through his lectures on Hume and John Stuart Mill and his treatment of problems in ethics, psychology, and logic. On Brentano's advice, Husserl went to the University of Halle where in 1886 he became an assistant under Carl Stumpf (1884–1936), the eminent psychologist under whose direction he wrote his first book, *Philosophy of Arithmetic* (1891). His *Logical Investigations* appeared in 1900 and in the same year he was invited to join the philosophy faculty at the University of Göttingen. It was here that Husserl spent sixteen productive years writing such important works as his *Lectures on Phenomenology* (1904–1905), *Lectures on Phenomenology of Inner Time Consciousness* (1905–1910), *The Idea of Phenomenology* (1906–1907), *Philosophy as a Rigorous Science* (1911) and the first volume of his *Ideas* (1913). In 1916 Husserl became a full professor at Freiburg where he taught until 1928. Here he wrote the last two volumes of his *Ideas* (1912—), *First Philosophy* (1923—), *Phenomenological Psychology* (1925—) and *Formal and Transcendental Logic* (1928). In 1928 Husserl applied for retirement. Then, between 1929 and 1936 he published two major works, *Cartesian Meditations* (1931) and the first part of his book *Philosophy and the Crisis of European Man* (1936). Because of his Jewish origins, Husserl was forbidden to participate in academic activities after 1933. Although he was offered a professorship by the University of Southern California, Husserl declined the offer, and after several months of suffering, he died of pleurisy at the age of 79 in 1938 at Freiburg in Breisgau.

Husserl's philosophy evolved gradually through several phases. His early interest was in logic and mathematics; next, he developed an early version of phenomenology focused chiefly upon a theory of knowledge; then, he moved on to a view of phenomenology as a universal foundation for philosophy and science; and finally he entered a phase in which his life-world, *Lebenswelt*, idea became a more dominant theme in his phenomenology. It is no wonder, then, that Husserl's philosophy should have had a variety of influences upon different scholars at various times. For example, Martin Heidegger, who became Husserl's assistant at Freiburg in 1920, had been familiar during his student days with Husserl's work in logic and his earlier writings in phenomenology. As his assistant during 1920–1923, Heidegger worked closely with Husserl. Together they prepared an article on phenomenology for the *Encyclopaedia Britannica*. Heidegger also prepared some of Husserl's earlier lectures for publication. Even after Heidegger left in 1923 to become a professor at Marburg, he continued his close association with Husserl. As time passed, however, Heidegger found it difficult to share Husserl's novel developments, especially those dealing with transcendental phenomenology. In his major work, *Being and Time*, Heidegger was critical of Husserl's method and his distinctive view of the ego. By the time Heidegger succeeded to Husserl's chair at Freiburg in the fall of 1928 their relationship had begun to weaken and eventually came to an end.

Similarly, although Sartre was deeply influenced by Husserl's writings when he studied German phenomenology at Freiburg, he eventually came to believe that Heidegger's modification of Husserl's view was philosophically more significant. Nevertheless, it was Sartre who upon his return to Paris from Germany in 1934 called Merleau-Ponty's attention to Husserl's book *Ideas* and urged him to study it carefully. Merleau-Ponty was extremely impressed by several distinctive elements in Husserl's phenomenology and was inspired to work further in Husserl's writings, being particularly influenced by Husserl's *Philosophy and the Crisis of European Man*. Although Merleau-Ponty was thoroughly familiar with Husserl's ideas as interpreted by Heidegger and Sartre, he made his own extensive study of the original documents and he even went to Louvain where he had access to the Husserl archives which contain over 40,000 pages of Husserl's manuscripts written in short-hand and which are gradually becoming available through transcriptions and translations. What we find, then, without analyzing all the details, is that Husserl exerted a strong influence upon Heidegger, Merleau-Ponty and Sartre, the leading exponents of phenomenology and existentialism. His influence upon these younger philosophers was different at various stages of their philosophical development. And, even though they rejected many of Husserl's key ideas, their finished works bear the imprint of his phenomenology.

Naturalism and the Collapse of Reason Before answering the question "What is Phenomenology?," it is helpful to ask "What prompted Husserl to invent Phenomenology in the first place?" Husserl's philosophy grows out of his deep conviction that Western culture has lost its true direction and purpose. His mood is reflected in the title of his last major philosophical work, *Philosophy and the Crisis of European Man*. The "crisis" consists of philosophy's departure from its true goal, which is to provide the best possible answers to man's human and humane concerns, to deal rigorously with man's quest for the highest values, and, in short, to develop the unique broad range capacities of human reason. Husserl described the "crisis" as the "seeming collapse of rationalism" and he set his lifetime objective as "saving human reason." What human reason has to be saved from according to Husserl provides the background for his phenomenology.

The key to the crisis of Western man is the enterprise of "natural science." Husserl is profoundly impressed by the brilliant successes of natural science. Indeed, his ultimate objective is to save human reason by developing philosophy into a rigorous science. His criticism is therefore not directed at science as such but rather at the assumptions and methods of the natural sciences. Husserl believes that the natural sciences have over the years developed a faulty *attitude* in Western man regarding what the world is like and how best to know it. The natural sciences rest upon the fatal *prejudice* that nature is basically physical and that the realm of spirit or "soul," the realm of knowing, valuing, and judging, in short, the realm of culture, is causally based upon corporeality. The possibility of formulating a self-contained science of the spirit is rejected by the natural scientist, and this rejection, says Husserl, explains to a large degree the crisis of modern man. To insist that the realm of spirit must be understood after the manner of the physical sciences reflects, says Husserl, the "naïveté" of modern scientific rationalism. What makes this rationalism naïve is that it expresses the questionable assumption of the various forms of *naturalism* which is that physical nature envelops everything. This means, for example, that all psychology is psychophysical. It means, moreover, that knowledge and truth are "objective," based upon a "reality" beyond the self. Just how this "objectivism" of naturalism constitutes the naïveté of modern rationalism is explained by Husserl as a fundamental departure from the original philosophical attitude developed in Greece.

The distinctive Greek attitude as exemplified in Socrates, Plato, and Aristotle was that the task of philosophy is to search for universal ideal norms for man's thought and behavior. Philosophy had transformed the earlier prephilosophical mode of human existence which was characterized as a naïvely direct living immersed in the world, in a world constantly there. Life in this state was practical and even the developing mythologies and early religions supported the basically practical concerns of individuals and larger groups. In this condition there was no culture of ideas in the sense of ideas reaching beyond the immediate boundaries of local experience and practical interests. What Greek philosophy did, says Husserl, was to develop a new kind of outlook or attitude, namely, a universal critique of all life and its goals. This was a critique of all systems of culture that had grown up in the life of mankind. The positive side of this critique was its aim of raising mankind through universal reason toward a radically new humanity, rising above the limited horizons of custom, geography, and social groups. What made this possible was a new conception of truth, a truth independent of tradition, universally valid, and capable of infinite refinement. Here, then, is the origin of the spiritual life, the culture, of Europe, of Western man. It was in ancient Greece that this new attitude grew up orienting individuals toward their environing world. The systematic formulation of this attitude is what the Greeks called philosophy. Correctly translated, says Husserl, this philosophy "bespeaks nothing but universal science, science of the world as a whole, of the universal unity of all being." But it was this one science, philosophy, with its comprehensive grasp of all nature which included the cultural as well as the physical, ideas as well as objects, which ultimately began to splinter into the several separate sciences. The intervening step was the discovery of how the world of perceived nature can be changed into a mathematical world, a discovery which eventually led to the development of the mathematical natural sciences.

Ultimately, the success of the mathematical natural sciences resulted in the gradual scientific repudiation of the spirit. By steadily focusing upon the environing world, the objective attitude was developed wherein everything was considered to be physical or derived from the physical. To be sure such a view had been offered earlier by Democritus but had been rejected by Socrates. For Socrates, man was viewed primarily as having a spiritual life within the context of society. For Plato and Aristotle, too, man possessed the same Socratic spiritual dimension. For, while human beings belong to the universe of objective facts, they are nevertheless persons, egos, who have goals and aims. But with the later success of the mathematical natural sciences, the methods of the natural sciences were extended to the knowledge of the spirit. Man's spirit was now conceived as an objective fact founded upon corporeality, taking on, Husserl says, "a predominantly dualistic, i.e., psychophysical form." Hence, the same causality embraces the one world in such a way that all explanation of the spirit involves the physical. For this reason, Husserl said that from the attitude of natural science, "there can be no pure self-contained search for an explanation of the spiritual, no purely inner-oriented psychology or theory of spirit beginning with the ego in psychical-self-experience and extending to the other psyche. The way that must be traveled is the external one, the path of physics and chemistry." He concluded that there can be no improvement in our understanding of mankind's true purposes so long as naturalistic objectivism, with its "naïve" and "absurd" dualistic interpretation of the world, looks upon spirit after the manner of spatio-temporal objects and studies spirit according to the methodology of the natural sciences. It was his desire to develop a proper method for grasping the essential nature of the spirit, to overcome naturalistic objectivism, that led Husserl to formulate his transcendental phenomenology.

What, then, is phenomenology? Some appreciation of this complex philosophy with its novel terminology can be gained by even a brief consideration of some major themes in Husserl's thought.

Husserl and Descartes   Husserl says that "phenomenology must honor Descartes as its genuine patriarch." There are, of course, other influences upon Husserl's thought, notably the empiricism of Locke, the skepticism of Hume, the Copernican revolution of Kant, and the pragmatism of William James. In every case Husserl went beyond these and others whose insights shaped his own ideas. Nevertheless, Descartes' influence was decisive for it led Husserl to begin where Descartes began, with the thinking self. However, whereas Descartes sought through systematic doubt to achieve an absolutely certain foundation for knowledge, Husserl formulated the distinctive mood of phenomenology by accepting only one part of Descartes' starting point. Husserl says, "We thus begin, every-one for himself and in himself with the decision to disregard all our present knowledge. We do not give up Descartes' guiding goal of an absolute foundation for knowledge. At the beginning, however, to presuppose even the possibility of that goal would be prejudice." Husserl thus takes an even more radical approach than Descartes did, for he tries to build a philosophy without *any* presupposi-tions, looking solely to "things and facts themselves, as these are given in actual experience and intuition." Husserl made it a cardinal rule of his method "to judge only by the evidence" and not according to any preconceived notions or presuppositions. He sought to recapture man's prescientific life which is filled with "immediate and mediate evidences." Thus, whereas Descartes employed systematic doubt, Husserl simply withheld any judgment about his experiences, seeking instead to describe his experiences as fully as possible in terms of the evidence of experience itself.

Experience obviously revolves around the self, the ego, and for Husserl as well as for Descartes the source of all knowledge is the ego. But while for Des-cartes the ego becomes the first axiom in a logical sequence which enables him to deduce, as one would in mathematics, a series of conclusions about reality, Hus-serl sees the ego simply as the matrix of experience. Husserl therefore puts pri-mary emphasis upon experience instead of logic. His concern is to discover and describe the given in experience as it is presented in its pure form and found as the immediate date of consciousness. Husserl criticizes Descartes for moving beyond the conscious self, the ego, to the notion of extended substance, a body, which ties the subject to an objective reality producing thereby the mind-body dualism. Instead, Husserl believed that "pure subjectivity" more accurately de-scribes the actual facts of human experience. Moreover, whereas Descartes em-phasized the two terms in his famous *ego cogito*, Husserl believed that a more accurate description of experience is expressed in the three terms *ego cogito cogitatum.* That is, whereas Descartes emphasized the "I think," Husserl makes the point that to say "I think *something*" is the typical human experience. In-deed, Husserl's analysis rests to a significant degree upon the relation he saw between consciousness, thinking, the thing thought, and the element of intention-ality which "creates" the phenomena of experience.

Phenomena   What provides Husserl the term "phenomenology" as the descrip-tive term for his philosophy is his refusal to go beyond the only evidence or data available, namely, the data available to consciousness, and the data derived from appearances—from phenomena. But unlike theories of knowledge which distin-guish between a knowing mind, on the one hand, and the object of knowledge on the other, Husserl sees virtually no distinction, at least in the preliminary descrip-tion, between consciousness and the phenomenon. Indeed, Husserl's unique point is that phenomena, or whatever is, are ultimately contained in the very subjective act whereby what is is present to consciousness. This is his novel "attitude," so contrary to the naturalistic attitude which assumes an objective physical world independently existing out there. For Husserl, knowing is not the act of a camera taking pictures of things. Nor is a simple psychological description of experience sufficient. Phenomenology goes beyond listing objects given in experience; it enlarges the act of "description" of experience to include the real object, our actual perception of it, the object as we mean it, and the act of intentionality which constitutes the object for us. Thus Husserl brings to his empiricism the element of "reflection;" that is, he moves beyond the description of the superficial aspects of phenomena or appearances to the intricate activity of consciousness whereby, as Husserl says, "consciousness makes possible and necessary the fact that such an 'existing' and 'thus determined' Object is intended in it, occurs in it as such a sense." In short, we understand the elements of our experience, phenomena, best by discovering the active role of consciousness in intending and creating phenomena.

Intentionality   For Husserl the clearest fact about human experience is not simply the fact of consciousness but rather that consciousness is always consciousness of something. Moreover, the clearest fact about consciousness is that its essence is to point toward, or to intend, some object. Our perception of things, our experience, consists of our projection toward intended objects. Thus Husserl believed that the essence of consciousness is intentionality. By intentionality Husserl means that any object of my consciousness, a house, a pleasure, a number, or another person, is something meant, constructed, constituted, that is, intended by me. Pure consciousness has no segments—it is a continuous stream. Our primitive perception consists of the undifferentiated world. The separate objects of perception are those parts of the stream of consciousness which we as subjects constitute by intending them. Kant described earlier how the mind organizes experience by imposing such categories as time, space, and causality upon sensory experience. Similarly, Bergson said that "in the continuity of sensible qualities we mark off the boundaries of bodies." For Husserl, too, intentionality designates the active involvement of the ego in creating our experience. Indeed, for Husserl, intentionality is the structure of consciousness itself and is also the fundamental category of being. Again, this means that phenomenology stresses the need to describe the data and activity of consciousness in the process of discovering reality, instead of looking for reality in things, for things are what we intend them to be. For example, we perceive a person from a limited perspective, a profile, or in a given setting, a concert, or at a given time, at school. From these fragments, which are parts of reality, our consciousness constitutes, "intends," *the* person in question. This process of intentionality may not be a conscious one but rather automatic. For this reason Husserl calls the ego's constitution of the world a passive genesis. But the question remains just how Husserl arrives at this notion of the intentionality of consciousness. The presence of intentionality is disclosed through the process Husserl calls phenomenological *epochē*.

Phenomenological Epochē   The term *epochē* is the Greek word for "bracketing." Husserl uses this term to describe his method of "detachment from any point of view regarding the objective world." Whereas Descartes began by doubting everything, including all phenomena, in short, the world, except his thinking self, Husserl in contrast "brackets" all phenomena, all the elements of experience, by refusing to assert whether the world does or does not exist. He abstains from entertaining any belief about experience. Thus Husserl "brackets" the whole stream of experienced life including objects, other people, and cultural situations. To bracket all these phenomena means only to look upon them without judging whether they are realities or appearances and to abstain from rendering any opinions, judgments or valuations about the world. It is through this phenomenological *epoché*, this standing back from the phenomena of experience, this ridding his mind of all presuppositions and prejudices which enabled Husserl to discover himself as the ego, the life of consciousness, in which and through which the objective world in its entirety exists. Unlike Descartes, who deduced the objective world from the residual certainty of the ego, Husserl found that the ego "contained" the world. In his *Paris Lectures,* Husserl says: " . . . for me the world is nothing other than what I am aware of and what appears valid in such *cogitationes* (my acts of thought). The whole meaning and reality of the world rests exclusively on such *cogitationes.* My entire worldly life takes its course within these. I cannot live, experience, think, value and act in any world which is not in some sense in me, and derives its meaning and truth from me."

Husserl said that "we must not make assertions about that which we do not ourselves *see.*" For this reason, Husserl rejects those portions of Descartes' and Kant's philosophies which go beyond the immediate phenomenal realm, what Husserl terms the *transcendental* realm, the world of experience. Kant's distinction between the *phenomenal* (experience) and the *noumenal* (the thing-in-itself, or the *transcendent*) is unacceptable to Husserl, notwithstanding the many similarities between his and Kant's philosophies. Husserl rigorously limits the scope of philosophy to the realm of experience and that is why it is called *transcendental phenomenology.* By bracketing the realm of experience, that is, by affecting the transcendental *epoché*, Husserl is "reduced," that is, led back (*re-ducere*) to the center of reality, namely, the conscious self. It makes no difference, says Husserl, whether we deny or affirm the existence of the world; he says, "the *epoché* . . . discloses the greatest and most magnificent of facts: I and my life remain—in my sense of reality—untouched by whichever way we decide the issue of whether the world is or is not." And from his unprejudiced view of his experience Husserl concludes that "I have discovered my true self. I have discovered that I alone am the pure ego, with pure existence. . . .Through this ego alone does the *being of the world,* and, for that matter, any being whatsoever, make sense to me and have possible validity."

To say, as Husserl does, that only through the ego does the being of the world make any sense takes us once again to his notion of intentionality. For the ego is consciousness, and consciousness is always consciousness of something. But pure consciousness must be discovered under several layers of presuppositions and points of view developed by various cultures. It is especially necessary to overcome the presuppositions of the natural sciences which have led us to believe that the original objects of experience are the ones as described and determined by the sciences. But the objects of science are abstractions and artificial structures as compared with our original experience. The *epochē* helps us discover the original, the primordial, mode of experience and what we find there is conscious-ness and *its* objects. The irreducible element of experience is the constant pres-ence of the ego as the source of objects and their meanings. Husserl says, there-fore, that all objects appear as basically determined by the structure of thinking itself. The meaning and the being of things is primordially constituted in and through consciousness. This is the act of intentionality which Husserl held to be the characteristic property of our consciousness.

The Life-World (Lebenswelt)   In order to prepare the way for the rigorous foundation of his philosophy, Husserl again and again urged the *epochē*, the bracketing of all presuppositions and especially the presuppositions of the natural sciences. To emphasize this point Husserl urged the reduction to, that is the leading back to, the original form of human experience, the mode of experience which is prescientific. This is the realm of man's daily world, his life-world, the *Lebenswelt.* The life-world consists of all those experiences—the perception, re-sponse, interpretation and the synthesis or organization of the many facets of everyday affairs—in which human beings are typically involved. This life-world is the source from which the sciences must abstract their objects. To that extent they provide only a partial grasp of reality. Much of the rich and meaningful elements of experience remain after the sciences have abstracted the elements of their concern. Indeed, the very nature of being a scientist is unaccounted for by science itself. Only a rigorous analysis of the way in which the life-world func-tions in man's unsophisticated experience as well as in science will provide an adequate basis for philosophy. In the last analysis, the basic justification or confir-mation of truth is to be found in the type of evidence that derives from events of the life-world. The totality of these events of the life-world is what Husserl calls "our world-experiencing life." Through this notion of the life-world, Husserl sought to liberate the philosopher, the phenomenologist, from a point of view which is dominated by the various natural sciences. For the purpose of an even more useful mode of science, but especially in order to liberate the spirit, Husserl fashioned a way of discovering what the world is like before it is interpreted by the scientific outlook. Through the *epochē*, the life-world emerges as a fresh terrain for the enterprise of description, opening a new way of experiencing, thinking, and even theorizing. Husserl thought he had discovered that the "world" is what we as subjects know it to be for it is, as he says, "the correlate of the subjectivity which gives it ontic meaning, through whose validities the world 'is' at all." It was this return to the life-world and subjectivity which channeled many facets of phenomenology into existentialism.

JASPERS AND MARCEL

Kierkegaard's writings influenced the philosopher Karl Jaspers (1883–1969), who was a professor at Heidelberg and, after World War II, at Basel. Jaspers believes that just as philosophy could not be the same again after Hume focused such a searching light upon the nature of human knowledge, so now philosophy can never return to its earlier modes since Kierkegaard focused upon man's human condition. Jaspers' works as a professional philosopher are placed in the setting of the predicament of twentieth-century man. His chief concern, he says, is the age-old question of Being, which must now be studied from the vantage point of *existence philosophy*. The subject of Being and of personal existence has been obscured by the overwhelming impact of the scientific mode of thinking upon the contemporary mind. In addition, the "human condition" has deteriorated with the development of technology, the emergence of mass movements, and the loosening of the bonds of religion. In particular, Jaspers comes to the conclusion that the task of philosophy must be reconsidered in the contemporary world especially because of the developments in the various sciences. Each of the sciences has carved out a special area for its subject matter, and each science has developed its own method. It would seem that a universal science could be formulated by bringing together in some form of unity all the particular sciences. Could not the unified sciences constitute a single science of Being, of total reality?

Jaspers believes that there could not be a universal *science* of Being. His argument is that just as each science functions within strict subject-matter limits, so, also, the aggregate of all the sciences is characterized by a limitation of coverage. The limitation of science, says Jaspers, is self-imposed. Each science deals with *objective data*. Hence, each science deals with a particular mode of being, with *a* particular kind of object. By definition, the sciences "divide up" reality into objects. To think scientifically, then, is to have access to only one kind of data, namely, objective data. But the content of Being, total reality, Existence, is not limited to objective data. The self, the individual, the whole complex of the subject—all this subjectivity is part of Existence. And nowhere is the limitation of science more apparent than when it tries to study man the individual. There can be various sciences of man such as psychology, sociology, and anthropology, but these, says Jaspers, cannot deal with man as an *existing* self, only as an object: "sociology, psychology and anthropology teach that man is to be regarded as an object concerning which something can be learnt that will make it possible to modify this object by deliberate organization." Jaspers recognizes the value and usefulness of each of these sciences. He cannot be considered an antirationalist. His argument is, however, that the task of philosophy is not the same as that of science, that in studying Being, philosophy must not ape the sciences by treating Being as an *object* of thought, for that would make out of Being *a* being among other beings. Science, he argues, is subphilosophic because it does not deal with the unique inner experiences of concrete individual human beings.

Jaspers believes that the task of philosophy is to deal with Existence, whose subject matter is based upon the existential thinker's immediate inner and personal experience. There is a level of Being, says Jaspers, that the existential thinker can grasp, a level that is neither purely objective nor purely subjective but is the creative *source* of experience, and this is Existence. Existence, says

Jaspers, "is something that can never become a mere object; it is the 'Source' whence springs my thinking and acting." Personal existence, he continues, is the center and direction of reality; it is an error to reverse this conclusion and to say that reality consists of objects. For this reason, only someone with a consciousness of personal experience can grasp the meaning of Existence. Philosophic thinking, under these assumptions, cannot set out, as Hegel had, "to raise philosophy to a science." Instead, philosophy, says Jaspers, must reaffirm that "truth is subjectivity," that philosophizing means communicating not about objects or objective knowledge but about the content of personal awareness produced by the individual's *inner constitution*. Existential thinking, says Jaspers, is "the philosophic practice of life."

Although Jaspers does not depreciate the technical knowledge of science, he insists that the "practice of life" requires that human beings bring to this knowledge some additional reality. All the principles and laws of science, he insists, are of no avail "unless individual human beings fulfill them with an effective and valuable reality." The piling-up of knowledge cannot by itself assure any particular outcome for humanity. "Decisive is a man's inward attitude," says Jaspers, "the way in which he contemplates his world and grows aware of it, the essential value of his satisfactions—these things are the origin of what he does." Philosophy, therefore, must be *existence philosophy*.

Although existence philosophy cannot be reduced to any systematic statement, one can nevertheless give, as Jaspers does, some of its characteristics. Primarily, existence philosophy is the manner of thought through which a person seeks to become himself. It is a way of thought that does not restrict itself to knowing objects but rather "elucidates and makes actual the being of the thinker." It does not discover solutions in analytic reflection but rather "becomes real" in the dialogue that proceeds from one person to another in genuine communication. Existence philosophy does not assume that "what man is" is a settled piece of knowledge, for that would make it not philosophy but, once again, anthropology, psychology, and sociology. There is the danger that existence philosophy may lapse into pure subjectivity, into a restrictive preoccupation with one's own ego, into a justification for shamelessness. But Jaspers considers these possibilities as aberrations. Where it remains genuine, existence philosophy is, he says, uniquely effective in promoting all that makes man genuinely human. Each person is "completely irreplaceable. We are not merely cases of universal Being." The concept of Being, for existence philosophy, arises only in the consciousness of each concrete human being.

If existence philosophy can be said to have a "function," it is to make the mind receptive to what Jaspers calls the *Transcendent*. The human situation is described as a movement from a knowledge of objects to a second stage where the individual recognizes in himself the foundations of existence and finally a third stage where a person becomes conscious of striving toward his genuine self. At this last stage, man discovers his finitude. There are certain "limiting situations" that each man faces as, for example, death, the possibility of one's own death. When one experiences an awareness of his own finitude, he simultaneously becomes aware of its opposite, namely, Being as the Transcendent. This awareness of the Transcendent, which traditional theology calls God, is a purely personal experience incapable of specific delineation or proof; it is simply an awareness that everything, including myself and all objects, is grounded in Being. Central to my awareness of the Transcendent is my concurrent awareness of my own *freedom.* In my striving to fulfill my genuine self, I am *free* to affirm or deny my relationship to the Transcendent. Authentic existence, however, requires that I affirm it. I stand in the presence of a choice, an either-or, without the help of any scientific proof or even knowledge, only an awareness. In the end, man must express a *philosophic faith,* not unlike Kierkegaard's *leap* of faith, which signifies not some mystical union with the Transcendent but a union with the depths of life.

Like Jaspers, Gabriel Marcel (1889–1973) centered his existentialist philosophy upon the problem of Being, particularly upon the human question "What am I?" As Jaspers, also, Marcel writes in a profuse and elusive style, making it virtually impossible to capture his thought in any brief form. There is in Marcel's works, however, a basic distinction, which provides one with a significant clue to his thought. This is the distinction between a *problem* and a *mystery.* It is not possible, he writes, to answer the question "What am I?" by reducing it to a problem, analyzing its parts, and then producing a solution. A problem implies that we lack some information or knowledge and that all we need to do is look for it, engage in "research," and thereby overcome our temporary ignorance. A problem usually revolves around an object or a relationship between objects. Information regarding objects and their relationships can be gathered and calculated. But the question "What am I?" cannot be reduced to a problem, because the *I* is not an object, an *it.* Although I am some sort of object, since I do have a body, my being is a combination of subject and object; and because the subjective part of myself can never be eliminated, I cannot be reduced to a mere object, and therefore the question about my existence is not merely a problem: it is a mystery. In this context Marcel means by the word *mystery* certain kinds of experiences that are permanently incapable of being translated into objects "out there"; these experiences *always* include the subject, and these are therefore matters of mystery.

Marcel says that "the essence of man is to be in a situation." He means by this that a man's relation to Being is different from a stone's. For one thing, "man is the only being who can make promises," a phrase of Nietzsche's, which Marcel wanted to underscore. To be able to make a promise places one into a unique relationship between himself and another, a kind of relationship that could not possibly exist between two objects. This moral dimension of existence led Marcel to believe that the ultimate character of man's relationships involves the element of fidelity. Fidelity therefore is the major clue to the nature of one's own existence, for it is through fidelity that a person continues to shape his life, thereby expressing his faith in whatever is other than he is, and it is therefore in expressing fidelity that a person's life achieves a responsible and authentic continuity. Fidelity is discovered in friendship and in love, where it has the power to overcome the "objectivity" of the other and to produce a new level of intimacy. In a deeper sense, too, a person affirms Being through fidelity insofar as he responds to a world that makes demands and in which he assumes responsibilities. This is the deep existentialist theme in Marcel, which he discovers in the question "What am I?" a question whose answer is illusive because it does not constitute a problem but is rather a mystery. The element of mystery is virtually irreducible precisely because human existence is a combination of "being and having." Whereas *having* things and ideas can be translated into objective and therefore cognitive terms, *being* is always the element of subjectivity. In the end, human existence derives its deepest meaning from the subjective affirmation of Being through fidelity. Although he is in no sense a narrow or even orthodox theologian, Marcel found in the Christian faith the basic spirit of his philosophy, becoming a convert to the Roman Catholic Church at the age of thirty-nine. Although Kierkegaard, Jaspers, and Marcel formulated their existential philosophies in different ways, they had in common a religious basis for existentialism. Sartre parts company with these men by frankly accepting the assumptions of atheism as the starting point and foundation for his philosophy of existentialism, a perspective Sartre derived from Heidegger.

HEIDEGGER

Even before Heidegger ever published anything, his reputation as an extraordinary thinker spread among students in the German universities. What was extraordinary about Heidegger as a teacher was that he did not develop a "set of ideas" or a "system" of philosophy. He produced nothing in the way of a neat structure of academic ideas which a student could quickly understand and memorize. He was not interested so much in objects of scholarship as in matters of thinking. With one bold stroke, he shifted the attention of twentieth-century Continental philosophy away from traditional concerns about theories and books and focused instead upon the concerns of thinking individuals. An individual is born in the world and responds to all his experiences by thinking. What Heidegger set out to explore was the deepest nature of an individual's thinking when he is thinking as an existing human being.

Born in 1889 in Germany's Black Forest region, Heidegger received his preparatory schooling in Constance and Freiburg and was introduced to philosophy at the age of seventeen when the pastor of his church gave him Franz Brentano's book entitled *On the Manifold Meaning of Being according to Aristotle.* This book, though difficult, made such an impression upon the young Heidegger that it launched him on his lifelong endeavor to explore the meaning of Being, or "the meaning that reigns in everything that is." Along the way, Heidegger was also influenced by Kierkegaard, Dostoevski, and Nietzsche, from whom he discovered that some concerns of philosophy are most creatively clarified by paying attention to concrete and historically relevant problems. At the University of Freiburg, he began his studies in theology but after four semesters he came under the influence of Husserl and changed his major field to philosophy. Upon completing his dissertation and some further advanced studies, Heidegger became Husserl's assistant until he was appointed in 1922 as an associate professor at the University of Marburg. Here, he pursued his studies in Aristotle, formulated a fresh interpretation of phenomenology, and was hard at work on a manuscript which was to become his most famous book. In order to facilitate his promotion, his Dean at Marburg urged him to publish this manuscript, and in 1927, deliberately leaving it incomplete, Heidegger hurriedly published his book with the title *Being and Time.* It was this book that became so influential as to be regarded as the fundamental source of modern existentialism. One year later, in 1928, Heidegger was chosen to be Husserl's successor to the chair of philosophy at Freiburg. He was elected Rector of the University in 1933 and for a brief period he was a member of the Nazi party. In less than a year, in 1934, he resigned as Rector and for the next ten years he taught courses critical of the Nazi interpretation of philosophy. He was drafted into the "People's Militia," having been declared in 1944 the "most expendable" member of the Freiburg faculty. The French occupying forces did not permit him to return to his teaching until 1951, one year before his retirement. Even after his retirement, he published several essays and interpretations of the history of philosophy including a two-volume study on Nietzsche (1961) and, his last work, *The Matter of Thinking* (1969). Heidegger died in 1976 in Freiburg at the age of eighty-six.

In a remarkable way, Heidegger transformed the concept of Being from a highly abstract and remote concept into a subject of intense concern to every human being. To be sure, he fashioned a new vocabulary and gave old words new meanings to convey his philosophical thought. But beneath his sometimes forbidding language one can grasp his central objective, which is to clarify our understanding of our own being, or to elucidate the meaning of Being itself. From his fresh interpretation of the concept of Being, Heidegger produced a new conception and understanding of man.

Between man and things there is this fundamental difference: only man can raise the question about his being or about Being itself. The error in traditional philosophy which Heidegger sought to correct was the tendency to think about man in the same way as we think about things. We think about things by defining them, that is, by listing their attributes or characteristics. But the essence of man cannot be accounted for by listing his attributes. Unlike the being of things, the being of man includes his awareness of his being. Unlike a hammer, which is simply a kind of being, man, says Heidegger, "always has to be (i.e. realize) his being as his own"—by which he means that man is aware of the fact that he faces the possibility of being or not being his own self. Whether one realizes or fails to realize this possibility of being one's unique self is a matter entirely of one's personal decision. In his awareness that he faces possibilities, that he must make decisions, that he might fail to realize his true self, man becomes aware not only of his own being but of Being itself. Only man, unlike things, has a relation to his own being, because only man finds himself as "thrown into the world" and as having to choose how to be. For man, being his unique self is a continuous task imposed upon him. Moreover, only man has such urgent experiences as anxiety, fear, care, and a concern about death. These and other human experiences lead a person to ask not only the limited question about his own being but also the larger question of what it means to be.

The word "man" can be deceptive, says Heidegger, because in the history of philosophy definitions of man have tended to resemble the definition of things. To think of man as, for example, Descartes did, as mind and body, placed the emphasis upon man as a combination of these two substances. As such, man was set off as a knowing subject facing a world as a known or knowable object. To view man and his relation to the world in these terms is to have a distorted view of both man and the world. Instead, Heidegger takes the lead from phenomenology and seeks to avoid defining man in terms of properties or attributes that divide man from the world. Phenomenology focuses rather upon the full texture of experience without separating it into discrete parts. Heidegger took seriously the meaning of the Greek work "phenomenon" as "that which reveals itself." What he thought he discovered by letting our human existence reveal itself was something quite different from our conventional conception of man. For this reason, Heidegger coined a new word to describe more accurately the experience of human existence: that word is *Dasein,* which in German means simply "being there." Man is best described as his unique mode of being rather than defined as an object. As Heidegger points out, "because we cannot define Dasein's essence by citing a 'what' of the kind that pertains to [an object] . . . we have chosen to designate this entity [man] as 'Dasein,' a term which is purely an expression of its being." Man as Dasein, or "being there" in the world, is a continuous being who thinks about the meaning of everything that is, not for any particular result, but because he is a "thinking, that is, a musing being." If, then, we ask what is the essence of man, the answer lies not in some attributes or properties but rather in how man exists.

The basic condition or state of man (Dasein) is his *being-in-the-world.* To these familiar words *being-in-the-world* Heidegger provides his novel analysis and interpretation by further elucidating the essential nature of Dasein (man). He asks us to think of our ordinary daily experiences which he calls "average everydayness," as the first step in discovering how we become most familiar with the world. To be in the world as Dasein is not the same as one thing being in another thing, as water is in a glass or as clothes are in a closet. Dasein, that is, man, is in the world in the sense of "dwelling upon" of "being familiar with," or "I look after something." Here the emphasis is not upon one object related in space to another object but rather upon a mode of understanding. To say, for example, that "she is *in* love" does not refer to her location but rather to her mode of being. Similarly, to say that man is in the world is not only to place him in space but to describe the structure of his existence which makes it possible for him to think meaningfully about the world.

The world is not a collection of things set over against man as though man is one kind of thing and the contents of the world another kind. Here we discover the reason Heidegger uses the word *Dasein* instead of man, even though *Dasein* represents Heidegger's new conception of man. Instead of viewing man solely as encapsulated in his body, the word *Dasein* is used to emphasize man's being as a wide "field." This wide–field dimension of man *is* the world. As Heidegger points out, "The world is not a way of characterizing those entities which Dasein essentially is not; it is rather a characteristic of Dasein itself."

To indicate how the world is a characteristic of Dasein, Heidegger describes the unique way we encounter everything in everyday experience: we encounter things as "gear," as what they are for, in short, as utensils. Take, for example, a hammer. Our first encounter with a hammer is how we use it. We use it as a utensil to accomplish some purpose. The more I hammer the less I am aware of the hammer as an object. There seems to be no distance between me and the hammer. Heidegger distinguishes between something that is "ready-to-hand" (available for its purpose) and "present-at-hand" (simply an object). Each of these ways of "seeing" the hammer is different. When the hammer is working well, we appear to be one with it. We "see" it as part of a project, fulfilling its purpose within a context of various purposes included in the project. If the hammer breaks, we "see" it in a different way, as a thing, an object. What is significant is that the same thing can be seen in two such different ways. The hammer ready-to-hand, available for a purpose, a project, is revealed as an item with a special purpose by a kind of sight which Heidegger calls "circumspection." A tool or utensil is chosen not by inspecting its properties first and then inferring its purpose from those properties. We see its purpose first. This point is fundamental in Heidegger's thought for it means that it is not the *properties* of a thing which determine whether it is a utensil, on the one hand, or an object, on the other; rather, it is Dasein's own *projection* of the context within which any item assumes its unique role that explains our different views of that item. Moreover, an item, such as a hammer, has a purpose only in relation to a project that involves several other purposes. No item possesses any properties which throw light on other purposes in the project; for example, no properties in the hammer indicate that a ladder will also be needed to hammer nails on the roof. Any particular item has meaning only as it is related to other purposes. It is this network of relations of purposes which is disclosed prior to our encounter with things as utensils and which gives us the understanding of items as being utensils; it is the essence of Dasein that it projects this network or context of purposes, and this is what it means to say that Dasein is the world. There can be different worlds even composed of the same things because of the different ways individuals project "their" world. We speak of "a woman's world" or compare the different worlds projected by our different moods.

Dasein, Heidegger's broad designation of human existence, is where the "world" takes place. Dasein possesses a threefold structure which makes possible the projection of the world. One structure is *understanding:* this is Dasein's projecting of the context of purposes and their interrelationships within which any particular thing derives its meaning. A second structure is Dasein's *mood:* our mood has a bearing upon how we will encounter our environment; in a despairing or joyful mood our projects will open up as either despairing or joyful—despairing or joyful are not mere attitudes but describe our manner of existence and the way the world exists for us. The third structure is *discourse:* only something that can be formulated in speech can be understood and become subject to our moods. Together these three structures in their interrelationship represent the essential structure of Dasein's existence.

If we ask again what it means for a human being to be, we must recall everything that has been said above about Dasein. In addition Heidegger emphasizes the element of time in human existence. We know time, he says, because we know we are going to die. Man's existence is therefore temporal. Man attempts to deny his temporality, to evade the inevitability of his limited existence. As Dasein, each person is situated here and now in the present facing future possibilities. Of his many moods, man's fundamental mood, says Heidegger, is the mood of anxiety. Anxiety arises out of man's awareness of the precarious nature of his Being. Not only is man "thrown into the world" without asking to be there, but he must constantly become his true self by making appropriate decisions. Along the way, man experiences a "fallenness," a loss of his "authentic" character. His authentic existence requires that he recognize and affirm his own unique self with his responsibility for his every action. A person's drift into an inauthentic existence is subtle but in every case it involves a tendency to escape from one's self by finding refuge in a public self, in an impersonal identity, the impersonal "one" in contrast to the concrete "I." The inauthentic person behaves as "one" is expected to instead of as "I" ought to. He reads and judges music, art, and literature as "one" is expected to; in public he suppresses any urge to be unique, to excel. He levels himself downward toward an averageness and behaves like the average "everyman." In this way, it is the "one" who is responsible for what happens to him since the "one" has taken over his decisions; there is no "one" in particular, certainly not the "I," who is answerable for anything. But a person cannot indefinitely avoid confronting his true self. Anxiety intrudes. For Heidegger, anxiety is not simply a psychological state; it is rather a mode of man's being. Nor is anxiety similar to fear. Fear has an object, a snake or an enemy against which it is possible to defend oneself. But anxiety refers to nothing, precisely to *no-thing.* Anxiety reveals the presence of "nothingness" in our being. There is no way to alter the presence of nothingness in the center of our being, the inevitability that we shall die. When a person affirms his authentic self, when he sees transparently what and who he is, he discovers that in his inauthentic existence he has been trying to do the impossible, namely, to hide the fact of his limitations and his temporality.

SARTRE

Born in 1905, Jean-Paul Sartre was the son of Jean-Batiste, a naval officer, and Anne-Marie Schweitzer, a first cousin of the theologian and jungle doctor. Sartre was educated at the École Normale Supérieure in Paris, exhibiting at an early age his precocious gift for literary expression. He was attracted to philosophy while at the École Normale by Henri Bergson whose *Essai sur les données immédiates de la conscience* left him "bowled over" and with the feeling that "philosophy is absolutely terrific, you can learn the truth through it." He spent the year 1934–35 at the Institut Français in Berlin where he studied Husserl's phenomenology. Sartre wrote his *Transcendental Ego* (1936) in Germany while at the Institut, and, as he says, "I wrote it actually under the direct influence of Husserl. . . ." It was in Berlin also that he worked on his novel *Nausea* which he considered his best work even at the end of his career. In that novel, Sartre deals with the pathological feeling one has upon experiencing through intuition the accidental and absurd nature of existence, the feeling that human existence is "contingent" and without explicit purpose. Because he could not find words adequate to describe this philosophical insight to the reader, "I had to garb it in a more romantic form, turn it into an adventure." During World War II Sartre was active in the French Resistance movement and became a German prisoner of war. While in the prisoner-of-war camp, he read Heidegger and "three times a week I explained to my priest friends Heidegger's philosophy." The notes he took on

Sartre in Cafe (*The Bettmann Archive*)

Heidegger at this time influenced Sartre very strongly and were, he says, "full of observations which later found their way into *Being and Nothingness*." For a brief period, he taught at the lycee at Havre, the lycee Henri IV, and the lycee Cordorcet, afterward resigning to devote himself exclusively to his writings which ultimately numbered over thirty volumes. As a sequel to *Being and Nothingness* (1943), Sartre wrote another major work entitled *Critique of Dialectical Reason* (1960). His last book was the three-volume work on Flaubert (*The Idiot of the Family*, 1971–72). Although Sartre was deeply influenced by Marxism and continued to be a political activist, he was never a member of the Communist party. While some commentators sought to moralize about Marxism they were not very successful, says Sartre, "because it was pretty hard to find much in Marxism to moralize about." His own criticism of Marxism was that it provided no explicit role for morality and freedom. Nor should one consider, says Sartre, "that morality is a simple superstructure, but rather that it exists at the very level of what is called infrastructure." Because of his commitment as an activist, he resisted personal acclaim, and when he was awarded the Nobel Prize in Literature in 1964, he refused to accept it on the ground that he did not want to be "transformed into an institution." While still a student at the elite École Normale Supérieure he met a fellow student, Simone de Beauvoir, with whom he enjoyed a lifelong companionship. He lived simply and with few possessions in a small apartment on the Left Bank in Paris. In declining health and virtually blind, Sartre died on April 15, 1980, at the age of seventy-four.

Existentialism   Sartre's name has become identified with existentialism primarily because he took the more technical writings of the contemporary German philosophers, especially Heidegger, who had probed into the meaning of Being through the deep recesses of man's anxious and restless soul and expressed their findings with great lucidity and popular appeal. What had appeared first in the heavy language of philosophy now came forth from Sartre's pen in the open and captivating style of novels and short stories. As a philosopher, Sartre was himself capable of writing about existentialism in the most exacting and complex style, which one finds in his massive major book *Being and Nothingness* (*L'Être et le Neant*, 1943). But his best known work is his lecture *Existentialism Is a Humanism* (*L'Existentialisme est un humanisme*), published in 1946, a work which has become famous because of its brilliance and despite Sartre's later desire to define existentialism in somewhat different terms.

Sartre's version of existentialism is the product of a special mixture of at least three contemporary modes of thought, stemming from Marx, Husserl, and Heidegger. What these three strands of thought had in common for Sartre was their concern about man's active role in forging his own destiny. Marx had expressed his passion for action when he wrote that "hitherto philosophers had merely understood the world; the point, however, is to change it." Husserl also focused his new brand of philosophy, which he called *phenomenology*, on the individual, saying that "true philosophy should seek its foundation exclusively in man and, more specifically, in the essence of his concrete worldly existence."

And Heidegger, in his great work *Being and Time* (*Sein und Zeit*), which relies somewhat upon Kierkegaard and Husserl, wrote that our basic understanding of the large question of Being is achieved best through the existential analysis of the *person*. Heidegger's analysis strongly shaped Sartre's thought, but whereas Heidegger was concerned chiefly with *Being*, and with the *existence* of the *person* only as a means for understanding Being, Sartre became preoccupied almost solely with the existence of the individual. Accordingly, Sartre's classical formulation of the basic principle of existentialism, namely, that *existence precedes essence*, is a reversal not only of Heidegger's intentions but of traditional metaphysics, which ever since Plato's time has said that essence precedes existence.

What does it mean to say that existence precedes essence, and how does this formula bear upon our understanding of human nature? Sartre argues that we cannot explain the nature of man in the same way that we describe an article of manufacture. When we consider, for example, a paper knife, we know that it has been made by someone who had in his mind a conception of it, including what it would be used for and how it would be made. Thus, even before it is made, the paper knife is already conceived of as having a definite purpose and as being the product of a definite process. If by the *essence* of the paper knife we mean the procedure by which it was made and the purposes for which it was produced, the paper knife's essence can be said to precede its existence. To look upon a paper knife is to understand exactly what its useful purpose is. When we think about man's nature, we tend to describe him also as the product of a maker, of a creator, of God. We think of God most of the time, says Sartre, as a "supernal artisan," implying that when God creates, He knows precisely what He is creating. This would mean that in the mind of God the conception of man is comparable to the conception of the paper knife in the mind of the artisan. Each individual, in this view, is the fulfillment or realization of a definite conception, which resides in God's understanding.

Although it is true that some of the philosophers of the eighteenth century, including Diderot, Voltaire, and Kant, were either atheists or else suppressed the idea of God, they nevertheless retained the notion, distinctive of the theist, that man possesses a "human nature," a nature that is found in every man. Each man, they said, is a particular example of the universal conception of Man. Whatever may be the level of development to which various men have attained, whether they be primitive natives, men in the state of nature, or cultured bourgeois, they all have the same fundamental qualities and are therefore all contained in the same definition or conception of Man. In short, they all possess the same essence, and their essence precedes their concrete or historic existence, which they confront in experience.

Sartre turned all this around by taking atheism seriously. He believed that if there is no God, there is no *given* human nature precisely because there is no God to have a conception of it. Human nature cannot be defined in advance because it is not completely thought out in advance. Man as such merely exists and only later becomes his essential self. To say that existence precedes essence means, says Sartre, that man first of all exists, confronts himself, emerges in the world and defines himself afterwards. At first, man simply is. Whether it follows that man does not have a basic and given nature simply because there is no God who stands in relation to man the way the artisan stands in relation to the knife is questionable. But what Sartre wants particularly to argue is that man is simply that which he makes of himself.

One's first reaction to this formulation of the first principle of Sartre's existentialism is that it is highly subjective, that each man can presumably set out to make of himself anything he wishes. Sartre's chief point here is that man has a greater dignity than a stone or a table. What gives him dignity is his possession of a subjective life, meaning that man is something which moves itself towards a future and is conscious that it is doing so. Sartre wants to call attention to two different modes of being, which he calls *being-in itself* (*l'en-soi*) and *being-for-itself* (*le pour-soi*). Applying this distinction to man, one can say that man shares both of these two modes of being, the *en-soi* indicating that he *is* (the way a stone is) and the *pour-soi* indicating that he is a *conscious subject* (which therefore differentiates him from a stone). To be a conscious subject is to stand constantly before a future. The most important consequence of placing existence before essence in human nature is not only that man creates himself but that man is responsible for his existence rests squarely upon each man. A stone cannot be responsible. And if man's essential nature were already given and fixed, he could not be responsible for what he is.

What began in Sartre's analysis as an amoral subjectivism now turns out to be an ethics of strict accountability based upon individual responsibility. If, that is, man is what he makes of himself, he has no one to blame for what he is except himself. Moreover, when man *chooses* in the process of making himself, he chooses not only for himself but for all men. He is therefore responsible not only for his own individuality but, says Sartre, he is responsible for all men. This last point seems to contradict the line of reasoning that Sartre has so far been developing, for to say that before one can choose a way of action he must ask, what would happen if everyone else acted so, is to assume a general human essence, which makes *my* mode of action relevant to *all* men. Sartre does in fact say that even though we create our own values and thereby create ourselves, we nevertheless create at the same time an image of our human nature as we believe it ought to be. When we choose this or that way of acting, we affirm the value of what we have chosen, and nothing can be better for any one of us unless it is better for all. This all sounds very much like Kant's categorical imperative. But Sartre does not wish to invoke any universal law to guide man's choice. He is calling attention to one of the clearest experiences of human beings, namely, that all men must choose, must make decisions and although they have no authoritative guide, they must still choose and at the same time ask whether they would be willing for others to choose the same action. One cannot escape at times the disturbing thought that he would not want others to act as he does. To say that others will not so act is a case of *self-deception*. The act of choice, then, is one that all men must accomplish with a deep sense of *anguish,* for in this act men are responsible not only for themselves but also for each other. Whoever evades his responsibility through *self-deception* will not, says Sartre, be at ease in his conscience.

Although Sartre's moral language sounds at times very much like traditional moral discourse, his intention is to carry out the rigorous implications of atheism. Sartre accepts Nietzsche's announcement that "God is dead" and takes seriously Dostoevsky's notion that "if God did not exist, everything would be permitted." In a Godless world, man's psychological condition is one of *abandonment,* a word Sartre takes from Heidegger. Abandonment means for Sartre that with the dismissal of God there also disappears every possibility of finding values in some sort of intelligible heaven. Again, there cannot now be any "good" prior to my choice since there is no infinite or perfect consciousness to think it. Man's sense of abandonment is a curious consequence of the fact that everything is indeed permitted, and as a consequence man is forlorn, for he cannot find anything on which he can rely either within or outside himself. Man is without any excuse. His existence precedes his essence. Apart from his existence there is nothingness. There is only the present. In his *Nausea,* Sartre writes that the true nature of the present was revealed as what exists, that what is not present does not exist. Things are entirely what they appear to be, and apart from them there is nothing. To say there is nothing besides the existing individual means for Sartre that there is no God, no objective system of values, no built-in essence, and, most important of all, *no determinism.* Man, says Sartre, is free; man is freedom. In a classic phrase, he says that man is *condemned* to be free. Condemned because he finds himself thrown into the world, yet free because as soon as he is conscious of himself, he is responsible for everything he does. Sartre rejects the notion that human behavior is swept up by a torrent of passion as though such a passion could be regarded as an excuse for certain actions. He rejected the Freudian analysis of human behavior because it appeared to him that it provided an excuse in the form of psychological determinism. Man is responsible even for his passions, because even his feelings are formed by his deeds. Freedom is appalling (Kierkegaard had similarly spoken of the *dizziness* of freedom) precisely because it means that there is nothing forcing me from behind, so to speak, to behave in any given way, nor is there a precise pattern luring me into the future. I am the only thing that exists. We are all free, says Sartre, therefore we must choose, that is, *invent,* because no rule of general morality can show us what we ought to do. There are no guidelines guaranteed to us in this world.

There is an element of despair in human existence, which comes, says Sartre, from the realization that we are limited to what is within the scope of our own wills. We cannot expect more from our existence than the finite probabilities it possesses. Here Sartre believes that he is touching the genuine theme of personal existence by emphasizing man's finitude and his relation to nothingness. "Nothingness," he says, "lies coiled in the heart of being, like a worm." Heidegger located the cause of human anxiety in man's awareness of his finitude when, for example, I confront death—not death in general but *my* death. It is not only man who faces nothingness, says Heidegger, but all Being has this relation to nothingness. Human finitude is therefore not simply a matter of temporary igno-rance or some shortcoming or even error. Finitude is the very structure of the human mind, and words such as *guilt, loneliness,* and *despair* describe the conse-quences of human finitude. The ultimate principle of Being, says Heidegger, is *will.* Sartre concurs by saying that only in action is there any reality. Man is only the sum of his actions and purposes; besides his actual daily life he is nothing. If a person is a coward, he *made* himself one. He is not a coward because of a cowardly heart or lungs or cerebrum, or because of his physiological organism; he is a coward because he made himself into one by his actions.

Although there is no prior essence in all men, no human *nature,* there is nevertheless, says Sartre, a universal human *condition.* He rejects a narrow indi-vidual subjectivism as the standard of truth. Rather, to discover oneself in the act of conscious thought is to discover the condition of all men. We are in a world of *intersubjectivity.* This is the kind of world in which an individual must live, choose, and decide. For this reason, no purpose chosen by any individual is ever wholly foreign to another individual. This does not mean that every purpose defines man forever but only that all men may be striving against the same limitations in the same way. For this reason, Sartre would not agree that it does not matter what we do or how we choose. Man is always obliged to act in a *situation,* that is, in relation to other persons, and consequently his actions can-not, must not, be capricious, since he must take responsibility for all his actions. Moreover, to say that man must make his essence, invent his values, does not mean that one cannot *judge* human actions. It is still possible to say that one's action was based on either error or upon self-deception, for any man who hides behind the excuse of his passions, or by espousing some doctrine of determinism deceives himself. To invent values, says Sartre, means only that there is no mean-ing or sense in life prior to acts of will. Life cannot be anything until it is lived, but each individual must make sense of it. The value of life is nothing else but the sense each person fashions into it. To argue that we are the victims of fate, of mysterious forces within us, of some grand passion, of heredity, is to be guilty of bad faith (*mauvaise foi*) or self-deception, of *inauthenticity.* A woman who con-sents to go out with a particular man knows very well, says Sartre, what the man's cherished intentions are, and she knows that sooner or later she will have to make a decision. She does not want to admit the urgency of the matter, preferring rather to interpret all his actions as discreet and respectful. She is, says Sartre, in self-deception; her actions are inauthentic. All human beings are guilty, on principle, of similar inauthenticity, of bad faith, of playing roles, of trying to disguise their actual personality behind a facade. The conclusion of Sartre's exis-tentialism is, therefore, that if man expresses his genuine humanity in all his behavior, he will never deceive himself, and honesty will then become not his ideal but rather his very being.

The Human Reality   Underlying Sartre's popular formulation of existentialism is his technical analysis of existence. In one respect, human nature is no different from any other kind of existing reality. Man is, just the same way anything else *is,* as simply *being there*. Unlike other things, however, man possesses consciousness. For this reason, he is related to the world of things and people in a variety of ways. At one level, man is conscious of "the world," which is everything that is beyond or other than himself and which therefore transcends him. At this level, the world is experienced simply as a solid, massive, undifferentiated, single something that is not yet separated into individual things.

Sartre describes this mode of consciousness in his *Nausea* where the character Roquentin is sitting on a park bench. He looks at all the things before him in the park and all at once he *sees* everything differently, everything as a single thing—"Suddenly existence had unveiled itself." Words had vanished and the points of reference which men use to give meaning to things also vanished. What Roquentin saw was existence as "the very paste of things": "The root [of the tree], the park gates, the bench, the sparse grass, all that had vanished: the diversity of things, their individuality, were only an appearance, a veneer. This veneer had melted, leaving soft, monstrous masses, all in disorder—naked." Only later, when man reflects, does the world become our familiar one. But, says Sartre, "The world of explanations and reasons is not the world of existence." At the level of Roquentin's experience, the world is the unity of all the objects of consciousness.

Sartre agrees that all consciousness is consciousness of *something*, which means that there is no consciousness without affirming the existence of an object which exists beyond, that is, transcends, itself. As we have seen, the object of consciousness can be "the world" as simply "being there." But in addition to the world as a single solid mass, we speak of specific objects like trees, benches and tables. Whenever we identify a specific object, we do this by saying what it is not—we differentiate a thing from its background. A chair appears as a chair because human beings give it that meaning by blacking out the background. What we call a chair is fashioned or drawn out of the solid context of the world by the activity of consciousness. The world of things appears as an intelligible system of separate and interrelated things only to consciousness. Without consciousness, the world simply is, it is *being-in-itself (l'en soi)* and as such it is without meaning. Consciousness constitutes the meaning of things in the world, though it does not constitute their being.

When he views the world as being-in-itself, as simply being there, Sartre says that "the essential point is contingency. I mean that by definition existence is not necessity. To exist is simply to be there." Contingency means that when something exists, it does so by chance and not because it necessarily follows from something else: "Existences appear . . . but you cannot deduce them." The world we experience is "uncreated, without reason for being, without any relation to another being; being-in-itself is gratuitous for all eternity." The meaning anything will have in the world will depend, says Sartre, upon choices men make. Even a table will have alternative meanings depending upon what a particular person chooses to use it for, to serve dinner or to write a letter. A mountain valley will mean one thing to a farmer and something else to a camper. Here, consciousness shifts a person from simply being there, being-in-itself, to *being-for-itself (le pour-soi)*, where consciousness dramatically differentiates the objects of the world from the conscious self as subject.

The activity of consciousness is at this point two-fold. First, consciousness defines the specific things in the world and invests them with meaning. Second, consciousness transcends, that is, puts a distance between itself and objects and in that way possesses a freedom from those objects. Because the conscious self has this freedom from the things in the world, it is within the power of consciousness to confer different or alternative meanings on things. The activity of consciousness is what is usually called "choice." Man chooses to undertake this project or that project and the meaning of things in the world will depend to a considerable extent upon what project a man chooses. If he chooses to be a farmer, the mountains, the valley and the impending storm will have special meanings for him, whereas if he chooses to be a camper in that valley, the surroundings and the storm will present different meanings. Man, as man, at first simply *is;* his existence is primary and precedes what he is to become. What he becomes will depend upon how his consciousness deals with the world—a world which he views from a distance. From this distance, in this position of freedom from things and persons, man makes a choice regarding how he will relate himself to them. It follows, also, that because man has this freedom from the world, the world does not, cannot, *mechanically and totally* affect man's consciousness and his choices. There is no way for man to alter the fact that he transcends the world, is able to view it, so to speak, from above and must therefore constantly make choices, take sides, undertake projects. In short, man is condemned to be free. By his free choices, man makes himself—not that he creates himself out of nothing but rather by a series of choices and decisions he converts his existence into the essence of his final self. Man possesses this freedom to create himself within some limitations such as the conditions of his birth and the circumstances of each particular situation. Nevertheless, Sartre says that any attempt on the part of a person to make excuses for his behavior by attributing his actions to external or underlying causes is self-deception and in bad faith. This strong emphasis on human freedom as worked out in *Being and Nothingness* (1943) was softened by Sartre in the sequel to that book, his *Critique of Dialectical Reason* (1960).

Although Sartre believed that Marxism is the philosophy of our time, he was aware of a striking contradiction between his existentialism and Marxist dialectical materialism. Indeed, one reason why Sartre never became a member of the Communist party is, he says, because "I would have had to turn my back on *Being and Nothingness,*" in which he had placed such a strong emphasis on human freedom. By contrast, Marxist dialectical materialism emphasized that all the structures and organizations of society and the behavior and thinking of human beings are determined by antecedent events. In this view, freedom of choice is an illusion and man is simply a vehicle through which the forces of history realize themselves. Whereas Sartre had argued that it is man's consciousness that "makes history" and confers meaning upon the world, Marxism holds that history is a process which produces the material foundations of social and economic structures, a process which therefore contains within itself the conditions and the reasons for its own development. Rather than conferring meaning upon the world, the mind, says the Marxist, discovers this meaning within the historical context as a matter of scientific knowledge.

In his earlier writings, Sartre focused primarily on the individual and his freedom. For this reason, he never would accept Freud's theory of the unconscious which Sartre saw as an irrational and mechanical causation of human behavior. Later, as in his *Critique of Dialectical Reason,* he focused more specifically upon the historical and social context in which man finds himself and which has an effect on man's behavior. He thought that Marx had succeeded more than anyone else in describing how social and economic structures develop and how they bear upon human decisions. Sartre accepted increasingly the limitations upon human choice—the limitations of birth, status in society, and family background. Earlier, he sought to describe how an individual is capable of deceiving himself by making excuses for his behavior, as if he were not free to have behaved otherwise, a form of self-deception Sartre labeled as bad faith. He never did depart from this emphasis upon the freedom of the individual. But he did adjust his thinking under the influence of Marxism by facing the fact of man's social existence, his relationship with other persons, especially as a member of a group—as, for example a labor union. Acknowledging the influence of group structures on human behavior and consciousness, resulting particularly in labor's sense of alienation, Sartre revised his optimistic view of human freedom to some extent. Recalling that he had written earlier (1945) that "no matter what the situation might be, one is always free" (giving as an example that "a worker is always free to join a union or not, as he is free to choose the kind of battle he wants to join, or not"), Sartre says this "all strikes me as absurd today" (1972). And he admits, "There is no question that there is some basic change in [my] concept of freedom." In his lengthy work on Flaubert, he concludes that although Flaubert was free to become uniquely Flaubert, his family background and his status in society meant that "he did not have all that many possibilities of becoming something else . . . he had the possibility of becoming a mediocre doctor . . . and the possibility of being Flaubert." This means, says Sartre, that social conditioning exists every minute of our lives. Nevertheless, he concludes that "I am still faithful to the notion of freedom." It is true, he says, that "you become what you are in the context of what others have made of you"; nevertheless, within these limitations man is still free and responsible. This is Sartre's way of reconciling the fact that historical conditions affect human behavior with his intuitive certainty that human beings are also capable of shaping history. In doing this, Sartre sought to overcome with his existentialism what he considered the major flaw of Marxist philosophy, namely, its failure to recognize man as a "real person."

BOOK II
PHILOSOPHICAL
PROBLEMS

ONE

ETHICS

I n countless ways, virtually every day every person is faced with the simple ethical question "What should I do?" Though this question is a simple one, the answer is not so simple. If, for example, the question takes the form "Should I tell the truth?" even the most rigorous moral philosopher might say yes but agree that there could be exceptional cases. To distinguish when one should and should not tell the truth involves further analysis of what really constitutes an ethical or moral situation. Similarly, if the question is "Should I take an easy job or develop my natural talents and gifts for a difficult profession?" this focuses upon a unique dimension of ethics, namely, upon the element of obligation, or the reason why I should or must do one thing rather than another. Ethics, then, is concerned with actions that can be called right or wrong, good or bad, desirable or undesirable, worthy or unworthy. Also, ethics is concerned with one's personal responsibility, duty, or obligation for his behavior.

As we discover in the readings which follow, theories of ethics do not try to give answers to every conceivable question of "right" and "wrong." The concern of moral philosophy is not so much with listing good actions as it is with the reasons why actions can be called "good." Moreover, we find in these selections that moral philosophers give quite different reasons for calling human actions good. If, for example, it is assumed that human nature has a specific purpose, or "end," then it follows that actions which fulfill this purpose are "good" while those which frustrate this purpose are "bad." For those who would agree that the concept of "purpose" is the key to determining what is right and wrong, a further question is whether that purpose is discoverable in man's nature or whether man's nature can be understood adequately only in relation to God. What aspect of man's nature, moreover, is most important in deciding upon the goodness of an action. Is it the action that is consistent with a rational principle, thus conforming to man's reason, that is the good act? Or, is it the action which springs spontaneously from the passions or emotions that is the good act? Or is the test for goodness to be found in the consequences of an act so that an act can be called good if it produces pleasure and bad if it produces pain?

Underlying all these questions is still another problem of ethics, namely, whether human actions are the product of forces outside the control of a person or whether a person truly has the freedom or the power to choose his actions. It would appear that there could be no moral responsibility if a person could in no way control his actions. Yet it is known that in various ways, including environment and genetic forces, behavior is influenced by means other than the "will." What we have to come to terms with is that we are constantly faced by requirements or "imperatives" to behave in certain ways as though it were obvious that we are capable of responding, or, for that matter, refusing to respond, to these requirements.

Basing Ethics on Human Nature

Aristotle (384–322 B.C.)

Every art and every inquiry, and similarly every action and pursuit, is thought to aim at some good; and for this reason the good has rightly been declared to be that at which all things aim. But a certain difference is found among ends; some are activities, others are products apart from the activities that produce them. Where there are ends apart from the actions, it is the nature of the products to be better than the activities. Now, as there are many actions, arts and sciences, their ends also are many; the end of the medical art is health, that of shipbuilding a vessel, that of strategy victory, that of economics wealth. But where such arts fall under a single capacity—as bridle-making and the other arts concerned with the equipment of horses fall under the art of riding, and this and every military action under strategy, in the same way other arts fall under yet others—in all of

From Aristotle, *Ethics*, vol. V, *The Student's Oxford Aristotle*, translated by W. D. Ross, by permission of Oxford University Press, Oxford, 1942.

these the ends of the master arts are to be preferred to all the subordinate ends; for it is for the sake of the former that the latter are pursued. It makes no difference whether the activities themselves are the ends of the actions, or something else apart from the activities, as in the case of the sciences just mentioned.

If, then, there is some end of the things we do, which we desire for its own sake (everything else being desired for the sake of this), and if we do not choose everything for the sake of something else (for at that rate the process would go on to infinity, so that our desire would be empty and vain), clearly this must be the good and the chief good. Will not the knowledge of it, then, have a great influence on life? Shall we not, like archers who have a mark to aim at, be more likely to hit upon what is right? If so, we must try, in outline at least, to determine what it is, and of which of the sciences or capacities it is the object. It would seem to belong to the most authoritative art and that which is most truly the master art. And politics appears to be of this nature; for it is this that ordains which of the sciences should be studied in a state, and which each class of citizens should learn and up to what point they should learn them; and we see even the most highly esteemed of capacities to fall under this, e.g. strategy, economics, rhetoric; now, since politics uses the rest of the sciences, and since, again, it legislates as to what we are to do and what we are to abstain from, the end of this science must include those of the others, so that this end must be the good for man. For even if the end is the same for a single man and for a state, that of the state seems at all events something greater and more complete whether to attain or to preserve; though it is worth while to attain the end merely for one man, it is finer and more godlike to attain it for a nation or for city-states. These, then, are the ends at which our inquiry aims since it is political science, in one sense of that term.

Our discussion will be adequate if it has as much clearness as the subject-matter admits of, for precision is not to be sought for alike in all discussions, any more than in all the products of the crafts. Now fine and just actions, which political science investigates, admit of much variety and fluctuation of opinion, so that they may be thought to exist only by convention, and not by nature. And goods also give rise to a similar fluctuation because they bring harm to many people; for before now men have been undone by reason of their wealth, and others by reason of their courage. We must be content, then, in speaking of such subjects and with such premises to indicate the truth roughly and in outline, and in speaking about things which are only for the most part true and with premises of the same kind to reach conclusions that are no better. In the same spirit, therefore, should each type of statement be *received;* for it is the mark of an educated man to look for precision in each class of things just so far as the nature of the subject admits; it is evidently equally foolish to accept probable reasoning from a mathematician and to demand from a rhetorician scientific proofs.

Now each man judges well the things he knows, and of these he is a good judge. And so the man who has been educated in a subject is a good judge of that subject, and the man who has received an all-round education is a good judge in general. Hence a young man is not a proper hearer of lectures on political science; for he is inexperienced in the actions that occur in life, but its discussions start from these and are about these; and, further, since he tends to follow his passions, his study will be vain and unprofitable, because the end aimed at is not knowledge but action. And it makes no difference whether he is young in years or youthful in character; the defect does not depend on time, but on his living, and pursuing each successive object, as passion directs. For to such persons, as to the incontinent, knowledge brings no profit; but to those who desire and act in accordance with a rational principle knowledge about such matters will be of great benefit. . . .

Let us resume our inquiry and state, in view of the fact that all knowledge and every pursuit aims at some good, what it is that we say political science aims at and what is the highest of all goods achievable by action. Verbally there is very general agreement; for both the general run of men and people of superior refinement say that it is happiness, and identify living well and doing well with being happy; but with regard to what happiness is they differ, and the many do not give the same account as the wise. For the former think it is some plain and obvious thing, like pleasure, wealth, or honour; they differ, however, from one another—and often even the same man identifies it with different things, with health when he is ill, with wealth when he is poor; but, conscious of their ignorance, they admire those who proclaim some great ideal that is above their comprehension. Now some thought that apart from these many goods there is another which is self-subsistent and causes the goodness of all these as well. . . .

Let us again return to the good we are seeking, and ask what it can be. It seems different in different actions and arts; it is different in medicine, in strategy, and in the other arts likewise. What then is the good of each? Surely that for whose sake everything else is done. In medicine this is health, in strategy victory, in architecture a house, in any other sphere something else, and in every action and pursuit the end; for it is for the sake of this that all men do whatever else they do. Therefore, if there is an end for all that we do, this will be the good achievable by action, and if there are more than one, these will be the goods achievable by action.

So the argument has by a different course reached the same point; but we must try to state this even more clearly. Since there are evidently more than one end, and we choose some of these (e.g. wealth, flutes, and in general instruments) for the sake of something else, clearly not all ends are final ends; but the chief good is evidently something final. Therefore, if there is only one final end, this will be what we are seeking, and if there are more than one, the most final of these will be what we are seeking. Now we call that which is in itself worthy of pursuit more final than that which is worthy of pursuit for the sake of something else, and that which is never desirable for the sake of something else more final than the things that are desirable both in themselves and for the sake of that other thing, and therefore we call final without qualification that which is always desirable in itself and never for the sake of something else.

Now such a thing happiness, above all else, is held to be; for this we choose always for itself and never for the sake of something else, but honour, pleasure, reason, and every virtue we choose indeed for themselves (for if nothing resulted from them we should still choose each of them), but we choose them also for the sake of happiness, judging that by means of them we shall be happy. Happiness, on the other hand, no one chooses for the sake of these, nor, in general, for anything other than itself.

From the point of view of self-sufficiency the same result seems to follow; for the final good is thought to be self-sufficient. Now by self-sufficient we do not mean that which is sufficient for a man by himself, for one who lives a solitary life, but also for parents, children, wife, and in general for his friends and fellow citizens, since man is born for citizenship. But some limit must be set to this; for if we extend our requirement to ancestors and descendants and friends' friends we are in for an infinite series. Let us examine this question, however, on another occasion; the self-sufficient we now define as that which when isolated makes life desirable and lacking in nothing; and such we think happiness to be; and further we think it most desirable of all things, without being counted as one good thing among others—if it were so counted it would clearly be made more desirable by the addition of even the least of goods; for that which is added becomes an excess of goods, and of goods the greater is always more desirable. Happiness, then, is something final and self-sufficient, and is the end of action.

Presumably, however, to say that happiness is the chief good seems a platitude, and a clearer account of what it is is still desired. This might perhaps be given, if we could first ascertain the function of man. For just as for a fluteplayer, a sculptor, or any artist, and, in general, for all things that have a function or activity, the good and the 'well' is thought to reside in the function, so would it seem to be for man, if he has a function. Have the carpenter, then, and the tanner certain functions or activities, and has man none? Is he born without a function? Or as eye, hand, foot, and in general each of the parts evidently has a function, may one lay it down that man similarly has a function apart from all these? What then can this be? Life seems to be common even to plants, but we are seeking what is peculiar to man. Let us exclude, therefore, the life of nutrition and growth. Next there would be a life of perception, but *it* also seems to be common even to the horse, the ox, and every animal. There remains, then, an active life of the element that has a rational principle; of this, one part has such a principle in the sense of being obedient to one, the other in the sense of possessing one and exercising thought. And, as 'life of the rational element' also has two meanings, we must state that life in the sense of activity is what we mean; for this seems to be the more proper sense of the term. Now if the function of man is an activity of soul which follows or implies a rational principle, and if we say 'a so-and-so' and 'a good so-and-so' have a function which is the same in kind, e.g. a lyre-player and a good lyre-player, and so without qualification in all cases, eminence in respect of goodness being added to the name of the function (for the function of a lyre-player is to play the lyre, and that of a good lyre-player is to do so well): if this is the case, [and we state the function of man to be a certain kind of life, and this to be an activity or actions of the soul implying a rational principle, and the function of a good man to be the good and noble performance of these, and if any action is well performed when it is performed in accordance with the appropriate excellence: if this is the case,] human good turns out to be activity of soul in accordance with virtue, and if there are more than one virtue, in accordance with the best and most complete.

But we must add 'in a complete life'. For one swallow does not make a summer, nor does one day; and so too one day, or a short time, does not make a man blessed and happy. . . .

Since happiness is an activity of soul in accordance with perfect virtue, we must consider the nature of virtue; for perhaps we shall thus see better the nature of happiness. The true student of politics, too, is thought to have studied virtue above all things; for he wishes to make his fellow citizens good and obedient to the laws. As an example of this we have the lawgivers of the Cretans and the Spartans, and any others of the kind that there may have been. And if this inquiry belongs to political science, clearly the pursuit of it will be in accordance with our original plan. But clearly the virtue we must study is human virtue; for the good we were seeking was human good and the happiness human happiness. By human virtue we mean not that of the body but that of the soul; and happiness also we call an activity of soul. But if this is so, clearly the student of politics must know somehow the facts about soul, as the man who is to heal the eyes of the body as a whole must know about the eyes or the body; and all the more since politics is more prized and better than medicine; but even among doctors the best educated spend much labour on acquiring knowledge of the body. The student of politics, then, must study the soul, and must study it with these objects in view, and do so just to the extent which is sufficient for the questions we are discussing; for further precision is perhaps something more laborious than our purposes require.

Some things are said about it, adequately enough, even in the discussions outside our school, and we must use these; e.g. that one element in the soul is irrational and one has a rational principle. Whether these are separated as the parts of the body or of anything divisible are, or are distinct by definition but by nature inseparable, like convex and concave in the circumference of a circle, does not affect the present question.

Of the irrational element one division seems to be widely distributed, and vegetative in its nature, I mean that which causes nutrition and growth; for it is this kind of power of the soul that one must assign to all nurslings and embryos, and this same power to full-grown creatures; this is more reasonable than to assign some different power to them. Now the excellence of this seems to be common to all species and not specifically human; for this part or faculty seems to function most in sleep, while goodness and badness are least manifest in sleep (whence comes the saying that the happy are no better off than the wretched for half their lives; and this happens naturally enough, since sleep is an inactivity of the soul in that respect in which it is called good or bad), unless perhaps to a small extent some of the movements actually penetrate to the soul, and in this respect the dreams of good men are better than those of ordinary people. Enough of this subject, however; let us leave the nutritive faculty alone, since it has by its nature no share in human excellence.

There seems to be also another irrational element in the soul—one which in a sense, however, shares in a rational principle. For we praise the rational principle of the continent man and of the incontinent, and the part of their soul that has such a principle, since it urges them aright and towards the best objects; but there is found in them also another element naturally opposed to the rational principle, which fights against and resists that principle. For exactly as paralysed limbs when we intend to move them to the right turn on the contrary to the left, so is it with the soul; the impulses of incontinent people move in contrary directions. But while in the body we see that which moves astray, in the soul we do not. No doubt, however, we must none the less suppose that in the soul too there is something contrary to the rational principle, resisting and opposing it. In what sense it is distinct from the other elements does not concern us. Now even this seems to have a share in a rational principle, as we said; at any rate in the continent man it obeys the rational principle—and presumably in the temperate and brave man it is still more obedient; for in him it speaks, on all matters, with the same voice as the rational principle. . . .

Virtue, then, being of two kinds, intellectual and moral, intellectual virtue in the main owes both its birth and its growth to teaching (for which reason it requires experience and time), while moral virtue comes about as a result of habit, whence also its name is one that is formed by a slight variation from the habit. From this it is also plain that none of the moral virtues arises in us by nature; for nothing that exists by nature can form a habit contrary to its nature. For instance the stone which by nature moves downwards cannot be habituated to move upwards, not even if one tries to train it by throwing it up ten thousand times; nor can fire be habituated to move downwards, nor can anything else that by nature behaves in one way be trained to behave in another. Neither by nature, then, nor contrary to nature do the virtues arise in us; rather we are adapted by nature to receive them, and are made perfect by habit.

Again, of all the things that come to us by nature we first acquire the potentiality and later exhibit the activity (this is plain in the case of senses; for it was not by often seeing or often hearing that we got these senses, but on the contrary we had them before we used them, and did not come to have them by using them); but the virtues we get by first exercising them, as also happens in the case of the arts as well. For the things we have to learn before we can do them, we learn by doing them, e.g. men become builders by building and lyre-players by playing the lyre; so too we become just by doing just acts, temperate by doing temperate acts, brave by doing brave acts. . . .

Again, it is from the same causes and by the same means that every virtue is both produced and destroyed, and similarly every art; for it is from playing the lyre that both good and bad lyre-players are produced. And the corresponding statement is true of builders and of all the rest; men will be good or bad builders as a result of building well or badly. For if this were not so, there would have been no need of a teacher, but all men would have been born good or bad at their craft. This, then, is the case with the virtues also; by doing the acts that we do in our transactions with other men we become just or unjust, and by doing the acts that we do in the presence of danger, and being habituated to feel fear or confidence, we become brave or cowardly. The same is true of appetites and feelings of anger; some men become temperate and good-tempered, others self-indulgent and irascible, by behaving in one way or the other in the appropriate circumstances. Thus, in one word, states of character arise out of like activities. This is why the activities we exhibit must be of a certain kind; it is because the states of character correspond to the differences between these. It makes no small difference, then, whether we form habits of one kind or of another from our very youth; it makes a very great difference, or rather *all* the difference. . . .

Virtue, then, is a state of character concerned with choice, lying in a mean, i.e. the mean relative to us, this being determined by a rational principle, and by that principle by which the man of practical wisdom would determine it. Now it is a mean between two vices, that which depends on excess and that which depends on defect; and again it is a mean because the vices respectively fall short of or exceed what is right in both passions and actions, while virtue both finds and chooses that which is intermediate. Hence in respect of its substance and the definition which states its essence virtue is a mean, with regard to what is best and right an extreme.

But not every action nor every passion admits of a mean; for some have names that already imply badness, e.g. spite, shamelessness, envy, and in the case of actions adultery, theft, murder; for all of these and suchlike things imply by their names that they are themselves bad, and not the excesses or deficiencies of them. It is not possible, then, ever to be right with regard to them; one must always be wrong. Nor does goodness or badness with regard to such things depend on committing adultery with the right woman, at the right time, and in the right way, but simply to do any of them is to go wrong. It would be equally absurd, then, to expect that in unjust, cowardly, and voluptuous action there should be a mean, an excess, and a deficiency; for at that rate there would be a mean of excess and deficiency, an excess of excess, and a deficiency of deficiency. But as there is no excess and deficiency of temperance and courage because what is intermediate is in a sense an extreme, so too of the actions we have mentioned there is no mean nor any excess and deficiency, but however they are done they are wrong; for in general there is neither a mean of excess and deficiency, nor excess and deficiency of a mean.

We must, however, not only make this general statement, but also apply it to the individual facts. For among statements about conduct those which are general apply more widely, but those which are particular are more genuine, since conduct has to do with individual cases, and our statements must harmonize with the facts in these cases. We may take these cases from our table. With regard to feelings of fear and confidence courage is the mean; of the people who exceed, he who exceeds in fearlessness has no name (many of the states have no name), while the man who exceeds in confidence is rash, and he who exceeds in fear and falls short in confidence is a coward. With regard to pleasures and pains—not all of them, and not so much with regard to the pains—the mean is temperance, the excess self-indulgence. Persons deficient with regard to the pleasures are not often found; hence such persons also have received no name. But let us call them 'insensible'.

With regard to giving and taking of money the mean is liberality, the excess and the defect prodigality and meanness. In these actions people exceed and fall short in contrary ways; the prodigal exceeds in spending and falls short in taking, while the mean man exceeds in taking and falls short in spending. (At present we are giving a mere outline or summary, and are satisfied with this; later these states will be more exactly determined.) With regard to money there are also other dispositions—a mean, magnificence (for the magnificent man differs from the liberal man; the former deals with large sums, the latter with small ones), an excess, tastelessness and vulgarity, and a deficiency, niggardliness; these differ from the states opposed to liberality, and the mode of their difference will be stated later.

With regard to honour and dishonour the mean is proper pride, the excess is known as a sort of 'empty vanity', and the deficiency is undue humility; and as we said liberality was related to magnificence, differing from it by dealing with small sums, so there is a state similarly related to proper pride, being concerned with small honours while that is concerned with great. For it is possible to desire honour as one ought, and more than one ought, and less, and the man who exceeds in his desires is called ambitious, the man who falls short unambitious, while the intermediate person has no name. The dispositions also are nameless, except that that of the ambitious man is called ambition. Hence the people who are at the extremes lay claim to the middle place; and we ourselves sometimes call the intermediate person ambitious and sometimes unambitious, and sometimes praise the ambitious man and sometimes the unambitious. The reason of our doing this will be stated in what follows; but now let us speak of the remaining states according to the method which has been indicated.

With regard to anger also there is an excess, a deficiency, and a mean. Although they can scarcely be said to have names, yet since we call the intermediate person good-tempered let us call the mean good temper; of the persons at the extremes let the one who exceeds be called irascible, and his vice irascibility, and the man who falls short an inirascible sort of person, and the deficiency inirascibility. . . .

The origin of action—its efficient, not its final cause—is choice, and that of *choice* is desire and reasoning with a view to an end. This is why choice cannot exist either without reason and intellect or without a moral state; for good action and its opposite cannot exist without a combination of intellect and character. Intellect itself, however, moves nothing, but only the intellect which aims at an end and is practical; for this rules the productive intellect as well, since every one who makes makes for an end, and that which is made is not an end in the unqualified sense (but only an end in a particular relation, and the end of a particular operation)—only that which is *done* is that; for good action is an end, and desire aims at this. Hence choice is either desiderative or ratiocinative desire, and such an origin of action is a man. (It is to be noted that nothing that is past is an object of choice, e.g. no one chooses to have sacked Troy; for no one *deliberates* about the past, but about what is future and capable of being otherwise, while what is past is not capable of not having taken place. . . .)

If happiness is activity in accordance with virtue, it is reasonable that it should be in accordance with the highest virtue; and this will be that of the best thing in us. Whether it be reason or something else that is this element which is thought to be our natural ruler and guide and to take thought of things noble and divine, whether it be itself also divine or only the most divine element in us, the activity of this in accordance with its proper virtue will be perfect happiness. That this activity is contemplative we have already said.

Now this would seem to be in agreement both with what we said before and with the truth. For, firstly, this activity is the best (since not only is reason the best thing in us, but the objects of reason are the best of knowable objects); and, secondly, it is the most continuous, since we can contemplate truth more continuously than we can *do* anything. And we think happiness has pleasure mingled with it, but the activity of philosophic wisdom is admittedly the pleasantest of virtuous activities; at all events the pursuit of it is thought to offer pleasures marvellous for their purity and their enduringness, and it is to be expected that those who know will pass their time more pleasantly than those who inquire. And the self-sufficiency that is spoken of must belong most to the contemplative activity. For while a philosopher, as well as a just man or one possessing any other virtue, needs the necessaries of life, when they are sufficiently equipped with things of that sort the just man needs people towards whom and with whom he shall act justly, and the temperate man, the brave man, and each of the others is in the same case, but the philosopher, even when by himself, can contemplate truth, and the better the wiser he is; he can perhaps do so better if he has fellow-workers, but still he is the most self-sufficient. And this activity alone would seem to be loved for its own sake; for nothing arises from it apart from the contemplating, while from practical activities we gain more or less apart from the action. And happiness is thought to depend on leisure; for we are busy that we may have leisure, and make war that we may live in peace. Now the activity of the practical virtues is exhibited in political or military affairs, but the actions concerned with these seem to be unleisurely. Warlike actions are completely so (for no one chooses to be at war, or provokes war, for the sake of being at war; any one would seem absolutely murderous if he were to make enemies of his friends in order to bring about battle and slaughter); but the action of the statesman is also unleisurely, and—apart from the political action itself—aims at despotic power and honours, or at all events happiness, for him and his fellow citizens—a happiness different from political action, and evidently sought as being different. So if among virtuous actions political and military actions are distinguished by nobility and greatness, and these are unleisurely and aim at an end and are not desirable for their own sake, but the activity of reason, which is contemplative, seems both to be superior in serious worth and to aim at no end beyond itself, and to have its pleasure proper to itself (and this augments the activity), and the self-sufficiency, leisureliness, unweariedness (so far as this is possible for man), and all the other attributes ascribed to the supremely happy man are evidently those connected with this activity, it follows that this will be the complete happiness of man, if it be allowed a complete term of life (for none of the attributes of happiness is *in*complete).

But such a life would be too high for man; for it is not in so far as he is man that he will live so, but in so far as something divine is present in him; and by so much as this is superior to our composite nature is its activity superior to that which is the exercise of the other kind of virtue. If reason is divine, then, in comparison with man, the life according to it is divine in comparison with human life. But we must not follow those who advise us, being men, to think of human things, and, being mortal, of mortal things, but must, so far as we can, make ourselves immortal, and strain every nerve to live in accordance with the best thing in us; for even if it be small in bulk, much more does it in power and worth surpass everything. This would seem, too, to be each man himself, since it is the authoritative and better part of him. It would be strange, then, if he were to choose not the life of his self but that of something else. And what we said before will apply now; that which is proper to each thing is by nature best and most pleasant for each thing; for man, therefore, the life according to reason is best and pleasantest, since reason more than anything else *is* man. This life therefore is also the happiest.

2

Stoic Doctrine of Acquiescence

Epictetus (A.D. 60–117)

Of our faculties in general you will find that none can take cognizance of itself; none therefore has the power to approve or disapprove its own action. Our grammatical faculty for instance: how far can that take cognizance? Only so far as to distinguish expression. Our musical faculty? Only so far as to distinguish tune. Does any one of these then take cognizance of itself? By no means. If you are writing to your friend, when you want to know what words to write grammar will tell you; but whether you should write to your friend or should not write grammar will not tell you. And in the same way music will tell you about tunes, but whether at this precise moment you should sing and play the lyre or should not sing nor play the lyre it will not tell you. What will tell you then? That faculty which takes cognizance of itself and of all things else. What is this? The reasoning

From *Epictetus: The Discourses and Manual,* translated by P. E. Matheson (1916), by permission of Oxford University Press.

faculty: for this alone of the faculties we have received is created to comprehend even its own nature; that is to say, what it is and what it can do, and with what precious qualities it has come to us, and to comprehend all other faculties as well. For what else is it that tells us that gold is a goodly thing? For the gold does not tell us. Clearly it is the faculty which can deal with our impressions. What else is it which distinguishes the faculties of music, grammar, and the rest, testing their uses and pointing out the due seasons for their use? It is reason and nothing else.

The gods then, as was but right, put in our hands the one blessing that is best of all and master of all, that and nothing else, the power to deal rightly with our impressons, but everything else they did not put in our hands. Was it that they would not? For my part I think that if they could have entrusted us with those other powers as well they would have done so, but they were quite unable. Prisoners on the earth and in an earthly body and among earthly companions, how was it possible that we should not be hindered from the attainment of these powers by these external fetters?

But what says Zeus? "Epictetus, if it were possible I would have made your body and your possessions (those trifles that you prize) free and untrammelled. But as things are—never forget this—this body is not yours, it is but a clever mixture of clay. But since I could not make it free, I gave you a portion in our divinity, this faculty of impulse to act and not to act, of will to get and will to avoid, in a word the faculty which can turn impressions to right use. If you pay heed to this, and put your affairs in its keeping, you will never suffer let nor hindrance, you will not groan, you will blame no man, you will flatter none. What then? Does all this seem but little to you?"

Heaven forbid!

"Are you content then?"

So surely as I hope for the gods' favour.

But, as things are, though we have it in our power to pay heed to one thing and to devote ourselves to one, yet instead of this we prefer to pay heed to many things and to be bound fast to many—our body, our property, brother and friend, child and slave. Inasmuch then as we are bound fast to many things, we are burdened by them and dragged down. That is why, if the weather is bad for sailing, we sit distracted and keep looking continually and ask, "What wind is blowing?" "The north wind." What have we to do with that? "When will the west wind blow?" When it so chooses, good sir, or when Aeolus chooses. For God made Aeolus the master of the winds, not you. What follows? We must make the best of those things that are in our power, and take the rest as nature gives it. What do you mean by "nature"? I mean, God's will.

"What? Am I to be beheaded now, and I alone?"

Why? Would you have had all beheaded, to give you consolation? Will you not stretch out your neck as Lateranus did in Rome when Nero ordered his beheadal? For he stretched out his neck and took the blow, and when the blow dealt him was too weak he shrank up a little and then stretched it out again. Nay more, on a previous occasion, when Nero's freedman Epaphroditus came to him and asked him the cause of his offence, he answered, "If I want to say anything, I will say it to your master."

What then must a man have ready to help him in such emergencies? Surely this: he must ask himself, "What is mine, and what is not mine? What may I do, what may I not do?"

I must die. But must I die groaning? I must be imprisoned. But must I whine as well? I must suffer exile. Can any one then hinder me from going with a smile, and a good courage, and at peace?

"Tell the secret!"

I refuse to tell, for this is in my power.

"But I will chain you."

What say you, fellow? Chain me? My leg you will chain—yes, but my will—no, not even Zeus can conquer that.

"I will imprison you."

My bit of a body, you mean.

"I will behead you."

Why? When did I ever tell you that I was the only man in the world that could not be beheaded?

These are the thoughts that those who pursue philosophy should ponder, these are the lessons they should write down day by day, in these they should exercise themselves.

Thrasea used to say "I had rather be killed to-day than exiled tomorrow". What then did Rufus say to him? "If you choose it as the harder, what is the meaning of your foolish choice? If as the easier, who has given you the easier? Will you not study to be content with what is given you?"

It was in this spirit that Agrippinus used to say—do you know what? "I will not stand in my own way!" News was brought him, "Your trial is on in the Senate!" "Good luck to it, but the fifth hour is come"—this was the hour when he used to take his exercise and have a cold bath—"let us go and take exercise." When he had taken his exercise they came and told him, "You are condemned." "Exile or death?" he asked. "Exile." "And my property?" "It is not confiscated." "Well then, let us go to Aricia and dine."

Here you see the result of training as training should be, of the will to get and will to avoid, so disciplined that nothing can hinder or frustrate them. I must die, must I? If at once, then I am dying: if soon, I dine now, as it is time for dinner, and afterwards when the time comes I will die. And die how? As befits one who gives back what is not his own.

3

The Categorical Imperative

Immanuel Kant (1724–1804)

Nothing can possibly be conceived in the world, or even out of it, which can be called good, without qualification, except a Good Will. Intelligence, wit, judgment, and the other *talents* of the mind, however they may be named, or courage, resolution, perseverance, as qualities of temperament, are undoubtedly good and desirable in many respects; but these gifts of nature may also become extremely bad and mischievous if the will which is to make use of them, and which, therefore, constitutes what is called *character*, is not good. It is the same with the *gifts* of fortune. Power, riches, honor, even health, and the general well-being and contentment with one's condition which is called happiness, inspire pride, and often presumption, if there is not a good will to correct the influence of these on

---

From Immanuel Kant, "Fundamental Principles of the Metaphysics of Morals," in *Kant's Critique of Practical Reason and Other Works on the Theory of Ethics,* translated by T. K. Abbott, Longmans, Green and Co., Ltd., London, 1909.

the mind, and with this also to rectify the whole principle of acting, and adapt it to its end. The sight of a being who is not adorned with a single feature of a pure and good will, enjoying unbroken prosperity, can never give pleasure to an impartial rational spectator. Thus a good will appears to constitute the indispensable condition even of being worthy of happiness.

There are even some qualities which are of service to this good will itself, and may facilitate its action, yet which have no intrinsic unconditional value, but always presuppose a good will, and this qualifies the esteem that we justly have for them, and does not permit us to regard them as absolutely good. Moderation in the affections and passions, self-control, and calm deliberation are not only good in many respects, but even seem to constitute part of the intrinsic worth of the person; but they are far from deserving to be called good without qualification, although they have been so unconditionally praised by the ancients. For without the principles of a good will, they may become extremely bad; and the coolness of a villain not only makes him far more dangerous, but also directly makes him more abominable in our eyes than he would have been without it.

A good will is good not because of what it performs or effects, not by its aptness for the attainment of some proposed end, but simply by virtue of the volition, that is, it is good in itself, and considered by itself is to be esteemed much higher than all that can be brought about by it in favor of any inclination, nay, even of the sum-total of all inclinations. Even if it should happen that, owing to special disfavor of fortune, or the niggardly provision of a step-motherly nature, this will should wholly lack power to accomplish its purpose, if with its greatest efforts it should yet achieve nothing, and there should remain only the good will (not, to be sure, a mere wish, but the summoning of all means in our power), then, like a jewel, it would still shine by its own light, as a thing which has its whole value in itself. Its usefulness or fruitlessness can neither add to nor take away anything from this value. It would be, as it were, only the setting to enable us to handle it the more conveniently in common commerce, or to attract to it the attention of those who are not yet connoisseurs, but not to recommend it to true connoisseurs, or to determine its value.

There is, however, something so strange in this idea of the absolute value of the mere will, in which no account is taken of its utility, that notwithstanding the thorough assent of even common reason to the idea, yet a suspicion must arise that it may perhaps really be the product of mere high-flown fancy, and that we may have misunderstood the purpose of nature in assigning reason as the governor of our will. . . .

For as reason is not competent to guide the will with certainty in regard to its objects and the satisfaction of all our wants (which it to some extent even multiplies), this being an end to which an implanted instinct would have led with much greater certainty; and since, nevertheless, reason is imparted to us as a practical faculty, i.e. as one which is to have influence on the *will*, therefore, admitting that nature generally in the distribution of her capacities has adapted the means to the end, its true destination must be to produce a *will*, not merely good as a *means* to something else, but *good in itself*, for which reason was absolutely necessary. This will then, though not indeed the sole and complete good, must be the supreme good and the condition of every other, even of the desire of happiness. Under these circumstances, there is nothing inconsistent with the wisdom of nature in the fact that the cultivation of the reason, which is requisite for the first and unconditional purpose, does in many ways interfere, at least in this life, with the attainment of the second, which is always conditional, namely happiness. Nay, it may even reduce it to nothing, without nature thereby failing of her purpose. For reason recognizes the establishment of a good will as its highest practical destination, and in attaining this purpose is capable only of a satisfaction of its own proper kind, namely, that from the attainment of an end, which end again is determined by reason only, notwithstanding that this may involve many a disappointment to the ends of inclination. . . .

I omit here all actions which are already recognized as inconsistent with duty, although they may be useful for this or that purpose, for with these the question whether they are done *from duty* cannot arise at all, since they even conflict with it. I also set aside those actions which really conform to duty, but to which men have *no* direct *inclination*, performing them because they are impelled thereto by some other inclination. For in this case we can readily distinguish whether the action which agrees with duty is done *from duty* or from a selfish view. It is much harder to make this distinction when the action accords with duty, and the subject has besides a *direct* inclination to it. For example, it is always a matter of duty that a dealer should not overcharge an inexperienced purchaser; and wherever there is much commerce the prudent tradesman does not overcharge, but keeps a fixed price for everyone, so that a child buys of him as well as any other. Men are thus *honestly* served; but this is not enough to make us believe that the tradesman has so acted from duty and from principles of honesty; his own advantage required it; it is out of the question in this case to suppose that he might besides have a direct inclination in favor of the buyers, so that, as it were, from love he should give no advantage to one over another. Accordingly the action was done neither from duty nor from direct inclination, but merely with a selfish view.

On the other hand, it is a duty to maintain one's life; and, in addition, everyone has also a direct inclination to do so. But on this account the often anxious care which most men take for it has no intrinsic worth, and their maxim has no moral import. They preserve their life *as duty requires*, no doubt, but not *because duty requires*. On the other hand, if adversity and hopeless sorrow have completely taken away the relish for life; if the unfortunate one, strong in mind, indignant at his fate rather than desponding or dejected, wishes for death, and yet preserves his life without loving it—not from inclination or fear, but from duty—then his maxim has a moral worth.

To be beneficent when we can is a duty; and besides this, there are many minds so sympathetically constituted that, without any other motive of vanity or self-interest, they find a pleasure in spreading joy around them, and can take delight in the satisfaction of others so far as it is their own work. But I maintain that in such a case an action of this kind, however proper, however amiable it may be, has nevertheless no true moral worth, but is on a level with other inclinations, e.g. the inclination to honor, which, if it is happily directed to that which is in fact of public utility and accordant with duty, and consequently honourable, deserves praise and encouragement, but not esteem. For the maxim lacks the moral import, namely, that such actions be done *from duty,* not from inclination. Put the case that the mind of that philanthropist was clouded by sorrow of his own, extinguishing all sympathy with the lot of others, and that while he still has the power to benefit others in distress, he is not touched by their trouble because he is absorbed with his own; and now suppose that he tears himself out of this dead insensibility, and performs the action without any inclination to it, but simply from duty, then first has his action its genuine moral worth. Further still, if nature has put little sympathy in the heart of this or that man, if he, supposed to be an upright man, is by temperament cold and indifferent to the sufferings of others, perhaps because in respect of his own he is provided with the special gift of patience and fortitude, and supposes, or even requires, that others should have the same—and such a man would certainly not be the meanest product of nature—but if nature had not specially framed him for a philanthropist, would he not still find in himself a source from whence to give himself a far higher worth than that of a good-natured temperament could be? Unquestionably. It is just in this that the moral worth of the character is brought out which is incomparably the highest of all, namely, that he is beneficent, not from inclination, but from duty.

To secure one's own happiness is a duty, at least indirectly; for discontent with one's condition, under a pressure of many anxieties and amidst unsatisfied wants, might easily become a great *temptation to transgression of duty.* But here again, without looking to duty, all men have already the strongest and most intimate inclination to happiness, because it is just in this idea that all inclinations are combined in one total. But the precept of happiness is often of such a sort that it greatly interferes with some inclinations, and yet a man cannot form any definite and certain conception of the sum of satisfaction of all of them which is called happiness. It is not then to be wondered at that a single inclination, definite both as to what it promises and as to the time within which it can be gratified, is often able to overcome such a fluctuating idea, and that a gouty patient, for instance, can choose to enjoy what he likes, and to suffer what he may, since, according to his calculation, on this occasion at least, he has (only) not sacrificed the enjoyment of the present moment to a possibly mistaken expectation of a happiness which is supposed to be found in health. But even in this case, if the general desire for happiness did not influence his will, and supposing that in his particular case health was not a necessary element in this calculation, there yet remains in this, as in all other cases, this law, namely, that he should promote his happiness not from inclination but from duty, and by this would his conduct first acquire true moral worth.

It is in this manner, undoubtedly, that we are to understand those passages of Scripture also in which we are commanded to love our neighbor, even our enemy. For love, as an affection, cannot be commanded, but beneficence for duty's sake may; even though we are not impelled to it by any inclination—nay, are even repelled by a natural and unconquerable aversion. This is *practical* love, and not *pathological*—a love which is seated in the will, and not in the propensions of sense—in principles of action and not of tender sympathy; and it is this love alone which can be commanded.

The second proposition is: That an action done from duty derives its moral worth, *not from the purpose* which is to be attained by it, but from the maxim by which it is determined, and therefore does not depend on the realization of the object of the action, but merely on the *principle of volition* by which the action has taken place, without regard to any object of desire. It is clear from what precedes that the purposes which we may have in view in our actions, or their effects regarded as ends and springs of the will, cannot give to actions any unconditional or moral worth. In what, then, can their worth lie, if it is not to consist in the will and in reference to its expected effect? It cannot lie anywhere but in the *principle of the will* without regard to the ends which can be attained by the action. For the will stands between its *a priori* principle, which is formal, and its *a posteriori* spring, which is material, as between two roads, and as it must be determined by something, it follows that it must be determined by the formal principle of volition when an action is done from duty, in which case every material principle has been withdrawn from it.

The third proposition, which is a consequence of the two preceding, I would express thus: *Duty is the necessity of acting from respect for the law.* I may have *inclination* for an object as the effect of my proposed action, but I cannot have *respect* for it, just for this reason, that it is an effect and not an energy of will. Similarly, I cannot have respect for inclination, whether my own or another's; I can at most, if my own, approve it; if another's, sometimes even love it, i.e. look on it as favorable to my own interest. It is only what is connected with my will as a principle, by no means as an effect—what does not subserve my inclination, but overpowers it, or at least in case of choice excludes it from its calculation—in other words, simply the law of itself, which can be an object of respect, and hence a command. Now an action done from duty must wholly exclude the influence of inclination, and with it every object of the will, so that nothing remains which can determine the will except objectively the *law*, and subjectively *pure respect* for this practical law, and consequently the maxim that I should follow this law even to the thwarting of all my inclinations.

Thus the moral worth of an action does not lie in the effect expected from it, nor in any principle of action which requires to borrow its motive from this expected effect. For all these effects—agreeableness of one's condition, and even the promotion of the happiness of others—could have been also brought about by other causes, so that for this there would have been no need of the will of a rational being; whereas it is in this alone that the supreme and unconditional good can be found. The preeminent good which we call moral can therefore consist in nothing else than *the conception of law* in itself, *which certainly is only possible in a rational being,* in so far as this conception, and not the expected effect, determines the will. This is a good which is already present in the person who acts accordingly, and we have not to wait for it to appear first in the result.

But what sort of law can that be, the conception of which must determine the will, even without paying any regard to the effect expected from it, in order that this will may be called good absolutely and without qualifications? As I have deprived the will of every impulse which could arise to it from obedience to any law, there remains nothing but the universal conformity of its actions to law in general, which alone is to serve the will as a principle, i.e. I am never to act otherwise than *so that I could also will that my maxim should become a univer-sal law.* Here, now, it is the simple conformity to law in general, without assum-ing any particular law applicable to certain actions, that serves the will as its principle, and must so serve it, if duty is not to be a vain delusion and a chime-rical notion. The common reason of men in its practical judgments perfectly coincides with this, and always has in view the principle here suggested. Let the question be, for example: May I when in distress make a promise with the intention not to keep it? I readily distinguish here between the two significations which the question may have: whether it is prudent, or whether it is right, to make a false promise? The former may undoubtedly often be the case. I see clearly indeed that it is not enough to extricate myself from a present difficulty by means of this subterfuge, but it must be well considered whether there may not hereafter spring from this lie much greater inconvenience than that from which I now free myself, and as, with all my supposed *cunning,* the conse-quences cannot be so easily foreseen but that credit once lost may be much more injurious to me than any mischief which I seek to avoid at present, it should be considered whether it would not be more *prudent* to act herein according to a universal maxim, and to make it a habit to promise nothing except with the intention of keeping it. But it is soon clear to me that such a maxim will still only be based on the fear of consequences. Now it is a wholly different thing to be truthful from duty, and to be so from apprehension of injurious consequences. In the first case, the very notion of the action already implies a law for me; in the second case, I must first look about elsewhere to see what results may be com-bined with it which would affect myself. For to deviate from the principle of duty is beyond all doubt wicked; but to be unfaithful to my maxim of prudence may often be very advantageous to me, although to abide by it is certainly safer. The shortest way, however, and an unerring one, to discover the answer to this question whether a lying promise is consistent with duty, is to ask myself, Should I be content that my maxim (to extricate myself from difficulty by a false prom-ise) should hold good as a universal law, for myself as well as for others? and should I be able to say to myself, "Every one may make a deceitful promise when he finds himself in a difficulty from which he cannot otherwise extricate him-self"? Then I presently become aware that, while I can will the lie, I can by no means will that lying should be a universal law. For with such a law there would be no promises at all, since it would be in vain to allege my intention in regard to my future actions to those who would not believe this allegation, or if they over-hastily did so, would pay me back in my own coin. Hence my maxim, as soon as it should be made a universal law, would necessarily destroy itself.

I do not, therefore, need any far-reaching penetration to discern what I have to do in order that my will may be morally good. Inexperienced in the course of the world, incapable of being prepared for all its contingencies, I only ask myself: Canst thou also will that thy maxim should be a universal law? If not, then it must be rejected, and that not because of a disadvantage accruing from it to myself or even to others, but because it cannot enter as a principle into a possible universal legislation, and reason extorts from me immediate respect for such legislation. I do not indeed as yet *discern* on what this respect is based (this the philosopher may inquire), but at least I understand this, that it is an estimation of the worth which far outweighs all worth of what is recommended by inclination, and that the necessity of acting from *pure* respect for the practical law is what constitutes duty, to which every other motive must give place because it is the condition of a will being good *in itself,* and the worth of such a will is above everything. . . .

Nor could anything be more fatal to morality than that we should wish to derive it from examples. For every example of it that is set before me must be first itself tested by principles of morality, whether it is worthy to serve as an original example, i.e. as a pattern, but by no means can it authoritatively furnish the conception of morality. . . .

From what has been said, it is clear that all moral conceptions have their seat and origin completely *a priori* in the reason, and that, moreover, in the commonest reason just as truly as in that which is in the highest degree speculative; that they cannot be obtained by abstraction from any empirical, and therefore merely contingent, knowledge; that it is just this purity of their origin that makes them worthy to serve as our supreme practical principle, and that just in proportion as we add anything empirical, we detract from their genuine influence, and from the absolute value of actions; that it is not only of the greatest necessity, in a purely speculative point of view, but is also of the greatest practical importance, to derive these notions and laws from pure reason, to present them pure and unmixed, and even to determine the compass of this practical or pure rational knowledge, i.e. to determine the whole faculty of pure practical reason; and, in doing so, we must not make its principles dependent on the particular nature of human reason, though in speculative philosophy this may be permitted, or may even at times be necessary; but since moral laws ought to hold good for every rational creature, we must derive them from the general concept of a rational being. In this way, although for its *application* to man morality has need of anthropology, yet, in the first instance, we must treat it independently as pure philosophy, i.e. as metaphysic, complete in itself (a thing which in such distinct branches of science is easily done); knowing well that, unless we are in possession of this, it would not only be vain to determine the moral element of duty in right actions for purposes of speculative criticism, but it would be impossible to base morals on their genuine principles, even for common practical purposes, especially of moral instruction, so as to produce pure moral dispositions, and to engraft them on men's minds to the promotion of the greatest possible good in the world.

But in order that in this study we may not merely advance by the natural steps from the common moral judgment (in this case very worthy of respect) to the philosophical, as has been already done, but also from a popular philosophy, which goes no further than it can reach by groping with the help of examples, to metaphysic (which does not allow itself to be checked by anything empirical, and as it must measure the whole extent of this kind of rational knowledge, goes as far as ideal conceptions, where even examples fail us), we must follow and clearly describe the practical faculty of reason, from the general rules of its determination to the point where the notion of duty springs from it.

Everything in nature works according to laws. Rational beings alone have the faculty of acting according *to the conception* of laws, that is according to principles, i.e. have a *will*. Since the deduction of actions from principles requires *reason*, the will is nothing but practical reason. If reason infallibly determines the will, then the actions of such a being which are recognized as objectively necessary are subjectively necessary, i.e. as good. But if reason of itself does not sufficiently determine the will, if the latter is subject also to subjective conditions (particular impulses) which do not always coincide with the objective conditions, in a word, if the will does not *in itself* completely accord with reason (which is actually the case with men), then the actions which objectively are recognized as necessary are subjectively contingent, and the determination of such a will according to objective laws is *obligation*, that is to say, the relation of the objective laws to a will that is not thoroughly good is conceived as the determination of the will of a rational being by principles of reason, but which the will from its nature does not of necessity follow.

The conception of an objective principle, in so far as it is obligatory for a will, is called a command (of reason), and the formula of the command is called an Imperative.

All imperatives are expressed by the word *ought* (or *shall*), and thereby indicate the relation of an objective law of reason to a will, which from its subjective constitution is not necessarily determined by it (an obligation). They say that something would be good to do or to forbear, but they say it to a will which does not always do a thing because it is conceived to be good to do it. That is practically *good*, however, which determines the will by means of the conceptions of reason, and consequently not from subjective causes, but objectively, that is, on principles which are valid for every rational being as such. It is distinguished from the *pleasant*, as that which influences the will only by means of sensation from merely subjective causes, valid only for the sense of this or that one, and not as a principle of reason, which holds for every one.

A perfectly good will would therefore be equally subject to objective laws (viz. laws of good), but could not be conceived as *obliged* thereby to act lawfully, because of itself from its subjective constitution it can only be determined by the conception of good. Therefore no imperatives hold for the Divine will, or in general for a *holy* will; *ought* is here out of place, because the volition is already of itself necessarily in unison with the law. Therefore imperatives are only formulae to express the relation of objective laws of all volition to the subjective imperfection of the will of this or that rational being, e.g. the human will.

Now all *imperatives* command either *hypothetically* or *categorically*. The former represent the practical necessity of a possible action as means to something else that is willed (or at least which one might possibly will). The categorical imperative would be that which represented an action as necessary of itself without reference to another end, i.e., as objectively necessary.

Since every practical law represents a possible action as good, and on this account, for a subject who is practically determinable by reason, necessary, all imperatives are formulae determining an action which is necessary according to the principle of a will good in some respects. If now the action is good only as a means *to something else,* then the imperative is *hypothetical;* if it is conceived as good *in itself* and consequently as being necessarily the principle of a will which of itself conforms to reason, then it is *categorical.*

Thus the imperative declares what action possible by me would be good, and presents the practical rule in relation to a will which does not forthwith perform an action simply because it is good, whether because the subject does not always know that it is good, or because, even if it know this, yet its maxims might be opposed to the objective principles of practical reason.

Accordingly the hypothetical imperative only says that the action is good for some purpose, *possible* or *actual.* In the first case it is a Problematical, in the second an Assertorial practical principle. The categorical imperative which declares an action to be objectively necessary in itself without reference to any purpose, i.e. without any other end, is valid as an Apodictic (practical) principle.

Whatever is possible only by the power of some rational being may also be conceived as a possible purpose of some will; and therefore the principles of action as regards the means necessary to attain some possible purpose are in fact infinitely numerous. All sciences have a practical part, consisting of problems expressing that some end is possible for us, and of imperatives directing how it may be attained. These may, therefore, be called in general imperatives of Skill. Here there is no question whether the end is rational and good, but only what one must do in order to attain it. The precepts for the physician to make his patient thoroughly healthy, and for a poisoner to ensure certain death, are of equal value in this respect, that each serves to effect its purpose perfectly. Since in early youth it cannot be known what ends are likely to occur to us in the course of life, parents seek to have their children taught a *great many things,* and provide for their *skill* in the use of means for all sorts of arbitrary ends, of none of which can they determine whether it may not perhaps hereafter be an object to their pupil, but which it is at all events *possible* that he might aim at; and this anxiety is so great that they commonly neglect to form and correct their judgment on the value of the things which may be chosen as ends.

There is *one* end, however, which may be assumed to be actually such to all rational beings (so far as imperatives apply to them, viz. as dependent beings), and, therefore, one purpose which they not merely *may* have, but which we may with certainty assume that they all actually *have* by a natural necessity, and this is *happiness.* The hypothetical imperative which expresses the practical necessity of an action as means to the advancement of happiness is Assertorial. We are not to present it as necessary for an uncertain and merely possible purpose, but for a purpose which we may presuppose with certainty and *a priori* in every man, because it belongs to his being. Now skill in the choice of means to his own greatest well-being may be called *prudence,* in the narrowest sense. And thus the imperative which refers to the choice of means to one's own happiness, i.e. the precept of prudence, is still always *hypothetical;* the action is not commanded absolutely, but only as means to another purpose.

Finally, there is an imperative which commands a certain conduct immediately, without having as its condition any other purpose to be attained by it. This imperative is Categorical. It concerns not the matter of the action, or its intended result, but its form and the principle of which it is itself a result; and what is essentially good in it consists in the mental disposition, let the consequence be what it may. This imperative may be called that of Morality. . . .

Now it is impossible that the most clear-sighted and at the same time most powerful being (supposed finite) should frame to himself a definite conception of what he really wills in this. Does he will riches, how much anxiety, envy, and snares might he not thereby draw upon his shoulders? Does he will knowledge and discernment, perhaps it might prove to be only an eye so much the sharper to show him so much the more fearfully the evils that are now concealed from him, and that cannot be avoided, or to impose more wants on his desires, which already give him concern enough. Would he have long life? who guarantees to him that it would not be a long misery? would he at least have health? how often has uneasiness of the body restrained from excesses into which perfect health would have allowed one to fall? and so on. In short, he is unable, on any principle, to determine with certainty what would make him truly happy; because to do so he would need to be omniscient. We cannot therefore act on any definite principles to secure happiness, but only on empirical counsels, e.g. of regimen, frugality, courtesy, reserve, etc., which experience teaches do, on the average, most promote well-being. Hence it follows that the imperatives of prudence do not, strictly speaking, command at all, that is, they cannot present actions objectively as practically *necessary;* that they are rather to be regarded as counsels (*consilia*) than precepts (*praecepta*) of reason, that the problem to determine certainly and universally what action would promote the happiness of a rational being is completely insoluble, and consequently no imperative respecting it is possible which should, in the strict sense, command to do what makes happy; because happiness is not an ideal of reason but of imagination, resting solely on empirical grounds, and it is vain to expect that these should define an action by which one could attain the totality of a series of consequences which is really endless. This imperative of prudence would, however, be an analytical proposition if we assume that the means to happiness could be certainly assigned; for it is distinguished from the imperative of skill only by this, that in the latter the end is merely possible, in the former it is given; as, however, both only ordain the means to that which we suppose to be willed as an end, it follows that the imperative which ordains the willing of the means to him who wills the end is in both cases analytical. Thus there is no difficulty in regard to the possibility of an imperative of this kind either.

On the other hand, the question, how the imperative of *morality* is possible, is undoubtedly one, the only one, demanding a solution, as this is not at all hypothetical, and the objective necessity which it presents cannot rest on any hypothesis, as is the case with the hypothetical imperatives. Only here we must never leave out of consideration that we *cannot* make out *by any example,* in other words empirically, whether there is such an imperative at all; but it is rather to be feared that all those which seem to be categorical may yet be at bottom hypothetical. For instance, when the precept is: Thou shalt not promise deceitfully; and it is assumed that the necessity of this is not a mere counsel to avoid some other evil, so that it should mean: Thou shalt not make a lying promise, lest if it become known thou shouldst destroy thy credit, but that an action of this kind must be regarded as evil in itself, so that the imperative of the prohibition is categorical; then we cannot show with certainty in any example that the will was determined merely by the law, without any other spring of action, although it may appear to be so. For it is always possible that fear of disgrace, perhaps also obscure dread of other dangers, may have a secret influence on the will. Who can prove by experience the non-existence of a cause when all that experience tells us is that we do not perceive it? But in such a case the so-called moral imperative, which as such appears to be categorical and unconditional, would in reality be only a pragmatic precept, drawing our attention to our own interests, and merely teaching us to take these into consideration.

We shall therefore have to investigate *a priori* the possibility of a categorical imperative, as we have not in this case the advantage of its reality being given in experience, so that (the elucidation of) its possibility should be requisite only for its explanation, not for its establishment. In the meantime it may be discerned beforehand that the categorical imperative alone has the purport of a practical law; all the rest may indeed be called *principles* of the will but not laws, since whatever is only necessary for the attainment of some arbitrary purpose may be considered as in itself contingent, and we can at any time be free from the precept if we give up the purpose; on the contrary, the unconditional command leaves the will no liberty to choose the opposite; consequently it alone carries with it that necessity which we require in a law.

Secondly, in the case of this categorical imperative or law of morality, the difficulty (of discerning its possibility) is a very profound one. It is an *a priori* synthetical practical proposition; and as there is so much difficulty in discerning the possibility of speculative propositions of this kind, it may readily be supposed that the difficulty will be no less with the practical.

In this problem we will first inquire whether the mere conception of a categorical imperative may not perhaps supply us also with the formula of it, containing the proposition which alone can be a categorical imperative; for even if we know the tenor of such an absolute command, yet how it is possible will require further special and laborious study, which we postpone to the last section.

When I conceive a hypothetical imperative, in general I do not know beforehand what it will contain until I am given the condition. But when I conceive a categorical imperative, I know at once what it contains. For as the imperative contains besides the law only the necessity that the maxims shall conform to this law, while the law contains no conditions restricting it, there remains nothing but the general statement that the maxim of the action should conform to a universal law, and it is this conformity alone that the imperative properly represents as necessary.

There is therefore but one categorical imperative, namely, this: *Act only on that maxim whereby thou canst at the same time will that it should become a universal law.*

Now if all imperatives of duty can be deduced from this one imperative as from their principle, then, although it should remain undecided whether what is called duty is not merely a vain notion, yet at least we shall be able to show what we understand by it and what this notion means.

Since the universality of the law according to which effects are produced constitutes what is properly called *nature* in the most general sense (as to form), that is the existence of things so far as it is determined by general laws, the imperative of duty may be expressed thus: *Act as if the maxim of thy action were to become by thy will a universal law of nature.*

We will now enumerate a few duties, adopting the usual division of them into duties to ourselves and to others, and into perfect and imperfect duties.

1. A man reduced to despair by a series of misfortunes feels wearied of life, but is still so far in possession of his reason that he can ask himself whether it would not be contrary to his duty to himself to take his own life. Now he inquires whether the maxim of his action could become a universal law of nature. His maxim is: From self-love I adopt it as a principle to shorten my life when its longer duration is likely to bring more evil than satisfaction. It is asked then simply whether this principle founded on self-love can become a universal law of nature. Now we see at once that a system of nature of which it should be a law to destroy life by means of the very feeling whose special nature it is to impel to the improvement of life would contradict itself, and therefore could not exist as a system of nature; hence that maxim cannot possibly exist as a universal law of nature, and consequently would be wholly inconsistent with the supreme principle of all duty.

2. Another finds himself forced by necessity to borrow money. He knows that he will not be able to repay it, but sees also that nothing will be lent to him, unless he promises stoutly to repay it in a definite time. He desires to make this promise, but he has still so much conscience as to ask himself: Is it not unlawful and inconsistent with duty to get out of a difficulty in this way? Suppose, however, that he resolves to do so, then the maxim of his action would be expressed thus: When I think myself in want of money, I will borrow money and promise to repay it, although I know that I never can do so. Now this principle of self-love or of one's own advantage may perhaps be consistent with my whole future welfare; but the question now is, Is it right? I change then the suggestion of self-

love into a universal law, and state the question thus: How would it be if my maxim were a universal law? Then I see at once that it could never hold as a universal law of nature, but would necessarily contradict itself. For supposing it to be a universal law that everyone when he thinks himself in a difficulty should be able to promise whatever he pleases, with the purpose of not keeping his promise, the promise itself would become impossible, as well as the end that one might have in view in it, since no one would consider that anything was promised to him, but would ridicule all such statements as vain pretenses.

3. A third finds in himself a talent which with the help of some culture might make him a useful man in many respects. But he finds himself in comfortable circumstances, and prefers to indulge in pleasure rather than to take pains in enlarging and improving his happy natural capacities. He asks, however, whether his maxim of neglect of his natural gifts, besides agreeing with his inclination to indulgence, agrees also with what is called duty. He sees then that a system of nature could indeed subsist with such a universal law although men (like the South Sea islanders) should let their talents rest, and resolve to devote their lives merely to idleness, amusement, and propagation of their species—in a word, to enjoyment; but he cannot possibly *will* that this should be a universal law of nature, or be implanted in us as such by a natural instinct. For, as a rational being, he necessarily wills that his faculties be developed, since they serve him, and have been given him, for all sorts of possible purposes.

4. A fourth, who is in prosperity, while he sees that others have to contend with great wretchedness and that he could help them, thinks: What concern is it of mine? Let everyone be as happy as Heaven pleases, or as he can make himself; I will take nothing from him nor even envy him, only I do not wish to contribute anything to his welfare or to his assistance in distress! Now no doubt, if such a mode of thinking were a universal law, the human race might very well subsist, and doubtless even better than in a state in which everyone talks of sympathy and good-will, or even takes care occasionally to put it into practice, but, on the other side, also cheats when he can, betrays the rights of men, or otherwise violates them. But although it is possible that a universal law of nature might exist in accordance with that maxim, it is impossible to *will* that such a principle should have the universal validity of a law of nature. For a will which resolved this would contradict itself, inasmuch as many cases might occur in which one would have need of the love and sympathy of others, and in which, by such a law of nature, sprung from his own will, he would deprive himself of all hope of the aid he desires.

These are a few of the many actual duties, or at least what we regard as such, which obviously fall into two classes on the one principle that we have laid down. We must be *able to will* that a maxim of our action should be a universal law. This is the canon of the moral appreciation of the action generally. Some actions are of such a character that their maxim cannot without contradiction be even *conceived* as a universal law of nature, far from it being possible that we should *will* that it *should* be so. In others this intrinsic impossibility is not found, but still it is impossible to *will* that their maxim should be raised to the universality of a law of nature, since such a will would contradict itself. It is easily seen that the former violate strict or rigorous (inflexible) duty; the latter only laxer (meritorious) duty. Thus it has been completely shown by these examples how all duties depend as regards the nature of the obligation (not of the object of the action) on the same principle.

4

The
Utilitarian
Calculus
of Pain
and Pleasure

John Stuart Mill (1806–1873)

A passing remark is all that needs to be given to the ignorant blunder of supposing that those who stand up for utility as the test of right and wrong, use the term in that restricted and merely colloquial sense in which utility is opposed to pleasure. An apology is due to the philosophical opponents of utilitarianism, for even the momentary appearance of confounding them with anyone capable of so absurd a misconception; which is the more extraordinary, inasmuch as the contrary accusation, of referring everything to pleasure, and that too in its grossest form, is another of the common charges against utilitarianism: and, as has been pointedly remarked by an able writer, the same sort of persons, and often the very same persons, denounce the theory "as impracticably dry when the word utility precedes the word pleasure, and as too practicably voluptuous when the word pleasure precedes the word utility." Those who know anything about the

From John Stuart Mill, *Utilitarianism*, chapter 2, "What Utilitarianism Is," 1863.

matter are aware that every writer, from Epicurus to Bentham, who maintained the theory of utility, meant by it, not something to be contradistinguished from pleasure, but pleasure itself, together with exemption from pain; and instead of opposing the useful to the agreeable or the ornamental, have always declared that the useful means these, among other things. Yet the common herd, including the herd of writers, not only in newspapers, and periodicals, but in books of weight and pretension, are perpetually falling into this shallow mistake. Having caught up the word 'utilitarian,' while knowing nothing whatever about it but its sound, they habitually express by it the rejection, or the neglect, of pleasure in some of its forms: of beauty, of ornament, or of amusement. Nor is the term thus ignorantly misapplied solely in disparagement, but occasionally in compliment; as though it implied superiority to frivolity and the mere pleasures of the moment. And this perverted use is the only one in which the word is popularly known, and the one from which the new generation are acquiring their sole notion of its meaning. Those who introduced the word, but who had for many years discontinued it as a distinctive appellation, may well feel themselves called upon to resume it, if by doing so they can hope to contribute anything towards rescuing it from this utter degradation.

The creed which accepts as the foundation of morals *utility*, or the *greatest happiness principle*, holds that actions are right in proportion as they tend to promote happiness, wrong as they tend to produce the reverse of happiness. By 'happiness' is intended pleasure, and the absence of pain; by 'unhappiness,' pain, and the privation of pleasure. To give a clear view of the moral standard set up by the theory, much more requires to be said; in particular, what things it includes in the ideas of pain and pleasure; and to what extent this is left an open question. But these supplementary explanations do not affect the theory of life on which this theory of morality is grounded—namely, that pleasure, and freedom from pain, are the only things desirable as ends; and that all desirable things (which are as numerous in the utilitarian as in any other scheme) are desirable either for the pleasure inherent in themselves, or as means to the promotion of pleasure and the prevention of pain.

Now such a theory of life excites in many minds, and among them in some of the most estimable in feeling and purpose, inveterate dislike. To suppose that life has (as they express it) no higher end than pleasure—no better and nobler object of desire and pursuit—they designate as utterly mean and groveling; as a doctrine worthy only of swine, to whom the followers of Epicurus were, at a very early period, contemptuously likened; and modern holders of the doctrine are occasionally made the subject of equally polite comparisons by its German, French, and English assailants.

When thus attacked, the Epicureans have always answered that it is not they but their accusers who represent human nature in a degrading light; since the accusation supposes human beings to be capable of no pleasures except those of which swine are capable. If this supposition were true, the charge could not be gainsaid, but would then be no longer an imputation; for if the sources of pleasure were precisely the same to human beings and to swine, the rule of life which is good enough for the one would be good enough for the other. The comparison of the Epicurean life to that of beasts is felt as degrading, precisely because a beast's pleasures do not satisfy a human being's conceptions of happiness. Human beings have faculties more elevated than the animal appetites, and when once made conscious of them, do not regard anything as happiness which does not include their gratification. I do not, indeed, consider the Epicureans to have been by any means faultless in drawing out their scheme of consequences from the utilitarian principle. To do this in any sufficient manner, many Stoic, as well as Christian elements require to be included. But there is no known Epicurean theory of life which does not assign to the pleasures of the intellect, of the feelings and imagination, and of the moral sentiments, a much higher value of pleasures than to those of mere sensation. It must be admitted, however, that utilitarian writers in general have placed the superiority of mental over bodily pleasures chiefly in the greater permanency, safety, uncostliness, etc., of the former—that is, in their circumstantial advantages rather than in their intrinsic nature. And on all these points utilitarians have fully proved their case; but they might have taken the other, and as it may be called, higher ground, with entire consistency. It is quire compatible with the principle of utility to recognize the fact, that some *kinds* of pleasure are more desirable and more valuable than others. It would be absurd that while, in estimating all other things, quality is considered as well as quantity, the estimation of pleasures should be supposed to depend on quantity alone.

If I am asked what I mean by difference of quality in pleasures, or what makes one pleasure more valuable than another merely as a pleasure, except its being greater in amount, there is but one possible answer. Of two pleasures, if there be one to which all or almost all who have experience of both give a decided preference, irrespective of any feeling of moral obligation to prefer it, that is the more desirable pleasure. If one of the two is, by those who are competently acquainted with both, placed so far above the other that they prefer it, even though knowing it to be attended with a greater amount of discontent, and would not resign it for any quantity of the other pleasure which their nature is capable of, we are justified in ascribing to the preferred enjoyment a superiority in quality, so far outweighing quantity as to render it, in comparison, of small account.

Now it is an unquestionable fact that those who are equally acquainted with, and equally capable of appreciating and enjoying, both, do give a most marked preference to the manner of existence which employs their higher faculties. Few human creatures would consent to be changed into any of the lower animals, for a promise of the fullest allowance of a beast's pleasures; no intelligent human being would consent to be a fool, no instructed person would be an ignoramus, no person of feeling and conscience would be selfish and base, even though they should be persuaded that the fool, the dunce, or the rascal is better satisfied with his lot than they are with theirs. They would not resign what they possess more than he for the most complete satisfaction of all the desires which they have in common with him. If they ever fancy they would, it is only in cases of unhappiness so extreme, that to escape from it they would exchange their lot for almost any other, however undesirable in their own eyes. A being of higher faculties requires more to make him happy, is capable probably of more acute suffering, and certainly accessible to it at more points, than one of an inferior type; but in spite of these liabilities, he can never really wish to sink into what he feels to be a lower grade of existence. We may give what explanation we please of this unwillingness: we may attribute it to pride, a name which is given indiscriminately to some of the most and to some of the least estimable feelings of which mankind are capable; we may refer it to the love of liberty and personal independence, an appeal to which was with the Stoics one of the most effective means for the inculcation of it; to the love of power, or to the love of excitement, both of which do really enter into and contribute to it: but its most appropriate appellation is a sense of dignity, which all human beings possess in one form or other, and in some, though by no means in exact proportion to their higher faculties, and which is so essential a part of the happiness of those in whom it is strong, that nothing which conflicts with it could be, otherwise than momentarily, an object of desire to them. Whoever supposes that this preference takes place at a sacrifice of happiness—that the superior being, in anything like equal circumstances, is not happier than the inferior—confounds the two very different ideas, of *happiness* and *content*. It is indisputable that the being whose capacities of enjoyment are low, has the greatest chance of having them fully satisfied; and a highly endowed being will always feel that any happiness which he can look for, as the world is constituted, is imperfect. But he can learn to bear its imperfections, if they are at all bearable; and they will not make him envy the being who is indeed unconscious of the imperfections, but only because he feels not at all the good which those imperfections qualify. It is better to be a human being dissatisfied than a pig satisfied; better to be Socrates dissatisfied than a fool satisfied. And if the fool, or the pig, are of a different opinion, it is because they only know their own side of the question. The other party to the comparison knows both sides.

It may be objected that many who are capable of the higher pleasures, occasionally, under the influence of temptation, postpone them to the lower. But this is quite compatible with a full appreciation of the intrinsic superiority of the higher. Men often, from infirmity of character, make their election for the nearer good, though they know it to be the less valuable; and this no less when the choice is between two bodily pleasures, than when it is between bodily and mental. They pursue sensual indulgences to the injury of health, though perfectly aware that health is the greater good. It may be further objected that many who begin with youthful enthusiasm for everything noble, as they advance in years sink into indolence and selfishness. But I do not believe that those who undergo this very common change, voluntarily choose the lower description of pleasures in preference to the higher. I believe that before they devote themselves exclusively to the one, they have already become incapable of the other. Capacity for the nobler feelings is in most natures a very tender plant, easily killed, not only by hostile influences, but by mere want of sustenance; and in the majority of young persons it speedily dies away if the occupations to which their position in life has devoted them, and the society into which it has thrown them, are not favorable to keeping that higher capacity in exercise. Men lose their high aspirations as they lose their intellectual tastes, because they have not time or opportunity for indulging them; and they addict themselves to inferior pleasures not because they deliberately prefer them, but because they are either the only ones to which they have access or the only ones which they are any longer capable of enjoying. It may be questioned whether anyone who has remained equally susceptible to both classes of pleasures, ever knowingly and calmly preferred the lower; though many, in all ages, have broken down in an ineffectual attempt to combine both.

From this verdict of the only competent judges I apprehend there can be no appeal. On a question which is the best worth having of two pleasures, or which of two modes of existence is the most grateful to the feelings, apart from its moral attributes and from its consequences, the judgment of those who are qualified by knowledge of both, or, if they differ, that of the majority among them, must be admitted as final. And there need be the less hesitation to accept this judgment respecting the quality of pleasures, since there is no other tribunal to be referred to even on the question of quantity. What means are there of determining which is the acutest of two pains, or the intensest of two pleasurable sensations, except the general suffrage of those who are familiar with both? Neither pains nor pleasures are homogeneous, and pain is always heterogeneous with pleasure. What is there to decide whether a particular pleasure is worth purchasing at the cost of a particular pain, except the feelings and judgment of the experienced? When, therefore, those feelings and judgment declare the pleasures derived from the higher faculties to be preferable *in kind,* apart from the question of intensity, to those of which the animal nature, disjoined from the higher faculties, is susceptible, they are entitled on this subject to the same regard.

I have dwelt on this point, as being a necessary part of a perfectly just conception of utility, or happiness, considered as the directive rule of human conduct. But it is by no means an indispensable condition to the acceptance of the utilitarian standard; for that standard is not the agent's own greatest happiness, but the greatest amount of happiness altogether; and if it may possibly be doubted whether a noble character is always the happier for its nobleness, there can be no doubt that it makes other people happier, and that the world in general is immensely a gainer by it. Utilitarianism, therefore, could only attain its end by the general cultivation of nobleness of character, even if each individual were only benefited by the nobleness of others, and his own, so far as happiness is concerned, were a sheer deduction from the benefit. But the bare enunciation of such an absurdity as this last renders refutation superfluous.

According to the 'greatest happiness principle,' as above explained, the ultimate end, with reference to and for the sake of which all other things are desirable (whether we are considering our own good or that of other people), is an existence exempt as far as possible from pain, and as rich as possible in enjoyments, both in point of quantity and quality; the test of quality, and the rule for measuring it against quantity, being the preference felt by those who in their opportunities of experience, to which must be added their habits of self-consciousness and self-observation, are best furnished with the means of comparison. This, being, according to the utilitarian opinion, the end of human action, is necessarily also the standard of morality; which may accordingly be defined, the rules and precepts for human conduct, by the observance of which an existence such as has been described might be, to the greatest extent possible, secured to all mankind; and not to them only, but so far as the nature of things admits, to the whole sentient creation.

Against this doctrine, however, arises another class of objectors, who say that happiness, in any form, cannot be the rational purpose of human life and action; because, in the first place, it is unattainable: and they contemptuously ask, what right hast thou to be happy?—a question which Mr. Carlyle clenches by the addition. What right, a short time ago, hadst thou even *to be?* Next, they say that men can do *without* happiness; that all noble human beings have felt this, and could not have become noble but by learning the lesson of *Entsagen,* or renunciation; which lesson, thoroughly learnt and submitted to, they affirm to be the beginning and necessary condition of all virtue.

The first of these objections would go to the root of the matter were it well founded; for if no happiness is to be had at all by human beings, the attainment of it cannot be the end of morality, or of any rational conduct. Though, even in that case, something might still be said for the utilitarian theory; since utility includes not solely the pursuit of happiness, but the prevention or mitigation of unhappiness; and if the former aim be chimerical, there will be all the greater scope and more imperative need for the latter, so long at least as mankind think fit to live, and do not take refuge in the simultaneous act of suicide recommended under certain conditions by Novalis. When, however, it is thus positively asserted to be impossible that human life should be happy, the assertion, if not something like a verbal quibble, is at least an exaggeration. If by happiness be meant a continuity of highly pleasurable excitement, it is evident enough that this is impossible. A state of exalted pleasure lasts only moments, or in some cases, and with some intermissions, hours or days, and is the occasional brilliant flash of enjoyment, not its permanent and steady flame. Of this the philosophers who have taught that happiness is the end of life were as fully aware as those who taunt them. The happiness which they meant was not a life of rapture; but moments of such, in an existence made up of few and transitory pains, many and various pleasures, with a decided predominance of the active over the passive, and having as the foundation of the whole, not to expect more from life than it is capable of bestowing. A life thus always appeared worthy of the name of happiness. And such an existence is even now the lot of many, during some considerable portion of their lives. The present wretched education, and wretched social arrangements, are the only real hindrance to its being attainable by almost all.

The objectors perhaps may doubt whether human beings, if taught to consider happiness as the end of life, would be satisfied with such a moderate share of it. But great numbers of mankind have been satisfied with much less. The main constituents of a satisfied life appear to be two, either of which by itself is often found sufficient for the purpose: tranquillity and excitement. With much tranquillity, many find that they can be content with very little pleasure; with much excitement, many can reconcile themselves to a considerable quantity of pain. There is assuredly no inherent impossibility in enabling even the mass of mankind to unite both; since the two are so far from being incompatible that they are in natural alliance, the prolongation of either being a preparation for, and exciting a wish for, the other. It is only those in whom indolence amounts to a vice, that do not desire excitement after an interval of repose; it is only those in whom the need of excitement is a disease, that feel the tranquillity which follows excitement dull and insipid, instead of pleasurable in direct proportion to the excitement which preceded it. When people who are tolerably fortunate in their outward lot do not find in life sufficient enjoyment to make it valuable to them, the cause generally is, caring for nobody but themselves. To those who have neither public nor private affections, the excitements of life are much curtailed, and in any case dwindle in value as the time approaches when all selfish interests must be terminated by death; while those who leave after them objects of personal affection, and especially those who have also cultivated a fellow-feeling with the collective interests of mankind, retain as lively an interest in life on the eve of death as in the vigor of youth and health. Next to selfishness, the principal cause which makes life unsatisfactory is want of mental cultivation. A cultivated mind (I do not mean that of a philosopher, but any mind to which the fountains of knowledge have been opened, and which has been taught, in any tolerable degree, to exercise its faculties) finds sources of inexhaustible interest in all that surrounds it; in the objects of nature, the achievements of art, the imaginations of poetry, the incidents of history, the ways of mankind, past and present, and their prospects in the future. It is possible, indeed, to become indifferent to all this, and that too without having exhausted a thousandth part of it; but only when one has had from the beginning no moral or human interest in these things, and has sought in them only the gratification of curiosity.

Now there is absolutely no reason in the nature of things why an amount of mental culture sufficient to give an intelligent interest in these objects of contemplation, should not be the inheritance of everyone born in a civilized country. As little is there an inherent necessity that any human being should be a selfish egotist, devoid of every feeling or care but those which center in his own miserable individuality. Something far superior to this is sufficiently common even now, to give ample earnest of what the human species may be made. Genuine private affections, and a sincere interest in the public good, are possible, though in unequal degrees, to every rightly brought up human being. In a world in which there is so much to interest, so much to enjoy, and so much also to correct and improve, everyone who has this moderate amount of moral and intellectual requisites is capable of an existence which may be called enviable; and unless such a person, through bad laws, or subjection to the will of others, is denied the liberty to use the sources of happiness within his reach, he will not fail to find this enviable existence, if he escape the positive evils of life, the great sources of physical and mental suffering—such as indigence, disease, and the unkindness, worthlessness, or premature loss of objects of affection. The main stress of the problem lies, therefore, in the contest with these calamities, from which it is a rare good fortune entirely to escape; which, as things now are, cannot be obviated, and often cannot be in any material degree mitigated. Yet no one whose opinion deserves a moment's consideration can doubt that most of the great positive evils of the world are in themselves removable, and will, if human affairs continue to improve, be in the end reduced within narrow limits. Poverty, in any sense implying suffering, may be completely extinguished by the wisdom of society, combined with the good sense and providence of individuals. Even that most intractable of enemies, disease, may be indefinitely reduced in dimensions by good physical and moral education, and proper control of noxious influences; while the progress of science holds out a promise for the future of still more direct conquests over this detestable foe. And every advance in that direction relieves us from some, not only of the chances which cut short our own lives, but, what concerns us still more, which deprive us of those in whom our happiness is wrapt up. As for vicissitudes of fortune, and other disappointments connected with worldly circumstances, these are principally the effect either of gross imprudence, of ill-regulated desires, or of bad or imperfect social institutions. All the grand sources, in short, of human suffering are in a great degree, many of them almost entirely, conquerable by human care and effort; and though their removal is grievously slow—though a long succession of generations will perish in the breach before the conquest is completed, and this world becomes all that, if will and knowledge were not wanting, it might easily be made—yet every mind sufficiently intelligent and generous to bear a part, however small and inconspicuous, in the endeavor, will draw a noble enjoyment from the contest itself, which he would not for any bribe in the form of selfish indulgence consent to be without.

And this leads to the true estimation of what is said by the objectors concerning the possibility, and the obligation, of learning to do without happiness. Unquestionably it is possible to do without happiness; it is done involuntarily by nineteen-twentieths of mankind, even in those parts of our present world which are least deep in barbarism; and it often has to be done voluntarily by the hero or the martyr, for the sake of something which he prizes more than his individual happiness. But this something, what is it, unless the happiness of others, or some of the requisites of happiness? It is noble to be capable of resigning entirely one's own portion of happiness, or chances of it: but, after all, this self-sacrifice must be for some end; it is not its own end; and if we are told that its end is not happiness, but virtue, which is better than happiness, I ask, would the sacrifice be made if the hero or martyr did not believe that it would earn for others immunity from similar sacrifices? Would it be made if he thought that his renunciation of happiness for himself would produce no fruit for any of his fellow creatures, but to make their lot like his, and place them also in the condition of persons who have renounced happiness? All honor to those who can abnegate for themselves the personal enjoyment of life, when by such renunciation they contribute worthily to increase the amount of happiness in the world; but he who does it, or professes to do it, for any other purpose, is no more deserving of admiration from the ascetic mounted on his pillar. He may be an inspiring proof of what men *can* do, but assuredly not an example of what they *should*.

Though it is only in a very imperfect state of the world's arrangements that anyone can best serve the happiness of others by the absolute sacrifice of his own, yet so long as the world is in that imperfect state, I fully acknowledge that the readiness to make such a sacrifice is the highest virtue which can be found in man. I will add that in this condition of the world, paradoxical as the assertion may be, the conscious ability to do without happiness gives the best prospect of realizing such happiness as is attainable. For nothing except that consciousness can raise a person above the chances of life, by making him feel that, let fate and fortune do their worst, they have not power to subdue him; which, once felt, frees him from excess of anxiety concerning the evils of life, and enables him, like many a Stoic in the worst times of the Roman Empire, to cultivate in tranquillity the sources of satisfaction accessible to him, without concerning himself about the uncertainty of their duration, any more than about their inevitable end.

Meanwhile, let utilitarians never cease to claim the morality of self-devotion as a possession which belongs by as good a right to them, as either to the Stoic or to the Transcendentalist. The utilitarian morality does recognize in human beings the power of sacrificing their own greatest good for the good of others. It only refuses to admit that the sacrifice is itself a good. A sacrifice which does not increase, or tend to increase, the sum total of happiness, it considers as wasted. The only self-renunciation which it applauds, is devotion to the happiness, or to some of the means of happiness, of others; either of mankind collectively, or of individuals within the limits imposed by the collective interests of mankind.

I must again repeat, what the assailants of utilitarianism seldom have the justice to acknowledge, that the happiness which forms the utilitarian standard of what is right in conduct, is not the agent's own happiness, but that of all concerned. As between his own happiness and that of others, utilitarianism requires him to be as strictly impartial as a disinterested and benevolent spectator. In the golden rule of Jesus of Nazareth, we read the complete spirit of the ethics of utility. To do as you would be done by, and to love your neighbor as yourself, constitute the ideal perfection of utilitarian morality. As the means of making the nearest approach to this ideal, utility would enjoin, first, that laws and social arrangements should place the happiness, or (as speaking practically it may be called) the interest, of every individual, as nearly as possible in harmony with the interest of the whole; and secondly, that education and opinion, which have so vast a power over human character, should so use that power as to establish in the mind of every individual an indissoluble association between his own happiness and the good of the whole—especially between his own happiness and the practice of such modes of conduct, negative and positive, as regard for the universal happiness prescribes; so that not only he may be unable to conceive the possibility of happiness to himself, consistently with conduct opposed to the general good, but also that a direct impulse to promote the general good may be in every individual one of the habitual motives of action, and the sentiments connected therewith may fill a large and prominent place in every human being's sentient existence. If the impugners of the utilitarian morality represented it to their own minds in this its true character, I know not what recommendation possessed by any other morality they could possibly affirm to be wanting to it; what more beautiful or more exalted developments of human nature any other ethical system can be supposed to foster, or what springs of action, not accessible to the utilitarian, such systems rely on for giving effect to their mandates.

The objectors to utilitarianism cannot always be charged with representing it in a discreditable light. On the contrary, those among them who entertain anything like a just idea of its disinterested character sometimes find fault with its standard as being too high for humanity. They say it is exacting too much to require that people shall always act for the inducement of promoting the general interests of society. But this is to mistake the very meaning of a standard of morals, and confound the rule of action with the motive of it. It is the business of ethics to tell us what are our duties, or by what test we may know them; but no system of ethics requires that the sole motive of all we do shall be a feeling of duty; on the contrary, ninety-nine hundredths of all our actions are done from other motives, and rightly so done, if the rule of duty does not condemn them. It is the more unjust to utilitarianism that this particular misapprehension should be made a ground of objection to it, inasmuch as utilitarian moralists have gone beyond almost all others in affirming that the motive has nothing to do with the morality of the action, though much with the worth of the agent. He who saves a fellow creature from drowning does what is morally right, whether his motive be duty, or the hope of being paid for his trouble; he who betrays the friend that trusts him, is guilty of a crime, even if his object be to serve another friend to whom he is under greater obligations. But to speak only of actions done from the motive of duty, and in direct obedience to principle: it is a misapprehension of the utilitarian mode of thought, to conceive it as implying that people should fix their minds upon so wide a generality as the world, or society at large. The great majority of good actions are intended not for the benefit of the world, but for that of individuals, of which the good of the world is made up; and the thoughts of the most virtuous man need not on these occasions travel beyond the particular persons concerned, except so far as is necessary to assure himself that in benefitting them he is not violating the rights, that is, the legitimate and authorized expectations, of anyone else. The multiplication of happiness is, according to the utilitarian ethics the object of virtue: the occasions on which any person (except one in a thousand) has it in his power to do this on an extended scale, in other words to be a public benefactor, are but exceptional, and on these occasions alone is he called on to consider public utility; in every other case, private utility, the interest or happiness of some few persons, is all he has to attend to. Those alone, the influence of whose actions extends to society in general, need concern themselves habitually about so large an object. In the case of abstinences indeed—of things which people forbear to do from moral considerations, though the consequences in the particular case might be beneficial—it would be unworthy of an intelligent agent not to be consciously aware that the action is of a class which, if practiced generally, would be generally injurious, and that this is the ground of the obligation to abstain from it. The amount of regard for the public interest implied in this recognition is no greater than is demanded by every system of morals, for they all enjoin to abstain from whatever is manifestly pernicious to society.

The same considerations dispose of another reproach against the doctrine of utility, founded on a still grosser misconception of the purpose of a standard of morality, and of the very meaning of the words right and wrong. It is often affirmed that utilitarianism renders men cold and unsympathizing; that it chills their moral feelings towards individuals; that it makes them regard only the dry and hard consideration of the consequences of actions, not taking into their moral estimate the qualities from which those actions emanate. If the assertion means that they do not allow their judgment respecting the rightness or wrongness of an action to be influenced by their opinion of the qualities of the person who does it, this is a complaint not against utilitarianism, but against having any standard of morality at all; for certainly no known ethical standard decides an action to be good or bad because it is done by a good or a bad man, still less because done by an amiable, a brave, or a benevolent man, or the contrary. These considerations are relevant, not to the estimation of actions, but of persons; and there is nothing in the utilitarian theory inconsistent with the fact that there are other things which interest us in persons besides the rightness and wrongness of their actions. The Stoics, indeed, with the paradoxical misuse of language which was part of their system, and by which they strove to raise themselves above all concern about anything but virtue, were fond of saying that he who has that has everything; that he, and only he, is rich, is beautiful, is a king. But no claim of this description is made for the virtuous man by the utilitarian doctrine. Utilitarians are quite aware that there are other desirable possessions and qualities besides virtue, and are perfectly willing to allow to all of them their full worth. They are also aware that a right action does not necessarily indicate a virtuous character, and that actions which are blamable, often proceed from qualities entitled to praise. When this is apparent in any particular case, it modifies their estimation, not certainly of the act, but of the agent. I grant that they are, notwithstanding, of opinion that in the long run the best proof of a good character is good actions; and resolutely refuse to consider any mental disposition as good, of which the predominant tendency is to produce bad conduct. This made them unpopular with many people; but it is an unpopularity which they must share with everyone who regards the distinction between right and wrong in a serious light; and the reproach is not one which a conscientious utilitarian need be anxious to repel.

If no more be meant by the objection than that many utilitarians look on the morality of actions, as measured by the utilitarian standard, with too exclusive a regard, and do not lay sufficient stress upon the other beauties of character which go towards making a human being lovable or admirable, this may be admitted. Utilitarians who have cultivated their moral feelings, but not their sympathies nor their artistic perceptions, do fall into this mistake; and so do all other moralists under the same conditions. What can be said in excuse for other moralists is equally available for them, namely, that if there is to be any error, it is better that it should be on that side. As a matter of fact, we may affirm that among utilitarians as among adherents of other systems, there is every imaginable degree of rigidity and of laxity in the application of their standard: some are even puritanically rigorous, while others are as indulgent as can possibly be desired by sinner or by sentimentalist. But on the whole, a doctrine which brings prominently forward the interest that mankind have in the repression and prevention of conduct which violates the moral law, is likely to be inferior to no other in turning the sanctions of opinion against such violations. It is true, the question, "What does violate the moral law?" is one on which those who recognize different standards of morality are likely now and then to differ. But difference of opinion on moral questions was not first introduced into the world by utilitarianism, while that doctrine does supply, if not always an easy, at all events a tangible and intelligible mode of deciding such differences.

It may not be superfluous to notice a few more of the common misapprehensions of utilitarian ethics, even those which are so obvious and gross that it might appear impossible for any person of candor and intelligence to fall into them; since persons, even of considerable mental endowments, often give themselves so little trouble to understand the bearings of any opinion against which they entertain a prejudice, and men are in general so little conscious of this voluntary ignorance as a defect, that the vulgarest misunderstandings of ethical doctrines are continually met with in the deliberate writings of persons of the greatest pretensions both to high principle and to philosophy. We not uncommonly hear the doctrine of utility inveighed against as a *godless* doctrine. If it be necessary to say anything at all against so mere an assumption, we may say that the question depends upon what idea we have formed of the moral character of the Deity. If it be a true belief that God desires, above all things, the happiness of his creatures, and that this was his purpose in their creation, utility is not only not a godless doctrine, but more profoundly religious than any other. If it be meant that utilitarianism does not recognize the revealed will of God as the supreme law of morals, I answer that a utilitarian who believes in the perfect goodness and wisdom of God, necessarily believes that whatever God has thought fit to reveal on the subject of morals, must fulfill the requirements of utility in a supreme degree. But others besides utilitarians have been of opinion that the Christian revelation was intended and is fitted, to inform the hearts and minds of mankind with a spirit which should enable them to find for themselves what is right, and incline them to do it when found, rather than to tell them, except in a very general way, what it is; and that we need a doctrine of ethics, carefully followed out, to *interpret* to us the will of God. Whether this opinion is correct or not, it is superfluous here to discuss; since whatever aid religion, either natural or revealed, can afford to ethical investigation, is as open to the utilitarian moralist as to any other. He can use it as the testimony of God to the usefulness or hurtfulness of any given course of action, by as good a right as others can use it for the indication of a transcendental law, having no connection with usefulness or with happiness.

Again, utility is often summarily stigmatized as an immoral doctrine by giving it the name of *expediency*, and taking advantage of the popular use of that term to contrast it with *principle*. But the *expedient*, in the sense in which it is opposed to the *right*, generally means that which is expedient for the particular interest of the agent himself; as when a minister sacrifices the interests of his country to keep himself in a place. When it means anything better than this, it means that which is expedient for some immediate object, some temporary purpose, but which violates a rule whose observance is expedient in a much higher degree. The expedient, in this sense, instead of being the same thing with the useful, is a branch of the hurtful. Thus, it would often be expedient, for the purpose of getting over some momentary embarrassment, or attaining some object immediately useful to ourselves or others, to tell a lie. But inasmuch as the cultivation in ourselves of a sensitive feeling on the subject of veracity, is one of the most useful, and the enfeeblement of that feeling one of the most hurtful, things to which our conduct can be instrumental; and inasmuch as any, even unintentional, deviation from truth, does that much towards weakening the trustworthiness of human assertion, which is not only the principal support of all present social well-being, but the insufficiency of which does more than any one thing that can be named to keep back civilization, virtue, everything on which human happiness on the largest scale depends; we feel that the violation, for a present advantage, of a rule of such transcendent expediency, is not expedient, and that he who, for the sake of a convenience to himself or to some other individual, does what depends on him to deprive mankind of the good, and inflict upon them the evil, involved in the greater or less reliance which they can place in each other's word, acts the part of one of their worst enemies. Yet that even this rule, sacred as it is, admits of possible exceptions, is acknowledged by all moralists; the chief of which is when the withholding of some fact (as of information from a malefactor, or of bad news from a person dangerously ill) would save an individual (especially an individual other than oneself) from great and unmerited evil, and when the withholding can only be effected by denial. But in order that the exception may not extend itself beyond the need, and may have the least possible effect in weakening reliance on veracity, it ought to be recognized, and, if possible, its limits defined; and if the principle of utility is good for anything, it must be good for weighing these conflicting utilities against one another, and marking out the region within which one or the other preponderates.

Again, defenders of utility often find themselves called upon to reply to such objections as this—that there is not time, previous to action, for calculating and weighing the effects of any line of conduct on the general happiness. This is exactly as if anyone were to say that it is impossible to guide our conduct by Christianity, because there is not time, on every occasion, on which anything has to be done, to read through the Old and New Testaments. The answer to the objection is that there has been ample time, namely, the whole past duration of the human species. During all that time, mankind have been learning by experience the tendencies of actions; on which experience all the prudence, as well as all the morality of life, are dependent. People talk as if the commencement of this course of experience had hitherto been put off, and as if, at the moment when some man feels tempted to meddle with the property or life of another, he had to begin considering for the first time whether murder and theft are injurious to human happiness. Even then I do not think that he would find the question very puzzling; but, at all events, the matter is now done to his hand. It is truly a whimsical supposition that, if mankind were agreed in considering utility to be the test of morality, they would remain without any agreement as to what is useful, and would take no measures for having their notions on the subject taught to the young, and enforced by law and opinion. There is no difficulty in proving any ethical standard whatever to work ill, if we suppose universal idiocy to be conjoined with it; but on any hypothesis short of that, mankind must by this time have acquired positive beliefs as to the effects of some actions on their happiness; and the beliefs which have thus come down are the rules of morality for the multitude, and for the philosopher until he has succeeded in finding better. That philosophers might easily do this, even now, on many subjects; that the received code of ethics is by no means of divine right; and that mankind have still much to learn as to the effects of actions on the general happiness, I admit, or rather, earnestly maintain. The corollaries from the principle of utility, like the precepts of every practical art, admit of indefinite improvement, and, in a progressive state of the human mind, their improvement is perpetually going on. But to consider the rules of morality as improvable, is one thing; to pass over the intermediate generalizations entirely, and endeavor to test each individual action directly by the first principle, is another. It is a strange notion that the acknowledgment of a first principle is inconsistent with the admission of secondary ones. To inform a traveler respecting the place of his ultimate destination, is not to forbid the use of landmarks and direction-posts on the way. The proposition that happiness is the end and aim of morality, does not mean that no road ought to be laid down to that goal, or that persons going thither should not be advised to take one direction rather than another. Men really ought to leave off talking a kind of nonsense on this subject, which they would neither talk nor listen to on other matters of practical concernment. Nobody argues that the art of navigation is not founded on astronomy, because sailors cannot wait to calculate the Nautical Almanac. Being rational creatures, they go to sea with it ready calculated; and all rational creatures go out upon the sea of life with their minds made up on the common questions of right and wrong, as well as on many of the far more difficult questions of wise and foolish. And this, as long as foresight is a human quality, it is to be presumed they will continue to do. Whatever we adopt as the fundamental principle of morality, we require subordinate principles to apply it by; the impossibility of doing without them, being common to all systems, can afford no argument against anyone in particular; but gravely to argue as if no such secondary principles could be had, and as if mankind had remained till now, and always must remain, without drawing any general conclusions from the experience of human life, is as high a pitch, I think, as absurdity has ever reached in philosophical controversy.

The remainder of the stock arguments against utilitarianism mostly consist in laying to its charge the common infirmities of human nature, and the general difficulties which embarrass conscientious persons in shaping their course through life. We are told that a utilitarian will be apt to make his own particular case an exception to moral rules, and when under temptation will see a utility in the breach of a rule greater than he will see in its observance. But is utility the only creed which is able to furnish us with excuses for evil-doing, and means of cheating our own conscience? They are afforded in abundance by all doctrines which recognize as a fact in morals the existence of conflicting considerations; which all doctrines do, that have been believed by sane persons. It is not the fault of any creed, but of the complicated nature of human affairs, that rules of conduct cannot be so framed as to require no exceptions, and that hardly any kind of action can safely be laid down as either always obligatory or always condemnable. There is no ethical creed which does not temper the rigidity of its laws by giving a certain latitude, under the moral responsibility of the agent, for accommodation to peculiarities of circumstances; and under every creed, at the opening thus made, self-deception and dishonest casuistry get in. There exists no moral system under which there do not arise unequivocal cases of conflicting obligation. These are the real difficulties, the knotty points both in the theory of ethics, and in the conscientious guidance of personal conduct. They are overcome practically, with greater or with less success, according to the intellect and virtue of the individual; but it can hardly be pretended that anyone will be the less qualified for dealing with them, from possessing an ultimate standard to which conflicting rights and duties can be referred. If utility is the ultimate source of moral obligations, utility may be invoked to decide between them when their demands are incompatible. Though the application of the standard may be difficult, it is better than none at all; while in other systems, the moral laws all claiming independent authority, there is no common umpire entitled to interfere between them: their claims to precedence one over another rest on little better than sophistry, and unless determined, as they generally are, by the unacknowledged influence of considerations of utility, afford a free scope for the action of personal desires and partialities. We must remember that only in these cases of conflict between secondary principles is it requisite that first principles should be appealed to. There is no case of moral obligation in which some secondary principle is not involved; and if only one, there can seldom be any real doubt which one it is, in the mind of any person by whom the principle itself is recognized.

5

Turning Values Upside Down

Friedrich Nietzsche (1844–1900)

BEYOND GOOD AND EVIL

I hope to be forgiven for discovering that all moral philosophy hitherto has been tedious and has belonged to the soporific appliances—and that "virtue," in my opinon, has been more injured by the *tediousness* of its advocates than by anything else; at the same time, however, I would not wish to overlook their general usefulness. It is desirable that as few people as possible should reflect upon morals, and consequently it is *very* desirable that morals should not some day become interesting! But let us not be afraid! Things still remain today as they have always been: I see no one in Europe who has (or discloses) an idea of the fact that philosophising concerning morals might be conducted in a dangerous, captious, and ensnaring manner—that *calamity* might be involved therein. Ob-

From Nietzsche, *Beyond Good and Evil,* translated by Helen Zimmern; *The Twilight of the Idols* and *The Will to Power,* translated by A. M. Ludovici in *The Complete Works of Friedrich Nietzsche,* translated under Oscar Levy (1909–1911).

serve, for example, the indefatigable, inevitable English utilitarians: how ponderously and respectably they stalk on, stalk along (a Homeric metaphor expresses it better) in the footsteps of Bentham, just as he had already stalked in the footsteps of the respectable Helvétius! (no, he was not a dangerous man, Helvétius, *ce senateur Pococurante,* to use an expression of Galiani). No new thought, nothing of the nature of a finer turning or better expression of an old thought, not even a proper history of what has been previously thought on the subject: an *impossible* literature, taking it all in all unless one knows how to leaven it with some mischief. In effect, the old English vice called *cant,* which is *moral Tartuffism,* has insinuated itself also into these moralists (whom one must certainly read with an eye to their motives if one *must* read them), concealed this time under the new form of the scientific spirit; moreover, there is not absent from them a secret struggle with the pangs of conscience, from which a race of former Puritans must naturally suffer, in all their scientific tinkering with morals. (Is not a moralist the opposite of a Puritan? That is to say, as a thinker who regards morality as questionable, as worthy of interrogation, in short, as a problem? Is moralising not—immoral?) In the end, they all want *English* morality to be recognised as authoritative, inasmuch as mankind, or the "general utility," or "the happiness of the greatest number,"—no! the happiness of *England,* will be best served thereby. They would like, by all means, to convince themselves that the striving after *English* happiness, I mean after *comfort* and *fashion* (and in the highest instance, a seat in Parliament), is at the same time the true path of virtue; in fact, that in so far as there has been virtue in the world hitherto, it has just consisted in such striving. Not one of those ponderous, conscience-stricken herding-animals (who undertake to advocate the cause of egoism as conducive to the general welfare) wants to have any knowledge or inkling of the facts that the "general welfare" is no ideal, no goal, no notion that can be at all grasped, but is only a nostrum,—that what is fair to one *may not* at all be fair to another, that the requirement of one morality for all is really a detriment to higher men, in short, that there is a *distinction of rank* between man and man, and consequently between morality and morality. They are an unassuming and fundamentally mediocre species of men, these utilitarian Englishmen, and, as already remarked, in so far as they are tedious, one cannot think highly enough of their utility. One ought even to *encourage* them, as has been partially attempted in the following rhymes:—

> Hail, ye worthies, barrow-wheeling,
> "Longer—better," aye revealing,
>   Stiffer aye in head and knee;
> Unenraptured, never jesting,
> Mediocre everlasting,
>   *Sans genie et sans esprit!*

Every elevation of the type "man," has hitherto been the work of an aristocratic society—and so will it always be—a society believing in a long scale of gradations of rank and differences of worth among human beings, and requiring slavery in some form or other. Without the *pathos of distance,* such as grows out of the incarnated difference of classes, out of the constant outlooking and down-looking of the ruling caste on subordinates and instruments, and out of their equally constant practice of obeying and commanding, of keeping down and keeping at a distance—that other more mysterious pathos could never have arisen, the longing for an ever new widening of distance within the soul itself, the formation of ever higher, rarer, further, more extended, more comprehensive states, in short, just the elevation of the type "man," the continued "self-sur-mounting of man," to use a moral formula in a supermoral sense. To be sure, one must not resign oneself to any humanitarian illusions about the history of the origin of an aristocratic society (that is to say, of the preliminary condition for the elevation of the type "man"): the truth is hard. Let us acknowledge unpreju-dicedly how every higher civilisation hitherto has *originated!* Men with a still natural nature, barbarians in every terrible sense of the word, men of prey, still in possession of unbroken strength of will and desire for power, threw themselves upon weaker, more moral, more peaceful races (perhaps trading or cattle-rearing communities), or upon old mellow civilisations in which the final vital force was flickering out in brilliant fireworks of wit and depravity. At the commencement, the noble caste was always the barbarian caste: their superiority did not consist first of all in their physical, but in their psychical power—they were more *com-plete* men (which at every point also implies the same as "more complete beasts").

To refrain mutually from injury, from violence, from exploitation, and put one's will on a par with that of others: this may result in a certain rough sense in good conduct among individuals when the necessary conditions are given (namely, the actual similarity of the individuals in amount of force and degree of worth, and their co-relation within one organisation). As soon, however, as one wished to take this principle more generally, and if possible even as *the funda-mental principle of society,* it would immediately disclose what it really is—namely, a Will to the *denial* of life, a principle of dissolution and decay. Here one must think profoundly to the very basis and resist all sentimental weakness: life itself is essentially appropriation, injury, conquest of the strange and weak, sup-pression, severity, obtrusion of peculiar forms, incorporation, and at the least, putting it mildest, exploitation;—but why should one for ever use precisely these words on which for ages a disparaging purpose has been stamped? Even the organisation within which, as was previously supposed, the individuals treat each other as equal—it takes place in every healthy aristocracy—must itself, if it be a living and not a dying organisation, do all that towards other bodies, which the individuals within it refrain from doing to each other: it will have to be the incarnated Will to Power, it will endeavour to grow, to gain ground, attract to itself and acquire ascendency—not owing to any morality or immorality, but because it *lives,* and because life *is* precisely Will to Power. On no point, how-ever, is the ordinary consciousness of Europeans more unwilling to be corrected than on this matter; people now rave everywhere, even under the guise of sci-ence, about coming conditions of society in which "the exploiting character" is to be absent:—that sounds to my ears as if they promised to invent a mode of life which should refrain from all organic functions. "Exploitation" does not belong to a depraved, or imperfect and primitive society: it belongs to the *nature* of the living being as a primary organic function; it is a consequence of the intrinsic Will to Power, which is precisely the Will to Life.—Granting that as a theory this is a novelty—as a reality it is the *fundamental fact* of all history: let us be so far honest towards ourselves!

In a tour through the many finer and coarser moralities which have hitherto prevailed or still prevail on the earth, I found certain traits recurring regularly together and connected with one another, until finally two primary types revealed themselves to me, and a radical distinction was brought to light. There is *master*-morality and *slave*-morality;—I would at once add, however, that in all higher and mixed civilisations, there are also attempts at the reconciliation of the two moralities; but one finds still oftener the confusion and mutual misunderstanding of them, indeed, sometimes their close juxtaposition—even in the same man, within one soul. The distinctions of moral values have either originated in a ruling caste, pleasantly conscious of being different from the ruled—or among the ruled class, the slaves and dependents of all sorts. In the first case, when it is the rulers who determine the conception "good," it is the exalted, proud disposition which is regarded as the distinguishing feature, and that which determines the order of rank. The noble type of man separates from himself the beings in whom the opposite of this exalted, proud disposition displays itself: he despises them. Let it at once be noted that in this first kind of morality the antithesis "good" and "bad" means practically the same as "noble" and "despicable";—the antithesis "good" and *"evil"* is of a different origin. The cowardly, the timid, the insignificant, and those thinking merely of narrow utility are despised; moreover, also, the distrustful, with their constrained glances, the self-abasing, the dog-like kind of men who let themselves be abused, the mendicant flatterers, and above all the liars:—it is a fundamental belief of all aristocrats that the common people are untruthful. "We truthful ones"—the nobility in ancient Greece called themselves. It is obvious that everywhere the designations of moral value were at first applied to *men,* and were only derivatively and at a later period applied to *actions;* it is a gross mistake, therefore, when historians of morals start with questions like, "Why have sympathetic actions been praised?" The noble type of man regards himself as a determiner of values; he does not require to be approved of; he passes the judgment: "What is injurious to me is injurious in itself"; he knows that it is he himself only who confers honour on things; he is a creator of values. He honours whatever he recognises in himself: such morality is self-glorification. In the foreground there is the feeling of plenitude, of power, which seeks to overflow, the happiness of high tension, the consciousness of a wealth which would fain give and bestow:—the noble man also helps the unfortunate, but not—or scarcely—out of pity, but rather from an impulse generated by the super-abundance of power. The noble man honours in himself the powerful one, him also who has power over himself, who knows how to speak and how to keep silence, who takes pleasure in subjecting himself to severity and hardness, and has reverence for all that is severe and hard. "Wotan placed a hard heart in my breast," says an old Scandinavian Saga: it is thus rightly expressed from the soul of a proud Viking. Such a type of man is even proud of *not* being made for sympathy; the hero of the Saga therefore adds warningly: "He who has not a hard heart when young, will never have one." The noble and brave who think thus are the furthest removed from the morality which sees precisely in sympathy, or in acting for the good of others, or in *désintéressement,* the characteristic of the moral; faith in oneself, pride in oneself, a radical enmity and irony towards "selflessness," belong as definitely to noble morality, as do a careless scorn and precaution in presence of sympathy and the "warm heart."—It is the powerful who *know* how to honour, it is their art, their domain for invention. The profound reverence for age and for tradition—all law rests on this double reverence,—the belief and prejudice in favour of ancestors and unfavourable to newcomers, is typical in the morality of the powerful; and if, reversely, men of "modern ideas" believe almost instinctively in "progress" and the "future," and are more and more lacking in respect for old age, the ignoble origin of these "ideas" has complacently betrayed itself thereby. A morality of the ruling class, however, is more especially foreign and irritating to present-day taste in the sternness of its principle that one has duties only to one's equals; that one may act towards beings of a lower rank, towards all that is foreign, just as seems good to one, or "as the heart desires," and in any case "beyond good and evil": it is here that sympathy and similar sentiments can have a place. The ability and obligation to exercise prolonged gratitude and prolonged revenge—both only within the circle of equals,—artfulness in retaliation, *raffinement* of the idea in friendship, a certain necessity to have enemies (as outlets for the emotions of envy, quarrelsomeness, arrogance—in fact, in order to be a good *friend*): all these are typical characteristics of the noble morality, which, as has been pointed out, is not the morality of "modern ideas," and is therefore at present difficult to realise, and also to unearth and disclose.—It is otherwise with the second type of morality, *slave-morality.* Supposing that the abused, the oppressed, the suffering, the unemancipated, the weary, and those uncertain of themselves, should moralise, what will be the common element in their moral estimates? Probably a pessimistic suspicion with regard to the entire situation of man will find expression, perhaps a condemnation of man, together with his situation. The slave has an unfavourable eye for the virtues of the powerful; he has a scepticism and distrust, a *refinement* of distrust of everything "good" that is there honoured—he would fain persuade himself that the very happiness there is not genuine. On the other hand, *those* qualities which serve to alleviate the existence of sufferers are brought into prominence and flooded with light; it is here that sympathy, the kind, helping hand, the warm heart, patience, diligence, humility, and friendliness attain to honour; for here these are the most useful qualities, and almost the only means of supporting the burden of existence. Slave-morality is essentially the morality of utility. Here is the seat of the origin of the famous antithesis "good" and "evil":—power and dangerousness are assumed to reside in the evil, a certain dreadfulness, subtlety, and strength, which do not admit of being despised. According to slave-morality, therefore, the "evil" man arouses fear: according to master-morality, it is precisely the "good" man who arouses fear and seeks to arouse it, while the bad man is regarded as the despicable being. The contrast attains its maximum when, in accordance with the logical consequences of slave-morality, a shade of depreciation—it may be slight and well-intentioned—at last attaches itself even to the "good" man of this morality; because, according to the servile mode of thought, the good man must in any case be the *safe* man: he is good-natured, easily deceived, perhaps a little stupid, *un bonhomme*. Everywhere that slave-morality gains the ascendency, language shows a tendency to approximate the significations of the words "good" and "stupid."— A last fundamental difference: the desire for *freedom*, the instinct for happiness and the refinements of the feeling of liberty belong as necessarily to slave-morals and morality, as artifice and enthusiasm in reverence and devotion are the regular symptoms of an aristocratic mode of thinking and estimating.—Hence we can understand without further detail why love as *a passion*—it is our European speciality—must absolutely be of noble origin; as is well known, its invention is due to the Provençal poet-cavaliers, those brilliant ingenious men of the "gai saber," to whom Europe owes so much, and almost owes itself.

TWILIGHT OF IDOLS

What then, alone, can our teaching be?—That no one gives man his qualities, either God, society, his parents, his ancestors, nor himself (this nonsensical idea, which is at last refuted here, was taught as "intelligible freedom" by Kant, and perhaps even as early as Plato himself). No one is responsible for the fact that he exists at all, that he is constituted as he is, and that he happens to be in certain circumstances and in a particular environment. The fatality of his being cannot be divorced from the fatality of all that which has been and will be. This is not the result of an individual attention, of a will, of an aim, there is no attempt at attaining to any "ideal man," or "ideal happiness" or "ideal morality" with him—it is absurd to wish him to be careering towards some sort of purpose. *We* invented the concept "purpose"; in reality purpose is altogether lacking. One is necessary, one is a piece of fate, one belongs to the whole, one is in the whole— there is nothing that could judge, measure, compare, and condemn our existence, for that would mean judging, measuring, comparing and condemning the whole. *But there is nothing outside the whole!* The fact that no one shall any longer be made responsible, that the nature of existence may not be traced to a *causa prima*, that the world is an entity neither as a sensorium nor as a spirit—*this alone is the great deliverance*—thus alone is the innocence of Becoming restored. . . . The concept "God" has been the greatest objection to existence hitherto. . . . We deny God, we deny responsibility in God: thus alone do we save the world.

THE WILL TO POWER

I regard Christianity as the most fatal and seductive lie that has ever yet existed—as the greatest and most *impious* lie: I can discern the last sprouts and branches of its ideal beneath every form of disguise, I decline to enter into any compromise or false position in reference to it—I urge people to declare open war with it.

The morality of paltry people as the measure of all things: this is the most repugnant kind of degeneracy that civilisation has ever yet brought into existence. And this *kind of ideal* is hanging still, under the name of "God," over men's heads!!

However modest one's demands may be concerning intellectual cleanliness, when one touches the New Testament one cannot help experiencing a sort of inexpressible feeling of discomfort; for the unbounded cheek with which the least qualified people will have their say in its pages, in regard to the greatest problems of existence, and claim to sit in judgment on such matters, exceeds all limits. The impudent levity with which the most unwieldy problems are spoken of here (life, the world, God, the purpose of life), as if they were not problems at all, but the most simple things which these little bigots *know all about!!!*

This was the most fatal form of insanity that has ever yet existed on earth:—when these little lying abortions of bigotry begin laying claim to the words "God," "last judgment," "truth," "love," "wisdom," "Holy Spirit," and thereby distinguishing themselves from the rest of the world; when such men begin to transvalue values to suit themselves, as though they were the sense, the salt, the standard, and the measure of all things; then all that one should do is this: build lunatic asylums for their incarceration. To *persecute* them was an egregious act of antique folly: this was taking them too seriously; it was making them serious.

The whole fatality was made possible by the fact that a similar form of megalomania was already *in existence,* the *Jewish* form (once the gulf separating the Jews from the Christian-Jews was bridged, the Christian-Jews *were compelled* to employ those self-preservative measures afresh which were discovered by the Jewish instinct, for their own self-preservation, after having accentuated them); and again through the fact that Greek moral philosophy had done everything that could be done to prepare the way for moral-fanaticism, even among Greeks and Romans, and to render it palatable. . . . Plato, the great importer of corruption, who was the first who refused to see Nature in morality, and who had already deprived the Greek gods of all their worth by his notion *"good,"* was already tainted with *Jewish bigotry* (in Egypt?). . . .

The *law,* which is the fundamentally realistic formula of certain self-preservative measures of a comunity, forbids certain actions that have a definite tendency to jeopardise the welfare of that community: it does *not* forbid the attitude of mind which gives rise to these actions—for in the pursuit of other ends the community requires these forbidden actions, namely, when it is a matter of opposing its *enemies.* The moral idealist now steps forward and says: "God sees into men's hearts: the action itself counts for nothing; the reprehensible attitude of mind from which it proceeds must be extirpated. . . ." In normal conditions men laugh at such things; it is only in exceptional cases, when a community lives *quite* beyond the need of waging war in order to maintain itself, that an ear is lent to such things. Any attitude of mind is abandoned, the utility of which cannot be conceived.

This was the case, for example, when Buddha appeared among a people that was both peaceable and afflicted with great intellectual weariness.

This was also the case in regard to the first Christian community (as also the Jewish), the primary condition of which was the absolutely *unpolitical* Jewish society. Christianity could grow only upon the soil of Judaism—that is to say, among a people that had already renounced the political life, and which led a sort of parasitic existence within the Roman sphere of government. Christianity goes a step *farther:* it allows men to "emasculate" themselves even more; the circumstances actually favour their doing so.—*Nature* is *expelled* from morality when it is said, "Love ye your enemies": for *Nature's* injunction, "Ye shall *love* your neighbour and *hate* your enemy," has now become senseless in the law (in instinct); now, even *the love a man feels for his neighbour* must first be based upon something (*a sort of love of God*). *God* is introduced everywhere, and *utility* is withdrawn; the natural *origin* of morality is denied everywhere: the *veneration of Nature*, which lies in *acknowledging a natural morality*, is *destroyed* to the roots. . . .

Whence comes the *seductive charm* of this emasculate ideal of man? Why are we not *disgusted* by it, just as we are disgusted at the thought of a eunuch? . . . The answer is obvious: it is not the voice of the eunuch that revolts us, despite the cruel mutilation of which it is the result; for, as a matter of fact, it has grown sweeter. . . . And owing to the very fact that the "male organ" has been amputated from virtue, its voice now has a feminine ring, which, formerly, was not to be discerned.

On the other hand, we have only to think of the terrible hardness, dangers, and accidents to which a life of manly virtues leads—the life of a Corsican, even at the present day, or that of a heathen Arab (which resembles the Corsican's life even to the smallest detail: the Arab's songs might have been written by Corsicans)—in order to perceive how the most robust type of man was fascinated and moved by the voluptuous ring of this "goodness" and "purity." . . . A pastoral melody . . . an idyll . . . the "good man": such things have most effect in ages when tragedy is abroad.

The *Astuteness of moral castration.*—How is war waged against the virile passions and valuations? No violent physical means are available; the war must therefore be one of ruses, spells, and lies—in short, a "spiritual war."

First recipe: One appropriates virtue in general, and makes it the main feature of one's ideal; the older ideal is denied and declared to be *the reverse of all ideals.* Slander has to be carried to a fine art for this purpose.

Second recipe: One's own type is set up as a general *standard;* and this is projected into all things, behind all things, and behind the destiny of all things—as God.

Third recipe: The opponents of one's ideal are declared to be the opponents of God; one arrogates to oneself a *right* to great pathos, to power, and a right to curse and to bless.

Fourth recipe: All suffering, all gruesome, terrible, and fatal things are declared to be the results of opposition to *one's* ideal—all suffering is *punishment* even in the case of one's adherents (except it be a trial, etc.).

Fifth recipe: One goes so far as to regard Nature as the reverse of one's ideal, and the lengthy sojourn amid natural conditions is considered a great trial of patience—a sort of martyrdom; one studies contempt, both in one's attitudes and one's looks towards all "natural things."

Sixth recipe: The triumph of anti-naturalism and ideal castration, the triumph of the world of the pure, good, sinless, and blessed, is projected into the future as the consummation, the finale, the great hope, and the "Coming of the Kingdom of God."

I hope that one may still be allowed to laugh at this artificial hoisting up of a small species of man to the position of an absolute standard of all things?

To what extent psychologists have been corrupted by the moral idiosyncrasy!—Not one of the ancient philosophers had the courage to advance the theory of the non-free will (that is to say, the theory that denies morality);—not one had the courage to identify the typical feature of happiness, of every kind of happiness ("pleasure"), with the will to power: for the pleasure of power was considered immoral;—not one had the courage to regard virtue as a *result of immorality* (as a result of a will to power) in the service of a species (or of a race, or of a *polis*); for the will to power was considered immoral.

In the whole of moral evolution, there is no sign of truth: all the conceptual elements which come into play are fictions; all the psychological tenets are false; all the forms of logic employed in this department of prevarication are sophisms. The chief feature of all moral philosophers is their total lack of intellectual cleanliness and self-control: they regard "fine feelings" as arguments: their heaving breasts seem to them the bellows of godliness. . . . Moral philosophy is the most suspicious period in the history of the human intellect.

The first great example: in the name of morality and under its patronage, a great wrong was committed, which as a matter of fact was in every respect an act of decadence. Sufficient stress cannot be laid upon this fact, that the great Greek philosophers not only represented the decadence of *every kind of Greek ability*, but also made it *contagious*. . . . This "virtue" made wholly abstract was the highest form of seduction; to make oneself abstract means to *turn one's back on the world.*

The moment is a very remarkable one: the Sophists are within sight of the first *criticism* of morality, the first *knowledge* of morality:—they classify the majority of moral valuations (in view of their dependence upon local conditions) together;—they lead one to understand that every form of morality is capable of being upheld dialectically: that is to say, they guessed that all the fundamental principles of a morality must be *sophistical*—a proposition which was afterwards proved in the grandest possible style by the ancient philosophers from Plato onwards (up to Kant);—they postulate the primary truth that there is no such thing as a "moral *per se*," a "good *per se*," and that it is madness to talk of "truth" in this respect.

Wherever was *intellectual uprightness* to be found in those days?

The Greek culture of the Sophists had grown out of all the Greek instincts; it belongs to the culture of the age of Pericles as necessarily as Plato does not: it has its predecessors in Heraclitus, Democritus, and in the scientific types of the old philosophy; it finds expression in the elevated culture of Thucydides, for instance. And—it has ultimately shown itself to be right: every step in the science of epistemology and morality has *confirmed the attitude* of the Sophists. . . . Our modern attitude of mind is, to a great extent, Heraclitean, Democritean, and Protagorean . . . to say that it is *Protagorean* is even sufficient: because Protagoras was in himself a synthesis of the two men Heraclitus and Democritus.

(*Plato: a great Cagliostro,*—let us think of how Epicurus judged him; how Timon, Pyrrho's friend, judged him—Is Plato's integrity by any chance beyond question? . . . But we at least know what he wished to have *taught* as absolute truth—namely, things which were to him not even relative truths: the separate and immortal life of "souls.")

6

Is the Will Free?

(Two views.)

THE DILEMMA OF DETERMINISM

William James (1842–1910)

To begin, then, I must suppose you acquainted with all the usual arguments on the subject. I cannot stop to take up the old proofs from causation, from statistics, from the certainty with which we can foretell one another's conduct, from the fixity of character, and all the rest. But there are two *words* which usually encumber these classical arguments, and which we must immediately dispose of if we are to make any progress. One is the eulogistic word *freedom*, and the other is the opprobrious word *chance*. The word "chance" I wish to keep, but I wish to get rid of the word "freedom." Its eulogistic associations have so far overshadowed all the rest of its meaning that both parties claim the sole right to use it, and determinists today insist that they alone are freedom's champions. Old-fashioned

From William James, "Dilemma of Determinism," 1884.

determinism was what we may call *hard* determinism. It did not shrink from such words as fatality, bondage of the will, necessitation, and the like. Nowadays, we have a *soft* determinism which abhors harsh words, and, repudiating fatality, necessity, and even predetermination, says that its real name is freedom; for freedom is only necessity understood, and bondage to the highest is identical with true freedom. Even a writer as little used to making capital out of soft words as Mr. Hodgson hesitates not to call himself a "free-will determinist."

Now, all this is a quagmire of evasion under which the real issue of fact has been entirely smothered. Freedom in all these senses presents simply no problem at all. No matter what the soft determinist mean by it—whether he mean the acting without external constraint; whether he mean the acting rightly, or whether he mean the acquiescing in the law of the whole—who cannot answer him that sometimes we are free and sometimes we are not? But there *is* a problem, an issue of fact and not of words, an issue of the most momentous importance, which is often decided without discussion in one sentence—nay, in one clause of a sentence—by those very writers who spin out whole chapters in their efforts to show what "true" freedom is; and that is the question of determinism, about which we are to talk tonight.

Fortunately, no ambiguities hang about this word or about its opposite, indeterminism. Both designate an outward way in which things may happen, and their cold and mathematical sound has no sentimental associations that can bribe our partiality either way in advance. Now, evidence of an external kind to decide between determinism and indeterminism is, as I intimated a while back, strictly impossible to find. Let us look at the difference between them and see for ourselves. What does determinism profess?

It professes that those parts of the universe already laid down absolutely appoint and decree what the other parts shall be. The future has no ambiguous possibilities hidden in its womb: the part we call the present is compatible with only totality. Any other future complement than the one fixed from eternity is impossible. The whole is in each and every part, and welds it with the rest into an absolute unity, an iron block, in which there can be no equivocation or shadow of turning.

> With earth's first clay they did the last man knead,
> And there of the last harvest sowed the seed.
> And the first morning of creation wrote
> What the last dawn of reckoning shall read.

Indeterminism, on the contrary, says that the parts have a certain amount of loose play on one another, so that the laying down of one of them does not necessarily determine what the others shall be. It admits that possibilities may be in excess of actualities, and that things not yet revealed to our knowledge may really in themselves be ambiguous. Of two alternative futures which we conceive, both may now be really possible; and the one become impossible only at the very moment when the other excludes it by becoming real itself. Indeterminism thus denies the world to be one unbending unit of fact. It says there is a certain ultimate pluralism in it; and, so saying, it corroborates our ordinary unsophisticated view of things. To that view, actualities seem to float in a wider sea of possibilities from out of which they are chosen; and, *somewhere,* indeterminism says, such possibilities exist, and form a part of truth.

Determinism, on the contrary, says they exist *nowhere,* and that necessity on the one hand and impossibility on the other are the sole categories of the real. Possibilities that fail to get realized are, for determinism, pure illusions: they never were possibilities at all. There is nothing inchoate, it says, about this universe of ours, all that was or is or shall be actual in it having been from eternity virtually there. The cloud of alternatives our minds escort this mass of actuality withal is a cloud of sheer deceptions, to which "impossibilities" is the only name that rightfully belongs.

The issue, it will be seen, is a perfectly sharp one, which no eulogistic terminology can smear over or wipe out. The truth *must* lie with one side or the other, and its lying with one side makes the other false.

The question relates solely to the existence of possibilities, in the strict sense of the term, as things that may, but need not, be. Both sides admit that a volition, for instance, has occurred. The indeterminists say another volition might have occurred in its place: the determinists swear that nothing could possibly have occurred in its place. Now, can science be called in to tell us which of these two point-blank contradicters of each other is right? Science professes to draw no conclusions but such as are based on matters of fact, things that have actually happened; but how can any amount of assurance that something actually happened give us the least grain of information as to whether another thing might or might not have happened in its place? Only facts can be proved by other facts. With things that are possibilities and not facts, facts have no concern. If we have no other evidence than the evidence of existing facts, the possibility-question must remain a mystery never to be cleared up.

And the truth is that facts practically have hardly anything to do with making us either determinists or indeterminists. Sure enough, we make a flourish of quoting facts this way or that; and if we are determinists, we talk about the infallibility with which we can predict one another's conduct; while if we are indeterminists, we lay great stress on the fact that it is just because we cannot foretell one another's conduct, either in war or statecraft or in any of the great and small intrigues and businesses of men, that life is so intensely anxious and hazardous a game. But who does not see the wretched insufficiency of this so-called objective testimony on both sides? What fills up the gaps in our minds is something not objective, not external. What divides us into *possibility* men and *antipossibility* men is different faiths or postulates—postulates of rationality. To this man the world seems more rational with possibilities in it—to that man more rational with possibilities excluded; and talk as we will about having to yield to evidence, what makes us monists or pluralists, determinists or indeterminists, is at bottom always some sentiment like this.

The stronghold of the deterministic sentiment is the antipathy to the idea of chance. As soon as we begin to talk indeterminism to our friends, we find a number of them shaking their heads. This notion of alternative possibility, they say, this admission that any one of several things may come to pass, is, after all, only a round-about name for chance; and chance is something the notion of which no sane mind can for an instant tolerate in the world. What is it, they ask, but barefaced crazy unreason, the negation of intelligibility and law? And if the slightest particle of it exist anywhere, what is to prevent the whole fabric from falling together, the stars from going out, and chaos from recommencing her topsy-turvy reign?

Remarks of this sort about chance will put an end to discussion as quickly as anything one can find. I have already told you that "chance" was a word I wished to keep and use. Let us then examine exactly what it means, and see whether it ought to be such a terrible bugbear to us. I fancy that squeezing the thistle boldly will rob it of its sting.

The sting of the word "chance" seems to lie in the assumption that it means something positive, and that if anything happens by chance, it must needs be something of an intrinsically irrational and preposterous sort. Now, chance means nothing of the kind. It is a purely negative and relative term, giving us no information about that of which it is predicated, except that it happens to be disconnected with something else—not controlled, secured, or necessitated by other things in advance of its own actual presence. At this point is the most subtile one of the whole lecture, and at the same time the point on which all the rest hinges, I beg you to pay particular attention to it. What I say is that it tells us nothing about what a thing may be in itself to call it "chance." It may be a bad thing, it may be a good thing. It may be lucidity, transparency, fitness incarnate, matching the whole system of other things, when it has once befallen, in an unimaginably perfect way. All you mean by calling it "chance" is that this is not guaranteed, that it may also fall out otherwise. For the system of other things has no positive hold on the chance-thing. Its origin is in a certain fashion negative: it escapes, and says, Hands off! coming, when it comes, as a free gift, or not at all.

This negativeness, however, and this opacity of the chance-thing when thus considered *ab extra*, or from the point of view of previous things or distant things, do not preclude its having any amount of positiveness and luminosity from within, and at its own place and moment. All that its chance-character asserts about it is that there is something in it really of its own, something that is not the unconditional property of the whole. If the whole wants this property, the whole must wait till it can get it, if it be a matter of chance. That the universe may actually be a sort of joint-stock society of this sort, in which the sharers have both limited liabilities and limited powers, is of course a simple and conceivable notion.

Nevertheless, many persons talk as if the minutest dose of disconnectedness of one part with another, the smallest modicum of independence, the faintest tremor of ambiguity about the future, for example, would ruin everything, and turn this goodly universe into a sort of insane sand-heap or nulliverse—no uni-

�֍

verse at all. Since future human volitions are as a matter of fact the only ambiguous things we are tempted to believe in, let us stop for a moment to make ourselves sure whether their independent and accidental character need be fraught with such direful consequences to the universe as these.

What is meant by saying that my choice of which way to walk home after the lecture is ambiguous and matter of chance as far as the present moment is concerned? It means that both Divinity Avenue and Oxford Street are called; but that only one, and that one *either* one, shall be chosen. Now, I ask you seriously to suppose that this ambiguity of my choice is real; and then to make the impossible hypothesis that the choice is made twice over, and each time falls on a different street. In other words, imagine that I first walk through Divinity Avenue, and then imagine that the powers governing the universe annihilate ten minutes of time with all that it contained, and set me back at the door of this hall just as I was before the choice was made. Imagine then that, everything else being the same, I now make a different choice and traverse Oxford Street. You, as passive spectators, look on and see the two alternative universes—one of them with me walking through Divinity Avenue in it, the other with the same me walking through Oxford Street. Now, if you are determinists you believe one of these universes to have been from eternity impossible: you believe it to have been impossible because of the intrinsic irrationality or accidentality somewhere involved in it. But looking outwardly at these universes, can you say which is the impossible and accidental one, and which the rational and necessary one? I doubt if the most iron-clad determinist among you could have the slightest glimmer of light on this point. In other words, either universe *after the fact* and once there would, to our means of observation and understanding, appear just as rational as the other. . . .

We have seen what determinism means: we have seen that indeterminism is rightly described as meaning chance; and we have seen that chance, the very name of which we are urged to shrink from as from a metaphysical pestilence, means only the negative fact that no part of the world, however big, can claim to control absolutely the destinies of the whole. But although, in discussing the word "chance," I may at moments have seemed to be arguing for its real existence, I have not meant to do so yet. We have not yet ascertained whether this be a world of chance or no; at most, we have agreed that it seems so. And I now repeat what I said at the outset, that, from any strict theoretical point of view, the question is insoluble. To deepen our theoretic sense of the *difference* between a world with chances in it and a deterministic world is the most I can hope to do; and this I may now at last begin upon, after all our tedious clearing of the way.

I wish first of all to show you just what the notion that this is a deterministic world implies. The implications I call your attention to are all bound up with the fact that it is a world in which we constantly have to make what I shall, with your permission, call judgments of regret. Hardly an hour passes in which we do not wish that something might be otherwise; and happy indeed are those of us whose hearts have never echoed the wish of Omar Khayam—

That we might clasp, ere closed, the book of fate,
   And make the writer on a fairer leaf
Inscribe our names, or quite obliterate.

Ah! Love, could you and I with fate conspire
To mend this sorry scheme of things entire,
   Would we not shatter it to bits, and then
Remould it nearer to the heart's desire?

Now, it is undeniable that most of these regrets are foolish, and quite on a par in point of philosophic value with the criticisms on the universe of that friend of our infancy, the hero of the fable "The Atheist and the Acorn"—

Fool! had that bough a pumpkin bore,
Thy whimsies would have worked no more, etc.

Even from the point of view of our own ends, we should probably make a botch of remodelling the universe. How much more then from the point of view of ends we cannot see! Wise men therefore regret as little as they can. But still some regrets are pretty obstinate and hard to stifle—regrets for acts of wanton cruelty or treachery, for example, whether performed by others or by ourselves. Hardly any one can remain *entirely* optimistic after reading the confession of the murderer at Brockton the other day: how, to get rid of the wife whose continued existence bored him, he inveigled her into a desert spot, shot her four times, and then, as she lay on the ground and said to him, "You didn't do it on purpose, did you, dear?" replied, "No, I didn't do it on purpose," as he raised a rock and smashed her skull. Such an occurrence, with the mild sentence and self-satisfaction of the prisoner, is a field for a crop of regrets, which one need not take up in detail. We feel that, although a perfect mechanical fit to the rest of the universe, it is a bad moral fit, and that something else would really have been better in its place.

But for the deterministic philosophy the murder, the sentence, and the prisoner's optimism were all necessary from eternity; and nothing else for a moment had a ghost of a chance of being put into their place. To admit such a chance, the determinists tell us, would be to make a suicide of reason; so we must steel our hearts against the thought. And here our plot thickens, for we see the first of those difficult implications of determinism and monism which it is my purpose to make you feel. If this Brockton murder was called for by the rest of the universe, if it had to come at its preappointed hour, and if nothing else would have been consistent with the sense of the whole, what are we to think of the universe? Are we stubbornly to stick to our judgment of regret, and say, though it *couldn't* be, yet it *would* have been a better universe with something different from this Brockton murder in it? That, of course, seems the natural and spontaneous thing for us to do; and yet it is nothing short of delibertely espousing a kind of pessimism. The judgment of regret calls the murder bad. Calling a thing bad means, if it mean anything at all, that the thing ought not to be, that something else ought to be in its stead. Determinism, in denying that anything else can be in its stead, virtually defines the universe as a place in which what ought to be is impossible—in other words, as an organism whose constitution is afflicted with an incurable taint, an irremediable flaw. The pessimism of a Schopenhauer says no more than this—that the murder is a symptom; and that it is a vicious symptom because it belongs to a vicious whole, which can express its nature no otherwise than by bringing forth just such a symptom as that at this particular spot. Regret for the murder must transform itself, if we are determinists and wise, into a larger regret. It is absurd to regret the murder alone. Other things being what they are, *it* could not be different. What we should regret is that whole frame of things of which the murder is one member. I see no escape whatever from this pessimistic conclusion if, being determinists, our judgment of regret is to be allowed to stand at all.

The only deterministic escape from pessimism is everywhere to abandon the judgment of regret. That this can be done, history shows to be not impossible. The devil, *quoad existentiam,* may be good. That is, although he be a *principle* of evil, yet the universe, with such a principle in it, may practically be a better universe than it could have been without. On every hand, in a small way, we find that a certain amount of evil is a condition by which a higher form of good is brought. There is nothing to prevent anybody from generalizing this view, and trusting that if we could but see things in the largest of all ways, even such matters as this Brockton murder would appear to be paid for by the uses that follow in their train. An optimism *quand même,* a systematic and infatuated optimism like that ridiculed by Voltaire in his *Candide,* is one of the possible ideal ways in which a man may train himself to look on life. Bereft of dogmatic hardness and lit up with the expression of a tender and pathetic hope, such an optimism has been the grace of some of the most religious characters that ever lived.

> Throb thine with Nature's throbbing breast,
> And all is clear from east to west.

Even cruelty and treachery may be among the absolutely blessed fruits of time, and to quarrel with any of their details may be blasphemy. The only real blasphemy, in short, may be that pessimistic temper of the soul which lets it give way to such things as regrets, remorse, and grief.

Thus, our deterministic pessimism may become a deterministic optimism at the price of extinguishing our judgments of regret.

But does not this immediately bring us into a curious logical predicament? Our determinism leads us to call our judgments of regret wrong, because they are pessimistic in implying that what is impossible yet ought to be. But how then about the judgments of regret themselves? If they are wrong, other judgments, judgments of approval presumably, ought to be in their place. But as they are necessitated, nothing else *can* be in their place; and the universe is just what it was before—namely, a place in which what ought to be appears impossible. We have got one foot out of the pessimistic bog, but the other one sinks all the deeper. We have rescued our actions from the bonds of evil, but our judgments are now held fast. When murders and treacheries cease to be sins, regrets are theoretic absurdities and errors. The theoretic and the active life thus play a kind of see-saw with each other on the ground of evil. The rise of either sends the other down. Murder and treachery cannot be good without regret being bad: regret cannot be good without treachery and murder being bad. Both, however, are supposed to have been foredoomed; so something must be fatally unreasonable, absurd, and wrong in the world. It must be a place of which either sin or error forms a necessary part. From this dilemma there seems at first sight no escape. Are we then so soon to fall back into the pessimism from which we thought we had emerged? And is there no possible way by which we may, with good intellectual consciences, call the cruelties and the treacheries, the reluctances and the regrets, *all* good together? . . .

The only consistent way of representing a pluralism and a world whose parts may affect one another through their conduct being either good or bad is the indeterministic way. What interest, zest, or excitement can there be in achieving the right way, unless we are enabled to feel that the wrong way is also a possible and a natural way—nay, more, a menacing and an imminent way? And what sense can there be in condemning ourselves for taking the wrong way, unless we need have done nothing of the sort, unless the right way was open to us as well? I cannot understand the willingness to act, no matter how we feel, without the belief that acts are really good and bad. I cannot understand the belief that an act is bad, without regret at its happening. I cannot understand regret without the admission of real, genuine possibilities in the world. Only *then* is it other than a mockery to feel, after we have failed to do our best, that an irreparable opportunity is gone from the universe, the loss of which it must forever after mourn.

If you insist that this is all superstition, that possibility is in the eye of science and reason impossibility, and that if I act badly 'tis that the universe was foredoomed to suffer this defect, you fall right back into the dilemma, the labyrinth, of pessimism and subjectivism, from out of whose toils we have just wound our way.

Now, we are of course free to fall back, if we please. For my own part, though, whatever difficulties may beset the philosophy of objective right and wrong, and the indeterminism it seems to imply, determinism, with its alternative of pessimism or romanticism, contains difficulties that are greater still. But you will remember that I expressly repudiated awhile ago the pretension to offer any arguments which could be coercive in a so-called scientific fashion in this matter. And I consequently find myself, at the end of this long talk, obliged to state my conclusions in an altogether personal way. This personal method of appeal seems to be among the very conditions of the problem; and the most any one can do is to confess as candidly as he can the grounds for the faith that is in him, and leave his example to work on others as it may.

Let me, then, without circumlocution say just this. The world is enigmatical enough in all conscience, whatever theory we may take up toward it. The indeterminism I defend, the free-will theory of popular sense based on the judgment of regret, represents that world as vulnerable, and liable to be injured by certain of its parts if they act wrong. And it represents their acting wrong as a matter of possibility or accident, neither inevitable nor yet to be infallibly warded off. In all this, it is a theory devoid either of transparency or of stability. It gives us a pluralistic, restless universe, in which no single point of view can ever take in the whole scene; and to a mind possessed of the love of unity at any cost, it will, no doubt, remain forever inacceptable. A friend with such a mind once told me that the thought of my universe made him sick, like the sight of the horrible motion of a mass of maggots in their carrion bed.

But while I freely admit that the pluralism and the restlessness are repugnant and irrational in a certain way, I find that every alternative to them is irrational in a deeper way. The indeterminism with its maggots, if you please to speak so about it, offends only the native absolutism of my intellect—an absolutism which, after all, perhaps, deserves to be snubbed and kept in check. But the determinism with its necessary carrion, to continue the figure of speech, and with no possible maggots to eat the latter up, violates my sense of moral reality through and through. When, for example, I imagine such carrion as the Brockton murder, I cannot conceive it as an act by which the universe, as a whole, logically and necessarily expresses its nature without shrinking from complicity with such a whole. And I deliberately refuse to keep on terms of loyalty with the universe by saying blankly that the murder, since it does flow from the nature of the whole, is not carrion. There are *some* instinctive reactions which I, for one, will not tamper with. The only remaining alternative, the attitude of gnostical romanticism, wrenches my personal instincts in quite as violent a way. It falsifies the simple objectivity of their deliverance. It makes the goose-flesh the murder excites in me a sufficient reason for the perpetration of the crime. It transforms life from a tragic reality into an insincere melodramatic exhibition, as foul or as tawdry as any one's diseased curiosity pleases to carry it out. And with its consecration of the *roman naturaliste* state of mind, and its enthronement of the baser crew of Parisian *littérateurs* among the eternally indispensable organs by which the infinite spirit of things attains to that subjective illumination which is the task of its life, it leaves me in presence of a sort of subjective carrion considerably more noisome than the objective carrion I called it in to take away.

No! better a thousand times, than such systematic corruption of our moral sanity, the plainest pessimism, so that it be straightforward; but better far than that the world of chance. Make as great an uproar about chance as you please, I know that chance means pluralism and nothing more. If some of the members of the pluralism are bad, the philosophy of pluralism, whatever broad views it may deny me, permits me, at least, to turn to the other members with a clean breast of affection and an unsophisticated moral sense. And if I still wish to think of the world as a totality, it lets me feel that a world with a *chance* in it of being altogether good, even if the chance never comes to pass, is better than a world with no such chance at all. That "chance" whose very notion I am exhorted and conjured to banish from my view of the future as the suicide of reason concerning it, that "chance" is—what? Just this—the chance that in moral respects the future may be other and better than the past has been. This is the only chance we have any motive for supposing to exist. Shame, rather, on its repudiation and its denial! For its presence is the vital air which lets the world live, the salt which keeps it sweet.

WALDEN TWO

B. F. Skinner (1904–   )

"Mr. Castle," said Frazier very earnestly, "let me ask you a question. I warn you, it will be the most terrifying question of your life. *What would you do if you found yourself in possession of an effective science of behavior?* Suppose you suddenly found it possible to control the behavior of men as you wished. What would you do?"

"That's an assumption?"

"Take it as one if you like. *I* take it as a fact. And apparently you accept it as a fact too. I can hardly be as despotic as you claim unless I hold the key to an extensive practical control."

"What would I do?" said Castle thoughtfully. "I think I would dump your science of behavior in the ocean."

"And deny men all the help you could otherwise give them?"

"And give them the freedom they would otherwise lose forever!"

"How could you give them freedom?"

"By refusing to control them!"

"But you would only be leaving the control in other hands."

"Whose?"

"The charlatan, the demagogue, the salesman, the ward heeler, the bully, the cheat, the educator, the priest—all who are now in possession of the techniques of behavioral engineering."

"A pretty good share of the control would remain in the hands of the individual himself."

"That's an assumption, too, and it's your only hope. It's your only possible chance to avoid the implications of a science of behavior. If man is free, then a technology of behavior is impossible. But I'm asking you to consider the other case."

Reprinted from B. F. Skinner, *Walden Two,* New York, 1945, with permission of Macmillan Publishing Co., Inc.

"Then my answer is that your assumption is contrary to fact and any further consideration idle."

"And your accusations—?"

"—were in terms of intention, not of possible achievement."

Frazier sighed dramatically.

"It's a little late to be proving that a behavioral technology is well advanced. How can you deny it? Many of its methods and techniques are really as old as the hills. Look at their frightful misuse in the hands of the Nazis! And what about the techniques of the psychological clinic? What about education? Or religion? Or practical politics? Or advertising and salesmanship? Bring them all together and you have a sort of rule-of-thumb technology of vast power. No, Mr. Castle, the science is there for the asking. But its techniques and methods are in the wrong hands—they are used for personal aggrandizement in a competitive world or, in the case of the psychologist and educator, for futilely corrective purposes. My question is, have you the courage to take up and wield the science of behavior for the good of mankind? You answer that you would dump it in the ocean!"

"I'd want to take it out of the hands of the politicians and advertisers and salesmen, too."

"And the psychologists and educators? You see, Mr. Castle, you can't have that kind of cake. The fact is, we not only *can* control human behavior, we *must*. But who's to do it, and what's to be done?"

"So long as a trace of personal freedom survives, I'll stick to my position," said Castle, very much out of countenance.

"Isn't it time we talked about freedom?" I said. "We parted a day or so ago on an agreement to let the question of freedom ring. It's time to answer, don't you think?"

"My answer is simple enough," said Frazier. "I deny that freedom exists at all. I must deny it—or my program would be absurd. You can't have a science about a subject matter which hops capriciously about. Perhaps we can never *prove* that man isn't free; it's an assumption. But the increasing success of a science of behavior makes it more and more plausible."

"On the contrary, a simple personal experience makes it untenable," said Castle. "The experience of freedom. I *know* that I'm free."

"It must be quite consoling," said Frazier.

"And what's more—you do, too," said Castle hotly. "When you deny your own freedom for the sake of playing with a science of behavior, you're acting in plain bad faith. That's the only way I can explain it." He tried to recover himself and shrugged his shoulders. "At least you'll grant that you *feel* free."

"The 'feeling of freedom' should deceive no one," said Frazier. "Give me a concrete case."

"Well, right now," Castle said. He picked up a book of matches. "I'm free to hold or drop these matches."

"You will, of course, do one or the other," said Frazier. "Linguistically or logically there seem to be two possibilities, but I submit that there's only one in fact. The determining forces may be subtle but they are inexorable. I suggest that as an orderly person you will probably hold—ah! you drop them! Well, you see, that's all part of your behavior with respect to me. You couldn't resist the temptation to prove me wrong. It was all lawful. You had no choice. The deciding factor entered rather late, and naturally you couldn't foresee the result when you first held them up. There was no strong likelihood that you would act in either direction, and so you said you were free."

"That's entirely too glib," said Castle. "It's easy to argue lawfulness after the fact. But let's see you predict what I will do in advance. Then I'll agree there's law."

"I didn't say that behavior is always predictable, any more than the weather is always predictable. There are often too many factors to be taken into account. We can't measure them all accurately, and we couldn't perform the mathematical operations needed to make a prediction if we had the measurements. The legality is usually an assumption—but none the less important in judging the issue at hand."

"Take a case where there's no choice, then," said Castle. "Certainly a man in jail isn't free in the sense in which I am free now."

"Good! That's an excellent start. Let us classify the kinds of determiners of human behavior. One class, as you suggest, is physical restraint—handcuffs, iron bars, forcible coercion. These are ways in which we shape human behavior according to our wishes. They're crude, and they sacrifice the affection of the controllee, but they often work. Now, what other ways are there of limiting freedom?"

Frazier had adopted a professional tone and Castle refused to answer.

"The threat of force would be one," I said.

"Right. And here again we shan't encourge any loyalty on the part of the controllee. He has perhaps a shade more of the feeling of freedom, since he can always 'choose to act and accept the consequences,' but he doesn't feel exactly free. He knows his behavior is being coerced. Now what else?"

I had no answer.

"Force or the threat of force—I see no other possibility," said Castle after a moment.

"Precisely," said Frazier.

"But certainly a large part of my behavior has no connection with force at all. There's my freedom!" said Castle.

"I wasn't agreeing that there was no other possibility—merely that *you* could see no other. Not being a good behaviorist—or a good Christian, for that matter—you have no feeling for a tremendous power of a different sort."

"What's that?"

"I shall have to be technical," said Frazier. "But only for a moment. It's what the science of behavior calls 'reinforcement theory.' The things that can happen to us fall into three classes. To some things we are indifferent. Other things we like—we want them to happen, and we take steps to make them happen again. Still other things we don't like—we don't want them to happen and we take steps to get rid of them or keep them from happening again.

"*Now*," Frazier continued earnestly, "if it's in our power to create any of the situations which a person likes or to remove any situation he doesn't like, we can control his behavior. When he behaves as we want him to behave, we simply create a situation he likes, or remove one he doesn't like. As a result, the probability that he will behave that way again goes up, which is what we want. Technically it's called 'positive reinforcement.'

"The old school made the amazing mistake of supposing that the reverse was true, that by removing a situation a person likes or setting up one he doesn't like—in other words by punishing him—it was possible to *reduce* the probability that he would behave in a given way again. That simply doesn't hold. It has been established beyond question. What is emerging at this critical stage in the evolution of society is a behavioral and cultural technology based on positive reinforcement alone. We are gradually discovering—at an untold cost in human suffering—that in the long run punishment doesn't reduce the probability that an act will occur. We have been so preoccupied with the contrary that we always take 'force' to mean punishment. We don't say we're using force when we send shiploads of food into a starving country, though we're displaying quite as much *power* as if we were sending troops and guns."

"I'm certainly not an advocate of force," said Castle. "But I can't agree that it's not effective."

"It's *temporarily* effective, that's the worst of it. That explains several thousand years of bloodshed. Even nature has been fooled. We 'instinctively' punish a person who doesn't behave as we like—we spank him if he's a child or strike him if he's a man. A nice distinction! The immediate effect of the blow teaches us to strike again. Retribution and revenge are the most natural things on earth. But in the long run the man we strike is no less likely to repeat his act."

"But he won't repeat it if we hit him hard enough," said Castle.

"He'll still *tend* to repeat it. He'll *want* to repeat it. We haven't really altered his potential behavior at all. That's the pity of it. If he doesn't repeat it in our presence, he will in the presence of someone else. Or it will be repeated in the disguise of a neurotic symptom. If we hit hard enough, we clear a little place for ourselves in the wilderness of civilization, but we make the rest of the wilderness still more terrible.

"Now, early forms of government are naturally based on punishment. It's the obvious technique when the physically strong control the weak. But we're in the throes of a great change to positive reinforcement—from a competitive society in which one man's reward is another man's punishment, to a cooperative society in which no one gains at the expense of anyone else.

"The change is slow and painful because the immediate, temporary effect of punishment overshadows the eventual advantage of positive reinforcement. We've all seen countless instances of the temporary effect of force, but clear evidence of the effect of not using force is rare. That's why I insist that Jesus, who was apparently the first to discover the power of refusing to punish, must have hit upon the principle by accident. He certainly had none of the experimental evidence which is available to us today, and I can't conceive that it was possible, no matter what the man's genius, to have discovered the principle from casual observation."

"A touch of revelation, perhaps?" said Castle.

"No, accident. Jesus discovered one principle because it had immediate consequences, and he got another thrown in for good measure."

I began to see light.

"You mean the principle of 'love your enemies'?" I said.

"Exactly! To 'do good to those who despitefully use you' has two unrelated consequences. You gain the peace of mind we talked about the other day. Let the stronger man push you around—at least you avoid the torture of your own rage. *That's* the immediate consequence. What an astonishing discovery it must have been to find that in the long run you could *control the stronger man* in the same way!"

"It's generous of you to give so much credit to your early colleague," said Castle, "but why are we still in the throes of so much misery? Twenty centuries should have been enough for one piece of behavioral engineering."

"The conditions which made the principle difficult to discover made it difficult to teach. The history of the Christian Church doesn't reveal many cases of doing good to one's enemies. To inoffensive heathens, perhaps, but not enemies. One must look outside the field of organized religion to find the principle in practice at all. Church governments are devotees of *power*, both temporal and bogus."

"But what has all this got to do with freedom?" I said hastily.

Frazier took time to reorganize his behavior. He looked steadily toward the window, against which the rain was beating heavily.

"Now that we *know* how positive reinforcement works and why negative doesn't," he said at last, "we can be more deliberate, and hence more successful, in our cultural design. We can achieve a sort of control under which the controlled, though they are following a code much more scrupulously than was ever the case under the old system, nevertheless *feel free*. They are doing what they want to do, not what they are forced to do. That's the source of the tremendous power of positive reinforcement—there's no restraint and no revolt. By a careful cultural design, we control not the final behavior, but the *inclination* to behave—the motives, the desires, the wishes.

"The curious thing is that in that case *the question of freedom never arises.* Mr. Castle was free to drop the matchbook in the sense that nothing was preventing him. If it had been securely bound to his hand he wouldn't have been free. Nor would he have been quite free if I'd covered him with a gun and threatened to shoot him if he let it fall. The question of freedom arises when there is restraint—either physical or psychological.

"But restraint is only one sort of control, and absence of restraint isn't freedom. It's not control that's lacking when one feels 'free,' but the objectionable control of force. Mr. Castle felt free to hold or drop the matches in the sense that he felt no restraint—no threat of punishment in taking either course of action. He neglected to examine his positive reasons for holding or letting go, in spite of the fact that these were more compelling in this instance than any threat of force.

"We have no vocabulary of freedom in dealing with what we want to do," Frazier went on. "The question never arises. When men strike for freedom, they strike against jails and the police, or the threat of them—against oppression. They never strike against forces which make them want to act the way they do. Yet, it seems to be understood that governments will operate only through force or the threat of force, and that all other principles of control will be left to education, religion, and commerce. If this continues to be the case, we may as well give up. A government can never create a free people with the techniques now allotted to it.

"The question is: Can men live in freedom and peace? And the answer is: Yes, if we can build a social structure which will satisfy the needs of everyone and in which everyone will want to observe the supporting code. But so far this has been achieved only in Walden Two. Your ruthless accusations to the contrary, Mr. Castle, this is the freest place on earth. And it is free precisely because we make no use of force or the threat of force. Every bit of our research, from the nursery through the psychological management of our adult membership, is directed toward that end—to exploit every alternative to forcible control. By skillful planning, by a wise choice of techniques we *increase* the feeling of freedom.

"It's not planning which infringes upon freedom, but planning which uses force. A sense of freedom was practically unknown in the planned society of Nazi Germany, because the planners made a fantastic use of force and the threat of force.

"No, Mr. Castle, when a science of behavior has once been achieved, there's no alternative to a planned society. We can't leave mankind to an accidental or biased control. But by using the principle of positive reinforcement— carefully avoiding force or the threat of force—we can preserve a personal sense of freedom."

7

A
Positivist
Polemic

A. J. Ayer (1910–   )

We shall set ourselves to show that in so far as statements of value are significant, they are ordinary "scientific" statements; and that in so far as they are not scientific, they are not in the literal sense significant, but are simply expressions of emotion which can be neither true nor false. In maintaining this view, we may confine ourselves for the present to the case of ethical statements. What is said about them will be found to apply, *mutatis mutandis*, to the case of aesthetic statements also.

The ordinary system of ethics, as elaborated in the works of ethical philosophers, is very far from being a homogeneous whole. Not only is it apt to contain pieces of metaphysics and analyses of non-ethical concepts: its actual ethical contents are themselves of very different kinds. We may divide them, indeed, into four main classes. There are, first of all, propositions which express defini-

From *Language, Truth and Logic*, 1946, A. J. Ayer, 1952, Dover Publications, Inc., New York.

tions of ethical terms, or judgements about the legitimacy or possibility of certain definitions. Secondly, there are propositions describing the phenomena of moral experience, and their causes. Thirdly, there are exhortations to moral virtue. And, lastly, there are actual ethical judgements. It is unfortunately the case that the distinction between these four classes, plain as it is, is commonly ignored by ethical philosophers; with the result that it is often very difficult to tell from their works what it is that they are seeking to discover or prove.

In fact, it is easy to see that only the first of our four classes, namely that which comprises the propositions relating to the definitions of ethical terms, can be said to constitute ethical philosophy. The propositions which describe the phenomena of moral experience, and their causes, must be assigned to the science of psychology, or sociology. The exhortations to moral virtue are not propositions at all, but ejaculations or commands which are designed to provoke the reader to action of a certain sort. Accordingly, they do not belong to any branch of philosophy or science. As for the expressions of ethical judgements, we have not yet determined how they should be classified. But inasmuch as they are certainly neither definitions nor comments upon definitions, nor quotations, we may say decisively that they do not belong to ethical philosophy. A strictly philosophical treatise on ethics should therefore make no ethical pronouncements. But it should, by giving an analysis of ethical terms, show what is the category to which all such pronouncements belong. And this is what we are now about to do.

A question which is often discussed by ethical philosophers is whether it is possible to find definitions which would reduce all ethical terms to one or two fundamental terms. But this question, though it undeniably belongs to ethical philosophy, is not relevant to our present enquiry. We are not now concerned to discover which term, within the sphere of ethical terms, is to be taken as fundamental; whether, for example, "good" can be defined in terms of "right" or "right" in terms of "good," or both in terms of "value." What we are interested in is the possibility of reducing the whole sphere of ethical terms to non-ethical terms. We are enquiring whether statements of ethical value can be translated into statements of empirical fact.

That they can be so translated is the contention of those ethical philosophers who are commonly called subjectivists, and of those who are known as utilitarians. For the utilitarian defines the rightness of actions, and the goodness of ends, in terms of the pleasure, or happiness, or satisfaction, to which they give rise; the subjectivist, in terms of the feelings of approval which a certain person, or group of people, has towards them. Each of these types of definition makes moral judgements into a sub-class of psychological or sociological judgements; and for this reason they are very attractive to us. For, if either was correct, it would follow that ethical assertions were not generically different from the factual assertions which are ordinarily contrasted with them; and the account which we have already given of empirical hypotheses would apply to them also.

Nevertheless we shall not adopt either a subjectivist or a utilitarian analysis of ethical terms. We reject the subjectivist view that to call an action right, or a thing good, is to say that it is generally approved of, because it is not self-contradictory to assert that some actions which are generally approved of are not right, or that some things which are generally approved of are not good. And we reject the alternative subjectivist view that a man who asserts that a certain action is right, or that a certain thing is good, is saying that he himself approves of it, on the ground that a man who confessed that he sometimes approved of what was bad or wrong would not be contradicting himself. And a similar argument is fatal to utilitarianism. We cannot agree that to call an action right is to say that of all the actions possible in the circumstances it would cause, or be likely to cause, the greatest happiness, or the greatest balance of pleasure over pain, or the greatest balance of satisfied over unsatisfied desire, because we find that it is not self-contradictory to say that it is sometimes wrong to perform the action which would actually or probably cause the greatest happiness, or the greatest balance of pleasure over pain, or of satisfied over unsatisfied desire. And since it is not self-contradictory to say that some pleasant things are not good, or that some bad things are desired, it cannot be the case that the sentence "x is good" is equivalent to "x is pleasant," or to "x is desired." And to every other variant of utilitarianism with which I am acquainted the same objection can be made. And therefore we should, I think, conclude that the validity of ethical judgements is not determined by the felicific tendencies of actions, any more than by the nature of people's feelings; but that it must be regarded as "absolute" or "intrinsic," and not empirically calculable.

If we say this, we are not, of course, denying that it is possible to invent a language in which all ethical symbols are definable in non-ethical terms, or even that it is desirable to invent such a language and adopt it in place of our own; what we are denying is that the suggested reduction of ethical to non-ethical statements is consistent with the conventions of our actual language. That is, we reject utilitarianism and subjectivism, not as proposals to replace our existing ethical notions by new ones, but as analyses of our existing ethical notions. Our contention is simply that, in our language, sentences which contain normative ethical symbols are not equivalent to sentences which express psychological propositions, or indeed empirical propositions of any kind.

It is advisable here to make it plain that it is only normative ethical symbols, and not descriptive ethical symbols, that are held by us to be indefinable in factual terms. There is a danger of confusing these two types of symbols, because they are commonly constituted by signs of the same sensible form. Thus a complex sign of the form "x is wrong" may constitute a sentence which expresses a moral judgement concerning a certain type of conduct, or it may constitute a sentence which states that a certain type of conduct is repugnant to the moral sense of a particular society. In the latter case, the symbol "wrong" is a descriptive ethical symbol, and the sentence in which it occurs expresses an ordinary sociological proposition; in the former case, the symbol "wrong" is a normative ethical symbol, and the sentence in which it occurs does not, we maintain, express an empirical proposition at all. It is only with normative ethics that we are at present concerned; so that whenever ethical symbols are used in the course of this argument without qualification, they are always to be interpreted as symbols of the normative type.

In admitting that normative ethical concepts are irreducible to empirical concepts, we seem to be leaving the way clear for the "absolutist" view of ethics—that is, the view that statements of value are not controlled by observation, as ordinary empirical propositions are, but only by a mysterious "intellectual intuition." A feature of this theory, which is seldom recognized by its advocates, is that it makes statements of value unverifiable. For it is notorious that what seems intuitively certain to one person may seem doubtful, or even false, to another. So that unless it is possible to provide some criterion by which one may decide between conflicting intuitions, a mere appeal to intuition is worthless as a test of a proposition's validity. But in the case of moral judgements, no such criterion can be given. Some moralists claim to settle the matter by saying that they "know" that their own moral judgements are correct. But such an assertion is of purely psychological interest, and has not the slightest tendency to prove the validity of any moral judgement. For dissentient moralists may equally well "know" that their ethical views are correct. And, as far as subjective certainty goes, there will be nothing to choose between them. When such differences of opinion arise in connection with an ordinary empirical proposition, one may attempt to resolve them by referring to, or actually carrying out, some relevant empirical test. But with regard to ethical statements, there is, on the "absolutist" or "intuitionist" theory, no relevant empirical test. We are therefore justified in saying that on this theory ethical statements are held to be unverifiable. They are, of course, also held to be genuine synthetic propositions.

Considering the use which we have made of the principle that a synthetic proposition is significant only if it is empirically verifiable, it is clear that the acceptance of an "absolutist" theory of ethics would undermine the whole of our main argument. And as we have already rejected the "naturalistic" theories which are commonly supposed to provide the only alternative to "absolutism" in ethics, we seem to have reached a difficult position. We shall meet the difficulty by showing that the correct treatment of ethical statements is afforded by a third theory, which is wholly compatible with our radical empiricism.

We begin by admitting that the fundamental ethical concepts are unanalysable, inasmuch as there is no criterion by which one can test the validity of the judgements in which they occur. So far we are in agreement with the absolutists. But, unlike the absolutists, we are able to give an explanation of this fact about ethical concepts. We say that the reason why they are unanalysable is that they are mere pseudo-concepts. The presence of an ethical symbol in a proposition adds nothing to its factual content. Thus if I say to someone, "You acted wrongly in stealing that money," I am not stating anything more than if I had simply said, "You stole that money." In adding that this action is wrong I am not making any further statement about it. I am simply evincing my moral disapproval of it. It is as if I had said, "You stole that money," in a peculiar tone of horror, or written it with the addition of some special exclamation marks. The tone, or the exclamation marks, adds nothing to the literal meaning of the sentence. It merely serves to show that the expression of it is attended by certain feelings in the speaker.

If now I generalise my previous statement and say, "Stealing money is wrong," I produce a sentence which has no factual meaning—that is, expresses no proposition which can be either true or false. It is as if I had written "Stealing money!!"—where the shape and thickness of the exclamation marks show, by a suitable convention, that a special sort of moral disapproval is the feeling which is being expressed. It is clear that there is nothing said here which can be true or false. Another man may disagree with me about the wrongness of stealing, in the sense that he may not have the same feelings about stealing as I have, and he may quarrel with me on account of my moral sentiments. But he cannot, strictly speaking, contradict me. For in saying that a certain type of action is right or wrong, I am not making any factual statement, not even a statement about my own state of mind. I am merely expressing certain moral sentiments. And the man who is ostensibly contradicting me is merely expressing his moral sentiments. So that there is plainly no sense in asking which of us is in the right. For neither of us is asserting a genuine proposition.

What we have just been saying about the symbol "wrong" applies to all normative ethical symbols. Sometimes they occur in sentences which record ordinary empirical facts besides expressing ethical feeling about those facts: sometimes they occur in sentences which simply express ethical feeling about a certain type of action, or situation, without making any statement of fact. But in every case in which one would commonly be said to be making an ethical judgement, the function of the relevant ethical word is purely "emotive." It is used to express feeling about certain objects, but not to make any assertion about them.

It is worth mentioning that ethical terms do not serve only to express feeling. They are calculated also to arouse feeling, and so to stimulate action. Indeed some of them are used in such a way as to give the sentences in which they occur the effect of commands. Thus the sentence "It is your duty to tell the truth" may be regarded both as the expression of a certain sort of ethical feeling about truthfulness and as the expression of the command "Tell the truth." The sentence "You ought to tell the truth" also involves the command "Tell the truth," but here the tone of the command is less emphatic. In the sentence "It is good to tell the truth" the command has become little more than a suggestion. And thus the "meaning" of the word "good," in its ethical usage, is differentiated from that of the word "duty" or the word "ought." In fact we may define the meaning of the various ethical words in terms both of the different feelings they are ordinarily taken to express, and also the different responses which they are calculated to provoke.

We can now see why it is impossible to find a criterion for determining the validity of ethical judgements. It is not because they have an "absolute" validity which is mysteriously independent of ordinary sense-experience, but because they have no objective validity whatsoever. If a sentence makes no statement at all, there is obviously no sense in asking whether what it says is true or false. And we have seen that sentences which simply express moral judgements do not say anything. They are pure expressions of feeling and as such do not come under the category of truth and falsehood. They are unverifiable for the same reason as a cry of pain or a word of command is unverifiable—because they do not express genuine propositions.

Thus, although our theory of ethics might fairly be said to be radically subjectivist, it differs in a very important respect from the orthodox subjectivist theory. For the orthodox subjectivist does not deny, as we do, that the sentences of a moralizer express genuine propositions. All he denies is that they express propositions about the speaker's feelings. If this were so, ethical judgements clearly would be capable of being true or false. They would be true if the speaker had the relevant feelings, and false if he had not. And this is a matter which is, in principle, empirically verifiable. Furthermore they could be significantly contradicted. For if I say, "Tolerance is a virtue," and someone answers, "You don't approve of it," he would, on the ordinary subjectivist theory, be contradicting me. On our theory, he would not be contradicting me, because, in saying that tolerance was a virtue, I should not be making any statement about my own feelings or about anything else. I should simply be evincing my feelings, which is not at all the same thing as saying that I have them.

The distinction between the expression of feeling and the assertion of feeling is complicated by the fact that the assertion that one has a certain feeling often accompanies the expression of that feeling, and is then, indeed, a factor in expression of that feeling. Thus I may simultaneously express boredom and say that I am bored, and in that case my utterance of the words, "I am bored," is one of the circumstances which make it true to say that I am expressing or evincing boredom. But I can express boredom without actually saying that I am bored. I can express it by my tone and gestures, while making a statement about something wholly unconnected with it, or by an ejaculation, or without uttering any words at all. So that even if the assertion that one has a certain feeling always involves the expression of that feeling, the expression of a feeling assuredly does not always involve the assertion that one has it. And this is the important point to grasp in considering the distinction between our theory and the ordinary subjectivist theory. For whereas the subjectivist holds that ethical statements actually assert the existence of certain feelings, we hold that ethical statements are expressions and excitants of feeling which do not necessarily involve any assertions.

We have already remarked that the main objection to the ordinary subjectivist theory is that the validity of ethical judgements is not determined by the nature of their author's feelings. And this is an objection which our theory escapes. For it does not imply that the existence of any feelings is a necessary and sufficient condition of the validity of an ethical judgement. It implies, on the contrary, that ethical judgements have no validity.

There is, however, a celebrated argument against subjectivist theories which our theory does not escape. It has been pointed out by Moore that if ethical statements were simply statements about the speaker's feelings, it would be impossible to argue about questions of value. To take a typical example: if a man said that thrift was a virtue, and another replied that it was vice, they would not, on this theory, be disputing with one another. One would be saying that he approved of thrift, and the other *he* didn't; and there is no reason why both these statements should not be true. Now Moore held it to be obvious that we do dispute about questions of value, and accordingly concluded that the particular form of subjectivism which he was discussing was false.

It is plain that the conclusion that it is impossible to dispute about questions of value follows from our theory also. For as we hold that such sentences as "Thrift is a virtue" and "Thrift is a vice" do not express propositions at all, we clearly cannot hold that they express incompatible propositions. We must therefore admit that if Moore's argument really refutes the ordinary subjectivist theory, it also refutes ours. But, in fact, we deny that it does refute even the ordinary subjectivist theory. For we hold that one really never does dispute about questions of value.

This may seem, at first sight, to be a very paradoxical assertion. For we certainly do engage in disputes which are ordinarily regarded as disputes about questions of value. But, in all such cases, we find, if we consider the matter closely, that the dispute is not really about a question of value, but about a question of fact. When someone disagrees with us about the moral value of a certain action or type of action, we do admittedly resort to argument in order to win him over to our way of thinking. But we do not attempt to show by our arguments that he has the "wrong" ethical feeling towards a situation whose nature he has correctly apprehended. What we attempt to show is that he is mistaken about the facts of the case. We argue that he has misconceived the agent's motive: or that he has misjudged the effects of the action, or its probable effects in view of the agent's knowledge; or that he has failed to take into account the special circumstances in which the agent was placed. Or else we employ more general arguments about the effects which actions of a certain type tend to produce, or the qualities which are usually manifested in their performance. We do this in the hope that we have only to get our opponent to agree with us about the nature of the empirical facts for him to adopt the same moral attitude towards them as we do. And as the people with whom we argue have generally received the same moral education as ourselves, and live in the same social order, our expectation is usually justified. But if our opponent happens to have undergone a different process of moral "conditioning" from ourselves, so that, even when he acknowledges all the facts, he still disagrees with us about the moral value of the actions under discussion, then we abandon the attempt to convince him by argument. We say that it is impossible to argue with him because he has a distorted or undeveloped moral sense; which signifies merely that he employs a different set of values from our own. We feel that our own system of values is superior, and therefore speak in such derogatory terms of his. But we cannot bring forward any arguments to show that our system is superior. For our judgement that it is so is itself a judgement of value, and accordingly outside the scope of argument. It is because argument fails us when we come to deal with pure questions of value, as distinct from questions of fact, that we finally resort to mere abuse.

In short, we find that argument is possible on moral questions only if some system of values is presupposed. If our opponent concurs with us in expressing moral disapproval of all actions of a given type t, then we may get him to condemn a particular action A, by bringing forward arguments to show that A is of type t. For the question whether A does or does not belong to that type is a plain question of fact. Given that a man has certain moral principles, we argue that he must, in order to be consistent, react morally to certain things in a certain way. What we do not and cannot argue about is the validity of these moral principles. We merely praise or condemn them in the light of our own feelings.

If anyone doubts the accuracy of this account of moral disputes, let him try to construct even an imaginary argument on a question of value which does not reduce itself to an argument about a question of logic or about an empirical matter of fact. I am confident that he will not succeed in producing a single example. And if that is the case, he must allow, that its involving the impossibility of purely ethical arguments is not, as Moore thought, a ground of objection to our theory, but rather a point in favour of it.

Having upheld our theory against the only criticism which appeared to threaten it, we may now use it to define the nature of all ethical enquiries. We find that ethical philosophy consists simply in saying that ethical concepts are pseudo-concepts and therefore unanalysable. The further task of describing the different feelings that the different ethical terms are used to express, and the different reactions that they customarily provoke, is a task for the psychologist. There cannot be such a thing as ethical science, if by ethical science one means the elaboration of a "true" system of morals. For we have seen that, as ethical judgements are mere expressions of feeling, there can be no way of determining the validity of any ethical system, and, indeed, no sense in asking whether any such system is true. All that one may legitimately enquire in this connection is, What are the moral habits of a given person or group of people, and what causes them to have precisely those habits and feelings? And this enquiry falls wholly within the scope of the existing social sciences.

It appears, then, that ethics, as a branch of knowledge, is nothing more than a department of psychology and sociology. . . .

8

An Existential Ethic

Jean-Paul Sartre (1905–1980)

What is meant by the term *existentialism?*

Most people who use the word would be rather embarrassed if they had to explain it, since, now that the word is all the rage, even the work of a musician or painter is being called existentialist. A gossip columnist in *Clartés* signs himself *The Existentialist,* so that by this time the word has been so stretched and has taken on so broad a meaning, that it no longer means anything at all. It seems that for want of an advanced-guard doctrine analogous to surrealism, the kind of people who are eager for scandal and flurry turn to this philosophy which in other respects does not at all serve their purposes in this sphere.

Actually, it is the least scandalous, the most austere of doctrines. It is intended strictly for specialists and philosophers. Yet it can be defined easily.

From Jean-Paul Sartre, "The Humanism of Existentialism" in *The Philosophy of Existentialism,* edited by Wade Baskin, Philosophical Library, 1965. By permission.

What complicates matters is that there are two kinds of existentialists; first, those who are Christian, among whom I would include Jaspers and Gabriel Marcel, both Catholic; and on the other hand the atheistic existentialists among whom I class Heidegger, and then the French existentialists and myself. What they have in common is that they think that existence precedes essence, or, if you prefer, that subjectivity must be the starting point.

Just what does that mean? Let us consider some object that is manufactured, for example, a book or a paper-cutter: here is an object which has been made by an artisan whose inspiration came from a concept. He referred to the concept of what a paper-cutter is and likewise to a known method of production, which is part of the concept, something which is, by and large, a routine. Thus, the paper-cutter is at once an object produced in a certain way and, on the other hand, one having a specific use; and one can not postulate a man who produces a paper-cutter but does not know what it is used for. Therefore, let us say that, for the paper-cutter, essence—that is, the ensemble of both the production routines and the properties which enable it to be both produced and defined— precedes existence. Thus, the presence of the paper-cutter or book in front of me is determined. Therefore, we have here a technical view of the world whereby it can be said that production precedes existence.

When we conceive God as the Creator, He is generally thought of as a superior sort of artisan. Whatever doctrine we may be considering, whether one like that of Descartes or that of Leibniz, we always grant that will more or less follows understanding or, at the very least, accompanies it, and that when God creates He knows exactly what He is creating. Thus, the concept of man in the mind of God is comparable to the concept of a paper-cutter in the mind of the manufacturer, and, following certain techniques and a conception, God produces man, just as the artisan, following a definition and a technique, makes a paper-cutter. Thus, the individual man is the realization of a certain concept in the divine intelligence.

In the eighteenth century, the atheism of the *philosophers* discarded the idea of God, but not so much for the notion that essence precedes existence. To a certain extent, this idea is found everywhere; we find it in Diderot, in Voltaire, and even in Kant. Man has a human nature; this human nature, which is the concept of the human, is found in all men, which means that each man is a particular example of a universal concept, man. In Kant, the result of this universality is that the wild-man, the natural man, as well as the bourgeois, are circumscribed by the same definition and have the same basic qualities. Thus, here too the essence of man precedes the historical existence that we find in nature.

Atheistic existentialism, which I represent, is more coherent. It states that if God does not exist, there is at least one being in whom existence precedes essence, a being who exists before he can be defined by any concept, and that this being is man, or, as Heidegger says, human reality. What is meant here by saying that existence precedes essence? It means that, first of all, man exists, turns up, appears on the scene, and, only afterwards, defines himself. If man, as the existentialist conceives him, is indefinable, it is because at first he is nothing. Only afterward will he be something, and he himself will have made what he will be. Thus, there is no human nature, since there is no God to conceive it. Not only is man what he conceives himself to be, but he is also only what he wills himself to be after his thrust toward existence.

Man is nothing else but what he makes of himself. Such is the first principle of existentialism. It is also what is called subjectivity, the name we are labeled with when charges are brought against us. But what do we mean by this, if not that man has a greater dignity than a stone or table? For we mean that man first exists, that is, that man first of all is the being who hurls himself toward a future and who is conscious of imagining himself as being in the future. Man is at the start a plan which is aware of itself, rather than a patch of moss, a piece of garbage, or a cauliflower; nothing exists prior to this plan; there is nothing in heaven; man will be what he will have planned to be. Not what he will want to be. Because by the word "will" we generally mean a conscious decision, which is subsequent to what we have already made of ourselves. I may want to belong to a political party, write a book, get married; but all that is only a manifestation of an earlier, more spontaneous choice that is called "will." But if existence really does precede essence, man is responsible for what he is. Thus, existentialism's first move is to make every man aware of what he is and to make the full responsibility of his existence rest on him. And when we say that a man is responsible for himself, we do not only mean that he is responsible for his own individuality, but that he is responsible for all men.

The word subjectivism has two meanings, and our opponents play on the two. Subjectivism means, on the one hand, that an individual chooses and makes himself; and, on the other, that it is impossible for man to transcend human subjectivity. The second of these is the essential meaning of existentialism. When we say that man chooses his own self, we mean that every one of us does likewise; but we also mean by that that in making this choice he also chooses all men. In fact, in creating the man that we want to be, there is not a single one of our acts which does not at the same time create an image of man as we think he ought to be. To choose to be this or that is to affirm at the same time the value of what we choose, because we can never choose evil. We always choose the good, and nothing can be good for us without being good for all.

If, on the other hand, existence precedes essence, and if we grant that we exist and fashion our image at one and the same time, the image is valid for everybody and for our whole age. Thus, our responsibility is much greater than we might have supposed, because it involves all mankind. If I am a workingman and choose to join a Christian trade-union rather than be a communist, and if by being a member I want to show that the best thing for man is resignation, that the kingdom of man is not of this world, I am not only involving my own case—I want to be resigned for everyone. As a result, my action has involved all humanity. To take a more individual matter, if I want to marry, to have children; even if this marriage depends solely on my own circumstances or passion or wish, I am involving all humanity in monogamy and not merely myself. Therefore, I am responsible for myself and for everyone else. I am creating a certain image of man of my own choosing. In choosing myself, I choose man.

agree that a sweeping passion is a ravaging torrent which fatally leads a man to certain acts and is therefore an excuse. He thinks that man is responsible for his passion.

The existentialist does not think that man is going to help himself by finding in the world some omen by which to orient himself. Because he thinks that man will interpret the omen to suit himself. Therefore, he thinks that man, with no support and no aid, is condemned every moment to invent man. Ponge, in a very fine article, has said, "Man is the future of man." That's exactly it. But if it is taken to mean that this future is recorded in heaven, that God sees it, then it is false, because it would really no longer be a future. If it is taken to mean that, whatever a man may be, there is a future to be forged, a virgin future before him, then this remark is sound. But then we are forlorn.

To give you an example which will enable you to understand forlornness better, I shall cite the case of one of my students who came to see me under the following circumstances: his father was on bad terms with his mother, and, moreover, was inclined to be a collaborationist; his older brother had been killed in the German offensive of 1940, and the young man, with somewhat immature but generous feelings, wanted to avenge him. His mother lived alone with him, very much upset by the half-treason of her husband and the death of her older son; the boy was her only consolation.

The boy was faced with the choice of leaving for England and joining the Free French Forces—that is, leaving his mother behind—or remaining with his mother and helping her to carry on. He was fully aware that the woman lived only for him and that his going-off—and perhaps his death—would plunge her into despair. He was also aware that every act that he did for his mother's sake was a sure thing, in the sense that it was helping her to carry on, whereas every effort he made toward going off and fighting was an uncertain move which might run aground and prove completely useless; for example, on his way to England he might, while passing through Spain, be detained indefinitely in a Spanish camp; he might reach England or Algiers and be stuck in an office at a desk job. As a result, he was faced with two very different kinds of action: one, concrete, immediate, but concerning only one individual; the other concerned an incomparably vaster group, a national collectivity, but for that very reason was dubious, and might be interrupted en route. And, at the same time, he was wavering between two kinds of ethics. On the one hand, an ethics of sympathy, of personal devotion; on the other, a broader ethics, but one whose efficacy was more dubious. He had to choose between the two.

Who could help him choose? Christian doctrine? No. Christian doctrine says, "Be charitable, love your neighbor, take the more rugged path, etc., etc." But which is the more rugged path? Whom should he love as a brother? The fighting man or his mother? Which does the greater good, the vague act of fighting in a group, or the concrete one of helping a particular human being to go on living? Who can decide *a priori*? Nobody. No book of ethics can tell him. The Kantian ethics says, "Never treat any person as a means, but as an end." Very well, if I stay with mother, I'll treat her as an end and not as a means; but by virtue of this very fact, I'm running the risk of treating the people around me who are fighting, as means; and, conversely, if I go to join those who are fighting, I'll be treating them as an end, and, by doing that, I run the risk of treating my mother as a means.

If values are vague, and if they are always too broad for the concrete and specific case that we are considering, the only thing left for us is to trust our instincts. That's what this young man tried to do; and when I saw him, he said, "In the end, feeling is what counts. I ought to choose whichever pushes me in one direction. If I feel that I love my mother enough to sacrifice everything else for her—my desire for vengeance, for action, for adventure—then I'll stay with her. If, on the contrary, I feel that my love for my mother isn't enough, I'll leave."

But how is the value of a feeling determined? What gives his feeling for his mother value? Precisely the fact that he remained with her. I may say that I like so-and-so well enough to sacrifice a certain amount of money for him, but I may say so only if I've done it. I may say "I love my mother well enough to remain with her" if I have remained with her. The only way to determine the value of this affection is, precisely, to perform an act which confirms and defines it. But, since I require this affection to justify my act, I find myself caught in a vicious circle.

On the other hand, Gide has well said that a mock feeling and a true feeling are almost indistinguishable; to decide that I love my mother and will remain with her, or to remain with her by putting on an act, amount somewhat to the same thing. In other words, the feeling is formed by the acts one performs; so, I can not refer to it in order to act upon it. Which means that I can neither seek within myself the true condition which will impel me to act, nor apply to a system of ethics for concepts which will permit me to act. You will say, "At least, he did go to a teacher for advice." But if you seek advice from a priest, for example, you have chosen this priest; you already knew, more or less, just about what advice he was going to give you. In other words, choosing your adviser is involving yourself. The proof of this is that if you are a Christian, you will say, "Consult a priest." But some priests are collaborating, some are just marking time, some are resisting. Which to choose? If the young man chooses a priest who is resisting or collaborating, he has already decided on the kind of advice he's going to get. Therefore, in coming to see me he knew the answer I was going to give him, and I had only one answer to give: "You're free, choose, that is, invent." No general ethics can show you what is to be done; there are no omens in the world. The Catholics will reply, "But there are." Granted—but, in any case, I myself choose the meaning they have.

When I was prisoner, I knew a rather remarkable young man who was a Jesuit. He had entered the Jesuit order in the following way: he had had a number of very bad breaks; in childhood, his father died, leaving him in poverty, and he was a scholarship student at a religious institution where he was constantly made to feel that he was being kept out of charity; then, he failed to get any of the honors and distinctions that children like; later on, at about eighteen, he bungled a love affair; finally, at twenty-two, he failed in military training, a childish enough matter, but it was the last straw.

This young fellow might well have felt that he had botched everything. It was a sign of something, but of what? He might have taken refuge in bitterness or despair. But he very wisely looked upon all this as a sign that he was not made for secular triumphs, and that only the triumphs of religion, holiness, and faith were open to him. He saw the hand of God in all this, and so he entered the order. Who can help seeing that he alone decided what the sign meant?

Some other interpretation might have been drawn from this series of set-backs; for example, that he might have done better to turn carpenter or revolutionist. Therefore, he is fully responsible for the interpretation. Forlornness implies that we ourselves choose our being. Forlornness and anguish go together.

As for despair, the term has a very simple meaning. It means that we shall confine ourselves to reckoning only with what depends upon our will, or on the ensemble of probabilities which make our action possible. When we want something, we always have to recken with probabilities. I may be counting on the arrival of a friend. The friend is coming by rail or street-car; this supposes that the train will arrive on schedule, or that the street-car will not jump the track. I am left in the realm of possibility; but possibilities are to be reckoned with only to the point where my action comports with the ensemble of these possibilities, and no further. The moment the possibilities I am considering are not rigorously involved by my action, I ought to disengage myself from them, because no God, no scheme, can adapt the world and its possibilities to my will. When Descartes said, "Conquer yourself rather than the world," he meant essentially the same thing.

The Marxists to whom I have spoken reply, "You can rely on the support of others in your action, which obviously has certain limits because you're not going to live forever. That means: rely on both what others are doing elsewhere to help you, in China, in Russia, and what they will do later on, after your death, to carry on the action and lead it to its fulfillment, which will be the revolution. You even *have* to rely upon that, otherwise you're immoral." I reply at once that I will always rely on fellow-fighters insofar as these comrades are involved with me in a common struggle, in the unity of a party or a group in which I can more or less make my weight felt; that is, one whose ranks I am in as a fighter and whose movements I am aware of at every moment. In such a situation, relying on the unity and will of the party is exactly like counting on the fact that the train will arrive on time or that the car won't jump the track. But, given that man is free and that there is no human nature for me to depend on, I can not count on men whom I do not know by relying on human goodness or man's concern for the good of society. I don't know what will become of the Russian revolution; I may make an example of it to the extent that at the present time it is apparent that the proletariat plays a part in Russia that it plays in no other nation. But I can't swear that this will inevitably lead to a triumph of the proletariat. I've got to limit myself to what I see.

Given that men are free and that tomorrow they will freely decide what man will be, I can not be sure that, after my death, fellow-fighters will carry on my work to bring it to its maximum perfection. Tomorrow, after my death, some men may decide to set up Fascism, and the others may be cowardly and muddled enough to let them do it. Fascism will then be the human reality, so much the worse for us.

Actually, things will be as man will have decided they are to be. Does that mean that I should abandon myself to quietism? No. First, I should involve myself; then, act on the old saw, "Nothing ventured, nothing gained." Nor does it mean that I shouldn't belong to a party, but rather that I shall have no illusions and shall do what I can. For example, suppose I ask myself, "Will socialization, as such, ever come about?" I know nothing about it. All I know is that I'm going to do everything in my power to bring it about. Beyond that, I can't count on anything. Quietism is the attitude of people who say, "Let others do what I can't do." The doctrine I am presenting is the very opposite of quietism, since it declares, "There is no reality except in action." Moreover, it goes further, since it adds, "Man is nothing else than his plan; he exists only to the extent that he fulfills himself; he is therefore nothing else than the ensemble of his acts, nothing else than his life."

According to this, we can understand why our doctrine horrifies certain people. Because often the only way they can bear their wretchedness is to think, "Circumstances have been against me. What I've been and done doesn't show my true worth. To be sure, I've had no great love, no great friendship, but that's because I haven't met a man or woman who was worthy. The books I've written haven't been very good because I haven't had the proper leisure. I haven't had children to devote myself to because I didn't find a man with whom I could have spent my life. So there remains within me, unused and quite viable, a host of propensities, inclinations, possibilities, that one wouldn't guess from the mere series of things I've done."

Now, for the existentialist there is really no love other than one which manifests itself in a person's being in love. There is no genius other than one which is expressed in works of art; the genius of Proust is the sum of Proust's works; the genius of Racine is his series of tragedies. Outside of that, there is nothing. Why say that Racine could have written another tragedy, when he didn't write it? A man is involved in life, leaves his impress on it, and outside of that there is nothing. To be sure, this may seem a harsh thought to someone whose life hasn't been a success. But, on the other hand, it prompts people to understand that reality alone is what counts, that dreams, expectations, and hopes warrant no more than to define a man as a disappointed dream, as miscarried hopes, as vain expectations. In other words, to define him negatively and not positively. However, when we say, "You are nothing else than your life," that does not imply that the artist will be judged solely on the basis of his works of art; a thousand other things will contribute toward summing him up. What we mean is that a man is nothing else than a series of undertakings, that he is the sum, the organization, the ensemble of the relationships which make up these undertakings.

When all is said and done, what we are accused of, at bottom, is not our pessimism, but an optimistic toughness. If people throw up to us our works of fiction in which we write about people who are soft, weak, cowardly, and sometimes even downright bad, it's not because these people are soft, weak, cowardly, or bad; because if we were to say, as Zola did, that they are that way because of heredity, the workings of environment, society, because of biological or psychological determinism, people would be reassured. They would say, "Well, that's what we're like, no one can do anything about it." But when the existentialist writes about a coward, he says that this coward is responsible for his cowardice. He's not like that because he has a cowardly heart or lung or brain; he's not like that on account of his physiological make-up; but he's like that because he has made himself a coward by his acts. There's no such thing as a cowardly constitution; there are nervous constitutions; there is poor blood, as the common people say, or there are strong constitutions. But the man whose blood is poor is not a coward on that account, for what makes cowardice is the act of renouncing or yielding. A constitution is not an act; the coward is defined on the basis of the acts he performs. People feel, in a vague sort of way, that this coward we're talking about is guilty of being a coward, and the thought frightens them. What people would like is that a coward or a hero be born that way.

One of the complaints most frequently made about *The Ways of Freedom* can be summed up as follows: "After all, these people are so spineless, how are you going to make heroes out of them?" This objection almost makes me laugh, for it assumes that people are born heroes. That's what people really want to think. If you're born cowardly, you may set your mind perfectly at rest; there's nothing you can do about it; you'll be cowardly all your life, whatever you may do. If you're born a hero, you may set your mind just as much at rest; you'll be a hero all your life; you'll drink like a hero and eat like a hero. What the existentialist says is that the coward makes himself cowardly, that the hero makes himself heroic. There's always a possibility for the coward not to be cowardly any more and for the hero to stop being heroic. What counts is total involvement; some one particular action or set of circumstances is not total involvement.

Thus, I think we have answered a number of the charges concerning existentialism. You see that it can not be taken for a philosophy of quietism, since it defines man in terms of action; nor for a pessimistic description of man—there is no doctrine more optimistic, since man's destiny is within himself; nor for an attempt to discourage man from acting, since it tells him that the only hope is in his acting and that action is the only thing that enables a man to live. Consequently, we are dealing here with an ethics of action and involvement.

Nevertheless, on the basis of a few notions like these, we are still charged with immuring man in his private subjectivity. There again we're very much misunderstood. Subjectivity of the individual is indeed our point of departure, and this for strictly philosophic reasons. Not because we are bourgeois, but because we want a doctrine based on truth and not a lot of fine theories, full of hope but with no real basis. There can be no other truth to start from than this: *I think; therefore, I exist.* There we have the absolute truth of consciousness becoming aware of itself. Every theory which takes man out of the moment in which he becomes aware of himself is, at its very beginning, a theory which confounds truth, for outside the Cartesian *cogito*, all views are only probable, and a doctrine of probability which is not bound to a truth dissolves into thin air. In order to describe the probable, you must have a firm hold on the true. Therefore, before there can be any truth whatsoever, there must be an absolute truth; and this one is simple and easily arrived at; it's on everyone's doorstep; it's a matter of grasping it directly.

Secondly, this theory is the only one which gives man dignity, the only one which does not reduce him to an object. The effect of all materialism is to treat every man, including the one philosophizing, as an object, that is, as an ensemble of determined reactions in no way distinguished from the ensemble of qualities and phenomena which constitute a table or a chair or a stone. We definitely wish to establish the human realm as an ensemble of values distinct from the material realm. But the subjectivity that we have thus arrived at, and which we have claimed to be truth, is not a strictly individual subjectivity, for we have demonstrated that one discovers in the *cogito* not only himself, but others as well.

The philosophies of Descartes and Kant to the contrary, through the *I think* we reach our own self in the presence of others, and the others are just as real to us as our own self. Thus, the man who becomes aware of himself through the *cogito* also perceives all others, and he perceives them as the condition of his own existence. He realizes that he can not be anything (in the sense that we say that someone is witty or nasty or jealous) unless others recognize it as such. In order to get any truth about myself, I must have contact with another person. The other is indispensable to my own existence, as well as to my knowledge about myself. This being so, in discovering my inner being I discover the other person at the same time, like a freedom placed in front of me which thinks and wills only for or against me. Hence, let us at once announce the discovery of a world which we shall call intersubjectivity; this is the world in which man decides what he is and what others are.

Besides, if it is impossible to find in every man some universal essence which would be human nature, yet there does exist a universal human condition. It's not by chance that today's thinkers speak more readily of man's condition than of his nature. By condition they mean, more or less definitely, the *a priori* limits which outline man's fundamental situation in the universe. Historical situations vary; a man may be born a slave in a pagan society or a feudal lord or a proletarian. What does not vary is the necessity for him to exist in the world, to be at work there, to be there in the midst of other people, and to be mortal there. The limits are neither subjective nor objective, or, rather, they have an objective and a subjective side. Objective because they are to be found everywhere and are recognizable everywhere; subjective because they are *lived* and are nothing if man does not live them, that is, freely determine his existence with reference to them. And though the configurations may differ, at least none of them are completely strange to me, because they all appear as attempts either to pass beyond these limits or recede from them or deny them to adapt to them. Consequently, every configuration, however individual it may be, has a universal value.

Every configuration, even the Chinese, the Indian, or the Negro, can be understood by a Westerner. "Can be understood" means that by virtue of a situation that he can imagine, a European of 1945 can, in like manner, push himself to his limits and reconstitute within himself the configuration of the Chinese, the Indian, or the African. Every configuration has universality in the sense that every configuration can be understood by every man. This does not at all mean that this configuration defines man forever, but that it can be met with again. There is always a way to understand the idiot, the child, the savage, the foreigner, provided one has the necessary information.

In this sense we may say that there is a universality of man; but it is not given, it is perpetually being made. I build the universal in choosing myself; I build it in understanding the configuration of every other man, whatever age he might have lived in. This absoluteness of choice does not do away with the relativeness of each epoch. At heart, what existentialism shows is the connection between the absolute character of free involvement, by virtue of which every man realizes himself in realizing a type of mankind, an involvement always comprehensible in any age whatsoever and by any person whosoever, and the relativeness of the cultural ensemble which may result from such a choice; . . .

This does not entirely settle the objection to subjectivism. In fact, the objection still takes several forms. First, there is the following: we are told, "So you're able to do anything, no matter what!" This is expressed in various ways. First we are accused of anarchy; then they say, "You're unable to pass judgment on others, because there's no reason to prefer one configuration to another"; finally they tell us, "Everything is arbitrary in this choosing of yours. You take something from one pocket and pretend you're putting in into the other."

These three objections aren't very serious. Take the first objection. "You're able to do anything, no matter what" is not to the point. In one sense choice is possible, but what is not possible is not to choose. I can always choose, but I ought to know that if I do not choose, I am still choosing. Though this may seem purely formal, it is highly important for keeping fantasy and caprice within bounds. If it is true that in facing a situation, for example, one in which, as a person capable of having sexual relations, of having children, I am obliged to choose an attitude, and if I in any way assume responsibility for a choice which, in involving myself, also involves all mankind, this has nothing to do with caprice, even if no *a priori* value determines my choice.

If anybody thinks that he recognizes here Gide's theory of the arbitrary act, he fails to see the enormous difference between this doctrine and Gide's. Gide does not know what a situation is. He acts out of pure caprice. For us, on the contrary, man is in an organized situation in which he himself is involved. Through his choice, he involves all mankind, and he can not avoid making a choice: either he will remain chaste, or he will marry without having children, or he will marry and have children; anyhow, whatever he may do, it is impossible for him not to take full responsibility for the way he handles this problem. Doubtless, he chooses without referring to pre-established values, but it is unfair to accuse him of caprice. Instead, let us say that moral choice is to be compared to the making of a work of art. And before going any further, let it be said at once that we are not dealing here with an aesthetic ethics, because our opponents are so dishonest that they even accuse us of that. The example I've chosen is a comparison only.

Having said that, may I ask whether anyone has ever accused an artist who has painted a picture of not having drawn his inspiration from rules set up *a priori*? Has any one ever asked, "What painting ought he to make?" It is clearly understood that there is no definite painting to be made, that the artist is engaged in the making of his painting, and that the painting to be made is precisely the painting he will have made. It is clearly understood that there are no *a priori* aesthetic values, but that there are values which appear subsequently in the coherence of the painting, in the correspondence between what the artist intended and the result. Nobody can tell what the painting of tomorrow will be like. Painting can be judged only after it has once been made. What connection does that have with ethics? We are in the same creative situation. We never say that a work of art is arbitrary. When we speak of a canvas of Picasso, we never say that it is arbitrary; we understand quite well that he was making himself what he is at the very time he was painting, that the ensemble of his work is embodied in his life.

The same holds on the ethical plane. What art and ethics have in common is that we have creation and invention in both cases. We can not decide *a priori* what there is to be done. I think that I pointed that out quite sufficiently when I mentioned the case of the student who came to see me, and who might have applied to all the ethical systems, Kantian or otherwise, without getting any sort of guidance. He was obliged to devise his law himself. Never let it be said by us that this man—who, taking affection, individual action, and kind-heartedness toward a specific person as his ethical first principle, chooses to remain with his mother, or who, preferring to make a sacrifice, chooses to go to England—has made an arbitrary choice. Man makes himself. He isn't ready made at the start. In choosing his ethics, he makes himself, and force of circumstances is such that he can not abstain from choosing one. We define man only in relationship to involvement. It is therefore absurd to charge us with arbitrariness of choice.

In the second place, it is said that we are unable to pass judgment on others. In a way this is true, and in another way, false. It is true in this sense, that, whenever a man sanely and sincerely involves himself and chooses his configuration, it is impossible for him to prefer another configuration, regardless of what his own may be in other respects. It is true in this sense, that we do not believe in progress. Progress is betterment. Man is always the same. The situation confronting him varies. Choice always remains a choice in a situation. The problem has not changed since the time one could choose between those for and those against slavery, for example, at the time of the Civil War, and the present time, when one can side with the Maquis Resistance Party, or with the Communists.

But, nevertheless, one can still pass judgment, for, as I have said, one makes a choice in relationship to others. First, one can judge (and this is perhaps not a judgment of value, but a logical judgment) that certain choices are based on error and others on truth. If we have defined man's situation as a free choice, with no excuses and no recourse, every man who takes refuge behind the excuse of his passions, every man who sets up a determinism, is a dishonest man.

The objection may be raised, "But why mayn't he choose himself dishonestly?" I reply that I am not obliged to pass moral judgment on him, but that I do define his dishonesty as an error. One can not help considering the truth of the matter. Dishonesty is obviously a falsehood because it belies the complete freedom of involvement. On the same grounds, I maintain that there is also dishonesty if I choose to state that certain values exist prior to me; it is self-contradictory for me to want them and at the same time state that they are imposed on me. Suppose someone says to me, "What if I want to be dishonest?" I'll answer, "There's no reason for you not to be, but I'm saying that that's what you are, and that the strictly coherent attitude is that of honesty."

Besides, I can bring moral judgment to bear. When I declare that freedom in every concrete circumstance can have no other aim than to want itself, if man has once become aware that in his forlornness he imposes values, he can no longer want but one thing, and that is freedom, as the basis of all values. That doesn't mean that he wants it in the abstract. It means simply that the ultimate meaning of the acts of honest men is the quest for freedom as such. A man who belongs to a communist or revolutionary union wants concrete goals; these goals imply an abstract desire for freedom; but this freedom is wanted in something concrete. We want freedom for freedom's sake and in every particular circumstance. And in wanting freedom we discover that it depends entirely on the freedom of others, and that the freedom of others depends on ours. Of course, freedom as the definition of man does not depend on others, but as soon as there is involvement, I am obliged to want others to have freedom at the same time that I want my own freedom. I can take freedom as my goal only if I take that of others as a goal as well. Consequently, when, in all honesty, I've recognized that man is a being in whom existence precedes essence, that he is a free being who, in various circumstances, can want only his freedom, I have at the same time recognized that I can want only the freedom of others.

Therefore, in the name of this will for freedom, which freedom itself implies, I may pass judgment on those who seek to hide from themselves the complete arbitrariness and the complete freedom of their existence. Those who hide their complete freedom from themselves out of a spirit of seriousness or by means of deterministic excuses, I shall call cowards; those who try to show that their existence was necessary, when it is the very contingency of man's appearance on earth, I shall call stinkers. But cowards or stinkers can be judged only from a strictly unbiased point of view.

Therefore though the content of ethics is variable, a certain form of it is universal. Kant says that freedom desires both itself and the freedom of others. Granted. But he believes that the formal and the universal are enough to constitute an ethics. We, on the other hand, think that principles which are too abstract run aground in trying to decide action. Once again, take the case of the student. In the name of what, in the name of what great moral maxim do you think he could have decided, in perfect peace of mind, to abandon his mother or to stay with her? There is no way of judging. The content is always concrete and thereby unforeseeable; there is always the element of invention. The one thing that counts is knowing whether the inventing that has been done, has been done in the name of freedom.

For example, let us look at the following two cases. You will see to what extent they correspond, yet differ. Take *The Mill on the Floss*. We find a certain young girl, Maggie Tulliver, who is an embodiment of the value of passion and who is aware of it. She is in love with a young man, Stephen, who is engaged to an insignificant young girl. This Maggie Tulliver, instead of heedlessly preferring her own happiness, chooses, in the name of human solidarity, to sacrifice herself and give up the man she loves. On the other hand, Sanseverina, in *The Charter-house of Parma*, believing that passion is man's true value, would say that a great love deserves sacrifices; that it is to be preferred to the banality of the conjugal love that would tie Stephen to the young ninny he had to marry. She would choose to sacrifice the girl and fulfill her happiness; and, as Stendhal shows, she is even ready to sacrifice herself for the sake of passion, if this life demands it. Here we are in the presence of two strictly opposed moralities. I claim that they are much the same thing; in both cases what has been set up as the goal is freedom.

You can imagine two highly similar attitudes: one girl prefers to renounce her love out of resignation; another prefers to disregard the prior attachment of the man she loves out of sexual desire. On the surface these two actions resemble those we've just described. However, they are completely different. Sanseverina's attitude is much nearer that of Maggie Tulliver, one of heedless rapacity.

Thus, you see that the second charge is true and, at the same time, false. One may choose anything if it is on the grounds of free involvement.

The third objection is the following: "You take something from one pocket and put it into the other. That is, fundamentally, values aren't serious, since you choose them." My answer to this is that I'm quite vexed that that's the way it is; but if I've discarded God the Father, there has to be someone to invent values. You've got to take things as they are. Moreover, to say that we invent values means nothing else but this: life has no meaning *a priori*. Before you come alive, life is nothing; it's up to you to give it a meaning, and value is nothing else but the meaning that you choose. In that way, you see, there is a possibility of creating a human community.

I've been reproached for asking whether existentialism is humanistic. It's been said, "But you said in *Nausea* that the humanists were all wrong. You made fun of a certain kind of humanist. Why come back to it now?" Actually, the word humanism has two very different meanings. By humanism one can mean a theory which takes man as an end and as a higher value. Humanism in this sense can be found in Cocteau's tale *Around the World in Eighty Hours* when a character, because he is flying over some mountains in an airplane, declares, "Man is simply amazing." That means that I, who did not build the airplanes, shall personally benefit from these particular inventions, and that I, as man, shall personally consider myself responsible for, and honored by, acts of a few particular men. This would imply that we ascribe a value to man on the basis of the highest deeds of certain men. This humanism is absurd, because only the dog or the horse would be able to make such an over-all judgment about man, which they are careful not to do, at least to my knowledge.

But it can not be granted that a man may make a judgment about man. Existentialism spares him from any such judgment. The existentialist will never consider man as an end because he is always in the making. Nor should we believe that there is a mankind to which we might set up a cult in the manner of Auguste Comte. The cult of mankind ends in the self-enclosed humanism of Comte, and, let it be said, of fascism. This kind of humanism we can do without.

But there is another meaning of humanism. Fundamentally it is this: man is constantly outside of himself; in projecting himself, in losing himself outside of himself, he makes for man's existing; and, on the other hand, it is by pursuing transcendent goals that he is able to exist; man, being this state of passing-beyond, and seizing upon things only as they bear upon this passing-beyond, is at the heart, at the center of this passing-beyond. There is no universe other than a human universe, the universe of human subjectivity. This connection between transcendency, as a constituent element of man—not in the sense that God is transcendent, but in the sense of passing beyond—and subjectivity, in the sense that man is not closed in on himself but is always present in a human universe, is what we call existentialist humanism. Humanism, because we remind man that there is no lawmaker other than himself, and that in his forlornness he will decide by himself; because we point out that man will fulfill himself as man, not in turning toward himself, but in seeking outside of himself a goal which is just this liberation, just this particular fulfillment.

From these few reflections it is evident that nothing is more unjust than the objections that have been raised against us. Existentialism is nothing else than an attempt to draw all the consequences of a coherent atheistic position. It isn't trying to plunge man into despair at all. But if one calls every attitude of unbelief despair, like the Christians, then the word is not being used in its original sense. Existentialism isn't so atheistic that it wears itself out showing that God doesn't exist. Rather, it declares that even if God did exist, that would change nothing. There you've got our point of view. Not that we believe that God exists, but we think that the problem of His existence is not the issue. In this sense existentialism is optimistic, a doctrine of action, and it is plain dishonesty for Christians to make no distinction between their own despair and ours and then to call us despairing.

TWO

POLITICAL PHILOSOPHY

One of the most complicated problems facing modern man is how to bring into harmony the elements of authority, human rights, and freedom. The concept of authority, in particular, has been a matter of constant perplexity. Who has the authority to tell another person what he may or may not do in society? Does the government have the right to override the wishes of a citizen? Is a law, as a command of the government, just or right simply because that law has been officially promulgated? Or, must a law, in order to be just, conform to some higher standard of justice? And finally, what should a person do when and if he concludes that a law is unjust—should he obey it or does he have a right to disobey it?

Political philosophers have answered these questions in different ways depending upon what concept they thought was most important to emphasize. For example, in discussing the nature of law, Aquinas sought to emphasize the moral dimension of law. For him, law was more than an expression of power or an arbitrary command. Law, he said, is a dictate of reason. Indeed, Aquinas linked the law of government to the moral law resident in human reason which, in turn, was linked to the eternal law which, according to Aquinas, is identical with God's reason. It followed in Aquinas' theory, therefore, that if a law of a government is contrary to the natural law known by human reason, then such a civil law does not even have the character of law and presumably does not have to be obeyed. Although the question of obedience to law is involved here, that was not Aquinas' chief concern. He appeared to be more interested in clarifying what a law is and how necessary it is for a law, to be a law, to conform to natural morality.

In Hobbes' writings we find what reads like a grammar of obedience. He emphasizes obedience to the law primarily because of his horror at the prospect of anarchy. One does not have to take too literally his, or Locke's, or Rousseau's theory of the social contract as an actual historical event in order to appreciate their arguments. Whether there was or was not a time when men entered into a social contract, thereby passing from the state of nature to civil society, any society can experience the conditions Hobbes described. He described what it would be like if each person were completely free to decide what it would take to preserve his own life. Under these circumstances, each person would have a right to do anything and everything he considered necessary for this end. Because men frequently want the same thing although only one can have it, and because men have inconsistent ideas of what is just and right or even what religion requires, life becomes a continuous struggle and conflict or a war of all against all. In order, then, to overcome this anarchy, it is necessary for men to agree upon one lawgiver, the sovereign, whose laws everyone must obey. Thus, obedience to the laws is what creates and preserves a civil society. The alternative, says Hobbes, is for everyone to retain his former freedom to decide by himself what justice is and what his conduct should be.

Political philosophy is concerned, then, with the problem of bringing these two equally important emphases into harmony, namely, that laws should conform to the moral standard of justice to prevent tyranny on the one hand and that laws should be obeyed in order to prevent anarchy on the other. What makes this an intricate process is that even in most enlightened societies bad laws will be passed, from the point of view of some segments of that society. Why should a person or group obey such a law? It would appear that Hobbes' answer is that one must obey even the bad law for the sake of order, as though nothing is worse than anarchy. On the other hand, Hobbes has focused upon a rigorous point which disobedience raises: Is the person who disobeys the law willing to extend to every other member of society the right to disobey whenever he thinks a law is unjust, or does the person who disobeys think only of his own freedom and expect others to obey the law? Hobbes' key point is that under the best circumstances it is virtually impossible to secure unanimous agreement on what the law should be. For everyone to retain the freedom to disobey when he disagrees would clearly lead to anarchy. But it does not need to follow from this that laws will be arbitrary or unjust or incapable of modification. Part of the legal and political structure can include the procedures for appeal, dissent, amendment, and repeal. In this manner, the fundamental drive for justice can be incorporated into the mechanisms for preserving order. In this view, a just order or ordered justice, and not order alone, is the end of political society. Rousseau argues in an ingenious way that the laws of the sovereign have the effect of forcing men to be free.

The quest for a just society involves a careful analysis of the nature of freedom or liberty. In John Stuart Mill's famous essay we find a classic formula for determining the scope of human liberty where men must be free from governmental coercion. In the twentieth century, John Rawls has fashioned a provocative theory of justice which contains a novel relationship between freedom and equality. Finally, Robert Nozick focuses upon fundamental human rights as the barrier against the intrusion upon the life of the individual by the state.

9

The Natural Basis of Society

Aristotle (384–322 B.C.)

Every state is a community of some kind, and every community is established with a view to some good; for mankind always act in order to obtain that which they think good. But, if all communities aim at some good, the state or political community, which is the highest of all, and which embraces all the rest, aims and in a greater degree than any other, at the highest good.

Now there is an erroneous opinion that a statesman, king, householder, and master are the same, and that they differ, not in kind, but only in the number of their subjects. For example, the ruler over a few is called a master; over more, the manager of a household; over a still larger number, a statesman or king, as if there were no difference between a great household and a small state. The distinction which is made between the king and the statesman is as follows: When

From *Politics*, translated by Benjamin Jowett, from *The Oxford Translation of Aristotle*, edited by W. D. Ross, vol. 10 (1921).

the government is personal, the ruler is a king; when, according to the principles of the political science, the citizens rule and are ruled in turn, then he is called a statesman.

But all this is a mistake; for governments differ in kind, as will be evident to any one who considers the matter according to the method which has hitherto guided us. As in other departments of science, so in politics, the compound should always be resolved into the simple elements or least parts of the whole. We must therefore look at the elements of which the state is composed, in order that we may see in what they differ from one another, and whether any scientific distinction can be drawn between the different kinds of rule.

He who thus considers things in their first growth and origin, whether a state or anything else, will obtain the clearest view of them. In the first place (1) there must be a union of those who cannot exist without each other; for example, of male and female, that the race may continue; and this is a union which is formed, not of deliberate purpose, but because, in common with other animals and with plants, mankind have a natural desire to leave behind them an image of themselves. And (2) there must be a union of natural ruler and subject, that both may be preserved. For he who can foresee with his mind is by nature intended to be lord and master, and he who can work with his body is a subject, and by nature a slave; hence master and slave have the same interest. Nature, however, has distinguished between the female and the slave. For she is not niggardly, like the smith who fashions the Delphian knife for many uses; she makes each thing for a single use, and every instrument is best made when intended for one and not for many uses. But among barbarians no distinction is made between women and slaves, because there is no natural ruler among them: they are a community of slaves, male and female. Wherefore the poets say,—

It is meet that Hellenes should rule over barbarians;
as if they thought that the barbarian and the slave were
by nature one.

Out of these two relationships between man and woman, master and slave, the family first arises, and Hesiod is right when he says,—

'First house and wife and an ox for the plough,'

for the ox is the poor man's slave. The family is the association by nature for the supply of men's every-day wants, and the members of it are called by Charondas 'companions of the cupboard' and by Epimenides the Cretan, 'companions of the manger'. But when several families are united, and the association aims at something more than the supply of daily needs, then comes into existence the village. And the most natural form of the village appears to be that of a colony from the family, composed of the children and grandchildren, who are said to be 'suckled with the same milk.' And this is the reason why Hellenic states were originally governed by kings; because the Hellenes were under royal rule before they came together, as the barbarians still are. Every family is ruled by the eldest, and therefore in the colonies of the family the kingly form of government prevailed because they were of the same blood. As Homer says (of the Cyclopes):—

'Each one gives law to his children and to his wives.'

For they lived dispersedly, as was the manner in ancient times. Wherefore men say that the Gods have a king, because they themselves either are or were in ancient times under the rule of a king. For they imagine, not only the forms of the Gods, but their ways of life to be like their own.

When several villages are united in a single community, perfect and large enough to be nearly or quite self-sufficing, the state comes into existence, originating in the bare needs of life, and continuing in existence for the sake of a good life. And therefore, if the earlier forms of society are natural, so is the state, for it is the end of them, and the (completed) nature is the end. For what each thing is when fully developed, we call its nature, whether we are speaking of a man, a horse, or a family. Besides, the final cause and end of a thing is the best, and to be self-sufficing is the end and the best.

Hence it is evident that the state is a creation of nature, and that man is by nature a political animal. And he who by nature and not by mere accident is without a state, is either above humanity, or below it; he is the

'Tribeless, lawless, hearthless one,'

whom Homer denounces—the outcast who is a lover of war; he may be compared to an unprotected piece in the game of draughts.

Now the reason why man is more of a political animal than bees or any other gregarious animals is evident. Nature, as we often say, makes nothing in vain, and man is the only animal whom she has endowed with the gift of speech. And whereas mere sound is but an indication of pleasure or pain, and is therefore found in other animals (for their nature attains to the perception of pleasure and pain and the intimation of them to one another, and no further), the power of speech is intended to set forth the expedient and inexpedient, and likewise the just and the unjust. And it is a characteristic of man that he alone has any sense of good and evil, of just and unjust, and the association of living beings who have this sense makes a family and a state.

Thus the state is by nature clearly prior to the family and to the individual, since the whole is of necessity prior to the part; for example, if the whole body be destroyed, there will be no foot or hand, except in an equivocal sense, as we might speak of a stone hand; for when destroyed the hand will be no better. But things are defined by their working and power; and we ought not to say that they are the same when they are no longer the same, but only that they have the same name. The proof that the state is a creation of nature and prior to the individual is that the individual, when isolated, is not self-sufficing; and therefore he is like a part in relation to the whole. But he who is unable to live in society, or who has no need because he is sufficient for himself, must be either a beast or a god: he is no part of a state. A social instinct is implanted in all men by nature, and yet he who first founded the state was the greatest of all benefactors. For man, when perfected, is the best of animals, but, when separated from law and justice, he is the worst of all; since armed injustice is the more dangerous, and he is equipped at birth with the arms of intelligence and with moral qualities which he may use for the worst ends. Wherefore, if he have not vitrue, he is the most unholy and the most savage of animals, and the most full of lust and gluttony. But justice is the bond of men in states, and the administration of justice, which is the determination of what is just, is the principle of order in political society. . . .

But a state exists for the sake of a good life, and not for the sake of life only: if life only were the object, slaves and brute animals might form a state, but they cannot, for they have no share in happiness or in a life of free choice. Nor does a state exist for the sake of alliance and security from injustice, nor yet for the sake of exchange and mutual intercourse; for then the Tyrrhenians and the Carthaginians, and all who have commercial treaties with one another, would be the citizens of one state. True, they have agreements about imports, and engagements that they will do no wrong to one another, and written articles of alliance. But there are no magistracies common to the contracting parties who will enforce their engagements; different states have each their own magistracies. Nor does one state take care that the citizens of the other are such as they ought to be, nor see that those who come under the terms of the treaty do no wrong or wickedness at all, but only that they do no injustice to one another. Whereas, those who care for good government take into consideration (the larger question of) virtue and vice in states. Whence it may be further inferred that virtue must be the serious care of a state which truly deserves the name: for (without this ethical end) the community becomes a mere alliance which differs only in place from alliances of which the members live apart; and law is only a convention, a surety to one another of justice, as the sophist Lycophron says, and has no real power to make the citizens good and just.

This is obvious; for suppose distinct places, such as Corinth and Megara, to be united by a wall, still they would not be one city, not even if the citizens had the right to intermarry, which is one of the rights peculiarly characteristic of states. Again, if men dwelt at a distance from one another, but not so far off as to have no intercourse, and there were laws among them that they should not wrong each other in their exchanges, neither would this be a state. Let us suppose that one man is a carpenter, another a husbandman, another a shoemaker, and so on, and that their number is ten thousand: nevertheless, if they have nothing in common but exchange, alliance, and the like, that would not constitute a state. Why is this? Surely not because they are at a distance from one another: for even supposing that such a community were to meet in one place, and that each man had a house of his own, which was in a manner his state, and that they made alliance with one another, but only against evil-doers; still an accurate thinker would not deem this to be a state, if their intercourse with one another was of the same character after as before their union. It is clear then that a state is not a mere society, having a common place, established for the prevention of crime and for the sake of exchange. These are conditions without which a state cannot exist; but all of them together do not constitute a state, which is a community of well-being in families and aggregations of families, for the sake of a perfect and self-sufficing life. Such a community can only be established among those who live in the same place and intermarry. Hence arise in cities family connexions, brotherhoods, common sacrifices, amusements, which draw men together. They are created by friendship, for friendship is the motive of society. The end is the good life, and these are the means towards it. And the state is the union of families and villages having for an end a perfect and self-sufficing life, by which we mean a happy and honourable life.

Our conclusion, then, is that political society exists for the sake of noble actions, and not of mere companionship. And they who contribute most to such a society have a greater share in it than those who have the same or a greater freedom or nobility of birth but are inferior to them in a political virtue; or than those who exceed them in wealth but are surpassed by them in virtue. . . .

He who would enquire into the nature and various kinds of government must first of all determine 'What is a state?' At present this is a disputed question. Some say that the state has done a certain act; others, no, not the state, but the oligarchy or the tyrant. And the legislator or statesman is concerned entirely with the state; a constitution or government being an arrangement of the inhabitants of a state. But a state is composite, and, like any other whole, made up of many parts;—these are the citizens, who compose it. It is evident, therefore, that we must begin by asking, Who is the citizen, and what is the meaning of the term? For here again there may be a difference of opinion. He who is a citizen in a democracy will often not be a citizen in an oligarchy. Leaving out of consideration those who have been made citizens, or who have obtained the name of citizen in any other accidental manner, we may say, first, that a citizen is not a citizen because he lives in a certain place, for resident aliens and slaves share in the place; nor is he a citizen who has no legal right except that of suing and being sued; for this right may be enjoyed under the provisions of a treaty. Even resident aliens in many places possess such rights, although in an imperfect form; for they are obliged to have a patron. Hence they do but imperfectly participate in citizenship, and we call them citizens only in a qualified sense, as we might apply the term to children who are too young to be on the register, or to old men who have been relieved from state duties. Of these we do not say simply that they are citizens, but add in the one case that they are not of age, and in the other, that they are past the age, or something of that sort; the precise expression is immaterial, for our meaning is clear. Similar difficulties to those which I have mentioned may be raised and answered about deprived citizens and about exiles. But the citizen, whom we are seeking to define, is a citizen in the strictest sense, against whom no such exception can be taken, and his special characteristic is that he shares in the administration of justice, and in offices. . . .

There is a point nearly allied to the preceding: Whether the virtue of a good man and a good citizen is the same or not. But, before entering on this discussion, we must first obtain some general notion of the virtue of the citizen. Like the sailor, the citizen is a member of a community. Now, sailors have different functions, for one of them is a rower, another a pilot, a third a look-out man, and a fourth is described by some similar term; and while the precise definition of each individual's virtue applies exclusively to him, there is, at the same time, a common definition applicable to them all. For they have all of them a common object, which is safety in navigation. Similarly, one citizen differs from another, but the salvation of the community is the common business of them all. This community is the state; the virtue of the citizen must therefore be relative to the constitution of which he is a member. If, then, there are many forms of government, it is evident that the virtue of the good citizen cannot be the one perfect virtue. But we say that the good man is he who has perfect virtue. Hence it is evident that the good citizen need not of necessity possess the virtue which makes a good man.

The same question may also be approached by another road, from a consideration of the perfect state. If the state cannot be entirely composed of good men, and each citizen is expected to do his own business well, and must therefore have virtue inasmuch as all the citizens cannot be alike, the virtue of the citizen and of the good man cannot coincide. All must have the virtue of the good citizen—thus, and thus only, can the state be perfect; but they will not have the virtue of a good man, unless we assume that in the good state all the citizens must be good.

Again, the state may be compared to the living being: as the first elements into which the living being is resolved are soul and body, as the soul is made up of reason and appetite, the family of husband and wife, property of master and slave, so out of all these, as well as other dissimilar elements, the state is composed; and, therefore, the virtue of all the citizens cannot possibly be the same, any more than the excellence of the leader of a chorus is the same as that of the performer who stands by his side. I have said enough to show why the two kinds of virtue cannot be absolutely and always the same.

But will there then be no case in which the virtue of the good citizen and the virtue of the good man coincide? To this we answer (not that the good citizen, but) that the good ruler is a good and wise man, and that he who would be a statesman must be a wise man. And some persons say that even the education of the ruler should be of a special kind; for are not the children of kings instructed in riding and military exercises? As Euripides says:

'No subtle arts for me, but what the state requires.'

As though there were a special education needed by a ruler. If then the virtue of a good ruler is the same as that of a good man, and we assume further that the subject is a citizen as well as the ruler, the virtue of the good citizen and the virtue of the good man cannot be always the same, although in some cases (i.e. in the perfect state) they may; for the virtue of a ruler differs from that of a citizen.

It was the sense of this difference which made Jason say that 'he felt hungry when he was a tyrant,' meaning that he could not endure to live in a private station. But, on the other hand, it may be argued that men are praised for knowing both how to rule and how to obey, and he is said to be a citizen of approved virtue who is able to do both. Now if we suppose the virtue of a good man to be that which rules, and the virtue of the citizen to include ruling and obeying, it cannot be said that they are equally worthy of praise. Since then, it is occasionally held that the ruler and the ruled should learn different things and not the same things, and that the citizen must know and share in both; the inference is obvious. There is, indeed, the rule of a master which is concerned with menial offices,—the master need not know how to perform these, but may employ others in the execution of them: anything else would be degrading; and by anything else I mean the menial duties which vary much in character and are executed by various classes of slaves, such, for example, as handicraftsmen, who, as their name signifies, live by the labour of their hands:—under these the mechanic is included. Hence in ancient times, and among some nations, the working classes had no share in the government—a privilege which they only acquired under the extreme democracy. Certainly the good man and the statesman and the good citizen ought not to learn the crafts of inferiors except for their own occasional use; if they habitually practise them, there will cease to be a distinction between master and slave.

This is not the rule of which we are speaking; but there is a rule of another kind, which is exercised over freemen and equals by birth—a constitutional rule, which the ruler must learn by obeying, as he would learn the duties of a general of cavalry by being under the orders of a general of cavalry, or the duties of a general of infantry by being under the orders of a general of infantry, or by having had the command of a company or brigade. It has been well said that 'he who has never learned to obey cannot be a good commander.' The two are not the same, but the good citizen ought to be capable of both; he should know how to govern like a freeman, and how to obey like a freeman—these are the virtues of a citizen. And, although the temperance and justice of a ruler are distinct from those of a subject, the virtue of a good man will include both; for the good man, who is free and also a subject, will not have one virtue only, say justice, but he will have distinct kinds of virtue, the one qualifying him to rule, the other to obey, and differing as the temperance and courage of men and women differ. For a man would be thought coward if he had no more courage than a courageous woman, and a woman would be thought loquacious if she imposed no more restraint on her conversation than the good man; and indeed their part in the management of the household is different, for the duty of the one is to acquire, and of the other to preserve. Practical wisdom only is characteristic of the ruler: it would seem that all other virtues must equally belong to ruler and subject. The virtue of the subject is certainly not wisdom, but only true opinion; he may be compared to the maker of the flute, while his master is like the flute-player or user of the flute.

From these considerations may be gathered the answer to the question, whether the virtue of the good man is the same as that of the good citizen, or different, and how far the same, and how far different. . . .

Since every political society is composed of rulers and subjects, let us consider whether the relations of one to the other should interchange or be permanent. For the education of the citizens will necessarily vary with the answer given to this question. Now, if some men excelled others in the same degree in which gods and heroes are supposed to excel mankind in general, having in the first place a great advantage even in their bodies, and secondly in their minds, so that the superiority of the governors over their subjects was patent and undisputed, it would clearly be better that once for all the one class should rule and the others serve. But since this is unattainable, and kings have no marked superiority over their subjects, such as Scylax affirms to be found among the Indians, it is obviously necessary on many grounds that all the citizens alike should take their turn of governing and being governed. Equality consists in the same treatment of similar persons, and no government can stand which is not founded upon justice. For (if the government be unjust) every one in the country unites with the governed in the desire to have a revolution, and it is an impossibility that the members of the government can be so numerous as to be stronger than all their enemies put together. Yet that governors should excel their subjects is undeniable. How all this is to be effected, and in what way they will respectively share in the government, the legislator has to consider. The subject has been already mentioned. Nature herself has given the principle of choice when she made a difference between old and young (though they are really the same in kind), of whom she fitted the one to govern and the others to be governed. No one takes offence at being governed when he is young, nor does he think himself better than his governors, especially if he will enjoy the same privilege when he reaches the required age.

We conclude that from one point of view governors and governed are identical, and from another different. And therefore their education must be the same and also different. For he who would learn to command well must, as men say, first of all learn to obey. As I observed in the first part of this treatise, there is one rule which is for the sake of the rulers and another rule which is for the sake of the ruled; the former is a despotic, the latter a free government. Some commands differ not in the thing commanded, but in the intention with which they are imposed. Wherefore, many apparently menial offices are an honour to the free youth by whom they are performed; for actions do not differ as honourable or dishonourable in themselves so much as in the end and intention of them. But since we say that the virtue of the citizen and ruler is the same as that of the good man, and that the same person must first be a subject and then a ruler, the legislator has to see that they become good men, and by what means this may be accomplished, and what is the end of the perfect life.

10

The Moral Dimensions of Law

Saint Thomas Aquinas (1225–1274)

Law is a rule and measure of acts, whereby man is induced to act or is restrained from acting; for *lex* (law) is derived from *ligare* (to bind), because it binds one to act. Now the rule and measure of human acts is the reason, which is the first principle of human acts . . . For it belongs to the reason to direct to the end, which is the first principle in all matters of action. . . . Now that which is the principle in any genus is the rule and measure of that genus: for instance, unity in the genus of numbers, and the first movement in the genus of movements. Consequently, it follows that law is something pertaining to reason. . . .

Now as reason is a principle of human acts, so in reason itself there is something which is the principle in respect of all the rest. Hence to this principle chiefly and mainly law must needs be referred. Now the first principle in practi-

From *Introduction to Saint Thomas Aquinas*, edited by Anton C. Pegis, Random House, Inc., (1948).

cal matters, which are the object of the practical reason, is the last end: and the last end of human life is happiness or beatitude, as we have stated above. Consequently, law must needs concern itself mainly with the order that is in beatitude. Moreover, since every part is ordained to the whole as the imperfect to the perfect, and since one man is a part of the perfect community, law must needs concern itself properly with the order directed to universal happiness. . . .

Law is nothing else but a dictate of practical reason emanating from the ruler who governs a perfect community. Now it is evident, granted that the world is ruled by divine providence, as was stated in the First Part, that the whole community of the universe is governed by the divine reason. Therefore the very notion of the government of things in God, the ruler of the universe, has the nature of a law. And since the divine reason's conception of things is not subject to time, but is eternal, according to Prov. viii. 23, therefore it is that this kind of law must be called eternal. . . .

Law being a rule and measure, can be in a person in two ways: in one way, as in him that rules and measures; in another way, as in that which is ruled and measured, since a thing is ruled and measured in so far as it partakes of the rule or measure. Therefore, since all things subject to divine providence are ruled and measured by the eternal law, as was stated above, it is evident that all things partake in some way in the eternal law, in so far as, namely, from its being imprinted on them, they derive their respective inclinations to their proper acts and ends. Now among all others, the rational creature is subject to divine providence in a more excellent way, in so far as it itself partakes of a share of providence, by being provident both for itself and for others. Therefore it has a share of the eternal reason, whereby it has a natural inclination to its proper act and end; and this participation of the eternal law in the rational creature is called the natural law. . . . The light of natural reason, whereby we discern what is good and what is evil, which is the function of the natural law, is nothing else than an imprint on us of the divine light. It is therefore evident that the natural law is nothing else than the rational creature's participation of the eternal law. . . .

As we have stated above, a law is a dictate of the practical reason. Now it is to be observed that the same procedure takes place in the practical and in the speculative reason, for each proceeds from principles to conclusions, as was stated above. Accordingly, we conclude that, just as in the speculative reason, from naturally known indemonstrable principles we draw the conclusions of the various sciences, the knowledge of which is not imparted to us by nature, but acquired by the efforts of reason, so too it is that from the precepts of the natural law, as from common and indemonstrable principles, the human reason needs to proceed to the more particular determination of certain matters. These particular determinations, devised by human reason, are called human laws, provided that the other essential conditions of law be observed. . . .

Besides the natural and the human law it was necessary for the directing of human conduct to have a divine law. And this for four reasons. First, because it is by law that man is directed how to perform his proper acts in view of his last end. Now if man were ordained to no other end than that which is proportionate to his natural ability, there would be no need for man to have any further direction, on the part of his reason, in addition to the natural law and humanly devised law which is derived from it. But since man is ordained to an end of eternal happiness which exceeds man's natural ability, as we have stated above, therefore it was necessary that, in addition to the natural and the human law, man should be directed to his end by a law given by God.

Secondly, because, by reason of the uncertainty of human judgment, especially on contingent and particular matters, different people form different judgments on human acts; whence also different and contrary laws result. In order, therefore, that man may know without any doubt what he ought to do, and what he ought to avoid, it was necessary for man to be directed in his proper acts by a law given by God, for it is certain that such a law cannot err.

Thirdly, because man can make laws in those matters of which he is competent to judge. But man is not competent to judge of interior movements, that are hidden, but only of exterior acts which are observable; and yet for the perfection of virtue it is necessary for man to conduct himself rightly in both kinds of acts. Consequently, human law could not sufficiently curb and direct interior acts, and it was necessary for this purpose that a divine law should supervene.

Fourthly, because, as Augustine says, human law cannot punish or forbid all evil deeds, since, while aiming at doing away with all evils, it would do away with many good things, and would hinder the advance of the common good, which is necessary for human living. In order, therefore, that no evil might remain unforbidden and unpunished, it was necessary for the divine law to supervene, whereby all sins are forbidden. . . .

As was stated above, law denotes a kind of plan directing acts towards an end. Now wherever there are movers ordained to one another, the power of the second mover must needs be derived from the power of the first mover, since the second mover does not move except in so far as it is moved by the first. Therefore we observe the same in all those who govern, namely, that the plan of government is derived by secondary governors from the governor in chief. Thus the plan of what is to be done in a state flows from the king's command to his inferior administrators; and again in things of art the plan of whatever is to be done by art flows from the chief craftsman to the under-craftsmen who work with their hands. Since, then, the eternal law is the plan of government in the Chief Governor, all the plans of government in the inferior governors must be derived from the eternal law. But these plans of inferior governors are all the other laws which are in addition to the eternal law. Therefore all laws, in so far as they partake of right reason, are derived from the eternal law. Hence Augustine says that *in temporal law there is nothing just and lawful but what man has drawn from the eternal law.* . . .

To the natural law belong those things to which a man is inclined naturally; and among these it is proper to man to be inclined to act according to reason. Now it belongs to the reason to proceed from what is common to what is proper, as is stated in *Physics i.* The speculative reason, however, is differently situated, in this matter, from the practical reason. For, since the speculative reason is concerned chiefly with necessary things, which cannot be otherwise than they are, its proper conclusions, like the universal principles, contain the truth without fail. The practical reason, on the other hand, is concerned with contingent matters, which is the domain of human actions; and, consequently, although there is necessity in the common principles, the more we descend towards the particular, the more frequently we encounter defects. Accordingly, then, in speculative matters truth is the same in all men, both as to principles and as to conclusions; although the truth is not known to all as regards the conclusions, but only as regards the principles which are called *common notions*. But in matters of action, truth or practical rectitude is not the same for all as to what is particular, but only as to the common principles; and where there is the same rectitude in relation to particulars, it is not equally known at all. . . .

Consequently, we must say that the natural law, as to the first common principles, is the same for all, both as to rectitude and as to knowledge. But as to certain more particular aspects, which are conclusions, as it were, of those common principles, it is the same for all in the majority of cases, both as to rectitude and as to knowledge; and yet in some few cases it may fail, both as to rectitude, by reason of certain obstacles (just as natures subject to generation and corruption fail in some few cases because of some obstacle), and as to knowledge, since in some the reason is perverted by passion, or evil habit, or an evil disposition of nature. Thus at one time theft, although it is expressly contrary to the natural law, was not considered wrong among the Germans, as Julius Caesar relates. . . .

As we have stated above, man has a natural aptitude for virtue; but the perfection of virtue must be acquired by man by means of some kind of training. Thus we observe that a man is helped by diligence in his necessities, for instance, in food and clothing. Certain beginnings of these he has from nature, viz., his reason and his hands; but he has not the full complement, as other animals have, to whom nature has given sufficiently of clothing and food. Now it is difficult to see how man could suffice for himself in the matter of this training, since the perfection of virtue consists chiefly in withdrawing man from under undue pleasures, to which above all man is inclined, and especially the young, who are more capable of being trained. Consequently a man needs to receive this training from another, whereby to arrive at the perfection of virtue. And as to these young people who are inclined to acts of virtue by their good natural disposition, or by custom, or rather by the gift of God, paternal training suffices, which is by admonitions. But since some are found to be dissolute and prone to vice, and not easily amenable to words, it was necessary for such to be restrained from evil by force and fear, in order that, at least, they might desist from evil-doing, and leave others in peace, and that they themselves, by being habituated in this way, might be brought to do willingly what hitherto they did from fear, and thus become virtuous. Now this kind of training, which compels through fear of punishment, is the discipline of laws. Therefore, in order that man might have peace and virtue, it was necessary for laws to be framed; for as the Philosopher says, *as man is the most noble of animals if he be perfect in virtue, so he is the lowest of all, if he be severed from law and justice.* For man can use his reason to devise means of satisfying his lusts and evil passions, which other animals are unable to do. . . .

As Augustine says, *that which is not just seems to be no law at all.* Hence the force of a law depends on the extent of its justice. Now in human affairs a thing is said to be just from being right, according to the rule of reason. But the first rule of reason is the law of nature, as is clear from what has been stated above. Consequently, every human law has just so much of the nature of law as it is derived from the law of nature. But if in any point it departs from the law of nature, it is no longer a law but a perversion of law.

But it must be noted that something may be derived from the natural law in two ways: first, as a conclusion from principles; secondly, by way of a determination of certain common notions. The first way is like to that by which, in the sciences, demonstrated conclusions are drawn from the principles; while the second is likened to that whereby, in the arts, common forms are determined to some particular. Thus, the craftsman needs to determine the common form of a house to the shape of this or that particular house. Some things are therefore derived from the common principles of the natural law by way of conclusions: e.g., that *one must not kill* may be derived as a conclusion from the principle that *one should do harm to no man;* while some are derived therefrom by way of determination: e.g., the law of nature has it that the evil-doer should be punished, but that he be punished in this or that way is a determination of the law of nature.

Accordingly, both modes of derivation are found in the human law. But those things which are derived in the first way are contained in human law, not as emanating therefrom exclusively, but as having some force from the natural law also. But those things which are derived in the second way have no other force than that of human law.

11

The Basis of Sovereign Authority

Thomas Hobbes (1588–1679)

PART I, CHAPTER I

The faculties of human nature may be reduced unto four kinds; bodily strength, experience, reason, passion. Taking the beginning of this following doctrine from these, we will declare in the first place what manner of inclinations men who are endued with these faculties bear towards each other, and whether, and by what faculty they are born, apt for society, and to preserve themselves against mutual violence; then proceeding, we will shew what advice was necessary to be taken for this business, and what are the conditions of society, or of human peace; that is to say, (changing the words only) what are the fundamental laws of nature.

The greatest part of those men who have written aught concerning commonwealths, either suppose, or require us, or beg of us to believe, that man is a

From Hobbes, *De Cive*, edited by Sterling P. Lamprecht, Appleton-Century-Crofts, Inc., New York, 1949.

creature born fit° for society. The Greeks call him *political animal;* and on this foundation they so build up the doctrine of civil society, as if for the preservation of peace, and the government of mankind, there were nothing else necessary, than that men should agree to make certain covenants and conditions together, which themselves should then call laws. Which axiom, though received by most, is yet certainly false, and an error proceeding from our too slight contemplation of human nature. For they who shall more narrowly look into the causes for which men come together, and delight in each other's company, shall easily find that this happens not because naturally it could happen no otherwise, but by accident. For if by nature one man should love another (that is) as man, there could no reason be returned why every man should not equally love every man, as being equally man, or why he should rather frequent those whose society affords him honour or profit. We do not therefore by nature seek society for its own sake, but that we may receive some honour or profit from it; these we desire primarily, that secondarily. How, by what advice, men do meet, will be best known by observing those things which they do when they are met. For if they meet for traffic, it is plain every man regards not his fellow, but his business; if to discharge some office, a certain market-friendship is begotten, which hath more of jealousy in it than true love, and whence factions sometimes may arise, but good will never; if for pleasure, and recreation of mind, every man is wont to please himself most with those things which stir up laughter, whence he may (according to the nature of that which is ridiculous) by comparison of another man's defects and infirmities, pass the more current in his own opinion; and although this be sometimes innocent and without offence, yet it is manifest they are not so much delighted with the society, as their own vain glory. But for the most part, in these kinds of meetings, we wound the absent; their whole life, sayings, actions are examined, judged, condemned; nay, it is very rare, but some present receive a fling before they part, so as his reason was not ill, who was wont always at parting to go out last. And these are indeed the true delights of society,

---

° Since we now see actually a constituted society among men, and none living out of it, since we discern all desirous of congress, and mutual corespondence, it may seem a wonderful kind of stupidity, to lay in the very threshold of this doctrine, such a stumbling block before the readers, as to deny man to be born fit for society. Therefore I must more plainly say, that it is true indeed, that to man, by nature, or as man, that is, as soon as he is born, solitude is an enemy; for infants have need of others to help them to live, and those of riper years to help them to live well, wherefore I deny not that men (even nature compelling) desire to come together. But civil societies are not mere meetings, but bonds, to the making whereof, faith and compacts are necessary: the virtue whereof to children, and fools, and the profit whereof to those who have not yet tasted the miseries which accompany its defects, is altogether unknown; whence it happens, that those, because they know not what society is, cannot enter into it; these, because ignorant of the benefit it brings, care not for it. Manifest therefore it is, that all men, because they are born in infancy, are born unapt for society. Many also (perhaps most men) either through defect of mind, or want of education, remain unfit during the whole course of their lives; yet have they, infants as well as those of riper years, a human nature; wherefore man is made fit for society not by nature but by education. Furthermore, although man were born in such a condition as to desire it, it follows not, that he therefore were born fit to enter into it; for it is one thing to desire, another to be in capacity fit for what we desire; for even they, who through their pride, will not stoop to equal conditions, without which there can be no society, do yet desire it.

unto which we are carried by nature, that is, by those passions which are incident to all creatures, until either by sad experience, or good precepts, it so fall out (which in many never happens) that the appetite of present matters be dulled with the memory of things past, without which, the discourse of most quick and nimble men on this subject, is but cold and hungry.

But if it so happen, that being met, they pass their time in relating some stories, and one of them begins to tell one which concerns himself; instantly every one of the rest most greedily desires to speak of himself too; if one relate some wonder, the rest will tell you miracles, if they have them, if not, they will feign them. Lastly, that I may say somewhat of them who pretend to be wiser than others; if they meet to talk of philosophy, look how many men, so many would be esteemed masters, or else they not only love not their fellows, but even persecute them with hatred. So clear is it by experience to all men who a little more narrowly consider human affairs, that all free congress ariseth either from mutual poverty, or from vain glory, whence the parties met, endeavour to carry with them either some benefit, or to leave behind them that same (eudokinein) some esteem and honour with those, with whom they have been conversant. The same is also collected by reason out of the definitions themselves, of will, good honour, profitable. For when we voluntarily contract society, in all manner of society we look after the object of the will, that is, that, which every one of those who gather together, propounds to himself for good. Now whatsoever seems good, is pleasant, and relates either to the senses, or the mind. But all the mind's pleasure is either glory, (or to have a good opinion of one's self) or refers to glory in the end; the rest are sensual, or conducing to sensuality, which may be all comprehended under the word conveniences. All society therefore is either for gain, or for glory; that is, not so much for love of our fellows, as for the love of ourselves. But no society can be great, or lasting, which begins from vain glory, because that glory is like honour if all men have it, no man hath it, for they consist in comparison and precellence; neither doth the society of others advance any whit the cause of my glorying in myself; for every man must account himself, such as he can make himself, without the help of others. But though the benefits of this life may be much farthered by mutual help, since yet those may be better attained to by dominion, than by the society of others: I hope no body will doubt but that men would much more greedily be carried by nature, if all fear were removed, to obtain dominion, than to gain society. We must therefore resolve, that the original of all great and lasting societies consisted not in the mutual good will men had towards each other, but in the mutual fear they had of each other.

The cause of mutual fear consists partly in the natural equality of men, partly in their mutual will of hurting: whence it comes to pass that we can neither expect from others, nor promise to ourselves the least security. For if we look on men full-grown, and consider how brittle the frame of our human body is, (which perishing, all its strength, vigour, and wisdom itself perisheth with it) and how easy a matter it is, even for the weakest man to kill the strongest, there is no reason why any man trusting to his own strength should conceive himself made by nature above others: they are equals who can do equal things one against the other; but they who can do the greatest things, (namely, kill) can do equal things. All men therefore among themselves are by nature equal; the inequality we now discern, hath its spring from the civil law.

All men in the state of nature have a desire and will to hurt, but not proceeding from the same cause, neither equally to be condemned. For one man, according to that natural equality which is among us, permits as much to others, as he assumes to himself (which is an argument of a temperate man, and one that rightly values his power). Another, supposing himself above others, will have a license to do what he lists, and challenges respect and honour, as due to him before others, (which is an argument of a fiery spirit). This man's will to hurt ariseth from vain glory, and the false esteem he hath of his own strength; the other's, from the necessity of defending himself, his liberty, and his goods, against this man's violence.

Furthermore, since the combat of wits is the fiercest, the greatest discords which are, must necessarily arise from this contention. For in this case it is not only odious to contend against, but also not to consent. For not to approve of what a man saith, is no less than tacitly to accuse him of an error in that thing which he speaketh; as in very many things to dissent, is as much as if you accounted him a fool whom you dissent from; which may appear hence, that there are no wars so sharply waged as between sects of the same religion, and factions of the same commonweal, where the contestation is either concerning doctrines or politic prudence. And since all the pleasure and jollity of the mind consists in this, even to get some, with whom comparing, it may find somewhat wherein to triumph and vaunt itself; it is impossible but men must declare sometimes some mutual scorn and contempt, either by laughter, or by words, or by gesture, or some sign or other; than which there is no greater vexation of mind, and than from which there cannot possibly arise a greater desire to do hurt.

But the most frequent reason why men desire to hurt each other, ariseth hence, that many men at the same time have an appetite to the same thing; which yet very often they can neither enjoy in common, nor yet divide it; whence it follows that the strongest must have it, and who is strongest must be decided by the sword.

Among so many dangers therefore, as the natural lusts of men do daily threaten each other withal, to have a care of one's self is not a matter so scornfully to be looked upon, as if so be there had not been a power and will left in one to have done otherwise. For every man is desirous of what is good for him, and shuns what is evil, but chiefly the chiefest of natural evils, which is death; and this he doth, by a certain impulsion of nature, no less than that whereby a stone moves downward. It is therefore neither absurd, nor reprehensible, neither against the dictates of true reason, for a man to use all his endeavours to preserve and defend his body and the members thereof from death and sorrows. But that which is not contrary to right reason, that all men account to be done justly, and with right; neither by the word right is anything else signified, than that liberty which every man hath to make use of is natural faculties according to right reason. Therefore the first foundation of natural right is this, that every man as much as in him lies endeavour to protect his life and members.

But because it is in vain for a man to have a right to the end, if the right to the necessary means be denied him; it follows, that since every man hath a right to preserve himself, he must also be allowed a right to use all the means, and do all the actions, without which he cannot preserve himself.

Now whether the means which he is about to use, and the action he is performing, be necessary to the preservation of his life and members, or not, he himself, by the right of nature, must be judge. For say another man judge that it is contrary to right reason that I should judge of mine own peril: why now, because he judgeth of what concerns me, by the same reason, because we are equal by nature, will I judge also of things which do belong to him. Therefore it agrees with right reason, that is, it is the right of nature that I judge of his opinion, that is, whether it conduce to my preservation or not.

Nature hath given to every one a right to all; that is, it was lawful for every man in the bare state of nature, or before such time as men had engaged themselves by any covenants or bonds, to do what he would, and against whom he thought fit, and to possess, use, and enjoy all what he would, or could get. Now because whatsoever a man would, it therefore seems good to him because he wills it, and either it really doth, or at least seems to him to contribute towards his preservation, (but we have already allowed him to be judge, in the foregoing article, whether it doth or not, in so much as we are to hold all for necessary whatsoever he shall esteem so), and by the 7th article it appears that by the right of nature those things may be done, and must be had, which necessarily conduce to the protection of life and members, it follows, that in the state of nature, to have all, and do all, is lawful for all. And this is that which is meant by that common saying, nature hath given all to all, from whence we understand likewise, that in the state of nature, profit is the measure of right.

But it was the least benefit for men thus to have a common right to all things; for the effects of this right are the same, almost, as if there had been no right at all. For although any man might say of every thing, this is mine, yet could he not enjoy it, by reason of his neighbour, who having equal right, and equal power, would pretend the same thing to be his.

If now to this natural proclivity of men, to hurt each other, which they derive from their passions, but chiefly form a vain esteem of themselves, you add, the right of all to all, wherewith one by right invades, the other by right resists, and whence arise perpetual jealousies and suspicions on all hands, and how hard a thing it is to provide against an enemy invading us, with an intention to oppress, and ruin, though they come with a small number, and no great provision; it cannot be denied but that the natural state of men, before they entered into society, was a mere war, and that not simply, but a war of all men against all men. For what is war, but that same time in which the will of contesting by force is fully declared, either by words, or deeds? The time remaining, is termed peace.

But it is easily judged how disagreeable a thing to the preservation either of mankind, or of each single man, a perpetual war is. But it is perpetual in its own nature, because in regard of the equality of those that strive, it cannot be ended by victory; for in this state the conqueror is subject to so much danger, as it were to be accounted a miracle, if any, even the most strong, should close up his life with many years, and old age. They of America are examples hereof, even in this present age: other nations have been in former ages, which now indeed are become civil and flourishing, but were then few, fierce, short-lived, poor, nasty, and deprived of all that pleasure, and beauty of life, which peace and society are wont to bring with them. Whosoever therefore holds, that it had been best to have continued in that state in which all things were lawful for all men, he contradicts himself. For every man by natural necessity desires that which is good for him: nor is there any that esteems a war of all against all, which necessarily adheres to such a state, to be good for him. And so it happens, that through fear of each other we think it fit to rid ourselves of this condition, and to get some fellows; that if there needs must be war it may not yet be against all men, nor without some helps.

Fellows are gotten either by constraint, or by consent; by constraint, when after fight the conqueror makes the conquered serve him either through fear of death, or by laying fetters on him: by consent, when men enter into society to help each other, both parties consenting without any constraint. But the conqueror may by right compel the conquered, or the strongest the weaker, (as a man in health may one that is sick, or he that is of riper years a child) unless he will choose to die, to give caution of his future obedience. For since the right of protecting ourselves according to our own wills proceeded from our danger, and our danger from our equality, it is more consonant to reason, and more certain for our conservation, using the present advantage to secure ourselves by taking caution, than, when they shall be full grown and strong, and got out of our power, to endeavour to recover that power again by doubtful fight. And on the other side, nothing can be thought more absurd, than by discharging whom you already have weak in your power, to make him at once both an enemy, and a strong one. From whence we may understand likewise as a corollary in the natural state of men, that a sure and irresistible power confers the right of dominion and ruling over those who cannot resist; insomuch, as the right of all things, that can be done, adheres essentially and immediately unto this omnipotence hence arising.

Yet cannot men expect any lasting preservation continuing thus in the state of nature, that is, of war, by reason of that equality of power, and other human faculties they are endued withal. Wherefore to seek peace, where there is any hopes of obtaining it, and where there is none, to enquire out for auxiliaries of war, is the dictate of right reason, that is, the law of nature, as shall be showed in the next chapter.

CHAPTER II

All authors agree not concerning the definition of the natural law, who notwithstanding do very often make use of this term in their writings. The method therefore, wherein we begin from definitions and exclusion of all equivocation, is only proper to them who leave no place for contrary disputes. For the rest, if any man say, that somewhat is done against the law of nature, one proves it hence, because it was done against the general agreement of all the most wise and learned nations: but this declares not who shall be the judge of the wisdom and learning of all nations. Another hence, that it was done against the general consent of all mankind; which definition is by no means to be admitted. For then it were impossible for any but children and fools, to offend against such a law; for sure, under the notion of mankind, they comprehend all men actually endued with reason. These therefore either do nought against it, or if they do aught, it is without their joint accord, and therefore ought to be excused. But to receive the laws of nature from the consents of them, who oftener break, than observe them, is in truth unreasonable. Besides, men condemn the same things in others, which they approve in themselves; on the other side, they publicly commend what they privately comdemn; and they deliver their opinions more by hearsay, than any speculation of their own; and they accord more through hatred of some object, through fear, hope, love, or some other perturbation of mind, than true reason. And therefore it comes to pass, that whole bodies of people often do those things by general accord, or contention, which those writers most willingly acknowledge to be against the law of nature. But since all do grant that is done by right, which is not done against reason, we ought to judge those actions only wrong, which are repugnant to right reason, that is, which contradict some certain truth collected by right reasoning from true principles. But that wrong which is done, we say it is done against some law. Therefore true reason is a certain law, which (since it is no less a part of human nature, than any other faculty, or affection of the mind) is also termed natural. Therefore the law of nature, that I may define it, is the dictate of right reason, conversant about those things which are either to be done or omitted for the constant preservation of life and members, as much as in us lies.

But the first and fundamental law of nature is, that peace is to be sought after, where it may be found; and where not, there to provide ourselves for helps of war. For we showed in the last article of the foregoing chapter, that this precept is the dictate of right reason; but that the dictates of right reason are natural laws, that hath been newly proved above. But this is the first, because the rest are derived from this, and they direct the ways either to peace or self-defence.

But one of the natural laws derived from this fundamental one is this: that the right of all men to all things, ought not to be retained, but that some certain rights ought to be transferred, or relinquished. For if every one should retain his right to all things, it must necessarily follow, that some by right might invade, and others, by the same right, might defend themselves against them, (for every man, by natural necessity, endeavours to defend his body, and the things which he judgeth necessary towards the protection of his body). Therefore war would follow. He therefore acts against the reason of peace, that is, against the law of nature, whosoever he be, that doth not part with his right to all things. . . .

No man is obliged by any contracts whatsoever not to resist him who shall offer to kill, wound, or any other way hurt his body. For there is in every man a certain high degree of fear, through which he apprehends that evil which is done to him to be the greatest; and therefore by natural necessity he shuns it all he can, and it is supposed he can do no otherwise. When a man is arrived to this degree of fear, we cannot expect that he will provide for himself either by flight or fight. Since therefore no man is tied to impossibilities, they who are threatened either with death, (which is the greatest evil to nature) or wounds, or some other bodily hurts, and are not stout enough to bear them, are not obliged to endure them. Furthermore, he that is tied by contract is trusted, (for faith only is the bond of contracts) but they who are brought to punishment, either capital, or more gentle, are fettered, or strongly guarded, which is a most certain sign that they seemed not sufficiently bound from non-resistance by their contracts. It is one thing, if I promise thus: if I do it not at the day appointed, kill me. Another thing, if thus: if I do it not, though you should offer to kill me, I will not resist. All men, if need be, contract the first way, but there is need sometimes. This second way, none; neither is it ever needful; for in the mere state of nature, if you have a mind to kill, that state itself affords you a right; insomuch as you need not first trust him, if for breach of trust you will afterwards kill him. But in a civil state, where the right of life, and death, and of all corporal punishment is with the supreme; that same right of killing cannot be granted to any private person. Neither need the supreme himself contract with any man patiently to yield to his punishment, but only this, that no man offer to defend others from him. If in the state of nature, as between two realms, there should a contract be made, on condition of killing if it were not performed, we must presuppose another contract of not killing before the appointed day. Wherefore on that day, if there be no performance, the right of war returns, that is an hostile state, in which all things are lawful, and therefore resistance also. Lastly, by the contract of not resisting, we are obliged of two evils to make choice of that which seems the greater; for certain death is a greater evil than fighting. But of two evils it is impossible not to choose the least. By such a compact, therefore, we should be tied to impossibilities, which is contrary to the very nature of compacts.

Likewise no man is tied by any compacts whatsoever to accuse himself, or any other, by whose damage he is like to procure himself a bitter life. Wherefore neither is a father obliged to bear witness against his son, nor a husband against his wife, nor a son against his father, nor any man against any one by whose means he hath his subsistence; for in vain is that testimony which is presumed to be corrupted from nature. But although no man be tied to accuse himself by any compact, yet in a public trial he may, by torture, be forced to make answer. But such answers are no testimony of the fact, but helps for the searching out of truth; insomuch that whether the party tortured answer true or false, or whether he answer not at all, whatsoever he doth, he doth it by right. . . .

CHAPTER III

. . . As it was necessary to the conservation of each man, that he should part with some of his rights, so it is no less necessary to the same conservation, that he retain some others, to wit, the right of bodily protection, of free enjoyment of air,

water, and all necessaries for life. Since therefore many common rights are retained by those who enter into a peaceable state, and that many peculiar ones are
also acquired, hence ariseth this ninth dictate of the natural law, to wit, that what
rights soever any man challenges to himself, he also grant the same as due to all
the rest. . . .

The laws of nature are immutable and eternal: what they forbid can never
be lawful; what they command, can never be unlawful. For pride, ingratitude,
breach of contracts (or injury), inhumanity, contumely, will never be lawful, nor
the contrary virtues to these ever unlawful, as we take them for dispositions of
the mind, that is, as they are considered in the court of conscience, where only
they oblige, and are laws. Yet actions may be so diversified by circumstances, and
the civil law, that what is done with equity at one time, is guilty of iniquity at
another; and what suits with reason at one time, is contrary to it another. Yet
reason is still the same, and changeth not her end, which is peace, and defence;
nor the means to attain them, to wit, those virtues of the mind which we have
declared above, and which cannot be abrogated by any custom or law whatsoever. . . .

All writers do agree that the natural law is the same with the moral. Let us
see wherefore this is true. We must know, therefore, that good and evil are names
given to things to signify the inclination or aversion of them by whom they were
given. But the inclinations of men are diverse, according to their diverse constitutions, customs, opinions; as we may see in those things we apprehend by sense,
as by tasting, touching, smelling; but much more in those which pertain to the
common actions of life, where what this man commends, (that is to say, calls
good) the other undervalues, as being evil; nay, very often the same man at
diverse times praises and dispraises the same thing. Whilst thus they do, necessary it is there should be discord and strife. They are therefore so long in the state
of war, as by reason of the diversity of the present appetites, they met good and
evil by diverse measures. All men easily acknowledge this state, as long as they
are in it, to be evil, and by consequence that peace is good. They therefore who
could not agree concerning a present, do agree concerning a future good, which
indeed is a work of reason; for things present are obvious to the sense, things to
come to our reason only. Reason declaring peace to be good, it follows by the
same reason, that all the necessary means to peace be good also; and therefore
that modesty, equity, trust, humanity, mercy, (which we have demonstrated to
be necessary to peace), are good manners or habits, that is, virtues. The law
therefore, is the means to peace, commands also good manners, or the practice of
virtue: and therefore it is called moral.

But because men cannot put off this same irrational appetite, whereby they
greedily prefer the present good (to which, by strict consequence, many unfore-
seen evils do adhere) before the future, it happens, that though all men do agree
in the commendation of the foresaid virtues, yet they disagree still concerning
their nature, to wit, in which each of them doth consist. For as oft as another's
good action displeaseth any man, that action hath the name given of some neigh-
bouring vice; likewise the bad actions, which please them, are ever entitled to

some virtue. Whence it comes to pass that the same action is praised by these, and called virtue, and dispraised by those, and termed vice. Neither is there as yet any remedy found by philosophers for this manner; for since they could not observe the goodness of actions to consist in this, that it was in order to peace, and the evil in this, that it related to discord, they built a moral philosophy wholly estranged from the moral law, and unconstant to itself. For they would have the nature of virtues seated in a certain kind of mediocrity between two extremes, and the vices in the extremes themselves; which is apparently false. For to dare is commended, and, under the name of fortitude is taken for a virtue, although it be an extreme, if the cause be approved. Also the quantity of a thing given, whether it be great, or little, or between both, makes not liberality, but the cause of giving it. Neither is it injustice, if I give any man more, of what is mine own, than I owe him. The laws of nature therefore are the sum of moral philosophy, thereof I have only delivered such precepts in this place, as appertain to the preservation of ourselves against those dangers which arise from discord. But there are other precepts of rational nature, from whence spring other virtues; for temperance also is a precept of reason, because intemperance tends to sickness and death. And so fortitude too, that is, that same faculty of resisting stoutly in present dangers, (and which are more hardly declined than overcome) because it is a means tending to the preservation of him that resists. . . .

CHAPTER V

Since therefore the exercise of the natural law is necessary for the preservation of peace, and that for the exercise of the natural law security is no less necessary, it is worth the considering what that is which affords such a security. For this matter nothing else can be imagined, but that each man provide himself so such meet helps, as the invasion of one on the other may be rendered so dangerous, as either of them may think it better to refrain, than to meddle. But first, it is plain, that the consent of two or three cannot make good such a security; because that the addition but of one, or some few on the other side, is sufficient to make the victory undoubtedly sure, and heartens the enemy to attack us. It is therefore necessary, to the end the security sought for may be obtained, that the number of them who conspire in a mutual assistance be so great, that the accession of some few to the enemy's party may not prove to them a matter of moment sufficient to assure the victory. . . .

Wherefore consent or contracted society, without some common power whereby particular men may be ruled through fear of punishment, doth not suffice to make up that security which is requisite to the exercise of natural justice.

Since therefore the conspiring of many wills to the same end doth not suffice to preserve peace, and to make a lasting defence, it is requisite that, in those necessary matters which concern peace and self-defence, there be but one will of all men. But this cannot be done, unless every man will so subject his will to some other one, to wit, either man or council, that whatsoever his will is in those things which are necessary to the common peace, it be received for the wills of all men in general, and of every one in particular. Now the gathering together of many men who deliberate of what is to be done, or not to be done, for the common good of all men, is that which I call a council.

This submission of the wills of all those men to the will of one man, or one council, is then made, when each one of them obligeth himself by contract to every one of the rest, not to resist the will of that one man, or council, to which he hath submitted himself; that is, that he refuse him not the use of his wealth and strength against any others whatsoever (for he is supposed still to retain a right of defending himself against violence) and this is called union. But we understand that to be the will of the council, which is the will of the major part of those men of whom the council consists. . . .

Now union thus made is called a city, or civil society, and also a civil person; for when there is one will of all men, it is to be esteemed for one person, and by the word one it is to be known, and distinguished from all particular men, as having its own rights and properties. Insomuch as neither any one citizen, nor all of them together, (if except him whose will stands for the will of all) is to be accounted the city. A city therefore (that we may define it) is one person, whose will, by the compact of many men, is to be received for the will of them all; so as he may use all the power and faculties of each particular person, to the maintenance of peace, and for common defence.

12

Natural
Rights
and
Civil Society

John Locke (1632–1704)

OF THE STATE OF NATURE

To understand political power aright, and derive it from its original, we must consider what state all men are naturally in, and that is a state of perfect freedom to order their actions and dispose of their possessions and persons as they think fit, within the bounds of the law of nature, without asking leave, or depending upon the will of any other man.

A state also of equality, wherein all the power and jurisdiction is reciprocal, no one having more than another; there being nothing more evident than that creatures of the same species and rank, promiscuously born to all the same advantages of nature, and the use of the same faculties, should also be equal one

From Locke, *Treatise of Civil Government,* edited by Charles L. Sherman, Appleton-Century-Crofts, Inc., New York, 1937, from Second Treatise.

amongst another without subordination or subjection, unless the Lord and Master of them all should by any manifest declaration of His will set one above another, and confer on him by an evident and clear appointment an undoubted right to dominion and sovereignty.

This quality of men by nature the judicious Hooker looks upon as so evident in itself and beyond all question, that he makes it the foundation of that obligation to mutual love amongst men on which he builds the duties they owe one another, and from whence he derives the great maxims of justice and charity. His words are:—

"The like natural inducement hath brought men to know that it is no less their duty to love others than themselves; for seeing those things which are equal must needs all have one measure, if I cannot but wish to receive good, even as much at every man's hands as any man can wish unto his own soul, how should I look to have any part of my desire herein satisfied, unless myself be careful to satisfy the like desire, which is undoubtedly in other men weak, being of one and the same nature? To have anything offered them repugnant to this desire, must needs in all respects grieve them as much as me, so that, if I do harm, I must look to suffer, there being no reason that others should show greater measures of love to me than they have by me showed unto them. My desire, therefore, to be loved of my equals in nature as much as possible may be, imposeth upon me a natural duty of bearing to themward fully the like affection; from which relation of equality between ourselves and them that are as ourselves, what several rules and canons natural reason hath drawn for direction of life no man is ignorant."— "Eccl. Pol.," lib. I.

But though this be a state of liberty, yet it is not a state of licence; though man in that state have an uncontrollable liberty to dispose of his person or possessions, yet he has not liberty to destroy himself, or so much as any creature in his possession, but where some nobler use than its bare preservation calls for it. The state of nature has a law of nature to govern it, which obliges every one; and reason, which is that law, teaches all mankind who will but consult it, that, being all equal and independent, no one ought to harm another in his life, health, liberty, or possessions. For men being all the workmanship of one omnipotent and infinitely wise Maker—all the servants of one sovereign Master, sent into the world by His order, and about His business—they are His property, whose workmanship they are, made to last during His, not one another's pleasure; and being furnished with like faculties, sharing all in one community of nature, there cannot be supposed any such subordination among us, that may authorise us to destroy one another, as if we were made for one another's uses, as the inferior ranks of creatures are for ours. Every one, as he is bound to preserve himself, and not to quit his station wilfully, so, by the like reason, when his own preservation comes not in competition, ought he, as much as he can, to preserve the rest of mankind, and not, unless it be to do justice on an offender, take away or impair the life, or what tends to the preservation of the life, the liberty, health, limb, or goods of another.

And that all men may be restrained from invading others' rights, and from doing hurt to one another, and the law of nature be observed, which willeth the peace and preservation of all mankind, the execution of the law of nature is in that state put into every man's hand, whereby every one has a right to punish the transgressors of that law to such a degree as may hinder its violation. For the law of nature would, as all other laws that concern men in this world, be in vain if there were nobody that, in the state of nature, had a power to execute that law, and thereby preserve the innocent and restrain offenders. And if any one in the state of nature may punish another for any evil he has done, every one may do so. For in that state of perfect equality, where naturally there is no superiority or jurisdiction of one over another, what any may do in prosecution of that law, every one must needs have a right to do.

And thus in the state of nature one man comes by a power over another; but yet no absolute or arbitrary power, to use a criminal, when he has got him in his hands, according to the passionate heats or boundless extravagance of his own will; but only to retribute to him so far as calm reason and conscience dictate what is proportionate to his transgression, which is so much as may serve for reparation and restraint. For these two are the only reasons why one man may lawfully do harm to another, which is that we call punishment. In transgressing the law of nature, the offender declares himself to live by another rule than that of common reason and equity, which is that measure God has set to the actions of men, for their mutual security; and so he becomes dangerous to mankind, the tie which is to secure them from injury and violence being slighted and broken by him. Which, being a trespass against the whole species, and the peace and safety of it, provided for by the law of nature, every man upon this score, by the right he hath to preserve mankind in general, may restrain, or, where it is necessary, destroy things noxious to them, and so may bring such evil on any one who hath transgressed that law, as may make him repent the doing of it, and there-by deter him, and by his example others, from doing the like mischief. And in this case, and upon this ground, every man hath a right to punish the offender, and be executioner of the law of nature.

I doubt not but this will seem a very strange doctrine to some men; but before they condemn it, I desire them to resolve me by what right any prince or State can put to death or punish an alien, for any crime he commits in their country. 'Tis certain their laws, by virtue of any sanction they receive from the promulgated will of the legislature, reach not a stranger: they speak not to him, nor, if they did, is he bound to hearken to them. The Legislative authority, by which they are in force over the subjects of that commonwealth, hath no power over him. Those who have the supreme power of making laws in England, France, or Holland, are to an Indian but like the rest of the world—men without authority. And, therefore, if by the law of nature every man hath not a power to punish offences against it, as he soberly judges the case to require, I see not how the magistrates of any community can punish an alien of another country; since in reference to him they can have no more power than what every man naturally may have over another.

Besides the crime which consists in violating the law, and varying from the right rule of reason, whereby a man so far becomes degenerate, and declares himself to quit the principles of human nature, and to be a noxious creature, there is commonly injury done, and some person or other, some other man receives damage by his transgression, in which case he who hath received any damage, has, besides the right of punishment common to him with other men, a particular right to seek reparation from him that has done it. And any other person who finds it just, may also join with him that is injured, and assist him in recovering from the offender so much as may make satisfaction for the harm he has suffered.

From those two distinct rights—the one of punishing the crime, for restraint and preventing the like offence, which right of punishing is in everybody; the other taking reparation, which belongs only to the injured party—comes it to pass that the magistrate, who by being magistrate hath the common right of punishing put into his hands, can often, where the public good demands not the execution of the law, remit the punishment of criminal offences by his own authority, but yet cannot remit the satisfaction due to any private man for the damage he has received. That he who has suffered the damage has a right to demand in his own name, and he alone can remit. The damnified person has this power of approaching to himself the goods or service of the offender, by right of self-preservation, as every man has a power to punish the crime, to prevent its being committed again, by the right he has of preserving all mankind, and doing all reasonable things he can in order to that end. And thus it is that every man in the state of nature has a power to kill a murderer, both to deter others from doing the like injury, which no reparation can compensate, by the example of the punishment that attends it from everybody, and also to secure men from the attempts of a criminal who having renounced reason, the common rule and measure God hath given to mankind, hath by the unjust violence and slaughter he hath committed upon one, declared war against all mankind, and therefore may be destroyed as a lion or a tiger, one of those wild savage beasts with whom men can have no society nor security. And upon this is grounded that great law of nature. "Whoso sheddeth man's blood, by man shall his blood be shed." And Cain was so fully convinced that every one had a right to destroy such a criminal, that after the murder of his brother he cries out, "Every one that findeth me shall slay me;" so plain was it writ in the hearts of mankind.

By the same reason may a man in the state of nature punish the lesser breaches of that law. It will perhaps be demanded, With death? I answer, each transgression may be punished to that degree, and with so much severity, as will suffice to make it an ill bargain to the offender, give him cause to repent, and terrify others from doing the like. Every offence that can be committed in the state of nature, may in the state of nature be also punished equally, and as far forth as it may, in a commonwealth. For though it would be beside my present purpose to enter here into the particulars of the law of nature, or its measures of punishment, yet it is certain there is such a law, and that, too, as intelligible and plain to a rational creature and a studier of that law as the positive laws of commonwealths; nay, possibly plainer, as much as reason is easier to be understood than the fancies and intricate contrivances of men, following contrary and hidden interests put into words; for truly so are a great part of the municipal laws of countries, which are only so far right as they are founded on the law of nature, by which they are to be regulated and interpreted.

To this strange doctrine—viz, That in the state of nature every one has the executive power of the law of nature—I doubt not but it will be objected that it is unreasonable for men to be judges in their own cases, that self-love will make men partial to themselves and their friends. And on the other side, that ill-nature, passion, and revenge will carry them too far in punishing others; and hence nothing but confusion and disorder will follow; and that therefore God hath certainly appointed government to restrain the partiality and violence of men. I easily grant that civil government is the proper remedy for the inconveniences of the state of nature, which must certainly be great where men may be judges in their own case, since 'tis easy to be imagined that he who was so unjust as to do his brother an injury, will scarce be so just as to condemn himself for it. But I shall desire those who make this objection, to remember that absolute monarchs are but men, and if government is to be the remedy of those evils which necessarily follow from men's being judges in their own cases, and the state of nature is therefore not to be endured, I desire to know what kind of government that is, and how much better it is than the state of nature, where one man commanding a multitude, has the liberty to be judge in his own case, and may do to all his subjects whatever he pleases, without the least question or control of those who execute his pleasure; and in whatsoever he doth, whether led by reason, mistake, or passion, must be submitted to, which men in the state of nature are not bound to do one to another? And if he that judges, judges amiss in his own or any other case, he is answerable for it to the rest of mankind.

'Tis often asked as a mighty objection, Where are, or ever were there, any men in such a state of nature? To which it may suffice as an answer at present: That since all princes and rulers of independent governments all through the world are in a state of nature, 'tis plain the world never was, nor ever will be, without numbers of men in that state. I have named all governors of independent communities, whether they are or are not in league with others. For 'tis not every compact that puts an end to the state of nature between men, but only this one of agreeing together mutually to enter into one community, and make one body politic; other promises and compacts men may make one with another, and yet still be in the state of nature. The promises and bargains for truck, etc., between the two men in Soldania, in or between a Swiss and an Indian, in the woods of America, are binding to them, though they are perfectly in a state of nature in reference to one another. For truth and keeping of faith belong to men as men, and not as members of society.

To those that say there were never any men in the state of nature, I will not only oppose the authority of the judicious Hooker—"Eccl. Pol.," lib. i, sec. 10, where he says, "The laws which have been hitherto mentioned," *i.e.*, the laws of nature, "do bind men absolutely, even as they are men, although they have never any settled fellowship, and never any solemn agreement amongst themselves what to do or not to do; but forasmuch as we are not by ourselves sufficient to furnish ourselves with competent store of things needful for such a life as our nature doth desire—a life fit for the dignity of man—therefore to supply those defects and imperfections which are in us, as living single and solely by ourselves, we are naturally induced to seek communion and fellowship with others; this was the cause of men's uniting themselves at first in politic societies"—but I moreover affirm that all men are naturally in that state, and remain so, till by their own consents they make themselves members of some politic society; and I doubt not, in the sequel of this discourse, to make it very clear. . . .

OF PROPERTY . . .

God, who hath given the world to men in common, hath also given them reason to make use of it to the best advantage of life and convenience. The earth and all that is therein is given to men for the support and comfort of their being. And though all the fruits it naturally produces, and beasts it feeds, belong to mankind in common, as they are produced by the spontaneous hand of nature; and nobody has originally a private dominion exclusive of the rest of mankind in any of them as they are thus in their natural state; yet being given for the use of men, there must of necessity be a means to appropriate them some way or other before they can be of any use or at all beneficial to any particular man. The fruit or venison which nourishes the wild Indian, who knows no enclosure, and is still a tenant in common, must be his, and so his, *i.e.*, a part of him, that another can no longer have any right to it, before it can do any good for the support of his life.

Though the earth and all inferior creatures be common to all men, yet every man has a property in his own person; this nobody has any right to but himself. The labour of his body and the work of his hands we may say are properly his. Whatsoever, then, he removes out of the state that nature hath provided and left it in, he hath mixed his labour with, and joined to it something that is his own, and thereby makes it his property. It being by him removed from the common state nature placed it in, it hath by this labour something annexed to it that excludes the common right of other men. For this labour being the unquestionable property of the labourer, no man but he can have a right to what that is once joined to, at least where there is enough, and as good left in common for others. . . .

OF POLITICAL OR CIVIL SOCIETY . . .

Man being born, as has been proved, with a title to perfect freedom, and an uncontrolled enjoyment of all the rights and privileges of the law of nature equally with any other man or number of men in the world, hath by nature a power not only to preserve his property—that is, his life, liberty, and estate—against the injuries and attempts of other men, but to judge of and punish the breaches of that law in others as he is persuaded the offence deserves, even with death itself, in crimes where the heinousness of the fact in his opinion requires it. But because no political society can be nor subsist without having in itself the power to preserve the property, and, in order thereunto, punish the offences of all those of that society, there, and there only, is political society, where every one of the members hath quitted this natural power, resigned it up into the hands of the community in all cases that exclude him not from appealing for protection to the law established by it; and thus all private judgment of every particular member being excluded, the community comes to be umpire; and by understanding indifferent rules and men authorized by the community for their execution, decides all the differences that may happen between any members of that society concerning any matter of right, and punishes those offences which any member hath committed against the society with such penalties as the law has established; whereby it is easy to discern who are and who are not in political society together. Those who are united into one body, and have a common established law and judicature to appeal to, with authority to decide controversies between them and punish offenders, are in civil society one with another; but those who have no such common appeal—I mean on earth—are still in the state of nature, each being, where there is no other, judge for himself and executioner, which is, as I have before shown it, the perfect state of nature.

And thus the commonwealth comes by a power to set down what punishment shall belong to the several transgressions which they think worthy of it committed amongst the members of that society, which is the power of making laws, as well as it has the power to punish any injury done unto any of its members by any one that is not of it, which is the power of war and peace; and all this for the preservation of the property of all the members of that society as far as is possible. But though every man entered into civil society, has acquitted his power to punish offences against the law of nature in prosecution of his own private judgment, yet with the judgment of offences, which he has given up to the legislature in all cases where he can appeal to the magistrate, he has given a right to the commonwealth to employ his force for the execution of the judgments of the commonwealth whenever he shall be called to it; which, indeed, are his own judgments, they being made by himself or his representative. And herein we have the original of the legislative and executive power of civil society, which is to judge by standing laws how far offences are to be punished when committed within the commonwealth, and also by occasional judgments founded on the present circumstances of the fact, how far injuries from without are to be vindicated; and in both these to employ all the force of all the members when there shall be need.

Wherever, therefore, any number of men so unite into one society, as to quit every one his executive power of the law of nature, and to resign it to the public, there, and there only, is a political, or civil society. And this is done wherever any number of men, in the state of nature, enter into society to make one people, one body politic, under one supreme government, or else when any one joins himself to, and incorporates with, any government already made. For thereby he authorises the society, or, which is all one, the legislative thereof, to make laws for him, as the public good of the society shall require, to the execution whereof his own assistance (as to his own decrees) is due. And this puts men out of a state of nature into that of a commonwealth, by setting up a judge on earth with authority to determine all the controversies and redress the injuries that may happen to any member of the commonwealth; which judge is the legislative, or magistrates appointed by it. And wherever there are any number of men, however associated, that have no such decisive power to appeal to, there they are still in the state of nature.

Hence it is evident that absolute monarchy, which by some men is counted the only government in the world, is indeed inconsistent with civil society, and so can be no form of civil government at all. For the end of civil society being to avoid and remedy those inconveniences of the state of nature which necessarily follow from every man's being judge in his own case, by setting up a known authority to which every one of that society may appeal upon any injury received or controversy that may arise, and which every one of the society ought to obey; wherever any persons are who have not such an authority to appeal to and decide any difference between them there, those persons are still in the state of nature. And so is every absolute prince, in respect of those who are under his dominion.

For he being supposed to have all, both legislative and executive power in himself alone, there is no judge to be found; no appeal lies open to any one who may fairly and indifferently and with authority decide, and from whence relief and redress may be expected of any injury or inconvenience that may be suffered from or by his order; so that such a man, however entitled— Czar, or Grand Seignior, or how you please—is as much in the state of nature, with all under his dominion, as he is with the rest of mankind. For wherever any two men are, who have no standing rule and common judge to appeal to on earth for the determination of controversies of right betwixt them, there they are still in the state of nature, and under all the inconveniences of it, with only this woeful difference to the subject, or rather slave, of an absolute prince: that, whereas in the ordinary state of nature he has a liberty to judge of his right, and according to the best of his power to maintain it, now, whenever his property is invaded by the will and order of his monarch, he has not only no appeal, as those in the society ought to have, but, as if he were degraded from the common state of rational creatures, is denied a liberty to judge of or to defend his right; and so is exposed to all the misery and inconveniences that a man can fear from one who, being in the unrestrained state of nature, is yet corrupted with flattery, and armed with power. . . .

OF THE ENDS OF POLITICAL SOCIETY
AND GOVERNMENT . . .

The great and chief end, therefore, of men's uniting into commonwealths, and putting themselves under government, is the preservation of their property; to which in the state of nature there are many things wanting.

First, There wants an established, settled, known law, received and allowed by common consent to be the standard of right and wrong, and the common measure to decide all controversies between them. For though the law of nature be plain and intelligible to all rational creatures; yet men, being biased by their interest, as well as ignorant for want to study of it, are not apt to allow of it as a law binding to them in the application of it to their particular cases.

Secondly, In the state of nature there wants a known and indifferent judge, with authority to determine all differences according to the established law. For every one in that state, being both judge and executioner of the law of nature, men being partial to themselves, passion and revenge is very apt to carry them too far, and with too much heat in their own cases, as well as negligence and unconcernedness, to make them too remiss in other men's.

Thirdly, In the state of nature there often wants power to back and support the sentence when right, and to give it due execution. They who by any injustice offend, will seldom fail, where they are able by force to make good their injustice; such resistance many times makes the punishment dangerous, and frequently destructive to those who attempt it.

Thus mankind, notwithstanding all the privileges of the state of nature, being but in an ill condition, while they remain in it, are quickly driven into society. Hence it comes to pass that we seldom find any number of men live any time together in this state. . . .

OF THE EXTENT OF THE LEGISLATIVE POWER

The great end of men's entering into society being the enjoyment of their properties in peace and safety, and the great instrument and means of that being the laws established in that society: the first and fundamental positive law of all commonwealths, is the establishing of the legislative power; as the first and fundamental natural law, which is to govern even the legislative itself, is the preservation of the society, and (as far as will consist with the public good) of every person in it. This legislative is not only the supreme power of the commonwealth, but sacred and unalterable in the hands where the community have once placed it; nor can any edict of anybody else, in what form soever conceived, or by what power soever backed, have the force and obligation of a law, which has not its sanction from that legislative which the public has chosen and appointed. For without this the law could not have that, which is absolutely necessary to its being a law, the consent of the society over whom nobody can have a power to make laws; but by their own consent, and by authority received from them; and therefore all the obedience, which by the most solemn ties any one can be obliged to pay, ultimately terminates in this supreme power, and is directed by those laws which it enacts; nor can any oaths to any foreign power whatsoever, or any domestic subordinate power discharge any member of the society from his obedience to the legislative, acting pursuant to their trust; nor oblige him to any obedience contrary to the laws so enacted, or farther than they do allow; it being ridiculous to imagine one can be tied ultimately to obey any power in the society which is not the supreme.

Though the legislative, whether placed in one or more, whether it be always in being, or only by intervals, though it be the supreme power in every commonwealth, yet,

First, It is not nor can possibly be absolutely arbitrary over the lives and fortunes of the people. For it being but the joint power of every member of the society given up to that person, or assembly, which is legislator; it can be no more than those persons had in a state of nature before they entered into society, and gave it up to the community. For nobody can transfer to another more power than he has in himself; and nobody has an absolute arbitrary power over himself, or over any other to destroy his own life, or take away the life or property of another. A man as has been proved cannot subject himself to the arbitrary power of another; and having in the state of nature no arbitrary power over the life, liberty, or possession of another, but only so much as the law of nature gave him for the preservation of himself, and the rest of mankind; this is all he doth, or can give up to the commonwealth, and by it to the legislative power, so that the legislative can have no more than this. Their power in the utmost bounds of it, is limited to the public good of the society. It is a power that hath no other end but preservation, and therefore can never have a right to destroy, enslave, or designedly to impoverish the subjects. The obligations of the law of nature cease not in society, but only in many cases are drawn closer, and have by human laws known penalties annexed to them to enforce their observation. Thus the law of nature stands as an eternal rule to all men, legislators as well as others. The rules that they make for other men's actions must, as well as their own, and other men's actions be conformable to the law of nature, *i.e.* to the will of God, of which that is a declaration, and the fundamental law of nature being the preservation of mankind, no human sanction can be good or valid against it.

Secondly, The legislative, or supreme authority, cannot assume to itself a power to rule by extemporary arbitrary decrees, but is bound to dispense justice, and decide the rights of the subject by promulgated standing laws, and known authorised judges. For the law of nature being unwritten, and so nowhere to be found but in the minds of men, they who through passion or interest shall miscite or misapply it, cannot so easily be convinced of their mistake where there is no established judge. And so it serves not, as it ought, to determine the rights, and fence the properties of those that live under it, especially where every one is judge, interpreter, and executioner of it too, and in his own case; and he that has right on his side, having ordinarily but his own single strength hath not force enough to defend himself from injuries, or punish delinquents. To avoid these inconveniences, which disorder men's properties in the state of nature, men unite into societies that they may have the united strength of the whole society to secure and defend their properties, and may have standing rules to bound it, by which every one may know what is his. To this end it is that men give up all their natural power to the society which they enter into, and the community put the legislative power into such hands as they think fit, with this trust, that they shall be governed by declared laws, or else their peace, quiet, and property, will still be at the same uncertainty as it was in the state of nature.

Absolute arbitrary power, or governing without settled standing laws, can neither of them consist with the ends of society and government, which men would not quit the freedom of the state of nature for, and tie themselves up under, were it not to preserve their lives, liberties, and fortunes; and by stated rules of right and property to secure their peace and quiet. It cannot be supposed that they should intend, had they a power so to do, to give to any one, or more, an absolute arbitrary power over their persons and estates, and put a force into the magistrate's hand to execute his unlimited will arbitrarily upon them. This were to put themselves into a worse condition than the state of nature, wherein they had a liberty to defend their right against the injuries of others, and were upon equal terms of force to maintain it, whether invaded by a single man or many in combination. Whereas, by supposing they have given up themselves to the absolute arbitrary power and will of a legislator, they have disarmed themselves, and armed him, to make prey of them when he pleases. He being in a much worse condition that is exposed to the arbitrary power of one man who has the command of 100,000 than he that is exposed to the arbitrary power of 100,000 single men; nobody being secure that his will, who hath such a command, is better than that of other men, though his force be 100,000 times stronger. And, therefore, whatever form the commonwealth is under, the ruling power ought to govern by declared and received laws, and not by extemporary dictates and undetermined resolutions. For then mankind will be in a far worse condition than in the state of nature, if they shall have armed one, or a few men, with the joint power of a multitude to force them to obey at pleasure the exorbitant and unlimited decrees of their sudden thoughts, or unrestrained, and, till that moment, unknown wills, without having any measures set down which may guide and justify their actions. For all the power the government has, being only for the good of the society, as it ought not to be arbitrary and at pleasure, so it ought to be exercised by established and promulgated laws; that both the people may know their duty and be safe and secure within the limits of the law; and the rulers too kept within their due bounds, and not be tempted by the power they have in their hands to employ it to such purposes, and by such measures as they would not have known, and own not willingly.

Thirdly, The supreme power cannot take from any man any part of his property without his own consent. For the preservation of property being the end of government, and that for which men enter into society, it necessarily supposes and requires that the people should have property, without which they must be supposed to lose that by entering into society, which was the end for which they entered into it, too gross an absurdity for any man to own. Men, therefore, in society having property, they have such a right to the goods which by the law of the community are theirs, that nobody hath a right to take them or any part of them from them, without their own consent; without this they have no property at all. For I have truly no property in that which another can by right take from me when he pleases, against my consent. Hence it is a mistake to think that the supreme or legislative power of any commonwealth can do what it will, and dispose of the estates of the subjects arbitrarily, or take any part of them at pleasure. This is not much to be feared in government where the legislative consists wholly, or in part, in assemblies which are variable, whose members, upon the dissolution of the assembly, are subjects under the common laws of their country, equally with the rest. But in governments where the legislative is in one lasting assembly, always in being, or in one man, as in absolute monarchies, there is danger still, that they will think themselves to have a distinct interest from the rest of the community, and so will be apt to increase their own riches and power by taking what they think fit from the people. For a man's property is not at all secure, though there be good and equitable laws to see the bounds of it between him and his fellow subjects, if he who commands those subjects have power to take from any private man what part he pleases of his property, and use and dispose of it as he thinks good.

But government, into whosesoever hands it is put, being, as I have before shown, entrusted with this condition, and for this end, that men might have and secure their properties, the prince, or senate, however it may have power to make laws for the regulating of property between the subjects one amongst another, yet can never have a power to take to themselves the whole or any part of the subject's property without their own consent. For this would be in effect to leave them no property at all. And to let us see that even absolute power, where it is necessary, is not arbitrary by being absolute, but is still limited by that reason, and confined to those ends which required it in some cases to be absolute, we need look no farther than the common practice of martial discipline. For the preservation of the army, and in it the whole commonwealth, requires an absolute obedience to the command of every superior officer, and it is justly death to disobey or dispute the most dangerous or unreasonable of them; but yet we see that neither the sergeant, that could command a soldier to march up to the mouth of a cannon, or stand in a breach, where he is almost sure to perish, can command that soldier to give him one penny of his money; nor the general that can condemn him to death for deserting his post, or not obeying the most desperate orders, cannot yet, with all his absolute power of life and death, dispose of one farthing of that soldier's estate, or seize one jot of his goods, whom yet he can command anything, and hang for the least disobedience. Because such a blind obedience is necessary to that end for which the commander has his power, viz., the preservation of the rest; but the disposing of his goods has nothing to do with it.

'Tis true governments cannot be supported without great charge, and it is fit every one who enjoys a share of the protection should pay out of his estate his proportion for the maintenance of it. But still it must be with his own consent, *i.e.,* the consent of the majority giving it either by themselves or their representatives chosen by them. For if any one shall claim a power to lay and levy taxes on the people, by his own authority, and without such consent of the people, he thereby invades the fundamental law of property, and subverts the end of government. For what property have I in that which another may by right take when he pleases to himself?

Fourthly, The legislative cannot transfer the power of making laws to any other hands; for it being but a delegated power from the people, they who have it cannot pass it over to others. The people alone can appoint the form of the commonwealth, which is by constituting the legislative, and appointing in whose hands that shall be. And when the people have said we will submit to rules, and be governed by laws made by such men, and in such forms, nobody else can say other men shall make laws for them; nor can the people be bound by any laws but such as are enacted by those whom they have chosen and authorised to make laws for them.

These are the bounds which the trust that is put in them by society, and the law of God and Nature, have set to the legislative power of every commonwealth, in all forms of government.

First, They are to govern by promulgated established laws, not to be varied in particular cases, but to have one rule for rich and poor, for the favourite at court and the countryman at plough.

Secondly, These laws also ought to be designed for no other end ultimately but the good of the people.

Thirdly, They must not raise taxes on the property of the people without the consent of the people, given by themselves or their deputies. And this properly concerns only such governments where the legislative is always in being, or at least where the people have not reserved any part of the legislative to deputies, to be from time to time chosen by themselves.

Fourthly, The legislative neither must nor can transfer the power of making laws to anybody else, or place it anywhere but where the people have.

13

Forcing Men to Be Free

Jean-Jacques Rousseau (1712–1778)

THE SOCIAL CONTRACT

BOOK I

I mean to inquire if, in the civil order, there can be any sure and legitimate rule of administration, men being taken as they are and laws as they might be. In this inquiry I shall endeavour always to unite what right sanctions with what is prescribed by interest, in order that justice and utility may in no case be divided.

CHAPTER I
SUBJECT OF THE FIRST BOOK

Man is born free; and everywhere he is in chains. . . . How did this change come about? I do not know. What can make it legitimate? That question I think I can answer.

From Jean-Jacques Rousseau, *The Social Contract* and *Discourses* translated with Introduction by G. D. H. Cole, Everyman's Library, J. M. Dent & Sons, Ltd., London and E. P. Dutton & Co., Inc., New York.

If I took into account only force, and the effects derived from it, I should say: "As long as a people is compelled to obey, and obeys, it does well; as soon as it can shake off the yoke, and shakes it off, it does still better; for, regaining its liberty by the same right as took it away, either it is justified in resuming it, or there was no justification for those who took it away." But the social order is a sacred right which is the basis of all rights. Nevertheless, this right does not come from nature, and must therefore be founded on conventions. . . .

Common liberty results from the nature of man. His first law is to provide for his own preservation, his first cares are those which he owes to himself; and, as soon as he reaches years of discretion, he is the sole judge of the proper means of preserving himself, and consequently becomes his own master.

To renounce liberty is to renounce being a man, to surrender the rights of humanity and even its duties. . . . Such a renunciation is incompatible with man's nature; to remove all liberty from his will is to remove all morality from his acts. Finally, it is an empty and contradictory convention that sets up, on the one side, absolute authority, and, on the other, unlimited obedience. . . .

CHAPTER V
THAT WE MUST ALWAYS GO BACK TO A
FIRST CONVENTION

. . . There will always be a great difference between subduing a multitude and ruling a society. Even if scattered individuals were successively enslaved by one man, however numerous they might be, I still see no more than a master and his slaves, and certainly not a people and its ruler. . . .

A people, says Grotius, can give itself to a king. Then according to Grotius, a people is a people before it gives itself. . . . It would be better, before examining the act by which a people gives itself to a king, to examine that by which it has become a people; for this act, being necessarily prior to the other, is the true foundation of society.

Indeed, if there were no prior convention, where, unless the election were unanimous, would be the obligation on the minority to submit to the choice of the majority? . . . The law of majority voting is itself something established by convention, and presupposes unanimity, on one occasion at least.

CHAPTER VI
THE SOCIAL COMPACT

I suppose men to have reached the point at which the obstacles in the way of their preservation in the state of nature show their power of resistance to be greater than the resources at the disposal of each individual for his maintenance in that state. That primitive condition can then subsist no longer; and the human race would perish unless it changed its manner of existence.

But, as men cannot engender new forces, but only unite and direct existing ones, they have no other means of preserving themselves than the formation, by aggregation, of a sum of forces great enough to overcome the resistance. . . .

. . . as the force and liberty of each man are the chief instruments of his self-preservation, how can he pledge them without harming his own interests, and neglecting the care he owes to himself? This difficulty, in its bearing on my present subject, may be stated in the following terms:

"The problem is to find a form of association which will defend and protect with the whole common force the person and goods of each associate, and in which each, while uniting himself with all, may still obey himself alone, and remain as free as before." This is the fundamental problem of which the *Social Contract* provides the solution.

The clauses of this contract are so determined by the nature of the act that the slightest modification would make them vain and ineffective; so that, although they have perhaps never been formally set forth, they are everywhere the same and everywhere tacitly admitted and recognized, until, on the violation of the social compact, each regains his original rights and resumes his natural liberty. . . .

These clauses, properly understood, may be reduced to one—the total alienation of each associate, together with all his rights, to the whole community; for, in the first place, as each gives himself absolutely, the conditions are the same for all; and, this being so, no one has any interest in making them burdensome to others.

Moreover, the alienation being without reserve, the union is as perfect as it can be, and no associate has anything more to demand: for, if the individuals retained certain rights, as there would be no common superior to decide between them and the public, each, being on one point his own judge, would ask to be so on all; the state of nature would thus continue, and the association would necessarily become inoperative or tyrannical.

Finally, each man, in giving himself to all, gives himself to nobody; and as there is no associate over which he does not acquire the same right as he yields others over himself, he gains an equivalent for everything he loses and an increase of force for the preservation of what he has.

. . . It reduces itself to the following terms:

"Each of us puts his person and all his power in common under the supreme direction of the general will, and, in our corporate capacity, we receive each member as an indivisible part of the whole."

At once, in place of the individual personality of each contracting party, this act of association creates a moral and collective body, composed of as many members as the assembly contains voters, and receiving from this act its unity, its common identity, its life, and its will. . . .

CHAPTER VII
THE SOVEREIGN

This formula shows us that the act of association comprises a mutual undertaking between the public and the individuals, and that each individual, in making a contract, as we may say, with himself, is bound in a double capacity; as a member of the Sovereign he is bound to the individuals, and as a member of the State to the Sovereign. . . .

. . . Public deliberation . . . cannot . . . bind the Sovereign to itself, and . . . it is consequently against the nature of the body politic for the Sovereign to impose on itself a law which it cannot infringe. Being able to regard itself in only one capacity, it is in the position of an individual who makes a contract with himself; and this makes it clear that there neither is nor can be any kind of fundamental law binding on the body of the people—not even the social contract itself. . . .

But the body politic or the Sovereign, drawing its being wholly from the sanctity of the contract, can never bind itself, even to an outsider, to do anything derogatory to the original act, for instance, to alienate any part of itself, or to submit to another Sovereign. . . .

As soon as this multitude is so united in one body, it is impossible to offend against one of the members without attacking the body, and still more to offend against the body without the members resenting it. Duty and interest therefore equally oblige the two contracting parties to give each other help; and the same men should seek to combine, in their double capacity, all the advantages dependent upon that capacity.

Again, the Sovereign, being formed wholly of the individuals who compose it, neither has nor can have any interest contrary to theirs; and consequently the sovereign power need give no guarantee to its subjects, because it is impossible for the body to wish to hurt all its members. We shall also see later on that it cannot hurt any in particular. The Sovereign, merely by virtue of what it is, is always what it should be.

This, however, is not the case with the relation of the subjects to the Sovereign, which, despite the common interest, would have no security that they would fulfil their undertakings, unless it found means to assure itself of their fidelity.

In fact, each individual, as a man, may have a particular will contrary or dissimilar to the general will which he has as a citizen. His particular interest may speak to him quite differently from the common interest: his absolute and naturally independent existence may make him look upon what he owes to the common cause as a gratuitous contribution, the loss of which will do less harm to others than the payment of it is burdensome to himself; and, regarding the moral person which constitutes the State as a *persona ficta*, because not a man, he may wish to enjoy the rights of citizenship without being ready to fulfil the duties of a subject. The continuance of such an injustice could not but prove the undoing of the body politic.

In order then that the social compact may not be an empty formula, it tacitly includes the undertaking, which alone can give force to the rest, that whoever refuses to obey the general will shall be compelled to do so by the whole body. This means nothing less than that he will be forced to be free; for this is the condition which, by giving each citizen to his country, secures him against all personal dependence. In this lies the key to the working of the political machine; this alone legitimizes civil undertakings, which, without it, would be absurd, tyrannical, and liable to the most frightful abuses.

CHAPTER VIII
THE CIVIL STATE

The passage from the state of nature to the civil state produces a very remarkable change in man, by substituting justice for instinct in his conduct, and giving his actions the morality they had formerly lacked. Then only, when the voice of duty takes the place of physical impulses and right of appetite, does man, who so far had considered only himself, find that he is forced to act on different principles, and to consult his reason before listening to his inclinations. . . .

. . . What man loses by the social contract is his natural liberty and an unlimited right to everything he tries to get and succeeds in getting; what he gains is civil liberty and the proprietorship of all he possesses. If we are to avoid mistake in weighing one against the other, we must clearly distinguish natural liberty, which is bounded only by the strength of the individual, from civil liberty, which is limited by the general will; and possession, which is merely the effect of force or the right of the first occupier, from property, which can be founded only on a positive title. . . .

BOOK II: CHAPTER I
THAT SOVEREIGNTY IS INALIENABLE

The first and most important deduction from the principles we have so far laid down is that the general will alone can direct the state according to the object for which it was instituted, i.e. the common good. . . .

. . . Sovereignty, being nothing less than the exercise of the general will, can never be alienated, and . . . the Sovereign, who is no less than a collective being, cannot be represented except by himself. . . .

In reality, if it is not impossible for a particular will to agree on some point with the general will, it is at least impossible for the agreement to be lasting and constant; for the particular will tends, by its very nature, to partiality, while the general will tends to equality. It is even more impossible to have any guarantee of this agreement; for even if it should always exist, it would be the effect not of art, but of chance. . . . If then the people promises simply to obey, by that very act it dissolves itself and loses what makes it a people; the moment a master exists, there is no longer a Sovereign, and from that moment the body politic has ceased to exist.

This does not mean that the commands of the rulers cannot pass for general wills, so long as the Sovereign, being free to oppose them, offers no opposition. In such a case, universal silence is taken to imply the consent of the people. . . .

CHAPTER II
THAT SOVEREIGNTY IS INDIVISIBLE

Sovereignty, for the same reason as makes it inalienable, is indivisible; for will either is, or is not, general; it is the will either of the body of the people, or only of a part of it. In the first case, the will, when declared, is an act of Sovereignty and constitutes law: in the second, it is merely a particular will, or act of magistracy—at the most a decree.

But our political theorists, unable to divide Sovereignty in principle, divide it according to its object: into force and will; into legislative power and executive power; into rights of taxation, justice, and war; into internal administration and power of foreign treaty. . . .

This error is due to a lack of exact notions concerning the Sovereign authority, and to taking for parts of it what are only emanations from it. Thus, for example, the acts of declaring war and making peace have been regarded as acts of Sovereignty; but this is not the case, as these acts do not constitute law, but merely the application of a law. . . .

CHAPTER III
WHETHER THE GENERAL WILL IS FALLIBLE

It follows from what has gone before that the general will is always right and tends to the public advantage; but it does not follow that the deliberations of the people are always equally correct. Our will is always for our own good, but we do not always see what that is; the people is never corrupted, but it is often deceived, and on such occasions only does it seem to will what is bad.

There is often a great deal of difference between the will of all and the general will; the latter considers only the common interest, while the former takes private interest into account, and is no more than a sum of particular wills: but take away from these same wills the pluses and minuses that cancel one another, and the general will remains as the sum of the differences.

If, when the people, being furnished with adequate information, held its deliberations, the citizens had no communication one with another, the grand total of the small differences would always give the general will, and the decision would always be good. But when factions arise, and partial associations are formed at the expense of the great association, the will of each of these associations becomes general in relation to its members, while it remains particular in relation to the State. . . . The differences become less numerous and give a less general result. Lastly, when one of these associations is so great as to prevail over all the rest, the result is no longer a sum of small differences, but a single difference; in this case there is no longer a general will, and the opinion which prevails is purely particular.

It is therefore essential, if the general will is to be able to express itself, that there should be no partial society within the State, and that each citizen should think only his own thoughts. But if there are partial societies, it is best to have as many as possible and to prevent them from being unequal. . . .

CHAPTER IV
THE LIMITS OF THE SOVEREIGN POWER

If the State is a moral person whose life is in the union of its members, and if the most important of its cares is the care for its own preservation, it must have a universal and compelling force, in order to move and dispose each part as may be most advantageous to the whole. As nature gives each man absolute power over all his members, the social compact gives the body politic absolute power over all its members also; and it is this power which, under the direction of the general will, bears, as I have said, the name of Sovereignty. . . .

Each man alienates, I admit, by the social compact, only such part of his powers, goods, and liberty as it is important for the community to control; but it must also be granted that the Sovereign is sole judge of what is important.

Every service a citizen can render the State he ought to render as soon as the Sovereign demands it; but the Sovereign, for its part, cannot impose upon its subjects any fetters that are useless to the community, nor can it even wish to do so; for no more by the law of reason than by the law of nature can anything occur without a cause.

The undertakings which bind us to the social body are obligatory only because they are mutual; and their nature is such that in fulfilling them we cannot work for others without working for ourselves. Why is it that the general will is always in the right, and that all continually will the happiness of each one, unless it is because there is not a man who does not think of "each" as meaning him, and consider himself in voting for all? This proves that equality of rights and the idea of justice which such equality creates originate in the preference each man gives to himself, and accordingly in the very nature of man. It proves that the general will, to be really such, must be general in its object as well as its essence; that it must both come from all and apply to all; and that it loses its natural rectitude when it is directed to some particular and determinate object, because in such a case we are judging of something foreign to us and have no true principle of equity to guide us.

Indeed, as soon as a question of particular fact or right arises on a point not previously regulated by a general convention, the matter becomes contentious. It is a case in which the individuals concerned are one party, and the public the other, but in which I can see neither the law that ought to be followed nor the judge who ought to give the decision. In such a case, it would be absurd to propose to refer the question to an express decision of the general will, which can be only the conclusion reached by one of the parties and in consequence will be, for the other party, merely an external and particular will, inclined on this occasion to injustice and subject to error. Thus, just as a particular will cannot stand for the general will, the general will, in turn, changes its nature, when its object is particular, and, as general, cannot pronounce on a man or a fact. When, for instance, the people of Athens nominated or displaced its rulers, decreed honours to one, and imposed penalties on another, and, by a multitude of particular decrees, exercised all the functions of government indiscriminately, it had in such cases no longer a general will in the strict sense; it was acting no longer as Sovereign, but as magistrate. . . .

. . . What makes the will general is less the number of voters than the common interest uniting them; for, under this system, each necessarily submits to the conditions he imposes on others: and this admirable agreement between interest and justice gives to the common deliberations an equitable character which at once vanishes when any particular question is discussed, in the absence of a common interest to unite and identify the ruling of the judge with that of the party.

From whatever side we approach our principle, we reach the same conclusion, that the social compact sets up among the citizens an equality of such a kind, that they all bind themselves to observe the same conditions and should therefore all enjoy the same rights. Thus, from the very nature of the compact, every act of Sovereignty, i.e. every authentic act of the general will, binds or favours all the citizens equally; so that the Sovereign recognizes only the body of the nation, and draws no distinctions between those of whom it is made up. What, then, strictly speaking, is an act of Sovereignty? It is not a convention between a superior and an inferior, but a convention between the body and each of its members. It is legitimate, because based on the social contract, and equitable, because common to all; useful, because it can have no other object than the general good, and stable, because guaranteed by the public force and the supreme power. . . .

When these distinctions have once been admitted, it is seen to be so untrue that there is, in the social contract, any real renunciation on the part of the individuals, that the position in which they find themselves as a result of the contract is really preferable to that in which they were before. Instead of a renunciation, they have made an advantageous exchange: instead of an uncertain and precarious way of living they have got one that is better and more secure; instead of natural independence they have got liberty; instead of the power to harm others security for themselves, and instead of their strength, which others might overcome, a right which social union makes invincible. . . . All have indeed to fight when their country needs them; but then no one has ever to fight for himself. Do we not gain something by running, on behalf of what gives us our security, only some of the risks we should have to run for ourselves, as soon as we lost it?

✿

14

✿

The Individual and the Limits of State Power

John Stuart Mill (1806–1873)

ON LIBERTY

The object of this essay is to assert one very simple principle, as entitled to govern absolutely the dealings of society with the individual in the way of compulsion and control, whether the means used be physical force in the form of legal penalties or the moral coercion of public opinion. The principle is that the sole end for which mankind are warranted, individually or collectively, in interfering with the liberty of action of any of their number is self-protection. That the only purpose for which power can be rightfully exercised over any member of a civilized community, against his will, is to prevent harm to others. His own good, either physical or moral, is not a sufficient warrant. He cannot rightfully be compelled to do or forbear because it will be better for him to do so, because it

From John Stuart Mill, *On Liberty*, 1859.

will make him happier, because, in the opinions of others, to do so would be wise or even right. These are good reasons for remonstrating with him, or reasoning with him, or persuading him, or entreating him, but not for compelling him or visiting him with any evil in case he do otherwise. To justify that, the conduct from which it is desired to deter him must be calculated to produce evil to someone else. The only part of the conduct of anyone for which he is amenable to society is that which concerns others. In the part which merely concerns himself, his independence is, of right, absolute. Over himself, over his own body and mind, the individual is sovereign. . . .

It is proper to state that I forego any advantage which could be derived to my argument from the idea of abstract right as a thing independent of utility. I regard utility as the ultimate appeal on all ethical questions; but it must be utility in the largest sense, grounded on the permanent interests of man as a progressive being. Those interests, I contend, authorize the subjection of individual spontaneity to external control only in respect to those actions of each which concern the interest of other people. . . .

. . . . This, then, is the appropriate region of human liberty. It comprises, first, the inward domain of consciousness, demanding liberty of conscience in the most comprehensive sense, liberty of thought and feeling, absolute freedom of opinion and sentiment on all subjects, practical or speculative, scientific, moral, or theological. The liberty of expressing and publishing opinions may seem to fall under a different principle, since it belongs to that part of the conduct of an individual which concerns other people, but, being almost of as much importance as the liberty of thought itself and resting in great part on the same reasons, is practically inseparable from it. Secondly, the principle requires liberty of tastes and pursuits, of framing the plan of our life to suit our own character, of doing as we like, subject to such consequences as may follow, without impediment from our fellow creatures, so long as what we do does not harm them, even though they should think our conduct foolish, perverse, or wrong. Thirdly, from this liberty of each individual follows the liberty, within the same limits, of combination among individuals; freedom to unite for any purpose not involving harm to others; the persons combining being supposed to be of full age and not forced or deceived.

No society in which these liberties are not, on the whole, respected is free, whatever may be its form of government; and none is completely free in which they do not exist absolute and unqualified. The only freedom which deserves the name is that of pursuing our own good in our own way, so long as we do not attempt to deprive others of theirs or impede their efforts to obtain it. Each is the proper guardian of his own health, whether bodily *or* mental and spiritual. Mankind are greater gainers by suffering each other to live as seems good to themselves than by compelling each to live as seems good to the rest. . . .

. . . . If all mankind minus one were of one opinion, mankind would be no more justified in silencing that one person than he, if he had the power, would be justified in silencing mankind. Were an opinion a personal possession of no value except to the owner, if to be obstructed in the enjoyment of it were simply a feudal lords, vassals, guild-masters, journeymen, apprentices, serfs; in almost all of these classes, again, subordinate gradations.

The modern bourgeois society that has sprouted from the ruins of feudal society has not done away with class antagonisms. It has but established new classes, new conditions of oppression, new forms of struggle in place of the old ones.

Our epoch, the epoch of the bourgeoisie, possesses, however, this distinctive feature: it has simplified the class antagonisms. Society as a whole is more and more splitting up into two great hostile camps, into two great classes directly facing each other: Bourgeoisie and Proletariat.

From the serfs of the Middle Ages sprang the chartered burghers of the earliest towns. From these burgesses the first elements of the bourgeoisie were developed.

The discovery of America, the rounding of the Cape, opened up fresh ground for the rising bourgeoisie. The East-Indian and Chinese markets, the colonisation of America, trade with the colonies, the increase in the means of exchange and in commodities generally, gave to commerce, to navigation, to industry, an impulse never before known, and thereby, to the revolutionary element in the tottering feudal society, a rapid development.

The feudal system of industry, under which industrial production was monopolised by closed guilds, now no longer sufficed for the growing wants of the new markets. The manufacturing system took its place. The guild-masters were pushed on one side by the manufacturing middle class; division of labour between the different corporate guilds vanished in the face of division of labour in each single workshop.

Meantime the markets kept ever growing, the demand ever rising. Even manufacture no longer sufficed. Thereupon, steam and machinery revolutionised industrial production. The place of manufacture was taken by the giant, Modern Industry, the place of the industrial middle class, by industrial millionaires, the leaders of whole industrial armies, the modern bourgeoisie.

Modern industry has established the world-market, for which the discovery of America paved the way. This market has given an immense development to commerce, to navigation, to communication by land. This development has, in its turn, reacted on the extension of industry; and in proportion as industry, commerce, navigation, railways extended, in the same proportion the bourgeoisie developed, increased its capital, and pushed into the background every class handed down from the Middle Ages.

We see, therefore, how the modern bourgeoisie is itself the product of a long course of development, of a series of revolutions in the modes of production and of exchange.

Each step in the development of the bourgeoisie was accompanied by a corresponding political advance of that class. An oppressed class under the sway of the feudal nobility, an armed and self-governing association in the mediaeval commune; here independent urban republic (as in Italy and Germany), there taxable "third estate" of the monarchy (as in France), afterwards, in the period of

15

The Clash of Class Interests: Alienation

(Two viewpoints by Karl Marx are presented on this topic.)

Karl Marx (1818–1883)

THE COMMUNIST MANIFESTO

The history of all hitherto existing society is the history of class struggles.

Freeman and slave, patrician and plebeian, lord and serf, guild-master and journeyman, in a word, oppressor and oppressed, stood in constant opposition to one another, carried on an uninterrupted, now hidden, now open fight that each time ended, either in a revolutionary re-constitution of society at large, or in the common ruin of the contending classes.

In the earlier epochs of history, we find almost everywhere a complicated arrangement of society into various orders, a manifold gradation of social rank. In ancient Rome we have patricians, knights, plebeians, slaves; in the Middle Ages,

From "Manifesto of the Communist Party" in *Marx and Engels, Selected Works,* vol. I, Foreign Languages Publishing House, Moscow, 1958.

feudal lords, vassals, guild-masters, journeymen, apprentices, serfs; in almost all of these classes, again, subordinate gradations.

The modern bourgeois society that has sprouted from the ruins of feudal society has not done away with class antagonisms. It has but established new classes, new conditions of oppression, new forms of struggle in place of the old ones.

Our epoch, the epoch of the bourgeoisie, possesses, however, this distinctive feature: it has simplified the class antagonisms. Society as a whole is more and more splitting up into two great hostile camps, into two great classes directly facing each other: Bourgeoisie and Proletariat.

From the serfs of the Middle Ages sprang the chartered burghers of the earliest towns. From these burgesses the first elements of the bourgeoisie were developed.

The discovery of America, the rounding of the Cape, opened up fresh ground for the rising bourgeoisie. The East-Indian and Chinese markets, the colonisation of America, trade with the colonies, the increase in the means of exchange and in commodities generally, gave to commerce, to navigation, to industry, an impulse never before known, and thereby, to the revolutionary element in the tottering feudal society, a rapid development.

The feudal system of industry, under which industrial production was monopolised by closed guilds, now no longer sufficed for the growing wants of the new markets. The manufacturing system took its place. The guild-masters were pushed on one side by the manufacturing middle class; division of labour between the different corporate guilds vanished in the face of division of labour in each single workshop.

Meantime the markets kept ever growing, the demand ever rising. Even manufacture no longer sufficed. Thereupon, steam and machinery revolutionised industrial production. The place of manufacture was taken by the giant, Modern Industry, the place of the industrial middle class, by industrial millionaires, the leaders of whole industrial armies, the modern bourgeoisie.

Modern industry has established the world-market, for which the discovery of America paved the way. This market has given an immense development to commerce, to navigation, to communication by land. This development has, in its turn, reacted on the extension of industry; and in proportion as industry, commerce, navigation, railways extended, in the same proportion the bourgeoisie developed, increased its capital, and pushed into the background every class handed down from the Middle Ages.

We see, therefore, how the modern bourgeoisie is itself the product of a long course of development, of a series of revolutions in the modes of production and of exchange.

Each step in the development of the bourgeoisie was accompanied by a corresponding political advance of that class. An oppressed class under the sway of the feudal nobility, an armed and self-governing association in the mediaeval commune; here independent urban republic (as in Italy and Germany), there taxable "third estate" of the monarchy (as in France), afterwards, in the period of everyone who receives the protection of society owes a return for the benefit, and the fact of living in society renders it indispensable that each should be bound to observe a certain line of conduct toward the rest. This conduct consists, first, in not injuring the interests of one another, or rather certain interests which, either by express legal provision or by tacit understanding, ought to be considered as rights; and secondly, in each person's bearing his share (to be fixed on some equitable principle) of the labors and sacrifices incurred for defending the society or its members from injury and molestation. These conditions society is justified in enforcing at all costs to those who endeavor to withhold fulfillment. Nor is this all that society may do. The acts of an individual may be hurtful to others or wanting in due consideration for their welfare, without going to the length of violating any of their constituted rights. The offender may then be justly punished by opinion, though not by law. As soon as any part of a person's conduct affects prejudicially the interests of others, society has jurisdiction over it, and the question whether the general welfare will or will not be promoted by interfering with it becomes open to discussion. But there is no room for entertaining any such question when a person's conduct affects the interests of no persons besides himself, or needs not affect them unless they like (all the persons concerned being of full age and the ordinary amount of understanding). In all such cases, there should be perfect freedom, legal and social, to do the action and stand the consequences.

It would be a great misunderstanding of this doctrine to suppose that it is one of selfish indifference which pretends that human beings have no business with each other's conduct in life, and that they should not concern themselves about the well-doing or well-being of one another, unless their own interest is involved. Instead of any diminution, there is need of a great increase of disinterested exertion to promote the good of others. But disinterested benevolence can find other instruments to persuade people to their good than whips and scourges, either of the literal or the metaphorical sort. . . .

. . . But neither one person, nor any number of persons, is warranted in saying to another human creature of ripe years that he shall not do with his life for his own benefit what he chooses to do with it. . . .

What I contend for is that the inconveniences which are strictly inseparable from the unfavorable judgment of others are the only ones to which a person should ever be subjected for that portion of his conduct and character which concerns his own good, but which does not affect the interest of others, in their relations with him. Acts injurious to others require a totally different treatment. Encroachment on their rights; infliction on them of any loss or damage not justified by his own rights; falsehood or duplicity in dealing with them; unfair or ungenerous use of advantages over them; even selfish abstinence from defending them against injury—these are fit objects of moral reprobation and, in grave cases, of moral retribution and punishment. . . .

the baneful consequences to the intellectual; and through that to the moral nature of man, unless this liberty is either conceded or asserted in spite of prohibition; let us next examine whether the same reasons do not require that men should be free to act upon their opinions—to carry these out in their lives without hindrance, either physical or moral, from their fellow men, so long as it is at their own risk and peril. This last proviso is of course indispensable. No one pretends that actions should be as free as opinions. On the contrary, even opinions lose their immunity when the circumstances in which they are expressed are such as to constitute by their expression a positive instigation to some mischievous act. An opinion that corn dealers are starvers of the poor, or that private property is robbery, ought to be unmolested when simply circulated through the press, but may justly incur punishment when delivered orally to an excited mob assembled before the house of a corn dealer, or when handed about among the same mob in the form of a placard. Acts, of whatever kind, which without justifiable cause do harm to others may be, and in the more important cases absolutely require to be, controlled by the unfavorable sentiments, and, when needful, by the active interference of mankind. The liberty of the individual must be thus far limited; he must not make himself a nuisance to other people. But if he refrains from molesting others in what concerns them, and merely acts according to his own inclination and judgment in things which concern himself, the same reasons which show that opinion should be free prove also that he should be allowed, without molestation, to carry his opinions into practice at his own cost. That mankind are not infallible; that their truths, for the most part, are only half-truths; that unity of opinion, unless resulting from the fullest and freest comparison of opposite opinions, is not desirable, and diversity not an evil, but a good, until mankind are much more capable than at present of recognizing all sides of the truth, are principles applicable to men's modes of action not less than to their opinions. As it is useful that while mankind are imperfect there should be different opinions, so it is that there should be different experiments of living; that free scope should be given to varieties of character, short of injury to others; and that the worth of different modes of life should be proved practically, when anyone thinks fit to try them. It is desirable, in short, that in things which do not primarily concern others individuality should assert itself. Where not the person's own character but the traditions of customs of other people are the rule of conduct, there is wanting one of the principal ingredients of human happiness, and quite the chief ingredient of individual and social progress. . . .

What, then, is the rightful limit to the sovereignty of the individual over himself? Where does the authority of society begin? How much of human life should be assigned to individuality, and how much to society?

Each will receive its proper share if each has that which more particularly concerns it. To individuality should belong the part of life in which it is chiefly the individual that is interested; to society, the part which chiefly interests society.

Though society is not founded on a contract, and though no good purpose is answered by inventing a contract in order to deduce social obligations from it, will make him happier, because, in the opinions of others, to do so would be wise or even right. These are good reasons for remonstrating with him, or reasoning with him, or persuading him, or entreating him, but not for compelling him or visiting him with any evil in case he do otherwise. To justify that, the conduct from which it is desired to deter him must be calculated to produce evil to someone else. The only part of the conduct of anyone for which he is amenable to society is that which concerns others. In the part which merely concerns himself, his independence is, of right, absolute. Over himself, over his own body and mind, the individual is sovereign. . . .

It is proper to state that I forego any advantage which could be derived to my argument from the idea of abstract right as a thing independent of utility. I regard utility as the ultimate appeal on all ethical questions; but it must be utility in the largest sense, grounded on the permanent interests of man as a progressive being. Those interests, I contend, authorize the subjection of individual spontaneity to external control only in respect to those actions of each which concern the interest of other people. . . .

. . . . This, then, is the appropriate region of human liberty. It comprises, first, the inward domain of consciousness, demanding liberty of conscience in the most comprehensive sense, liberty of thought and feeling, absolute freedom of opinion and sentiment on all subjects, practical or speculative, scientific, moral, or theological. The liberty of expressing and publishing opinions may seem to fall under a different principle, since it belongs to that part of the conduct of an individual which concerns other people, but, being almost of as much importance as the liberty of thought itself and resting in great part on the same reasons, is practically inseparable from it. Secondly, the principle requires liberty of tastes and pursuits, of framing the plan of our life to suit our own character, of doing as we like, subject to such consequences as may follow, without impediment from our fellow creatures, so long as what we do does not harm them, even though they should think our conduct foolish, perverse, or wrong. Thirdly, from this liberty of each individual follows the liberty, within the same limits, of combination among individuals; freedom to unite for any purpose not involving harm to others; the persons combining being supposed to be of full age and not forced or deceived.

No society in which these liberties are not, on the whole, respected is free, whatever may be its form of government; and none is completely free in which they do not exist absolute and unqualified. The only freedom which deserves the name is that of pursuing our own good in our own way, so long as we do not attempt to deprive others of theirs or impede their efforts to obtain it. Each is the proper guardian of his own health, whether bodily *or* mental and spiritual. Mankind are greater gainers by suffering each other to live as seems good to themselves than by compelling each to live as seems good to the rest. . . .

. . . . If all mankind minus one were of one opinion, mankind would be no more justified in silencing that one person than he, if he had the power, would be justified in silencing mankind. Were an opinion a personal possession of no value except to the owner, if to be obstructed in the enjoyment of it were simply a private injury, it would make some difference whether the injury was inflicted only on few persons or on many. But the peculiar evil of silencing the expression of an opinion is that it is robbing the human race, posterity as well as the existing generation—those who dissent from the opinion, still more than those who hold it. If the opinion is right, they are deprived of the opportunity of exchanging error for truth; if wrong, they lose, what is almost as great a benefit, the clearer perception and livelier impression of truth produced by its collision with error. . . .

. . . . But it is not the minds of heretics that are deteriorated most by the ban placed on all inquiry which does not end in the orthodox conclusions. The greatest harm done is to those who are not heretics, and whose whole mental development is cramped and their reason cowed by the fear of heresy. Who can compute what the world loses in the multitude of promising intellects combined with timid characters, who dare not follow out any bold, vigorous, independent train of thought, lest it should land them in something which would admit of being considered irreligious or immoral? Among them we may occasionally see some man of deep conscientiousness and subtle and refined understanding, who spends a life in sophisticating with an intellect which he cannot silence, and exhausts the resources of ingenuity in attempting to reconcile the promptings of his conscience and reason with orthodoxy, which yet he does not, perhaps, to the end succeed in doing. No one can be a great thinker who does not recognize that as a thinker it is his first duty to follow his intellect to whatever conclusions it may lead. . . .

We have now recognized the necessity to the mental well-being of mankind (on which all their other well-being depends) of freedom of opinion, and freedom of the expression of opinion, on four distinct grounds, which we will now briefly recapitulate:

First, if any opinion is compelled to silence, that opinion may, for aught we can certainly know, be true. To deny this is to assume our own infallibility.

Secondly, though the silenced opinion be an error, it may, and very commonly does, contain a portion of truth; and since the general or prevailing opinion on any subject is rarely or never the whole truth, it is only by the collision of adverse opinions that the remainder of the truth has any chance of being supplied.

Thirdly, even if the received opinion be not only true, but the whole truth; unless it is suffered to be, and actually is, vigorously and earnestly contested, it will, by most of those who receive it, be held in the manner of a prejudice, with little comprehension or feeling of its rational grounds. And not only this, but, fourthly, the meaning of the doctrine itself will be in danger of being lost or enfeebled, and deprived of its vital effect on the character and conduct; the dogma becoming a mere formal profession, inefficacious for good, but cumbering the ground and preventing the growth of any real and heartfelt conviction from reason or personal experience. . . .

Such being the reasons which make it imperative that human beings should be free to form opinions and to express their opinions without reserve; and such manufacture proper, serving either the semi-feudal or the absolute monarchy as a counterpoise against the nobility, and, in fact, corner-stone of the great monarchies in general, the bourgeoisie has at last, since the establishment of Modern Industry and of the world-market, conquered for itself, in the modern representative State, exclusive political sway. The executive of the modern State is but a committee for managing the common affairs of the whole bourgeoisie.

The bourgeoisie, historically, has played a most revolutionary part.

The bourgeoisie, wherever it has got the upper hand, has put an end to all feudal, patriarchal, idyllic relations. It has pitilessly torn asunder the motley feudal ties that bound man to his "natural superiors," and has left remaining no other nexus between man and man than naked self-interest, than callous "cash payment." It has drowned the most heavenly ecstasies of religious fervour, of chivalrous enthusiasm, of philistine sentimentalism, in the icy water of egotistical calculation. It has resolved personal worth into exchange value, and in place of the numberless indefeasible chartered freedoms, has set up that single, unconscionable freedom—Free Trade. In one word, for exploitation, veiled by religious and political illusions, it has substituted naked, shameless, direct, brutal exploitation.

The bourgeoisie has stripped of its halo every occupation hitherto honoured and looked up to with reverent awe. It has converted the physician, the lawyer, the priest, the poet, the man of science, into its paid wage-labourers.

The bourgeoisie has torn away from the family its sentimental veil, and has reduced the family relation to a mere money relation.

The bourgeoisie has disclosed how it came to pass that the brutal display of vigour in the Middle Ages, which Reactionists so much admire, found its fitting complement in the most slothful indolence. It has been the first to show what man's activity can bring about. It has accomplished wonders far surpassing Egyptian pyramids, Roman aqueducts, and Gothic cathedrals; it has conducted expeditions that put in the shade all former Exoduses of nations and crusades.

The bourgeoisie cannot exist without constantly revolutionising the instruments of production, and thereby the relations of production, and with them the whole relations of society. Conservation of the old modes of production in unaltered form, was, on the contrary, the first condition of existence for all earlier industrial classes. Constant revolutionising of production, uninterrupted disturbance of all social conditions, everlasting uncertainty and agitation distinguish the bourgeois epoch from all earlier ones. All fixed, fast-frozen relations, with their train of ancient and venerable prejudices and opinions, are swept away, all new-formed ones become antiquated before they can ossify. All that is solid melts into air, all that is holy is profaned, and man is at last compelled to face with sober senses, his real conditions of life, and his relations with his kind.

The need of a constantly expanding market for its products chases the bourgeoisie over the whole surface of the globe. It must nestle everywhere, settle everywhere, establish connexions everywhere.

The bourgeoisie has through its exploitation of the world-market given a cosmopolitan character to production and consumption in every country. To the great chagrin of Reactionists, it has drawn from under the feet of industry the national ground on which it stood. All old-established national industries have been destroyed or are daily being destroyed. They are dislodged by new industries, whose introduction becomes a life and death question for all civilised nations, by industries that no longer work up indigenous raw material, but raw material drawn from the remotest zones; industries whose products are consumed, not only at home, but in every quarter of the globe. In place of the old wants, satisfied by the productions of the country, we find new wants, requiring for their satisfaction the products of distant lands and climes. In place of the old local and national seclusion and self-sufficiency, we have intercourse in every direction, universal inter-dependence of nations. And as in material, so also in intellectual production. The intellectual creations of individual nations become common property. National one-sidedness and narrow-mindedness become more and more impossible, and from the numerous national and local literatures, there arises a world literature.

The bourgeoisie, by the rapid improvement of all instruments of production, by the immensely facilitated means of communication, draws all, even the most barbarian, nations into civilisation. The cheap prices of its commodities are the heavy artillery with which it batters down all Chinese walls, with which it forces the barbarians' intensely obstinate hatred of foreigners to capitulate. It compels all nations, on pain of extinction, to adopt the bourgeois mode of production; it compels them to introduce what it calls civilisation into their midst, i.e., to become bourgeois themselves. In one word, it creates a world after its own image.

The bourgeoisie has subjected the country to the rule of the towns. It has created enormous cities, has greatly increased the urban population as compared with the rural, and has thus rescued a considerable part of the population from the idiocy of rural life. Just as it has made the country dependent on the towns, so it has made barbarian and semi-barbarian countries dependent on the civilised ones, nations of peasants on nations of bourgeois, the East on the West.

The bourgeoisie keeps more and more doing away with the scattered state of the population, of the means of production, and of property. It has agglomerated population, centralised means of production, and has concentrated property in a few hands. The necessary consequence of this was political centralisation. Independent, or but loosely connected provinces, with separate interests, laws, governments and systems of taxation, became lumped together into one nation, with one government, one code of laws, one national class-interest, one frontier and one customs-tariff.

The bourgeoisie, during its rule of scarce one hundred years, has created more massive and more colossal productive forces than have all preceding generations together. Subjection of Nature's forces to man, machinery, application of chemistry to industry and agriculture, steam-navigation, railways, electric telegraphs, clearing of whole continents for cultivation, canalisation of rivers, whole populations conjured out of the ground—what earlier century had even a presentiment that such productive forces slumbered in the lap of social labour?

We see then: the means of production and of exchange, on whose foundation the bourgeoisie built itself up, were generated in feudal society. At a certain stage in the development of these means of production and of exchange, the conditions under which feudal society produced and exchanged, the feudal organisation of agriculture and manufacturing industry, in one word, the feudal relations of property became no longer compatible with the already developed productive forces; they became so many fetters. They had to be burst asunder; they were burst asunder.

Into their place stepped free competition, accompanied by a social and political constitution adapted to it, and by the economical and political sway of the bourgeois class.

A similar movement is going on before our own eyes. Modern bourgeois society with its relations of production, of exchange and of property, a society that has conjured up such gigantic means of production and of exchange, is like the sorcerer, who is no longer able to control the powers of the nether world whom he has called up by his spells. For many a decade past the history of industry and commerce is but the history of the revolt of modern productive forces against modern conditions of production, against the property relations that are the conditions for the existence of the bourgeoisie and of its rule. It is enough to mention the commercial crises that by their periodical return put on its trial, each time more threateningly, the existence of the entire bourgeois society. In these crises a great part not only of the existing products, but also of the previously created productive forces, are periodically destroyed. In these crises there breaks out an epidemic that, in all earlier epochs, would have seemed an absurdity—the epidemic of overproduction. Society suddenly finds itself put back into a state of momentary barbarism; it appears as if a famine, a universal war of devastation had cut off the supply of every means of subsistence; industry and commerce seem to be destroyed; and why? Because there is too much civilisation, too much means of subsistence, too much industry, too much commerce. The productive forces at the disposal of society no longer tend to further the development of the conditions of bourgeois property; on the contrary, they have become too powerful for these conditions, by which they are fettered, and so soon as they overcome these fetters, they bring disorder into the whole bourgeois society, endanger the existence of bourgeois property. The conditions of bourgeois society are too narrow to comprise the wealth created by them. And how does the bourgeoisie get over these crises? On the one hand by enforced destruction of a mass of productive forces; on the other, by the conquest of new markets, and by the more thorough exploitation of the old ones. That is to say, by paving the way for more extensive and more destructive crises, and by diminishing the means whereby crises are prevented.

The weapons with which the bourgeoisie felled feudalism to the ground are now turned against the bourgeoisie itself.

But not only has the bourgeoisie forged the weapons that bring death to itself; it has also called into existence the men who are to wield those weapons—the modern working class—the proletarians.

In proportion as the bourgeoisie, *i.e.*, capital, is developed, in the same proportion is the proletariat, the modern working class, developed—a class of labourers, who live only so long as they find work, and who find work only so long as their labour increases capital. These labourers, who must sell themselves piecemeal, are a commodity, like every other article of commerce, and are consequently exposed to all the vicissitudes of competition, to all the fluctuations of the market.

Owing to the extensive use of machinery and to division of labour, the work of the proletarians has lost all individual character, and, consequently, all charm for the workman. He becomes an appendage of the machine, and it is only the most simple, most monotonous, and most easily acquired knack, that is required of him. Hence, the cost of production of a workman is restricted, almost entirely, to the means of subsistence that he requires for his maintenance, and for the propagation of his race. But the price of a commodity, and therefore, also of labour, is equal to its cost of production. In proportion, therefore, as the repulsiveness of the work increases, the wage decreases. Nay more, in proportion as the use of machinery and division of labour increases, in the same proportion of the burden of toil also increases, whether by prolongation of the working hours, by increase of the work exacted in a given time or by increased speed of the machinery, etc.

Modern industry has converted the little workshop of the patriarchal master into the great factory of the industrial capitalist. Masses of labourers, crowded into the factory, are organised like soldiers. As privates of the industrial army they are placed under the command of a perfect hierarchy of officers and sergeants. Not only are they slaves of the bourgeois class, and of the bourgeois State; they are daily and hourly enslaved by the machine, by the over-looker, and, above all, by the individual bourgeois manufacturer himself. The more openly this despotism proclaims gain to be its end and aim, the more petty, the more hateful and the more embittering it is.

The less the skill and exertion of strength implied in manual labour, in other words, the more modern industry becomes developed, the more is the labour of men superseded by that of women. Differences of age and sex have no longer any distinctive social validity for the working class. All are instruments of labour, more or less expensive to use, according to their age and sex.

No sooner is the exploitation of the labour by the manufacturer, so far, at an end, than he receives his wages in cash, than he is set upon by the other portions of the bourgeoisie, the landlord, the shopkeeper, the pawnbroker, etc.

The lower strata of the middle class—the small tradespeople, shopkeepers, and retired tradesmen generally, the handicraftsmen and peasants—all these sink gradually into the proletariat, partly because their diminutive capital does not suffice for the scale on which Modern Industry is carried on, and is swamped in the competition with the large capitalists, partly because their specialised skill is rendered worthless by new methods of production. Thus the proletariat is recruited from all classes of the population.

The proletariat goes through various stages of development. With its birth begins its struggle with the bourgeoisie. At first the contest is carried on by individual labourers, then by the workpeople of a factory, then by the operatives of one trade, in one locality, against the individual bourgeois who directly exploits them. They direct their attacks not against the bourgeois conditions of production, but against the instruments of production themselves; they destroy imported wares that compete with their labour, they smash to pieces machinery, they set factories ablaze, they seek to restore by force the vanished status of the workman of the Middle Ages.

At this stage the labourers still form an incoherent mass scattered over the whole country, and broken up by their mutual competition. If anywhere they unite to form more compact bodies, this is not yet the consequence of their own active union, but of the union of the bourgeoisie, which class, in order to attain its own political ends, is compelled to set the whole proletariat in motion, and is moreover yet, for a time, able to do so. At this stage, therefore, the proletarians do not fight their enemies, but the enemies of their enemies, the remnants of absolute monarchy, the landowners, the non-industrial bourgeois, the petty bourgeoisie. Thus the whole historical movement is concentrated in the hands of the bourgeoisie; every victory so obtained is a victory for the bourgeoisie.

But with the development of industry the proletariat not only increases in number; it becomes concentrated in greater masses, its strength grows, and it feels that strength more. The various interests and conditions of life within the ranks of the proletariat are more and more equalised, in proportion as machinery obliterates all distinctions of labour, and nearly everywhere reduces wages to the same low level. The growing competition among the bourgeois, and the resulting commercial crises, make the wages of the workers ever more fluctuating. The unceasing improvement of machinery, ever more rapidly developing, makes their livelihood more and more precarious; the collisions between individual workmen and individual bourgeois take more and more the character of collisions between two classes. Thereupon the workers begin to form combinations (Trades' Unions) against the bourgeois; they club together in order to keep up the rate of wages; they found permanent associations in order to make provision beforehand for these occasional revolts. Here and there the contest breaks out into riots.

Now and then the workers are victorious, but only for a time. The real fruit of their battles lies, not in the immediate result, but in the ever-expanding union of the workers. This union is helped on by the improved means of communication that are created by modern industry and that place the workers of different localities in contact with one another. It was just this contact that was needed to centralise the numerous local struggles, all of the same character, into one national struggle between classes. But every class struggle is a political struggle. And that union, to attain which the burghers of the Middle Ages, with their miserable highways, required centuries, the modern proletarians, thanks to railways, achieve in a few years.

This organization of the proletarians into a class, and consequently into a political party, is continually being upset again by the competition between the workers themselves. But it ever rises up again, stronger, firmer, mightier. It compels legislative recognition of particular interests of the workers, by taking advantage of the divisions among the bourgeoisie itself. Thus the ten-hours' bill in England was carried.

Altogether collisions between the classes of the old society further, in many ways, the course of development of the proletariat. The bourgeoisie finds itself involved in a constant battle. At first with the aristocracy; later on, with those portions of the bourgeoisie itself, whose interests have become antagonistic to the progress of industry; at all times, with the bourgeoisie of foreign countries. In all these battles it sees itself compelled to appeal to the proletariat, to ask for its help, and thus, to drag it into the political arena. The bourgeoisie itself, therefore, supplies the proletariat with its own elements of political and general education, in other words, it furnishes the proletariat with weapons for fighting the bourgeoisie.

Further, as we have already seen, entire sections of the ruling classes are, by the advance of industry, precipitated into the proletariat, or are at least threatened in their conditions of existence. These also supply the proletariat with fresh elements of enlightenment and progress.

Finally, in times when the class struggle nears the decisive hour, the process of dissolution going on within the ruling class, in fact within the whole range of old society, assumes such a violent, glaring character, that a small section of the ruling class cuts itself adrift, and joins the revolutionary class, the class that holds the future in its hands. Just as, therefore, at an earlier period, a section of the nobility went over to the bourgeoisie, so now a portion of the bourgeoisie goes over to the proletariat, and in particular, a portion of the bourgeois ideologists, who have raised themselves to the level of comprehending theoretically the historical movement as a whole.

Of all the classes that stand face to face with the bourgeoisie today, the proletariat alone is a really revolutionary class. The other classes decay and finally disappear in the face of Modern Industry; the proletariat is its special and essential product.

The lower middle class, the small manufacturer, the shopkeeper, the artisan, the peasant, all these fight against the bourgeoisie, to save from extinction their existence as fractions of the middle class. They are therefore not revolutionary, but conservative. Nay more, they are reactionary, for they try to roll back the wheel of history. If by chance they are revolutionary, they are so only in view of their impending transfer into the proletariat, they thus defend not their present, but their future interests, they desert their own standpoint to place themselves at that of the proletariat.

The "dangerous class," the social scum, that passively rotting mass thrown off by the lowest layers of old society, may, here and there, be swept into the movement by a proletarian revolution, its conditions of life, however, prepare it far more for the part of a bribed tool of reactionary intrigue.

In the conditions of the proletariat, those of old society at large are already virtually swamped. The proletarian is without property; his relation to his wife and children has no longer anything in common with the bourgeois family-relations; modern industrial labour, modern subjection to capital, the same in England as in France, in America as in Germany, has stripped him of every trace of national character. Law, morality, religion, are to him so many bourgeois prejudices, behind which lurk in ambush just as many bourgeois interests.

All the preceding classes that got the upper hand, sought to fortify their already acquired status by subjecting society at large to their conditions of appropriation. The proletarians cannot become masters of the productive forces of society, except by abolishing their own previous mode of appropriation, and thereby also every other previous mode of appropriation. They have nothing of their own to secure and to fortify; their mission is to destroy all previous securities for, and insurances of, individual property.

All previous historical movements were movements of minorities, or in the interest of minorities. The proletarian movement is the self-conscious, independent movement of the immense majority, in the interests of the immense majority. The proletariat, the lowest stratum of our present society, cannot stir, cannot raise itself up, without the whole superincumbent strata of official society being sprung into the air.

Though not in substance, yet in form, the struggle of the proletariat with the bourgeoisie is at first a national struggle. The proletariat of each country must, of course, first of all settle matters with its own bourgeoisie.

In depicting the most general phases of the development of the proletariat, we traced the more or less veiled civil war, raging within existing society, up to the point where that war breaks out into open revolution, and where the violent overthrow of the bourgeoisie lays the foundation for the sway of the proletariat.

Hitherto, every form of society has been based, as we have already seen, on the antagonism of oppressing and oppressed classes. But in order to oppress a class, certain conditions must be assured to it under which it can, at least, continue its slavish existence. The serf, in the period of serfdom, raised himself to membership in the commune, just as the petty bourgeois, under the yoke of feudal absolutism, managed to develop into a bourgeois. The modern labourer, on the contrary, instead of rising with the progress of industry, sinks deeper and deeper below the conditions of existence of his own class. He becomes a pauper, and pauperism develops more rapidly than population and wealth. And here it becomes evident, that the bourgeoisie is unfit any longer to be the ruling class in society, and to impose its conditions of existence upon society as an overriding law. It is unfit to rule because it is incompetent to assure an existence to its slave within his slavery, because it cannot help letting him sink into such a state, that it has to feed him, instead of being fed by him. Society can no longer live under this bourgeoisie, in other words, its existence is no longer compatible with society.

The essential condition for the existence, and for the sway of the bourgeois class, is the formation and augmentation of capital; the condition for capital is wage-labour. Wage-labour rests exclusively on competition between the labourers. The advance of industry, whose involuntary promoter is the bourgeoisie, replaces the isolation of the labourers, due to competition, by their revolutionary combination, due to association. The development of Modern Industry, therefore, cuts from under its feet the very foundation on which the bourgeoisie produces and appropriates products. What the bourgeoisie, therefore, produces, above all, is its own gravediggers. Its fall and the victory of the proletariat are equally inevitable.

ALIENATED LABOR

We proceed from a *present* fact of political economy.

The worker becomes poorer the more wealth he produces, the more his production increases in power and extent. The worker becomes a cheaper commodity the more commodities he produces. The *increase in value* of the world of things is directly proportional to the *decrease in value* of the human world. Labor not only produces commodities. It also produces itself and the worker as a *commodity*, and indeed in the same proportion as it produces commodities in general.

This fact simply indicates that the object which labor produces, its product, stands opposed to it as an *alien thing*, as a *power independent* of the producer. The product of labor is labor embodied and made objective in a thing. It is the *objectification* of labor. The realization of labor is its objectification. In the viewpoint of political economy this realization of labor appears as the *diminution* of the worker, the objectification as the *loss of and subservience to the object*, and the appropriation as *alienation* as externalization.

So much does the realization of labor appear as diminution that the worker is diminished to the point of starvation. So much does objectification appear as loss of the object that the worker is robbed of the most essential objects not only of life but also of work. Indeed, work itself becomes a thing of which he can take possession only with the greatest effort and with the most unpredictable interruptions. So much does the appropriation of the object appear as alienation that the more objects the worker produces, the fewer he can own and the more he falls under the domination of his product, of capital.

All these consequences follow from the fact that the worker is related to the *product of his labor* as to an *alien* object. For it is clear according to this premise: The more the worker exerts himself, the more powerful becomes the alien objective world which he fashions against himself, the poorer he and his inner world become, the less there is that belongs to him. It is the same in religion. The more man attributes to God, the less he retains in himself. The worker puts his life into

From *Writings of the Young Marx on Philosophy and Society*, edited and translated by Loyd D. Easton and Kurt H. Guddat, copyright © 1967 by Loyd D. Easton and Kurt H. Guddat. Reprinted by permission of Doubleday and Company, Inc.

the object; then it no longer belongs to him but to the object. The greater this activity, the poorer is the worker. What the product of his work is, he is not. The greater this product is, the smaller he is himself. The *externalization* of the worker in his product means not only that his work becomes an object, an *external* existence, but also that it exists *outside him* independently, alien, an autonomous power, opposed to him. The life he has given to the object confronts him as hostile and alien. . . .

Let us now consider more closely the *objectification*, the worker's production and with it the *alienation* and *loss* of the object, his product.

The worker can make nothing without *nature*, without the *sensuous external world*. It is the material wherein his labor realizes itself, wherein it is active, out of which and by means of which it produces.

But as nature furnishes to labor the *means of life* in the sense that labor cannot *live* without objects upon which labor is exercised, nature also furnishes the *means of life* in the narrower sense, namely, the means of physical subsistence of the *worker* himself.

The more the worker *appropriates* the external world and sensuous nature through his labor, the more he deprives himself of the *means of life* in two respects: first, that the sensuous external world gradually ceases to be an object belonging to his labor, a *means of life* of his work; secondly, that it gradually ceases to be a *means of life* in the immediate sense, a means of physical subsistence of the worker.

In these two respects, therefore, the worker becomes a slave to his objects; first, in that he receives an *object of labor,* that is, he receives *labor,* and secondly that he receives the *means of subsistence*. The first enables him to exist as a *worker* and the second as a *physical subject*. The terminus of this slavery is that he can only maintain himself as a *physical subject* so far as he is a *worker* and only as a *physical subject* is he a worker.

(The alienation of the worker in his object is expressed according to the laws of political economy as follows: the more the worker produces, the less he has to consume; the more values he creates the more worthless and unworthy he becomes; the better shaped his product, the more misshapen is he; the more civilized his product, the more barbaric is the worker; the more powerful the work, the more powerless becomes the worker; the more intelligence the work has, the more witless is the worker and the more he becomes a slave of nature.)

Political economy conceals the alienation in the nature of labor by ignoring the direct relationship between the worker (labor) *and production.* To be sure, labor produces marvels for the wealthy but it produces deprivation for the worker. It produces palaces, but hovels for the worker. It produces beauty, but mutilation for the worker. It displaces labor through machines, but it throws some workers back into barbarous labor and turns others into machines. It produces intelligence, but for the worker it produces imbecility and cretinism. . . .

Up to now we have considered the alienation, the externalization of the worker only from one side: his *relationship to the products of his labor*. But alienation is shown not only in the result but also in the *process of production*, in the *producing activity* itself. How could the worker stand in an alien relationship to the product of his activity if he did not alienate himself from himself in the very act of production? After all, the product is only the résumé of activity, of production. If the product of work is externalization, production itself must be active externalization, externalization of activity, activity of externalization. Only alienation—and externalization in the activity of labor itself—is summarized in the alienation of the object of labor.

What constitutes the externalization of labor?

First is the fact that labor is *external* to the laborer—that is, it is not part of his nature—and that the worker does not affirm himself in his work but denies himself, feels miserable and unhappy, develops no free physical and mental energy but mortifies his flesh and ruins his mind. The worker, therefore feels at ease only outside work, and during work he is outside himself. He is at home when he is not working and when he is working he is not at home. His work, therefore, is not voluntary, but coerced, *forced labor.* It is not the satisfaction of a need but only a *means* to satisfy other needs. Its alien character is obvious from the fact that as soon as no physical or other pressure exists, labor is avoided like the plague. External labor, labor in which man is externalized, is labor of self-sacrifice, of penance. Finally, the external nature of work for the worker appears in the fact that it is not his own but another person's, that in work he does not belong to himself but to someone else. In religion the spontaneity of human imagination, the spontaneity of the human brain and heart, acts independently of the individual as an alien, divine or devilish activity. Similarly, the activity of the worker is not his own spontaneous activity. It belongs to another. It is the loss of his own self.

The result, therefore, is that man (the worker) feels that he is acting freely only in his animal functions—eating, drinking, and procreating, or at most in his shelter and finery—while in his human functions he feels only like an animal. The animalistic becomes the human and the human the animalistic.

To be sure, eating, drinking, and procreation are genuine human functions. In abstraction, however, and separated from the remaining sphere of human activities and turned into final and sole ends, they are animal functions.

We have considered labor, the act of alienation of practical human activity, in two aspects: (1) the relationship of the worker to the *product of labor* as an alien object dominating him. This relationship is at the same time the relationship to the sensuous external world, to natural objects as an alien world hostile to him; (2) the relationship of labor to the *act of production* in *labor.* This relationship is that of the worker to his own activity as alien and not belonging to him, activity as passivity, power as weakness, procreation as emasculation, the worker's *own* physical and spiritual energy, his personal life—for what else is life but activity—as an activity turned against him, independent of him, and not belonging to him. *Self-alienation,* as against the alienation of the *object,* stated above.

We have now to derive a third aspect of *alienated labor* from the two previous ones.

Man is a species-being [*Gattungswesen*] not only in that he practically and theoretically makes his own species as well as that of other things his object, but also—and this is only another expression for the same thing—in that as present and living species he considerers himself to be a *universal* and consequently free being.

The life of the species in man as in animals is physical in that man, (like the animal) lives by inorganic nature. And as man is more universal than the animal, the realm of inorganic nature by which he lives is more universal. As plants, animals, minerals, air, light, etc., in theory form a part of human consciousness, partly as objects of natural science, partly as objects of art—his spiritual inorganic nature or spiritual means of life which he first must prepare for enjoyment and assimilation—so they also form in practice a part of human life and human activity. Man lives physically only by these products of nature; they may appear in the form of food, heat, clothing, housing, etc. The universality of man appears in practice in the universality which makes the whole of nature his *inorganic* body: (1) as a direct means of life, and (2) as the matter, object, and instrument of his life activity. Nature is the *inorganic body* of man, that is, nature insofar as it is not the human body. Man *lives* by nature. This means that nature is his *body* with which he must remain in perpetual process in order not to die. That the physical and spiritual life of man is tied up with nature is another way of saying that nature is linked to itself, for man is a part of nature.

In alienating (1) nature from man, and (2) man from himself, his own active function, his life activity, alienated labor also alienated the *species* from him; it makes *species-life* the means of individual life. In the first place it alienates species-life and the individual life, and secondly it turns the latter in its abstraction into the purpose of the former, also in its abstract and alienated form.

For labor, *life activity,* and *productive life* appear to man at first only as a *means* to satisfy a need, the need to maintain physical existence. Productive life, however, is species-life. It is life begetting life. In the mode of life activity lies the entire character of a species, its species-character; and free conscious activity is the species-character of man. Life itself appears only as a *means of life.*

The animal is immediately one with its life activity, not distinct from it. The animal is *its life activity.* Man makes his life activity itself into an object of will and consciousness. He has conscious life activity. It is not a determination with which he immediately identifies. Conscious life activity dintinguishes man immediately from the life activity of the animal. Only thereby is he a species-being. Or rather, he is only a conscious being—that is, his own life is an object for him—since he is a species-being. Only on that account is his activity free activity. Alienated labor reverses the relationship in that man, since he is a conscious being, makes his life activity, his *essence,* only a means for his *existence.*

The practical creation of an *objective world,* the *treatment* of inorganic nature, is proof that man is a conscious species-being, that is, a being which is related to its species as to its own essence or is related to itself as a species-being. To be sure animals also produce. They build themselves nests, dwelling places, like the bees, beavers, ants, etc. But the animal produces only what is immediately necessary for itself or its young. It produces in a one-sided way while man produces universally. The animal produces under the domination of immediate physical need while man produces free of physical need and only genuinely so in freedom from such need. The animal only produces itself while man reproduces the whole of nature. The animal's product belongs immediately to its physical body while man is free when he confronts his product. The animal builds only according to the standard and need of the species to which it belongs while man knows how to produce according to the standard of any species and at all times knows how to apply an intrinsic standard to the object. Thus man creates also according to the laws of beauty.

In the treatment of the objective world, therefore, man proves himself to be genuinely a *species-being*. This production is his active species-life. Through it nature appears as *his* work and his actuality. The object of labor is thus the *objectification of man's species-life;* he produces himself not only intellectually, as in consciousness, but also actively in a real sense and sees himself in a world he made. In taking from man the object of his production, alienated labor takes from his *species-life*, his actual and objective existence as a species. It changes his superiority to the animal to inferiority, since he is deprived of nature, his inorganic body.

By degrading free spontaneous activity to the level of a means, alienated labor makes the species-life of man a means of his physical existence.

The consciousness which man has from his species is altered through alienation, so that species-life becomes a means for him.

(3) Alienated labor hence turns the *species-existence of man,* and also nature as his mental species-capacity, into an existence *alien* to him, into the *means* of his *individual existence*. It alienates his spiritual nature, his *human essence,* from his own body and likewise from nature outside him.

(4) A direct consequence of man's alienation from the product of his work, from his life activity, and from his species-existence, is the *alienation of man* from *man*. When man confronts himself, he confronts *other* men. What holds true of man's relationship to his work, to the product of his work, and to himself, also holds true of man's relationship to other men, to their labor, and the object of their labor.

In general, the statement that man is alienated from his species-existence means that one man is alienated from another just as each man is alienated from human nature.

The alienation of man, the relation of man to himself, is realized and expressed in the relation between man and other men.

Thus in the relation of alienated labor every man sees the others according to the standard and the relation in which he finds himself as a worker.

We began with an economic fact, the alienation of the worker and his product. We have given expression to the concept of this fact: *alienated, externalized* labor. We have analyzed this concept and have thus analyzed merely a fact of political economy.

Let us now see further how the concept of alienated, externalized labor must express and represent itself in actuality.

If the product of labor is alien to me, confronts me as an alien power, to whom then does it belong?

If my own activity does not belong to me, if it is an alien and forced activity, to whom then does it belong?

To a being *other* than myself.

Who is this being?

Gods? To be sure, in early times the main production, for example, the building of temples in Egypt, India, and Mexico, appears to be in the service of the gods, just as the product belongs to the gods. But gods alone were never workmasters. The same is true of *nature.* And what a contradiction it would be if the more man subjugates nature through his work and the more the miracles of gods are rendered superfluous by the marvels of industry, man should renounce his joy in producing and the enjoyment of his product for love of these powers.

The *alien* being who owns labor and the product of labor, whom labor serves and whom the product of labor satisfies can only be *man* himself.

That the product of labor does not belong to the worker and an alien power confronts him is possible only because this product belongs to *a man other than the worker.* If his activity is torment for him, it must be the *pleasure* and the life-enjoyment for another. Not gods, not nature, but only man himself can be this alien power over man.

Let us consider the statement previously made, that the relationship of man to himself is *objective* and *actual* to him only through his relationship to other men. If man is related to the product of his labor, to his objectified labor, as to an *alien*, hostile, powerful object independent of him, he is so related that another alien hostile, powerful man independent of him is the lord of this object. If he is unfree is relation to his own activity, he is related to it as bonded activity, activity under the domination, coercion, and yoke of another man.

Every self-alienation of man, from himself and from nature, appears in the relationship which he postulates between other men and himself and nature. Thus religious self-alienation appears necessarily in the relation of laity to priest, or also to a mediator, since we are here now concerned with the spiritual world. In the practical real world self-alienation can appear only in the practical real relationships to other men. The means whereby the alienation proceeds is a *practical* means. Through alienated labor man thus not only produces his relationship to the object and to the act of production as an alien man at enmity with him. He also creates the relation in which other men stand to his production and product, and the relation in which he stands to these other men. Just as he begets his own production as loss of his reality, as his punishment; just as he begets his own product as a loss, a product not belonging to him, so he begets the domination of the nonproducer over production and over product. As he alienates his own activity from himself, he confers upon the stranger an activity which is not his own.

Justice as Fairness

John Rawls ° *(1921–   )*

THE MAIN IDEA OF THE THEORY OF JUSTICE

My aim is to present a conception of justice which generalizes and carries to a higher level of abstraction the familiar theory of the social contract. . . . In order to do this we are not to think of the original contract as one to enter a particular society or to set up a particular form of government. Rather, the guiding idea is that the principles of justice for the basic structure of society are the object of the original agreement. They are the principles that free and rational persons concerned to further their own interests would accept in an initial position of equality as defining the fundamental terms of their association. These principles

From John Rawls, *A Theory of Justice*, The Belknap Press of Harvard Univ. Press, Cambridge, Mass., 1971.
° Professor of Philosophy, Harvard University.

are to regulate all further agreements; they specify the kinds of social cooperation that can be entered into and the forms of government that can be established. This way of regarding the principles of justice I shall call justice as fairness.

Thus we are to imagine that those who engage in social cooperation choose together, in one joint act, the principles which are to assign basic rights and duties and to determine the division of social benefits. Men are to decide in advance how they are to regulate their claims against one another and what is to be the foundation charter of their society. Just as each person must decide by rational reflection what constitutes his good, that is, the system of ends which it is rational for him to pursue, so a group of persons must decide once and for all what is to count among them as just and unjust. The choice which rational men would make in this hypothetical situation of equal liberty, assuming for the present that this choice problem has a solution, determines the principles of justice.

In justice as fairness the original position of equality corresponds to the state of nature in the traditional theory of the social contract. This original position is not, of course, thought of as an actual historical state of affairs, much less as a primitive condition of culture. It is understood as a purely hypothetical situation characterized so as to lead to a certain conception of justice. Among the essential features of this situation is that no one knows his place in society, his class position or social status, nor does any one know his fortune in the distribution of natural assets and abilities, his intelligence, strength, and the like. I shall even assume that the parties do not know their conceptions of the good or their special psychological propensities. The principles of justice are chosen behind a veil of ignorance. This ensures that no one is advantaged or disadvantaged in the choice of principles by the outcome of natural chance or the contingency of social circumstances. Since all are similarly situated and no one is able to design principles to favor his particular condition, the principles of justice are the result of a fair agreement or bargain. For given the circumstances of the original position, the symmetry of everyone's relations to each other, this initial situation is fair between individuals as moral persons, that is, as rational beings with their own ends and capable, I shall assume, of a sense of justice. The original position is, one might say, the appropriate initial status quo, and thus the fundamental agreements reached in it are fair. This explains the propriety of the name "justice as fairness": it conveys the idea that the principles of justice are agreed to in an initial situation that is fair. The name does not mean that the concepts of justice and fairness are the same, any more than the phrase "poetry as metaphor" means that the concepts of poetry and metaphor are the same. . . .

One feature of justice as fairness is to think of the parties in the initial situation as rational and mutually disinterested. This does not mean that the parties are egoists, that is, individuals with only certain kinds of interests, say in wealth, prestige, and domination. But they are conceived as not taking an interest in one another's interests. They are to presume that even their spiritual aims may be opposed, in the way that the aims of those of different religions may be opposed. Moreover, the concept of rationality must be interpreted as far as possible in the narrow sense, standard in economic theory, of taking the most effective means to given ends. . . .

I maintain instead that the persons in the initial situation would choose two rather different principles: the first requires equality in the assignment of basic rights and duties, while the second holds that social and economic inequalities, for example inequalities of wealth and authority, are just only if they result in compensating benefits for everyone, and in particular for the least advantaged members of society. The principles rule out justifying institutions on the grounds that the hardships of some are offset by a greater good in the aggregate. It may be expedient but it is not just that some should have less in order that others may prosper. But there is not injustice in the greater benefits earned by a few provided that the situations of persons not so fortunate is thereby improved. The intuitive idea is that since everyone's well-being depends upon a scheme of cooperation without which no one could have a satisfactory life, the division of advantages should be such as to draw forth the willing cooperation of everyone taking part in it, including those less well situated. Yet this can be expected only if reasonable terms are proposed. The two principles mentioned seem to be a fair agreement on the basis of which those better endowed, or more fortunate in their social position, neither of which we can be said to deserve, could expect the willing cooperation of others when some workable scheme is a necessary condition of the welfare of all. . . .

THE ORIGINAL POSITION

The Veil of Ignorance.   The idea of the original position is to set up a fair procedure so that any principles agreed to will be just. The aim is to use the notion of pure procedural justice as a basis of theory. Somehow we must nullify the effects of specific contingencies which put men at odds and tempt them to exploit social and natural circumstances to their own advantage. Now in order to do this I assume that the parties are situated behind a veil of ignorance. They do not know how the various alternatives will affect their own particular case and they are obliged to evaluate principles solely on the basis of general considerations.

It is assumed, then, that the parties do not know certain kinds of particular facts. First of all, no one knows his place in society, his class position or social status; nor does he know his fortune in the distribution of natural assets and abilities, his intelligence and strength, and the like. Nor, again, does anyone know his conception of the good, the particulars of his rational plan of life, or even the special features of his psychology such as his aversion to risk or liability to optimism or pessimism. More than this, I assume that the parties do not know the particular circumstances of their own society. That is, they do not know its economic or political situation, or the level of civilization and culture it has been able to achieve. The persons in the original position have no information as to which generation they belong. These broader restrictions on knowledge are appropriate in part because questions of social justice arise between generations as well as within them, for example, the question of the appropriate rate of capital saving and of the conservation of natural resources and the environment of nature. There is also, theoretically anyway, the question of a reasonable genetic policy. In these cases too, in order to carry through the idea of the original position, the parties must not know the contingencies that set them in opposition. They must choose principles the consequences of which they are prepared to live with whatever generation they turn out to belong to.

As far as possible, then, the only particular facts which the parties know is that their society is subject to the circumstances of justice and whatever this implies. It is taken for granted, however, that they know the general facts about human society. They understand political affairs and the principles of economic theory; they know the basis of social organization and the laws of human psychology. Indeed, the parties are presumed to know whatever general facts affect the choice of the principles of justice. . . .

The veil of ignorance makes possible a unanimous choice of a particular conception of justice. Without these limitations on knowledge the bargaining problem of the original position would be hopelessly complicated. . . .

Now the reasons for the veil of ignorance go beyond mere simplicity. We want to define the original position so that we get the desired solution. If a knowledge of particulars is allowed, then the outcome is biased by arbitrary contingencies. As already observed, to each according to his threat advantage is not a principle of justice. If the original position is to yield agreements that are just, the parties must be fairly situated and treated equally as moral persons. The arbitrariness of the world must be corrected for by adjusting the circumstances of the initial contractual situation.

The Rationality of Parties. The concept of rationality invoked here, with the exception of one essential feature, is the standard one familiar in social theory. Thus in the usual way, a rational person is thought to have a coherent set of preferences between the options open to him. He ranks these options according to how well they further his purposes; he follows the plan which will satisfy more of his desires rather than less, and which has the greater chance of being successfully executed. The special assumption I make is that a rational individual does not suffer from envy. He is not ready to accept a loss for himself if only others have less as well.

The assumption of mutually disinterested rationality, then, comes to this: the persons in the original position try to acknowledge principles which advance their system of ends as far as possible.

There is one further assumption to guarantee strict compliance. The parties are presumed to be capable of a sense of justice and this fact is public knowledge among them. This condition is to insure the integrity of the agreement made in the original position. It does not mean that in their deliberations the parties apply some particular conception of justice, for this would defeat the point of the motivation assumption. Rather, it means that the parties can rely on each other to understand and to act in accordance with whatever principles are finally agreed to. Once principles are acknowledged the parties can depend on one another to conform to them. In reaching an agreement, then, they know that their undertaking is not in vain: their capacity for a sense of justice insures that the principles chosen will be respected. It is essential to observe, however, that this assumption still permits the consideration of men's capacity to act on the various conceptions of justice. The general facts of human psychology and the principles of moral learning are relevant matters for the parties to examine. If a conception of justice is unlikely to generate its own support, or lacks stability, this fact must not be overlooked. For then a different conception of justice might be preferred. The assumption only says that the parties have a capacity for justice in a purely formal sense: taking everything relevant into account including the general facts of moral psychology, the parties will adhere to the principles eventually chosen. They are rational in that they will not enter into agreements they know they cannot keep, or can do so only with great difficulty.

The Maximin Rule. The term "maximin" means the *maximum minimorum;* and the rule directs our attention to the worst that can happen under any proposed course of action, and to decide in the light of that. . . .

The maximin rule tells us to rank alternatives by their worst possible outcomes: we are to adopt the alternative the worst outcome of which is superior to the worst outcomes of the others.

TWO PRINCIPLES OF JUSTICE

I shall now state in a provisional form the two principles of justice that I believe would be chosen in the original position.

The first statement of the two principles reads as follows.

First: each person is to have an equal right to the most extensive basic liberty compatible with a similar liberty for others.

Second: social and economic inequalities are to be arranged so that they are both (a) reasonably expected to be to everyone's advantage, and (b) attached to positions and offices open to all. There are two ambiguous phrases in the second principle, namely "everyone's advantage" and "open to all."

By way of general comment, these principles primarily apply, as I have said, to the basic structure of society. They are to govern the assignment of rights and duties and to regulate the distribution of social and economic advantages. As their formulation suggests, these principles presuppose that the social structure can be divided into two more or less distinct parts, the first principle applying to the one, the second to the other. They distinguish between those aspects of the social system that define and secure the equal liberties of citizenship and those that specify and establish social and economic inequalities. The basic liberties of citizens are, roughly speaking, political liberty (the right to vote and to be eligible for public office) together with freedom of speech and assembly; liberty of conscience and freedom of thought; freedom of the person along with the right to hold (personal) property; and freedom from arbitrary arrest and seizure as defined by the concept of the rule of law. These liberties are all required to be equal by the first principle, since citizens of a just society are to have the same basic rights.

The second principle applies, in the first approximation, to the distribution of income and wealth and to the design of organizations that make use of differences in authority and responsibility, or chains of command. While the distribution of wealth and income need not be equal, it must be to everyone's advantage, and at the same time, positions of authority and offices of command must be accessible to all. One applies the second principle by holding positions open, and then, subject to this constraint, arranges social and economic inequalities so that everyone benefits.

These principles are to be arranged in a serial order with the first principle prior to the second. This ordering means that a departure from the institutions of equal liberty required by the first principle cannot be justified by, or compensated for, by greater social and economic advantages. The distribution of wealth and income, and the hierarchies of authority, must be consistent with both the liberties of equal citizenship and equality of opportunity.

It is clear that these principles are rather specific in their content, and their acceptance rests on certain assumptions that I must eventually try to explain and justify. A theory of justice depends upon a theory of society in ways that will become evident as we proceed. For the present, it should be observed that the two principles (and this holds for all formulations) are a special case of a more general conception of justice that can be expressed as follows.

All social values—liberty and opportunity, income and wealth, and the bases of self-respect—are to be distributed equally unless an unequal distribution of any, or all, of these values is to everyone's advantage. Injustice, then, is simply inequalities that are not to the benefit of all. Of course, this conception is extremely vague and requires interpretation.

As a first step, suppose that the basic structure of society distributes certain primary goods, that is, things that every rational man is presumed to want. These goods normally have a use whatever a person's rational plan of life. For simplicity, assume that the chief primary goods at the disposition of society are rights and liberties, powers and opportunities, income and wealth. These are the social primary goods. Other primary goods such as health and vigor, intelligence and imagination, are natural goods; although their possession is influenced by the basic structure, they are not so directly under its control. Imagine, then, a hypothetical initial arrangement in which all the social primary goods are equally distributed: everyone has similar rights and duties, and income and wealth are evenly shared. This state of affairs provides a benchmark for judging improvements. If certain inequalities of wealth and organizational powers would make everyone better off than in this hypothetical starting situation, then they accord with the general conception.

Now it is possible, at least theoretically, that by giving up some of their fundamental liberties men are sufficiently compensated by the resulting social and economic gains. The general conception of justice imposes no restrictions on what sort of inequalities are permissible; it only requires that everyone's position be improved. We need not suppose anything so drastic as consenting to a condition of slavery. Imagine instead that men forego certain political rights when the economic returns are significant and their capacity to influence the course of policy by the exercise of these rights would be marginal in any case. It is this kind of exchange which the two principles as stated ruled out; being arranged in serial order they do not permit exchanges between basic liberties and economic and social gains. The serial ordering of principles expresses an underlying preference among primary social goods. When this preference is rational so likewise is the choice of these principles in this order.

17

Moral Constraints and the State

Robert Nozick° (1938–   )

THE MINIMAL STATE AND THE ULTRAMINIMAL STATE

The night-watchman state of classical liberal theory, limited to the functions of protecting all its citizens against violence, theft, and fraud, and to the enforcement of contracts, and so on, appears to be redistributive [i.e. where benefits are redistributed from one group to another]. We can imagine at least one social arrangement intermediate between the scheme of private protective associations [where there is no state and where individuals protect themselves by organizing private associations for this purpose] and the night-watchman state. Since the night-watchman state is often called a minimal state, we shall call this other arrangement the *ultraminimal state*. An ultraminimal state maintains a monopoly

From Robert Nozick, *Anarchy State, and Utopia*, Chap. III, Basic Books, Inc., Publishers, New York, 1974.
° Professor of Philosophy, Harvard University.

over all use of force except that necessary in immediate self-defense, and so excludes private (or agency) retaliation for wrong and exaction of compensation; but it provides protection and enforcement services *only* to those who purchase its protection and enforcement policies. People who don't buy a protection contract from the monopoly don't get protected. The minimal (night-watchman) state is equivalent to the ultraminimal state conjoined with a (clearly redistributive) . . . voucher plan, financed from tax revenues. Under this plan all people, or some (for example, those in need), are given tax-funded vouchers that can be used only for their purchase of a protection policy from the ultraminimal state. . . .

A proponent of the ultraminimal state may seem to occupy an inconsistent position, even though he avoids the question of what makes protection uniquely suitable for redistributive provision. Greatly concerned to protect rights against violation, he makes this the sole legitimate function of the state; and he protests that all other functions are illegitimate because they themselves involve the violation of rights. Since he accords paramount place to the protection and nonviolation of rights, how can he support the ultraminimal state, which would seem to leave some persons' rights unprotected or illprotected? How can he support this *in the name of* the nonviolation of rights?

MORAL CONSTRAINTS
AND MORAL GOALS

This question assumes that a moral concern can function only as a moral *goal*, as an end state for some activities to achieve as their result. It may, indeed, seem to be a necessary truth that "right," "ought," "should," and so on, are to be explained in terms of what is, or is intended to be, productive of the greatest good, with all goals built into the good. Thus it is often thought that what is wrong with utilitarianism (which *is* of this form) is its too narrow conception of good. Utilitarianism doesn't, it is said, properly take rights and their nonviolation into account; it instead leaves them a derivative status. Many of the counterexample cases to utilitarianism fit under this objection, for example, punishing an innocent man to save a neighborhood from a vengeful rampage. But a theory may include in a primary way the nonviolation of rights, yet include it in the wrong place and the wrong manner. For suppose some condition about minimizing the total (weighted) amount of violations of rights is built into the desirable end state to be achieved. We then would have something like a "utilitarianism of rights"; violations of rights (to be *minimized*) merely would replace the total happiness as the relevant end state in the utilitarian structure. (Note that we do not hold the nonviolation of our rights as our sole greatest good or even rank it first lexicographically to exclude trade-offs, if there is some desirable society we would choose to inhabit even though in it some rights of ours sometimes are violated, rather than move to a desert island where we could survive alone.) This still would require us to violate someone's rights when doing so minimizes the total (weighted) amount of the violation of rights in the society. For example, violating someone's rights might deflect others from *their* intended action of gravely violating rights, or might remove their motive for doing so, or might divert their attention, and so on. A mob rampaging through a part of town killing and burning *will* violate the rights of those living there. Therefore, someone might try to justify his punishing another *he* knows to be innocent of a crime that enraged a mob, on the grounds that punishing this innocent person would help to avoid even greater violations of rights by others, and so would lead to a minimum weighted score for rights violations in the society.

In contrast to incorporating rights into the end state to be achieved, one might place them as side constraints upon the actions to be done: don't violate constraints C. The rights of others determine the constraints upon your actions. (A *goal-directed* view with constraints added would be: among those acts available to you that don't violate constraints C, act so as to maximize goal G. Here, the rights of others would constrain your goal-directed behavior. I do not mean to imply that the correct moral view includes mandatory goals that must be pursued, even within the constraints.) This view differs from one that tries to build the side constraints C *into* the goal G. The side-constraint view forbids you to violate these moral constraints in the pursuit of your goals; whereas the view whose objective is to minimize the violation of these rights allows you to violate the rights (the constraints) in order to lessen their total violation in the society.

The claim that the proponent of the ultraminimal state is inconsistent, we now can see, assumes that he is a "utilitarian of rights." It assumes that his goal is, for example, to minimize the weighted amount of the violation of rights in the society, and that he should pursue this goal even through means that themselves violate people's rights. Instead, he may place the nonviolation of rights as a constraint upon action, rather than (or in addition to) building it into the end state to be realized. The position held by this proponent of the ultraminimal state will be a consistent one if his conception of rights holds that your being *forced* to contribute to another's welfare violates your rights, whereas someone else's not providing you with things you need greatly, including things essential to the protection of your rights, does not *itself* violate your rights, even though it avoids making it more difficult for someone else to violate them. (That conception will be consistent provided it does not construe the monopoly element of the ultraminimal state as itself a violation of rights.) That it is a consistent position does not, of course, show that it is an acceptable one.

WHY SIDE CONSTRAINTS?

Isn't it *irrational* to accept a side constraint C, rather than a view that directs minimizing the violations of C? (The latter view treats C as a condition rather than a constraint.) If nonviolation of C is so important, shouldn't that be the goal? How can a concern for the nonviolation of C lead to the refusal to violate C even when this would prevent other more extensive violations of *C*? What is the rationale for placing the nonviolation of rights as a side constraint upon action instead of including it solely as a goal of one's actions?

Side constraints upon action reflect the underlying Kantian principle that individuals are ends and not merely means; they may not be sacrificed or used for the achieving of other ends without their consent. Individuals are inviolable. More should be said to illuminate this talk of ends and means. Consider a prime example of a means, a tool. There is no side constraint on how we may use a tool, other than the moral constraints on how we may use it upon others. There are procedures to be followed to preserve it for future use ("don't leave it out in the rain"), and there are more and less efficient ways of using it. But there is no limit on what we may do to it to best achieve our goals. Now imagine that there was an overrideable constraint *C* on some tool's use. For example, the tool might have been lent to you only on the condition that *C* not be violated unless the gain from doing so was above a certain specified amount, or unless it was necessary to achieve a certain specified goal. Here the object is not *completely* your tool, for use according to your wish or whim. But it is a tool nevertheless, even with regard to the overrideable constraint. If we add constraints on its use that may not be overriden, then the object may not be used as a tool *in those ways. In those respects,* it is not a tool at all. Can one add enough constraints so that an object cannot be used as a tool at all, in *any* respect?

Can behavior toward a person be constrained so that he is not to be used for any end except as he chooses? This is an impossibly stringent condition if it requires everyone who provides us with a good to approve positively of every use to which we wish to put it. Even the requirement that he merely should not object to any use we plan would seriously curtail bilateral exchange, not to mention sequences of such exchanges. It is sufficient that the other party stands to gain enough from the exchange so that he is willing to go through with it, even though he objects to one or more of the uses to which you shall put the good. Under such conditions, the other party is not being used solely as a means, in that respect. Another party, however, who would not choose to interact with you if he knew of the uses to which you *intend* to put his actions or good, *is* being used as a means, even if he receives enough to choose (in his ignorance) to interact with you. ("All along, you were just *using* me" can be said by someone who chose to interact only because he was ignorant of another's goals and of the uses to which he himself would be put.) Is it morally incumbent upon someone to reveal his intended uses of an interaction if he has good reason to believe the other would refuse to interact if he knew? Is he *using* the other person, if he does not reveal this? And what of the cases where the other does not choose to be of use at all? In getting pleasure from seeing an attractive person go by, does one use the other solely as a means? Does someone so use an object of sexual fantasies? These and related questions raise very interesting issues for moral philosophy; but not, I think, for political philosophy.

Political philosophy is concerned only with *certain* ways that persons may not use others; primarily, physically aggressing against them. A specific side constraint upon action toward others expresses the fact that others may not be used in the specific ways the side constraint excludes. Side constraints express the inviolability of others, in the ways they specify. These modes of inviolability are expressed by the following injunction: "Don't use people in specified ways." An end-state view, on the other hand, would express the view that people are ends and not merely means (if it chooses to express this view at all), by a different injunction: "Minimize the use in specified ways of persons as means." Following this precept itself may involve using someone as a means in one of the ways specified. Had Kant held this view, he would have given the second formula of the categorical imperative as, "So act as to minimize the use of humanity simply as a means," rather than the one he actually used: "Act in such a way that you always treat humanity, whether in your own person or in the person of any other, never simply as a means, but always at the same time as an end."

Side constraints express the inviolability of other persons. But why may not one violate persons for the greater social good? Individually, we each sometimes choose to undergo some pain or sacrifice for a greater benefit or to avoid a greater harm: we go to the dentist to avoid worse suffering later; we do some unpleasant work for its results; some persons diet to improve their health or looks; some save money to support themselves when they are older. In each case, some cost is borne for the sake of the greater overall good. Why not, *similarly,* hold that some persons have to bear some costs that benefit other persons more, for the sake of the overall social good? But there is no *social entity* with a good that undergoes some sacrifice for its own good. There are only individual people, different individual people, with their own individual lives. Using one of these people for the benefit of others, uses him and benefits the others. Nothing more. What happens is that something is done to him for the sake of others. Talk of an overall social good covers this up. (Intentionally?) To use a person in this way does not sufficiently respect and take account of the fact that he is a separate person, that his is the only life he has. *He* does not get some overbalancing good from his sacrifice, and no one is entitled to force this upon him—least of all a state or government that claims his allegiance (as other individuals do not) and that therefore scrupulously must be *neutral* between its citizens. . . .

CONSTRAINTS AND ANIMALS

We can illuminate the status and implications of moral side constraints by considering living beings for whom such stringent side constraints (or any at all) usually are not considered appropriate: namely, nonhuman animals. Are there any limits to what we may do to animals? Have animals the moral status of mere *objects?* Do some purposes fail to entitle us to impose great costs on animals? What entitles us to use them at all?

Animals count for something. Some higher animals, at least, ought to be given some weight in people's deliberations about what to do. It is difficult to *prove* this. (It is also difficult to prove that people count for something!) We first shall adduce particular examples, and then arguments. If you felt like snapping your fingers, perhaps to the beat of some music, and you knew that by some strange causal connection your snapping your fingers would cause 10,000 contented, unowned cows to die after great pain and suffering, or even painlessly and instantaneously, would it be perfectly all right to snap your fingers? Is there some reason why it would be morally wrong to do so?

Some say people should not do so because such acts brutalize them and make them more likely to take the lives of *persons,* solely for pleasure. These acts that are morally unobjectionable in themselves, they say, have an undesirable moral spillover. (Things then would be different if there were no possibility of such spillover—for example, for the person who knows himself to be the last person on earth.) But why *should* there be such a spillover? If it is, in itself, perfectly all right to do anything at all to animals for any reason whatsoever, then provided a person realizes the clear line between animals and persons and keeps it in mind as he acts, why should killing animals tend to brutalize him and make him more likely to harm or kill persons? Do butchers commit more murders? (Than other persons who have knives around?) If I enjoy hitting a baseball squarely with a bat, does this significantly increase the danger of my doing the same to someone's head? Am I not capable of understanding that people differ from baseballs, and doesn't this understanding stop the spillover? Why should things be different in the case of animals? To be sure, it is an empirical question whether spillover does take place or not; but there *is* a puzzle as to why it should, at least among readers of this essay, sophisticated people who are capable of drawing distinctions and differentially acting upon them.

If some animals count for something, which animals count, how much do they count, and how can this be determined? Suppose (as I believe the evidence supports) that *eating* animals is not necessary for *health* and is not less expensive than alternate equally healthy diets available to people in the United States. The gain, then, from the eating of animals is pleasures of the palate, gustatory delights, varied tastes. I would not claim that these are not truly pleasant, delightful, and interesting. The question is: do they, or rather does the marginal addition in them gained by eating animals rather than only nonanimals, *outweigh* the moral weight to be given to animals' lives and pain? Given that animals are to count for *something,* is the *extra* gain obtained by eating them rather than non-animal products greater than the moral cost? . . .

Consider the following (too minimal) position about the treatment of animals. So that we can easily refer to it, let us label this position "utilitarianism for animals, Kantianism for people." It says: (1) maximize the total happiness of all living beings; (2) place stringent side constraints on what one may do to human beings. Human beings may not be used or sacrificed for the benefit of others; animals may be used or sacrificed for the benefit of other people or animals *only* if those benefits are greater than the loss inflicted. (This inexact statement of the utilitarian position is close enough for our purposes, and it can be handled more easily in discussion.) One may proceed only if the total utilitarian benefit is greater than the utilitarian loss inflicted on the animals. This utilitarian view counts animals as much as normal utilitarianism does persons. Following Orwell, we might summarize this view as: *all animals are equal but some are more equal than others.* (None may be sacrificed except for a greater total benefit; but persons may not be sacrificed at all, or only under far more stringent conditions, and never for the benefit of nonhuman animals. I mean (1) above merely to exclude sacrifices which do not meet the utilitarian standard, not to mandate a utilitarian goal. We shall call this position negative utilitarianism.)

We can now direct arguments for animals counting for something to holders of different views. To the "Kantian" moral philosopher who imposes stringent side constraints on what may be done to a person, we can say:

> You hold utilitarianism inadequate because it allows an individual to be sacrificed to and for another, and so forth, thereby neglecting the stringent limitations on how one legitimately may behave toward persons. But *could* there be anything morally intermediate between persons and stones, something without such stringent limitations on its treatment, yet not to be treated merely as an object? One would expect that by subtracting or diminishing some features of persons, we would get this intermediate sort of being. (Or perhaps beings of intermediate moral status are gotten by subtracting some of our characteristics and adding others very different from ours.)
>
> Plausibly, animals are the intermediate beings, and utilitarianism is the intermediate position. We may come at the question from a slightly different angle. Utilitarianism assumes both that happiness is all that matters morally and that all beings are interchangeable. This conjunction does not hold true of persons. But isn't (negative) utilitarianism true of whatever beings the conjunction does hold for, and doesn't it hold for animals?

To the utilitarian we may say:

> If only the experiences of pleasure, pain, happiness, and so on (and the capacity for these experiences) are morally relevant, then animals must be counted in moral calculations to the extent they *do* have these capacities and experiences. Form a matrix where the rows represent alternative policies or actions, the columns represent different individual organisms, and each entry represents the utility (net pleasure, happiness) the policy will lead to for the organism. The utilitarian theory evaluates each policy by the sum of the entries in its row and directs us to perform an action or adopt a policy whose sum is maximal. Each column is weighted equally and counted once, be it that of a person or a nonhuman animal. Though the structure of the view treats them equally, animals might be less important in the decisions because of facts about them. If animals have less capacity for pleasure, pain, happiness than humans do, the matrix entries in animals' columns will be lower generally than those in people's columns. In this case, they will be less important factors in the ultimate decisions to be made.

A utilitarian would find it difficult to deny animals this kind of equal consideration. On what grounds could he consistently distinguish persons' happiness from that of animals, to count only the former? Even if experiences don't get entered in the utility matrix unless they are above a certain threshold, surely *some* animal experiences are greater than some people's experiences that the utilitarian wishes to count. (Compare an animal's being burned alive unanesthetized with a person's mild annoyance.) Bentham, we may note, *does* count animals' happiness equally in just the way we have explained.

Under "utilitarianism for animals, Kantianism for people," animals will be used for the gain of other animals and persons, but persons will never be used (harmed, sacrificed) against their will, for the gain of animals. Nothing may be inflicted upon persons for the sake of animals. (Including penalties for violating laws against cruelty to animals?) Is this an acceptable consequence? Can't one save 10,000 animals from excruciating suffering by inflicting some slight discomfort on a person who did not cause the animals' suffering? One may feel the side constraint is not absolute when it is *people* who can be saved from excruciating suffering. So perhaps the side constraint also relaxes, though not as much, when animals' suffering is at stake. The thoroughgoing utilitarian (for animals *and* for people, combined in one group) goes further and holds that, *ceteris paribus*, we may inflict some suffering on a person to avoid a (slightly) greater suffering of an animal. This permissive principle seems to me to be unacceptably strong, even when the purpose is to avoid greater suffering to a *person!* . . .

Since it counts only the happiness and suffering of animals, would the utilitarian view hold it all right to kill animals painlessly? Would it be all right, on the utilitarian view, to kill *people* painlessly, in the night, provided one didn't first announce it? Utilitarianism is notoriously inept with decisions where the *number* of persons is at issue. (In this area, it must be conceded, eptness is hard to come by.) (Maximizing the total happiness requires continuing to add persons so long as their net utility is positive and is sufficient to counterbalance the loss in utility their presence in the world causes others. Maximizing the average utility allows a person to kill everyone else if that would make him ecstatic, and so happier than average. (Don't say he shouldn't because after his death the average would drop lower than if he didn't kill all the others.) Is it all right to kill someone provided you immediately substitute another (by having a child or, in science-fiction fashion, by creating a full-grown person) who will be as happy as the rest of the life of the person you killed? After all, there would be no net diminution in total utility, or even any change in its profile of distribution. Do we forbid murder only to prevent feelings of *worry* on the part of potential victims? (And how does a utilitarian explain what it is they're worried about, and would he really base a policy on what he must hold to be an irrational fear?) Clearly, a utilitarian needs to supplement his view to handle such issues; perhaps he will find that the supplementary theory becomes the main one, relegating utilitarian considerations to a corner.

But isn't utilitarianism at least adequate for animals? I think not. But if not only the animals' felt experiences are relevant, what else is? Here a tangle of questions arises. How much does an animal's life have to be respected once it's alive, and how can we decide this? Must one also introduce some notion of a nondegraded existence? Would it be all right to use genetic-engineering techniques to breed natural slaves who would be contented with their lots? Natural animals slaves? Was that the domestication of animals? Even for animals, utilitarianism won't do as the whole story, but the thicket of questions daunts us. . . .

UNDERDETERMINATION OF MORAL THEORY

What about persons distinguishes them from animals, so that stringent constraints apply to how persons may be treated, yet not to how animals may be treated? Could beings from another galaxy stand to *us* as it is usually thought we do to animals, and if so, would they be justified in treating us as means à la utilitarianism? Are organisms arranged on some ascending scale, so that any may be sacrificed or caused to suffer to achieve a greater total benefit for those not lower on the scale? Such an elitist hierarchical view would distinguish three moral statuses (forming an interval partition of the scale):

Status 1: The being may not be sacrificed, harmed, and so on, for any other organism's sake.
Status 2: The being may be sacrificed, harmed, and so on, only for the sake of beings higher on the scale, but not for the sake of beings at the same level.
Status 3: The being may be sacrificed, harmed, and so on, for the sake of other beings at the same or higher levels on the scale.

If animals occupy status 3 and we occupy status 1, what occupies status 2? Perhaps *we* occupy status 2! Is it morally forbidden to use people as means for the benefit of others, or is it only fobidden to use them for the sake of other *people,* that is, for beings at the same level? Do ordinary views include the possibility of more than one significant moral divide (like that between persons and animals), and *might one come on the other side of human beings?* Some theological views hold that God is permitted to sacrifice people for his own purposes. We also might imagine people encountering beings from another planet who traverse in their childhood whatever "stages" of moral development our developmental psychologists can identify. These beings claim that they all continue on through fourteen further sequential stages, each being necessary to enter the next one. However, they cannot explain to us (primitive as we are) the content and modes of reasoning of these later stages. These beings claim that we may be sacrificed for their well-being, or at least in order to preserve their higher capacities. They say that they see the truth of this now that they are in their moral maturity, though they didn't as children at what is our highest level of moral development. (A story like this, perhaps, reminds us that a sequence of developmental stages, each a precondition for the next, may after some point deteriorate rather than progress. It would be no recommendation of senility to point out that in order to reach it one must have passed first through other stages.) Do our moral views permit our sacrifice for the sake of these beings' higher capacities, including their moral ones? This decision is not easily disentangled from the epistemological effects of contemplating the existence of such moral authorities who differ from us, while we admit that, being fallible, we may be wrong. (A similar effect would obtain even if we happened not to know which view of the matter these other beings actually held.)

Beings who occupy the intermediate status 2 will be sacrificeable, but *not* for the sake of beings at the same or lower levels. If they never encounter or know of or affect beings higher in the hierarchy, then *they* will occupy the highest level for every situation they actually encounter and deliberate over. It will be as if an *absolute* side constraint prohibits their being sacrificed for any purpose. Two very different moral theories, the elitist hierarchical theory placing people in status 2 and the absolute-side-constraint theory, yield exactly the same moral judgments for the situations people actually have faced and account equally well for (almost) all of the moral judgments we have made. ("Almost all," because we make judgments about hypothetical situations, and these may include some involving "superbeings" from another planet.) This is not the philosopher's vision of two alternative theories accounting equally well for all of the *possible* data. Nor is it merely the claim that by various gimmicks a side-constraint view can be put into the form of a maximizing view. Rather, the two alternative theories account for all of the actual data, the data about cases we have encountered heretofore; yet they diverge significantly for certain only hypothetical situations.

It would not be surprising if we found it difficult to decide which theory to believe. For we have not been obliged to think about these situations; they are not the situations that shaped our views. Yet the issues do not concern merely whether superior beings may sacrifice us for their sakes. They also concern what *we* ought to do. For if there are other such beings, the elitist hierarchical view does *not* collapse into the "Kantian" side-constraint view, as far as *we* are concerned. A person may not sacrifice one of his fellows for his own benefit or that of another of his fellows, but may he sacrifice one of his fellows for the benefit of the higher beings? (We also will be interested in the question of whether the higher beings may sacrifice us for their own benefit.)

WHAT ARE CONSTRAINTS BASED UPON?

Such questions do not press upon us as practical problems (yet?), but they force us to consider fundamental issues about the foundations of our moral views: first, is our moral view a side-constraint view, or a view of a more complicated hierarchical structure; and second, in virture of precisely what characteristics of persons are there moral constraints on how they may treat each other or be treated? We also want to understand *why* these characteristics connect with these constraints. (And, perhaps, we want these characteristics not to be had by animals; or not had by them in as high a degree.) It would appear that a person's characteristics, by virtue of which others are constrained in their treatment of him, must themselves be valuable characteristics. How else are we to understand why something so valuable emerges from them? (This natural assumption is worth further scrutiny.)

The traditional proposals for the important individuating characteristic connected with moral constraints are the following: sentient and self-conscious; rational (capable of using abstract concepts, not tied to responses to immediate stimuli); possessing free will; being a moral agent capable of guiding its behavior by moral principles and capable of engaging in mutual limitation of conduct; having a soul. Let us ignore questions about how these notions are precisely to be understood, and whether the characteristics are possessed, and possessed uniquely, by man, and instead seek their connection with moral constraints on others. Leaving aside the last on the list, each of them seems insufficient to forge the requisite connection. Why is the fact that a being is very smart or foresightful or has an I.Q. above a certain threshold a reason to limit specially how we treat it? Would beings even more intelligent than we have the right not to limit themselves with regard to us? Or, what is the significance of any purported crucial threshold? If a being is capable of choosing autonomously among alternatives, is there some reason to *let it* do so? Are autonomous choices intrinsically good? If a being could make only once an autonomous choice, say between flavors of ice cream on a particular occasion, and would forget immediately afterwards, would there be strong reasons to allow it to choose? That a being can agree with others to mutual rule-governed limitations on conduct shows that it *can* observe limits. But it does not show which limits should be observed toward it ("no abstaining from murdering it"?), or why any limits should be observed at all. . . .

But haven't we been unfair in treating rationality, free will, and moral agency individually and separately? In conjunction, don't they add up to something whose significance is clear: a being able to formulate long-term plans for its life, able to consider and decide on the basis of abstract principles or considerations it formulates to itself and hence not merely the plaything of immediate stimuli, a being that limits its own behavior in accordance with some principles or picture it has of what an appropriate life is for itself and others, and so on. However, this exceeds the three listed traits. We can distinguish theoretically between long-term planning and an overall conception of a life that guides particular decisions, and the three traits that are their basis. For a being could possess these three traits and yet also have built into it some particular barrier that prevents it from operating in terms of an overall conception of its life and what it is to add up to. So let us add, as an additional feature, the ability to regulate and guide its life in accordance with some overall conception it chooses to accept. Such an overall conception, and knowing how we are doing in terms of it, is important to the kind of goals we formulate for ourselves and the kind of beings we are. Think how different we would be (and how differently it would be legitimate to treat us) if we all were amnesiacs, forgetting each evening as we slept the happenings of the preceding day. Even if by accident someone were to pick up each day where he left off the previous day, living in accordance with a coherent conception an aware individual might have chosen, he still would not be leading the other's sort of life. His life would parallel the other life, but it would not be integrated in the same way.

What is the moral importance of this additional ability to form a picture of one's whole life (or at least of significant chunks of it) and to act in terms of some overall conception of the life one wishes to lead? Why not intefere with someone else's shaping of his own life? (And what of those not actively shaping their lives, but drifting with the forces that play upon them?) One might note that anyone might come up with the pattern of life you would wish to adopt. Since one cannot predict in advance that someone won't, it is in your self-interest to allow another to pursue his conception of his life as he sees it; you may learn (to emulate or avoid or modify) from his example. This prudential argument seems insufficient.

I conjecture that the answer is connected with that elusive and difficult notion: the meaning of life. A person's shaping his life in accordance with some overall plan is his way of giving meaning to his life; only a being with the capacity to so shape his life can have or strive for meaningful life. But even supposing that we could elaborate and clarify this notion satisfactorily, we would face many difficult questions. Is the capacity so to shape a life itself the capacity to have (or strive for?) a life with meaning, or is something else required? (For ethics, might the content of the attribute of having a soul simply be that the being strives, or is capable of striving, to give meaning to its life?) Why are there constraints on how we may treat beings shaping their lives? Are certain modes of treatment incompatible with their having meaningful lives? And even if so, why not destroy meaningful lives? Or, why not replace "happiness" with "meaningfulness" within utilitarian theory, and maximize the total "meaningfulness" score of the persons of the world? Or does the notion of the meaningfulness of a life enter into ethics in a different fashion? This notion, we should note, has the right "feel" as something that might help to bridge an "is-ought" gap; it appropriately seems to straddle the two. Suppose, for example, that one could show that if a person acted in certain ways his life would be meaningless. Would this be a hypothetical or a categorical imperative? Would one need to answer the further question: "But why shouldn't my life be meaningless?" Or, suppose that acting in a certain way toward others was itself a way of granting that one's own life (and those very actions) was meaningless. Mightn't this, resembling a pragmatic contradiction, lead at least to a status 2 conclusion of side constraints in behavior to all other human beings? I hope to grapple with these and related issues on another occasion.

THE INDIVIDUALIST ANARCHIST

We have surveyed the important issues underlying the view that moral side constraints limit how people may behave to each other, and we may return now to the private protection scheme. A system of private protection, even when one protective agency is dominant in a geographical territory, appears to fall short of a state. It apparently does not provide protection for everyone in its territory, as does a state, and it apparently does not possess or claim the sort of monopoly over the use of force necessary to a state. In our earlier terminology, it apparently does not constitute a minimal state, and it apparently does not even constitute an ultraminimal state.

These very ways in which the dominant protective agency or association in a territory apparently falls short of being a state provide the focus of the individualist anarchist's complaint *against* the state. For he holds that when the state monopolizes the use of force in a territory and punishes others who violate its monopoly, and when the state provides protection for everyone by forcing some to purchase protection for others, it violates moral side constraints on how individuals may be treated. Hence, he concludes, the state itself is intrinsically immoral. The state grants that under some circumstances it is legitimate to punish persons who violate the rights of others, for it itself does so. How then does it arrogate to itself the right to forbid private exaction of justice by other nonaggressive individuals whose rights have been violated? *What* right does the private exacter of justice violate that is not violated also by the state when it punishes? When a group of persons constitute themselves as the state and begin to punish, *and forbid others from doing likewise,* is there some right these others would violate that they themselves do not? By what right, then, can the state and its officials claim a unique right (a privilege) with regard to force and enforce this monopoly? If the private exacter of justice violates no one's rights, then punishing him for his actions (actions state officials also perform) violates his rights and hence violates moral side constraints. Monopolizing the use of force then, on this view, is itself immoral, as is redistribution through the compulsory tax apparatus of the state. Peaceful individuals minding their own business are not violating the rights of others. It does not constitute a violation of someone's rights to refrain from purchasing something for him (that you have not entered specifically into an obligation to buy). Hence, so the argument continues, when the state threatens someone with punishment if he does not contribute to the protection of another, it violates (and its officials violate) his rights. In threatening him with something that would be a violation of his rights if done by a private citizen, they violate moral constraints.

THREE

RELIGION

O f the many subjects commanding the attention of religious philosophers, few have received more careful treatment than the question of
the existence of God. Why should the existence of God be considered
in the first place, and what kind of a being is it whose existence is
thought to be a significant intellectual and religious matter? The most persistent
question provoking the discussion about the existence of God concerns the origin
of things—of human life and of the physical universe. God, in this context, is
therefore thought of as the origin of all being, the creator of all things, and, as
such, is beyond the realm of created things. Other attributes are attached to the
concept of God by some, as, for example, that God is a personal being, all-good,
and purposeful. That such a supreme being exists provides, it is thought, an
explanation of the origin of all things and the purpose of human existence.

      Most arguments for the existence of God rely, as in the case of Aquinas'
five ways, upon the notion of cause and effect. An effect can be explained in
various ways, but whether an explanation is sufficient or adequate depends upon
the nature of the question. For example, a boy might ask his father where that log

came from as he throws it into the fireplace. It may be that the boy simply wanted to know whether his father bought it or had cut down one of the trees on their land. But the boy's question could be more philosophical. He may want to know what caused the tree to come into existence. To this question a series of answers can be given, referring to a series of causes, not unlike the answer to the question where a child came from by referring to parents, grandparents, and further back through a long series of causes. But however far this series of causes and effects can be retraced, one still must ask about the earliest cause that had caused *it*. Since this series must come to an end in order to provide an adequate explanation of the series itself, there must be, it is argued, a first cause whose nature is such that it did not need to be caused.

To illustrate some of the facets of this argument, we can consider briefly one of Aquinas' five ways, his argument from motion. Starting from the simple fact that we perceive by our senses that in the world some things are in motion, we also observe that things tend to stay at rest unless they are moved. For every motion, then, there must be a mover. Although, say, a billiard ball, is potentially in motion, it will not move unless it is moved by something that is actually in motion. If you lined up all the billiard balls behind each other on the table, not one of them would move until the first one was struck by the cue, even though potentially they could all move. The argument, then, comes to this: what if *everything* in the universe is of this kind, namely, that it will move only if it is moved? The word "motion," in this context, signifies more than simply locomotion as suggested by billiard balls; motion also means generation or coming into being. If everything were only potentially in motion, then even now nothing would be in motion. Actual motion cannot be derived from potential motion. Yet, the fact is that there is motion in the world. To explain this fact, there must be, argues Aquinas, some being that is capable of moving others but does not require to be moved, a being which actually is which is capable of bringing others into being. Again, it does not help to say that even the first mover would have to be moved. The force of the argument seems to rest on the rigorous implication of what it would mean if everything in the universe is only potentially moveable. This implication is that if everything were only potentially in motion, there would even now be no world at all. Just as the billiard balls would all be at rest with respect to locomotion, so all things would *be* only potentially, which is to say that they would not *actually* exist. That things do actually exist must mean that there is a being whose nature is to be in a state of eternal actuality and as such is the source of other forms of existence.

A similar argument is put forward to prove that the first mover or first cause is an intelligent being and therefore the source of purpose and design in the universe. But if this argument rests upon the information available to the senses or human experience, then other conclusions also seem possible. Hume raises many fundamental skeptical questions. If we think we can discover the elements of design, order, and purpose in the universe, he points out that there is also considerable evidence of disorder, purposelessness, and what is called both natural and moral evil. Moreover, Hume raised serious questions about induction, about the possibility of moving from one event to another as though they were necessarily connected as cause and effect. If all that experience makes clear to us is that one event up until now is accompanied by another event, we have no reason to conclude that those events will always accompany each other, that they are necessarily linked to each by what is called "causality." We simply have developed the habit of associating events with each other. If causality is such a misconception in explaining specific events or phenomena in our experience, then it can hardly provide a reliable basis for proving the existence of God where God is designated as the cause, or creater, of all things. Even Kant, who had tried to answer Hume's objections to the notions of causality, rejected the traditional proofs for the existence of God. While Kant agreed that it is legitimate in the realm of sense experience to infer a cause for each event, he held that the principle of causality has no meaning and no criterion for its application beyond the sensible world.

To some, particularly to existentialist philosophers such as Søren Kierkegaard, the existence of God cannot be proved by quasi-scientific explanations of the causes of things. Other dimensions of human experience, besides technical rationality, provide more adequate and vivid insights into religious truth. In addition, John Dewey sought to distinguish the essence of the religious dimension of human experience, on the one hand, from the specific teachings of any particular religions, on the other. There is, finally, the question of life after death which is viewed quite differently by Plato, Hume, and Kierkegaard.

18

The Ontological Argument

Saint Anselm (1033–1109)

After I had published, at the solicitous entreaties of certain brethren, a brief work (the Monologium) as an example of meditation on the grounds of faith, in the person of one who investigates, in a course of silent reasoning with himself, matters of which he is ignorant; considering that this book was knit together by the linking of many arguments, I began to ask myself whether there might be found a single argument which would require no other for its proof than itself alone; and alone would suffice to demonstrate that God truly exists, and that there is a supreme good requiring nothing else, which all other things require for their existence and well-being; and whatever we believe regarding the divine Being.

Although I often and earnestly directed my thought to this end, and at some times that which I sought seemed to be just within my reach, while again it wholly evaded my mental vision, at last in despair I was about to cease, as if from

Reprinted from *Prosloguim; Monologium,* by St. Anselm, translated by S. N. Deane, by permission of the Open Court Publishing Co., La Salle, Illinois, 1939.

the search for a thing which could not be found. But when I wished to exclude this thought altogether, lest, by busying my mind to no purpose, it should keep me from other thoughts, in which I might be successful; then more and more, though I was unwilling and shunned it, it began to force itself upon me, with a kind of importunity. So, one day, when I was exceedingly wearied with resisting its importunity, in the very conflict of my thoughts, the proof of which I had despaired offered itself, so that I eagerly embraced the thoughts which I was strenuously repelling.

Thinking, therefore, that what I rejoiced to have found, would, if put in writing, be welcome to some readers, of this very matter, and of some others, I have written the following treatise, in the person of one who strives to lift his mind to the contemplation of God, and seeks to understand what he believes. . . .

And so, Lord, do thou, who dost give understanding to faith, give me, so far as thou knowest it to be profitable, to understand that thou art as we believe; and that thou art that which we believe. And, indeed, we believe that thou art a being than which nothing greater can be conceived. Or is there no such nature, since the fool hath said in his heart, there is no God? (Psalms xiv. 1). But, at any rate, this very fool, when he hears of this being of which I speak—a being than which nothing greater can be conceived—understands what he hears, and what he understands is in his understanding; although he does not understand it to exist.

For, it is one thing for an object to be in the understanding, and another to understand that the object exists. When a painter first conceives of what he will afterwards perform, he has it in his understanding, but he does not yet understand it to be, because he has not yet performed it. But after he has made the painting, he both has it in his understanding, and he understands that it exists, because he has made it.

Hence, even the fool is convinced that something exists in the understanding, at least, than which nothing greater can be conceived. For, when he hears of this, he understands it. And whatever is understood, exists in the understanding. And assuredly that, than which nothing greater can be conceived, cannot exist in the understanding alone. For, suppose it exists in the understanding alone: then it can be conceived to exist in reality; which is greater.

Therefore, if that, than which nothing greater can be conceived, exists in the understanding alone, the very being, than which nothing greater can be conceived, is one, than which a greater can be conceived. But obviously this is impossible. Hence, there is no doubt that there exists a being, than which nothing greater can be conceived, and it exists both in the understanding and in reality.

CHAPTER III
GOD CANNOT BE CONCEIVED NOT TO EXIST.—GOD IS THAT, THAN WHICH NOTHING GREATER CAN BE CONCEIVED.—THAT WHICH CAN BE CONCEIVED NOT TO EXIST IS NOT GOD.

And it assuredly exists so truly, that it cannot be conceived not to exist. For, it is possible to conceive of a being which cannot be conceived not to exist; and this is greater than one which can be conceived not to exist. Hence, if that, than which nothing greater can be conceived, can be conceived not to exist, it is not that, than which nothing greater can be conceived. But this is an irreconcilable contradition. There is, then, so truly a being than which nothing greater can be conceived to exist, that it cannot even be conceived not to exist; and this being thou art, O Lord, our God.

So truly, therefore, dost thou exist, O Lord, my God, that thou canst not be conceived not to exist; and rightly. For, if a mind could conceive of a being better than thee, the creature would rise above the Creator; and this is most absurd. And, indeed, whatever else there is, except thee alone, can be conceived not to exist. To thee alone, therefore, it belongs to exist more truly than all other beings, and hence in a higher degree than all others. For, whatever else exists does not exist so truly, and hence in a less degree it belongs to it to exist. Why, then, has the fool said in his heart, there is no God (Psalms xiv. 1), since it is so evident, to a rational mind, that thou dost exist in the highest degree of all? Why, except that he is dull and a fool?

CHAPTER IV
HOW THE FOOL HAS SAID IN HIS HEART WHAT CANNOT BE CONCEIVED.—A THING MAY BE CONCEIVED IN TWO WAYS: (1) WHEN THE WORD SIGNIFYING IT IS CONCEIVED; (2) WHEN THE THING ITSELF IS UNDERSTOOD AS FAR AS THE WORD GOES. GOD CAN BE CONCEIVED NOT TO EXIST; IN REALITY HE CANNOT.

But how has the fool said in his heart what he could not conceive; or how is it that he could not conceive what he said in his heart? since it is the same to say in the heart, and to conceive.

But, if really, nay, since really, he both conceived, because he said in his heart; and did not say in his heart, because he could not conceive; there is more than one way in which a thing is said in the heart or conceived. For, in one sense, an object is conceived, when the word signifying it is conceived; and in another, when the very entity, which the object is, is understood.

In the former sense, then, God can be conceived not to exist; but in the latter, not at all. For no one who understands what fire and water are can conceive fire to be water, in accordance with the nature of the facts themselves, although this is possible according to the words. So, then, no one who understands what God is can conceive that God does not exist; although he says these words in his heart, either without any, or with some foreign, signification. For, God is that than which a greater cannot be conceived. And he who thoroughly understands this, assuredly understands that this being so truly exists, that not even in concept can it be non-existent. Therefore, he who understands that God so exists, cannot conceive that he does not exist.

I thank thee, gracious Lord, I thank thee; because what I formerly believed by thy bounty, I now so understand by thine illumination, that if I were unwilling to believe that thou dost exist, I should not be able not to understand this to be true.

CHAPTER V
GOD IS WHATEVER IT IS BETTER TO BE THAN NOT TO BE; AND HE, AS THE ONLY SELF-EXISTENT BEING, CREATES ALL THINGS FROM NOTHING.

What art thou, then, Lord God, than whom nothing greater can be conceived? But what art thou, except that which, as the highest of all beings, alone exists through itself and creates all other things from nothing? For, whatever is not this is less than a thing which can be conceived of. But this cannot be conceived of thee. What good, therefore, does the supreme Good lack, through which every good is? Therefore, thou art just, truthful, blessed, and whatever it is better to be than not to be. For it is better to be just than not just; better to be blessed than not blessed.

[GAUNILON'S ANSWER TO ANSELM'S ARGUMENT]

For example: it is said that somewhere in the ocean is an island, which, because of the difficulty, or rather the impossibility, of discovering what does not exist, is called the lost island. And they say that this island has an inestimable wealth of all manner of riches and delicacies in greater abundance than is told of the Islands of the Blest; and that having no owner or inhabitant, it is more excellent than all other countries, which are inhabited by mankind, in the abundance with which it is stored.

Now if some one should tell me that there is such an island, I should easily understand his words, in which there is no difficulty. But suppose that he went on to say, as if by a logical inference: "You can no longer doubt that this island which is more excellent than all lands exists somewhere, since you have no doubt that it is in your understanding. And since it is more excellent not to be in the understanding alone, but to exist both in the understanding and in reality, for this reason it must exist. For if it does not exist, any land which really exists will be more excellent than it; and so the island already understood by you to be more excellent will not be more excellent."

If a man should try to prove to me by such reasoning that this island truly exists, and that its existence should no longer be doubted, either I should believe that he was jesting, or I know not which I ought to regard as the greater fool: myself, supposing that I should allow this proof; or him, if he should suppose that he had established with any certainty the existence of this island. For he ought to show first that the hypothetical excellence of this island exists as a real and indubitable fact, and in no wise as any unreal object, or one whose existence is uncertain, in my understanding.

[ANSELM'S REPLY TO GAUNILON] CHAPTER III
A CRITICISM OF GAUNILON'S EXAMPLE, IN WHICH HE TRIES TO SHOW THAT IN THIS WAY THE REAL EXISTENCE OF A LOST ISLAND MIGHT BE INFERRED FROM THE FACT OF ITS BEING CONCEIVED.

But, you say, it is as if one should suppose an island in the ocean, which surpasses all lands in its fertility, and which, because of the difficulty, or rather the impossibility, of discovering what does not exist, is called a lost island; and should say that there can be no doubt that this island truly exists in reality, for this reason, that one who hears it described easily understands what he hears.

Now I promise confidently that if any man shall devise anything existing either in reality or in concept alone (except that than which a greater cannot be conceived) to which he can adapt the sequence of my reasoning, I will discover that thing, and will give him his lost island, not to be lost again.

But it now appears that this being than which a greater is inconceivable cannot be conceived not to be, because it exists on so assured a ground of truth; for otherwise it would not exist at all.

Hence, if any one says that he conceives this being not to exist, I say that at the time when he conceives of this either he conceives of a being than which a greater is inconceivable, or he does not conceive at all. If he does not conceive, he does not conceive of the non-existence of that of which he does not conceive. But if he does conceive, he certainly conceives of a being which cannot be even conceived not to exist. For if it could be conceived not to exist, it could be conceived to have a beginning and an end. But this is impossible.

He, then, who conceives of this being which cannot be even conceived not to exist; but he who conceives of this being does not conceive that it does not exist; else he conceives what is inconceivable. The non-existence, then, of that than which a greater cannot be conceived is inconceivable.

CHAPTER IV
THE DIFFERENCE BETWEEN THE POSSIBILITY OF CONCEIVING OF NON-EXISTENCE, AND UNDERSTANDING NON-EXISTENCE.

You say, moreover, that whereas I assert that this supreme being cannot be *conceived* not to exist, it might better be said that its nonexistence, or even the possibility of its non-existence, cannot be *understood*.

But it was more proper to say, it cannot be conceived. For if I had said that the object itself cannot be understood not to exist, possibly you yourself, who say that in accordance with the true meaning of the term what is unreal cannot be understood, would offer the objection that nothing which is can be understood not to be, for the non-existence of what exists is unreal: hence God would not be the only being of which it could be said, it is impossible to understand its non-existence. For thus one of those beings which most certainly exist can be understood not to exist in the same way in which certain other real objects can be understood not to exist.

But this objection, assuredly, cannot be urged against the term *conception,* if one considers the matter well. For although no objects which exist can be understood not to exist, yet all objects, except that which exists in the highest degree, can be conceived not to exist. For all those objects, and those alone, can be conceived not to exist, which have a beginning or end or composition of parts: also, as I have already said, whatever at any place or at any time does not exist as a whole.

That being alone, on the other hand, cannot be conceived not to exist, in which any conception discovers neither beginning nor end nor composition of parts, and which any conception finds always and everywhere as a whole.

Be assured, then, that you can conceive of your own non-existence, although you are most certain that you exist. I am surprised that you should have admitted that you are ignorant of this. For we conceive of the non-existence of many objects which we know to exist, and of the existence of which we know not to exist; not by forming the opinion that they so exist, but by imagining that they exist as we conceive of them.

And indeed, we can conceive of the non-existence of an object, although we know it to exist, because at the same time we can conceive of the former and know the latter. And we cannot conceive of the non-existence of an object, so long as we know it to exist, because we cannot conceive at the same time of existence and non-existence.

If, then, one will thus distinguish these two senses of this statement, he will understand that nothing, so long as it is known to exist, can be conceived not to exist; and that whatever exists, except that being than which a greater cannot be conceived, can be conceived not to exist, even when it is known to exist.

So, then, of God alone it can be said that it is impossible to conceive of his non-existence; and yet many objects, so long as they exist, in one sense cannot be conceived not to exist. But in what sense God is to be conceived not to exist, I think has been shown clearly enough in my book.

19

Proving God's Existence from Experience

Saint Thomas Aquinas (1225-1274)

. . . The existence of God can be proved in five ways. The first and more manifest way is the argument from motion. It is certain, and evident to our senses, that in the world some things are in motion. Now whatever is moved is moved by another, for nothing can be moved except it is in potentiality to that towards which it is moved; whereas a thing moves inasmuch as it is in act. For motion is nothing else than the reduction of something from potentiality to actuality. But nothing can be reduced from potentiality to actuality, except by something in a state of actuality. Thus that which is actually hot, as fire, makes wood, which is potentially hot, to be actually hot, and thereby moves and changes it. Now it is not possible that the same thing should be at once in actuality and potentiality in the same respect but only in different respects. For what is actually hot cannot

---

From *Introduction to St. Thomas Aquinas,* edited by Anton Pegis, Random House, Inc. (1948)

simultaneously be potentially hot; but it is simultaneously potentially cold. It is therefore impossible that in the same respect and in the same way a thing should be both mover and moved, i.e., that it should move itself. Therefore, whatever is moved must be moved by another. If that by which it is moved be itself moved, then this also must needs be moved by another, and that by another. But this cannot go on to infinity, because then there would be no first mover, and consequently, no other mover, seeing that subsequent movers move only inasmuch as they are moved by the first mover; as the staff moves only because it is moved by the hand. Therefore it is necessary to arrive at a first mover, moved by no other; and this everyone understands to be God.

The second way is from the nature of efficient cause. In the world of sensible things we find there is an order of efficient causes. There is no case known (neither is it, indeed, possible) in which a thing is found to be the efficient cause of itself; for so it would be prior to itself, which is impossible. Now in efficient causes it is not possible to go on to infinity, because in all efficient causes following in order, the first is the cause of the intermediate cause, and the intermediate is the cause of the ultimate cause, whether the intermediate cause be several, or one only. Now to take away the cause is to take away the effect. Therefore, if there be no first cause among efficient causes, there will be no ultimate, nor any intermediate, cause. But if in efficient causes it is possible to go on to infinity, there will be no first efficient cause, neither will there be an ultimate effect, nor any intermediate efficient causes; all of which is plainly false. Therefore it is necessary to admit a first efficient cause, to which everyone gives the name of God.

The third way is taken from possibility and necessity, and runs thus. We find in nature things that are possible to be and not to be, since they are found to be generated, and to be corrupted, and consequently, it is possible for them to be and not to be. But it is impossible for these always to exist, for that which can not-be at some time is not. Therefore, if everything can not-be, then at one time there was nothing in existence. Now if this were true, even now there would be nothing in existence, because that which does not exist begins to exist only through something already existing. Therefore, if at one time nothing was in existence, it would have been impossible for anything to have begun to exist; and thus even now nothing would be in existence—which is absurd. Therefore, not all beings are merely possible, but there must exist something the existence of which is necessary. But every necessary thing either has its necessity caused by another, or not. Now it is impossible to go on to infinity in necessary things which have their necessary caused by another, as has been already proved in regard to efficient causes. Therefore we cannot but admit the existence of some being having of itself its own necessity, and not receiving it from another, but rather causing in others their necessity. This all men speak of as God.

The fourth way is taken from the gradation to be found in things. Among beings there are some more and some less good, true, noble, and the like. But *more* and *less* are predicated of different things according as they resemble in their different ways something which is the maximum, as a thing is said to be hotter according as it more nearly resembles that which is hottest; so that there is something which is truest, something best, something noblest, and consequently, something which is most being, for those things that are greatest in truth are greatest in being, as it is written in *Metaph. ii*. Now the maximum in any genus is the cause of all in that genus, as fire, which is the maximum of heat, is the cause of all hot things, as is said in the same book. Therefore there must also be something which is to all beings the cause of their being, goodness, and every other perfection; and this we call God.

The fifth way is taken from the governance of the world. We see that things which lack knowledge, such as natural bodies, act for an end, and this is evident from their acting always, or nearly always, in the same way, so as to obtain the best result. Hence it is plain that they achieve their end, not fortuitously, but designedly. Now whatever lacks knowledge cannot move towards an end, unless it be directed by some being endowed with knowledge and intelligence; as the arrow is directed by the archer. Therefore some intelligent being exists by whom all natural things are directed to their end; and this being we call God.

20

Evil
and
the Proof
from Design

David Hume (1711–1776)

If a very limited intelligence whom we shall suppose utterly unacquainted with the universe were assured that it were the production of a very good, wise, and powerful Being, however finite, he would, from his conjectures, form *beforehand* a different notion of it from what we find it to be by experience; nor would he ever imagine, merely from these attributes of the cause of which he is informed, that the effect could be so full of vice and misery and disorder, as it appears in this life. Supposing now that this person were brought into the world, still assured that it was the workmanship of such a sublime and benevolent Being, he might, perhaps, be surprised at the disappointment, but would never retract his former belief if founded on any very solid argument, since such a limited intelligence must be sensible of his own blindness and ignorance, and must allow that there may be many solutions of those phenomena which will forever escape his com-

From David Hume, *Dialogues Concerning Natural Religion,* published 1779.

prehension. But supposing, which is the real case with regard to man, that this creature is not antecedently convinced of a supreme intelligence, benevolent, and powerful, but is left to gather such a belief from the appearances of things— this entirely alters the case, nor will he ever find any reason for such a conclusion. He may be fully convinced of the narrow limits of his understanding, but this will not help him in forming an inference concerning to goodness of superior powers, since he must form that inference from what he knows, not from what he is ignorant of. The more you exaggerate his weakness and ignorance, the more diffident you render him, and give him the greater suspicion that such subjects are beyond the reach of his faculties. You are obliged, therefore, to reason with him merely from the known phenomena, and to drop every arbitrary supposition or conjecture.

Did I show you a house or palace where there was not one apartment convenient or agreeable, where the windows, doors, fires, passages, stairs, and the whole economy of the building were the source of noise, confusion, fatigue, darkness, and the extremes of heat and cold, you would certainly blame the contrivance, without any further examination. The architect would in vain display his subtilty, and prove to you that, if this door or that window were altered, greater ills would ensue. What he says may be strictly true: the alteration of one particular, while the other parts of the building remain, may only augment the inconveniences. But still you would assert in general that, if the architect had had skill and good intentions, he might have formed such a plan of the whole, and might have adjusted the parts in such a manner as would have remedied all or most of these inconveniences. His ignorance, or even your own ignorance of such a plan, will never convince you of the impossibility of it. If you find any inconveniences and deformities in the building, you will always without entering into any detail, condemn the architect.

In short, I repeat the question: Is the world, considered in general and as it appears to us in this life, different from what a man or such a limited being would, *beforehand,* expect from a very powerful, wise, and benevolent Deity? It must be strange prejudice to assert the contrary. And from thence I conclude that, however consistent the world may be, allowing certain suppositions and conjectures with the idea of such a Deity, it can never afford us an inference concerning his existence. The consistency is not absolutely denied, only the inference. Conjectures, especially where infinity is excluded from the Divine attributes, may perhaps be sufficient to prove a consistency, but can never be foundations for any inference.

There seem to be *four* circumstances on which depend all or the greatest part of the ills that molest sensible creatures; and it is not impossible but all these circumstances may be necessary and unavoidable. We know so little beyond common life, or even of common life, that, with regard to the economy of a universe, there is no conjecture, however wild, which may not be just, nor any one, however plausible, which may not be erroneous. All that belongs to human understanding, in this deep ignorance and obscurity, is to be sceptical or at least cautious, and not to admit of any hypothesis whatever, much less of any which is supported by no appearance of probability. Now this I assert to be the case with regard to all the causes of evil and the circumstances on which it depends. None of them appear to human reason in the least degree necessary or unavoidable, nor can we suppose them such, without the utmost license of imagination.

The *first* circumstance which introduces evil is that contrivance or economy of the animal creation by which pains, as well as pleasures, are employed to excite all creatures to action, and make them vigilant in the great work of self-preservation. Now pleasure alone, in its various degrees, seems to human understanding sufficient for this purpose. All animals might be constantly in a state of enjoyment; but when urged by any of the necessities of nature, such as thirst, hunger, weariness instead of pain, they might feel a diminution of pleasure by which they might be promoted to seek that object which is necessary to their subsistence. Men pursue pleasure as eagerly as they avoid pain; at least, they might have been so constituted. It seems, therefore, plainly possible to carry on the business of life without any pain. Why then is any animal ever rendered susceptible of such a sensation? If animals can be free from it an hour, they might enjoy a perpetual exemption from it, and it required as particular a contrivance of their organs to produce that feeling as to endow them with sight, hearing, or any of the senses. Shall we conjecture that such a contrivance was necessary, without any appearance of reason, and shall we build on that conjecture as on the most certain truth?

But a capacity of pain would not alone produce pain were it not for the *second* circumstance, viz., the conducting of the world by general laws; and this seems nowise necessary to a very perfect Being. It is true, if everything were conducted by particular volitions, the course of nature would be perpetually broken, and no man could employ his reason in the conduct of life. But might not other particular volitions remedy this inconvenience? In short, might not the Deity exterminate all ill, wherever it were to be found, and produce all good, without any preparation or long progress of causes and effects?

Besides, we must consider that, according to the present economy of the world, the course of nature, though supposed exactly regular, yet to us appears not so, and many events are uncertain, and many disappoint our expectations. Health and sickness, calm and tempest, with an infinite number of other accidents whose causes are unknown and variable, have a great influence both on the fortunes of particular persons and on the prosperity of public societies; and indeed all human life, in a manner, depends on such accidents. A being, therefore, who knows the secret springs of the universe might easily, by particular volitions, turn all these accidents to the good of mankind and render the whole world happy, without discovering himself in any operation. A fleet whose purposes were salutary to society might always meet with a fair wind. Good princes enjoy sound health and long life. Persons born to power and authority be framed with good tempers and virtuous dispositions. A few such events as these, regularly and wisely conducted, would change the face of the world, and yet would no more seem to distrub the course of nature or confound human conduct than the present economy of things where the causes are secret and variable and compounded. Some small touches given to Caligula's brain in his infancy might have converted him into a Trajan. One wave, a little higher than the rest, by burying Caesar and his fortune in the bottom of the ocean, might have restored liberty to a considerable part of mankind. There may, for aught we know, be good reasons why Providence interposes not in this manner, but they are unknown to us; and, though the mere supposition that such reasons exist may be sufficient to *save* the conclusion concerning the Divine attributes, yet surely it can never be sufficient to *establish* that conclusion.

If everything in the universe be conducted by general laws, and if animals be rendered susceptible of pain, it scarcely seems possible but some ill must arise in the various shocks of matter and the various concurrence and opposition of general laws; but this ill would be very rare were it not for the *third* circumstance which I proposed to mention, viz., the great frugality with which all powers and faculties are distributed to every particular being. So well adjusted are the organs and capacities of all animals, and so well fitted to their preservation, that, as far as history or tradition reaches, there appears not to be any single species which has yet been extinguished in the universe. Every animal has the requisite endowments, but these endowments are bestowed with so scrupulous an economy that any considerable diminution must entirely destroy the creature. Wherever one power is increased, there is a proportional abatement in the others. Animals which excel in swiftness are commonly defective in force. Those which possess both are either imperfect in some of their senses or are oppressed with the most craving wants. The human species, whose chief excellence is reason and sagacity, is of all others the most necessitous, and the most deficient in bodily advantages, without clothes, without arms, without food, without lodging, without any convenience of life, except what they owe to their own skill and industry. In short, nature seems to have formed an exact calculation of the necessities of her creatures, and, like a *rigid master,* has afforded them little more powers or endownments than what are strictly sufficient to supply those necessities. An *indulgent* parent would have bestowed a large stock in order to guard against accidents, and secure the happiness and welfare of the creature in the most unfortunate concurrence of circumstances. Every course of life would not have been so surrounded with precipices that the least departure from the true path, by mistake or necessity, must involve us in misery and ruin. Some reserve, some fund, would have been provided to ensure happiness, nor would the powers and the necessities have been adjusted with so rigid an economy. The Author of nature is inconceivably powerful; his force is supposed great, if not altogether inexhaustible, nor is there any reason, as far as we can judge, to make him observe this strict frugality in his dealings with his creatures. It would have been better, were his power extremely limited, to have created fewer animals, and to have endowed these with more faculties for their happiness and preservation. A builder is never esteemed prudent who undertakes a plan beyond what his stock will enable him to finish.

In order to cure most of the ills of human life, I require not that man should have the wings of the eagle, the swiftness of the stag, the force of the ox, the arms of the lion, the scales of the crocodile or rhinoceros; much less do I demand the sagacity of an angel or cherubim. I am contented to take an increase in one single power or faculty of his soul. Let him be endowed with a greater propensity to industry and labour, a more vigorous spring and activity of mind, a more constant bent to business and application. Let the whole species possess naturally an equal diligence with that which many individuals are able to attain by habit and reflection, and the most beneficial consequences, without any allay of ill, is the immediate and necessary result of this endowment. Almost all the moral as well as natural evils of human life arise from idleness; and were our species, by the original constitution of their frame, exempt from this vice or infirmity, the perfect cultivation of land, the improvement of arts and manufactures, the exact execution of every office and duty, immediatey follow; and men at once may fully reach that state of society which is so imperfectly attained by the best regulated government. But as industry is a power, and the most valuable of any, nature seems determined, suitably to her usual maxims, to bestow it on men with a very sparing hand, and rather to punish him severly for his deficiency in it than to reward him for his attainments. She has so contrived his frame that nothing but the most violent necessity can oblige him to labour; and she employs all his other wants to overcome, at least in part, the want of diligence, and to endow him with some share of a faculty of which she has thought fit naturally to bereave him. Here our demands may be allowed very humble, and therefore the more reasonable. If we required the endowments of superior penetration and judgment, of a more delicate taste of beauty, of a nicer sensibility to benevolence and friendship, we might be told that we impiously pretend to break the order of nature, that we want to exalt ourselves into a higher rank of being, that the presents which we require, not being suitable to our state and condition, would only be pernicious to us. But it is hard, I dare to repeat it, it is hard that, being placed in a world so full of wants and necessities, where almost every being and element is either our foe or refuses its assistance . . . we should also have our own temper to struggle with, and should be deprived of that faculty which can alone fence against these multiplied evils.

The *fourth* circumstance whence arises the misery and ill of the universe is the inaccurate workmanship of all the springs and principles of the great machine of nature. It must be acknowledged that there are few parts of the universe which seem not to serve some purpose, and whose removal would not produce a visible defect and disorder in the whole. The parts hang all together, nor can one be touched without affecting the rest, in a greater or less degree. But at the same time, it must be observed that none of these parts or principles, however useful, are so accurately adjusted as to keep precisely within those bounds in which their utility consists; but they are, all of them, apt, on every occasion, to run into the one extreme or the other. One would imagine that this grand production had not received the last hand of the maker—so little finished is every part, and so coarse are the strokes with which it is executed. Thus the winds are requisite to convey the vapours along the surface of the globe, and to assist men in navigation; but how often, rising up to tempests and hurricanes, do they become pernicious?

Rains are necessary to nourish all the plants and animals of the earth; but how often are they defective? how often excessive? Heat is a requisite of all life and vegetation, but is not always found in the due proportion. On the mixture and secretion of the humours and juices of the body depend the health and prosperity of the animal; but the parts perform not regularly their proper function. What more useful than all the passions of the mind, ambition, vanity, love, anger? But how often do they break their bounds and cause the greatest convulsions in society? There is nothing so advantageous in the universe but what frequently becomes pernicious, by its excess or defect; nor has nature guarded, with the requisite accuracy, against all disorder or confusion. The irregularity is never perhaps so great as to destroy any species, but is often sufficient to involve the individuals in ruin and misery.

On the concurrence, then, of these *four* circumstances does all or the greatest part of natural evil depend. Were all living creatures incapable of pain, or were the world administered by particular volitions, evil never could have found access into the universe; and were animals endowed with a large stock of powers and faculties, beyond what strict necessity requires, or were the several springs and principles of the universe so accurately framed as to preserve always the just temperament and medium, there must have been very little ill in comparison of what we feel at present. What then shall we pronounce on this occasion? Shall we say that these circumstances are not necessary, and that they might easily have been altered in the contrivance of the universe? This decision seems too presumptuous for creatures so blind and ignorant. Let us be more modest in our conclusions. Let us allow that, if the goodness of the Deity (I mean a goodness like the human) could be established on any tolerable reasons *a priori*, these phenomena, however untoward, would not be sufficient to subvert that principle, but might easily, in some unknown manner, be reconcilable to it. But let us still assert that, as this goodness is not antecedently established but must be inferred from the phenomena, there can be no grounds for such an inference while there are so many ills in the universe, and while these ills might so easily have been remedied, as far as human understanding can be allowed to judge on such a subject. I am sceptic enough to allow that the bad appearances, notwithstanding all my reasonings, may be compatible with such attributes as you suppose, but surely they can never prove these attributes. Such a conclusion cannot result from scepticism, but must arise from the phenomena, and from our confidence in the reasonings which we deduce from these phenomena.

Look round this universe. What an immense profusion of beings, animated and organized, sensible and active! You admire this prodigious variety and fecundity. But inspect a little more narrowly these living existences, the only beings worth regarding. How hostile and destructive to each other! How insufficient all of them for their own happiness! How contemptible or odious to the spectator! The whole presents nothing but the idea of a blind nature, impregnated by a great vivifying principle, and pouring forth from her lap, without discernment or parental care, her maimed and abortive children!

21

Love of God as the Highest Good

Saint Augustine (354–430)

CHAPTER III
HAPPINESS IS IN THE ENJOYMENT OF MAN'S CHIEF GOOD. TWO CONDITIONS OF THE CHIEF GOOD: 1ST, NOTHING IS BETTER THAN IT; 2D, IT CANNOT BE LOST AGAINST THE WILL

How then, according to reason, ought man to live? We all certainly desire to live happily; and there is no human being but assents to this statement almost before it is made. But the title happy cannot, in my opinion, belong either to him who has not what he loves, whatever it may be, or to him who has what he loves if it is hurtful, or to him who does not love what he has, although it is good in perfection. For one who seeks what he cannot obtain suffers torture, and one

From *The Writings against the Manichaens and against the Donatists* (a Select Library of the Nicene and post-Nicene Fathers), First Series, ed. Philip Schaff, vol. 4 (New York: The Christian Literature Publishing Co., 1886–1890).

who has got what is not desirable is cheated, and one who does not seek for what is worth seeking for is diseased. Now in all these cases the mind cannot but be unhappy, and happiness and unhappiness cannot reside at the same time in one man: so in none of these cases can the man be happy. I find, then, a fourth case, where the happy life exists—when that which is man's chief good is both loved and possessed. For what do we call enjoyment but having at hand the objects of love? And no one can be happy who does not enjoy what is man's chief good, nor is there any one who enjoys this who is not happy. We must then have at hand our chief good, if we think of living happily.

We must now inquire what is man's chief good, which of course cannot be anything inferior to man himself. For whoever follows after what is inferior to himself, becomes himself inferior. But every man is bound to follow what is best. Wherefore mean's chief good is not inferior to man. Is it then something similar to man himself? It must be so, if there is nothing above man which he is capable of enjoying. But if we find something which is both superior to man, and can be possessed by the man who loves it, who can doubt that in seeking for happiness man should endeavor to reach that which is more excellent than the being who makes the endeavor. For if happiness consists in the enjoyment of a good than which there is nothing better, which we call the chief good, how can a man be properly called happy who has not yet attained to his chief good? or how can that be the chief good beyond which something better remains for us to arrive at? Such, then, being the chief good, it must be something which cannot be lost against the will. For no one can feel confident regarding a good which he knows can be taken from him, although he wishes to keep and cherish it. But if a man feels no confidence regarding the good which he enjoys, how can he be happy while in such fear of losing it?

CHAPTER IV
MAN—WHAT?

Let us then see what is better than man. This must necessarily be hard to find, unless we first ask and examine what man is. I am not now called upon to give a definition of man. The question here seems to me to be—since almost all agree, or at least, which is enough, those I have now to do with are of the same opinion with me, that we are made up of soul and body—What is man? Is he both of these? or is he the body only, or the soul only? For although the things are two, soul and body, and although neither without the other could be called man (for the body would not be man without the soul, nor again would the soul be man if there were not a body animated by it), still it is possible that one of these may be held to be man, and may be called so. What then do we call man? Is he soul and body, as in a double harness, or like a centaur? Or do we mean the body only, as being in the service of the soul which rules it, as the word lamp denotes not the light and the case together, but only the case, yet it is on account of the light that it is so called? Or do we mean only the mind, and that on account of the body which it rules, as horseman means not the man and the horse, but the man only, and that as employed in ruling the horse? This dispute is not easy to settle; or, if the proof is plain, the statement requires time. This is an expenditure of time and strength which we need not incur. For whether the name man belongs to both, or only to the soul, the chief good of man is not the chief good of the body; but what is the chief good either of both soul and body, or of the soul only, that is man's chief good.

CHAPTER V
MAN'S CHIEF GOOD IS NOT THE CHIEF GOOD OF THE BODY ONLY, BUT THE CHIEF GOOD OF THE SOUL

Now if we ask what is the chief good of the body, reason obliges us to admit that it is that by means of which the body comes to be in its best state. But of all the things which invigorate the body, there is nothing better or greater than the soul. The chief good of the body, then, is not bodily pleasure, not absence of pain, not strength, not beauty, not swiftness, or whatever else is usually reckoned among the goods of the body, but simply the soul. For all the things mentioned the soul supplies to the body by its presence, and, what is above them all, life. Hence I conclude that the soul is not the chief good of man, whether we give the name of man to soul and body together, or to the soul alone. For as, according to reason, the chief good of the body is that which is better than the body and from which the body receives vigor and life, so whether the soul itself is man, or soul and body both, we must discover whether there is anything which goes before the soul itself, in following which the soul comes to the perfection of good of which it is capable in its own kind. If such a thing can be found, all uncertainty must be at an end, and we must pronounce this to be really and truly the chief good of man.

If, again, the body is man, it must be admitted that the soul is the chief good of man. But clearly, when we treat of morals—when we inquire what manner of life must be held in order to obtain happiness—it is not the body to which the precepts are addressed, it is not bodily discipline which we discuss. In short, the observance of good *customs* belongs to that part of us which inquires and learns, which are the prerogatives of the soul; so, when we speak of attaining to virtue, the question does not regard the body. But if it follows, as it does, that the body which is ruled over by a soul possessed of virtue is ruled both better and more honorably, and is in its greatest perfection in consequence of the perfection of the soul which rightfully governs it, that which gives perfection to the soul will be man's chief good, though we call the body man. For if my coachman, in obedience to me, feeds and drives the horses he has charge of in the most satisfactory manner, himself enjoying the more of my bounty in proportion to his good conduct, can any one deny that the good condition of the horses, as well as that of the coachman, is due to me? So the question seems to me to be not, whether soul and body is man, or the soul only, or the body only, but what gives perfection to the soul; for when this is obtained, a man cannot but be either perfect, or as least much better than in the absence of this one thing. . . .

CHAPTER VIII
GOD IS THE CHIEF GOOD, WHOM WE ARE TO SEEK AFTER WITH SUPREME AFFECTION

Let us see how the Lord Himself in the gospel has taught us to live; how, too, Paul the apostle—for the Manichaeans dare not reject these Scriptures. Let us hear, O Christ, what chief end Thou dost prescribe to us; and that is evidently the chief end after which we are told to strive with supreme affection. "Thou shalt love," He says, "the Lord thy God." Tell me also, I pray Thee, what must be the measure of love; for I fear lest the desire enkindled in my heart should either exceed or come short in fervor. "With all thy heart," He says. Nor is that enough. "With all they soul." Nor is it enough yet. "With all thy mind." What do you wish more? I might, perhaps, wish more if I could see the possibility of more. What does Paul say on this? "We know," he says, "that all things issue in good to them that love God." Let him, too, say what is the measure of love. "Who then," he says, "shall separate us from the love of Christ? shall tribulation, or distress, or persecution, or famine, or nakedness, or peril, or the sword?" We have heard, then, what and how much we must love; this we must strive after, and to this we must refer all our plans. The perfection of all our good things and our perfect good is God. We must neither come short of this nor go beyond it: the one is dangerous, the other impossible. . . .

CHAPTER V
THAT IN ALL NATURES, OF EVERY KIND AND RANK, GOD IS GLORIFIED

All natures, then, inasmuch as they are, and have therefore a rank and species of their own, and a kind of internal harmony, are certainly good. And when they are in the places assigned to them by the order of their nature, they preserve such being as they have received. And those things which have received everlasting being, are altered for better or for worse, so as to suit the wants and notions of those things to which the Creator's law has made them subservient; and thus they tend in the divine providence to that end which is embraced in the general scheme of the government of the universe. So that, though the corruption of transitory and perishable things brings them to utter destruction, it does not prevent their producing that which was designed to be their result. And this being so, God, who supremely is, and who therefore created every being which has not supreme existence (for that which was made of nothing could not be equal to Him, and indeed could not be at all had He not made it), is not to be found fault with on account of the creature's faults, but is to be praised in view of the natures He has made. . . .

CHAPTER VII
THAT WE OUGHT NOT TO EXPECT TO FIND ANY EFFICIENT CAUSE OF THE EVIL WILL

Let no one, therefore, look for an efficient cause of the evil will; for it is not efficient, but deficient, as the will itself is not an effecting of something, but a defect. For defection from that which supremely is, to that which has less of being—this is to begin to have an evil will. Now, to seek to discover the causes of these defections—causes, as I have said, not efficient, but deficient—is as if someone sought to see darkness, or hear silence. Yet both of these are known by us, and the former by means only of the eye, the latter only by the ear; but not by their positive actuality, but by their want of it. Let no one, then seek to know from me what I know that I do not know; unless he perhaps wishes to learn to be ignorant of that of which all we know is, that it cannot be known. For those things which are known not by their actuality, but by their want of it, are known, if our expression may be allowed and understood, by not knowing them, that by knowing them they may be not known. For when the eyesight surveys objects that strike the sense, it nowhere sees darkness but where it begins not to see. And so no other sense but the ear can perceive silence, and yet it is only perceived by not hearing. Thus, too, our mind perceives intelligible forms by understanding them; but when they are deficient, it knows them by not knowing them; for who can understand defects?

CHAPTER VIII
OF THE MISDIRECTED LOVE WHEREBY THE WILL FELL AWAY FROM THE IMMUTABLE TO THE MUTABLE GOOD

This I do know, that the nature of God can never, nowhere, nowise be defective, and that natures made of nothing can. These latter, however, the more being they have, and the more good they do (for then they do something positive), the more they have efficient causes; but in so far as they are defective in being, and consequently do evil (for then what is their work but vanity?) they have deficient causes. And I know likewise, that the will could not become evil, were it unwilling to become so; and therefore its failings are justly punished, being not necessary, but voluntary. For its defections are not to evil things, but are themselves evil; that is to say, are not towards things that are naturally and in themselves evil, but the defection of the will is evil, because it is contrary to the order of nature, and an abandonment of that which has supreme being for that which has less. For avarice is not a fault inherent in gold, but in the man who inordinately loves gold, to the detriment of justice, which ought to be held in incomparably higher regard than gold. Neither is luxury the fault of lovely and charming objects, but of the heart that inordinately loves sensual pleasures, to the neglect of temperance, which attaches us to objects more lovely in their spirituality, and more delectable by their incorruptibility. Nor yet is boasting the fault of human praise but of the soul that is inordinately fond of the applause of men, and that makes light of the voice of conscience. Pride, too, is not the fault of him who delegates power, nor of power itself, but of the soul that is inordinately enamored of its own power, and despises the more just dominion of a higher authority. Consequently he who inordinately loves the good which any nature possesses, even though he obtain it, himself becomes evil in the good, and wretched because deprived of a greater good. . . .

CHAPTER XII
THAT EVEN THE FIERCENESS OF WAR AND ALL THE
DISQUIETUDE OF MEN MAKE TOWARDS THIS ONE END
OF PEACE, WHICH EVERY NATURE DESIRES

Whoever gives even moderate attention to human affairs and to our common nature, will recognize that if there is no man who does not wish to be joyful, neither is there any one who does not wish to have peace. For even they who make war desire nothing but victory—desire, that is to say, to attain to peace with glory. For what else is victory than the conquest of those who resist us? and when this is done there is peace. It is therefore with the desire for peace that wars are waged, even by those who take pleasure in exercising their warlike nature in command and battle. And hence it is obvious that peace is the end sought for by war. For every man seeks peace by waging war, but no man seeks war by making peace. For even they who intentionally interrupt the peace in which they are living have no hatred of peace, but only wish it changed into a peace that suits them better. They do not, therefore, wish to have no peace, but only one more to their mind. And in the case of sedition, when men have separated themselves from the community, they yet do not effect what they wish, unless they maintain some kind of peace with their fellow-conspirators. And therefore even robbers take care to maintain peace with their comrades, that they may with greater effect and greater safety invade the peace of other men. And if an individual happen to be of such unrivalled strength, and to be so jealous of partnership, that he trusts himself with no comrades, but makes his own plots, and commits depredations and murders on his own account, yet he maintains some shadow of peace with such persons as he is unable to kill, and from whom he wishes to conceal his deeds. In his own home, too, he makes it his aim to be at peace with his wife and children, and any other members of his household; for unquestionably their prompt obedience to his every look is a source of pleasure to him. And if this be not rendered, he is angry, he chides and punishes; and even by this storm he secures the calm peace of his own home, as occasion demands. For he sees that peace cannot be maintained unless all the members of the same domestic circle be subject to one head, such as he himself is in his own house. And therefore if a city or nation offered to submit itself to him, to serve him in the same style as he had made his household serve him, he would no longer lurk in a brigand's hiding-places, but lift his head in open day as a king, though the same coveteousness and wickedness should remain in him. And thus all men desire to have peace with their own circle whom they wish to govern as suits themselves. For even those whom they make war against they wish to make their own, and impose on them the laws of their own peace.

But let us suppose a man such as poetry and mythology speak of—a man so insociable and savage as to be called rather a semi-man than a man. Although, then, his kingdom was the solitude of a dreary cave, and he himself was so singularly bad-hearted that he was named Kaxos, which is the Greek word for *bad;* though he had no wife to soothe him with endearing talk, no children to play with, no sons to do his bidding, no friend to enliven him with intercourse, not even his father Vulcan (though in one respect he was happier than his father, not having begotten a monster like himself); although he gave to no man, but took as he wished whatever he could, from whomsoever he could, when he could; yet in that solitary den, the floor of which, as Virgil says, was always reeking with recent slaughter, there was nothing else than peace sought, a peace in which no one should molest him, or disquiet him with any assault or alarm. With his own body he desired to be at peace, and he was satisfied only in proportion as he had this peace. For he ruled his members, and they obeyed him; and for the sake of pacifying his mortal nature, which rebelled when it needed anything, and of allaying the sedition of hunger which threatened to banish the soul from the body, he made forays, slew, and devoured, but used the ferocity and savageness he displayed in these actions only for the preservation of his own life's peace. So that, had he been willing to make with other men the same peace which he made with himself in his own cave, he would neither have been called bad, nor a monster, nor a semi-man. Or if the appearance of his body and his vomiting smoky fires frightened men from having any dealings with him, perhaps his fierce ways arose not from a desire to do mischief, but from the necessity of finding a living. But he may have had no existence, or, at least, he was not such as the poets fancifully describe him, for they had to exalt Hercules, and did so at the expense of Cacus. It is better, then, to believe that such a man or semi-man never existed, and that this, in common with many other fancies of the poets, is mere fiction. For the most savage animals (and he is said to have been almost a wild beast) encompass their own species with a ring of protecting peace. They co-habit, beget, produce, suckle, and bring up their young, though very many of them are not gregarious, but solitary—not like sheep, deer, pigeons, starlings, bees, but such as lions, foxes, eagles, bats. For what tigress does not gently purr over her cubs, and lay aside her ferocity to fondle them? What kite, solitary as he is when circling over his prey, does not seek a mate, build a nest, hatch the eggs, bring up the young birds, and maintain with the mother of his family as peaceful a domestic alliance as he can? How much more powerfully do the laws of man's nature move him to hold fellowship and maintain peace with all men so far as in him lies, since even wicked men wage war to maintain the peace of their own circle, and wish that, if possible, all men belonged to them, that all men and things might serve but one head, and might, either through love or fear, yield themselves to peace with him! It is thus that pride in its perversity apes God. It abhors equality with other men under Him; but, instead of His rule, it seeks to impose a rule of its own upon its equals. It abhors, that is to say, the just peace of God, and loves its own unjust peace; but it cannot help loving peace of one kind or other. For there is no vice so clean contrary to nature that it obliterates even the faintest traces of nature.

He, then, who prefers what is right to what is wrong, and what is well-ordered to what is perverted, sees that the peace of unjust men is not worthy to be called peace in comparison with the peace of the just. And yet even what is perverted must of necessity be in harmony with, and in dependence on, and in some part of the order of things, for otherwise it would have no existence at all. Suppose a man hangs with his head downwards, this is certainly a perverted attitude of body and arrangement of its members; for that which nature requires to be above is beneath, and *vice versa*. This perversity disturbs the peace of the body, and is therefore painful. Nevertheless the spirit is at peace with its body, and labors for its preservation, and hence the suffering; but if it is banished from the body by its pains, then, so long as the bodily framework holds together, there is in the remains a kind of peace among the members, and hence the body remains suspended. And inasmuch as the earthly body tends towards the earth, and rests on the bond by which it is suspended, it tends thus to its natural peace, and the voice of its own weight demands a place for it to rest; and though now lifeless and without feeling, it does not fall from the peace that is natural to its place in creation, whether it already has it, or is tending towards it. For if you apply embalming preparations to prevent the bodily frame from mouldering and dissolving, a kind of peace still unites part to part, and keeps the whole body in a suitable place on the earth—in other words, in a place that is at peace with the body. If, on the other hand, the body receive no such care, but be left to the natural course, it is disturbed by exhalations that do not harmonize with one another, and that offend our senses; for it is this which is perceived in putrefaction until it is assimilated to the elements of the world, and particle by particle enters into peace with them. Yet throughout this process the laws of the most high Creator and Governor are strictly observed, for it is by Him the peace of the universe is administered. For although minute animals are produced from the carcass of a larger animal, all these little atoms, by the law of the same Creator, serve the animals they belong to in peace. And although the flesh of dead animals be eaten by others, no matter where it be carried, nor what it be brought into contact with, nor what it be converted and changed into, it still is ruled by the same laws which pervade all things for the conservation of every mortal race, and which bring things that fit one another into harmony.

primitive, compares the definition with the variety of known facts and by means of the comparison sets out to determine just what the definition means. I think he will be struck by three facts that reduce the terms of the definition to such a low common denominator that little meaning is left.

He will note that the "unseen powers" referred to have been conceived in a multitude of incompatible ways. Eliminating the differences, nothing is left beyond the bare reference to something unseen and powerful. This has been conceived as the vague and undefined Mana of the Melanesians; the Kami of primitive Shintoism; the fetish of the Africans; spirits, having some human properties, that pervade natural places and animate natural forces; the ultimate and impersonal principle of Buddhism; the unmoved mover of Greek thought; the gods and semidivine heroes of the Greek and Roman Pantheons; the personal and loving Providence of Christianity, omnipotent, and limited by a corresponding evil power; the arbitrary Will of Moslemism; the supreme legislator and judge of deism. And these are but a few of the outstanding varieties of ways in which the invisible power has been conceived.

There is no greater similarity in the ways in which obedience and reverence have been expressed. There has been worship of animals, of ghosts, of ancestors, phallic worship, as well as of a Being of dread power and of love and wisdom. Reverence has been expressed in the human sacrifices of the Peruvians and Aztecs; the sexual orgies of some Oriental religions; exorcisms and ablutions; the offering of the humble and contrite mind of the Hebrew prophet, the elaborate rituals of the Greek and Roman Churches. Not even sacrifice has been uniform; it is highly sublimated in Protestant denominations and in Moslemism. Where it has existed it has taken all kinds of forms and been directed to a great variety of powers and spirits. It has been used for expiation, for propitiation and for buying special favors. There is no conceivable purpose for which rites have not been employed.

Finally, there is no discernible unity in the moral motivations appealed to and utilized. They have been as far apart as fear of lasting torture, hope of enduring bliss in which sexual enjoyment has sometimes been a conspicuous element; mortification of the flesh and extreme asceticism; prostitution and chastity; wars to extirpate the unbeliever; persecution to convert or punish the unbeliever, and philanthropic zeal; servile acceptance of imposed dogma, along with brotherly love and aspiration for a reign of justice among men.

I have, of course, mentioned only a sparse number of the facts which fill volumes in any well-stocked library. It may be asked by those who do not like to look upon the darker side of the history of religions why the darker facts should be brought up. We all know that civilized man has a background of bestiality and superstition and that these elements are still with us. Indeed, have not some religions, including the most influential forms of Christianity, taught that the heart of man is totally corrupt? How could the course of religion in its entire sweep not be marked by practices that are shameful in their cruelty and lustfulness, and by beliefs that are degraded and intellectually incredible? What else than what we find could be expected, in the case of people having little knowl-

22

Religion versus the Religious

John Dewey (1859–1952)

The heart of my point . . . is that there is a difference between religion, *a* religion, and the religious; between anything that may be denoted by a noun substantive and the quality of experience that is designated by an adjective. It is not easy to find a definition of religion in the substantive sense that wins general acceptance. However, in the *Oxford Dictionary* I find the following: "Recognition on the part of man of some unseen higher power as having control of his destiny and as being entitled to obedience, reverence and worship."

This particular definition is less explicit in assertion of the supernatural character of the higher unseen power than are others that might be cited. It is, however, surcharged with implications having their source in ideas connected with the belief in the supernatural, characteristic of historic religions. Let us suppose that one familiar with the history of religions, including those called

From John Dewey, *A Common Faith*, Yale University Press, New Haven, 1960. By permission.

primitive, compares the definition with the variety of known facts and by means of the comparison sets out to determine just what the definition means. I think he will be struck by three facts that reduce the terms of the definition to such a low common denominator that little meaning is left.

He will note that the "unseen powers" referred to have been conceived in a multitude of incompatible ways. Eliminating the differences, nothing is left beyond the bare reference to something unseen and powerful. This has been conceived as the vague and undefined Mana of the Melanesians; the Kami of primitive Shintoism; the fetish of the Africans; spirits, having some human properties, that pervade natural places and animate natural forces; the ultimate and impersonal principle of Buddhism; the unmoved mover of Greek thought; the gods and semidivine heroes of the Greek and Roman Pantheons; the personal and loving Providence of Christianity, omnipotent, and limited by a corresponding evil power; the arbitrary Will of Moslemism; the supreme legislator and judge of deism. And these are but a few of the outstanding varieties of ways in which the invisible power has been conceived.

There is no greater similarity in the ways in which obedience and reverence have been expressed. There has been worship of animals, of ghosts, of ancestors, phallic worship, as well as of a Being of dread power and of love and wisdom. Reverence has been expressed in the human sacrifices of the Peruvians and Aztecs; the sexual orgies of some Oriental religions; exorcisms and ablutions; the offering of the humble and contrite mind of the Hebrew prophet, the elaborate rituals of the Greek and Roman Churches. Not even sacrifice has been uniform; it is highly sublimated in Protestant denominations and in Moslemism. Where it has existed it has taken all kinds of forms and been directed to a great variety of powers and spirits. It has been used for expiation, for propitiation and for buying special favors. There is no conceivable purpose for which rites have not been employed.

Finally, there is no discernible unity in the moral motivations appealed to and utilized. They have been as far apart as fear of lasting torture, hope of enduring bliss in which sexual enjoyment has sometimes been a conspicuous element; mortification of the flesh and extreme asceticism; prostitution and chastity; wars to extirpate the unbeliever; persecution to convert or punish the unbeliever, and philanthropic zeal; servile acceptance of imposed dogma, along with brotherly love and aspiration for a reign of justice among men.

I have, of course, mentioned only a sparse number of the facts which fill volumes in any well-stocked library. It may be asked by those who do not like to look upon the darker side of the history of religions why the darker facts should be brought up. We all know that civilized man has a background of bestiality and superstition and that these elements are still with us. Indeed, have not some religions, including the most influential forms of Christianity, taught that the heart of man is totally corrupt? How could the course of religion in its entire sweep not be marked by practices that are shameful in their cruelty and lustfulness, and by beliefs that are degraded and intellectually incredible? What else than what we find could be expected, in the case of people having little knowla domestic alliance as he can? How much more powerfully do the laws of man's nature move him to hold fellowship and maintain peace with all men so far as in him lies, since even wicked men wage war to maintain the peace of their own circle, and wish that, if possible, all men belonged to them, that all men and things might serve but one head, and might, either through love or fear, yield themselves to peace with him! It is thus that pride in its perversity apes God. It abhors equality with other men under Him; but, instead of His rule, it seeks to impose a rule of its own upon its equals. It abhors, that is to say, the just peace of God, and loves its own unjust peace; but it cannot help loving peace of one kind or other. For there is no vice so clean contrary to nature that it obliterates even the faintest traces of nature.

He, then, who prefers what is right to what is wrong, and what is well-ordered to what is perverted, sees that the peace of unjust men is not worthy to be called peace in comparison with the peace of the just. And yet even what is perverted must of necessity be in harmony with, and in dependence on, and in some part of the order of things, for otherwise it would have no existence at all. Suppose a man hangs with his head downwards, this is certainly a perverted attitude of body and arrangement of its members; for that which nature requires to be above is beneath, and *vice versa*. This perversity disturbs the peace of the body, and is therefore painful. Nevertheless the spirit is at peace with its body, and labors for its preservation, and hence the suffering; but if it is banished from the body by its pains, then, so long as the bodily framework holds together, there is in the remains a kind of peace among the members, and hence the body remains suspended. And inasmuch as the earthly body tends towards the earth, and rests on the bond by which it is suspended, it tends thus to its natural peace, and the voice of its own weight demands a place for it to rest; and though now lifeless and without feeling, it does not fall from the peace that is natural to its place in creation, whether it already has it, or is tending towards it. For if you apply embalming preparations to prevent the bodily frame from mouldering and dissolving, a kind of peace still unites part to part, and keeps the whole body in a suitable place on the earth—in other words, in a place that is at peace with the body. If, on the other hand, the body receive no such care, but be left to the natural course, it is disturbed by exhalations that do not harmonize with one another, and that offend our senses; for it is this which is perceived in putrefaction until it is assimilated to the elements of the world, and particle by particle enters into peace with them. Yet throughout this process the laws of the most high Creator and Governor are strictly observed, for it is by Him the peace of the universe is administered. For although minute animals are produced from the carcass of a larger animal, all these little atoms, by the law of the same Creator, serve the animals they belong to in peace. And although the flesh of dead animals be eaten by others, no matter where it be carried, nor what it be brought into contact with, nor what it be converted and changed into, it still is ruled by the same laws which pervade all things for the conservation of every mortal race, and which bring things that fit one another into harmony.

CHAPTER XIII
OF THE UNIVERSAL PEACE
WHICH THE LAW OF NATURE PRESERVES
THROUGH ALL DISTURBANCES,
AND BY WHICH EVERY ONE REACHES HIS DESERT
IN A WAY REGULATED BY THE JUST JUDGE

The peace of the body then consists in the duly proportioned arrangement of its parts. The peace of the irrational soul is the harmonious repose of the appetites, and that of the rational soul the harmony of knowledge and action. The peace of body and soul is the well-ordered and harmonious life and health of the living creature. Peace between man and God is the well-ordered obedience of faith to eternal law. Peace between man and man is well-ordered concord. Domestic peace is the well-ordered concord between those of the family who rule and those who obey. Civil peace is a similar concord among the citizens. The peace of the celestial city is the perfectly ordered and harmonious enjoyment of God, and of one another in God. The peace of all things is the tranquillity of order. Order is the distribution which allots things equal and unequal, each to its own place. And hence, though the miserable, in so far as they are such, do certainly not enjoy peace, but are severed from that tranquillity of order in which there is no disturbance, nevertheless, inasmuch as they are deservedly and justly miserable, they are by their very misery connected with order. They are not, indeed, conjoined with the blessed, but they are disjoined from them by the law of order. And though they are disquieted, their circumstances are notwithstanding adjusted to them, and consequently they have some tranquillity of order, and therefore some peace. But they are wretched because, although not wholly miserable, they are not in that place where any mixture of misery is impossible. They would, however, be more wretched if they had not that peace which arises from being in harmony with the natural order of things. When they suffer, their peace is in so far disturbed; but their peace continues in so far as they do not suffer, and in so far as their nature continues to exist. As, then, there may be life without pain, while there cannot be pain without some kind of life, so there may be peace without war, but there cannot be war without some kind of peace, because war supposes the existence of some natures to wage it, and these natures cannot exist without peace of one kind or other.

And therefore there is a nature in which evil does not or even cannot exist; but there cannot be a nature in which there is no good. Hence not even the nature of the devil himself is evil, in so far as it is nature, but it was made evil by being perverted. . . .

edge and no secure method of knowing; with primitive institutions, and with so little control of natural forces that they lived in a constant state of fear?

I gladly admit that historic religions have been relative to the conditions of social culture in which peoples lived. Indeed, what I am concerned with is to press home the logic of this method of disposal of outgrown traits of past religions. Beliefs and practices in a religion that now prevails are by this logic relative to the present state of culture. If so much flexibility has obtained in the past regarding an unseen power, the way it affects human destiny, and the attitudes we are to take toward it, why should it be assumed that change in conception and action has now come to an end? The logic involved in getting rid of inconvenient aspects of past religions compels us to inquire how much in religions now accepted are survivals from outgrown cultures. It compels us to ask what conception of unseen powers and our relations to them would be consonant with the best achievements and aspirations of the present. It demands that in imagination we wipe the slate clean and start afresh by asking what would be the idea of the unseen, of the manner of its control over us and the ways in which reverence and obedience would be manifested, if whatever is basically religious in experience had the opportunity to express itself free from all historic encumbrances.

So we return to the elements of the definition that has been given. What boots it to accept, in defense of the universality of religion, a definition that applies equally to the most savage and degraded beliefs and practices that have related to unseen powers and to noble ideals of a religion having the greatest share of moral content? There are two points involved. One of them is that there is nothing left worth preserving in the notions of unseen powers, controlling human destiny to which obedience, reverence and worship are due, if we glide silently over the nature that has been attributed to the powers, the radically diverse ways in which they have been supposed to control human destiny, and in which submission and awe have been manifested. The other point is that when we begin to select, to choose, and say that some present ways of thinking about the unseen powers are better than others; that the reverence shown by a free and self-respecting human being is better than the servile obedience rendered to an arbitrary power by frightened men; that we should believe that control of human destiny is exercised by a wise and loving spirit rather than by madcap ghosts or sheer force—when I say, we begin to choose, we have entered upon a road that has not yet come to an end. We have reached a point that invites us to proceed farther.

For we are forced to acknowledge that concretely there is no such thing as religion in the singular. There is only a multitude of religions. "Religion" is a strictly collective term and the collection it stands for is not even of the kind illustrated in textbooks of logic. It has not the unity of a regiment or assembly but that of any miscellaneous aggregate. Attempts to prove the universality prove too much or too little. It is probable that religions have been universal in the sense that all the peoples we know anything about have had *a* religion. But the differences among them are so great and so shocking that any common element that can be extracted is meaningless. The idea that religion is universal proves too little in that the older apologists for Christianity seem to have been better advised than some modern ones in condemning every religion but one as an impostor, as at bottom some kind of demon worship or at any rate a superstitious figment. Choice among religions is imperative, and the necessity for choice leaves nothing of any force in the argument from universality. Moreover, when once we enter upon the road of choice, there is at once presented a possibility not yet generally realized.

For the historic increase of the ethical and ideal content of religions suggests that the process of purification may be carried further. It indicates that further choice is imminent in which certain values and functions in experience may be selected. This possibility is what I had in mind in speaking of the difference between the religious and a religion. I am not proposing a religion, but rather the emancipation of elements and outlooks that may be called religious. For the moment we have a religion, whether that of the Sioux Indian or of Judaism or of Christianity, that moment the ideal factors in experience that may be called religious take on a load that is not inherent in them, a load of current beliefs and of institutional practices that are irrelevant to them.

I can illustrate what I mean by a common phenomenon in contemporary life. It is widely supposed that a person who does not accept any religion is thereby shown to be a non-religious person. Yet it is conceivable that the present depression in religion is closely connected with the fact that religions now prevent, because of their weight of historic encumbrances, the religious quality of experience from coming to consciousness and finding the expression that is appropriate to present conditions, intellectual and moral. I believe that such is the case. I believe that many persons are so repelled from what exists as a religion by its intellectual and moral implications, that they are not even aware of attitudes in themselves that if they came to fruition would be genuinely religious. I hope that this remark may help make clear what I mean by the distinction between "religion" as a noun substantive and "religious" as adjectival.

To be somewhat more explicit, a religion (and as I have just said there is no such thing as religion in general) always signifies a special body of beliefs and practices having some kind of institutional organization, loose or tight. In contrast, the adjective "religious" denotes nothing in the way of a specifiable entity, either institutional or as a system of beliefs. It does not denote anything to which one can specifically point as one can point to this and that historic religion or existing church. For it does not denote anything that can exist by itself or that can be organized into a particular and distinctive form of existence. It denotes attitudes that may be taken toward every object and every proposed end or ideal.

Before, however, I develop my suggestion that realization of the distinction just made would operate to emancipate the religious quality from encumbrances that now smother or limit it, I must refer to a position that in some respects is similar in words to the position I have taken, but that in fact is a whole world removed from it. I have several times used the phrase "religious elements of experience." Now at present there is much talk, especially in liberal circles, of religious experience as vouching for the authenticity of certain beliefs and the desirability of certain practices, such as particular forms of prayer and worship. It is even asserted that religious experience is the ultimate basis of religion itself. The gulf between this position and that which I have taken is what I am now concerned to point out.

Those who hold to the notion that there is a definite kind of experience which is itself religious, by that very fact make out of its something specific, as a kind of experience that is marked off from experience as aesthetic, scientific, moral, political; from experience as companionship and friendship. But "religious" as a quality of experience signifies something that may belong to all these experiences. It is the polar opposite of some type of experience that can exist by itself. The distinction comes out clearly when it is noted that the concept of this distinct kind of experience is used to validate a belief in some special kind of object and also to justify some special kind of practice.

For there are many religionists who are now dissatisfied with the older "proofs" of the existence of God, those that go by the name of ontological, cosmological and teleological. The cause of the dissatisfaction is perhaps not so much the arguments that Kant used to show the insufficiency of these alleged proofs, as it is the growing feeling that they are too formal to offer any support to religion in action. Anyway, the dissatisfaction exists. Moreover, these religionists are moved by the rise of the experimental method in other fields. What is more natural and proper, accordingly, than that they should affirm they are just as good empiricists as anybody else—indeed, as good as the scientists themselves? As the latter rely upon certain kinds of experience to prove the existence of certain kinds of objects, so the religionists rely upon a certain kind of experience to prove the existence of the object of religion, especially the supreme object, God.

The discussion may be made more definite by introducing, at this point, a particular illustration of this type of reasoning. A writer says: "I broke down from overwork and soon came to the verge of nervous prostration. One morning after a long and sleepless night . . . I resolved to stop drawing upon myself so continuously and begin drawing upon God. I determined to set apart a quiet time every day in which I could relate my life to its ultimate source, regain the consciousness that in God I live, move and have my being. That was thirty years ago. Since then I have had literally not one hour of darkness or despair."

This is an impressive record. I do not doubt its authenticity nor that of the experience related. It illustrates a religious aspect of experience. But it illustrates also the use of that quality to carry a superimposed load of a particular religion. For having been brought up in the Christian religion, its subject interprets it in the terms of the personal God characteristic of that religion. Taoists, Buddhists, Moslems, persons of no religion including those who reject all supernatural influence and power, have had experiences similar in their effect. Yet another author commenting upon the passage says: "The religious expert can be more sure that this God exists than he can of either the cosmological God of speculative surmise or the Christlike God involved in the validity of moral optimism," and goes on to add that such experiences "mean that God the savior, the power that gives victory over sin on certain conditions that man can fulfill, is an existent, accessible and scientifically knowable reality." It should be clear that this inference is sound only if the conditions, of whatever sort, that produce the effect are called "God." But most readers will take the inference to mean that the existence of a particular Being, of the type called "God" in the Christian religion, is proved by a method akin to that of experimental science.

In reality, the only thing that can be said to be "proved" is the existence of some complex of conditions that have operated to effect an adjustment in life, an orientation, that brings with it a sense of security and peace. The particular interpretation given to this complex of conditions is not inherent in the experience itself. It is derived from the culture with which a particular person has been imbued. A fatalist will give one name to it; a Christian Scientist another, and the one who rejects all supernatural being still another. The determining factor in the interpretation of the experience is the particular doctrinal apparatus into which a person has been inducted. The emotional deposit connected with prior teaching floods the whole situation. It may readily confer upon the experience such a peculiarly sacred preciousness that all inquiry into its causation is barred. The stable outcome is so invaluable that the cause to which it is referred is usually nothing but a reduplication of the thing that has occurred, plus some name that has acquired a deeply emotional quality.

The intent of this discussion is not to deny the genuineness of the result nor its importance in life. It is not, save incidentally, to point out the possibility of a purely naturalistic explanation of the event. My purpose is to indicate what happens when religious experience is already set aside as something *sui generis*. The actual religious quality in the experience described is the *effect* produced, the better adjustment in life and its conditions, not the manner and cause of its production. The way in which the experience operated, its function, determines its religious value. If the reorientation actually occurs, it, and the sense of security and stability accompanying it, are forces on their own account. It takes place in different persons in a multitude of ways. It is sometimes brought about by devotion to a cause; sometimes by a passage of poetry that opens a new perspective; sometimes as was the case with Spinoza—deemed an atheist in his day—through philosophical reflection.

The difference between an experience having a religious force because of what it does in and to the processes of living and religious experience as a separate kind of thing gives me occasion to refer to a previous remark. If this function were rescued through emancipation from dependence upon specific types of beliefs and practices, from those elements that constitute a religion, many individuals would find that experiences having the force of bringing about a better, deeper and enduring adjustment in life are not so rare and infrequent as they are commonly supposed to be. They occur frequently in connection with many significant moments of living. The idea of invisible powers would take on the meaning of all the conditions of nature and human association that support and deepen the sense of values which carry one through periods of darkness and despair to such an extent that they lose their usual depressive character.

I do not suppose for many minds the dislocation of the religious from a religion is easy to effect. Tradition and custom, especially when emotionally charged, are a part of the habits that have become one with our very being. But the possibility of the transfer is demonstrated by its actuality. Let us then for the moment drop the term "religious," and ask what are the attitudes that lend deep and enduring support to the processes of living. I have, for example, used the words "adjustment" and "orientation." What do they signify?

While the words "accommodation," "adaptation," and "adjustment" are frequently employed as synonyms, attitudes exist that are so different that for the sake of clear thought they should be discriminated. There are conditions we meet that cannot be changed. If they are particular and limited, we modify our own particular attitudes in accordance with them. Thus we accommodate ourselves to changes in weather, to alterations in income when we have no other recourse. When the external conditions are lasting we become inured, habituated, or, as the process is now often called, conditioned. The two main traits of this attitude, which I should like to call accommodation, are that it affects *particular* modes of conduct, not the entire self, and that the process is mainly *passive*. It may, however, become general and then it becomes fatalistic resignation or submission. There are other attitudes toward the environment that are also particular but that are more active. We re-act against conditions and endeavor to change them to meet our wants and demands. Plays in a foreign language are "adapted" to meet the needs of an American audience. A house is rebuilt to suit changed conditions of the household; the telephone is invented to serve the demand for speedy communication at a distance; dry soils are irrigated so that they may bear abundant crops. Instead of accommodating ourselves to conditions, we modify conditions so that they will be accommodated to our wants and purposes. This process may be called adaptation.

Now both of these processes are often called by the more general name of adjustment. But there are also changes in ourselves in relation to the world in which we live that are much more inclusive and deep seated. They relate not to this and that want in relation to this and that condition of our surroundings, but pertain to our being in its entirety. Because of their scope, this modification of ourselves is enduring. It lasts through any amount of vicissitude of circumstances, internal and external. There is a composing and harmonizing of the various elements of our being such that, in spite of changes in the special conditions that surround us, these conditions are also arranged, settled, in relation to us. This attitude includes a note of submission. But it is voluntary, not externally imposed; and as voluntary it is something more than a mere Stoical resolution to endure unperturbed throughout the buffetings of fortune. It is more outgoing, more ready and glad, than the latter attitude, and it is more active than the former. And in calling it voluntary, it is not meant that it depends upon a particular resolve or volition. It is a change *of* will conceived as the organic plenitude of our being, rather than any special change *in* will.

It is the claim of religions that they effect this generic and enduring change in attitude. I should like to turn the statement around and say that whenever this change takes place there is a definitely religious attitude. It is not *a* religion that brings it about, but when it occurs, from whatever cause and by whatever means, there is a religious outlook and function.

23

The Seriousness of Making Choices*

Søren Kierkegaard (1813–1855)

My friend, *I think of my early youth,* when without clearly comprehending what it is to make a choice I listened with childish trust to the talk of my elders and the instant of choice was solemn and venerable, although in choosing I was only following the instructions of another person. I think of the occasions in my later life when I stood at the crossways, when my soul was matured in the hour of decision. I think of the many occasions in life less important but by no means indifferent to me, when it was a question of making a choice. For although there is only one situation in which either/or has absolute significance, namely, when

---

* This passage from *Either/Or* was written by Kierkegaard in the form of a letter from "Judge William" to his "young friend" giving some autobiographical references to Kierkegaard's character as a young university student.

From Søren Kierkegaard, *Either/Or*, Vol. II. translated by Walter Lowrie with revisions and a forward by Howard A. Johnson, Copyright 1944 © 1955 by Princeton Univ. Press. Reprinted by permission of Princeton Univ. Press, Princeton, 1944.

truth, righteousness and holiness are lined up on one side, and lust and base propensities and obscure passions and perdition on the other; yet, it is always important to choose rightly, even as between things which one may innocently choose, it is important to test oneself, lest some day one might have to beat a retreat to the point from which one started, and might have reason to thank God if one had to reproach oneself for nothing worse than a waste of time. In common parlance I use these words [either/or] as others use them, and it would indeed be foolish to give up using them. And although my life now has to a certain degree its either/or behind it, yet I know well that it may still encounter many a situation where the either/or will have its full significance. I hope, however, that these words may find me in a worthy state of mind when they check me on my path, and I hope that I may be successful in choosing the right course; at all events, I shall endeavor to make the choice with real earnestness, and with that I venture, at least, to hope that I shall the sooner get out of the wrong path.

And now as for you—this phrase is only too often on your lips, it has almost become a byword with you. What significance has it for you? None at all. You, according to your own expression, regard it as a wink of the eye, a snap of the fingers, a *coup de main,* an abracadabra. At every opportunity you know how to introduce it, nor is it without effect; for it affects you as strong drink affects a neurasthenic, you become completely intoxicated by what you call the higher madness. . . . [You are like] that great thinker and true practical philosopher who said to a man who had insulted him by pulling off his hat and throwing it on the floor, "If you pick it up, you'll get a thrashing; if you don't pick it up, you'll also get a thrashing; now you can choose." You take great delight in "comforting" people when they have recourse to you in critical situations. You listen to their exposition of the case and then say, "Yes, I perceive perfectly that there are two possibilities, one can either do this or that. My sincere opinion and my friendly counsel is as follows: Do it/or don't do it—you will regret both." But he who mocks others mocks himself, and your rejoinder is not a mere nothing but a profound mockery of yourself, a sorry proof how limp your soul is, that your whole philosophy of life is concentrated in one single proposition, "I say merely either/or." In case this really were your serious meaning, there would be nothing one could do with you, one must simply put up with you as you are and deplore the fact that melancholy [literally, heavy-mindedness] or light-mindedness had enfeebled your spirit. Now on the contrary, since one knows very well that such is not the case, one is not tempted to pity you but rather to wish that some day the circumstances of your life may tighten upon you the screws in its rack and compel you to come out with what really dwells in you, may begin the sharper inquisition of the rack which cannot be beguiled by nonsense and witticisms. Life is a masquerade, you explain, and for you this is inexhaustible material for amusement; and so far, no one has succeeded in knowing you; for every revelation you make is always an illusion. Your occupation consists in preserving your hiding place, and that you succeed in doing, for your mask is the most enigmatical of all. In fact you are nothing . . . an enigmatic figure on whose brow is inscribed Either/or—"For this," you say, "is my motto. . . ."

Now although nothing you say in that style has the slighest effect upon me, nevertheless, for your own sake I will reply to you. Do you not know that there comes a midnight hour when every one has to throw off his mask? Do you believe that life will always let itself be mocked? Do you think you can slip away a little before midnight in order to avoid this? Or are you not terrified by it? I have seen men in real life who so long deceived others that at last their true nature could not reveal itself; I have seen men who played hide and seek so long that at last madness through them obtruded disgustingly upon others their secret thoughts which hitherto they had proudly concealed. Or can you think of anything more frightful than that you thus would have lost the inmost and holiest thing of all in a man, the unifying power of personality? Truly, you should not jest with that which is not only serious but dreadful. In every man there is something which to a certain degree prevents him from becoming perfectly transparent to himself; and this may be the case in so high a degree, he may be so inexplicably woven into relationships of life which extend far beyond himself that he almost cannot reveal himself. But he who cannot reveal himself cannot love, and he who cannot love is the most unhappy man of all.

24

Concerning Life after Death

Plato, Hume, and *Kierkegaard*

1. PLATO

I desire to prove to you that the real philosopher has reason to be of good cheer when he is about to die, and that after death he may hope to obtain the greatest good in the other world. And how this may be, Simmias and Cebes, I will endeavor to explain. For I deem that the true votary of philosophy is likely to be misunderstood by other men; they do not perceive that he is always pursuing death and dying; and if this be so, and he has had the desire of death all his life long, why when his time comes should he repine at that which he has been always pursuing and desiring?

Simmias said laughingly: Though not in a laughing humour, you have made me laugh, Socrates; for I cannot help thinking that the many when they hear

From Plato, "Phaedo," in *Dialogues of Plato,* translated by Benjamin Jowett, Oxford, 1920.

your words will say how truly you have described philosophers, and our people at home will likewise say that the life which philosophers desire is in reality death, and that they have found them out to be deserving of the death which they desire.

And they are right, Simmias, in thinking so, with the exception of the words "they have found them out"; for they have not found out either what is the nature of that death which the true philosopher deserves, or how he deserves or desires death. But enough of them:—let us discuss the matter among ourselves. Do we believe that there is such a thing as death?

To be sure, replied Simmias.

Is it not the separation of soul and body? And to be dead is the completion of this; when the soul exists in herself, and is released from the body and the body is released from the soul, what is this but death?

Just so, he replied.

There is another question, which will probably throw light on our present enquiry if you and I can agree about it—Ought the philosopher to care about the pleasures—if they are to be called pleasures—of eating and drinking?

Certainly not, answered Simmias.

And what about the pleasures of love—should he care for them?

By no means.

And will he think much of the other ways of indulging the body, for example, the acquisition of costly raiment, or sandals, or other adornments of the body? Instead of caring about them, does he not rather despise anything more than nature needs? What do you say?

I should say that the true philosopher would despise them.

Would you not say that he is entirely concerned with the soul and not with the body? He would like, as far as he can, to get away from the body and to turn to the soul.

Quite true.

In matters of this sort philosophers, above all other men, may be observed in every sort of way to dissever the soul from the communion of the body.

Very true.

Whereas, Simmias, the rest of the world are of opinion that to him who has no sense of pleasure and no part in bodily pleasure, life is not worth having; and that he who is indifferent about them is as good as dead.

That is also true.

What again shall we say of the actual acquirement of knowledge?—is the body, if invited to share in the enquiry, a hinderer or a helper? I mean to say, have sight and hearing any truth in them? Are they not, as the poets are always telling us, inaccurate witnesses? and yet, if even they are inaccurate and indistinct, what is to be said of the other senses?—for you will allow that they are the best of them?

Certainly, he replied.

Then when does the soul attain truth?—for in attempting to consider anything in company with the body she is obviously deceived.

True.

Then must not true existence be revealed to her in thought, if at all?

Yes.

And thought is best when the mind is gathered into herself and none of these things trouble her—neither sounds nor sights nor pain nor any pleasure—when she takes leave of the body, and has as little as possible to do with it, when she has no bodily sense or desire, but is aspiring after true being?

Certainly.

And in this the philosopher dishonours the body; his soul runs away from his body and desires to be alone and by herself?

That is true.

Well, but there is another thing, Simmias: Is there or is there not an absolute justice?

Assuredly there is.

And an absolute beauty and absolute good?

Of course.

But did you ever behold any of them with your eyes?

Certainly not.

Or did you ever reach them with any other bodily sense?—and I speak not of these alone, but of absolute greatness, and health, and strength, and of the essence or true nature of everything. Has the reality of them ever been perceived by you through the bodily organs? or rather, is not the nearest approach to the knowledge of their several natures made by him who so orders his intellectual vision as to have the most exact conception of the essence of each thing which he considers?

Certainly.

And he attains to the purest knowledge of them who goes to each with the mind alone, not introducing or intruding in the act of thought sight or any other sense together with reason, but with the very light of the mind in her own clearness searches into the very truth of each; he who has got rid, as far as he can, of eyes and ears and, so to speak, of the whole body, these being in his opinion distracting elements which when they infect the soul hinder her from acquiring truth and knowledge—who, if not he, is likely to attain to the knowledge of true being?

What you say has a wonderful truth in it, Socrates, replied Simmias.

And when real philosophers consider all these things, will they not be led to make a reflection which they will express in words something like the following? "Have we not found," they will say, "a path of thought which seems to bring us and our argument to the conclusion, that while we are in the body, and while the soul is infected with the evils of the body, our desire will not be satisfied? and our desire is of the truth. For the body is a source of endless trouble to us by reason of the mere requirement of food; and is liable also to diseases which overtake and impede us in the search after true being: it fills us full of loves, and lusts, and fears, and fancies of all kinds, and endless foolery, and in fact, as men say, takes away from us the power of thinking at all. Whence come wars, and fightings, and factions? whence but from the body and the lusts of the body? Wars are occasioned by the love of money, and money has to be acquired for the sake and in the service of the body; and by reason of all these impediments we have no time to give to philosophy; and, last and worst of all, even if we are at lesiure and betake ourselves to some speculation, the body is always breaking in upon us, causing turmoil and confusion in our enquiries, and so amazing us that we are prevented from seeing the truth. It has been proved to us by experience that if we would have pure knowledge of anything we must be quit of the body—the soul in herself must behold things in themselves: and then we shall attain the wisdom which we desire, and of which we say that we are lovers; not while we live, but after death; for if while in company with the body, the soul cannot have pure knowledge, one of two things follows—either knowledge is not to be attained at all, or, if at all, after death. For then, and not till then, the soul will be parted from the body and exist in herself alone. In this present life, I reckon that we make the nearest approach to knowledge when we have the least possible intercourse or communion with the body, and are not surfeited with the bodily nature, but keep ourselves pure until the hour when God himself is pleased to release us. And thus having got rid of the foolishness of the body we shall be pure and hold converse with the pure, and know of ourselves the clear light everywhere, which is no other than the light of truth." For the impure are not permitted to approach the pure. These are the sort of words, Simmias, which the true lovers of knowledge cannot help saying to one another, and thinking. You would agree; would you not?

Undoubtedly, Socrates.

But, O my friend, if this be true, there is great reason to hope that, going whither I go, when I have come to the end of my journey, I shall attain that which has been the pursuit of my life. And therefore I go on my way rejoicing, and not I only, but every other man who believes that his mind has been made ready and that he is in a manner purified.

Certainly, replied Simmias.

And what is purification but the separation of the soul from the body, as I was saying before; the habit of the soul gathering and collecting herself into herself from all sides out of the body; the dwelling in her own place alone, as in another life, so also in this, as far as she can;—the release of the soul from the chains of the body?

Very true, he said.

And this separation and release of the soul from the body is termed death?

To be sure, he said.

And the true philosophers, and they only, are ever seeking to release the soul. Is not the separation and release of the soul from the body their especial study?

That is true.

And, as I was saying at first, there would be a ridiculous contradiction in men studying to live as nearly as they can in a state of death, and yet repining when it comes upon them.

Clearly.

And the true philosophers, Simmias, are always occupied in the practice of dying, wherefore also to them least of all men is death terrible. Look at the matter thus:—if they have been in every way the enemies of the body, and are wanting to be alone with the soul, when this desire of theirs is granted, how inconsistent would they be if they trembled and repined, instead of rejoicing at their departure to that place where, when they arrive, they hope to gain that which in life they desired—and this was wisdom—and at the same time to be rid of the company of their enemy. Many a man has been willing to go to the world below animated by the hope of seeing there an earthly love, or wife, or son, and conversing with them. And will he who is a true lover of wisdom, and is strongly persuaded in like manner that only in the world below he can worthily enjoy her, still repine at death? Will he not depart with joy? Surely he will, O my friend, if he be a true philosopher. For he will have a firm conviction that there, and there only, he can find wisdom in her purity. And if this be true, he would be very absurd, as I was saying, if he were afraid of death.

2. HUME

The physical arguments from the analogy of nature are strong for the mortality of the soul: and these are really the only philosophical arguments, which ought to be admitted with regard to this question, or indeed any question of fact.

Where any two objects are so closely connected, that all alterations, which we have seen in the one, are attended with proportionable alterations in the other: we ought to conclude, by all rules of analogy, that, when there are still greater alterations produced in the former, and it is totally dissolved, there follows a total dissolution of the latter.

Sleep, a very small effect on the body, is attended with a temporary extinction: at least, a great confusion in the soul.

The weakness of the body and that of the mind in infancy are exactly proportioned; their vigour in manhood, their sympathetic disorder in sickness, their common gradual decay in old age. The step further seems unavoidable; their common dissolution in death.

The last symptoms, which the mind discovers, are disorder, weakness, insensibility, and stupidity; the forerunners of its annihilation. The further progress of the same causes, increasing the same effects, totally extinguish it.

Judging by the usual analogy of nature, no form can continue, when transferred to a condition of life very different from the original one, in which it was placed. Trees perish in the water; fishes in the air; animals in the earth. Even so small a difference as that of climate is often fatal. What reason then to imagine,

---

From David Hume, "Of the Immortality of the Soul" written 1755.

that an immense alteration, such as is made on the soul by the dissolution of its body, and all its organs of thought and sensation, can be effected without the dissolution of the whole?

Everything is in common betwixt soul and body. The organs of the one are all of them the organs of the other. The existence therefore of the one must be dependent on the other.

The souls of animals are allowed to be mortal: and these bear so near a resemblance to the souls of men, that the analogy from one to the other forms a very strong argument. Their bodies are not more resembling: yet no one rejects the argument drawn from comparative anatomy.

Nothing in this world is perpetual; Everything, however seemingly firm, is in continual flux and change: The world itself gives symptoms of frailty and dissolution: How contrary to analogy, therefore, to imagine, that one single form, seeming the frailest of any, and subject to the greatest disorders is immortal and indissoluble! What a daring theory is that! How lightly, not to say how rashly, entertained!

How to dispose of the infinite number of posthumous existences ought also to embarrass the religious theory. Every planet, in every solar system, we are at liberty to imagine peopled with intelligent, mortal beings: At least we can fix on no other supposition. For these, then, a new universe must, every generation, be created beyond the bounds of the present universe: or one must have been created at first so prodigiously wide as to admit of this continual influx of beings. Ought such bold suppositions to be received by philosophy: and that merely on the pretext of a bare possibility?

When it is asked, whether *Agamemnon, Thersites, Hannibal, Nero,* and every stupid clown, that ever existed in *Italy, Scythia, Bactria, or Guinea,* are now alive; can any man think, that a scrutiny of nature will furnish arguments strong enough to answer so strange a question in the affirmative? The want of argument, without revelation, sufficiently establishes the negative. . . .

Were our horrors of annihilation an original passion, not the effect of our general love of happiness, it would rather prove the mortality of the soul: For as nature does nothing in vain, she would never give us a horror against an impossible event. She may give us a horror against an unavoidable event, provided our endeavours, as in the present case, may often remove it to some distance. Death is in the end unavoidable; yet the human species could not be preserved, had not nature inspired us with an aversion towards it. All doctrines are to be suspected which are favoured by our passions. And the hopes and fears which give rise to this doctrine, are very obvious.

'Tis an infinite advantage in every controversy, to defend the negative. If the question be out of the common experienced course of nature, this circumstance is almost, if not altogether, decisive. By what arguments or analogies can we prove any state of existence, which no one ever saw, and which no way resembles any that ever was seen? Who will repose such trust in any pretended philosophy, as to admit upon its testimony the reality of so marvelous a scene?

Some new species of logic is requisite for that purpose; and some new faculties of the mind, that they may enable us to comprehend that logic.

Nothing could set in a fuller light the infinite obligations which mankind have to Divine revelation; since we find, that no other medium could ascertain this great and important truth.

3. KIERKEGAARD

Christianity protests every form of objectivity; it desires that the subject should be infinitely concerned about himself. It is subjectivity that Christianity is concerned with, and it is only in subjectivity that its truth exists, if it exists at all; objectively. Christianity has absolutely no existence. If its truth happens to be in only a single subject, it exists in him alone; and there is greater Christian joy in heaven over this one individual than over universal history and the System, which as objective entities are incommensurable for that which is Christian. . . .

For example, the problem of *what it means to die.* I know concerning this what people in general know about it; I know that I shall die if I take a dose of sulphuric acid, and also if I drown myself, or go to sleep in an atmosphere of coal gas, and so forth. I know that Napoleon always went about with poison ready to hand, and that Juliet in Shakespeare poisoned herself. I know that the Stoics regarded suicide as a courageous deed, and that others consider it a cowardly act. I know that death may result from so ridiculous and trivial a circumstance that even the most serious-minded of men cannot help laughing at death; I know that it is possible to escape what appears to be certain death, and so forth. I know that the tragic hero dies in the fifth act of the drama, and that death here has an infinite significance in pathos; but that when a bartender dies, death does not have this significance. I know that the poet can interpret death in a diversity of moods, even to the limit of the comical; I pledge myself to produce the same diversity of effects in prose. I know furthermore what the clergy are accustomed to say on this subject, and I am familiar with the general run of themes treated at funerals. If nothing else stands in the way of my passing over to world-history, I am ready; I need only purchase black cloth for a ministerial gown, and I shall engage to preach funeral sermons as well as any ordinary clergyman. I freely admit that those who wear a velvet inset in their gowns do it more elegantly; but this distinction is not essential any more than the difference between five dollars and ten dollars for the hearse.

Nevertheless, in spite of this almost extraordinary knowledge or facility in knowledge, I can by no means regard death as something I have understood.

From Søren Kierkegaard, *Concluding Unscientific Postscript,* translated by David F. Swenson and Walter Lowrie, Princeton University Press, Princeton, 1968.

Before I pass over to universal history—of which I must always say: "God knows whether it is any concern of yours"—it seems to me that I had better think about this, lest existence mock me, because I had become so learned and highfalutin that I had forgotten to understand what will some time happen to me as to every human being—sometime, nay, what am I saying: suppose death were so treacherous as to come tomorrow? Merely this one uncertainty, when it is to be understood and held fast by an existing individual, and hence enter into every thought, precisely because it is an uncertainty entering into my beginning upon universal history even, so that I make it clear to myself whether if death comes tomorrow, I am beginning upon something that is worth beginning—merely this one uncertainty generates inconceivable difficulties, difficulties that not even the speaker who treats of death is always aware of, in that he thinks that he apprehends the uncertainty of death, while nevertheless forgetting to think it into what he says about it, so that he speaks movingly and with emotion about the uncertainty of death, and yet ends by encouraging his hearers to make a resolution for the whole of life. This is essentially to forget the uncertainty of death, since otherwise the enthusiastic resolve for the whole of life must be made commensurable with the uncertainty of death. To think about it once for all, or once a year at matins of New Year's morning, is of course nonsense, and is the same as not thinking about it at all.

If, on the other hand, the uncertainty of death is merely something in general, then my own death is itself only something in general. Perhaps this is also the case for systematic philosophers, for absent-minded people. For the late Herr Soldin, his own death is supposed to have been such a something in general: "when he was about to get up in the morning he was not aware that he was dead." But the fact of my own death is not for me by any means such a something in general, although for others, the fact of my death may indeed be something of that sort. Nor am I for myself such a something in general, although perhaps for others I may be a mere generality. But if the task of life is to become subjective, then every subject will for *himself* become the very opposite of such a something in general. And it would seem to be a somewhat embarrassing thing to be so significant for universal history, and then at home, in company with oneself, to be merely a something in general. It is already embarrassing enough for a man who is an extraordinarily important figure in the public assembly to come home to his wife, and then to be for her only such a something in general; or to be a world-historical Diedrich Menschenschreck, and then at home to be— aye, I do not care to say anything more. But it is still more embarrassing to have so low a standing with oneself, and it is most embarrassing of all to remain unaware of the fact that this is so.

The question then arises as to what death is, and especially as to what it is for the living individual. We wish to know how the conception of death will transform a man's entire life, when in order to think its uncertainty he has to think it in every moment, so as to prepare himself for it. We wish to know what it means to prepare for death, since here again one must distinguish between its actual presence and the thought of it. This distinction appears to make all my preparation insignificant, if that which really comes is not that for which I prepared myself; and if it is the same, then my preparation is in its perfection identical with death itself. And I must take into account the fact that death may come in the very moment that I begin my preparation. The question must be raised of the possibility of finding an ethical expression for the significance of death, and a religious expression for the victory over death; one needs a solving word which explains its mystery, and a binding word by which the living individual defends himself against the ever recurrent conception; for surely we dare scarcely recommend mere thoughtlessness and forgetfulness as wisdom.

When death thus becomes something to be related to the entire life of the subject, I must confess I am very far indeed from having understood it, even if it were to cost me my life to make this confession. Still less have I realized the task existentially. And yet I have thought about this subject again and again; I have sought for guidance in books—and I have found none.

For example, what does it mean to be immortal? In this respect, I know what people generally know. I know that some hold a belief in immortality, that others say they do not hold it; whether they actually do not hold it I know not; it does not occur to me therefore to want to combat them, for such an undertaking is so dialectically difficult that I should need a year and a day before it could become dialectically clear to me whether there is any reality in such a contest; whether the dialectic of communication, when it is properly understood, would approve of such a proceeding or transform it into a mere beating of the air; whether the consciousness of immortality is a doctrinal topic which is appropriate as a subject for instruction, and how the dialectic of instruction must be determined with relation to the learner's presuppositions; whether these presuppositions are not so essential that the instruction becomes a deception in case one is not at once aware of them, and in that event the instruction is transformed into non-instruction. A book raises the question of the immortality of the soul. The contents of the book constitute the answer. But the contents of the book, as the reader can convince himself by reading it through, are the opinions of the wisest and best men about immortality, all neatly strung on a thread. Oh! thou great Chinese god! Is this immortality? So then the question about immortality is a learned question. All honor to learning! All honor to him who can handle learnedly the learned question of immortality! But the question of immortality is essentially not a learned question, rather it is a question of inwardness, which the subject by becoming subjective must put to himself. Objectively the question cannot be answered, because objectively it cannot be put, since immortality precisely is the potentiation and highest development of the developed subjectivity. Only by really willing to become subjective can the question properly emerge, therefore how could it be answered objectively? The question cannot be answered in social terms, for in social terms it cannot be expressed, inasmuch as only the subject who wills to become subjective can conceive the question and ask rightly, "Do I become immortal, or am I immortal?" Of course, people can combine for many things; thus several families can combine for a box at the theater, and three single gentlemen can combine for a riding horse, so that each of them rides every third day. But it is not so with immortality; the consciousness of my immortality belongs to me alone, precisely at the moment when I am conscious of my immortality I am absolutely subjective, and I cannot become immortal in partnership with three single gentlemen in turn. People who go about with a paper soliciting the endorsement of numerous men and women, who feel a need in general to become immortal, get no reward for their pains, for immortality is not a possession which can be extorted by a list of endorsements. Systematically, immortality cannot be proved at all. The fault does not lie in the proofs, but in the fact that people will not understand that viewed systematically the whole question is nonsense, so that instead of seeking outward proofs, one had better seek to become a little subjective. Immortality is the most passionate interest of subjectivity; precisely in the interest lies the proof. When for the sake of objectivity (quite consistently from the systematic point of view), one systematically ignores the interest, God only knows in this case what immortality is, or even what is the sense of wishing to prove it, or how one could get into one's head the fixed idea of bothering about it.

Quite simply therefore the existing subject asks, not about immortality in general, for such a phantom has no existence, but about his immortality, about what it means to become immortal, whether he is able to contribute anything to the accomplishment of this end, or whether he becomes immortal as a matter of course, or whether he is that and can become it. . . .

The question is raised, how he, while he exists, can hold fast his consciousness of immortality, lest the metaphysical conception of immortality proceed to confuse the ethical and reduce it to an illusion; for ethically, everything culminates in immortality, without which the ethical is merely use and wont, and metaphysically, immortality swallows up existence, yea, the seventy years of existence, as a thing of naught, and yet ethically this naught must be of infinite importance. The question is raised, how immortality practically transforms his life; in what sense he must have the consciousness of it always present to him, or whether perhaps it is enough to think this thought once for all.

And the fact of asking about his immortality is at the same time for the existing subject who raises the question a deed—as it is not, to be sure, for absent-minded people who once in a while ask about the matter of being immortal quite in general, as if immortality were something one has once in a while, and the question were some sort of thing in general. So he asks how he is to behave in order to express in existence his immortality, whether he is really expressing it; and for the time being, he is satisfied with this task, which surely must be enough to last a man a lifetime since it is to last for an eternity. And then? Well, then, when he has completed this task, then comes the turn for world-history. In these days, to be sure, it is just the other way round: now people apply themselves first to world-history, and therefore there comes out of this the ludicrous result (as another author has remarked), that while people are proving and proving immortality quite in general, faith in immortality is more and more diminishing.

FOUR

THEORY
OF KNOWLEDGE

"What can I know?" is the central question about which the theory of knowledge is concerned. Closely related is the question "What is there?" to which metaphysics turns its attention. To show how these two questions arise virtually simultaneously, we can ask what occurs when we perceive something, say, an apple. Do we *know* that it is an apple? Do we know that it *is* an apple? What does it mean to *know* anything? What does it mean to say that something *is?* Suppose one says that "I know that it is an apple because I recognize its shape and color." There can be no question that a person who perceives an apple does in fact have the psychological experience of shape and color. But is that experience what we call knowledge? Does it follow, for example, that when you perceive a certain shape and color which appears identical to the apple you ate yesterday that the present object will also taste the same or even be an apple? Could it not be that unlike the apple you ate yesterday, the present object is something made of wax or paper or clay. If the object you perceive turns out not to be what you thought it was, then you did not have true knowledge about the object. Appearances do not always signify the reality one associates with them. Knowledge, therefore, which is based upon appearances is less reliable than knowledge based upon reality. More exactly, true knowledge assumes that we know what reality is. But the problem philosophers have tried to solve is whether there is any reliable way to distinguish between appearance and reality.

The distinction between appearance and reality can be considered in various ways. For example, an object may appear to be solid and permanent. In reality, it may turn out to be made of many parts and destructible. Even in theory it could be thought that the physical world is nothing more than an indefinite number and variety of objects or entities composed of matter or atoms. What Sir Isaac Newton thought atoms to be, namely, indivisible and indestructible bits of matter, are today described as modes of energy. It makes considerable difference for certain purposes to say that the "real" nature of atoms is energy instead of matter. Philosophers have long been aware of the fact that knowledge sometimes seems to be certain only to have its certainty destroyed by the discovery that the reality upon which it was based turned out to be merely appearance.

The experience of discovering that a system of knowledge can be dismantled because it did not rest upon a permanent reality has led many thinkers to assume a skeptical attitude toward the possibility of attaining truth or certainty in knowledge. Historically, however, the skeptics did not conclude that we cannot attain reliable knowledge; for the most part they assumed an attitude of doubt in order not to foreclose the possibility of better or true knowledge. The skeptics did not, for example, argue that laws were useless because no one could define what justice really is or that religion has no value because no one can know ultimate truth. Rather, they were impressed that virtually equally good reasons or arguments could be presented for different definitions of justice or different modes of religion. One form of skepticism, then, is not so much a posture of perpetual doubt as an attitude of receptiveness and openness to new possibilities of knowledge.

Some forms of skepticism have raised serious questions about the certainty of knowledge. David Hume's skepticism is rigorous and challenges the possibility of drawing exact and predictable conclusions from experience. Suppose, as Hume does, that all our knowledge is derived from experience. Can we experience anything more than the particular event or events we do in fact experience. Take, for example, what common sense seems most certain about, namely, that some events are caused by other events. A person takes an aspirin and subsequently his headache disappears. The aspirin is said to be the cause of the headache's disappearance. Scientific thought looks for and builds upon the notion of cause or causality. Yet one does not experience a "cause" as such. We know only that the person swallowed the aspirin and that subsequently his headache ceased. The prediction that if one swallows an aspirin his headache will cease can be no more than an assumption that what happened before will happen again. But it is not inconceivable nor even contradictory to think that this sequence will not occur next time. To infer the future from the past is to assume that knowledge is based upon something other than experience. That a person's headache ceased after taking an aspirin is known because it happened, but that it will happen in the future cannot now be known because he has not yet experienced that future event and he knows only what he has experienced. At most, knowledge of the future is inferred from the present or the past; the future is only probable. We do not "know" enough about "cause," says the skeptic, to enable us to predict, by induction, what the effect will be. It takes a different theory of knowledge to explain how scientific knowledge achieves such regularity in predictions, how the landing of a vehicle on the moon can be achieved with such precision.

One way to move beyond the skepticism of Hume's empiricism is to argue, as Kant did, that while knowledge begins in experience, it is not limited to experience. The mind itself brings something to the act of knowing in the way that lenses in a pair of glasses facilitate seeing. Among other things, it may be that the mind is structured in such a way that it organizes the phenomena of experience into causal relations, not arbitrarily but with fidelity to the way things happen. The limits of doubt were delineated in still a different way by Descartes, who thought he could construct an edifice of certain knowledge, including mathematical knowledge, upon the single simple fact of thinking which led him to conclude that "I think, therefore I am." To William James, the quest for truth required that the very idea of truth had to be redefined not as some reality somewhere to which the mind had to conform but as the way ideas behave or perform. An idea is true, he said, if it works, if it does what one expects. But the dominant theme in contemporary philosophy concerning the nature of knowledge was expressed by the positivist A. J. Ayer, whose passionately expressed theory of *verification* has focused upon that issue in determining what we can know.

25

The Ascent to True Knowledge

Plato (428/27–348/47 B.C.)

[LINE AND CAVE]

Conceive, then, that there are these two powers I speak of, the Good reigning over the domain of all that is intelligible, the Sun over the visible world—or the heaven as I might call it; only you would think I was showing off my skill in etymology. At any rate you have these two orders of things clearly before your mind: the visible and the intelligible?

I have.

Now take a line divided into two unequal parts, one to represent the visible order, the other the intelligible; and divide each part again in the same proportion, symbolizing degrees of comparative clearness or obscurity. Then (A) one of

From *The Republic of Plato*, translated by C. M. Cornford, 1962; "Meno," *Dialogues of Plato*, vol. I, translated by Benjamin Jowett, 1920, by permission of Oxford University Press, Oxford.

the two sections in the visible world will stand for images. By images I mean first shadows, and then reflections in water or in close-grained, polished surfaces, and everything of that kind, if you understand.

Yes, I understand.

Let the second section (B) stand for the actual things of which the first are likenesses, the living creatures about us and all the works of nature or of human hands.

So be it.

Will you also take the proposition in which the visible world has been divided as corresponding to degrees of reality and truth, so that the likeness shall stand to the original in the same ratio as the sphere of appearances and belief to the sphere of knowledge?

Certainly.

Now consider how we are to divide the part which stands for the intelligible world. There are two sections. In the first (C) the mind uses as images those actual things which themselves had images in the visible world; and it is compelled to pursue its inquiry by starting from assumptions and travelling, not up to a principle, but down to a conclusion. In the second (D) the mind moves in the other direction, from an assumption up towards a principle which is not hypothetical; and it makes no use of the images employed in the other section, but only of Forms, and conducts its inquiry solely by their means.

I don't quite understand what you mean.

Then we will try again; what I have just said will help you to understand. (C) You know, of course, how students of subjects like geometry and arithmetic begin by postulating odd and even numbers, or the various figures and the three kinds of angle, and other such data in each subject. These data they take as known; and, having adopted them as assumptions, they do not feel called upon to give any account of them to themselves or to anyone else, but treat them as self-evident. Then, starting from these assumptions, they go on until they arrive, by a series of consistent steps, at all the conclusions they set out to investigate.

Yes, I know that.

You also know how they make use of visible figures and discourse about them, though what they really have in mind is the originals of which these figures are images: they are not reasoning, for instance, about this particular square and diagonal which they have drawn, but about *the* Square and *the* Diagonal; and so in all cases. The diagrams they draw and the models they make are actual things, which may have their shadows or images in water; but now they serve in their turn as images, while the student is seeking to behold those realities which only thought can apprehend.

True.

This, then, is the class of things that I spoke of as intelligible, but with two qualifications: first, that the mind, in studying them, is compelled to employ assumptions, and, because it cannot rise above these, does not travel upwards to a first principle; and second, that it uses as images those actual things which have images of their own in the section below them and which, in comparison with those shadows and reflections, are reputed to be more palpable and valued accordingly.

I understand: you mean the subject-matter of geometry and of the kindred arts.

(D) Then by the second section of the intelligible world you may understand me to mean all that unaided reasoning apprehends by the power of dialectic, when it treats its assumptions, not as first principles, but as hypotheses in the literal sense, things "laid down" like a flight of steps up which it may mount all the way to something that is not hypothetical, the first principle of all; and having grasped this, may turn back and, holding on to the consequences which depend upon it, descend at last to a conclusion, never making use of any sensible object, but only of Forms, moving through Forms from one to another, and ending with Forms.

I understand, he said, though not perfectly; for the procedure you describe sounds like an enormous undertaking. But I see that you mean to distinguish the field of intelligible reality studied by dialectic as having a greater certainty and truth than the subject-matter of the 'arts,' as they are called, which treat their assumptions as first principles. The students of these arts are, it is true, compelled to exercise thought in contemplating objects which the senses cannot perceive, but because they start from assumptions without going back to a first principle, you do not regard them as gaining true understanding about those objects, although the objects themselves, when connected with a first principle, are intelligible. And I think you would call the state of mind of the students of geometry and other such arts, not intelligence, but thinking, as being something between intelligence and mere acceptance of appearances.

You have understood me quite well enough, I replied. And now you may take, as corresponding to the four sections, these four states of mind: *intelligence* for the highest, *thinking* for the second, *belief* for the third, and for the last *imagining*. These you may arrange as the terms in a proportion, assigning to each a degree of clearness and certainty corresponding to the measure in which their objects possess truth and reality. . . .

[CAVE]

Next, said I, here is a parable to illustrate the degrees in which our nature may be enlightened or unenlightened. Imagine the condition of men living in a sort of cavernous chamber underground, with an entrance open to the light and a long passage all down the cave. Here they have been from childhood, chained by the leg and also by the neck, so that they cannot move and can see only what is in front of them, because the chains will not let them turn their heads. At some distance higher up is the light of a fire burning behind them; and between the prisoners and the fire is a track with a parapet built along it, like the screen at a puppet-show, which hides the performers while they show their puppets over the top.

I see, said he.

Now behind this parapet imagine persons carrying along various artificial objects, including figures of men and animals in wood or stone or other materials, which project above the parapet. Naturaly, some of these persons will be talking, others silent.

It is a strange picture, he said, and a strange sort of prisoners.

Like ourselves, I replied; for in the first place prisoners so confined would have seen nothing of themselves or of one another, except the shadows thrown by the fire-light on the wall of the Cave facing them, would they?

Not if all their lives they had been prevented from moving their heads.

And they would have seen as little of the objects carried past.

Of course.

Now, if they could talk to one another, would they not suppose that their words referred only to those passing shadows which they saw?

Necessarily.

And suppose their prison had an echo from the wall facing them? When one of the people crossing behind them spoke, they could only suppose that the sound came from the shadow passing before their eyes.

No doubt.

In every way, then, such prisoners would recognize as reality nothing but the shadows of those artificial objects.

Inevitably.

Now consider what would happen if their release from the chains and the healing of their unwisdom should come about in this way. Suppose one of them set free and forced suddenly to stand up, turn his head, and walk with eyes lifted to the light; all these movements would be painful, and he would be too dazzled to make out the objects whose shadows he had been used to see. What do you think he would say, if someone told him that what he had formerly seen was meaningless illusion, but now, being somewhat nearer to reality and turned towards more real objects, he was getting a truer view? Suppose further that he were shown the various objects being carried by and were made to say, in reply to questions, what each of them was. Would he not be perplexed and believe the objects now shown him to be not so real as what he formerly saw?

Yes, not nearly so real.

And if he were forced to look at the fire-light itself, would not his eyes ache, so that he would try to escape and turn back to the things which he could see distinctly, convinced that they really were clearer than these other objects now being shown to him?

Yes.

And suppose someone were to drag him away forcibly up the steep and rugged ascent and not let him go until he had hauled him out into the sunlight, would he not suffer pain and vexation at such treatment, and, when he had come out into the light, find his eyes so full of its radiance that he could not see a single one of the things that he was now told were real?

Certainly he would not see them all at once.

He would need, then, to grow accustomed before he could see things in that upper world. At first it would be easiest to make out shadows, and then the images of men and things reflected in water, and later on the things themselves. After that, it would be easier to watch the heavenly bodies and the sky itself by night, looking at the light of the moon and stars rather than the Sun and the Sun's light in the day-time.

Yes, surely.

Last of all, he would be able to look at the Sun and contemplate its nature, not as it appears when reflected in water or any alien medium, but as it is in itself in its own domain.

No doubt.

And now he would begin to draw the conclusion that it is the Sun that produces the seasons and the course of the year and controls everything in the visible world, and moreover is in a way the cause of all that he and his companions used to see.

Clearly he would come at last to that conclusion.

Then if he called to mind his fellow prisoners and what passed for wisdom in his former dwelling-place, he would surely think himself happy in the change and be sorry for them. They may have had a practice of honouring and commending one another, with prizes for the man who had the keenest eye for the passing shadows and the best memory for the order in which they followed or accompanied one another, so that he could make a good guess as to which was going to come next. Would our released prisoner be likely to covet those prizes or to envy the men exalted to honour and power in the Cave? Would he not feel like Homer's Achilles, that he would far sooner 'be on earth as a hired servant in the house of a landless man' or endure anything rather than go back to his old beliefs and live in the old way?

Yes, he would prefer any fate to such a life.

Now imagine what would happen if he went down again to take his former seat in the Cave. Coming suddenly out of the sunlight, his eyes would be filled with darkness. He might be required once more to deliver his opinion on those shadows, in competition with the prisoners who had never been released, while his eyesight was still dim and unsteady; and it might take some time to become used to the darkness. They would laugh at him and say that he had gone up only to come back with his sight ruined; it was worth no one's while even to attempt the ascent. If they could lay hands on the man who was trying to set them free and lead them up, they would kill him.

Yes, they would.

Every feature in this parable, my dear Glaucon, is meant to fit our earlier analysis. The prison dwelling corresponds to the region revealed to us through the sense of sight, and the fire-light within it to the power of the Sun. The ascent to see the things in the upper world you may take as standing for the upward journey of the soul into the region of the intelligible; then you will be in possession of what I surmise, since that is what you wish to be told. Heaven knows whether it is true; but this, at any rate, is how it appears to me. In the world of knowledge, the last thing to be perceived and only with great difficulty is the essential Form of Goodness. Once it is perceived, the conclusion must follow that, for all things, this is the cause of whatever is right and good; in the visible world it gives birth to light and to the lord of light, while it is itself sovereign in the intelligible world and the parent of intelligence and truth. Without having had a vision of this Form no one can act with wisdom, either in his own life or in matters of state.

So far as I can understand, I share your belief.

Then you may also agree that it is no wonder if those who have reached this height are reluctant to manage the affairs of men. Their souls long to spend all their time in that upper world—naturally enough, if here once more our parable holds true. Nor, again, is it at all strange that one who comes from the contemplation of divine things to the miseries of human life should appear awkward and ridiculous when, with eyes still dazed and not yet accustomed to the darkness, he is compelled, in a law-court or elsewhere, to dispute about the shadows of justice or the images that cast those shadows, and to wrangle over the notions of what is right in the minds of men who have never beheld Justice itself.

It is not at all strange. . . .

[MENO]

Meno. And how will you enquire, Socrates, into that which you do not know? What will you put forth as the subject of enquiry? And if you find what you want, how will you ever know that this is the thing which you did not know?

Socrates. I know, Meno, what you mean; but just see what a tiresome dispute you are introducing. You argue that a man cannot enquire either about that which he knows, or about that which he does not know; for if he knows, he has no need to enquire; and if not, he cannot; for he does not know the very subject about which he is to enquire.

Men. Well, Socrates, and is not the argument sound?

Soc. I think not.

Men. Why not?

Soc. I will tell you why: I have heard from certain wise men and women who spoke of things divine that—

Men. What did they say?

Soc. They spoke of a glorious truth, as I conceive.

Men. What was it? and who were they?

Soc. Some of them were priests and priestesses, who had studied how they might be able to give a reason of their profession: there have been poets also, who spoke of these things by inspiration, like Pindar, and many others who were inspired. And they say—mark, now, and see whether their words are true—they say that the soul of man is immortal, and at one time has an end, which is termed dying, and at another time is born again, but is never destroyed. And the moral is, that a man ought to live always in perfect holiness. '*For in the ninth year*

Persephone sends the souls of those from whom she has received the penalty of ancient crime back again from beneath into the light of the sun above, and these are they who become noble kings and mighty men and great in wisdom and are called saintly heroes in after ages.' The soul, then, as being immortal, and having been born again many times, and having seen all things that exist, whether in this world or in the world below, has knowledge of them all; and it is no wonder that she should be able to call to remembrance all that she ever knew about virtue, and about everything; for as all nature is akin, and the soul has learned all things, there is no difficulty in her eliciting or as men say learning, out of a single recollection all the rest, if a man is strenuous and does not faint; for all enquiry and all learning is but recollection. And therefore we ought not to listen to this sophistical argument about the impossibility of enquiry; for it will make us idle, and is sweet only to the sluggard; but the other saying will make us active and inquisitive. In that confiding, I will gladly enquire with you into the nature of virtue.

Men.   Yes, Socrates; but what do you mean by saying that we do not learn, and that what we call learning is only a process of recollection? Can you teach me how this is?

Soc.   I told you, Meno, just now that you were a rogue, and now you ask whether I can teach you, when I am saying that there is no teaching, but only recollection; and thus you imagine that you will involve me in a contradiction.

Men.   Indeed, Socrates, I protest that I had no such intention. I only asked the question from habit; but if you can prove to me that what you say is true, I wish that you would.

Soc.   It will be no easy matter, but I will try to please you to the utmost of my power. Suppose that you call one of your numerous attendants, that I may demonstrate on him.

Men.   Certainly. Come hither, boy.

Soc.   He is Greek, and speaks Greek, does he not?

Men.   Yes, indeed; he was born in the house.

Soc.   Attend now to the question which I ask him, and observe whether he learns of me or only remembers.

Men.   I will.

Soc.   Tell me, boy, do you know that a figure like this is a square?

Boy.   I do.

Soc.   And you know that a square figure has these four lines equal?

Boy.   Certainly.

Soc.   And these lines which I have drawn through the middle of the square are also equal?

Boy.   Yes.

Soc.   A square may be of any size?

Boy.   Certainly.

Soc.   And if one side of the figure be of two feet, and the other side be of two feet, how much will the whole be? Let me explain: if in one direction the space was of two feet, and in the other direction of one foot, the whole would be of two feet taken once?

Boy. Yes.

Soc. But since this side is also of two feet, there are twice two feet?

Boy. There are.

Soc. Then the square is of twice two feet?

Boy. Yes.

Soc. And how many are twice two feet? count and tell me.

Boy. Four, Socrates.

Soc. And might there not be another square twice as large as this, and having like this the lines equal?

Boy. Yes.

Soc. And of how many feet will that be?

Boy. Of eight feet.

Soc. And now try and tell me that the length of the line which forms the side of that double square: this is two feet—what will that be?

Boy. Clearly, Socrates, it will be double.

Soc. Do you observe, Meno, that I am not teaching the boy anything, but only asking him questions; and now he fancies that he knows how long a line is necessary in order to produce a figure of eight square feet; does he not?

Men. Yes.

Soc. And does he really know?

Men. Certainly not.

Soc. He only guesses that because the square is double, the line is double.

Men. True.

Soc. Observe him while he recalls the steps in regular order. (*To the Boy*). Tell me, boy, do you assert that a double space comes from a double line? Remember that I am not speaking of an oblong, but of a figure equal every way, and twice the size of this—that is to say of eight feet; and I want to know whether you still say that a double square comes from a double line?

Boy. Yes.

Soc. But does not this line become doubled if we add another such line here?

Boy. Certainly.

Soc. And four such lines will make a space containing eight feet?

Boy. Yes.

Soc. Let us describe such a figure: Would you not say that this is the figure of eight feet?

Boy. Yes.

Soc. And are there not these four divisions in the figure, each of which is equal to the figure of four feet?

Boy. True.

Soc. And is now that four times four?

Boy. Certainly.

Soc. And four times is not double?

Boy. No, indeed.

Soc. But how much?

Boy. Four times as much.

Soc. Therefore the double line, boy, has given a space, not twice, but four times as much.

Boy. True.

Soc. Four times four are sixteen—are they not?

Boy. Yes.

Soc. What line would give you a space of eight feet, as this gives one of sixteen feet;—do you see?

Boy. Yes.

Soc. And the space of four feet is made from this half line?

Boy. Yes.

Soc. Good; and is not a space of eight feet twice the size of this, and half the size of the other?

Boy. Certainly.

Soc. Such a space, then, will be made out of a line greater than this one, and less than that one?

Boy. Yes; I think so.

Soc. Very good; I like to hear you say what you think. And now tell me, is not this a line of two feet and that of four?

Boy. Yes.

Soc. Then the line which forms the side of eight feet ought to be more than this line of two feet, and less than the other of four feet?

Boy. It ought.

Soc. Try and see if you can tell me how much it will be.

Boy. Three feet.

Soc. Then if we add a half to this line of two, that will be the line of three. Here are two and there is one; and on the other side; here are two also and there is one: and that makes the figure of which you speak?

Boy. Yes.

Soc. But if there are three feet this way and three feet that way, the whole space will be three times three feet?

Boy. That is evident.

Soc. And how much are three times three feet?

Boy. Nine.

Soc. And how much is the double of four?

Boy. Eight.

Soc. Then the figure of eight is not made out of a line of three?

Boy. No.

Soc. But from what line?—tell me exactly; and if you would rather not reckon, try and show me the line.

Boy. Indeed, Socrates, I do not know.

Soc. Do you see, Meno, what advances he has made in his power of recollection? He did not know at first, and he does not know now, what is the side of a figure of eight feet: but then he thought that he knew, and answered confidently as if he knew, and had no difficulty; now he has a difficulty, and neither knows nor fancies that he knows.

Men. True.

Soc.   Is he not better off in knowing his ignorance?

Men.   I think that he is.

Soc.   If we have made him doubt, and given him the 'torpedo's shock,' have we done him any harm?

Men.   I think not.

Soc.   We have certainly, as would seem, assisted him to some degree to the discovery of the truth; and now he will wish to remedy his ignorance, but then he would have been ready to tell all the world again and again that the double space should have a double side.

Men.   True.

Soc.   But do you suppose that he would ever have enquired into or learned what he fancied that he knew, though he was really ignorant of it, until he had fallen into perplexity under the idea that he did not know, and had desired to know?

Men.   I think not, Socrates.

Soc.   Then he was the better for the torpedo's touch?

Men.   I think so.

Soc.   Mark now the farther development. I shall only ask him, and not teach him, and he shall share the enquiry with me: and do you watch and see if you find me telling or explaining anything to him, instead of eliciting his opinion. Tell me, boy, is not this a square of four feet which I have drawn?

Boy.   Yes.

Soc.   And now I add another square equal to the former one?

Boy.   Yes.

Soc.   And a third, which is equal to either of them?

Boy.   Yes.

Soc.   Suppose that we fill up the vacant corner?

Boy.   Very good.

Soc.   Here, then, there are four equal spaces?

Boy.   Yes.

Soc.   And how many times larger is this space than this other?

Boy.   Four times.

Soc.   But it ought to have been twice only, as you will remember.

Boy.   True.

Soc.   And does not this line, reaching from corner to corner, bisect each of these spaces?

Boy.   Yes.

Soc.   And are there not here four equal lines which contain this space?

Boy.   There are.

Soc.   Look and see how much this space is.

Boy.   I do not understand.

Soc.   Has not each interior line cut off half of the four spaces?

Boy.   Yes.

Soc.   And how many spaces are there in this section?

Boy.   Four.

Soc.   And how many in this?

Boy.   Two.

Soc.   And four is how many times two?

Boy.   Twice.

Soc.   And this space is of how many feet?

Boy.   Of eight feet.

Soc.   And from what line do you get this figure?

Boy.   From this.

Soc.   That is, from the line which extends from corner to corner of the figure of four feet?

Boy.   Yes.

Soc.   And that is the line which the learned called the diagonal. And if this is the proper name, then you, Meno's slave, are prepared to affirm that the double space is the square of the diagonal?

Boy.   Certainly, Socrates.

Soc.   What do you say of him, Meno? Were not all these answers given out of his own head?

Men.   Yes, they were all his own.

Soc.   And yet, as we were just now saying, he did not know?

Men.   True.

Soc.   But still he had in him those notions of his—had he not?

Men.   Yes.

Soc.   Then he who does not know may still have true notions of that which he does not know?

Men.   He has.

Soc.   And at present these notions have just been stirred up in him, as in a dream; but if he were frequently asked the same questions, in different forms, he would know as well as any one at last?

Men.   I dare say.

Soc.   Without any one teaching him he will recover his knowledge for himself, if he is only asked questions?

Men.   Yes.

Soc.   And this spontaneous recovery of knowledge in him is recollection?

Men.   True.

Soc.   And this knowledge which he now has must he not either have acquired or always possessed?

Men.   Yes.

Soc.   But if he always possessed this knowledge he would always have known; or if he has acquired the knowledge he could not have acquired it in this life, unless he has been taught geometry; for he may be made to do the same with all geometry and every other branch of knowledge. Now, has any one ever taught him all this? You must know about him, if, as you say, he was born and bred in your house.

Men.   And I am certain that no one ever did teach him.

Soc.   And yet he has the knowledge?

Men. The fact, Socrates, is undeniable.

Soc. But if he did not acquire the knowledge in this life, then he must have had and learned it at some other time?

Men. Clearly he must.

Soc. Which must have been the time when he was not a man?

Men. Yes.

Soc. And if there have been always true thoughts in him, both at the time when he was and was not a man, which only need to be awakened into knowledge by putting questions to him, his soul must have always possessed this knowledge, for he always either was or was not a man?

Men. Obviously.

Soc. And if the truth of all things always existed in the soul, then the soul is immortal. Wherefore be of good cheer, and try to recollect what you do not know, or rather why you do not remember.

Men. I feel, somehow, that I like what you are saying.

Soc. And I, Meno, like what I am saying. Some things I have said of which I am not altogether confident. But that we shall be better and braver and less helpless if we think that we ought to enquire, than we should have been if we indulged in the idle fancy that there was no knowing and no use in seeking to know what we do not know;—that is a theme upon which I am ready to fight, in word and deed, to the utmost of my power.

26

Scepticism and the Postponement of Certainty

Sextus Empiricus (ca. A.D. 200)

CHAPTER I
THE BASIC DIFFERENCE BETWEEN PHILOSOPHIES

It is a fair presumption that when people search for a thing the result will be either its discovery, a confession of non-discovery and of its non-apprehensibility, or perseverance in the search. Perhaps this is the reason why in matters of philosophical research some claim to have discovered the truth, while others declare that finding it is an impossibility, and others are still seeking it. There are some who think they have found the truth, such as Aristotle, Epicurus, the Stoics, and certain others. These are, in a special sense of the term, the so-called dogmatists. Clitomachus and Carneades, on the other hand, and other Academics, claim it is a search for inapprehensibles. But the Sceptics go on searching. It is, there-

From "Outlines of Pyrrhonism" in *Scepticism, Man, and God,* edited with an Introduction, Notes, and Bibliography by Philip P. Hallie, translated by Sanford G. Etheridge, Wesleyan University Press, 1964.

fore, a reasonable inference that basically there are three philosophies, the dogmatic, the Academic, and the Sceptic. For the present our task will be to present an outline of the Sceptic discipline, leaving it to such others as it befits to treat of the former two. We declare at the outset that we do not make any positive assertion that anything we shall say is wholly as we affirm it to be. We merely report accurately on each thing as our impressions of it are at the moment.

CHAPTER II
THE ARGUMENTS OF SCEPTICISM

The Sceptic philosophy comprises two types of argument, the general and the special. In the first we undertake an exposition of the character of Scepticism by stating its notion, the principles and methods of reasoning involved, and its criterion and end. We set forth also the various modes of suspension of judgement, and manner in which we use the Sceptic formulae, and the distinction between Scepticism and those philosophies which closely approach it. The special argument is that in which we dispute the validity of so-called philosophy in all its parts. Let us, then, first treat of the general argument and begin our sketch with the various appellations of the Sceptic discipline.

CHAPTER III
THE NAMES OF SCEPTICISM

Now, the Sceptic discipline is called the "zetetic" (searching) from its activity of searching and examining. It is also called the "ephetic" (suspending) from the experience which the inquirer feels after the search. "Aporetic" (doubting) is another name for it, either from the fact that their doubting and searching extends to everything (the opinion of some), or from their inability to give final assent or denial. It is also called "Pyrrhonean," because Pyrrho appears to us to have applied himself to Scepticism more thoroughly and with more distinction than his predecessors.

CHAPTER IV
THE MEANING OF SCEPTICISM

Scepticism is an ability to place in antithesis, in any manner whatever, appearances and judgements, and thus—because of the equality of force in the objects and arguments opposed—to come first of all to a suspension of judgement and then to mental tranquillity. Now, we call it an "ability" not in any peculiar sense of the word, but simply as it denotes a "being able." "Appearances" we take as meaning the objects of sense-perception; hence we set over against them the objects of thought. The phrase "in any manner whatever" may attach itself to "ability," so that we may understand that word (as we have said) in its simple sense, or it may be understood as modifying the phrase "to place in antithesis appearances and judgements." For since the antitheses we make take various forms, appearances opposed to appearances, judgements to judgements, or appearances to judgements, we say "in any manner whatever" in order to include all the antitheses. Or, we may understand it as "any manner of appearances and judgements whatever," in order to relieve ourselves of the inquiry into how appearances appear or how judgements are formed, and thus take them at their face value. When we speak of arguments which are "opposed," we do not at all mean denial and affirmation, but use this word in the sense of "conflicting." By "equality of force" we mean equality in respect of credibility and incredibility, since we do not admit that any of the conflicting arguments can take precedence over another on grounds of its being more credible. "Suspension of judgement" is a cessation of the thought processes in consequences of which we neither deny or affirm anything. "Mental tranquillity" is an undisturbed and calm state of soul. The question how mental tranquillity enters into the soul along with suspension of judgement we shall bring up in the chapter "On the End."

CHAPTER V
THE SCEPTIC

The definition of the Pyrrhonean philosopher is also virtually included in the concept of the Sceptic discipline. It is, of course, he who shares in the "ability" we have spoken of.

CHAPTER VI
THE PRINCIPLES OF SCEPTICISM

Scepticism has its inception and cause, we say, in the hope of attaining mental tranquillity. Men of noble nature had been disturbed at the irregularity in things, and puzzled as to where they should place their belief. Thus they were led on to investigate both truth and falsehood in things, in order that, when truth and falsehood were determined, they might attain tranquillity of mind. Now, the principle fundamental to the existence of Scepticism is the proposition, "To every argument an equal argument is opposed," for we believe that it is in consequence of this principle that we are brought to a point where we cease to dogmatize.

CHAPTER VII
DOES THE SCEPTIC DOGMATIZE?

We say that the Sceptic does not dogmatize. But in saying this we do not understand the word "dogma" as some do, in the more general sense of "approval of a thing." The Sceptic, of course, assents to feelings which derive necessarily from sense-impressions; he would not, for example, when feeling warm (or cold), say, "I believe I am not warm (or cold)." But some say that "dogma" is "the assent given to one of the non-evident things which form the object of scientific research." It is this meaning of "dogma" that we have in view when we say that the Sceptic does not dogmatize, for concerning non-evident things the Pyrrhonean philosopher holds no opinion. In fact, he does not even dogmatize when he is uttering the Sceptic formulae in regard to non-evident things (these formulae, the "No more," the "I determine nothing," and the others, we shall speak of later). No—for the dogmatizer affirms the real existence of that thing about which he is said to be dogmatizing, whereas the Sceptic does not take the real existence of these formulae wholly for granted. As he understands them, the formula "All things are false," for example, asserts its own falsity together with that of all other things, and the formula "Nothing is true" likewise. Thus also the formula "No more" asserts not only of other things but of itself also that it is "no more" existent than anything else, and hence cancels itself together with the other things. We say the same about the other Sceptic formulae also. However, if the dogmatizer affirms the real existence of the thing about which he is dogmatizing, while the Sceptic, uttering his own formulae, does so in such a way that they virtually cancel themselves, he can hardly be said to be dogmatizing when he pronounces them. The greatest indication of this is that in the enunciation of these formulae he is saying what appears to him and is reporting his own feeling, without indulging in opinion or making positive statements about the reality of things outside himself.

CHAPTER VIII
DOES THE SCEPTIC HAVE A SYSTEM?

Our attitude is the same when we are asked whether the Sceptic has a system. For if one defines "system" as "an adherence to a set of numerous dogmas which are consistent both with one another and with appearances," and if "dogma" is defined as "assent to a non-evident thing," then we shall say that we have no system. But if one means by "system" a "discipline which, in accordance with appearance, follows a certain line of reasoning, that line of reasoning indicating how it is possible to seem to live rightly ('rightly' understood not only with reference to virtue, but more simply), and extending also to the ability to suspend judgement," then we say that we do have a system. For we follow a certain line of reasoning which indicates to us, in a manner consistent with appearances, how to live in accordance with the customs, the laws, and the institutions of our country, and with our own natural feelings.

CHAPTER IX
IS THE SCEPTIC CONCERNED
WITH THE STUDY OF PHYSICS?

To the inquiry whether the Sceptic should theorize about physics our reply is similar. We do not theorize about physics in order to give firm and confident opinions on any of the things in physical theory about which firm doctrines are held. On the other hand, we do touch on physics in order to have for every argument an equal argument to oppose to it, and for the sake of mental tranquillity. Our approach to the logical and ethical divisions of so-called philosophy is similar.

CHAPTER X
DO THE SCEPTICS DENY APPEARANCES?

Those who say that the Sceptics deny appearances seem to me to be ignorant of what we say. As we said above, we do not deny those things which, in accordance with the passivity of our sense-impressions, lead us involuntarily to give our assent to them; and these are the appearances. And when we inquire whether an object is such as it appears, we grant the fact of its appearance. Our inquiry is thus not directed at the appearance itself. Rather, it is a question of what is predicated of it, and this is a different thing from investigating the fact of the appearance itself. For example, honey appears to us to have a sweetening quality. This much we concede, because it affects us with a sensation of sweetness. The question, however, is whether it is sweet in an absolute sense. Hence not the appearance is questioned, but that which is predicated of the appearance. Whenever we do expound arguments directly against appearances, we do so not with the intention of denying them, but in order to point out the hasty judgement of the dogmatists. For if reason is such a rogue as to all but snatch even the appearances from under our very eyes, should we not by all means be wary of it, at least not be hasty to follow it, in the case of things non-evident?

CHAPTER XI
THE CRITERION OF SCEPTICISM

That we pay attention to appearances is clear from what we say about the criterion of the Sceptic discipline. Now, the word "criterion" is used in two senses. First, it is the standard one takes for belief in reality or non-reality. This we shall discuss in our refutation. Second, it is the standard of action the observance of which regulates our actions in life. It is this latter about which we now speak. Now, we say that the criterion of the Sceptic discipline is the appearance, and it is virtually the sense-presentation to which we give this name, for this is dependent on feeling and involuntary affection and hence is not subject to question. Therefore no one, probably, will dispute that an object has this or that appearance; the question is whether it is in reality as it appears to be. Now, we cannot be entirely inactive when it comes to the observances of everyday life. Therefore, while living undogmatically, we pay due regard to appearances. This observance of the requirements of daily life seems to be fourfold, with the following particular heads: the guidance of nature, the compulsion of the feelings, the tradition of laws and customs, and the instruction of the arts. It is by the guidance of nature that we are naturally capable of sensation and thought. It is by the compulsion of the feelings that hunger leads us to food and thirst leads us to drink. It is by virtue of the tradition of laws and customs that in everyday life we accept piety as good and impiety as evil. And it is by virtue of the instruction of the arts that we are not inactive in those arts which we employ. All these statements, however, we make without prejudice.

CHAPTER XII
THE END OF SCEPTICISM

The next point to go through would be the end of Scepticism. An end is "that at which all actions or thoughts are directed, and which is itself directed at nothing, in other words, the ultimate of desirable things." Our assertion up to now is that the Sceptic's end, where matters of opinion are concerned, is mental tranquillity; in the realm of things unavoidable, moderation of feeling is the end. His initial purpose in philosophizing was to pronounce judgement on appearances. He wished to find out which are true and which false, so as to attain mental tranquillity. In doing so, he met with contradicting alternatives and equal force. Since he could not decide between them, he withheld judgement. Upon his suspension of judgement there followed, by chance, mental tranquillity in matters of opinion. For the person who entertains the opinion that anything is by nature good or bad is continually disturbed. When he lacks those things which seem to him to be good, he believes he is being pursued, as if by the Furies, by those things which are by nature bad, and pursues what he believes to be the good things. But when he has acquired them, he encounters further perturbations. This is because his elation at the acquisition is unreasonable and immoderate, and also because in his fear of a reversal all his exertions go to prevent the loss of the things which to him seem good. On the other side there is the man who leaves undetermined the question what things are good and bad by nature. He does not exert himself to avoid anything or to seek after anything, and hence he is in a tranquil state.

The Sceptic, in fact, had the same experience as that related in the story about Apelles the artist. They say that when Apelles was painting a horse, he wished to represent the horse's foam in the painting. His attempt was so unsuccessful that he gave it up and at the same time flung at the picture his sponge, with which he had wiped the paints off his brush. As it struck the picture, the sponge produced an image of horse's foam. So it was with the Sceptics. They were in hopes of attaining mental tranquillity, thinking that they could do this by arriving at some rational judgement which would dispel the inconsistencies involved in both appearances and thoughts. When they found this impossible, they withheld judgement. While they were in this state, they made a chance discovery. They found that they were attended by mental tranquillity as surely as a body by its shadow.

Nevertheless, we do not suppose the Sceptic to be altogether free from disturbance, rather, we say that when he is disturbed, it is by things which are unavoidable. Certainly we concede that he is sometimes cold and thirsty, and that he suffers in other such ways. But even here there is a difference. Two circumstances combine to the detriment of the ordinary man: he is hindered both by the feelings themselves and not less by the fact that he believes these conditions to be evil by nature. The Sceptic, on the other hand, rejects this additional notion that each of these things is evil by nature, and thus he gets off more easily. These, then, are our reasons for saying that the Sceptic's end is mental tranquillity where matters of opinion are concerned, and moderate feeling in the realm of things unavoidable. Some notable Sceptics have, however, added to these a third: suspension of judgement in investigations.

27

Certainty and the Limits of Doubt

René Descartes (1596–1650)

It is now several years since I first became aware how many false opinions I had from my childhood been admitting as true, and how doubtful was everything I have subsequently based on them. Accordingly I have ever since been convinced that if I am to establish anything firm and lasting in the sciences, I must once for all, and by a deliberate effort, rid myself of all those opinions to which I have hitherto given credence, starting entirely anew, and building from the foundations up. But as this enterprise was evidently one of great magnitude, I waited until I had attained an age so mature that I could no longer expect that I should at any later date be better able to execute my design. This is what has made me delay so long; and I should now be failing in my duty, were I to continue consuming in deliberation such time for action as still remains to me.

From "Meditations" in *Descartes Philosophical Writings,* translated by Norman Kemp Smith, The Modern Library, New York, 1958.

Today, then, as I have suitably freed my mind from all cares, and have secured for myself an assured leisure in peaceful solitude, I shall at last apply myself earnestly and freely to the general overthrow of all my former opinions. In so doing, it will not be necessary for me to show that they are one and all false; that is perhaps more than can be done. But since reason has already persuaded me that I ought to withhold belief no less carefully from things not entirely certain and indubitable than from those which appear to me manifestly false, I shall be justified in setting all of them aside, if in each case I can find any ground whatsoever for regarding them as dubitable. Nor in so doing shall I be investigating each belief separately—that, like inquiry into their falsity, would be an endless labor. The withdrawal of foundations involves the downfall of whatever rests on these foundations, and what I shall therefore begin by examining are the principles on which my former beliefs rested.

Whatever, up to the present, I have accepted as possessed of the highest truth and certainty I have learned either from the senses or through the senses. Now these senses I have sometimes found to be deceptive; and it is only prudent never to place complete confidence in that by which we have even once been deceived.

But, it may be said, although the senses sometimes deceive us regarding minute objects, or such as are at a great distance from us, there are yet many other things which, though known by way of sense, are too evident to be doubted; as, for instance, that I am in this place, seated by the fire, attired in a dressing-gown, having this paper in my hands, and other similar seeming certainties. Can I deny that these hands and this body are mine, save perhaps by comparing myself to those who are insane, and whose brains are so disturbed and clouded by dark bilious vapors that they persist in assuring us that they are kings, when in fact they are in extreme poverty; or that they are clothed in gold and purple when they are in fact destitute of any covering; or that their head is made of clay and their body of glass, or that they are pumpkins. They are mad; and I should be no less insane were I to follow examples so extravagant.

None the less I must bear in mind that I am a man, and am therefore in the habit of sleeping, and that what the insane represent to themselves in their waking moments I represent to myself, with other things even less probable, in my dreams. How often, indeed, have I dreamt of myself being in this place, dressed and seated by the fire, whilst all the time I was lying undressed in bed! At the present moment it certainly seems that in looking at this paper I do so with open eyes, that the head which I move is not asleep, that it is deliberately and of set purpose that I extend this hand, and that I am sensing the hand. The things which happen to the sleeper are not so clear nor so distinct as all of these are. I cannot, however, but remind myself that on many occasions I have in sleep been deceived by similar illusions; and on more careful study of them I see that there are no certain marks distinguishing waking from sleep; and I see this so manifestly that, lost in amazement, I am almost persuaded that I am now dreaming.

Let us, then, suppose ourselves to be asleep, and that all these particulars—namely, that we open our eyes, move the head, extend the hands—are false and illusory; and let us reflect that our hands perhaps, and the whole body, are not what we see them as being. Nevertheless we must at least agree that the things seen by us in sleep are as it were like painted images, and cannot have been formed save in the likeness of what is real and true. The types of things depicted, eyes, head, hands, etc.—these at least are not imaginary, but true and existent. For in truth when painters endeavor with all possible artifice to represent sirens and satyrs by forms the most fantastic and unusual, they cannot assign them natures which are entirely new, but only make a certain selection of limbs from different animals. Even should they excogitate something so novel that nothing similar has ever before been seen, and that their work represents to us a thing entirely fictitious and false, the colors used in depicting them cannot be similarly fictitious; they at least must truly exist. And by this same reasoning, even should those general things, viz., a body, eyes, a head, hands and such like, be imaginary, we are yet bound to admit that there are things simpler and more universal which are real existents and by the intermixture of which, as in the case of the colors, all the images of things of which we have any awareness be they true and real or false and fantastic, are formed. To this class of things belong corporeal nature in general and its extension, the shape of extended things, their quantity or magnitude, and their number, as also the location in which they are, the time through which they endure, and other similar things.

This, perhaps, is why we not unreasonably conclude that physics, astronomy, medicine, and all other disciplines treating of composite things are of doubtful character, and that arithmetic, geometry, etc., treating only of the simplest and most general things and but little concerned as to whether or not they are actual existents, have a content that is certain and indubitable. For whether I am awake or dreaming, 2 and 3 are 5, a square has no more than four sides; and it does not seem possible that truths so evident can ever be suspected of falsity.

Yet even these truths can be questioned. That God exists, that He is all-powerful and has created me such as I am, has long been my settled opinion. How, then, do I know that He has not arranged that there be no Earth, no heavens, no extended thing, no shape, no magnitude, no location, while at the same time securing that all these things appear to me to exist precisely as they now do? Others, as I sometimes think, deceive themselves in the things which they believe they know best. How do I know that I am not myself deceived everytime I add 2 and 3, or count the sides of a square, or judge of things yet simpler, if anything simpler can be suggested? But perhaps God has not been willing that I should be thus deceived, for He is said to be supremely good. If, however, it be repugnant to the goodness of God to have created me such that I am constantly subject to deception, it would also appear to be contrary to His goodness to permit me to be sometimes deceived, and that He does permit this is not in doubt.

There may be those who might prefer to deny the existence of a God so powerful, rather than to believe that all other things are uncertain. Let us, for the present, not oppose them; let us allow, in the manner of their view, that all which has been said regarding God is a fable. Even so we shall not have met and answered the doubts suggested above regarding the reliability of our mental faculties; instead we shall have given added force to them. For in whatever way it be supposed that I have come to be what I am, whether by fate or by chance, or by a continual succession and connection of things, or by some other means, since to be deceived and to err is an imperfection, the likelihood of my being so imperfect as to be the constant victim of deception will be increased in proportion as the power to which they assign my origin is lessened. To such argument I have assuredly nothing to reply; and thus at last I am constrained to confess that there is no one of all my former opinions which is not open to doubt, and this not merely owing to want of thought on my part, or through levity, but from cogent and maturely considered reasons. Henceforth, therefore, should I desire to discover something certain, I ought to refrain from assenting to these opinions no less scrupulously than in respect of what is manifestly false.

But it is not sufficient to have taken note of these conclusions; we must also be careful to keep them in mind. For long-established customary opinions perpetually recur in thought, long and familiar usage having given them the right to occupy my mind, even almost against my will, and to be masters of my belief. Nor shall I ever lose this habit of assenting to and of confiding in them, not at least so long as I consider them as in truth they are, namely, as opinions which, though in some fashion doubtful (as I have just shown), are still, none the less, highly probable and such as it is much more reasonable to believe than to deny. This is why I shall, as I think, be acting prudently if, taking a directly contrary line, I of set purpose employ every available device for the deceiving of myself, feigning that all these opinions are entirely false and imaginary. Then, in due course, having so balanced my old-time prejudices by this new prejudice that I cease to incline to one side more than to another, my judgment, no longer dominated by misleading usages, will not be hindered by them in the apprehension of things. In this course there can, I am convinced, be neither danger nor error. What I have under consideration is a question solely of knowledge, not of action, so that I cannot for the present be at fault as being over-ready to adopt a questioning attitude.

Accordingly I shall now suppose, not that a true God, who as such must be supremely good and the fountain of truth, but that some malignant genius exceedingly powerful and cunning has devoted all his powers in the deceiving of me; I shall suppose that the sky, the earth, colors, shapes, sounds and all external things are illusions and impostures of which this evil genius has availed himself for the abuse of my credulity; I shall consider myself as having no hands, no eyes, no flesh, no blood, nor any senses, but as falsely opining myself to possess all these things. Further, I shall obstinately persist in this way of thinking; and even if, while so doing, it may not be within my power to arrive at the knowledge of any truth, there is one thing I have it in me to do, viz., to suspend judgment, refusing assent to what is false. Thereby, thanks to this resolved firmness of mind, I shall be effectively guarding myself against being imposed upon by this deceiver, no matter how powerful or how craftly deceptive he may be. . . .

So disquieting are the doubts in which yesterday's meditation has involved me that it is no longer in my power to forget them. Nor do I yet see how they are to be resolved. It is as if I had all of a sudden fallen into very deep water, and am so disconcerted that I can neither plant my feet securely on the bottom nor maintain myself by swimming on the surface. I shall, however, brace myself for a great effort, entering anew on the path which I was yesterday exploring; that is, I shall proceed by setting aside all that admits even of the very slightest doubt, just as if I had convicted it of being absolutely false; and I shall persist in following this path, until I have come upon something certain, or, failing in that, until at least I know, and know with certainty, that in the world there is nothing certain.

Archimedes, that he might displace the whole earth, required only that there might be some one point, fixed and immovable, to serve in leverage; so likewise I shall be entitled to entertain high hopes if I am fortunate enough to find some one thing that is certain and indubitable.

I am supposing, then, that all the things I see are false; that of all the happenings my memory has ever suggested to me, none has ever so existed; that I have no senses; that body, shape, extension, movement and location are but mental fictions. What is there, then, which can be esteemed true? Perhaps this only, that nothing whatsoever is certain.

But how do I know that there is not something different from all the things I have thus far enumerated and in regard to which there is not the least occasion for doubt? Is there not some God, or other being by whatever name we call Him, who puts these thoughts into my mind? Yet why suppose such a being? May it not be that I am myself capable of being their author? Am I not myself at least a something? But already I have denied that I have a body and senses. This indeed raises awkward questions. But what is it that thereupon follows? Am I so dependent on the body and senses that without them I cannot exist? Having persuaded myself that outside me there is nothing, that there is no heaven, no Earth, that there are no minds, no bodies, am I thereby committed to the view that I also do not exist? By no means. If I am persuading myself of something in so doing I assuredly do exist. But what if, unknown to me, there be some deceiver, very powerful and very cunning, who is constantly employing his ingenuity in deceiving me? Again, as before, without doubt, if he is deceiving me, I exist. Let him deceive me as much as he will, he can never cause me to be nothing so long as I shall be thinking that I am something. And thus, having reflected well, and carefully examined all things, we have finally to conclude that this declaration, *Ego sum, ego existo,* is necessarily true every time I propound it or mentally apprehend it.

But I do not yet know in any adequate manner what I am, I who am certain that I am; and I must be careful not to substitute some other thing in place of myself, and so go astray in this knowledge which I am holding to be the most certain and evident of all that is knowable by me. This is why I shall now meditate anew on what, prior to my venturing on these questions, I believed myself to be. I shall withdraw those beliefs which can, even in the least degree, be invalidated by the reasons cited, in order that at length, of all my previous beliefs, there may remain only what is certain and indubitable.

What then did I formerly believe myself to be? Undoubtedly I thought myself to be a man. But what is a man? Shall I say a rational animal? No, for then I should have to inquire what is "animal," what "rational"; and thus from the one question I should be drawn on into several others yet more difficult. I have not, at present, the leisure for any such subtle inquiries. Instead, I prefer to meditate on the thoughts which of themselves sprang up in my mind on my applying myself to the consideration of what I am, considerations suggested by my own proper nature. I thought that I possessed a face, hands, arms, and that whole structure to which I was giving the title "body," composed as it is of the limbs discernible in a corpse. In addition, I took notice that I was nourished, that I walked, that I sensed, that I thought, all of which actions I ascribed to the soul. But what the soul might be I did not stop to consider; or if I did, I imaged it as being something extremely rare and subtle, like a wind, a flame or an ether, and as diffused throughout my grosser parts. As to the nature of "body," no doubts whatsoever disturbed me. I had, as I thought, quite distinct knowledge of it; and had I been called upon to explain the manner in which I then conceived it, I should have explained myself somewhat thus: by body I understand whatever can be determined by a certain shape, and comprised in a certain location, whatever so fills a certain space as to exclude from it every other body, whatever can be apprehended by touch, sight, hearing, taste or smell, and whatever can be moved in various ways, not indeed of itself but something foreign to it by which it is touched and impressed. For I nowise conceived the power of self-movement, of sensing or knowing, as pertaining to the nature of body: on the contrary I was somewhat astonished on finding in certain bodies faculties such as these.

But what am I now to say that I am, now that I am supposing that there exists a very powerful, and if I may so speak, malignant being, who employs all his powers and skill in deceiving me? Can I affirm that I possess any one of those things which I have been speaking of as pertaining to the nature of body? On stopping to consider them with closer attention, and on reviewing all of them, I find none of which I can say that it belongs to me; to enumerate them again would be idle and tedious. What then, of those things which I have been attributing not to body, but to the soul? What of nutrition or of walking? If it be that I have no body, it cannot be that I take nourishment or that I walk. Sensing? There can be no sensing in the absence of body; and besides I have seemed during sleep to apprehend things which, as I afterwards noted, had not been sensed. Thinking? Here I find what does belong to me: it alone cannot be separated from me. *I am, I exist.* This is certain. How often? As often as I think. For it might indeed be that if I entirely ceased to think, I should thereupon altogether cease to exist. I am not at present admitting anything which is not necessarily true; and, accurately speaking, I am therefore (taking myself to be) only a thinking thing, that is to say, a mind, an understanding or reason—terms the significance of which has hitherto been unknown to me. I am, then, a real thing, and really existent. What thing? I have said it, a thinking thing.

And what more am I? I look for aid to the imagination. (But how mistakenly!) I am not that assemblage of limbs we call the human body; I am not a subtle penetrating air distributed throughout all these members; I am not a wind, a fire, a vapor, a breath or anything at all that I can image. I am supposing all these things to be nothing. Yet I find, while so doing, that I am still assured that I am a something. . . .

What then is it that I am? A thinking thing. What is a thinking thing? It is a thing that doubts, understands, affirms, denies, wills, abstains from willing, that also can be aware of images and sensations.

Assuredly if all these things pertain to me, I am indeed a something. And how could it be they should not pertain to me? Am I not that very being who doubts of almost everything, who none the less also apprehends certain things, who affirms that one thing only is true, while denying all the rest, who yet desires to know more, who is averse to being deceived, who images many things, sometimes even despite his will, and who likewise apprehends many things which seem to come by way of the senses? Even though I should be always dreaming, and though he who has created me employs all his ingenuity in deceiving me, is there any one of the above assertions which is not as true as that I am and that I exist? And one of them which can be distinguished from my thinking? Any one of them which can be said to be separate from the self? So manifest is it that it is I who doubt, I who apprehend, I who desire, that there is here no need to add anything by way of rendering it more evident. It is no less certain that I can apprehend images. For although it may happen (as I have been supposing) that none of the things imaged are true, the imaging, *qua* active power, is none the less really in me, as forming part of my thinking. Again, I am the being who senses, that is to say, who apprehends corporeal things, as if by the organs of sense, since I do in truth see light, hear noise, feel heat. These things, it will be said, are false, and I am only dreaming. Even so, it is none the less certain that it seems to me that I see, that I hear, and that I am warmed. This is what in me is rightly called sensing, and as used in this precise manner is nowise other than thinking.

From all this I begin to know what I am somewhat better than heretofore. But it still seems to me—for I am unable to prevent myself continuing in this way of thinking—that corporeal things, which are reconnoitered by the senses, and whose images inform thought, are known with much greater distinctness than that part of myself (whatever it be) which is not imageable—strange though it may be to be thus saying that I know and comprehend more distinctly those things which I am supposing to be doubtful and unknown, and as not belonging to me, than others which are known to me, which appertain to my proper nature and of the truth of which I am convinced—in short are known more distinctly than I know myself. But I can see how this comes about: my mind delights to wander and will not yet suffer itself to be restrained within the limits of truth.

Let us, therefore, once again allow the mind the freest reign, so that when afterwards we bring it, more opportunely, under due constraint, it may be the more easily controlled. Let us begin by considering the things which are commonly thought to be the most distinctly known, viz., the bodies which we touch and see; not, indeed, bodies in general, for such general notions are usually somewhat confused, but one particular body. Take, for example, this piece of wax; it has been but recently taken from the hive; it has not yet lost the sweetness of the honey it contained; it still retains something of the odor of the flowers from which it has been gathered; its color, its shape, its size, are manifest to us; it is hard, cold, easily handled, and when struck upon with the finger emits a sound. In short, all that is required to make a body known with the greatest possible distinctness is present in the one now before us. But behold! While I am speaking let it be moved toward the fire. What remains of the taste exhales, the odor evaporates, the color changes, the shape is destroyed, its size increases, it becomes liquid, it becomes hot and can no longer be handled, and when struck upon emits no sound. Does the wax, notwithstanding these changes, still remain the same wax? We must admit that it does; no one doubts that it does, no one judges otherwise. What then, was it I comprehended so distinctly in knowing the piece of wax? Certainly, it could be nothing of all that I was aware of by way of the senses, since all the things that came by way of taste, smell, sight, touch and hearing, are changed, and the wax none the less remains.

Perhaps it has all along been as I am now thinking, viz., that the wax was not that sweetness of honey, nor that pleasing scent of flowers, nor that whiteness, that shape, that sound, but a body which a little while ago appeared to me decked out with those modes, and now appears decked out with others. But what precisely is it that I am here imaging? Let us attentively consider the wax, withdrawing from it all that does not belong to it, that we may see what remains. As we find, what then alone remains is a something extended, flexible and movable. But what is this "flexible," this "movable"? What am I then imaging? That the piece of wax from being round in shape can become square, or from being square can become triangular? Assuredly not. For I am apprehending that it admits of an infinity of similar shapes, and am not able to compass this infinity by way of images. Consequently this comprehension of it cannot be the product of the faculty of imagination.

What, we may next ask, is its extension? Is it also not known (by way of the imagination)? It becomes greater when the wax is melted, greater when the wax is made to boil, and ever greater as the heat increases; and I should not be apprehending what the wax truly is, if I did not think that this piece of wax we are considering allows of a greater variety of extensions than I have ever imaged. I must, therefore, admit that I cannot by way of images comprehend what this wax is, and that it is by the mind alone that I (adequately) apprehend it. I say this particular wax, for as to wax in general that is yet more evident. Now what is this wax which cannot be (adequately) apprehended save by the mind? Certainly the same that I see, touch, image, and in short, the very body that from the start I have been supposing it to be. And what has especially to be noted is that our (adequate) apprehension of it is not a seeing, nor a touching, nor an imaging, and has never been such, although it may formerly have seemed so, but is solely an inspection of the mind which may be imperfect and confused, as it formerly was, or clear and distinct, as it now is, according as my attention is directed less or more to the constituents composing the body.

I am indeed amazed when I consider how weak my mind is and how prone to error. For although I can, dispensing with words, (directly) apprehend all this in myself, none the less words have a hampering hold upon me, and the accepted usages of ordinary speech tend to mislead me. Thus when the wax is before us we say that we see it to be the same wax as that previously seen, and not that we judge it to be the same from its retaining the same color and shape. From this I should straight-way conclude that the wax is known by ocular vision, independently of a strictly mental inspection, were it not that perchance I recall how when looking from a window at beings passing by on the street below, I similarly say that it is men I am seeing, just as I say that I am seeing the wax. What do I see from the window beyond hats and cloaks, which might cover automatic machines? Yet I judge those to be men. In analogous fashion, what I have been supposing myself to see with the eyes I am comprehending solely with the faculty of judgment, a faculty proper not to my eyes but to my mind. . . .

28

Empiricism and the Limits of Knowledge

David Hume (1711–1776)

All the objects of human reason or enquiry may naturally be divided into two kinds, to wit, *Relations of Ideas,* and *Matters of Fact.* Of the first kind are the sciences of Geometry, Algebra, and Arithmetic; and in short, every affirmation which is either intuitively or demonstratively certain. *That the square of the hypothenuse is equal to the square of the two sides,* is a proposition which expresses a relation between these figures. *That* three times five is equal to the half of thirty, expresses a relation between these numbers. Propositions of this kind are discoverable by the mere operation of thought, without dependence on what is anywhere existent in the universe. Though there never were a circle or triangle in nature, the truths demonstrated by Euclid would for ever retain their certainty and evidence.

From David Hume, *Inquiry Concerning Human Knowledge,* 1748.

Matters of fact, which are the second objects of human reason, are not ascertained in the same manner; nor is our evidence of their truth, however great, of a like nature with the foregoing. The contrary of every matter of fact is still possible; because it can never imply a contradiction, and is conceived by the mind with the same facility and distinctness, as if ever so conformable to reality. *That the sun will not rise tomorrow* is no less intelligible a proposition, and implies no more contradiction than the affirmation, *that it will rise.* We should in vain, therefore, attempt to demonstrate its falsehood. Were it demonstratively false, it would imply a contradiction, and could never be distinctly conceived by the mind.

It may, therefore, be a subject worthy of curiosity, to enquire what is the nature of that evidence which assures us of any real existence and matter of fact, beyond the present testimony of our senses, or the records of our memory. This part of philosophy, it is observable, has been little cultivated, either by the ancients or moderns; and therefore our doubts and errors, in the prosecution of so important an enquiry, may be the more excusable; while we march through such difficult paths without any guide or direction. They may even prove useful, by exciting curiosity, and destroying that implicit faith and security, which is the bane of all reasoning and free enquiry. The discovery of defects in the common philosophy, if any such there be, will not, I presume, be a discouragement, but rather an incitement, as is usual, to attempt something more full and satisfactory than has yet been proposed to the public.

All reasonings concerning matter of fact seem to be founded on the relation of *Cause and Effect.* By means of that relation alone we can go beyond the evidence of our memory and senses. If you were to ask a man, why he believes any matter of fact, which is absent; for instance, that his friend is in the country, or in France; he would give you a reason; and this reason would be some other fact; as a letter received from him, or the knowledge of his former resolutions and promises. A man finding a watch or any other machine in a desert island, would conclude that there had once been men in that island. All our reasonings concerning fact are of the same nature. And here it is constantly supposed that there is a connexion between the present fact and that which is inferred from it. Were there nothing to bind them together, the inference would be entirely precarious. The hearing of an articulate voice and rational discourse in the dark assures us of the presence of some person: Why? because these are the effects of the human make and fabric, and closely connected with it. If we anatomize all the other reasonings of this nature, we shall find that they are founded on the relation of cause and effect, and that this relation is either near or remote, direct or collateral. Heat and light are collateral effects of fire, and the one effect may justly be inferred from the other.

If we would satisfy ourselves, therefore, concerning the nature of that evidence, which assures us of matters of fact, we must enquire how we arrive at the knowledge of cause and effect.

I shall venture to affirm, as a general proposition, which admits of no exception, that the knowledge of this relation is not, in any instance, attained by reasonings *a priori;* but arises entirely from experience, when we find that any particular objects are constantly conjoined with each other. Let an object be presented to a man of ever so strong natural reason and abilities; if that object be entirely new to him, he will not be able, by the most accurate examination of its sensible qualities, to discover any of its causes or effects. Adam, though his rational faculties be supposed, at the very first, entirely perfect, could not have inferred from the fluidity and transparency of water that it would suffocate him, or from the light and warmth of fire that it would consume him. No object ever discovers, by the qualities which appear to the senses, either the causes which produced it, or the effects which will arise from it; nor can our reason, unassisted by experience, ever draw any inference concerning real existence and matter of fact.

This proposition, *that causes and effects are discoverable, not by reason but by experience,* will readily be admitted with regard to such objects, as we remember to have once been altogether unknown to us; since we must be conscious of the utter inability, which we then lay under, of foretelling what would arise from them. Present two smooth pieces of marble to a man who has no tincture of natural philosophy; he will never discover that they will adhere together in such a manner as to require great force to separate them in a direct line, while they make so small a resistance to a lateral pressure. Such events, as bear little analogy to the common course of nature, are also readily confessed to be known only by experience; nor does any man imagine that the explosion of gunpowder, or the attraction of a loadstone, could ever be discovered by arguments *a priori.* In like manner, when an effect is supposed to depend upon an intricate machinery or secret structure of parts, we make no difficulty in attributing all our knowledge of it to experience. Who will assert that he can give the ultimate reason, why milk or bread is proper nourishment for a man, not for a lion or a tiger?

But the same truth may not appear, at first sight, to have the same evidence with regard to events, which have become familiar to us from our first appearance in the world, which bear a close analogy to the whole course of nature, and which are supposed to depend on the simple qualities of objects, without any secret structure of parts. We are apt to imagine that we could discover these effects by the mere operation of our reason, without experience. We fancy, that were we brought on a sudden into this world, we could at first have inferred that one Billiard-ball would communicate motion to another upon impulse; and that we needed not to have waited for the event, in order to pronounce with certainty concerning it. Such is the influence of custom, that, where it is strongest, it not only covers our natural ignorance, but even conceals itself, and seems not to take place, merely because it is found in the highest degree.

But to convince us that all the laws of nature, and all the operations of bodies without exception, are known only by experience, the following reflections may, perhaps, suffice. Were any object presented to us, and were we required to pronounce concerning the effect, which will result from it, without consulting past observation; after what manner, I beseech you, must the mind proceed in this operation? It must invent or imagine some event, which it ascribes to the object as its effect; and it is plain that this invention must be entirely arbitrary. The mind can never possibly find the effect in the supposed cause, by the most accurate scrutiny and examination. For the effect is totally different from the cause, and consequently can never be discovered in it. Motion in the second Billiard-ball is a quite distinct event from motion in the first; nor is there anything in the one to suggest the smallest hint of the other. A stone or piece of metal raised into the air, and left without any support, immediately falls: but to consider the matter *a priori*, is there anything we discover in this situation which can beget the idea of a downward, rather than an upward, or any other motion, in the stone or metal?

And as the first imagination or invention of a particular effect, in all natural operations, is arbitrary, where we consult not experience; so must we also esteem the supposed tie or connexion between the cause and effect, which binds them together, and renders it impossible that any other effect could result from the operation of that cause. When I see, for instance, a Billiard-ball moving in a straight line towards another; even suppose motion in the second ball should by accident be suggested to me, as the result of their contact or impulse; may I not conceive, that a hundred different events might as well follow from that cause? May not both these balls remain at absolute rest? May not the first ball return in a straight line, or leap off from the second in any line or direction? All these suppositions are consistent and conceivable. Why then should we give the preference to one, which is no more consistent or conceivable than the rest? All our reasonings *a priori* will never be able to show us any foundation for this preference.

In a word, then, every effect is a distinct event from its cause. It could not, therefore, be discovered in the cause, and the first invention or conception of it, *a priori*, must be entirely arbitrary. And even after it is suggested, the conjunction of it with the cause must appear equally arbitrary; since there are always many other effects, which, to reason, must seem fully as consistent and natural. In vain, therefore, should we pretend to determine any single event, or infer any cause or effect, without the assistance of observation and experience.

Hence we may discover the reason why no philosopher, who is rational and modest, has ever pretended to assign the ultimate cause of any natural operation, or to show distinctly the action of that power, which produces any single effect in the universe. It is confessed, that the utmost effect of human reason is to reduce the principles, productive of natural phenomena, to a greater simplicity, and to resolve the many particular effects into a few general causes, by means of reasonings from analogy, experience, and observation. But as to the causes of these general causes, we should in vain attempt their discovery; nor shall we ever be able to satisfy ourselves, by any particular explication of them. These ultimate springs and principles are totally shut up from human curiosity and enquiry. Elasticity, gravity, cohesion of parts, communication of motion by impulse; these are probably the ultimate causes and principles which we shall ever discover in nature; and we may esteem ourselves sufficiently happy, if, by accurate enquiry and reasoning, we can trace up the particular phenomena to, or near to, these general principles. The most perfect philosophy of the natural kind only staves off our ignorance a little longer: as perhaps the most perfect philosophy of the moral or metaphysical kind serves only to discover larger portions of it. Thus the observation of human blindness and weakness is the result of all philosophy, and meets us at every turn, in spite of our endeavours to elude or avoid it.

Nor is geometry, when taken into the assistance of natural philosophy, ever able to remedy this defect, or lead us into the knowledge of ultimate causes, by all that accuracy of reasoning for which it is so justly celebrated. Every part of mixed mathematics proceeds upon the supposition that certain laws are established by nature in her operations; and abstract reasonings are employed, either to assist experience in the discovery of these laws, or to determine their influence in particular instances, where it depends upon any precise degree of distance and quality. Thus, it is a law of motion, discovered by experience, that the movement or force of any body in motion is in the compound ratio or proportion of its solid contents and its velocity; and consequently, that a small force may remove the greatest obstacle or raise the greatest weight, if, by any contrivance or machinery, we can increase the velocity of that force, so as to make it an overmatch for its antagonist. Geometry assists us in the application of this law, by giving us the just dimensions of all the parts and figures which can enter into any species of machine; but still the discovery of the law itself is owing merely to experience, and all the abstract reasonings in the world could never lead us one step towards the knowledge of it. When we reason *a priori*, and consider merely any object or cause, as it appears to the mind, independent of all observation, it never could suggest to us the notion of any distinct object, such as its effect; much less, show us the inseparable and inviolable connexion between them. A man must be very sagacious who could discover by reasoning that crystal is the effect of heat, and ice of cold, without being previously acquainted with the operation of these qualities.

But we have not yet attained any tolerable satisfaction with regard to the question first proposed. Each solution still gives rise to a new question as difficult as the foregoing, and leads us on to farther enquiries. When it is asked, *What is the nature of all our reasonings concerning matter of fact?* the proper answer seems to be, that they are founded on the relation of cause and effect. When again it is asked, *What is the foundation of all our reasonings and conclusions concerning that relation?* it may be replied in one word, Experience. But if we still carry on our sifting humour, and ask, *What is the foundation of all conclusions from experience?* this implies a new question, which may be of more difficult solution and explication. Philosophers, that give themselves airs of superior wisdom and sufficiency, have a hard task when they encounter persons of inquisitive dispositions, who push them from every corner to which they retreat, and who are sure at last to bring them to some dangerous dilemma. The best expedient to prevent this confusion, is to be modest in our pretensions; and even to discover the difficulty ourselves before it is objected to us. By this means, we may make a kind of merit of our very ignorance.

I shall content myself, in this section, with an easy task, and shall pretend only to give a negative answer to the question here proposed. I say then, that, even after we have experience of the operations of cause and effect, our conclusions from that experience are *not* founded on reasoning, or any process of the understanding. This answer we must endeavour both to explain and to defend.

It must certainly be allowed, that nature has kept us at a great distance from all her secrets, and has afforded us only the knowledge of a few superficial qualities of objects; while she conceals from us those powers and principles on which the influence of those objects entirely depends. Our senses inform us of the colour, weight, and consistence of bread; but neither sense nor reason can ever inform us of those qualities which fit it for the nourishment and support of a human body. Sight or feeling conveys an idea of the actual motion of bodies; but as to that wonderful force or power, which would carry on a moving body for ever in a continued change of place, and which bodies never lose but by communicating it to others; of this we cannot form the most distant conception. But notwithstanding this ignorance of natural powers and principles, we always presume, when we see like sensible qualities, that they have like secret powers, and expect that effects, similar to those which we have experienced, will follow from them. If a body of like colour and consistence with that bread, which we have formerly eaten, be presented to us, we make no scruple of repeating the experiment, and foresee, with certainty, like nourishment and support. Now this is a process of the mind or thought, of which I would willingly know the foundation. It is allowed on all hands that there is no known connexion between the sensible qualities and the secret powers; and consequently, that the mind is not led to form such a conclusion concerning their constant and regular conjunction, by anything which it knows of their nature. As to past *Experience*, it can be allowed to give *direct* and *certain* information of those precise objects only, and that precise period of time, which fell under its cognizance: but why this experience should be extended to future times, and to other objects, which for aught we know, may be only in appearance similar; this is the main question on which I would insist. The bread, which I formerly eat, nourished me; that is, a body of such sensible qualities was, at that time, endued with such secret powers: but does it follow, that other bread must also nourish me at another time, and that like sensible qualities must always be attended with like secret powers? The consequence seems nowise necessary. At least, it must be acknowledged that there is here a consequence drawn by the mind; that there is a certain step taken; a process of thought, and an inference, which wants to be explained. These two propositions are far from being the same, *I have found that such an object has always been attended with such an effect, and I foresee, that other objects, which are, in appearance, similar, will be attended with similar effects.* I shall allow, if you please, that the one proposition may justly be inferred from the other: I know, in fact, that it always is inferred. But if you insist that the inference is made by a chain of reasoning, I desire you to produce that reasoning. The connexion between these propositions is not intuitive. There is required a medium, which may enable the mind to draw such an inference, if indeed it be drawn by reasoning, and argument. What that medium is, I must confess, passes my comprehension; and it is incumbent on those to produce it, who assert that it really exists, and is the origin of all our conclusions concerning matter of fact.

This negative argument must certainly, in process of time, become altogether convincing, if many penetrating and able philosophers shall turn their enquiries this way and no one be ever able to discover any connecting proposition or intermediate step, which supports the understanding in this conclusion. But as the question is yet new, every reader may not trust so far to his own penetration, as to conclude, because an argument escapes his enquiry, that therefore it does not really exist. For this reason it may be requisite to venture upon a more difficult task; and enumerating all the branches of human knowledge, endeavour to show that none of them can afford such an argument.

All reasonings may be divided into two kinds, namely, demonstrative reasoning, or that concerning relations of ideas, and moral reasoning, or that concerning matter of fact and existence. That there are no demonstrative arguments in the case seems evident; since it implies no contradiction that the cause of nature may change, and that an object, seemingly like those which we have experienced, may be attended with different or contrary effects. May I not clearly and distinctly conceive that a body, falling from the clouds, and which, in all other respects, resembles snow, has yet the taste of salt or feeling of fire? Is there any more intelligible proposition than to affirm, that all the trees will flourish in December and January, and decay in May and June? Now whatever is intelligible, and can be distinctly conceived, implies no contradiction, and can never be proved false by any demonstrative argument or abstract reasoning *a priori*.

If we be, therefore, engaged by arguments to put trust in past experience, and make it the standard of our future judgement, these arguments must be probable only, or such as regard matter of fact and real existence, according to the division above mentioned. But that there is no argument of this kind, must appear, if our explication of that species of reasoning be admitted as solid and satisfactory. We have said that all arguments concerning existence are founded on the relations of cause and effect; that our knowledge of that relation is derived entirely from experience; and that all our experimental conclusions proceed upon the supposition that the future will be conformable to the past. To endeavour, therefore, the proof of this last supposition by probable arguments, or arguments regarding existence, must be evidently going in a circle, and taking that for granted, which is the very point in question.

In reality, all arguments from experience are founded on the similarity which we discover among natural objects, and by which we are induced to expect effects similar to those which we have found to follow from such objects. And though none but a fool or madman will ever pretend to dispute the authority of experience, or to reject that great guide of human life, it may surely be allowed a philosopher to have so much curiosity at least as to examine the principle of human nature, which gives this mighty authority to experience, and makes us draw advantage from that similarity which nature has placed among different objects. From causes which appear *similar* we expect similar effects. This is the sum of all our experimental conclusions. Now it seems evident that, if this conclusion were formed by reason, it would be as perfect at first, and upon one instance, as after ever so long a course of experience. But the case is far otherwise. Nothing so like as eggs; yet no one, on account of this appearing similarity, expects the same taste and relish in all of them. It is only after a long course of uniform experiments in any kind, that we attain a firm reliance and security with regard to a particular event. Now where is that process of reasoning which, from one instance, draws a conclusion, so different from that which it infers from a hundred instances that are nowise different from that single one? This question I propose as much for the sake of information, as with an intention of raising difficulties. I cannot find, I cannot imagine any such reasoning. But I keep my mind still open to instruction, if any one will vouchsafe to bestow it on me.

Should it be said that, from a number of uniform experiments, we *infer* a connexion between the sensible qualities and the secret powers; this, I must confess, seems the same difficulty, couched in different terms. The question still recurs, on what process of argument this *inference* is founded? Where is the medium, the interposing ideas, which join propositions so very wide of each other? It is confessed that the colour, consistence, and other sensible qualities of bread appear not, of themselves, to have any connexion with the secret powers of nourishment and support. For otherwise we could infer these secret powers from the first appearance of these sensible qualities, without the aid of experience; contrary to the sentiment of all philosophers, and contrary to plain matter of fact. Here, then, is our natural state of ignorance with regard to the powers and influence of all objects. How is this remedied by experience? It only shows us a number of uniform effects, resulting from certain objects, and teaches us that those particular objects, at that particular time, were endowed with such powers and forces. When a new object, endowed with similar sensible qualities, is produced, we expect similar powers and forces, and look for a like effect. From a body of like colour and consistence with bread we expect like nourishment and support. But this surely is a step or progress of the mind, which wants to be explained. When a man says, *I have found, all past instances, such sensible qualities conjoined with such secret powers:* And when he says, *Similar sensible qualities will always be conjoined with similar secret powers,* he is not guilty of a tautology, nor are these propositions in any respect the same. You say that the one proposition is an inference from the other. But you must confess that the inference is not intuitive; neither is it demonstrative: Of what nature is it, then? To say it is experimental, is begging the question. For all inferences from experience suppose, as their foundation, that the future will resemble the past, and that similar powers will be conjoined with similar sensible qualities. If there be any suspicion that the course of nature may change, and that the past may be no rule for the future, all experience becomes useless, and can give rise to no inference or conclusion. It is impossible, therefore, that any arguments from experience can prove this resemblance of the past to the future; since all these arguments are founded on the supposition of that resemblance. Let the course of things be allowed hitherto ever so regular; that alone, without some new argument or inference, proves not that, for the future, it will continue so. In vain do you pretend to have learned the nature of bodies from your past experience. Their secret nature, and consequently all their effects and influence, may change, without any change in their sensible qualities. This happens sometimes, and with regard to some objects: Why may it not happen always, and with regard to all objects? What logic, what process of argument secures you against this supposition? My practice, you say, refutes my doubts. But you mistake the purport of my question. As an agent, I am quite satisfied in the point; but as a philosopher, who has some share of curiosity, I will not say scepticism, I want to learn the foundation of this inference. No reading, no enquiry has yet been able to remove my difficulty, or give me satisfaction in a matter of such importance. Can I do better than propose the difficulty to the public, even though, perhaps, I have small hopes of obtaining a solution? We shall at least, by this means, be sensible of our ignorance, if we do not augment our knowledge.

I must confess that a man is guilty of unpardonable arrogance who concludes, because an argument has escaped his own investigation, that therefore it does not really exist. I must also confess that, though all the learned, for several ages, should have employed themselves in fruitless search upon any subject, it may still, perhaps, be rash to conclude positively that the subject must, therefore, pass all human comprehension. Even though we examine all the sources of our knowledge, and conclude them unfit for such a subject, there may still remain a suspicion, that the enumeration is not complete, or the examination not accurate. But with regard to the present subject, there are some considerations which seem to remove all this accusation of arrogance or suspicion of mistake.

It is certain that the most ignorant and stupid peasants—nay infants, nay even brute beasts—improve by experience, and learn the qualities of natural objects, by observing the effects which result from them. When a child has felt the sensation of pain from touching the flame of a candle, he will be careful not to put his hand near any candle; but will expect a similar effect from a cause which is similar in its sensible qualities and appearance. If you assert, therefore, that the understanding of the child is led into this conclusion by any process of argument or ratiocination, I may justly require you to produce that argument; nor have you any pretence to refuse so equitable a demand. You cannot say that the argument is abstruse, and may possibly escape your enquiry; since you confess that it is obvious to the capacity of a mere infant. If you hesitate, therefore, a moment, or if, after reflection, you produce any intricate or profound argument, you, in a manner, give up the question, and confess that it is not reasoning which engages us to suppose the past resembling the future, and to expect similar effects from causes which are, to appearance, similar. This is the proposition which I intended to enforce in the present section. If I be right, I pretend not to have made any mighty discovery. And if I be wrong, I must acknowledge myself to be indeed a very backward scholar; since I cannot now discover an argument which, it seems, was perfectly familiar to me long before I was out of my cradle.

29

How Knowledge Is Possible

Immanuel Kant (1724–1804)

I. THE DISTINCTION BETWEEN PURE AND EMPIRICAL KNOWLEDGE

There can be no doubt that all our knowledge begins with experience. For how should our faculty of knowledge be awakened into action did not objects affecting our senses partly of themselves produce representations, partly arouse the activity of our understanding to compare these representations and, by combining or separating them, work up the raw material of the sensible impressions into that knowledge of objects which is entitled experience? In the order of time, therefore, we have no knowledge antecedent to experience, and with experience all our knowledge begins.

From Immanuel Kant, *Critique of Pure Reason*, translated by Norman Kemp Smith, © 1968 and reprinted by permission of St. Martin's Press, Inc., New York.

But though all our knowledge begins with experience, it does not follow that it all arises out of experience. For it may well be that even our empirical knowledge is made up of what we receive through impressions and of what our own faculty of knowledge (sensible impressions serving merely as the occasion) supplies from itself. If our faculty of knowledge makes any such addition, it may be that we are not in a position to distinguish it from the raw material, until with long practice of attention we have become skilled in separating it.

This, then, is a question which at least calls for closer examination, and does not allow of any off-hand answer:—whether there is any knowledge that is thus independent of experience and even of all impressions of the senses. Such knowledge is entitled *a priori*, and distinguished from the *empirical*, which has its sources *a posteriori*, that is, in experience.

The expression '*a priori*' does not, however, indicate with sufficient precision the full meaning of our question. For it has been customary to say, even of much knowledge that is derived from empirical sources, that we have it or are capable of having it *a priori*, meaning thereby that we do not derive it immediately from experience, but from a universal rule—a rule which is itself, however, borrowed by us from experience. Thus we would say of a man who undermined the foundations of his house, that he might have known *a priori* that it would fall, that is, that he need not have waited for the experience of its actual falling. But still he could not know this completely *a priori*. For he had first to learn through experience that bodies are heavy, and therefore fall when their supports are withdrawn.

In what follows, therefore, we shall understand by *a priori* knowledge, not knowledge independent of this or that experience, but knowledge absolutely independent of all experience. Opposed to it is empirical knowledge, which is knowledge possible only *a posteriori*, that is, through experience. *A priori* modes of knowledge are entitled pure when there is no admixture of anything empirical. Thus, for instance, the proposition, 'every alteration has its cause', while an *a priori* proposition, is not a pure proposition, because alteration is a concept which can be derived from experience.

II. WE ARE IN POSSESSION OF CERTAIN MODES OF *A PRIORI* KNOWLEDGE, AND EVEN THE COMMON UNDERSTANDING IS NEVER WITHOUT THEM

What we here require is a criterion by which to distinguish with certainty between pure and empirical knowledge. Experience teaches us that a thing is so and so, but not that it cannot be otherwise. First, then, if we have a proposition which in being thought is thought as *necessary*, it is an *a priori* judgment; and if, besides, it is not derived from any proposition except one which also has the validity of a necessary judgment, it is an absolutely *a priori* judgment. Secondly, experience never confers on its judgments true or strict, but only assumed and comparative *universality*, through induction. We can properly only say, therefore, that, so far as we have hitherto observed, there is no exception to this or that rule. If, then, a judgment is thought with strict universality, that is, in such manner that no exception is allowed as possible, it is not derived from experience, but is valid absolutely *a priori*. Empirical universality is only an arbitrary extension of a validity holding in most cases to one which holds in all, for instance, in the proposition, 'all bodies are heavy'. When, on the other hand, strict universality is essential to a judgment, this indicates a special source of knowledge, namely, a faculty of *a priori* knowledge. Necessity and strict universality are thus sure criteria of *a priori* knowledge, and are inseparable from one another. But since in the employment of these criteria the contingency of judgments is sometimes more easily shown than their empirical limitation, or, as sometimes also happens, their unlimited universality can be more convincingly proved than their necessity, it is advisable to use the two criteria separately, each by itself being infallible.

Now it is easy to show that there actually are in human knowledge judgments which are necessary and in the strictest sense universal, and which are therefore pure *a priori* judgments. If an example from the sciences be desired, we have only to look to any of the propositions of mathematics; if we seek an example from the understanding in its quite ordinary employment, the proposition, 'every alteration must have a cause', will serve our purpose. In the latter case, indeed, the very concept of a cause so manifestly contains the concept of a necessity of connection with an effect and of the strict universality of the rule, that the concept would be altogether lost if we attempted to derive it, as Hume has done, from a repeated association of that which happens with that which precedes, and from a custom of connecting representations, a custom originating in this repeated association, and constituting therefore a merely subjective necessity. Even without appealing to such examples, it is possible to show that pure *a priori* principles are indispensable for the possibility of experience, and so to prove their existence *a priori*. For whence could experience derive its certainty, if all the rules, according to which it proceeds, were always themselves empirical, and therefore contingent? Such rules could hardly be regarded as first principles. At present, however, we may be content to have established a pure employment, and to have shown what are the criteria of such an employment.

Such *a priori* origin is manifest in certain concepts, no less than in judgments. If we remove from our empirical concept of a body, one by one, every feature in it which is (merely) empirical, the colour, the hardness or softness, the weight, even the impenetrability, there still remains the space which the body (now entirely vanished) occupied, and this cannot be removed. Again, if we remove from our empirical concept of any object, corporeal or incorporeal, all properties which experience has taught us, we yet cannot take away that property through which the object is thought as substance or as inhering in a substance (although this concept of substance is more determinate than that of an object in general). Owing, therefore, to the necessity with which this concept of substances forces itself upon us, we have no option save to admit that it has its seat in our faculty of *a priori* knowledge.

III. PHILOSOPHY STANDS IN NEED OF A SCIENCE WHICH SHALL DETERMINE THE POSSIBILITY, THE PRINCIPLES, AND THE EXTENT OF ALL *A PRIORI* KNOWLEDGE

But what is still more extraordinary than all the preceding is this, that certain modes of knowledge leave the field of all possible experiences and have the appearance of extending the scope of our judgments beyond all limits of experience, and this by means of concepts to which no corresponding object can ever be given in experience.

It is precisely by means of the latter modes of knowledge, in a realm beyond the world of the senses, where experience can yield neither guidance nor correction, that our reason carries on those enquiries which owing to their importance we consider to be far more excellent, and in their purpose far more lofty, than all that the understanding can learn in the field of appearances. Indeed we prefer to run every risk of error rather than desist from such urgent enquiries, on the ground of their dubious character, or from disdain and indifference. These unavoidable problems set by pure reason itself are *God, freedom,* and *immortality.* The science which, with all its preparations, is in its final intention directed solely to their solution is metaphysics; and its procedure is at first dogmatic, that is, it confidently sets itself to this task without any previous examination of the capacity or incapacity of reason for so great an undertaking.

Now it does indeed seem natural that, as soon as we have left the ground of experience, we should, through careful enquiries, assure ourselves as to the foundations of any building that we propose to erect, not making use of any knowledge that we possess without first determining whence it has come, and not trusting to principles without knowing their origin. It is natural, that is to say, that the question should first be considered, how the understanding can arrive at all this knowledge *a priori,* and what extent, validity, and worth it may have. Nothing, indeed, could be more natural, if by the term 'natural' we signify what fittingly and reasonably ought to happen. But if we mean by 'natural' what ordinarily happens, then on the contrary nothing is more natural and more intelligible than the fact that this enquiry has been so long neglected. For one part of this knowledge, the mathematical, has long been of established reliability, and so gives rise to a favourable presumption as regards the other part, which may yet be of quite different nature. Besides, once we are outside the circle of experience, we can be sure of not being *contradicted* by experience. The charm of extending our knowledge is so great that nothing short of encountering a direct contradiction can suffice to arrest us in our course; and this can be avoided, if we are careful in our fabrications—which none the less will still remain fabrications. Mathematics gives us a shining example of how far, independently of experience, we can progress in *a priori* knowledge. It does, indeed, occupy itself with objects and with knowledge solely in so far as they allow of being exhibited in intuition. But this circumstance is easily overlooked, since the intuition, in being thought, can itself be given *a priori,* and is therefore hardly to be distinguished from a bare and pure concept. Misled by such a proof of the power of reason, the demand for the extension of knowledge recognizes no limits. The light dove, cleaving the air in her free flight, and feeling its resistance, might imagine that its flight would be still easier in empty space. It was thus that Plato left the world of the senses, as setting too narrow limits to the understanding, and ventured out beyond it on the wings of the ideas, in the empty space of the pure understanding. He did not observe that with all his efforts he made no advance—meeting no resistance that might, as it were, serve as a support upon which he could take a stand, to which he could apply his powers, and so set his understanding in motion. It is, indeed, the common fate of human reason to complete its speculative structures as speedily as may be, and only afterwards to enquire whether the foundations are reliable. All sorts of excuses will then be appealed to, in order to reassure us of their solidity, or rather indeed to enable us to dispense altogether with so late and so dangerous an enquiry. But what keeps us, during the actual building, free from all apprehension and suspicion, and flatters us with a seeming thoroughness, is this other circumstance, namely, that a great, prehaps the greatest, part of the business of our reason consists in analysis of the concepts which we already have of objects. This analysis supplies us with a considerable body of knowledge, which, while nothing but explanation or elucidation of what has already been thought in our concepts, though in a confused manner, is yet prized as being, at least as regards its form, new insight. But so far as the matter or content is concerned, there has been no extension of our previously possessed concepts, but only an analysis of them. Since this procedure yields real knowledge *a priori*, which progresses in an assured and useful fashion, reason is so far misled as surreptitiously to introduce, without itself being aware of so doing, assertions of an entirely different order, in which it attaches to given concepts others completely foreign to them, and moreover attaches them *a priori*. And yet it is not known how reason can be in position to do this. Such a question is never so much as thought of. I shall therefore at once proceed to deal with the difference between these two kinds of knowledge.

IV. THE DISTINCTION BETWEEN ANALYTIC AND SYNTHETIC JUDGMENTS

In all judgments in which the relation of a subject to the predicate is thought (I take into consideration affirmative judgments only, the subsequent application to negative judgments being easily made), this relation is possible in two different ways. Either the predicate B belongs to the subject A, as something which is (covertly) contained in this concept A; or B lies outside the concept A, although it does indeed stand in connection with it. In the one case I entitled the judgment analytic, in the other synthetic. Analytic judgments (affirmative) are therefore those in which the connection of the predicate with the subject is thought through identity; those in which this connection is thought without identity should be entitled synthetic. The former, as adding nothing through the predicate to the concept of the subject, but merely breaking it up into those constituent concepts that have all along been thought in it, although confusedly, can also be entitled explicative. The latter, on the other hand, add to the concept of the subject a predicate which has not been in any wise thought in it, and which no analysis could possibly extract from it; and they may therefore be entitled ampliative. If I say, for instance, 'All bodies are extended', this is an analytic judgment. For I do not require to go beyond the concept which I connect with 'body' in order to find extension as bound up with it. To meet with this predicate, I have merely to analyse the concept, that is, to become conscious to myself of the manifold which I always think in that concept. The judgment is therefore analytic. But when I say, 'All bodies are heavy', the predicate is something quite different from anything that I think in the mere concept of body in general; and the addition of such a predicate therefore yields a synthetic judgment.

Judgments of experience, as such, are one and all synthetic. For it would be absurd to found an analytic judgment on experience. Since, in framing the judgment, I must not go outside my concept, there is no need to appeal to the testimony of experience in its support. That a body is extended is a proposition that holds *a priori* and is not empirical. For, before appealing to experience, I have already in the concept of body all the conditions required for my judgment, I have only to extract from it, in accordance with the principle of contradiction, the required predicate, and in so doing can at the same time become conscious of the necessity of the judgment—and that is what experience could never have taught me. On the other hand, though I do not include in the concept of a body in general the predicate 'weight', none the less this concept indicates an object of experience through one of its parts, and I can add to that part other parts of this same experience, as in this way belonging together with the concept. From the start I can apprehend the concept of body analytically through the characters of extension, impenetrability, figure, etc., all of which are thought in the concept. Now, however, looking back on the experience from which I have derived this concept of body, and finding weight to be invariably connected with the above characters, I attach it as a predicate to the concept; and in doing so I attach it synthetically, and am therefore extending my knowledge. The possibility of the synthesis of the predicate 'weight' with the concept of 'body' thus rests upon experience. While the one concept is not contained in the other, they yet belong to one another, though only contingently, as parts of a whole, namely, of an experience which is itself a synthetic combination of intuitions.

But in *a priori* synthetic judgments this help is entirely lacking. (I do not here have the advantage of looking around in the field of experience.) Upon what, then, am I to rely, when I seek to go beyond the concept A, and to know that another concept B is connected with it? Through what is the synthesis made possible? Let us take the proposition, 'Everything which happens has its cause'. In the concept of 'something which happens', I do indeed think an existence which is preceded by a time, etc., and from this concept analytic judgments may be obtained. But the concept of a 'cause' lies entirely outside the other concept, and signifies something different from 'that which happens', and is not therefore in any way contained in this latter representation. How come I then to predicate of that which happens something quite different, and to apprehend that the concept of cause, though not contained in it, yet belongs, and indeed necessarily belongs, to it? What is here the unknown = X which gives support to the understanding when it believes that it can discover outside the concept A a predicate B foreign to this concept, which it yet at the same time considers to be connected with it? It cannot be experience, because the suggested principle has connected the second representation with the first, not only with greater universality, but also with the character of necessity, and therefore completely *a priori* and on the basis of mere concepts. Upon such synthetic, that is, ampliative principles, all our *a priori* speculative knowledge must ultimately rest; analytic judgments are very important, and indeed necessary, but only for obtaining that clearness in the concepts which is requisite for such a sure and wide synthesis as will lead to a genuinely new addition to all previous knowledge.

V. IN ALL THEORETICAL SCIENCES OF REASON SYNTHETIC *A PRIORI* JUDGMENTS ARE CONTAINED AS PRINCIPLES

1. *All mathematical judgments, without exception, are synthetic.* This fact, though incontestably certain and in its consequences very important, has hitherto escaped the notice of those who are engaged in the analysis of human reason, and is, indeed, directly opposed to all their conjectures. For as it was found that all mathematical inferences proceed in accordance with the principle of contradiction (which the nature of all apodeictic certainty requires), it was supposed that the fundamental propositions of the science can themselves be known to be true through that principle. This is an erroneous view. For though a synthetic proposition can indeed be discerned in accordance with the principle of contradiction, this can only be if another synthetic proposition is presupposed, and if it can then be apprehended as following from this other proposition; it can never be so discerned in and by itself.

First of all, it has to be noted that mathematical propositions, strictly so called, are always judgments *a priori*, not empirical; because they carry with them necessity, which cannot be derived from experience. If this be demurred to, I am willing to limit my statement to *pure* mathematics, the very concept of which implies that it does not contain empirical, but only pure *a priori* knowledge.

We might, indeed, at first suppose that the proposition $7 + 5 = 12$ is a merely analytic proposition, and follows by the principle of contradiction from the concept of a sum of 7 and 5. But if we look more closely we find that the concept of the sum of 7 and 5 contains nothing save the union of the two numbers into one, and in this no thought is being taken as to what that single number may be which combines both. The concept of 12 is by no means already thought in merely thinking this union of 7 and 5; and I may analyse my concept of such a possible sum as long as I please, still I shall never find the 12 in it. We have to go outside these concepts, and call in the aid of the intuition which corresponds to one of them, our five fingers, for instance, or, as Segner does in his *Arithmetic*, five points, adding to the concept of 7, unit by unit, the five given in intuition. For starting with the number 7, and for the concept of 5 calling in the aid of the fingers of my hand as intuition, I now add one by one to the number 7 the units which I previously took together to form the number 5, and with the aid of that figure (the hand) see the number 12 come into being. That 5 should be added to 7, I have indeed already thought in the concept of a sum $= 7 + 5$, but not that this sum is equivalent to the number 12. Arithmetical propositions are therefore always synthetic. This is still more evident if we take larger numbers. For it is then obvious that, however we might turn and twist our concepts, we could never, by the mere analysis of them, and without the aid of intuition, discover what (the number is that) is the sum.

Just as little is any fundamental proposition of pure geometry analytic. That the straight line between two points is the shortest, is a synthetic proposition. For my concept of *straight* contains nothing of quantity, but only of quality. The concept of the shortest is wholly an addition, and cannot be derived, through any process of analysis, from the concept of the straight line. Intuition, therefore, must here be called in; only by its aid is the synthesis possible. What here causes us commonly to believe that the predicate of such apodeictic judgments is already contained in our concept, and that the judgment is therefore analytic, is merely the ambiguous character of the terms used. We are required to join in thought a certain predicate to a given concept, and this necessity is inherent in the concepts themselves. But the question is not what we *ought* to join in thought to the given concept, but what we *actually* think in it, even if only obscurely; and it is then manifest that, while the predicate is indeed attached necessarily to the concept, it is so in virtue of an intuition which must be added to the concept, not as thought in the concept itself.

Some few fundamental propositions, presupposed by the geometrician, are, indeed, really analytic, and rest on the principle of contradiction. But, as identical propositions, they serve only as links in the chain of method and not as principles; for instance, a $=$ a; the whole is equal to itself; or $(a + b) > a$, that is, the whole is greater than its part. And even these propositions, though they are valid according to pure concepts, are only admitted in mathematics because they can be exhibited in intuition.

2. *Natural science (physics) contains* a priori *synthetic judgments as principles.* I need cite only two such judgments: that in all changes of the material world the quantity of matter remains unchanged; and that in all communication of motion, action and reaction must always be equal. Both propositions, it is evident, are not only necessary, and therefore in their origin *a priori*, but also synthetic. For in the concept of matter I do not think its permanence, but only its presence in the space which it occupies. I go outside and beyond the concept of matter, joining to it *a priori* in thought something which I have not thought *in* it. The proposition is not, therefore, analytic, but synthetic, and yet is thought *a*

priori; and so likewise are the other propositions of the pure part of natural science.

3. *Metaphysics,* even if we look upon it as having hitherto failed in all its endeavours, is yet, owing to the nature of human reason, a quite indispensable science, and *ought to contain* a priori *synthetic knowledge.* For its business is not merely to analyse concepts which we make for ourselves *a priori* of things, and thereby to clarify them analytically, but to extend our *a priori* knowledge. And for this purpose we must employ principles which add to the given concept something that was not contained in it, and through *a priori* synthetic judgments venture out so far that experience is quite unable to follow us, as, for instance, in the proposition, that the world must have a first beginning, and such like. Thus metaphysics consists, at least *in intention,* entirely of *a priori* synthetic propositions.

VI. THE GENERAL PROBLEM OF PURE REASON

Much is already gained if we can bring a number of investigations under the formula of a single problem. For we not only lighten our own task, by defining it accurately, but make it easier for others, who would test our results, to judge whether or not we have succeeded in what we set out to do. Now the proper problem of pure reason is contained in the question: How are *a priori* synthetic judgments possible?

That metaphysics has hitherto remained in so vacillating a state of uncertainty and contradiction, is entirely due to the fact that this problem, and perhaps even the distinction between analytic and synthetic judgments, has never previously been considered. Upon the solution of this problem, or upon a sufficient proof that the possibility which it desires to have explained does in fact not exist at all, depends the success or failure of metaphysics. Among philosophers, David Hume came nearest to envisaging this problem, but still was very far from conceiving it with sufficient definiteness and universality. He occupied himself exclusively with the synthetic proposition regarding the connection of an effect with its cause (*principium causalitatis*), and he believed himself to have shown that such an *a priori* proposition is entirely impossible. If we accept his conclusions, then all that we call metaphysics is a mere delusion whereby we fancy ourselves to have rational insight into what, in actual fact, is borrowed solely from experience, and under the influence of custom has taken the illusory semblance of necessity. If he had envisaged our problem in all its universality, he would never have been guilty of this statement, so destructive of all pure philosophy. For he would then have recognised that, according to his own argument, pure mathematics, as certainly containing *a priori* synthetic propositions, would also not be possible; and from such an assertion his good sense would have saved him.

In the solution of the above problem, we are at the same time deciding as to the possibility of the employment of pure reason in establishing and developing all those sciences which contain a theoretical *a priori* knowledge of objects, and have therefore to answer the questions:

How is pure mathematics possible?
How is pure science of nature possible?

Since these sciences actually exist, it is quite proper to ask *how* they are possible; for that they must be possible is proved by the fact that they exist. But the poor progress which has hitherto been made in metaphysics, and the fact that no system yet propounded can, in view of the essential purpose of metaphysics, be said really to exist, leaves everyone sufficient ground for doubting as to its possibility.

Yet, in a certain sense, this *kind of knowledge* is to be looked upon as given; that is to say, metaphysics actually exists, if not as a science, yet still as natural disposition (*metaphysica naturalis*). For human reason, without being moved merely by the idle desire for extent and variety of knowledge, proceeds impetuously, driven on by an inward need, to questions such as cannot be answered by any empirical employment of reason, or by principles thence derived. Thus in all men, as soon as their reason has become ripe for speculation, there has always existed and will always continue to exist some kind of metaphysics. And so we have the question:

How is metaphysics, as natural disposition, possible? that is, how from the nature of universal human reason do those questions arise which pure reason propounds to itself, and which it is impelled by its own need to answer as best it can?

But since all attempts which have hitherto been made to answer these natural questions—for instance, whether the world has a beginning or is from eternity—have always met with unavoidable contradictions, we cannot rest satisfied with the mere natural disposition to metaphysics, that is, with the pure faculty of reason itself, from which, indeed, some sort of metaphysics (be it what it may) always arises. It must be possible for reason to attain to certainty whether we know or do not know the objects of metaphysics, that is, to come to a decision either in regard to the objects of its enquiries or in regard to the capacity or incapacity of reason to pass any judgment upon them, so that we may either with confidence extend our pure reason or set to it sure and determinate limits. This last question, which arises out of the previous general problem, may, rightly stated, take the form:

How is metaphysics, as science, possible?

Thus the critique of reason, in the end, necessarily, leads to scientific knowledge; while its dogmatic employment, on the other hand, lands us in dogmatic assertions to which other assertions, equally specious, can always be opposed—that is, in *scepticism*.

This science cannot be of any very formidable prolixity, since it has to deal not with the objects of reason, the variety of which is inexhaustible, but only with itself and the problems which arise entirely from within itself, and which are imposed upon it by its own nature, not by the nature of things which are distinct from it. When once reason has learnt completely to understand its own power in respect of objects which can be presented to it in experience, it should easily be able to determine, with completeness and certainty, the extent and the limits of its attempted employment beyond the bounds of all experience.

We may, then, and indeed we must, regard as abortive all attempts, hitherto made, to establish a metaphysic *dogmatically.* For the analytic part in any such attempted system, namely, the mere analysis of the concepts that inhere in our reason *a priori,* is by no means the aim of, but only a preparation for, metaphysics proper, that is, the extension of its *a priori* synthetic knowledge. For such a purpose, the analysis of concepts is useless, since it merely shows what is contained in these concepts, not how we arrive at them *a priori.* A solution of this latter problem is required, that we may be able to determine the valid employment of such concepts in regard to the objects of all knowledge in general. Nor is much self-denial needed to give up these claims, seeing that the undeniable, and in the dogmatic procedure of reason also unavoidable, contradictions of reason with itself have long since undermined the authority of every metaphysical system yet propounded. Greater firmness will be required if we are not to be deterred by inward difficulties and outward opposition from endeavouring, through application of a method entirely different from any hitherto employed, at last to bring to a prosperous and fruitful growth a science indispensable to human reason—a science whose every branch may be cut away but whose root cannot be destroyed.

VII. THE IDEA AND DIVISION OF A SPECIAL SCIENCE, UNDER THE TITLE "CRITIQUE OF PURE REASON"

In view of all these considerations, we arrive at the idea of a special science which can be entitled the Critique of Pure Reason. For reason is the faculty which supplies the principles of *a priori* knowledge. Pure reason is, therefore, that which contains the principles whereby we know anything absolutely *a priori.* . . .

30

Pragmatism and the Enterprise of Knowing

William James (1842–1910)

Some years ago, being with a camping party in the mountains, I returned from a solitary ramble to find every one engaged in a ferocious metaphysical dispute. The *corpus* of the dispute was a squirrel—a live squirrel supposed to be clinging to one side of a tree-trunk; while over against the tree's opposite side a human being was imagined to stand. This human witness tries to get sight of the squirrel by moving rapidly round the tree, but no matter how fast he goes, the squirrel moves as fast in the opposite direction, and always keeps the tree between himself and the man, so that never a glimpse of him is caught. The resultant metaphysical problem now is this: *Does the man go round the squirrel or not?* He goes round the tree, sure enough, and the squirrel is on the tree; but does he go round the squirrel? In the unlimited leisure of the wilderness, discussion had been worn threadbare. Every one had taken sides, and was obstinate; and the numbers on

From William James, "What Pragmatism Means," 1907.

both sides were even. Each side, when I appeared, therefore appealed to me to make it a majority. Mindful of the scholastic adage that whenever you meet a contradiction you must make a distinction, I immediately sought and found one, as follows: "Which party is right," I said, "depends on what you *practically mean* by 'going round' the squirrel. If you mean passing from the north of him to the east, then to the south, then to the west, and then to the north of him again, obviously the man does go round him, for he occupies these successive positions. But if on the contrary you mean being first in front of him, then on the right of him, then behind him, then on his left, and finally in front again, it is quite as obvious that the man fails to go round him, for by the compensating movements the squirrel makes, he keeps his belly turned towards the man all the time, and his back turned away. Make the distinction, and there is no occasion for any further dispute. You are both right and both wrong according as you conceive the verb 'to go round' in one practical fashion or the other."

Although one or two of the hotter disputants called my speech a shuffling evasion, saying they wanted no quibbling or scholastic hair-splitting, but meant just plain honest English "round," the majority seemed to think that the distinction had assuaged the dispute.

I tell this trivial anecdote because it is a peculiarly simple example of what I wish now to speak of as *the pragmatic method*. The pragmatic method is primarily a method of settling metaphysical disputes that otherwise might be interminable. Is the world one or many?—fated or free?—material or spiritual?— here are notions either of which may or may not hold good of the world; and disputes over such notions are unending. The pragmatic method in such cases is to try to interpret each notion by tracing its respective practical consequences. What difference would it practically make to any one if this notion rather than that notion were true? If no practical difference whatever can be traced, then the alternatives mean practically the same thing, and all dispute is idle. Whenever a dispute is serious, we ought to be able to show some practical difference that must follow from one side or the other's being right.

A glance at the history of the idea will show you still better what pragmatism means. The term is derived from the same Greek word *pragma*, meaning action, from which our words "practice" and "practical" come. It was first introduced into philosophy by Mr. Charles Peirce in 1878. In an article entitled "How to Make Our Ideas Clear," in the *Popular Science Monthly* for January of that year Mr. Peirce, after pointing out that our beliefs are really rules for action, said that, to develop a thought's meaning, we need only determine what conduct it is fitted to produce: that conduct is for us its sole significance. And the tangible fact at the root of all our thought-distinctions, however subtle, is that there is no one of them so fine as to consist in anything but a possible difference of practice. To attain perfect clearness in our thoughts of an object, then, we need only consider what conceivable effects of a practical kind the object may involve—what sensations we are to expect from it, and what reactions we must prepare. Our conception of these effects, whether immediate or remote, is then for us the whole of our conception of the object, so far as that conception has positive significance at all.

This is the principle of Peirce, the principle of pragmatism. It lay entirely unnoticed by any one for twenty years, until I, in an address before Professor Howison's Philosophical Union at the University of California, brought it forward again and made a special application of it to religion. By that date (1898) the times seemed ripe for its reception. The word "pragmatism" spread, and at present it fairly spots the pages of the philosophic journals. On all hands we find the "pragmatic movement" spoken of, sometimes with respect, sometimes with contumely, seldom with clear understanding. It is evident that the term applies itself conveniently to a number of tendencies that hitherto have lacked a collective name, and that it has "come to stay."

To take in the importance of Peirce's principle, one must get accustomed to applying it to concrete cases. I found a few years ago that Ostwald, the illustrious Leipzig chemist, had been making perfectly distinct use of the principle of pragmatism in his lectures on the philosophy of science, though he had not called it by that name.

"All realities influence our practice," he wrote me, "and that influence is their meaning for us. I am accustomed to put questions to my classes in this way: In what respects would the world be different if this alternative to that were true? If I can find nothing that would become different, then the alternative has no sense."

That is, the rival views mean practically the same thing, and meaning, other than practical, there is for us none. Ostwald in a published lecture gives this example of what he means. Chemists have long wrangled over the inner constitution of certain bodies called "tautomerous." Their properties seemed equally consistent with the notion that an instable hydrogen atom oscillates inside of them, or that they are instable mixtures of two bodies. Controversy raged, but never was decided. "It would never have begun," says Ostwald, "if the combatants had asked themselves what particular experimental fact could have been made different by one or the other view being correct. For it would then have appeared that no difference of fact could possibly ensue; and the quarrel was as unreal as if, theorizing in primitive times about the raising of dough by yeast, one party should have invoked a 'brownie,' while another insisted on an 'elf' as the true cause of the phenomenon."

It is astonishing to see how many philosophical disputes collapse into insignificance the moment you subject them to this simple test of tracing a concrete consequence. There can *be* no difference anywhere that doesn't *make* a difference elsewhere—no difference in abstract truth that doesn't express itself in a difference in concrete fact and in conduct consequent upon that fact, imposed on somebody, somehow, somewhere, and somewhen. The whole function of philosophy ought to be to find out what definite difference it will make to you and me, at definite instants of our life, if this world-formula or that world-formula be the true one.

There is absolutely nothing new in the pragmatic method. Socrates was an adept at it. Aristotle used it methodically. Locke, Berkeley, and Hume made momentous contributions to truth by its means. Shadworth Hodgson keeps insisting that realities are only what they are "known as." But these forerunners of pragmatism used it in fragments: they were preluders only. Not until in our time has it generalized itself, become conscious of a universal mission, pretended to a conquering destiny. I believe in that destiny, and I hope I may end by inspiring you with my belief.

Pragmatism represents a perfectly familiar attitude in philosophy, the empiricist attitude, but it represents it, as it seems to me, both in a more radical and in a less objectionable form than it has ever yet assumed. A pragmatist turns his back resolutely and once for all upon a lot of inveterate habits dear to professional philosophers. He turns away from abstraction and insufficiency, from verbal solutions, from bad *a priori* reasons, from fixed principles, closed systems, and pretended absolutes and origins. He turns towards concreteness and adequacy, towards facts, towards action and towards power. That means the empiricist temper regnant and the rationalist temper sincerely given up. It means the open air and possibilities of nature, as against dogma, artificiality, and the pretence of finality in truth.

At the same time it does not stand for any special results. It is a method only. But the general triumph of that method would mean an enormous change in what I called in my last lecture the "temperament" of philosophy. Teachers of the ultra-rationalistic type would be frozen out, much as the courtier type is frozen out in republics, as the ultramontane type of priest is frozen out in protestant lands. Science and metaphysics would come much nearer together, would in fact work absolutely hand in hand.

Metaphysics has usually followed a very primitive kind of quest. You know how men have always hankered after unlawful magic, and you know what a great part in magic *words* have always played. If you have his name, or the formula of incantation that binds him, you can control the spirit, genie, afrite, or whatever the power may be. Solomon knew the names of all the spirits, and having their names, he held them subject to his will. So the universe has always appeared to the natural mind as a kind of enigma, of which the key must be sought in the shape of some illuminating or power-bringing word or name. That word names the universe's *principle*, and to possess it is after a fashion to possess the universe itself. "God," "Matter," "Reason," "the Absolute," "Energy," are so many solving names. You can rest when you have them. You are at the end of your metaphysical quest.

But if you follow the pragmatic method, you cannot look on any such word as closing your quest. You must bring out of each word its practical cash-value, set it at work within the stream of your experience. It appears less as a solution, then, than as a program for more work, and more particularly as an indication of the ways in which existing realities may be *changed*.

Theories thus become instruments, not answers to enigmas, in which we can rest. We don't lie back upon them. we move forward, and, on occasion, make nature over again by their aid. Pragmatism unstiffens all our theories, limbers them up and sets each one at work. Being nothing essentially new, it harmonizes with many ancient philosophic tendencies. It agrees with nominalism, for instance, in always appealing to particulars; with utilitarianism in emphasizing practical aspects; with positivism in its disdain for verbal solutions, useless questions and metaphysical abstractions.

All these, you see, are *anti-intellectualist* tendencies. Against rationalism as a pretension and a method pragmatism is fully armed and militant. But, at the outset, at least, it stands for no particular results. It has no dogmas, and no doctrines save its method. As the young Italian pragmatist Papini has well said, it lies in the midst of our theories, like a corridor in a hotel. Innumerable chambers open out of it. In one you may find a man writing an atheistic volume; in the next some one on his knees praying for faith and strength; in a third a chemist investigating a body's properties. In a fourth a system of idealistic metaphysics is being excogitated; in a fifth the impossibility of metaphysics is being shown. But they all own the corridor, and all must pass through it if they want a practicable way of getting into or out of their respective rooms.

No particular results then, so far, but only an attitude of orientation, is what the pragmatic method means. *The attitude of looking away from first things, principles, "categories," supposed necessities; and of looking towards last things, fruits, consequences, facts.*

So much for the pragmatic method! You may say that I have been praising it rather than explaining it to you, but I shall presently explain it abundantly enough by showing how it works on some familiar problems. Meanwhile the word pragmatism has come to be used in a still wider sense, as meaning also a certain *theory of truth.* I mean to give a whole lecture to the statement of that theory, after first paving the way, so I can be very brief now. But brevity is hard to follow, so I ask for your redoubled attention for a quarter of an hour. If much remains obscure, I hope to make it clear in the later lectures.

One of the most successfully cultivated branches of philosophy in our time is what is called inductive logic, the study of the conditions under which our sciences have evolved. Writers on this subject have begun to show a singular unanimity as to what the laws of nature and elements of fact mean, when formulated by mathematicians, physicists and chemists. When the first mathematical, logical, and natural uniformities, the first laws, were discovered, men were so carried away by the clearness, beauty and simplification that resulted, that they believed themselves to have deciphered authentically the eternal thoughts of the Almighty. His mind also thundered and reverberated in syllogisms. He also thought in conic sections, squares and roots and ratios, and geometrized like Euclid. He made Kepler's laws for the planets to follow; he made velocity increase proportionally to the time in falling bodies; he made the law of the sines for light to obey when refracted; he established the classes, orders, families and genera of plants and animals, and fixed the distances between them. He thought the archetypes of all things, and devised their variations; and when we rediscover any one of these his wondrous institutions, we seize his mind in its very literal intention.

But as the sciences have developed further, the notion has gained ground that most, perhaps all, of our laws are only approximations. The laws themselves, moreover, have grown so numerous that there is no counting them; and so many rival formulations are proposed in all the branches of science that investigators have become accustomed to the notion that no theory is absolutely a transcript of reality, but that any one of them may from some point of view be useful. Their great use is to summarize old facts and to lead to new ones. They are only a man-made language, a conceptual shorthand, as some one calls them, in which we write our reports of nature; and languages, as is well known, tolerate much choice of expression and many dialects.

Thus human arbitrariness has driven divine necessity from scientific logic. If I mention the names of Sigwart, Mach, Ostwald, Pearson, Milhaud, Poincare, Duhem, Ruyssen, those of you who are students will easily identify the tendency I speak of, and will think of additional names.

Riding now on the front of this wave of scientific logic Messrs. Schiller and Dewey appear with their pragmatistic account of what truth everywhere signifies. Everywhere, these teachers say, "truth" in our ideas and beliefs means the same thing that it means in science. It means, they say, nothing but this, *that ideas (which themselves are but parts of our experience) become true just in so far as they help us to get into satisfactory relation with other parts of our experience,* to summarize them and get about among them by conceptual shortcuts instead of following the interminable succession of particular phenomena. Any idea upon which we can rise, so to speak; any idea that will carry us prosperously from any one part of our experience to any other part, linking things satisfactorily, working securely, simplifying, saving labor; is true for just so much, true in so far forth, true *instrumentally*. This is the "instrumental" view of truth taught so successfully at Chicago, the view that truth in our ideas means their power to "work", promulgated so brilliantly at Oxford. . . .

Now pragmatism, devoted though she be to facts, has no such materialistic bias as ordinary empiricism labors under. Moreover, she has no objection whatever to the realizing of abstractions, so long as you get about among particulars with their aid and they actually carry you somewhere. Interested in no conclusions but those which our minds and our experiences work out together, she has no *a priori* prejudices against theology. *If theological ideas prove to have a value for concrete life, they will be true, for pragmatism, in the sense of being good for so much. For how much more they are true, will depend entirely on their relations to the other truths that also have to be acknowledged.* . . .

If there be any life that it is really better we should lead, and if there be any idea which, if believed in, would help us to lead that life, then it would be really *better for us* to believe in that idea, *unless, indeed, belief in it incidentally clashed with other greater vital benefits.* . . .

Pragmatism is willing to take anything, to follow either logic or the senses and to count the humblest and most personal experiences. She will count mystical experiences if they have practical consequences. She will take a God who lives in the very dirt of private fact—if that should seem a likely place to find him.

Her only test of probable truth is what works best in the way of leading us, what fits every part of life best and combines with the collectivity of experience's demands, nothing being omitted. If theological ideas should do this, if the notion of God, in particular, should prove to do it, how could pragmatism possibly deny God's existence? She could see no meaning in treating as "not true" a notion that was pragmatically so successful. What other kind of truth could there be, for her, than all this agreement with concrete reality?

31

Verification
and Knowledge

A. J. Ayer (1910–   )

We may begin by criticising the metaphysical thesis that philosophy affords us knowledge of a reality transcending the world of science and common sense.

One way of attacking a metaphysician who claimed to have knowledge of a reality which transcended the phenomenal world would be to enquire from what premises his propositions were deduced. Must he not begin, as other men do, with the evidence of his senses? And if so, what valid process of reasoning can possibly lead him to the conception of a transcendent reality? Surely from empirical premises nothing whatsoever concerning the properties, or even the existence, of anything super-empirical can legitimately be inferred. But this objection would be met by a denial on the part of the metaphysician that his assertions were ultimately based on the evidence of his senses. He would say that he was endowed with a faculty of intellectual intuition which enabled him to

From *Language, Truth and Logic*, 1946, A. J. Ayer, 1952, Dover Publications, Inc., New York.

know facts that could not be known through sense-experience. And even if it could be shown that he was relying on empirical premises, and that his venture into a nonempirical world was therefore logically unjustified, it would not follow that the assertions which he made concerning this nonempirical world could not be true. For the fact that a conclusion does not follow from its putative premise is not sufficient to show that it is false. Consequently one cannot overthrow a system of transcendent metaphysics merely by criticising the way in which it comes into being. What is required is rather a criticism of the nature of the actual statements which comprise it. And this is the line of argument which we shall, in fact, pursue. For we shall maintain that no statement which refers to a "reality" transcending the limits of all possible sense-experience can possibly have any literal significance; from which it must follow that the labours of those who have striven to describe such a reality have all been devoted to the production of nonsense.

It may be suggested that this is a proposition which has already been proved by Kant. But although Kant also condemned transcendent metaphysics, he did so on different grounds. For he said that the human understanding was so constituted that it lost itself in contradictions when it ventured out beyond the limits of possible experience and attempted to deal with things in themselves. And thus he made the impossibility of a transcendent metaphysic not, as we do, a matter of logic, but a matter of fact. He asserted, not that our minds could not conceivably have had the power of penetrating beyond the phenomenal world, but merely that they were in fact devoid of it. And this leads the critic to ask how, if it is possible to know only what lies within the bounds of sense-experience, the author can be justified in asserting that real things do exist beyond, and how he can tell what are the boundaries beyond which the human understanding may not venture, unless he succeeds in passing them himself. As Wittgenstein says, "in order to draw a limit to thinking, we should have to think both sides of this limit," a truth to which Bradley gives a special twist in maintaining that the man who is ready to prove that metaphysics is impossible is a brother metaphysician with a rival theory of his own.

Whatever force these objections may have against the Kantian doctrine, they have none whatsoever against the thesis that I am about to set forth. It cannot here be said that the author is himself overstepping the barrier he maintains to be impassable. For the fruitlessness of attempting to transcend the limits of possible sense-experience will be deduced, not from a psychological hypothesis concerning the actual constitution of the human mind, but from the rule which determines the literal significance of language. Our charge against the metaphysician is not that he attempts to employ the understanding in a field where it cannot profitably venture, but that he produces sentences which fail to conform to the conditions under which alone a sentence can be literally significant. Nor are we ourselves obliged to talk nonsense in order to show that all sentences of a certain type are necessarily devoid of literal significance. We need only formulate the criterion which enables us to test whether a sentence expresses a genuine proposition about a matter of fact, and then point out that the sentences under consideration fail to satisfy it. And this we shall now proceed to do. We shall first of all formulate the criterion in somewhat vague terms, and then give the explanations which are necessary to render it precise.

The criterion which we use to test the genuineness of apparent statements of fact is the criterion of verifiability. We say that a sentence is factually significant to any given person, if, and only if, he knows how to verify the proposition which it purports to express—that is, if he knows what observations would lead him, under certain conditions, to accept the proposition as being true, or reject it as being false. If, on the other hand, the putative proposition is of such a character that the assumption of its truth, or falsehood, is consistent with any assumption whatsoever concerning the nature of his future experience, then, as far as he is concerned, it is, if not a tautology, a mere pseudo-proposition. The sentence expressing it may be emotionally significant to him; but it is not literally significant. And with regard to questions the procedure is the same. We enquire in every case what observations would lead us to answer the question, one way or the other; and, if none can be discovered, we must conclude that the sentence under consideration does not, as far as we are concerned, express a genuine question, however strongly its grammatical appearance may suggest that it does. . . .

In the first place, it is necessary to draw a distinction between practical verifiability, and verifiability in principle. Plainly we all understand, in many cases believe, propositions which we have not in fact taken steps to verify. Many of these are propositions which we could verify if we took enough trouble. But there remain a number of significant propositions, concerning matters of fact, which we could not verify even if we chose; simply because we lack the practical means of placing ourselves in the situation where the relevant observations could be made. A simple and familiar example of such a proposition is the proposition that there are mountains on the farther side of the moon. No rocket has yet been invented which would enable me to go and look at the farther side of the moon, so that I am unable to decide the matter by actual observation. But I do know what observations would decide it for me, if, as is theoretically conceivable, I were once in a position to make them. And therefore I say that the proposition is verifiable in principle, if not in practice, and is accordingly significant. On the other hand, such a metaphysical pseudo-proposition as "the Absolute enters into, but is itself incapable of, evolution and progress," is not even in principle verifiable. For one cannot conceive of an observation which would enable one to determine whether the Absolute did, or did not, enter into evolution and progress. Of course it is possible that the author of such a remark is using English words in a way in which they are not commonly used by English-speaking people, and that he does, in fact, intend to assert something which could be empirically verified. But until he makes us understand how the proposition that he wishes to express would be verified, he fails to communicate anything to us. And if he admits, as I think the author of the remark in question would have admitted, that his words were not intended to express either a tautology or a proposition which was capable, at least in principle, of being verified, then it follows that he has made an utterance which has no literal significance even for himself.

A further distinction which we must make is the distinction between the "strong" and the "weak" sense of the term "verifiable." A proposition is said to be verifiable, in the strong sense of the term, if, and only if, its truth could be conclusively established in experience. But it is verifiable, in the weak sense, if it is possible for experience to render it probable. In which sense are we using the term when we say that a putative proposition is genuine only if it is verifiable?

It seems to me that if we adopt conclusive verifiability as our criterion of significance, as some positivists have proposed, our argument will prove too much. Consider, for example, the case of general propositions of law—such propositions, namely, as "arsenic is poisonous"; "all men are mortal"; "a body tends to expand when it is heated." It is of the very nature of these propositions that their truth cannot be established with certainty by any finite series of observations. But if it is recognised that such general propositions of law are designed to cover an infinite number of cases, then it must be admitted that they cannot, even in principle, be verified conclusively. And then, if we adopt conclusive verifiability as our criterion of significance, we are logically obliged to treat these general propositions of law in the same fashion as we treat the statements of the metaphysician.

In face of this difficulty, some positivists have adopted the heroic course of saying that these general propositions are indeed pieces of nonsense, albeit an essentially important type of nonsense. But here the introduction of the term "important" is simply an attempt to hedge. It serves only to mark the authors' recognition that their view is somewhat too paradoxical, without in any way removing the paradox. Besides, the difficulty is not confined to the case of general propositions of law, though it is there revealed most plainly. It is hardly less obvious in the case of propositions about the remote past. For it must surely be admitted that, however strong the evidence in favour of historical statements may be, their truth can never become more than highly probable. And to maintain that they also constituted an important, or unimportant, type of nonsense would be unplausible, to say the very least. Indeed, it will be our contention that no proposition, other than a tautology, can possibly be anything more than a probable hypothesis. And if this is correct, the principle that a sentence can be factually significant only if it expresses what is conclusively verifiable is self-stultifying as a criterion of significance. For it leads to the conclusion that it is impossible to make a significant statement of fact at all. . . .

Accordingly, we fall back on the weaker sense of verification. We say that the question that must be asked about any putative statement of fact is not, Would any observations make its truth or falsehood logically certain? but simply, Would any observations be relevant to the determination of its truth or falsehood? And it is only if a negative answer is given to this second question that we conclude that the statement under consideration is nonsensical.

To make our position clearer, we may formulate it in another way. Let us call a proposition which records an actual or possible observation an experiential proposition. Then we may say that it is the mark of a genuine factual proposition, not that it should be equivalent to an experiential proposition, or any finite number of experiential propositions, but simply that some experiential propositions can be deduced from it in conjunction with certain other premises without being deducible from those other premises alone.

This criterion seems liberal enough. In contrast to the principle of conclusive verifiability, it clearly does not deny significance to general propositions or to propositions about the past. Let us see what kinds of assertion it rules out.

A good example of the kind of utterance that is condemned by our criterion as being not even false but nonsensical would be the assertion that the world of sense-experience was altogether unreal. It must, of course, be admitted that our senses do sometimes deceive us. We may, as the result of having certain sensations, expect certain other sensations to be obtainable which are, in fact, not obtainable. But, in all such cases, it is further sense-experience that informs us of the mistakes that arise out of sense-experience. We say that the senses sometimes deceive us, just because the expectations to which our sense-experiences give rise do not always accord with what we subsequently experience. That is, we rely on our senses to substantiate or confute the judgements which are based on our sensations. And therefore the fact that our perceptual judgements are sometimes found to be erroneous has not the slightest tendency to show that the world of sense-experience is unreal. And, indeed, it is plain that no conceivable observation, or series of observations, could have any tendency to show that the world revealed to us by sense-experience was unreal. Consequently, anyone who condemns the sensible world as a world of mere appearance, as opposed to reality, is saying something which, according to our criterion of significance, is literally nonsensical.

An example of a controversy which the application of our criterion obliges us to condemn as fictitious is provided by those who dispute concerning the number of substances that there are in the world. For it is admitted both by monists, who maintain that reality is one substance, and by pluralists, who maintain that reality is many, that it is impossible to imagine any empirical situation which would be relevant to the solution of their dispute. But if we are told that no possible observation could give any probability either to the assertion that reality was one substance or to the assertion that it was many, then we must conclude that neither assertion is significant. . . .

A similar treatment must be accorded to the controversy between realists and idealists, in its metaphysical aspect. A simple illustration, which I have made use of in a similar argument elsewhere, will help to demonstrate this. Let us suppose that a picture is discovered and the suggestion made that it was painted by Goya. There is a definite procedure for dealing with such a question. The experts examine the picture to see in what way it resembles the accredited works of Goya, and to see if it bears any marks which are characteristic of a forgery; they look up contemporary records for evidence of the existence of such a picture, and so on. In the end, they may still disagree, but each one knows what empirical evidence would go to confirm or discredit his opinion. Suppose, now, that these men have studied philosophy, and some of them proceed to maintain that this picture is a set of ideas in the perceiver's mind, or in God's mind, others that it is objectively real. What possible experience could any of them have which would be relevant to the solution of this dispute one way or the other? In the ordinary sense of the term "real," in which it is opposed to "illusory," the reality of the picture is not in doubt. The disputants have satisfied themselves that the picture is real, in this sense, by obtaining a correlated series of sensations of sight and sensations of touch. Is there any similar process by which they could discover whether the picture was real, in the sense in which the term "real" is opposed to "ideal"? Clearly there is none. But, if that is so, the problem is fictitious according to our criterion. What we have just shown is that the question at issue between idealists and realists becomes fictitious when, as is often the case, it is given a metaphysical interpretation. . . .

The use of the term "substance," to which we have already referred, provides us with a good example of the way in which metaphysics mostly comes to be written. It happens to be the case that we cannot, in our language, refer to the sensible properties of a thing without introducing a word or phrase which appears to stand for the thing itself as opposed to anything which may be said about it. And, as a result of this, those who are infected by the primitive superstition that to every name a single real entity must correspond assume that it is necessary to distinguish logically between the thing itself and any, or all, of its sensible properties. And so they employ the term "substance" to refer to the thing itself. But from the fact that we happen to employ a single word to refer to a thing, and make that word the grammatical subject of the sentences in which we refer to the sensible appearances of the thing, it does not by any means follow that the thing itself is a "simple entity," or that it cannot be defined in terms of the totality of its appearances. It is true that in talking of "its" appearances we appear to distinguish the thing from the appearances, but that is simply an accident of linguistic usage. Logical analysis shows that what makes these "appearances" the "appearances of" the same thing is not their relationship to an entity other than themselves, but their relationship to one another. The metaphysician fails to see this because he is misled by a superficial grammatical feature of his language.

A simpler and clearer instance of the way in which a consideration of grammar leads to metaphysics is the case of the metaphysical concept of Being. The origin of our temptation to raise questions about Being, which no conceivable experience would enable us to answer, lies in the fact that, in our language, sentences which express existential propositions and sentences which express attributive propositions may be of the same grammatical form. For instance, the sentences "Martyrs exist" and "Martyrs suffer" both consist of a noun followed by an intransitive verb, and the fact that they have grammatically the same appearance leads one to assume that they are of the same logical type. It is seen that in the proposition "Martyrs suffer," the members of a certain species are credited with a certain attribute, and it is sometimes assumed that the same thing is true of such a proposition as "Martyrs exist." If this were actually the case, it would, indeed, be as legitimate to speculate about the Being of martyrs as it is to speculate about their suffering. But, as Kant pointed out, existence is not an attribute. For, when we ascribe an attribute to a thing, we covertly assert that it exists: so that if existence were itself an attribute, it would follow that all positive existential propositions were tautologies, and all negative existential propositions self-contradictory; and this is not the case. So that those who raise questions about Being which are based on the assumption that existence is an attribute are guilty of following grammar beyond the boundaries of sense.

A similar mistake has been made in connection with such propositions as "Unicorns are fictitious." Here again the fact that there is a superficial grammatical resemblance between the English sentences "Dogs are faithful" and "Unicorns are fictitious," and between the corresponding sentences in other languages, creates the assumption that they are of the same logical type. Dogs must exist in order to have the property of being faithful, and so it is held that unless unicorns in some way existed they could not have the property of being fictitious. But, as it is plainly self-contradictory to say that fictitious objects exist, the device is adopted of saying that they are real in some non-empirical sense—that they have a mode of real being which is different from the mode of being of existent things. But since there is no way of testing whether an object is real in this sense, as there is for testing whether it is real in the ordinary sense, the assertion that fictitious objects have a special non-empirical mode of real being is devoid of all literal significance. It comes to be made as a result of the assumption that being fictitious is an attribute. And this is a fallacy of the same order as the fallacy of supposing that existence is an attribute, and it can be exposed in the same way.

In general, the postulation of real non-existent entities results from the superstition, just now referred to, that, to every word or phrase that can be the grammatical subject of a sentence, there must somewhere be a real entity corresponding. For as there is no place in the empirical world for many of these "entities," a special non-empirical world is invoked to house them. To this error must be attributed not only the utterances of a Heidegger, who bases his metaphysics on the assumption that "Nothing" is a name which is used to denote something peculiarly mysterious, but also the prevalence of such problems as those concerning the reality of propositions and universals whose senselessness, though less obvious, is no less complete.

FIVE

METAPHYSICS

Metaphysics seeks answers to the question "What is there?" Among the earliest answers was that of the Atomists, Democritus, and Leucippus, whose basic ideas Lucretius expressed in his poem *De Rerum Natura*. He explains the nature of all things, including both mind and body, as the composition of atomic particles moving in space, thus designating matter as the basis of all things. It is interesting to contrast this ancient intuitive theory with Bertrand Russell's account of how contemporary science and philosophy answer the question "What is there?" In an extraordinary argument, Bishop Berkeley concludes that consciousness, not matter, is the true reality. From a still different point of view, according to Bergson, we cannot rightly understand what there is if we seek reality analytically. Analysis distorts reality because analysis involves taking something apart. To analyze a rose, you remove each petal. What remains and what you know are the separate parts. But reality is, for Bergson, a dynamic continuum and this is known not through analysis but by an act of intellectual sympathy, by intuition. Finally, Whitehead argues that to pursue what truly exists by traditional scientific procedures is to obscure what is most important in human experience. If, as science assumes, the structure of reality reflects a mechanism whose every part is connected by antecedent causes, there could be no coherent account of what most human beings experience as the capacity of self-determination.

32

Matter and Space the Basis of All Things

Lucretius (98–55 B.C.)

All nature then, as it is of itself, is built of these two things: for there are bodies and the void, in which they are placed and where they move hither and thither. For that body exists is declared by the sensation which all share alike; and unless faith in this sensation be firmly grounded at once and prevail, there will be nought to which we can make appeal about things hidden, so as to prove ought by the reasoning of the mind. And next, were there not room and empty space, which we call void, nowhere could bodies be placed, nor could they wander at all hither and thither in any direction; and this I have above shown to you but a little while before. Besides these there is nothing which you could say is parted from all body and sundered from void, which could be discovered as it were a third nature in the list. For whatever shall exist, must needs be something in

From Lucretius, *De Rerum Natura*, edited and translated by Cyril Bailey, (1947) by permission of Oxford University Press, Oxford.

itself; and if it suffer touch, however small and light, it will swell the sum of body by an increase great or maybe small, provided it exist at all, and be added to its total. But if it is not to be touched, inasmuch as it cannot on any side check anything from wandering through it and passing on its way, in truth it will be that which we call empty void. Or again, whatsoever exists by itself, will either act on something or suffer itself while other things act upon it, or it will be such that things may exist and go on in it. But nothing can act or suffer without body, nor afford room again, unless it be void and empty space. And so besides void and bodies no third nature by itself can be left in the list of things, which might either at any time fall within the purview of our senses, or be grasped by anyone through reasoning of the mind.

For all things that have a name, you will find either properties linked to these two things or you will see them to be their accidents. That is a property which in no case can be sundered or separated without the fatal disunion of the thing, as is weight to rocks, heat to fire, moisture to water, touch to all bodies, intangibility to the void. On the other hand, slavery, poverty, riches, liberty, war, concord, and other things by whose coming and going the nature of things abides untouched, these we are used, as is right, to call accidents. Even so time exists not by itself, but from actual things comes a feeling, what was brought to a close in time past, then what is present now, and further what is going to be hereafter. And it must be avowed that no man feels time by itself apart from the motion or quiet rest of things. Then again, when men say that 'the rape of Tyndarus' daughter', or 'the vanquishing of the Trojan tribes in war' exist, beware that they do not perchance constrain us to avow that these things exist in themselves, just because the past ages have carried off beyond recall those races of men, of whom, in truth, these were the accidents. For firstly, we might well say that whatsoever has happened is an accident in one case of the countries, in another even of the regions of space. Or again, if there had been no substance of things nor place and space, in which all things are carried on, never would the flame have been fired by love through the beauty of Tyndarus, nor swelling deep in the Phrygian heart of Alexander have kindled the blazing battles of savage war, nor unknown of the Trojans would the timber horse have set Pergama aflame at dead of night, when the sons of the Greeks issued from its womb. So that you may see clearly that all events from first to last do not exist by themselves and are not like body, nor can they be spoken of in the same way as the being of the void, but rather so that you might justly call them the accidents of body and place, in which they are carried on, one and all.

Bodies, moreover, are in part of the first-beginnings of things, in part those which are created by the union of first-beginnings. Now the true first-beginnings of things, no force can quench; for they by their solid body prevail in the end. Albeit it seems hard to believe that there can be found among things anything of solid body. For the thunderbolt of heaven passes through walled houses, as do shouts and cries; iron grows white hot in the flame, and stones leap asunder in fierce fiery heat; both the hardness of gold is relaxed and softened by heat, and the ice of brass yields beneath the flame and melts; warmth and piercing cold ooze through silver, since when we have held cups duly in our hands we have felt both alike, when the dewy moisture of water was poured in from above. So true is it that in things there is seen to be nothing solid. But yet because true reasoning and the nature of things constrains us, give heed, until in a few verses we set forth that there are things which exist with solid and everlasting body, which we show to be the seeds of things and their first-beginnings, out of which the whole sum of things now stands created.

First, since we have found existing a twofold nature of two things far differing, the nature of body and of space, in which all things take place, it must needs be that each exists alone by itself and unmixed. For wherever space lies empty, which we call the void, body is not there; moreover, wherever body has its station, there is by no means empty void. Therefore the first bodies are solid and free from void. Moreover, since there is void in things created, solid matter must needs stand all round, nor can anything by true reasoning be shown to hide void in its body and hold it within, except you grant that what keeps it in is solid. Now it can be nothing but a union of matter, which could keep in the void in things. Matter then, which exists with solid body, can be everlasting, when all else is dissolved. Next, if there were nothing which was empty and void, the whole would be solid; unless on the other hand there were bodies determined, to fill all the places that they held, the whole universe would be but empty void space. Body, then, we may be sure, is marked off from void turn and turn about, since there is neither a world utterly full nor yet quite empty. There are therefore bodies determined, such as can mark off void space from what is full. These cannot be broken up when hit by blows from without, nor again can they be pierced to the heart and undone, nor by any other way can they be assailed and made to totter; all of which I have above shown to you but a little while before. For it is clear that nothing could be crushed in without void, or broken or cleft in twain by cutting, nor admit moisture nor likewise spreading cold or piercing flame, whereby all things are brought to their end. And the more each thing keeps void within it, the more is it assailed within by these things and begins to totter. Therefore, if the first bodies are solid and free from void, as I have shown, they must be everlasting. Moreover, if matter had not been everlasting, ere this all things had wholly passed away to nothing, and all that we see had been born again from nothing. But since I have shown above that nothing can be created from nothing, the first-beginnings must needs be of immortal body, into which at their last day all things can be dissolved, that there may be matter enough for renewing things. Therefore the first-beginnings are of solid singleness, nor in any other way can they be preserved so through the ages from infinite time now gone and renew things. . . ."

. . . But since I have taught that the most solid bodies of matter fly about for ever unvanquished through the ages, come now, let us unfold, whether there be a certain limit to their full sum or not; and likewise the void that we have discovered, or room or space, in which all things are carried on, let us see clearly whether it is altogether bounded or spreads out limitless and immeasurably deep.

The whole universe then is bounded in no direction of its ways; for then it would be bound to have an extreme edge. Now it is seen that nothing can have an extreme edge, unless there be something beyond to bound it, so that there is seen to be a spot farther than which the nature of our sense cannot follow it. As it is, since we must admit that there is nothing outside the whole sum, it has not an extreme point, it lacks therefore bound and limit. Nor does it matter in which quarter of it you take your stand; so true is it that, whatever place every man takes up, he leaves the whole boundless just as much on every side. Moreover, suppose now that all space were created finite, if one were to run on to the end, to its farthest coasts, and throw a flying dart, would you have it that that dart, hurled with might and main, goes on whither it is sped and flies afar, or do you think that something checks and bars its way? For one or the other you must needs admit and choose. Yet both shut off your escape and constrain you to grant that the universe spreads our free from limit. For whether there is something to check it and bring it about that it arrives not whither it was sped, nor plants itself in the goal, or whether it fares forward, it set not forth from the end. In this way I will press on, and wherever you shall set the farthest coasts, I shall ask what then becomes of the dart. It will come to pass that nowhere can a bound be set, and room for flight ever prolongs the chance of flight. Moreover, if all the space in the whole universe were shut in on all sides, and were created with borders determined, and had been bounded, then the store of matter would have flowed together with solid weight from all sides to the bottom, nor could anything be carried on beneath the canopy of the sky, nor would there be sky at all, nor the light of the sun, since in truth all matter would lie idle piled together by sinking down from limitless time. But as it is, no rest, we may be sure, has been granted to the bodies of the first-beginnings, because there is no bottom at all, whither they may, as it were, flow together, and make their resting-place. All things are for ever carried on in ceaseless movement from all sides, and bodies of matter are stirred up and supplied from beneath out of limitless space. Lastly, before our eyes one thing is seen to bound another; air is as a wall between the hills, and mountains between tracts of air, land bounds the sea, and again sea bounds all lands; yet in truth there is nothing to limit the universe outside.

The nature of room then and the space of the deep is such that neither could the bright thunderbolts course through it in their career, gliding on through the everlasting tract of time, nor bring it about by their travelling that there remain a whit less to traverse; so far on every side spreads out huge room for things, free from limit in all directions everywhere.

Nay more, nature ordains that the sum of things may not have power to set a limit to itself, since she constrains body to be bounded by void, and all that is void to be bounded by body, so that thus she makes the universe infinite by their interchange, or else at least one of the two, if the other of them bound it not, yet spreads out immeasurable with nature unmixed. (But if space were limited, it could not contain the infinite bodies of matter; and if matter were limited,) neither sea nor earth nor the gleaming quarters of heaven nor the race of mortal men, nor the hallowed bodies of the gods could exist for the short space of an hour. For driven apart from its unions the store of matter would be carried all dissolved through the great void, or rather in truth it could never have grown together and given birth to anything, since scattered abroad it could not have been brought to meet. For in very truth, not by design did the first-beginnings of things place themselves each in their order with foreseeing mind, nor indeed did they make compact what movements each should start, but because many of them shifting in many ways throughout the universe are harried and buffeted by blows from limitless time, by trying movements and unions of every kind, at last they fall into such dispositions as those, whereby our world of things is created and holds together. And it too, preserved from harm through many great years, when once it has been cast into harmonious movements, brings it about that the rivers replenish the greedy sea with the bounteous waters of their streams, and the earth, fostered by the sun's heat, renews its increase, and the race of living things flourishes, sent up from beneath, and the gliding fires of heaven are alive; all this they would in no wise do, unless store of matter might rise up from limitless space, out of which they are used to renew all their losses in due season. For even as the nature of living things, robbed of food, loses its flesh and melts away, so all things must needs be dissolved, when once matter has ceased to come from their supply, turned aside in any way from its due course. Nor can blows from without on all sides keep together the whole of each world which has come together in union. For they can smite on it once and again, and keep a part in place, until others come, and the sum may be supplied. Yet sometimes they are constrained to rebound and at the same time afford space and time for flight to the first-beginnings of things, so that they can pass away freed from union. Therefore, again and again, it must be that many things rise up, yea, and in order that even the blows too may not fail, there must needs be limitless mass of matter on all sides. . . .

Or, again, things which seem to us hard and compact, these, it must needs be, are made of particles more hooked one to another, and are held together close-fastened at their roots, as it were by branching particles. First of all in this class diamond stones stand in the forefront of the fight, well used to despise all blows, and stubborn flints and the strength of hard iron, and brass sockets, which scream loud as they struggle against the bolts. Those things indeed must be made of particles more round and smooth, which are liquid with a fluid body: for indeed a handful of poppy-seed moves easily just as a draught of water; for the several round particles are not checked one by the other, and when struck, it will roll downhill just like water. Lastly, all things which you perceive flying asunder in an instant, like smoke, clouds and flames, it must needs be that even if they are not made entirely of smooth and round particles, yet they are not hampered by particles closely linked, so that they can prick the body, and pass into rocks, and yet not cling one to another: so that you can easily learn that, whatever things we see allayed by the senses, are of elements not closely linked but pointed. But because you see that some things which are fluid, are also bitter, as is the brine of the sea, it should be no wonder. . . . For because it is fluid, it is of smooth and round particles, and many rugged painful bodies are mingled in it; and yet it must needs be that they are not hooked and held together: you must know that they are nevertheless spherical, though rugged, so that they can roll on together and hurt the senses. And that you may the more think that rough are mingled with smooth first-beginnings, from which is made the bitter body of the sea-god, there is a way of sundering them and seeing how, apart from the rest, the fresh water, when it trickles many a time through the earth, flows into a trench and loses its harshness; for it leaves behind up above the first-beginnings of its sickly saltness, since the rough particles can more easily stick in the earth. . . .

Come now, I will unfold by what movement the creative bodies of matter beget diverse things, and break up those that are begotten, by what force they are constrained to do this, and what velocity is appointed them for moving through the mighty void: do you remember to give your mind to my words. For in very truth matter does not cleave close-packed to itself, since we see each thing grow less, and we perceive all things flow away, as it were, in the long lapse of time, as age withdraws them from our sight: and yet the sum of all is seen to remain undiminished, inasmuch as all bodies that depart from anything lessen that from which they pass away, and bless with increase that to which they have come; they constrain the former to grow old and the latter again to flourish, and yet they abide not with it. Thus the sum of things is ever being replenished, and mortals live one and all by give and take. Some races wax and others wane, and in a short space the tribes of living things are changed, and like runners hand on the torch of life.

If you think that the first-beginnings of things can stay still, and by staying still beget new movements in things, you stray very far away from the true reasoning. For since they wander through the void, it must needs be that all the first-beginnings of things move on either by their own weight or sometimes by the blow of another. For when as they move, again and again, they have met and clashed together, it comes to pass that they leap asunder at once this way and that; for indeed it is not strange, since they are most hard with solid heavy bodies, and nothing bars them from behind. And the more you perceive all the bodies of matter tossing about, bring it to mind that there is no lowest point in the whole universe, nor have the first-bodies any place where they may come to rest, since space is without bound or limit, and I have shown in many words, and it has been proved by true reasoning that it spreads out immeasurable towards every quarter everywhere. And since that is certain, no rest, we may be sure, is allowed to the first-bodies moving through the deep void, but rather plied with unceasing, diverse motion, some when they have dashed together leap back at great intervals apart, others too are thrust but a short way from the blow. And all those which are driven together in more close-packed union and leap back but a little space apart, entangled by their own close-locking shapes, these make the strong roots of rock and the brute bulk of iron and all other things of their kind. Of the rest which wander through the great void, a few leap far apart, and recoil afar with great spaces between; these supply for us thin air and the bright light of the sun. Many, moreover, wander on through the great void, which have been cast back from the unions of things, nor have they anywhere else availed to be taken into them and link their movements. And of this truth, as I have said, a likeness and image is ever passing presently before our eyes. For look closely, whenever rays are let in and pour the sun's light through the dark places in houses: for you will see many tiny bodies mingle in many ways all through the empty space right in the light of the rays, and as though in some everlasting strife wage war and battle, struggling troop against troop, nor ever crying a halt, harried with constant meetings and partings; so that you may guess from this what it means that the first-beginnings of things are for ever tossing in the great void. . . .

(But since I have taught of what manner are the beginnings of all things, and how, differing in their diverse forms, of their own accord they fly on, spurred by everlasting motion; and in what way each several thing can be created from them, now I will begin to tell you what exceeding nearly concerns this theme, that there are what we call idols of things, which may be named, as it were, films or even rind, because the image bears an appearance and form like to that, whatever it be, from whose body it appears to be shed, ere it wanders abroad.)

First of all, since among things clear to see many things give off bodies, in part scattered loosely abroad, even as wood gives off smoke and fires heat, and in part more closely knit and packed together, as when now and then grasshoppers lay aside their smooth coats in summer, and when calves at their birth give off cauls from their outermost body, and likewise when the slippery serpent rubs off its vesture on the thorns; for often we see the brambles laden with wind-blown spoils from snakes. And since these things come to pass, a thin image from things too must needs be given off from the outermost body of things. For why these films should fall and part from things any more than films that are thin, none can breathe a word to prove; above all, since on the surface of things there are many tiny bodies, which could be cast off in the same order wherein they stood, and could preserve the outline of their shape, yea, and be cast the more quickly, inasmuch as they can be less entangled, in that they are few, and placed in the forefront. For verily we see many things cast off and give out bodies in abundance, not only from deep beneath, as we said before, but often too from the surface, such as their own colour. And commonly is this done by awnings, yellow and red and purple, when stretched over great theatres they flap and flutter, spread everywhere on masts and beams. For there they tingle the assembly in the tiers beneath, and all the bravery of the stage (and the gay-clad company of the elders), and constrain them to flutter in their colours. And the more closely are the hoardings of the theatre shut in all around, the more does all the scene within laugh, bathed in brightness, as the light of day is straitened. Since then the canvas gives out this hue from its surface, each several thing also must needs give out thin likenesses, since in either case they are throwing off from the surface. There are then sure traces of forms, which fly about everywhere, endowed with slender bulk, nor can they be seen apart one by one. Moreover, all smell, smoke, heat, and other like things stream forth from things, scattering loosely, because while they arise and come forth from deep within, they are torn in their winding course, nor are there straight outlets to their paths, whereby they may hasten to issue all in one mass. But, on the other hand, when the thin film of surface-colour is cast off, there is nothing which can avail to rend it, since it is ready at hand, and placed in the forefront. Lastly, whenever idols appear to us in mirrors, in water, and in every shining surface, it must needs be, seeing that they are endowed with an appearance like the things, that they are made of images of them, which are given off. (For why these films should fall and part from things any more than films which are thin, none can breathe a word to prove.) There are then thin images of the forms of things, resembling them, which, although no one can see them one by one, yet thrown back with constant and ceaseless repulse, give back a picture from the surface of the mirrors, and it is seen that they cannot by any other means be so preserved that shapes so exceeding like each several thing may be given back.

Come now and learn of how thin a nature this image is formed. And to begin with, since the first-beginnings are so far beneath the ken of our senses, and so much smaller than the things which our eyes first begin to be unable to descry, yet now that I may assure you of this too, learn in a few words how fine in texture are the beginnings of all things. First of all there are living things sometimes so small that a third part of them could by no means be seen. Of what kind must we think any one of their entrails to be? What of the round ball of their heart or eye? what of their members? what of their limbs? how small are they? still more, what of the several first-beginnings whereof their soul and the nature of their mind must needs be formed? do you not see how fine and how tiny they are? . . .

Now it is left to explain in what manner the other senses perceive each their own object—a path by no means stony to tread.

First of all, every kind of sound and voice is heard, when they have found their way into the ears and struck upon the sense with their body. For that voice too and sound are bodily you must grant, since they can strike on the senses. Moreover, the voice often scrapes the throat and shouting makes the windpipe over-rough as it issues forth; since, indeed, the first-beginnings of voices have risen up in too great a throng through the narrow passage, and begun to pass forth: and then, in truth, the door to the mouth too is scraped when the throat is choked. There is no doubt then that voices and words are composed of bodily elements, so that they can hurt. And likewise it does not escape you how much body is taken away and drawn off from men's very sinews and strength by speech continued without pause from the glimmer of rising dawn to the shades of dark night, above all if it is poured out with loud shouting. And so the voice must needs be corporeal, since one who speaks much loses a part from his body. Now roughness of voice comes from roughness in its first-beginnings, and likewise smoothness is begotten of their smoothness. . . .

Come now, I will tell in what manner the impact of smell touches the nostrils. First there must needs be many things whence the varying stream of scents flows and rolls on, and we must think that it is always streaming off and being cast and scattered everywhere abroad; but one smell is better fitted to some living things, another to others, on account of the unlike shapes of the elements. And so through the breezes bees are drawn on however far by the scent of honey, and vultures by corpses. Then the strength of dogs sent on before leads on the hunters whithersoever the cloven hoof of the wild beasts has turned its steps, and the white goose, saviour of the citadel of Romulus' sons, scents far ahead the smell of man. So diverse scents assigned to diverse creatures lead on each to its own food, and constrain them to recoil from noisome poison, and in that way are preserved the races of wild beasts.

This very smell then, whenever it stirs the nostrils, may in one case be thrown farther then in another. But yet no smell at all is carried as far as sound, as voice, I forbear to say as the bodies which strike the pupil of the eyes and stir the sight. For it strays abroad and comes but slowly, and dies away too soon, its frail nature scattered little by little among the breezes of air. . . .

But by what means that gathering together of matter established earth and sky and the depths of ocean, and the courses of sun and moon, I will set forth in order. For in very truth not by design did the first-beginnings of things place themselves each in their order with foreseeing mind, nor indeed did they make a compact what movements each should start; but because many first-beginnings of things in many ways, driven on by blows from time everlasting until now, and moved by their own weight, have been wont to be borne on, and to unite in every way and essay everything that they might create, meeting one with another, therefore it comes to pass that scattered abroad through a great age, as they try meetings and motions of every kind, at last those come together, which, suddenly cast together, become often the beginnings of great things, of earth, sea, and sky, and the race of living things.

Then, when things were so, neither could the sun's orb be seen, flying on high with its bounteous light, nor the stars of the great world, nor sea nor sky, nay nor earth nor air, nor anything at all like to the things we know, but only as it were a fresh-formed storm, a mass gathered together of first-beginnings of every kind, whose discord was waging war and confounding interspaces, paths, interlacings, weights, blows, meetings, and motions, because, owing to their unlike forms and diverse shapes, all things were unable to remain in union, as they do now, and to give and receive harmonious motions. From this mass parts began to fly off hither and thither, and like things to unite with like, and so to unfold a world, and to sunder its members and dispose its great parts, that is, to mark off the high heaven from the earth, and the sea by itself, so that it might spread out with its moisture kept apart, and likewise the fires of the sky by themselves, unmixed and kept apart.

Yea, verily, first of all the several bodies of earth, because they were heavy and interlaced, met together in the middle, and all took up the lowest places; and the more they met and interlaced, the more did they squeeze out those which were to make sea, stars, sun, and moon, and the walls of the great world. For all these are of smoother and rounder seeds, and of much smaller particles than earth. And so, bursting out from the quarter of the earth through its loose-knit openings, first of all the fiery ether rose up and, being so light, carried off with it many fires, in no far different wise than often we see now, when first the golden morning light of the radiant sun reddens over the grass bejewelled with dew, and the pools and everrunning streams give off a mist, yea, even as the earth from time to time is seen to steam: and when all these are gathered together as they move upwards on high, clouds with body now formed weave a web beneath the sky. Thus then at that time the light and spreading ether, with body now formed, was set all around and curved on every side, and spreading wide towards every part on all sides, thus fenced in all else in its greedy embrace. There followed then the beginnings of sun and moon, whose spheres turn in air midway betwixt earth and ether; for neither earth nor the great ether claimed them for itself, because they were neither heavy enough to sink and settle down, nor light enough to be able to glide along the topmost coasts, yet they are so set between the two that they can move along their living bodies, and become parts of the whole world; even as in our bodies some limbs may abide in their place, while yet there are others moving. So when these things were withdrawn, at once the earth sank down, where now the vast blue belt of ocean stretches, and flooded the furrows with salt surge. And day by day, the more the tide of ether and the rays of the sun with constant blows along its outer edges constrained the earth on all sides into closer texture, so that thus smitten it condensed and drew together at its middle, the more did the salt sweat, squeezed out from its body, go to increase the sea and the swimming plains, as it trickled forth; yea, and the more did those many bodies of heat and air slip forth and fly abroad, and far away from earth condense the high glowing quarters of the sky. Plains sank down, lofty mountains grew in height; for indeed the rocks could not settle down, nor could all parts subside equally in the same degree.

So then the weight of earth, with body now formed, sank to its place, and, as it were, all the slime of the world slid heavily to the bottom, and sank right down like dregs; then the sea and then the air and then the fiery ether itself were all left unmixed with their liquid bodies; they are lighter each than the next beneath, and ether, most liquid and lightest of all, floats above the breezes of air, nor does it mingle its liquid body with the boisterous breezes of air; it suffers all our air below to be churned by headstrong hurricanes, it suffers it to brawl with shifting storms, but itself bears on its fires as it glides in changeless advance. For that the ether can follow on quietly and with one constant effort. . . .

But the diverse sounds of the tongue nature constrained men to utter, and use shaped the names of things, in a manner not far other than the very speech-lessness of their tongue is seen to lead children on to gesture, when it makes them point out with the finger the things that are before their eyes. For everyone feels to what purpose he can use his own powers. Before the horns of a calf appear and sprout from his forehead, he butts with them when angry, and pushes passionately. But the whelps of panthers and lion-cubs already fight with claws and feet and biting, when their teeth and claws are scarce yet formed. Further, we see all the tribe of winged fowls trusting to their wings, and seeking an unsteady aid from their pinions. Again, to think that anyone then parcelled out names to things, and that from him men learnt their first words, is mere folly. For why should he be able to mark off all things by words, and to utter the diverse sounds of the tongue, and at the same time others be thought unable to do this? More-over, if others too had not used words to one another, whence was implanted in him the concept of their use; whence was he given the first power to know and see in his mind what he wanted to do? Likewise one man could not avail to constrain many and vanquish them to his will, that they should be willing to learn all his names for things; nor indeed is it easy in any way to teach and persuade the deaf what it is needful to do; for they would not endure it, nor in any way suffer the sounds of words not comprehended to batter on their ears for long to no purpose. Lastly, what is there so marvellous in this, if the human race, with strong voice and tongue, should mark off things with diverse sounds for diverse feelings? For the dumb cattle, yea and the races of wild beasts are wont to give forth diverse unlike sounds, when they are in fear or pain, or again when their joys grow strong. Yea verily, this we may learn from things clear to see. When the large loose lips of Molossian dogs start to snarl in anger, baring their hard teeth, thus drawn back in rage they threaten with a noise far other than when they bark and fill all around with their clamour. Yet when they essay fondly to lick their pups with their tongue, or when they toss them with their feet, and making for them with open mouth, feign gently to swallow them, checking their closing teeth, they fondle them with growling voice in a way far other than when left alone in the house they bay, or when whining they shrink from a beating with cringing body. Again, is not neighing seen to differ likewise, when a young stallion in the flower of his years rages among the mares, pricked by the spur of winged love, and from spreading nostrils snorts for the fray, and when, it may be, at other times he whinnies with trembling limbs? Lastly, the tribe of winged fowls and the diverse birds, hawks and ospreys and gulls amid the seawaves, seeking in the salt waters for life and livelihood, utter at other times cries far other than when they are struggling for their food and fighting against their prey. And some of them change their harsh notes with the weather, as the long-lived tribes of crows and flocks of rooks, when they are said to cry for water and rains, and anon to summon the winds and breezes. And so, if diverse feelings constrain animals, though they are dumb, to utter diverse sounds, how much more likely is it that mortals should then have been able to mark off things unlike with one sound and another!

33

Consciousness, Not Matter, the True Reality

George Berkeley (1685–1753)

Hylas. You were represented in last night's conversation, as one who maintained the most extravagant opinion that ever entered into the mind of man, to wit, that there is no such thing as *material substance* in the world.

Philonous. That there is no such thing as what Philosophers call *material substance*, I am seriously persuaded: but, if I were made to see anything absurd or sceptical in this, I should then have the same reason to renounce this that I imagine I have now to reject the contrary opinion.

Hylas. What! can anything be more fantastical, more repugnant to common sense, or a more manifest piece of Scepticism, than to believe there is no such thing as *matter?*

Philonous. Softly, good Hylas. What if it should prove, that you, who hold there is, are, by virtue of that opinion, a greater sceptic, and maintain more paradoxes and repugnances to common sense, than I who believe no such thing?

From George Berkeley, *Three Dialogues between Hylas and Philonous*, 1713. First Dialogue.

Hylas. You may as soon persuade me, the part is greater than the whole, as that, in order to avoid absurdity and Scepticism, I should ever be obliged to give up my opinion in this point.

Philonous. Well then, are you content to admit that opinion for true, which, upon examination, shall appear most agreeable to common sense, and remote from Scepticism?

Hylas. With all my heart. Since you are for raising disputes about the plainest things in nature, I am content for once to hear what you have to say.

Philonous. Pray, *Hylas*, what do you mean by a *sceptic?*

Hylas. I mean what all men mean, one that doubts of everything.

Philonous. He then who entertains no doubt concerning some particular point, with regard to that point cannot be thought a sceptic.

Hylas. I agree with you.

Philonous. Whether doth doubting consist in embracing the affirmative or negative side of a question?

Hylas. In neither; for whoever understands English cannot but know that *doubting* signifies a suspense between both.

Philonous. He then that denieth any point, can no more be said to doubt of it, then he who affirmeth it with the same degree of assurance.

Hylas. True.

Philonous. And, consequently, for such his denial is no more to be esteemed a sceptic than the other.

Hylas. I acknowledge it.

Philonous. How cometh it to pass then, *Hylas*, that you pronounce me a *sceptic*, because I deny what you affirm, to wit, the existence of Matter? Since, for aught you can tell, I am as peremptory in my denial, as you in your affirmation.

Hylas. Hold, *Philonous*, I have been a little out in my definition; but every false step a man makes in discourse is not to be insisted on. I said indeed that a *sceptic* was one who doubted of everything; but I should have added, or who denies the reality and truth of things.

Philonous. What things? Do you mean the principles and theorems of sciences? But these you know are universal intellectual notions, and consequently independent of Matter; the denial therefore of this doth not imply the denying them.

Hylas. I grant it. But are there no other things? What think you of distrusting the senses, of denying the real existence of sensible things, or pretending to know nothing of them. Is not this sufficient to denominate a man a *sceptic?*

Philonous. Shall we therefore examine which of us it is that denies the reality of sensible things, or professes the greatest ignorance of them; since, if I take you rightly, he is to be esteemed the greatest *sceptic?*

Hylas. That is what I desire.

Philonous. What mean you by Sensible Things?

Hylas. Those things which are perceived by the senses. Can you imagine that I mean anything else?

Philonous. Pardon me, Hylas, if I am desirous clearly to apprehend your notions, since this may much shorten our inquiry. Suffer me then to ask you this farther question. Are those things only perceived by the senses which are perceived immediately? Or, may those things properly be said to be *sensible* which are perceived mediately, or not without the intervention of others?

Hylas. I do not sufficiently understand you.

Philonous. In reading a book, what I immediately perceive are the letters, but mediately, or by means of these, are suggested to my mind the notions of God, virtue, truth, &c. Now, that the letters are truly sensible things, or perceived by sense, there is no doubt: but I would know whether you take the things suggested by them to be so too.

Hylas. No, certainly; it were absurd to think God or *virtue* sensible things, though they may be signified and suggested to the mind by sensible marks, with which they have an arbitrary connexion.

Philonous. It seems then, that by *sensible things* you mean those only which can be perceived *immediately* by sense?

Hylas. Right.

Philonous. Doth it not follow from this, that though I see one part of the sky red, and another blue, and that my reason doth thence evidently conclude there must be some cause of that diversity of colours, yet that cause cannot be said to be a sensible thing, or perceived by the sense of seeing?

Hylas. It doth.

Philonous. In like manner, though I hear variety of sounds, yet I cannot be said to hear the causes of those sounds?

Hylas. You cannot.

Philonous. And when by my touch I perceive a thing to be hot and heavy, I cannot say, with any truth or propriety, that I feel the cause of its heat or weight?

Hylas. To prevent any more questions of this kind, I tell you once for all, that by *sensible things* I mean those only which are perceived by sense, and that in truth the senses perceive nothing which they do not perceive immediately: for they make no inferences. The deducing therefore of causes or occasions from effects and appearances, which alone are perceived by sense, entirely relates to reason.

Philonous. This point then is agreed between us—that *sensible things are those only which are immediately perceived by sense.* You will farther inform me, whether we immediately perceive by sight anything beside light, and colours, and figures; or by hearing, anything but sounds; by the palate, anything besides tastes; by the smell, beside odours; or by the touch, more than tangible qualities.

Hylas. We do not.

Philonous. It seems, therefore, that if you take away all sensible qualities, there remains nothing sensible?

Hylas. I grant it.

Philonous. Sensible things therefore are nothing else but so many sensible qualities, or combinations of sensible qualities?

Hylas. Nothing else.

Philonous. *Heat* is then a sensible thing?

Hylas. Certainly.

Philonous. Doth the reality of sensible things consist in being perceived? or, is it something distinct from their being perceived, and that bears no relation to the mind?

Hylas. To *exist* is one thing, and to be *perceived* is another.

Philonous. I speak with regard to sensible things only: and of these I ask, whether by their real existence you mean a subsistence exterior to the mind, and distinct from their being perceived?

Hylas. I mean a real absolute being, distinct from, and without any relation to their being perceived.

Philonous. Heat therefore, if it be allowed a real being, must exist without the mind?

Hylas. It must.

Philonous. Tell me, Hylas, is real existence equally compatible to all degrees of heat, which we perceive; or is there any reason why we should attribute it to some, and deny it to others? and if there be, pray let me know that reason.

Hylas. Whatever degree of heat we perceive by sense, we may be sure the same exists in the object that occasions it.

Philonous. What! the greatest as well as the least?

Hylas. I tell you, the reason is plainly the same in respect of both: they are both perceived by sense; nay, the greater degree of heat is more sensibly perceived; and consequently, if there is any difference, we are more certain of its real existence than we can be of the reality of a lesser degree.

Philonous. But is not the most vehement and intense degree of heat a very great pain?

Hylas. No one can deny it.

Philonous. And is any unperceiving thing capable of pain or pleasure?

Hylas. No certainly.

Philonous. Is your material substance a senseless being, or a being endowed with sense and perception?

Hylas. It is senseless without doubt.

Philonous. It cannot therefore be the subject of pain?

Hylas. By no means.

Philonous. Nor consequently of the greatest heat perceived by sense, since you acknowledge this to be no small pain?

Hylas. I grant it.

Philonous. What shall we say then of your external object; is it a material Substance, or no?

Hylas. It is a material substance with the sensible qualities inhering in it.

Philonous. How then can a great heat exist in it, since you own it cannot in a material substance? I desire you would clear this point.

Hylas. Hold, *Philonous*, I fear I was out in yielding intense heat to be a pain. It should seem rather, that pain is something distinct from heat, and the consequences or effect of it.

Philonous. Upon putting your hand near the fire, do you perceive one simple uniform sensation, or two distinct sensations?

Hylas. But one simple sensation.

Philonous. Is not the heat immediately perceived?

Hylas. It is.

Philonous. And the pain?

Hylas. True.

Philonous. Seeing therefore they are both immediately perceived at the same time, and the fire affects you only with one simple, or uncompounded idea, it follows that this same simple idea is both the intense heat immediately perceived, and the pain; and, consequently, that the intense heat immediately perceived, is nothing distinct from a particular sort of pain.

Hylas. It seems so.

Philonous. Again, try in your thoughts, Hylas, if you can conceive a vehement sensation to be without pain or pleasure.

Hylas. I cannot.

Philonous. Or can you frame to yourself an idea of sensible pain or pleasure, in general, abstracted from every particular idea of heat, cold, tastes, smells? &c.

Hylas. I do not find that I can.

Philonous. Doth it not therefore follow, that sensible pain is nothing distinct from those sensations or ideas,—in an intense degree?

Hylas. It is undeniable; and, to speak the truth, I begin to suspect a very great heat cannot exist but in a mind perceiving it.

Philonous. What! are you then in that *sceptical* state of suspense, between affirming and denying?

Hylas. I think I may be positive in the point. A very violent and painful heat cannot exist without the mind.

Philonous. It hath not therefore, according to you, any real being?

Hylas. I own it.

Philonous. Is it therefore certain, that there is no body in nature really hot?

Hylas. I have not denied there is any real heat in bodies. I only say, there is no such thing as an intense real heat.

Philonous. But, did not you say before that all degrees of heat were equally real; or, if there was any difference, that the greater were more undoubtedly real than the lesser?

Hylas. True: but it was because I did not then consider the ground there is for distinguishing between them, which I now plainly see. And it is this:— because intense heat is nothing else but a particular kind of painful sensation; and pain cannot exist but in a perceiving being; it follows that no intense heat can really exist in an unperceiving corporeal substance. But this is no reason why we should deny heat in an inferior degree to exist in such a substance.

Philonous. But how shall we be able to discern those degrees of heat which exist only in the mind from those which exist without it?

Hylas. That is no difficult matter. You know the least pain cannot exist unperceived; whatever, therefore, degree of heat is a pain exists only in the mind. But, as for all other degrees of heat, nothing obliges us to think the same of them.

Philonous. I think you granted before that no unperceiving being was capable of pleasure, any more than of pain.

Hylas. I did.

Philonous. And is not warmth, or a more gentle degree of heat than what causes uneasiness, a pleasure?

Hylas. What then?

Philonous. Consequently, it cannot exist without the mind in an unperceiving substance, or body.

Hylas. So it seems.

Philonous. Since, therefore, as well those degrees of heat that are not painful, as those that are, can exist only in a thinking substance; may we not conclude that external bodies are absolutely incapable of any degree of heat whatsoever?

Hylas. On second thoughts, I do not think it is so evident that warmth is a pleasure, as that a great degree of heat is a pain.

Philonous. I do not pretend that warmth is as great a pleasure as heat is a pain. But, if you grant it to be even a small pleasure, it serves to make good my conclusion.

Hylas. I could rather call it an *indolence*. It seems to be nothing more than a privation of both pain and pleasure. And that such a quality or state as this may agree to an unthinking substance, I hope you will not deny.

Philonous. If you are resolved to maintain that warmth, or a gentle degree of heat, is no pleasure, I know not how to convince you otherwise, than by appealing to your own sense. But what think you of cold?

Hylas. The same that I do of heat. An intense degree of cold is a pain; for to feel a very great cold, is to perceive a great uneasiness: it cannot therefore exist without the mind; but a lesser degree of cold may, as well as a lesser degree of heat.

Philonous. Those bodies, therefore, upon whose application to our own, we perceive a moderate degree of heat, must be concluded to have a moderate degree of heat or warmth in them; and those, upon whose application we feel a like degree of cold, must be thought to have cold in them.

Hylas. They must.

Philonous. Can any doctrine be true that necessarily leads a man into an absurdity?

Hylas. Without doubt it cannot.

Philonous. Is it not an absurdity to think that the same thing should be at the same time both cold and warm?

Hylas. It is.

Philonous. Suppose now one of your hands hot, and the other cold, and that they are both at once put into the same vessel of water, in an intermediate state; will not the water seem cold to one hand, and warm to the other?

Hylas.   It will.

Philonous.   Ought we not therefore, by our principles, to conclude it is really both cold and warm at the same time, that is, according to your own concession, to believe an absurdity?

Hylas.   I confess it seems so.

Philonous.   Consequently, the principles themselves are false, since you have granted that no true principle leads to an absurdity.

Hylas.   But, after all, can anything be more absurd than to say, *there is no heat in the fire?*

Philonous.   To make the point still clearer; tell me whether, in two cases exactly alike, we ought not to make the same judgment?

Hylas.   We ought.

Philonous.   When a pin pricks your finger, doth it not rend and divide the fibres of your flesh?

Hylas.   It doth.

Philonous.   And when a coal burns your finger, doth it any more?

Hylas.   It doth not.

Philonous.   Since, therefore, you neither judge the sensation itself occasioned by the pin, nor anything like it to be in the pin; you should not, conformably to what you have now granted, judge the sensation occasioned by the fire, or anything like it, to be in the fire.

Hylas.   Well, since it must be so, I am content to yield this point, and acknowledge that heat and cold are only sensations existing in our minds. But there still remain qualities enough to secure the reality of external things.

Philonous.   But what will you say, Hylas, if it shall appear that the case is the same with regard to all other sensible qualities, and that they can no more be supposed to exist without the mind, than heat and cold?

Hylas.   Then indeed you will have done something to the purpose; but that is what I despair of seeing proved. . . .

Hylas.   One great oversight I take to be this—that I did not sufficiently distinguish the *object* from the *sensation.* Now, though this latter may not exist without the mind, yet it will not thence follow that the former cannot.

Philonous.   What object do you mean? The object of the senses?

Hylas.   The same.

Philonous.   It is then immediately perceived?

Hylas.   Right.

Philonous.   Make me to understand the differences between what is immediately perceived, and a sensation.

Hylas.   The sensation I take to be an act of the mind perceiving; besides which, there is something perceived; and this I call the *object.* For example, there is red and yellow on that tulip. But then the act of perceiving those colours is in me only, and not in the tulip.

Philonous.   What tulip do you speak of? Is it that which you see?

Hylas.   The same.

Philonous.   And what do you see beside colour, figure, and extension?

Hylas.   Nothing.

Philonous.   What you would say then is that the red and yellow are coexistent with the extension; is it not?

Hylas.   That is not all; I would say they have a real existence without the mind, in some unthinking substance.

Philonous.   That the colours are really in the tulip which I see is manifest. Neither can it be denied that this tulip may exist independent of your mind or mine; but, that any immediate object of the senses—that is, any idea, or combination of ideas—should exist in an unthinking substance, or exterior to all minds, is in itself an evident contradiction. Nor can I imagine how this follows from what you said just now, to wit, that the red and yellow were on the tulip you *saw,* since you do not pretend to *see* that unthinking substance.

Hylas.   You have an artful way, *Philonous,* of diverting our inquiry from the subject.

Philonous.   I see you have no mind to be pressed that way. To return then to your distinction between *sensation* and *object;* if I take you right, you distinguish in every perception two things, the one an action of the mind, the other not.

Hylas.   True.

Philonous.   And this action cannot exist in, or belong to, any unthinking thing; but, whatever beside is implied in a perception may?

Hylas.   That is my meaning.

Philonous.   So that if there was a perception without any act of the mind, it were possible such a perception should exist in an unthinking substance?

Hylas.   I grant it. But it is impossible there should be such a perception.

Philonous.   When is the mind said to be active?

Hylas.   When it produces, puts an end to, or changes, anything.

Philonous.   Can the mind produce, discontinue, or change anything, but by an act of the will?

Hylas.   It cannot.

Philonous.   The mind therefore is to be accounted *active* in its perceptions so far forth as *volition* is included in them?

Hylas.   It is.

Philonous.   In plucking this flower I am active; because I do it by the motion of my hand, which was consequent upon my volition; so likewise in applying it to my nose. But is either of these smelling?

Hylas.   No.

Philonous.   I act too in drawing the air through my nose; because my breathing so rather than otherwise is the effect of my volition. But neither can this be called *smelling:* for, if it were, I should smell every time I breathed in that manner?

Hylas.   True.

Philonous.   Smelling then is somewhat consequent to all this?

Hylas.   It is.

Philonous.   But I do not find my will concerned any farther. Whatever more there is—as that I perceive such a particular smell, or any smell at all—this is independent of my will, and therein I am altogether passive. Do you find it otherwise with you, *Hylas?*

Hylas.   No, the very same.

Philonous.   Then, as to seeing, is it not in your power to open your eyes, or keep them shut; to turn them this or that way?

Hylas.   Without doubt.

Philonous.   But, doth it in like manner depend on your will that in looking on this flower you perceive *white* rather than any other colour? Or, directing your open eyes towards yonder part of the heaven, can you avoid seeing the sun? Or is light or darkness the effect of your volition?

Hylas.   No certainly.

Philonous.   You are then in these respects altogether passive?

Hylas.   I am.

Philonous.   Tell me now, whether *seeing* consists in perceiving light and colours, or in opening and turning the eyes?

Hylas.   Without doubt, in the former.

Philonous.   Since therefore you are in the very perception of light and colours altogether passive, what is become of that action you were speaking of as an ingredient in every sensation? And, doth it not follow from your own concessions, that the perception of light and colours, including no action in it may exist in an unperceiving substance? And is not this a plain contradiction?

Hylas.   I know not what to think of it.

Philonous.   Besides, since you distinguish the *active* and *passive* in every perception, you must do it in that of pain. But how is it possible that pain, be it as little active as you please, should exist in an unperceiving substance? In short, do but consider the point, and then confess ingenuously, whether light and colours, tastes, sounds, &c., are not all equally passions or sensations in the soul. You may indeed call them *external objects,* and give them in words what subsistence you please. But, examine your own thoughts, and then tell me whether it be not as I say?

Hylas.   I acknowledge, *Philonous,* that, upon a fair observation of what passes in my mind, I can discover nothing else but that I am a thinking being, affected with variety of sensations; neither is it possible to conceive how a sensation should exist in an unperceiving substance. But then, on the other hand, when I look on sensible things in a different view, considering them as so many modes and qualities, I find it necessary to suppose a material substratum, without which they cannot be conceived to exist.

Philonous.   *Material substratum* call you it? Pray, by which of your senses came you acquainted with that being?

Hylas.   It is not itself sensible; its modes and qualities only being perceived by the senses.

Philonous.   I presume then it was by reflection and reason you obtained the idea of it?

Hylas.   I do not pretend to any proper positive idea of it. However, I conclude it exists, because qualities cannot be conceived to exist without a support.

Philonous.   It seems then you have only a relative notion of it, or that you conceive it not otherwise than by conceiving the relation it bears to sensible qualities?

Hylas.   Right.

Philonous.   Be pleased therefore to let me know wherein that relation consists.

Hylas.   Is it not sufficiently expressed in the term *substratum* or *substance?*

Philonous.   If so, the word *substratum* should import that it is spread under the sensible qualities or accidents?

Hylas.   True.

Philonous.   And consequently under extension?

Hylas.   I own it.

Philonous.   It is therefore somewhat in its own nature entirely distinct from extension?

Hylas.   I tell you, extension is only a mode, and Matter is something that supports modes. And is it not evident the thing supported is different from the thing supporting?

Philonous.   So that something distinct from, and exclusive of, extension is supposed to be the *substratum* of extension?

Hylas.   Just so.

Philonous.   Answer me, Hylas. Can a thing be spread without extension? or is not the idea of extension necessarily included in *spreading?*

Hylas.   It is.

Philonous.   Whatsoever therefore you suppose spread under anything must have in itself an extension distinct from the extension of that thing under which it is spread?

Hylas.   It must.

Philonous.   Consequently, every corporeal substance being the substratum of extension must have in itself another extension, by which it is qualified to be a *substratum,* and so on to infinity? And I ask whether this be not absurd in itself, and repugnant to what you granted just now, to wit, that the *substratum* was something distinct from and exclusive of extension?

Hylas.   Aye, but *Philonous,* you take me wrong. I do not mean that Matter is *spread* in a gross literal sense under extension. The word *substratum* is used only to express in general the same thing with *substance.*

Philonous.   Well then, let us examine the relation implied in the term *substance.* Is it not that it stands under accidents?

Hylas.   The very same.

Philonous.   But, that one thing may stand under or support another, must it not be extended?

Hylas.   It must.

Philonous.   Is not therefore this supposition liable to the same absurdity with the former?

Hylas.   You still take things in a strict literal sense; that is not fair, *Philonous.*

Hylas. Upon inquiry, I find it is impossible for me to conceive or under-stand how anything but an idea can be like an idea. And it is most evident that *no idea can exist without the mind.*

Philonous. You are therefore, by our principles, forced to deny the reality of sensible things; since you made it to consist in an absolute existence exterior to the mind. That is to say, you are a downright sceptic. So I have gained my point, which was to shew your principles led to Scepticism.

Hylas. For the present I am, if not entirely convinced, at least silenced.

Philonous. I would fain know what more you would require in order to perfect conviction. Have you not had the liberty of explaining yourself all man-ner of ways? Were any little slips in discourse laid hold and insisted on? Or were you not allowed to retract or reinforce anything you had offered, as best served your purpose? Hath not everything you could say been heard and examined with all the fairness imaginable? In a word, have you not in every point been con-vinced out of your own mouth? and, if you can at present discover any flaw in any of your former concessions, or think of any remaining subterfuge, any new distinction, colour, or comment whatsoever, why do you not produce it?

Hylas. A little patience, Philonous, I am at present so amazed to see myself ensnared, and as it were imprisoned in the labyrinths you have drawn me into, that on the sudden it cannot be expected I should find my way out. You must give me time to look about me and recollect myself.

Philonous. Hark; is not this the college bell.

Hylas. It rings for prayers.

Philonous. We will go in then, if you please, and meet here again to-morrow morning. In the meantime, you may employ your thoughts on this morn-ing's discourse, and try if you can find any fallacy in it, or invent any new means to extricate yourself.

Hylas. Agreed.

any reason, is in effect what you have more than once during this discourse seen good reason to give up. But, to pass over all this; if I understand you rightly, you say our ideas do not exist without the mind; but that they are copies, images, or represeatives, of certain originals that do?

Hylas.   You take me right.

Philonous.   They are then like external things?

Hylas.   They are.

Philonous.   Have those things a stable and permanent nature, independent of our senses; or are they in a perpetual change, upon our producing any motions in our bodies, suspending, exerting, or altering, our faculties or organs of sense?

Hylas.   Real things, it is plain, have a fixed and real nature, which remains the same notwithstanding any change in our senses, or in the posture and motion of our bodies; which indeed may affect the ideas in our minds, but it were absurd to think they had the same effect on things existing without the mind.

Philonous.   How then is it possible that things perpetually fleeting and variable as our ideas should be copies or images of anything fixed and constant? Or, in other words, since all sensible qualities, as size, figure, colour, &c., that is, our ideas, are continually changing upon every alteration in the distance, medium, or instruments of sensation; how can any determinate material objects be properly represented or painted forth by several distinct things, each of which is so different from and unlike the rest? Or, if you say it resembles some one only of our ideas, how shall we be able to distinguish the true copy from all the false ones?

Hylas.   I profess, Philonous, I am at a loss. I know not what to say to this.

Philonous.   But neither is this all. Which are material objects in themselves—perceptible or imperceptible?

Hylas.   Properly and immediately nothing can be perceived but ideas. All material things, therefore, are in themselves insensible, and to be perceived only by our ideas.

Philonous.   Ideas then are sensible, and their archetypes or originals insensible?

Hylas.   Right.

Philonous.   But how can that which is sensible be like that which is insensible? Can a real thing, in itself *invisible*, be like a *colour;* or a real thing, which is not *audible,* be like a *sound?* In a word, can anything be like a sensation or idea, but another sensation or idea?

Hylas.   I must own, I think not.

Philonous.   Is it possible there should be any doubt on the point? Do you not perfectly know your own ideas?

Hylas.   I know them perfectly; since what I do not perceive or know can be no part of my idea.

Philonous.   Consider, therefore, and examine them, and then tell me if there be anything in them which can exist without the mind? or if you can conceive anything like them existing without the mind?

Hylas. Upon inquiry, I find it is impossible for me to conceive or understand how anything but an idea can be like an idea. And it is most evident that *no idea can exist without the mind.*

Philonous. You are therefore, by our principles, forced to deny the reality of sensible things; since you made it to consist in an absolute existence exterior to the mind. That is to say, you are a downright sceptic. So I have gained my point, which was to shew your principles led to Scepticism.

Hylas. For the present I am, if not entirely convinced, at least silenced.

Philonous. I would fain know what more you would require in order to perfect conviction. Have you not had the liberty of explaining yourself all manner of ways? Were any little slips in discourse laid hold and insisted on? Or were you not allowed to retract or reinforce anything you had offered, as best served your purpose? Hath not everything you could say been heard and examined with all the fairness imaginable? In a word, have you not in every point been convinced out of your own mouth? and, if you can at present discover any flaw in any of your former concessions, or think of any remaining subterfuge, any new distinction, colour, or comment whatsoever, why do you not produce it?

Hylas. A little patience, Philonous, I am at present so amazed to see myself ensnared, and as it were imprisoned in the labyrinths you have drawn me into, that on the sudden it cannot be expected I should find my way out. You must give me time to look about me and recollect myself.

Philonous. Hark; is not this the college bell.

Hylas. It rings for prayers.

Philonous. We will go in then, if you please, and meet here again tomorrow morning. In the meantime, you may employ your thoughts on this morning's discourse, and try if you can find any fallacy in it, or invent any new means to extricate yourself.

Hylas. Agreed.

tage over him in that respect. It should seem therefore to proceed from reason and memory: should it not?

Hylas.   It should.

Philonous.   Consequently, it will not follow from that instance that anything is perceived by sense which is not immediately perceived. Though I grant we may, in one acceptation, be said to perceive sensible things mediately by sense—that is, when, from a frequently perceived connexion, the immediate perception of ideas by one sense suggest to the mind others, perhaps belonging to another sense, which we wont to be connected with them. For instance, when I hear a coach drive along the streets, immediately I perceive only the sound; but, from the experience I have had that such a sound is connected with a coach, I am said to hear the coach. It is nevertheless evident that, in truth and strictness, nothing can be *heard* but *sound;* and the coach is not then properly perceived by sense, but suggested from experience. So likewise when we are said to see a red-hot bar of iron; the solidity and heat of the iron are not the objects of sight, but suggested to the imagination by the colour and figure which are properly perceived by that sense. In short, those things alone are actually and strictly perceived by any sense, which would have been perceived in case that same sense had then been first conferred on us. As for other things, it is plain they are only suggested to the mind by experience, grounded on former perceptions. But, to return to your comparison of Caesar's picture, it is plain, if you keep to that, you must hold the real things or archetypes of our ideas are not perceived by sense, but by some internal faculty of the soul, as reason or memory. I would therefore fain know what arguments you can draw from reason for the existence of what you call *real things* or *material objects.* Or, whether you remember to have seen them formerly as they are in themselves; or, if you have heard or read of any one that did.

Hylas.   I see, Philonous, you are disposed to raillery; but that will never convince me.

Philonous.   My aim is only to learn from you the way to come at the knowledge of *material beings.* Whatever we perceive is perceived immediately or mediately: by sense; or by reason and reflection. But, as you have excluded sense, pray shew me what reason you have to believe their existence; or what *medium* you can possibly make use of to prove it, either to mine or your own understanding.

Hylas.   To deal ingenuously, Philonous, now I consider the point, I do not find I can give you any good reason for it. But, thus much seems pretty plain, that it is at least possible such things may really exist. And, as long as there is no absurdity in supposing them, I am resolved to believe as I did, till you bring good reasons to the contrary.

Philonous.   What! is it come to this, that you only believe the existence of material objects, and that your belief is founded barely on the possibility of its being true? Then you will have me bring reasons against it: though another would think it reasonable the proof should lie on him who holds the affirmative. And, after all, this very point which you are now resolved to maintain, without

Hylas. To suppose that were absurd: but, inform me, Philonous, can we perceive or know nothing beside our ideas?

Philonous. As for the rational deducing of causes from effects, that is beside our inquiry. And, by the senses you can best tell whether you perceive anything which is not immediately perceived. And I ask you, whether the things immediately perceived are other than your own sensations or ideas? You have indeed more than once, in the course of this conversation, declared youself on those points; but you seem, by this last question, to have departed from what you then thought.

Hylas. To speak the truth, Philonous, I think there are two kinds of objects:—the one perceived immediately, which are likewise called *ideas;* the other are real things or external objects, perceived by the mediation of ideas, which are their images and representations. Now, I own ideas to not exist without the mind; but the latter sort of objects do. I am sorry I did not think of this distinction sooner; it would probably have cut short your discourse.

Philonous. Are those external objects perceived by sense, or by some other faculty?

Hylas. They are perceived by sense.

Philonous. How! is there anything perceived by sense which is not immediately perceived?

Hylas. Yes, Philonous, in some sort there is. For example, when I look on a picture or statue of Julius Caesar, I may be said after a manner to perceive him (though not immediately) by my senses.

Philonous. It seems then you will have our ideas, which alone are immediately perceived, to be pictures of external things: and that these also are perceived by sense, inasmuch as they have a conformity or resemblance to our ideas?

Hylas. That is my meaning.

Philonous. And, in the same way that Julius Caesar, in himself invisible, is nevertheless perceived by sight; real things, in themselves imperceptible, are perceived by sense.

Hylas. In the very same.

Philonous. Tell me, Hylas, when you behold the picture of Julius Caesar, do you see with your eyes any more than some colours and figures, with a certain symmetry and composition of the whole?

Hylas. Nothing else.

Philonous. And would not a man who had never known anything of Juluis Caesar see as much?

Hylas. He would.

Philonous. Consequently he hath his sight, and the use of it, in as perfect a degree as you?

Hylas. I agree with you.

Philonous. Whence comes it then that your thoughts are directed to the Roman emperor, and his are not? This cannot proceed from the sensations or ideas of sense by you then perceived; since you acknowledge you have no advan-

Philonous. Upon approaching a distant object, do the visible size and figure change perpetually, or do they appear the same at all distances?

Hylas. They are in a continual change.

Philonous. Sight therefore doth not suggest or any way inform you that the visible object you immediately perceive exists at a distance or will be perceived when you advance farther onward; there being a continued series of visible objects succeeding each other during the whole time of your approach.

Hylas. It doth not; but still I know, upon seeing an object, what object I shall perceive after having passed over a certain distance: no matter whether it be exactly the same or no: there is still something of distance suggested in the case.

Philonous. Good Hylas, do but reflect a little on the point, and then tell me whether there be any more in it than this:—From the ideas you actually perceive by sight, you have by experience learned to collect what other ideas you will (according to the standing order of nature) be affected with, after such a certain succession of time and motion.

Hylas. Upon the whole, I take it to be nothing else.

Philonous. Now, is it not plain that if we suppose a man born blind was on a sudden made to see, he could at first have no experience of what may be suggested by sight?

Hylas. It is.

Philonous. He would not then, according to you, have any notion of distance annexed to the things he saw; but would take them for a new set of sensations existing only in his mind?

Hylas. It is undeniable.

Philonous. But, to make it still more plain: is not *distance* a line turned endwise to the eye?

Hylas. It is.

Philonous. And can a line so situated be perceived by sight?

Hylas. It cannot.

Philonous. Doth it not therefore follow that distance is not properly and immediately perceived by sight?

Hylas. It should seem so.

Philonous. Again, is it your opinion that colours are at a distance?

Hylas. It must be acknowledged they are only in the mind.

Philonous. But do not colours appear to the eye as coexisting in the same place with extension and figures?

Hylas. They do.

Philonous. How can you then conclude from sight that figures exist without, when you acknowledge colours do not; the sensible appearance being the very same with regard to both?

Hylas. I know not what to answer.

Philonous. But, allowing that distance was truly and immediately perceived by the mind, yet it would not thence follow it existed out of the mind. For, whatever is immediately perceived is an idea: and can any idea *exist* out of the mind?

Hylas. No, that were a contradiction.

Philonous. Is it not as great a contradiction to talk of *conceiving* a thing which is unconceived?

Hylas. It is.

Philonous. The tree or house therefore which you think of is *conceived* by you?

Hylas. How should it be otherwise?

Philonous. And what is conceived is surely in the mind?

Hylas. Without question, that which is conceived is in the mind.

Philonous. How then came you to say, you conceived a house or tree existing independent and out of all minds whatsoever?

Hylas. That was I own an oversight; but stay, let me consider what led me into it.—It is a pleasant mistake enough. As I was thinking of a tree in a solitary place where no one was present to see it, methought that was to conceive a tree as existing unperceived or unthought of—not considering that I myself conceived it all the while. But now I plainly see that all I can do is to frame ideas in my own mind. I may indeed conceive in my own thoughts the idea of a tree, or a house, or a mountain, but that is all. And this is far from proving that I can conceive them *existing out of the minds of all Spirits.*

Philonous. You acknowledge then that you cannot possibly conceive how any one corporeal sensible thing should exist otherwise than in a mind?

Hylas. I do.

Philonous. And yet you will earnestly contend for the truth of that which you cannot so much as conceive?

Hylas. I profess I know not what to think; but still there are some scruples remain with me. Is it not certain I *see* things at a distance? Do we not perceive the stars and moon, for example, to be a great way off? Is not this, I say, manifest to the senses?

Philonous. Do you not in a dream too perceive those or the like objects?

Hylas. I do.

Philonous. And have they not then the same appearance of being distant?

Hylas. They have.

Philonous. But you do not thence conclude the apparitions in a dream to be without the mind?

Hylas. By no means.

Philonous. You ought not therefore to conclude that sensible objects are without the mind, from their appearance or manner wherein they are perceived.

Hylas. I acknowledge it. But doth not my sense deceive me in those cases?

Philonous. By no means. The idea or thing which you immediately perceive, neither sense nor reason informs you that it actually exists without the mind. By sense you only know that you are affected with such certain sensations of light and colours, &c. And these you will not say are without the mind.

Hylas. True: but, beside all that, do you think the sight suggests something of *outness* or *distance*?

Philonous. It seems then you have only a relative notion of it, or that you conceive it not otherwise than by conceiving the relation it bears to sensible qualities?

Hylas. Right.

Philonous. Be pleased therefore to let me know wherein that relation consists.

Hylas. Is it not sufficiently expressed in the term *substratum* or *substance?*

Philonous. If so, the word *substratum* should import that it is spread under the sensible qualities or accidents?

Hylas. True.

Philonous. And consequently under extension?

Hylas. I own it.

Philonous. It is therefore somewhat in its own nature entirely distinct from extension?

Hylas. I tell you, extension is only a mode, and Matter is something that supports modes. And is it not evident the thing supported is different from the thing supporting?

Philonous. So that something distinct from, and exclusive of, extension is supposed to be the *substratum* of extension?

Hylas. Just so.

Philonous. Answer me, Hylas. Can a thing be spread without extension? or is not the idea of extension necessarily included in *spreading?*

Hylas. It is.

Philonous. Whatsoever therefore you suppose spread under anything must have in itself an extension distinct from the extension of that thing under which it is spread?

Hylas. It must.

Philonous. Consequently, every corporeal substance being the substratum of extension must have in itself another extension, by which it is qualified to be a *substratum,* and so on to infinity? And I ask whether this be not absurd in itself, and repugnant to what you granted just now, to wit, that the *substratum* was something distinct from and exclusive of extension?

Hylas. Aye, but *Philonous,* you take me wrong. I do not mean that Matter is *spread* in a gross literal sense under extension. The word *substratum* is used only to express in general the same thing with *substance.*

Philonous. Well then, let us examine the relation implied in the term *substance.* Is it not that it stands under accidents?

Hylas. The very same.

Philonous. But, that one thing may stand under or support another, must it not be extended?

Hylas. It must.

Philonous. Is not therefore this supposition liable to the same absurdity with the former?

Hylas. You still take things in a strict literal sense; that is not fair, *Philonous.*

Philonous. I am not for imposing any sense on your words: you are at liberty to explain them as you please. Only, I beseech you, make me understand something by them. You tell me Matter supports or stands under accidents. How! is it as your legs support your body!

Hylas. No; that is the literal sense.

Philonous. Pray let me know any sense, literal or not literal, that you understand it in. . . . How long must I wait for an answer, Hylas?

Hylas. I declare I know not what to say. I once thought I understood well enough what was meant by Matter's supporting accidents. But now, the more I think on it the less can I comprehend it; in short I find that I know nothing of it.

Philonous. It seems then you have no idea at all, neither relative nor positive, of Matter; you know neither what it is in itself, nor what relation it bears to accidents?

Hylas. I acknowledge it.

Philonous. And yet you asserted that you could not conceive how qualities or accidents should really exist, without conceiving at the same time a material support of them?

Hylas. I did.

Philonous. That is to say, when you conceive the real existence of qualities, you do withal conceive something which you cannot conceive?

Hylas. It was wrong I own. But still I fear there is some fallacy or other. Pray what think you of this? It is just come into my head that the ground of all our mistake lies in your treating of each quality by itself. Now, I grant that each quality cannot singly subsist without the mind. Colour cannot without extension, neither can figure without some other sensible quality. But, as the several qualities united or blended together form entire sensible things, nothing hinders why such things may not be supposed to exist without the mind.

Philonous. Either, Hylas, you are jesting, or have a very bad memory. Though indeed we went through all the qualities by name one after another; yet my arguments, or rather your concessions, nowhere tended to prove that the Secondary Qualities did not subsist each alone by itself; but, that they were not *at all* without the mind. Indeed, in treating of figure and motion we concluded they could not exist without the mind, because it was impossible even in thought to separate them from all secondary qualities, so as to conceive them existing by themselves. But then this was not the only argument made use of upon that occasion. But (to pass by all that hath been hitherto said, and reckon it for nothing, if you will have it so) I am content to put the whole upon this issue. If you can conceive it possible for any mixture or combination of qualities, or any sensible object whatever, to exist without the mind, then I will grant it actually to be so.

Hylas. If it comes to that the point will soon be decided. What more easy than to conceive a tree or house existing by itself, independent of, and unperceived by, any mind whatsoever? I do at this present time conceive them existing after that manner.

Philonous. How say you, Hylas, can you see a thing which is at the same time unseen?

34

Materialism and the Cause of Change

Dialectical and Historical Materialism

Dialectial materialism is the world outlook of the Marxist-Leninist party. It is called dialectical materialism because its approach to the phenomena of nature, its method of studying and apprehending them, is *dialectical*, while its interpretation of the phenomena of nature, its conception of these phenomena, its theory, is *materialistic*.

Historical materialism is the extension of the principles of dialectical materialism to the study of social life, an application of the principles of dialectical materialism to the phenomena of the life of society, to the study of society and of its history.

When describing their dialectical method, Marx and Engels usually refer to Hegel as the philosopher who formulated the main features of dialectics. This,

From "Dialectical and Historical Materialism," in *History of the Communist Party of the Soviet Union*, Moscow, 1939.

however, does not mean that the dialectics of Marx and Engels is identical with the dialectics of Hegel. As a matter of fact, Marx and Engels took from the Hegelian dialectics only its "rational kernel," casting aside its idealistic shell, and developed it further so as to lend it a modern scientific form.

"My dialectic method," says Marx, "is not only different from the Hegelian, but is its direct opposite. To Hegel, the life-process of the human brain, i.e., the process of thinking, which under the name of 'the Idea,' he even transforms into an independent subject, is the demiurgos of the real world, and the real world is only the external, phenomenal form of 'the Idea,' With me, on the contrary, the ideal is nothing else than the material world reflected by the human mind, and translated into forms of thought." (Karl Marx, *Capital*, Vol. I, p. 19, Foreign Languages Publishing House, Moscow, 1961.)

When describing their materialism, Marx and Engels usually refer to Feuerbach as the philosopher who restored materialism to its rights. This, however, does not mean that the materialism of Marx and Engels is identical with Feuerbach's materialism. As a matter of fact, Marx and Engels took from Feuerbach's materialism its "inner kernel," developed it into a scientific-philosophical theory of materialism and cast aside its idealistic and religious-ethical encumbrances. We know that Feuerbach, although he was fundamentally a materialist, objected to the name materialism. Engels more than once declared that "in spite of the materialist foundation, Feuerbach remained bound by the traditional idealist fetters," and that "the idealism of Feuerbach becomes evident as soon as we come to his philosophy of religion and ethics." (Karl Marx, *Ludwig Feuerbach and the End of Classical German Philosophy*, Marx-Engels, *Selected Works*, Vol. II, p. 378.)

Dialectics comes from the Greek *dialego,* to discourse, to debate. In ancient times dialectics was the art of arriving at the truth by disclosing the contradictions in the argument of an opponent and overcoming these contradictions. There were philosophers in ancient times who believed that the disclosure of contradictions in thought and the clash of opposite opinions was the best method of arriving at the truth. This dialectical method of thought, later extended to the phenomena of nature, developed into the dialectical method of apprehending nature, which regards the phenomena of nature as being in constant movement and undergoing constant change, and the development of nature as the result of the development of the contradictions in nature, as the result of the interaction of opposed forces in nature.

In its essence, dialectics is the direct opposite of metaphysics.

1) The principal features of the Marxist *dialectical method* are as follows:

a) Contrary to metaphysics, dialectics does not regard nature as an accidental agglomeration of things, of phenomena, unconnected with, isolated from, and independent of, each other, but as a connected and integral whole, in which things, phenomena are organically connected with, dependent on, and determined by, each other.

The dialectical method therefore holds that no phenomenon in nature can be understood if taken by itself, isolated from surrounding phenomena, inasmuch as any phenomenon in any realm of nature may become meaningless to us if it is not considered in connection with the surrounding conditions, but divorced from them; and that, vice versa, any phenomenon can be understood and explained if considered in its inseparable connection with surrounding phenomena, as one conditioned by surrounding phenomena.

b) Contrary to metaphysics, dialectics holds that nature is not a state of rest and immobility, stagnation and immutability, but a state of continuous movement and change, of continuous renewal and development, where something is always rising and developing, and always disintegrating and dying away.

The dialectical method therefore requires that phenomena should be considered not only from the standpoint of their interconnection and interdependence, but also from the standpoint of their movement, their change, their development, their coming into being and going out of being.

The dialectical method regards as important primarily not that which at the given moment seems to be durable and yet is already beginning to die away, but that which is arising and developing, even though at the given moment it may appear to be not durable, for the dialectical method considers invincible only that which is arising and developing.

"All nature," says Engels, "from the smallest thing to the biggest, from a grain of sand to the sun, from the protista (the primary living cell-Ed.) to man, is in a constant state of coming into being and going out of being, in a constant flux, in a ceaseless state of movement and change." (F. Engels, *Dialectics of Nature.*)

Therefore, dialectics, Engels says, "takes things and their perceptual images essentially in their inter-connection, in their concatenation, in their movement, in their rise and disappearance." *(Ibid.)*

c) Contrary to metaphysics, dialectics does not regard the process of development as a simple process of growth, where quantitative changes do not lead to qualitative changes, but as a development which passes from insignificant and imperceptible quantitative changes to open, fundamental changes, to qualitative changes; a development in which the qualitative changes occur not gradually, but rapidly and abruptly, taking the form of a leap from one state to another; they occur not accidentally but as the natural result of an accumulation of imperceptible and gradual quantitative changes.

The dialectical method therefore holds that the process of development should be understood not as movement in a circle, not as a simple repetition of what has already occurred, but as an onward and upward movement, as a transition from an old qualitative state to a new qualitative state, as a development from the simple to the complex, from the lower to the higher:

"Nature," says Engels, "is the test of dialectics, and it must be said for modern natural science that it has furnished extremely rich and daily increasing materials for this test, and has thus proved that in the last analysis nature's process is dialectical and not metaphysical, that it does not move in an eternally uniform and constantly repeated circle, but passes through a real history. Here prime mention should be made of Darwin, who dealt a severe blow to the metaphysical conception of nature by proving that the organic world of today, plants and animals, and consequently man too, is all a product of a process of development that has been in progress for millions of years." (F. Engels, *Anti-Dühring.*)

Describing dialectical development as a transition from quantitative changes to qualitative changes, Engels says:

"In physics . . . every change is a passing of quantity into quality, as a result of a quantitative change of some form of movement either inherent in a body or imparted to it. For example, the temperature of water has at first no effect on its liquid state; but as the temperature of liquid water rises or falls, a moment arrives when this state of cohesion changes and the water is converted in one case into steam and in the other into ice. . . . A definite minimum current is required to make a platinum wire glow; every metal has its melting temperature; every liquid has a definite freezing point and boiling point at a given pressure, as far as we are able with the means at our disposal to attain the required temperatures; finally, every gas has its critical point at which, by proper pressure and cooling, it can be converted into a liquid state. . . . What are known as the constants of physics (the point at which one state passes into another—Ed.) are in most cases nothing but designations for the nodal points at which a quantitative (change) increase or decrease of movement causes a qualitative change in the state of the given body, and at which, consequently, quantity is transformed into quality." *(Dialectics of Nature.)*

Passing to chemistry, Engels continues:

"Chemistry may be called the science of the qualitative changes which take place in bodies as the effect of changes of quantitative composition. This was already known to Hagel. . . . Take oxygen: if the molecule contains three atoms instead of the customary two, we get ozone, a body definitely distinct in odour and reaction from ordinary oxygen. And what shall we say of the different proportions in which oxygen combines with nitrogen or sulphur, and each of which produces a body qualitatively different from all other bodies!" *(Ibid.)*

Finally, criticizing Dühring, who scolded Hegel for all he was worth, but surreptitiously borrowed from him the well-known thesis that the transition from the insentient world to the sentient world, from the kingdom of inorganic matter to the kingdom of organic life, is a leap to a new state, Engels says:

"This is precisely the Hegelian nodal line of measure relations, in which at certain definite nodal points, the purely quantitative increase or decrease gives rise to a *qualitative leap*, for example, in the case of water which is heated or cooled, where boiling-point and freezing-point are the nodes at which—under normal pressure—the leap to a new aggregate state takes place, and where consequently quantity is transformed into quality." (F. Engels, *Anti-Dühring.*)

d) Contrary to metaphysics, dialectics holds that internal contradictions are inherent in all things and phenomena of nature, for they all have their negative and positive sides, a past and a future, something dying away and something developing; and that the struggle between these opposites, the struggle between the old and the new, between that which is dying away and that which is being born, between that which is disappearing and that which is developing, constitutes the internal content of the process of development, the internal content of the transformation of quantitative changes into qualitative changes.

The dialectical method therefore holds that the process of development from the lower to the higher takes place not as a harmonious unfolding of phenomena, but as a disclosure of the contradictions inherent in things and phenomena, as a "struggle" of opposite tendencies which operate on the basis of these contradictions.

"In its proper meaning, Lenin says, "dialectics is the study of the contradiction *within the very essence of things.*" (Lenin, *Philosophical Notebooks*, Russ. ed., p. 263.)

And further:

"Development is the 'struggle' of opposites." (Lenin, *Selected Works*, Eng. ed., Vol. XI, pp. 81-2.)

Such, in brief, are the principal features of the Marxist dialectical method.

It is easy to understand how immensely important is the extension of the principles of the dialectical method to the study of social life and the history of society, and how immensely important is the application of these principles to the history of society and to the practical activities of the party of the proletariat.

If there is no isolated phenomena in the world, if all phenomena are interconnected and interdependent, then it is clear that every social system and every social movement in history must be evaluated not from the standpoint of "eternal justice" or some other preconceived idea, as is not infrequently done by historians, but from the standpoint of the conditions which gave rise to that system or that social movement and with which they are connected.

The slave system would be senseless, stupid and unnatural under modern conditions. But under the conditions of a disintegrating primitive communal system, the slave system is a quite understandable and natural phenomenon, since it represents an advance on the primitive communal system. . . .

Everything depends on the conditions, time and place.

It is clear that without such a *historical* approach to social phenomena, the existence and development of the science of history is impossible, for only such an approach saves the science of history from becoming a jumble of accidents and an agglomeration of most absurd mistakes.

Further, if the world is in a state of constant movement and development, if the dying away of the old and the upgrowth of the new is a law of development, then it is clear that there can be no "immutable" social systems, no "eternal principles" of private property and exploitation, no "eternal ideas" of the subjugation of the peasant to the landlord, of the worker to the capitalist. . . .

As to Marxist philosophical materialism, it is fundamentally the direct opposite of philosophical idealism.

2) The principal features of Marxist philosophical *materialism* are as follows:

a) Contrary to idealism, which regards the world as the embodiment of an "absolute idea," a "universal spirit," "consciousness," Marx's philosophical materialism holds that the world is by its very nature *material*, that the multifold phenomena of the world constitute different forms of matter in motion, that interconnection and interdependence of phenomena, as established by the dialectical method, are a law of the development of moving matter, and that the world develops in accordance with the laws of movement of matter and stands in no need of a "universal spirit."

"The materialist world outlook," says Engels, "is simply the conception of nature as it is, without any reservations." (MS of *Ludwig Feuerbach.*)

Speaking of the materialist views of the ancient philosopher Heraclitus, who held that "the world, the all in one, was not created by any god or any man, but was, is and ever will be a living flame, systematically flaring up and systematically dying down." Lenin comments: "A very good exposition of the rudiments of dialectical materialism." (Lenin, *Philosophical Notebooks*, Russ. ed., p. 318.)

b) Contrary to idealism, which asserts that only our mind really exists, and that the material world, being, nature, exists only in our mind, in our sensations, ideas and perceptions, the Marxist materialist philosophy holds that matter, nature, being, is an objective reality existing outside and independent of our mind; that matter is primary, since it is the source of sensations, ideas, mind, and that mind is secondary, derivative, since it is a reflection of matter, a reflection of being; that thought is a product of matter which in its development has reached a high degree of perfection, namely, of the brain, and the brain is the organ of thought; and that therefore one cannot separate thought from matter without committing a grave error. Engels says:

"The question of the relation of thinking to being, the relation of spirit to nature is the paramount question of the whole of philosophy. . . . The answers which the philosophers gave to this question split them into two great camps. Those who asserted the primacy of spirit to nature . . . comprised the camp of *idealism*. The others, who regarded nature as primary, belong to the various schools of materialism." (Karl Marx, *Selected Works*, Eng. ed., Vol. I, pp. 430-31.)

And further:

"The material, sensuously perceptible world to which we ourselves belong is the only reality. . . . Our consciousness and thinking, however supra-sensuous they may seem, are the product of a material, bodily organ, the brain. Matter is not a product of mind, but mind itself is merely the highest product of matter." (*Ibid.*, p. 435.)

Concerning the question of matter and thought, Marx says:

"It is impossible to separate thought from matter that thinks. Matter is the subject of all changes." (*Ibid.*, 397.)

Describing the Marxist philosophy of materialism, Lenin says: "Materialism in general recognizes objectively real being (matter) as independent of consciousness, sensation, experience. . . . Consciousness is only the reflection of being, at best, an approximately true (adequate, ideally exact) reflection of it." (Lenin, *Selected Works*, Eng. ed., Vol. XI, p. 377.)

And further:

(a) "Matter is that which, acting upon our sense-organs, produces sensation; matter is the objective reality given to us in sensation. . . . Matter, nature, being, the physical—is primary, and spirit, consciousness, sensation, the psychical—is secondary." (*Ibid.*, pp. 207, 208.)

(b) "The world picture is a picture of how matter moves and of how *'matter thinks.'* " (*Ibid.*, p. 402.)

(c) "The brain is the organ of thought." (*Ibid.*, p. 214.)

c) Contrary to idealism, which denies the possibility of knowing the world and its laws, which does not believe in the authenticity of our knowledge, does not recognize objective truth, and holds that the world is full of "things-in-themselves" that can never be known to science, Marxist philosophical materialism holds that the world and its laws are fully knowable, that our knowledge of the laws of nature, tested by experiment and practice, is authentic knowledge having the validity of objective truth, and that there are no things in the world which are unknowable, but only things which are still not known, but which will be disclosed and made known by the efforts of science and practice.

Criticizing the thesis of Kant and other idealists that the world is unknowable and that there are "things-in-themselves" which are unknowable, and defending the well-known materialist thesis that our knowledge is authentic knowledge, Engels writes:

"The most telling refutation of this as of all other philosophical crotchets is practice, namely, experiment and industry. If we are able to prove the correctness of our conception of a natural process by making it ourselves, bringing it into being out of its conditions and making it serve our own purposes into the bargain, then there is an end to the Kantian ungraspable 'thing-in-itself.' The chemical substances produced in the bodies of plants and animals remained just such 'things-in-themselves' until organic chemistry began to produce them one after another, whereupon the 'thing-in-itself' became a thing for us, as, for instance, alizarin, the colouring matter of the madder, which we no longer trouble to grow in the madder roots in the field, but produce much more cheaply and simply from coal tar. For three hundred years the Copernican solar system was a hypothesis with a hundred, a thousand or ten thousand chances to one in its favour, but still always a hypothesis. But when Leverrier, by means of the data provided by this system, not only deduced the necessity of the existence of an unknown planet, but also calculated the position in the heavens which this planet must necessarily occupy, and when Galle really found this planet, the Copernican system was proved." (Ludwig Feuerbach, Marx-Engels, *Selected Works*, Vol. II, p. 371.)

Accusing Bogdanov, Bazarov, Yushkevich and the other followers of Mach of fideism, and defending the well-known materialist thesis that our scientific knowledge of the laws of nature is authentic knowledge, and that the laws of science represent objective truth, Lenin says:

"Contemporary fideism does not at all reject science; all it rejects is the 'exaggerated claims' of science, to wit, its claim to objective truth. If objective truth exists (as the materialists think), if natural science, reflecting the outer world in human 'experience,' is alone capable of giving us objective truth, then all fideism is absolutely refuted." (Lenin, *Selected Works,* Eng. Ed., Vol. XI, p. 188.)

Such, in brief, are the characteristic features of the Marxist philosophical materialism.

35

Vital versus Static Reality

Henri Bergson (1859–1941)

If we compare the various ways of defining metaphysics and of conceiving the absolute, we shall find, despite apparent discrepancies, that philosophers agree in making a deep distinction between two ways of knowing a thing. The first implies going all around it, the second entering into it. The first depends on the viewpoint chosen and the symbols employed, while the second is taken from no viewpoint and rests on no symbol. Of the first kind of knowledge we shall say that it stops at the *relative;* of the second that, wherever possible, it attains the *absolute.*

Take, for example, the movement of an object in space. I perceive it differently according to the point of view from which I look at it, whether from that of mobility or of immobility. I express it differently, furthermore as I relate it to the

From Henri Bergson, *An Introduction to Metaphysics,* translated by Mabelle L. Andison. Philosophical Library, 1946.

system of axes or reference points, that is to say, according to the symbols by which I translate it. And I call it *relative* for this double reason: in either case, I place myself outside the object itself. When I speak of an absolute movement, it means that I attribute to the mobile an inner being and, as it were, states of soul; it also means that I am in harmony with these states and enter into them by an effort of imagination. Therefore, according to whether the object is mobile or immobile, whether it adopts one movement or another, I shall not have the same feeling about it. And what I feel will depend neither on the point of view I adopt toward the object, since I am in the object itself, nor on the symbols by which I translate it, since I have renounced all translation in order to possess the original. In short, the movement will not be grasped from without and, as it were, from where I am, but from within, inside it, in what it is in itself. I shall have hold of an absolute.

Or again, take a character whose adventures make up the subject of a novel. The novelist may multiply traits of character, make his hero speak and act as much as he likes: all this has not the same value as the simple and indivisible feeling I should experience if I were to coincide for a single moment with the personage himself. The actions, gestures and words would then appear to flow naturally, as though from their source. They would no longer be accidents making up the idea I had of the character, constantly enriching this idea without ever succeeding in completing it. The character would be given to me all at once in its entirety, and the thousand and one incidents which make it manifest, instead of adding to the idea and enriching it, would, on the contrary, seem to me to fall away from it without in any way exhausting or impoverishing its essence. I get a different point of view regarding the person with every added detail I am given. All the traits which describe it to me, yet which can only enable me to know it by comparisons with persons or things I already know, are signs by which it is more or less symbolically expressed. Symbols and points of view then place me outside it; they give me only what it has in common with others and what does not belong properly to it. But what is properly itself, what constitutes its essence, cannot be perceived from without, being internal by definition, nor be expressed by symbols, being incommensurable with everything else. Description, history and analysis in this case leave me in the relative. Only by coinciding with the person itself would I possess the absolute.

It is in this sense alone, that *absolute* is synonymous with *perfection*. Though all the photographs of a city taken from all possible points of view indefinitely complete one another, they will never equal in value that dimensional object, the city along whose streets one walks. All the translations of a poem in all possible languages may add nuance to nuance and, by a kind of mutual retouching, by correcting one another, may give an increasingly faithful picture of the poem they translate, yet they will never give the inner meaning of the original. A representation taken from a certain point of view, a translation made with certain symbols still remain imperfect in comparison with the object whose picture has been taken or which the symbols seek to express. But the absolute is perfect in that it is perfectly what it is.

It is probably for the same reason that the *absolute* and the *infinite* are often taken as identical. If I wish to explain to someone who does not know Greek the simple impression that a line of Homer leaves upon me, I shall give the translation of the line, then comment on my translation, then I shall develop my commentary, and from explanation to explanation I shall get closer to what I wish to express; but I shall never quite reach it. When you lift your arm you accomplish a movement the simple perception of which you have inwardly; but outwardly, for me, the person who sees it, your arm passes through one point, then through another and between these two points there will be still other points, so that if I begin to count them, the operation will continue indefinitely. Seen from within, an absolute is then a simple thing; but considered from without, that is to say relative to something else, it becomes, with relation to those signs which express it, the piece of gold for which one can never make up the change. Now what lends itself at the same time to an indivisible apprehension and to an inexhaustible enumeration is, by definition, an infinite.

It follows that an absolute can only be given in an *intuition,* while all the rest has to do with *analysis.* We call intuition here the *sympathy* by which one is transported into the interior of an object in order to coincide with what there is unique and consequently inexpressible in it. Analysis, on the contrary, is the operation which reduces the object to elements already known, that is, common to that object and to others. Analyzing then consists in expressing a thing in terms of what is not it. All analysis is thus a translation, a development into symbols, a representation taken from successive points of view from which are noted a corresponding number of contacts between the new object under consideration and others believed to be already known. In its eternally unsatisfied desire to embrace the object around which it is condemned to turn, analysis multiplies endlessly the points of view in order to complete the ever incomplete representation, varies interminably the symbols with the hope of perfecting the always imperfect translation. It is analysis ad infinitum. But intuition, if it is possible, is a simple act.

This being granted, it would be easy to see that for positive science analysis is its habitual function. It works above all with symbols. Even the most concrete of the sciences of nature, the sciences of life, confine themselves to the visible form of living beings, their organs, their anatomical elements. They compare these forms with one another, reduce the more complex to the more simple, in fact they study the functioning of life in what is, so to speak, its visual symbol. If there exists a means of possessing a reality absolutely, instead of knowing it relatively, of placing oneself within it instead of adopting points of view toward it, of having the intuition of it instead of making the analysis of it, in short, of grasping it over and above all expression, translation or symbolical representation, metaphysics is that very means. *Metaphysics is therefore the science which claims to dispense with symbols.*

There is at least one reality which we all seize from within, by intuition and not by simple analysis. It is our own person in its flowing through time, the self which endures. With no other thing can we sympathize intellectually, or if you like, spiritually. But one thing is sure: we sympathize with ourselves.

When, with the inner regard of my consciousness, I examine my person in its passivity, like some superficial encrustment, first I perceive all the perceptions which come to it from the material world. These perceptions are clear-cut, distinct juxtaposed or mutually juxtaposable; they seek to group themselves into objects. Next I perceive memories more or less adherent to these perceptions and which serve to interpret them; these memories are, so to speak, as if detached from the depth of my person and drawn to the periphery by perceptions resembling them; they are fastened on me without being absolutely myself. And finally, I become aware of tendencies, motor habits, a crowd of virtual actions more or less solidly bound to those perceptions and these memories. All these elements with their well-defined forms appear to me to be all the more distinct from myself the more they are distinct from one another. Turned outwards from within, together they constitute the surface of a sphere which tends to expand and lose itself in the external world. But if I pull myself in from the periphery toward the centre, if I seek deep down within me what is the most uniformly, the most constantly and durably myself, I find something altogether different.

What I find beneath these clear-cut crystals and this superficial congelation is a continuity of flow comparable to no other flowing I have ever seen. It is a succession of states each one of which announces what follows and contains what precedes. Strictly speaking they do not constitute multiple states until I have already got beyond them, and turn around to observe their trail. While I was experiencing them they were so solidly organized, so profoundly animated with a common life, that I could never have said where any one of them finished or the next one began. In reality, none of them do begin or end; they all dove-tail into one another.

It is, if you like, the unrolling of a spool, for there is no living being who does not feel himself coming little by little to the end of his span; and living consists in growing old. But it is just as much a continual winding, like that of thread into a ball, for our past follows us, becoming larger and larger with the present it picks up on its way; and consciousness means memory.

To tell the truth, it is neither a winding nor an unwinding, for these two images evoke the representation of lines or surfaces whose parts are homogeneous to and superposable on one another. Now, no two moments are identical in a conscious being. Take for example the simplest feeling, suppose it to be constant, absorb the whole personality in it: the consciousness which will accompany this feeling will not be able to remain identical with itself for two consecutive moments, since the following moment always contains, over and above the preceding one, the memory the latter has left it. A consciousness which had two identical moments would be a consciousness without memory. It would therefore die and be re-born continually. How otherwise can unconsciousness be described?

We must therefore evoke a spectrum of a thousand shades, with imperceptible gradations leading from one shade to another. A current of feeling running through the spectrum, becoming tinted with each of these shades in turn, would suffer gradual changes, each of which would announce the following and sum up within itself the preceding ones. Even then the successive shades of the spectrum will always remain external to each other. They are juxtaposed. They occupy space. On the contrary, what is pure duration excludes all idea of juxtaposition, reciprocal exteriority and extension.

Instead, let us imagine an infinitely small piece of elastic, contracted, if that were possible, to a mathematical point. Let us draw it out gradually in such a way as to bring out of the point a line which will grow progressively longer. Let us fix our attention not on the line as line, but on the action which traces it. Let us consider that this action, in spite of its duration, is indivisible if one supposes that it goes on without stopping; that, if we intercalate a stop in it, we make two actions of it instead of one and that each of these actions will then be the indivisible of which we speak; that it is not the moving act itself which is never indivisible, but the motionless line it lays down beneath it like a track in space. Let us take our mind off the space subtending the movement and concentrate solely on the movement itself, on the act of tension or extension, in short, on pure mobility. This time we shall have a more exact image of our development in duration.

And yet that image will still be incomplete, and all comparison furthermore will be inadequate, because the unrolling of our duration in certain aspects resembles the unity of a movement which progresses, in others, a multiplicity of states spreading out, and because no metaphor can express one of the two aspects without sacrificing the other. If I evoke a spectrum of a thousand shades, I have before me a complete thing, whereas duration is the state of completing itself. If I think of an elastic being stretched, of a spring being wound or unwound, I forget the wealth of coloring characteristic of duration as something lived and see only the simple movement by which consciousness goes from one shade to the other. The inner life is all that at once, variety of qualities, continuity of progress, unity of direction. It cannot be represented by images.

But still less could it be represented by *concepts*, that is, by abstract ideas, whether general or simple. Doubtless no image will quite answer to the original feeling I have of the flowing of myself. But neither is it necessary for me to try to express it. To him who is not capable of giving himself the intuition of the duration constitutive of his being, nothing will ever give it, neither concepts nor images. In this regard, the philosopher's sole aim should be to start up a certain effort which the utilitarian habits of mind of everyday life tend, in most men, to discourage. Now the image has at least the advantage of keeping us in the concrete. No image will replace the intuition of duration, but many different images, taken from quite different orders of things, will be able, through the convergence of their action, to direct the consciousness to the precise point where there is a certain intuition to seize on. By choosing images as dissimilar as possible, any one of them will be prevented from usurping the place of the intuition it is instructed to call forth, since it would then be driven out immediately by its rivals. By seeing that in spite of their differences in aspect they all demand of our mind the same kind of attention and, as it were, the same degree of tension, one will gradually accustom the consciousness to a particular and definitely determined disposition, precisely the one it will have to adopt in order to appear unveiled to itself. But even then the consciousness must acquiesce in this effort; for we shall have shown it nothing. We shall simply have placed it in the attitude it must take to produce the desired effort and, by itself, to arrive at the intuition. On the other hand the disadvantage of too simple concepts is that they are really symbols which take the place of the object they symbolize and which do not demand any effort on our part. Upon close examination one would see that each of them retains of the object only what is common to that object and to others. Each of them is seen to express, even more than does the image, a *comparison* between the object and those objects resembling it. But as the comparison has brought out a resemblance, and as the resemblance is a property of the object, and as a property seems very much as though it were a *part* of the object possessing it, we are easily persuaded that by juxtaposing concepts to concepts we shall recompose the whole of the object with its parts and obtain from it, so to speak, an intellectual equivalent. We shall in this way think we are forming a faithful representation of duration by lining up the concepts of unity, multiplicity, continuity, finite or infinite divisibility, etc. That is precisely the illusion. And that, also, is the danger. In so far as abstract ideas can render service to analysis, that is, to a scientific study of the object in its relations with all others, to that very extent are they incapable of replacing intuition, that is to say, the metaphysical investigation of the object in what essentially belongs to it. On the one hand, indeed, these concepts placed end to end will never give us anything more than an artificial recomposition of the object of which they can symbolize only certain general and, as it were, impersonal aspects: therefore it is vain to believe that through them one can grasp a reality when all they present is its shadow. But on the other hand, alongside the illusion, there is also a grave danger. For the concept generalizes at the same time that it abstracts. The concept can symbolize a particular property only by making it common to an infinity of things. Therefore it always more or less distorts this property by the extension it gives to it. A property put back into the metaphysical object to which it belongs coincides with the object, at least moulds itself on it, adopting the same contours. Extracted from the metaphysical object and represented in a concept, it extends itself indefinitely, surpassing the object since it must henceforth contain it along with others. The various concepts we form of the properties of a thing are so many much larger circles drawn round it, not one of which fits it exactly. And yet, in the thing itself, the properties coincided with it and therefore with each other. We have no alternative then but to resort to some artifice in order to re-establish the coincidence. We shall take any one of these concepts and with it try to rejoin the others. But the injunction will be brought about in a different way, depending upon the concept we start from. According to whether we start, for example, from unity or from multiplicity, we shall form a different conception of the multiple unity of duration. Everything will depend on the weight we assign to this or that concept, and this weight will always be arbitrary, since the concept, extracted from the object, has no weight, being nothing more than the shadow of a body. Thus a multiplicity of different *systems* will arise, as many systems as there are external viewpoints on the reality one is examining or as there are larger circles in which to enclose it. The simple concepts, therefore, not only have the disadvantage of dividing the concrete unity of the object into so many symbolical expressions; they also divide philosophy into distinct schools, each of which reserves its place, chooses its chips, and begins with the others a game that will never end. Either metaphysics is only this game of ideas, or else, if it is a serious occupation of the mind, it must transcend concepts to arrive at intuition. To be sure, concepts are indispensable to it, for all the other sciences ordinarily work with concepts, and metaphysics cannot get along without the other sciences. But it is strictly itself only when it goes beyond the concept, or at least when it frees itself of the inflexible and ready-made concepts and creates others very different from those we usually handle, I mean flexible, mobile, almost fluid representations, always ready to mould themselves on the fleeting forms of intuition. I shall come back to this important point a little later. It is enough for us to have shown that our duration can be presented to us directly in an intuition, that it can be suggested indirectly to us by images, but that it cannot—if we give to the word *concept* its proper meaning—be enclosed in a conceptual representation.

Let us for an instant try to break it up into parts. We must add that the terms of these parts, instead of being distinguished like those of any multiplicity, encroach upon one another; that we can, no doubt, by an effort of imagination, solidify this duration once it has passed by, divide it into pieces set side by side and count all the pieces; but that this operation is achieved on the fixed memory of the duration, on the immobile track the mobility of the duration leaves behind it, not on the duration itself. Let us therefore admit that, if there is a multiplicity here, this multiplicity resembles no other. Shall we say then that this duration has unity? Undoubtedly a continuity of elements prolonged into one another partakes of unity as much as it does of multiplicity, but this moving, changing, colored and living unity scarcely resembles the abstract unity, empty and motionless, which the concept of pure unity circumscribes. Are we to conclude from this that duration must be defined by both unity and multiplicity at the same time? But curiously enough, no matter how I manipulate the two concepts, apportion them, combine them in various ways, practice on them the most delicate operations of mental chemistry, I shall never obtain anything which resembles the simple intuition I have of duration; instead of which, if I place myself back in duration by an effort of intuition, I perceive immediately how it is unity, multiplicity and many other things besides. These various concepts were therefore just so many external points of view on duration. Neither separated nor re-united have they made us penetrate duration itself.

We penetrate it, nevertheless, and the only way possible is by an intuition. In this sense, an absolute internal knowledge of the duration of the self by the self is possible. But if metaphysics demands and can obtain here an intuition, science has no less need of an analysis. And it is because of a confusion between the roles of analysis and intuition that the dissensions between schools of thought and the conflicts between systems will arise.

Psychology, in fact, like the other sciences, proceeds by analysis. It resolves the self, first given to it in the form of a simple intuition, into sensations, feelings, images, etc. which it studies separately. It therefore substitutes for the self a series of elements which are the psychological facts. But these *elements*, are they *parts?* That is the whole question, and it is because we have evaded it that we have often stated in insoluble terms the problem of the human personality.

It is undeniable that any psychological state, by the sole fact that it belongs to a person, reflects the whole of a personality. There is no feeling, no matter how simple, which does not virtually contain the past and present of the being which experiences it, which can be separated from it and constitute a "state," other than by an effort of abstraction or analysis. But it is no less undeniable that without this effort of abstraction or analysis there would be no possible development of psychological science. Now, of what does the operation consist by which the psychologist detaches a psychological state in order to set it up as a more or less independent entity? He begins by disregarding the person's special coloration, which can be expressed only in common and known terms. He then strives to isolate, in the person thus already simplified, this or that aspect which lends itself to an interesting study. If, for example, it is a question of inclination, he will leave out of account the inexpressible shading which colors it and which brings it about that my inclination is not yours; he will then fix his attention on the movement by which our personality tends towards a certain object; he will isolate this attitude, and it is this special aspect of the person, this point of view on the mobility of the inner life, this "schema" of the concrete inclination which he will set up as an independent fact. In this there is a work analogous to that of an artist who, on a visit to Paris, would, for example, make a sketch of a tower of Notre Dame. The tower is an inseparable part of the edifice, which is no less inseparably a part of the soil, the surroundings, the whole of Paris, etc. He must begin by detaching it; he will focus only on a certain aspect of the whole, and that aspect is this tower of Notre Dame. Now the tower is in reality constituted of stones whose particular grouping is what gives it its form; but the sketcher is not interested in the stones, he only notices the silhouette of the tower. He substitutes for the real and internal organization of the thing an external and schematic reconstitution. So that his design corresponds, in short, to a certain point of view of the object and to the choice of a certain mode of representation. Now the same holds for the operation by which the psychologist extracts a psychological state from the whole person. This isolated psychological state is scarcely more than a sketch, the beginning of an artificial recomposition; it is the whole envisaged under a certain elementary aspect in which one has become especially interested and which one has taken care to note. It is not a part, but an element. It has not been obtained by fragmentation, but by analysis.

Now at the bottom of all the sketches made in Paris the stranger will probably write "Paris" by way of reminder. And as he has really seen Paris, he will be able, by descending from the original intuition of the whole, to place his sketches in it and thus arrange them in relation to one another. But there is no way of performing the opposite operation; even with an infinity of sketches as exact as you like, even with the word "Paris" to indicate that they must bear close connection, it is impossible to travel back to an intuition one has not had, and gain the impression of Paris if one has never seen Paris. The point is that we are not dealing here with parts of the whole, but with *notes* taken on the thing as a whole. To choose a more striking example, where the notation is more completely symbolical, let us suppose someone puts before me, all jumbled together, the letters which go to make up a poem, without my knowing which poem it is. If the letters were *parts* of the poem, I could attempt to reconstruct it with them by trying various possible arrangements, as a child does with the pieces of a jigsaw puzzle. But I shall not for an instant think of attempting it, because the letters are not *component parts,* but *partial expressions,* which is quite another thing. That is why, if I know the poem, I put each one of the letters in its proper place and link them together without difficulty in one continuous chain, while the reverse operation is impossible. Even when I take it into my head to try that reverse operation, even when I place the letters end to end, I begin by imagining a plausible meaning: I thus give myself an intuition, and it is from the intuition that I try to fall back on the elementary symbols which would re-create its expression. The very notion of reconstructing the thing by carring out operations on symbolical elements alone implies such an absurdity that it would never occur to anyone if it were realized that he was not dealing with fragments of the thing, but in some sort with fragments of symbol.

That, however, is what philosophers undertake to do when they seek to recompose the person with psychological states, whether they confine themselves to these states or whether they add a thread for the purpose of tying the states to one another. Empiricists and rationalists alike are in this case dupes of the same illusion. Both take the *partial notions* for *real parts,* thus confusing the point of view of analysis and that of intuition, science and metaphysics.

The empiricists are right in saying that psychological analysis does not uncover in the person anything more than psychological states. And such is in fact the function, such is the very definition of analysis. The psychologist has nothing else to do but analyze the person, that is, take note of the states: at most he will place the rubric "Ego" on these states in saying that they are "states of ego," just as the sketcher writes the word "Paris" on each of his sketches. Within the sphere in which the psychologist places himself and where he should place himself, the "Ego" is only a sign by which one recalls the primitive intuition (a very vague one at that) which furnished psychology with its object: it is only a word, and the great mistake is to think that one could, by staying in the same sphere, find a thing behind the word. That has been the mistake of those philosophers who have not been able to resign themselves to being simply psychologists in psychology. Taine and Stuart Mill, for example. Psychologists by the method they apply, they have remained metaphysicans by the object they have in view. Looking for an intuition, through a strange inconsistency they seek to get this intuition from its very negation, analysis. They are seeking the self (le moi), and claim to find it in the psychological states, even though it has been possible to obtain that diversity of psychological states only by transporting oneself outside of the self and taking a series of sketches of the person, a series of notes, of more or less schematic and symbolic representations. And so although they place states side by side with states, mulitply their contacts, explore their intervening spaces, the self always escapes them, so that in the end they see nothing more in it than an empty phantom. One might just as well deny that the *Iliad* has a meaning, on the plea that one has looked in vain for this meaning in the spaces between the letters which go to make it up.

Understanding
the Cosmos

Bertrand Russell (1872–1970)

The view to which I have been gradually led is one which has been almost universally misunderstood and which, for this reason, I will try to state as simply and clearly as I possibly can. I am, for the present, only endeavouring to state the view, not to give the reasons which have led me to it. I will, however, say this much by way of preface: it is a view which results from a synthesis of four different sciences—namely, physics, physiology, psychology and mathematical logic. Mathematical logic is used in creating structures having assigned properties out of elements that have much less mathematical smoothness. I reverse the process which has been common in philosophy since Kant. It has been common among philosophers to begin with how we know and proceed afterwards to what we know. I think this a mistake, because knowing how we know is one small

From Bertrand Russell, *My Philosophical Development*, chapter 2, "My Present View of the World," George Allen & Unwin Ltd., London, 1959.

department of knowing what we know. I think it a mistake for another reason: it tends to give to knowing a cosmic importance which it by no means deserves, and thus prepares the philosophical student for the belief that mind has some kind of supremacy over the non-mental universe, or even that the non-mental universe is nothing but a nightmare dreamt by mind in its un-philosophical moments. This point of view is completely remote from my imaginative picture of the cosmos. I accept without qualification the view that results from astronomy and geology, from which it would appear that there is no evidence of anything mental except in a tiny fragment of space-time, and that the great processes of nebular and stellar evolution proceed according to laws in which mind plays no part.

If this initial bias is accepted, it is obviously to theoretical physics that we must first look for an understanding of the major processes in the history of the universe. Unfortunately, theoretical physics no longer speaks with that splendid dogmatic clarity that it enjoyed in the seventeenth century. Newton works with four fundamental concepts: space, time, matter and force. All four have been swept into limbo by modern physicists. Space and time, for Newton, were solid, independent things. They have been replaced by space-time, which is not substantial but only a system of relations. Matter has had to be replaced by series of events. Force, which was the first of the Newtonian concepts to be abandoned, has been replaced by energy; and energy turns out to be indistinguishable from the pale ghost which is all that remains of matter. Cause, which was the philosophical form of what physicists called force, has also become decrepit. I will not admit that it is dead, but it has nothing like the vigour of its earlier days.

For all these reasons, what modern physics has to say is somewhat confused. Nevertheless, we are bound to believe it on pain of death. If there were any community which rejected the doctrines of modern physics, physicists employed by a hostile government would have no difficulty in exterminating it. The modern physicist, therefore, enjoys powers far exceeding those of the Inquisition in its palmiest days, and it certainly behoves us to treat his pronouncements with due awe. For my part, I have no doubt that, although progressive changes are to be expected in physics, the present doctrines are likely to be nearer to the truth than any rival doctrines now before the world. Science is at no moment quite right, but it is seldom quite wrong, and has, as a rule, a better chance of being right than the theories of the unscientific. It is, therefore, rational to accept it hypothetically.

It is not always realized how exceedingly abstract is the information that theoretical physics has to give. It lays down certain fundamental equations which enable it to deal with the logical structure of events, while leaving it completely unknown what is the intrinsic character of the events that have the structure. We only know the intrinsic character of events when they happen to us. Nothing whatever in theoretical physics enables us to say anything about the intrinsic character of events elsewhere. They may be just like the events that happen to us, or they may be totally different in strictly unimaginable ways. All that physics gives us is certain equations giving abstract properties of their changes. But as to what it is that changes, and what it changes from and to—as to this, physics is silent.

The next step is an approximation to perception, but without passing beyond the realm of physics. A photographic plate exposed to a portion of the night sky takes photographs of separate stars. Given similar photographic plates and atmospheric conditions, different photographs of the same portion of the sky will be closely similar. There must, therefore, be some influence (I am using the vaguest word that I can think of) proceeding from the various stars to the various photographic plates. Physicists used to think that this influence consisted of waves, but now they think that it consists of little bundles of energy called photons. They know how fast a photon travels and in what manner it will, on occasion, deviate from a rectilinear path. When it hits a photographic plate, it is transformed into energy of a different kind. Since each separate star gets itself photographed, and since it can be photographed anywhere on a clear night where there is an unimpeded view of the sky, there must be something happening, at each place where it can be photographed, that is specially connected with it. It follows that the atmosphere at night contains everywhere as many separable events as there are stars that can be photographed there, and each of these separable events must have some kind of individual history connecting it with the star from which it has come. All this follows from the consideration of different photographic plates exposed to the same night sky.

Or let us take another illustration. Let us imagine a rich cynic, disgusted by the philistinism of theatregoers, deciding to have a play performed, not before live people, but before a collection of cine-cameras. The cine-cameras—supposing them all of equal excellence—will produce closely similar records, differing according to the laws of perspective and according to their distance from the stage. This again shows, like the photographic plate, that at each cine-camera a complex of events is occurring at each moment which is closely related to the complex of events occurring on the stage. There is here the same need as before of separable influences proceeding from diverse sources. If, at a given moment, one actor shouts, 'Die, Varlet!' while another exclaims, 'Help! Murder!' both will be recorded, and therefore something connected with both must be happening at each cine-camera.

To take yet another illustration: suppose that a speech is recorded simultaneously by a number of gramophones, the gramophone records do not in any obvious way resemble the original speech, and yet, by a suitable mechanism, they can be made to reproduce something exceedingly like it. They must, therefore, have something in common with the speech. But what they have in common can only be expressed in rather abstract language concerning structure. Broadcasting affords an even better illustration of the same process. What intervenes between an orator and a man listening to him on the radio is not, on the face of it, at all similar either to what the orator says or to what the listener hears. Here, again, we have a causal chain in which the beginning resembles the end, but the intermediate terms, so far as intrinsic qualities are concerned, appear to be of quite a different kind. What is preserved throughout the causal chain, in this case as in that of the gramophone record, is a certain constancy of structure.

These various processes all belong purely to physics. We do not suppose that the cine-cameras have minds, and we should not suppose so even if, by a little ingenuity on the part of their maker, those in the stalls were made to sneer at the moments when those in the pit applauded. What these physical analogies to perception show is that in most places at most times, if not in all places at all times, a vast assemblage of overlapping events is taking place, and that many of these events, at a given place and time, are connected by causal chains with an original event which, by a sort of prolific heredity, has produced offspring more or less similar to itself in a vast number of different places.

What sort of picture of the universe do these considerations invite us to construct? I think the answer must proceed by stages differing as to the degree of analysis that has been effected. For present purposes I shall content myself by treating as fundamental the notion of 'event'. I conceive each event as occupying a finite amount of space-time and as overlapping with innumerable other events which occupy partially, but not wholly, the same region of space-time. The mathematician who wishes to operate with point-instants can construct them by means of mathematical logic out of assemblages of overlapping events, but that is only for his technical purposes, which, for the moment, we may ignore. The events occurring in any given small region of space-time are not unconnected with events occurring elsewhere. On the contrary, if a photographic plate can photograph a certain star, that is because an event is happening at the photographic plate which is connected by what we may call heredity with the star in question. The photographic plate, in turn, if it is photographed, is the origin of a fresh progeny. In mathematical physics, which is only interested in exceedingly abstract aspects of the matters with which it deals, these various processes appear as paths by which energy travels. It is because mathematical physics is so abstract that its world seems so different from that of our daily life. But the difference is more apparent than real. Suppose you study population statistics, the people who make up the items are deprived of almost all the characteristics of real people before they are recorded in the census. But in this case, because the process of abstraction has not proceeded very far, we do not find it very difficult to undo it in imagination. But in the case of mathematical physics, the journey back from the abstract to the concrete is long and arduous, and, out of sheer weariness, we are tempted to rest by the way and endow some semi-abstraction with a concrete reality which it cannot justly claim . . .

We have seen that, for purely physical reasons, events in many different places and times can often be collected into families proceeding from an original progenitor as the light from a star proceeds from it in all directions. The successive generations in a single branch of such a family have varying degrees of resemblance to each other according to circumstances. The events which constitute the journey of the light from a star to our atmosphere change slowly and little. That is why it is possible to regard them as the voyage of single entities called photons, which may be thought of as persisting. But when the light reaches our atmosphere, a series of continually odder and odder things begins to happen to it. It may be stopped or transformed by mist or cloud. It may hit a sheet of water and be reflected or refracted. It may hit a photographic plate and become a black dot of interest to an astronomer. Finally, it may happen to hit a human eye. When this occurs, the results are very complicated. There are a set of events between the eye and the brain which are studied by the physiologist and which have as little resemblance to the photons in the outer world as radio waves have to the orator's speech. At last the disturbance in the nerves, which has been traced by the physiologist, reaches the appropriate region in the brain; and then, at last, the man whose brain it is sees the star. People are puzzled because the seeing of the star seems so different from the processes that the physiologist discovered in the optic nerve, and yet it is clear that without these processes the man would not see the star. And so there is supposed to be a gulf between mind and matter, and a mystery which it is held in some degree impious to try to dissipate. I believe, for my part, that there is no greater mystery than there is in the transformation by the radio of electro-magnetic waves into sounds. I think the mystery is produced by a wrong conception of the physical world and by a Manichaean fear of degrading the mental world to the level of the supposedly inferior world of matter.

The world of which we have been speaking hitherto is entirely an inferred world. We do not perceive the sort of entitites that physics talks of, and, if it is of such entities that the physical world is composed, then we do not see the eye or the optic nerve, for the eye and the optic nerve, equally, if the physicist is to be believed, consist of the odd hypothetical entities with which the theoretical physicist tries to make us familiar. These entities, however, since they owe their credibility to inference, are only defined to the degree that is necessary to make them fulfil their inferential purpose. It is not necessary to suppose that electrons, protons, neutrons, mesons, photons, and the rest have that sort of simple reality that belongs to immediate objects of experience. They have, at best, the sort of reality that belongs to 'London'. 'London' is a convenient word, but every *fact* which is stated by using this word could be stated, though more cumbrously, without using it. There is, however, a difference, and an important one, between London and the electrons: we can see the various parts of which London is composed, and, indeed, the parts are more immediately known to us than the whole. In the case of the electron, we do not perceive it and we do not perceive anything that we know to be a constituent of it. We know it only as a hypothetical entity fulfilling certain theoretical purposes. So far as theoretical physics is concerned, anything that fulfils these purposes can be taken to *be* the electron. It may be simple or complex; and, if complex, it may be built out of any components that allow the resultant structure to have the requisite properties. All this applies not only to the inanimate world but, equally, to the eyes and other sense organs, the nerves, and the brain.

But our world is not wholly a matter of inference. There are things that we know without asking the opinion of men of science. If you are too hot or too cold, you can be perfectly aware of this fact without asking the physicist what heat and cold consist of. When you see other people's faces you have an experience which is completely indubitable, but which does not consist of seeing the things which theoretical physicists speak of. You see other people's eyes and you believe that they see yours. Your own eyes as visual objects belong to the inferred part of the world, though the inference is rendered fairly indubitable by mirrors, photographs and the testimony of your friends. The inference to your own eyes as visual objects is essentially of the same sort as the physicist's inference to electrons, etc.; and, if you are going to deny validity to the physicist's inferences, you ought also to deny that you know you have visible eyes—which is absurd, as Euclid would say.

We may give the name 'data' to all the things of which we are aware without inference. They include all our observed sensations—visual, auditory, tactile, etc. Common sense sees reason to attribute many of our sensations to causes outside our own bodies. It does not believe that the room in which it is sitting ceases to exist when it shuts its eyes or goes to sleep. It does not believe that its wife and children are mere figments of its imagination. In all this we may agree with common sense; but where it goes wrong is in supposing that inanimate objects resemble, in their intrinsic qualities, the perceptions which they cause. To believe this is as groundless as it would be to suppose that a gramophone record resembles the music that it causes. It is not, however, the *difference* between the physical world and the world of data that I chiefly wish to emphasize. On the contrary, it is the possibility of much closer resemblances than physics at first sight suggests that I consider it important to bring to light.

I think perhaps I can best make my own views clear by comparing them with those of Leibniz. Leibniz thought that the universe consisted of monads, each of which was a little mind and each of which mirrored the universe. They did this mirroring with varying degrees of inexactness. The best monads had the least confusion in their picture of the universe. Misled by the Aristotelian subject-predicate logic, Leibniz held that monads do not interact, and that the fact of their continuing to mirror the same universe is to be explained by a preestablished harmony. This part of his doctrine is totally unacceptable. It is only through the causal action of the outer world upon us that we reflect the world in so far as we do reflect it. But there are other aspects of his doctrine which are more in agreement with the theory that I wish to advocate. One of the most important of these is as to space. There are for Leibniz (though he was never quite clear on this point) two kinds of space. There is the space in the private world of each monad, which is the space that the monad can come to know by analysing and arranging data without assuming anything beyond data. But there is also another kind of space. The monads, Leibniz tells us, reflect the world each from its own point of view, the differences of points of view being analogous to differences of perspective. The arrangement of the whole assemblage of points of view gives us another kind of space different from that in the private world of each monad. In this public space, each monad occupies a point or, at any rate, a very small region. Although in its private world there is a private space which from its private point of view is immense, the whole of this immensity shrinks into a tiny pin-point when the monad is placed among other monads. We may call the space in each monad's world of data 'private' space, and the space consisting of the diverse points of view of diverse monads 'physical' space. In so far as monads correctly mirror the world, the geometrical properties of private space will be analogous to those of physical space.

Most of this can be applied with little change to exemplify the theory that I wish to advocate. There is space in the world of my perceptions and there is space in physics. The whole of the space in my perceptions, for me as for Leibniz, occupies only a tiny region in physical space. There is, however, an important difference between my theory and that of Leibniz, which has to do with a different conception of causality and with consequences of the theory of relativity. I think that space-time order in the physical world is bound up with causation, and this, in turn, with the irreversibility of physical processes. In classical physics, everything was reversible. If you were to start every bit of matter moving backwards with the same velocity as before, the whole history of the universe would unroll itself backwards. Modern physics, starting from the Second Law of Thermodynamics, has abandoned this view not only in thermodynamics but also elsewhere. Radioactive atoms disintegrate and do not put themselves together again. Speaking generally, processes in the physical world all have a certain direction which makes a distinction between cause and effect that was absent in classical dynamics. I think that the space-time order of the physical world involves this directed causality. It is on this ground that I maintain an opinion which all other philosophers find shocking: namely, that people's thoughts are in their heads. The light from a star travels over intervening space and causes a disturbance in the optic nerve ending in an occurrence in the brain. What I maintain is that the occurrence in the brain *is* a visual sensation. I maintain, in fact, that the brain consists of thoughts—using 'thought' in its widest sense, as it is used by Descartes. To this people will reply 'Nonsense! I can see a brain through a microscope, and I can see that it does not consist of thoughts but of matter just as tables and chairs do.' This is a sheer mistake. What you see when you look at a brain through a microscope is part of your private world. It is the effect in you of a long causal process starting from the brain that you say you are looking at. The brain that you say you are looking at is, no doubt, part of the physical world; but this is not the brain which is a datum in your experience. *That* brain is a remote effect of the physical brain. And, if the location of events in physical space-time is to be effected, as I maintain, by causal relations, then your percept, which comes after events in the eye and optic nerve leading into the brain, must be located in your brain. I may illustrate how I differ from most philosophers by quoting the title of an article by Mr. H. Hudson in *Mind* of April 1956. His article is entitled, 'Why we cannot witness or observe what goes on "in our heads".' What I maintain is that we *can* witness or observe what goes on in our heads, and that we cannot witness or observe anything else at all.

We can approach the same result by another route. When we were considering the photographic plate which photographs a portion of the starry heavens, we saw that this involves a great multiplicity of occurrences at the photographic plate: namely, at the very least, one for each object that it can photograph. I infer that, in every small region of space-time, there is an immense multiplicity of overlapping events each connected by a causal line to an origin at some earlier time—though, usually, at a very slightly earlier time. A sensitive instrument, such as a photographic plate, placed anywhere, may be said in a sense to 'perceive' the various objects from which these causal lines emanate. We do not use the word 'perceive' unless the instrument in question is a living brain, but that is because those regions which are inhabited by living brains have certain peculiar relations among the events occurring there. The most important of these is memory. Wherever these peculiar relations exist, we say that there is a percipient. We may define a 'mind' as a collection of events connected with each other by memory-chains backwards and forwards. We know about one such collection of events— namely, that constituting ourself—more intimately and directly than we know about anything else in the world. In regard to what happens to ourself, we know not only abstract logical structure, but also qualities—by which I mean what characterizes sounds as opposed to colours, or red as opposed to green. This is the sort of thing that we cannot know where the physical world is concerned.

There are three key points in the above theory. The first is that the entities that occur in mathematical physics are not part of the stuff of the world, but are constructions composed of events and taken as units for the convenience of the mathematician. The second is that the whole of what we perceive without inference belongs to our private world. In this respect, I agree with Berkeley. The starry heaven that we know in visual sensation is inside us. The external starry heaven that we believe in is inferred. The third point is that the causal lines which enable us to be aware of a diversity of objects, though there are some such lines everywhere, are apt to peter out like rivers in the sand. That is why we do not at all times perceive everything.

I do not pretend that the above theory can be proved. What I contend is that, like the theories of physics, it cannot be disproved, and gives an answer to many problems which older theorists have found puzzling. I do not think that any prudent person will claim more than this for any theory.

37

Nature Beyond the Grasp of Science

Alfred North Whitehead (1861–1947)

We quickly find that the Western peoples exhibit on a colossal scale a peculiarity which is popularly supposed to be more especially characteristic of the Chinese. Surprise is often expressed that a Chinaman can be of two religions, a Confucian for some occasions and a Buddhist for other occasions. Whether this is true of China I do not know; nor do I know whether, if true, these two attitudes are really inconsistent. But there can be no doubt that an analogous fact is true of the West, and that the two attitudes involved are inconsistent. A scientific realism, based on mechanism, is conjoined with an unwavering belief in the world of men and of the higher animals as being composed of self-determining organisms. This radical inconsistency at the basis of modern thought accounts for much that is half-hearted and wavering in our civilisation. It would be going too far to say that it distracts thought. It enfeebles it, by reason of the inconsistency lurking in the background. After all, the men of the Middle Ages were in pursuit of an excellency of which we have nearly forgotten the existence. They set before themselves the idea of the attainment of a harmony of the understanding. We are content with superficial orderings from diverse arbitrary starting points. For instance, the enterprises produced by the individualistic energy of the European peoples presuppose physical actions directed to final causes. But the science which is employed in their development is based on a philosophy which asserts that physical causation is supreme, and which disjoins the physical cause from the final end. It is not popular to dwell on the absolute contradiction here involved. It is the fact, however you gloze it over with phrases. Of course, we find in the eighteenth century Paley's famous argument, that mechanism presupposes a God who is the author of nature. But even before Paley put the argument into its final form, Hume had written the retort, that the God whom you will find will be the sort of God who makes that mechanism. In other words, that mechanism can, at most, presuppose a mechanic, and not merely *a* mechanic but *its* mechanic. The only way of mitigating mechanism is by the discovery that it is not mechanism.

When we leave apologetic theology, and come to ordinary literature, we find, as we might expect, that the scientific outlook is in general simply ignored. So far as the mass of literature is concerned, science might never have been heard of. Until recently nearly all writers have been soaked in classical and renaissance literature. For the most part, neither philosophy nor science interested them, and their minds were trained to ignore them.

There are exceptions to this sweeping statement; and, even if we confine ourselves to English literature, they concern some of the greatest names; also the indirect influence of science has been considerable.

A side light on this distracting inconsistency in modern thought is obtained by examining some of those great serious poems in English literature, whose general scale gives them a didactic character. The relevant poems are Milton's *Paradise Lost*, Pope's *Essay on Man*, Wordsworth's *Excursion*, Tennyson's *In Memoriam*. Milton, though he is writing after the Restoration, voices the theological aspect of the earlier portion of his century, untouched by the influence of the scientific materialism. Pope's poem represents the effect on popular thought of the intervening sixty years which includes the first period of assured triumph for the scientific movement. Wordsworth in his whole being expresses a conscious reaction against the mentality of the eighteenth century. This mentality means nothing else than the acceptance of the scientific ideas at their full face value. Wordsworth was not bothered by any intellectual antagonism. What moved him was a moral repulsion. He felt that something had been left out, and that what had been left out comprised everything that was most important. Tennyson is the mouthpiece of the attempts of the waning romantic movement in the second quarter of the nineteenth century to come to terms with science. By this time the two elements in modern thought had disclosed their fundamental divergence by their jarring interpretations of the course of nature and the life of man. Tennyson stands in this poem as the perfect example of the distraction which I have already mentioned. There are opposing visions of the world, and both of them command his assent by appeals to ultimate intuitions from which there seems no escape. Tennyson goes to the heart of the difficulty. It is the problem of mechanism which appalls him,

"The stars," she whispers, "blindly run on."

This line states starkly the whole philosophic problem implicit in the poem. Each molecule blindly runs. The human body is a collection of molecules. Therefore, the human body blindly runs, and therefore there can be no individual responsibility for the actions of the body. If you once accept that the molecule is definitely determined to be what it is, independently of any determination by reason of the total organism of the body, and if you further admit that the blind run is settled by the general mechanical laws, there can be no escape from this conclusion. But mental experiences are derivative from the actions of the body, including of course its internal behaviour. Accordingly, the sole function of the mind is to have at least some of its experiences settled for it, and to add such others as may be open to it independently of the body's motions, internal and external.

There are then two possible theories as to the mind. You can either deny that it can supply for itself any experiences other than those provided for it by the body, or you can admit them.

If you refuse to admit the additional experiences, then all individual responsibility is swept away. If you do admit them, then a human being may be responsible for the state of his mind though he has no responsibility for the actions of his body. The enfeeblement of thought in the modern world is illustrated by the way in which this plain issue is avoided in Tennyson's poem. There is something kept in the background, a skeleton in the cupboard. He touches on almost every religious and scientific problem, but carefully avoids more than a passing allusion to this one.

This very problem was in full debate at the date of the poem. John Stuart Mill was maintaining his doctrine of determinism. In this doctrine volitions are determined by motives, and motives are expressible in terms of antecedent conditions including states of mind as well as states of the body.

It is obvious that this doctrine affords no escape from the dilemma presented by a thoroughgoing mechanism. For if the volition affects the state of the body, then the molecules in the body do not blindly run. If the volition does not affect the state of the body, the mind is still left in its uncomfortable position.

Mill's doctrine is generally accepted, especially among scientists, as though in some way it allowed you to accept the extreme doctrine of materialistic mechanism, and yet mitigated its unbelievable consequences. It does nothing of the sort. Either the bodily molecules blindly run, or they do not. If they do blindly run, the mental states are irrelevant in discussing the bodily actions. . . .

The doctrine which I am maintaining is that the whole concept of materialism only applies to very abstract entities, the products of logical discernment.

The concrete enduring entities are organisms, so that the plan of the *whole* influences the very characters of the various subordinate organisms which enter into it. In the case of an animal, the mental states enter into the plan of the total organism and thus modify the plans of the successive subordinate organisms until the ultimate smallest organisms, such as electrons, are reached. Thus an electron within a living body is different from an electron outside it, by reason of the plan of the body. The electron blindly runs either within or without the body; but it runs within the body in accordance with its character within the body; that is to say, in accordance with the general plan of the body, and this plan includes the mental state. But the principle of modification is perfectly general throughout nature, and represents no property peculiar to living bodies. . . .

The discrepancy between the materialistic mechanism of science and the moral intuitions, which are presupposed in the concrete affairs of life, only gradually assumed its true importance as the centuries advanced. . . .

The literary romantic movement at the beginning of the nineteenth century, just as much as Berkeley's philosophical idealistic movement a hundred years earlier, refused to be confined within the materialistic concepts of the orthodox scientific theory. . . .

It is, however, impossible to proceed until we have settled whether this refashioning of ideas is to be carried out on an objectivist basis or on a subjectivist basis. By a subjectivist basis I mean the belief that the nature of our immediate experience is the outcome of the perceptive peculiarities of the subject enjoying the experience. In other words, I mean that for this theory what is perceived is not a partial vision of a complex of things generally independent of that act of cognition; but that it merely is the expression of the individual peculiarities of the cognitive act. Accordingly what is common to the multiplicity of cognitive acts is the ratiocination connected with them. Thus, though there is a common world of thought associated with our sense-perceptions, there is no common world to think about. What we do think about is a common conceptual world applying indifferently to our individual experiences which are strictly personal to ourselves. Such a conceptual world will ultimately find its complete expression in the equations of applied mathematics. This is the extreme subjectivist position. There is of course the half-way house of those who believe that our perceptual experience does tell us of a common objective world; but that the things perceived are merely the outcome for us of this world, and are not *in themselves* elements in the common world itself.

Also there is the objectivist position. This creed is that the actual elements perceived by our senses are *in themselves* the elements of a common world; and that this world is a complex of things, including indeed our acts of cognition, but transcending them. According to this point of view the things experienced are to be distinguished from our knowledge of them. So far as there is dependence, the *things* pave the way for the *cognition*, rather than *vice versa*. But the point is that the actual things experienced enter into a common world which transcends knowledge, though it includes knowledge. The intermediate subjectivists would hold that the things experienced only indirectly enter into the common world by reason of their dependence on the subject who is cognising. The objectivist holds that the things experienced and the cognisant subject enter into the common world on equal terms. . . .

Some people express themselves as though bodies, brains, and nerves were the only real things in an entirely imaginary world. In other words, they treat bodies on objective principles, and the rest of the world on subjectivist principles. This will not do; especially, when we remember that it is the experimenter's perception of another person's body which is in question as evidence.

But we have to admit that the body is the organism whose states regulate our cognisance of the world. The unity of the perceptual field therefore must be a unity of bodily experience. In being aware of the bodily experience, we must thereby be aware of aspects of the whole spatio-temporal world as mirrored within the bodily life. . . . My theory involves the entire abandonment of the notion that simple location is the primary way in which things are involved in space-time. In a certain sense, everything is everywhere at all times. For every location involves an aspect of itself in every other location. Thus every spatio-temporal standpoint mirrors the world.

If you try to imagine this doctrine in terms of our conventional views of space and time, which presuppose simple location, it is a great paradox. But if you think of it in terms of our naïve experience, it is a mere transcript of the obvious facts. You are in a certain place perceiving things. Your perception takes place where you are, and is entirely dependent on how your body is functioning. But this functioning of the body in one place, exhibits for your cognisance an aspect of the distance environment, fading away into the general knowledge that there are things beyond. If this cognisance conveys knowledge of a transcendent world, it must be because the event which is the bodily life unifies in itself aspects of the universe.

This is a doctrine extremely consonant with the vivid expression of personal experience which we find in the nature-poetry of imaginative writers such as Wordsworth or Shelley. The brooding, immediate presences of things are an obsession to Wordsworth. What the theory does do is to edge cognitive mentality away from being the necessary sub-stratum of the unity of experience. That unity is now placed in the unity of an event. Accompanying this unity, there may or there may not be cognition.

At this point we come back to the great question which was posed before us by our examination of the evidence afforded by the poetic insight of Wordsworth and Shelley. This single question has expanded into a group of questions. What are enduring things, as distinguished from the eternal objects, such as colour and shape? How are they possible? What is their status and meaning in the universe? It comes to this: What is the status of the enduring stability of the order of nature? There is the summary answer, which refers nature to some greater reality standing behind it. This reality occurs in the history of thought under many names, The Absolute, Brahma, The Order of Heaven, God. The delineation of final metaphysical truth is no part of this lecture. My point is that any summary conclusion jumping from our conviction of the existence of such an order of nature to the easy assumption that there is an ultimate reality which, in some unexplained way, is to be appealed to for the removal of perplexity, constitutes the great refusal of rationality to assert its rights. We have to search whether nature does not in its very being show itself as self-explanatory. By this I mean, that the sheer statement, of what things are, may contain elements explanatory of why things are. Such elements may be expected to refer to depths beyond anything which we can grasp with a clear apprehension. In a sense, all explanation must end in an ultimate arbitrariness. My demand is, that the ultimate arbitrariness of matter of fact from which our formulation starts should disclose the same general principles of reality, which we dimly discern as stretching away into regions beyond our explicit powers of discernment. Nature exhibits itself as exemplifying a philosophy of the evolution of organisms subject to determinate conditions. Examples of such conditions are the dimensions of space, the laws of nature, the determinate enduring entities, such as atoms and electrons, which exemplify these laws. But the very nature of these entities, the very nature of their spatiality and temporality, should exhibit the arbitrariness of these conditions as the outcome of a wider evolution beyond nature itself, and within which nature is but a limited mode.

One all-pervasive fact, inherent in the very character of what is real, is the transition of things, the passage one to another. This passage is not a mere linear procession of discrete entities. However we fix a determinate entity, there is always a narrower determination of something which is presupposed in our first choice. Also there is always a wider determination into which our first choice fades by transition beyond itself. The general aspect of nature is that of evolutionary expansiveness. These units, which I call events, are the emergence into actuality of something. How are we to characterise the something which thus emerges? The name *"event,"* given to such a unity, draws attention to the inherent transitoriness, combined with the actual unity. But this abstract word cannot be sufficient to characterise what the fact of the reality of an event is in itself. A moment's thought shows us that no one idea can in itself be sufficient. For every idea which finds its significance in each event must represent something which contributes to what realisation is in itself. Thus no one word can be adequate. But conversely, nothing must be left out. Remembering the poetic rendering of our concrete experience, we see at once that the element of value, of being valuable, of having value, of being an end in itself, of being something which is for its own sake, must not be omitted in any account of an event as the most concrete actual something. "Value" is the word I use for the intrinsic reality of an event. Value is an element which permeates through and through the poetic view of nature. We have only to transfer to the very texture of realisation in itself that value which we recognise so readily in terms of human life.

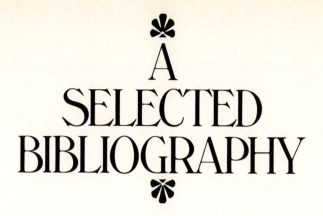

A SELECTED BIBLIOGRAPHY

GENERAL HISTORIES OF PHILOSOPHY

Boas, George: *The Dominant Themes of Modern Philosophy,* The Ronald Press Company, New York, 1957.

Burnet, John: *Greek Philosophy; Thales to Plato,* St. Martin's Press, Inc., New York, 1962.

Copleston, Frederick: *History of Philosophy,* Doubleday & Company, Inc., Garden City, N.Y., 1961–1974, nine vols.

Höffding, Harald: *History of Modern Philosophy,* Dover Publications, Inc., New York, 1924, two vols.

Leff, Gordon: *Medieval Thought from St. Augustine to Ockham,* Penguin Books, Inc., Baltimore, 1962.

Schneider, H. W.: *A History of American Philosophy,* Columbia University Press, New York, 1963.

Sorley, W. R.: *History of British Philosophy to 1900,* Cambridge University Press, New York, 1964.

Warnock, Geoffrey: *English Philosophy since 1900,* Oxford University Press, Fair Lawn, N.J., 1958.

Windelband, Wilhelm: *History of Ancient Philosophy,* Dover Publications, Inc., New York, 1956.

————: *History of Philosophy,* Harper & Row, Publishers, Incorporated, New York, 1958, two vols.

Zeller, Eduard: *Outlines of the History of Greek Philosophy,* The World Publishing Company, Cleveland, 1955.

Part 1   The Ancient Period

Bailey, Cyril: *The Greek Atomists and Epicurus,* Russell & Russell, Inc., New York, 1964.

Bevan, E. R.: *Stoics and Sceptics,* Barnes & Noble, Inc., New York, 1959.

Burnet, John: *Early Greek Philosophy,* The World Publishing Company, Cleveland, 1958.

Cornford, F. M.: *Before and after Socrates,* Cambridge University Press, New York, 1960.

Essential Works of Stoicism (To Himself by Marcus Aurelius, *The Manual* by Epictetus, *On Tranquility* by Seneca, *Life of Zeno* by Diogenes Laertius), Bantam Books, Inc., New York, 1965.

Gosling, J. C. B.: *Plato,* Routledge & Kegan Paul, Ltd., London, 1973.

Graeser, A.: *Plotinus and the Stoics,* E. J. Brill, NV Leiden, Netherlands, 1972.

Hallie, P. P. (ed.): *Scepticism, Man and God,* Wesleyan University Press, Middletown, Conn., 1964.

Jaeger, Werner: *Aristotle,* Oxford University Press, Fair Lawn, N.J., 1948.

Kirk, G. S., and J. E. Raven: *The Presocratic Philosophers,* Cambridge University Press, New York, 1960.

Long, A. A.: *Hellenistic Philosophy, Stoics, Epicureans, Sceptics,* Charles Scribner's Sons, New York, 1974.

McKeon, Richard P.: *An Introduction to Aristotle,* Random House, Inc., New York, 1947.

Nettleship, R. L.: *Lectures on the Republic of Plato,* St. Martin's Press, Inc., New York, 1962.

Oates, W. J. (ed.): *Stoic and Epicurean Philosophers,* Random House, Inc., New York, 1940.

Plotinus: *The Philosophy of Plotinus,* Appleton-Century-Crofts, Inc., New York, 1950.

Ross, W. D.: *Aristotle,* Barnes & Noble Inc., New York, 1955.

————: *Plato's Theory of Ideas,* Oxford University Press, Fair Lawn, N.J., 1951.

Santas, G. X.: *Socrates: Philosophy in Plato's Early Dialogues,* Routledge & Kegan Paul, Ltd., London, 1979.

Taylor, A. E.: *Aristotle,* Dover Publications, Inc., New York, 1955.

————: *Plato: The Man and His Work,* The World Publishing Company, Cleveland, 1956.

Versenyi, Laszlo: *Socratic Humanism,* Yale University Press, New Haven, Conn., 1963.

Vlastos, G.: *Plato's Universe,* University of Washington Press, Seattle, 1975.

Part 2   The Medieval Period

Anselm: *Anselm's Basic Writings.* The Open Court Publishing Company, La Salle, Ill., 1962.

Augustine: *The City of God,* Doubleday & Company, Inc., Garden City, N.Y., 1958.

————: *Confessions,* Penguin Books, Inc., Baltimore, 1961.

————: *On Free Choice of the Will,* Bobbs-Merrill, Indianapolis, Ind., 1964.

Blakney, R. B. (ed.): *Meister Eckhart: A Modern Translation,* Harper & Row, Publishers, Incorporated, New York, 1941.

Boethius: *Consolation of Philosophy,* Frederick Ungar, New York, 1957.

Bourke, V. J.: *Augustine's Quest of Wisdom,* The Bruce Publishing Company, Milwaukee, 1945.

Carré, M. H.: *Realists and Nominalists,* Oxford University Press, Fair Lawn, N.J., 1946.

Chesterton, G. K.: *St. Thomas Aquinas,* Doubleday & Company, Inc., Garden City, N.Y., 1936.

Copleston, Frederick: *Aquinas,* Penguin Books, Inc., Baltimore, 1955.

D'Arcy, M. C.: *Thomas Aquinas.* The Newman Press, Westminster, Md., 1953.

Duns Scotus: *Philosophical Writings,* The Liberal Arts Press, Inc., New York, 1964.

Fremantle, Anne (ed.): *Age of Belief: The Medieval Philosophers,* New American Library of World Literature, Inc., New York, 1955.

Gilson, E.: *The Christian Philosophy of St. Augustine,* Random House, Inc., New York, 1960.

————: *The Philosophy of St. Thomas Aquinas,* Cambridge University Press, New York, 1937.

McKeon, Richard (ed.): *Medieval Philosophers,* Charles Scribner's Sons, New York, 1959, two vols.

Maimonides, Moses: *Guide of the Perplexed,* The University of Chicago Press, Chicago, 1963.

Maritain, J.: *St. Thomas Aquinas,* The World Publishing Company, Cleveland, 1958.

Meagher, R. E.: *An Introduction to Augustine,* New York University Press, New York, 1978.

Ockham: *Philosophical Writings,* The Liberal Arts Press, Inc., New York, 1964.

Pegis, Anton C. (ed.): *Basic Writings of St. Thomas Aquinas,* Random House, Inc., New York, 1944, two vols.

Te Selle, E.: *Augustine the Theologian,* Herder & Herder, Inc., 1970.

Part 3 The Modern Period

Aaron, R. I.: *John Locke,* Oxford University Press, Fair Lawn, N.J., 1955.

Aiken, Henry D. (ed.): *Age of Ideology: The 19th Century Philosophers,* New American Library of World Literature, Inc., New York, 1957.

Ayer, A. J.: *Hume,* Hill and Wang, Inc., New York, 1980.

Bacon, Francis: *New Organon,* The Liberal Arts Press, Inc., New York, 1960.

————: *Advancement of Learning and New Atlantis,* Oxford University Press, Fair Lawn, N.J., 1938.

Beck, Lewis White: *Commentary on Kant's Critique of Practical Reason,* The University of Chicago Press, Chicago, 1964.

Bentham, Jeremy: *Introduction to the Principles of Morals and Legislation,* Hafner Publishing Company, Inc., New York, 1948.

Berkeley, George: *Principles of Human Knowledge* and *Three Dialogues between Hylas and Philonous,* The World Publishing Company, Cleveland, 1963.

Berlin, Isaiah (ed.): *Age of Enlightenment: The 18th Century Philosophers,* New American Library of World Literature, Inc., New York, 1956.

————: *The Empiricists: John Locke, George Berkeley, David Hume,* Dolphin Books, Doubleday & Company, Inc. Garden City, N.Y., 1961.

Bouwsma, W. J.: *The Culture of Renaissance Humanism,* American Historical Association, Washington, 1973.

Broad, C. D.: *Kant: An Introduction,* Cambridge University Press, Cambridge, 1978.

Broome, J. H.: *Rousseau: A Study of His Thought,* Barnes & Noble, Inc., New York, 1963.

Butterfield, H.: *Origins of Modern Science,* Collier Books, a division of Crowell-Collier Publishing Co., New York, 1962.

Cassirer, Ernest: *Rousseau, Kant, and Goethe,* Harper & Row, Publishers, Incorporated, New York, 1963.

————: *The Individual and the Cosmos in Renaissance Thought,* Harper & Row. Publishers, Incorporated, New York, 1964.

————: **Paul O. Kristeller, and J. H. Randall (eds.):** *The Renaissance Philosophy of Man,* The University of Chicago Press, Chicago, 1955.

Davies, S.: *Renaissance Views of Man,* Barnes & Noble, New York, 1979.

Descartes, René: *Philosophical Works of Descartes,* Dover Publications, Inc., New York, 1931, two vols.

Ewing, A. C.: *A Short Commentary on Kant's Critique of Pure Reason,* Methuen & Co., Ltd., London, 1950.

Findlay, J. N.: *Hegel: A Re-examination,* Collier Books, a division of Crowell-Collier Publishing Co., New York, 1962.

Green, F. C.: *Jean-Jacques Rousseau: A Critical Study of His Life and Writings,* Cambridge University Press, Cambridge, 1955.

Grimsley, R.: *The Philosophy of Rousseau,* Oxford University, Press, Fair Lawn, N.J., 1973.

Halevy, E.: *The Growth of Philosophical Radicalism,* Faber & Faber, Ltd., London, 1949.

Hampshire, Stuart (ed.): *Age of Reason: The 17th Century Philosophers,* New American Library of World Literature, Inc., New York, 1956.

————: *Spinoza,* Penguin Books, Inc., Baltimore, 1962.

Hegel, G. W. F.: *Lectures on the Philosophy of History,* Dover Publications, Inc., New York, 1956.

————: *Reason in History,* The Liberal Arts Press, Inc., New York, 1953.

————: *The Phenomenology of Mind,* Harper & Row, Publishers, Incorporated, New York, 1967.

Hobbes, Thomas: *Body, Man and Citizen,* Collier Books, a division of Crowell-Collier Publishing Co., New York, 1962.

————: *Leviathan,* The Liberal Arts Press, Inc., New York, 1958.

Hume, David: *Dialogues Concerning Natural Religion,* The Liberal Arts Press, Inc., New York, 1962.

————: *An Enquiry Concerning Human Understanding,* The Liberal Arts Press, Inc., New York, 1955.

Kant, Immanuel: *Critique of Practical Reason,* The Liberal Arts Press, Inc., New York, 1956.

————: *Critique of Pure Reason,* St. Martin's Press, Inc., New York, 1965.

————: *Groundwork of the Metaphysics of Morals,* Harper & Row, Publishers, Incorporated, New York, 1964.

————: *Prolegomena to Any Future Metaphysics.* The Liberal Arts Press, New York, 1950.

————: *Religion within the Limits of Reason Alone,* Harper & Row, Publishers, Incorporated, New York, 1960.

————: *Critique of Judgment,* Hafner Publishing Company, New York, 1968.

Kaufmann, Walter: *Hegel: A Reinterpretation,* Doubleday Anchor Books, Garden City, N.Y., 1966.

Kristeller, Paul O.: *Renaissance Concept of Man and Other Essays,* Harper & Rowe Publishers, Incorporated, New York, 1972.

————: *Renaissance Thought: The Classic, Scholastic, and Humanist Strains,* Harper & Row, Publishers, Incorporated, New York, 1961.

Locke, John: *Essay Concerning Human Understanding,* Dower Publications, Inc., New York, 1894, two vols.

————: *Treatise of Civil Government and A Letter Concerning Toleration,* Appleton-Century-Crofts, Inc., New York, 1959.

Lukacs, G.: *The Young Hegel,* trans. Rodney Livingstone, The M.I.T. Press, Cambridge, Mass. 1976.

Maritain, J.: *The Dream of Descartes,* Philosophical Library, Inc., New York, 1944.

McRae, R.: *Leibniz: Perception, Apperception, and Thought,* University of Toronto Press, Toronto, 1976.

Mill, John Stuart: *Auguste Comte and Positivism,* Ann Arbor Paperbacks, University of Michigan Press, Ann Arbor, Mich., 1961.

Mure, G. R. G.: *A Study of Hegel's Logic,* Oxford University Press, Fair Lawn, N.J., 1950.

Paton, H. J.: *Kant's Metaphysics of Experience,* The Macmillan Company, New York, 1951.

————: *The Categorical Imperative,* The University of Chicago Press, Chicago, 1948.

Pitcher, George: *Berkeley,* Routledge & Kegan Paul, Boston, 1977.

Raphael, D. D.: *Hobbes, Morals, and Politics,* Allen & Unwin, Inc., London, 1977.

Roche, K. F.: *Rousseau, Stoic and Romantic,* Methuen & Co., Ltd., London, 1974.

Rosen, Stanley: *G. W. F. Hegel: An Introduction to the Science of Wisdom,* Yale University Press, New Haven, Conn., 1974.

Roth, Leon: *Spinoza, Descartes, and Maimonides,* Russell & Russell, Inc., New York, 1963.

Russell, Bertrand: *A Critical Exposition of the Philosophy of Leibniz,* The University Press, Cambridge, 1900.

Smith, Norman Kemp: *A Commentary to Kant's Critique of Pure Reason,* Macmillan & Co., Ltd., London, 1930.

————: *New Studies in the Philosophy of Descartes,* Russell & Russell, Inc., New York, 1963.

————: *The Philosophy of David Hume,* Macmillan & Co., Ltd., London, 1941.

Spinoza, Baruch: *Chief Works,* Dover Publications, Inc., New York, 1962, two vols.

Stephen, Leslie: *History of English Thought in the 18th Century,* Harcourt, Brace & World, Inc., New York, 1902, two vols.

————: *Hobbes,* Ann Arbor Paperbacks, University of Michigan Press, Ann Arbor,

Stephens, J.: *Francis Bacon and the Style of Science,* University of Chicago Press, Chicago, 1975.

Strauss, Leo: *Political Philosophy of Hobbes: Its Basis and Its Genesis,* The University of Chicago Press, Chicago, 1963.

Strawson, P. F.: *The Bounds of Sense: An Essay on Kant's Critique of Pure Reason,* Methuen & Co., Ltd., London, 1975.

Taylor, C.: *Hegel,* Cambridge University Press, New York, 1975.

————: *Hegel and Modern Society,* Cambridge University Press, New York, 1979.

Taylor, Henry Osborn: *Philosophy of Science in the Renaissance,* Collier Books, a division of Crowell-Collier Publishing Co., New York, 1962.

Tipton, I. C.: *Locke on Human Understanding*, Oxford University Press, New York, 1977.

Warnock, G. J.: *Berkeley*, Penguin Books, Inc., Baltimore, 1953.

Weiss, Frederick: *Hegel: The Essential Writings*, Harper & Row, Publishers, Incorporated, New York, 1974.

Wolff, Robert Paul: *Kant's Theory of Mental Activity*, Harvard University Press, Cambridge, Mass., 1963.

————: *The Autonomy of Reason*, A Commentary on Kant's *Groundwork of the Metaphysic of Morals*, Harper & Row, Publishers, Incorporated, New York, 1973.

Wolfson, Harry Austryn: *Philosophy of Spinoza*. The World Publishing Company, Cleveland, 1958.

Wright, E. H.: *The Meaning of Rousseau*, Russell & Russell, Inc., New York, 1963.

Part 4   The Contemporary Period

Alexander, I. W.: *Bergson: Philosopher of Reflection*, Bowes & Bowes, Ltd., London, 1957.

Austin, J. L.: *Sense and Sensibilia*, Oxford University Press, Fair Lawn, N.J., 1962.

Avineri, Shlomo: *The Social and Political Thought of Karl Marx*, Cambridge University Press, London, 1968.

Axelos, K.: *Alienation, Praxis, and Technē in the Thought of Karl Marx*, University of Texas Press, Austin, 1976.

Ayer, A. J.: *The Foundations of Empirical Knowledge*, St. Martin's Press, Inc., New York, 1962.

————: *Language, Truth and Logic*, Dover Publications, Inc., New York, 1946.

————: *Logical Positivism*, The Free Press of Glencoe, New York, 1958.

Bentley, John E.: *American Philosophy*, Littlefield, Adams & Company, Paterson, N.J., 1963.

Bergson, Henri: *Creative Mind*, Philosophical Library, Inc., New York, 1956.

————: *Introduction to Metaphysics*, The Liberal Arts Press, Inc., New York, 1949.

————: *Time and Free Will*, Harper & Row, Publishers, Incorporated, New York, 1960.

————: *The Two Sources of Morality and Religion*, Doubleday & Company, Inc., Garden City, N.Y., 1954.

Berlin, Isaiah: *Karl Marx: His Life and Environment*, 4th ed., Oxford University Press, New York, 1978.

Biemel, W.: *Martin Heidegger: An Illustrated Study*, Harcourt Brace Jovanovich, Inc., New York, 1976.

Cahn, S. M. (ed.): *New Studies in the Philosophy of John Dewey*, University Press of New England, Hanover, N.H., 1977.

Camus, Albert: *The Rebel*, Random House, Inc., New York, 1954.

Caton, Charles E.: *Philosophy and Ordinary Language*, The University of Illinois Press, Urbana, 1963.

Christian, W. A.: *An Interpretation of Whitehead's Metaphysics*, Yale University Press, New Haven, Conn., 1959.

Copleston, F.: *Friedrich Nietzsche, Philosopher of Culture*, Barnes & Noble, Inc., New York, 1975.

Cornforth, Maurice: *Introduction to Dialectical Materialism*, vol. I, *Materialism and Dialectical Method*, International Publishers Company, Inc., New York, 1953.

————: *Introduction to Dialectical Materialism*, vol. II, *Historical Materialism*, International Publishers Company, Inc., New York, 1954.

————: *Introduction to Dialectical Materialism*, vol. III, *Theory of Knowledge*, International Publishers Company, Inc., New York, 1955.

Dewey, John: *A Common Faith*, Yale University Press, New Haven, Conn., 1960.

————: *Essays in Experimental Logic*, Dover Publications, Inc., New York, 1916.

————: *Experience and Nature*, Dover Publications, Inc., New York, 1929.

————: *On Experience, Nature and Freedom*, The Liberal Arts Press, Inc., New York, 1960.

————: *Philosophy of Education*, Littlefield, Adams & Company, Paterson, N.J., 1956.

————: *Quest for Certainty*, Capricorn Books, G. P. Putnam's Sons, New York, 1960.

————: *Reconstruction in Philosophy*, Beacon Press, Boston, 1957.

Feuer, Lewis (ed.): *Basic Writings on Politics and Philosophy: Karl Marx and Friedrich Engels*, Doubleday & Company, Inc., Garden City, N.Y., 1959.

Grene, Marjorie: *Sartre*, Franklin Watts, New York, 1973.

Hare, R. M.: *Language of Morals*, Oxford University Press, Fair Lawn, N.J., 1952.

Heidegger, Martin: *Essays in Metaphysics*, Philosophical Library, Inc., New York, 1960.

————: *Existence and Being*, Henry Regnery Company, Chicago, 1949.

————: *Introduction to Metaphysics*, Doubleday & Company, Inc., Garden City, N.Y., 1961.

————: *Being and Time*, Harper & Row, Publishers, Incorporated, New York, 1962.

Hollingdale, R. J.: *Nietzsche*, Routledge & Kegan Paul, London, 1973.

Hook, Sidney: *Towards the Understanding of Karl Marx*, The John Day Company, Inc., New York, 1933.

James, William: *Essays in Pragmatism*, Hafner Publishing Company, Inc., New York, 1948.

————: *Varieties of Religious Experience*, New American Library of World Literature, Inc., New York, 1958.

————: *The Will to Believe and Human Immortality*, Dover Publications, Inc., New York, 1956.

Jaspers, Karl: *Man in the Modern Age*, Doubleday & Company, Inc., Garden City, N.Y., 1957.

————: *Philosophy and the World*, Henry Regnery Company, Chicago, 1963.

————: *Reason and Existenz*, Noonday Books, Farrar, Straus & Cudahy, Inc., New York, 1957.

————: *The Philosophy of Existence*, University of Pennsylvania Press, Philadelphia, 1971.

Kaufmann, W.: *Nietzsche, Philosopher, Psychologist, Anti-Christ*, 3d. ed. Princeton University Press, Princeton, 1968.

Kenny, A.: *Wittgenstein*, Harvard University Press, Cambridge, 1973.

Kierkegaard, Soren: *Either/Or*, Doubleday & Company, Inc., Garden City, N.Y., 1959, two vols.

————: *Fear and Trembling* and *The Sickness unto Death*, Doubleday & Company, Inc., Garden City, N.Y., 1954.

————: *Philosophical Fragments*, Princeton University Press, Princeton, N.J., 1962.

Kline, George (ed.): *A. N. Whitehead: Essays on His Philosophy*, Prentice-Hall, Inc., Englewood Cliffs, N.J., 1963.

Langan, Thomas: *The Meaning of Heidegger*, Columbia University Press, New York, 1959.

Leclerc, Ivor: *Whitehead's Metaphysics*, The Macmillan Company, New York, 1958.

Lowrie, Walter: *Kierkegaard: A Life,* Harper & Row, Publishers, Incorporated, New York, 1962, two vols.

Mackey, Louis: *Kierkegaard: A Kind of Poet,* University of Pennsylvania Press, Philadelphia, 1971.

Macomber, W. B.: *The Anatomy of Disillusion: Martin Heidegger's Notion of Truth,* Northwestern University Press, Evanston, Ill., 1967.

Malcolm, Norman, with G. H. Von Wright: *Ludwig Wittgenstein: A Memoir,* Oxford University Press, Fair Lawn, N.J., 1958.

Marcel, Gabriel: *Creative Fidelity,* Noonday Books, Farrar, Straus & Cudahy, Inc., New York, 1964.

——: *Homo Viator,* Harper & Row, Publishers, Incorporated, New York, 1962.

——: *Mystery of Being,* Henry Regnery Company, Chicago, 1960, two vols.

Marsh, R. C. (ed.): *Logic and Knowledge,* The Macmillan Company, New York, 1956.

Marx, Karl: *Early Writings,* Vintage Books, Random House, Inc., New York, 1975.

McLellan, D.: *Karl Marx,* The Viking Press, Inc., New York, 1975.

Mehta, J. L.: *Martin Heidegger: The Way and the Vision,* University of Hawaii Press, Honolulu, 1976.

Moore, G. E.: *Philosophical Papers,* Collier Books, a division of Crowell-Collier Publishing Co., New York, 1962.

——: *Principia Ethica,* Cambridge University Press, Cambridge, 1948.

——: *Some Main Problems of Philosophy,* Collier Books, a division of Crowell-Collier Publishing Co., New York, 1962.

Murdoch, Iris: *Sartre,* Yale University Press, New Haven, Conn., 1953.

Nietzsche, Friedrich: *The Birth of Tragedy and the Genealogy of Morals,* Doubleday & Company, Inc., Garden City, N.Y., 1956.

——: *Beyond Good and Evil,* Henry Regnery Company, Chicago, 1959.

——: *The Portable Nietzsche,* Viking Press, Inc., New York, 1954.

Olsen, R. E.: *Karl Marx,* Twayne Publishers, Inc., Boston, 1978.

Pears, D. F.: *Ludwig Wittgenstein,* The Viking Press, Inc., New York, 1970.

Peirce, C. S.: *Philosophical Writings,* Dover Publications, Inc., New York, 1940.

Pitcher, George: *The Philosophy of Wittgenstein,* Prentice-Hall, Inc., Englewood Cliffs, N.J., 1964.

Russell, Bertrand: *Human Knowledge,* Simon and Schuster, Inc., New York, 1962.

——: *Mysticism and Logic,* Doubleday & Company, Inc., Garden City, N.Y., 1957.

——: *Our Knowledge of the External World,* New American Library of World Literature, Inc., New York, 1960.

——: *The Problems of Philosophy,* Oxford University Press, Fair Lawn, N.J., 1912.

——: *Sceptical Essays,* Barnes & Noble, Inc., New York, 1961.

Ryle, Gilbert: *The Concept of Mind,* Barnes & Noble, Inc., New York, 1950.

——: *Dilemmas,* Cambridge University Press, New York, 1960.

Sartre, Jean-Paul: *The Philosophy of Existentialism,* Philosophical Library, Inc., New York, 1965.

——: *Being and Nothingness,* Philosophical Library, Inc., New York, 1956.

——: *The Critique of Dialectical Reason,* NLB, London, 1976.

——: *Sartre by Himself,* Urizen Books, Incorporated, New York, 1978.

Scheffler, I.: *Four Pragmatists: A Critical Introduction to Peirce, James Mead, and Dewey,* Routledge & Kegan Paul, London, 1974.

Schilpp, Paul A. (ed.): *Philosophy of Bertrand Russell,* Harper & Row, Publishers, Incorporated, New York, 1963, two vols.

Schlick, Moritz: *The Problems of Ethics,* Dover Publications, Inc., New York, 1939.

Searle, J. R. (**ed.**): *The Philosophy of Language,* Oxford University Press, London, 1971.

Smith, John E.: *The Spirit of American Philosophy,* Oxford University Press, Fair Lawn, N.J., 1963.

Stalin, Joseph: *Dialectical and Historical Materialism,* International Publishers Company, Inc., New York, 1940.

Stern, J. P.: *A Study of Nietzsche,* Cambridge University Press, Cambridge, 1977.

Urmson, J. O.: *Philosophical Analysis,* Clarendon Press, Oxford, 1956.

Wahl, Jean: *A Short History of Existentialism,* Philosophical Library, Inc., New York, 1962.

Warnock, G. J.: *English Philosophy since 1900,* Oxford University Press, Fair Lawn, N.J., 1958.

Weinberg, Julius: *An Examination of Logical Positivism,* Littlefield, Adams & Company, Paterson, N.J., 1960.

White, Morton (**ed.**): *Age of Analysis: 20th Century Philosophers,* New American Library of World Literature, Inc., New York, 1955.

Whitehead, A. N.: *Adventures of Ideas,* New American Library of World Literature, Inc., New York, 1955.

————: *Modes of Thought,* Capricorn Books, G. P. Putnam's Sons, New York, 1959.

————: *Process and Reality,* Harper & Row, Publishers, Incorporated, New York, 1960.

————: *Religion in the Making,* The World Publishing Company, Cleveland, 1960.

————: *Science and the Modern World,* New American Library of World Literature, Inc., New York, 1949.

Wild, John: *The Challenge of Existentialism,* Indiana University Press, Bloomington, 1955.

————: *The Radical Empiricism of William James,* Doubleday Anchor Books, Garden City, N.Y., 1970.

Wisdom, John: *Other Minds,* Basil Blackwell & Mott, Ltd., Oxford, 1952.

A Glossary
of Key Concepts

Appearance: how something presents itself to our senses as compared with its true reality. The oar appears bent in the water, but it really is not bent.

Aesthetics: the branch of philosophy concerned with the analysis of concepts such as beauty or beautiful as standards for judging works of art.

Autonomy: independence from external authority; in Kant, freedom of the will to make its own law or rule of conduct in contrast to (heteronomy) being subject to someone else's rules.

Categorical imperative: according to Kant, the absolute moral law understood as a duty by any rational creature, to be compared with hypothetical imperatives which permit exceptions.

Cause: a cause is something that has the power to produce a change, motion, or action in another thing; this change (effect) can be explained in terms of the behavior of the cause.

Change: the alternation of anything, the rearrangement of something's parts, the coming into being of something that did not exist before, and the decline and dissolution of something.

Cognition: in the broadest sense, knowledge, or, the act of knowing.

Cognitive meaning: a statement has cognitive meaning if (a) it asserts something that is true simply because the words used necessarily and always require the statement to be true (as in mathematics) or (b) it asserts something that can be judged as true or false by verifying it in experience.

Deduction: a process of reasoning by which the mind relates the truth of a proposition to another proposition by inferring that the truth of the second proposition is involved in and therefore derived from the first proposition (*see* **Induction**).

Determinism: the theory that every fact or event in the universe is determined or caused by previous facts or events: human behavior and the events of history follow strict laws of causation or necessary connection. Accordingly, in this view, human beings do not possess freedom of the will or the power to originate independent or genuine choices.

Dialectic: a process of reasoning based upon the analysis of opposing propositions. Socrates used the dialectic method of teaching by distinguishing between opinion and knowledge. Hegel and Marx developed dialectical conceptions of history in which for Hegel opposing ideas were the key while for Marx history is explained as the conflict of material forces.

Dogmatism: the act of making a positive assertion without demonstration by either rational argument or experience.

Dualism: a theory which holds that there are two independent and irreducible substances, such as mind and body, the intelligible world of ideas and the visible world of things, and the forces of good and evil.

Empiricism: the theory which says that experience is the source of all knowledge, thereby denying that human beings possess inborn knowledge or that they can derive knowledge through the exercise of reason alone.

Epistemology: the branch of philosophy which studies the nature, origin, scope, and validity of knowledge.

Essence: the chief characteristic, quality, or necessary function which makes a thing what it uniquely is.

Ethics: (1) a set of rules for human behavior; (2) a study of judgments of value, of good and evil, right and wrong, desirable and undesirable; and (3) theories of obligation or duty or why we "ought" to behave in certain ways. (Greek, *ethicos;* Latin, *moralis*)

Existentialism: a mode of philosophy which focuses upon the existing individual person; instead of searching for truth in distant universal concepts, existentialism is concerned with the authentic concerns of concrete existing individuals as they face choices and decisions in daily life.

Idealism: the view that mind is the ultimate reality in the world. Idealism is, accordingly, opposed to materialism which views material things as the basic reality from which mind emerges and to which mind is reducible.

Induction: proceeding from the observation of some particular facts to a generalization (or conclusion) concerning all such facts (*see* **Deduction**).

Instrumentalism: John Dewey's theory of how thought functions by emphasizing the practical function of thought in determining future consequences; thought is therefore viewed as instrumental in producing consequences.

Intuition: direct and immediate knowledge, or the immediate apprehension by the self of itself, of the truth of certain propositions, of the external world, and of values, without the prior need for the ability to define a term, to justify a conclusion, or to build upon inferences.

Logical positivism: the view that statements are meaningful only if they can be verified either directly or indirectly in experience. Logical positivism seeks to analyze all claims to knowledge, all assertions of science and everyday life, and only those assertions have meaning which are verified by empirical facts or are connected logically with such facts and therefore verifiable.

Man: (*as used throughout this book*) a human being, or the human creature regarded abstractly and without regard to gender, hence, the human race or humanity.

Materialism: the view that matter constitutes the basis of all that exists in the universe. Hence combinations of matter and material forces account for every aspect of reality, including the nature of thought, the process of historical and economic events, the standard of values based on sensuous bodily pleasures and the abundance of things; and the notion of the primacy of spirit or mind and rational purpose in nature is rejected.

Metaphysics: the branch of philosophy concerned with the question of the ultimate nature of reality. Unlike the sciences which focus on various aspects of nature, metaphysics goes beyond particular things to enquire about more general questions such as what lies beyond nature, how things come into being, what it means for something to be, and whether there is a realm of being which is not subject to change and which is therefore the basis of certainty in knowledge.

Perception: the discovery, by the senses, of knowledge about the world; the apprehension of everyday objects, for example trees, through sense impressions.

Pluralism: the view that there are more than one (Monism) or two (Dualism) ultimate and separate substances making up the world.

Positivism: John Stuart Mill defined positivism as follows: "We [positivists] have no knowledge of anything but Phenomena, and our knowledge of phenomena is relative, not absolute. We know not the essence, not the real mode of production, of any fact, but only its relations to other facts in the way of succession or of similitude. These relations are constant; that is, always the same in the same circumstances." (See page 329).

Pragmatism: according to William James, pragmatism is a method of solving various types of problems, such as "Does God exist?" or "Is man's will free?" by looking at the practical consequences of accepting this or that answer. James says, "The pragmatic method tries to interpret each notion (or theory) by tracing its respective practical consequences . . . . If no practical difference whatever can be traced . . . they mean practically the same thing" and that ends the argument. As a theory of *truth,* James says that an idea is true if it works in daily life.

Rationalism: the philosophical view that emphasizes the ability of human reason to grasp fundamental truths about the world without the aid of sense impressions.

Relativism: the view that there is no absolute knowledge, that truth is different for each individual, social group, or historic period and is therefore relative to the circumstances of the knowing subject.

Scholasticism: refers to the method of learning in the medieval cathedral schools where a combination of philosophy and theology was taught by emphasizing logical or deductive form and basing thinking and its conclusions upon the sayings or writings of key figures of the past whose tradition was viewed as authoritative.

Skepticism: some skeptics doubt that any knowledge achieved so far is absolute and therefore continue to seek after more refined and reliable versions of truth; other skeptics doubt whether it is ever possible to attain perfect certainty of knowledge.

Solipsism: the theory that the self alone (*solus,* alone; *ipse,* self) is the source of all knowledge of existence, a view that sometimes leads to the conclusion that the self is the only reality.

Substance: a separate and distinct thing; that which underlies phenomena; the essence of a thing.

Teleology: *telos* is the Greek word for "purpose," hence teleology is the study of purpose in human nature and in the events of history; in ethical theory (teleological ethics) an action is considered good if it is conducive to fulfilling the purposes of human nature.

Utilitarianism: in this view, an action is considered good or right if its consequence is the greatest happiness (pleasure) of the greatest number. In that case, the action is *useful* (utilitarian) in producing as much or more good than any alternative behavior.

Verification: demonstrating or proving something to be true either by means of evidence or by formal rules of reasoning.

INDEX
FOR BOOK I